WORLD PRESS
ENCYCLOPEDIA

WORLD PRESS
ENCYCLOPEDIA

Edited by
GEORGE THOMAS KURIAN

Indexed by
Marjorie B. Bank
and James Johnson

FACTS ON FILE, Inc.
460 Park Avenue South
New York, N.Y. 10016

WORLD PRESS ENCYCLOPEDIA

George Thomas Kurian

©1982 copyright by Facts On File, Inc.

Published by Facts On File, Inc.
460 Park Ave. South, New York, N.Y. 10016

Library of Congress Cataloging in Publication Data

Kurian, George Thomas
  World press encyclopedia.

  Bibliography: p.
  Includes index.
  1. Liberty of the press. 2. Government and the press.
I. Title.
PN4735.K87   070   80-25120
ISBN 0-87196-392-2 Volume I   AACR1
ISBN 0-87196-497-X Volume II
ISBN 0-87196-621-2 2 Volume set

Printed in the United States of America
9 8 7 6 5 4 3 2 1

Table of Contents

SECTION III:
Smaller & Developing Press Systems

SECTION IV:
Minimal & Underdeveloped Press Systems

APPENDICES

Editorial Advisory Panel Members and Contributors

Paul Ashdown	Associate Professor School of Journalism University of Tennessee	Ireland
Raymond J. Boston	Director of Studies Center for Journalism Studies University College Cardiff, England	*Editorial Adviser*
Susan Bruce	Graduate College of Journalism & Communications University of Florida	Brazil
Min Chen	Visiting Assistant Professor California State University-Chico	China
James Chu	Director Center for Information & Communication Studies California State University-Chico	China
Carman Cumming	Professor School of Journalism Carleton University Ottawa, Canada	Canada
Marlene Cuthbert	Communication Specialist Caribbean Regional Communications Service Study University of the West Indies Kingston, Jamaica	Jamaica
S. Watson Dunn	Professor of Marketing University of Missouri-Columbia	International Advertising
Charles R. Eisendrath	Professor Department of Communication University of Michigan	France
Harold A. Fisher	Director School of Journalism Bowling Green State University	Belgium, Denmark, Egypt, Ethiopia, Lebanon, Malawi, Norway, Portugal, Switzerland, Uganda, Zambia, Zimbabwe *Editorial Adviser*
Jonathan Gunter	International Communication Specialist	International Information Politics
Cynthia Hill	Research Associate School of Journalism Louisiana State University	Philippines
Peter Johansen	Professor School of Journalism Carleton University Ottawa, Canada	Canada

Mark Journey	Undergraduate Student College of Journalism & Communications University of Florida	Brazil
John J. Karch	Professor Department of International Studies National War College	USSR
Wilfred H. Kesterton	Professor School of Journalism Carleton University Ottawa, Canada	Canada
Robert P. Knight	Professor School of Journalism University of Missouri	Chile
Pnina Lahav	Visiting Professor School of Law Boston University	Comparative Press Laws
Jae-won Lee	Director Political Communication Program Cleveland State University	South Korea
John A. Lent	Professor Department of Journalism Temple University	Japan, Thailand *Editorial Adviser*
Robert Lindsay	Professor School of Journalism & Mass Communication University of Minnesota	*Editorial Adviser*
Ralph Lowenstein	Dean College of Journalism & Communications University of Florida	*Editorial Adviser*
L. John Martin	Dean School of Journalism University of Maryland	*Editorial Adviser*
John C. Merrill	Director School of Journalism Louisiana State University	South Africa, The World's Elite Newspapers *Editorial Adviser*
Colleen C. Moore	Research Associate School of Journalism Louisiana State University	Papua New Guinea
Samuel R. Moore	Research Associate School of Journalism Louisiana State University	Israel
Allan Morantz	Free-lance writer specializing in labor- management relations	Canada
Whitney R. Mundt	Associate Professor School of Journalism Louisiana State University	India *Editorial Adviser*
John Spicer Nichols	Assistant Professor Pennsylvania State University	Cuba, El Salvador, Honduras, Guatemala, Nicaragua
Robert L. Nwank wo	Chairperson Department of Communication Arts & Sciences Howard University	Nigeria

Christine L. Ogan	Assistant Professor School of Journalism Indiana University	Turkey
Emmanuel Paraschos	Director Graduate Program Department of Journalism University of Arkansas-Little Rock	Greece
Elliott S. Parker	Associate Professor Department of Journalism Central Michigan University	Hong Kong, Indonesia, Malaysia, Singapore, Taiwan
Robert N. Pierce	Director of Graduate Studies College of Journalism & Communications University of Florida	Brazil, Colombia, Panama, Haiti, Costa Rica, Dominican Republic, Venezuela
William E. Porter	Professor Department of Communication The University of Michigan	Italy
Brian Priestly	Reader in Journalism Department of Journalism University of Canterbury Christchurch, New Zealand	New Zealand
Kuldip Rampal	Assistant Professor Central Missouri State University	Press Councils of the World
Robert Rupert	Professor School of Journalism Carleton University Ottawa, Canada	Canada
Charles T. Salmon	Doctoral Candidate School of Journalism and Mass Communication University of Minnesota	El Salvador
Henry F. Schulte	Dean Samuel Newhouse School of Public Communications Syracuse University	Spain
Michael Sewell	Professor Department of Journalism Texas Wesleyan College	Mexico
G. Paul Smeyak	Professor College of Journalism & Communications University of Florida	Guyana
Aviam Soifer	Professor of Law Boston University School of Law	United States: Press Laws Section
Lowndes F. Stephens	Professor School of Journalism University of South Carolina	*Editorial Adviser*
Leonard Sussman	Director Freedom House	*Editorial Adviser*
Callix Udofia	Doctoral Candidate Department of Mass Communications Wayne State University	Ghana

Paul S. Underwood   Professor
School of Journalism
The Ohio State University

Albania, Austria, Bulgaria,
Czechoslovakia, East Germany,
Hungary, Libya, Poland, Rumania,
Yugoslavia
Editorial Adviser

James W. Welke   Chairperson
Department of Journalism
    & Telecommunications
University of Wyoming

United Kingdom

Sally White   Executive Assistant to the Managing
     Director
THE AGE
Melbourne, Australia

Australia

Jan Wieten   Professor
Vakgroep Massacommunicatie
    Faculteit der Sociale Wetenschappen
Universiteit van Amsterdam
Amsterdam, The Netherlands

The Netherlands

Dennis L. Wilcox   Associate Professor
Department of Journalism & Mass
    Communications
San Jose State University

Tanzania, Kenya
Editorial Adviser

Rodolfo A. Windhausen   Latin America Desk
Associated Press
New York, N.Y.

Argentina

Preface

The *WORLD PRESS ENCYCLOPEDIA* is a definitive survey of the state of the press in 180 countries of the world. It brings together in an easily consultable form available information and statistics on the history and operation of the world's press as well as the political and economic climate in which it functions. In both scope and size, it is the most comprehensive survey of the world's press *ever* attempted.

The press is one of the most influential and visible institutions in the modern world and it performs a critical function in the dissemination of information—the more complex the society the more complex this function. Formerly only a messenger conveying the news, the press has increasingly become a gatekeeper determining what is news and what is not out of the vast quantities of information available to it on a daily basis. The media must not only report the news but also mediate it; they not only purvey the news but interpret it. All editors must constantly make editorial decisions that determine the news mix and content. However objective, they must downplay some news items and play up others, thus imposing their own news values on their readers. In a Berkeleian sense, the way an event is perceived is as important as the event itself. The quality of the press is thus critical if only because it affects the way we perceive the world around us.

The press is also one of the levers of power in the modern world. The relationship between news and power is perceived perhaps more clearly by politicians than by editors and by dictators than by democratic leaders. In the architecture of power the press may be compared to windows—it lets the sunlight into the dark recesses and crevices of government. Sunlight, as Justice Brandeis reminded us, is the best disinfectant in the world and a free and vigilant press is the best deterrent to the abuses of authority every devised.

Further, the press is an opinion maker and molder in a world where public opinion is the ultimate tribunal. The press can crystallize and guide public opinion or arouse passions; it can build reputations or demolish them; it can construct bridges of understanding or reinforce chauvinism and prejudices; it can promote rational debate on issues or inflame them with emotions. Although it no longer enjoys a monopoly in this respect, the press is still the world's best platform and bully pulpit.

Given the importance of the subject, it is surprising that there is less information on the workings of the press worldwide than on any comparable institution. The press has not been the subject of an intensive international survey, although there have been excellent studies on a few national and regional presses. In fact, the field of comparative media studies is of quite recent origin. Holding a mirror to the world, the press itself has apparently shunned the limelight of inquiry.

When this work was first suggested, there was almost universal agreement that such a project was badly needed and overdue. But the question was: Can it be done? Can available information—sparse, uneven, in many cases unreliable and outdated—be organized to meet the rigorous standards of presentation demanded of a reference book? The publication of this book supplies the answer.

As a source book on the international press, the *WORLD PRESS ENCYCLOPEDIA* attempts to compare national news media in terms of both performance and environment. The organization of the data is designed to enable journalists and students of journalism to gain new insights into the historical evolution, present structure and future trends of each national press as well as to discern cross-national patterns. While reviewers are entitled to judge this edition on its own merits, I am inclined to look upon it as a beginning, a base on which to build in the coming years. It is hoped that future editions will be, where possible, expanded and improved, and, where necessary, corrected.

The *WORLD PRESS ENCYCLOPEDIA* considers the press on four levels:

On the economic level, as a business institution and a profit-making activity, as a consumer of goods and services and as an employer.

On the political level, as the fourth estate, often in conflict with the other three, often muzzled and unfree, but nonetheless helping to mold public opinion and serving the public's right to know.

On the professional level, as an occupation with its own ethics and standards, and in relation to other sectors of the mass media.

On the philosophical level, as an intellectual activity, as a marketplace of ideas and opinions, dealing with the very raw materials of history.

It is this last level that distinguishes the press from other businesses and purely economic activities. It is the source of its strength, because the press has to strive at all times to maintain the rigorous standards of objectivity and honesty that an intellectual enterprise demands. It also helps to make the press the terror of errant governments, forcing them to move against the news media more cautiously than they do in the case of other sectors of national life. A vigorous editor can be a thorn in the flesh of the powers that be, telling the truth about the emperor's new clothes. Invariably the press functions in an adversarial capacity and sometimes in the capacity of a devil's advocate. The result is that journalism has become a dangerous profession throughout the world. Each year the annual reports of the International Press Institute and Amnesty International contain longer and longer lists of journalists arrested and beaten, newspapers confiscated, newspaper offices bombed and correspondents expelled. Nothing attests so clearly to the power of the press as these lists.

This encyclopedia has no ideological ax to grind. Its purpose is, as indeed the purpose of every reference book should be, to organize and present facts faithfully and accurately. The authors have tried to avoid polemics, although the temptation to be drawn into controversy is always great in any discussion of such a sensitive subject as the press. The merits of the press of each country are assessed in purely functional terms. Such issues as censorship and ownership are discussed in reference to their impact on the *quality of journalism*, the central concept which this work examines. The quality of journalism, in turn, is an essential building block of a larger and even more significant concept—the quality of the intellectual environment. A vigorous press is the product —not the producer—of a thriving intellectual environment in which the spirit of unfettered inquiry prevails.

Nevertheless, as readers will quickly per-

ceive, there is a philosophical bias in this work in favor of a free press. Such a bias is unavoidable and even inherent in a comparative study of the press. The articles themselves bear out the relationship between political freedom and press freedom. In a sense, every country gets the press it deserves. An unfree country cannot afford the luxury of a free press or it will soon cease to be unfree. Similarly, the citizens of a democratic country cannot exercise all their political rights without access to a free press.

The encyclopedia also takes a look at the information-poor countries of the world, represented by the 65 countries in Section IV. Just as in other areas where the division between rich and poor is marked, the information-poor are growing poorer while the information-rich are being overwhelmed by a flood of publications and broadcasting services. It must be remembered that out of a global population of 4.2 billion, some three billion never read a newspaper or watch a television set and some two billion never listen to a radio. Unfortunately for those with little or no access to information, most of the press growth in recent decades has taken place in countries where there already was a strong press. The establishment of a viable press system in countries without one seems an appropriate agenda for the last two decades of the 20th century.

The *WORLD PRESS ENCYCLOPEDIA* is a collective effort. Without the dedication and participation of its 46 contributors this work would not have been possible. Cheerfully putting up with the importunities of a nagging editor, they have helped to put together what I hope will be a standard reference book on the world's press.

This is the third major reference book I have undertaken for Facts on File Publications in association—a very productive association, I must add—with Edward W. Knappman, its executive vice president. This project itself is a tribute to his vision and commitment, both of which sustained it during the long and difficult gestation extending over two years. His ideas and suggestions, kneaded into every facet of the work, have enriched it far more than can be acknowledged in a brief preface. My thanks are also due to Joe Reilly, who oversaw the task of copyediting with a cheerfulness and perceptiveness that made it a pleasure to work with him. In addition I would like to thank Marjorie Bank and James Johnson for the preparation of the index. My acknowledgements would not be complete without mention of Charles Miller and Linda O'Brien, who lent their excellent copyediting skills to the project.

The publishers and I have made every effort to make this work as authoritative, accurate and useful as possible. Nevertheless, inadequacies and shortcomings are inevitable in a work of this size and I must assume full responsibility for them. If they are brought to my attention, it will be possible to correct them in the next edition.

GEORGE THOMAS KURIAN

November 1981

Notes, Definitions & Classification System

The data presented in the *WORLD PRESS ENCYCLOPEDIA* vary in vintage because of the uneven availability of up-to-date information. Every effort has been made to present the most recent information. In most cases the data reflect the state of the press in the late 1970s, that is in 1978 and 1979. Wherever possible 1980 data have been included either in the data sheet or in the text.

The encyclopedia is divided into four sections. The first, called The International Press, comprises six chapters dealing with certain aspects of the international press situation that needed to be discussed more fully and brought into sharper focus. The second, titled The World's Developed Press Systems, consists of profiles of eighty-two major countries. The next two sections, Smaller and Developing Press Systems and Minimal and Underdeveloped Press Systems, profile respectively 33 middle-level countries and 65 mini-countries. Because each section is alphabetized independently without cross-references, readers are advised to refer to the master list in the Table of Contents when looking up a particular country.

It has been found impossible to achieve a completely satisfactory solution to the problem of transliterating names of newspapers and magazines from such languages as Arabic and Chinese. In all such cases we have followed the most common usage.

The question of definitions of such key terms as newspaper, periodical, nondaily etc. also proved a nagging one, especially when putting together information drawn from disparate sources. Because of the bulk of the statistical data was taken from UNESCO publications, it seemed logical to use that body's definitions throughout the work. As defined by UNESCO:

Newspapers of General Interest are publications devoted primarily to the recording of current events.

Daily Newspapers are newspapers of general interest published as least four times a week.

Nondaily Newspapers are newspapers of general interest published three times a week or less, including Sunday and weekend editions of daily newpapers.

Periodicals are publications of general interest (other than daily newspapers and nondaily newspapers) containing news and/or specialized information.

Circulation may refer to certified circulation, reported circulation, copies printed, copies distributed or copies sold.

Copies per 1,000 People may or may not refer to actual readership.

Information in each country section has been arranged according to a standard, but not rigidly uniform, pattern. This classification system, outlined below, has been adhered to throughout all the A section countries except where the need for clarity or the nature or absence of information required some modification in the scheme. Such an organization is also designed to provide a comparative framework essential to the study of international institutions.

Basic Data
Background & General Characteristics

General Description
The Nature of the Audience: Literacy, Affluence, Population Distribution, Language Distribution
Quality of Journalism: General Comments
Historical Traditions
Distribution by Language, Ethnic & Religious Orientation, Political Ideology, Geography
Size: Regular/Tabloid; Average Number of Pages per Issue
A.M., P.M.; Sunday Newspaper; Magazine Sections
Foreign Language Press
Minority-owned Press; Other Special-Interest Press
Number of Cities with Newspapers/with Competing Newspapers
Number of Newspapers by Circulation

Groups (below 10,000; 10,000 to 25,000; 25,000 to 50,000; 50,000 to 100,000; 100,000 to 500,000; 500,000 to 1,000,000; over 1,000,000)

10 Largest Newspapers by Circulation

Three Most Influential Newspapers

Economic Framework

Overview of the Economic Climate & Its Influence on Media

Newspapers in the Mass Media Milieu: Print Media versus Electronic Media

Types of Ownership: Individual, Corporate, Government, Ruling Political Party, Opposition Party

Types of Newspapers: Elite, Popular, Yellow

Concentration in Ownership: Newspaper Chains & Cross-Ownership; Decline or Growth in Competition; Monopolies; Antitrust Legislation in Force

Distribution Networks: Concentration in Distribution

Newsprint Availability: Policies Relating to Newsprint Import & Allocation; Average Cost of Newsprint per Ton

Advertisers' Influence on Editorial Policies: Ad Ratio

Influence of Special-Interest Lobbies on Editorial Policies

Industrial Relations: Strikes, 1975-; Major Labor Unions; Influence of Unions on Press Freedom; Total Employment and Average Wage Scales; "Reporter Power"

Circulation Patterns; Average Price & Recent Price Hikes; Percentage of Circulation Accounted for by the Top 10

Distribution of Printing Methods (Offset etc.); Impact of New Printing & Editing Technologies

Press Laws

Constitutional Provisions & Guarantees Relating to Media

Summary of Press Laws in Force

Registration & Licensing of Newspapers & Journalists

Compulsory Posting of Bonds

Press-related Laws, such as Sunshine Laws, Shield Laws, Libel Laws, Laws against Blasphemy & Obscenity, Official Secrets Acts

Laws Protecting Privacy of Non-official Citizens

Independence of the Judiciary: General Comments

Censorship

Agency Concerned with Monitoring the Press

Pre-publication Censorship Procedures; Modes of Compliance

Case Studies

Composition, Functions & Operations of Press/Media Councils

Administrative Rules Restricting Officials from Giving Information to the Press; Freedom of Information Acts

State-Press Relations

Organization & Functions of Information Ministry/Department

The Right to Criticize Government: Theory & Practice

Managed News

Editorial Influence on Government Policies: Case Studies

Suspension & Confiscation of Newspapers, 1970-

Jailings of Newsmen, 1970-

State Control over the Press through Subsidies, Allocation of Newsprint, Advertising Support, Labor Union Manipulation, Import Licenses for Printing Equipment, Licensing of Journalists

Attitude Toward Foreign Media

Accreditation Procedures for Foreign Correspondents

Special Visas for Foreign Correspondents

Prior Approval for Cables

Bannings & Jailings of Foreign Correspondents, 1970-

Import Restrictions on Foreign Publications: Ban on Sales

Foreign Ownership of Domestic Media

Foreign Propaganda & Its Impact on Domestic Media

Domestic Contacts with International Press Organizations

Government Stand on UNESCO Declaration of 1979

News Agencies

Domestic News Agencies: Organization;
Relations with the State; Number of
Subscribers; Rate Data
Foreign News Bureaus: Number of
Subscribers; Exclusive Contracts with
State
Issues Related to News Flow

Electronic News Media

State Policies Relating to Radio & TV
News

Education & Training

Review of Education in Journalism:
Degrees Granted

Journalistic Awards & Prizes
Major Journalistic Associations &
Organizations

Summary

Conclusions
Trends & Prospects for the Media: Outlook
for the 1980s

Chronology

Highlights of Press History during the
Past Five Years

Bibliography

SECTION I
The International Press

THE WORLD PRESS: A STATISTICAL PROFILE

by George Kurian

The press is the youngest of the four estates. The earliest newspapers were founded in the 17th century in Europe, more than 150 years after Gutenberg. They first appeared in Germany where the oldest German newspaper, *Avisa Relation oder Zeitung,* was published in 1609. Other European countries followed in rapid succession. The first Dutch newspaper, *Nieuwe Tijdingen,* appeared in 1616; the first English newspaper, Nathaniel Butter's *Weekly Newes,* in 1622; and the first French newspaper, *Gazette,* in 1631. All these newspapers, however, were nondailies; the daily was a still later phenomenon. The first English daily newspaper, the *Daily Courant,* did not appear until 1702.

By the early 19th century newspapers had been established in all the major capitals of Europe and North America. But it was not until the beginning of the 20th century that the true mass-circulation dailies came into existence. Their rise was helped by dramatic breakthroughs in printing and telecommunication technologies, the establishment of news agencies and the extension of literacy.

The years immediately following World War I have been described as the heyday of the print media. Although they continued to expand in the newly independent countries of Asia and Africa, their growth slowed after World War II as the changing economics of newspaper publishing forced the weaker ones to close. Faced with increasing competition from the electronic media for both markets and audiences, the press experienced its most critical decline in the 1950s and 1960s. Although the decline was halted in the 1970s, the press has been unable to recapture its media dominance. In terms of both numbers and circulation, the press today stands more or less where it did in the early 1950s. The gains in some countries are offset by losses in others. On the basis of current statistics the world's press is expected to grow only slightly during the 1980s.

Dailies & Circulation Figures

According to UNESCO, 8,210 daily newspapers were published in 152 countries in 1978 as compared to 7,680 newspapers in 146 countries in 1969. While this represents a gain of 530 newspapers over a 10-year period, fewer newspapers were being published in 1978 per one million inhabitants: 1.92 as compared to 2.12 in 1969. In terms of circulation, the picture is even less encouraging. While total circulation reached an all-time high of 443 million in 1978, per capita circulation edged up only slightly to 136 from 130 per 1,000 inhabitants. Not only does this growth rate lag behind the electronic media, but it also falls short of major demographic and economic indicators such as population, GNP and literacy. Further, although there was no country without a publication of some kind, 28 countries reported no dailies at all.

A major characteristic of the world press is its heavy concentration, in terms of both circulation and numbers, among the top 10 countries. In terms of number of newspapers, the top 10 account for 63 percent of the total, while in terms of circulation the top 10 account for an even greater share of 68 percent.

The Top 10 National Presses

No. of Dailies		Circulation	
United States	1,815	Soviet Union	100,928,000
India	835	United States	61,222,000
Soviet Union	691	Japan	57,820,000
Turkey	437	United Kingdom	21,700,000
West Germany	334	West Germany	19,298,000
Brazil	280	France	11,341,000
Mexico	256	India	9,383,000
Japan	180	Poland	8,429,000
Indonesia	172	Italy	6,296,000
Argentina	164	South Korea	6,010,000

Assuming an average household of four persons, a circulation rate of 250 per 1,000 inhabitants would indicate a saturation point, the level at which an entire population is being reached by a medium. Twenty-one countries in the world have reached this level, all in Europe except for Japan, Israel, Australia, New Zealand and Hong Kong. Significantly, all these countries exhibit high penetration by radio and television as well. At the other end of the scale some 30 countries have circulations of less than 10 per

Dailies & Circulation by Region

Major Regions	Number of Dailies 1969	Number of Dailies 1978	Growth Index 1978 (1969 = 100)	Total (Million)	Circulation Per 1,000 Inhabitants 1969	Circulation Per 1,000 Inhabitants 1978	Growth Index 1978 (1969 = 100)
Africa	210	180	86	9	19	21	110
North America	1,880	1,950	104	67	295	281	95
Latin America	1,160	1,085	93	25	61	72	118
Asia (excluding Arab States)	NA	2,300		106	NA	73	—
Arab States		110		5		30	
Europe	1,800	1,740	97	127	259	264	102
Oceania	114	110	96	6	296	268	90
USSR	630	690	109	102	321	394	123
Developed Countries		4,700		366		321	
Developing Countries		3,510		77		36	
World		8,210		443		136	

Source: other than Growth Index: UNESCO *Statistical Yearbook, 1978*.

Nondailies by Region

Major Regions	No. of Countries Reporting	No. of Nondailies
Africa	30	433
North America	16	11,060
South America	9	1,022
Asia	23	6,385
Europe	30	6,821
Oceania	15	756
USSR	1	7,237
World	124	33,714

Periodicals by Region

Major Regions	No. of Countries Reporting	No. of Periodicals
Africa	15	863
North America	14	12,947
South America	8	3,550
Asia	24	41,164
Europe	27	70,602
Oceania	11	8,415
USSR	1	4,772
World	100	142,313

Newsprint Production & Consumption by Region (1977)

Major Region	Production (million metric tons)	Consumption Total (million metric tons)	Consumption Per Inhabitant (kg.)
Africa	0.3	0.3	0.8
North America	11.4	10.2	42.5
Latin America	0.3	0.9	2.6
Asia (Excluding Arab States)	3.9	4.4	1.9
Arab States	0.0	0.1	0.8
Europe	5.0	6.2	13.0
Oceania	0.5	0.6	28.0
USSR	1.4	1.1	4.4
Developed Countries	20.8	20.7	18.2
Developing Countries	1.9	3.1	1.0
World	22.7	23.8	5.8

Source: UNESCO *Statistical Yearbook, 1978.*

1,000, the so-called information-poverty level, a concept that is now fairly well established in media studies. All but eight of these countries are in Africa, historically the continent where the media are the weakest in the world. These information-poor countries illustrate the relationship between general economic underdevelopment and media underdevelopment. A healthy media can flourish only in a healthy economy. It cannot be sustained without the necessary infrastructure, including a literacy rate of at least 25 percent, availability of printing equipment and newsprint, proper telecommunication facilities, training programs for journalists at the university level, and a well-developed distribution network. Such an infrastructure cannot be built up overnight but takes massive investments and a new set of priorities on the part of developing countries.

More than 25 percent of the world's dailies are in English. Next to English the greatest number of dailies appear in Chinese, followed by German and Spanish. In most countries the dailies are small, having only four to six pages per issue. Only in some 25 nations can dailies be found with 12 pages or more per issue.

Newsprint

Despite 50 percent increase in production over the past decade, newsprint is in short supply and consequently is becoming more and more expensive. It is produced in only 36 countries and of these only six—Canada, Finland, Sweden, Norway, the Soviet Union and New Zealand—are exporters. The United States, the world's largest consumer, uses more than three times it own annual production. Practically no newsprint is produced in Africa. Only four countries in Asia and 12 in Europe produce enough for their domestic needs.

According to the Canadian Pulp and Paper Association, worldwide newsprint demand increased 3.7 percent in 1980 to 24.6 million metric tons, roughly equal to production. The manufacturing capacity expanded to 26.5 million metric tons. Canada was the largest producer with 8.7 million metric tons, the Unites States second with 3.7 million metric tons and Japan third with 2.5 million metric tons. The United States accounted for 41 percent of worldwide demand with Japan a distant second at 10 percent. Worldwide production and both total and per capita consumption by regions are documented in the accompanying table.

News Agencies

News agencies may be described as the sluice gates that control the flow of news, particularly across national borders. In 1980 there were 174 news agencies in the world in 93 countries, including 60 Third World countries. Eighty-seven countries covered in this work have no news agencies; of these 25 have populations of more than 1 million. (A complete listing of news agencies with ratings is given in Appendix III.) News agencies serve not only the press but also radio and television broadcasters with domestic and foreign news. In 50 countries news agencies are directly controlled and operated by the state; in others they are either cooperatively owned and controlled by the media or are autonomous public corporations established by the state. There are vast differences in scale of operations among news agencies; some are no more than glorified government information offices.

Of the 174 agencies, only some 20 may be described as major in the sense of possessing the capability to gather and transmit information across national borders. Of these the most important are the so-called Big Five— AP, UPI, Reuters, AFP and Tass—who dominate the field through sheer size and technological superiority. Each of the Big Five has offices in between 100 and 200 countries and large numbers of full-time and part-time correspondents. Each issues news 24 hours a day in all the major languages. In many Third World countries one or more of the Big Five have entered into exclusive contracts with the national news agencies for the supply and exchange of news. Despite UNESCO-led efforts to dilute the virtual monopoly of the Big Five, both technology and economics have tended to reinforce it. The spectacular technical developments in the collection and transmission of news, particularly via satellites, have favored the larger news agencies with the know-how and the capital. The prohibitive costs of foreign operations also make it difficult for smaller agencies to compete with the Big Five or to establish new bureaus. It has been estimated that it costs AP an average of $300,000 per year to maintain *one* correspondent overseas. The very economics of news gathering seem to be working against UNESCO's New International Information Order.

Radio & Television

Radio and television are considered together in this work because they constitute the electronic media as opposed to the print media. Radio is not only the largest single medium in the world, with a constituency of over one billion, but it is also the most versatile. Even with refined jamming techniques it can transcend national borders and defy the censors. It is cheap even in countries that require periodical payment of license fees. It does not require the total concentration of a television set or newspaper and can be listened to even while driving or working. Television, on the other hand, has an unrivalled immediacy and impact, which none of the other media can match. While the print media appeal only to the elite and the literate,

radio and television can reach the semiliterates and even illiterates. Indeed, according to David Lerner, radio and television are the principal instruments of modernization in developing societies.

The electronic media are subject to state legislation in almost all countries. Originally, such control was necessary for technical reasons, particularly the allocation of frequencies, but later, as the impact of broadcasting became more clearly understood, it became a matter of political convenience. The majority of the states operate or directly control radio and television services, which are financed either by state funds or through license fees. In other countries the services are operated by autonomous corporations that enjoy some measure of freedom in day-to-day operations. In still others the pattern is mixed with private commercial companies, universities, religious organizations and private foundations operating services side by side or in competition with state or autonomous services. In only a few countries, such as the United States, are the services operated almost entirely by private commercial companies and financed solely through advertising revenues. But even in the United States, the principal foreign short-wave broadcasting is conducted by the government through its Voice of America.

The number of radio receivers is less than 100 per 1,000 in all but 17 African countries, five Latin American countries, and 19 Asian countries. Television has spread to more countries in the 1970s but there are still no television services in 20 African and 10 Asian countries. In only three African countries—Djibouti, Reunion and Ivory Coast— does the number of television receivers exceed 30 per 1,000. The number of television receivers is less than 100 per 1,000 in 18 Latin American and 19 Asian countries.

Patterns of Ownership & Control

Media ownership patterns vary widely depending primarily on the political complexion of the state and the type of national economy. Private ownership of the media is becoming increasingly limited to Western democracies; political and economic pressures have been too severe to enable privately owned papers to survive in the Third World. Even as private media succumb to state pressures, new patterns of ownership are emerging.

Number of Radio Broadcasting Transmitters by Region

Major Regions	1965	1970	1975	1977
Africa	500	680	730	790
North America	6,170	6,770	8,530	9,190
Latin America	3,470	4,140	4,200	4,210
Asia (excluding Arab States)	1,330	1,830	2,630	3,600
Arab States	160	220	250	300
Europe	4,170	5,240	5,980	6,190
Oceania	290	310	330	380
USSR	410	3,030	3,300	3,500
Developed Countries	11,670	16,200	19,100	20,360
Developing Countries	4,730	5,900	6,700	7,640
World	16,400	22,100	25,800	28,000

Number of Radio Receivers by Region

Major Regions	Total (Millions)				Per 1,000 Inhabitants			
	1965	1970	1975	1977	1965	1970	1975	1977
Africa	10	16	28	31	33	45	70	73
North America	251	306	424	466	1,173	1,353	1,793	1,942
Latin America	34	51	81	87	138	180	249	252
Asia (excluding Arab States)	40	56	102	133	39	48	77	92
Arab States	6	10	17	19	59	83	120	130
Europe	110	138	155	182	249	299	327	381
Oceania	3	8	13	17	189	428	606	773
USSR	74	95	122	134	319	390	480	515
Developed Countries	460	572	770	869	449	533	687	762
Developing Countries	64	100	161	189	42	58	83	89
World	524	672	931	1,058	207	241	303	325

Number of Television Transmitters by Region

Major Regions	1965	1970	1975	1977
Africa	100	140	230	250
North America	2,820	3,850	4,360	4,420
Latin America	250	460	640	650
Asia (excluding Arab States)	1,070	3,730	6,630	8,930
Arab States	75	120	180	190
Europe	3,550	7,900	14,900	16,300
Oceania	80	230	370	440
USSR	650	1,340	1,800	1,840
Developed Countries	8,100	16,900	27,580	31,250
Developing Countries	450	800	1,420	1,650
World	8,550	17,700	29,000	32,900

Number of Television Sets by Region

Major Regions	Total (Millions)				Per 1,000 Inhabitants			
	1965	1970	1975	1977	1965	1970	1975	1977
Africa	0.6	1.2	2.5	4.7	1.9	3.4	6.2	11
North America	76.0	92.0	133.0	145.0	355.0	407.0	562.0	604
Latin America	8.0	17.0	27.0	31.0	32.0	60.0	83.0	90
Asia (excluding Arab States)	18.8	26.0	35.7	42.0	18.0	22.0	27.0	29
Arab States	0.9	1.9	3.4	5.2	8.4	15.0	24.0	36
Europe	59.0	90.0	114.0	126.0	132.0	196.0	241.0	264
Oceania	2.4	3.5	5.5	5.9	137.0	200.0	258.0	268
USSR	16.0	35.0	55.0	62.0	69.0	144.0	216.0	238
Developed Countries	170.0	244.0	344.0	368.0	166.0	277.0	298.0	322
Developing Countries	11.0	22.0	40.0	51.0	7.3	13.0	21.0	24
World	181.0	266.0	374.0	419.0	72.0	96.0	122.0	128

Among the more common is the ostensibly private newspaper subsidized by the state or the ruling political party. It is expected that 80 percent of the national media will be state owned or controlled by the end of the century.

Implicit in the question of ownership is that of press freedom. In 1981, according to Freedom House, the print media are regarded as free in 51 nations (33 percent), partly free in 38 (25 percent) and not free in 66 (42 percent). The broadcast media are listed as free in 36 countries (23 percent), partly free in 34 (22 percent) and not free in 85 (55 percent). Thus in only 23 percent of the countries of the world are both the print and broadcast media regarded as free, down from 24 percent in 1980.

INTERNATIONAL INFORMATION POLITICS*

By Jonathan F. Gunter

In recent years media coverage of world events and the politicalization of the media have become a growing source of friction between Third World countries and the nations of the West, particularly the United States.

•As the Somoza regime in Nicaragua came under increasing pressure from the Sandinista rebels, Western media coverage of the situation became more critical of Somoza. Nicaragua's official and pro-government media responded with a campaign to discredit the Western press. American TV viewers soon witnessed the grim sight of a U.S. cameraman being murdered at point-blank range by one of Somoza's troops—even as he waved a white flag.

•After Iranian militants seized the U.S. Embassy in Teheran, demonstrations before American TV cameras became a daily cathartic ritual for the Iranians and a nightly ordeal for TV viewers in the United States. Many Americans became greatly upset with the U.S. news media when the militants succeeded in trading film footage of the hostages for the broadcast of a statement conveying their views.

•As Fidel Castro's new high-powered transmitters began to interfere with programs in the United States and to extend broadcasts throughout the Caribbean and Central America, the Reagan Administration's response was initiation of Radio Free Cuba, to "tell the truth" about life under Castro.

Pre-dating these episodes is a long-standing controversy over the way media organizations in the West have covered news in the developing nations. For nearly a quarter century this controversy and the related issue of the free flow of information have been debated in various international forums —the United Nations, UNESCO and the movement of non-aligned nations. Part of the problem stems from the different roles the media play in the West and in the Third World.

Perspectives on the Role of Media

Since the end of World War II over a hundred poor nations (comprising two-thirds of the world's population) have emerged. The overriding concern of all these countries is economic, social and political development. The developed nations, which are committed to the concepts of individual liberty and private enterprise, suddenly command a small minority of the votes in one-vote per country international organizations.

The movement of non-aligned nations began in the mid-1950s when the eighty-five nations now in this grouping resolved not to become "pawns" in the struggle between East and West, and to develop a "third way" of government and of development. Recently, many have questioned what ties could possibly bind Communist Cuba with capitalist and democratic Venezuela. The answer is underdevelopment, the conditions it imposes and the demands it creates.

Communications and Development

The communications media have become major instruments for promoting develop-

*This chapter draws upon *The United States and the Debate on the World Information Order,* a report to the U.S. International Communications Agency and the Ford Foundation. Contributions of Tim Logue, Mark Kieffer and Donna Freeman-Jones are acknowledged, as is advice from some 30 others. An expanded treatment of this topic, edited by Dr. Gunter, is scheduled to be published by Pergamon Press in 1982.

ment. The media's impact over the last 25 years has been greatly extended by the vast increase in the size of audiences as a result of technological advances. Communications infrastructure has been vigorously expanded through the efforts of international organizations, private enterprise and bilateral assistance programs. Aided by the "transistor revolution," radio has become the world's dominant mass medium, reaching even the rural populations in the Third World. Television has also been undergoing an enormous expansion, although from a much narrower, urban base. The emergence of direct satellite broadcasting in the 1980s will accelerate the pace of TV and radio penetration. While print media have grown much more slowly and from a small, elite base, their content is reflected in the broadcast media. International wire service copy, for example, is heavily used in broadcast news in the developing world. As the mass media continue to grow in coming years, there may be increasing pressure to orient media toward development (as defined by governments) and away from anything deemed politically disruptive.

The media influence development in many ways. They can change attitudes, teach new knowledge and alter behavior (although these capabilities were exaggerated by early U.S. researchers). India's Satellite Instructional Television Experiment (SITE) was the most dramatic case to date of a government using "big media" to further population, health, agricultural and educational programs. Although technologically more modest, Tanzania's radio campaigns mobilized two million villagers to combat local health problems. Under the concept of "development journalism," pioneered by the Press Foundation of Asia, print media have been employed to generate public support for sacrifice and national service.

Yet for every conscious developmental application of media, there are thousands of instances of influence by messages designed to entertain or to sell—either a product or a way of life. Many such messages come from developed countries (particularly the United States) in the form of advertisements, TV shows and movies. While such "unintended" developmental impacts were judged positive by early (U.S.) researchers, such as Wilbur Schramm and Daniel Lerner, later (mostly non-U.S.) researchers have been far less sanguine. Even Lerner himself changed his view of a "revolution of rising expectations" into concern over a "revolution of rising frustra-

tions." Many Third World governments, fearing "rising frustrations," have tried (with widely varying success) to use media to stimulate participation in development.

In many countries there has seemed to be no realistic opportunity for the establishment of a private media sector (although MIT's Ithiel de Sola Pool argues that private broadcast media—but possibly not print—are economically viable in any country). Markets for advertising and sources of private capital seem to be extremely limited in those countries that see the greatest need for mobilizing media to aid development. In most of Latin America (the richest continent of the developing world) the print and broadcast media are largely in private hands (although the telecommunications infrastructure is almost completely under state control). In Africa and developing Asia, private broadcast media are extremely rare, and private print media generally serve only the urban populations. In the developing world view, public financing of the media imposes a responsibility on them to serve the goals of national development, as specified by government. Additional reasons for controlling the media are the maintenance of social and political order and the protection of institutional interests.

America's Unique Media System

In order to grasp the reaction by Third World critics to U.S. media policies and products, the unique nature of this country's media must be considered. The independence of American media is based upon the First Amendment to the Constitution, which says that Congress shall pass no laws to abridge freedom of speech or of the press. This grew out of the British tradition of allowing the press to act as an independent watchdog and check on government. Historically, the law has been interpreted to mean that communications should be largely a nongovernmental activity in the United States.

More than that of any other major country in the world, America's communications system is based on free enterprise. Very few countries share the Anglo-American concept of the press acting as a monitor of government actions. In the vast majority of countries, including America's Western allies, telecommunications industries are in public hands. In most countries, also including the industrialized nations of the West, broadcasting is both publicly owned and operated.

In several Western countries, the press receives direct government subsidies. In the United States, the funds government allocates to public broadcasting are a small fraction of those that private enterprise invests in commercial broadcasting. The only major subsidies to the private media are indirect, such as preferential postal rates for publications and no charge to broadcasters for use of public airwaves—a limited resource —although such use falls under government regulation.

George Gerbner, dean of the University of Pennsylvania's Annenberg School, has stressed that the production of news has become a highly selective, highly synthetic manufacturing process. In the United States, some observers contend, decisions regarding what to communicate (and what to ignore) and how to communicate are made on the basis of commercial criteria. To speak in traditional terms of "free speech" in the United States (or "free flow" internationally) may be at odds with the economic and technological realities, i.e., the growth of media conglomerates, sometimes associated with "speech" and "flow."

The American private media have acknowledged, in some instances, a coincidence between American ideals, commercial self-interest and the appropriate direction for world communications. For instance, a *Washington Post* editorial on July 22, 1976, entitled "UNESCO's Assault on News," responding to a UNESCO-sponsored conference on communications, argued:

> Now, this newspaper, which offers its news product for foreign sale, has an undeniable self-interest in nourishing an international climate in which the commercial opportunities for Western media are maintained. But this, of course, is no different from the vested interest that the American media—being free, competitive institutions —have in maintaining the same commercial opportunities at home. It is a simple matter of principle coinciding with commercial self-interest, and the principle involved here, of course, was set forth at a rather early stage in our history, in the First Amendment to the Constitution. And if it is a sound principle for us in this country, it follows, or so it seems to us, that it is also a good rule to apply to the communication of ideas abroad....

The coincidence between principle and self-interest is not always a "simple matter." The ultimate ramifications of this extension of the First Amendment have been questioned by U.S. Supreme Court Chief Justice Warren Burger.

In a separate but concurring opinion on a case in which corporations' rights of free speech were upheld by the court, *First National Bank of Boston* v. *Bellotti*, Chief Justice Burger noted the growth of U.S. media corporations horizontally (e.g., the growing number of chains) and vertically (e.g., newspaper ownership of paper mills and transportation) and into non-media markets as well. He added:

> In terms of "unfair advantages in the political process" and "corporate domination of the electoral process"...it could be argued that such media conglomerates as I describe pose a much more realistic threat to valid interest than do appellants and similar entities not regularly concerned with shaping popular opinion on public issues....In Tornillo, for example, we noted the serious contentions advanced that a result of the growth of modern media empires "has been to place in a few hands the power to inform the American people and shape public opinion."*

Thus, the fruitful coincidence between principle and commercial self-interest cited by the *Washington Post* has been a subject of discussion in the highest court in the land. In countries receiving massive amounts of U.S. technology and information but moving towards quite different perspectives on the social role of media, even deeper and more bitter conflicts would seem likely.

The United Nations

In the early years of the United Nations, the primary concern was the dichotomy between the communist East and the capitalist West. The colonial empires of the Western nations were only beginning to break up. The United Nations had a much smaller membership (in 1945 there were 50 members, today 149) and for the most part Western ideals predominated. Debates on news and information during this earlier period and the treaties, declarations and conventions that grew out of them relate to the present and the future in a very real way. They are frequently

---

*"First National Bank of Boston et al., Apellants v. Francis X. Bellotti etc., et al.," *Supreme Court Reporter,* vol. 98, no. 14 (May 15, 1978), pp. 1426–27.

invoked by governments to support or refute positions taken in current debates. Although these documents may not always carry the rule of law, they do have moral and psychological weight in the eyes of policy makers throughout the world.

U.N. Documents Concerning Information

The U.N. Charter contains broad statements supporting fundamental principles of human rights, including those of freedom of speech and information. These rights have been further elaborated in subsequent U.N. documents. The charter, however, also emphasizes national sovereignty as being vital to the maintenance of peace and security.

The U.N. Declaration on Freedom of Information (United Nations General Assembly Resolution 59 [1]), issued in 1946, made the first reference to the flow of information:

> all states should proclaim policies under which the *free flow of information* within countries and across frontiers, will be protected. The right to seek and transmit information should be insured in order to enable the public to ascertain facts and appraise events....

Two years later the United Nations held the Freedom of Information Conference in Geneva, where differing views arose on how "freely" information should flow. The United States called for "free and unrestricted flow." The Soviets maintained that no true freedom of communications existed in the West so long as the means to communicate were controlled by a small wealthy group. A middle position called for a formula that would seek to control the flow of information in specified cases involving a potential violation of national sovereignty. Even today, after years of deliberation, agreement has not been reached on a draft Convention on Freedom of Information because of conflicting legal and ideological positions.

Of particular importance among past U.N. actions is the Universal Declaration of Human Rights passed by the General Assembly (UNGA) in 1948 by a vote of 48 states for, none against and eight abstentions (six Eastern bloc nations, South Africa and Saudi Arabia). Although the declaration is not legally binding, it carries great moral and psychological weight with U.N. members. Article 19 of this document has often been referred to in numerous international forums,

particularly UNESCO. It reads, "Everyone has the right to freedom of opinion and expression; this right includes freedom to hold opinions...and to seek, receive and impart information and ideas through any media and regardless of frontiers." Article 2 extends the document's affirmation of basic human rights to every individual "without distinction of any kind," including the "limitation of sovereignty."

In an effort to confer legal status on some of the principles of the Universal Declaration, the International Covenant on Civil and Political Rights was adopted by the General Assembly in 1966 following years of deliberation. In Article 19 of the covenant, rights of freedom of expression and opinion are reaffirmed, although with the stipulation that these rights carry with them certain duties and responsibilities, including respect for the rights of others and protection of national security and domestic order. Article 20 of the same document outlaws war propaganda and any national or religious activities that are designed to incite conflict or violence. The United States has not ratified this covenant, although many other nations have.

Numerous other resolutions and conventions adopted by the General Assembly are often invoked during the discussions of various international organizations. Among these are Resolution 110 (II), passed in 1947, which condemns all forms of conflict-inciting propaganda and the International Convention on Elimination of Racial Discrimination, passed in 1963, whose Article 4 condemns all manner of racist propaganda.

U.N. Activities Concerning Peaceful Uses of Outer Space

With the launching of Sputnik I, the first space satellite, the United Nations became directly involved in questions relating to the free flow of information. Soon after the formation of the Committee on Peaceful Uses of Outer Space (COPUOS) in 1959, two subcommittees, one on scientific and technological aspects and one on legal affairs, were established. It is in these subcommittees, which operate on a consensus basis, that most of the debate on information issues has transpired.

Article 1 of the U.N. Outer Space Treaty of 1967, produced in a spirit of cooperation, declared that outer space was to remain "the province of all mankind," to which all nations were to have equal access. However, a controversy began when the talks turned towards communications via direct broadcast satellites (DBS), which many nations have viewed as a symbol of modern mass media, controlled by the most technically advanced countries, particularly the United States. Ironically, DBS was the subject of debate long before its technology became operational.

In 1969, during COPUOS's annual session, the positions of the major parties in the debates over DBS began to take shape. The Soviets took the stand that countries should be legally bound to obtain "prior consent" from receiving governments before broadcasting from space via satellite. The United States opposed this notion as contrary to Article 19 of the Universal Declaration of Human Rights and as a threat to the free flow of information.

As a result of a joint Swedish-Canadian initiative, an ad hoc Working Group on Direct Broadcast Satellites was formed that year to consider the technical, legal and political aspects of DBS. However, the group reached no consensus on the establishment of legal instruments for regulation of DBS. Some participants felt that widespread application of such technology would not come until 1980 and thus the call for regulation of DBS was premature.

Nonetheless, in 1972 the debate over DBS began to intensify as the USSR introduced a proposal to the General Assembly calling for a binding convention of principles on television transmissions from satellites. In essence, this was a call for a more "regulatory" response to DBS than previous policies, which had been characterized by a Western laissez faire attitude. Some delegations agreed that this was necessary since the Outer Space Treaty had not dealt with outer space activities whose direct effects would be essentially felt on earth.

The United States raised strong objections to the Soviet proposals, calling them premature and unduly restrictive. Consistent with previous—and present—U.S. policy, it was felt that any outside regulations whatsoever would constitute a threat to the unrestricted flow of information. Much to the Americans' dismay, however, the desire to establish some regulatory principles concerning DBS extended far beyond the Soviet Union. By a vote of 102 to one, with the United States the lone dissenter, the General Assembly called

on COPUOS to "elaborate principles governing the use by States of artificial earth satellites for direct television broadcasting with a view toward concluding an international agreement or agreements." Behind this near unanimous vote was the fear, widely expressed by a large number of states, that the United States would employ its tremendous technological advantage for political, cultural or commercial purposes.

The United States continues to maintain that regulations should be allowed to evolve as the technology develops. The Soviets, numerous Third World countries—particularly Argentina and Brazil—and even some more moderate developed countries—Canada and Sweden—have pressed for some degree of control over DBS. The debates concerning DBS center around the conflict between two concepts: the free flow of information and national sovereignty. On the one hand, the less developed states worry that their entire system—economic, social and political—will be undermined by a flood of foreign television messages (these would be broadcast from space and would supposedly be less susceptible to control and, therefore, more potentially harmful than messages transmitted by other means of broadcasting). On the other hand, the United States is committed politically and philosophically to the unrestricted exchange of information, which it considers necessary for the full development of all states.

UNESCO

The United Nations Educational, Scientific and Cultural Organization has long been involved in communications-related issues. In fact, UNESCO in recent years has become a forum for debates on the world "information order." The organization speaks on these issues through many voices. The Biennial General Conferences of UNESCO are attended by official delegations from all the member nations. At the General Conferences the member states determine the activities to be carried out by the UNESCO Secretariat during the next two years, including research, field projects, meetings of experts, regional conferences and seminars. Participants in these activities come from the UNESCO Secretariat, member states, the academic community and a variety of other professional fields.

Background 1945–1969

UNESCO's involvement with the media in news and culture is mandated in Article 1, Section 2 of the UNESCO Constitution, which states that the organization will "collaborate in the work of advancing the mutual knowledge and understanding of peoples, through all means of mass communication and to that end, recommend such international agreements as may be necessary to promote the free flow of ideas by word or image." Thus, the framers of UNESCO's Constitution intended the organization to propagate the concept of the free flow of information, reflecting, as was the case in the United Nations during its early years, the powerful influence of Western ideas in international forums. This influence was enhanced in UNESCO by the absence of the Soviet Union, which boycotted the organization until 1954.

UNESCO's principal labors in the information field during the 1950s involved the provision of technical assistance to help build communications infrastructures in the developing world. However, Western models were nearly always used and in many cases they proved unworkable. Through most of the 1960s the prevailing philosophy in UNESCO was "more and more media are a good thing." Behind this sentiment was the assumption that exposure to mass media would create attitudes favorable to modernization and development. In general, UNESCO continued to place more emphasis on the development of communications infrastructures than on communications content.

Although dependence on Western media models and products did not become a major issue until the 1970s, there were inklings of what was to come in the early 1960s. UNESCO convened regional meetings on news and information flow in Bangkok (1960), Santiago (1961), and Paris (1962). At these meetings, the problems of regional information dissemination came strongly to the fore, but the focus was on the quantity of news provided rather than the quality. All three meetings recommended the establishment of regional news agencies. (Interestingly, a Latin American news agency had been proposed as early as 1934.)

Support for the free flow of information continued to characterize most UNESCO statements throughout the 1960s. For example, in 1966 Article VIII of the UNESCO Declaration of Principles of International Cultural Cooperation stated that "broad dissemination of ideas and knowledge, based on the freest exchange and discussion, is essential to create activity the pursuit of truth and the development of the personality."

UNESCO Activities Concerning Information Issues, 1969–1976

At a 1969 UNESCO meeting of experts in Montreal, reference was made to the "two-way circulation of news" and "the balanced circulation of news," terminology that would become very familiar at subsequent UNESCO meetings. Participants suggested that measures be taken to encourage flow from the Third World to the West and to eliminate the barriers which had prevented this.

In 1970 the 16th General Conference of the organization authorized the director general "to help member states in the formulation of their mass communication policies." At this conference a group of developing countries, under the leadership of the Indian delegation, expressed concern over what they felt was an imbalance in the world flow of information.

In the 1970s concerns were voiced in both UNESCO and the United Nations regarding the possibility of direct television broadcasting via satellites to home receivers. Fear grew among numerous Third World countries and, in some cases, developed countries that with its powerful media and advanced technology such broadcasting by the United States would have a harmful impact on local cultures and media systems. During the 17th UNESCO General Conference in 1972, the Soviet Union, in response to these growing concerns, submitted a resolution calling for a "Declaration of Guiding Principles on the Use of Satellite Broadcasting for the Free Flow of Information, the Spread of Education and Cultural Exchange." At the same time, the Soviets presented their own draft declaration, whose Article IX called for the principle of prior consent to be applied to broadcasts from satellites. The final vote clearly indicated that support for a declaration of principles, albeit not so restrictive as the Soviets desired, was not limited to Communist-bloc states. The resolution was adopted by a vote of 55 to seven with 22 abstentions. The United States voted against it.

Another Soviet-sponsored resolution—

strongly supported by Third World members —called upon the director general to prepare a declaration on "the fundamental principles governing the use of the mass media with a view to strengthening peace and understanding and combating war propaganda, racialism, and apartheid." This mass media draft declaration was to become a hotly debated issue in the years ahead.

At the 18th UNESCO General Conference in 1974, the theme of "free flow" was again discussed and the view was expressed that free flow had little to offer those who lack the means to communicate. It was felt that before states could participate equally in the flow, they would have to be on a "free and equal footing." Thus, there was a call for practical action to strengthen and expand communication capabilities and to help correct imbalances.

The conference also considered the first draft of the mass media declaration, written by a Swedish international law expert and initially discussed at a March 1974 meeting of nongovernmental experts. Since no agreement was reached, it was decided that a decision on the mass media draft declaration should be delayed. The conference then passed a resolution calling for an intergovernmental meeting of experts to study the issue.

In response to that resolution an intergovernmental group of experts met in Paris in December 1975 to draft an acceptable mass media declaration. At this meeting, which was notable for the withdrawal of the U.S. delegation and 12 other Western delegations following the introduction of the "Zionism/Racism" issue into the discussions, a draft was approved, but it was unacceptable to the Americans and others. In particular, Article XII of the draft, which asserted that "States are responsible for the activities in the international sphere of all mass media under their jurisdiction," was seen as contrary to the Western tradition of independent and private media. In view of the First Amendment to the Constitution, the U.S. government could not accept responsibility for the international activities of private American media enterprises, because it could exercise no control over them.

As part of the preparation for the 19th General Conference, the ministerial-level Intergovernmental Conference on Communications Policies in Latin America and the Caribbean convened in Costa Rica in July 1976. (Latin America is the one region of the developing world with vigorous private press and broadcasting systems.) Predictably, the meeting took place in an atmosphere of tension caused by open hostility between UNESCO staff and both the representatives of the Inter-American Press Association (the trade association of the hemisphere's press) and many U.S. press representatives involved in Latin American affairs. Nevertheless, the resulting recommendations seemed to most Western observers to be less adversarial than those of earlier meetings. A proposal on a journalistic code of ethics was killed and proposals on regional news agencies were modified to include language protecting existing agencies. But many U.S. and Latin American observers and participants still regarded the recommendations as an implicit threat to freedom of the press.

19th UNESCO General Conference, Nairobi, 1976

Debates over the world information order rose to a high pitch at the 19th General Conference in 1976 in Nairobi. Sharp criticism of the mass media draft declaration was expressed by Western diplomats, politicians and journalists. On the other side, proponents of the declaration repeated and intensified criticisms voiced at earlier UNESCO meetings alleging an imbalance in information flow and a distortion and a cultural bias in news reporting and in books, films, magazines, TV programs, etc., from the West.

Although some opponents of the draft declaration concurred in the view that there was an imbalance in the world information flow and a need for constructive action to correct it, they were not prepared to accept what they perceived as an overly restrictive regime. Again, as in previous UNESCO meetings, it was the clause mandating governmental responsibility "for the activities in the international sphere of all mass media under their jurisdiction" that stirred the most controversy. However, a decision on the mass media draft declaration was deferred when a commission voted 78 to 15 to table it. In its place, the participants adopted a resolution inviting the director general to hold further consultations with experts for the purpose of preparing a final draft mass media declaration that would meet with the largest possible agreement.

Also passed at the Nairobi Conference was

a resolution introduced by Tunisia that called for international cooperation in the development of communications, and pleaded a special case for the news agencies' pool that had just been formed by the non-aligned countries. The United States and other Western countries saw this as an opportunity to put aside contentious ideological issues and to demonstrate Western commitment to practical measures. In a speech to the conference on November 1, Ambassador John Reinhardt, head of the U.S. delegation stated, "We believe that the United States and other nations in which are found highly developed mass media facilities and capabilities should endeavor to make available, through bilateral and multilateral channels, both private and governmental, assistance to other states in helping to develop their mass media."

An outgrowth of the Nairobi Conference was the establishment of the International Commission for the Study of Communication Problems. Chosen as its head was Sean MacBride of Ireland, winner of both the Lenin and Nobel prizes. Fifteen other members were selected from a broad range of countries, relevant professional backgrounds and ideological persuasions. Former broadcaster and Columbia School of Journalism Dean Elie Abel was the American voice on the MacBride Commission, as it became known. As UNESCO's director general, Amadou-Mahtar M'Bow, stated on December 14, 1977 in Paris, the commission had a mandate to "search for general agreement on the manner in which men should organize free and balanced exchanges of information and for ways and means whereby the communication media may contribute more effectively to the progress of peoples and their mutual understanding."

At the commission's first meeting in late 1977, as he related in an article entitled "Communications in the Service of Mankind" in the spring 1978 issue of *Irish Broadcasting Review,* MacBride posed four key questions:

What is meant by free and balanced flow of information?

What does a "new world information order" mean, and what is its inter-relationship with the new international economic order?

How may the "right to communicate," with all its ethical and legal implications, be achieved as a new line of thought and action in the whole communication field?

How can the objectivity and independence of the media be assured and protected?

After several contentious sessions in various parts of the world, the commissioners disagreed vehemently over the tone of an interim report drafted by the UNESCO Secretariat. Western commission members generally considered the draft to favor regulated, government media over independent, private media and public funding over advertising.

20th UNESCO General Conference, Paris, 1978

The commissioners' disagreements were reflected in the 20th General Conference discussion of the report and in a resolution proposed by the United States, France, Sri Lanka, Tunisia and Venezuela calling upon the commission to "propose concrete and practical measures leading to the establishment of a more just and effective world information order."

A major accomplishment of the conference was the unanimous passage of the mass media declaration, which had been six tedious years in the making. Because of the concerted efforts and cooperation of the U.S. media, the State Department and the U.S. National Commission for UNESCO, the United States was able to join the consensus. U.S. media representatives were present in the official American delegation and in private advisory capacities.

After intensive negotiations the objectionable phrase regarding government jurisdiction over media was finally removed from the text. Instead of previous formulations on righting "imbalances" in information flow, the final version mentioned "the creation of conditions for a free flow and wider and more balanced dissemination of information."

A final outcome of the 1978 conference was a resolution initiated by the United States and aimed at establishing a structure for coordinating aid in communications. The UNESCO director general was asked to convene a planning meeting and to enlist the support of other international organizations in the formation of this structure.

International Program for the Development of Communications (IPDC)

The U.S. conception of the coordinating structure for assistance called for equal participation by all international agencies involved in the field: the United Nations Development Program, UNESCO, the International Telecommunication Union, the World Bank, etc. The UNESCO Secretariat, not surprisingly, conceived of its own role as being central to the enterprise. Having been given the lead in creating the program, UNESCO has been able to ensure that its council and executive director will respond to the director general. UNESCO and the developing countries have called for donations in addition to the regular contributions to UNESCO's budget, but the major Western countries have not responded.

In 1980 the MacBride Commission issued its final report, entitled *Many Voices, One World,* a lengthy and comprehensive document. Many of the conclusions are sympathetic to the positions of the West, including the need for access to a diversity of news sources and for freedom of speech and opinion. On the other hand, advertising—seen by U.S. media as the main financial base of their independence—is attacked. Concentration of private ownership is criticized while governmental monopoly is condoned. Themes such as an international code of ethics and measures that are supposed to protect journalists also appear in the report, although Western members of the UNESCO commission viewed such themes as covers for governmental supervision.

21st UNESCO General Conference, Belgrade, 1980

At the Belgrade Conference in 1980 participants passed a resolution praising the MacBride Commission report and urging member states to disseminate the report and to study means of creating a new world information and communications order. The statutes of the IPDC Council firmly establishing UNESCO's control were also enacted. The U.S. delegation issued a statement deploring the political overtones of many of the studies to be undertaken by the Secretariat in the next two years. Interestingly, the U.S. National News Council published a report ("Report on News Coverage of Belgrade UNESCO Conference," mimeo, 1981) criticizing U.S. media coverage of the Belgrade Conference and of UNESCO in general:

> Without questioning the sincerity or even the validity of the apprehensions held by American editors and publishers on the direction in which UNESCO is moving—many of which concerns are fully shared by the National News Council—it is nevertheless rele-

vant to observe that the seeming reflections of these apprehensions in the decision of American newspapers on what to print in their news columns about UNESCO is inconsistent with the spirit of detachment that is invariably set forth as the touchstone of sound news judgement.

Recent Developments

The Belgrade Conference convinced many Western media leaders that the compromise approach pursued in the late 1970s was not productive. The hope that developing countries would moderate their ideological zeal in return for financial and technical assistance from the West seems to have faded. Some have argued that aid has not been forthcoming on a large enough scale to test the compromise approach.

In any event, developments since the Belgrade Conference have not been encouraging. In February 1981 UNESCO held a consultative meeting on protection of journalists, which proposed an international commission be established to ensure that journalists adhered to generally accepted rules of professional ethics. The commission would issue identity cards and suggest procedures that nations could incorporate into their legislation.

Understandably, these proposals created great apprehension among the Western media. Even more troublesome was the failure of UNESCO to inform Western media representatives of the meeting or to invite them to it. Only after the application of great pressure were Western media representatives allowed to participate.

In May 1981 the media staged their own meeting under the auspices of Tufts University's Murrow Center for Public Diplomacy. UNESCO Director General M'Bow was invited to the meeting, and a heated exchange is said to have ensued. The meeting produced a UNESCO-style declaration embodying the principles of independent media and resolving to resist attempts by UNESCO to challenge these principles.

The Declaration of Talloires (site of the meeting) was characterized by its framers as a statement of principles on which there would never be compromise. A few months later the U.S. House of Representatives also developed a resolution opposing UNESCO's actions in the area of press freedom. Given the present mood in both Congress and the executive, U.S. attitudes toward UNESCO will most likely harden over the next few years.

The Non-Aligned Movement

Communications issues were prominent among the topics discussed at the Fourth Conference of Heads of State or Government of Non-Aligned Countries, held in Algiers on September 5–9, 1973. Representatives of 75 member nations, 24 observer nations and three guest nations (Austria, Finland and Sweden) reviewed worldwide political, economic and cultural trends since the previous summit. Under the topic "Preservation and Development," the conferees stated that "it is an established fact that the activities of imperialism are not confined solely to the political and economic fields, but also cover the cultural and social fields," and stressed "the need to reaffirm national cultural identity and eliminate harmful consequences of the colonial era." Articles 13 and 14 of the conference's Action Program for Economic Cooperation specifically refer to communications:

xiii) Developing countries should take concerted action in the field of mass communications on the following lines in order to promote a greater interchange of ideas among themselves:
a.) Reorganize existing communication channels which are the legacy of the colonial past, and which have hampered free, direct and fast communications among them;
b.) Initiate joint action for the revision of existing multilateral agreements with a view to reviewing press cable rates and facilitating faster and cheaper intercommunication;
c.) Take urgent steps to expedite the process of collective ownership of communications satellites and evolve a code of conduct for directing their use;
d.) Promote increased contact between the mass media, universities, libraries, planning and research bodies and other institutions so as to enable developing countries to exchange experience and expertise and share ideas.
xiv) Non-aligned countries should exchange and disseminate information concerning their mutual achievements in all fields through newspapers and periodicals, radio, television and the news media of their respective countries. They should formulate plans for sharing experience in this field, inter alia through reciprocal visits of delegations from information media and through exchange of radio and television programs, films, books, photographs, and through cultural events and art festivals.

Tanjug's Non-Aligned News Agencies Pool

In response to the Algiers Summit resolutions and after consulting with several national news agencies, Tanjug, the Yugoslav news agency, initiated a Non-Aligned News Agencies Pool on January 20, 1975. The first reports were issued in French, Spanish and English. In a spirit of cooperation, the agencies involved in the first transmission asked all non-aligned nations to join the pool. At the end of one year the pool had 26 members and had relayed 3,500 news items. Within three years over 40 national agencies were participating in the mutual exchange and it had received encouragement from the United Nations, UNESCO, the World Bank, the Associated Press and the United Press International.

After the Algiers Summit and the commencement of the news agencies pool, steps were taken to coordinate and implement the activities of the non-aligned movement. In May 1975 representatives of 14 non-aligned countries met in Belgrade to prepare the agenda for a Non-Aligned Symposium on Information to be held in Tunis in March 1976. An organization committee (composed of representatives from Mexico, Tunisia, Sri Lanka, Cuba and Yugoslavia) for the symposium agreed upon discussion topics and submitted them to the Fifth Ministerial (Foreign Ministers) Conference, held in Lima on August 25–30, 1975. The agenda for Tunis included discussion of methods for furthering an exchange of information between countries, the role of information organs in promoting cultural interchange and the role of infrastructures in reinforcing economic and social cooperation. Resolution VI from the Lima Conference, entitled "Cooperation in the Field of Diffusion of Information and Mass Communication Media," supported the Non-Aligned News Agencies Pool and recommended that a meeting of government representatives and press agencies be called to draft a constitution for the pool. India offered to host the meeting in New Delhi in 1976. The 81 countries at the Lima Conference named Tunisia as coordinating country.

The Tunis Symposium

Delegates from 38 member states and 13

observer nations attended the Tunis Symposium, held on March 26–30, 1976. The final report, entitled "The Emancipation of the Mass Media in Non-Aligned Countries," contained suggestions for a study of the potential for mass media self-reliance within the non-aligned countries, for the creation of regional exchange centers for journalists and technologies, and for the future development of an appropriate infrastructure capable of communication production and distribution. The Tunis Symposium critically evaluated the immense problems faced by the non-aligned countries, especially at the structural-operational level of communications development.

The issues addressed in the final report to the conference represented the first attempt to deal in practical terms with the problem of distribution of Third World-generated news. Much previous discussion had centered on the need for balance in communications flow and the communications rights of the less developed countries. During the "Development Decade" of the 1960s, the emphasis had been on the establishment of production facilities and the training of producers. Third World critics have felt that Western aid-providing nations often underplayed the problems of news distribution, especially among the less developed nations. On an international scale, the establishment by many Third World countries of national news agencies was one answer to the problem of production, and the pool provided a complementary solution to the problem of international distribution. The symposium urged the upcoming summit at Colombo to establish specialized entities for mapping out strategies, consolidating diverse projects, and drafting and integrating general regulations.

The New Delhi Conference

Over 60 states and organizations (including the United Nations) were represented at the New Delhi Ministerial Conference, held on July 8–13, 1976. Thirty-one managers of news agencies and 33 information ministers met for the first time to take an in-depth look at communications policy for the non-aligned nations. The group received a progress report from Tanjug on the Non-Aligned News Agencies Pool, a review of the Tunis Symposium report and a recommendation to set up a Coordination Committee for the news pool,

and discussed methods for improving communications facilities in the non-aligned countries. India was designated to head a Coordination Committee for the news pool and convened the first session immediately after the six-day New Delhi Conference.

One of the final acts of the conference was to adopt the New Delhi Declaration, which asserted a worldwide information imbalance and expressed the non-aligned nations' commitment to change the situation. The conference resolutions reveal a desire to find common approaches to such questions as the right to information, the right to communicate and the functioning of satellite communications. The conferees also decided to set up a committee of experts to study the possibilities for cooperation in such fields as telecommunications facilities, satellite communications and shortwave radio transmissions.

The Colombo Summit

On August 15–19, 1976 the leaders of 84 non-aligned nations assembled in Colombo, Sri Lanka to consider the recommendations made at New Delhi as well as those adopted at ministerial meetings held since the last summit in Algiers in 1973. The heads of state not only endorsed the declarations and decisions made at New Delhi but also approved a constitution for the Non-Aligned News Agencies Pool, giving formal approval to the experiment begun by Tanjug a year and a half earlier.

According to its constitution, the aim of the pool is to provide objective information with an emphasis on progressive social, economic, political and cultural development. The pool is not to act as an international news agency, nor is any participant to have a dominant role. Each country is to bear the cost of its participation. In day-to-day operation, the participating news agencies, can if they choose, send dispatches to one or more of the agencies (such as Tanjug) that has volunteered to be a regional redistribution center. Additionally, there are provisions for coordinating the exchange of features, photographs and specialized economic and cultural information as well as journalists and technical personnel.

The Colombo Summit also approved the establishment of a Coordinating Committee of the Press Agencies Pool of Non-Aligned Countries and an Inter-Governmental Coordinating Council for the Coordination of Information in the Non-Aligned Countries.

Three major documents—the Action Program for Economic Cooperation, the Political Declaration and the Economic Declaration—were produced at the summit. The Political Declaration states that "a new international order in the fields of information and mass communication is as vital as a new international economic order," and notes with concern "the vast and evergrowing gap between communication capacities in non-aligned countries and the advanced countries." The declaration also asserts that "the emancipation and development of national media is an integral part of the overall struggle for political, economic and social independence for a large majority of the peoples of the world who should not be denied the right to inform and be informed objectively and correctly."

Tunisia was also given a mandate by the summit to take the "international information order" question to the upcoming UNESCO General Conference in Nairobi. At Nairobi a "compromise" Tunisian Resolution expressed support for the Non-Aligned News Agencies Pool and directed UNESCO to aid it.

In the years following the Colombo Summit, the pace of non-aligned gatherings on information quickened. In 1977 broadcasting organizations gathered in the first of a series of meetings to examine both general topics and specific arrangements for cooperative program exchange and training. Telecommunications specialists also met on several occasions, largely in preparation for the 1979 General World Administrative Radio Conference, which made technical regulatory decisions concerning the range of radio communications services. Since the Colombo Summit the non-aligned news agencies have also met on a continuing basis, largely to stimulate the growth of their news pool.

The Havana Summit, 1979

The Havana Summit strained the cohesiveness of the movement as no other summit had. President Fidel Castro, assuming the leadership of the non-aligned movement, tried to impose a pro-Soviet position on the conference. More moderate leaders, including President Tito of Yugoslavia, urged a traditional neutral stand between East and West. Despite the conflict the conference managed to develop a resolution on "cooperation in the Field of Information and the

media." In addition to several organizational matters relating to committees concerned with communications, the resolution called for lower transmission rates, a non-aligned documentation center, and a united front and the election of a chairman from a non-aligned country at the World Administrative Radio Conference (WARC).

Recent Developments

The non-aligned countries were not successful in electing their candidate chairman of WARC. However, negotiations over the election of a chairman delayed the opening of the conference for three days. The non-aligned nations also greatly affected the agenda for radio regulatory conferences in the 1980s by calling for meetings on specific issues. A working-level meeting after the Havana Summit led to a broadcast cooperation agreement between Cuba and Nicaragua. Another such meeting produced a news agency exchange accord between Vietnam and India.

While many Western observers tend to discount the impact of the movement in the communications field, organizing efforts continue. The movement's efforts have clearly gone beyond UNESCO and the United Nations and into the world radio conferences. Like those in the past, the next summit, scheduled for Baghdad in 1982, will undoubtedly consider communications issues.

Basic Unresolvable Issues

Debates on information flow in the United Nations and UNESCO and within the non-aligned movement have focused on three basic issues: conflicting news values, allegations of distortion and imbalance and dependence on Western media institutions.

What is news?

The underlying controversy may actually involve the definition of news itself. Americans and many others tend to believe that their concept of detached "objectivity" and independence from government is acultural and merits universal acceptance. Third World spokesmen (mostly academics and government spokesmen) counter that other cultures have different conceptions of the common good of the relationship between media and government, and the nature of news.

Gerald Long, former chief of Reuters and currently managing director of London's Times Newspapers, observed in an article entitled "News Value Social Values" in *Issues in Communications* (1:1977):

It is pointless to try to separate, in any society, what are called its news values and its general values, national or international. The values which are called news values will have been formed by the various processes in the society that form values.

Thus, different cultures and societies can be expected to have different "news values," quite apart from any institutional aims, such as promoting official policies or maximizing advertising revenues.

Distortion and Imbalance

A logical extension of the above issue is the judging of news content. The essence of many criticisms is that a distorted and imbalanced image of events in the Third World is conveyed by an excessive focus upon the sensational, the violent and the trivial. The more important stories, critics allege, of efforts to promote national unity and development under difficult conditions go largely unreported in the West.

In response, defenders of Western media point out that development programs are often not newsworthy. They note that sensational and violent events are reported in the West because readers demand such coverage and cite content analyses by Western researchers that demonstrate Western media news content is not imbalanced or negative. Studies have concluded that editors in the developing world generally share the editorial inclinations of their counterparts in the West. Third World spokesmen disagree, citing studies (often UNESCO-funded) with critical conclusions.

It seems highly unlikely that the issue will be decided through news content analysis. The perception of bias on the part of the critics and the dedication of Western journalists to their news values and professional identities will fuel the debate for years to come.

Dependence upon Western Media Institutions

Both the news values and content issues derive from the global structure of news flow. There is little argument over the prominence of the four Western wire services (the Associated Press, United Press International, Reuters and Agence France-Presse). The influence of the Voice of America and the British Broadcasting Corporation (BBC) External Services is also acknowledged by Western media spokesmen. The roles of Western TV organizations have grown immensely as portable video equipment and proliferating transmission facilities have made on-the-spot coverage possible from most countries.

Western media leaders have expressed general support for the development of new media voices in world news flow, and in fact, news agencies and broadcasting organizations in the developing world have grown and extended their overseas influence. Several such organizations have benefited from technical cooperation arrangements with major Western media institutions.

Still, the problem of gaining acceptance internationally and competing against well-funded and well-staffed Western media is indeed formidable. It is also widely acknowledged that Western assistance to date has not materialized on a scale matching the magnitude of the problem. In difficult economic times, however, this may be too much to expect.

Much of the dependence on Western media organizations results from economic disparities. If developing countries had the resources to build worldwide news organizations with highly trained and highly paid writers, photographers, editors and producers, they obviously could minimize their dependence. However, such prospects seem remote indeed.

Conclusion

Asked how the new information order would be created, a leading proponent responded, "By discussing it." There followed a tacit admission that most Third World political leaders and media practitioners had yet to get the message.

Although disconcerting for weary Western media defenders, the controversy over world news flow seems destined to become a permanent feature in North-South relations. Within every North-South crisis, there now lurks the possibility of a media "subcrisis." Before long this may become accepted and acceptable, however. Ten years from now, observers looking back may wonder why there was surprise and indignation when media coverage became controversial at the global level.

COMPARATIVE PRESS LAWS

by Pnina Lahav

The history and development of press law, particularly in Western and Western-influenced societies, has been shaped largely by the interplay between competing political philosophies.* In the early stages of development, following the invention of the printing press in the 15th century, press laws were predicated on an authoritarian theory. The theory was dominated by the principle of government control over both the form and content of newspapers and served to keep the ruling elite and their world view in power.

The advent of the Enlightenment gave rise to an alternative, libertarian theory. The libertarians thought that the press should be free of governmental control and developed justifications for press freedom based on the need for self-fulfillment and the search for truth as the basis of self-rule. As the basis of self-rule, they believed that a free marketplace of ideas would facilitate this search. With varying degrees of success, this theory has managed to displace—or at least contend with—authoritarianism.

More recently, particularly in the 20th century as the press has evolved into a network of mass communications, a theory of social responsibility has been developed to accommodate the growing power of the press to notions of civil morality. Today, these three theories share an uneasy coexistence, and the influence of each can be detected in various legal systems.

A fourth model of contemporary press law, the Marxist-Leninist, is built on a different philosophy. Within this framework the state monopoly over the means of production includes the printing press. Hence, the state controls all publications. Furthermore, under Leninist doctrine freedom of the press is limited to those who accept the legitimacy and hegemony of the Communist Party. Such freedom is denied to those who criticize the very foundations of the Party's ideology. Insofar as this review is limited to a discussion of press laws in liberal-democratic regimes, however, this alternative philosophy is only noted in passing.

A classic example of authoritarian press laws is the regulatory regime introduced by Britain into many of its colonies. This system was designed to establish absolute control over the printing press and the newspaper. Two aspects of the regulations are particularly illuminating. First, both the printing press and the newspaper depended on a permit issued by an administrative official for their legitimate operation. Further, the permit could be either suspended or revoked at any time and for any reason. Reg. 94, Defense (Emergency) Regulations of *The Palestine Gazette,* Supp. 2, 1079 (1945), for example, reads:

> (1) No newspaper shall be printed or published unless the proprietor thereof shall have obtained a permit under the hand of the District Commissioner of the District in which the newspaper is being, or is to be, printed.
> (2) The District Commissioner, in his discretion and without assigning any reason therefor, may grant or refuse any such permit and may attach conditions thereto and may at any time suspend or revoke any such permit or vary or delete any conditions attached to the permit or attach new conditions thereto.

These regulations are still part of Israeli law.

Second, control over the content of the publications was sought through the establishment of a censor who was vested with broad discretion to delete any material from the publication. Reg. 87 of the same law states:

> The Censor may by order prohibit generally or specially the publishing in publications of matter the publishing of which, in his opinion, would be, or be likely to be or become, prejudicial to the defence of Palestine or to the public safety or to public order.

---

*The following analysis relies heavily on Siebert, Peterson and Schram, *Four Theories of the Press* (1956). This article is based on my forthcoming book, *Press Law in Democracy,* which analyzes the comparative aspects of press laws.

Violation of the permit requirement or the censorship regulations constituted a criminal offense. Furthermore, even an indication by the newspaper that the censor had deleted some information was prohibited (Reg. 94(3), 87(2), and 98 respectively). The regulations pertaining to censorship, while part of Israeli law, by no means reflected a voluntary agreement between the press and the government. Government's grip over the press was thus made absolute, since even the fact that there was a policy disagreement between it and a newspaper could not be disclosed.

An early triumph of the libertarian over the authoritarian theory of the press is the 18th century British doctrine against prior restraint found in Blackstone's *Commentaries*. The doctrine provides that legal limitations over press freedom cannot be applied before publication. It thus questions the licensing and censoring mechanisms that typify authoritarian regimes. It reads in part:

> The liberty of the press is indeed essential to the nature of a free state; but this consists in laying no *previous* restraint upon publications, and not in freedom from censure for criminal matter when published. Every freeman has an undoubted right to lay what sentiments he pleases before the public; to forbid this is to destroy the freedom of the press; but if he publishes what is improper, mischievous, or illegal, he must take the consequence of his own temerity.

Blackstone's theory has been adopted by most common-law systems. For example, it is a part of American law (*New York Times* v. *United States*, 403 U.S. 713, 1971, per curiam), and it is a part of Israeli law (*Kol-Haam* v. *Minister of the Interior*, 1 Selected Judgements of the Supreme Court of Israel, 1948-53, p. 90). In different forms, the libertarian attack on censorship and other forms of prior restraint is also part of civil law of such countries as West Germany and Sweden. Article 5(1) of the Basic Law of the Federal Republic of Germany, for example, provides specifically that "there shall be no censorship." Article 1 of the Swedish Freedom of the Press Act embodies similar provisions.

Blackstone's doctrine is important because it reflects the basic libertarian philosophy that the regimentation of expression through licensing and prior suppression of expression are invariably detrimental to society. More specifically, the doctrine parallels libertarian philosophy in its assertion of individualism. It declares that a person should not be told in advance what he or she may think or say, but that he or she should be expected to be accountable for the consequences of his or her expression. The doctrine thus at once rejects paternalism and affirms individualism through the approval of subsequent punishment.

Concomitantly, and perhaps more importantly, Blackstone's theory reflects an important shift in the legal treatment of the press. The rejection of prior restraints as legitimate tools was simultaneously a rejection of executive fiat and caprice. Through these administrative measures public officials could exercise unchecked power over the press, as the British colonial measures in Palestine illustrate. Blackstone's insistence that the state can exercise legitimate control over expression only through the criminal law established the courts as checks over executive discretion. It also interjected important requirements of due process into any attempt to suppress such expression. Thus, Blackstone's theory was also a product of libertarianism in its assertion of the importance of free expression through the elimination of censorship. Moreover, by emphasis on the criminal law as the only legitimate method of control over the press, the theory affirmed the libertarian belief in the power of reason—embodied in the courts and safeguarded by notions of due process—over arbitrary will.

However, only Blackstone's theory and its continental European counterparts constituted only a first step in the ascendance of the libertarian theory. Through the criminal law, governments possessed ample power and means to suppress objectionable expression. One such means was the doctrine of seditious libel which treated criticism of the government as subversive. This doctrine did not lose its strength under Blackstone's influence. A good example of a seditious libel statute is the Sedition Act passed by the U.S. Congress in 1798 (1 Stat. 596). Section 2 of that act states:

> That if any person shall write, print, utter or publish, or shall cause or procure to be written, printed, uttered or published, or shall knowingly and willingly assist or aid in writing, printing, uttering or publishing any false, scandalous and malicious writing or writings against the government of the United States, or either house of the Congress of the Unied States; or the President of the United States, with intent to defame the said government, or either house of the said Congress, or the said President, or to bring them, or either of them, into contempt or

disrepute; or to excite against them, or either or any of them, the hatred of the good people of the United States, or to stir up sedition within the United States, or to excite any unlawful combinations therein, for opposing or resisting any law of the United States, or any act of the President of the United States, done in pursuance of any such law, or of the powers in him vested by the constitution of the United States, or to resist, oppose, or defeat any such law or act, or to aid, encourage or abet any hostile designs of any foreign nation against the United States, their people or government, then such person, being thereof convicted before any court of the United States having jurisdiction thereof, shall be punished by a fine not exceeding two thousand dollars, and by imprisonment not exceeding two years.

The notion that criticism of the government or of public officials could amount to a criminal offense persisted through the 19th and 20th centuries. In fact, provisions to this effect remain on the statute books of many constitutional democracies. It is included, for example, in §134-36, Penal Law, Laws of the State of Israel 5737-1977. In Sweden, the crime of seditious libel was abolished only in 1976.

The most radical rejection of the doctrine of seditious libel, and indeed the most radical affirmation of the libertarian credo, appeared in the opinion of the U.S. Supreme Court in *New York Times* v. *Sullivan* (376 U.S. 254, 1964). A police officer from the state of Alabama sued *The New York Times* for having published an allegedly defamatory advertisement depicting police behavior during the black struggle for civil rights in a false and negative light. The Supreme Court overruled the Alabama court's decision against the newspaper. In a dictum the Court declared the Alien and Sedition Act unconstitutional. It then proceeded to outline the immunity of public criticism of the government from both criminal and civil actions. Page 270 of the decision states:

> We consider this case against the background of a profound national commitment to the principle that debate on public issues should be uninhibited, robust, and wide open, and that it may well include vehement, caustic and sometimes unpleasantly sharp attacks on government and public officials.

Hence, the Court concluded that the newspaper could not be held liable unless the allegedly defamatory statements were made with "actual malice," i.e., with knowledge that the statements were false or with reckless disregard of their truth.

The libertarian theory, springing from the individualism of the Enlightenment, however, does not distinguish between freedom of the press and general freedom of expression. Consequently, journalists as journalists do not enjoy any particular privileges. The right to freedom of expression that they enjoy is neither separate from nor superior to the right of free expression enjoyed by other members of the community. As a result, the libertarian theory is not prepared to concede any social function to the press and would not grant any special privileges to it.

The theory of social responsibility shares the libertarian antipathy toward authoritarianism. It recognizes that governmental monopoly over expression is detrimental to freedom and the good of society. It also recognizes the social importance of the press as an educational and informative medium.

In contrast, however, the theory of social responsibility concludes that the social dimensions of the press justify a special legal status. The issue of the reporter's privilege—the legal recognition that a reporter is immune from the general legal obligation to disclose information—illustrates this. The justifications advanced in defense of the reporter's privilege point to the connection between the public need to know and the special status of the press. The main justification for a reporter's privilege has been the protection of sources in order to provide the public with trustworthy information.

Courts have had difficulties in recognizing even a qualified privilege. Many states in the United States, however, have passed statutes recognizing a qualified privilege for reporter's news, and it is not surprising that the trend has been spreading into other democracies. In Japan, the case of the *Hokkaido Shimbun*, decided by the Sapporo High Court on August 31, 1979 (937 Hanrei Jiho 16) and followed by the Supreme Court decree of March 6, 1980 (956 Hanrei Jiho 32) moved in this direction. For Israel, this was paralleled in Hershkovitz, Reporters' Privilege, 1 Mechkarey Mishpat 251 of 1980. In the United Kingdom, the case of *British Steel Corporation* v. *Granada Television Ltd.*, (3 W.L.R. 774, 1980) is similar to the United States case of *Branzburg* v. *Hayes* (408 U.S. 665, 1972).

The freedom of information acts passed in recent decades in such countries as France, Sweden and the United States also reflect the theory of social responsibility in their recognition of "the public right to know." This right is the foundation of the theory since it provides the missing link between the citizen's need to know and the growing alienation of government bureaucracy in modern society. Although the freedom of information acts do not grant the press a legal status, their recognition that modern society depends on the press for information has hastened the institutionalization of special privileges for journalists.

The other side of the theory of social responsibility is the imposition of legal obligations on journalists. This is hardly surprising. The recognition that journalists perform important social functions, coupled with the realization that the mass media exert political influence even when they possess no special legal status, logically leads to their regulation in a fashion similar to that of other professions such as law and medicine. Indeed, the developing disagreement around the UNESCO proposals to regulate the mass media—supported by the developing countries and the socialist block and opposed by the Western liberal democracies—is a perfect illustration of this particular side of the theory.

We have thus far presented each of the major theories of the press separately, as ideal types. However, the illustrations presented have already made it clear that one theory alone animates any legal system. At most it may be argued that a legal system contains strong elements that strongly reflect one theory, but one could quite easily find contradictory illustrations in that very same system. The legal systems of the United States and Israel are good examples. In the United States, the so-called Pentagon Papers Case clearly constituted a triumph of the libertarian theory. There, in the case of *New York Times Co.* v. *The United States* the Supreme Court refused to enjoin the newspaper from publishing information classified by the government as top secret. Yet, in the case of *The United States* v. *Progressive, Inc.* (467 F. Supp. 990, W.D. Wis.,1979), decided by a lower federal court several years after the Pentagon Papers case, a newspaper was enjoined from publishing an article based on information that had not been previously classified. In this case a rehearing was denied (486 F. Supp. 5, 1979) and the case was dismissed without opinion (610 F. 2d 819, 7th Cir. 1979).

The tension between authoritarian and libertarian press theories was manifest not only in the conflicting results but also in the legal doctrines used by the courts. While the Pentagon Papers court employed various versions of the "clear and present danger" test, the Progressive court adopted the "bad tendency" test—a doctrine closely related to the authoritarian philosophy of the press. Furthermore, in *Morland* v. *Sprecher* (443 U.S. 709, 1979) the United States Supreme Court declined to order expedient review of the Progressive case, in contrast to its treatment of the Pentagon Papers case.

The same type of conflict is apparent in Israel. On the one hand, Israel's legal system is replete with authoritarian statutes that allow the executive vast discretion in censoring, suspending and issuing permits for newspapers. On the other hand, as early as the case of *Kol-Haam* v. *Minister of The Interior* in 1953, Israel's High Court of Justice held that the principle of freedom of expression and freedom of the press is an integral part of Israel's legal system and that the Minister of Interior cannot suspend a newspaper unless it is demonstrated that its content will probably pose a substantial danger to the nation's security.

Such contradictions can be found in every liberal-democratic legal system where all three theories compete in various forms. Each country has its own unique combination, peculiar to its own history, philosophy and political culture. The particular combination, the causes that contributed to its formation and the results in terms of the freedom enjoyed by the particular national press have not yet been adequately researched. Here lies the challenge to scholars of comparative press laws.

Two other related aspects of national press law deserve special attention: positive law's commitment to the principle of free expression and the phenomenon of special statutes for the press. Both present some interesting comparative jurisprudential problems.

One major difference between the various press laws is the constitutional system in which they operate. Some countries such as West Germany, Japan, the United States and Sweden guarantee freedom of the press. These countries also recognize the mechanism of the judicial review of statutory constitutionalism. These countries differ, however, in the quality of their commitment to free expression. One type of commitment is blank and unqualified. For example, Article 21 of the Japanese constitution provides that "Freedom of assembly and association as well as speech, press and all other forms of expression are guaranteed." The First Amendment of the U.S. Constitution provides the same right.

In contrast, West Germany's Basic Law is qualified. It recognizes in advance the legitimacy of laws that would restrict the freedom of the press. Article 5, on freedom of expression, declares that:

(1) Everyone shall have the right freely to express and disseminate his opinion by speech, writing and pictures and freely to inform himself from generally accessible sources. Freedom of the press and freedom of reporting by means of broadcasts and films are guaranteed. There shall be no censorship. (2) These rights are limited by the provisions of the general laws, the provisions of law for the protection of youth, and by the right to inviolability of personal honor.

The extent to which this variable influences press freedom in a particular country and how it relates to theories of press freedom poses another question. In his article "The Jurisprudence of Free Speech in the United States and the Federal Republic of Germany," in volume 53 (1980) of *Southern California Law Review* Kommers demonstrates that the press law of West Germany is stricter than its American counterpart. It would be interesting to try to disentangle the various philosophical, institutional and normative variables that may explain this phenomenon.

However, it is not clear whether constitutional guarantees and judicial review explain the different degrees of press freedom in the democracies. In countries that have neither a written constitution nor judicial review such as England and Israel, freedom of the press is recognized as a principle that guides the courts in interpreting statutes that limit press freedom. An interesting and perhaps crucial variable may thus be the degree of judicial activism practiced in the various legal systems. This issue needs more extensive research before it can be fully understood.

It does seem, however, that the level of judicial activism—the willingness of the court to shape policy through both legal and extralegal means—is related to the degree of freedom extended to the press by any particular legal system. For instance, Rabban's "The First Amendment in its Forgotten Years," vol. 90 (1981) of the *Yale Law Jour-nal*, concludes that despite the presence of the First Amendment in the United States Constitution, and despite the availability of judicial review, an American jurisprudence of free speech did not begin to develop until the 20th Century. It was not until the emergence of an activist judiciary that meaningful doctrines of press protection appeared.

Another interesting topic for comparison is the nature and form of press statutes themselves. Continental European countries such as France, West Germany and Sweden have special press statutes that amount to a comprehensive regulation of the press. Typically, such statutes regulate the enterprise of publication and include measures dealing with registration, proprietory rights of the publisher and accountability of the editor. Historically, some press statutes authorized suspension of newspapers and specified other criminal offences that pertain specifically to the press.

In certain respects, some contemporary press statutes differ. The Swedish and West German press statutes merely regulate some aspects of the press, but are very libertarian in the sense that they contain no provisions designed to suppress freedom. In West Germany, press statutes are part of the law of the states [länder]; there is no federal press law. On the other hand, the French and the Israeli press laws contain classic authoritarian measures including the administrative power to suspend newspapers. Most common law systems such as the British and the American contain no special press statutes.

Several explanations for these differences are available. First, on the European continent the movement toward codification has always been far stronger than in the common law world. The case of Israel is peculiar here since Israel received its press law during British rule over Palestine. While the British did not have a press law at home, they did enact ones in colonies such as Cyprus, India and Palestine. Another explanation for the absence of press statutes in most of the common law systems is an Anglo-American refusal to recognize a difference between the rights of individuals and newspapers to freedom of expression. Thus, in the Anglo-American systems the press is regulated by different statutes directed at individual behavior. No special statute purports to regulate it as such. Yet another difference was the predominant influence of the authoritarian theory during the period when most press laws were enacted in Europe. This neglected interrelationship between authoritarianism, the movement toward codification and the emergence of press laws is worth exploring further.

This brings us back to the three competing philosophies of press law. In the United States, for example, the theory of social responsibility has produced some legislation dealing specifically with the press. One illustration is reporters' privilege statutes. These define the term press and regulate press privilege much like European continental statutes. These "mini-press-statutes" contain both libertarian and nonlibertarian elements. Their content is libertarian since they strengthen press freedom by shielding the newsgathering process for state intervention. They are nonlibertarian in that they distinguish between the journalist and the ordinary citizen. They provide a definition of the press that sets journalists into a privileged class enjoying broader rights to free expression. Paradoxically, the recognition of the important function of the press also leads to demands for state control, as the UNESCO proposal illustrates so well.

In this context, libertarians are caught in a bind. They recognize the social function of the press and sanction some statutory privileges that will attach to it, but they cannot accept licensing or other authoritarian regulatory measures. Contemporary press laws thus function in a dialectic between the contradictory poles of authoritarianism and libertarianism. They may yet yield a synthesis in some form of social responsibility, the contours and content of which is still in the making.

PRESS COUNCILS OF THE WORLD

by Kuldip R. Rampal

Press Councils of the World: An Overview

The development of the press-council concept in many countries sees press freedom intertwined in varying degrees with the emergence of the social responsibility theory of the press in the 20th century. Although a socially responsible press can mean different things to different people, one common requirement throughout these "free press" countries* is that the press, while remaining free, be fair and responsive to its readers. This requirement seems to be a natural consequence of the importance the mass media have acquired in influencing people's lives.

Governmental and private commissions, investigating press performance in various nations, have voiced a need for regulation to guard against abuses not covered by press laws. The American Commission on the Freedom of the Press (1945–47), the Royal Commission on the Press in England (1947–49), the Indian Press Commission (1952–54) and the South African Press Commission (1951–62) provide but a few examples in which voluntary regulation was suggested to correct press abuses. Voluntary regulation was prescribed in light of the fact that governmental intervention in press affairs would violate press-freedom guarantees.

At least 14 "free press" countries have functioning arbitration boards, called press councils, to resolve free-press–fair-press conflicts; they are Austria, Denmark, Finland, West Germany, Israel, South Korea, the Netherlands, New Zealand, Norway, South Africa, Taiwan, Sweden, the United Kingdom and the United States. An examination of their composition and procedures demonstrates how press councils strive to foster a fair and responsible press.

What are Press Councils?

There is no single definition that can be applied to every press council. Generally, however, press councils are created by and for the press; journalists and publishers voluntarily cooperate with them to ensure a proper relationship between the press on the one hand and the State and the society on the other. The councils can be likened to medical or bar associations, which enforce professional ethics, except that press-council decisions are generally non-binding.

The concept of the press council is not new. It began in 1916 when the first Scandinavian press council was established in Sweden to serve as an intermediary between news media and the public. Since then 17 other nations have established press councils, the 27-year-old British Press Council standing out as quite successful. In early 1980 the press councils of Sri Lanka and the Philippines were under state control. The Turkish Press Council, established in 1960, was dissolved in 1968. The Press Council of India, founded in 1965 under the Press Council Act of that year, was abolished in January 1976.

Most of the remaining 14 press councils were established voluntarily by publishers and journalists, or jointly by both. In Great Britain, Israel and South Africa, governmental criticism of the press paved the way for the creation of the councils. The National News Council (NNC) of the United States was established by independent foundations in 1973. As a result, it does not have the status of a media-established press council. The councils of South Korea and Taiwan were established by newspaper organizations to circumvent laws providing for press regulation in these countries.

It can be said that press councils are

---

*Here a "free press" country is defined as any nation where independence and critical ability of the press is guaranteed, except for minimal libel and obscenity laws. The degree of press freedom can vary from country to country, but the definition assumes that there is no outright control of the press by the government.

established more readily in those countries that do not have the legal institution of the right to reply, for which they try to offer a substitute. This is made evident by the fact that the primary objective of every press council is to make the press responsive to the readers' complaints and, where justified, publicize their rebuttals. Faced with access-to-the-press-issues, legal institutions have also suggested a recourse to councils. For example, in *Miami Herald Publishing Co. v. Tornillo*, the U.S. Supreme Court suggested that perhaps the NNC could resolve press fairness issues and accommodate the conflicting interests. It should be added, however, that there are countries—for example Austria and West Germany—which have both the right of reply and press councils, which indicates that such councils have tasks other than simply securing reader access.

Membership

Journalists and publishers constitute the majority membership in most press councils. Exceptions are Denmark and the Netherlands: press members on the Danish Press Council are drawn only from publishers and chief editors (who are often publishers themselves), while the Dutch Press Council, on the other hand, draws its members only from the journalists.

Laymen serve on most of the councils. A press council, it is believed, can command a greater public confidence if it has members who are qualified to speak for the public at large. In fact, the chairman is usually a well-known jurist. Laymen, elected or appointed, usually account for from 20 percent to 33 percent of the total membership. However, again there are exceptions: the Korean council membership is 46 percent laymen, while the majority in the United States and the Netherlands are laymen. The Austrian and German Press Councils consist exclusively of press members.

There is a wide variation in the size of press councils, as the following table shows.

Of significance is that part of a council membership that examines complaints against the press. This body may be either the press council itself or a specialized committee set up by it. Membership of the specialized committees—used by Great Britain, Israel and the United States—are diversified to include both professionals and laymen.

Size of Press Councils	
Country	**Members**
Israel	80
Great Britain	31
West Germany	20
U.S.A.	18
South Africa	18
Finland	13
South Korea	13
Austria	10
Taiwan	9
Norway	7
Sweden	6
Netherlands	5
Denmark	4
New Zealand	4

Independence of members responsible for examining complaints is ensured as, for example, indicated by Article 3 (2) of the rules of procedure of the Austrian Press Council:

In performing their duties, members (and substitute members) of the Austrian Press Council shall be completely free, equal and independent and shall not be bound by any directives from the associations which delegated them or from any other insitutions. They shall act solely according to their consciences and in conformity with the law.

Functions

Among the tasks of press councils are, in general, the preservation of freedom of the press and the maintenance of professional standards. Thus, the press councils are machinery for both self-defense and self-control. This dual function emerges particularly clearly from the rules of procedure of the Austrian Press Council, Article 2:

The Austrian Press Council shall have the following tasks:
(a) protecting the freedom of the press;
(b) ascertaining and seeking to eliminate abuses in journalism, particularly with regard to crime and sex reporting, as well as cases of invasion of privacy for the sole purpose of sensationalism; to that end it shall draw up guidelines and principles or take decisions as provided for [elsewhere in the rules].

The emphasis may be placed on either the self-control or self-defense function, depending on the country. The Scandinavian press councils, for example, are primarily concerned with protecting individual privacy and the rights of persons under trial for criminal offenses. Self-control is also the paramount concern of the Korean, Taiwanese, South African and Dutch press councils.

Other councils have equally important objectives in addition to their self-control function. The German Press Council represents the press to its government and parliament, especially in legislative bills affecting the press. The British and New Zealand councils are asked to deal with complaints about the conduct of persons or organizations towards the press, although most councils take on this task.

Press councils also strive to engage in such activities as ensuring a flow of information; preventing press concentration and monopoly whenever they threaten to stifle diversity of opinion; promoting education and research in journalism; promoting technical improvements; and representing the press at national and international forums.

Purview

With the exception of West Germany, Finland, Taiwan and the United States, all press councils limit their purview to problems affecting newspapers. The West German Press Council also includes magazines. The Finnish and Taiwan Press Councils extend their mandates to radio and television. The National News Council of the United States has limited its scope to national news media, except when it deems local coverage to be of national significance as news or for journalism. It concerns itself with editorial comment only insofar as allegations of fact are in dispute.

Although not always specified in their charters, most press councils also bring within their purview the working methods and activities of journalists. The Dutch Press Council concerns itself with the professional ethics of journalists only, not of publishers, but the Danish council limits itself to publishers', not journalists', professional ethics.

Basis of Press Self-Control

Press councils usually judge complaints against the press on the basis of a national code of conduct for the press, set up by the press rather than by the press council. Denmark, Finland, Norway, South Korea and Sweden use this method. A number of councils, including Austria, Israel, Taiwan and West Germany, have drawn up codes of press ethics on which they base their free-press-fair-press decisions. Others, like Great Britain, New Zealand and the United States, have preferred to proceed by building a record of "case law" and measure the complaints against established precedents. The Dutch Press Council makes reference to the code of the International Federation of Journalists (IFJ) adopted at the Bordeaux Congress in 1954.

Press Codes Not Designed by Press Council.

The Danish, Norwegian and Swedish ethical codes describe at length the publication and professional rules, with emphasis on policy regarding the reporting of trials and police investigations. The Danish code is approved only by the publishers and editors; the journalists do not have a written code of their own yet. A pocket-sized copy of the Swedish code of ethics is given to every journalist taking his first job. Similarly, a summarized copy of the Norwegian code is included on the Norwegian press card, headed: "Journalist, be careful!" The ethical codes of the United Nations and the IFJ, the Finnish Journalists' Rules and the Finnish Broadcasting Company's Rules of Programme Making guide the work of the Finnish Press Council. The South Korean Press Council exists to measure press performance against the country's Press Code of Ethics and the Standard of Conduct for Newspapermen. These codes bear the approval of the country's journalists, editors and publishers.

Press Codes Designed by Press Council.

The Israel Press Council's Code of Professional Ethics is a comprehensive statement of good journalistic practice, with its emphasis on accuracy and responsibility. Similarly, the South African council's Code of Conduct asks all concerned with the press to observe the very highest standards in the performance of the duty of newspapers to inform the public truthfully and to comment fairly. The Austrian and German councils, on the other hand, operated for many years without referring to any single code. It is interesting to note that the Austrian Press Council in 1971 and the German Press Council in 1973 developed codes of ethics from their experience in deciding free-press–fair-press issues. This trend might be followed by other councils that have not formulated their own code of ethics. Already, from various "statements of principles" issued by the National News Council of the United States, a code of ethics for the press appears to be emerging.

Case Method Procedure.

The British Press Council has refused to draft or refer to any code since it was established in 1953, in the belief that no code can cover every complaint. However, while maintaining its flexibility in entertaining free-press–fair-press questions, the council's adjudications in a previous case provide invaluable guidance in deciding cases of a similar kind. Thus, an unwritten code is emerging from the council's adjudications, as its first chairman, Lord Devlin, indicates:

> The Press Council has not, unlike many other professional bodies, drafted a code. It has, whether it realised it or not, adopted the methods of generations of judges who produced the common law of England. They let it grow out of the decisions they gave.

The New Zealand Press Council and the NNC of the United States also do not base their decisions on any recognized code. Following the British practice, both consider each complaint on its own merits and hope to establish a body of professional journalistic standards in the course of pronouncing decisions. Meanwhile the New Zealand council is looking for answers or support from the British council's "case law" in settling its free-press–fair-press complaints.

Investigation of Complaints

The press council usually takes its first step toward considering a problem when someone files a complaint, even if not personally affected by the publication. In general, complaints are against sensationalism, violation of individual privacy, factual mistakes and nonpublication of letters to the editor. Most press councils, including those of Austria, Finland, Germany, Israel, South Korea and the United States, can also initiate complaints against the press. Councils

usually decline to adjudicate on a complaint if it merits judicial inquiry, but when they do decide to consider matters that might become the subject of litigation, they require the complainant to sign a waiver of legal action. In Sweden, however, legal action following an adjudication by the press council is possible.

The press councils of Great Britain, New Zealand and the United States do not hear a dispute until the parties involved have tried to reach reconciliation. The first step of most others, after accepting a complaint, is to bring direct reconciliation between the complainant and the medium involved.

If a direct settlement cannot be reached, a hearing is scheduled. All parties are given adequate notice and a full opportunity to present relevant evidence and to cross-examine witnesses. To preserve the informality and flexibility of their proceedings, press councils do not allow legal representation or apply systems of legal proof. An exception is the NNC of the United States, which allows each party the right to engage counsel.

Generally, initial investigation into complaints is conducted by specialized committees of the press councils. To insure that the council's findings are not used in any court litigation, the hearings are usually held in private. The American NNC holds its hearings in public. Generally, the specialized committees limit their investigations to evidence furnished by the parties involved.

The findings and recommendations of the specialized committee are sent to the press council, which can make a decision based on the committee's recommendation, or proceed toward an independent adjudication on the basis of its own investigation.

The Executive Committee of the Israel Press Council and the Complaints Committee of the German Press Council have been delegated the authority to decide complaints in the name of their councils. However, if any member of the German Complaints Committee objects to its decision, the case is sent to the press council for adjudication. In Sweden, the Press Ombudsman independently investigates complaints and has the authority to refer the unsettled cases to the press council.

The press council renders a decision by a written opinion, which includes a statement of facts, a ruling for one of the parties, and a discussion of the considerations on which the ruling is based. Most councils require a simple majority of the votes cast to reach a decision. However, the German council requires a majority of two-thirds and the Austrian council three-fourths. Both parties in a complaint and all members of the news media within the council's purview are notified of the decision and are requested to publicize it.

The annual number of complaints examined by the press councils varies from one country to another. Most hear fewer than 100, although the U.S. and German councils examine about 150. Only the British and Swedish councils hover around the 400 mark. However, less than one-third of the complaints examined result in a decision in Britain, Germany, Sweden and the United States.

Sanctions

Reproof or censure of a news medium or journalist held to be at fault is the only sanction of a majority of the press councils. In addition, the particular medium involved and the country's press in general are expected to publicize the council's decision. It is from this publicity that the press council derives its real power.

The councils of Germany and Finland also expect the medium involved to redress its wrongs. The Israeli council goes a step further by asking a public apology and retraction from the newspaper at fault, and usually getting it. The Korean council, in addition to censuring a guilty publication, news agency or journalist, can also impose exclusion of a journalist from the profession when the press codes are seriously violated. The councils of Sweden and South Africa can impose fines for violating ethical codes. Since 1969 the Swedish Press Council has the power to impose fines, starting at 1,000 Swedish kronor (about $230) on a newspaper, on an ascending scale determined by the number of complaints upheld against it in any one year. However, a person cannot collect damages through the Press Council. In early 1975 the South African Press Council's 13-year-old Code of Conduct was backed up with strong punitive measures by the Newspaper Press Union, the organization of newspaper publishers. Now the council reprimand any proprietor, editor or journalist found guilty of an infringement of the code. In addition it can impose a maximum fine of 10,000 rand (about $14,000) on the proprietor of a publication in which the transgression of the code has occurred. The findings and verdict of the

Press Council are expected to be given wide publicity. The council can also cause a correction to be published where necessary, but its decisions can be appealed to the country's courts.

The National News Council of the United States does not admonish or censure the news organization against which a complaint has been upheld. In pronouncing its decision, the council simply states that the complaint was warranted or unwarranted. There is no requirement for the press to publish adverse rulings of the council. However, the NNC hopes that its moral force would encourage the news medium at fault to publicize its findings.

Are Press Councils Necessary?

A review of the press councils' experience points to various advantages and disadvantages of a typical council, that is, the council created voluntarily by the press. The good points, as the following discussion shows, seem to outweigh the bad, suggesting that a press council might prove to be useful for a press lacking credibility with the government and the public.

Among the advantages are:

1. The press council provides an efficient recourse for a reader who previously could take his free-press–fair-press grievance only to the courts. A letter to the press council activates its grievance-hearing mechanism and relief can be obtained without involving lengthy, costly and often ineffective legal proceedings.

2. The press council provides an independent forum for discussion of media responsibility and performance, so that a government agency will not be needed to conduct such debate. A number of press councils—for example, in Great Britain, Germany, Israel, the Netherlands and South Korea—demonstrate that this forum can be provided quite successfully.

3. A respected press council with members of stature can protect the interests of the press as few other groups can. The British Press Council, for one, has been active in seeking the reform of the law of libel, and clarification of the legal situation with regard to "confidential information." The German council is consulted by the government in drafting any bills affecting the press. The council has succeeded in securing a shield law for the press.

4. Appraisal of the press's conduct by an independent and detached press council will tend to increase its credibility. The reader is likely to have a greater belief in newspapers' accuracy and fairness if printed or pictorial matter is subject to censure by the press council in case found untrue or unfair.

5. By enforcing a self-promulgated or a media-promulgated code of ethics, the press council brings journalism closer to true "professionalism." The press council expects those within its purview to live up to certain stated standards. Thus, this accountability to the professional organization may raise the status of the journalist.

6. The press council provides the editor with guidelines within which he and competing editors must try to operate. Thus, the council cuts down on excessive competition without necessarily hurting the editor's enthusiasm for "exclusives."

7. Formulation of journalistic standards by the press councils at national levels might be helpful in codifying rules for press behavior at an international level. An international code of ethics can be particularly useful in combating propaganda, racism and national stereotypes. At the same time, it might aid the free flow of information in this era of satellite broadcasting.

Among the disadvantages are:

1. By becoming a leveling-down instrument, the press council might constitute a risk to popular and underground newspapers, which are often the refuge of the press's more audacious expressions of freedom. An institutionalized yardstick for press operations is naturally going to have a sharper definition of "responsible" and "irresponsible" journalism.

2. The press council has the potential of turning into a machinery for self-censorship, as shown by the experience of the South African Press Council, which has recently acquired severe penal provisions.

3. Faced with institutionalized dictates and standards, the editors and journalists will be careful to conform. No editor or journalist likes to see himself publicly censured by a press council. Consequently, an unsubstantiated story, although newsworthy, might not make the next day's headlines.

4. There is lack of due process since, generally, there is no appeal against the adjudication of the press council. With the exception of Sweden and South Africa, an appeal, when it is accepted, must be considered by the same body that heard the case in the first instance. Lack of due process becomes more prominent when the press council can initiate a complaint against the press, thus taking on the role of investigator, prosecutor and judge.

A Comparison of National Press Councils Around the World*

Country	Sponsoring organizations	Functions	Purview	Basis of procedure	Sanctions	Source of funding	Success
Austria	Newspaper journalists & publishers	Adjudicates complaints & defends press freedom	Newspapers & periodicals	Press Council's code of ethics	Publicity	Member press organizations	Considered effective
Denmark	Newspaper chief editors & publishers	Adjudicates complaints	Newspapers	Press code of ethics	Publicity	Member press organization	Considered weak
Finland	Newspaper journalists & publishers; Broadcast journalists; the Finnish Broadcasting Corporation	Adjudicates complaints & defends press freedom	Newspapers, periodicals, radio & TV	Press code of ethics	Publicity	Member press organizations. Some government funds	Considered effective
West Germany	Newspaper journalists and publishers, Magazine publishers	Adjudicates complaints & defends press freedom, prevents press monopoly	Newspapers & periodicals	Press Council's code of ethics	Publicity, corrections expected	Member press organizations	Considered effective
Israel	Newspaper journalists & publishers	Adjudicates complaints, defends press freedom, other	Newspapers	Press Council's code of ethics	Publicity, retraction expected	Member press organizations	Considered effective
South Korea	Newspaper journalists & publishers, news agencies	Implements professional codes	Newspapers & news agencies	Press codes of ethics	Reprimand, publicity	Member press organizations	Considered effective
Netherlands	Newspaper journalists	Adjudicates complaints	Newspaper journalists	Makes reference to the code of the IFJ	Publicity	Member press organization	Considered effective
New Zealand	Newspaper journalists & publishers	Adjudicates complaints, defends press freedom, other	Newspapers	"case law"	Publicity	Member press organization	Considered effective
Norway	Newspaper journalists & publishers	Adjudicates complaints	Daily & periodical press	Press code of ethics	Publicity	Member press organizations	Considered effective

*Based on Press Councils of the World: Role and Experience, doctoral dissertation by author, University of Missouri at Columbia, 1976.

A Comparison of National Press Councils Around the World*

Country	Sponsoring organizations	Functions	Purview	Basis of procedure	Sanctions	Source of funding	Success
South Africa	Newspaper journalists & publishers	Adjudicates complaints & defends press freedom	Newspapers & periodicals	Press code of conduct	Reprimand, fine, correction & publicity	Member publishers' association	Considers itself effective but government dissatisfied with the Council
Sweden	Newspaper journalists & publishers	Adjudicates complaints	Newspapers	Press code of ethics	Fine, publicity	Member press organizations & fines	Considered effective
Taiwan	Newspaper journalists & publishers, broadcasters & news agencies of Taipei	Adjudicates complaints, research in self-regulation	Newspapers, news agencies & broadcast stations of Taipei	Press code of ethics, will enforce its own ethical codes	Correction, publicity	Member media organizations	Considered weak
United Kingdom	Newspaper journalists & publishers of Britain & Scotland, periodical publishers	Adjudicates complaints defends press freedom, other	Newspapers	"case law"	Publicity	Member press organizations	Considered effective
United States	Private philanthropic foundations	Adjudicates complaints, defends press freedom	National news media	"case law"	Publicity	Philanthropic foundations; some funding from the media	Considered weak

*Based on *Press Councils of the World: Role and Experience*, doctoral dissertation by author, University of Missouri at Columbia, 1976.

THE WORLD'S ELITE NEWSPAPERS

by John C. Merrill

Criticism of the press abounds throughout the world today, pointing out low professional standards, trivial subject matter, sensationalized treatment, news gaps and stereotypes and all kinds of "irresponsible" journalistic activities. There are, indeed, rather bleak and disheartening aspects of the world's press today in spite of the significant quantitative growth of the modern mass media, which is defined in great detail in this press encyclopedia. Mediocre and sensational international journalism threaten to extinguish reasoned discourse and thoughtful interaction in most parts of the world.

The General Press Context

Gossipy journalism abounds. Stories about celebrities and their private lives share inordinate space and time in the mass media. Sordid details of criminal activities are presented *ad nauseam* in the world's press. And there are, as critics from developing nations enjoy telling us, notable gaps in the general coverage of the world's news. Flippant and unsavory aspects of the news—especially in the nonaligned world—are played up while the continuing positive developmental news is ignored or soft-pedaled. Coups, earthquakes, hurricanes, assassinations, sports events, activities of celebrities, criminals, eccentrics and other atypical persons tend to get excessive coverage.

A very small portion of the newspaper journalism of the world concerns the intricacies of politics, international relations, economics, education, the sciences, literature, the arts and religion. Very little foreign news is carried in most papers. In short, so the litany of criticism goes, the world's press virtually ignores the sensitive, progressive, cultural and developmental news and views, and instead plays up the "downbeat" and destructive aspects of the world around us.

The person who spends much time viewing the world press finds it hard to deny the general validity of such criticism. The world's press is basically an unsynthesized hodgepodge of blood and gore, overstatement, sex and sexual innuendo, lurid pictures, gaudy headlines (often now in color), superficial stories vying with each other for attention and increasing deserts of advertising stretching through the pages with little relief.

The vast majority of the world's newspapers are entertainment/play-oriented and cater in varying degrees to the superficial whims of mass audiences. Although this press orientation is (or may be) psychologically refreshing to the readers who would like to escape the efforts of thinking and concern, it provides little hope for those millions scattered about the globe who want and need more from their newspapers. It is sad—at least to many of us—that so many newspapers fill their columns with shallow, often inconsequential and incoherent stories when world conditions call for a more thoughtful world citizenry and more responsible journalism. Even if news is regarded as simply a playful exercise at which the multitudes enjoy themselves, we cannot escape the fact that the real events behind the verbal images are often of vital significance and need to be confronted and dealt with realistically and intelligently.

A steady diet of sensation may satiate the mass appetite for vicarious and effortless "adventure," but it does little to create a body of common knowledge or well-informed people. The great network of newspapers spread across the globe is not significantly concerned with serious thought or with thoughtful readers; it is primarily a popular press, calling the people of the world to play and feast on froth. It does not call on them to think, to assess, to become concerned, involved or empathic. Such "supermarket" journalism shows no discernment in selection, in assessment of editorial matter, in meaning or interpretation. It is vulgar in the truest sense of the word—speaking to masses of semiliterates who feel they need to read something called a "newspaper" but who have no desire to understand the vital issues of the day, and even less desire to concern themselves with these issues. Moreover, far too many "thoughtful" newspapers are mainly inane instruments of national propaganda, seeking to create barriers to understanding by presenting unreal and alarmist news without interpretation, without context and often with no follow-up. Instead of conveying enlightenment, the press systems in many countries tend too often to be press agents for individual nations or special groups. A serious observer must acknowledge that, taken as a whole, the world's press is doing little to supplant ignorance with knowledge, bewilderment with understanding, irrationalism with reason, provincialism with cosmopolitanism, social friction with peace and harmony, and a loss of faith with constructive ideals and ideas.

The Elite Minority

In the midst of this vast desert of global mediocrity, there is a remnant of hope—a handful of newspapers that seek quality, erudition, reasoned analysis and reliable news. Their number is not large, their overall impact probably not very great, and their share of the world's readers is miniscule. Yet their philosophy is important, their standards are high, their staffs are dedicated and thoughtful, and their influence is far greater than their circulation would indicate.

These are "elite"—or "quality," or "class" —newspapers, whose standards of editorial practice are conditioned more by intellectual orientation and idealistic vision than by a desire for mammoth circulation or impressive profits. Serious in tone and lacking in the flippancy so common in modern journalism, they are the optimistic papers of the world. They invite the reader to consider ideas critically, to dissect issues, to try to solve problems. They are basically optimistic: if they were not they would not take serious things so seriously. Nor would they have so much respect for their readers. These few notable newspapers, found mainly in some 15 to 20 of the world's nations, often struggling against great odds, comprise the cream of the international press.

What characterizes the elite press? They are concerned, knowledgeable and serious, the papers that thoughtful people and opinion leaders in all countries read seriously, the papers found in every good library the world over. Such papers appeal to reason and logic, not to prejudices and emotion. They are relatives of one another, regardless of place of publication or language. They have the same concerns no matter what their circulations may be or what their ideological or political contexts. All strive, wherever they may be, for a dignified world community of thoughtfulness and cooperation, of sensitivity and humanity. Like individuals, they may not always live up to their ideals, but they always have that basic *concern* for quality, enlightenment, credibility and wisdom.

While it is true to a degree that "the press rightly holds up a mirror to society," as a noted British journalist has remarked, a quality or elite paper must do more. It must judge events and not simply report them, have definite opinions and express them courageously. The elite paper, even if it believed it could do so, would not be satisfied merely to "reflect" society; its mission is far greater than that. It sees itself as a leader, an interpreter, a pioneer into the frontiers of human and international relations. More than attempting simply to reflect society in all of its imperfections, the elite newspaper hopes to present such news and views to reform society, or at least portions of it. The aim of the elite press, then, is directing in a reasonable way, instead of reflecting in a fragmented and distorted way.

The elite papers continually sort and coordinate the endless stream of news reports, attempting to arrange them so as to give meaning to the news, for these papers realize that news items out of context are only confusing to the reader. As the editors of Switzerland's first-rate *Neue Zürcher Zeitung* have put it, a newspaper should offer "a picture of events, not a blurred mosaic, and to the extent that a newspaper is able to make events clearer and easier to understand, to that extent does it fulfill its mission." *The New York Times'* James Reston echoes this important point when he says that "the news we have to report and explain these days...is more intricate and many-sided." He continues, "It does not fit easily into the short news story with the punch lead. It often defies accurate definition in very short space. Very often it rebels against our passion for what is bright and brief."

Looking a little further at the elite press, still rather generally, we will note that this small group of dailies (and some few weeklies) will not appeal to the typical reader looking over a wide assortment of journals at a newsstand. First of all, the makeup or physical appearance of these elite papers will not attract him. For example, the *Neue Zürcher Zeitung,* without a doubt one of the two or three best papers in the world, has a rather dull, ultraserious tone to its page makeup. Headlines are small, pictures are few, and there are no comics, no entertainment (or very little), no crossword puzzles, no women's page. Another top-ranking elite daily, *Le Monde* of Paris, also is in staid typographical dress and is "top-heavy with analytical writing at the expense of the 'All-we-want-is-the-facts-Ma'am' school."

Not all elite papers are as typographically and editorially conservative in tone as these two tabloids of Switzerland and France; the few quality dailies of Scandinavia (*Berlingske Tidende* of Copenhagen, for instance) are much more sprightly, both in dress and in editorial character. It can definitely be said, however, that there is little in any of the elite papers of the general levity, splash, crackle and pop that characterizes the general press of the world. The elite press actually attempts to do what the Commission on Freedom of the Press said the press should do for society in its 1947 report—"to present a truthful, comprehensive, and intelligent account of the day's events in a context which gives them meaning." With intelligent realism, editors of the elite papers realize, however, that the most difficult standard to meet is that of "comprehensiveness." The realities of publishing—time, space, money, staff—predicate against comprehensive coverage by any one newspaper, even the massive *New York Times.* But the elite paper, through intelligent editing, tries to compensate for this intrinsic shortcoming.

Many readers will smile condescendingly at this idealistic and optimistic thesis, and will argue that the small core of thoughtful and intellectual figures and journals through the years has done little or nothing to raise the hopes and exalt the reason of the masses. These critics would be hard put to prove that these isolated figures and journals have not propelled the world toward reason, but we will grant the general validity of their objection.

However, it should be stressed at this point that prior to this century the serious voices speaking to mass audiences were virtually nonexistent. Isolated intellectual spoke to

isolated intellectual usually in an intranational or intracultural context. No truly international newspapers were to be found, and when excellent ones did exist within countries, there was slight chance of their being read abroad except in a few academic centers.

Today, on the other hand, a larger slice of the world's population is literate, even well educated. And of this educated group more and more persons are able to read foreign languages or have access to serious journals —like *World Press Review* (formerly *Atlas*) of the United States—which give them a rich diet of informed world news and views in translation. In addition, each year more general magazines and newspapers quote in part or in whole from foreign journals. In other words, serious journalism is crossing national borders in an ever-increasing flow and more and more people are being exposed to it directly, through translation or through opinion leaders in their respective countries. One elite paper quotes another, and a "quality journalism" spreads across nations and across languages and develops a common denominator, not of popular *event/reportorial* journalism, but of *idea/interpretation* journalism that is a catalyst to world reason.

This cooperation of the press of the world in an effort to achieve understanding and international stability should not be simply idealistic theorizing; it should be expected of more and more newspapers as literacy increases and education expands, and as editors and publishers see the good that quality journalism can do. Clarence K. Streit, an American journalist with an outstanding career, has asked if it is too much to expect the press to help in giving publicity to "reasonable men" who are trying to avoid "the twin dangers of war and endless tension... by appeal to sober common sense." From the elite newspapers of the world would come a resounding "No, it is not too much to expect!"

The Elite Press: Types

In every major country one newspaper, and often two or three, will stand out as a journal of elite opinion, catering to the intelligentsia and the opinion leaders, however variously defined. Well informed on government matters, they achieve a reputation for reliability, for expert knowledge, and even for presenting the most accurate image of governmental thinking. Although their circulations are seldom larger than 300,000, their influence is tremendous, for they are read regularly by public officials, scholars, journalists, theologians, lawyers, judges and business leaders. And what is more, they are read in other countries by those persons whose business it is to keep up with world affairs. Even papers like *Pravda* and *Izvestia* are read seriously by persons in the free world who consider these journals as accurately reflecting official viewpoints of the Soviet Union. And, no doubt, Soviet officials, regardless of their feelings about Western journalistic bias and capitalistic exploitation of the press, peruse *The New York Times* and the London *Times* regularly for their picture of the United States and Britain.

As is true with so many really important institutions and concepts, the elite press is difficult to define. Its nature is rather tenuous, ephemeral, temporary and, most of all, relative. Part of it speaks coldly, with detached scientific precision; another part involves itself with the reader in a warm and personal manner. While one part snarls, another purrs. One part, trying for quantity as well as quality, submerges the reader in a flood of facts; another carefully sifts through the news and thoughtfully offers the reader a coherent and rich diet of significance. But regardless of the differences among the elite newspapers, they are all serious, concerned, intelligent and articulate.

It is quite obvious that there are types or natures of quality and of prestige among the world's papers, and these distinctions make categorizing and defining extremely difficult. Some papers, quite qualitative in one sense, are so vastly different from other papers (also qualitative)) that it is difficult to talk of them in the same context, or to judge them against the same set of criteria. First of all, elite papers fall into the two main types or contexts already mentioned: (1) libertarian, or those published in a free or open society, and (2) authoritarian, or those published in a restricted or closed society. Certainly it is unwise, or at least disconcerting, to try to compare meaningfully the elite paper of Context 1 with the elite paper of Context 2.

Then, in each of these two basic contexts there are other "sub-contexts" into which elite papers might fall, and one paper can be found in more than one context at one time: (3) daily, (4) weekly, (5) specialized, and (6) general. Of course, there are other contexts, for example a semiweekly in a quasi-authori-

tarian country; but these six contexts are quite useful in talking about elite newspapers.

Two elite daily papers, moreover, may be of very distinct natures, perhaps with Contexts 5 and 6 different, or perhaps, 1 and 2. For example, the daily *The Wall Street Journal* and the daily Baltimore *Sun* little resemble one another because one is a specialized, and the other is a general, journal. Nor would the *Berlingske Tidende* of Denmark (published for the serious general reader in an open society) be of the same nature as the very prestigious *Komsomolskaya Pravda* of Russia (published for the Young Communists in a closed society). Wilbur Schramm of Stanford University has even pointed out that great differences exist among free-society elite papers and gives the examples of (1) the "analytical" types such as *Le Monde* and the *Frankfurter Allgemeine,* and (2) the "news-oriented" types such as *The New York Times.*

In comparing elite papers it is obviously advantageous (really indispensable) to use the context method. Correlation of several contexts places newspapers of relative similitude before us. For example, if we are considering general daily papers of a conservative leaning we must include in the list *Svenska Dagbladet* of Stockholm, the *Chicago Tribune, The Times* of London, *The Scotsman* of Edinburgh, the *Corriere della Sera* of Milan, and the *Frankfurter Allgemeine* of Frankfurt am Main. Their free-world counterparts among the liberal dailies would include *The Guardian* of Manchester and London, *Dagens Nyheter* of Stockholm, the *Post-Dispatch* of St. Louis, *Le Monde* of Paris, *Neue Zürcher Zeitung* of Zurich, and *Süddeutsche Zeitung* of Munich.

A list of general-discussion weekly elite papers would include *Die Zeit* of Hamburg, *Weltwoche* of Zurich, *Sunday Times* of London, and *France Observateur* of Paris.

Of course, in order to compare the great variety of quality newspapers intelligently, one must have at hand certain basic data about these publications. In addition, one must read the papers with some regularity or keep up with appraisals of them presented by knowledgeable press observers.

The word "prestige" is likely to be used synonymously with "quality" when referring to an admired newspaper, and there is perhaps no reason to quibble with this. However, it might be helpful to make a distinction between a quality and a prestige paper for the sake of discussion. A very simple distinction might be this:

Quality: a good, influential, *free* newspaper
Prestige: a good, influential, *restricted* newspaper

Prestige papers, in the above sense, would include official government organs such as *Pravda* in the USSR or *El Nacional* in Mexico, or perhaps *Osservatore Romano* of Vatican City. These are good papers, to be sure, but they are "kept" organs operating in the strict confines of some official policy. They are influential, but their appeal to the intellectual elite is a narrow, specialized, ideological appeal. Their basic nature is quite different from that of a free elite journal (or quality paper) such as Switzerland's *Neue Zürcher Zeitung,* Sweden's *Dagens Nyheter,* or West Germany's *Die Welt.* It seems that some confusion could be removed if one would talk of the free elite as the quality paper and the authoritarian elite as the prestige paper.

The free-press elite newspapers, contrary to the "official" or managed prestige papers of the more regimented societies, are papers that strive to open minds and stimulate discussion and intelligent reflection. Whether they are called "conservative" or "liberal" in their own societies is of no consequence. These labels have little or nothing to do with quality journalism or with the elite press; they are simply tags, having some vague meaning within their societal fabric but little or none elsewhere. The quality of the liberal *Guardian* is no better than the quality of the conservative *Times,* and both the conservative *Frankfurter Allgemeine* and the more liberal *Süddeutsche Zeitung* of West Germany are quality dailies. Many persons in the United States equate all quality papers and all intellectuals with liberalism. This is unfortunate and quite erroneous and simply shows an illiberalism of thought; it is unheard of in Europe, where liberalism is more along classic lines, closely connected with the open mind and the progressive spirit and a sense of tolerance—not with one's purported position on a left-right continuum.

Without a doubt, the ideological position that a press critic sees himself as taking affects his evaluation of a particular newspaper. This is a quite human tendency, although it evidences considerable lack of sophistication. Liberals should read quality newspapers of all ideological persuasions if they are to be truly liberal, and conservatives should do the same thing if they are to be truly conservative. With persons, as with newspapers, the tag that one carries should

have little or nothing to do with his quality or with the sincerity with which he seeks the truth.

Dr. Robert Desmond, formerly of the University of California, has pointed out that newspapers can be no better than the persons who read them. It is unfortunate, he says, that "if a newspaper honestly supports, editorially, either a liberal or a conservative outlook, those holding the contrary view abuse it unmercifully, and rarely even credit it with sincerity." Perhaps Dr. Desmond has exaggerated the seriousness of this problem, for if what he says is true, the effectiveness of the quality press is limited by the closed minds of serious readers who are unwilling to break through the curtain of labels and seek enlightenment from all sources.

If one characteristic of an enlightened quality newspaper is its seeking the truth wherever it may be found, it is not unreasonable to expect the same of an enlightened intellectual. The quality papers fight mental and emotional rigidity; they try to break down prejudices and to open minds. This is why they are great.

"Free Elite": Traits

Although the effort has just been made to explain the distinctions among the various types of press "elite," it should be said that this writer is primarily concerned with the elite of the libertarian nations—the "free" elite—which, as has been pointed out, may be distinguished rather easily from the elite of the authoritarian nations by considering their political and social setting. These free elite will be referred to as "quality" (rather than "prestige") papers. However, most writers do not make such a distinction, and it is quite common to find the leading serious papers of the world (regardless of where they are) referred to by an assortment of terms used interchangeably.

The British call these papers quality or class papers, distinguishing them from popular or mass papers. The French often refer to them as *journaux de prestige,* while Germans frequently allude to them as *Weltblätter,* stressing their international reputation. In the United States there seems to be no standard name—serious, quality, and prestige being adjectives usually applied to them. Here and there they are also referred to as great, intellectual, international, and elite.

Quite obviously these terms can reasonably be used synonymously to talk about this type of newspaper, but it would seem useful to differentiate, at least, among those of a free and of an authoritarian society. This is the reason an elite paper in Paraguay or in the Soviet Union is called a prestige paper, while one in a country like Britain, Japan or the United States is referred to as a quality paper. Both types can be considered as part of the elite press although they are certainly of distinct natures.

Even though the prestige papers of the closed society are quite different from the quality papers of the open society, they would still appear to have a considerable amount of reasonableness and national and international concern; for this reason a paper like *Pravda,* appealing to opinion leaders with a serious turn of mind, can be accommodated under the label "elite" as well as can a paper like *The Times* of London. Many persons will, if they are of the Western world, disagree with this premise, saying that *Pravda* and its ilk, because of their doctrinaire orientation and attachment to one party, cannot contribute to reason. From a nonauthoritarian perspective, this is quite true, but a communist might just as well say that since the Western capitalistic newspaper is tied to the vested interests of "big business," it is not really free and cannot present news and views without considerable bias, subjectivity, prejudice and selfish motivation.

Both viewpoints are to some degree valid and invalid. At any rate, there is no cause for rejecting the premise that within the sober, influential press of any political system there is a certain respect and concern with seriousness, humanity, and social progress. Of course, the emphasis here is on the free elite press, since the writer is convinced that these papers are the ones which offer the greatest hope for personal, national and international discourse and liberalizing "mind-opening." Nevertheless, however superior we may think the libertarian elite to be, this seems little justification for dismissing the entire government-controlled press of the world as no more than propaganda and unreasonable journalism.

While we are concerned with the free elite newspaper, we recognize the importance, leadership, seriousness and considerable reasonableness of the authoritarian elite. The purpose here is to highlight the free elite and to discuss the characteristics or criteria by which it is judged. Marks of the authoritarian elite, touched on lightly in the preceding section, will receive little further attention.

Therefore, let us proceed with a discussion of the free elite of the world and attempt to determine the characteristics that define them. These papers will generally be referred to as quality papers except where they are given some alternate name by other writers.

Even though it is obvious that quality newspapers have many natures, there is a certain character they all have in common. The overall tone and style, plus the interest and emphasis that the quality papers share with one another, make them a recognizable segment of the total press system.

If a reader looks through several copies of a few of the quality papers, he will find an obvious emphasis on idea-oriented news— stories that bear a significance beyond the straight facts (or bits of information) which they carry. They are articles that present the news "as a piece," relating the varying stories in a subtle (not always immediately recognizable) fashion. The economic stories relate to the political, the political to the cultural and social, and so on. Even the so-called human interest item (when it appears) puts the spotlight briefly on an important social (in a broad sense) point of contention, and taken together with the edition's total editorial focus, helps set the tone of the national and international events.

A quality paper's popularity is not built on voyeurism, sensationalism or prurience. It offers its readers facts (in a meaningful context), ideas, interpretation; in short, it presents a continuing education. It gives its reader the feeling that he is getting a synthesized look at the most significant happenings and thinking of the day. The reader of the quality paper, unlike the reader of many of the popular and general "middle-area" papers, does not feel like a news-scrap collector; rather he has at hand carefully selected and written stories that mean something, that present background and point out trends, that give insights into personalities who run the world or who might step into such positions tomorrow.

The respected publisher of Buenos Aires' *La Prensa,* Dr. Gainza Paz, in a speech in New York in 1965, had the following comments to make about a quality paper's relation to its readers:

We know the responsibility of all good editors: to stimulate reader interest in the progress and development of their country. We also know that we ought to find ways of awakening that interest, despite the fact that sometimes uninformed readers appear to be indifferent.

We also know that newspapers should interpret the news without bias, and without fear of giving conflicting viewpoints. And most importantly...a paper should express its own view clearly and without concern for the consequences.

But even beyond its duty to inform, beyond its editorial policy, no matter how courageous that may be, the true journalist must somehow create a bond of confidence between the readers and the newspaper. Only then can he expect to have their support in defense of a press freedom that guarantees the people's right to know.

Although the quality paper reflects a serious and intellectual orientation, its editors and chief writers seek a minimum of specialized jargon and strive always for clarity of expression. The editors, however, realize (unlike their counterparts on many mass papers) that technical, specialized and scientific words are often better than lay terms, and that if they are to educate, they must use these more difficult (but more precise) expressions.

The late French writer and journalist, Albert Camus, perhaps has provided as clear a view of the philosophy of quality journalism as has been given. With several others he founded in Paris the newspaper *Combat* in 1944, and made it in many ways the prototype of what he meant by an elite or quality journal. He attacked most newspapers as being too popularized, commercial, insincere, unconcerned, and careless with the truth. The press generally, he believed, was seeking to please rather than to enlighten.

Camus defined a good journalist in this way: "One who, first of all, is supposed to have ideas. Next, his task is to inform the public on events which have just taken place. He is a sort of day-to-day historian whose prime concern is the truth." He elaborated on this, however, by saying that the "first news" is not always the best news and that "it is better to come in second and report the truth than to be first and false." He reprimanded the popular papers for their gaudy makeup and sensational content, saying that they were overly concerned with colorful details and eye-catching layout. Taking issue with those who said that this is the kind of journalism the public wants, he said: "No, this is what the public has been taught to want over a period of twenty years, which

isn't at all the same thing.... But if a score of newspapers spew forth the same mediocrity and distortion every day, the public will breathe in this poisoned air and be unable to get along without it."

Camus recommended that serious and responsible newspapers make some sacrifices in profits and in readership in order to provide daily reflection and the scrupulous reporting necessary to keep high-level journalistic standards. What he advocated, he illustrated in *Combat*—makeup and content which were serious but not academic, dignified but lively. Virtue, to Camus, was by no means boring, and he demanded conciseness of expression, a feeling for form, a nonrigidity in style, incisive interpretation, and a piercing wit. He had several little catchwords to illustrate his journalistic principles. To define an editorial, he would say, "One idea, two examples, three pages," and to report a news item, "Facts, local color, juxtapositions."

In 1955, long after the *Combat* period, Camus renewed his ties with journalism by writing regularly for the weekly serious paper of Paris, *L'Express* (now a magazine). What Camus left behind him for the world of quality journalism is a legacy of values which, in a way, might serve to guide the free elite papers of the world. Jean Daniel, writing about Camus in 1964, noted that his main contribution was critical reporting, which Daniel defined in this way: "A passionately dedicated effort to eliminate passion from reporting; in other words, complete candor as to the limitations of the observer in his understanding of the phenomenon observed. It is an attitude of respect toward those to whom one is responsible for communicating the journalistic fact, once that fact has been defined."

One of the chief concerns of the free elite—and Camus would have considered it so—is the editorial page or section. Editorials, essays, cartoons, columns, and letters to the editor are not bland "stay-out-of-trouble" types; rather, they are strong, vital, outspoken, knowledgeable, thoughtful, and thought-provoking. They are often critical of government, regardless of what government or party is in power. The free elite takes very seriously its place as critic of government and of excesses in other institutions of society. It also offers what Roy E. Larsen has called "a platform for debate, a forum for the expression of people's viewpoints and ideas."

Elite newspapers, of all the many types,

seem most concerned about the future, about the implications of current events in days to come. They are insightful and predictive because of their concern and knowledge. Andrew Sharf, in a book written in 1964 analyzing the behavior of the British press during the rise of Hitler, repeatedly praised the three quality papers—*The Times, The Guardian,* and *The Daily Telegraph*—for their general coverage of the news from Germany during the 1930s. Although he singled out *The Guardian* as the most astute and the only one that consistently saw clearly what was happening in Germany, and pointed to the direct connection between anti-Semitism and the Nazis' other policies, Sharf noted that the accuracy and completeness of German coverage was outstanding in all three papers.

In one sense, the elite press serves as the true conscience of a nation, and even, to a large degree, as the conscience of the world. Even many papers which are not very well known internationally like to consider themselves part of their national conscience. Undoubtedly key staff members, especially policy-making editors (such as John W. Dafoe of the *Winnipeg Free Press* in Canada, 1901–44) largely forge the quality of a paper and see to it that there is a continuity of editorial policy.

What exactly is meant by "editorial policy"? Although it is broad and complex, there are certain things that can be said about it which might be helpful to an understanding of it. It has to do with consistency in outlook and in publishing practices; it is the course a newspaper chooses to follow as it answers the two all-important questions: What shall we print? How shall we print it? Editorial policy is composed of the practices, rules, and principles which the paper sets as a guide and standard for itself. As such, it really governs every aspect of the newspaper from the type of staff sought, the kind of news dealt with, the ideological orientation embraced and even the size of type used in printing.

Seldom are the most important elements of a paper's editorial policy expressed in writing; they are simply understood. The staff member (as does the reader) comes to know through experience the editorial policy of the paper. Usually the policy of a paper is established when the paper is founded; there is a certain permanence and stability about it, although it would be wrong to think that it does not change over the years. So far as a quality paper is concerned, an inflexible editorial policy is no sign of excellence. (Even the traditional *Times* of London cleared its front page of advertising for news in the spring of 1966.)

In countries which have several or many national dailies, one would expect to find a larger quality press—at least in the sense of dealing largely with national and international topics. In Britain, for example, the national serious dailies have almost completely taken over the job of informing the public on major topics, leaving most of the provincial press with the responsibility of dealing with provincial matters. In the United States, on the other hand, where there is really no national press, every paper (with the exception of many grass-roots weeklies) feels it must be something to everybody. Consequently, most general American dailies are unfocused, undisciplined in basic journalistic philosophy, offering up all types of disorganized bits and snippets of entertainment, comics, puzzles, fiction, columns, sensational or conflict-oriented news, and fair portions of undigested (and usually bland) local editorial opinion or comment.

In fairness, it must be said that most of these middle-area general United States dailies provide more news about world affairs than most of their counterparts in other nations; but it is so scattered among all the other assorted journalistic goodies that its importance and impact is lost on the average American reader.

The international elite paper must evidence a *cosmopolitanism* quite alien to mass papers and only occasionally approached in middle-area general appeal papers. Concern for news and views of other countries is a definite characteristic of the elite paper; thus the emphasis on international trade, political relations, cross-cultural economic, social, scientific and educational affairs. The elite paper not only takes its serious national affairs seriously, but also deems it important to inform its readers of the salient international affairs and the concerns of other nations. The elite paper is able to see the world as a piece, not simply as a hodgepodge of nationalistic states isolated and unimportant to one another. Unlike the popular paper, it would not cause the kind of reaction that stimulated Reinhold Niebuhr to indict a segment of the press in a 1950 lecture:

Nothing is more disconcerting to an American visitor in Britain than to find that the afternoon press in that country has no other news from this country than little snippets of sensational items which cannot possibly give the reader a balanced view of our nation. I would not claim that our papers of similar stripe do any better for Britain or for any other continental nation.

The elite press would not have affected Dr. Niebuhr as did the popular British afternoon papers. The elite papers would have given him a heavy diet of news and views of four main types: (1) politics/international relations, (2) business/economics, (3) education/science/culture and (4) the humanities with emphasis on the fine arts, literature, philosophy and religion. Dr. Niebuhr or any other reader of the elite paper would have received much more, however, than serious facts and opinion.

- An aura of *dignity and stability* is a characteristic of the elite paper. This manifests itself not only in a conservative, soft-sell makeup but also in a rather heavy, semi-academic writing style that approaches the type one finds in such journals as London's *Economist*. In the elite paper there is an overriding tone of seriousness, of respect for the reader's intelligence and store of knowledge; there is an absence of sensation or hysteria that tends to dominate the general newspaper press of the world. The elite paper has a clearer conception of what is really significant and vital than do other types of papers. It has a serious-minded and moral approach to news that keeps it digging and interested in the news at any cost. All of this, of course, makes the quality press *reliable*.

- The elite paper is *courageous*. The mere fact that it has foregone the temptation to popularize, to sensationalize, to build up a large readership shows that it has courage. It dares to give the readers a thoughtful and heavy portion of news and views; it constantly attempts to lead, not follow, public opinion. This, in itself, takes courage. It has a reputation for speaking out on issues when it is not popular to do so; is forward-looking, progressive, and eager to change when the change is in accord with society's best interests, regardless of whether it is considered (or considers itself) liberal or conservative (or something else).

- The elite paper is *responsible:* responsible to its readers. In a free society, of course, this makes it also responsible to its government and to people everywhere. Its main job is, as *The New York Times'* James

Reston has said, "to get all the facts the people need to reach correct judgments." (Authoritarian prestige papers like *Pravda* or *Ren-min Rih-pao* [*People's Daily*] are also responsible, but their responsibility is of a different nature, being directed toward the system and emphasizing the solidarity of the state rather than considering the individual citizen as the object of its responsibility. In a sense, the authoritarian elite paper's responsibility is one of party-government-people consensus, a sort of responsibility for conformity and harmony, not a responsibility which enthrones honesty and pluralistic discourse.)

If Reston is right, then the free elite press should be *reliable;* the readers should be able to trust it. It must be adequate to a free people's needs. Often indictments are made of a nation's press and these would evidently, in their generalized form, include the quality or elite papers, for it must be remembered that they are available to a nation's readers.

Some Specific Surveys: Quality

Before surveying some specific studies of criteria of the quality press, it should be reemphasized that elite papers are written and edited for the discerning reader, the inquisitive reader, the knowledgeable reader, the thoughtful reader, the issue-oriented (not fact-oriented) reader. The quality paper, in short, is designed for the person who takes serious things seriously and is conscientiously seeking the truth.

Many persons, most, in fact, do not take serious things seriously, and they have their press. The person who reads the London *Daily Mirror* or the Sunday *News of the World* may want or need these trivial forays into a crazy-quilt world of gaudiness and news anarchy. Thus, the popular press has its place, serves its purpose, but it should be recognized for what it is. Admittedly, the reader of the *Daily Mirror* may also be a reader of an elite paper in his more serious moments, but the point is that he knows the difference. His journalistic habits are consciously schizophrenic. But he probably is not a typical newspaper reader, for there is reason to believe that serious persons, opinion leaders, intellectuals would not be comfortable reading the *Daily Mirror*. However, if a single person does read both types of papers, he knows they are of quite different characters, speak different languages, have different goals and address different audiences, or at least appeal to the different tastes or sensibilities of an individual.

Let us turn now to several studies and discussions (since 1959) that have dealt with the marks of the free elite. Many other articles and books have approached quality journalism and its characteristics from a variety of perspectives during this same period, and even before, but the four studies which follow reflect the thinking of scholars and practicing journalists of many nations relative to the marks or characteristics of the quality, or free elite, newspapers.

In 1959 Wilbur Schramm, of Stanford University's Institute for Communications Research, wrote that a prestige or quality newspaper (in a democratic nation) is privately owned, but that "it may or may not speak for a political party"; he pointed out that *Dagens Nyheter* of Sweden, for example, usually follows the Liberal party line. In addition, such a quality paper may or may not have an official quality (the London *Times,* for instance, is often considered the unofficial voice of the British government, although it is completely independent). But Schramm believes one thing is certain: in a democracy the quality newspaper speaks for its owner and publisher. Schramm emphasizes that neither size nor circulation—nor great financial prosperity—determine a prestige paper. He says that the main distinguishing characteristics (aside from the type of readers) are content and the newspaper's relation to its public.

The great newspapers of the world, writes Schramm, tend to focus on the big events of the day—news of national and international scope at the expense of local news, human interest items, sensational content; and they try to treat these larger events at greater length than do other papers. The quality papers also tend to deal with the news more thoughtfully, to stress political and economic affairs, the serious side of social problems, and scientific developments. Schramm says that the quality papers attract influential readers by the breadth and depth of their coverage, and tend to be independent and often critical of government. No central authority controls their policy, and they serve as observers and critics of their governments rather than as representatives.

In 1961 the U.S. magazine *Saturday Review* undertook a mail-questionnaire survey of all deans, full professors and associate professors in the 46 schools accredited by the American Council on Education for Journalism. Object: to discover which of the 119 American dailies with circulations of 100,000 or more were most highly regarded by these journalism educators and what criteria were used in rating a daily paper. Selecting from the replies of the 125 respondents, here are the 10 main criteria used to adjudge an American daily as superior:

1. Completeness of coverage in foreign and international affairs, business, the arts, science and education
2. Concern with interpretive pieces, backgrounding articles and depth-news articles
3. Typographical and general editorial dignity
4. Lack of sensationalism
5. Depth and analytical perception of stories
6. Absence of hysteria and cultural tone
7. Thorough and impartial news coverage and serious-minded, moral approach to news
8. Imagination, decency, interest in democratic problems and humanity
9. Excellent editorial page
10. Orientation that rises above provincialism and sensationalism

In the summer of 1964 a survey of a panel of 26 professors of international communication in the United States was conducted to help determine criteria used, in this case, to rate a newspaper in the top 20 quality papers of the world. In addition, names of newspapers so considered were solicited. The newspapers actually listed by the panel of specialists are named in the next section of this essay, but it is appropriate here to give the most significant criteria for judging a quality paper in an international context. These are given below in the order corresponding to the panel's opinion of their importance.

The most important criterion in the panel's view was an emphasis on political, economic and cultural news and views. A long tradition of freedom and editorial courage was considered second most important. (This, of course, would eliminate highly controlled newspapers of the authoritarian nations from a roster of quality papers.) The third criterion of political and economic independence was closely related to the second. A strong editorial page and/or section given over to opinion and interpretive essays was named as fourth most important for a quality paper, followed by staff enterprise in obtaining and writing news and commentary.

Other criteria thought by the panel very important for determining a quality paper: large proportion of space given to world affairs; lack of provincialism; consistently good writing in all sections of the paper; high regard by opinion leaders and by other serious publications; large, well-educated staff; typographical and printing excellence and general makeup dignity; de-emphasis of sensational news and pictures; high overall quality of coverage on world, national and local levels; active integrity; consistent opposition to intolerance and unfairness; active community leadership, comprehensive news coverage in its pre-empted area; and influence with the decision makers and policymakers at home and in other countries.

The panel's criteria indicate that its members felt a quality paper must stress politics, economics and culture, and that this emphasis must extend to the international scene, not simply to the country where it is published. Cosmopolitanism, then, was considered to be very important, along with editorial courage and an impact on the opinion leaders of its own nation and of other nations. A dignity of page makeup as well as a large, enterprising, well-educated staff rounds out the basic image of a quality paper as seen by the 1964 American panel. Underlying implications here are that the quality paper must be supranational in circulation and scope, literate, courageous, forceful, free, knowledgeable, stimulating, credible, sober, socially concerned, world conscious, and dignified. It is little wonder that the group of international quality newspapers is small.

One other survey should be mentioned. In late 1965, the present writer sent a brief questionnaire to 185 editors in the United States, Britain, West Germany, Denmark, Switzerland, Italy, Japan, Mexico, Australia and India. The purpose of this survey was to follow up the author's 1964 survey and to get some comment from an international panel relative to the world's leading elite newspapers—this time from newspaper editors instead of journalism professors. Questionnaires were sent to editors of newspapers (with more than 50,000 circulation) chosen at random. Ninety-two were returned (a very

high response) and after an additional group of forms was mailed to other editors and the total return numbered exactly 100, the seeking of completed questionnaires stopped, although response from Indian and Australian editors was disproportionately small.

The returns from various countries were: United States, 18; West Germany, 14; Britain, 12; Japan, 12; Switzerland, 11; Italy, 10; Mexico, 9; Denmark, 8; Australia, 4; India, 2.

Admittedly, this is a small sample, but the intent was not to take a statistically reliable survey (and claim any scientific validity for it), but to elicit some comments (hopefully representative) from respondents in ten free-world countries. This, it is felt, was accomplished with some comments more incisive and more frank than had been anticipated.

The questionnaire had only two brief parts: (1) the editors were asked to name five dailies of the world (no more than one from a single country) which they considered good examples of leading quality, influential, or elite newspapers, and (2) they were asked to give at least five main determinants or characteristics which they used in deciding on the five dailies.

Instead of summarizing in detail the criteria deemed important in classifying a quality newspaper by the international panel of editors, it will suffice here to say that their standards of evaluation included all those mentioned by Schramm (1959), the *Saturday Review* survey (1961), and my survey of U.S. professors teaching international communications (1964). This, of course, did not come as a surprise, but did reinforce the previous surveys—or, said another way, it extended or projected these criteria into an international context. It showed that newsmen in diverse countries (nonauthoritarian) tend to have a common set of standards which they use in determining the leading newspapers of the world.

It should be noted at this point that many of these editors stated their evaluative criteria in various terms, but it was quite clear that the basic values were the same and the variously worded responses could quite easily be structured as to common or standard themes.

What were these main themes or criteria considered most important by the international panel for determining a leading quality paper? They have been grouped in five rather large categories, and although they reiterate in large part what has already been said, their presentation should serve well to summarize and conclude this chapter. Marks of the free elite are these:

1. Independence; financial stability; integrity; social concern; good writing and editing.
2. Strong opinion and interpretive emphasis; world consciousness; nonsensationalism in articles and makeup.
3. Emphasis on politics, international relations, economics, social welfare, cultural endeavors, education and science.
4. Concern with getting, developing, and keeping a large, intelligent, well-educated, articulate and technically proficient staff.
5. Determination to serve and help expand a well-educated, intellectual readership at home and abroad; desire to appeal to, and influence, opinion leaders everywhere.

The Elite: A Look at Names

After considering the criteria just discussed, one may wonder if any newspaper in the world really qualifies for membership in the elite international press. The answer to such a question is that if all the characteristics and standards are not applied too stringently to a newspaper at all times, certainly there are journals which would qualify for membership. Of course, the whole matter is one of "degree" of achievement, concern, independence, cosmopolitanism, rationality, social responsibility, seriousness and the like. One must attune himself to "continuum thinking" (thinking in gradations or degrees, not "black-white" thinking) and not to compartmentalized and undynamic thought when considering the subject of quality journalism. However, if a person takes continuum thinking too far and falls under the spell of extreme relativity, he cannot adjudge or criticize newspapers for fear of making unwarranted evaluations.

Journalists, educators and interested laymen should not shirk from making judgments and from trying to determine for themselves excellence among newspapers, even to the establishing of a "hierarchy," however difficult and subjective this enterprise may be. Granted the complexity of such a venture, it should be remembered that historians (and many others) classify statesmen, military leaders, universities, philosophers, writers and even nations as great, second-rate, mediocre and so forth. There appears equal justification in classifying newspapers. At any rate, it is done every day by an assortment of people, many of whom, unfortunately, do offer their judgments out of an empty chamber of ignorance.

Persons in any country who study the press of the world and seriously attempt to compare newspapers, analyze their contents and criticize them should be encouraged, not discouraged. Perspectives may be different among students of the press, values and standards may vary somewhat (although not substantially, as was seen in the last section of this essay), but they make their opinions known out of a concern, an interest and a constantly growing fund of knowledge. Usually the statements and appraisals coming from press critics bring no real surprises, but occasionally a writer will overturn rather well-established beliefs and challenge prevalent conceptions with his opinions.

Critics who are interested in the world press, who attempt constantly to keep up with it, who read numerous newspapers in the native language or in translation, or who receive impressions about them from respected persons who do—these people would seem to be as well qualified as any to criticize, rank and pass judgment on newspapers. Those who belittle such critics and such labors as senseless and valueless because of the subjectivity involved only evidence an ignorance of the serious critic and of the whole realm of criticism and evaluation in every area. Certainly a critic such as John Tebbel is qualified to appraise the press as he does in this case:

> There are more "serious" newspapers in the United Kingdom, in the manner of *The New York Times*. The quality of the daily London *Times*, *The Daily Telegraph*, the…*Guardian*, and the *Financial Times*, and the Sunday edition of *The Telegraph*, along with the *Sunday Times* and *The Observer* (to name some of the best), is matched in America only by *The New York Times*, *The Wall Street Journal*, and *The Christian Science Monitor*. In some respects, notably political analysis and critical writing, these "serious" British papers are in general better than most of ours, and more comprehensive in their coverage than all save the Gray Lady of Forty-third Street.

The serious student of the international press may be exemplified by Dr. Robert W. Desmond, who since the early 1930's, when he wrote his doctoral dissertation at the London School of Economics on the world press, has been conscientiously studying and evaluating the world press, evidenced by his pioneering book *The Press and World Affairs* (1937). In a letter to this writer, Dr. Desmond wrote:

You and I think we know something about the papers (foreign papers), and we do...we are at the mercy of others for most of what we know. We have to talk with persons who do know the papers, who do read them, who do have the language, who do themselves also (preferably) know the best of the U.S. press (and the worst, too, perhaps) so that they have a standard of comparison and judgment. I know I always ask people in other countries and from other countries, persons whose judgment and opinion I respect, to comment—and I try to keep up to date that way, also, on changes such as do occur now and then, where a paper that once didn't rate may now have advanced (or another declined in quality) so the order is different. This sort of ranking is subjective, but when you get enough witnesses and enough evidence it becomes pretty satisfactory, I would say. So our judgments—that is, what we say—may have to be second or third hand, but they are not without validity, even so.

In spite of the fact that there will always be some who will not grant any validity or value to classification or ranking surveys, and will consider arguments such as Dr. Desmond's as inadequate, there is good reason to believe that international press scholarship and the tremendous growth in journalism literature since World War II have given a sound foundation on which to build a valid set of standards for judging newspaper quality and for naming certain papers to the elite fraternity. Let us then consider some surveys that have been made to determine members of the elite press.

In 1951 in a study for UNESCO, the late Jacques Kayser, who enjoyed an international reputation as a press researcher, selected seventeen newspapers as major dailies for a comparative analysis. The following list indicates that Kayser was thinking of major papers, not necessarily of the elite papers, and that he was also considering those which fall in many spots along an authoritarian-libertarian continuum:

Borba (Belgrade), *Times of India* (Bombay), *La Nación* (Buenos Aires), *Al Misri* (Cairo), *Hürriyet* (Istanbul), *Rand Daily Mail* (Johannesburg), *Daily Express* (London), *La Prensa* (Mexico City), *Corriere della Sera* (Milan), *Pravda* (Moscow), *Daily News* (New York), *Le Parisien Libéré* (Paris), *Rudé Právo* (Prague), *O Estado de São Paulo* (Brazil), *Ta Kung Pao* (Shanghai), *Dagens Nyheter* (Stockholm), and the *Daily Telegraph* (Sydney).

Noteworthy is the fact that when compared with more recent lists of quality papers only six of Dr. Kayser's dailies would be considered as members of the elite club: *Times of India, La Nación, Corriere della Sera, Pravda, O Estado de São Paulo* and *Dagens Nyheter*. But Kayser's list, as noted above, was not intended to include only quality papers, but others which he felt would be representative of various segments of the press of the nations of various political orientations.

Then, in 1959, Wilbur Schramm did another comparative study (of one day during the 1956 Suez Crisis) in which he chose important dailies that he felt were representative of world journalism. It is interesting that three of the five communist papers on Schramm's list were also on Kayser's. Here are Schramm's dailies, with the communist papers listed first; Schramm refers to all of them as great papers and says that they fall into the class which is usually called the prestige papers:

Pravda, Trybuna Ludu (Warsaw), *Rudé Právo* (Prague), *Borba, Ren-min Rih-pao* (Peking); *Le Monde* (Paris), *Frankfurter Allgemeine Zeitung* (Frankfurt am Main), *Dagens Nyheter, Al Ahram* (Cairo), *Asahi Shimbun* (Tokyo), *La Prensa* (Buenos Aires), *Times of India, The Times* (London), and *The New York Times*.

Schramm's list appears to be much more in line with informed thinking than Kayser's as to what is an elite paper. For example, Schramm's papers include the London *Times, The New York Times, La Prensa* of Buenos Aires, *Ren-min Rih-pao* of Peking, the *Frankfurter Allgemeine Zeitung* and *Le Monde*, all omitted from Kayser's 1951 study.

In 1961 Edward L. Bernays, a New York public relations counsel, conducted a national poll of 1,596 U.S. daily newspaper publishers on their ranking of the top 10 foreign papers. He also asked for their ranking of the top 10 domestic newspapers. The fact that only 7.2 percent ranked foreign papers as opposed to 17.2 percent ranking U.S. papers indicates perhaps, among other possibilities, the low degree of familiarity American publishers have with the foreign press. What were the foreign papers thought most important by the American publishers who responded? They follow in order of the percentage of publishers listing them:

The Guardian (Britain), *The Times* (Britain), *La Prensa* (Argentina), *Toronto Daily Star* (Canada), *The Daily Telegraph* (England), *Le Monde* (France), *Mainichi* (Japan), *Le Figaro* (France), *The Observer* (Britain), *France-Soir* (France), *Asahi Shimbun* (Japan) and the *Montreal Star* (Canada).

This listing by U.S. publishers is quite interesting. First of all, it indicates that English-language papers were considered most prominently in the 10, probably because the publishers read, or felt they read, them. It is unusual that two Canadian dailies made the list. And it is strange indeed that Britain's ultraserious weekly *Observer* (the only weekly in the list) and France's outstanding mass or popular (sensational) *France-Soir* tied for eighth place. It should be noted, however, that with the exception of *France-Soir,* all the papers named are usually considered as quality or elite journals. Unlike Kayser and Schramm, the American publishers omitted completely any communist paper from their list.

According to the Bernays poll, runner-up newspapers receiving at least three percent of the votes, were:

Dagens Nyheter, Paris *Herald-Tribune* (in a sense not a foreign newspaper), *Berliner Morgenpost, The Times of India, El Mercurio* (Santiago, Chile), *Frankfurter Allgemeine, Neue Zürcher Zeitung, Aftenposten* (Oslo), *El Tiempo* (Bogotá, Colombia), *Il Messaggero* (Rome), *La Nación* (Buenos Aires) and *The Scotsman* (Edinburgh).

In the Bernays poll, the top 10 United States papers listed in order of frequency of publishers' mention, and using the same judgmental standard as for the foreign papers, were:

The New York Times, St. Louis Post-Dispatch, The Christian Science Monitor, Milwaukee Journal, Louisville Courier-Journal, New York *Herald Tribune, The Washington Post, Los Angeles Times, Chicago Tribune* and *Kansas City Star.*

Notice how the above correspond with the top 10 of the *Saturday Review* poll the same year (1961):

The New York Times, The Christian Science Monitor, The Wall Street Journal, St. Louis Post-Dispatch, Milwaukee Journal, The Washington Post, New York *Herald Tribune, Louisville Courier-Journal, Chicago Tribune* and *The* (Baltimore) *Sun.*

In 1962 this writer, in a chapter for a new journalism textbook, presented a list of daily papers that appeared to him at the time to be gravitating toward the top of the elite pyramid. This list was composed of both libertarian and authoritarian elite, and was limited to non-U.S. papers. Dailies appearing in this 1962 list follow:

Neue Zürcher Zeitung, The Guardian, The Times, Le Monde, Pravda, Scotsman, Izvestia, Asahi Shimbun, Le Figaro, El Tiempo, Frankfurter Allgemeine, La Nación, Journal de Genève, The Hindu, Corriere della Sera, Süddeutsche Zeitung, Nieuwe Rotterdamse Courant, Berlingske Tidende, Die Welt, Excélsior, The Globe and Mail and *Ren-min Rih-pao (People's Daily).*

Some of these dailies had not appeared in any of the lists already mentioned, but were thought to be extremely qualitative and prestigious journals. For example, it seemed to the writer at the time that such dailies as *The Hindu* of Madras, *Süddeutsche Zeitung* of Munich, *Nieuwe Rotterdamse Courant* of Rotterdam, *Berlingske Tidende* of Copenhagen, *Die Welt* of Hamburg and *Izvestia* of the Soviet Union should definitely be considered among the truly great papers of the world.

In 1963 the faculty of the School of Journalism, Syracuse University (New York), determined a list of the 10 leading dailies of the world, using stylistic quality, journalistic courage, editorial independence and decency as principal evaluative criteria. The Syracuse University list presented the newspapers in the following order:

Neue Zürcher Zeitung, Frankfurter Allgemeine Zeitung, The New York Times, The Christian Science Monitor, The Guardian (London/Manchester), *Le Monde, Asahi Shimbun, La Prensa* (Buenos Aires), *The Times* (London) and *Dagens Nyheter* (Stockholm).

In the summer of 1964 a survey was made in the United States by the writer and was intended to elicit a ranking of elite dailies of the world from 26 professors of international communications from as many schools of journalism throughout the country. The criteria of evaluation used by respondents were given earlier, and only the names of the papers and their ranking will be given here. The top 10:

1. *The New York Times* (United States)
2. *The Times* (Britain)
3. *The Christian Science Monitor* (United States)
4. *The Guardian* (Britain)
5. *Le Monde* (France)
6. *Neue Zürcher Zeitung* (Switzerland)
7. *The Washington Post* (United States)
8. *La Prensa* (Argentina)
9. *Asahi Shimbun* (Japan)
10. *Frankfurter Allgemeine* (West Germany)

In addition to the first 10, the U.S. faculty panel named the following among the world's best dailies:

Dagens Nyheter (Stockholm), *Corriere della Sera* (Milan), *Berlingske Tidende* (Copenhagen), *La Nación* (Buenos Aires), *Times of India* (Bombay), *Die Welt* (Hamburg), *Excélsior* (Mexico City), *Journal de Genève*, *The Scotsman* (Edinburgh), *Nieuwe Rotterdamse Courant* (Rotterdam), *The Sun* (Baltimore), *Süddeutsche Zeitung* (Munich), *Aftenposten* (Oslo), *O Estado de São Paulo* (Brazil), *Svenska Dagbladet* (Stockholm), *Die Presse* (Vienna), *Izvestia* (Moscow), *Los Angeles Times* (United States), *El Tiempo* (Bogotá), *Pravda* (Moscow), *Courier-Journal* (Louisville), *Milwaukee Journal* (United States), New York *Herald Tribune* (United States), *Minneapolis Morning Tribune* (United States), *Winnipeg Free Press* (Canada), *The Globe and Mail* (Toronto), *The Daily Telegraph* (London), *The Age* (Melbourne), *La Stampa* (Turin) and *Helsingin Sanomat* (Helsinki).

In late 1965 I followed up this survey of American journalism professors with an international survey of newspaper editors. Questionnaires were received from 100 editors in 10 countries (including the United States), on which this international panel ranked what they considered were the top five quality dailies of the world, naming no more than one from any one country. Asking for no more than one daily from any country may have distorted the survey somewhat, but it forced the respondents to think of top newspapers in at least five nations and

tended to disperse the papers to a degree not found in some of the other surveys.

So far as is known, this survey was the largest such poll conducted through 1965 and tended to reinforce opinions made by independent students and smaller samples of respondents. No real surprises came from the 1965 survey, although it is interesting to note that U.S. papers tended to be a little lower in the list than in several previous studies. Two factors could account for this: (1) this was an international survey, whereas most of the others were conducted among Americans, and (2) the request that no more than one paper from any one country be listed may have eliminated the naming of additional U.S. papers by respondents.

At any rate, here are the 10 dailies of the world that received the most mentions by the international panel of editors, presented in the order of frequency of mention:

1. *The New York Times* (United States)
2. *Neue Zürcher Zeitung* (Switzerland)
3. *The Guardian* (Britain)
4. *Le Monde* (France)
5. *The Times* (Britain)
6. *Asahi Shimbun* (Japan)
7. *Dagens Nyheter* (Sweden)
8. *Excélsior* (Mexico)
9. *Corriere della Sera* (Milan)
10. *Frankfurter Allgemeine Zeitung* (West Germany)

The second 10 dailies getting the most mentions by the international panel were:

O Estado de São Paulo (Brazil), *St. Louis Post-Dispatch* (United States), *Die Welt* (West Germany), *The Christian Science Monitor* (United States), *Times of India*, *Globe and Mail* (Canada), *The Washington Post* (United States), *The Daily Telegraph* (Britain), *Berlingske Tidende* (Denmark) and *La Prensa* (Argentina).

A book written in 1965 by Danish writers Steen Albrectsen and Niels Holst included a list of leading non-Danish dailies considered by the authors to be most important. This list showed a significant overlapping with the list obtained through the international survey just mentioned. The Albrectsen-Holst list follows:

La Prensa (Argentina); *Le Soir* and *Het Laatste Nieuws* (Belgium); *The Times, The Guardian,* and *The Telegraph* (Britain); *Helsingin Sanomat* and *Uusi Suomi* (Finland); *Combat, Le Figaro,* and *Le Monde* (France); *Algemeen Handelsblad, de Telegraaf* and *Nieuwe Rotterdamse Courant* (Holland); *Corriere della Sera* and *Il Messaggero* (Italy); *Asahi Shimbun* and *Mainichi* (Japan); *Borba* (Yugoslavia); *People's Daily* (China); *Aftenposten, Arbeiderbladet,* and *Dadbladet* (Norway); *The Christian Science Monitor, The* (Baltimore) *Sun,* New York *Herald Tribune, The New York Times, St. Louis Post-Dispatch, The Washington Post* and *Chicago Tribune* (United States); *Osservatore Romano* (Vatican City); *Frankfurter Allgemeine, Süddeutsche Zeitung,* and *Die Welt* (West Germany); *Neues Deutschland* (East Germany), and *Die Presse* (Austria).

Another list of great newspapers should be mentioned: the dailies included in Heinz-Dietrich Fischer's 1966 book, *Die grossen Zeitungen.* In this attractive paperback published in Munich, Fischer gives brief "portraits" of 13 leading or great newspapers of the world but makes no attempt to rank them. Fischer's newspapers include representatives from the communist as well as the non-communist world, and it is interesting that all of them appear in one or more of the lists already given in this chapter. Without a doubt, they are all at the very top levels of the world's elite press. Fischer quite logically includes the communist world's two most prestigious dailies—Russia's *Pravda* and Red China's *Ren-min Rih-pao* (People's Daily). *The New York Times* represents North America, and *La Prensa* of Buenos Aires represents South America. All the rest of Fischer's papers are from Europe—*Berlingske Tidende* (Denmark), *Neue Zürcher Zeitung* (Switzerland), *The Times* (Britain), *Die Presse* (Austria), *Corriere della Sera* (Italy), *Svenska Dagbladet* (Sweden), *Le Monde* (France), and *Die Welt* and *Frankfurter Allgemeine* (Germany).

Perhaps the heavy weighting of these outstanding newspapers toward Europe is natural, considering Fischer's nationality and the tendency of European intellectuals to have an affinity for European serious journalism. Although from an American perspective the Fischer book seems too European, there is absolutely no cause to argue with the papers he selected for discussion. It should be noted that seven of the 11 free-world papers in Fischer's list were in the top papers of my 1965 survey of editors in 10 countries.

Although there is some disharmony or variation in the newspapers various persons or groups would place in the elite category,

and while rankings are not correlated perfectly, it should appear obvious (and rather surprising) that such a high degree of consistency and agreement exists in regard to which newspapers should have places in the world's elite press. Even the same newspapers, although their rank order presents some variation, tend to appear again and again in about the same position on a scale of quality. For something as subjective as evaluating journalistic greatness or eliteness, this would lead one to grant some validity or meaning to such listings and rankings by individual writers and survey panels.

One last listing of great newspapers should be mentioned. A colleague, Dr. Harold Fisher of Bowling Green (Ohio) State University, and I wrote a book titled *The World's Great Dailies: Profiles of 50 Newspapers,* published by Hastings House in 1980. Both of us having studied world newspapers for many years and having visited most of them, we decided to select arbitrarily the 50 examples of "great newspapers." No survey techniques were used.

A few of the dailies that are profiled in the book were dropped in 1980—e.g., *Excélsior* of Mexico, *La Prensa* and *La Nación* of Argentina (due to their becoming more and more governmental bulletin boards), and certain dailies (e.g. *El País* of Spain and the *Straits Times* of Singapore) were added. The 50 profiles contained in the book (with the exception of the post-Franco *El País*) are all of dailies named as the top newspapers in several of the surveys already cited here.

Patterns and Trends

Although the elite press of the world has been referred to as a "community," it is clearly an uneven, multifaceted one. A seriousness of tone and purpose and a high readership among influential persons are about the only common denominators of the elite press. The membership of the elite, because of differences in language, economic stability, freedom from government control, and basic philosophy, is splintered and fragmented and suffers from too little rapport and theoretical consensus. Thus, the world's elite press is heterogeneous and pluralistic in spite of its commonalities of seriousness, general civility, and influence. Struggling against great obstacles everywhere but with renewed hope and vigor, it is developing unevenly throughout the world. It falls roughly into at least three major patterns.

The first pattern is primarily *political* or *ideological.* Elite papers tend either toward separation from government or toward integration with government. While the free elite see themselves as independent agents, standing aloof from, and unaffected by, government, the authoritarian elite envision themselves as partners in government, cooperative agents of their regimes, bent on carrying forth the socio-political system of their people.

Both groups of elite papers are dedicated to their philosophies and take their responsibilities, as they see them, quite seriously. It should be noted, however, that such a binary classification of the world's elite is too simple in reality and that all papers everywhere are free to varying degrees and restricted to varying degrees, although the character of the freedom and the restraint may differ significantly.

Many students of the press place considerable emphasis on social responsibility in determining the elite status of a newspaper. To what degree is the paper socially responsible? The answer to this question, to many, will largely determine the quality or eliteness of a newspaper. In the United States and other Western democracies social responsibility is thought of generally in terms of nonauthoritarianism or freedom from government control. In other words, social responsibility is the press utopia into which only libertarian-oriented papers may pass. This, however, seems much too simple a theory, and is unsatisfactory in the modern world of fragmented and pluralistic serious journalism.

It is this writer's contention that all conscientious and serious newspapers, regardless of what nation or political ideology they may represent, are socially responsible. This idea was put forth in a paper in early 1965 and met with considerable objection from some quarters. However, it was also embraced by large numbers of persons who had previously failed to challenge the concept of press social responsibility being connected only to a libertarian press. Why cannot the authoritarian press or the communist press claim to be socially responsible also? In fact, in certain respects, a newspaper would be more "responsible" if some type of governmental supervision existed; indeed, reporters could be kept from nosing about in critical areas during critical times. And, as the Russians are quick to point out, the amount of sensational material in the press could be controlled or eliminated altogether. Government activities could always be supported

and public policy could be pushed on all occasions. The press could be more educational in the sense that more news of art exhibits, concerts and national progress could be stressed. In short, the press would eliminate the negative and stress the positive. Then, with one voice the press of the nation would be responsible to its society; and the definition of "responsible" would be functional—defined and carried out in the context of the existing government and social structure.

A second important pattern among the world's elite, and one that is even more ragged than the political one just mentioned, is that of *economic diversity.*

This pattern, of course, is related to the political context, but actually it is quite different. For example, one elite paper in a libertarian nation can run into dire financial difficulties while another in the same country prospers and grows. An elite paper is not determined by how much property it owns or the profit it makes. Elite papers throughout the world exemplify a wide range of economic development and prosperity, but their overriding concern with serious news and views manifests itself quite apart from such differences in economic health.

Naturally, there is a point below which an elite paper (or any paper) may not fall and keep up its desired level of quality. Certainly it must have facilities for good printing. It must be able to pay enough to get conscientious, well-educated staff members. It must be able to receive a variety of services from news agencies, and to collect much national and world news with its own correspondents. It must, therefore, either have a rather sizable circulation, or it must develop a special elite readership that will offset a small circulation. Although some elite papers like *Asahi Shimbun* of Japan and *Pravda* of the Soviet Union have tremendous circulations, most of the world's elite have only modest ones. The elite newspaper (especially in a libertarian nation) runs the risk of lowering its quality when it makes a bid for larger readership, at least unless it does it very slowly. For it is the popular or mass press that is after the big circulations; the elite press is after thoughtful and discerning readers. Unfortunately for international rationality, the public, as Leo Rosten has said, "chooses the frivolous as against the serious, the lurid as against the tragic, the trivial as against fact, the diverting as against the significant." Rosten points out that very few people in any society "have reasonably good taste or care deeply about ideas" and that even fewer appear to be "equipped—by temperament and capacity, rather than education—to handle ideas with both skill and pleasure." The elite press is unwilling to sacrifice its high purpose for a larger circulation which it might obtain by being more lively and readable in the sense of the popular press. Elite newspapers recognize that their readership will probably be small, but they know that it is unusually potent, sapient and prestigious. It should be mentioned, however, that there are some few elite papers—in nations such as Sweden, where the whole public is literate and uncommonly serious—which manage to be rational and serious and at the same time furnish all types of reading material.

The third pattern of the elite press is *geographical*. And this, of course, is closely related to national development. Most of the elite are published in developed or modern countries, although there are a few that represent the developing (modernizing) or transitional nations. Europe and North America are the principal homes of the elite newspapers. This is not surprising since these two continents are the most industrialized, the most technological and the most literate of all the continents. As the economic bases become stabilized and literate and well-educated populations of other continents grow, the evenness of dispersion of the elite press throughout the world should improve significantly. At present, however, elite newspapers are scattered about the earth in a very uneven fashion. This pattern of clusters and vast gaps greatly hinders the total impact of concerned journalism in the world as a whole. It might be well to look more closely at this geographical pattern of the world's elite press.

Asia, with the exception of China, Japan and India, is virtually without an elite press. Of the three, Japan stands out for its great progress in quality journalism, and popular journalism too, for that matter. *Asahi Shimbun* is without a doubt the best quality daily in Japan and shows that an elite paper can, with editorial flexibility and sagacity, develop a large circulation within a free-market press. *Pravda* and its counterpart in Peking, *Ren-min Rih-pao,* of course have fewer problems building circulation since Communist party members and many others find that they need to have these daily journals of guidance and news. In India, the problems of the elite papers are much more acute than in either the USSR, China or Japan. There are

many reasons for this, but the chief one is probably the problem of too many languages. At present the major elite papers of India are published in English, understood only by the educated, who are found mainly in a few of the large cities. And, even within the English-reading public, the circulation of the English elite is segmented since there are three very important elite dailies in the country—*The Statesman* of Calcutta, *The Hindu* of Madras and the *Times of India* of Bombay. The vernacular languages of India, of which Hindi is the official one, have not caught on as press languages. Although there are a few well-written and well-edited papers in some of these dialects, they have little or no national or international prestige. To the language problem facing the development of the Indian elite press must be added these (generally applicable throughout Southeast Asia): low literacy rate, underdeveloped educational system, scarcity of training facilities and trained journalists, and old and inadequate printing equipment.

In Africa, with the exception of Egypt in the extreme northeast and the Republic of South Africa in the far south, there is no significant elite press; and even in these two republics considerable governmental sensitivity has hindered development of a truly quality press. Egypt, with its nationalized newspapers, would, from a Western viewpoint, have to take second place to South Africa as a libertarian press nation with elite papers of a pluralistic nature.

In South Africa, for example, in spite of government uneasiness concerning what it feels are press "excesses," the papers, especially those in English, show clearly that processes of inquiry and criticism are still at work, only slightly hampered, and able to explore those facets of a regime considered very sensitive. Johannesburg's morning *Rand Daily Mail* is a good example. It has consistently presented facts and opinion that have irritated the government, and has given its readers healthy portions of national and foreign news. Although most Afrikaans-language papers present a rather narrow pro-government picture, an important exception is *Die Burger* of Cape Town, committed generally to the policies of the Nationalist Party but often refreshingly independent and unconventional. It is also interesting that in South Africa the freest papers, generally the English-language papers, have the largest circulations. For instance, the Johannesburg *Star* has a circulation of almost double the combined circulations of the city's two Afrikaans papers, the *Transvaler* and the *Vaderland*.

The Egyptian press (which might better be considered part of the Middle Eastern press) has slowly but increasingly become a government-controlled press. In 1956 came the biggest blow to press freedom: President Nasser transferred the ownership of all papers to the National Union (the government party) in order to assure popular support for his regime. And in 1960 the Egyptian papers were placed in groups or units, each having an administrative council appointed by the government. *Al Ahram* gives a good selection of news and features, and uses UPI and Reuters and other foreign agencies (and many interpretive articles on international affairs) to keep its cosmopolitan tone. Probably the most influential papers of the Arab world are still found in Egypt.

In the neighboring Middle East the press systems are mainly transitional, caught between the severe problems of many parts of Asia on one side and of Africa on the other. One hindrance to elite-press development in this area is that these nations cannot decide whether to have their press systems (and governments) veer toward libertarianism or authoritarianism. Governments through the region are generally suspicious of the press and sensitive to its criticism. The press of Israel is probably improving faster than any other in the Middle East, and has been called the most "internationally minded in the world." For instance, *Ma'ariv* of Tel Aviv subscribes to Reuters, UPI, AP, and the London *Daily Telegraph* services and has several correspondents and their families in foreign capitals. And this paper, although the country's largest, is not as serious as others such as the staid *Ha'aretz*.

Latin America, in spite of awesome economic and literacy problems, has somehow managed to develop a rather sizable group of elite newspapers. Without a doubt, this region of the world has a far more advanced press than is generally found in Asia and Africa. One obvious explanation for this is the fact that Spanish is the almost common language of the press in Latin America, whereas in both Asia and Africa the polyglot of languages and dialects makes the development of newspapers of substantial influence and circulation extremely difficult, if not impossible.

Many Latin American dailies meet the demands (more difficult as controls mount) of serious readers for percipient journalism; almost every major nation south of the United States has at least one journal which is in, or aspires to, the elite press. Argentina has its *La Nación* and *La Prensa,* Chile its *Mercurio,* Peru its *Comercio,* Colombia its *Tiempo,* and Mexico its *Excélsior, Novedades* and *El Universal.* These and many other thoughtful dailies of Latin America do an outstanding job of providing large proportions of scientific and humanistic news and views, with much emphasis on foreign affairs. Perhaps the Latin American elite press, like its ancestral press of Iberia, places undue stress on philosophical, theological and literary discussion, but this is simply an intellectual Latin proclivity and the elite press does well to serve it.

In Oceania, Australia alone has a press which includes newspapers of the elite type. Barriers to press growth in this sprawling island region are mainly (1) small populations, (2) technological underdevelopment, (3) scarcity of trained journalists and (4) geographical isolation from the mainstream of international concerns. In Australia several papers might be included among the elite and several others are aspirants. *The Age* of Melbourne is usually considered the most serious and influential with the country's power elite. Even a paper like the same city's *Herald,* an afternoon journal that does not avoid some appeal to all classes, furnishes a substantial diet of serious material. Its economic coverage and its weekly book page are especially laudable. *The Australian,* begun in 1964, has become an excellent national daily, with offices in several cities.

In North America (above the Mexican border) the elite press thrives. Whereas Canadian elite tend to cluster in the southern part of that country, especially in Toronto and Montreal, the elite of the United States are rather well dispersed nationwide. *The Globe and Mail* of Toronto is Canada's only truly national daily. The same city's *Daily Star* is the country's largest and contains much serious material, although it displays it in a rather sensational manner. Canadian newspaper makeup is much closer to that typically found in the United States than it is to that of Britain. Montreal's evening *La Presse,* a comprehensive afternoon daily with an exceptionally fine weekend edition, is the largest French-language daily in the Western Hemisphere. In Winnipeg, Manitoba, the *Free Press* provides excellent international coverage and national coverage of the central and western portions of Canada.

Although there are elite and near-elite papers in every major section of the United States, most of them are concentrated along the East Coast, in the Middle West and around the fringes of the South. In the East are such sophisticated dailies as *The New York Times, The Washington Post, The Christian Science Monitor, The* (Baltimore) *Sun* and *The Miami Herald.* In the Middle West a few of the leaders among the elite are the *St. Louis Post-Dispatch,* the *Minneapolis Tribune, The Des Moines Register* and *The Milwaukee Journal.* In Kentucky, there is *The Courier-Journal* of Louisville; in Georgia, *The Atlanta Constitution.* Quality papers of national and international prestige tend to fade out in the plains and mountain areas of the West. Along the West Coast, there are several good dailies but the *Los Angeles Times* is easily the best.

If the press of North America is well developed and the elite papers numerous, the press of Europe (Western Europe) might be said to be overdeveloped and the elite papers very numerous. From Scandinavia to Spain and from Britain to Russia, elite dailies (and weeklies) spread their serious journalism into every corner of the continent and, increasingly, into distant lands. The elite dailies of Europe are probably the most erudite and knowledgeable in the world, providing insights available nowhere else.

All types of quality papers are to be found in Europe. There are the free elite of most of Western Europe, led by the superserious *Neue Zürcher Zeitung* of Switzerland, *Le Monde* of France, *The Times* and *The Guardian* of Britain and *Frankfurter Allgemeine* of West Germany. There are the "new" free elite of Spain such as *ABC, La Vanguardia Española* and *El País;* and the communist elite such as *Pravda* and *Izvestia* of Russia and *Borba* and *Politika* of Yugoslavia. There are the dailies of Scandinavia such as Oslo's *Aftenposten,* Copenhagen's *Berlingske Tidende* and Stockholm's *Dagens Nyheter;* these combine a rather flashy typographical dress with a heavy diet of serious news and views. There are also such dailies as *Die Welt* of Bonn and *Corriere della Sera* of Milan, which are able to combine a modern demeanor with strong thoughtfulness. And, of course, there is the stolid drabness of ultra-seriousness to be found in the daily of Vatican City, *Osservatore Romano.* The European elite press offers the reader a wide selection of packaging and political orientation; there is a paper whose journalistic style and philosophy, as well as size, layout and typographical tone, appeal to any kind of

reflective newspaper reader.

In addition to the elite daily papers it should be remembered that many excellent elite weekly papers exist in a number of countries (most of them in Europe), and reinforce the international concern and reasonableness of the elite dailies. No one should minimize the extremely high-level journalism of such papers as the London *Observer* and *Sunday Times, Weltwoche* of Zurich, *Embros* of Athens, *Le Canard Enchaîné* of Paris, *Die Zeit* of Hamburg, *Christ und Welt* of Stuttgart, *Rheinische Merkur* of Cologne, *Jeune Afrique* of Tunis and *The Nation* of Rangoon.

And, of course, adding to reasonable and serious international journalism, though probably not as substantially as the elite newspapers, are the well-edited weekly newsmagazines of the *Time/Newsweek/U.S. News & World Report* variety sprinkled around the world—notably *Der Spiegel* of West Germany, *L'Express* of France, *Tiempo* of Mexico, *Link* of India, *Veritas* of Argentina, *Reporter* of Kenya, *Akis* of Turkey and *Shukan Asahi* of Japan.

It is interesting to note that in the areas of the world where daily journalism is most advanced and there are many elite newspapers, there are also the largest numbers of journalism schools, press institutes and training programs of one type or another. This concern with or emphasis on journalism education is coupled with a high development of education generally. In the developing nations, such as those of Asia and Africa, the little emphasis on media training that has been begun is still concerned chiefly with the technical aspects of journalism: typesetting, printing, newsprint acquisition and the overcoming of basic economic handicaps. On the other hand, in the more advanced nations, where the elite press is strongest, these elemental problems are secondary in journalism education and a concern with editorial quality, ethical standards and social responsibility come in for more consideration. This nontechnical and noneconomic emphasis or approach inevitably results in a higher quality journalism.

This article has said very little about the natures of individual papers except in the general way of noting common denominators of emphasis and characteristics of makeup and content. Many of the elite papers, however, have been written about by various authors. Two of the most convenient books are: J.C. Merrill, *The Elite Press* (Pitman Publishing Corp., 1968); and J.C. Merrill and Harold Fisher, *The World's Great Dailies* (New York: Hastings House, 1980).

INTERNATIONAL ADVERTISING

by S. Watson Dunn

Until the latter part of the 20th century advertising was associated mainly with the capitalist countries of the world—and especially with New York's Madison Avenue. However, by the 1970s advertising had become truly international, with many centers of professional excellence having been established around the world. By 1980 almost half of the free world's advertising (over 100 billion U.S. dollars) was placed outside the United States, and advertising had become a well-established and accepted marketing and communications tool in the USSR and the People's Republic of China as well as in the capitalist countries. Multinational companies and their agencies had learned how to conduct multinational campaigns that speeded introduction of new products around the world. The proliferation of commercial media substantially increased availabilities for advertisers in various countries to reach desired audiences.

Many large multinational firms gain a higher percentage of their sales and profits from foreign than from domestic markets. For example, Colgate-Palmolive had over 60 percent of its 1979 sales outside its home country, the United States. And it spent approximately 55 percent of its total worldwide advertising budget of $273 million in foreign advertising. What is probably the world's largest advertiser, Unilever, headquartered partly in the United Kingdom and partly in the Netherlands, had an even higher percentage of its advertising expenditures outside its home countries. Unilever's U.S. subsidiary, Lever Brothers, is one of the largest advertisers in the United States. Such foreign-owned retailers as Gimbels and A & P are major United States advertisers. Advertising agencies have also been expanding their international activities. For example, J. Walter Thompson placed approximately 53 percent of its total advertising outside its home base in the United

States. Most of the large U.S.-based agencies expanded overseas when it became clear that their clients needed worldwide advertising service. By 1974, however, the largest agency in the world was Dentsu, which is based in Tokyo.

Certain corporations, agencies and media have, of course, long had important international operations. For example, Cockerill of Belgium put up its first foreign manufacturing plant (textile machinery in Prussia) in 1915. U.S.-made Singer sewing machines and International Harvester farm machinery were sold in many foreign countries in the 19th century. J. Walter Thompson was the first U.S. agency to establish a foreign subsidiary when it opened an office in London in 1899. *Reader's Digest* with its home office in the United States and *The Economist* in the United Kingdom have both had success at selling advertising space in their foreign editions.

Scope of Advertising Around the World

Total advertising expenditures for 1977 were estimated by Starch INRA Hooper to be over $70 billion U.S. The United States was the world leader, with Japan second and West Germany third. (See Table 2 for a summary of advertising expenditures in the measured media [print, television and radio] in the 50 leading world countries.) The total figure includes, in addition, the measured media, direct advertising, exhibitions, demonstrations, displays, point-of-sale displays, outdoor and transportation posters, sales promotion and cinema in most countries. Starch/INRA Hooper found it much easier to establish the accuracy of the measured than of these other media to verify expenditures in the developed as compared with the developing countries.

On a per capita basis the following countries had the highest expenditures for advertising:

Table 1
Countries with Highest Per Capita Ad Expenditures

Country	Per capita advertising (US$)
United States	175.83
Sweden	157.08
Switzerland	120.08
Bermuda	118.33
Norway	105.73

The lowest per capita expenditures took place in the least developed countries. For example Ethiopia had $.04, Nepal $0.05, Bangladesh $0.10 and India $0.026.

Definition of International Advertising

International advertising has changed substantially in the latter part of the 20th century and these changes have led to some confusion about what should be included as "international." Part of this confusion stems from the fact that many business firms have subsidiaries in various countries through which they manufacture and market their product. Other firms depend primarily on export of their product to a foreign country, and they depend on importers and distributors in foreign markets to take care of it in each market. Many of our largest corporations do both. Others, like Pepsi-Cola and McDonald's, have franchisees in foreign markets who are responsible for producing and selling their product in that country under franchise arrangements. Yet the parent company keeps control over the advertising and expects all foreign franchises to follow certain specified guidelines. In the case of Pepsi-Cola's marketing in the USSR the amount of Pepsi bottled and sold is dependent on the amount of Russian vodka that is imported and sold by Pepsi-Cola in the United States.

U.S. magazines like *Newsweek* and *Reader's Digest* sell advertising in their foreign as well as their domestic editions. To the publishers, this is international advertising since it is placed in the overseas rather than the domestic editions. Most newspapers have their circulation concentrated primarily within the country where the editorial offices are located. There are, however, exceptions such as the *International Herald-Tribune*, published in Paris primarily for readers in Western European countries but owned by three U.S. media firms: Washington Post, New York Times and Whitney Communications. Several radio stations in Europe beam the major part of their broadcasts to foreign countries and advertising on these can properly be called international.

To an advertising agency manager, all the advertising placed by its foreign branches can properly be called "international" even though the client might be a multinational one based in the agency's home country.

What is included in "international" thus depends at least partly on one's point of view. It must include the advertising of various multinational corporations (or as the United Nations and some other organizations prefer to call them, "transnational"), the advertising used to promote goods and services in the export market, and the activities of the various service firms needed to service international advertising—advertising agencies, media, research firms, television and film production firms, graphic arts firms, and many others.

Reasons for the Growth of International Advertising

As we have noted, international advertising, by any definition, has grown rapidly since World War II. Following are the most important reasons for this growth:

Rise of the Multinational Corporation

Multinational corporations include not only large industrial concerns like General Electric and Caterpillar but also banks, retail concerns, insurance companies, public accounting firms, research organizations, fast-food franchisers, hotels, airlines and many others. The rapid growth of such firms has aroused some critics who are afraid that they are becoming too powerful and that there is no supranational body to curb any excesses. Thus we have seen studies and proposals from the United Nations and the European Economic Community regarding multinationals. According to *Fortune,* the 500 leading multinationals based outside the United States now have total sales of around one trillion U.S. dollars. In the late 1970s U.S. corporation investments abroad totaled over $100 billion and accounted for over $200 billion in production of goods and services.

Defenders of the multinationals emphasize the economic and social contributions of these firms to the countries in which they operate. For example, the chief executive officer of one of the largest U.S. multinationals, Caterpillar Tractor, has maintained that expansion of the firm has helped add jobs in both the United States and abroad. When Caterpillar had no foreign subsidiaries, it employed 25,000 people; 7,500 of those jobs dealt with exports. After establishing 11 new factories abroad, Caterpillar's employment in the United States had jumped to 63,000, with 24,000 of these working in export or international areas. However, both the critics and the defenders of multinationals agree that the growth of multinational firms has been a major factor in stimulating growth of international advertising. By their ability to choose the best markets of the world for their manufacturing, their financing, their purchase of raw materials and their marketing, these companies can operate on a scale of efficiency far greater than many of the domestically bound corporations.

Increase in Foreign Trade

Small as well as large corporations have increased their trade with foreign countries. By 1980 U.S. exports of goods and services reached an estimated 12.2 percent of GNP, imports an estimated 12.3 percent. The combined total of 24.5 percent of GNP is twice the comparable figure for 1970. According to data compiled by the U.S. government, the number of jobs dependent on export trade from the United States is roughly equal to the number of jobs displaced by imports.

Foreign trade has increased at a comparable rate in most other countries. According to the General Agreement on Tariffs and Trade, headquartered in Geneva, Switzerland, world trade increased substantially faster than world population during the 1970s.

This trade has been encouraged by several trade agreements completed in the 1960s and 1970s. These have been directed toward lowering tariffs, eliminating quotas and stimu-

lating competition. Agreements in Western Europe have undoubtedly attracted the greatest interest. Among the most important were the Brussels Treaty of 1948, the Organization for European Economic Cooperation in 1948, the Benelux customs agreement of 1948, the Council of Europe in 1949 and, most important, the European Economic Community (European Common Market) established by the Treaty of Rome in 1957 and followed by the European Free Trade Association in 1958.

The EEC stimulated the nine Western European countries involved, by the gradual elimination of tariffs, allowing free movement of goods, capital and labor across national boundaries, establishment of a social fund to assist families of workers injured by increased commercial competition, and establishment of two investment funds—one to channel constructive capital into backward areas of EEC and the other to do the same for underdeveloped regions in overseas territories of the nine countries.

Improvement in Communications and Transportation

In the 1920s Alfred Sloan and his fellow executives at General Motors traveled to Germany to consummate that company's first major overseas venture—purchase of Adam Opel A.G. The round-trip ocean-liner crossing took approximately two weeks and they spent several weeks on the continent. They could communicate to the home office only by cable or letter. Today jet travel makes it possible for an executive to cross the Atlantic in a relatively few hours to attend a single meeting. And if he likes he can make the round trip in a single day. With direct dialing, telex and other improved communications, large amounts of information can be quickly and inexpensively transmitted back and forth between an overseas subsidiary and a home office. If necessary, data may be digested by digital computers and critical operating data can be transmitted quickly to the proper executives.

Neither the modern sophisticated multinational corporations nor the many organizations serving them could operate effectively without these developments. Modern developments in communications and transportation have brought the business world much closer.

Table 2

1977 Advertising Expenditures in 50 Countries— in Total Measured Media (a), in Print Media, in Television and in Radio

	Total Measured Media Advertising Expenditures (a) (In Millions of U.S. Dollars)		Print Expenditures		Television Expenditures		Radio Expenditures	
	1976	1977	1976	1977	1976	1977	1976	1977
Argentina	$ 367.5	$ 382.2	$ 172.3	$ 181.6	$ 140.8	$ 120.9	$ 33.2	$ 51.3
Australia	1,116.0	1,186.4	534.3	594.1	334.7	339.6	104.7	110.7
Austria	251.9	306.9	155.9	187.8	58.6	72.2	22.1	29.2
Belgium	219.6	295.4	159.4	216.4	7.9 (b)	22.0 (b)	0.6 (c)	1.0 (c)
Brazil	1,206.5	1,610.9	384.9	483.8	506.9	697.1	246.1	337.6
Canada	1,737.3 (d)	1,699.8 (d)	931.2	935.5	368.9	353.5	268.7	252.8
Colombia	77.5	167.8 (g)	19.6	36.4 (g)	35.0	91.0 (g)	17.8	29.0 (g)
Cyprus	2.4	3.2	0.8	1.0	1.0	1.4	0.3	0.5
Denmark	315.9	444.6	303.4	430.1	(e)	(e)	(e)	(e)
Dominican Republic	29.4 (f)	41.1	9.5	12.3	15.5	18.8	3.8	6.3
Egypt	45.7	36.7	34.0	20.1	4.4	8.9	1.1	1.1
Finland	271.7	380.7	218.9	320.2	42.5	44.1	(e)	(e)
France	1,574.1	1,720.0	968.5	972.0	230.0	279.5	146.6	184.9
Greece	61.6	71.9	27.7	34.8	28.7	31.3	3.1	4.5
India	121.4	143.8	74.2	88.6	1.2	2.2	7.3	9.2
Indonesia	50.9	63.3	28.5	35.5	6.4	7.9	3.9	4.6
Ireland	49.7	62.6	25.3	33.4	15.4	19.7	4.5	5.9
Israel	55.1	81.3	44.3	62.1	(e)	(e)	5.2	8.0
Italy	581.0	648.7	342.0	409.6	100.0	112.1	48.0	57.2
Japan	3,714.7 (d)(f)	4,779.0 (d)(f)	1,782.4	2,255.5	1,697.7	2,218.2	234.6	305.3
Kenya	9.3	10.7	5.2	6.1	0.2	0.2	1.7	2.0
Lebanon	23.2	13.6	11.9	6.3	5.8	4.9	(e)	2.2
Malaysia	42.1 (f)	45.6 (f)	28.5	30.9	7.3	7.8	2.2	2.4
Malta	2.4	2.1	1.1	1.1	1.0	0.8	0.3	0.1
Mexico	451.8 (f)	298.3 (f)	57.7	37.3	298.0	202.0	72.1	46.6

							Co:	
Nepal	0.5	0.5	0.4	0.4	(e)	(e)		0.1
Netherlands	817.8	1,031.0	696.6	859.8	71.8	74.1	7.9	9.9
New Zealand	121.2	176.8	86.5	107.6	15.6	45.1	14.5	21.8
Nigeria	38.9	42.3	18.6	20.9	4.5	4.4	8.6	10.1
Norway	240.5	376.3	227.1	364.1	(e)	(e)	(e)	(e)
Pakistan	13.5	16.9	3.0	4.8	6.0	7.0	1.7	1.8
Philippines	59.0	81.4	26.2	34.5	16.5	22.4	14.6	16.5
Puerto Rico	96.3 (d)(f)	130.6 (d)(f)	35.9	38.9	42.7	62.7	17.7	29.0
Singapore	50.3	53.7	40.0	40.0	6.4	9.6	0.8	1.4
South Africa	274.6	307.1	204.1	233.6	(e)	6.9	41.6	42.0
South Korea	175.3	189.0	77.9	76.3	54.7	75.0	36.1	32.1
Spain	521.0	551.3	275.6	283.5	137.4	157.5	45.3	53.4
Sri Lanka	4.2	5.1 (f)	3.1	3.9	(e)	(e)	0.6	0.9
Surinam	1.5 (f)	1.9 (f)	0.6	0.7	0.3	0.4	0.6	0.8
Sweden	392.4	532.8	365.7	494.6	(e)	(e)	(e)	(e)
Switzerland	523.2	550.4	455.7	468.9	41.2	49.0	(e)	(e)
Syria	10.0	17.3	4.0	6.0	3.5	6.0	0.2	0.4
Taiwan	94.9	118.4	35.1	45.4	42.0	52.4	8.8	10.3
Thailand	79.9	99.2 (g)	14.7	25.5 (g)	40.4	42.0 (g)	9.2	12.5 (g)
Trinidad & Tobago	10.9	12.7	4.0	4.6	4.1	5.0	2.4	2.6
Turkey	209.0	107.0	77.0	41.0	92.0	36.0	16.0	5.0
United Kingdom	2,051.3	2,568.9	1,379.4	1,709.6	544.3	702.2	37.2	45.9
United States	22,254.0 (d)	25,269.0 (d)	12,820.0	14,605.0	6,721.0	7,612.0	2,330.0	2,634.0
Venezuela	240.1	280.2	93.1	108.7	79.6	92.7	41.7	48.8
West Germany	2,482.4	3,148.9	1,930.2	2,485.1	335.0	386.7	80.4	109.0

*Less than $0.05 million.

Source: Starch INRA Hooper

(a) Reported advertising expenditures in print, "outdoor and transportation," cinema, radio and television, where these media are available for advertising.
(b) Television not available for advertising in Belgium. Expenditure for Tele-Luxembourg.
(c) Radio not available for advertising in Belgium. Expenditure for Radio-Luxembourg.
(d) Expenditure for cinema not reported.
(e) Medium not available for advertising.
(f) Expenditure for "outdoor and transportation" not reported.
(g) 1978 data.

Improvement in Living Standards

Even though much poverty remains in the world, living standards improved dramatically during the 1960s and 1970s. This betterment brought many into the middle class and increased both their ability and desire to own what they had previously considered luxuries. As a result of the increase in discretionary income of large numbers of people, advertising budgets were increased. By 1980 per capita GNP was quite comparable in such developed countries as the United States, Sweden, West Germany, Canada and Denmark.

Institutions of International Advertising

Like advertising in most developed countries, international advertising is carried out primarily by the advertising agencies, advertisers, advertising media and the various institutions that serve them.

Table 3

World's Top 50 Ad Agencies in 1979

Figures shown here in millions are based on total equity interest in foreign shops. AA must stress that this table represents only estimates due to reporting procedures of a few agencies that varied slightly from those requested.

Rank	Agency	Gross Income	Billings	Rank	Agency	Gross Income	Billings
1.	Dentsu	$352.8	$2,437	30.	Intermarco-Farner	43.5	291.6
2.	J. Walter Thompson	253.9	1,693	31.	Dai-Ichi Kikaku	38.4	272.6
3.	McCann-Erickson	252.3	1,687	32.	KM&G Intl.	37.7	245.1
4.	Young & Rubicam	247.6	1,921	33.	Tokyu	34.4	239.9
5.	Ogilvy & Mather	206.2	1,393	34.	Yomiko	30.7	172.9
6.	Ted Bates	181.0	1,177	35.	Cunningham & Walsh	29.3	225.2
7.	SSC&B	153.2	1,021.6	36.	Publicis Conseil	29.2	201.2
8.	BBDO	144.8	985.5	37.	Ross Roy	26.9	179.0
9.	Leo Burnett	141.1	950.7	38.	Asahi Kokoku Sha	26.0	165.4
10.	Foote, Cone & Belding	137.6	918.1	39.	Campbell-Mithun	23.8	158.4
11.	*D'Arcy-MacManus & Masius	128.0	853.6	40.	MPM/Casabranca	23.1	86.7
12.	Hakuhodo	127.4	896.3	41.	Wunderman, Ricotta & Kline	22.7	151.2
13.	Grey Advertising	106.3	710.0	42.	TBWA	22.6	150.8
14.	Doyle Dane Bernbach	104.0	701.0	43.	Dai-Ichi	22.2	158.1
15.	†Benton & Bowles	95.4	640.4	44.	Alcantara Machado Periscinoto	20.8	83.1
16.	Campbell-Ewald	84.2	561.9	45.	Asahi Tsushin	20.8	143.9
17.	Compton	77.7	524.6	46.	††Groupe Roux Seguela Cayzac & Goudard	18.9	97.3
18.	Eurocom	77.2	519.7	47.	William Wilkens & Co.	18.6	93.7
19.	Dancer Fitzgerald Sample	68.4	469.9	48.	Nationwide Ad Service	18.2	69.8
20.	Naito Issui Sha	65.0	370.3	49.	Orikomi	18.1	134.6
21.	N W Ayer	63.9	428.4	50.	GGK	17.8	118.4
22.	Daiko Advertising	62.5	491.8				
23.	Wells, Rich, Greene	56.6	377.6				
24.	Marsteller	54.3	362.5				
25.	Needham, Harper & Steers	50.4	336.2				
26.	Kenyon & Eckhardt	49.2	328.3				
27.	Norman, Craig & Kummel	48.0	323.1				
28.	William Esty Co.	45.6	304.0				
29.	Bozell & Jacobs Intl.	45.2	304.0				

*D'Arcy-MacManus & Masius figures exclude de Garmo, which was merged into the D'Arcy New York office in January.

†Figures include 20% ownership in Gestion et Recherche Publicitaire, a French agency group comprising B&B Publicite, Feldman, Calleux and Concurrence.

††Groupe RSCG includes the main Paris agency, RSCG, plus Chevassus & Vadon, Dire, Immediat and four smaller units.

Source: *Advertising Age,* April 30, 1980, p. 265.

Advertising Agencies

As the accompanying table indicates, most advertising agencies around the world have a significant portion of their billings (amount of advertising placed in media for their clients) in foreign markets. These branches normally solicit accounts from the country in which they are located in addition to serving multinational clients in all other countries where they operate. For example, J. Walter Thompson handles the advertising of Kraft Foods in most countries where Kraft markets. On the other hand, it does the advertising for Kellogg's cereals in the United Kingdom, while another large agency, Leo Burnett, handles this account in the United States.

The services of the advertising agency have been spelled out by the American Association of Advertising agencies. These apply just as much to foreign as to U.S. agencies:
1. A study of the client's product or service in order to determine its inherent advantages and disadvantages and the relation to the competition.
2. An analysis of present and potential markets for which the product or service is adapted.
3. A knowledge of the factors of distribution and sales and their method of operation.
4. A knowledge of all the available media and means that can profitably be used to carry the interpretation of the product or service to consumer, wholesaler, dealer, contractor or others.
5. Formulation of a definite plan and presentation of this plan to the client.
6. Execution of this plan through (a) writing, designing and illustrating the advertisements; (b) contracting for the space, time or other means of advertising; (c) incorporation of the message in mechanical form and forwarding it to the media; (d) checking and verifying insertions, displays and so forth; (e) auditing charges and billing for the service, space and preparation.
7. Cooperation with the client's sales force.

Advertising agencies in most countries represent a collection of skilled specialists who are hired by clients to perform the services outlined above. Although the number of specialized departments varies widely from agency to agency—depending on size, type of accounts and management philosophy—the following would normally be found in most agencies:

1. Planning. Most agencies work jointly with the client in developing the plan on the basis of the best information available to both. Some agencies have a plans board, others accomplish the planning function through informal meetings. An important part of planning is preparation of the advertising budget.
2. Copy. In most agencies the copy department is one of the largest. Its function is to plan and prepare advertising copy for all media, although some agencies have separate departments for preparing television and broadcast commercials. Copy, art and production are often coordinated under a creative director.
3. Art. The principal art function of most agencies is to lay out the advertisement, that is, arrange the various elements in a given space so that the ad will attract the attention of the right audience and communicate what the planners had in mind. The art department also arranges for finished artwork, usually prepared by an outside studio. For television, the storyboard corresponds to the layout in the printed ad since it indicates what scenes will be shot and how the audio is coordinated with the video.
4. Production. After the copy has been written and the layout and illustrations approved, the advertisement is usually turned over to the production department. This department maintains contact with printers, typographers, photoengravers and other specialists. In the case of the broadcast media the agency may produce its own programs and commercials but the tendency in recent years has been to contract with "package" organizations for casting, filming, videotaping, audio and all other elements of the finished product.
5. Media. The media department plans the placement of ads in the various media and makes sure that the plan is carried out. It is expected to see that the media plan conveys the campaign's communication and marketing objectives. After the agency makes its media recommendations and these are approved by the client, the media department prepares an advertising schedule showing the publications and dates of printing of the ad and the times and stations of television or radio presentations. It then makes contracts and finally pays the bill received from the media. An agency, unlike a client, is normally eligible

for a commission on the space it buys (about 15 percent in most countries).

6. Research. Agency planners and clients alike have a constant need for all sorts of information. Most agencies do some research on their own and the larger ones will have research departments. In most cases, large surveys and the field work involved are contracted to an outside research firm.

7. Sales promotion. Many agencies work with clients and dealers in planning retail promotions, contests, sampling programs, point-of-purchase material and other forms of promotion that help make the advertising productive. Some departments create sales promotion material and work with the sales and marketing departments of client firms.

8. Public Relations. Many larger agencies help work out their public relations or public affairs programs, sometimes through a department within the agency and sometimes by coordinating efforts with a public relations firm that is owned by the same parent organization as the advertising agency. Public relations departments are concerned with all activities which will help build a favorable corporate image.

Advertising agencies that expand into foreign markets may choose any of several alternative methods of entry. One is to establish a new branch in the country—usually in its main business center. This is the way most U.S. agencies expanded abroad in the period before World War II. It is also the way the world's largest agency, Densu, has normally moved into foreign markets. Another alternative is to find an already established overseas agency and purchase an interest in it. This has been a common method for U.S. agencies expanding into the West European and Far Eastern Markets in the 1960s and 1970s. When the dollar was a strong currency and many others were weak, this was an attractive way of establishing a beachhead in many foreign markets.

Another alternative is to set up joint agencies in one or more foreign countries. These are usually separate entities controlled by the domestic agency and at least one foreign agency. Some of these joint ventures operate in several countries although more commonly they are confined to a single country. This has provided a viable approach for entering markets like Japan, where the government has been reluctant to approve wholly owned subsidiaries.

Yet another alternative is to join an agency network system. There are now in Europe, for example, several networks of agencies that have formed integrated groups to offer local services, talents and ideas on an organized and regular exchange basis. Still another possibility is to work through affiliate agencies abroad. This is often done where the domestic agency has good media files and specialized personnel that can be used by the foreign agency. It is an approach popular with large agencies where a particular market is not large enough for them to set up a full-fledged branch office or even a joint venture.

Advertisers

Most advertisers operating in a foreign market will use an agency for the duties outlined above. There are exceptions, however, such as a few retail chains (Gimbels and Bergners in the United States, McDonald's in various foreign countries) that handle much of their own advertising. Even large international industrial firms like Colgate-Palmolive often have an international advertising manager to coordinate the advertising in different countries. However, the exact form of an international firm's advertising organization depends on a wide variety of factors (e.g., nature of the product marketed, market characteristics, management philosophy and the like). The goal of the organization is to find a structure that enables the company to respond to relevant differences in market environment. At the same time the company wants to extend valuable knowledge, experience and know-how from its headquarters to the entire corporate system. There is often a conflict between centralizing knowledge of the firm and its operations and adapting response to local situations that can create tension in the international organization.

Firms like Caterpillar with a single or simplified worldwide product line (tractors in the case of Caterpillar) have found that a central worldwide advertising department works well. Among the most important duties of an international advertising executive are the following:

1. Planning the campaign. This is usually the advertising manager's most important

job. To do this he will depend on input from his research worldwide and the information he receives from the firm's representative in various markets. If the firm is a large one, it is likely that there will be an advertising manager in each country and probably one also for an important regional office like that for Western Europe and the Far East.

2. Helping select and evaluate the work of the firm's agencies. Some U.S. firms, such as Ford, tend to use the same agency worldwide. Others, like Procter & Gamble, tend to give local managers more autonomy and thus have a bigger job in working with and evaluating agencies around the world.

3. Advising top executives on advertising matters and related problems. This requires knowledge of all phases of marketing and communication.

4. Coordinating advertising and other marketing functions. In some cases (such as ITT, with a wide variety of products and services, including telecommunications, food, hotels, and insurance sold worldwide) the advertising director is also director of public affairs and is expected to coordinate the two functions. In this case public affairs includes all those activities that help improve the company's relations with such publics as government, media and labor unions as well as potential customers for the firm's products and services.

Some companies allow considerable autonomy to the regional and national advertising managers in the hope that they can adapt advertising strategy to the local market, by building close relations with the firm's agencies and the media.

A variation of the organizational and international advertising function is the brand manager approach. In such a system the emphasis is on the product, with the one brand manager responsible for its worldwide marketing. This type of organization, however, is more common in domestic than in international marketing.

Advertising Media

As already noted, media tend to be somewhat less international than their agencies or advertisers. Some, however, have international sales and marketing organizations which attempt to solicit advertising in various offices around the world. Leading U.S. publishers like *Reader's Digest* and McGraw-Hill have sales offices in most major business centers of the world. These have little to do with editorial material. And such European publishing organizations as *The Economist* and *L'Express* have sales offices in the United States.

The largest of the international research firms, A.C. Nielsen Company, was strongly entrenched in the foreign market before World War II. It depends on its mainly 100-percent-owned affiliates around the world to provide information to advertisers, agencies and media in most major business centers. On the other hand, other leading advertising and media research firms, such as Gallup and Starch INRA Hooper, tend to work through affiliated research organizations in various foreign markets.

Advertising Associations

The principal worldwide organization for the advertising industry is the International Advertising Association (IAA), with headquarters in New York. It has members and chapters throughout the world and serves as a medium for exchange of information, ideas and techniques and as a representative of the industry on the international front.

Regulation of International Advertising

Executives who work for international advertisers, agencies or media have been concerned (and in many cases confused) by the wide variety of regulations they face from one country or region to another. For example, Gillette officials in Britain were surprised when that country's regulatory board (Advertising Standards Authority) turned down a television commercial based on a funeral theme (burial of an old method of shaving). This was felt to be in bad taste. The authority finally approved a revised commercial suggesting burial but no funeral or even such accoutrements as pallbearers and hearse.

Although regulation of advertising is generally on the increase, there are some cases where the opposite trend is in effect. In the EEC strong effort is being made to "harmonize" laws among the nine members and to drop or relax some of the more restrictive practices in the hope that the industry will do a better job of regulating itself.

Part of the trend toward more regulation is attributable to the criticism of the multinational corporations. It is in advertising that such corporations most often show their face to the man in the street and it is advertising that is thus likely to arouse indignation among critics of business. Part of it is due merely to political, cultural and religious upheavals around the world. Because of this increase in regulation and the confusion it has engendered, the whole subject of regulation has been examined carefully. The following discussion is based on these studies.

General Trends

Regulators almost everywhere are very much concerned about certain types of advertising message content. Advertising-control groups and individuals outside the United States are more concerned than those in this country with advertising that insults intelligence, uses foreign languages, offends or corrupts morals (especially children's), compares products, encourages energy consumption, or generally misleads. A rising force in the regulation of advertising has been the worldwide consumer movement. These are groups who seek to increase the rights and powers of buyers in relation to sellers and are actively insisting that the consumer has a basic right to safety, information, choice, and redress in case of wrongdoing. In Austria and Switzerland, for example, foreign expressions are allowed in commercials only if they are readily intelligible to a general audience. And in West Germany, foreign brand names are forbidden if they would cause confusion regarding the origin of the product. Thus a German advertisement could be run in English for a product made in the United States or the United Kingdom, but not for one made locally.

There is generally a stronger trend toward regulation of advertising in countries that are more economically developed. Thus one finds more stringent regulations in Sweden and Belgium than in Italy or Spain. In the more affluent nations, the anti-advertising forces are more militant and better organized, and they not only have greater government support but also receive considerable cooperation from many managers who run

the very businesses that are sometimes criticized.

Some of the differences in regulation among countries is due to basic legal philosophy. The United Kingdom, for example, is a common-law country (law based on precedents and previous legal decisions) while most of the continental countries have legal systems based on code law (a strict and fairly literal interpretation of what is legal and what is not). In common-law countries, for example, ownership of a trademark is determined by priority of use, in code-law countries by priority in registration.

Types of Regulatory Problems

Content of the Advertising Message. Resolution (72) 8 on Consumer Protection Against Misleading Advertising passed by the Committee of Ministers of the Council of Europe in 1972 attempted to define the areas in which advertising is likely to mislead:
1. The nature, composition, origin, quantity, dates of manufacture, or properties of the goods or, so far as is relevant, services described by the advertisements
2. The total price actually to be paid by the consumer for the goods and services offered, or any favorable comparison made by the advertiser with other prices
3. The identity, qualifications or competence of the producers of goods, traders or suppliers of services

The Council of Europe has had almost as much trouble as the Federal Trade Commission and the various U.S. courts in agreeing on a workable definition of "misleading advertising." The British Trade Descriptions Act takes a commonsense approach by emphasizing what might mislead a "reasonable person" to "a reasonable degree." This would seem to allow some product puffer (e.g., Coca Cola's "refreshes best"). The assumption here, as in the United States, is that the consumer knows the message comes from a partisan source and does not take the claims literally.

In France, whether the message is legally misleading may well depend on how the product is distributed. For example, Carter-Wallace, a large U.S.-based pharmaceutical house, sold its Arrid Extra Dry deodorant through department stores but had to distribute its Carter's Little Liver Pills through pharmacies, thus bringing them under France's very strict drug marketing laws. A seller of cosmetics can avoid much regulation if he can make sure his product is not considered a proprietary drug. Penalties for false and misleading advertising are especially stringent in such countries as France and West Germany. In the latter, the laws cover deception in both words and pictures in regard to the advertiser or his business, the qualities, origin, manufacture or price of goods or service sold, buying of the product, awards conferred on products, and size of the seller's stocks. Omissions, ambiguous statements, deceptive uses of type faces or demonstrations, or partly true statements are considered misleading. Sellers in Germany must notify the authorities in advance if they plan to have a sale. In recent years the German courts have softened their traditionally hard line on comparisons in advertising ("Our product is better") and allow them when sufficiently justified by the consuming public's need for adequate information.

In general, comparative claims are more likely to be considered deceptive in most other countries than the United States, where the policy of the FTC is to encourage comparisons that can be verified by evidence. Testimonials by professionals such as doctors or dentists, or by consumers, cannot be used in many countries if they imply comparisons with competing products. The right of defense (droit de response) is considered an acceptable justification for comparative advertising in France.

The EEC Commission on Misleading and Unfair Advertising has proposed that "comparative advertising shall be allowed as long as it compares material and verifiable details, and is neither misleading nor unfair." This would require Belgium, France, Italy and Luxembourg to remove their restrictions on such advertising.

Decency and Sexism in Advertising: These are also general areas of concern to regulators in many countries. As a study on this area of regulation by Jean Boddewyn for the IAA noted:

Laws, regulations and voluntary guidelines applying to advertising are seldom easy to interpret. This is even truer in the matter of the elusive concept of decency and sexism—two related topics because they're frequently associated with sexual appeals and with women.

"Decency" refers to advertising that con-

forms to standards generally accepted by a country or culture. Problems typically concern such sensitive issues in some countries as contraception, use of tasteless images, vulgar language or offensive appeals, promotion of "very personal" products and services such as undergarments, feminine hygiene goods, contraceptives and massages, advertising of cigarettes, alcoholic beverages, pornographic materials, violence or sex-ridden films or comic books.

"Sexism" in advertising applies to the exploitation of sexual appeals, situations, poses and dress. It includes the overuse of young, attractive women in ads or the use of women in situations not related to use of the product or service. Clearly this is, as in the case of decency, a very subjective problem, viewed differently from one culture to another.

Key factors in defining the role of decency and sexism, according to the IAA study, were the following: (1) religion and related value systems that vary from one country to another (e.g., French commercials show brassieres modeled by live models and allow considerable nudity, but prohibit advertising of contraceptives; Japan allows seminudity; Saudi Arabia and Kuwait restrict irrelevant use of women as glamor symbols; Spain has recently lifted its ban on contraceptive advertising); (2) the law that usually parallels moral standards by banning certain types of sex and violence in ads and in several countries bans discriminatory statements in advertisements soliciting applicants for jobs; in many cases the law includes health-related products (e.g., cosmetics, medicines and aphrodisiacs); (3) activism of religious and feminist groups (many Moslem countries, such as Iran and Saudi Arabia, are strongly resisting invasion of Western advertising themes and creative approaches); (4) media control: in many countries (Mexico and Taiwan, for example) a strong pre-clearance system by the media exists; in general, TV and radio commercials are more restricted than print ads and direct mail, which are more selective in their audiences; (5) advertising self-regulation, where used, as a factor preventing strong government regulation.

According to the IAA survey, respondents generally rated decency and sexism in advertising as one of the minor issues. However, Canada, Indonesia, Thailand and Venezuela considered it to be a major issue with considerable importance, just slightly less emphasis being put on it in Chile, Japan and

Nigeria. It is undoubtedly true, however, that the laws and self-regulation have blunted much of what might be serious criticism.

Products whose advertising is regulated in advertising are the following, listed in order of importance as indicated by the IAA study: female (nonprescription) contraceptives, male contraceptives, feminine hygiene products, female undergarments, hemorrhoid remedies, male hygiene products, deodorants, perfumes and beauty care products. Sexist situations most likely to be regulated were ads using a woman as an attention getter although she has no relevance to the product, ads showing a woman in a lewd and salacious way, ads presenting use of a product as apt to confer power of seduction, and ads that sytematically associate a product or service with only one sex when it is used by both. The survey indicated that decency and sexism will remain something of a source of complaint, owing to a wide variety of cultural standards. There appears to be relative permissiveness in *sexual* matters but some tendency to become more sensitive in the *sexist* area.

Information in Advertisements: Some organizations have proposed that the advertising tax should be based on the amount of information in a firm's advertising (the more information, the less the tax). When Pepsi-Cola is promoted in Germany, each advertisement must include the phrase "contains caffeine." In other countries such a qualifying statement is not needed.

The European Association of Advertising Agencies objects to requiring specific information in advertisements primarily because consumers need certain kinds of information in connection with buying some products, but very little with others. Certain media lend themselves to providing a wealth of information; certain others, such as radio and television, lend themselves more to image building. Many advertisements are most effective for both the seller and the prospective buyer when they contain one or two main points.

In certain countries the regulators are willing to trade advertising-information requirements for more information on the label. Some marketers are trying to standardize labels across national lines, but this attempt has met with only limited support so far—even in the EEC, where it has the most support.

In most countries, labeling of certain specific products is controlled more than that of others. The problem is that some of the

distinctions among products make little sense to marketers. For example beverages in France are divided into categories according to their alcohol content. In the highest categories, such as whiskey and cognac, no advertising is allowed, whereas in the case of aperitifs one can show the bottle and the name and address of the marketer—but no selling copy. Where products are classified as "medical" in France, advertising takes place only in the medical journals, not in the general media.

Use of Foreign Languages: Although in most countries there is relatively little use of foreign languages in advertising, this has become a matter of concern to many advertisers and to the International Advertising Association. Foreign languages are used mainly for the following:

1. Reaching special target audiences, such as ads for employment where language is needed
2. Addition of credibility and/or prestige to the advertisement, say, the use of French for perfumes or English for sophisticated equipment
3. Reaching special national or foreign ethnic groups; for example, the Malay, Chinese, Malaysian, or the variety of nationalities in the Middle East

In general, liberalism prevails in the use of foreign languages, but there are exceptions. Only Australia, Colombia, France, Malaysia, Quebec Province (Canada) and Venezuela may be considered very restrictive (with the Philippines moving in that direction).

Such restrictions are based on one of two motivations: (1) economic or national considerations and (2) consumer protection. They are more common in television, radio, cinema and outdoor advertising than in the print and direct media. Since broadcasting networks are few and often government run, they are controllable. Some countries, moreover, are trying to provide jobs to local personnel such as announcers, actors, musicians and writers. The Actors' and Announcers' Equity Association of Australia imposes a limit of 20 percent of foreign materials with no talent content. It will accept foreign talent if local performers are paid an equivalent fee. Foreign-company and foreign-brand names can be used everywhere except in Mexico where the equivalent Spanish name must be adjoined. Foreign-prepared materials can generally be used but there are restrictions in Peru and a few other countries. In certain countries (particularly the non-Western ones) there have been occasional clashes with ethnic and cultural groups, some of which are pressuring the government to remove what they consider colonial relics of dependence on foreign powers. The Philippine government, for instance, encourages the use of Tagalog "due to a desire for preserving the national heritage and independence from foreigners."

The rise of consumer protectionism, together with an increasing number of poorly labeled imported products is leading some governments to require that information be provided in the consumers' native language. Thus in Austria and Switzerland, foreign expressions are allowed in broadcast commercials only if they are readily intelligible to a general audience.

Advertising to Children: Advertising directed primarily at children constitutes a major issue in the United States and to a lesser extent in 37 other countries of the world, according to an IAA study. Consumerist groups in several countries are especially concerned with children, and they have asked supernational bodies such as the EEC Commission, the OECD Committee on Consumer Policy and UNESCO to study the subject and prepare regulatory proposals. Canada's Quebec Province has banned ads directed primarily to children on radio and television. Industry itself has developed voluntary guidelines in such countries as Australia, Canada, the Philippines, South Africa, Spain and the United Kingdom. The code of the International Chamber of Commerce also addresses this problem.

The main arguments for regulating ads to children are:

1. Such ads create wants among children which parents cannot or should not gratify.
2. They teach children overly materialistic views.
3. They encourage consumption of "junk" foods, sweets and candy.
4. They take advantage of children's natural credibility and lack of experience.
5. They exploit children's difficulty in distinguishing between broadcast program material and the advertising messages.

Industry typically counters that children are exposed to much advertising on media and programs not specifically directed to children, that children have to learn something of how to buy anyway, and that there is little evidence that watching these commercials is a direct cause of any bad habits or antisocial behavior.

The aforementioned IAA study of children's advertising around the world cites as its major findings:

1. Children's advertising is only a minor problem in most countries, but is expected to increase in importance during the 1980s.
2. Most countries currently allow television and radio commercials directed to children, but 12 countries have media or self-regulatory requirements that children's ads be distinguished from program and editorial content. Canada and the United States restrict the time devoted to children's ads.
3. One is less likely to find special restrictions applying to children in the broadcast than in other media.
4. Outside of tobacco and alcoholic products, drugs and medicines, less than one-third of the countries restrict advertising of special products to children.
5. About 40 percent of the countries require pre-clearance of TV and radio ads for children.
6. Most nations allow premiums, gifts and contests for children.
7. Most countries that allow comparative ads are more restrictive when such ads are directed to children.
8. In a few countries children cannot be shown in advertisements unless they are clearly related to the product or service promoted.

Energy and Advertising: Although major energy crises have occurred in recent years, in many countries the advertising of energy-consuming products has generally not been affected substantially. In general, countries have been more likely to control energy through higher prices, extra taxes, performance standards on automobiles, tax credit incentives for insulation, and educational campaigns to discourage waste.

A 1974 international energy program ratified by some twenty OECD countries led to the creation of the International Energy Agency. This required governments to draft national contingency plans for restricting the demand for oil. In 1979 the EEC started a harmonization program to standardize information regarding energy on labels and in advertising.

The most active countries in regulating energy advertising have been the United

Kingdom and the United States. Home insulation materials are the principal target of such regulations. According to a study of this problem by the IAA, most advertising and marketing people around the world expect that means other than advertising regulations will be used to achieve energy conservation.

Trademarks: Many companies have been blocked from using a valuable trade name or symbol when they enter a foreign market. Budweiser, the largest selling beer brand in the United States, could not be marketed in most of Europe until recently because of prior registration of the mark by a brewery in Czechoslovakia. After developing "Pearl Drops" as a successful entry into the highly competitive and lucrative dentifrice market in the United States, Carter-Wallace sought to use it in England. Because Pearl Drops soap was registered by Unilever, the company was blocked from using its own product.

According to U.S. trademarks lawyer Sidney A. Diamond, major American companies seeking protection for their brands in foreign markets must frequently file in 50 to 100 countries. Approximately 200 countries are prepared to receive applications for trademark registration and to issue registration certifications, but if everything is in order the company looking for protection must then file a separate application in each individual country, in each case hiring a local attorney or agent to prepare the proper legal documents in the proper language.

Advertisers have been encouraged by the results of a conference in Vienna in 1973, when representatives from 50 countries adopted the text of an international trademark registration treaty that would simplify procedures for obtaining legal protection for trademarks, including trade names, symbols or characters, and themes or slogans.

Sales Promotion: To encourage distributors to promote—and consumers to try their products or services and to help support their advertising—a number of business firms use such forms of sales promotion as free samples, coupons providing free trial at reduced prices, contests, and premiums attached to the product. An IAA survey shows some form of promotion control in 38 countries. It complements studies by the OECD and EEC, both of which have also considered restrictions on promotions.

While most forms of sales promotion are readily accepted by both consumers and advertisers in the United States, this is by no means always the case elsewhere. Competition in the form of games, prizes, contests, lotteries, and the like is restricted on moral grounds in many countries, although not on a consistent basis. Some countries, such as Norway, permit games of skill but not of chance; others allow games of chance provided they are taxed. A third group—including the United States and Sweden—objects to competition being linked to proof of purchase. A fourth type of regulation (in Japan, for instance) covers prizes.

Premiums present a special case in that they tend to be more controversial than most other sales promotion methods. Advertisers claim that premiums stimulate competition and thus benefit consumers, that they force competitors to lower their prices, that they provide free merchandise for many consumers and that they help distributors take full advantage of the advertising. However, critics claim goods and services should be sold on their own merit, that premiums tend to divert attention from the product and what it will do for them, and that the system is an uneconomic and wasteful form of promotion.

Practically all countries condemn misleading or deceptive presentation in advertising of premium, gift and competition offers—in varying degrees. The United States and the United Kingdom are generally most lenient in the use of premiums, gifts and contests, but Scandinavian countries, Belgium, France and West Germany are negative toward premiums because they think such offers tend to distract consumers from the merits of goods or services and are "overattractive."

Sales promotion depends partly on the extent to which consumerism is a force in the country. In the United States and the United Kingdom there is an attempt to make sure the offering is not misleading and if not is relatively free from regulation. On the other hand, in certain other countries the consumer is not considered quite so knowledgeable and the government takes on the job of protecting him from himself by limiting his chances to go wrong.

Efforts to regulate promotion are opposed by advertising groups in most countries on the grounds that they will result in all countries agreeing to be regulated as much as those that are now most strictly controlled.

Government Pre-Clearance of Advertising

If an advertisement is false, misleading, deceptive or unfair, it can be challenged after the fact in most countries. If the complaint is valid some sort of cease-and-desist injunction will normally follow. However, this procedure is considered in many countries as being too cumbersome and slow, since the harm has already been done. Much better, they say, is a system of pre-clearance ("pre-vetting" in Britain) involving some mandatory requirement that advertising materials be approved before the ads are released to the media.

Most advertising professionals oppose such an approach, since they feel it threatens their freedom of expression and their creativity. It could also lead to costly delays and arguments with whatever bureaucracy which enforces the regulations.

However, pre-clearance exists in many countries; in quite a few the media may refuse proposed ads. In some there is a mandatory government pre-clearance arrangement, in others pre-screening is voluntary. In general, the professionals favor the latter. In many countries the voluntary system exists only in the sense that pre-clearance is not required, but elsewhere it is used to forestall proposals for government-mandated pre-clearance. To all practical purposes, voluntary pre-clearance is really mandatory in Australia and Canada.

An IAA survey of pre-clearance in 42 countries revealed that:

1. About 60 percent of the countries have one or more government pre-clearance requirements applying to such health-related products as prescription drugs, over-the-counter drugs, medicated toiletries and cosmetics. These requirements are based on the idea that the consumer needs special protection in buying such products. There is also opposition to making illness a business in some countries (such as Denmark) and advertising is viewed as leading to unnecessary use of drugs.
2. About 40 percent of pre-clearance requirements apply to promotional practices such as games, lotteries and contests.
3. Almost a third of the countries have special pre-clearances for the broadcast media. In some 10 countries, for example, including Canada, the United Kingdom and France, all broadcast ads have to be pre-cleared. In such countries as France, the government owns the stations and so does all the pre-screening.
4. A smaller but growing number of countries are moving toward mandatory pre-clearance for all food and drink advertisements, particularly if they include some sort of therapeutic claims.
5. Advertisements for cigarettes, alcoholic beverages, financial services, tourism and real estate, together with advertisements directed at children, are favorite targets for pre-clearance requirements.
6. Cinema advertising requires pre-clearance in 23 percent of the countries, including Egypt, India, Kenya and Malaysia. Developing countries are especially concerned with violence, sedition, nudity and the promotion of Western values.

The IAA study indicated that a little less than one-third of the countries anticipated greater pre-clearance requirements in the near future. The most likely candidates were considered to be foods, tobacco, liquor, feminine hygiene products and ads to children. Some view guidelines of do's and don'ts as substitutes for pre-clearance (such as the proposed ban in Belgium of expressions like "natural" and "healthy").

Self-Regulation of Advertising

Advertising is regulated through a variety of means, including legal regulation as interpreted by the courts and governmental administrative agencies, and self-regulation by the industry. More indirect control comes through lobbying of consumer or business groups and from taxation of certain types of advertising. In Denmark, Norway and Sweden the Consumer Ombudsman applies the laws regulating advertising and tries to get advertisers to comply with both national law and codes of the International Chamber of Commerce.

As of 1979, according to the IAA, the various industry, trade and advertising associations had developed codes of ethics and guidelines in at least 35 countries. These are most effective in those countries where the advertising industry is well developed. At a minimum such countries subscribe to the International Chamber of Commerce codes of practice in marketing, marketing research, sales promotion, and advertising. Courts use them as reference in Belgium, France, Germany and the Scandinavian countries.

Begun in 1937, the ICC codes are fairly general, emphasizing principles rather than specifics. More explicit provisions are found in national voluntary codes such as those of Argentina, Canada, Germany, South Africa and Spain. These are usually issued by industry-wide organizations and are supported by large segments of their corporate memberships.

Most codes are based at least in part on the ICC codes, and on the experience of such long-time self-regulators as the United Kingdom. The self-regulatory mechanism in the United States (the National Advertising Review Board and the National Advertising Division of the Better Business Bureaus) is based primarily on the U.K.'s widely respected Advertising Standards Authority.

The EEC Commission has acknowledged the role of self-regulation but in general seems to prefer to limit its role to "advisory" and to depend more on legal regulation. Consumer groups are also generally lukewarm toward self-regulation, since they suspect that too much soft-pedaling of restraints and whitewashing of violations will result. Even businessmen are not wholly supportive of self-regulation. Many like to operate with minimum restraint and prefer to trust the judgment of their lawyers.

Advertising and the Media

There is little evidence that the editorial and entertainment content of media are influenced by the growth of international advertising. This is true even though media in almost every country are heavily dependent on the multinational corporations for much of their advertising revenue. There are, however, differences in media dependence on advertising from one country to another. In most of the developing countries, as well as the United States, television depends heavily on advertising revenue. In those countries where television is government subsidized or owned, the high cost of programming and transmission requires that the revenue come from a mixture of advertising, government tax on television sets, appropriations from general tax revenues and contributions from private industry or the public.

The print media are not as dependent on advertising revenues as the broadcast media. In some countries the readers pay most of the publication's production cost, while in others the advertisers pay all or most of it. We find particularly wide variations in the magazine field, since most countries have controlled- or free-circulation magazines that are supported entirely from advertising revenue. These are particularly common in certain technical and industrial fields, where important readerships can be covered very comprehensively through free circulation. Such complete coverage can then be sold to adver-

tisers who are anxious to reach these homogeneous audiences. We find also in most countries some magazines that accept no advertising, being supported entirely through circulation or through dues in a particular association that sponsors the publication.

According to a study of international advertising conducted by the UNESCO Commission on Transactional Corporations and published in 1979, there is a discernible trend throughout the world toward more commercialization of the communications media. In the print media this seems to be reflected primarily in a substantial increase in commercial as compared with noncommercial content. In the case of television, commercial time is increasing as a percentage of total broadcast time, but it is still far less than the total percentage of newspaper or magazine advertising content. However, these percentages are not comparable: in the print media, the reader can decide whether or not to read a particular item—commercial or noncommercial, while in the broadcast media control is in the hands of the broadcaster and the audience cannot exercise the same degree of choice. Many countries consequently group television commercials within a few time periods of the day and keep the rest of the programming free from all advertising. This is a common pattern in Western Europe.

On the other hand, several countries, including the United Kingdom, allow commercials during breaks between programs, but do not have advertiser-sponsored programs or interrupt the program with commercials. Still others follow the example of the United States, allowing commercials to be placed within the programs, advertisers to sponsor programs, and broadcasters to decide where and how often the commercials will be shown. However, in the United States and Japan, the self-regulatory bodies attempt to keep the amount of time in commercials within certain limits and try to set forth rules for what is proper in radio-TV advertising content.

The UNESCO study also looked at the worldwide tendency toward more commercial television: the mounting costs associated with operating stations and networks have caused governments to turn more to advertisers for revenue.

Some critics are concerned that the increasing involvement of advertisers—particularly the multinational companies—could lead to certain undesirable effects. For one thing, publishers and broadcasters are encouraged to aim for mass appeal since large audiences are more saleable to advertisers. However, there is evidence that just the opposite is taking place in the print media of Western Europe and the United States, where the specialized publications are prospering more than those that seek to attract mass audiences. In the case of the broadcast media there is also incentive to specialize but no evidence that this is taking place to any great extent. In most of the Western European countries, for example, television broadcasters do not have to cater to advertisers since they typically have a waiting list of private companies trying to buy television time. In several EEC countries, in fact, advertisers like Procter & Gamble have launched a campaign to encourage telecasters to allot more time to advertising.

There is also the danger that advertisers may influence the editorial viewpoint or news coverage in the media by withdrawing or threatening to withdraw advertising. However, in practice, as the UNESCO study points out, this is obviously short-sighted, since the main aim of advertisers is to reach large groups of potential customers. In those countries where regulations and the professional standards of journalists are weak, the potential is probably greatest for advertiser influence on editorial policy.

One advertising medium that has attracted considerable attention from consumer groups and consequent regulation is outdoor display —store or factory signs, messages on billboards, painted bulletins, posters, painted walls, metallic and electric signs, handbills, transit advertising, and vehicles equipped with loudspeakers. According to an IAA study of this medium published in 1979, all but four countries have formal restrictions on such advertising. The most common reasons for such regulations are:

1. Promotion of traffic safety by not distracting drivers.
2. Environmental protection or the prevention of visual pollution.
3. Esthetic considerations, to keep signs away from major monuments or important tourist attractions.
4. Bad taste: such advertising will be seen by all and cannot easily be screened.
5. Taxation: this is looked on as another source of revenue.
6. Energy savings: billboards are aimed at *automobile drivers*.

According to the IAA study, local or municipal regulations are more likely to regulate outdoor advertising than federal laws. This seems to reflect the idea that outdoor display is to a great extent a local zoning problem. The developing nations tend to be more restrictive in what can be shown on billboards, with emphasis on avoiding pornographic or obscene material—particularly in Muslim and Catholic countries. The United States, being heavily motorized, has more highway restrictions than most, but is not particularly severe in its restrictions on content.

Advertising and the Communications Mix

Many advertisers and their agencies have tried to standardize their advertising strategy from one market to another. It makes eminent sense to many of them to exploit successes and failures at home in promoting products or services in a foreign market. Unfortunately, however, what succeeds or fails in one country may do just the reverse in another. Marketing executives often fail to account for the differences in advertising media, cultural characteristics, languages, economics and distribution systems when they try to transfer a marketing project. According to a study by this author, advertising was more difficult to transfer successfully than sales promotion, partly because advertising is more influenced by cultural differences. The problems of working out the major communication mix are most likely to occur in the areas of creating the message and choosing the communications media.

Creative Strategy

Some creative approaches seem to be much more transferable than others. Pepsi-Cola learned that its theme "Come alive" was interpreted in some countries as "Arise from the dead." Colgate-Palmolive learned that the young lady who throws kisses to young men in U.S. television commercials to sell Ultra-Brite dentifrice caused adverse reaction in many European countries, and that it was better to modify this theme. "Give your mouth sex appeal" was considered bad taste in certain markets. Coca-Cola found it easier to transfer the theme "Things go better with Coke" than "It's the real thing." The barriers to effective international communication through advertising are many, and experienced marketing people learn through experience or research to anticipate some of the problems in creating effective messages for a foreign market. The following appear to be the most important criteria for determining when the creative strategy can be transferred from one country to another:

1. Availability and acceptance of the media; what types of audiences read or view the media?
2. Product position; is the product sold to the same type of market and for the same purpose as in the domestic market?
3. Economic climate; is the foreign market comparable economically to the domestic market?
4. Cultural patterns; how similar is the culture of the country to that of the domestic culture? This is especially important in the case of culture-bound products like food and clothing.
5. Legal restrictions; are there restrictions on what can be said in an advertisement that are not present in the domestic market?
6. Consumerism; is there an active consumer movement that might attack some of the contents of the advertising message?
7. Political climate; are there sensitive national issues that might cause difficulty in a particular country?

Media Strategy

Another of the major problems involved in implementing advertising strategy is working out an effective mix of the media for each country. Many international firms find that they do not have proper media coverage of prospective buyers in many of the markets they want to reach. Often they find it difficult to evaluate the media because of insufficient media research or even reliable scientific circulation dates. Many U.S. advertisers, who depend heavily on television in their home market, are dismayed when they find they cannot buy TV time for commercial purposes in such important markets as Sweden and Belgium, or that they have to take their chances on allotments of scarce time in such important markets as France and West Germany. (By contrast they find that advertising in the cinema—a relatively minor medium in the United States—is an

important channel to markets in many countries.)

Table 1 shows the expenditures in the "measured media" (print, television and radio) in most of the major markets of the world. It is evident that there are wide variations in the proportions divided to each medium—even among such comparable countries as the United Kingdom or developing countries such as Egypt and Turkey. As one would expect in a country like Denmark, where television is not available, print expenditures represent a very high proportion of total measured media expenditures. Moreover, in some areas the media tend to follow cultural rather than political lines. People who identify themselves with the French or the German or the Arab cultural patterns will probably read much the same publications although they may live in several different countries.

There is also a difference in media coverage within relatively comparable countries. For example, one finds many national media in the United Kingdom but much fewer in Italy—another EEC country of somewhat comparable population. Consequently, an advertiser might use a few newspapers to blanket the entire United Kingdom, but not Italy. In the United States and most developed countries, television is a mass medium with well over 90 percent of the homes having a television set in working order. But while television can be used in the United States as a national network medium or as a national spot medium where time is bought market by market, this is much more difficult to do in most other countries, where television tends to be national. (In the developing nations television is also somewhat selective.)

Such common yardsticks for measuring media efficiency as the milline rate (advertising line rate multiplied by one million and divided by circulation) are of limited benefit in many countries. Whereas in the United States rates are usually set by quantity and quality of the audience reached by a publication or a broadcast program, in many countries these are set by the government on the basis of other criteria. Advertising rates are firm in some countries, open to bargaining in others.

There are several important international media, but these have not prospered in proportion to the growth of international advertising. For example, U.S. magazines like *Playboy* and *Cosmopolitan* have turned to local editions in many European countries—

an approach carried out earlier by *Reader's Digest*. International advertisers tend to prefer national media to reach mass audiences but often use international media to reach upper-income markets or specialized groups such as engineers or business executives.

Role of Advertising Research

Advertisers have a wealth of media and market data in most of the developed countries, much less in the developing countries. Many U.S. research firms like A.C. Nielsen have major branches abroad, and most business centers have a large number of local research firms. However, the lack of good information is still a common complaint from national advertisers. Even companies that are avid testers of creative and media strategy in the United States often do little when they move into a foreign market. The following seem to be the principal reasons for the slow growth of advertising research by multinational corporations, agencies and media:

1. The expense of good research
2. Skepticism regarding the quality of foreign research personnel and their organizations
3. Difficulty of communicating with local researchers and respondents
4. Doubt as to the validity of testing techniques that work in one country but are yet to be tried in another
5. Lack of research by much of competition

It must be kept in mind also that multinational advertisers who could justify a large media study in a large market such as the United States or Japan find it much more difficult to justify one in a small market like the Netherlands or Greece. The chances are that it will cost almost as much to make the study in the small market as in the large one.

Advertising in Socialist Countries

Karl Marx wrote that capital invested in "trade" was part of the "dead expense of the capitalistic economic system." Consequently, one might be suprised that his socialist followers have in recent years started to use advertising domestically and have welcomed advertising from other countries. Although socialist leaders tend to criticize capitalist economies for using advertising and public relations to excess, they contend now that their own socialist machinery utilizes advertising in a controlled market and that consequently advertising tends to aid in the development of their planned economy.

The bellwether of socialist policy is the Soviet Union. Adertising was virtually unknown there until the early 1960s, when it was recognized for the first time as economically worthwhile. The volume of advertising in both Russia and the other Eastern-bloc countries is still quite low in comparison with Western levels, but it is on the rise. Advertising in the broadcast and print media was estimated by the Soviet Ministry of Trade at approximately $300 million in 1975. According to the head of the American Business Press, "The decision made by the state-controlled economy of the U.S.S.R. that it needs advertising is not an emotional one; it is rather based on sound economic reasons." In Russia all foreign advertising (import and export) is handled by one state-run advertising agency, Vneshtorgreklama. Advertising in Yugoslavia is somewhat more available to foreign businesses than in the USSR. There one finds brands like Coca-Cola, Schweppes and Brown & Decker advertised regularly on television.

The world's largest market in terms of population, the People's Republic of China, had become by 1980 the number-one trading partner for the United States among communist bloc nations. It has established a large promotion organization, Shanghai Advertising Corporation, to oversee advertising operations within China. The Peking government has contracted with two large U.S. agencies to handle Chinese advertising in such overseas markets as the United States, the Far East and Europe.

Summary

In the 1970s world advertising expenditures grew rapidly with the total by the late 1970s reaching an estimated 80 billion U.S. dollars. The United States was by far the world leader, Japan second and West Germany third. This figure covered both the firms' exports and the products of their subsidiaries abroad. Reasons for the growth were the rise of the multinationals, worldwide improvement in living standards, higher overseas profits and improvement in communications and transportation.

The institutions are much the same from

country to country with advertising agencies, advertising divisions of business firms and the advertising media being the most important groups almost everywhere. The techniques are also similar but there are differences that cause serious problems—perhaps the most important of these being creative and media strategy. The lack of information from research or other credible sources presents a serious problem for both U.S. and many international advertisers and their agencies. The increase in regulations poses a further serious problem for most international advertisers, who must keep abreast of the change in these and their wide differences from country to country.

The future of international advertising appears to be greatly promising, due to several factors: (1) continued growth of multinational corporations; (2) improvements in advertising techniques in many countries; (3) expansion of media availabilities for advertisers in most markets; (4) improvement in living standards in many of the poorer countries of the world.

SECTION II:
The World's Developed Press Systems

ALBANIA

by Paul Underwood

BASIC DATA

Population: 2,655,000 (1980)	**Number of Periodicals:** 51
Area: 28,749 sq. km. (11,100 sq. mi.)	**Number of Radio Stations:** 5
GNP: 15.4 billion lek (US$2.2 billion) (1979)	**Number of Television Stations:** 1
Literacy Rate: 70%	**Number of Radio Receivers:** 173,000
Language(s): Albanian	**Radio Receivers per 1,000:** 70
Number of Dailies: 2	**Number of Television Sets:** 5,000
Aggregate Circulation: 115,000	**Television Sets per 1,000:** 2
Circulation per 1,000: 45	**Total Annual Newsprint Consumption:** NA
Number of Nondailies: 10	**Per Capita Newsprint Consumption:** NA
Aggregate Circulation: 140,000	**Total Newspaper Ad Receipts:** NA
Circulation per 1,000: 63	**As % of All Ad Expenditures:** NA

Background & General Characteristics

Albania is the smallest country in Eastern Europe and probably the poorest and least developed nation on the continent. It has been Communist ruled since the end of World War II; its leaders openly identify themselves with Stalinism and have successfully resisted any change in the tight control they exert on virtually all aspects of life. Contacts with the outside world are held to an absolute minimum.

Rugged mountains divided by rivers running west to the Adriatic Sea characterize most of the country, except for a marshy and malarial coastal plain. The Albanians historically have been mountain people, inhabiting the highlands. Their origins are a matter of dispute but it is widely believed that they are predominantly descendants of the ancient Illyrians, who ruled the eastern Adriatic shores before the Romans and became incorporated into Rome's empire.

Their language is also a puzzle. It owes much of its vocabulary to Latin and other languages, including Greek and old Slav dialects. But the grammar and pronunciation have remained largely indigenous. Some authorities have argued that even the name

Albanian is foreign, holding that it came from a Greco-Roman city of Albanopolis, or Albanum.

Ethnically, almost all the people are Albanian, the major exception being some Greeks who maintain their own language and customs in villages along the Greek-Albanian border. Albanians have been divided, both historically and linguistically, into two groups: the Ghegs north of the Shkumbi River and the Tosks to the south. Until relatively recent times the Ghegs were an essentially tribal society while the Tosk area was characterized by large semi-feudal land holdings. The modern Albanian language, which has been developed only since 1909, is based largely on the Tosk dialect.

The regime of Communist Party chief Enver Hoxha closed all churches and other religious institutions in the country in the late 1960s. Prior to that time the population had been listed as about 70 percent Moslem, 20 percent Greek Orthodox and 10 percent Roman Catholic.

About 60 percent of the population is under 30 years of age. The regime has devoted considerable attention to education but the literacy rate is still estimated to be only about 70 percent. Agriculture remains the mainstay of the economy, although industrialization has been a priority and by now about a third of the population is urban.

All aspects of economic life, even the smallest shops, are nationalized. Standards of living have improved in recent years, but figures for significant yardsticks—the per capita consumption of energy, the availability of social services, the consumption of consumer durables—are the lowest in Europe.

The press is undoubtedly the most limited, the most strictly controlled of all the European Communist-ruled states. Its function is limited to political indoctrination in furtherance of the ruling Party's aim to reconstruct the political and social life of the country. No variation is permitted.

Albania has never had a free press. For most of its known history it has been subject to a variety of conquerors. After the Romans came the Goths, the Vandals, the Byzantines, various Slav states and then the Turks. The great Albanian hero Skanderbeg was able to unite all the various tribes in 1443 to fight the Turks and establish an independent state, but it lasted only until 1478.

The Venetians, who had established themselves along the coast, were forced to evacuate what is now the city of Durres in 1501. The Turks found the people of the north an even harder nut to crack and eventually agreed to allow them considerable autonomy in return for supplying troops for the Sultan's armies. It was in this area, in the city of Scutari, that the country's first printing press was established in 1563. It bore no fruit, however. The Turks suppressed the Albanian language and forbade the publication of any works in Albanian. The only writings of this period that are known were produced by Albanians who had fled before the advancing Turks and taken refuge in other countries. There was a particularly active settlement in Italy, which produced religious works in Albanian, written in a number of different scripts.

The Turks first opened schools in the country in 1860, but these were reserved for Moslems and Turkish was the language of instruction. The Orthodox Church was also permitted to operate schools but used Greek. Not until 1878, when it appeared the European powers might take the country away from Constantinople and distribute its territories to Christian states in the area, did the situation change. In that year the Sultan lifted the ban on Albanian printing and schools. Constantin Christophorides developed an alphabet using Latin letters that quickly came into common use. Schools were opened and primitive news sheets began to appear. The Turks became alarmed at the rapid tempo of this cultural revival and in 1886 reimposed the ban on Albanian publications and schools. But activity did not cease in the communities outside the homeland. By 1908, more than 30 Albanian newspapers and periodicals were being published abroad, including seven in Bulgaria, seven in Italy, four in Egypt, four in Romania, three in Belgium and one each in Austria-Hungary, Greece, Britain and the United States.

The Young Turk revolt in Constantinople in 1908 gave another boost to Albanian nationalism. It led to a great outburst of educational and organizational activities. Within 10 months the Albanians had established 14 night schools, 34 day schools and a teachers' training institution. They also set up four printing presses and began issuing 17 newspapers, as well as other publications.

Alarmed by these developments and signs of disaffection in other parts of the empire, the Young Turks went back to the old forced Ottomanization program. This led to a series of revolts that finally won Albanian autonomy, and in 1912 a national congress proclaimed the independence of the land. This was confirmed the following year by the major European powers.

The powers selected a prince to rule the new nation but he was unable to win the loyalty of the people or bring stability to the country, which literally began to fall apart. The chaos became complete when, with the outbreak of World War I, at least seven foreign armies moved in to occupy various parts of the state.

Proposals to partition the land between Greece, Yugoslavia and Italy were beaten down at the Versailles Peace Conference by determined Albanian resistance, backed by President Woodrow Wilson. Nationalist leaders at home began a reorganization that culminated in an election in 1920 of a national assembly. In that same year, Italian occupation forces were withdrawn and Albania was admitted to the League of Nations.

Political turmoil continued, however. Two main factions were liberals, led by Bishop Fan Noli, and conservative landowners, led by Ahmed Zog. Zog became premier in 1922 but in 1924 was forced to leave the country. Noli assumed the premiership but a few months later Zog, with an army composed partly of Yugoslav troops, drove out Noli and the liberals and made himself president.

A 1925 constitution concentrated state power in Zog's hands but, somewhat surprisingly, promised freedom of the press. It has been suggested that Zog felt newspapers could help in the imposition of central authority.

Despite the turmoil and the illiteracy and poverty that characterized the country—the value of all Albanian exports in 1921 had amounted to only $420,000—the press continued to grow. Weekly papers had been published, at least off and on, since 1908. In 1913 the country's first daily, called *Taraboshi,* appeared in Scutari. About 60 newspapers had been founded by 1925, and the climate generated by the new constitution encouraged others. By 1929 almost all major towns and cities had their own papers.

In the meantime, Zog had made himself king and introduced a new constitution that gave him almost unlimited power. He remodeled the nation's legal codes, following Western European patterns, and instituted a land reform program. But the poverty of the country forced him to look for financial help. The Mussolini regime in Italy came to the rescue, and Zog soon was in an Italian stranglehold.

Zog found that a free press could be a weapon against him as well as a useful tool, and in 1931 he began a crackdown that soon squelched all criticism. The three Tirana dailies became nothing but government mouthpieces. These, plus a few regional weeklies, were all that were permitted to remain in operation. None were large. The most important, the daily *Arbenia* of Tirana, had a circulation of only about 2,800.

The Italians finally invaded Albania in 1939, forced Zog into exile and annexed the country. They immediately suppressed all existing papers and limited the press to one daily, called *Fashizma,* and three provincial weeklies.

A few months later World War II broke out. Guerrilla bands representing various political points of view fought the Italians and each other. Eventual victory went to the Communists, led by Hoxha, who were aided and supported by the Yugoslav Partisans. In 1945, the Western allies recognized the provisional government Hoxha had set up, on condition that it hold free elections.

A bloody purge of all opposition led to the election of a Communist-dominated national assembly, and in 1946, Albania was declared a People's Republic. A United Nations report later asserted that between 1945 and 1956, 50,000 political opponents had been arrested, of whom 16,000 had been killed in prisons or concentration camps.

The Albanian guerrillas, like their Yugoslav counterparts, had established papers in their hideouts during the war. With their victory in 1944 they seized control of all media and turned press facilities over to their own publications. Their three main publications were *Zeri i Popullit* ("Voice of the People"), *Bashkimi* ("Unity") and *Kustrimi i lirse* ("Call of Freedom"). The first two remain the nation's principal dailies.

Zeri i Popullit is the organ of the Albanian Workers Party, which is what the Communists call themselves. It is the *Pravda* of Albania. *Bashkimi* is technically the mouthpiece of the Democratic Front, the Party's mass political organization, but it is essentially the voice of the government. There have been several significant changes in Albania's international orientation since the war, but the composition and functions of the media have remained virtually unchanged.

Because of her poverty, Albania has been forced into the role of a client state. Until 1948 the regime was largely controlled by the Yugoslavs. After the break between Moscow and Belgrade, Hoxha seized the opportunity to shake off these ties and align himself with Moscow. This link was broken in the early 1960s as the Albanians turned to China for support. And this alliance, in turn, came to an end in 1978 when Peking shut off its aid.

Throughout all this period the press has grown in numbers and circulation, but its mobilization role has remained unchanged. For example, in the late 1960s a number of local papers were established and the use of wall newspapers fostered for the specific purpose of furthering an "ideological and cultural revolution" Hoxha had decided to wage.

All information media are controlled by the Party, either directly or indirectly through the government or affiliated organizations. No other orientation is permitted. All are published in Albanian, except for one fortnightly in Greek. The only publications in other languages are periodicals designed to serve as propaganda organs abroad. Copies of the two Tirana dailies are available in some European capitals but very little is known outside the country about the regional papers. Some of them apparently are little more than news sheets.

Both *Zeri i Popullit* and *Bashkimi* are full-size papers. They normally publish only four pages a day. Both *Zeri i Popullit* and *Bashkimi* publish six days a week, skipping Mondays. The first is by far the larger, with a circulation of about 110,000. *Bashkimi* claims 35,000. *Puna* ("Labor"), which is the organ of the Central Council of Albanian Trade Unions, appeared as a daily for a time in the mid-1970s but has now reverted to its previous twice-weekly pattern.

More than 50 specialized periodicals are published for various segments of the society. Some of the more important are *Drita*, the weekly organ of Albanian Artists and Authors, *10 Korriku* ("10th of July"), the weekly organ of the political department of the army, and *Zeri i Rinise* ("Voice of Youth"), the twice-weekly publication of the Central Committee of the Union of Albanian Youth.

Local newspapers are published in Durres, Fier, Saranda, Shkoder, Kruje, Kukes, Berat, Gjirokaster and Korce. The latter is a twice-weekly publication of the local Party organization and claims a circulation of 4,000. No statistics are available on any of the others, which apparently are all weeklies or fortnightlies. A United Nations publication in the mid-1970s listed the total circulation of all nondailies in the country at 140,000 copies.

Economic Framework

The Albanian economy is almost completely nationalized. All trade and industry is socialized and about 99 percent of all the arable land is in the hands of collective or state farms. The regime has been pushing industrialization with the help of its various patron states, with emphasis on agriculture, electric power generation, engineering and non-ferrous metallurgy. Acceptance of any credits from the West or establishment of joint companies are barred by the 1976 constitution.

Albania does not produce newsprint. All must be imported, and is distributed as the regime sees fit.

Overall, resources are slim and the media's share is correspondingly limited. Radio has become of increasing importance in recent years. One of the gifts of the Chinese to Albania was a powerful broadcasting sta-

tion, which the Chinese used to relay their own propaganda into Europe. Now, of course, the Albanians have it to use for their own purposes.

Radio may have the wider audience but print is still the most important medium to the regime. The reason is that in its internal propaganda Tirana relies heavily on Party activists who push the Party line on a face-to-face basis among the people. The press is the principal transmission belt between the leadership and these activists.

Hoxha himself has been quoted as saying, "Without the press there can be no education of the masses; without the press there can be no conscientious mobilization of them, organization or solution to the problems of the economic and cultural construction in the new socialist society."

Press Laws & State-Press Relations

The Albanian constitution forbids private ownership of any medium. All are owned and controlled by the state or Party, either directly or through affiliated organizations.

Press content is intensely serious, pushing the Party doctrine in an extremely forceful manner but within a nationalist framework. A Polish literary magazine once accused the Albanian media of speaking what the author called "Tiranese," which he characterized as "a total disregard of facts, a free transposition of cause and effect, separating words from their real meanings and calling things by names totally alien to them, a whole line of reasoning based on a wholly arbitrary interpretation of reality."

As far as can be determined from the fragmentary information available, control of the media in the Albanian system is vested in the Party, rather than in the government machinery. Decisions involving the media are implemented by the Central Committee's Agitation and Propaganda section. This section controls and directs subordinate agitprop units set up on all levels of the government and Party structures. Control is assured by the fact that all media employees, ordinary journalists as well as editors, must be Party members. Any ideological misstep would bring immediate disciplining by the Party, expulsion from which would mean the loss of one's job, if not worse.

As a result, the press prints only what is passed down to it, although it may explain policies or directives in local terms. Local newspapers also reportedly pay considerable attention to problems specific to their regions.

The same is generally true of the wall newspapers that became a feature of the cultural revolution of the late 1960s. These are written by Party agitators or other local Party representatives and are used to campaign for greater productivity, to give a local angle on some policy decision, to combat continuing religious influence and the like.

The Albanian constitution guarantees to all citizens "freedom of the spoken and written word." Legal codes contain the usual prohibition against libel and the publication of military or official secrets. Religion and religious subjects have been banned since the regime declared the country an atheistic state, although continuing attacks in the press indicate that religious feeling is still quite strong.

Censorship

Apparently there is no formal censorship organization in the Albanian structure. The tight control that exists is maintained by the Party through its Agitation and Propaganda units on all levels. Experience has shown that the slightest deviation from the established Party line, or even questioning of it, brings instant dismissal, even for persons holding top-level jobs.

Two members of the Party's Central Committee, Fadel Pacrami and Todi Libonja, who had earlier served at different times as chief editors of *Zeri i Popullit*, were expelled both from the Committee and the Party in 1972. Apparently they had advocated a relaxation of the regime's pressure-packed drive for ideological purity that was a feature of the cultural revolution.

The problem, as official accounts indicated, was that the nation's youth were already following a different drummer. They apparently were wearing their hair long and dressing in "mod" styles, an abomination to a regime that bans even chewing gum. The youths were also accused of indulging in "unworthy behavior." This included what was described as "irresponsible" conduct on the job, as well as leaving work without authorization, defying parents and teachers, indulging in vulgar language and skipping school. At the same time writers and artists came under attack for "bourgeois and alien" trends in their work.

The whole affair suggested that Albanians have conisderably more access to knowledge about the rest of the world and are more receptive to foreign influences than had been generally recognized abroad.

Attitude Toward Foreign Media

No Western correspondents have been based regularly in Albania so little is known about accreditation procedures. The only permanent foreign news bureaus have been those of Communist agencies, which are arranged under special agreements.

Foreign newsmen who want to visit Albania must apply to the Foreign Ministry for special visas. Some applications have been granted, but in some cases approval has taken a year or more. Such visits are strictly supervised and newsmen are restricted as to what they may see and to whom they may talk.

Applications from U.S. newsmen are not answered. Up to 1981 only one American correspondent had ever succeeded in getting permission to visit and that was in the 1950s.

Except for certain categories of books, foreign publications are banned. Nevertheless, the regime has blamed some of its troubles with the youth and the intellectuals on foreign television, books and tourists.

Owners of TV sets in the eastern part of the country can watch Yugoslav TV if they have special antennas, and those along the Adriatic coast can pick up Italian TV, at least at night. Complaints appearing in the press suggest that such antennas are not uncommon.

As a Communist nation, Albania supports UNESCO's positions on the media.

News Agencies

The Albanian Telegraph Agency, an arm of the government, has a monopoly on the distribution of both foreign and domestic news. It has bureaus in various parts of the country and, like Tass in the Soviet Union, is the sole provider of government announcements and communiques. It has access to foreign news through a broadcast monitoring operation and through exchange arrangements with foreign agencies, including Italy's ANSA, Yugoslavia's Tanjug and Peking's Hsinhua. Its service is available in some neighboring countries, where it is distributed in French as well as Albanian.

The *Europa Yearbook* for 1980 lists two foreign agencies as having bureaus in Tirana: the Bulgarian Telegraph Agency (BTA) and Hsinhua. There is no indication whether the 1978 cancellation of aid by the Chinese has yet affected relations between Hsinhua and ATA, but there is little doubt that it will sooner or later.

Electronic News Media

All broadcasting is operated by Albanian Radio and Television, a state-run organization under the Council of Ministers. It is headed by a Directorate of Broadcasting.

An experimental TV station began operations in Tirana in 1960 but by 1969 was still on the air only three days a week for three hours at a stretch. A new French-built facility was opened in 1971 and has been offering about four and a half hours of black and white programming daily, primarily news, sports, music and education. Retransmitters are located at Berat, Pogradac and Kukes.

The radio service, thanks to the Chinese gift of equipment, is much more developed in both domestic and foreign services. In fact Albania ranks eighth in the world among international broadcasters in terms of number of hours of external programming. It broadcasts in 19 languages, including Albanian.

Radio Tirana's installations include four medium-wave transmitters and 41 shortwave transmitters, ranging in power up to 500 kilowatts. Domestically its broadcast day is 18 hours long. Local stations in Kukes, Shkoder, Korce and Gjirokaster, all operating medium-wave transmitters, are on the air for about six hours daily.

As in all less developed countries, radios are much more common than TV sets, if for no other reason than price. Available statistics list only about 4,000 to 4,500 TV receivers in the country. These figures are not up to date. They reflect the situation as it was in the mid-1970s, but there apparently has not been a significant increase since; travelers report seeing very few TV sets or signs of them even today.

Control over the broadcast operations is assured through the same mechanisms as the print media. Not only are all personnel government employees, they are also Party members and subject to Party discipline.

Education & Training

There are no specialized journalism schools in Albania. Journalists receive training and political indoctrination in Party schools, where the main emphasis is on ideology. This used to be standard procedure in most of Europe's Communist-ruled states but by now many have added journalism on the undergraduate or postgraduate level.

A union of journalists to which, presumably, all Albanian newspeople belong, publishes a satirical fortnightly journal in Tirana called *Hosteni* ("The Goad").

Summary

There are no indications that media conditions might change, in the near future at least. The Albanian leadership appears determined to keep tight control and maintain what it sees as the ideological purity of its policies. However, Hoxha and his chief aides are aging. How much longer they will be in power is a question. An infusion of new blood in the leadership stratum could weaken its militancy and give the media a little more room.

Furthermore, with education spreading and with more and more people having access to radio and TV, the regime almost certainly will face increasing difficulties in trying to insulate the people from outside influences and maintain its tough, xenophobic line. The problems with the youth it complained of in the 1970s may have been only a foretaste of the future.

CHRONOLOGY

1972   Fadel Pacrami and Todi Libonja, chief editors of *Zeri i Popullit,* expelled from Communist Party.

1976   New constitution promulgated, guarantees freedom of speech.

BIBLIOGRAPHY

Holuj, Tadeusz. "Albanian Twaddle." *Zycie Literackie,* Krakow, Poland, September 10, 1968, p. 5.

Merrill, John C., Bryan, Carter R., and Alisky, Marvin. *The Foreign Press.* Baton Rouge, La., 1970.

Olson, Kenneth E. *The History Makers.* Baton Rouge, La., 1966.

Pano, Nicholas C. "The Albanian Cultural Revolution." *Problems of Communism,* July-August 1974, p. 44.

Prifti, Peter R. *Socialist Albania since 1944.* Cambridge, Mass., 1978.

_____. "Albania's Expanding Horizons." *Problems of Communism,* January-February 1972, p. 30.

Pribichevich, Stoyan. *World Without End.* New York, 1939.

Radio Free Europe. "Anti-Liberalism Campaign Claims First Victims." *RFE Research Report,* July 26, 1973.

Schopflin, George, ed. *The Soviet Union and Eastern Europe.* New York, 1970.

Skendi, Stavro. *Albania.* New York, 1956.

Stankovic, Slobodan. "Yugoslav Paper Hails Albania's Alleged Change in Attitude Toward Europe." *RFE Background Report,* June 12, 1975.

Stavrianos, L. S. *The Balkans since 1453.* New York, 1966.

Wolff, Robert Lee. *The Balkans in Our Time.* Cambridge, Mass., 1956.

Zanga, Louis. "Albanian Leadership at the Crossroads." *RFE Research Report,* November 6, 1974.

ARGENTINA

by Rodolfo Windhausen

BASIC DATA

Population: 27,002,000
Area: 2,771,300 sq. km. (1,079,965 sq. mi.)
GNP: 45 trillion pesos (US$ 45 billion) (1978)
Literacy Rate: 85%
Language(s): Spanish
Number of Dailies: 142
   Aggregate Circulation: 2,682,000
   Circulation per 1,000: 103
Number of Nondailies: 63
   Aggregate Circulation: NA
   Circulation per 1,000: NA
Number of Periodicals: 1,360
Number of Radio Stations: 163

Number of Television Stations: 75
Number of Radio Receivers: 10 million
   Radio Receivers per 1,000: 384
Number of Television Sets: 4.6 million
   Television Sets per 1,000: 177
Total Annual Newsprint Consumption: 120,800 metric tons
   Per Capita Newsprint Consumption: 4.6 kg. (10.1 lb.)
Total Newspaper Ad Receipts: 47.21 billion pesos (US$172.3 million) (1976)
   As % of All Ad Expenditures: 46.9

Background & General Characteristics

The newspaper industry in Argentina clearly has been shaped by the country's high rates of literacy (94.8 percent) and per capita income—4.01 million pesos ($2,100 +) —both among the highest in Latin America. Other factors, such as a large urban population (79 percent) and a uniform, mandatory use of Spanish as the official language, have also contributed substantially to Argentina's leading role in the Latin American press.

The size of the press is in line with the concentration of population in the eastern plains—the "humid pampa."—which also created a sociopolitical pattern of predominance for the Buenos Aires and Sante Fe provinces, Argentina's traditional outlets to the Atlantic Ocean. Other large urban centers in the interior—Cordoba, Mendoza and Tucuman, for example—also developed their own political, economic and social influence. Subsequently, the press in those areas developed some regional influence. In general, however, the press reflects the historic predominance of Buenos Aires and its surrounding areas. Even the term "national press"— or worse, "Argentine press"—is often reserved for Buenos Aires-based newspapers

and magazines. In contrast, some newspapers in the interior have managed in recent years to overcome the increasing competition of the electronic media and serve as fair examples of regional press development, which is hard to find in South America.

The "porteño" (Buenos Aires-based) newspapers traditionally bear the self-appointed burden of being spokesmen for political events and ideologies nationwide. Furthermore, the older the newspaper, the more staunchly conservative its editorial policies: *La Nación* and *La Prensa* are both well over 100 years old and strongholds of "porteño" rightist ideologies.

Conversely, claims for decentralization and federalism have found their way into the interior press, although not necessarily in a radical fashion.

In addition, the size of the country, its large, sparsely populated areas and its lack of communications also shaped the distribution of the press well into the 1950s, particularly in remote regions like Patagonia. This pattern has hardly changed in recent years in spite of evident progress in air and surface communications.

In the 1960s a UNESCO-sponsored survey of Latin American dailies rated at least two major Argentine papers among the most remarkable in the continent. One of them, *La Gaceta de Tucumán*, was not based in Buenos Aires. One U.S. specialist in "elite journalism," John C. Merrill, has repeatedly rated Argentine newspapers as examples, citing their emphasis on foreign affairs and cosmopolitan view of world events.

In the last decade, however, both censorship and economic restraints derived from the world's highest inflation rate have substantially affected the Argentine press. This is particularly evident in its coverage of the recurrent wave of international terrorism and Argentina's own alleged human rights violations. Not only has coverage been restricted in this and other fields, but the quality of language—once a matter of pride and a long-established tradition in the Argentine press—has also greatly deteriorated. In some cases, the latter has forced Argentine newsmen to create a sort of elliptical Spanish to describe otherwise clear developments, so as to avoid a mounting governmental or self-imposed censorship. The Argentine press today seems increasingly infested with bureaucratic jargon and a multiplicity of euphemisms.

Historically, yet another factor must be taken into account. The influence of Spanish and British patterns (a somewhat unlikely combination) is still very strong in several ways. From the Spaniards, conquerors and colonizers of the country, comes what has been called an "undue stress on philosophical, theological and literary discussion." This characteristic has played a substantial role in shaping the Argentine press. From the British, Argentina inherited such things as layout patterns molded on those of the traditional London newspapers—together with some European liberal ideas.

Curiously, the Argentine press has been consistent in its anti-American position by rejecting many U.S. methods of journalism, particularly the "both sides of the story" practice and the "sources said" device. This trend is also noticeable in the increasing use of European wire services, in spite of the predominance of The Associated Press and United Press International as the two basic sources of foreign news coverage.

Uniform use of the Spanish language in Argentina has facilitated press distribution throughout the country, although sales of the "national" newspapers in the interior have remained consistently low in relative terms. The ethnic and religious press is even more limited, perhaps due to the deeply rooted liberal stand for separation of state and church, plus the fact that ethnic minorities have become increasingly integrated in recent years. The strong and influential Catholic Church owns and operates at least one large Buenos Aires-based newspaper and is known to have interests in others in the interior. But both their influence and circulation are limited.

The decrease of immigration—in fact, there has been a rather alarming trend to emigrate in recent years—has also contributed to diminishing the once influential German-, Jewish- and English-language press. (Other ethnic papers are printed in Italian and Arabic.) Foreign language publications still play a role in preserving certain cultural patterns for immigrant families, but as the assimilation process increases, their real influence becomes weaker. It should be noted, however, that the oldest English newspaper, the *Buenos Aires Herald,* has been a staunch and influential opponent to both left- and right-wing extremisms in the 1970s. At one point, it became a major source of information even for Argentine newsmen, since it successfully defied censorship and published otherwise unprintable reports on human rights violations.

In general, the Argentine morning newspapers follow the European-U.S. standards of size. The regular format is still the more usual for morning papers, while tabloid is reserved mostly for the evening, mass-circulation press. Some remarkable exceptions, however, should be noted, namely *Clarín* of Buenos Aires, the country's most widely circulated morning newspaper, still loyal to its confused tabloid format. Some interior-based newspapers also prefer to run tabloid, but mainly for economic reasons stemming from their relatively low circulation and advertising income.

The average number of pages in the "national" press is about 36 pages per weekday issue and up to some 64 pages for weekend editions. In general, these figures exclude special sections or supplements and Sunday magazines. The latter average 32 pages in tabloid format and are sold jointly with the regular Sunday edition. Their content consists mainly of features emphasizing arts and entertainment news, celebrity interviews and home and living articles.

An important characteristic of the Sunday editions in Argentina's most influential newspapers is the long-established tradition of the literary section. Highly cosmopolitan in both their approach and their lists of contributors, these sections largely remain an oasis of language quality and, in some cases—although publishers admit they are not profitable as advertising sources—their existence or survival is deemed a matter of prestige. Not surprisingly, these literary sections—as well as some Sunday magazines—have independent staffs or managing editors, loosely dependent on or linked to the publisher instead of being under direct editorial supervision.

In general, the Argentine press, despite recent shortcomings and the country's political turmoil, has managed to survive by playing a low-keyed role, or by adopting a lukewarm attitude toward the military in power. It has seemingly preserved its basic features: a cosmopolitan approach in its treatment of foreign news, a preference for intellectual topics and a reluctance to venture into revolutionary format or layout changes.

In 1978 some 307 Argentine cities had newspapers (although many were less dailies than community newsletters). Eight large urban centers have well established, regularly competing newspapers with average circulations of *not less* than 60,000 copies a day. (Many other small towns have competing newspapers too, but their aggregate circulation is too low to be analyzed here). Those cities, each with more than 250,000 inhabitants, are Buenos Aires, La Plata, Mar del Plata, Córdoba, Rosario, Mendoza, Santa Fe and Tucumán. (In the last the recent closure of a competing newspaper has created a current monopoly in favor of the oldest existing publication). As of March 1980, the number of newspapers by circulation groups listed by the Argentine Instituto Verificador de Circulaciones (IVC), was as follows:

Number of Newspapers by Circulation Groups	
Below 10,000 copies	14
10,000 to 25,000	9
25,000 to 50,000	7
50,000 to 100,000	5
100,000 to 500,000	3
500,000 to 1,000,000	1
Over 1,000,000	none

It should be noted, however, that the IVC—roughly an equivalent to the Audit Bureau of Circulation of the United States or France's Office de Justification de la Diffusion—lists only the net paid circulation figures *declared* by its members, which amount to approximately 50 percent of Argentina's total existing newspapers.

10 Largest Newspapers by Circulation (January 1980)	
1. *Clarín* (Buenos Aires)	525,279
2. *La Razón* (Buenos Aires)	309,713
3. *La Nación* (Buenos Aires)	233,780
4. *Diario Popular* (La Plata)	109,312
5. *La Capital* (Rosario)	72,885
6. *La Gaceta* (Tucumán)	70,535
7. *Los Andes* (Mendoza)	57,396
8. *La Voz del Interior* (Córdoba)	54,339
9. *El Día* (La Plata)	55,330
10. *La Capital* (Mar del Plata)	38,517

The three most influential Buenos Aires newspapers have traditionally been *Clarín*, *La Nación* and *La Prensa*, although *La Opinión* also played an important role between 1971 and 1977 when it was put under direct governmental control. Its closure has deprived Argentina, since 1980, of one of the best examples of quality press in South America.

In the interior of the country, the three most influential newspapers—excluding those of Buenos Aires province—are Mendoza's *Los Andes*, Tucumán's *La Gaceta*, Córdoba's *La Voz del Interior* or Rosario's *La Capital*. The last, founded in 1867, is the oldest newspaper in the country. Though these papers have a limited area of distribution, their influence is considerable and their editorials often reflect the viewpoints and concerns of the large communities they serve. Thus, the Córdoba and Rosario dailies are spokesmen for the agro-industrial complex in their provinces, whereas the same happens in Mendoza, a wine- and oil-producing region, and in Tucumán, site of sugar-cane processing, the country's oldest manufacturing industry.

In addition, Argentina has a solid magazine market, which in general has experienced a steadier growth than that of newspapers. In 1978, there were 633 such periodicals in Argentina, ranging from general news magazines to highly specialized publications. Their annual circulation amounted to 63.1 million copies in Buenos Aires and 94.1 million in the interior. According to the Argentine Institute of Statistics and Censuses, 136 foreign publications in various languages were also being sold throughout the country at that time. The leading news-magazine is *Gente y la Actualidad*—known simply as *Gente*—published by Editorial Atlántida, with an average monthly circulation of 250,000 copies (four editions).

The special interest press had some 150 publications in Buenos Aires alone in 1978. Their coverage ranges from agriculture to business and industry interests. In some cases, they also serve as in-house organs for chambers of commerce or industrial complexes throughout the country. Many have circulations restricted to members of those groups; some are published irregularly.

Economic Framework

From a staggering world record of inflation—over 400 percent in 1975—Argentina managed to slow down to about 170 percent between 1977 and 1979. In 1980, however, the International Labor Organization statistics still placed Argentina among nations with the world's highest inflation rates. The efforts of the military government could not stop a real-wage loss of 40 percent between 1976, when it took office, and 1978. Nor could a surprising 267 percent net capital inflow in 1978–79 prevent an overall unstable economic situation.

Argentina's economic ills have also clearly influenced the media. The effects of the military regime's economic policy include disappearance of many small publications, staff reductions, and postponement of necessary investments in other media. The situation has also increased the phenomenon of double, even triple, employment among journalists. Financial difficulties may have been behind the scenes in the takeover of one of Argentina's largest publishing houses, Editorial Abril, by Italy's celebrated publishing complex Rizzoli—a process begun in 1978 and only recently completed. Further, increasing production costs—mainly in newsprint—have periodically forced newspapers to raise prices per copy, even at the risk of losing circulation, and to impose frequent hikes in advertising rates.

Stagnation of circulation may also be related to the parallel increase of electronic media exposure among people who would otherwise have been more inclined to read newspapers and magazines. Radio and television have increased their growth since the late 1970s while the print media have remained within their relatively low circulation figures or even lost readership. By mid-1980, with the establishment of regular color broadcasts, television clearly showed a growing popularity. In fact, the repeal of customs restrictions for the importation of color TV sets has caused such an overflow that the government has been forced to reimpose them to prevent local manufacturers and importers from going bankrupt. Limitations and taxes were reinstated for Argentine tourists returning home to stop the uncontrollable influx of electronic-media appliances.

The military government's own policy of promoting the development of the broadcasting media has also contributed to the sudden radio and television vogue. New microwave and satellite communications have helped radio and television alike to reach remote areas and incorporate stations into nationwide networks. Radio stations in particular have shown an increase in sophisticated use of FM broadcasts, renewal or replacement of old equipment and, simultaneously, a military-sponsored increase in the so-called "low power stations" in border areas. The last, a long-cherished military project, is basically intended to counter foreign radio broadcasts—mainly from neighboring countries. But a certain side effect will be to deprive the print media of marginal areas for potential readership. Competition with live coverage of news events by radio and TV has now become a real problem that Argentina's press finds hard to cope with.

This competition, in turn, may well be a major factor in pushing some of the country's largest newspapers to incorporate computer technology into their newsrooms. In 1980 plans for fully computerized news processing and editing were completed by *La Nación* and *Clarín* in Buenos Aires, while at least one large provincial newspaper—*La Gaceta* in Tucumán—had already begun its breakthrough switchover to video terminals to complement its offset printing facilities.

A minor side effect of the entire economic situation has had a positive aspect of sorts. An artificially low rate of exchange has allowed the Argentine press, radio and TV to increase their use of foreign correspondents and improve their coverage of world news events. Through special-assignment and traveling correspondents or freelance overseas-based newsmen, the Argentine media have begun to recover their tradition of interest in world affairs. This process has been favored by the overvalued peso and the lifting of formerly strict barriers that limited currency exchange. Thus, while local salaries of journalists remained relatively high, the Argentine media owners found it increasingly inexpensive to pay for the regular services of Spanish-speaking newsmen who provide them exclusive information from abroad. At the same time, many media can now afford to base their own correspondents in foreign countries—even with offices—particularly in the Western Hemisphere. But then again, this field also shows competition between print and electronic media, since rates for satellite communications affect overall budgets minimally but clearly favor the latter for foreign news coverage.

Print media ownership in Argentina has been evolving from a typically individual or "one family" control into corporate shape. Individual ownership, although still existent, remains largely confined to minor, irregular publications. All of the big newspapers and magazines are now published by large corporations, mostly "sociedades anónimas." As with many other Western countries, the real form of corporate operation ownership remains under a veil of secrecy. In Argentina, the names of shareholders are kept from public scrutiny—as are the frequent but unpublished nonjournalistic investments of media owners. Legal regulations protect shareholder anonymity, and the media "trade" organizations have firmly opposed any attempt to change the status quo.

Argentina has, in general, all types of newspapers ranging from the elite to the yellow. Although the latter are kept at bay by severe "public morality" measures, as well as by the stern censorship regulations, many evening dailies, such as Buenos Aires' *Crónica* and Córdoba's *Córdoba*, publish sex- and violence-related news items.

Concentration in ownership has been prevented legally, especially by the anti-monopoly laws and occasional governmental "reminders" through decrees. Frequent attempts by newspaper publishers to obtain broadcasting licences have faced opposition from the military-controlled Comité Federal de Radiodifusión (COMFER), the government licensing agency. Anti-trust legislation also plays an important role in preventing concentration of distribution networks. However, the recent Foreign Investment Law—far less rigid than previous regulations—has raised fears that troubled Argentine publishers may feel tempted to sell to foreign corporations or let their publications be effectively controlled by non-Argentine investors.

The distribution networks have increased their reliance on air freight for delivery into the country's major provincial capitals. Again, Buenos Aires-based distribution demonstrates the country's uneven dependence on the federal district for a truly *national* press. Even major provincial newspapers are forced to hire services of Buenos Aires-based distributors to sell their editions in the capital.

Newsprint availability has undergone major changes. A complex web of regulations, based on circulation figures to establish each newspaper's needs, was used in the 1970s as a means of exerting pressure and wielding political control over opposition print media. But in 1972, the military government of General Alejandro A. Lanusse initiated a program to reduce Argentina's traditional dependence on foreign newsprint supplies, mainly from Canada, Chile, Sweden and the United States. Although hindered and delayed by bureaucratic problems, the project was finally completed by President Jorge R. Videla's regime. It worked as the establishment of a large mixed-ownership corporation, Papel Prensa S.A., designed to produce approximately 75 percent of Argentina's newsprint from the rich forests in the northeast and in the delta of the River Plate. Its plant in San Pedro, near Buenos Aires, inaugurated on September 27, 1978, was designed to produce 105,000 metric tons annually.

The company was created by the government and the country's three largest newspapers—*La Nación, Clarín* and *La Razón*—but the military regime established the rules of the game. It reserved for itself 25 percent of the shares, plus the right to select shareholders of the preferred class "A" stock, and thus maintain a political control over the corporation. The three private newspapers hold a joint 65 percent of the shares and in 1977 were authorized by the government to manage the company. (The remaining 10 percent of Papel Prensa's shares is in the hands of an estimated 30,000 small investors favored with tax deductions.)

Barely three months after the plant went on stream, protests arose among other publishers when a ruling established that newspapers must buy 50 percent of their supplies from Papel Prensa. *La Prensa*, not a corporation shareholder, charged that the price of $750 dollars per metric ton was "considerably higher" than the world price in 1979. Subsequently, *La Nación, Clarín* and *La*

Razón withdrew from Argentina's largest publishers' organization, ADEPA, in the wake of the dispute.

And, despite charges of monopoly and fears of a newsprint overflow, construction on yet another plant began in May 1979 in Tucumán. This second Argentine newsprint factory is owned by Papel del Tucumán, a corporation founded by a group of provincial newspapers led by Tucumán's La Gaceta as an entirely private operation. It differs from the government-dominated company in several respects, not the least of which being the use of sugar-cane bagasse instead of wood pulp, to take advantage of the leftovers from the province's 16 sugar mills.

But a major problem is yet to be solved. Argentina's per capita rate of newsprint consumption—some 10 kilograms annually a decade ago—had begun to decrease in the late 1970s. Papel Prensa's output will be matched by Papel del Tucumán when the latter operates at full capacity from mid-1982 on. Analysts of the Argentine newsprint market have warned there could be a surplus in the short run, causing a major drop in prices and subsequent losses due to growing production costs. The surplus could cause the bankruptcy of both newsprint producers or put them under severe financial stress—forcing the government to subsidize the country's newborn newsprint industry.

Advertisers' influence on editorial policies is not always easily noticeable in most Argentine newspapers. However, some interest groups have a way of sneaking in their viewpoints through articles and news items in sympathetic media. The long-established relationship between cattle-raising associations and conservative newspapers like *La Nación* or *La Prensa* is reflected in the two papers' ideological stand—and certainly receptive to the big-ranch owners' ads. A similar parallel between the defense of industrial interests and a clear preference of advertisers can be noticed in *Clarín* and other newspapers. Open demands for editorial support, however, are far less common.

The ad ratio as compared to news space varies enormously from one newspaper to another. Financially stronger publications, however, are in a better position to limit or reduce their amount of advertising and favor occasional allocation of more space to news. But in general an average of 55 percent of space for advertising can be considered fairly accurate.

The special interest lobbies' influence has also varied along with the country's unstable political situation in the past decade. In the Peronist-dominated period of 1973–76, large labor organizations could exert pressure, under a union-oriented government that did not hesitate to put any media out of business with closure threats or censorship. Conversely, the business and industrial organizations regained prominence in periods of military government. The military's banning of strikes and union activities in 1976 put a stop to the politically motivated walkouts that were common in the Peronist regime. A freeze on wages following the coup was reinforced in November 1979 with the long-awaited new labor law that banned all union political activities and prohibited national labor organizations—especially the country's major union, the Confederación General del Trabajo (CGT).

Not that CGT, organized in the 1940s by Peronist union leaders, had ever played a prominent role in promoting freedom of the press. On the contrary, its leaders remained consistently opposed to lifting censorship or other controls. The innumerable work stoppages to show "support" for the Peronist rulers affected the media throughout the early 1970s, although, curiously enough, the largest news union organizations were members of CGT.

The banning of nearly all labor associations since 1976 has put most journalistic trade unions under severe stress. Their leaders—many of them jailed—were affected by a freeze on their banking accounts in the wake of the military takeover. The Federación Argentina de Trabajadores de Prensa (FATPREN), which had attempted with mixed results to encompass all the press workers in Argentina, was put under audit and control by the military government, as were scores of other unions. FATPREN had some 35 affiliated unions.

With the suspension of collective bargaining, most newsmen have had to look for their own individual arrangements with publishers. Regulations of the Estatuto del Periodista, however, create certain complications. This Peronist-inspired law (passed first in 1944 as a decree and continued in 1949 by a Peronist-controlled Congress) calls for six months' pay in case of severance, plus a complicated tabulation of the average salary earned in the years a journalist has served in a news organization. Actually the law is one of the world's most advanced in protecting of journalists against arbitrary dismissals, and has been effective in preventing major lay-offs during inflationary times like the mid-1970s. Nevertheless, newsmen frequently negotiate the amount of their severance for a sort of "cash average" from the publishers or other media owners. Unions, being sharply restricted, have been forced to tolerate these arrangements without protest.

Reliable, accurate figures on total employment in the Argentine newspaper industry have never been entirely disclosed and seem to be part of the same veil of secrecy that covers media ownership. However, the Ministry of Labor had over 9,500 professional journalists registered by the end of the 1970s. The number does not include other journalists and freelance writers, since Argentine law requires that a journalist be employed by a social-security-tax-withholding medium for a minimum of two years, in order to hold a professional-journalist card issued by the labor ministry. The official figures also are known to include many non-editorial managers and other people within the media but without real journalistic functions. (This means that in many cases, possession of a professional-journalist card is of little use in gaining effective access to governmental sources of information.)

Periodic price hikes are so frequent—sometimes occurring monthly—that the average price of a newspaper in 1980, around 800 pesos (or 90 cents), has been quickly outdated and will continue along this path in the foreseeable future.

The impact of new technologies is being clearly felt by the Argentine newspaper industry. *Clarin* has already expressed increasing preference for the offset printing method, but as with most of its counterparts in the Buenos Aires press, it has been lagging behind several regional newspapers from the interior which have managed to switch over to this system earlier and faster. Perhaps a major but never clearly revealed reason for the provincial newspapers' quicker changes has been their relatively less costly operations and their smaller overall size.

Fully computerized news editing systems have also been introduced already by the provincial press leaders, or are about to be completed within the next few years. In Buenos Aires, competition between the U.S. and European technologies has also played a role in delaying otherwise quick decisions for a change in this field, at least in *La Nación* and *Clarin,* among the major newspapers. But the provincial press breakthrough has already put Argentina's newspaper industry on a new path in printing and editing techniques.

Press Laws

The Argentine Constitution, largely based on the United States model, contains provisions guaranteeing Argentines the right to publish their ideas "without previous censorship." But the charter's writers failed to specify sanctions for violations, and the country's own political instability has substantially contributed to constitutional weaknesses throughout this century. The "freedom of printing" provision, drawn up to prevent monopolies and restrictions that were common in Argentina during the 19th century, has been largely disregarded.

In line with Argentina's constantly changing political situation, the nation's Supreme Court has followed a somewhat erratic course in its rulings on press freedom in the last few decades. The court's justices, appointed with obvious political aims by the executive of recent de facto governments, have frequently yielded to the authoritarian regimes. More than once, their task has been simply confined to upholding or justifying the executive viewpoint and its recurrent, abusive utilization of the president's "exceptional powers" under the state-of-siege constitutional regulations.

In 1973 the Peronist government increased manipulation of the press through a series of decrees aimed at controlling its opponents and discouraging "unfavorable" news-agency reporting in the midst of a major political crisis. Ironically, the controversial National Security Law, passed by a Peronist-controlled Congress in 1974, survived the 1976 military coup and became the main tool for media control and suppression of dissent. The law, still in force, establishes an unprecedented joint penal liability. Its Article 3 punishes both news writers *and* publishers (or their equivalents in other media) with prison from two to five years if they "inform or disseminate facts, images or news" on any attempt "to alter or suppress the nation's constitutional order and social peace." Clearly intended to forbid independent, censor-free reporting on terrorist activities, the provision has proven the most effective way to hamper freedom of the press. The very ambiguity of its wording gave room to ample interpretation by the judiciary of what may be considered an attempt to change the status quo. Furthermore, the National Security Law provides no definition of terms such as "ideological premises," or sets no limitations on the judges' power to rule on security matters. Anything and everything, eventually, may be considered an attempt against the country's "social peace."

Clearly, the threat inherent in this law has been largely responsible for the Argentine media's self-restraint, particularly on terrorism and left-wing ideologies and human rights violations. Publishers, managing editors, news writers and reporters will not print any facts related to such matters without official clearance—usually in the form of a communiqué or statement carried by the government-controlled news agency, Télam. Even then, the official version is printed with very little or no comment.

Certain national security matters, protected by an Official Secrets Act, are kept from public scrutiny and are not published in the Boletín Oficial, a record of public laws. Those items include not only military budget, armament and defense or intelligence matters but also have been extended in some cases to so-called "strategic" subjects, such as mineral resources and certain industrial data.

While there are no specific regulations for the licensing of newspapers in Argentina—except the obvious Code of Commerce provisions on incorporation and other non-journalistic trade rules—licensing of individual journalists is in the hands of the Ministry of Labor. Other press-related laws are included in the Penal Code, which protects the right to privacy by tracing a clear distinction between "insult" and actual libel. The latter is an injury to reputation and may result from news stories that allege crime, fraud, dishonesty or immoral conduct. The burden of the proof is on the defendant and, as in many other countries, the publisher of an allegedly libelous story must be able to prove it true. Constitutional provisions also protect certain public officials, such as congressmen. And, although libel suits have frequently been brought to the attention of the courts, mainly by politicians who felt damaged in their reputation by press stories, cases are usually settled by the parties. Judges can impose a retraction on publishers of libelous items, but seldom do. Since the established procedure calls for a "conciliatory hearing" as part of the libel process, and since this takes a long time, the suit rarely goes beyond that point.

The government operates no newspapers of its own, but in the 1970s, both the civilian Peronist regime and the military put some opposition-controlled or financially troubled newspapers under direct audit or management. The measure—called "intervención"—was applied in the cases of La Opinión and Mendoza newspapers. The former's editor, Jacobo Timerman, was the subject of a much publicized arrest and subsequent deportation, which caused an uproar of international protests. Timerman had been accused of alleged links with left-wing organizations—never proved. His newspaper, one of the most influential in Latin America in the past decade, was finally auctioned off by the government in 1980.

A previous and much-opposed "intervención" had put all privately owned radio and television stations under direct governmental control and administration. The decision was taken on grounds of an allegedly imminent takeover by U.S. networks—also never proved, or even publicly disclosed. The unadmitted reason for hitting the private sector, however, seems more likely to have been to gain control over the increasingly influential electronic media.

During the brief Peronist administration of 1973-76, a daily newspaper, Mayoria, was published with the party's financial support in Buenos Aires (Peronism had gained ideological control over newsmen in other publications, too), while left-wing Peronist internal groups put out political magazines such as El Descamisado. All of them have been banned or closed down by the military government.

Currently, only one major influential medium—Clarin—shows a clear linkage to a large political party. Founded in 1945 by Roberto Noble and now the most widely circulated newspaper in Argentina, Clarin is clearly aligned with Movimiento de Integración y Desarrollo (MID), a center-to-left political group led by economist Rogelio Frigerio and former President Arturo Frondizi. Frigerio is known to be Clarin's major stockholder. MID's ideology leaks not only from editorials but is also evident in the newspaper's special sections on industrial and technological affairs. A minority political group, MID advocates a strong, continued industrialization of Argentina—a line of thought locally known as "desarrollismo" ("developmentalism"). Its internal struggles are displayed in the newspaper's front pages with lengthy, detailed (and often boring) coverage.

Otherwise, *La Nación* and *La Prensa* follow an overall conservative line but have no evident links to any particular right-wing political party, while the evening daily *Crónica* takes a generally populist, pro-Peronist political posture. Among the provincial publications, *La Nueva Provincia* of Bahía Blanca is an outspoken rightist daily that has recently—and quite openly—supported some rebel elements of that ideology within the army.

Political compromises related to judicial appointments are known to have influenced Argentine judges in recent years. However, the common pattern in the judiciary's relationship with authoritarian regimes is to take accommodating attitudes immediately following any given change of government, then pursue more independent rulings. For example, in 1978—two years after the military takeover—in a government case against *La Prensa* for alleged violation of Article 212 of the Penal Code, which punishes dissemination of "subversive" propaganda, a federal judge acquitted the newspaper. An appeals court upheld the judge's decision and went further, criticizing the military government in its attempt to punish the newspaper. (It had published a story on a press conference, held in Rome, by members of an Argentine terrorist group.) The court even noted that the Penal Code is not "intended to prosecute the right to information," and pointed out that, instead, the government should have tried the members of the group for a crime whose effects were to take place within Argentina.

Further, in 1979 the Argentine Supreme Court found no evidence of the alleged financial links between Jacob Timerman, publisher of *La Opinión*, and terrorist groups. The justices found no reason for his continued house arrest and ordered his immediate release. The ruling, however, was ignored for months by President Videla's regime, but it reportedly caused an abortive coup led by a right-wing senior officer. Finally a "compromise solution" was reached, and Videla expelled Timerman—after stripping him of his Argentine citizenship.

The *La Prensa* and Timerman cases are far from being the only instances of Argentine judicial defiance of the military regime.

In 1979 a judge in the province of Santa Fe jailed and prosecuted Riobó Caputo, publisher of *El Litoral*, on grounds of an alleged violation of the National Security Law for publishing a news item—carried by United Press International's Spanish wire service—on a statement made in Nicaragua by an exiled leftist leader. Subsequently two editors of *La Opinión*, of the neighboring city of Rafaela, were also jailed on the same charge. On appeal a court ordered the release of Caputo along with a statement that the action against him had not affected "his good name and honor." Curiously dailies in Buenos Aires and other cities had published the same news item but no action had been taken.

The Argentine publishers' organization, ADEPA, of which Caputo is a member, protested his prosecution and jailing. So did the Inter-American Press Association (IAPA). The English language daily *Buenos Aires Herald* called the Santa Fe judge's action "an inexplicable blunder" and labeled the charge "ridiculous." With a touch of irony, the newspaper noted that unless Caputo was immediately released "hundreds of his fellow editors in Argentina will be conscience-bound to present themselves to the nearest police station and ask to be taken into custody."

The judge had considered the news item, in which a Peronist guerrilla leader predicted a resurgence of the terrorist movement in Argentina, a violation of the National Security Law's provisions on leftist ideological propaganda. Yet no other justice around the country deemed the publication a crime.

In matters related to freedom of the press, the Argentine judiciary's much-proclaimed independence is heavily influenced by political circumstances and pressures from military circles.

Censorship

The agency that monitors the Argentine press is the Secretaría de Información Pública, popularly known by its acronym, SIP. Its head is appointed by the executive, with a rank equivalent to that of a cabinet minister; he reports directly to the president and, ultimately, is responsible before the military junta, the top element in Argentina's current power structure.

Largely derived from the late-1940s Peronist system of media control, SIP not only manages and supervises voluminous release of official information but has also established a network of similar agencies in the provincial governments—thus creating a highly centralized nationwide information web. Its procedures, as well as its ties to other branches of the federal government, remain blurry, and many of its "directives"—usually in the form of "top secret" regulations and decrees—have been kept from public scrutiny. It is known, however, to function in close contact with the armed forces in matters related to "national security," which range from terrorism to labor unions and political party activities.

SIP regulates management and appointments at Télam, the official news agency that was founded in 1945 and has since become increasingly powerful as an instrument of censorship. Télam, also in charge of the government's advertising accounts, provides regular news service to some 90 percent of the Argentine media. Coupled with SIP directives, Télam handles information on terrorist attacks and left-wing organizations' activities, and even editorializes in its wire services with a strong anti-communist stand that follows the government line.

Besides authorizing or denying access to public sources of information, SIP also serves as the propaganda branch of the government. Its budget, whose figures are mostly kept secret, provides funds to produce brochures, booklets, reprints from public speeches and the like. In many cases bilingual and intended for distribution overseas, these publications are distributed through Argentine embassies and consulates.

Through the Comité Federal de Radiodifusión (COMFER), SIP also handles all matters related to electronic-media broadcasting, including the administration of the government-controlled private radio and TV stations. COMFER itself issues periodical lists of musical themes and performers whose recordings are banned. (These lists are known as "Boletines del COMFER.") In some cases, recording companies or the performers' agents have argued against the restrictions imposed and revisions of the measures have been granted. But in general, COMFER decisions stand.

Similarly, SIP is known to have blacklisted other artists whose names are not to be mentioned in newspapers and magazines— mostly internationally renowned writers and intellectuals who have expressed dissent or are engaged in so-called "subversive activities." Blacklisting applied to published works is routinely handled by the Secretaría de Comunicaciones, the governmental agency in charge of postal and telecommunications services. Circulation of books, brochures and newspapers or magazines—in Spanish or foreign languages—allegedly linked to left-wing ideologies has been restricted for years in the Argentine mail.

SIP's most important task in recent years has been an all-out effort to prevent publication of news items, in the independent press, about opposition and terrorist activities. Through its monopolistic reporting on terrorism and human rights, it has been successful in spreading fear among news editors and publishers, thus preventing publication of dissenting viewpoints in most of the Argentine media. This—accompanied by the simultaneous and frightening techniques of jailing and disappearances of journalists—has created a virtual monopoly for Télam as the "official" authority on most political events related to the government's anti-terrorist campaign.

In March 1976, hours after the military takeover, editors around the country were notified that their media were under "military censorship," which lasted for a few months. In 1978, to gain favor among the increasingly disgruntled publishers, the military government repealed several decrees of the Peronist regime. But censorship on most aspects remained harsh.

At the end of that year, the Inter-American Press Association awarded a controversial annual prize to Argentine journalists who had vanished. The award was strongly denounced by the Argentine publishers' organization *and* by the government—a surprising joint action under the circumstances. An IAPA special mission sent to Argentina had found "extremely difficult conditions" for the media in that country. Its report pointed out that "the most surprising facet of the profile is that for the most part the press of Argentina accepts the rules of censorship imposed directly or indirectly by the military government."

Restrictions on officials to give information to the press, in effect since 1976, have changed very little. SIP has reserved for itself, at both federal and provincial levels, the role of the government's sole voice. Minor exceptions are tolerated but confined to noncontroversial or nonpolitical matters. No freedom of information acts protect journalists, so access to official sources is channeled through the omnipresent SIP.

A good example of the amount of censorship in Argentine media is provided by the 1980–81 National Broadcasting Law (Ley Nacional de Radiodifusión) and its implementation. The law was worked out by representatives of COMFER, the armed forces and SIP. Delegates of private organizations were consulted but had no decision as to the final wording.

The law forbids reports on: astrology, occultism, fortune-telling, illegal medical practices "or similar expressions," indirect advertising, the eulogy of crime "or vices," and the exploitation of "perversion," "lust" and birth control. More important, the decree forces reporting of "subversive acts" to emphasize "the criminal nature of the facts." It also requires reporting national or local news prior to international events.

No media or press councils exist as such in Argentina. The press's own performance is hardly reviewed at all by news editors, although publishers have sometimes hinted at their disagreements on treatment of certain news events. Criticism among peers, however, is regarded as distasteful.

In the last three years, the situation of the Argentine press has prompted concern by international media organizations. The Argentine media have been consistently labeled "not free" by groups such as Freedom House, IAPA and the International Federation of Journalists. Ironically, this categorization has aroused the outrage of both censors and censored in Argentina—clear evidence of the state of journalism in that country.

State-Press Relations

The ever more powerful functions of SIP in the last four years have been concurrent with an increase on restrictions in the right to criticize government—although it should be mentioned that the short-lived 1973-76 Peronist constitutional regime exerted pressures on the Argentine media. However, the situation has become much worse since the 1976 military coup.

In theory, the media in Argentina are supposed to criticize the government and the performance of public officials. In practice, that is hardly the case. Like its predecessor, the authoritarian military regime deems any dissent as an attack on the "truth-holders," or as a means of favoring "subversive, anti-national" ideologies. Whereas the Peronist government saw criticism as attacks on "the will of the people," the military views the same dissent as an attempt to "destroy the foundations of national unity" or encompass it within the "subversive international campaign" linked to the communist "menace."

Nonetheless, the military government installed in 1976 has permitted some mild criticism of its economic policies, probably as a consequence of the armed forces' own disagreements on programs of economic "liberalization" developed by a civilian minister of economics. But it is hard to know how far to go. In 1980, when objections to the regime by some agrarian producers' organizations that threatened a walkout was echoed by the press, the Ministry of the Interior summoned one of the movement's leaders to warn him that his speeches could be considered "subversive." This pattern is constantly applied by the government as a means for suppression of dissent.

The hypersensitive official attitude toward criticism has also led, in recent times, to governmental manipulation of certain news, particularly that related to human rights violations. Télam deletes or minimizes "unfavorable" news reports from overseas in its national wire services. Its contracts with foreign news agencies—mainly European— authorize this veiled censorship. For instance, leases signed with Spain's EFE, France's AFP, West Germany's DPA and Italy's ANSA give Télam the power to "condense" or even delete such reports from its national wire services.

On terrorist-related news, all information is managed by Télam and SIP, which use only the military-command sources and their official version of any episodes involving "subversive" activities. Although many media disgruntledly carry them, no strong voices of opposition are heard in the Argentine press, with the exception of the outspoken denunciations in the English-language daily *Buenos Aires Herald*. The official version is hardly questioned or even given a balanced side by publication of the left-wing organizations' viewpoint or account; this would immediately subject editors and publishers to penalties under the National Security Law.

Thus editorial influence on government policies has remained confined to minor problems, such as municipal administration and community affairs. Major questioning on political, labor-unions or terrorist problems is kept aside and only low-keyed complaints are published from time to time— never with outright, clearly stated dissent. Once more, only the *Buenos Aires Herald*'s persistent denunciation of threats to its editors, Robert Cox and James Nielson, prompted some government action in 1979-80. This, however, was more related to mounting international pressure than to a willingness to admit any dissenting viewpoint on governmental policy.

During the 1970s suspensions and confiscations of newspapers were a common occurrence—particularly in the cases of *La Opinión* and *Crónica*. Most recently, Timerman's *La Opinión* has provided the best-known instance of confiscation by the government, which also put Timerman under house arrest without formal charges for some two years and his newspaper under direct military supervision. (Timerman himself has written that the government subjected him to electric-shock torture.) In the case of *Crónica* —whose publisher, Héctor Ricardo García, made a spectacular personal campaign to support Argentina's old claim for sovereignty over the Malvinas/Falkland Islands —was forced to change its name to *Ultima Hora*. For some time, García managed to keep the newly named publication afloat until *Crónica* was allowed to reappear as such.

Between 1973 and 1979, in the wake of the military campaign against terrorism, jailings and disappearances of newsmen, as well as death threats from either left- or right-wing organizations, became sadly commonplace in Argentina. The International Federation of Journalists (IFJ) has reported the disappearance of more than 100 newsmen, presumably killed by the security forces or paramilitary groups. Some 400 journalists were forced into exile at various times during the fierce, all-out anti-terrorist war. It has also been reported that some 67 news media were shut down, although this figure may be slightly exaggerated.

Nevertheless, the jailings and disappearances of newsmen, which were clearly aimed to intimidate the press, increased in the aftermath of the March 1976 military coup. The most notable cases reported have involved internationally-known literati, such as writers Haroldo Conti, Antonio Di Benedetto and Rodolfo Walsh, who were also newspapermen. Celebrated journalists like Rodolfo Guagnini, onetime news editor of *Clarin, La Opinión* and *El Cronista Comercial* (as well as a correspondent for left-leaning news organizations), have vanished without trace and are presumed dead. Others, like editor Horacio Agulla, of the now-defunct weekly magazine *Confirmado*, have been killed in the streets in broad daylight by unidentified gunmen. Still many others have been harassed constantly by the military regime's officials or warned to "keep quiet" under threats of a similar fate.

The Argentine publishers' organization,

ADEPA, reported three assassinations and 13 disappearances between 1976 and 1978 alone. The jailing of Di Benedetto, assistant managing editor of the prestigious conservative daily *Los Andes* of Mendoza and an acclaimed novelist, ended with his release and exile in Spain after a campaign led by the PEN Club International. Others, like *La Rioja*'s writer and newsman Daniel Moyano, managed to flee the country after a short arrest. Most of the vanished journalists ("desaparecidos") have been outspoken critics of the military campaign against terrorism. Others, however, were neutral but intended to live up to certain journalistic standards of impartiality that were deemed intolerable by either rightist or leftist organizations.

Some additional means of exerting pressure on Argentine newsmen include indirect or anonymous threats, bombings and brief kidnappings with torture. The indirect-threats system apparently developed only in 1980, when Molotov cocktails were thrown into the offices of an advertising company that handles the accounts of a politician in La Plata.

Despite this frightening a climate for the press, allocation of newsprint, advertising support from official bodies and subsidies were so arbitrarily managed as to arouse criticism by the otherwise obliging publishers' organization, ADEPA, which became particularly concerned over newsprint. The military government clearly showed its intention to create a virtual monopoly for the state-owned Papel Prensa corporation, through a 1980 decree imposing a 45 percent import duty on newsprint, intended to protect that corporation and the nascent Argentine newsprint industry. This outraged ADEPA, which denounced the measure as a means of placing the Argentine press at the mercy of a government-controlled enterprise. ADEPA also charged that many provincial newspapers "will have to die to enable Papel Prensa to live."

Attitude Toward Foreign Media

The Argentine government grants a one-year "transitory resident" visa to foreign correspondents. Renewable for another year on expiration, the visas authorize employment only for the purposes declared by the applicants and their media organizations. In some cases Argentine consulates may conduct a previous investigation of an applicant's background or require validation of the credentials submitted.

In general, the procedure is relatively expeditious when the applicant is an employee of Western media organizations, more complicated when the journalist works for media of the communist countries.

However, once a correspondent is fully accredited, there is no prior approval for cables or other forms of information that are sent abroad. Interviews with public officials are handled routinely by SIP, which usually requires that questions be written and submitted in advance. Not infrequently, questions on touchy political issues are deleted. Government protests over certain reporting, usually related to political or human rights issues, have been a common occurrence in recent times. The attitude toward foreign media, however, is much more restrained than toward local news organizations and journalists.

There were a few cases of expulsions of foreign journalists in the 1970s, mainly for political reasons. In the first half of the decade, the xenophobia of the Peronist government was reflected in frequent attacks on the foreign media through Télam. Balder de Goes, a correspondent for Brazil's *Jornal do Brasil,* was expelled as was Bolivian-born newsman A. Montesinos, who worked for Brazilian-born newsman A. Montesinos, who worked for Brazilian magazine *Veja.* In both cases, "biased" and "inaccurate" reporting were cited as reasons for the expulsions.

Members of the foreign press gather periodically at the Asociación de Corresponsales de la Prensa Extranjera (Foreign Press Correspondents Association), which hosts a prominent public figure—usually the president or a top cabinet minister—as guest speaker at its annual luncheon. That event has become a source of valuable information even for the local press, since senior Argentine officials are far more outspoken here than at any other time.

Western publications circulate freely in most cases, but erotic or pornographic material, regardless of origin, is banned and cannot circulate in the mail or be sold at newsstands. This measure is applied through the blacklists issued by the Secretaria de Communicaciones, or by municipal "morality" committees. Distribution of some publications in Spanish, mostly printed in Latin America, has been restricted in some other instances, as during the petty border disputes that frequently erupt between Argentina and her neighboring countries.

The government's stand on publications from communist countries is harsh. Their circulation is banned both in the mail and on newsstands.

In the early 1970s Peronist xenophobia led to a series of decrees affecting foreign newsagency reporting of Argentine affairs for domestic subscribers. In a bill intended to create a "National Press Law"—but finally never enacted—Peronism tried to impose drastic measures to curtail foreign ownership of Argentine media. By the same token, radio and TV stations were put under governmental control on alleged linkage to foreign media.

Legal regulations require participation of Argentine capital in media organizations, but in many cases this is minimal, with a cosmetic Argentine appearance in the form of figurehead boards of directors. In other instances, foreign publishing houses are known to have created dummy local corporations to hide their dependent Argentine publications, as happened when Italy's Rizzoli took over the former Editorial Abril through a group of Argentine straw men using the name Editorial Crea.

Foreign media organizations, like news agencies, are required to be incorporated under Argentine law in order to operate and conduct business within the country. They are also subject to the local labor and tax laws, regardless of the citizenship of their managers or staffers.

In general, the intensely nationalistic policies of the Argentine government and its suspicious attitude toward outside influences prevent a great deal of foreign propaganda. (Censorship has been very useful in this respect.) Control of overseas publications, however, seems to be more effective than that of radio broadcasts beamed into Argentina, particularly from neighboring countries.

Partly because of internal censorship, domestic media organizations have maintained or increased their contacts with international press organizations. ADEPA keeps in close touch with the Inter-American Press Association, of which it is a member, in spite of recent disagreements of IAPA's criticism of Argentine newspapers. Indeed, in the last few years the Argentine press seems greatly to have increased its dependence on special services provided by foreign news organizations. Many publications rely heavily on overseas news agencies for a supply of stories, features and analysis to counter—or try to counter—the severe restrictions of government censorship.

The Argentine government's stand on UNESCO's 1978 declaration has been blurry and ambiguous. On one side, it claims to support the need for a more balanced flow of information and is not entirely opposed to the idea of a nonaligned-nation "pool" of news agencies, since Télam itself has been a sort of pioneer among Latin American news agencies by creating its own links to European counterparts. The government seems to be equally sympathetic to the idea of licensing journalists. On the other hand, Argentina firmly proclaims an anti-communist stand that would prevent alliances with news agencies from socialist countries. Further, the government has frequently complained—rather swiftly—about what it deems "biased" or "negative" reporting on the country's political situation. To date, the trend seems to be to enhance Télam's operations in Latin America and the United States instead of joining nonaligned-nation news-agency pools.

News Agencies

The size and operations of Argentine news agencies have increased rapidly in the last decade. In 1978 there were eight, although only three of them—Télam, Noticias Argentinas and Saporiti—can be considered strictly as such.

Others were mainly designed to provide occasional, irregular features on given topics to minor subscribers. Actually, only Télam and Noticias Argentinas are in strong, steady competition for the growing Argentine media market. Further, their evolution proves the existence of a simmering confrontation between the state-owned media organizations and the private, independent press. To a certain extent, it also underlines the protracted differences between the provincial press—which played a key role in organizing and developing Noticias Argentinas—and a Buenos Aires-dominated official news network led by the government's Télam.

Télam's organization is clearly linked to the Argentine equivalent of a Ministry of Information, the Secretaría de Información Pública. Its managing news editor is appointed by the government by decree, as are the agency's staffers, after close scrutiny of each individual's political records. It reportedly employs 213 journalists, excluding technical and administrative personnel, and also handles the government's advertising and propaganda campaigns in all Argentine media. In 1980 the agency had its headquarters in Buenos Aires and 30 bureaus throughout the country, with 64 correspondents scattered in provincial capitals and towns. Every bureau is linked to the Buenos Aires headquarters by direct telex lines provided by the government on a 24-hour, 365-day basis. Télam also offers a complementary photo service to subscribers throughout Argentina.

Editing and processing are done in Buenos Aires, whence news items are bounced back to an estimated 90 percent of the private media—amounting to upwards of 300 newspapers and around a score of radio and TV stations, although many of these electronic outlets were under direct governmental control in the late 1970s.

Overseas, Télam has established offices in Brazil, Chile, Bolivia, Paraguay, Peru, Uruguay and the United States. Plans were being completed when this was written to open additional offices in Mexico and Venezuela.

The expansion of Télam has been favored by a series of restrictive measures—originally passed by the Peronist government—that ban foreign news-agency reporting of domestic issues. Earlier, AP and UPI had traditionally engaged in fierce competition for domination of the Argentine market. Their national wire services, complemented by a "package offer" that included radiophotos and foreign news wire services in Spanish, had prevented Télam from competing on its own. But when the foreign agencies were forced to close down their national news services, Télam became the obvious choice for most publishers.

Even so, the inaccurate wording of the decree that was intended to create a monopoly for Télam in national information permitted the establishment of Noticias Argentinas in 1973. Noticias Argentinas (NA) was created as a cooperative by several newspapers from Mendoza, Río Negro, Córdoba and Santa Fe. It hired most of the displaced newsmen who had served UPI and initially also used that agency's leased lines. To counter claims that NA was just an undercover agent for UPI, its founders took special care to stress the agency's "all-Argentine" capital and staff. However, it has remained linked to the U.S. agency through a contract to distribute UPI's Spanish wire service to Argentine subscribers—a total of 121 newspapers and broadcast stations. Early in 1981 negotiations were under way to switch over to AP's Spanish wire service for distribution.

The agency provides independently obtained information and frequently disclaims Télam's official viewpoint on political, human rights and terrorism matters. Much to the military government's dismay, it has posed a serious threat to Télam by constantly increasing the number of its subscribers. Probably for this reason, NA's newsmen have been periodically harassed by either federal police forces or paramilitary groups. Nevertheless, after some initial hesitation among provincial newspaper publishers who feared government retaliation, NA managed to persuade them—and the major Buenos Aires-based newspapers—that its services provided a balance to the pro-official Télam coverage of national events. The new agency soon equaled Télam in its share of Argentina's influential press, and because of its independent stand is still in a process of steady expansion.

News-agency rate data varies, but it can be safely averaged at 5,730 pesos ($300) to 9,550 pesos ($500) a month, depending on the total amount of service a subscriber demands. Special services and requests are billed separately.

Foreign news bureaus in Argentina have also increased in recent years. AP and UPI (although no longer permitted to report local news) have been operating in the country since the beginning of this century, as has Reuters through its subsidiary Spanish wire service, Latin. (Owing to financial difficulties, however, the latter reduced its operations in 1980). The major Western European news agencies also have offices and correspondents—if somewhat fewer in numbers—in Buenos Aires. Agence France-Presse, DPA, ANSA and EFE operate in Argentina, with the first and the last leading the standings in number of subscribers and influence. EFE in particular has thrived in the Argentine market, due largely to a long-established connection between many influential Buenos Aires newspapers and Spain.

Télam, as previously mentioned, has lease contracts to distribute EFE, AFP, DPA and ANSA's Spanish services to its domestic subscribers, thus creating fierce competition with the U.S. news agencies. This also allows Télam to filter touchy news items. ANSA provides a separate feature service on arts and entertainment, which is especially appreciated by Argentine editors, while EFE is

actually competing with AP and UPI in material of this kind that originates in the United States.

Figures on the actual number of news-agency subscribers are—as other data related to the media in Argentina—either hidden or distorted. AP, which maintains a six-man staff in Buenos Aires, claims a conservative 14 Argentine subscribers, but UPI boasts a total of 121. Actually, this report misleads, since it includes Noticias Argentinas' subscribers to its UPI foreign news service within Argentina. Curiously, AP's Spanish wire service is still confined to its traditional clients in the Argentine print media. AP has apparently been unable to attract the country's growing broadcasting market, which continues to deem the U.S. agency "too newspaper-inclined" in its foreign-news coverage. However, AP has managed to increase its clientele among magazines.

In general, the Argentine press depends on Western news services in Spanish for its coverage of foreign events, which have traditionally been a substantial part of the country's highly sophisticated and cosmopolitan journalism. National news coverage is protected: the local agencies share the domestic news market and have virtually established a monopoly on it.

In summary, news flow in Argentina is severely affected by the country's ever-changing political circumstances. While Télam provides the official version of any given political event, Noticias Argentinas's frequent recourse to unofficial sources keeps the balance somewhat even, although actual publication of independent reports is not always easy. Threats of censorship—backed by the National Security Law—have more than once prevented Argentine readers from hearing other voices in the media. All this helps to explain the sometimes unanimous tone of the Argentine press—all too often unanimous by Western standards.

Electronic News Media

State policies relating to radio and television news are closely in line with the military government's stand on control and censorship of print-media outlets in general.

Since the mid-1970s, when "intervención" was imposed on most of the private owners of radio and TV stations, the state has developed a monopoly on official information—which of course encompasses reporting on political issues—as a major weapon in an overall propaganda campaign. This can be dated as far back as the 1940s, when the system of "cadenas nacionales"—radio and TV broadcasting in a "chain" directed from Buenos Aires by the official Servicio Nacional de Radiodifusión—became very common, particularly in case of military coups, revolutions or major political events. More recently, the use of "cadenas" has increased for almost every single ceremony attended by the president, every minister's speech and all types of official activities (even including the much-publicized World Soccer Championship in 1978).

Simultaneously, the military government has used the audio-visual media under its control to launch a major propaganda effort to counter leftist terrorism and also to justify its own all-out war against that movement. Directives issued by SIP have barred or restricted very severely any reporting on terrorist activities. Instructions are often coupled to the elimination of names of alleged leftists from all news items, through COMFER blacklists.

Radio Nacional, the government's radio network, has 26 stations throughout the country plus a foreign broadcasting service in several languages; known as Radiodifusion Argentina al Exterior or RAE, it uses short-wave frequencies. There are four state-controlled television channels in Buenos Aires, one in Mar del Plata and one in Mendoza and 48 state-controlled relay television services in the major cities of the interior.

Appointments—and dismissals—of government-owned radio and TV news editors, anchormen and announcers are carefully screened. The entire process throughout the country is highly centralized and in various instances requires previous approval, from such agencies as the Administración General de Emisoras Comerciales (for privately owned stations) and COMFER and SIP (for the state-controlled federal network). In most cases, screening reportedly includes a secret investigation of any applicant's political background, through checks with the federal government's intelligence units.

Privately owned radio and TV stations have been less rigidly controlled, particularly since enactment of the 1980 National Broadcasting Law. However, this law establishes clearly the content and type of information that privately owned stations will be allowed to handle—and how. More blurry is the law's broad wording on what may (and by whom) be deemed "subversive" or "anti-national" news reporting. Still, most of Argentina's controversial political issues are barred.

However, the broadcasting law's most significant aspect is that it will return radio and TV stations previously under government control to private licensees. The reason for this is simply that government ownership costs too much. The stations will be offered to private bidders in public tender at a rate of approximately six per month. However, the government will directly control and manage at least one radio and one TV station in every province, through the newly created Servicio Oficial de Radiodifusión (SOR). (A so-called "National Plan of Broadcasting" is yet to establish the number and distribution of frequencies, which will reportedly reserve "the best" for the government's network.) In short, the government is far from eager to relinquish its total control over broadcasting in Argentina and will only permit operation by private licensees under the official rules of the game. This will mean ongoing news censorship—while the government simultaneously unloads a heavy burden on the federal budget.

Education & Training

Journalism education in Argentina faces two major problems. The first is a pervasively reluctant attitude of media owners to encourage and provide funds for the establishment or development of journalism schools, in line with a firm belief in the adage, "A journalist is born, not made by schools." The second is a hesitant and distrustful governmental policy on the matter.

Lack of support from media owners has actually closed down some schools in recent years, while the Ministry of Education's entangled bureaucratic process to validate the degrees granted by some others has not contributed to journalism education. Furthermore, no regulations require the media to hire journalism graduates, which makes choice of this career a high risk for potential job-seekers. In fact, many news editors and publishers show a rather contemptuous attitude toward degree holders, partly because most senior executives in the field began their careers without specialized studies in journalism schools.

The University of Buenos Aires' Students Guide of 1980 listed 15 journalism schools throughout the country. However, only nine of these offer degrees at a college level, that is with four years or more in their curricula and with degrees roughly equivalent to the U.S. master's degree. The rest mostly provide basic training with a high-school level diploma, although in some cases this allows a student to pursue studies and obtain an equivalent to the U.S. universities' bachelor of arts.

The curriculum itself varies enormously from one school to the other. Argentina's most prestigious journalism schools—recognized as such even by critics of formal journalistic training—are part of the national universities of La Plata and Córdoba. Lack of financial support has generally prevented the incorporation of modern audio-visual and computerized techniques, so journalism education remains largely within the limits of print-media training. Otherwise, study of the electronic media is mostly theoretical and based on imported—predominantly North American—translated textbooks.

There are no reliable statistics on the ratio of journalism graduates effectively hired by the Argentine media. In Tucumán, a journalism school sponsored and financed by the local newsmen's union had fewer than five percent of its graduates actually placed locally, although around 30 percent were hired by the provincial government's press offices in 1978.

Journalism awards are also scarce in Argentina, the only exception being the prestigious ADEPA annual journalism prizes granted in conjunction with the Rizzuto Foundation. These prizes—which include cash and a medal—are divided into various categories, and are generally considered a high honor by recipients. Some newspapers have also established local prizes, such as La Gaceta's annual award to nonprofessional photographers who provide newsworthy pictures published by the newspaper during the year.

Argentina's major journalistic associations are ADEPA, the publishers' organization, divided into specialized sister groups like AEDBA, of the Buenos Aires private print-media publishers, and ADIRA, AEDBA's provincial press counterpart. There are also a number of other media owners' organizations, such as the Asociación de la Prensa Técnica Argentina (APTA, the technical press publishers' lobby), and the Asociación Argentina de Editores de Revistas (AAER, the magazines group). All

are members of ADEPA. The electronic media owners have their Asociación de Radiodifusoras Privadas Argentinas (ARPA, for private radio stations) and the Asociación de Teleradiodifusoras Argentinas (ATA, for private TV stations licensees).

Associations of photographers, advertising copywriters, advertising agencies and other related trades also exist, as well as journalists' circles and clubs.

Summary

The overall picture of the Argentine media shows that the number of dailies, nondailies and TV-radio stations is in line with the country's relatively-higher development compared to the other Latin American nations. The picture is also deceptive if removed from its sociopolitical background, which shows a less impressive communications performance.

In 1978, according to UNESCO statistics, Argentina had a total daily press circulation of nearly 4.25 million and a readership rate of about 180 copies per 1,000 people—all well above Latin American levels. But the decline in both the quality and depth of news coverage in Argentina only underscores the superficiality of the statistics.

Self-censorship, a persistent reluctance to admit its own flaws and failures and a generally accommodating attitude toward the military government are the basic features of the Argentine press today. Lack of self-criticism and the country's persistent economic problems have also contributed to the decline of the once proud Argentine newspapers and magazines. Much of this also applies to the electronic media, although their record is somewhat more explicable in view of the much harsher governmental control.

Political circumstances of course cannot be ignored, since the country has undergone serious changes during the fierce, turbulent and often uncontrolled civil war of the 1970s. But the Argentine press's reluctance to report on human rights violations during the domestic conflict is difficult to explain—or justify. Newspaper owners have all too often accepted the official viewpoint, lest the military government close down their publications. Increasing international pressure has helped prevent further disappearances, kidnappings and murders of journalists, but very little credit for this can be given to the Argentine media, which consistently have preferred to align themselves with the government and accept the largely fictitious theory of a foreign "conspiracy" against the nation.

Instead of a combative, courageous stand to preserve their independence, many journalists and publishers, acting out of fear, preferred to remain silent and obey the rules imposed by the government. How much guilt can be placed on them—how much the press itself is to blame for the very existence of censorship—is yet to be determined, perhaps by history and time. But the signs for a possible acquittal are not good.

Unless major changes are introduced in this well-rooted stand, the prospects for a free press in Argentina are very dim in the near future. A sign of warning to the country as a whole may well be the minor increase in circulation—or its virtual paralysis—experienced by the private press in recent years. Statistics here reveal the Argentine reader's distaste for an astonishingly unanimous—and often boring—reportage on major political issues. Too frequently, the press has avoided any criticism of the government's propaganda and distorted interpretations of fact.

The repeal of Peronist-inspired decrees that had imposed restrictions on the press—hailed as a victory by hasty, over-optimistic media—was soon followed by much firmer censorship, which narrowed even more the margins of press freedom. To their surprise, many publishers looked back on the past with nostalgia.

The situation of the press in the 1980s will depend, to a large extent, on the country's political stability and, in the long run, on the solution of many a domestic problem. The prospects for the Argentine media as a whole seem promising only in the area of technological advances and the modernization, already under way, of the print media's processing methods. The final product, at any rate, will remain the same unless a turn of events eases present conditions.

This would require a firmer opposition to government press controls, a more definite and better articulated action on the publishers' side to defend freedom of expression and, above all, a major drive to rid the country of the oppressive climate that has prevented most Argentines to face the naked truth about their own culture and its place in the real world. This attitude would be especially necessary among journalists, who have already paid too high a price during the past internal turmoils and seem to have suffered more than enough.

CHRONOLOGY

1976 Military coup overthrows Peronist constitutional government. Media owners and editors are notified, in synchronized action, that they are under "military censorship." Kidnappings, disappearances and murders continue, increasing trend begun in previous years and affecting scores of people, including many prominent journalists. Blacklisting and dismissals begin.

1977 Celebrated Argentine publisher Jacobo Timerman, owner of *La Opinión* of Buenos Aires, arrested by military on charges of alleged link to financier related to Montoneros, Peronist left-wing organization. *La Opinión* is put thereafter under direct military control and administration.

Disappearances of journalists continue.

1978 Federal Appeals Court upholds judge's ruling in case against *La Prensa* for alleged violation of Penal Code involving wire report on exiled Montoneros press conference in Rome. Court states Penal Code is not intended to "prosecute the right to information."

Inter-American Press Association convention in Miami awards prize to Argentina's persecuted newspapermen. ADEPA, Argentine publishers' organization, rejects award on grounds it is part of "insidious" campaign by foreign press to discredit Argentina.

Horacio Agulla, editor of weekly *Confirmado*, killed in daylight in Buenos Aires by unidentified gunmen. ADEPA, at its annual meeting, reports 13 disappearances and three assassinations of journalists since 1976 military takeover.

In spite of Supreme Court ruling clearing him of all charges, Timerman remains in custody. More journalists kidnapped by unidentified plainclothesmen.

Military regime repeals Peronist-inspired censorship decrees in attempt to gain publishers' favor just before opening of World Soccer Championship.

Papel Prensa begins operations as first Argentine newsprint manufacturer.

1979 More journalists disappear or are kidnapped throughout country. ADEPA asks government to explain two cases in Buenos Aires and Salta. A staffer of Salta's *El Intransigente* killed by his captors.

Three major newspapers—*Clarin*, La Razón and *La Nación*—withdraw from ADEPA in dispute over Papel Prensa. Government had ordered that newspapers buy 50 percent of their newsprint supplies from the corporation, a ruling strongly opposed by ADEPA.

La Prensa accuses state-controlled corporation of surcharges well above international newsprint prices.

Papel del Tucumán, second Argentine newsprint mill, begins construction of plant in northwestern Argentina.

Riobó Caputo, publisher of Santa Fe's *El Litoral*, jailed (and later acquitted) on charges of alleged violation of National Security Law for publishing

report from abroad by a leftist leader.

Jacobo Timerman, stripped of citizenship, is expelled from Argentina after nearly two years under arrest.

Robert Cox, editor of English-language *Buenos Aires Herald*, leaves Argentina after repeated death threats for his campaign against human rights violations.

1980 James Neilson, Cox's successor at the *Herald*, also receives death threats and other pressures. ADEPA protests to government.

In Mendoza, retired army colonel threatens journalists in the daily *Los Andes* with revolver, in dispute over his performance as public official.

Government repeals 40-year-old half-fare discount for professional journalists in air and surface travel.

Advertising agency that handled accounts for *El Día* and *Diario Popular* of La Plata attacked.

Unidentified civilians confiscate editions of political magazine. Municipal ruling orders seizure of newsmagazines in Buenos Aires.

Government enacts the National Broadcasting Law, containing further censorship provisions and simultaneously announces auctions of *La Opinión* and *Mendoza*, two dailies under military control.

International Federation of Journalists (IFJ) reports in Brussels that 100 journalists have disappeared in Argentina since military takeover.

BIBLIOGRAPHY

Banco Interamericano de Desarrollo. *Progreso Económico y Social en América Latina.* Washington, D.C., 1979.

Buenos Aires Herald. Various editions.

Butler, David, Cox, Robert, et al. "Kafkaesque Prisoner." Newsweek, 5 March 1979.

CIESPAL. *Dos semanas en la prensa de América Latina.* Quito, Ecuador, 1966.

Clarin. Various editions.

Comité Federal de Radiodifusión (COMFER), Argentina. *Nómina de Emisoras de Radiodifusión.* Mimeographed. Buenos Aires, February 1979.

Ebert-Stiftung, Friedrich. *La estructura de poder de los medios de comunicación en cinco paises latinoamericanos.* Bonn, Germany, n.d.

Fischer, H. D., and Merrill, J. C. *International and Intercultural Communication.* New York, 1976.

"Guía del Estudiante 1980." Universidad de Buenos Aires. Buenos Aires, 1980.

Herrera, Mario. "El periodismo en la Argentina." In "Argentina ante el Mundo," BIR. Buenos Aires, 1976.

Hoeffel, Paul H. and Montalvo, Juan. "Missing or Dead in Argentina." The New York Times Magazine, 21 October 1979.

"How Argentina is consolidating Success." *Euromoney.* London, December 1978.

Instituto Verificador de Circulaciones, Informes Mensuales, 1980-81. Buenos Aires.

Inter-American Press Association. *IAPA News,* and *Updater,* 1978-80.

International Federation of Journalists. *Direct Line.* Monthly report. Brussels, Belgium, 1978-81.

Jordan, David C. "Argentina's Military Commonwealth." *Current History,* February 1979.

La Nación. Various editions.

La Prensa (Buenos Aires). Various editions.

"Las cifras del IVC." *HQD.* Buenos Aires, 1973.

"Los diarios, uno por uno: Intereses e Ideología." Cuestionario (Buenos Aires), September 1975.

Mara, Richard, and Nelson, James. "One generation of Argentines at War With Another." *The Sun,* (Baltimore), 18 January 1976.

Merrill, J. C. *The Elite Press: Great Newspapers of the World.* New York, 1968.

Ministry of Economy, Argentina. *"Economic Information on Argentina."* Buenos Aires, February–June 1979.

"Papel Prensa: Desbrozando el Camino" Carta Política (Buenos Aires), November 1978.

Reports on human rights in Argentina and data on journalists who disappeared. In publications of Organization of American States (1978-80), Council on Hemispheric Affairs, etc.

Roig, A. A. *La literatura y el periodismo mendocinos.* Mendoza, Argentina, n.d.

Secretaría de Información Pública, "Argentina," nos. 4, 5, 6. Buenos Aires, 1977.

_____. *"The Armed Forces and the Process of National Reorganization."* Buenos Aires n.d.

_____. *"The Political Thinking of the Argentine Government."* Buenos Aires, September 1977.

Smith, Peter H. "Argentina: The Uncertain Warriors." *Current History,* February 1980.

Télam. Descriptive brochure. Buenos Aires, n.d.

The New York Times. Various editions.

The Times of the Americas. On government media control in Latin America. 29 March 1978.

Timerman, Jacobo. *"Los limites del silencio en Argentina."* Opiniones (Coral Gables, Fla.), September 1980.

_____. "The Bodies Counted Are Our Own." *Columbia Journalism Review,* (May–June 1980).

UNESCO. *Conferencia Intergubernamental sobre Politicas de Comunicación en América Latina y el Caribe.* Mimeographed. Paris, 1976.

_____. *Cooperación Multilateral de las Agencias de Prensa.* Mimeographed. Paris, n.d.

"Veritas Ante Todo." *Veritas.* 48th anniversary edition. Buenos Aires, December 1978.

Wells, A. *Picture-tube Imperialism?* New York, 1972.

_____. *Mass Communications: A World View.* Palo Alto, California, 1974.

Wynia, Gary W. "Illusion and Reality in Argentina." *Current History,* February 1981.

AUSTRALIA

by Sally A. White

BASIC DATA

Population: 14,615,900 (est. 1980)
Area: 7,682,300 sq. km. (2,966,000 sq. mi.)
GNP: $A118.8 billion (US$132 billion)
Literacy Rate: 98.5%
Language(s): English
Number of Dailies: 54
  Aggregate Circulation: 4.3 million
  Circulation per 1,000: NA
Number of Nondailies: 463
  Aggregate Circulation: 3 million
  Circulation per 1,000: NA
Number of Periodicals: 1,400

Number of Radio Stations: 234
Number of Television Stations: 145
Number of Radio Receivers: 16.6 million
  Radio Receivers per 1,000: 1,130
Number of Television Sets: 5.5 million
  Television Sets per 1,000: 380
Total Annual Newsprint Consumption: 450,000 metric tons
  Per Capita Newsprint Consumption: 30.8 kg. (67.8 lb.)
Total Newspaper Ad Receipts: $A592.7 million (US$658.6 million) (1979)
  As % of All Ad Expenditures: 40% (1979)

Background & General Characteristics

When the "first fleet" arrived in Sydney Cove, New South Wales, in January 1788, it carried not only large numbers of convicts who had been "transported" from England but also a printing press. But no one among the convicts or the civil and military authorities could operate the press. It was not until 1803 that the young Australian quasi-colony's first newspaper was produced. A weekly, the *Sydney Gazette & New South Wales Advertiser* had as its editor one George Howe, a Creole convict and former typesetter for *The Times* of London, who had been transported two years earlier for robbery.

The *Sydney Gazette* served a tiny community of 10,000 people who had settled on a small strip of land on the continent's east coast. It was a modest publication of only four foolscap pages, selling for sixpence. As a government publication, it was much concerned with supporting the status quo. Howe's editorial policy was expressed firmly: "We open no channel to political discussion or personal misadversion; information is our only purpose."

The Australian newspaper industry is very different today. It services a population of just over 14.6 million, across the breadth of a huge land mass. Although there are only two daily papers circulating throughout the whole nation, there are 15 major dailies in the various state capitals and another 37 dailies in the bigger regional cities. There are also two local weekly national newsmagazines, nine Sunday papers, over 300 regional nondailies servicing country districts and about 150 papers published for the suburbs of major cities. The magazine and specialist press is ballooning, as new titles appear every week. Despite this apparent diversity, however, the main news outlets are owned by four groups, including a "big three": the Melbourne-based Herald & Weekly Times Ltd., and, in Sydney, Rupert Murdoch's News Corporation Ltd. and John Fairfax and Sons Ltd. Between them, the three groups have a controlling interest in every Australian metropolitan daily newspaper as well as interlocking interests in a complex variety of magazines, suburban and country papers and radio-TV outlets. The fourth media giant is Consolidated Press Holding Ltd., which used to own daily papers in Sydney but now concentrates on its substantial television and magazine properties.

Australian newspaper publishers have the happy advantage of operating in a society that is highly literate, largely English speaking, urbanized and relatively affluent.

While there is some debate about the levels of functional literacy in Australia—as yet, no authority is prepared to furnish exact literacy figures—the fact remains that Australians are voracious readers. Their book, magazine and newspaper readership levels are high by international standards.

On the surface, the demographic and readership patterns in Australia provide fertile ground for the nation's newspapers, setting the scene for a vigorous, diverse press. But while the quality of Australian journalism is nearly always competent, it is rarely excellent. Its traditional links with Britain are evident in the tightly written copy in the popular press and a sometimes ponderous self-consciousness in the so-called serious press. There remains very little top-quality investigative journalism despite the advent during the 1960s and 1970s of special investigative units in a few daily papers and weekly newsmagazines. The Australian daily press also remains generalist in approach. There have been some moves recently towards sectionalized newspapers, but career specialization among journalists, except in political and financial reporting, remains the exception rather than the rule.

While the 19th century witnessed the growth and community acceptance of a number of fiercely outspoken journals—like the weekly Sydney-based *Bulletin* or the daily *Age* in Melbourne, which espoused political causes with vehemence and effect—the Australian newspaper of the mid-20th century is more quiescent in both content and tone. No Australian daily newspaper aligns itself formally with any political party although many observers assert, with some justification, that the majority of dailies adopt a conservative political line. None of the main political parties regularly publishes a newspaper for the general market, although some parties do have holdings in a few radio stations.

Similarly, among the mass-circulation papers, one finds no overt connection with specific religious or ethnic groups, although there is a general tendency to uphold Australia's Anglo-Saxon, Christian traditions. This emphasis is possibly on the wane, following government initiatives during the 1970s aimed at fostering recognition of the multicultural basis of Australian society. Some mass-circulation papers are, for instance, including Moslem prayer times in their service information and many are paying greater attention to covering news generated within ethnic communities.

As an independent nation Australia is comparatively young. Federation of the various colonies only occurred in 1901, yet Australia's press has rapidly assumed a homogeneity of style. While Sydney and Melbourne retain their reputation as Australia's premier newspaper centers, a reputation bolstered by the fact that over one-third of the nation's population lives in these two state capitals, there is little significant difference in quality or tone of dailies throughout the country. Sydney's afternoon tabloids are a little more flamboyant in presentation than their daily counterparts elsewhere, but the distinction is marginal.

The pre-federation newspaper scene was very different. Rivalry between the various colonies gave rise to publications that aggressively promoted diverse political and economic philosophies. Competition was keen. Following the lifting of government censorship regulations in 1824, the way was cleared for the establishment of an articulate, competitive press despite attempts by the authorities to impose restrictions by way of heavy stamp duties during the late 1820s. By 1848 there were at least 11 daily newspapers being published and, following the discovery of gold in the 1850s, the industry expanded even more rapidly, particularly in the country areas. By 1886 Australia had 48 daily papers and the beginnings of a Sunday press. At this time, moreover, a distribution system through news agencies had been established for some 20 years. While most newspapers of the period were dominated by local news and a great deal of space was devoted to rural matters, overseas coverage was extensive in special supplements whenever the ships arrived bringing the latest news from Europe. There was also a high proportion of crime reporting, and as early as the mid-1830s some newspapers had shown tendencies to a form of "yellow" journalism—with sensationalized accounts of flogging, sadism and sex.

One characteristic of the 19th- and early 20th-century Australian press was the number of individual, and individualistic, owners. It was not until the 1920s that newspaper companies and newspaper chains began to emerge. However, from many of those companies sprang the publishing empires of individuals or families, and some leading publishing houses did not become publicly listed companies until after World War II.

The physical appearance of the Australian newspaper has also undergone transformation in the 20th century. In 1910 the *Sydney Sun* became the first daily to put news on the front page, and in 1922 the *Sun News Picto-*

rial in Melbourne became the country's first picture tabloid daily. Today many dailies, most regional newspapers and every suburban paper are tabloid. There are few regular, or "broadsheet," newspapers still published; those that remain are all morning dailies with the notable exception of *The Herald* in Melbourne.

Australian papers are subject to considerable seasonal variation in pagination figures. The traditional long summer vacation sees a marked decline in the size of dailies as both display and classified advertising volumes decline; thus average pagination figures are difficult to determine. However, as a general guideline, a typical small but healthy suburban newspaper has an average issue-size of 16 pages, while the metropolitan dailies vary in size between a seasonal low of 48 pages to the occasional 160 pages in a single print run achieved by the Melbourne *Age*.

Edition times are clearly delineated in the Australian industry. No Australian daily runs continuously from morning to evening. Final editions for most morning papers are off the press by 3:30 or 4 a.m. First editions for the afternoon papers are usually available by 11:30 a.m. and final editions are on the streets by 5 p.m.

The development of a varied Sunday press has been slow. A strong Sabbatarian following inhibited the establishment of any Sunday publication until the 1880s. Later, strong unionism proved a contributing factor toward making the economics of Sunday publication unattractive. Another cause was the absence of a home delivery distribution system on Sunday. Both factors are still applicable to varying degrees throughout the country, although there are now nine Sunday papers. Only one, *The Canberra Times,* is the Sunday issue of a seven-day publishing operation. All others are separate titles although the *Sunday Press* in Melbourne is a joint venture between separate publishers whose publications compete during the rest of the week. The use of full color or inserted color magazines is not a feature of the Australian Sunday press, nor is full color widely used in the dailies.

Like the daily press, the Sunday papers are dominated by the large media companies. It is in the foreign-language press, and to some extent in the specialist press, that the smaller publisher operates. The foreign-language press in Australia is growing in diversity, but the situation is fluid and some titles last only a few issues. Most publications are weeklies,

fortnightlies or monthlies, although the Italian and Yugoslav communities are served with biweekly publications and the Greek reader, by buying several separate titles, has access to a Greek-language newspaper six days a week. Owing to the flexibility of the market, accurate figures are difficult to obtain. The estimated number of foreign-language papers in 1980 was 80, with an approximate combined nationwide circulation of 500,000.

The foreign-language press situation has not always been as healthy as it appears currently, although it has had a history almost as long as white settlement. The first publication catering to a specific language group was the *German Australian Post,* which began publication in South Australia in 1848 and contained alternate columns of German and English copy. The oldest foreign language paper still in existence is *Le Courrier Australien,* first published in 1892.

In 1934 a federal law was enacted requiring that at least one-quarter of all copy in foreign-language publications be printed in English. This xenophobic and discriminatory law remained in force until 1956, by which time the numbers of postwar immigrants had made sufficient impact on the Australian economy and national perception to ensure a less chauvinistic attitude.

Despite the increasing emphasis on multiculturalism in Australian policy-making and the advertising boost to revenues generated by government decisions to publish migrant and welfare service information in foreign languages, many people involved with the foreign-language or ethnic press in Australia are pessimistic about its future. They assert that fragmentation, lack of reliable circulation audits and the fact that, historically, foreign-language newspapers have relied on continuing waves of first-generation immigrants mean that the role of the ethnic press in the overall Australian scene will remain peripheral.

The special interest press is, at first glance, extremely healthy in Australia. There are probably about 1,400 magazines on subjects ranging from Australian literature to motorcycles, from skin-diving to electronics. However, it remains a very risky enterprise, particularly because of the small population and high distribution costs. Like the foreign-language press, many of the special interest publications last for only a few issues. The specialist titles that remain on the market are frequently those produced by larger publishers such as Consolidated Press Ltd. or the Fairfax magazine subsidiary, *Sungravure*. These are able to rationalize resources and distribution costs.

In the late 1970s the traditionally stable women's magazine section of the specialist market came under pressure. Women's magazine circulation peaked in 1972, when the combined circulation was in excess of 2 million. But by 1978 the combined figure had dropped to 1,878,000: a loss of just over 200,000 copies a week despite the fact that four new titles had been launched.

Daily newspapers published in the five mainland capitals of Australia—Sydney, Melbourne, Brisbane, Adelaide and Perth—circulate in areas that contain more than 70 percent of the total Australian population. However, only three cities—Sydney, Melbourne and Adelaide—have competing daily newspapers. Perth and Brisbane, while without directly competing dailies, do have competition in the weekend market. Further, a small degree of competition arises because the major dailies, particularly those published in Sydney or Melbourne, have limited circulation in other capital cities.

Given the small Australian population, it is not surprising that no newspaper boasts a circulation of 1 million or over; only one, the *Sun News Pictorial,* tops the half-million mark with a circulation of 629,381. The rest of the top 10 dailies fall in the 100,000-500,000 bracket. In September 1980 circulation figures were:

10 Largest Dailies by Circulation	
1. Sun News Pictorial	629,381
2. The Herald	393,185
3. The Daily Mirror	358,907
4. The Sun	348,715
5. The Daily Telegraph	308,801
6. The Courier Mail	269,588
7. The Sydney Morning Herald	258,175
8. The West Australian	252,603
9. The Age	243,467
10. The Advertiser	227,708

The observation that high circulation figures do not necessarily indicate the influence of a given newspaper applies to some extent in Australia. Industry surveys have given *The Sydney Morning Herald* and *The Age* in Melbourne top position among the country's most influential dailies. The third position is filled in Sydney by the national daily, *The Australian,* which had a 1980 September circulation audit of 126,966, and in Melbourne by the top seller, the *Sun News Pictorial.*

Economic Framework

Like many developed nations, Australia was hit by an economic downturn in the 1970s. In 1976 and 1977 its rate of inflation was four to five percentage points above the rate for most industrial economies included in the Organization for Economic Cooperation and Development. Its comparative position, however, improved as the decade drew to a close, and in 1979 its inflation rate was almost two points lower than the OECD rate. Unemployment over the period fluctuated between five and six percent.

The newspaper industry, particularly the dailies, reflected the harder economic times. Profits fell in the mid-1970s and circulation dipped in most areas, although the situation improved marginally in 1979 and 1980. The effects of the general economic decline were compounded by the stresses placed on publishers by the high capital expenditure involved in the introduction of new technologies. Those publishers with interests in television were able to cushion the blow, for television remained the glamor medium for advertisers. An indication of the relative contributions of the various media at the time is the John Fairfax group figures for 1976. The company's five Sydney newspapers contributed 7.1 percent to after-tax profits, whereas the television holdings contributed 42.3 percent. In the 10 years to 1978, total advertising receipts for television increased 4.5 times; radio receipts were 3.3 times the 1968 figure and print receipts 3.5 times higher. However, in 1978 print still accounted for 48.7 percent of total advertising expenditure, and its share edged over 50 percent in 1980. A breakdown of the 1978 figures shows that one-third of total revenue was paid to newspapers. These included the metropolitan dailies, the Sunday press, regional dailies and suburbans. Magazines received 5.7 percent of the total and the specialist and rural press gained 3.3 percent. Some 15 percent of all print media revenue was derived from classified advertising.

As previously noted, the bulk of the print media is owned by four media companies—the Herald & Weekly Times Ltd., John Fairfax Ltd., News Corporation Ltd. and Consolidated Press Ltd. The last no longer publishes newspapers, having sold its Sydney daily papers to the News Limited group in 1972.

It has been asserted that Australia has the greatest concentration of media ownership among the world's democracies. Certainly, it has a high—and increasing—cross ownership between media companies. While there have been instances of minor divestiture and the advent of some new publishers, particularly in Western Australia, the trend from the mid-1960s has been towards concentration. In the mid-1960s the Fairfax group moved into the Melbourne market with purchase of some 50 percent of David Syme & Co. Ltd., publisher of *The Age*. In the early 1970s Consolidated Press sold its newspaper interests to News Limited, and throughout the country a number of smaller regional dailies, nondailies and suburban newspapers were purchased, either outright or partially, by the larger groups.

There has been no national research into the extent of concentration or cross ownership and, in the absence of tracing provisions for nominee or holding companies in the publishing industry, full details of the extent of cross ownership are elusive. Over the past 10 years there has been some political and academic criticism of interlocking ownership, but no national inquiry similar to the British Royal Commissions on the Press or the Canadian Senate inquiry, has been held. Following an unsuccessful takeover bid by Rupert Murdoch's News Corporation Ltd. for the Melbourne-based Herald & Weekly Times group in November 1979, there were renewed calls for such a national inquiry. The takeover bid had been thwarted by Queensland Newspapers, a partly owned subsidiary of the Herald & Weekly Times, and the John Fairfax group, both acquiring nearly 15 percent of the parent Herald company. The complexity of the interlocking holdings can be illustrated by the fact that the Herald & Weekly Times also owns some 14 percent of David Syme & Co. Ltd., its principal competitor in the Melbourne market and a 57-percent-owned subsidiary of the Fairfax group. Eleven months after the takeover bid, the Victoria government announced a limited inquiry into press ownership and control in that state.

There are no controls limiting holdings in print-media companies although certain provisions limit ownership of television and radio companies. These are imposed by federal legislation (see section on Electronic Media), whereas the print media come under the various state jurisdictions. Although a federal Trade Practices Act is aimed at curbing monopolies, it appears that, following amendments to the act in 1977, it has little application in the media area. The Trade Practices Commission, which administers the act, ruled it was unable to take action on the flurry of media share transactions in late 1979.

In addition to cross ownership, the major publishing companies cooperate in several areas. Distribution is one. Individual companies make their own transport arrangements, using either contract transport operators or their own fleets. The actual distribution is effected by news agents who act on a commission basis, billing customers and employing home-delivery labor. The publishers thereby retain ownership of the product and can set maximum retail prices. The publishing companies also cooperate in accrediting agencies to ensure reliability of service. The system was endorsed in 1980 by the Federal Trade Practices Commission, which ruled that it was in the public interest despite its anticompetitive elements. The bulk of physical distribution is by road for distances up to 500 kilometers (310 miles) from the publication point, although some copies of metropolitan dailies are air-freighted for distances up to 3,500 kilometers (2,170 miles).

On the face of it, the Australian newspaper industry has been disadvantaged by the physical characteristics of the country. Its vast distances contribute to high distribution costs and there are no native softwoods suitable for newsprint manufacture. However, the softwood problem no longer troubles the industry, as Australian Newsprint Mills, which is jointly owned by the Herald & Weekly Times Limited and the Fairfax group, has developed a process of manufacturing good quality newsprint from the native eucalyptus. In 1980 domestic newsprint consumption reached 500,000 tons, of which 450,000 tons was used by the newspaper industry. Of that amount some 280,000 tons were imported from New Zealand, Canada and Scandinavia. A new ANM mill, currently under construction at Albury on the New South Wales/Victoria border, will boost domestic output by 180,000 tons when it reaches full production in the mid-1980s. The commissioning of the Albury mill will lessen Australian mainland publishers' dependence on stability in the shipping industry. Currently all newsprint is shipped to the mainland, either from overseas or from ANM's mills in the island state of Tasmania.

Newsprint is not subject to government import or allocation regulations, although protective tariffs do apply to certain coated papers used in magazine publishing. Average newsprint costs in 1980 were $A420 (US$487) a ton and industry sources expect to pay an average of $A462 (US$536) a ton in 1981.

The Australian press suffers a noticeable lack of analysis of the working of the industry, particularly its professional aspects. There is only one journal, published intermittently, which addresses itself to professional journalism issues in any detail. Very few newspapers run regular media comment, although the financial press covers business aspects of the industry in some detail. On the whole, newspaper owners and senior management are reticent about discussing the industry in public. This absence of public debate means there are few contemporary and fully documented accounts of pressure by advertisers or special-interest lobbies. Industry sources suggest, in private, that country, suburban and special interest publications are more vulnerable to pressure from advertisers and lobbyists, but cases have occurred on metropolitan dailies. For instance, an advertising boycott by real estate agents during the 1950s of the now defunct *Argus* newspaper in Melbourne was resisted; however, some media observers believe the substantial revenue loss that resulted hastened the paper's demise. More recently an airline company briefly withdrew its display advertising from the Melbourne *Age* following publication of an investigative series on lax airport security.

Examples of lobby-group pressure are rarely mentioned, but since the late 1960s there has been a considerable increase in the number of professional lobbyists operating in the political arena, especially in the federal capital, Canberra. However, there are no registration regulations for lobbyists and the public has few avenues by which to discover which lobbyist is representing whom, and the press has not deemed lobbyist activity worthy of in-depth scrutiny.

During the period when newspapers were undergoing economic stress, they were also subjected to an increase in industrial disputes. This came about principally because the major Australian publishers wanted to utilize new printing and editing techniques and partly because the national wage-fixing mechanism was under pressure that had been intensified by the general economic downturn.

Australia is a highly unionized country. Only the smallest publishers can employ non-union labor. Industrial relations are covered by both federal and state jurisdictions and the major publishers must operate at these two levels.

The two main unions are the Printing and Kindred Industries Union, which, although a federal union, negotiates industrial agreements at state level; and the Australian Journalists' Association, which negotiates industrial agreements for journalists nationally. The PKIU has a total membership of 51,000. The percentage of membership employed in the newspaper industry is difficult to obtain, but the breakdown for the largest branch in New South Wales gives some indication: approximately one-seventh of the 21,000 NSW members work for newspaper companies. The AJA has a total membership of 10,000. The membership includes public relations professionals, book editors, news cameramen, electronic journalists and court reporters. Federal AJA officials estimate that 4,500 members are full-time or permanent casual employees in the newspaper industry.

In early 1981, the salary scale for metropolitan daily newspaper journalists ranged from $A218 (US$252.88) a week for those who had just completed training to $A448 (US$519.68) a week for senior journalists. Rates for regional and suburban papers are lower. Production union wage scales vary to some extent, but a compositor's wage in the capital cities ranges from $A260 (US$301.60) to $A270 (US$313.20) a week. In addition, night shift and weekend penalties, which range from 15 percent to 20 percent a shift, and a 17.5 percent holiday loading, apply to newspaper employees. Annual vacation and leave entitlements are fairly standard, most workers receiving 35 working days a year, which include public holidays.

Although the PKIU represents workers with some 37 specific trade skills within the printing industry, there are also many other unions whose members work in newspapers. They include the Federated Clerks Union, the Victorian Printers' Operatives, and various national or state unions covering electrical tradesmen, transport workers and other specialists.

In April 1975 national wage-fixing guidelines were established for all Australian wage and salary earners, whereby basic increases were made regularly, taking into account the rise in the cost-of-living index. Increases beyond these national wage adjustments had to be argued on the basis of changes in work value. However, for the newspaper industry, it was a time of change-over to new printing and editing techniques, and therefore changed work skills. The resolution of industrial matters during the changeover was not wholly smooth. Initially problems occurred concerning which group should keyboard copy, and later, disputes arose over pay and conditions that were sought because of changed work skills. In April 1975 printers in Fairfax's Sydney plant struck for 25 days, ostensibly in support of claims unrelated to the new technology, although the coming installation of new equipment undoubtedly added an anxiety factor. A further strike at Fairfax in 1976 lasted 56 days; this was specifically related to the keyboarding demarcation issue. One of the conditions of settlement of that dispute was referral to arbitration, and in August 1977 the NSW Industrial Court ruled that journalists could keyboard original copy but printers had keyboarding claims on other material. Seven months later, the main employers in Victoria reached agreement on the introduction of new technology with minimal unrest. However, all problems were not settled. Journalists in Sydney began operating visual display units, pending resolution of health and certain other questions. In June 1980 the journalists rejected an Arbitration Commission ruling on these matters and a six-week national strike followed. The strike ended when employers agreed to increase payments to journalists using the new equipment.

Most industrial disputes in the Australian newspaper industry have involved working conditions or salary claims. There have been no disputes like Britain's protracted "closed shop" dislocations, and only a few significant instances of production or journalists' unions using their industrial strength in attempts to influence editorial policy or content. The most notable exemption was a 28-hour strike by News Corporation Ltd. (then News Ltd.) journalists in December 1975. The journalists asserted that management had interfered grossly in the news coverage of the federal election following the controversial dismissal of the Australian Labor Party government by the governor general on November 11, 1975. Overall, however, "reporter power" has been low key and restricted to the achievement of minor working-condition concessions negotiated by reporter "house committees" in individual publishing offices.

As already noted, daily newspapers did not flourish in the late 1970s, either in profit or circulation terms. The only national news-

paper to increase its circulation in the last five years of the decade has been the business-oriented *Australian Financial Review.* The morning metropolitan papers edged ahead slightly, showing a 1.6 percent increase in 1979–80 over 1975–76; but the increase did not match the population growth. The metropolitan evening papers showed a net loss of 0.6 percent over the same period, and while most Sunday papers increased their circulations, the loss of one title out of 10 resulted in an overall reduction of 10.9 percent between 1976 and 1980.

Circulation losses, at least initially, were probably compounded by a shift away from the traditional Australian strategy of maintaining low cover prices despite rising costs. Several approaches to the Prices Justification Tribunal during the mid-1980s resulted in sharp increases. In 1977 *The Australian* lifted its cover price by 33 percent to 20 (US23) cents. The competing broadsheets did not follow suit until early 1980, when most lifted prices to 20 cents. Most tabloids also increased prices in early 1980 and most now sell for 15 (US17) or 20 (US23) cents. Sunday papers sell in the 30- to 60-cent (US35- to US66-cent) range.

In 1980 no leading publishers were receiving any cost benefit from the introduction of the new technology. Indeed, some were facing greater expenditure than previously budgeted. As in many other countries, it was the small publishers who pioneered the introduction of computer typesetting and enthusiastically embraced offset printing techniques. In early 1978 *The Dubbo Liberal* in the New South Wales country town of Dubbo became the first Australian newspaper to use CRTs for editorial input. The larger newspapers, particularly those with large classified advertising volumes, were slower to react although *The Australian* began editorial input with CRTs in 1979. Most large publishers plan to convert fully to computer setting and cold type by the mid-1980s. At present many leading newspapers still print on letterpress, although in 1979 there were some 100 offset presses in use throughout the country.

Press Laws

The Australian media operate in a legal environment that is complex, confusing and inhibiting. Local media commentators are fond of remarking that if the American press is free, the British press is half free and the Australian press is a quarter free. While this may be overstating the case, it is fair to say that Australian legislation relating to publication has developed in such a topsy-turvy fashion that a high degree of self-censorship, born of confused caution, is practiced by Australian journalists and publishers.

There is no constitutional guarantee of press freedom, although the widespread push for constitutional reform since the mid 1970s has included demands for the inclusion of basic rights, including freedom of the press, in either a remodeled federal constitution or a separate bill of rights.

The federal nature of the Australian political situation means that legislative responsibility for publication matters is divided between the federal, or Commonwealth, government and the various state Governments.

The powers of the Commonwealth touch the media in several areas. The Commonwealth has jurisdiction over imports and exports, and thus over the importation of books, newspapers and other printed matter, and over the prohibition of entry to those publications deemed obscene or seditious by Commonwealth authorities. Regulation of the broadcast spectrum is also a federal responsibility, so that both radio and television regulation are national issues. The Commonwealth's defense powers affect the media in that the federal government can censor material on security grounds. Its foreign-affairs powers give it jurisdiction to enforce adherence to international conventions relating to copyright, newspaper ethics and labor conditions. Because the federal government has power over conciliation and arbitration of interstate industrial disputes, and because many of the newspaper and printing unions are federal unions, Commonwealth legislation is relevant to many newspaper industrial matters. Finally, the Commonwealth has jurisdiction over marriage and divorce, and therefore has the power to regulate the reports of judicial proceedings concerning them.

The individual state legislatures deal with the majority of matters affecting day-to-day press activity. They are responsible for the general criminal law, including publication of obscene and seditious material, the general law of torts, including defamation, and registration of newspapers, printing presses and publishing companies. While Commonwealth law is uniform, the state regulations vary considerably, although they stem from the base of common law inherited from Britain. In a country where there is a considerable degree of circulation overlap across state borders, especially by the major metropolitan dailies, the state-to-state variation causes confusion. Since 1958 there have been attempts to bring uniformity by consensus in important areas of state private law, but many anomalies remain.

The most recent attempt to rationalize conflicting defamation laws was made in 1976, when the federal authorities commissioned a national inquiry into defamation and publication privacy by the Australian Law Reform Commission. In 1978 the commission presented its findings, including draft legislation on "unfair publication," to the federal government. In its report the commission noted that in most jurisdictions in Australia the content of defamation laws had been substantially unrevised during this century, and that it was not reasonable to expect publishers and journalists to know and apply eight separate defamation laws. The law, it said, was inefficient in vindicating reputation, impeded the flow of information on public affairs and imperfectly protected personal privacy. The thrust of the commission's recommendations, then, was to ensure uniformity of defamation laws throughout the country, to put the first privacy laws on the Australian statute books and to ease the existing restrictions on fair comment and investigative reporting in the public interest. However, no action has been taken on these recommendations.

The concept of legislation aimed at protecting confidentiality of news sources is unknown in Australia, although in some defamation actions a newspaper employee has the privilege of declining to name the author of the alleged defamatory material for which the publisher and editor have taken responsibility.

Defamation legislation preoccupies Australian journalists and publishers to a greater degree than the host of other legal requirements imposed on publication by either federal or state governments. However, many of the laws have a direct bearing on the practice of journalism in Australia. The Commonwealth Crimes Act is perhaps the most significant. The act covers publication of material by unlawful associations, official secrets and espionage. The official-secrets provision relates to disclosure of official information by people who are, or have been, Commonwealth officers where there is a duty not to disclose. Some legal authorities maintain that practically all information in the possession of the government is prima facie confidential. However, a 1980 ruling in the High Court, lifting an interlocutory injunction that sought to prevent publication of documents relating to Australian defense and foreign policy indicated that the judiciary's attitude toward excessively restrictive classification of government documents is more liberal than previously thought.

Seditious material is covered mainly by state legislation during peacetime and by federal powers on defense during wars. Historically, successful prosecutions during peacetime have been rare.

In the area of blasphemy, obscenity and sedition, both the federal and state governments have some jurisdiction. As well as its powers over the importation of obscene publications, the Commonwealth government can prevent domestic traffic in obscene material under its postal legislation. All newspapers and magazines must be registered if they wish to take advantage of concessional postal rates. Should they carry obscene or indecent matter, registration can be cancelled and copies held up or destroyed.

The states all have powers relating to obscenity, which vary considerably. In all states however, publication of obscene material is a summary offence, subject to trial before magistrates or justices of the peace, sitting without a jury, and with provision for seizure and destruction. Some states that require registration of publishers and distributors empower the courts to cancel registration if the publisher or printer is found guilty of publishing obscene matter.

Each state has some form of legislation relating to the registration of printing presses and/or newspapers. Several states require bonds from publishers to ensure compliance with libel laws. However, neither federally nor at state level is registration of journalists required.

In addition to legislation relating to the traditional matters of defamation, obscenity etc. Australian newspapers contend with a series of minor restrictions relating to advertising or reporting unlicensed lotteries, illegal gaming and betting and false or misleading advertising, all of which come under state jurisdiction, and therefore vary considerably.

Both federal and state governments have enacted legislation relating to political advertisements, articles and broadcasts, particularly in relation to electoral material. Again the actual requirements vary, but most require identification in some .form of the author of political advertisements and identification of paid election advertising.

The complexity and range of laws affecting the Australian press have been criticized for many years by both the legal and the journalistic profession. However, there is little hope that radical reform is imminent. Indeed, the Australian Press Council, which conducted a national survey of encroachments on press freedom, asserted that some 40 percent of restrictions notified during 1979–80 were initiated by lower-court magistrates or judges, an estimate indicating that the relationship between Australia's independent judiciary and its press remains uneasy.

Censorship

The legislative framework already described constitutes the principal inhibition on publication in Australia. In addition, the Australian press has adopted the British D-notice system of pre-censorship, whereby publishers agree to withhold, voluntarily, the publication of material that has been deemed sensitive by a joint industry-government committee. There are currently five D-notices in operation, most of which relate to strategic defense information. It is perhaps indicative of the quiescence of the Australian press and its public that there has been little sustained criticism of this type of censorship and very few cases of breach of a D-notice.

The most visible self-regulatory mechanisms are the Australian Press Council and the Advertising Standards Council. The Australian Press Council was established in 1976, after the publication of a discussion paper on press reform by the then media minister in the Labor government brought the specter of legislative restraint closer in the eyes of publishers. The council comprises 13 members, of whom one is an independent chairman. Six representatives come from the various publishers' groups, three are elected by the Australian Journalists' Association from among its ranks and three are public members appointed by the chairman. The council's first and present chairman is a former High Court judge. Its function is to hear and adjudicate public complaints about press performance, to monitor movements in media ownership and to establish guidelines and issue discussion papers on a range of professional matters. It has no punitive powers, as its sole sanction is publication of its findings through newspapers and its own annual reports. It is funded by participating newspaper companies and associations and the journalists' union.

Since its inception the council has been consistently criticized because one of the "big three," the John Fairfax group, is not a participating member. (However, as the council can adjudicate on reports in all print media, Fairfax publications have been the subject of complaints and have been more assiduous in reporting council findings than many of the participating newspapers.) A further blow to the council's public credibility was the withdrawal of another significant publisher, News Corporation Ltd., in 1979.

The Advertising Standards Council operates under the auspices of the Media Council of Australia. This council is a cooperative federal body that represents all media and is primarily concerned with the accreditation of advertising agencies and the formation of voluntary codes for the advertising of products such as alcohol, tobacco and therapeutic drugs. The council deals with public complaints about specific advertisements in all media. It does not report directly to the public but through its parent body. It is chaired by a former president of the Australian Conciliation and Arbitration Commission (or federal industrial court).

The establishment of the Press Council and the Advertising Standards Council was partly an industry response to the marked rise in consumer activity that occurred in Australia, as in many other developed countries, during the 1970s. But in general terms the rise of consumerism cannot be said to have greatly improved the public's access to information. Demands for such access have yet to be fully articulated. Media observers and civil rights activists have noted that Australia is a peculiarly closed society, considering its democratic system and its anti-authoritarian traditions. While politicians from both main parties have publically espoused the cause of freedom of information and promised legislative initiatives, no such legislation has been enacted at state or federal level. Throughout the mid-1970s, successive federal governments drafted and redrafted freedom of information legislation. A bill dubbed "The Freedom From Information Act" by both local and overseas critics will be debated in federal parliament in early 1981.

State-Press Relations

The federal government imposes no special restrictions on the entry of foreign correspondents. Like other resident aliens, they

1973 the country had no ministerial portfolio with responsibility for communication policies. The regulation of the electromagnetic spectrum was just one of the tasks of the minister for posts and telegraphs. The election of the Australian Labor party after 23 years of conservative government saw the appointment of a minister with special responsibility for the media, although delineation of federal/state jurisdictions limited the role. The return of the conservative Liberal/National party coalition in 1975 brought the temporary demise of the portfolio. It was revived in 1980 with the appointment of a minister for communications, but the Australian attitude to international communications issues, except in the purely technical area, remains the responsibility of the minister of foreign affairs.

It would be incorrect to assert that the Australian press suffers from direct government control. The right to criticize government is upheld in theory and in practice, although seldom welcomed. Journalists are not jailed although there are statutory provisions for imprisonment in cases of contempt of court and breach of parliamentary privilege. The most recent case of a reprimand occurred in 1978, when a Melbourne Sunday paper was called before the federal Parliament after it had published generalized but trenchant criticism of the behavior of some members of the House of Representatives. Surprisingly, there was little adverse reaction from other publishers.

Neither the Australian nor state governments exercise control through newsprint allocation, subsidies, licensing of journalists or import licenses for printing equipment.

There remain, however, several disquieting elements in press-state relations. One is the ban on reporting of election material by the electronic media from midnight on the Wednesday preceding an election to the end of voting at 8 p.m. on the Saturday of the poll. This severe restriction on reporting has been in force since 1942 and, despite mounting criticism from all media groups, there appears little hope of repeal in the near future. The as yet unsatisfactorily resolved freedom of information question, the growing number of lower-court closures and the slowness of defamation reform all constitute blots on Australia's press freedom record.

Attitude Toward Foreign Media

The federal government imposes no special restrictions on the entry of foreign correspondents. Like other resident aliens, they hold temporary residents' visas and there have been no recent cases where such visas have been refused or withdrawn.

Foreign publications, subject to the general laws on obscenity and sedition that apply to all print matter, have free entry; the only restriction on foreign media involvement is the limitation to 10 percent foreign holding in Australian media companies.

The Australian press has strong traditional links with international press freedom organizations such as the International Press Institute, the International Federation of Newspaper Publishers and the Commonwealth Press Union, and has worked actively to ensure that the Australian government adopts a firm stand against any international restrictions on the unfettered flow of information throughout the world. Australia has actively supported U.S. positions on the controversial UNESCO declarations on the media.

News Agencies

Australia has one national domestic news agency, Australian Associated Press, which services the majority of major and minor newspapers. Established in 1935, AAP is a cooperative of the main publishers with the exception of News Corporation Ltd. It furnishes such special services as parliamentary reporting, detailed sporting results and stock market reports to its subscribers and is expanding vigorously in most areas of domestic reporting. AAP also handles the bulk of foreign news entering the country. It receives and processes copy from Associated Press, Reuters, Agency France Presse, the U.K. Press Association and the New Zealand Press Association, as well as material from *The Times* of London and *The New York Times*. In 1980 AAP had 300 subscribers.

A number of overseas news agencies maintain bureaus in Australia, mainly in Canberra and Sydney. At the end of 1980 some 21 foreign correspondents or local reporters, working full time for overseas agencies, publications or radio services, were accredited to the Canberra parliamentary press gallery.

Electronic News Media

The principal legislation that governs radio and television services is the Broadcasting and Television Act of 1942. Other acts lay down license fee schedules, and the Parliamentary Proceedings Broadcasting Act of 1946 requires the noncommercial Australian Broadcasting Commission to broadcast the proceedings of the federal Parliament from one of the national broadcasting stations in each capital city and some specified regional cities.

The broadcasting act is administered by the Australian Broadcasting Tribunal, formerly the Australian Broadcasting Control Board. The tribunal conducts public inquiries on license renewal for both radio and television in the commercial and public fields. It may also conduct inquiries into the setting of standards of broadcasting performance in areas such as children's television and Australian content, alleged breaches of license conditions and any other aspect of broadcasting referred to it by the appropriate federal minister. In 1980, for instance, the tribunal was charged with conducting a public inquiry into the introduction of cable television services in Australia. It also has some research function, and reviews public complaints about electronic media performance.

Among the provisions of the Broadcasting and Television Act are certain restrictions on ownership of the electronic media, which, because of multiple media ownership patterns in Australia, indirectly affect the business operations of newspaper publishers. The legislation limits the number of prescribed and/or controlling interests in electronic media companies that may be acquired. In television a prescribed interest is more than five percent and a controlling interest is fixed at more than 15 percent. No individual or company can hold a prescribed interest in more than two television stations; these cannot be situated in the same metropolitan area.

In radio, a prescribed interest and a controlling interest are each described as any holding over 15 percent. No person or company can have a prescribed interest in more than eight stations throughout the country, more than four stations in any one state, more than four metropolitan stations, and more than one in any single metropolitan area.

These restrictions pose particular difficulties for Australian media companies because of the high degree of interlocking shareholding. In early 1981 the federal government indicated that the ownership provisions and the powers of the tribunal in relation to license hearings may be revised.

Education & Training

Traditionally the Australian newspaper industry has accepted responsibility for the training of journalists, artists and photographers. Until recent years the sole training method was the cadetship system, in which those leaving school at ages 17 or 18 entered the industry as cadets for three or four years. Their training was carried out on the job with some requirements in the journalists' industrial agreement for provision of formal lectures and counseling by the employers. The award also provides that cadets be granted time off on company time to pursue further nonjournalistic training at tertiary institutions. At the end of the cadetship period, trainees are automatically graded as journalists.

However, the expansion of tertiary institutions that occurred during the 1960s and 1970s has given rise to a second method of professional education. There are now 10 universities or colleges of advanced education that offer degree courses in communications. Most courses are of three years' duration. The practical journalism content of these courses varies considerably, and it is still true to say that newspaper employers are not fully convinced that the tertiary courses cater adequately to the industry's needs. However, there are increasing numbers of journalism or communications graduates entering the profession, as well as general graduates embarking on one-year cadetships that provide in-house training after graduation.

Just as journalism training courses have proliferated in recent years, so too have journalism awards. There is some industry anxiety that many of the newer awards are promotional in character and do not contribute significantly to the raising of professional standards. The two principal awards that are fully endorsed by all sectors of the industry are the annual Walkley Awards, granted to both print and electronic journalists in an extensive number of categories, and the Graham Perkin Journalist of the Year Award, which was instituted in 1976 to recognize the country's single most outstanding contribution to the profession.

Summary

By international criteria, Australia is well served by its press. Standards are relatively high and Australian journalists practice their craft in a basically unrestricted and unhostile environment. While the 1970s were a decade of economic strain within the newspaper industry, the difficulties attending the changes necessary to compete with alternative news sources were overcome with comparative ease.

The trends that began in the 1970s are likely to accelerate in the coming decade. There will be growing sophistication in printing techniques, including greater use of color and an increase in specialized reporting in both the newspaper and newsmagazine fields. It is probable that the Eighties will see a greater diversity of style as the serious and popular press target more specifically on sectors of the mass market, but it is highly unlikely that there will be any significant growth in the press's market share.

It is possible that media ownership patterns will be modified as public pressure intensifies against further ownership concentration. It is also possible, and some media commentators would say probable, that the Australian press will experience gradual erosion of its freedoms to report unless it takes more vigorous action to demonstrate its accountability to the community it serves.

CHRONOLOGY

1975

June	Federal minister for the media releases controversial discussion paper on press reform.
October	Six members of Australian Journalists' Association killed while on assignment in East Timor.
November	John Fairfax & Sons Ltd. become first large Australian publisher to announce new technology plans.
December	Journalists employed by national daily, *The Australian,* strike for 28 hours in protest against management interference in news coverage of federal election campaign.

1976

July	Australian Press Council established.
October–December	Printers employed by John Fairfax group in Sydney strike in support of claims relating to new technology issues.

1977

July	Prices Justification Tribunal allows 33 percent cover price

rise for *The Australian.*

August   NSW Industrial Court rules specific union rights in relation to keyboarding copy.

1978
March   Australia hosts first IPI General Assembly in Southern Hemisphere.

1979
November   News Corporation Ltd. makes unsuccessful takeover bid for Herald & Weekly Times group.

1980:
February   Trade Practices Commission rules in favor of continuance of distribution system through news-agency outlets regulated by newspaper publishers.
June–July   Newspaper journalists strike for six weeks in support of improved pay and conditions for operating CRTs.
October   Victoria state government announces inquiry into ownership and control of print media in Victoria.

BIBLIOGRAPHY

Australian Broadcasting Tribunal. *Annual Report 1978-1979.* Canberra, 1979

Australian Bureau of Statistics. *Monthly Summary of Statistics, Australia November-December 1980.* Canberra, 1980.

Australian Information Service. *The Media 1979.* Canberra, 1979.

Australian Law Reform Commission. *Report No. 11—Unfair Publication: Defamation and Privacy.* Canberra, 1979.

Best, Bruce. "The Other Press Barons." *The Age,* July 12, 1980.

Bosi, Pino. "Ethnic Press—A Question of Survival." *Media Information Australia,* no. 15, February 1980, p. 34.

Brown, Allan. "Takeovers, Mergers and Australian Newspapers." *Media Information Australia,* May 1980, p. 3.

Commercial Information Advisory Service of Australia. *Advertising Expenditure in Main Media.* Sydney, 1979.

Cordner, S., ed. *B & T Year Book 1980.* Sydney, 1980.

Deamer, Adrian. "Adrian Deamer on Self-Censorship." *The New Journalist,* no. 5, November-December 1972.

Frawley, Ray. "The Provincial Press." *Media Information Australia,* November 1979, p. 3.

Gee, M. *Media Guide.* 5th ed. Melbourne, November 1980.

Gordon, H. A. *An Eyewitness History of Australia.* Adelaide, 1976.

IPI Report. December 1980.

Lawson, Valerie, and Mawbey, Pam. "The Battle for Australia's Women." *Australian Financial Review,* February 22, 1980.

Macdonald, C. R. "Newspaper Advertising." *The Australian Director,* December 1979, p. 32

Mawbey, Pam. "Readers Choose Their Favorite Newspapers." *Australian Financial Review,* August 1, 1980.

——— "City Newspapers Find It Tougher." *Australian Financial Review,* December 4, 1977.

McGregor, Ken. "NSW Daily Newspaper Leads with Computers." *Australian Financial Review,* March 3, 1978.

McKeon, Ashley. "Troubled Australian Gains 33pc Price Rise." *Australian Financial Review,* July 4, 1977.

Mayer, H. *The Press in Australia.* Melbourne, 1964.

O'Hara, John. "The Print Revolution." *Sydney Morning Herald,* November 15, 1976.

Sawyer, G. *A Guide to Australian Law for Journalists, Authors, Printers and Publishers.* Melbourne, 1968.

Sprague, Holden W. *Australia Goes to Press.* Melbourne, 1962.

Status of the Media 1979. Sydney, 1979.

The New Journalist, no. 21, December 1975-January 1976.

Whitlock, Anthony. "Electronic Papers...of a Type." *The Age,* March 13, 1979.

Wilson, Nigel. "Newsagents Win the Right to Monopoly." *The Age,* February 1980.

Wiltshire, K. W., and Stokes, C.H. *Government Regulation and the Printed Media Industry.* Melbourne, 1977.

——— *Government Regulation and the Commercial Electronic Media.* Melbourne, 1976.

AUSTRIA

by Paul Underwood

BASIC DATA

Population: 7,491,000
Area: 83,916 sq. km. (32,400 sq. mi.)
GNP: 803 billion schillings (US$64.6 billion) (1979)
Literacy Rate: 98%
Language(s): German
Number of Dailies: 28
  Aggregate Circulation: 2.5 million
  Circulation per 1,000: 336
Number of Nondailies: 132
  Aggregate Circulation: NA
  Circulation per 1,000: NA
Number of Periodicals: 2,206

Number of Radio Stations: 1
Number of Television Stations: 1
Number of Radio Receivers: 2,266,220 (1979)
  Radio Receivers per 1,000: 306
Number of Television Sets: 2,097,550 (1979)
  Television Sets per 1,000: 283
Total Annual Newsprint Consumption: 144,800 metric tons (1977)
  Per Capita Newsprint Consumption: 19.3 kg. (42.5 lb.)
Total Newspaper Ad Receipts: 3.4 billion schillings (US$275.3 million) (1979)
  As % of All Ad Expenditures: 37.5 (1979)

Background & General Characteristics

Austria occupies a strategic position in the heart of Central Europe. Although its total area is only 32,400 square miles, it shares a common border with three Communist-ruled countries, Hungary, Czechoslovakia and Yugoslavia; with two members of the NATO alliance, West Germany and Italy, and with neutral Switzerland.

A small remnant of the old Hapsburg Empire, Austria has declared herself a neutral state. Her 7.4 million people are nearly all Austrian. German is their native language, and literacy is about 98 percent. The only significant ethnic minority is the bloc of 70,000 Slovenes who live in the province of Carinthia, just north of the Yugoslav border.

The first half of the 20th century proved a difficult period for Austria, but since World War II the country has enjoyed a remarkable degree of political stability. Although several of the nation's largest industrial enterprises are nationalized, the economy operates basically on private enterprise principles. Per capita income is somewhat lower than the average for Western Europe, but the economy is generally healthy and consumption rates are higher than in some neighboring states.

The city of Vienna, home to 1.8 million people—about a fourth of the total population—dominates the media scene as well as the political, social and economic life of the nation. The Viennese press accounts for about three-quarters of the total newspaper circulation.

Austrian newspapers can be divided into three distinct groups: the big, popular, mass-appeal dailies, all in Vienna; the provincial press, generally solid, sober and with strong ties to political parties; and a small number of independent, quality papers, of which the capital city's *Die Presse* and the *Salzburger Nachrichten* are probably the best known.

The mass-appeal dailies tend toward the sensational, but most provide fairly good coverage of international and domestic developments. All pay considerable attention to cultural events. Continued political party leanings, if not actual affiliations, are characteristic, even among the sensationalist papers.

Most of present-day Austria was a part of the old Roman Empire, which held the Danube as a frontier against the Germanic tribes to the north. The Roman city of Vindobona, which stood on the site of the center of present-day Vienna, was a military strongpoint on this frontier.

With the collapse of the empire the area became a battleground for all the various marauding peoples that swept over Central Europe. It finally reappeared in history when the western part was incorporated into Charlemagne's empire as a mark, or frontier. In succeeding centuries, its rulers gradually extended their dominions to the east and south, eventually becoming dukes of the Holy Roman Empire. In 1231 the dukedom became a Hapsburg posession, beginning a 640-year rule that made the family name virtually synonymous with Austria.

The first printing press was set up in Vienna in 1480, and by the end of the century news sheets recounting important or unusual events began to appear. The date of the first newspaper is a matter of dispute; there are claims for one as early as 1605. It is certain that one weekly was in operation by 1620 and that three more were published by 1660.

The most notable of these early publications was a twice-weekly paper called *Der Postalische Mercurius,* which was established in 1703. It became a daily in 1714 and 10 years later was made the official voice of the government. Renamed the *Wiener Zeitung,* it still appears in Vienna today under government auspices—the oldest operating newspaper in the world. For nearly a century and a half it held a monopoly on all newspaper advertising in the city.

The Hapsburgs, like most of their counterparts, were autocratic rulers who had no interest in press freedom. Strict censorship was the rule. And the unfavorable climate became even more oppressive as a result of the crown's support of the Counter-Reformation. For long periods of time, news sheets were the only print competition to the official daily.

Although newspapers could not prosper, the 18th century saw the birth of a number of weekly journals dealing with nonpolitical subjects. In 1781 one of the more enlightened of the Hapsburgs, Joseph II, abolished censorship and declared press freedom. This lasted only until his death nine years later. His successor immediately restored the old order.

Austria's first real experience with a free press came during the wave of revolutions that swept over Europe in 1848. An uprising in Vienna forced the lifting of censorship. Within a few weeks more than 200 papers, including 90 dailies, had been established.

Most of these were promptly put out of business when Hapsburg forces moved back in control.

One that did survive was *Die Presse.* It had been founded in the midst of the revolution but quickly established a reputation for coverage of international events. It became so popular that it eventually was able to break the *Wiener Zeitung*'s monopoly on advertising.

The restoration of Imperial rule brought back the old press controls. In fact, for a time all newspapers except the *Wiener Zeitung* were banned. In 1849 a new press law was issued that permitted resumption of publication but required precensorship and large deposits by publishers to ensure obedience. It also provided for punishments ranging up to suppression of papers in case of violations. A tax on advertising was imposed.

By 1850, 50 papers were being published in the country. Most of these managed to survive until 1862, when still another press law abolished censorship and the system of punishments, even though the press was still restricted in other ways. The response to the change was immediate. By the end of 1862, 345 periodicals of one kind or another were being published throughout the empire. A further easing came in 1869 when a new constitution was approved that guaranteed freedom of the press. It also provided for compulsory education. The freedoms were partly nullified, however, by press laws that permitted the government to keep a tight rein on papers, particularly those representing minority peoples of the empire.

Nevertheless, the last part of the 19th century witnessed the blossoming of the press. Compulsory education increased the number of potential readers. The spread of industrialization and the growth of the industrial proletariat led to the emergence of a political press, a continuing characteristic of Austria. One of Vienna's most respected papers, the *Arbeiter Zeitung,* dates back to this period. It was founded in 1889 and ever since has served as the principal voice of the Social Democrats.

Two of the outstanding papers of the period were non-party publications, however. Generally recognized as the country's best was the *Neue Freie Presse,* which was established in 1864 by part of the staff of the *Die Presse.* It enjoyed an international reputation and played a powerful role in internal affairs, even though its circulation did not reach 100,000 until 1910.

The other prominent non-party paper was

the *Neues Wiener Tagblatt.* It had a larger circulation than the *Neue Freie Presse* and was the nation's leader in advertising. However, it never gained much attention outside the capital, remaining a largely Vienna paper.

As in Germany, the turn of the century saw the emergence of new type of paper, the so-called *Boulevardblatter,* the mass-appeal picture press that thrived on sensation and scandal. Austria's outstanding example was the *Illustrierte Kronen-Zeitung,* which was founded at the end of the century and achieved an unprecedented 300,000 circulation.

World War I was a disaster for Austria. At the end, the empire was dismembered. The country was reduced to a small remnant of its former glory, with only seven million of the 43 million people Vienna had once ruled over. The economy had collapsed, and the loss of many of its natural markets made rebuilding a formidable task.

The Hapsburgs had given way to a republic. Politics grew increasingly violent. Private armies organized by both Right and Left battled in the streets. The newspapers, too, grew increasingly partisan. At least 25 dailies competed for readers in Vienna, and there were others in provincial centers.

The leading paper of the Social Democrats was again the *Arbeiter Zeitung,* which had a circulation of about 100,000. The most important voice of the Right was the *Reichspost,* published by the Christian Socialist Party, with 60,000. Both these two main parties established popular tabloids to attract more readers. The Social Democrats brought out *Das Kleine Blatt* in 1928 and the Christian Socialists *Das Kleine Volksblatt* the following year.

The continuing political conflict finally spelled the end of democratic rule. The government instituted rule by decree. Social Democratic papers were closed; licensing was reintroduced. The old imperial news agency, renamed the Amtliche Nachrichtenstelle, was put under tight government control. Precensorship and confiscations became common.

In the 1930s Nazism became a political force, agitating for union with Hitler's Germany. A new paper, the *Weiner Neuste Nachrichten,* became the voice of this movement, and was joined by others established in other cities. Alternative voices were limited to illegal underground publications, some printed inside the country and others smuggled in from abroad. The latter included a miniature edition of the *Arbeiter Zeitung,* printed in Brno, Czechoslovakia.

The government finally tried to curb the Nazis, but in 1938 Hitler's forces marched in to bring about the Anschluss, or union, of the two states. The press was an immediate victim.

The *Weiner Neueste Nachrichten* became the leading evening paper. The Nazis also published a Vienna edition of their own, *Volkischer Beobachter.* They took over the old *Reichspost,* and merged the *Neue Freie Presse* and the *Neues Wiener Tagblatt* into another mouthpiece. Four popular tabloids were merged into the *Kleine Kriegs Zeitung.* They incorporated the nation's news agency into the Deutsches Nachrichtenbüro, Hitler's news agency, and made all radio stations a part of the German network.

From that time on until the end of World War II the fate of the Austrian press mirrored that of the German press. With the defeat of the Nazis, Austria, like Germany, was occupied by the four major Allied powers: Britain, France, the Soviet Union and the United States. Each governed a specific zone of occupation as well as a sector of divided Vienna. They moved immediately to set up their own newspapers and soon began issuing licenses to prospective Austrian publishers.

Within a relatively short time a number of papers had appeared, some issued by the occupation forces, some by political parties and a few by independent publishers. The old *Arbeiter Zeitung* was reestablished. *Die Presse* was set up as a serious independent. The People's Party, the successor to the former Christian Socialists, published *Das Kleine Volksblatt* and the *Neue Wiener Tagszeitung.* A new title, *Neues Österreich,* represented the government coalition. The Communists had *Volkstimme* and *Der Abend.* Two of the most popular occupation papers were the British *Weltpresse* and the American *Kurier.* The latter, which was sold to an Austrian industrialist in 1954, is still one of the country's major dailies.

A new national news agency, the Austrian Press Agency (APA), was organized in 1946 as a cooperative venture of most of the nation's dailies.

Both independent and party papers appeared in the provinces as well. By 1948 Austria counted 33 dailies, 11 of them based in Vienna. Because of newsprint shortages papers were small, usually only a few pages on weekdays; but their combined circulations totalled more than 2,225,000 copies. The fol-

Most Important Dailies

Newspaper	Place of Publication	Political Orientation	Frequency	Circulation
Neue Kronen-Zeitung	Vienna	Independent but left leaning	Mon.–Thurs.	832,800
			Fri.–Sat.	951,300
			Sun.	1,370,000
Kurier	Vienna	Independent but right-of-center	Mon.–Thurs.	413,081
			Fri.	629,461
			Sat.	624,814
			Sun.	634, 519
Arbeiter Zeitung	Vienna	Socialist	Mon.–Sat.	104,341
			Sun.	120,548
Die Presse	Vienna	Independent but conservative	Mon.–Thurs.	56,242
			Fri.	66,408
			Sat.	73,426
Volkstimme	Vienna	Communist	Tues.–Sat.	42,816
			Sun.	80,404
Wiener Zeitung	Vienna; published by the Federal Administration; circulation not disclosed but believed to be about 40,000.			
Kleine Zeitung	Graz & Klagenfurt	Independent	Fri.	250,839
			All other days	215,128
Oberosterreichische Nachrichten	Linz	Independent	Mon.–Fri.	93,533
			Sat.	127,153
Neue Zeit	Graz	Socialist	Mon.–Thurs. & Sat.	78,850
			Fri.	89,125
Tiroler Tageszeitung	Innsbruck	Independent	Mon.–Fri.	84,012
			Sat.	94,233
Salzburger Nachrichten	Salzburg	Independent	Mon.–Fri.	56,074
			Sat.	88,407

lowing year, 1949, the old *Illustrierte Kronen-Zeitung* was revived under the title *Neue Kronen-Zeitung.* The rebuilding period was climaxed in 1955 with the signing of the Austrian State Treaty that ended the four-power occupation. Austria was at last on its own.

A handbook of the Austrian press listed 28 dailies published in 1979; seven of these are regional editions of other papers. All six of the capital's dailies are distributed nationally and some have satellite editions that are actually printed in provincial centers. All the dailies are published in German.

The weeklies, which number about 130, include several Catholic papers as well as one published in Czech for Czech-speaking people in the Vienna area. One of the Catholic weeklies, *Die Furche* of Vienna, is generally looked at as speaking for the nation's Roman Catholic hierarchy. Most of the other weeklies are purely regional in character and audience, except for some like Vienna's *Wochenpresse,* a combination newspaper/news magazine.

Of the other periodicals, more than 70 are published in minority and foreign languages. Many of these are for the information of visitors or other persons interested in developments in Austria, but they also include publications for the Slovene minority.

Generally speaking the party press has been losing ground to the independents, although circulations of most papers have increased in recent years after an uncomfortable period of decline.

All Austrian papers are tabloid or odd size. *Die Presse* is composed as a full sheet but the pages are only about three-quarters the usual size. The *Neue Kronen-Zeitung* is printed in tabloid format but the pages are only one-quarter full size instead of being half size. The number of pages varies widely from paper to paper but most average from 10 to 25 pages on weekdays, with larger editions on weekends. Neither *Die Presse* nor the *Neue Kronen-Zeitung* fit that pattern, however, largely because of their formats. *Die Presse* usually runs 10 to 14 pages, while the *Neue Kronen-Zeitung* can appear with 50 or more.

Most Austrian dailies are published in the morning, including all those in Vienna except *Kurier* and the *Neue Kronen-Zeitung,* which come out at noon.

All seven major cities—Vienna, Klagenfurt, Linz, Salzburg, Graz, Innsbruck and Breganz—have competing newspapers, either locally owned or branch editions of the Vienna dailies. Most dailies print regular editions Monday through Friday, with a larger weekend edition on Saturday (in a few cases on Fridays); most don't publish on Sundays. This accounts for much larger Sunday circulations of papers, such as the *Neue Kronen-Zeitung,* that do publish that day.

On the basis of weekday circulation alone, no Austrian daily falls below the 10,000 level and only one reports less than 25,000. Seven fall between 25,000 and 50,000, seven more between 50,000 and 100,000. Three publish from 100,000 to 500,000 copies; only the *Neue Kronen-Zeitung* exceeds that figure.

The three most influential papers, and the three most often quoted abroad, are *Die Presse,* the *Arbiter Zeitung* and the *Salzburger Nachrichten.*

Economic Framework

The Austrian economy functions on a private enterprise, free-market basis, even though important segments are nationalized. These actually operate in the fashion of private businesses. The nation is heavily dependent on foreign trade, both for markets for her manufactures and as sources for raw materials. As a rule she runs deficits in her trading accounts, which are usually offset by earnings from tourism and other sources. This dependence makes her particularly vulnerable to international business cycles, and the general business downturn resulting from the world energy crisis has caused some problems in recent years.

Beyond that, the biggest problem as far as the press is concerned is the fact that the growth of advertising has not kept pace with the rest of the economy. Newspapers do carry a few display ads, most of them for large Austrian or foreign firms, but the great bulk of the advertising is made up of small classifieds. This has left the press much too dependent on circulation for good health.

About a dozen noteworthy papers disappeared in the decade before 1975. Even so, fewer than a third of the dailies made a profit that year. The victims included the leading People's Party paper, the *Volksblatt,* and the *Express,* a mass-appeal paper that in the 1960s had been a rival of the *Neue Kronen-Zeitung* and *Kurier,* each selling over 300,000 copies. Its sales figures began to fall in the late 1960s. It was finally bought by the owners of the *Neue Kronen-Zeitung,* who kept it going for a while but in 1975 merged it with the *NKZ.* A government subsidy system, under a Press Promotion Law, was put into effect in an attempt to deal with the problem.

Newspapers are very important in Vienna. The consumption of newspapers in the capital averages more than 500 per thousand people, an impressive figure by any standard. But consumption in the provinces is much lower: as few as 116 per thousand in the Alpine areas of the Tyrol and Vorarlberg. In these areas, broadcasting is obviously the more important medium.

The position of broadcasting has certainly been aided by the development of an elaborate coaxial cable system capable of simultaneously handling all electronic traffic, including even computer exchanges, between major cities. Multiconductor cables branch from the coaxial line to service regional points. Microwave links are used where the terrain makes cable service too costly. As a result, telecommunication operations are generally excellent.

The Austrian press exhibits about every known type of ownership: individual, political party and government. None are directly tied to any commercial or industrial enterprises, although there is some cross interest. Most of the dailies fall into either the elite or popular class, although some of the latter range over toward yellow journalism.

Austria clearly has not been spared the trend toward press concentration that most Western countries have experienced in recent years, although there it has tended to take the form of control by political parties rather than the formation of chains. The disappearance of papers like the *Express* reflected the fragility of the economic base of the Vienna papers and the cutthroat competition this engenders. The disproportionate size of the big Vienna dailies—four of them account for about three-quarters of the country's daily sales—raises the frightening prospect of an unprecedented concentration should one of them collapse or some kind of merger be arranged. Fears of some such development are widespread; the man generally thought of as the possible future czar of the Austrian press is Kurt Kalk, the publisher of the *Neue Kronen-Zeitung*.

The Press Promotion law of 1975 was designed to give the government the power to help ailing newspapers by subsidizing their operations in part. The reasoning behind it was that in a democracy newspapers perform a public function, so the state should be interested in the continued operation of as many newspapers as possible in order to assure the widest diversity of opinions. Allocations are made by the government on the basis of recommendations by the federal chancellor in consultation with Verband Österreichischer Zeitungsherausgeber und Zeitungsverleger.

Austria is an important producer of newsprint—161,000 metric tons in 1978—and uses 90 percent of that total. The rest is exported. As with other commodities, the price tends to be that current in the European Economic Community, with which about half of Austria's foreign trade is conducted.

Since, with the exception of a couple of the Viennese dailies, the amount of space devoted to advertising in Austrian newspapers is relatively low—abou 25 percent—there is not much chance that individual advertisers would have a great deal of influence on editorial policies. The impact of political party ownership or affiliation is a much more important factor in the Austrian system.

Press Laws

Freedom of the press is guaranteed by the Federal Constitution, which says, in part: "Every person has the right of free expression of opinion in speech, writing, print and visual media within the limits of legal regulations. The press must not be subjected to censorship, nor restricted by rule of the licensing system."

The "legal regulations" noted above are spelled out in the press law of 1922 as amended. They include a kind of postpublication censorship, under which editors can be brought to trial for publishing pornography or libelous material or something that could be considered liable to corrupt minors.

Each paper is required to submit copies of every issue to the Ministry of Interior for review and each must have a "responsible" editor who can be held personally liable for any violation of the rules. Theoretically he could be sent to prison if convicted. It has been many years, however, since any editor

received a sentence more severe than a fine or confiscation of an offending issue.

Another provision provides for a right of reply. According to it, a person who feels himself the victim of an incorrect statement in the press can—and does—demand to have a formal reply of the same length printed in an equal position in a subsequent issue of the offending paper.

The press has been pushing for revision of the right of reply law as far as the equal length requirement is concerned. It also has been urging revision of the postcensorship measure as well as the addition to the press code of guarantees of freedom of circulation and opinion.

There has also been an effort to ensure what are called the "internal freedoms," as distinct from external freedom of the press. This involves the right of journalists to write and publish reports and commentaries without depending on instructions or directives from the publisher or any other policymaker. This has been done through the acceptance of "editorial statutes" by publishers and journalists working for individual publications. These usually provide, among other things, that a journalist cannot be compelled to change an article in any way that would alter the substance of what he wanted to say. However, they also reinforce the editor's right to decide what will or will not be published.

Austrian journalists are fortunate in another way. They have what appears to be an absolute right to refuse to disclose their sources or give evidence in any court, civil or criminal, or any administrative proceeding.

They are subject to the customary laws against libel, revealing military secrets, etc., in addition to the restrictions on pornography and materials considered damaging to minors. Newspapers still must be licensed, but bonds are not required.

There are also specific laws covering journalists in such matters as salary, holidays, severance pay, period of notice for dismissal and conditions of such dismissal or severance.

Censorship

There is no precensorship of the press, but there is a kind of postcensorship. The law not only permits the banning of material deemed pornographic or dangerous to minors but also anything interpreted as racial propaganda or as an excitement to political extremism as well as alleged libel.

Under the law, application for the banning of a specific issue of any periodical can be made, by any person who feels injured, to the Interior Ministry, which receives a copy of all publications distributed in the country, whether produced domestically or abroad. Bans have been ordered against a number of domestic publications over the years and occasionally even against imported periodicals. In many cases some moral justification for the bans could be argued, but not in all.

In the 1960s the International Press Institute reported the case of a Catholic weekly that had been seized twice on the application of a local bureaucrat whose financial transactions the paper had criticized. The bureaucrat had charged that the paper had libelled him in its articles. The courts later rescinded the ban, but the paper was not compensated for the damages it had suffered.

The Austrian Press Council was formed in 1961 to monitor press activities. It is made up of 10 representatives each of the Journalists' Trade Union and the Newspaper Publishers' and Editors' Association. The council is supposed to ensure that the freedoms guaranteed by the press laws are protected and to settle any complaints, both from within the press community and between the press and outside individuals or agencies, including the government. Discussions with the government usually involve such matters as taxes, possible legislation or executive actions affecting the press. The council deals with complaints from individuals concerning alleged violations of privacy rights by the press, untruthful reporting or other violations of the press code. It has no enforcement powers, but all newspapers carry reports of its proceedings and it has been remarkably successful in gaining voluntary acceptance of its judgments.

State-Press Relations

There are a variety of information offices for the press in Austria. Most departments of the federal government have press offices and all the provincial governments include information services. In addition, the two major political parties—the Socialists and the People's Party—operate quite efficient information offices. So does the Roman Catholic Church. An unusual government information office with the formidable title of Informationdienst für Bildungspolitik und Forschung ("Information Service on Questions of Education and Research") provides material on matters concerning cultural policy and science.

Austrian newspapers can and do criticize the government, particularly those representing whichever political party happens to be the opposition. They are the victims of "managed news" to about the same degree that the press of any Western democracy is. Skillful politicians have used and still use the press to push their plans and policies or to float "trial balloons," and Austria has had several particularly able political leaders in the years since World War II.

The press has considerable influence on government policies relating to information. For example, the 1975 law setting up the subsidy fund for ailing papers was pushed primarily by the newspapers, particularly the provincial publishers.

It is difficult to document specific actions taken in other areas that resulted primarily from press pressure. However, the press as a reflector of public opinion is a major political factor, especially since the parliamentary margins enjoyed by the party in power are never very large. One press historian has cited the case of a 1964 campaign conducted by the nation's independent papers aimed at a reform of the nation's broadcasting system and policies as an example of press influence, but actually this was a case in which the papers took the lead in focusing attention on an issue about which public opinion was already strong.

One newspaper in Austria definitely receives preferential treatment from the government. The *Wiener Zeitung,* the government's own, gets breaks on state advertising and other benefits. But this is nowhere near the issue that charges of political party preference have been at times in the past. Papers representing the party out of power have frequently complained about unfair treatment in the receipt of handouts, the issuance of licenses and other such areas.

Attitude Toward Foreign Media

Foreign correspondents do not need special accreditation or visas to work in Austria, although they should register with the various press offices if they wish to receive official announcements and other materials. No prior approval is needed for the filing of cables or any other copy to their home offices.

There are no import restrictions on foreign media, although, as indicated earlier, those too are subject to possible banning if they happen to violate one of the provisions of the press law.

Austrian newspapers are all home-grown and home-owned, but this is not true of the mass magazine field. Here the market is dominated by Austrian editions of various popular West German magazines. Thus the main radio and TV program weekly is a local edition of *Hör zu,* the product of the Springer group in West Germany. The two largest West German illustrated weeklies, *Bunte* and *stern* both took over Austrian publications in the 1960s and used them to develop Austrian editions, both of which sell from 150,000 to 200,000 copies a week. News magazines like France's *L'Express,* America's *Time* and *Newsweek* and particularly West Germany's *Der Spiegel* enjoy a wide readership throughout the country. One genuinely Austrian product that has so far successfully bucked the trend is the *Neue Illustrierte Wochenschau,* although its circulation has fallen to under 200,000 after having been above 250,000 only a few years ago.

However, the magazine with the largest circulation is not one usually thought of as a mass-appeal publication. It is a fortnightly called *Auto-Touring,* published by the Austrian Automobile, Motorcycle and Touring Club, which sells more than 500,000 copies an issue.

The various media organizations in Austria are members of or have some form of relationship with almost all international news bodies. Befitting the country's neutral stance, they attempt to remain on at least comfortable terms with both East and West. In UNESCO, Austria has generally voted with the Western nations on media issues, especially the 1978 UNESCO Declaration.

News Agencies

The national news agency is the Österreichische Presse-Agentur, known as APA. It is a cooperative owned jointly by all but one of the daily newspapers and the national broadcasting service. The exception among the newspapers is the *Neue Kronen-Zeitung.*

Set up with the approval of the Allied occupation forces in 1946, the APA supplies the newspapers and the broadcast service with news gathered by its own personnel and the principal world and European agencies. Headquartered in Vienna, it has bureaus in Salzburg, Linz, Graz, Innsbruck, Klagenfurt and Eisenstadt.

It does not have bureaus abroad but has a number of part-time correspondents in all major centers in Europe and the United States, Canada and Australia. It also does a great deal of monitoring of foreign broadcasts, particularly those of neighboring Communist-ruled countries, as well as of the news services of most of those states. As a result, its reports are closely watched by Western correspondents stationed in Vienna.

The agency distributes about 40,000 words a day on its regular news service wires, about half of it concerning domestic developments. It also distributes features and photos and offers a video-TV service for private subscribers, a telephone news bulletin service and other features. Official government announcements are first released through APA.

It has contracts for the supply of news with Reuters, AP, Agence France-Presse (AFP), Tass and Deutsche Presse-Agentur (dpa) and exchange agreements with other smaller agencies from countries as diverse as Israel and Japan. However, most of the items it relays from foreign agencies come from dpa, AP, Reuters and AFP. A 1976 study showed that even its own reports constituted a very small percentage of the foreign-news file; Dpa had a 29.2 percent share, AP 29.1, Reuters 22.5, AFP 15.9 and APA only 1.9 percent. Tass had an even smaller share, only 0.5 percent.

Reuters, dpa, AP, AFP, APA and Tass maintain full bureaus with their own communication links in Vienna, while a number of other agencies are represented by correspondents. These include Italy's ANSA, Spain's EFE, Czechoslovakia's CETEKA, Hungary's MTI and Yugoslavia's Tanjug. UPI for years operated a German-language service in Vienna that translated the European wire for Austrian subscribers; it ended in 1978.

Electronic News Media

All radio and TV programming in Austria is the responsibility of the Austrian broadcasting corporation (Österreichischer Rundfunk, or ORF). The ORF is a public corporation, shares of which are held by the provincial governments. Transmitting facilities are operated by the Post and Telegraph Administration, which is under the federal Ministry of Transport.

Operations are financed from advertising revenues and license fees, although the government subsidizes international shortwave broadcasting. Total time devoted to advertising can run as much as two hours a day on two of the three radio channels and to about 20 minutes a day on one of the two TV channels.

Austria has had TV broadcasting in black and white since 1957 and in color since 1969. The network includes more than 150 transmitters, but most of them are low-powered retransmitters needed to ensure good coverage in the mountainous areas of the country.

One of the TV channels carries a mixture of news, music and various kinds of entertainment programming. The second is more educational and cultural. The first channel is on the air a good part of the day, with morning programs for schools, for workers employed in the evenings and for coverage of special events. The regular service begins at 4 p.m. and generally lasts until midnight. The second channel operates mainly in the evenings.

The three radio channels likewise serve somewhat different audiences. The first provides general programming that emphasizes news and information, music, literature and science. The second combines national and regional programming, most of it devoted to information and popular entertainment. The third channel aims at younger listeners with lighter entertainment and popular music, interspersed with frequent news items.

The international shortwave service broadcasts in English, French, Spanish and German to North and South America, Africa, the Middle East, Asia and Australia.

Experimental radio broadcasting began in Austria in 1923, and the following year a public company generally known as RAVAG started a regular program service, financed by income from receiver licenses. Commercials were not introduced until 1937. Eighty-two percent of the shares in RAVAG—an acronym formed from elements of its proper name: Österreichische Radioverkehrs A.G.— were in public hands.

With the Anschluss, its facilities became part of the Nazi radio network while the company itself disappeared. The defeat of the Nazis and the occupation of the country brought new problems. Each of the four occupying powers established its own broadcasting organization in its zone of control.

Some of the programming was done by the occupation authorities, but most of it was Austrian and subject to varying degrees of censorship and control.

Repeated Austrian requests to have the responsibility for broadcasting placed in their hands were met only very gradually, but in 1953 an all-Austrian service went on the air, using the recently assigned VHF bands, and was networked simultaneously in all four zones. A year prior to the end of the occupation in 1955, the Federal Constitutional Court ruled that jurisdiction over broadcasting was a federal matter over which the provincial administration had no authority, setting the stage for developments in the immediate post-occupation period.

After considerable pulling and hauling, the government set up the special company to operate the broadcasting services, with the ownership divided between the federal administration and the provincial governments. The internal structure as originally conceived proved virtually unworkable. A kind of proportional representation on all levels of the system, reflecting the political situation in the country, led to a paralysis of programming. The financial condition of broadcasting became so bad that the third channel on radio had to be stopped for a year and a half beginning in 1962.

Public dismay and disgust was almost universal, but each of the two main parties was afraid any change would give the other an unfair advantage. In 1964 a plebiscite organized by the major daily newspapers in response to the public complaints called for a change. Parliament was obliged to bring the matter up for debate. The parties still could not agree on a workable solution, but the stalemate was finally broken by the national elections in 1966 which, for the first time since World War II, gave one of the two main parties—the People's Party—a clear majority in Parliament. It pushed its reform plan through the lawmaking process; the plan became effective January 1, 1967.

In essence, this revamped the old Austrian Broadcasting Company into a politically and economically independent organization, under the leadership of a superintendent general. Not only were its freedom and independence guaranteed but it had full control over its own finances. Organizational structure and program content were altered drastically and receiver license fees increased, ending the financial crunch that had crippled Austrian broadcasting since 1955. The system quickly became recognized as one of the most progressive in Europe.

Despite the improvements broadcasting remained a political football. The Socialists complained that the organization was too much a mouthpiece for conservative thought and when they, in turn, came to power in 1972 they proposed several different reform plans, at one time even suggesting the formation of a second, commercial broadcasting company set up in the form of a newspaper publishers' cooperative.

They finally settled on a simple revision of the broadcasting law, which aimed at greater democratization and independence for ORF by giving listeners and viewers a greater voice in program decisionmaking, and other similar changes. The law also guarantees the "objectivity and impartiality of reporting, due consideration of a diversity of opinions, consistent balancing of the programs and the independence of the institution's personnel and organs."

Commercials appear only on the first TV channel. They normally take the form of spots clumped together in five-minute blocks. However, ORF also broadcasts sponsored programs. The sponsor has no control over the program itself but does have the right to a brief announcement at the beginning and end of the program as well as a normal commercial spot ad.

The TV also carries a variety of official announcements as a kind of public service. These are usually inserted after a 6:55 p.m. break for commercials.

The radio service makes almost a feature of various kinds of messages. It permits advertising on both the second and third channels (the second carries local as well as national ads). And there are regular announcements about lost or stolen property, meetings, sports events, theater and movie offerings and even personal greetings. A small fee is charged for these, unless they are from religious, education or charitable groups. Radio also permits sponsored programs, under the same restrictions as television.

Responsibility for programming rests with a superintendent for the radio section and two for TV, one in charge of each of the two channels. There is also a superintendent for each of the provincial studios. A technical director and a commercial director are in charge of the technical and administrative affairs of the corporation.

The various superintendents are appointed by a Board of Trustees, composed of 30 mem-

bers. Six of them are named by the federal government, one by each of the provincial governments, one each by the federal chancellor, the finance minister and the minister of education and transport, five by the organization representing the radio and television subscribers and five by the Central Employees Council of the ORF.

Exercise of the federal government's legal supervision of the ORF is entrusted to a Commission for the Enforcement of the Radio and Television Act. This is made up of 17 public representatives, including nine judges, four members named by the Central Employees Council of the ORF and four named by the subscribers' organization.

Austrian broadcasting is at least partially dependent upon the West German broadcasting organizations for high-quality programming, through coproductions and the simultaneous transmission of plays and other shows. ORF has been able to hold such imports to about 40 percent of its total programming and, in recent years, has been successful in selling some of its own productions abroad to help the budget. Nevertheless, it has tended to run in the red more often than not since the early 1970s.

Austrian TV plays an important international role in at least two different ways. First, it is the major link between the Soviet bloc's Intervision network and Western Europe's Eurovision hookup. ORF coordinates the daily exchange of news film between the two networks as well as the relay of any special programs in either direction.

Second, ORF's audience in neighboring Eastern European countries is huge. It has been estimated that as many as 10 million viewers in Czechoslovakia, Hungary and Yugoslavia tune into ORF's transmitters at least some of the time. In Hungary the newspapers print the Austrian TV schedules alongside their own, and in the Czech city of Bratislava, only about 30 miles down the Danube from Vienna, so many rooftop aerials are directed toward the Austrian border that local wits refer to them as "the Vienna woods."

ORF soft-pedals its attraction for this audience, making no attempt to program specifically for it. However, in one case it does produce programs for a non-Austrian audience: the German-speaking inhabitants of the Italian province of the Alto-Adige. This area has been disputed by both countries ever since World War II; an agreement reached in 1974 allows ORF to relay its domestic radio and TV programs through the transmitter network of the Italian broadcasting service in that area.

Education & Training

There are no professional journalism schools in Austria. Most working journalists are university graduates who are trained on the job. However, both the University of Salzburg and the University of Vienna offer PhD programs in their mass communication research institutes.

In addition to the Austrian Press Council and the Journalists' Trade Union, there are five different associations of journalists, most of them organized along specialty lines. The Newspaper Publishers' and Editors' Association is primarily concerned with business and commercial questions. It also negotiates with the government on questions of concern to the papers.

Summary

In proportion to total population, Austria has fewer daily papers and lower total daily circulation than most European countries. Circulations have been rising, but not enough to change the situation markedly. With advertising still largely undeveloped, the financial basis of most of the dailies is shaky at best. It is generally believed that many of the party papers would have gone under by now were it not for the fact that they are supported by their organizations. There are also fears that one or more of the larger Vienna dailies could easily move into a financial tailspin and decline to such a point that it could not be salvaged by the official subsidy fund.

Another fear that has been voiced frequently in recent years is that West German interests might step in and take over segments of the press as they have done in the magazine field. At present the profits to be gained do not seem attractive enough for the West Germans. This could change, however, and they might be induced to move simply by the economies of scale.

Economics are also a problem for broadcasting. Austria is a small country, and the ORF has about reached the limits of possible funding from license fees: there are more than 25 TV sets for every 100 people. As a result the service has had to rely more and more on advertising for its revenue, and as in the case of the newspapers, there is not enough, particularly in times of economic difficulties.

In addition, a political threat hangs over the broadcasting operations. Austrians assume an air of doom and gloom when discussing these problems, but most seem to think the solution is political, not economic. This suggests the possibility that every time the party in power in the government changes, the broadcasting services will be overhauled and shaken up to suit the taste of the new ruling group.

CHRONOLOGY

1961 Austrian Press Council (Presserat) founded.
1972 Daily *Neue Vorarlberger Tagezeitung* founded.
1975 Nationalrat passes Press Promotion Law to extend subsidies to financially ailing newspapers.
Express merges with *Neue Kronen-Zeitung*.

BIBLIOGRAPHY

Austrian Newspaper Publishers' and Editors' Association. *Handbuch—Österreichs Presse, Werbung, Graphik.* Vienna, 1980.
Boyd-Barrett, Oliver. *The International News Agencies.* Beverly Hills, Calif., 1980.
Crankshaw, Edward. *The Fall of the House of Hapsburg.* New York, 1963.
The Europa Yearbook. London, 1980.
Federal Press Service. "The Mass Media in Austria." (A collection of handouts published by the Press Service as a part of a series called "*Austria Documentation.*") 1980.

Haacke, Wilmont. "The Austrian and Viennese Press." *Gazette,* 1968, p. 195.

International Press Institute. "Concentration of Press in Vienna Feared." *IPI Report,* March 1974, p. 3.

_____. *Government Pressures on the Press.* Zurich, 1955.

_____. *Professional Secrecy and the Journalist.* Zurich, 1962.

Merrill, John, Bryan, Carter R., and Alisky, Marvin. *The Foreign Press.* Baton Rouge, La., 1970.

Olson, Kenneth E. *The History Makers.* Baton Rouge, La., 1966.

Sanford, John. *The Mass Media of the German-Speaking Countries.* London, 1976.

Signitzer, Benno. "Austria: Media Dependence." *Journal of Communication,* Summer 1978, p. 79.

Smith, Anthony. "Europe's Changing Newspapers." *World Press Review,* February 1978, p. 24.

Tapie, Victor L. *The Rise and Fall of the Hapsburg Monarchy.* New York, 1971.

BANGLADESH

by George Kurian

BASIC DATA

Population: 89,284,000
Area: 142,500 sq. km. (55,019 sq. mi.)
GNP: 121.06 billion taka (US$ 7.8 billion) (1978)
Literacy Rate: 25%
Language(s): Bangla, English
Number of Dailies: 30
   Aggregate Circulation: 350,000
   Circulation per 1,000: 4
Number of Nondailies: NA
   Aggregate Circulation: NA
   Circulation per 1,000: NA
Number of Periodicals: 203

Number of Radio Stations: 6
Number of Television Stations: 3
Number of Radio Receivers: 1.2 million
   Radio Receivers per 1,000: 14
Number of Television Sets: 35,000
   Television Sets per 1,000: 0.42
Total Annual Newsprint Consumption: 9,300 metric tons
Per Capita Newsprint Consumption: 0.1 kg. (0.22 lb.)
Total Newspaper Ad Receipts: NA
   As % of All Ad Expenditures: NA

Background & General Characteristics

For some time before the struggle for independence, the privately owned press of East Pakistan (as Bangladesh was then known) was comparatively free. (For East Pakistani press, see the chapter on Pakistan.) The Yahya Khan regime had permitted free expression during the election campaign of 1970, and the 14 dailies and 50 periodicals published in the province took full advantage of it until the armed crackdown in late 1971.

After liberation in 1971, several new dailies appeared along with the older dailies that had been suppressed during the civil war. During the early years of independence the newspapers were adulatory in tone and even sycophantic in their references to Sheikh Mujibur Rahman. But by 1973 the picture was changing. Determined to eliminate a free press, Mujibur replaced the 1961 Pakistani Press Ordinance with the Printing Presses and Publications (Declaration and Registration) Act. Under this new act the newspapers were subject to prior approval by the government and prior licensing. Newspapers not so registered were denied newsprint and/or advertising allocations. The act was followed by the Special Powers Bill of 1974,

which made it an offense, punishable by five years' imprisonment and/or a fine, to "print, publish, or distribute prejudicial reports." Newsmen were required to identify all sources of information, and authorities were given the right to seize documents and newspapers, to ban publications and to search premises on the assumption that they contained documents classified as "harmful." Pre-censorship was instituted on all matters affecting state security and friendly relations with foreign powers. In less than half a year another piece of legislation was introduced to curb the press. The Newsprint Control Order of 1974 entrusted the Ministry of Commerce and Foreign Trade and the Ministry of Information and Broadcasting with control over the production and consumption of newsprint. A state of emergency, declared in 1974, empowered the government to regularly ban foreign periodicals. The culmination of the anti-media drive came in June 1975: 20 dailies and all political weeklies were banned, leaving only the government-owned *Observer* and *Dainik Bangla* and the party-owned *Bangladesh Times* and *Ittefaq* still publishing. Such drastic action was certainly overkill since, after the closure of *Ganakantha* in 1975, the entire press had virtually capitulated. By spring 1975, over 600 journalists had applied for membership in Mujibur's ruling party and pledged allegiance to it.

The assassination and overthrow of Sheikh Mujibur Rahman brought a brief respite for the troubled press. The new government under President Khondakar Mushtaque Ahmed returned *Ittefaq* and *Sangbad* to their owners and gradually permitted the others to resume publication. Another coup toppled Mushtaque within months, and a new government came to power with General Zia-ur Rahman in control. Zia-ur Rahman promised a more liberal stand toward the media without, however, rescinding any of the anti-media laws on the statute book. By this time, the press was more concerned with survival than with enlargement of press freedom and accepted with gratitude the small concessions from the state.

In late 1980 the Bangladeshi press comprised 30 dailies with an aggregate circulation of around 350,000. Given the population of 89 million people, this works out to a miniscule four per 1,000 inhabitants, placing Bangladesh in the bottom 20 in the world in this respect. Twenty-four of the dailies are published in Bangla, the national language, and six in English, the effective lingua franca. About one-third of all weeklies are published in English. The Bangla press is more colorful and lively, while the English-language press appears stilted.

Both Bangla and English dailies have eight to 10 pages per issue, but the size often shrinks when newsprint supplies run low. As befits a capital, Dacca is the center of all media activities, accounting for 13 (or 43 percent) of the dailies, followed by Chittagong as a distant second with seven. Of the provincial centers, Khulna has five dailies, Bogra two and Rajshahi, Jessore and Dinajpur one each. Of the six English-language dailies, three are published in Dacca, two in Chittagong and one in Khulna.

Among the privately owned Bangla papers, *Ittefaq* is by far the most influential, partly because of its large circulation (140,000) and partly because of its association with the Awami League in an earlier period. The paper was founded by the late Tofazzal Hossain, whose son, Anwar Hossain, is now the editor and publisher. The paper still sympathizes with the League, although the younger Hossain refuses to admit it. The paper generally follows an independent editorial policy and its comments on government policies are objective by Bangladeshi standards. *Ittefaq*'s wide readership cuts across class, party and religious lines.

Of the three conservative dailies, which support the Muslim League, *Azad* is the most influential and also enjoys the most circulation (30,000). *Dainik Bangla* (75,000) is a government-controlled daily that combines conservatism in religious matters with liberalism in politics. It has gained a wide readership among the more literate readers because it is edited by a prominent poet.

Of the English-language dailies, the *Observer* (70,000) and the *Times* (35,000) are owned and managed by a government-appointed board under the direction of the secretary of information. Their editorial policies generally reflect government views and they make extensive use of press releases and the state wire service. Although it has only half the circulation of the *Observer*, the *Times* has made rapid strides in recent years under the editorship of Enayetullah Khan, who also owns *Holiday*, considered the liveliest and most provocative English-language weekly in Dacca. It is being challenged by *New Nation*, a well-written journal produced by *Ittefaq*.

Economic Framework

An underdeveloped country in the classic sense of the term, Bangladesh appears to be permanently on the brink of economic collapse. This is hardly the kind of economic climate in which a vigorous press could flourish. Readership is a tiny minority, or, rather, a minority within a minority, since even large segments of the educated class cannot afford to buy newspapers regularly. The aggregate circulation of all Bangladesh dailies is less than that of a good-sized daily in the United States or Europe.

Economic and political realities have combined to drive the media into the hands of the government. Rather than the adversary role, they have been forced to assume the suppliant role. Of the popular papers, only the *Ittefaq* can survive without government subsidies and advertising. For most other papers, up to half a typical issue consists of official announcements. There are of course exceptions. *Sangbad*, for example, is funded by Ahmadul Kabir, a wealthy industrialist. *Dainik Banglar Mukh*, with a circulation of

7,000, is published by a young working journalist without any obvious connections. Most of the other non-government dailies are underwritten by political parties or by conservative religious organizations with political ambitions.

Economic conditions in Bangladesh do not favor the growth of monopolies or chain newspapers. There are few national newspapers because of the formidable costs and logistics of transportation. Further, although Bangladesh is a newsprint producer, frequent shortfalls in supply (sometimes artificially induced by the government) have caused newspapers to cut back rather than expand. Individual and aggregate circulations have not shown any appreciable increase over the years.

The press suffers under technical constraints as well. Many newspapers use handset type or, in some cases, obsolete linotype machines heavily damaged during the civil war.

Newspapers generally toe the government line, but the journalists are a different breed. Like most Bangladeshis, they display a wide range of vehement personal ideologies and resist all forms of regimentation. They are represented by a number of associations. The Jatiya Press Club of Dacca, despite its high-sounding name, is little more than a recreational association. Since 1973 no elections have been held for offices in either the Federal Union of Journalists or the Dacca Union of Journalists. Many of their members believe that these associations are run by leftists who do not represent their interests. The Association of Journalists, originally made up of newsmen stationed outside of Dacca, has even less influence.

The Ministry of Information and Broadcasting and the Newspaper Employees Wage Board issued wage and fringe-benefit scales for all newspaper and news agency employees by decree on April 30, 1977. The plan divided papers into four categories according to their annual gross revenue and set proportionate pay scales. Several newspaper owners still have not implemented these scales, claiming that they cannot afford the suggested compensation levels.

Press Laws & Censorship

All publication activity is subject to the Press and Publication Act of 1973 passed under Mujib. In order to start any new newspaper or journal, a registry number must be secured from the information ministry and broadcasting. This is nothing new in itself and, in fact, is one of the press-control mechanisms inherited from the British Raj. The application must be accompanied by evidence of sufficient capital and a pledge to obey the laws of the land. Although the law does not specify it, all applicants are subject to police investigation of their political persuasion and activities. The register number has to be shown on all copies of the newspaper, and four copies of each issue must be sent to a designated government agency for "verification."

Even outside of this Act, the press is subject to strict control. General censorship of all news has been in effect virtually from the time of independence through all the coups and changes of regimes. The government, however, denies the existence of formal censorship.

State-Press Relations

Even when the government does not exercise its formal censorship powers, papers are usually "guided" by the advice and briefings of the principal information officer of the Ministry of Information or by the external publicity division of the Ministry of Foreign Affairs. The President's Council of Advisors also controls editors informally by means of a journalistic code of ethics. Even the display of important government statements on the front pages of the *Times* and *Observer* must be uniform in size and wording. Both private and government papers reflect the same general policy in matters of national importance. An exception is the extensive reportage on economic development, including criticism of bureaucratic inefficiencies in dealing with the economy.

The government also controls the press by renting building space and presses to the papers, through grants of import licenses for printing equipment, by controlling the supply of newsprint at its source from the state-owned mill at Khulna, and through advertising support.

When newspapers step out of line, the authorities are quick to warn the offending editors. One such case was the warning issued to *Ittefaq* for reporting, against government advice, the arrest, detention and trial of A. B. M. Mahmud, the editor of the weekly

Wave. Suspensions and other harsher penalties, however, are extremely rare.

Attitude Toward Foreign Media

The Zia-ur Rahman regime maintained an open and liberal policy toward foreign correspondents in general. There were, however, exceptions. Larry Lipschultz of the *Far Eastern Economic Review* was expelled from the country for trying to cover the trial of A. B. M. Mahmud. A Dutch journalist, Peter Custers, was caught up in the politically motivated conspiracy trials of 1976. He was held without trial or access to legal counsel for nine months and later sentenced by a secret military tribunal to 14 years' imprisonment. He was eventually expelled after Dutch officials interceded on his behalf.

Special visas are not required for foreign correspondents; neither is prior approval required for cables.

Bangladesh has supported the UNESCO stand on a greater role for the state in national media, especially in developing countries.

News Agencies

There are two national news agencies: The Bangladesh Sangbad Sangstha, a government-owned service, and the Eastern News Agency, a private concern receiving government subsidy. Most newspapers use both services. BSS subscribes to UPI, Reuters, AFP and New China News Agency, while ENA subscribes to AP, Tass and Tanjug.

The majority of the foreign news is supplied by AFP and Reuters. ENA usually uses its own byline when it carries an AP item, but BSS usually credits UPI or Reuters as the source.

Electronic News Media

Radio and television programs are operated by Radio Bangladesh and the Bangladesh Television Corporation respectively. Both are state corporations, directly under the Ministry of Information and Broadcasting. Radio Bangladesh operates seven medium-wave transmitters, four shortwave transmitters and five FM transmitters. The main television transmitter is in Dacca.

Education & Training

Bangladeshi journalists constitute an important segment of the intelligentsia. Most of them come from the middle class and have at least a high school education; some have university degrees. A few have diplomas in journalism from Dacca University, but most depend on in-service training at their newspapers. The government provides additional training at the Bangladesh Press Institute. Formerly Bangladeshi journalism attracted people who had no other avenues of employment, but nowadays there is vigorous competition for the few jobs that are open in this field.

Summary

Like the country itself, the Bangladeshi press is very underdeveloped. Low literacy, political instability, primitive printing technologies, poor facilities for distribution and poor professional pay scales for journalists have combined to stunt the growth of the press from every side. The bleak picture is redeemed, however, by one factor: the natural love of the Bangladeshi for public debate and discussion, for which the press seems to provide the only avenue, even under a dictatorship.

CHRONOLOGY

1977	Press censorship reimposed; Peter Custers, a Dutch journalist, expelled from the country	after having been sentenced to 14 years' imprisonment.

BIBLIOGRAPHY

Johnson, B. C. *Bangladesh.* New York, 1975.

Wilcox, Wayne. *The Emergence of Bangladesh.* Washington, D.C., 1973.

Belgium

by Harold A. Fisher

BASIC DATA

Population: 9,841,654
Area: 30,513 sq. km. (11,778 sq. mi.)
GNP: BFr 3.15 trillion (US $107 billion) (1979)
Literacy Rate: Over 90%
Language(s): French, Flemish
Number of Dailies: 40
   Aggregate Circulation: 2,369,000 (1977)
   Circulation per 1,000: 241
Number of Nondailies: 5,942
   Aggregate Circulation: NA
   Circulation per 1,000: NA
Number of Periodicals: 5,942

Number of Radio Stations: 20
Number of Television Stations: 23
Number of Radio Receivers: 4,077,416 (1977)
   Radio Receivers per 1,000: 414
Number of Television Sets: 2,811,169 (1977)
   Television Sets per 1,000: 286
Total Annual Newsprint Consumption: 189,000 metric tons
Per Capita Newsprint Consumption: 18.5 kg. (40.7 lb.)
Total Newspaper Ad Receipts: BFr 4.8 billion (US $170.9 million) (1979)
   As % of All Ad Expenditures: 30.2 (1979)

Background & General Characteristics

Founded early in the 17th century, the newspaper industry in Belgium—together with that of Holland and Germany—represents one of history's longest press traditions. Nearly all Belgian papers seek to give serious coverage of the news. Nearly all are also journals of opinion with political party affiliations, but readers do not necessarily subscribe to a paper's party leanings. Most publications, even the major ones, are family operations; even when a paper has multiple ownership, family interests still tend to dominate. In recent years, the press has experienced serious financial difficulties, resulting in a steady decline in the number of dailies published. Meanwhile, radio and television have become increasingly popular means of information and entertainment for the Belgian public.

An average of about one in every four Belgian inhabitants typically buys and reads a newspaper each day. According to one reliable source, Belgian readers expect three things of their newspapers: (1) information to assist in their community living; (2) coverage of its regional, national and worldwide interests; and (3) material dealing with their specialized needs and tastes. Unfortunately, however, the exacting conditions of most Belgians' increasingly complex urban life leaves readers a decreasing proportion of time and energy for serious news. Consequently, their interest in political affairs, so long the principal coverage function of Belgian newspapers, has declined. Instead, there is a growing tendency to look to the media, including newspapers, for relaxation and amusement, and the press has at least partially obliged. To some extent, this popular-appeal factor is a matter of survival, as newspapers have had to struggle to maintain economic viability in recent years.

In general, Belgian newspaper readers are literate and quite well educated. Education is compulsory between six and 14 years of age in one of two education systems. In 1978 over 89,000 students were enrolled in the country's 19 universities, and over 375,000 post-secondary students were in technical schools.

The population is divided between two language groups: French in the Walloon region of the south and Flemish (a Dutch dialect) in the north. The capitol, Brussels, is composed of both groups; it is also a cosmopolitan city with many residents from other countries.

Generally speaking, the quality of Belgian journalism is high. The majority of the dailies provide good international, economic and financial coverage. Their makeup is generally dignified and interesting, their appearance pleasant. Because most Belgian papers seek to give serious news coverage, it is difficult to sort dailies into "popular" and "serious" categories. With tightening competition, the press has tried to become more interesting, lively and attractive to readers. Generally speaking, there are numerous pictures, bold-faced story leads, comic strips, crossword puzzles, feature pages and entertainment pages to liven up the serious approach to local, national and international news. No Belgian paper can be classified as sensational, but neither can any compete with the seriousness or quality of the French *Le Monde*, the German *Frankfurter Allegemeine* or the Swiss *Neue Zürcher Zeitung*.

Belgium's openness to public expression via the media has led to several alternative media experiments during the past decade. The alternative press approaches have been amateurish, low-circulation attempts to meet special interests. The *Journal d'Europe* was launched in 1972 to appeal to intellectual and international circles and to tackle sensitive taboo subjects such as abortion and women's liberation. Although popular for a while, it disappeared within a year. Another independent paper, *Notre Temps*, founded by the Information Study and Research Center of the Free University of Brussels, lasted three years.

A number of more radical alternative social-protest publications also came into being in the 1970s. *Agence de Presse Libération* was founded on the campus of Louvain University to supply the daily papers with information coming from militant groups fighting for social justice. It provided editorial fuel for other protest publications, such as *Alternative Libertaire, Kloak, Rictus* and *Le 22 Mars*. Papers aimed at making specific professions more aware of social and economic injustices even arose, among them *Les Cahiers Galilée* (for scientists) and *Hypothèse d'École* (for teachers). And the periodical *Le Zinjanthrope* was launched to make satirical criticism of the Right. But all these efforts ran into financial difficulty and, before long, ended in failure.

Prior to the publication of the earliest Bel-

gian newspaper, the merchants of Antwerp and Venice shared a news bulletin, the *Courante Bladen*. Then, in 1605, Abraham Verhoeven developed one of Europe's first true newspapers, *Nieuwe Tijdinghen*, a series of broadsheets containing news, illustrations and advertisements. *Nieuwe Tijdinghen* did not appear regularly at first, and its pages were neither numbered nor dated. Verhoeven had special correspondents who reported events from all over the world—including first-hand accounts of battles fought in Antwerp against the Dukes of Nassau. But the paper also suffered censorship at the hands of archducal leaders.

In 1649 Jean Mommaert II developed his *Courrier Véritable des Pays-Bas ou Relations Fideles Extraites de Diverses Lettres* ("True News from the Low Countries or Unvarnished Tales Copied from Various Letters"). This was Brussels' only daily newspaper until 1791. During that period, Martin Binnart began to edit a second daily, *Den Ordinarien Posten*, in Antwerp. In 1666 the *Gentsche Posttijdinghen* appeared in Ghent; later it was replaced by the *Gazette van Gent*. Two other papers were founded at this time, in Bruges and Liège. With the coming of the 18th century the number of newspapers increased steadily, but not without difficulty, as the region's Spanish and Austrian rulers were not anxious to see a Belgian press develop.

During the Brabant Revolution (1789–90), the loyalties of the public and the press were split. French authorities then in control banned some papers, while others were allowed to continue publishing because of their loyalty to France. During this period, one publication departed from normal Belgian press policies by printing the news without voicing its opinion; its only commentary related to what it chose to print and what to omit.

The ruling Austrian Empire expressed its distaste for newspapers with a political slant by imposing strict censorship from 1798 to 1814. After Napoleon's defeat, Belgium was made part of the Kingdom of the Netherlands. But the Dutch rulers proved as oppressive toward press freedom as their predecessors and once again daily papers were split into two camps, the anti-Dutch press and the pro-Dutch "Orangist" press. Pro-Dutch papers included the *Journal d'Anvers et de la Province*, the *Journal (Messager) de Gand*, the *Knout*, the *Lynx*, the *Echo*, the *National* and the *Gazette Générale des Pays-Bas*.

Several anti-Dutch publications proved to be forerunners of the modern Belgian press, among them the *Courrier de la Flandre, De Vaderlander, De Nieuwe Gazet, Le Catholique, Courrier de la Meuse, La Belge* and *L'Observateur.*

During this period the Dutch government prosecuted a journalist named L. DePotter for his outspoken articles in *Courrier des Pays-Bas.* Many newspapers reacted by circulating a petition in which 360,000 signers demanded freedom of the press. Holland's King William I responded by founding a government paper, *Le National,* and then by introducing a law further curbing press freedom. Thus the long battle for press liberty continued.

During the Revolution of 1830, which brought Belgium its independence, many journalists had opportunity to become members of the National Congress. In 1831, through their influence, the Belgian Constitution stipulated that the press would be free to publish what it wished and that no censorship could be imposed. One consequence was the emergence of Belgium's two main press factions, representing the country's leading political parties, the Liberal and the Catholic.

For the next half-century, other Belgian political parties proliferated. Newspapers grew in number and circulation as publications were founded to express a diversity of political outlooks. The French-language press flourished first; it was not until 1844, with the founding of *Het Handelsblad,* that the Flemish press also began to thrive.

In 1874 Belgium had 68 daily papers read by about 175,000 subscribers. Between that time and the outbreak of World War I, hundreds of new papers appeared in both the French- and Flemish-language presses. The hostilities of World War I sounded the death-knell for 909 daily and weekly papers with 464,606 subscribers. Then, after 1918, the Belgian press recovered and underwent a remarkable expansion. This advance was due almost entirely to improved printing and distribution techniques and to a compulsory education that was producing a more alert, politically minded readership. But World War II was also fatal for numerous dailies, so that, at the end of the hostilities in 1945, 32 French-language and 19 Flemish-language papers published by 42 ownership groups remained. Although there were numerous attempts after World War II to start up new papers, only six have survived and gained wide circulation: *Le Lanterne, Le Monde du*

Travail, De Nieuwe Gids, La Nouvelle Gazette, and *La Cité,* all founded in 1950.

Throughout its development, the experiences of the Belgian press helped establish its strongest traditions: constant struggle and vigilance against government censorship and controls; strong orientation to political party views; the establishment of numerous press voices; and a desire to furnish the reading public serious news and information.

Numerous considerations have restricted the size and circulation of the Belgian press during the past quarter-century, so that today only 40 newspapers remain, 26 published in French, 13 in Flemish and one in German. In addition, there are four financial papers, one official gazette, and the recent addition of *Le Semaine d'Anvers* to provide a French-language paper in Flanders.

Belgium lies along the border dividing German and French politico-legal traditions, representing a coalition of French (or Walloon) and Dutch (or Flemish) interests, the press thus is divided between French- and Flemish-language publications. Geographically, the French-language papers are found in the south in Wallonia near the French border while the Flemish-language publications are in Flanders, in areas contiguous with the German and Dutch borders. Brussels, divided between Flemish and Walloon interests, hosts French and Dutch-language papers, plus Belgium's only German-language daily. The 26 French-language papers publish a total of around 1.3 million copies daily, about 50,000 more than the 13 dailies of the Flemish-language press.

Because of Belgium's small size and bilingual division, there is no national daily and circulations of even the largest dailies are confined to their own language group. The larger dailies tend to circulate throughout the entire geographical area in which the paper's language holds sway. In 1979 the Belgian press had a total daily circulation of about 2,564,000 copies, of which about 1.3 million were in French, 1.25 million in Dutch and 13,500 in German. About 58 percent of that circulation was accounted for by the country's top ten dailies. One-third of Belgium's papers have daily circulations of less than 35,000. Except for the larger and specialized publications, weeklies tend to be much more local or provincial in their circulations. Recent heightened interest in local dailies and weeklies make them one of the bright areas for development in the Belgian press.

The country's predominant religion, Roman Catholicism, carries a strong influence in the press. Among the French-language Catholic papers are the provincial papers of the Vers l'Avenir group, including *L'Avenir du Luxembourg, Le Courrier de Verviers* and *Le Courrier*; and those of the Editions de la Libre Belgique, which encompasses *La Libre Belgique* and *Gazette de Liège*. The chief Dutch Catholic papers include those of the large circulation *Het Volk-De Nieuwe Gids* group and the Standaard group. The latter publishes *De Standaard, Het Nieuwsblad, De Gentenaar* and *Het Handelsblad*. The nation's only German-language paper, *Grenz-Echo*, is also part of the Catholic press.

While nearly all Belgian dailies are journals of opinion with political leanings, few are official political organs. Antwerp's *De Volksgazet* and Brussels' *Voorhuit* do represent the Belgian Socialist party in a semiofficial capacity. Papers unofficially identifying with Christian Democrat views include *Gazet Van Antwerpen, La Cité, Gazet van Mechelen* and *Vers l'Avenir*. Among dailies with Christian Social leanings are *Le Rappel, Le Journal de Mons, l'Echo du Centre, Het Belang van Limburg* and *Le Courrier de L'Escaut*.

Belgian dailies appear both in standard broadsheet and tabloid page sizes. Larger-size papers typically carry seven or eight columns to the page, while most tabloids have five columns. Depending on the publication, standard-page-size dailies typically run from 16 to 24 pages in length on weekdays.

Competing newspapers exist in seven Belgian cities. Twelve dailies are published in Brussels, six in Antwerp, three in Ghent, and two each in Charleroi, Liège, Tournai and Verviers.

Belgium also serves as the home of 14 specialized dailies (eight in French, three in Dutch and three bilingual), 506 weeklies, 345 semimonthlies, 2,060 monthlies, and 1,133 bimonthlies, plus 1,884 quarterlies and biannual publications. Some of the weeklies report high circulations, among them Antwerp's *Libelle/Rosita* (325,000), *TV Ekspres* and *TV Strip* (276,340), and Brussels' *BS* or *Bonne Soirée* (300,000), *Kwik/Zondag Nieuws* (287,355) and *Humo* (225,000). Though their circulation is lower, several high-quality weeklies are influential, among them *Panorama/Ons Land* (99,000) and *Le Soir Illustré*, the latter associated with the influential daily *Le Soir*; and the cultural periodicals *Knack* (80,000) and *Pourquoi*

Pas? (78,000). The women's magazine *Femmes d'Aujourd'hui* (170,612) is popular both in Belgium and in France. Some periodicals are printed both in Dutch and in French. One trilingual weekly, the special periodical *International Business Equipment* (56,000), is published in French, English and German.

Because there is no compulsory auditing of circulation figures, because Belgian papers normally do not make public their readership, and because circulation of newspapers is frequently reported by ownership groupings rather than by individual papers, accurate circulation data is difficult to secure. But some estimates can be pieced together from available information. *Le Soir* is the country's highest-circulation French daily (233,412 in 1978) while *Het Laatste Nieuws* (308,000 in 1978) is the most widely read of the Flemish-language dailies. The Standaard group, consisting of four papers, had a combined circulation of 312,062 in 1977. *Het Volk* claimed a circulation of 201,633 in 1978 and *Gazet van Antwerpen* 188,432. Other larger publications or group circulations are *La Meuse/La Lanterne* (160,283), the *La Dernière Heure* group of three papers (125,000) and the Vers l'Avenir group of four (108,402). Other groups and individual papers all report less than 100,000 total circulation, with one grouping of three claiming only 35,000 readers.

10 Largest Dailies by Circulation	
1. *Het Laatste Nieuws* (Flemish)	308,000
2. *Le Soir* (French)	233,412
3. *Het Volk* (Flemish)	201,633
4. *Gazet van Antwerpen* (Flemish)	188,432
5. *La Libre Belgique* (French)	125,000
6. *La Dernière Heure* (French)	125,000
7. *Het Belang van Limburg* (Flemish)	81,132
8. the Standaard group of *De Standard, Het Nieuwsblad, De Gentenaar* and *Het Handelsblad* (Flemish)	78,000 each
9. *Vers l'Avenir* (French)	57,079
10. *L'Avenir du Luxembourg* (French)	32,028

Although again difficult to determine because of ownership groupings and Belgium's Walloon-Flemish divisions, perhaps the nation's most influential dailies are the French-language *Le Soir* and the Flemish-language dailies *Het Laatste Nieuws* and *Het Volk-De Nieuwe Gids*. This assessment must be weighed in light of the fact that in Belgium influence is linked with special-interest groups.

Economic Framework

Belgium, one of Europe's most densely populated countries (322 per square kilometer), is primarily industrial, especially in the Flemish north. Agriculture contributes only about 2.5 percent to the GNP. Other than an abundance of coal, the country has few natural resources. Consequently, the economy must depend heavily on export trade.

High inflation, record unemployment and a decreased GNP led to a recession in 1974. Slowdowns in the steel and textile industries, excessive public spending, the weakness of the Belgian franc, and further unemployment—especially in the Walloon areas—have continued to mar Belgium's economic health. In 1978 a program of large-scale foreign borrowing was undertaken by the government in an effort to reduce inflation. In 1979 the government nearly collapsed amid disagreements over economic austerity measures. The continuing economic problems contributed to the fall of two governments in 1980; the coalition of Christian Democrats and Socialists that emerged after the second 1980 crisis promised reduced government spending, tax reforms, assistance to small companies and pay cuts for all officials.

The worsening economic situation over the past quarter-century has led to closure of numerous newspapers, a growing concentration of publication ownership, lowered circulation of newspapers and periodicals, more advertising, and concentration of maximum profitmaking. And, amid the increasingly difficult economic problems for print-media circulations, more and more Belgians have been attracted to radio and television for their information and entertainment.

During the past decade, other problems have arisen to besiege especially the French-language press: cutbacks in circulation across the border into France, increasing penetration of foreign newspapers and a growing readership of provincial papers. By 1974 the readership of French-language papers in Flanders fell to the point where the last major daily had to close down. To fill that void, *La Semaine d'Anvers* has since been founded.

Conditions during the past 30 years have forced technological and editorial amalgamations of dailies into newspaper groups in both the national and provincial press, resulting in a growing concentration of ownership. The larger, more influential groups have been on the French-language side. The Rossel group owns *Le Soir* and several smaller papers. As already mentioned, the Vers l'Avenir company publishes four Catholic papers, while the Editions de la Libre Belgique owns three dailies. Another grouping is *Le Peuple, Le Travail* and *Le Monde du Travail*. Still others under group ownership are *La Nouvelle Gazette, La Province* and *Le Progres*; and *Le Rappel, L'Echo de Centre* and *Le Journal de Mons*. These groups are expanding; in 1976, for example, three Belgian groups bought capital shares of the large circulation weekly *Femmes d'Aujourd'hui*, formerly owned by the French company Hachette.

On the Flemish-language side, The Standaard group, which suffered financial collapse in 1976 only to be rescued by government aid, has consisted of four papers, *De Standaard* and *Het Nieuwsblad* in Brussels, *De Gentenaar* in Ghent and *Het Handelsblad* in Antwerp. Another group is composed of *Het Volk* in Ghent, *De Nieuwe Gids* in Brussels, *La Cité* (a Walloon paper), a publishing house and two weekly papers, *Samedi* in Brussels and *Zondagsblad* in Ghent. *Het Laatste Nieuws* (Brussels) and *De Nieuwe Gazet* (Antwerp) have formed a partnership called the Hoste group, but each paper has kept its own editorial independence. And the *Gazet van Antwerpen* owns the *Gazet van Mechelen* in Malines. Taken together, there are 19 press consortiums and six associated companies.

Amid the increased concentration of ownership and decreased newspaper titles, two new papers have come into being. After the last French-language paper in Flanders had disappeared in 1974, *La Semaine d'Anvers* was founded to fill the gap. The other new paper, *De Morgen,* was started in Antwerp in December 1978, to recapture the readership of the Belgian Socialist party's semiofficial organ *De Volksgazet* (75,560 in 1977), which had failed in July of that year.

Despite the gain of two new dailies, the failure of the press continues: in June 1979 Brussels was told the Socialist *La Peuple* had gone into liquidation. Today, there are just 40 general newspapers left, plus four financial papers and one official gazette. Two of the financial-economic-commercial papers are published in Antwerp, *De Financieel Economische Tijd* (14,800) and *Lloyd Anversois* (9,750). The other two originate in Brussels: *Courrier de la Bourse et de la Banque* (20,000) and *L'Echo de la Bourse* (25,000).

Belgium produces about half of the newsprint it uses. Despite the decreasing number of dailies, consumption and import of newsprint have risen steadily in recent years. About 77 million metric tons were imported in 1965; by 1977, imports totaled over 129 million tons. During the same period, consumption rose from 133.4 million to 189.2 million tons. In 1977 per capita consumption of newsprint was about 18.5 kilograms.

Advertising as a means of financial support for the Belgian media has been on the rise. The increase of expenditures for advertising in all media for a single year, 1978 over 1977, was nearly 10 percent. However, the print press has been getting smaller and smaller proportions of the total advertising expenditures. In 1970 over 57 percent of advertising revenue was spent on publicity via the print media; by 1975 the proportion was 53.5 percent, and by 1978 down to 48.8 percent. Meanwhile, radio, magazines, outdoor and direct-mail advertising have been rising dramatically. Newspapers now get about 28 percent of commercial advertising monies.

Advertisers have no direct impact on editorial policies, but because of economic necessity, newspapers and periodicals have allocated more space to ads, thus decreasing the size of the "news hole." The amount of advertising varies widely according to individual papers. An economic paper, *De Nieuwe Gids* of Brussels, for example, has very little advertising, while others, such as *Het Laatste Nieuws* and *Le Soir*, may devote 50 percent or more of their space to paid space.

Generally speaking, however, circulation of dailies has been negatively affected by hikes in the prices asked for newspapers. In 1977 several leading newspapers experienced a brief stoppage because of a strike. Disputes with the Socialist union, Fédération Générale du Travail, prevented publication of the March 10, 1977 issues of the Brussels dailies *Le Soir, L'Echo de la Bourse, La Dernière Heure, Het Laatste Nieuws* and *De Standaard*. The French-speaking Belgian radio and television services went silent for about eight hours for the same reason. But the strike was settled quickly.

Journalists have entered into several collective bargaining agreements to stabilize relations with their employers. A national convention between publishers and professional journalists is renewed regularly. The National Federation of Weekly Newspapers has bargaining agreements with the unions of professional journalists. All these agreements are regularly updated.

As is the case elsewhere in Europe, Belgian newspapers have rapidly been adopting the newer technologies of electronic newsrooms and offset printing. The costs of conversion to these new technologies have played a large part in forcing amalgamation into newspaper groups and acceptance of government aid in several forms. So far, however, the new technology has done nothing to cut down the need for editorial manpower, because the volume of news has been increasing rapidly.

Press Laws

The long tradition of press freedom in Belgium is rooted in Articles 14 and 18 of the Belgian Constitution formulated by the Constituent Assembly in 1830. Article 14 stipulates freedom of belief, worship and of expression of opinions on all subjects, "with the exception of any misdemeanors committed in the implementation of such freedom." Article 18 relates more specifically to the press: "The press is free; censorship may never be established; no deposit in earnest of good faith may be demanded from writers, editors or printers. When the author is known and is resident in Belgium, the publisher, printer or distributor may not be prosecuted."

These two articles make clear that (1) every Belgian is free to express his/her opinions; (2) no censorship may ever be established; and (3) there are no rules to restrict newspaper publications, except that the responsible editor's personal name and address (not that of a corporation) must be printed in every issue.

While the history of Belgian information has been guided by these unrestrictive principles of freedom, certain restrictions within this framework have been devised to preserve order and, especially, to protect individuals. These rulings are primarily set forth in the country's civil and penal codes and in its special rulings on radio and television broadcasting.

Both the civil and penal regulations are as binding on journalists as they are on other citizens. About 20 such rulings limit unrestricted press freedom. For example, under Article 1832 of the Civil Code, a journalist (or any other citizen) may be prosecuted if he/she has caused material or moral prejudice to another and has failed to make adequate reparations. Article 253 prohibits the publication of divorce-court proceedings, that being considered a private matter in Belgium, where privacy is highly respected. The penal code prohibits advertising of illegal lotteries, maneuvers to influence stock and currency prices, illustrations that offend public decency and materials that wrongfully discredit the state or public confidence in the national currency. There has also been a law on the books since 1852, protecting the Belgian king, royal family and foreign heads of state from press abuse. In practice, however, the press has impinged on this last restriction without having sanctions imposed on it.

In Belgium, the person charged receives maximum rights and protection provided they are not abused. Abuse of those rights by the press has been considered a press misdemeanor, defined by the Court of Cassation in 1870 as "an act prejudicial to the rights of society at large, or of individual citizens, by the abuse or misuse of the expression of opinion in writings that are printed or published." A press misdemeanor implies there has been an infringement of the law through published writing. This ruling is particularly effective for the preservation of copyrighted materials. However, the assize courts in Belgium have yet to deal with a press case. Lower courts have settled misdemeanor charges, and where newspapers have been found guilty, they have, at maximum, been required to pay damages and to publish, at their own expense, the results of the decision in a certain number of publications.

The individual in Belgium is further protected by a 1961 right-to-reply ruling. Any person has the right, within three months, to reply in a publication which has published mistakes about him/her or has impugned personal honor. The law states that the reply may not occupy more than twice the original space, but the paper or periodical may refuse to publish the reply if it does not relate to the incriminating text, is injurious, contrary to law, unnecessarily involves a third party or uses a language other than that of the periodical concerned. Any publisher refusing to publish the reply under those conditions may be fined.

Belgian journalists and newspapers jealously guard their freedom rights. They have set up organizations such as the Association des Journalistes Professionnels de Belgique (AJPB). Press organizations were instrumental in the passing of legislation in 1963 that protects the rank and title of the professional journalist. The law prohibits legislators from creating any specific order or system of journalists; rather, its stated purpose is to give newsmen a definite rank and title and to provide legal protection for the same. The law specifies that the title of professional journalist may be used only by people over 21 years of age who enjoy full civil and political rights, who do not take part in commercial activity other than that of a newspaper or news agency and whose main source of income comes through the exercise of their journalistic profession. The journalist must have received regular pay for at least two years as an editor, sub-editor, photographer, news cameraman or correspondent for the news media. Anyone illegally using the title is subject to fines. But holding the rank and title does not require the journalist to engage in press activities.

Belgian law also serves to govern the obligations and protect the rights of journalists as they appear in the statutes of the AJPB. Obligations of the journalist in those rules include respecting the truth regardless of its consequences; upholding of freedom of information, commentary and criticism; publishing of information from known sources only; honesty in procuring and publishing information; refraining from plagiarism, slander, libel and unfounded accusations; and rejecting pressure to serve as a publicity agent or a propagandist. Declared rights of the professional journalist include free access to all sources of information, the right to investigate, the right to confidentiality, the right to refuse to express opinions which go against his convictions or his conscience, the right to collective bargaining and to a personal salary that is sufficient to guarantee his financial independence, and the right to be informed of decisions affecting the life of his newspaper or publication.

Newspapers and journalists are not licensed in Belgium, nor is there any compulsory posting of bonds.

Belgium's judiciary system is basically independent and based on the constitutional division of power between the legislative, executive and judicial bodies, each of which acts independently. Judges are appointed by the crown for life and they cannot be removed except by judicial sentence.

Censorship

Article 18 of the Belgian Constitution says, in part, that "no form of censorship may ever be instituted." Belgian abhorrence of censorship, expressed so strongly in the constitution, undoubtedly goes back to the unpleasant history of strict press control experienced in the 18th and 19th centuries under the domination of the Austrians and the French. Censorship will be tolerated and freedom of the press suspended, as declared by a 1916 decree, only in the time of war or during a siege. The press was heavily censored during World War II until Belgium was again liberated in 1944.

There are no rules that restrict officials from giving information to the press. Rather, officials see the press as an opportunity to reach the public.

State-Press Relations

In Belgium, the media relate on the governmental level to the Belgian Information and Documentation Institute (INBEL), set up in 1962. It serves both as official government spokesman and, at the same time, as a state information bureau independent of political pressures. INBEL is run by a board of directors representing a wide range of public opinion. It gets its budget from two ministries: the Ministry for Internal Affairs contributes half and the Ministry for Foreign Affairs the other. So far, however, the government has asked Parliament to grant subsidies annually without dictating to INBEL how it should operate. Further, both the general public and the press keep a watchful eye to assure there is no government interference in communications.

The government does remain uneasy about leaks of official information. In 1975, when the *La Dernière Heure* published important facts about the arrest of a high Ministry of Interior official, police searched the offices of several of its editors.

A number of governmental bureaus, such as the departments of National Defense, Public Works and Foreign Affairs, have their own press and information services, established primarily for informing the public of their activities. While the state, therefore, has a real presence in Belgium's informational structures (over and above access to the media), it uses its own services on a random basis to speak directly to the public or to get its opinion. But it has seldom interfered directly in the operations of the press or the electronic media. In general, it seeks to aid the press and to safeguard press freedom.

And that posture has led to a dilemma. Recently, the state has found itself in the paradoxical situation of wanting to help protect a pluralistic press while offering financial aid to keep certain newspapers solvent. The press has also contributed to the dilemma by asking government to be selective in dispensing its aid.

Government aid to the press in the past decade has been in the form of VAT and other tax concessions; direct grants; postal, telephone, telegraph and rail concessions; and government advertising in newspapers. Preferential postal rates for papers alone amount to over BFr 3 billion (over $100 million) per year. The government's real dilemma in providing the aid is that, theoretically, the bigger the newspaper, the more help it should receive. However, such a policy only widens the gap between the economically viable and the indebted papers, causing bankruptcies and destroying the plurality on which Belgium's press freedom is based. Also, by providing support, the government obliges some papers to stay in business, thus making a strong political statement about what should constitute the press in a country where newspapers have strong party, lingual and ethnic affiliations.

At first the government refused to look into this problem. Then, in 1972, the Belgian delegate at the Council of Europe indicated his government intended to take measures to ensure the survival of a politically oriented press. Parliamentary and press disputes arose over which criteria should govern apportionment of subsidies. Finally, in 1974, it was agreed that direct aid would go only to newspaper companies (not editorial offices) that published at least one daily of 7,500 circulation for 250 days per year and that aid would be apportioned to French and Flemish papers according to a quota related to their editorial, technical and financial independence. Under this system, Flemish-language dailies received about twice as much as comparable French dailies. This situation prevailed between 1974 and 1978 as inflation spiraled. Meantime, too, the newspaper syndicates had undue influence and the Socialist members of Parliament put so much pressure on the system in 1977 that the criteria governing independence were dropped. Large papers benefited more than smaller, politically oriented ones.

In the meantime, the government asked the press associations to offer their suggestions for solution. But it has been slow to accept association ideas that a press fund be set up or the feasibility of a press council be studied.

A new 1978 law covering aid to the press did not change the BFr 200 million ($67 million) offered for aid annually, but it did provide some new criteria for selective support of papers with low circulations and budgets, but which still have a certain number of journalists, editorial and feature pages and an agreed-upon percentage of space given to advertising. If a paper refuses a grant, that sum is returned to the Treasury for reapportionment. The new system favors smaller, financially troubled dailies. But it does not provide for continuing inflation, nor are publishers required to furnish proof of financial need. And, because of forms of indirect aid favoring larger papers, the new system does not provide equity to all the press. Thus, as of this writing, the government continues to distribute support unevenly and the danger of interference remains.

Attitude Toward Foreign Media

Belgium has become a business and news center of significance to the entire world. The nation plays a key role in the European Economic Community. Brussels serves as a locus for the Coal and Steel Community, the Common Market, NATO and the International Confederation of Trade Unions, and for African trade. As a result, Belgium is headquarters for many international press and media organizations. And they have found a welcome with few restrictions. No special visas or accreditation procedures apply to foreign journalists.

Some of the international organizations with Belgian offices include the International Press Association (API), the International Federation of Journalists (FIJ), the International Federation of Editors of Journals and Publications (FIED), the Organisation Mondiale de la Presse Periodique (World Organization of the Periodical Press), the Union Mondiale de le Presse Feminine (World Union of the Women's Press), the International Association of Journalists of the Women's Press, the European Alliance of News Agencies, the Association of European Journalists, the European Union of Radio Broadcasting (UER) and the European Center for Public Relations (CERP). Most have

offices in the government's Press Building or in the International Press Center (IPC), where the Committee of the EEC Newspaper Publishers Association also has its offices. The IPC also houses offices for individual international news agencies and for correspondents of individual foreign dailies headquartered in Brussels. IPC offers meeting rooms, the Lionel Bertelson Library, an auditorium equipped for simultaneous translations and a press club for its tenants. IPC was provided by the Belgian government to be operated as a nonprofit association designed to make representatives of the international press feel welcome.

In addition, the technical operations of the European Broadcasting Union (EBU) and Eurovision are located in Brussels, where electronic-media experts from several nations form a multilingual specialist team.

Like journalists from other countries, foreign newspapers circulate freely in Belgium. The increasing sales of French dailies has caused a crisis in the French-language press. Because of Belgium's small size, the national radio and television service faces strong competition from stations in neighboring countries. Much of the television news comes from the Eurovision network.

Although the Belgian government has taken no official stance on the issue, the press stands on the side of free flow of information in the UNESCO-sponsored push for a balanced information flow. Recently, Max Snijders, the Belgian member of the International Press Institute, said there is little evidence to sustain the assertion that the flow is all from rich countries. As evidence, he recalled that New Zealand has more TV imports than Malaysia, Canada more than Argentina, Colombia and Mexico together, Israel more than Iraq, and Nigeria more than Ghana. He showed that an unbalanced flow does not automatically lead to cultural domination. He predicted that a Third World news agency would not succeed in increasing the output of development news. And he warned that the UNESCO-sponsored code of ethics for journalists would have a tendency to become institutionalized by governments. At the same time, he urged that journalists in developing countries be involved in national development campaigns.

News Agencies

Agence Belga (Agence Télégraphique

Belge de Presse), located in Brussels, serves as the nation's national news agency. It has branch offices in Antwerp, Zaire and Benin. Founded in 1920 and largely owned by dailies, it distributes about 50,000 words daily in Flemish and French. About half of its dispatches cover foreign news. Agence Belga has exchange agreements with Agence France-Presse, Reuters and several other services.

Two smaller agencies also operate. Agence Day and the Centre d'Information de Presse (CIP), a Catholic agency, provide specialized news items.

Numerous foreign bureaus have branch offices or regional headquarters in the country. In addition to wire services already mentioned, news agencies with Brussels offices include Agence Zaire-Presse (AZAP), EFE (Spain), Novosti and Tass (USSR), ANSA (Italy), ANP (Netherlands), ADN (German Democratic Republic), AP and UPI (U.S.A.), CTK (Czechoslovakia), DPA (Federal Republic of Germany), Jiji Tsushin-sha and Kyodo Tsushin (Japan), TANJUG (Yugoslavia), and Tunis Afrique Presse (TAP).

Electronic News Media

Broadcasting began in Belgium in the 1920s. In 1930 Parliament set up a semi-independent public broadcasting service, Institut National de Radiodiffusion with a 10-member managing board and the Belgian minister for posts, telegraph and telephone as its chairman. For a while, some private radio stations were also allowed to operate, but World War II ended their existence as the Belgian government-in-exile set up the Office de Radiodiffusion Nationale Belge (RNB) in London. After the war a new law amalgamated the two organizations. Shortly thereafter, TV commenced.

Then, in 1960, a new statute established two national broadcasting institutes, the Flemish-language Belgische Radio et Televisie (BRT) and the French-speaking Radio-Télévision Belge de la Communaute Culturelle Française (RTBF). The law gave the two bodies statutory autonomy. Directors were to be appointed by Parliament and the board was no longer chaired by a government minister. However, the state could still exercise a measure of a priori control over the board, and the two institutes remained subject to certain other government supervision, including appointment and hiring of personnel and sanction of budget proposals.

But the law also enshrined some important new principles, among them the insistence of Article 28 on rigorous objectivity in the sphere of news and information: "news broadcasts...shall be done in a spirit of rigorous objectivity and without any prior government censorship." Anything contrary to law, offensive to public decency, insulting to heads of states or officials of foreign countries, or of commercial publicity nature was banned.

Another clause of Article 28 did allow political parties, trade unions, religious and other special-interest groups to utilize the institutes' radio and TV services for broadcasts according to equality rulings established by the government. The institutes were required to broadcast 10 hours of official announcements each month free of charge. Article 28 also established a Common Services Institute, a coordinating public utility legally in charge of technical, administrative and financial services.

The overall purpose of the 1960 statute was to safeguard the institutes' independence from government interference or from becoming its instruments of propaganda.

In 1977 a new law invalidated the Common Services Institute and rescinded the government-announcements provision of the 1960 law. It also set up a German-language radio and TV broadcasting center. RTBF was freed to draw up and fill its own program schedule. It now has its own press officer. As of late 1979, BRT was still primarily operating by the 1960 provisions.

In Belgium, the electronic media do not compete with the print press for advertising revenue. However, as elsewhere, Belgians have increasingly depended on TV and radio for their news and information, and this phenomenon has adversely affected newspaper readership and circulation. In 1977 there were 415 radio receivers per 1,000 inhabitants, or one for each 2.5 persons. The number of television-receiver licenses grew from 163 per 1,000 in 1965 to 286 per 1,000 in 1977. By 1978, over half of all TV receivers were color sets.

Both BRT and RTBF feature regional news and educational programs, and the BRT broadcasts a heavy diet of newsreels, current events and television news documentaries. However, both BRT and RTBF officials and many Belgian viewers are troubled by increasing competition from foreign stations. Three-fourths of Belgian TV sets are now linked to cable, which brings the average viewer a choice of 13 channels (four Belgian, three German, three French, two Dutch and one Luxembourg). As a result, for example, RTBF's two channels are watched by only 43 percent of the French-speaking audience. By EEC agreement allowing free flow of goods and services across borders, the foreign channels can transmit commercials, but Belgian law forbids BRT and RTBF the same privilege. As of this writing, RTBF has filed suit to stop foreign commercials. There has also been pressure to allow commercials on the national broadcasts.

The 1970s also witnessed the rise of "free" or pirate radio stations that operate in protest of RTBF/BRT's monopoly of broadcasting. Such stations usually broadcast clandestinely with low power, their support coming from people who seek programming alternatives to those offered by the official stations. These operations desire to return to the system that prevailed prior to World War II, when private radio stations operated alongside national radio. The persistence of these "free" station operations will probably eventually force Parliament to consider whether private stations should again be allowed to function legally.

Education & Training

In the past, Belgian journalists learned their trade on the job while working as apprentices. Since World War II, two streams of journalistic training have developed. Belgium has official state universities and free universities, the latter supported by borough or provincial authorities, or by private sources such as the Catholic Church. Immediately after the war, the free universities of Louvain and Brussels introduced some basic journalism courses. Several years later the state universities of Ghent and Liege began to provide communications training. Most state schools offer degrees after a three-year course of study. A few universities have developed doctoral programs in mass communications, but only a handful of students have received such degrees. Universities specialize in print or electronic journalism or in research, depending on their resources. The first university courses were taught by practitioners; today, many of the faculty lack lengthy practical experience.

The second approach requires up to four years of non-university education in special institutes or media-education centers. Most institutes offer technical training in a wide range of skills ranging from press, radio and television techniques to public relations, films and the visual arts. In many cases, media professionals teach evening classes. Typical of this approach are the Institut pour Journalistes de Belgique and the Centre Belge de Relations Publiques, the latter sponsored by the European Public Relations Center.

In recent years, many institutes have been founded. For example, there are now 14 academies just for teaching film-making techniques. As a result, between the products of these institutes and the graduates of university training there are more candidates than job opportunities. Increasingly, journalists and media specialists require both broad theoretical knowledge and practical skills. Consequently, a growing number of institute trainees are acquiring university degrees before seeking employment.

Belgium's proclivity for associations extends to the media. In 1979 the two main journalistic professional associations, the Association Générale de la Belge and the Union Professionelle de la Presse Belge joined into a single bilingual Association des Professionnels de Belgique (AJPB) with alternating French- and Flemish-speaking presidents. The stated purpose of the AJPB is to uphold and promote the professional interests of its members by protecting the rights of the press, by negotiating in behalf of journalists, by working for legislation favorable to journalists and by setting up and observing a professional code of ethics. The AJPB has several regional sections.

In addition, numerous other specialized media associations flourish. There are associations for the legal press, for press photographers, for TV news, for music, art, film and drama critics, for writers and for specialized correspondents. Political correspondents have organized themselves into four party-oriented associations. The periodical press has established several more associations. Newspaper owners and publishers have six associations of their own, and public relations specialists have formed two more for themselves. Many of the national associations relate to the numerous international bodies located in the country.

Summary

The presence in Belgium of two ethnic communities, Dutch (Flemish) and French (Walloon), has divided the media into two entities serving both language groups. Until recently there has been little crossover between the two. The press of each community has tried to provide serious quality news, but papers have historically had political leanings. While the press has a long tradition of freedom, it now faces not only financial difficulty but—because of government aid—the danger of losing that freedom itself. Numerous papers have failed, so that only 40 remain. Papers form into groups to survive. To aid the financially troubled print media, the state has provided support in the form of concessions, grants and advertising, but in the administration of such help, the government has necessarily had to make some decisions that influence if not reduce press independence. Meanwhile the public is increasingly drawn to radio, television and foreign electronic-media programs via cable for its information and entertainment.

The future of the Belgian media relates to economics and developing technology. With rising print costs, only the largest newspaper groups may be able to survive. But both the press and the government seem determined to preserve press plurality. Eventually, the residual resistance to commercial advertising on radio and television will be overcome and then the electronic media will also compete for publicity revenues. Thus the future of the Belgian press—and of all Belgian media—appears to be largely dependent on where new technologies will lead and what alternative solutions to economic problems can be developed.

CHRONOLOGY

1977   Eight dailies and French-speaking Belgian RTBF engage in one-day stoppage in dispute with Socialist Fédération Générale du Travail.

New law allows broadcasting entities greater freedom in programming, rescinds government-announcement requirements and eliminates Common Services Institute.

1978   Advertising expenditures in print media increase 10 percent over 1977. New law provides new criteria for government aid to press; it seeks to help papers with low circulations, but still fails to provide aid equity or to cover effects of inflation.

1979   The two main journalists' associations, one French and one Flemish, join forces in new single organization, Association des Journalistes Professionnels de Belgique.

BIBLIOGRAPHY

"A Quick Look Around: Belgium." *IPI Report,* 21:11 (November 1972), p. 7.

Belgian Information and Documentation Institute. *The Topical Press Under The Sign of Freedom.* Brussels, 1967.

"Belgian Stoppage." *IPI Report,* 26:4 (April 1977), p. 2.

"Belgian Television: Spoiled for Choice." *The Economist,* March 3, 1979, pp. 75–76.

Europa Yearbook: Vol. 1. "Belgium." London, 1980.

Fisher, Harold. *The EBU: Model for Regional Cooperation in Broadcasting.* Journalism Monograph No. 68. Lexington, Ky., 1980.

"IPI Activity in Belgium Reviewed." *IPI Report,* 22:5-6 (May–June 1973), 9.

Merrill, John, Bryan, Carter, and Alisky, Marvin. *The Foreign Press.* Baton Rouge, La., 1970.

"News of the World Press: Belgium." *IPI Report,* 21:10 (October 1972), 2.

"Press Vital for Civil Liberty." *IPI Report,* 26:5 (May–June 1977), 17, 20.

"Rating Films on TV." *Journal of Communication,* 27:4 (Autumn 1977) 48–53.

"The Press Under Pressure: Belgium." *IPI Report,* 24:1 (January 1975), 12.

UNESCO. *Statistical Yearbook, 1978–1979.* Paris, 1980.

Van Bol, Jean-Marie. *The Policy Surrounding Social Communications in Belgium.* Brussels, 1979.

"Who's Afraid of Handouts?" *IPI Report,* 26:5 (May–June 1977), 21–22.

"World Press Freedom Review, 1979." *IPI Report,* 28:12 (December 1979), 12.

BOLIVIA

by George Kurian

BASIC DATA

Population: 5,286,000 (1980)
Area: 1,908,160 sq. km. (736,741 sq. mi.)
GNP: 90 billion pesos (US$4.5 billion) (1978)
Literacy Rate: 35–40%
Language(s): Spanish
Number of Dailies: 13
  Aggregate Circulation: 150,000
  Circulation per 1,000: 26
Number of Nondailies: 13
  Aggregate Circulation: 78,000
  Circulation per 1,000: 15
Number of Periodicals: 18

Number of Radio Stations: 125
Number of Television Stations: 1
Number of Radio Receivers: 3,500,000
  Radio Receivers per 1,000: 74
Number of Television Sets: 265,000
  Television Sets per 1,000: 8
Total Annual Newsprint Consumption: 4,700
  metric tons (1978)
  Per Capita Newsprint Consumption: 0.9 kg.
  (2.0 lb.)
Total Newspaper Ad Receipts: NA
  As % of All Ad Expenditures: NA

Background & General Characteristics

The earliest Bolivian newspapers appeared shortly after printing presses were brought to La Paz and Sucre (then known as Chuquisaca) in 1825 and freedom of expression was granted by the constitution of 1826. For the next few decades, official news bulletins and religious publications were published at irregular intervals. Along with the news, the newspapers contained excerpts of learned debates and articles on law, economics and politics. The internal disturbances of the 1830s and 1840s and the 30 years of civil disorder that followed were not favorable to the growth of a press. During this period two papers, *El Comercio* of La Paz and *El Cruzado* of Sucre, served the entire nation. The press revived during the 1870s but still served only the educated elite, who constituted a virtual nation within a nation. It was not until the mid-20th century that a true national press could claim to have been established in the country.

The relative recency of the press is best illustrated by the age of the newspapers. Of the six La Paz dailies being published in 1980, the oldest, *El Diario*, was founded in 1904. The next oldest paper, *Ultima Hora*, was founded 35 years later. *Presencia*, the third oldest, was founded in 1952. The 1960s witnessed the founding of two more dailies, *Hoy* and *Jornada*. The most recent daily, *La Voz del Pueblo*, was founded only in 1974. *El Diario, Hoy* and *Presencia* are morning papers; the others are evening tabloids. All describe themselves as independents except *Presencia*, which is Catholic.

The provincial press is centered around three cities: Cochabamba, Oruro and Santa Cruz. Cochabamba has three dailies, of which *Los Tiempos*, published by three generations of the Canelas family, is the best known; the other two are *Prensa Libre* and *Clarin*. Oruro and Santa Cruz have two dailies each, *El Expreso* and *La Patria* in the former and *El Comercio* and *El Deber* in the latter. All provincial papers describe themselves as independent.

Presencia, with a circulation of 70,000, has edged out *El Diario* to become the largest selling newspaper in the country. *Hoy,* the third morning daily, has a circulation of 40,000. The evening papers have much smaller circulations; *Ultima Hora,* the leading tabloid, has a circulation of only 20,000. *Los Tiempos* is the best-selling provincial paper, with sales of 30,000 per issue. Aggregate circulation of the Bolivian press was reported in 1977 to be close to 300,000, or 60 per 1,000 inhabitants. Circulation figures show wide fluctuations because some provincial papers do not report them in some years. Per capita circulation is about average for Latin America; it is higher than Paraguay and Guatemala but lower than Ecuador, Colombia and Brazil. Over all, Bolivia ranks 80th in the world in this respect. It must be remembered that the reading public is limited to the Spanish-speaking whites and mestizos; the Quechua- or Aymara-speaking Indians, who constitute the majority of the population, are, as UNESCO describes them, "practically untouched by the press."

Surprisingly, the Bolivian press has achieved an influence and reputation out of all proportion to its size. If asked to name the 20 most influential newspapers in the Spanish-speaking world, most media watchers will include at least two Bolivian newspapers, *Presencia* and *El Diario,* and possibly three, adding *Los Tiempos. Presencia* is an unusual paper because it is owned by the Catholic Church. Its consistent defense of social justice in Bolivia and neighboring countries has made it an authentic voice of the Bolivian masses.

Because of the shortage of qualified reporters, local news predominates in most newspapers. Only *Presencia* and *El Diario* provide adequate coverage of international news. The format varies; for morning papers it is the standard 22″ x 15″ and for evening papers the 15″ x 11″ tabloid size. Typical weekday editions are about 10 pages. Only La Paz and Cochabamba papers use pictures regularly. Gossip columns and cartoons are extremely popular and take up considerable space.

The nondaily and periodical press is comparatively weak in Bolivia. UNESCO reports only 13 nondailies and 18 periodicals, none with large circulations.

Economic Framework

The press is entirely in private hands. Apart from *Presencia,* owned by the Catholic Church, most of the others are owned by wealthy families with strong political connections. At the same time, for historical reasons a party press has not developed in the country and the state has little or no direct involvement in the media, except in television. Stable patterns of ownership have contributed to a strong and economically viable press. Except for the geographical concentration in the capital, monopolies and chains are absent. No single newspaper—not even *Presencia* or *El Diario*—dominates the market. Newcomers are able to gain entry, as was illustrated in 1974 when *La Voz del Pueblo* was founded.

Nevertheless, economic constraints have kept the Bolivian press in a depressed and underdeveloped state. Because they have no out-of-town correspondents and cannot afford subscription rates of wire services, the smaller newspapers simply copy items from the metropolitan papers without attribution. While the principal source of newspaper revenue is from advertising, there are few large or regular advertisers. Because of low salary scales of newspaper staffs, journalism is not considered an attractive profession and even full-fledged journalists find it necessary to moonlight. Except for *El Diario* and *Presencia* in La Paz and *Los Tiempos* in Cochabamba, newspapers are still being printed by letterpress. Distribution is another problem, one that has hampered the development of La Paz papers as true national newspapers. Transportation systems are largely inadequate to ensure same-day delivery of papers outside of the city of publication.

Journalists and publishers are represented by two associations: Asociación Nacional de Periodistas and Asociación Nacional de Prensa. Strikes have been rare in recent years because of governmental restrictions on union activities.

Press Laws, Censorship & State-Press Relations

For most of its history the Bolivian press had to contend with an adversary, if not hostile, government. The University of Missouri Press Freedom Index rated Bolivia near the bottom of the category in the late 1960s. Kim Hill and Patricia Hurley in their 30-year survey of press freedom in Latin America rated Bolivia average only during 1960 to 1965 and consigned it to the poor category during other periods.

On the same scale Bolivia will probably rank much worse since the 1980 coup, which brought General Luis Garcia Meza to power. Within hours of his seizure of power General Garcia arrested 25 journalists, suspended most dailies for several days and stationed troops in editorial offices. Many journalists fled the country or sought refuge in foreign embassies. Radio Fides, the Catholic Church-owned radio station, was attacked by armed men and most of its equipment destroyed. Newspapers were punished not only for publishing news the government considered offensive but also for not reporting news it considered important. On December 29, 1980 the minister of the interior ordered the closing of *Presencia* because of alleged slurs against Bolivian womanhood.

For the Bolivian press, such repression is nothing new. In the years following World War II it has enjoyed a brief interlude of relative freedom only under President Victor Paz Estenssoro and his successor Rene Barrientos Ortuno. During the early 1960s the Bolivian press would freely criticize both the president and the government and boldly publish articles on government corruption and political blundering. This period came to an end with the rise to the presidency of Luis Siles Salinas. In 1967 a law was enacted that required that newspapers reserve space (and broadcasting stations time) for employees who disagree with editorial policy, that only workers' associations could publish Monday editions of newspapers, and that all newspapers must publish (and radio stations broadcast) communiques by labor unions. For the first time in Bolivian history the government directly entered newspaper publishing with a short-lived daily called *Prensa*. What little freedom remained to the press came under attack under Siles' successor, the left-leaning Gen. Juan Jose Torres. He instituted "cooperatization" of the press by "encouraging" workers to take over newspaper establishments. *El Diario,* for example, was not only taken over by the workers but the owning Carrasco family members were made virtual prisoners in their apartment over the paper's editorial offices.

Some normalcy returned when Col. Hugo Banzer overthrew Torres, but frequent clashes and skirmishes underlined the precariousness of the truce. One of the most serious of such incidents occurred in 1976 when *Los Tiempos* and other newspapers charged the junta with responsibility for the assassination of Gen. Joaquin Zenteno Anaya, Bolivian ambassador to France, by unknown assailants on the streets of Paris. The Banzer regime responded by threatening to muzzle the press. Invoking the Military Penal Code, the government said that "all press or radio comment injurious to the dignity of the country, the president of the republic, the commander in chief of the armed forces, Gen. Hugo Banzer Suarez, members of the institution, or any dignitary of state, or which contravenes high nationalistic values, shall be considered as a grave offense and subject to the severest penalties." The warning brought about an immediate reaction from the press and radio associations: a call for a 24-hour general strike, which was carried out nationwide. The incident ended with a communique in which the government "reiterated its continued will to respect freedom of the press and the press and radio organizations on their part acknowledged their responsibility to respect constituted authorities and national institutions."

As in several other Latin American countries during the troubled 1960s and 1970s, newspapers and journalists became prime targets for both left-wing and right-wing terrorists. Disappearances of journalists, bombings of printing plants and editorial offices, and assassinations of prominent editors became frequent. In one such incident in 1970 Alfredo Alexander, the publisher of *Ultima Hora* and *Hoy,* and his wife were killed when a package delivered to their home exploded as they were opening it.

All these alarms and excursions notwithstanding, the Bolivian press enjoys complete constitutional protection on paper. It is also one of the few presses in this region that has not witnessed large-scale government involvement. In short, the press is tough and hardy and has learned the arts of survival in difficult political climates. As the Inter-American Press Association said, "Bolivia is one of the few countries in the Western Hemisphere where the situation of the press is *not* determined by the nature of the government."

Attitude Toward Foreign Media

Following the 1980 coup, which was condemned by most free nations of the world, government relations with the foreign media worsened. A number of incidents occurred in which foreign reporters were arrested, mistreated and expelled from the country. On August 25, 1980 the military authorities arrested Albert Brun, an AFP correspondent, who was accused of communicating with opposition leaders by telephone. Government officials admitted having copies of Brun's dispatches and records of his telephone conversations. After three days in jail Brun was expelled from the country. During the same period, Mary Helen Spooner, correspondent of the London *Financial Times* and *The Economist,* was arrested for having written an unpublished article alleging that members of the government were involved in illicit drug trafficking. She was released when two representatives of the *Financial Times* traveled to Bolivia and apologized for the alleged insults.

While these incidents reflect the Garcia regime's sensitivity to international public opinion, they are unusual in Bolivian press history. Previous regimes had permitted considerable latitude to foreign reporters and there are no standing administrative restrictions on cables or visas of foreign correspondents. In fact the Bolivian press has been long active in the Inter-American Press Association, the principal watchdog of press freedom in the Western Hemisphere.

While the present Garcia regime's stand is unclear, Bolivia has generally followed the IPI and IAPA guidelines regarding state-press relations and opposed the statist elements in the 1978 UNESCO Declaration on the Media.

News Agencies

Bolivia has no national news agency. Eight foreign news agencies are represented in La Paz, including UPI, AP, Reuters-Latin and Tass.

Electronic News Media

In 1980 there were 125 radio stations in Bolivia, compared to 88 in 1973. The most powerful is the Radio Illimani—the Voice of Bolivia—located in La Paz and operated by the government. The majority of the private stations are commercial, but there are a number of them run by the Catholic Church and religious orders, such as Maryknoll, Jesuits and the Oblate Fathers. The industry is regu-

lated by the Directorate General of Radio Communications. Most programs are in Spanish.

Television is conducted by the state-run Empresa Nacional de Television Boliviana, which operates stations in La Paz, Oruro, Cochabamba, and Santa Cruz. News and information make up 24 percent of television programming.

Education & Training

A three-year course in journalism has been offered since 1968 at the Universidad Catolica Boliviana in La Paz and the school of journalism at Santa Cruz. A similar program has been more recently introduced at the National University at La Paz.

Along with some of its neighbors, Bolivia has introduced government licensing or certification for all working journalists, under the auspices of the College of Journalists. The government also maintains a National Register of Professional Journalists. To be listed in the Register, one must be a graduate of an approved journalism program or possess professional experience for specified number of years.

Summary

Although La Paz boasts of two of the finest newspapers in the continent, the Bolivian press as a whole has not registered much growth in the past three decades. During the 1970s it had to contend with hostile governments and was able to survive only because of the instability of the revolving-door regimes and their lack of a consistent media policy. In between regimes the press is usually able to recoup its losses and prepare itself for the next onslaught. The pattern is not likely to be radically different in the 1980s.

CHRONOLOGY

1974 *La Voz del Pueblo* founded.
1976 Banzer regime threatens to muzzle press, alleging insults to the junta, but climbs down in the face of a nationwide strike.
1980 Following the coup led by General Luis Garcia Meza, 25 jour-

nalists are arrested and most dailies suspended for days.
Radio Fides attacked and destroyed by armed men.
Minister of the interior orders closure of *Presencia* and arrest of its publisher, Huascar Cajias.

BIBLIOGRAPHY

Hill, K. Q., and Hurley, P. A. "Freedom of the Press in Latin America: A Thirty-Year Survey." *Latin American Research Review,* 15:2, 1980.

Knudson, J. W. *The Press and the Bolivian National Revolution.* Minneapolis, 1973.
Mitchell, C. *The Legacy of Populism in Bolivia.* New York, 1978.

BRAZIL

by Mark Journey, Susan Bruce and Robert N. Pierce

BASIC DATA

Population: 120,386,000
Area: 8,521,100 sq. km. (3,289,144 sq. mi.)
GNP: Cr$8.86 trillion (US$207.27 billion) (1979)
Literacy Rate: 83%
Language(s): Portuguese
Number of Dailies: 299
  Aggregate Circulation: 4,895,000
  Circulation per 1,000: 45
Number of Nondailies: 788
  Aggregate Circulation: 2,969,000
  Circulation per 1,000: 27
Number of Periodicals: 1,255
Number of Radio Stations: 1,071

Number of Television Stations: 92
Number of Radio Receivers: 45 million
  Radio Receivers per 1,000: 374
Number of Television Sets: 18 million
  Television Sets per 1,000: 150
Total Annual Newsprint Consumption: 179,900 metric tons
  Per Capita Newsprint Consumption: 1.5 kg. (3.3 lb.)
Total Newspaper Ad Receipts: Cr$13.26 billion (US$311.9 million)
  As % of All Ad Expenditures: 18.9

Background & General Characteristics

Much as a psychiatrist would describe a schizophrenic, Brazilians speak of their country as *os dois Braseis*—("the two Brazils"). They are referring to two distinct national faces, one resplendent with some of the most vibrant sophistication in the world, the other pitted, scarred and twisted with poverty and misery that surpasses that of some of the most backward nations. For a Brazilian to recognize the split is to be ambivalent himself, on the one hand pointing with pride, on the other venting disgust.

The contradictions abound also in Brazil's mass media. There is a responsible, courageous, independent press, ranking among the world's best; the largest television market in South America (ninth in the world); the fourth largest privately owned TV network in the world, smaller only than the three major U.S. systems; and an enormous radio, film and magazine market. At the same time, the media have undergone the most systematic controls in the hemisphere outside Cuba. One-third of the population is illiterate; and journalism is mostly limited to urban centers, forsaking the vast peasantry.

The concept of mass communication has been difficult to realize in a country whose official literacy rate stands so low, even ebbing to 50 percent in the destitute Northeast. Thirty years ago, when the national rate was much worse, one legislator remarked that the only way to raise literacy was to make it a prerequisite for the two things that are consuming interests to practically all Brazilians, soccer and carnival.

But a 10-year-old government program called MOBRAL (Brazilian Literacy Movement) has made impressive attempts to stamp out illiteracy and ease the difficult transformation for many rural Brazilians into a modern, competitive society. Hampered by a high dropout rate (50–60 percent) and a shoestring budget, the program nevertheless has survived longer than any other such Brazilian effort and has brought schools and teachers to areas where none existed. Extensive, elaborately produced television and radio programs also have stimulated literacy training.

A larger obstacle to the growth of Brazil's communication market is the country's principal illness—hunger. Malnutrition has resulted in bad vision and limited mental capacity for some peasants. The lower class includes 70 percent of the population, the upper class only five percent. When the majority of Brazilians make less than two dollars, a day few can spend 30 cents for a newspaper.

Massive immigration to the cities by peasants fleeing drought and depleted farms has made Brazil a country of large cities. São Paulo has eight million inhabitants, Rio 5.5 million, and at least four more—Belo Horizonte, Recife, Salvador and Porto Alegre—have more than a million. Thus media production is concentrated in a few centers, and vast stretches of the country must rely on the urban output.

Language diversity does not pose a major problem for media dissemination, as Portuguese is universally understood. A great number of ethnic groups, such as German, Japanese, Italian and Hispanic Americans, have strong representation, along with daily use of their language. Publications are to be found in these and other languages, but they are always supplementary to those printed in Portuguese.

The quality of Brazil's journalism has undergone one of the world's most dramatic transformations. Until the 1950s considered to be among the most undeveloped systems, the Brazilian media have since reached international prominence. Two of its newspapers are the only Latin American ones listed in *The World's Great Dailies,* its magazines are frequently quoted abroad, and its television industry has become an exporter of programs.

Even though professional stature has come late to Brazilian journalists, they have been actively involved in the nation's development for nearly two centuries. During most of this time the dominant tone of journalism has been a struggle against some form of government.

Busy making their fortunes, early settlers in the Portuguese colony (discovered in 1500) did little to challenge a royal prohibition from the motherland against printing. However, a few clandestine publications were circulated by such secret societies as the Freemasons.

In 1808 the Portuguese royal family and supporters arrived in Brazil to escape the Napoleonic invasion. The first legal newspaper, *A Gazeta do Rio de Janeiro,* appeared. Consisting mainly of official announcements and court gossip, it was printed on a press brought from Portugal. Later that year, a

monthly opposition opinion journal, the *Correio Brasiliense,* emerged. It was printed in England and smuggled into the growing colony.

Immediately a royal censor was placed in charge of preventing the publication of any material against religion, the government or good manners. Two significant characteristics of the Brazilian media were already becoming apparent:
1. The patronizing role of the government, confident it knew what was best for the reading public.
2. Cross-currents of liberalism and authoritarianism in the media.

The arrival of the royal family brought with it the opening of Brazil's harbors for trade with all friendly nations. Ships from all over Europe dropped their anchors in Brazil's ports and the young colony's population was overwhelmed with news. New ideas, especially those of the French and American revolutions, began exciting some urban sophisticates, and the pressure for mass communication began to build. Before long, ideas of Brazil's own independence spread among the colonists, the press being instrumental in fanning the flames.

The king was soon summoned back to Portugal in 1820, leaving his son, Dom Pedro, to fill his shoes. However, giving way to pressure by the elite, Dom Pedro declared Brazil independent in 1822, and became emperor.

Under Dom Pedro's son, Dom Pedro II, the struggling nation prospered and became more unified during the latter part of the century. Dom Pedro II's moderate policies and technical innovations also led to a healthy press development. During these initial boom years, increasing specialization developed in the printed media, reflecting the nation's social complexity and diversity. Periodicals on medicine, law, dentistry, literature, music and economics were published alongside foreign-language newspapers, which served European immigrants' needs.

But undoubtedly the most socially significant press remained the political newspapers, which were noted for their angry campaigns against slavery. Gradually the liberal press swayed Brazilian public opinion as hundreds of articles were published attacking large slaveowning ranchers and recounting episodes of torture and brutality inflicted upon the black man. The campaign led to abolition in 1888.

As in other South American countries, the press took on a literary facade, contributing to the acceptance of culture by the masses. Like Europeans of the time, Brazilians greatly enjoyed the publication of fascicles in local newspapers. Some of the great novelists published chapters of their latest books in the Brazilian press, often read aloud to illiterate yet enthralled crowds. Gradually foreign literature began to replace national, and by the early 20th century the market was flooded with this foreign "canned" material —a process that has been continued in all forms of the Brazilian media.

Toward the end of the 19th century, there was a growing movement to replace Brazil's constitutional monarchy with a republican form of government. Editors openly advocated a change in government. Newspapers such as *A República* and *O Manifesto Repúblicano* appeared. A coup d'etat was staged in 1889, creating the new republic.

But the first years of the republic were not easy, as Brazilians became increasingly aware of their backwardness compared with Europe and the United States. All over the world rapid change was taking place as a result of the technical and industrial revolution. The press became a capitalist enterprise, and advertising helped to establish a consumer society.

Brazil, however, seemed locked into a coffee monoculture, and development and industrialization occurred almost exclusively in the temperate south. Transportation facilities were built, but not in great enough numbers.

The economy and social climate grew shaky. Between 1906 and 1929 the country faced crisis after crisis. Finally Getulio Vargas, a superb propagandist, came to office in 1930 and gradually consolidated his power until he was able to establish a dictatorial regime in 1937. One scholar describes him as having,

like Pedro II,...a consuming ambition to modernize Brazil, but unlike the emperor he saw no reason to tolerate diversity of ideas. While instituting strict censorship of the media, he also exercised positive as well as negative control by exploiting mass communication for propaganda. Like others adroit political leaders of his time such as Roosevelt, Mussolini, Hitler and Perón, he saw the opportunity to use radio as a personal channel to the minds of his people.

Although radio had been officially introduced in Brazil in 1922, its expansion was slow because of equipment costs. But by the time Vargas came to power there were radio transmitters in all of Brazil's major cities. He quickly realized not only its potential as a propaganda tool but also as an instrument for negative criticism of his regime—if not controlled with an iron fist.

Consequently, on December 30, 1939, the Department of Press and Propaganda (DIP) was created to exert prior censorship of everything from the media to the theater. So all-embracing were the controls that the saying spread: "Don't speak—Getulio will do it for you; don't think—the DIP will do it for you."

Tension grew and in 1945 Vargas was deposed, and a new, more liberal constitution guaranteed the press, politicians and the masses complete freedom of expression. Unfortunately, the two decades that followed gave way to what in many cases was blatant irresponsibility on the part of the press.

These days were embarrassing to anyone who believed in an objective press. Newspapers did not discuss economic policies or political debates in a rational manner, but instead slandered elected officials and their private lives or character.

In some cases politicians fought back vehemently. João Goulart, who was president until the military took over in 1964, organized a massive propaganda campaign to disseminate his leftist ideology and promote his projects and policies. In some cases he manipulated government loans to bring opposition papers to heel.

The newspaper industry which has emerged in recent years from this heritage has been shaped by the political events both before and after the 1964 coup that brought the military to power (the latter phase will be detailed later). However, the press has also had a professional and an economic life that can be described somewhat apart from Brazil's political milieu.

The number of newspapers in Brazil has grown from 50 in 1831 to more than 1,400 today, including 338 dailies and 1,075 non-dailies. Circulation of all papers totals more than four million, a small figure compared with a population of 120 million. Only 3.5 copies of dailies are sold per 100 population, far below the 10 estimated by UNESCO as the minimum for takeoff into modernity.

About half the newspapers are published in state capitals, and about 95 percent of the total circulation is there. Many journalists are concerned about the scarcity and weakness of community newspapers. Those that exist have been known to reprint material without permission from major São Paulo and Rio newspapers, with a smattering of local news.

Massive media ownership groups are common. The best-known, now defunct, was Francisco de Assis Chateaubriand's Associated Daily Newspapers and Broadcasting Stations. It included 32 newspapers, 10 television stations, 23 radio stations, many periodicals and a news agency. Most newspapers are privately owned and express the views of their owners, although some are mouthpieces for political parties. Some powerful owners publish a variety of types of papers to get the attention of all social classes.

In no aspect is the prosperity of Brazilian newspapers more evident than in the physical form. Nearly all the daily newspapers are standard size, and the typical number of pages is among the highest of any country except the United States. *O Estado de S. Paulo* usually has more than 100 pages and on special occasions has approached 500. Most of the large papers have Sunday editions, and four-color magazine sections on agriculture, literature, tourism and women's interests are common. The weekly press, mostly political and satirical papers, tends to be tabloid in page size and has far less advertising than the dailies.

The news content and style of major newspapers somewhat resembles that of large papers in the United States. Excellent foreign coverage produced by overseas correspondents and enterprising domestic stories dominate the front pages. Financial and cultural sections are also common in these papers, along with sports sections that emphasize soccer. These sections run between four and six pages. In smaller towns, local and national news often overshadows international coverage. The very small papers, like country weeklies in the United States, often play up human interest, crime, and wedding and funeral stories on page one.

The best-known specialized newspaper is *Gazeta Mercantil*, headquartered in São Paulo with an edition in Rio. Its enterprise and reliability as a business paper have won it wide influence. Two sports newspapers, both with circulations of more than 30,000, are published: *A Gazeta Esportiva* of São Paulo and *Jornal dos Esportes* of Rio.

The most prominent foreign-language newspaper has long been the *Brazil Herald,* which serves the English-reading population (both foreigners and Brazilians) with a circulation of about 30,000. It is published in Rio and owned by a Brazilian company. The same company is publishing a daring experiment in an English-language paper in São Paulo. This is the *Latin American Daily Post,* started in 1979 with the goal of being circulated throughout the hemisphere much as the *International Herald Tribune* of Paris serves Europe and the Middle East. By 1980 it had achieved sales of 30,000, of which 70 percent were in Brazil, but its managers are working steadily to increase the circulation in other countries.

Other foreign-language newspapers in Brazil include the *Deutsche Nachrichten* in São Paulo, for German residents, and the *Diário Nippak,* serving the large Japanese community.

Important Dailies in Brazil		
São Paulo		
Folha de São Paulo	Independent	300,000 (daily) 320,000 (Sunday)
O Estado de São Paulo	Independent	210,000 (daily) 270,000 (Sunday)
Rio de Janeiro		
O Dia	Popular Labor	320,000 (daily) 250,000 (Sunday)
Jornal do Brazil	Catholic conservative	170,000 (daily) 260,000 (Sunday)
O Globo	Conservative, pro-government	250,000 (daily) 305,000 (Sunday)
Recife		
Diario de Pernambuco	Independent	36,200 (daily) 62,000 (Sunday)
Porto Alegre		
Correio de Povo	Independent, conservative	81,500 (daily) 142,500 (Sunday)

Cities having newspapers total 398. Of these, 161 have competing newspapers of all periodicities. Those having competing dailies total 48.

Number of Newspapers by Circulation Groups

100,000–500,000	11
50,000–100,000	10
25,000–50,000	30
10,000–25,000	20
under 10,000	267

Largest Newspapers by Circulation

O Dia, Rio de Janeiro (morning)	320,000
Folha de São Paulo (morning)	300,000
O Globo, Rio de Janeiro (afternoon)	250,000
O Estado de S. Paulo, São Paulo (morning)	210,000
Jornal do Brasil, Rio de Janeiro (morning)	170,000
Folha da Tarde, São Paulo (afternoon)	160,000
Diário Popular, São Paulo (afternoon)	150,000
Noticias Populares, São Paulo (morning)	140,000
Jornal da Tarde, São Paulo (afternoon)	120,000
Estado de Minas, Belo Horizonte (morning)	110,000

Founded in 1875, *O Estado de S. Paulo* ("The State of São Paulo") has grown to be Brazil's most prestigious newspaper within and outside the country; it is widely considered the best in Latin America. Under three generations of the Mesquita family, *O Estado* has become an institution in Brazil, much as *The New York Times* is in the United States. In the words of its editors, which few would disagree with, "For a century, this paper has been a bulwark in the cause of freedom in Brazil, having fought fearlessly and tirelessly for the ideals of democracy ever since its founding." *O Estado* probably has the best political coverage and clearly the most complete international section, subscribing to seven international news agencies and keeping correspondents in 12 foreign cities. Sober in appearance, it is also Latin America's bulkiest newspaper, with an average of 60 pages on weekdays and 250 on Sundays, heavily laden with industrial advertising.

O Estado has won citations from such groups as the International Newspaper Editors' Foundation, Golden Quill of Freedom, Mergenthaler and Theodore Brent International awards. Its director, Julio Mesquita Neto, grandson of the founder, was first president of LATIN, the Latin American news agency.

O Estado's daily, *Jornal da Tarde* ("Evening Journal"), has a circulation of 120,000 and is a forward-looking paper that seeks a different public with its varied and innovative design and typefaces. It sometimes fills much of the front page with a single headline and a picture, although the effect is not one of sensationalism. *Jornal da Tarde* selects several of the day's most interesting items and then tries to give them the country's best in-depth coverage.

Both newspapers are produced in a new ultra-modern complex on the outskirts of São Paulo. The Mesquita family empire also includes a news agency; an important radio station, Eldorado; and the Eldorado musical recording business.

O Estado has its critics. Some leftists complain that it does not go as far as it could in advocating socioeconomic improvements in Brazil. These intellectuals claim it could use its vast influence more positively. For many years the paper was a favorite target for student demonstrators, who saw it as a symbol of the establishment.

According to its editor, Boris Casoy, *Folha de São Paulo* ("São Paulo Leaflet") was the only newspaper in 1979 to make a profit in Brazil. It now exceeds *O Estado* in circulation weekdays but falls behind it on Sundays because of *O Estado*'s large amount of classified advertising. It does not have *O Estado*'s wide recognition, but since it became financially and politically independent in 1975 it has drawn steadily more readers from all sectors.

The paper's third page, carrying letters to the editor, has been a resounding success. According to Casoy, "We represent opinions of all sectors of Brazilian society, all philosophical thoughts, from the extreme right to the extreme left. The only prerequisite is quality."

Established in 1921, the paper is one of several in the *Folha* group. It has 11 bureaus in Brazil and seven overseas.

In international reputation, *Jornal do Brasil* ("Journal of Brazil") is most often considered alongside *O Estado de S. Paulo*, particularly because of its seriousness and its forthright defense of its freedom. Even though its reputation inside Brazil does not surpass several other papers and its circulation is somewhat lower, it has perhaps the best coverage of national political news through its Brasilia bureau, and is read by politicians, businessmen and intellectuals in Rio. Since its founding in 1891, it has maintained a Catholic and mildly conservative position. It also has won several international awards, and its executives are active in hemispheric associations.

The color Sunday magazine of *Jornal do Brasil* is the only one of its kind in the country, similar to *The New York Times* Sunday magazine. The paper has 14 foreign correspondents, operates a national news service and has a large, modern building in the outskirts of Rio.

Magazine publishing is vibrant and prosperous in Brazil, and unlike the United States it still has highly successful general and family magazines, in addition to a vast array of specialized ones. Production and printing are among the best in the world, showing evidence of Brazilians' flair for visual design.

Three newsmagazines stand out among many dealing with public affairs. *Veja* ("Look"), the best known, has a circulation of 300,000 and is similar in appearance and content to *Time* magazine. Nearly half its circulation is handled by subscription. *Veja* is put out by the country's largest publishing house Abril ("April") Cultural and Industrial Company, which produces other widely sold magazines, including such women's periodicals as *Capricho, Claudia* and *Manequim.* Its other titles cover a complete range of specializations, besides many comic books and musical records.

Another news magazine, *Visão,* is related to the hemispheric magazine in Spanish, *Visión.* It has 140,000 circulation and is sold amost entirely by subscription.

The third newsmagazine is *Isto E* ("This Is It"), which has rapidly gained popularity since it changed from a monthly to a weekly in 1977 and took on a more direct political character. *Isto E* is more analytical and opinionated and boasts a more creative style than the other two. Begun in 1976, it has increased its circulation to 125,000. Its editor is Mino Carta, one of the country's most notable journalists and former editor of *Jornal da Tarde.* The magazine has strongly opposed the government's policies on nuclear energy—a controversial subject.

Other popular magazines include *Manchete* ("Headline") and *O Cruzerio* ("Southern Cross"), similar to the former *Life* and *Look; Reader's Digest* in Portuguese; and *Nova,* Brazil's version of *Cosmopolitan.*

Homen ("Men") and *Playboy* are soft-core sex magazines.

Economic Framework

Brazil's economic boom of 1967-73 excited almost as much admiration abroad as the postwar West German recovery, but in the middle and late 1970s the pace of growth severely slackened. This was mostly because of international petroleum prices (Brazil is the poorest in energy production among the large Latin American countries). Inflation, earlier somewhat controlled, multiplied each year.

The government took drastic steps to cope with the problems, including a massive program of producing fuel alcohol and hydroelectricity. This, along with currency devaluation to maintain industrial exports, managed to head off collapse of economic growth, which stayed several percentage points ahead of population increase.

Thus despite deep concern among publishers that their livelihood would shrivel, the climate for mass media remained economically healthy. Television continued to grow faster than other media, although newspapers, radio and magazines all brought in good returns.

Most media are privately owned, since—aside from educational television and radio—the government has refrained from getting deeply involved in such ownership. Newspapers generally express the views of their owners, although some are mouthpieces of political parties. Some powerful owners publish a variety of types of papers to get the attention of all social classes. Even when the government's puppet political party, Arena, was the only one allowed except for a token opposition, it did not acquire a large apparatus of mass communication.

Despite the strong influence chain ownership has had on the media, competition remains active in all major cities of Brazil. Cross-channel ownership has been the chief concern of the government in this regard, and official pressure was largely responsible for the dismantling of the Assis Chateaubriand combine of newspapers and broadcast stations.

One of Brazil's curses has always been inadequate communication with its vast interior, and distribution of all types of goods remains over-concentrated on the Atlantic coast despite governmental experiments such as moving the capital inland to Brasilia and building a highway across the Amazon basin. This has had its effect on the distribution of newspapers. While the country's intricate network of airline routes can take small shipments of papers to outlying cities, the movement of large amounts by truck is effectively restricted to the coastal area.

Newsprint production in Brazil is the highest in Latin America, even surpassing that of Chile, which exports large amounts. However, Brazilian production falls far short of demand, with 40 percent being imported. This reflects the huge size of the country rather than its sophistication, as the per capita consumption of newsprint is on a par with the less developed countries of the region, ranging at slightly less than three kilograms per person, as compared with 45 in the United States.

Another anomaly exists in regard to advertising. While the placement of advertisements is booming in the major newspapers, it appeals, like the papers themselves, primarily to the upper economic classes. Furthermore, television is taking away most mass-market advertising from other media, and the thriving advertising agencies that throng the business buildings of Rio and São Paulo cater largely to TV. They also concentrate on the part of the country southward from Rio, which makes up two-thirds of the national market.

Special-interest influences count for relatively little in the modern Brazilian media, as they tend to be financially independent to a degree that they do not have to rely on outside help. However, the political interests of the owners often play a strong role, particularly in the case of the Marinhos of the daily *O Globo* and the Rede Globo broadcast network, who are avid supporters of the military regime.

The major newspapers generally are strong enough to resist any possibility of advertiser domination. In fact, the only advertisers posing a potential threat of this type are the government-owned commercial firms.

Labor relations within the media have generally been peaceful for two reasons:

1. The government has kept labor unions tightly controlled since the 1964 coup, although restrictions have begun to ease up. Because of the pressure few unions have developed much independence or initiative;

an exception is the citywide syndicate in São Paulo, which has fiercely guarded any prerogatives it could achieve.

2. Thanks to the earlier economic boom, employees of the media have been notably well paid, particularly in comparison with other developing countries. Among top executives and journalists the pay often surpasses the level found in the United States.

Brazilian media also have, as a general rule, some of the best production equipment in the world. Newspapers have been rapidly adopting offset printing and computerized typesetting and word transmission. Spacious and efficient new plants have become the rule rather than the exception.

Press Laws

The military forces that came to power in 1964 quickly let the media know they would not tolerate opposition. They almost immediately stripped hundreds of prominent politicians and some civilians of their political rights for at least 10 years. These *cassados,* as they were called, could not hold public office, could not vote or belong to political parties, and were not allowed to be quoted by the media. Several journalists were among the *cassados.*

Until the late 1960s and early 1970s the media did not feel the censor's pen. However, by the early 1970s regulations existed covering virtually all aspects of press control, in some cases with vague decrees that could be interpreted in numerous ways. The reason the new regulations came about as decrees was to avoid their having to pass through the legislative process.

Although media legislation was not subject to uniform codification, the military did, with one decree after another, try to regulate the media completely. Consequently, there were dozens of regulations on the subject, but the most significant were the Press Law, decreed in 1967, Institutional Act 5 (IA5) of 1968 and the National Security Law of 1969.

Brazil's Press Law was one of the most all-encompassing of its kind, setting standards for everything from news agencies to television. The seven areas dealt with were freedom of thought and expression, registration of mass communication enterprises, abuses of freedom of expression, the right of response, criminal procedures and responsibilities, civil responsibilities, and general matters. Although it specifically guaranteed freedom of thought through the dissemination of information without prior censorship, everyone was responsible under the law for abuses committed. In addition the law stated that there would be no toleration of propaganda for war, political or social subversion, and race or class prejudice.

This seemingly inoffensive law had a catch. Censorship could be exerted on any books, newspapers or other periodicals, national or foreign, that were offensive to morals and social customs. These included publications that offended "internal and external security"; distorted facts that provoked social alarm or disturbed public order; caused distrust or a credit rupture of the banking system, enterprises or private individuals; damaged the credit of any governmental body; or disturbed commodity or stock markets.

But the government's most often-used and most threatening tools for repression were IA5 and the National Security Law. IA5 gave the president the power to suspend the political rights of any citizen, dismiss anyone from his or her job and effectively declare someone a non-person with virtually no private or public rights. The section that made journalists especially fearful was Article 10 of the act, which canceled a person's right to habeas corpus in cases of political crimes against national security, economic and social order and the popular economy. One *cassado* said, "The IA5 itself was a coup within a coup. It was a weapon of the military to freely alter situations." Basically violators of the vague, all-encompassing Press Law were punished under the severe provisions of IA5.

Soon after the publication of this act people were arrested without charge, intimidating many journalists and editorial writers. Brazilians during this period lived with an inordinate fear of the police, knowing they could be harassed, detained or arrested at any time.

The government was also given an extraordinary amount of power via a provision in the National Security Law of 1969 that made it a crime for anyone to practice "adverse psychological warfare." It was considered a crime to disseminate doctrines or ideas incompatible with the constitution; divulge by any means of mass communication false or tendentious news, or true information cut short or distorted so as to create or attempt to create ill will among the people against the

constituted authorities; offend the honor or dignity of the president, vice president, or presidents of the Senate, Chamber of Deputies or Supreme Court; defame an institution or person who exercises public authority or office (making, for example, an accusation of wrongful arrest extremely dangerous); support collective civil disobenience; or to cause animosity among the armed forces or between them and other groups.

Violators could be fined and/or sentenced up to 20 years in prison. If a mass media was the guilty party the penalties were increased. If someone died as a result of an alleged violation, prosecutors could ask for capital punishment.

While in theory journalists were allowed to investigate public officials and criticize politicians or their policies, criminal sanctions were provided against those who violated privacy laws or maliciously slandered a person. There was much leeway for judges to decide whether journalists had committed such violations.

A blanket of controls was spread over all forms of the media, including the music industry, the theater, and other forms of entertainment. Controls took the forms of prior censorship, self-censorship, withholding of government advertising, and "recommendations" of what not to print. These "recommendations" by the censors, in effect, prohibited mentioning a wide range of items such as the stealing of radioactive materials at a nuclear power plant and even the name of the anti-government archbishop of Recife, Dom Helder Camara.

In a seemingly nationalistic attempt to avoid any form of "cultural imperialism," the Brazilian government also prohibited any foreigners or foreign corporations from owning any mass media enterprise. In fact, foreigners, including those who were naturalized, could not be partners or even hold stock in the media. The only media exempted from this regulation were enterprises that dealt with scientific, technical or artistic information. Technical or hardware supply contracts for radio or TV enterprises with foreign organizations were subject to approval by the National Council of Telecommunications. That body was created in 1962 to issue authorizations and permits for telecommunication services and to supervise the activities of government-granted concessions. It was made up of the heads of federal agencies in charge of postal, telegraph, and telex systems. Directors also came from the ministries of Interior, Education, Foreign Affairs, Industry, Trade and Defense.

As in the cases of the press and periodicals, television and radio owners had to be native Brazilians. However, to further control these enterprises the government also demanded that the directors and managers of concessionaire enterprises be Brazilians. Foreigners could, however, be granted exemptions by the government for a limited time if they were residents of Brazil. A National Code of Telecommunication was created to spell out these regulations.

Censorship

According to the constitution, the government has the right to examine any publication, entertainment, or television or radio show before it is presented to the public. Federal police are given 20 days to examine books and 48 hours for periodicals to decide whether the material is fit to be read by the public.

At the height of government censorship, about 90 censors were responsible for seeing that none of the stringent media laws were violated by Brazil's almost 3,000 newspapers, magazines and broadcast stations—and also by more than 6,000 books and about 800 films and song titles, plays, concerts and paintings.

Few newspapers were actually subjected to prior censorship, but the simple threat of it was quite effective. However, entire editions were confiscated and presses were held up for changes in material; the government also canceled advertising and private corporations decided it was no longer prudent to advertise in certain newspapers or periodicals. Economic loss forced many papers to close.

Few papers in the country suffered as strict control as the São Paulo archdiocesan newspaper, *O São Paulo,* a small (circulation around 20,000) yet influential weekly. It was subject to prior censorship as late as 1978; even passages from the Bible were on occasion deleted. Many of the censored articles were written by the main contributor and driving force behind the paper, Cardinal Archbishop Paulo Evaristo Arns, head of the largest archdiocese in the world. Through *O São Paulo,* Arns, (who has a doctorate from the Sorbonne) has consistently protested the torture of prisoners in his area and the socio-economic position of the poor in Brazil. In addition to suffering censorship (*O São Paulo* had the unusual practice of leaving its censored columns totally blank in the distributed copy of the paper), Cardinal Arns saw his radio station's license suspended in 1973.

Though censorship has been lifted from *O São Paulo,* Arns's paper always tries to push the government a little bit further with information he thinks his parishioners should know.

The experience of *Opinião,* a slightly leftist journal, is in many ways typical of what befell many of the offbeat, highly politicized weeklies. *Opinião* was started in 1972 by Fernando Gasparian, to "give dissident young people an outlet for expression other than terrorism," as he said. Like many other Brazilian industrialists, Gasparian was also concerned with protecting local and private enterprises against growing pressure from Brazilian state-run companies and foreign multinational corporations.

Soon the Rio tabloid was in disfavor with the government. One of *Opinião's* investigations dealt with the large investments of U.S. private companies in Brazil. The government quickly cracked down on this type of reporting, perhaps fearing it might discourage further foreign investment. After only two months of publication, *Opinião's* editors were told they would have to send all copy off to Brasilia before the paper could be printed. Articles were cut drastically. To survive financially and perhaps hoping to improve credibility with the government, *Opinião* began printing reprints from prestigious newspapers around the world. Many of these articles were also cut. It was not uncommon for half or more of the copy sent to Brasilia to be killed without explanation.

Once in 1973 when censors failed to return all copy by press deadline, Gasparian ordered the presses to roll. He and two of his editors were arrested and 17,000 copies of the weekly were confiscated.

But the final blow came when censors started demanding dummy editions a week prior to publication along with the usual copy. Gasparian complained vehemently that the new policy would strangle his paper, making it impossible to cover late-breaking news. He also went to court to challenge the government's use of censorship, arguing that it had never been authorized by law. Surprisingly, the federal appeals court agreed, and ordered the censors to withdraw. But President Medici overruled the court, citing IA5 in his decision.

Finally, *Opinião* and its idealistic young journalists gave in to the government's pressure. From one hour to another it was losing ads such as those of the state's Getulio Vargas Foundation. The last edition came out April 1, 1977, Gasparian vowing not to publish again until censorship was abolished.

Other newspapers of the so-called alternative or midget press faced similar harassment. These are usually political and satirical weeklies or monthlies of tabloid size and are quite popular in Brazil. The alternative publication with the largest readership is the hilarious, irreverent weekly *Pasquim* (circulation 100,000). Seventy percent of its sales, as with most of the alternate press, are on newsstands. Translated "The Lampoon," *Pasquim* has often been at odds with the government. Once the whole staff was thrown in jail, but volunteers continued publishing the papers.

Another important tabloid that has survived in spite of the government is the highly political *Movimento* (circulation 32,000). Its editor is Raimundo Pereira (formerly the editor of *Opinião),* and it publishes articulate, sophisticated articles on Brazil's social, political and economic situation. Like *Opinião,* the São Paulo-based weekly was heavily censored. In five editions in 1976 censors cut 108 articles, 70 photographs, 49 cartoons and 39 illustrations. And because censorship in Brazil was so erratic, *Movimento* was prohibited from mentioning many topics that mainstream newspapers were free to cover. Due to censorship and harassment both *Movimento* and *Pasquim* suffered financial losses and reduced readership.

One of the most celebrated cases of censorship was that imposed on the prestigious *O Estado de S. Paulo*—the only major Brazilian newspaper ever to have a censor on its ground (from 1972 to 1975). In the early 1970s, while almost all other newspapers had been intimidated to the point of practicing self-censorship—sometimes taking greater precautions than government censors—*O Estado* remained a citadel of press freedom. Despite extreme government pressure, *O Estado* continued to report on political developments, the military and the presidential succession (a prohibited topic), which was to come in 1974.

But government harassment was not new to *O Estado* in its more than one century of existence under the guidance of the Mesquita family. On January 4, 1975, when the paper celebrated its centennial of its founding its masthead read only: "95th year." That was because after 10 years of opposition from the *O Estado,* former president Vargas ousted the Mesquita family from control and directed the paper from 1940 to 1945 through a government puppet-trustee. These five years are not counted in its history.

Interestingly, *O Estado* supported the coup of 1964 and even discussed it in the newsroom with the plotters. Though the paper's editorial policy was basically conservative and favored most of the economic goals of the military, it criticized the new government's tactics. Tensions therefore increased and for a while *O Estado,* like other Brazilian newspapers, was informed by telephone what not to print. Finally in 1972 Julio Mesquita, the paper's director, told the government: "If you want to censor *O Estado,* come and do it yourself. We will not censor our newspaper." The censors arrived. Usually just the major news pages and editorials were read, but in a business with continual tight deadlines, the added step of censorship, with its attendant complications, could be maddening.

To illustrate to its readers that material was being censored, *O Estado* began printing lengthy descriptions of certain flowers and then poetry, sometimes on the front page. For a while the paper received numerous letters praising its sudden cultural interest. But the public finally caught on when *O Estado*'s sister paper, *Jornal da Tarde,* replaced deleted columns with recipes.

Then, on January 3, 1975, Editor in Chief Oliveiros Ferreira received a phone call: "Senhor Oliveiros, tonight the censors aren't coming." And in fact they did not. The paper went to press. On January 4, another call: "Senhor Oliveiros, as an homage to *O Estado de São Paulo,* which is one hundred years old today, we won't be coming any more." And he hung up.

State-Press Relations

The end of censorship in 1975 for *O Estado,* the newsweekly *Veja* and the Porto de Alegre daily *Correio do Povo* can be seen now as the beginning of a new era offering hope of life for those newspapers that had survived the rigors of government harassment. Soon the movement toward liberalization in all phases of Brazilian public life became known as the *Abertura* ("opening-up").

Various theories have been advanced as to why the *Abertura* came about. Some say President Ernesto Geisel (1974–79) was personally against censorship and the overly harsh political line that had preceded his administration. Some hold that international ridicule and criticism had pressured the military into adopting a softer strategy. (Journalists, lawyers and many international organizations such as the Inter-American Press Association had complained bitterly against controls over the media and other institutions.) Others feel that reason was strictly economic. In 1973 the so-called economic miracle had ended and the economy was in trouble. To attract foreign investment and generate more activity at home, a more liberal and open exchange of ideas and commodities was needed.

Censorship, harassment and torture by no means ended overnight. The *Abertura* might better be described as a lessening of government pressure. As President Geisel said: "It's necessary to do things slowly, in steps and securely." Journalists and newspapers still were not free to print what they pleased.

Even torture was not abolished instantly. One of the most celebrated of such cases ended with the death of journalist Vladimir Herzog. It became a cause célébre in the press, and opponents of the military and its tactics rallied in protest.

Herzog, a former BBC employee who had become news director of a São Paulo educational TV station, went to officials one morning in November 1975 in response to a call about his connection with the banned Communist party. That afternoon the 39-year-old journalist was dead. Authorities said he had hanged himself from the bars of a prison cell window, and denied his wife's request for an independent autopsy. No one publicly accused the security forces of torturing Herzog to death, but the church, the press and lawyers made it clear they did not believe the government's story. It was pointed out that the bar Herzog was hung from was actually lower than his height. Also, friends said he never used the type of cloth belt shown around his neck.

Hundreds crowded in and around São Paulo's massive Catholic cathedral, where Cardinal Arns performed a memorial service. Professors joined thousands of students in a protest strike.

Finally, in a suit filed by Herzog's wife, a federal judge in 1978 rejected the official reports and asked for a new investigation.

The next year the government was charged with his death and the doctor who performed the autopsy was indicted with criminal falsification of the autopsy report.

Nonetheless, although tales of abuse and harassment continued to crop up during the late 1970s, censorship was obviously fading and a liberalization process was oozing into the system.

Another major step to improve the political climate came on December 31, 1978, when the dangerous IA5 was revoked—lifting a great weight from Brazilians. Earlier, in June, the three remaining publications under prior political censorship—*Movimento, O São Paulo* and the Rio daily *Tribuna da Imprensa*—had been freed of this burden. In January 1979 a new National Security Law was written, abrogating the death penalty, perpetual imprisonment and banishment. The right of habeas corpus was restored for political detainees. The president was given the power (with approval of a constitutional council, of which he is chairman) to implement emergency measures where public order is gravely disturbed in specific regions. Among other things a state of emergency can be called for 90 days, and a state of siege for 180 days—the latter including the powers of detention and censorship.

The new president, João Baptista Figueiredo continued the *Abertura* process. Soon after taking office in 1979 he granted hundreds of exiled politicians total amnesty. Many have returned to Brazil. Brazilians are now talking about open municipal and gubernatorial elections in 1982 and even a general presidential election in 1984. The two-party system (one pro-government party and one in opposition) established in 1964 has now expanded to include others such as the growing Labor Party. Virtually all the major newspapers feel free from censorship these days. Said one editor: "We can finally search for the truth without fear."

Other media forms have also felt the effects of the *Abertura*. Beginning in 1979 television news broadcasts were aired without prior censorship. Bookstores began stocking numerous previously banned titles by such authors as Fidel Castro, Che Guevara, Lenin and Mao Tse-tung. Banned pieces are playing at theaters, and versions of songs previously outlawed have recently been released. Many formerly banned foreign magazines such as *Der Spiegel* and *Playboy* are being sold openly. There are still some protests from the theatrical, musical and film artists that their professions are not yet free enough. But the government has proposed several conferences with representatives from these areas to discuss the problems and offer solutions.

Several anti-communist groups, however, oppose the new *Abertura* process. Newsstands selling outspoken alternative newspapers and magazines have been victimized recently by planted bombs, attributed to these extremist conservative groups. As a result many newsstands have backed down from displaying or selling alternative publications. Midget-press news offices have also been bombed. Though vehemently criticized by the public and government, these anti-*Abertura* groups have succeeded at lowering alternative-press circulations.

There still exists much confusion and disagreement as to what controls of the media can be relaxed. Some of the smaller midget-press publications were seized in 1980, although prior censorship has totally ceased. Most of these confiscations were done so on "offensive-to-morality-and-good-manners" grounds. But this, too, is a vague term, and official uncertainty was reflected in the December 1980 resignation of the minister of social communications and the disbanding of that ministry.

Attitude Toward Foreign Media

Foreign correspondents working in Brazil, to the frustration of much of the military and the federal police, have never been as restricted as members of the domestic media. Theoretically they have to abide by the same laws as Brazilian journalists but no one would argue that they often are allowed to publish articles that would be unthinkable if written by local newsmen. Normally the worst penalties to befall a correspondent have been interrogation or the threat of legal penalties. Employees of *Time, The New York Times,* the Associated Press, and Agence France-Presse have been arrested.

Perhaps the most brutal punishment alleged to have occurred was the torture of Frederick Morris, a former Methodist missionary, who occasionally contributed articles to *Time* and the Associated Press. Morris was held 17 days in jail in Recife, where he said he was tortured with electrodes placed on various parts of his body. After the American consul intervened he was ousted from the country.

On another occasion, François Pelou, correspondent for Agence France-Presse, was expelled from Brazil on the charge that he had violated the country's national security law in connection with the kidnapping of Swiss Ambassador Enrico Bucher by Brazilian terrorists in 1970. The Foreign Ministry issued a statement that said Pelou had been asked to give information of vital importance to the investigation and had failed to do so. Police said Pelou should have contacted them as soon as he received negotiating demands from the terrorists and thus helped them with the investigation. They also maintained that Pelou's publication of the demands was illegal.

Pelou was held incommunicado for 27 hours and later his credentials as a correspondent were canceled, forcing him to leave the country. Some foreign observers saw the action as a new clampdown on correspondents, imposing on them the same controls as on Brazilian journalists, but such a concerted effort did not materialize.

Foreign magazines have also been censored by cutting articles from them or simply prohibiting their sale in the country. The Brazilian military claims that it is curbing the importation of foreign periodicals to preserve national morality or because the magazines contain subversive material. In 1973 the ban fell on 48 foreign magazines, including *Playboy* and the West German weekly *Der Spiegel.* The decree was signed by the federal police chief, General Nilo Canepa, and it stipulated that editors or publishers of national magazines and distributors of foreign periodicals would have to register the title, contents and publishing schedules. In addition, three copies of each magazine were to be sent to federal police censorship offices around the country.

Brazilian journalists have contact with various international press organizations, but by far the most important link is with the Inter-American Press Association. Largely because of the influential Mesquita family, owners of *O Estado,* and Manoel F. do Nascimento Brito, director of Rio's *Jornal do Brasil,* IAPA has vigorously protested government harassment of Brazilian journalists. Although IAPA has no formal power to curb such abuses, its complaints receive much publicity both in the United States and Latin America. Undoubtedly many arrests have been prevented and journalists' stays in jail have been shortened because IAPA stepped in.

When the movement for a "new world information order" burgeoned in UNESCO, Brazil sought to identify itself as a leader of the non-aligned nations in protest against major-power domination. However, the involvement died out quickly as the unnatural kinship of a right-wing dictatorship with socialist ideologies became apparent.

News Agencies

Brazil's principal national news agencies are the Agência Nacional in Brasilia, Agência Meridional (the oldest) in Rio and Agência Noticiosa Brastele, also in Rio. In addition, the major newspapers such as *O Estado* and *Jornal do Brasil* maintain national news networks and sell their service to papers in other cities.

The chief international agencies maintain offices in São Paulo and Rio. The fact that Brazil is the Western Hemisphere's only Portuguese-speaking country poses a problem for these agencies, and the large newspapers maintain sizable staffs of translators.

Brazilian papers have developed the unusual practice of not identifying the supplier of their foreign-agency news, even when they have paid fully for it. Editors justify this by pointing out that they rewrite the stories while translating them, thus changing them into a staff product. Nevertheless, the large papers are heavy consumers of agency material. *O Estado* subscribes to AP, UPI, Reuters, AFP, ANSA, dpa and the New York Times News Service, besides having agreements with several supplemental suppliers. *Jornal do Brasil* has a similar range. Both papers also maintain their own staffs of foreign correspondents, averaging about 15.

Electronic News Media

Of all the media, radio has been the most important form of communication because it can reach rural areas. Receivers are also cheap and even the poorest families own them. In 1979 Brazil had over 1,000 radio stations, of which one-fourth were in the state of São Paulo.

The government grants concessions to establish stations. It owns about 75 stations run by various ministries, and the Catholic church operates about 200, the major ones being Radio Vera Cruz and Nove de Julho.

The government stations are financed by subsidies from the state budget and function on the same basis and with the same status as privately owned stations.

The major stations are Radio Nacional, Globo, Eldorado, Jornal do Brasil and Mundial in Rio; and Radio Bandeirantes, Difusora, Eldorado, Cultura, Record and Excelsior in São Paulo. In 1972 the government's Radio Nacional began its international short-wave program, copied from Voice of America, and began broadcasting in six languages.

All stations are required to broadcast the government Voice of Brazil between seven and eight p.m.—commonly referred to as the "hour of silence" because of its unpopularity.

Television, begun in 1950, is still too expensive for most Brazilians but many people share sets. It is not uncommon to see dozens of people at a neighbor's house for the prime-time soap operas, which are immensely popular. The number of stations has grown to nearly 100, operated also under government concessions. Most of the stations are found along the coast, particularly in the south, but there are numerous repeater stations in the interior. TV coverage extends to approximately 12 million Brazilians.

Almost all the stations are privately owned, but the government has one station in Brasilia and another in Paraná. There are also educational stations in Rio and São Paulo.

The major networks are Rede Globo, Rede Bandeirantes and Rede Record. Rede Globo is by far the richest and most popular. It captures close to 70 percent of the TV audience even though it has been broadcasting only 15 years. Owner Roberto Marinho entered into an agreement with Time Inc. from which Rede Globo received much of its early funding and equipment. They no longer are connected. Globo was the first TV network in the world to produce and show the U.S. children's program "Sesame Street" in a foreign language. There has been much objection to the network on the grounds that with its large economic resources it should produce a better quality of content.

A major TV network, Tupi, shut down operations and declared bankruptcy in 1980. The government divided its stations into two new potential networks. Though competition is fierce the two leading candidates to operate the stations are Rio's *Jornal do Brasil* and the Sao Paulo-based Abril Corporation.

Brazil was the first South American country to introduce color, when it adopted the PAL-M system in 1972.

Political campaigning was banned from Brazil's television and radio in 1977. Many Brazilian broadcasters belong to the Brazilian Association of Radio and TV Broadcasters, or Diarios e Emissoras Associadas.

The Brazilian Telecommunications Enterprise is responsible for Brazil's participation in the International System of Communication and the International Telecommunication Satellite Organization.

Education & Training

It was not until the mid-1960s that Brazilians could learn the journalistic profession at a university. Previously, journalism was practiced mostly by amateurs, and in many instances reporters had to hold two jobs to support themselves. Thus there were few persons who prided themselves on being professionals, and lawyers and politicians used newspapers to express their opinions, while literary figures often had their short stories or chapters of their books published in the daily press. Radio and television were even later in developing professional independence, even though many of their early workers had been involved in theater or the arts.

Although universities had offered journalism courses in one form or another for more than 30 years, the first comprehensive school was not established until 1967, at the University of São Paulo. Under the military government, laws quickly defined the type of curriculum to be taught at journalism schools. They set policy for various media and established terms of salary, working hours and social security. Public relations professionals also were covered, but the rules for broadcast employees were less comprehensive.

The School of Communications and Arts at the University of São Paulo offers all types of journalism courses relating to newspaper reporting and editing, cinema, radio and television, public relations, advertising, tourism and library sciences, in addition to courses in drama, music and plastic arts. The curriculum is similar to that offered at more than 50 journalism schools elsewhere in the country.

São Paulo's school also offers advanced courses leading to master's and doctoral degrees. The first doctorates were conferred in 1973.

Brazilian journalism schools also try to get students to take courses outside their major field, such as history or political science. Most universities have special agreements with newspapers and broadcasters, allowing students to gain practical experience. The major difficulty facing Brazilian journalism schools today is finding high-quality teachers. Often working journalists are hired to teach.

Summary

After nearly two centuries of fitful professional progress and governmental repression, the Brazilian press is emerging from its most severe period of controls, which began with the military coup in 1964. The military has achieved its primarily political goal of calming and dignifying public life, and its liberalization (*Abertura*) is going forward in an orderly manner on schedule.

One of the loudest complaints from journalists is that much of the old, repressive legislation regarding media still exists even though it is not being exercised as it was in the early 1970s. However, in 1980 the government proposed a revision of the Press Law. Some journalists fear it still will be too restrictive.

Many Brazilians fear also that as the economy continues to worsen the government may find it necessary to crack down in order to get the country back on its feet. Reducing inflation and cleaning up the extensive corruption in the system were the motivations behind the 1964 coup. Both remain severe today.

The somewhat simplistic phrase Brazilian cynics use referring to the military is also applicable to many of the leaders of the "new" political movements: "They all come from the same sack of flour."

But there is tremendous hope among Brazilians that the dark days of the 1960s and early 1970s are gone forever, that the direction toward democracy will continue, and that the goal be achieved.

CHRONOLOGY

1975	Censorship of *O Estado de S. Paulo* ends.		Last censorship of newspapers lifted.
	Death of reporter Vladimir Herzog in São Paulo jail stirs nationwide protest.	**1979**	National Security Law rewritten, ending death penalty, life imprisonment and exile.
1977	*Isto E,* enterprising news magazine, founded.		*Latin American Post,* daily designed for all Latin America, founded in São Paulo.
	Opinião, widely respected opposition weekly, dies as result of government harassment.		Television censorship lifted.
1978	Institutional Act 5, most oppressive law controlling media, revoked.	**1980**	Ministry of Communications disbanded.

BIBLIOGRAPHY

Anuário Brasileiro de Media. Sao Paulo, yearly.

Camargo, Nelly, and Noya Pinto, Virgilio B. *Communication Policies in Brazil.* Paris, 1975.

De Melo, Jose Marques. *Comunicacão, Opinião, Desenvolvimento.* Petropolis, Brazil, 1971.

_____. *Subdesenvolvimento, Urbanizãcao e Comunicacao* Petropolis, Brazil, 1976.

Haring, C. H. *Empire in Brazil.* New York, 1958.

Lancelloti, Silvio. *Communications in Brazil.* Sao Paulo, n.d.

Pierce, Robert N. *Keeping the Flame.* New York, 1979.

Segismundo, Fernando. *Imprensa Brasileira.* Rio de Janeiro, 1962.

Weil, Thomas E., et al. *Area Handbook for Brazil.* Washington, D.C., 1975.

BULGARIA

by Paul Underwood

BASIC DATA

Population: 8,848,000 (1980)
Area: 111,852 sq. km. (43,186 sq. mi.)
GNP: 21.75 billion leva (US$24.8 billion)
Literacy Rate: 95%
Language(s): Bulgarian
Number of Dailies: 13
   Aggregate Circulation: 5.496 million
   Circulation per 1,000: 624
Number of Nondailies: 33
   Aggregate Circulation: 949,000
   Circulation per 1,000: 108
Number of Periodicals: 1,470

Number of Radio Stations: 5
Number of Television Stations: 8
Number of Radio Receivers: 2,624,000 (1979)
   Radio Receivers per 1,000: 298
Number of Television Sets: 1,631,427 (1979)
   Television Sets per 1,000: 185
Total Annual Newsprint Consumption: 41,400
   metric tons (1977)
   Per Capita Newsprint Consumption: 4.7 kg.
   (10.4 lb.)
Total Newspaper Ad Receipts: NA
   As % of All Ad Expenditures: NA

Background & General Characteristics

Bulgaria is one of the smaller of the Eastern European Soviet bloc states and one that does not have a common border with the Soviet Union. Nevertheless, it is generally regarded as Moscow's most loyal and most reliable ally. Its nearly nine million people occupy an area of about 43,000 square miles south of the Danube River, extending from the center of the Balkan Peninsula eastward to the Black Sea. Predominately agricultural before World War II, Bulgaria has undergone rapid industrialization, particularly since the 1960s, although farm products are still a mainstay of the economy.

The population is about 85 percent Bulgarian. The largest minority group is Turkish—about nine percent of the total. There are also small communities of Armenians, Gypsies, Greeks and Macedonians. Literacy is about 95 percent. The national language is Bulgarian, one of the Slav group, and the Cyrillic alphabet is used.

Living standards have improved markedly in recent years but still lag behind the more industrialized Soviet bloc states, particularly in consumption of consumer durables.

The area around the capital city of Sofia, near the Yugoslav border, forms the population, communication and economic center of the country, but other cities, including Plovdiv, Pleven, Pernik, Burgas and Ruse, also have become industrially and commercially important.

The Bulgarian media system is based on the Soviet model, with newspapers primarily serving an agitation and propaganda role for the ruling Communist Party and government. They have not been doing a very good job, however. Even the Party's Politburo complained in 1977 of "hackneyed style, grayness and monotony," as well as delayed distribution. *Rabotnichesko Delo* ("Workers' Cause"), the Bulgarian equivalent of Moscow's *Pravda,* has specifically been taken to task for alleged shortcomings in its propaganda efforts.

The original Bulgars were a Turkic tribe living in southern Russia in the 7th century A.D. Under pressure from other tribes they split into two groups, one of which moved west along the north shore of the Black Sea to settle near the mouth of the Danube River, on the border of the Byzantine Empire. Soon they began raiding into the empire and in 680 A.D. moved across the river in force. They defeated several armies sent by Constantinople to root them out, and in 681 a peace treaty recognized their conquest of the territory between the Danube and the foothills of the Balkan Mountains.

Their numbers could not have been large, and over the years they mingled with both the original Thracian inhabitants of the area and the Slav peoples who had moved in. By the 8th century they had forgotten their own language and customs and had become indistinguishable from the Slavs. Only their name remained.

The Bulgars spent the first two hundred years after their arrival in this new homeland fending off attacks by the Byzantines. Finally, in the 10th century, they were able to establish an empire of their own that stretched from the Black Sea to the Adriatic. This collapsed before long, and the country fell under Byzantine rule. In the 13th century another Bulgarian Empire flourished, but it in turn fell to the Serbs. Then, in the 14th century, the armies of the Turkish sultans swept over the peninsula, and Bulgaria, along with other Balkan states, fell under the Ottoman yoke, which in Bulgaria's case was not lifted until the last half of the 19th century.

The Bulgars had already made at least one great contribution to Slav culture. Back in the 9th century, two Greek Orthodox monks named Cyril and Methodius had been sent to what is now part of Czechoslovakia to convert the Slavs in that area. They invented an alphabet for those people by modifying old Greek letters and adapted the dialect of the Macedonian Slavs into a common Slav church language, into which they translated all the Orthodox holy books. Cyril and Methodius lost the conversion battle to supporters of Roman Catholicism, but their disciples found refuge in Bulgaria, which had only just accepted Orthodox Christianity. And it was from Bulgaria that this new written language went forth to become the ecclesiastical language of all Slavs under the Orthodox Church. From it developed Slavonic, the only literary language of the East Slavs until the 18th century and modern Cyrillic alphabets.

As with many of Europe's subject peoples, a nationalist revival started in Bulgaria in the 18th century. A monk named Father Paissi, who lived in the monastic colony of Mt. Athos, off the coast of Greece, wrote a book bearing the resounding title *Slavo-Bulgarian History of the Peoples, Tsars and Saints of Bulgaria and of Everything That Has Happened There*. His book was not printed until 1844 but it circulated in thousands of manuscript copies all over the country. Its effect was so powerful that a modern historian has described it as "the Gospel of the Bulgarian renewal."

Bulgarian patriots began establishing schools in which the language of instruction was Bulgarian rather than Turkish or Greek, the principal languages of administration and commerce. Grammars and dictionaries were written and a literary language evolved, derived from dialects of eastern Bulgaria.

A Bulgarian press emerged, but not inside the country; the Turks would not allow that. The first Bulgarian magazine was established in Smyrna, Turkey, in 1844 and the first newspaper in Leipzig, Germany, in 1846. Within a short time neighboring Rumania became a center of Bulgarian publishing, the products of which were smuggled across the border.

Missionary-educators from other countries, particularly the U.S., came to help. Their efforts led to the establishment of more schools and eventually to the founding of the famous Roberts College in Constantinople. The country was experiencing a rapid growth of commerce and handicrafts, accompanied by the rise of a new class of monied men and merchants. These people organized themselves into guilds for collective action, not only to further the interests of their own particular group but also to help in the national awakening effort. These guilds built schools and provided them with books in Bulgarian. Their members bought the newspapers and journals printed abroad. Bulgarian youths were sent to study in neighboring countries— Serbia, Greece and, above all, Russia.

Revolts against Turkish rule erupted again and again from 1834 on. In 1875 the people of Herzegovina, in what is now Yugoslavia, rose in revolt against the Turks. Bulgarian revolutionaries seized the opportunity and scheduled an uprising of their own on May 13, 1876. It actually started early, on May 2, in a small town in central Bulgaria. Mistakes by the rebels allowed the Turks to overwhelm villages one by one and crush the revolt. Turkish retribution was terrible. Thousands were slaughtered.

Nonetheless, this failure led directly to an independent Bulgaria, thanks in part to an American news correspondent named Januarius Aloysius MacGahan. MacGahan had made a name for himself covering stories in Europe for the *New York Herald*. Reports of

Turkish atrocities following the revolt swept over Europe and became a political issue in Britain, where the Conservative Disraeli government, fearing the spread of Russian influence, strongly supported Turkey. The London *Daily News,* a voice of the opposition Liberals, hired MacGahan to go to Bulgaria to investigate the reports. The gory details of his dispatches forced the Disraeli government to back away from its support of Turkey. The Russians declared war on Turkey in 1877, and a peace treaty the following year established Bulgaria as an autonomous province with an elected prince. The Congress of Berlin the following year greatly reduced the size of the new state but did not change its autonomous status.

MacGahan died of typhoid fever at the start of the peace negotiations but his memory lived on in the hearts of the Bulgarians, who still every year lay a wreath on his tomb in the little Ohio town of New Lexington, where he had been born.

Meanwhile, a national assembly called to organize a government for the new state adopted a very liberal constitution guaranteeing civil rights and elected a German nobleman, Alexander of Battenburg, as first prince. Troubles erupted immediately. A new Parliament had divided into liberal and conservative wings, with the liberals, who had pushed the new constitution, in the majority. Moreover, Alexander openly disapproved of the constitution.

This struggle continued for years. Partly as a result, the first newspapers printed inside the new country were strictly political organs. The liberals established *Nezavisimost* and the conservatives *Vitocha.* Other papers also came on the scene, and by 1881 nineteen, all weeklies, were being published in various parts of the country.

In that year Alexander staged a coup and ruled by decree until 1885. All liberal newspapers were suppressed. Then, in 1885, a revolt broke out in the Turkish-ruled province of Eastern Rumelia, which was inhabited by Bulgars who wanted to join the new state. Alexander succeeded in achieving this union under a plan approved by the great powers. Nevertheless, he was overthrown in a military coup and deposed.

The real winner in this situation was a young politician named Stephan Stambulov, who had organized a new party, the Nationalists. He staged a countercoup and within days was master of the country. A new prince, Ferdinand of Saxe-Colburg-Gotha,

was chosen. Stambulov became premier and was the real ruler of the country for more than a decade. Never hesitating to use force and even brutality to achieve his aims, he effectively muzzled the press through fear and strict precensorship. During his tenure in office *Svaboda,* which had been the name of one of the old exile papers, was set up as the government's official organ and became the country's first daily.

Ferdinand had been working behind the scenes all this time to enhance his own power and in 1894 he dismissed Stambulov and his supporters in the administration. The following year Stambulov was assassinated in the streets of Sofia. As a means of maintaining his rule, the prince deliberately set political leaders and groups warring with each other. Before long Bulgaria had more political parties than any other country in the Balkans. The number of papers naturally increased, although most of them were small sheets, published weekly or even less frequently. With the exception of *Svaboda,* even papers in Sofia were relatively tiny, appearing two or three times a week, with circulations of two or three thousand at best.

Ferdinand began a policy of economic development, including the building of railroads, that paid off handsomely. By 1908, the prince felt strong enough to declare the final and complete independence of the country from Turkey. More prosperous newspapers appeared, most of them still organs of the many political groups, but the turn of the century saw the establishment of the first aimed at providing broad news coverage. *Vetcherna Poschta* ("Evening Courier") began operations in 1900. It was followed in 1903 by *Dnevnik* ("Journal"). The success of these papers, whose circulations soon reached the unheard of level of 15,000, forced the political papers to improve their general coverage and add more popular features.

With the growth of the economy, advertising developed. By 1911, a total of 239 papers were being published. Most of them were weeklies, but Sofia, Plovdiv and Varna all boasted dailies, some with circulations as high as 30,000.

Beginning in 1912, Bulgaria became involved in three wars in quick succession: the First and Second Balkan Wars and World War I. In the last one it was allied with the losing German-Austro-Hungarian side and suffered severe hardships. The supply of newsprint became short. Most provincial papers, as well as some in the capital city, disappeared. Those that survived had to cut the number of pages drastically. All were subject to tight military censorship. Still, circulations increased to a peak of 50,000 copies.

At the end of the war Ferdinand was forced to abdicate in favor of his son, Boris, and a new government was formed by Alexander Stambuliski, the leader of the Agrarian Party. He pushed through a fairly comprehensive program of social reform but also dealt roughly with his opponents, shutting down the university in Sofia and abolishing press freedom.

The bureaucratic-military oligarchy that had ruled before the war had no intention of relinquishing its powers if it could help, and in 1923 Stambuliski was overthrown by an army coup. Reaction and terrorism characterized the next few years, but the combination of the throne, the army and the bureaucracy maintained the status quo until the outbreak of World War II.

The economy was in a disastrous state, and newspapers were a primary victim. Few people had money; there was no advertising to speak of. Papers were started and went out of business with monotonous regularity. In 1934 a group of army officers, disgusted with the failure of the parties to bring order, staged another coup, installing a dictatorial regime that the king gradually converted into a personal dictatorship.

Conditions did improve somewhat, and the press began to make a modest comeback. More or less stable independent and party papers began to appear again after 1935. By the outbreak of World War II a few had improved sufficiently to be taken seriously in other European capitals.

Once again Bulgaria entered a war on what was to be the losing side. In 1941 she declared war on Britain and the United States but, significantly, not on the Soviet Union. Nazi troops moved in to use the territory as a base of operations against Greece and Yugoslavia, and for the next three years the Bulgarian press was under stringent controls.

Opposition quickly developed inside the country, however. In 1942 representatives of the Communists, the Social Democrats, the left wing of the Agrarians, and an army-intellectual group known as Zveno—after a journal that had been published in Sofia—formed the Fatherland Front to coordinate opposition activities. Partisan guerrillas, mostly under Communist control, began to

strike against the Nazis. As early as 1943 the Front began to circulate news bulletins in Sofia and elsewhere throughout the country.

By 1944, with Soviet armies nearing the Balkans, the position of the Sofia regime was in jeopardy. Peace overtures were made to the Western powers, but the Soviet Union at that point declared war on Bulgaria. In September the Fatherland Front staged a successful coup and established a coalition government. This included only two Communists—one of them held the Ministry of Interior portfolio and so controlled the police.

Under this cover the Communists established a People's Militia, which terrorized the country with mass arrests, as well as People's Courts, which condemned thousands to death or imprisonment. They next moved to expel all independent-minded people from the Fatherland Front. Following a plebiscite in September 1946, the monarchy was abolished and Bulgaria proclaimed a People's Republic, under the control of the Communists and their remaining allies.

The election of a new Parliament was held in 1947 in an atmosphere of terror. Even so, opposition groups won 30 percent of the vote. It was the last time even a "tolerated" opposition was permitted. A new constitution based on the Soviet model was approved in December of that year.

The Communists had closed down all the party press, and now it was the turn of the independent papers. Publishing establishments became the property of the state and were turned over to the party or its tools to operate.

In addition to *Rabotnichesko Delo,* which had been the party's underground paper since 1927, *Otechestven Front* ("Fatherland Front") was set up ostensibly as the organ of National Council of the Front; it actually served as the voice of the government. Other papers represented the Communist youth organization, the trade union's Central Council, the army and the Communists' farm organizations.

The new constitution guaranteed freedom of speech, press and assembly, but with the usual Communist proviso that these could not be exercised contrary to the state and public order. Controls were as tight as anywhere in the Soviet bloc.

There was no relaxation of terror until after the death of Stalin in 1953. Then articles began to appear in the press urging officials to show more concern for the welfare of the masses and to encourage greater public participation. So-called "small freedoms" were extended to writers and intellectuals.

In April 1956 Vladimir Topencharov, then chairman of the Bulgarian Press Association and chief editor of *Otechestven Front,* published an article criticizing his paper's failure to carry out its proper role and accusing Party leaders of estranging themselves from the people. "Contact between the paper and its readers has been lost," he wrote. "Original ideas were replaced by repetition of what had already been said. Difficult questions were avoided....Statistics were never revealed. This meant that our press never talked of any failures, except those of minor importance."

Rabotnichesko Delo slapped back a few weeks later, attacking Topencharov on the grounds that his ideas indicated "a hidden desire to see the Party's role discontinued and have the country run by the press." And the paper made it clear the Party had not fundamentally changed any of its ideas by asserting that the main duty of the press was "the clarification of correct Party and government policy and the influencing of the labor force for the attainment of these policies."

The ferment continued throughout 1957 until the regime cracked down, purging advocates of relaxation from various unions and associations. Topencharov was demoted to deputy editor and finally fired, along with his successor as editor. Nevertheless, individual Bulgarian newsmen remained more open in discussions with Western reporters than most of their colleagues in the bloc.

Another slight easing took place in 1965 at the time of a still mysterious plot against the regime. This too was brief; by 1966 the reins were tightened again. Since then Communist-ruled Bulgaria has continued to inch forward toward a better, more efficient society, even a freer one. But the pace is slow in terms of both expectations and the progress in some of the other Eastern European states. The regime clings to the old monolithic theory of state and society by which the power of the Party should not only be maintained but even increased.

Eight of the country's 13 dailies are published in Sofia. Seven of these are distributed nationally, including the three generally considered the nation's most important: *Rabotnichesko Delo, Otechestven Front* and *Narodna Mladezh,* the main youth paper. Five others are published in the provincial centers of Plovdiv, Russe, Burgas, Varna and Blagoevrad.

Of the 33 nondailies, 10 are weeklies and the rest appear at least twice a week. The only papers not published in Bulgarian are one weekly published in Greek and another in Armenian. The Orthodox Church also has at least one paper. The only political ideology permitted is Communist.

Bulgarian newspapers are printed in full-size format but the average number of pages and number of issues per week has varied. Up till 1974 all dailies except *Rabotnichesko Delo* published six days a week with four pages an issue. The Party daily appeared every day of the week and after 1969 printed six pages an issue. In the early 1970s a few others also began to print six-page issues once or twice a week. But in February 1974 all except *Rabotnichesko Delo* not only dropped any extra pages but began appearing only five days a week, apparently as a newsprint-saving device. Later that same year even the Party paper reduced its Monday issue to four pages instead of the usual six. Early in 1976, things returned almost to the old pattern. However, *Rabotnichesko Delo* continued to print one issue a week of only four pages. Later that year it expanded its Friday issue to eight pages, the first time any daily had reached that size except on special occasions. The other dailies returned to the old six-day-week schedule.

Another change came in January 1978 when all the dailies cancelled one issue a week. *Rabotnichesko Delo* stopped appearing on Sundays, for the first time. The others went back to five-issues-a-week schedules. However, *Rabotnichesko Delo* had added more pages, printing eight twice a week, six four times a week and four only once a week. Later that same year *Otechestven Front* began printing a 12-page issue on Fridays.

Since then, *Rabotnichesko Delo* has shifted its day off from Sundays to Mondays. It and *Narodna Mladezh* are the only two that appear on Sundays; neither print special sections on that day.

Most of the dailies are published in the morning. *Otechestven Front* publishes both morning and evening editions, and Sofia has a popular evening paper called *Vecherni Novini* ("Evening News").

Sofia is the only city that has more than one daily. Even there, papers are not thought of as competing with one another. As in other Communist-ruled states, each paper is designed for a specific audience and does not struggle with others for increased circulation or advertising.

Rabotnichesko Delo has by far the largest circulation of any of the Bulgarian papers: 850,000 copies. *Otechestven Front* claims 280,000; *Narodna Mladezh* and *Trud* ("Labor"), the organ of the Central Council of Trade Unions, each have 250,000. Two agricultural papers, *Koopernativno Selo* ("Cooperative Farming"), the organ of the Ministry of Agriculture, and *Zemedelsko Zname* ("Agrarian Banner"), the organ of the captive Agrarian People's Party, claim 130,000 and 165,000 respectively. *Vecherni Novini* has 125,000. The only Sofia paper with fewer is *Narodna Armiya* ("People's Army"), the organ of the Ministry of National Defense. It claims 55,000.

None of the provincial dailies exceed 50,000. The closest is *Narodno Delo* ("People's Cause") of Varna, which lists its circulation at 49,500. *Otechestven Glas* ("Voice of the Fatherland") of Plovdiv is next, with 37,500. The others all fall between 25,000 and 37,000.

Bulgarian statistics list more than 1,700 periodicals published in the country. These apparently include a large number of very small provincial papers. (In 1974 a Party spokesman said there were 450 of these.) Most of them consist of only two pages and are published only once or twice a month.

Economic Framework

The Bulgarian economy is essentially the centrally controlled command system characteristic of the Soviet bloc, with a frosting of reform. Since 1965, reform measures have included rationalization of some categories of prices and the establishment of vertically integrated trusts, on the East German model, that have the effect of decentralizing some powers from government ministries to the trusts. Growth has been relatively impressive.

Average incomes and personal savings have increased sharply in the last two decades. Coupled with the virtual eradication of illiteracy—about 20 to 25 percent at the end of World War II—it would seem this should have brought a commensurate increase in newspaper circulations and even advertising. This has not happened, however. *Rabotnichesko Delo* has increased its circulation by about 300,000 in the last 15 years, but the others have remained about where they were or even declined. The lack of growth in circulations is probably best explained by the fact that, as the Party has admitted, the general

public finds the newspapers dull and not very useful.

As in most Communist-ruled countries, the print media are considered of primary importance, if for no other reason than their role as the principal relayer of doctrine and policy from the Party leadership to the rank and file of members. Furthermore, polls indicate people generally prefer the press as a source of information even though they don't think much of its quality.

Private ownership of any medium is forbidden by the constitution. Broadcasting is a government function. All newspapers and periodicals are owned by the Party or government or associated organizations; they also own the publishing organizations. Distribution is in the hands of the government.

Newspapers do not compete with one another. All are part of a general plan that envisions a specific audience for each publication. The papers are all deadly serious, although in recent years some of the dailies have begun to provide somewhat lighter fare in the form of cultural pieces and humorous features.

Bulgaria has its own newsprint-manufacturing enterprises but it does not supply separate statistics on production, even to the United Nations. Up to now output evidently has not been sufficient to meet demand, since some supplies have had to be imported. A new wood-processing combine in Silistra, on which construction began in 1972, was scheduled to produce as much as 60,000 tons annually by 1982.

Among the dailies, only *Vecherni Novini* gives much space to ads, and even it in the past has seldom devoted more than a quarter to a third of a page of them. This may change somewhat if the papers continue to be allowed to add pages. But under the system there is no way in which advertisers or any special interests other than the Party could influence editorial policies.

Active journalists must be members of the Party. Judging from the complaints that have been made by editors, the number of those so qualified who also are well trained is relatively small. Many of those who do meet all the standards apparently do not remain in the profession because of the low pay scales.

In 1974, an editor disclosed that the average wage for a journalist with five years' experience was 105 leva a month, the equivalent of $90.30 at the official exchange rate. Of course this does not tell the whole story since that journalist would also receive subsidized housing, medical care, etc. However, it is significant that the figure was only 25 leva above the official minimum wage.

Bulgarian newspapermen have complained for several years that the print shops and processes that produce the dailies were in urgent need of modernization. Conditions for some of the smaller papers generally are described as primitive. A proposed new head-quarters building for *Rabotnichesko Delo,* which has been talked about at least since 1977, may incorporate some of the new electronic technology that has become common in the West.

Press Laws

Both the postwar 1947 constitution and a new one promulgated in 1971 guaranteed freedom of the press, along with freedoms of speech, assembly, meetings and demonstrations. But other articles specify the sole right of the state to develop and control the media. Since the government is given this authority to develop the media, there is no need for any licensing or registration procedure.

The nation's legal codes contain the usual prohibition against the divulging of official secrets and against libel and pornography. The libel law has created some problems for journalists. There have been quite a few complaints that individuals or enterprises criticized by the media have retaliated by suing the author of the article.

There are no such things as sunshine laws. Articles in *Bulgarski Zhurnalist,* the organ of the Bulgarian Union of Journalists, have charged that the secrecy imposed by the bureaucracy with regard to production figures and other data has reached "grotesque" proportions. One described practices of this kind as "an attempt to shut the Bulgarian journalists' mouth by inappropriate means." This declaring any kind of figure a "state secret," the article continued, threatens every Bulgarian journalist, making him "a potential candidate for prison."

Censorship

Officially there is no censorship; a variety of rules add up to the same thing. For example, in general only the national news agency's account of a major international event may be printed, and it must appear verbatim. Since the agency is an arm of the government, this means that only the official view gets published. In addition, all papers must provide space for any government announcement and all Central Committee directives must be printed without alteration.

Beyond these rules, the party relies for control on the fact that all working journalists are Party members, subject to Party discipline. A misstep could mean expulsion and the loss of one's job. That sort of thing occurs, as the Topencharov case proved. In 1975 several members of the editorial staff of the country's leading literary magazine, *Septemvri,* were dismissed after the magazine had published a story about the experiences of Bulgarians who had spent 20 years in Soviet forced-labor camps.

As a general rule, any announcement of such removals merely notes that so-and-so has been dismissed for publishing articles not in line with government or party policy.

State-Press Relations

Ostensibly the media are controlled by the Committee for the Press and the Committee on Art and Culture, which are attached to the government's Council of Ministers. Actually, however, the work of these two agencies is supervised by the Department for Mass Information of the Party's Central Committee. This department takes its orders from the Party's Politboro, which dictates the broad outlines of media and propaganda policy.

No criticism of government or basic Party policy is tolerated; the Soviet Union must always be presented as the great friend and benefactor of the country. Most news is managed to some degee, although certain subjects are treated in a generally objective manner. These include such matters as environmental pollution, many aspects of science, and some social problems, such as drunkenness, a major concern in the country.

International affairs are a different matter. Ties with the Soviet Union are always seen as unshakable, while the West is the embodiment of ever-threatening bourgeois capitalism. The official attitude toward the West has improved in recent years, moving from overt hostility to limited tolerance, but calls for vigilance against the machinations of its representatives are still standard fare in Bulgarian publications.

In such a system editorial actions can have no effect on policymaking; quite the reverse is the fact. On the whole, the press has been a docile instrument of the Party and government. There have been no scandals, no papers suspended. A few have been confiscated from time to time; in 1977 one issue of *Narodna Mladezh,* the official youth paper, was seized because it had published articles by two authors under official disapproval. No journalists have been jailed for editorial failings in recent years, as far as is known. The control by the Party and the government is virtually absolute.

Attitude Toward Foreign Media

Foreign news people wishing to report on Bulgaria must apply for special visas. Accreditation is granted by the Press Department of the Foreign Ministry. No prior approval is required for the sending of copy abroad. Correspondents whose stories displease the authorities can be expelled. A more likely result would be that the offending correspondent would not receive a visa if he or she ever applied again. No official ban is announced in such cases; the applicant just never receives an answer.

No recent cases of either expulsion or visa problems have been revealed, but this may be due as much to the fact that few Western newspeople visit Bulgaria as to tolerance on the part of the regime.

Until 1977 most Western publications, except for a restricted list of books, were banned from the country. In that year the regime began to permit the importation of some Western newspapers and magazines, which could be found on sale in newsstands and in the large hotels in the cities and the resort areas along the Black Sea coast. The numbers are not large; these are for the benefit of the tourist trade, which the regime has worked hard at building up. Nevertheless, all these publications are carefully scanned for material the regime considers objectionable, and specific issues are sometimes banned. For example, in 1977 copies of the Paris newspaper *Le Monde* containing the text of the Charter 77 proclamation of Czech dissidents were seized at the airport in Sofia.

The fact that the majority of Bulgarians don't appear to have a very good opinion of the nation's press, plus the regime's constant harping on the dangers of ideological subversion from the West suggest that foreign propaganda, particularly broadcasting, must have a considerable audience inside the country. But except for some changes in their own broadcasting programming clearly designed for greater audience appeal, there is little indication of any direct impact on the media.

Critics of the press, however, have frequently charged, as a Central Committee secretary did in a 1978 report, that the inadequate performance of the media "leaves room for foreign ideological influence." Surprisingly, the deputy editor of *Rabotnichesko Delo,* in a 1978 article in the monthly *Bulgarski Zhurnalist* criticizing the quality of editorials in the Bulgarian press, suggested that Western newspapers could provide "excellent examples" of how an editorial should be written.

Some of the newly available foreign periodicals have come under fire as not "sympathetic to our way of life." But most of the published complaints about foreign propaganda have concerned either such international broadcasting organizations as Radio Free Europe or materials brought in by people traveling as tourists. An article in *Narodna Mladezh* in the fall of 1977 reported that 680 magazines and 49 novels judged pornographic, 24 Bibles and three New Testaments, as well as "several magazines full of vulgar slanders of and attacks on our country" had been seized at various border points during the current tourist season.

The Bulgarian media are supposed to have as close as possible ties to Soviet journalism, in keeping with the regime's theme of close coordination between the two countries. Officials have also suggested the encouragement of wider contacts with the West, clearly because they see propaganda possibilities in such contacts. But almost all serious ties are with the Soviet and East-bloc organizations, such as the International Union of Journalists headquartered in Prague, Czechoslovakia.

Internationally, Bulgaria is an unwavering supporter of the Soviet Union, giving unquestioning backing to all Moscow's initiatives. Their official stand supporting the 1978 UNESCO declaration was no exception.

News Agencies

Like the Soviet Union, Bulgaria has two news agencies, the Bulgarska Telegrafitscheka Agentzia (BTA) and the Sofia-Press Agency (Sofiapres). BTA is an arm of the state and the official voice of the government. Sofiapres is assigned the task of preparing and distributing propaganda abroad.

BTA is the sole source for both foreign and domestic news for the nation's media. It has correspondents in major provincial centers and abroad, although it relies heavily on Tass for both international coverage and stories about Soviet affairs. It also has exchange agreements with about 35 other foreign agencies, including Agence France-Presse, Reuters, Associated Press and United Press International. BTA correspondents are frequently sent on special assignments to cover events in other countries considered of special interest.

BTA maintains a photo service and exchanges photos with foreign agencies. In addition, it is responsible for four publicly distributed weekly bulletins. One of these is an illustrated periodical of general interest, one deals with foreign affairs, another with culture and the third with science and technology. The present BTA traces its ancestry back to 1898.

Sofiapres was founded in 1967 by the Union of Bulgarian Writers, the Journalists' Union and the Union of Bulgarian Artists. It is described as an autonomous body, but it has been assigned by the Party to prepare articles and films for foreign media. It also publishes books, magazines, journals, newspapers and pamphlets in a variety of foreign languages to be distributed to foreign audiences.

Official statistics for 1980 listed only four foreign news bureaus in Sofia and one of those represented Novesti, the Soviet equivalent of Sofiapres. The only Western agency represented was Agence France-Presse. Correspondents of other agencies and newspapers who are headquartered in nearby countries make periodic visits to Bulgaria.

Electronic News Media

Broadcasting became a state monopoly under the control of the Minister of Culture in 1948. It is now controlled by the Council of Ministers' Committee for Art and Culture under the supervision of the Party's Department of Mass Information.

Before 1977 broadcast administration was centralized in a Committee for Television and Radio. Since then the two have been split into separate legal entities subordinate to the Committee for Art and Culture. They are known simply as Bulgarian Radio and Bulgarian Television.

The radio operates three domestic channels and a foreign broadcast service. Most of the programming originates with the Sofia station, which, of course, is the principal center. However, three others—at Plovdiv, Varna and Stara Zagora—also transmit popular programs. One of the three channels operates 24 hours a day.

Beginning in the early 1970s, Bulgarian radio made a concerted effort to brighten up its programming, which has been widely criticized as dull and pompous. Reaction to the changes has been mixed, but there is no doubt authorities are making an effort to respond to listener wishes, particularly those of the youth, whose lack of interest and disaffection had become a source of concern to the regime.

Experimental television broadcasts began in 1954 and a regular service was put into operation in 1959. Color was introduced in 1977.

All broadcasting is supported by license fees and official subsidies. Advertising is permitted, but very little is carried.

Except for some radio programming in Macedonian and Turkish, virtually all broadcasting is in Bulgarian, although during the tourist season some stations in the Black Sea area broadcast news bulletins and weather information in several different languages, including English and French.

Broadcast programming, like the content of the print media, is heavily larded with propaganda. Nearly a third of the TV broadcast day is devoted to news and matters of political concern. There have been a few Western imports that don't fit the pattern, like some of the internationally famous series from the BBC. But on the whole the Bulgarians have been more reluctant than even some of their Soviet-bloc neighbors to carry Western programming. Most of what they do use comes to them via the bloc's Intervision network; some of their news film is supplied by UPI and Visnews.

The international shortwave programs are broadcast in Arabic, English, Esperanto, French, German, Greek, Italian, Serbo-Croatian, Spanish and Turkish, as well as Bulgarian. There are other programs for Bulgarians living abroad that are broadcast on medium wave.

Education & Training

The only journalism program in any Bulgarian institution of higher learning is a four-year one offered at Sofia University. The Department of Journalism there is attached to the Faculty of Philology, a situation the leadership of the Journalists' Union has been trying to change for some years. It wants a separate faculty of journalism and has repeatedly described the education and training of newcomers to the profession as inadequate. At present the department is reported to have around 900 students on all levels.

The union, the only major journalist group in the country, sponsors seminars of its own on special topics important to the news media. It represents Bulgarian journalism in relations with other countries and publishes not only *Bulgarski Zhurnalist* but also another periodical, *Pogled*. It is also responsible for setting up professional and ethical standards for newspeople.

Summary

Although Bulgaria has not experienced any sensational or dramatic upheavals, the nation has undergone profound social change. From being predominantly rural, the population has become predominantly urban. The percentage of the work force engaged in agriculture has declined from more than 80 percent in 1948 to about 30 percent. Not only has illiteracy been virtually eliminated, but the country now stands fifth in the world in terms of the ratio of university-level students to total population.

These changes have produced a younger generation whose experience differs significantly from its elders. They have also produced a society in which the need for useful information has greatly increased, as well as the pressure for greater participation in public life. The longer the Party tries to maintain its monolithic role, the greater the chance for some kind of trouble.

The saving grace may lie in the fact that the leadership can't last much longer—their average age is in the seventies. But their successors will have to do something about meeting the society's needs, one of which is a more responsive press.

CHRONOLOGY

1974	All dailies except *Rabotnichesko Delo* change frequency of issue to five days a week.
1977	Government relaxes restrictions on import of Western publications.

Narodna Mladezh banned temporarily.

1978	*Rabotnichesko Delo* stops publication on Sundays.

BIBLIOGRAPHY

Brown, J. F. *Bulgaria Under Communist Rule*. New York, 1970.

Dvornik, Francis. *The Slavs in European History and Civilization*. New Brunswick, N.J., 1962.

International Press Institute. *The Press In Authoritarian Countries*. Zurich, 1959.

Merrill, John C., Bryan, Carter R., and Alisky, Marvin. *The Foreign Press*. Baton Rouge, La., 1970.

Olson, Kenneth E. *The History Makers*. Baton Rouge, La., 1966.

Paulu, Burton. *Broadcasting in Eastern Europe*. Minneapolis, 1974.

Portal, Roger. *The Slavs: A Cultural and Historical Survey of the Slavonic Peoples*. New York, 1969.

Radio Free Europe. "Bulgarian Radio Increases Broadcast Time and Expands Program Variety." *RFE Situation Report*, January 9, 1975.

_____. "Closer Contacts Between Bulgarian and Soviet Journalists Unions." *RFE Situation Report*, January 3, 1974.

_____. "Committee on Television and Radio Reorganized." *RFE Situation Report*, May 5, 1977.

_____. "Ideological Work Discussed by Journalists." *RFE Situation Report*, July 12, 1974.

_____. "Komsomol Daily on Basket Three." *RFE Situation Report,* August 25, 1977.

_____. "More Complaints About the Information Media." *RFE Situation Report,* May 16, 1974.

_____. "New CC Department for Mass Information Media." *RFE Situation Report,* August 22, 1974.

_____. "A New Look for Rabotnichesko Delo and Other Sofia Dailies." *RFE Situation Report,* February 13, 1978.

_____. "Politburo Directive Calls for Improvement in Rabotnichesko Delo." *RFE Situation Report,* February 9, 1977.

_____. "Provincial Press Discussed." *RFE Situation Report,* October 31, 1974.

_____. "Rabotnichesko Delo Joins in Newsprint Saving Measures." *RFE Situation Report,* November 28, 1974.

_____. "Readers' Reactions to Journalism and Journalists." *RFE Situation Report,* June 15, 1973.

_____. "Sofia Dailies to Help Save Newsprint." *RFE Situation Report,* October 31, 1974.

Schopflin, George, ed. *The Soviet Union and Eastern Europe.* New York, 1970.

Selucky, Radislav. *Economic Reforms in Eastern Europe.* New York, 1972.

Stavrianos, L. S. *The Balkans Since 1453.* New York, 1966.

CANADA

by Carman Cumming, Peter Johansen, W. H. Kesterton, Allan Morantz and Robert Rupert

BASIC DATA

Population: 23,671,000 (est., 1979)
Area: 9,977,000 sq. km. (3,851,122 sq. mi.)
GNP: $260,305,000,000 (US$222,821,080,000) (est., 1979)
Literacy Rate: NA
Language(s): English, French
Number of Dailies: 117
   Aggregate Circulation: 5,203,538
   Circulation per 1,000: 220
Number of Nondailies: 1,090
   Aggregate Circulation: 10,096,706
   Circulation per 1,000: 421
Number of Periodicals: 878 (1977)

Number of Radio Stations: 1,207
Number of Television Stations: 1,100
Number of Radio Receivers: 7,437,000
   Radio Receivers per 1,000: 314 (est.)
Number of Television Sets: 7,388,000
   Television Sets per 1,000: 312 (est.)
Total Annual Newsprint Consumption: 970,870 metric tons (1979)
   Per Capita Newsprint Consumption: 41 kg. (90.2 lb) (1979)
Total Newspaper Ad Receipts: $1,002,000,000 (US$857,712,000) (est., 1979)
As % of All Ad Expenditures: 30.7

Background & General Characteristics

When the first Canadian newspaper was published in Halifax, Nova Scotia in 1752, Britain's North American colonies were ruled in an authoritarian manner. As a result, the early press supported the government, a condition no doubt encouraged by the printing patronage provided most printers of the day. But as the public voiced increasing discontent with their non-democratic rulers, the 19th-century press openly joined the debate. There were vigorously partisan journals on both the reformist and conservative sides; others attempted a moderate course. All this initiated a freedom from government interference that continues, with some notable exceptions, to this day.

The Canadian nation has a strong preference for private enterprise, tempered by public ownership in those areas thought to be poorly serviced by profit-motivated entrepreneurs. Transportation and communications have traditionally been seen as an important part of the public sector—the Canadian National Railway, Air Canada, provincially owned telephone systems and so on. A notable instance of this public-ownership course occurred in 1932; the government thought broadcasting ought to be at least partly under public ownership, so that sparsely populated regions would be serviced and programming would not be dictated entirely by what was popular and cheap. The Canadian Broadcasting Corporation continues today as an agency funded principally by government appropriations, amounting in 1979-80 to $477 million (US$408 million).

But for the most part, the media are privately owned. This is true without exception of Canada's daily-newspaper industry. As such, dailies reflect the widespread business trend toward an increasingly oligopolistic pattern of ownership. The range of editorial viewpoint of Canada's 117 privately owned dailies is more limited than might otherwise be the case. Unlike the European press, with its wide range of political views, the Canadian daily typically and traditionally supports one of the two largest political parties, although the traditions withered in the elections of the 1970s. Only sporadically has there been endorsement of the smaller parties of the left and right, and some newspapers in smaller communities consistently avoid endorsing any party or candidate during election campaigns.

By contrast, the news columns are not usually partisan, but rather reflect the "objective" style that emerged in the United States in the late 19th century; this is also the reporting strategy adopted by Canada's principal wire services, Canadian Press and United Press Canada. There is an increasing use of interpretative reporting, but this is characterized more by a disdain for all the principal political parties than by support for any one of them. In only one recent case—that of the short-lived Montreal daily *Le Jour*—was there a consistent political coloration of the sort familiar to European readers. *Le Jour,* predictably, was not published primarily to turn a profit; it was an organ of the Quebec separatist party, the Parti Quebecois.

Private ownership combines with yet another reality of Canadian life, the generally small population base of the country, to diminish the amount of competition in much of Canadian commerce. The press is not immune. In mid-1980, 99 communities had daily newspapers. Of these, 14 had more than one, but in most cases there was no genuine competition. In five cities the two papers are published by the same company, and in three other communities, "competition" is between English and French dailies, which effectively means monopolies in the respective linguistic markets. There is genuine English-language competition only in St. John's, Toronto, Edmonton and Calgary. French-language competition prevails in Montreal and Quebec City.

The small population base also means that, by world standards, newspapers have fairly small circulations. Although at an average 36 pages, the typical daily is large enough, especially considering its average newsstand price of just 23 (US20) cents, well over half the dailies have circulations under 25,000. Only one can claim an average daily circulation in excess of 500,000 (see accompanying tables). Small-circulation bases translate into a lack of resources to cover both the immediate community and the broader nation and world.

Nonetheless, some newspapers are fairly sizable and a few are looked to for their leadership role. In Anglophone Canada, the elite newspaper is the Toronto *Globe and Mail,* which styles itself "Canada's national newspaper." Although it tends to display a Toronto focus inconsistent with its broader pretentions, the daily launched satellite editions, printed in Calgary and Montreal, in late 1980; it is expected these editions will give greater attention to non-Toronto news. The *Globe*'s counterpart in Francophone Canada, Montreal's *Le Devoir* (circulation 42,482), attempts to emulate the European tradition of a literary newspaper more given to analysis and comment than to factual reportage. The *Toronto Star,* by virtue of its large circulation and its superiority as a mass-appeal journal, is also influential.

A distinguished political scientist, Donald Smiley, suggests three other dominant factors that have an impact on Canada's media. He terms these the "three axes of Canadian federalism"—the relationships between the French and English cultures, between Canada and the United States, and among the provinces and regions (especially the heartland provinces of Ontario and Quebec against the others).

Consider first Canada's biculturalism. According to the 1971 census, 45 percent of the population is of British origin, 29 percent of French and the remainder of other descents, none of which is very large. This cultural cleavage is reinforced by a geographical one—most Francophones live in the province of Quebec. (Significant settlements in parts

Number of Newspapers By Circulation Groups	
Below 10,000	43
10,000 to 25,000	32
25,000 to 50,000	18
50,000 to 100,000	8
100,000 to 500,000	15
Over 500,000	1

Largest Newspapers By Circulation*	
Toronto Star	506,525
Le Journal de Montreal	315,335
Globe and Mail (Toronto)	284,702
Toronto Sun	248,863
Vancouver Sun	234,270
Montreal Gazette	219,932
La Presse (Montreal)	189,914
Edmonton Journal	179,290
Hamilton Spectator	147,996
Winnipeg Free Press	145,196

*Average daily circulation, calculated over 6 or 7 days/week. Based on August 1980 *Canadian Advertising Rates and Data*.
NOTE: The total circulation represents 47.5 percent of daily circulation in Canada.

of Ontario and New Brunswick are greatly outnumbered by Anglophones.) Without this geographical concentration, it is unlikely French Canada would have persisted as a cultural entity.

Accordingly Canada's media system is in effect, two systems, split along the linguistic lines that divide the country in other important ways. Studies show that the French- and English-language media view the world in quite different ways. Both French-language dailies and the Canadian Press wire service in French give much greater attention to domestic news, but this occurs almost entirely because of a preoccupation with Quebec's regional and provincial affairs. A similar emphasis has been found in the French-language news of CBC television, although it is thought that the ongoing expansion of the network to areas outside Quebec will force it to adopt a more cosmopolitan flavor, and there is some evidence to suggest this has occurred. But when the same stories do get covered by Francophone and Anglophone media, they are reported and commented upon from different perspectives. And English and French journalists appear to have differing notions of what their role should be, the Francophones being substantially more likely to adopt a guiding rather than informing function.

The second principal factor of the three mentioned above is the influence of the United States. Two-thirds of the Canadian people live within 100 miles of the border. This permits an easy trans-border flow of ideas and culture, resulting from—and resulting in—considerable parallel evolution in social, economic, political and judicial structures. There are substantial linkages in economic ownership, trade, labor unions, government bodies, and so on.

Of course this produces a considerable interest in and exposure to U.S. media. Television signals spill over the border. Some 70 percent of Canadians have access to at least one U.S. channel, and about three-quarters of English Canadians' television time is spent watching U.S. programs. Hollywood films dominate the Canadian cinemas. About 95 percent of feature films in Canada originate outside the country, and of the film rental payments sent abroad, all but five percent go to the United States. American magazines outsell Canadian ones, and U.S. book imports make up two-thirds of total book sales.

Even in daily newspapers, up to 18 percent of all news is about the United States—this represents up to half of all foreign news printed—and most news of other foreign countries originates with the American wire services. It is impossible to study the press of Canada without taking the U.S. presence into account.

Of course, not all prominent features of the American press have migrated north. In Canada there is no strong tradition of a Sunday newspaper; the Saturday paper fulfills that function, containing as it does such features as extended news commentary, rotogravures and comics. (At one time, the only Sunday paper in English-speaking Canada was the *Victoria Colonist,* and that British Columbia publication did not produce a Monday edition.) Recently, several Sunday papers have been introduced. They range from the Toronto competitors—the *Sun* and the *Star*—to such smaller enterprises as the Kamloops, B.C. *Daily Sentinel* (circulation 10,590). Morning papers are also more American than Canadian, although the comparatively healthy condition of the U.S. morning dailies has had some impact on Canadian publishers; the *Ottawa Journal,* for example, switched to mornings in September 1979, a year before its death, in its struggle for profitability. Montreal's *La Presse,* long an afternoon paper, went to morning publication in late 1980.

The third factor influencing Canadian media—regionalism—has recently taken on increasing visibility, as Canada's ten provinces assert their right to wrestle additional constitutional power from Ottawa. One political scientist, Richard Simeon, predicts that the country is moving toward a situation in which the provinces will be the dominant governments. The recent rise in regional self-assertion is closely linked to the postwar demands for greater autonomy by Quebec, but it is also grounded in real differences in the provinces' historical development, religious and ethnic composition, urbanization, economic development and resources.

In terms of the media, the common regional complaint is that content is directed by an Ontario-centered elite working in Toronto, the principal English-speaking city. The regions especially fault the CBC and the nationally distributed consumer magazines. Critics say these media offer little material originating in the hinterlands. A recent study of the CBC's English TV Network, for instance, reports that only one-tenth of prime-time programming was produced outside Toronto. Moreover, when the regions *are* depicted, they are frequently shown in a predictably stereotyped way. As newspaper columnist Don McGillivray wrote after a trip to Nova Scotia:

> More than one Nova Scotian described to me the stock opening of the typical Canadian Broadcasting Corporation program on their province. "You see a broken-down old fisherman rowing along in a dory. Then slowly he passes a factory that has been shut down. That's how they see our province in Upper Canada."

These complaints echo the concerns of developing countries in recent debates about international communication flow.

Certainly the media infrastructures are more highly developed in the elite provinces. The headquarters of the two principal chains, for example, are both located in Toronto; so too are the news operation of the English-language radio and television networks and the national news agency, Canadian Press. Among dailies the province of Ontario has 45 of the country's 117. The next largest number, the 19 dailies of British Columbia, is less than half that. Other provinces have dailies in a descending scale: Quebec, 11; Alberta, nine; Manitoba, eight; Nova Scotia, seven; New Brunswick, six; Saskatchewan, five; Newfoundland and Prince Edward Island, three each; Yukon territory, one. (All but 15, incidentally, are of broadsheet size.) The distribution of dailies reflects the population and urbanization of the various provinces, of course, but it also skews the resources on which Canadian Press relies for much of its news copy.

On the nondaily newspaper level, there are almost 1,100 publications. While some of these, like *Native Press* of Yellowknife, Northwest Territories, cater to special readerships, the vast majority are general-circulation newspapers aimed for either small-town readers or the subcommunities of large urban centers. Of the 15 dailies that have appeared since 1965, 10 were originally weeklies.

Much of the ethnic press in Canada is published on a weekly basis. There are only three foreign-language dailies: the Italian *Corriere Canadese* in Toronto (circulation 24,849), and the *Chinese Express* (Toronto, circulation not available) and *Chinese Times* (Vancouver, circulation 3,131). A recent listing of ethnic newspapers in *Canadian Advertising Rates & Data* shows a total of 36 different ethnic-group publications. Some

groups, such as the Danes, publish only one periodical; others publish more, the largest number being 24 for the Italian community

At least one study, done by Douglas Baer, has shown that newspaper readership in Canada generally follows the pattern found in U.S. studies. That is, reading is heaviest among males, older people and those with high incomes; it peaks with those who have one or two years of post-secondary education; and it is significantly greater among Anglophones than Francophones. A daily average of 40 minutes is spent reading a newspaper.

Economic Framework

With the important exception of the CBC, Canadian media are financially supported by advertising revenue and subscription fees. For most, the former is far more significant. The average daily newspaper, for example, relies on advertising for about 70 percent of its revenue, and ads make up 56 percent of its total pages. Total advertising expenditures in 1979 were an estimated $3,007,600,000 (US$2,574,505,600), of which newspapers, broadcasting and periodicals accounted for 74.5 percent.

This reliance on advertising creates two practical problems for the media. First, it ties their income rather closely to the economy in general, so that economic downturns are generally paralleled by sluggish spending by advertisers. Recessions affect new construction, for instance, and this in turn affects real estate listings, a valuable source of newspaper advertising. Second, the overflow of American mass media into Canada reduces the volume of advertisements that multinational corporations feel they have to place in Canadian media. On a per capita basis, therefore, advertisers in Canada spend only 70 percent of what they spend in the United States. Together, these two factors mean that the Canadian media must endure cyclical swings in income, and even at the best of times do not match the potential of U.S. counterparts.

This gives rise to great competition for the scarce resources that are available. While the daily papers trebled their net ad revenue between 1969 and 1979 (from $269 (US$230) million to $836 (US$716) million, according to figures prepared by the Canadian Daily Newspaper Publishers Association), their overall share of the total ad revenues has slipped from 29.2 percent to 27.8 percent. The chief beneficiaries are radio and especially television, whose combined share increased from 23.5 to 28.0 percent. Also benefiting were the periodicals, with a smaller jump from 11.3 to 13.2 percent of total advertising expenditures. But the most seriously disadvantaged medium must surely be the weekly press. In the decade of the 1970s, their circulation more than doubled, while that of the dailies increased by a mere nine percent. But weeklies' slice of the total advertising pie slipped by 0.3 percent.

Partly because of the comparative loss of both dailies and weeklies, the newspaper industry has not been able to increase its advertising rates as quickly as broadcasters have. Statistics reported by the Radio Bureau of Canada (1980) show that between 1974 and 1979 TV rates jumped 58 percent and radio rates 55 percent; by contrast, newspaper rates increased only 39 percent.

From the point of view of circulation growth, however, the position of newspapers vis-a-vis their media competitors is not bad. In 13 major markets, television ratings—as measured by the average quarter-hour adult audience in prime time—actually decreased in the period 1974-79 by four percent. Consumer magazines increased their circulation by the same percentage. But daily circulation climbed by seven percent (Radio Bureau of Canada, 1980). Considering all dailies, circulation grew by 15 percent in the decade 1969-79, and the number of copies per 1,000 population edged up from 224 to 229. The one sour note: the number of copies per 100 households fell from 85 to 72.

The search for both readers and advertisers is especially keen in competitive newspaper markets. If the rivals have not tried to attract specialized markets, the smaller paper almost inevitably finds it impossible to survive. In the national capital, for example, the *Ottawa Journal* died in 1980 because its smaller circulation made it less attractive to advertisers than the larger *Citizen*. Based on their transient line rates, a full-page ad in the *Journal* cost roughly 40 percent more per thousand readers than in the *Citizen*.

Hand in hand with the consolidation of newspapers in communities has come the equally worrisome trend of ownership concentration, which has proceeded in the past decade at an alarming pace. In a 1970 report, the Senate Committee on Mass Media noted that 49 dailies, representing 44.7 percent of the national circulation at the time, were in the hands of three principal chains: Southam,

FP, and Thomson. In early 1980 the Thomson organization purchased the eight newspapers of the FP group. By August 1980 it had sold one (the Calgary *Herald,* now renamed the *Sun*), merged two (the Victoria *Times* and *Colonist*) and ceased publishing a fourth (the *Ottawa Journal*). On the day the *Journal*'s closing was announced, the Southam group closed its money-losing *Winnipeg Tribune,* and the two groups reorganized joint business ventures in Vancouver and Montreal. At this point, just two firms shared 48 percent of the total daily circulation. Eight smaller chains, all regionally concentrated, held an additional 28 percent.

Compounding the problem is the fact that both the giants have extensive holdings elsewhere. Southam has indirect broadcasting interests, through its shares in Selkirk Communications, although these operate in no communities where it publishes dailies. Southam also publishes more than 70 trade journals and owns 50 trade shows. More problematic is the Thomson organization, whose major interests include oil and gas, insurance, travel and trucking. In the case of both chains, the potential exists that the news can be slanted to protect the parent organization's other interests. In the Thomson empire, a special worry is its 75 percent interest in Hudson Bay Company, a giant department store chain; retail advertising is especially important to newspaper revenues, and some observers foresee Thomson's retailing division unfairly placing its ads to bolster Thomson newspapers.

The newspaper shufflings of August 1980 led the federal government to establish a royal commission to investigate the newspaper industry; its report is expected by mid-1981. At the same time, another government body is seeking to learn whether the Thomson and Southam groups are guilty of creating monopolies to the public's detriment, and whether they conspired to unduly lessen competition. Both are criminal offenses. Most observers do not expect this investigation will lead to convictions, however. They point to a previous case involving K. C. Irving, who owned all five English-language dailies in New Brunswick. In 1971 he was charged with creating a monopoly, because his papers constituted 97 percent of the total daily circulation in the province. Moreover, Irving held extensive interests in such areas as oil and gas, pulp and paper, and transportation. A lower-court conviction was overturned in 1976 by the Supreme Court of Canada, which stated that mere control did not prove that Irving acted to the public detriment, a condition difficult to demonstrate in a craft like journalism. The Irving family continues to own the five newspapers.

Not all aspects of media ownership are negative, of course. One benefit seems to be that large organizations are better able to cope with recent technological changes, which by now are widely disseminated in Canada. Almost all dailies, for example, are printed offset; only about a dozen still employ letterpress technology. The *Globe and Mail* began satellite transmission of facsimile pages from Toronto to Calgary and Montreal in late 1980. The *Edmonton Journal* is using lasers to cut printing plates. Almost every large- and medium-size paper now makes use of computers for both editorial and business purposes. The greater assets and borrowing capacity of chains makes acquisition of such technology more manageable. The chain can also monitor experiments at one daily for the benefit of its other properties, as Southam is doing with the Edmonton paper's laser plate-making.

Another benefit of large enterprises is their ability to withstand pressure from special interests or advertisers. Neo-Marxist writers such as Wallace Clement point to instances of advertiser influence on news content, but these examples tend to be dated. A survey of daily managing editors suggests little influence from publishers on stories affecting major advertisers, with the percentage responding "never" higher among those owned by chains—60 percent as opposed to 37.5 percent among the independents. Nonetheless, as the Senate Report on Mass Media has noted, advertisers do not have to manipulate the media, "because broadly speaking the advertisers, their agencies, and the media owners are all the same kind of people, doing the same kind of thing, within the same kind of private-enterprise rationale."

Lack of competition within communities has led, perhaps, to a greater uniformity of newspapers in Canada than in Britain or the United States. Most appeal to the mass of readers, rather than to either an elite or yellow-journalism audience. This arises from most communities having only one newspaper, which attempts to appeal to a broad cross-section of the population. The *Globe and Mail* is the only elite daily in English; in French, Montreal's *Le Devoir* is the recognized intellectual paper. The French-language system has a proportionately higher number of sensationalist papers. In English-speaking Canada the *Toronto Sun* is the most notable in the sensationalist category, but it is tame compared to the most notorious of the British tabloids. The *Sun* has recently introduced similar dailies in the Alberta cities of Edmonton and Calgary.

Labor relations in Canada's press must be seen in the wider North American context: the same issues and trends that determine the economics of newspaper publishing in the United States exist in Canada. Almost all organized employees in the industry are members of international unions with headquarters—and most decision-making—in the United States. Only in the province of Quebec, with its predominantly French-speaking population, are there substantive differences in the labor-relations environment.

In all, there are about 22,000 employees in the Canadian newspaper industry, and about one-third (almost all of them on dailies) are union members. French-language journalists are members of the Fédération nationale des communications, an affiliate of the Confédération des syndicats nationaux, a militant union central. In the rest of Canada the newspaper industry has been organized by international unions based in the United States. As with almost every other international union in Canada, the press unions have made concessions to the nationalist yearnings of some members. In the early seventies the Newspaper Guild—formerly called the American Newspaper Guild—established a "Canadian region" with a director and at least two seats for Canadian representatives on its 15-member International Executive Board. The Canadian section of the union has autonomy in determining social and political policy for its members.

The Guild, which began the 1970s with about 3,400 members, represented about 4,300 reporters and other nontechnical employees by 1980. That figure has fluctuated; in the late 1970s the Guild lost about 630 members due to the various mergers and closings. Although the first Guild contract had been signed with *Toronto Star* in 1949, success with Canada's wire service, the Canadian Press, had to wait much longer. After an acrimonious failure to win its first Canadian Press contract in 1950, a foothold was finally gained after a strike at the end of 1976. A major problem for the Wire Service Guild, however, is the absence of a strong union security clause—a problem imported from the United States, where the Guild has repeatedly failed in its efforts to negotiate union security with Associated Press and United Press International.

The International Typographical Union, which appeared to be headed into a merger with the Guild in the early eighties, represented 7,300 Canadian workers in 1970 and 7,800 members by the end of that decade. While technological change has hit hard at the ITU, the union has been able to offset the loss partially by organizing workers in Quebec and also in some non-technical departments. The International Printing and Graphic Communications Union has 10,800 members in Canada, while the Graphic Arts International Union claims a membership of 13,000.

During the past decade the major labor-relations issues in the Canadian newspaper industry have been technological change and "manning." These issues are so basic, inspiring the survival instinct of both labor and management, as to have caused strikes that have been long, bitter, and sometimes fatal.

Ever since newspaper publishers decided to embrace the technology available to them for newsrooms and pressrooms, the unions, particularly those representing tradesmen, perceived themselves as being under a well orchestrated attack. For the most part, they have been able to maintain a tenuous solidarity. The most prominent, if not the biggest, strike (the union claimed it was a lockout) concerning technological change occurred at the Ottawa Journal in 1976 when the International Typographical Union local walked out. Four years later the newspaper folded. While many of the technology-related problems were eventually resolved in collective bargaining, it was with considerable difficulty and acrimony and long after the dispute had taken its toll.

At the end of the decade, as technological change came to be more of an established fact and less of an issue, "manning" took its place. This was initiated by management. Publishers felt manning levels in the pressroom were too high and too rigid, leading to inefficient operations. The switch from hot-metal production to cold type meant fewer press operators were needed. The union thought this unacceptable and fought to maintain existing levels. The most costly strike over manning, at least in the long term, was at the Montreal Star. The strike lasted eight months, cost the owners, the FP Publications chain, $7 (US$5.99) million, and more significantly, led directly to the previously viable Star's death seven months later. In the end, contracts favorable to the unions were signed. The rival Gazette, now the sole surviving English-language daily in Montreal, published throughout the long strike and promptly agreed to the same terms. Star management would later admit to having been mistaken in trying to weather such a lengthy strike. The manning issue and job security were also at the center of an eight-month strike at Pacific Press, affecting both the Vancouver Sun and the Province.

Confrontation in English-speaking Canada generally involved the mechanical newspaper unions. But in Quebec the most bitter disputes occurred in the journalists' union, where the issue was "reporter power." While it has not been of paramount concern in the rest of Canada, giving reporters and copy editors greater control in a newspaper's editorial operation has been a central issue for the French-speaking reporter. Three major strikes occurred at French-language newspapers over this question. The August 1977 walkout at Quebec City's Le Soleil lasted ten months; the strikes beginning that October at Montreal's La Presse and Montreal Matin both lasted seven months. Montreal Matin ceased publishing shortly afterwards. These strikes had some success. Reporters and copy editors, especially at Le Soleil, now have an effective voice in determining editorial content and appointments. Unionized journalists at Le Devoir form the majority of the paper's news committee, which meets weekly to discuss performance and plan news coverage. "Reporter power" and concentration of newspaper ownership remain major issues in French-speaking Quebec.

The contrasting preoccupations of the French- and English-language newspaper employee illustrate the gulf (which also exists at the grassroots level) in ideological orientation between the two. The Newspaper Guild supports the notion of "reporter power" as does the Fédération nationale des communications. But while the Francophone newspaper employee has actively pursued this goal, the vast majority of Anglophones may accept the notion on paper but have not given it high priority in collective bargaining. "Reporter power" at Anglophone newspapers is generally limited to "ethics committees," which insure, for example, that advertisements are clearly identified, and to clauses giving the journalists the right to withdraw their bylines.

Press Laws

Canada's press operates under a libertarian system, free of licensing in the Miltonian *Areopagitica* sense, subject to little prior *publishing* restraint, and unencumbered by draconian censorship provisions. Some provinces do require newspapers to register with an appropriate government department, but that requirement is a precondition of certain libel defense pleadings available to newspapers rather than a device of government to impose control on the print media. Although in 1807 John Ryan was made to post a £200 bond to guarantee the docility of the pioneer *Royal Gazette and Newfoundland Advertiser*, today's newspapers are not so circumscribed. The Newspaper Stamp Acts are only a memory of a distant colonial past.

The press of Canada is comparable to that of the United States in its freedom from governmental shackles. But no First Amendment infuses Canadian media with the positive spirit of liberty that manifests itself in the American no-malice libel defense or in journalists' demands for shield laws or investigation of government under the Freedom of Information Act. The Canadian Bill of Rights, passed in 1960, states that "[i]t is hereby recognized and declared that in Canada there have existed and shall continue to exist without discrimination by reason of race, national origin, color, religion or sex, the following human rights and fundamental freedoms, namely...(f) freedom of the press." This provision is not enshrined in the Constitution. It is a legislative enactment of the federal Parliament that can be repealed by the federal Parliament. It is limited in application and lacks punitive sanctions. As of 1980 the only decision determined by the Bill of Rights had been a verdict in a case unconnected with the press.

Canada's hope for a press that is responsible as well as free depends on the journalists' sense of what is true, fair and socially desirable, under due process of law. The laws with special application to the press are those dealing with contempt of court, civil defamation, criminal libel, obscenity, copyright, privacy and government secrecy.

Contempt laws do not apply exclusively to the press, of course, but because of the nature of their calling journalists are more likely to suffer contempt sanctions than are most of their fellow citizens. Except in the matter of photography in the courtroom or of a reporter's refusal to divulge sources, the media are less likely to be convicted of contempt "in the face of the court" than of *constructive* contempt—contempt "not in the face of the court." Offenses of both kinds may involve scandalizing the court or prejudicing a fair trial. The journalist may commit the crime of prejudicing by reporting false "facts" about a case, publishing facts ruled inadmissible on a *voir dire* hearing or for other reasons, and publishing comment on *sub judice* matter.

Criminal punishments for contempt may be applied when legal prohibitions are violated. Section 470 of the Criminal Code forbids, during a preliminary inquiry, publication of a confession or even of the fact that a confession has been made. Under Section 467, *if the defendant so requests,* the court will forbid publication of most of the information concerning a preliminary inquiry except the charge, the name of the accused and what might be called the dramatis personae of the inquiry.

Canada has no shield laws to protect journalists from having to disclose sources or information to courts, parliamentary bodies or properly constituted committees of inquiry. On the other hand, although there has been agitation for such a law, no law forbids publication of the names of persons charged with crimes, as the law does in Sweden. What is permitted is contemporaneous, fair and accurate reports of open court proceedings and evidence given in open court. Trial by newspaper and other media is unknown in Canada, where no cases comparable to the Bruno Richard Hauptmann and Sheppard trials have occurred.

In recent times criminal law has rarely been resorted to in cases of defamation. More often plaintiffs have sued under civil-law enactments, relying on provincial statutes and common law for the decisions reached. Alberta, Manitoba, New Brunswick, Nova Scotia and Prince Edward Island find it unnecessary to distinguish between libel and slander; they have defamation acts. British Columbia, Saskatchewan and Ontario have libel and slander acts, but as of July 1980 Saskatchewan was undertaking a wholesale revision of its act, which was to be renamed "Defamation Act." Newfoundland, more reliant on common law, has a Slander Act only. Quebec has a Newspaper Registration Act and a Press Act. Manitoba has a Newspaper Act in addition to its Defamation Act.

In Canada the three requirements to maintain a libel action are: proof of *publication* of the words complained of; *defamation* (that is, whether those words are capable of defamatory meaning); and *identification* of the alleged libelee. The three main defenses available to defendant journalists are pleas of truth, fair comment and privilege. In Canada's nine common-law provinces, *proved* truth provides an absolute defense against a libel claim, but in Quebec a plea of truth must be accompanied by a plea of public benefit. Except in fair, accurate and contemporaneous reportage of *trials,* journalists do not enjoy absolute privilege (that is, privilege that cannot be destroyed by malice on the part of the press) but only *qualified* privilege (that is, privilege that such malice does destroy).

Apologies and retractions may mitigate damages assessed against a journalist, provided certain conditions are fulfilled. The libelous statement must not impute a criminal conviction or criminal offense, and must not be motivated by malice. Apologies and retractions must meet statutory requirements of prominence and timing. If the court finds such an apology acceptable it will award only *special* damages and not *general* damages.

Criminal libel, provided for by the federally enacted Criminal Code, includes defamatory, seditious and blasphemous libel. Defamatory libel charges are answerable by the same defenses of truth, fair comment, and privilege as are civil libel claims, but, as with Quebec civil libel, a plea of truth must, to succeed, be accompanied by proof of public benefit. The code provides severer penalties for defamatory libel when the charge is known to be false, and for defamatory libel used as an extortion tool, than for defamatory libel not so qualified.

Seditious-libel law, rarely invoked in peacetime, is designed to punish advocacy of the use of force, without the authority of law, to accomplish governmental change in Canada. But an accompanying proviso is that the section does not forbid debate and argument designed to improve governance and achieve constitutional or other political reform.

Blasphemous-libel law, dormant in Canada since the 1930s, is defined only in terms of *intention* to publish blasphemy, and blasphemy is not defined in the Criminal Code. The law presumably relies on the popular definition contemporaneous with the trial that considers the charge. This section of the code also has an ameliorating provision, to prevent the punitive section from inhibiting religious discussion carried on in good faith and in temperate language. In recent years it has become more difficult to prove seditious or blasphemous libel.

For a long time obscenity was defined thus by the common law, or Hicklin test: "whether the tendency of the matter charged as obscenity is to deprave and corrupt those whose minds are open to such immoral influences and into whose hands a publication of this sort may fall." In 1959, however, a new section of the Criminal Code was enacted. It labeled as obscene any publication whose dominant trait is the undue exploitation of sex or crime, horror, cruelty or violence. Intended by its authors to supplement the Hicklin test, the Criminal Code definition has, through court decisions, replaced it. It is notable that obscenity convictions in Canada have not been imposed for factual writing so that daily and weekly newspapers and family magazines have been virtually untouched by the law.

Canadian copyright is determined by Canada's Copyright Act, a 1921 instrument that has long been slated for thoroughgoing revision. Additionally, Canada adheres to the Rome Revision of the Berne or International Copyright Convention and in 1963 it became a signatory of the Geneva or Universal Copyright Convention. A copyright agreement with the United States is significant for the reciprocal arrangements it embodies. Of importance to the journalist is the fact that news is not copyrightable, but that the form of the news report and the language with which that news is clothed do enjoy copyright. In conformity with Berne Convention conditions, except for serial stories and tales, articles from one newspaper may be freely reproduced by other newspapers—unless such borrowing has been expressly forbidden —although the sources of such articles must be indicated.

In 1974 Canada's federal Parliament enacted a Protection of Privacy Act, criminal legislation almost exclusively concerned with electronic surveillance. British Columbia, Manitoba and Saskatchewan also have privacy acts, but the legislation has produced little case law and none press related.

Unlike the United States, Canada has an Official Secrets Act. Section 4 of the Act makes it a crime to either communicate or receive information to which a government official or civil servant has become privy by virtue of his or her office, a provision that inhibits the press in its investigative function. There have been few prosecutions and fewer convictions under the act. No journalists have been prosecuted, although in 1978 editor Peter Worthington and publisher Douglas Creighton were charged after the *Toronto Sun* published a secret federal police document related to Soviet espionage in Canada. However, a preliminary inquiry did not establish a *prima facie* case against the accused and the charges were not pursued.

As of mid-1980 Canada had no Freedom of Information Act, although throughout the 1970s increasing efforts were made to enact such legislation. A 1979 Freedom of Information Bill died with the short-lived Conservative government that sponsored it. During a long period of active discussion leading to the aborted legislation, attention focused on two issues: what areas should be properly exempted from disclosure; and whether, to compel disclosure, the American device of judicial review should be chosen in preference to an agency responsible to Parliament. In the summer of 1980 the newly returned Liberal government, previously unsympathetic to the judicial review device, introduced a bill that would also rely on judicial review as a means of compelling disclosure.

Censorship

No bodies with true censorship powers restrain the press of Canada. This does not mean that censorship is unknown: in the words of one observer, Don C. Pember, "In many cases punishment after publication imposes effective censorship on freedom of expression." This retroactive effect is to be noted in what the Criminal Code calls "Offences Tending To Corrupt Public Morals" (the obscenity laws) and in national security (the seditious-libel law and Official Secrets Act).

Prior restraint is applied less often to Canadian journalism to prohibit publication than to deny access to publishable material. It is expected that a future Freedom of Information Act will reduce censorship of this kind. It is to be noted, however, that the Freedom of Information Act will be ineffective unless it is matched by such measures as a liberalizing of the Official Secrets Act and by the repeal of a subsection of the

Federal Court Act that asserts the principle of ministerial privilege in withholding certain kinds of evidence in court.

In the 1970s the Quebec, Ontario, Alberta and Windsor (Ontario) Press Councils came into being. These are not *censor*ship bodies, however, their power being to *censure*. They may reprimand but not impose punitive sanctions or otherwise punish journals or reporters who offend against what the councils adjudge to be the dictates of ethical and responsible journalism.

State-Press Relations

Canadian newspapers, serving a small and scattered population, were slower than those in some other Western countries to escape political influence. As late as the early 20th century firm links remained between many newspapers and supporting political parties. Informal alliances were detectable even at mid-century. In recent decades, though, the principle of media independence has become fixed. The general stance of government was set out by then Secretary of State John Roberts at a 1978 UNESCO conference:

Canadians do not believe that either politicians or public servants should have anything to do or say in the management, direction or correction of the media. Quite the contrary. In their view, only a free press can guarantee that the decisions of the state power are in harmony with the wishes of the people.

Despite this stance, Canadian governments have maintained a strong interest in some media, particularly radio, television and films. The interest traditionally has been linked with pressure to strengthen national culture in the face of potential American domination. Also, governments in recent years have developed increasingly sophisticated mechanisms to influence the media through public relations and advertising programs. In a sense, growing independence at the reporting level has been matched by government efforts to influence or circumvent an often critical press.

Historically, in the absence of a constitutional guarantee of press freedom, journalistic independence from government has been defined by two major cases in which governments sought to circumscribe the press. Both occurred at the provincial level and began in the 1930s. The most striking of the two was the Alberta Press Act, introduced in 1937 by a Social Credit government locked in conflict with financial and newspaper interests in the province. The act, passed by the legislature but never actually put into effect, would have given the government extraordinary power over the press. Newspapers would have been required to publish corrections whenever the government decided there had been an erroneous or incomplete report. The government could also demand that a newspaper disclose a source of information. And, if a paper contravened these regulations, the government would have had the right to close it down, to ban a particular reporter from writing, or even to prohibit publication of information from a particular source.

The legislation was struck down when the Supreme Court of Canada, backed by the Judicial Committee of the Privy Council of England, declared it beyond provincial jurisdiction. The decision then came to be seen as a guarantor of press independence, although some have argued that it is at best a flawed instrument, since it hinges not on the question of press freedom but on the issue of jurisdiction, and in that area builds on doubtful premises.

The second notable case is that of the so-called Quebec Padlock Law, also passed in 1937 and remaining in effect for two decades. Directed against subversion, the law in practice allowed the provincial attorney general to be both prosecutor and judge in suppressing anyone considered to be a Communist. The act also made it illegal to publish "any newspaper, periodical, pamphlet, circular, document, or writing whatsoever propagating or tending to propagate communism or bolshevism." The act was invoked repeatedly, and on one occasion in 1948 was used to close two newspapers. Like the Alberta Press Act, the Padlock Law was eventually ruled by the Supreme Court to be beyond provincial powers. But again the decision turned on jurisdictional questions rather than the essential issues of individual or press liberty.

A third and more recent case raising questions of political interference centered on a radical Vancouver newspaper called *Georgia Straight*. In the late 1960s the paper experienced a series of conflicts that led, among other things, to suspension of its municipal distributer's license and to an unusual conviction for defamatory libel. It has been argued that the episode dramatized serious gaps in press freedom, and underscored the need for firmer guarantees of free expression.

While these cases were all localized, a much wider and more difficult chapter in government-media relations came in 1970 with the so-called October Crisis, in which terrorists of the Front de liberation du Quebec (FLQ) kidnapped and later killed a Quebec cabinet minister, and also kidnapped a British diplomat. The federal government reacted to the crisis by invoking the War Measures Act, suspending civil liberties in some areas and setting up a mechanism for the jailing without charge of more than 400 suspected Quebec separatists, some of them journalists. Censorship provisions of the act were not invoked, but a form of censorship was implied, since the act provided a jail term of up to five years for anyone who communicated a statement on behalf of the terrorists. Shortly after the act was invoked the federal justice minister stated that a "fair and accurate" report of an FLQ communiqué, or a fair comment on it, would not violate the act. This left open the question of what constituted fair comment, and throughout the crisis there was confusion and ambiguity about media vulnerability to prosecution, with some consequent overreaction. The media were said by some to have given in to government pressure to support a repressive measure.

After the crisis, instances of alleged harassment of newsmen were reported, in a document entitled *Dossier Z*, by the Federation professionnelle des journalistes du Quebec. The document reported, for instance, that the editors of a community newspaper in Hull had been jailed for 13 days after printing the FLQ manifesto. It also quoted journalist Pierre Pascau of Montreal radio station CKLM as saying he had held back from broadcasting parts of an FLQ communiqué following a direct warning by the Quebec justice minister.

While the October crisis amounted to no more than a minor incident in comparison to terrorist problems in many countries, it indicated the extent of the government's ability to curb the press, even in peacetime. In addition, Parliament and the provincial legislatures retain the right to censure a newspaper or journalist. The power is rarely exercised, although in one 1975 case the Montreal *Gazette* was called before a parliamentary committee to defend a report alleging premature disclosure of budget secrets. The committee found the *Gazette*'s allegations unfounded, and said the report "fell short of the standards to be expected of a newspaper," but it took no action beyond this rebuke.

In general, no federal department in Canada has an exclusive role in dealing with the media. In recent years, in both Conservative and Liberal governments, a single minister has held the post of secretary of state and minister of communications, and has reported to Parliament for a variety of media or cultural agencies such as the Canadian Broadcasting Corporation, the National Film Board and the Canadian Film Development Corporation. However, instances of direct interference are exceptions. More common, and perhaps more notable, is a pattern of generalized government influence on media, often exercised in the name of cultural protectionism and with the media's willing compliance. Postal rates, for instance, have traditionally favored newspapers and magazines. Other measures have been aimed at requiring Canadian ownership of Canadian media, or at ensuring Canadian advertising expenditures go to Canadian media. In recent years, government advertising has become a crucial factor for some publications. Grants from government support many other publications or quasi-publications. (Even the national news agency, the Canadian Press, accepted direct government subsidies for several years after its formation in 1917.) This kind of support has led to instances of pressure, in the form of threats to cut off grants or advertising. In 1975, for instance, the federal finance minister cancelled an ad his department had placed in a short-lived Quebec separatist daily, Le Jour, on the grounds that the government should not support a paper that "proposes the destruction of Canada." The action was condemned by papers across the country, but the minister held to his decision. In 1980 the left-wing magazine Canadian Dimension charged the government with a "crude attempt at official censorship" when the revenue department withdrew its tax status as a charitable institution on the grounds that its aims were not educational, but rather to "promote a particular political ideology." The magazine sued to have the tax status reinstated and the case was still before the courts in late 1980.

Canadian magazines have had a heavier dose of protectionism than newspapers, on the assumption that unprotected publications would not be able to compete with American rivals able to print Canadian editions at relatively small cost. This problem was studied intensively by a 1960-61 federal commission, which recommended—among other things—tax measures designed to discourage Canadian companies from advertising in American periodicals aimed at the Canadian market. This proposal was implemented in 1965, although the Canadian editions of Time and Reader's Digest were in effect ruled to be Canadian publications and were therefore excluded. Five years later, another federal study showed the two magazines were taking in more than half of the country's consumer magazine advertising. Another five years of controversy led to legislation in 1976 specifying that publications to be considered Canadian must be 75 percent Canadian owned and must contain at least 80 percent Canadian content. Thereafter Reader's Digest converted its Canadian edition to Canadian ownership; Time chose to close its Canadian edition, although it still prints and solicits advertising in Canada.

Governmental and other public bodies have also from time to time shown concern about the high level of ownership concentration in the newspaper industry, although little action has resulted. One of the most intensive studies of Canada's mass media, undertaken in the late 1960s by the Special Senate Committee on Mass Media, focused particularly on this problem. Its prime recommendation, never adopted, called on the government to set up a press ownership review board, to represent the public interest in future takeovers and mergers. The report also called for creation of a Publications Development Loan Fund, to encourage and support alternate publications, and this recommendation was also ignored. Another recommendation for creation of press councils apparently had some effect: such councils are now operating in Quebec, Ontario, and Alberta.

Since the election in Quebec of a separatist Parti Quebecois government in 1976, considerable attention has been given to proposals for making the Quebec media more responsive to the French-language milieu. The provincial government has pressed for jurisdiction over broadcasting and has talked of encouraging creation of a Quebec news agency to replace the French-language service of the Canadian Press. There have also been proposals for imposing a residency requirement on managers of Quebec newspapers, and for creation of a board to rule on transfers of newspaper ownership. None of these ideas had been implemented at the start of the 1980s, however.

The tension between the Quebec and federal governments has also led to extensive advertising campaigns by both in support of their opposing views. In 1980 total federal advertising alone was estimated at $40 to $50 million (US$34 to US$42 million), and a significant part of this was allocated either to "national unity" advertising or to "lifestyles" ads, advocating more healthful living. Budgets for government information work also rose rapidly in the 1960s and early 1970s, although they tapered off toward the end of the decade amid continuing criticism that information services lacked coordination and coherent policy objectives. At the start of the 1980s, however, federal information services were much larger but still suffering from the same problems. The whole apparatus numbered about 1,000 information officers, all but 250 in Ottawa, working for some 65 departments or agencies. The annual cost of the federal program was officially estimated at $119 (US$101) million, although unofficial estimates, including sectors not solely concerned with information, put the total in the area of $250 (US$212) million. Renewed efforts were also being made to coordinate information activities under the Privy Council, and to bring federal advertising programs under a cabinet committee on information.

As in other Western societies, complaints are regularly aired in the media about government attempts to manipulate or manage them. These complaints emerge most often at election time and often focus on the staging of media events, or the well-timed release of favorable information. However, one observer has commented that while journalists complain about managed news, they could hardly exist without it: "The press gets really angry only when there is not enough managed news—as for example when the Prime Minister declines to hold a news conference." Traditionally, Canadian journalists have had ready access to politicians, although the contacts have become more formal in recent years, despite protests from the media. In 1976, for instance, the Ottawa press corps reacted angrily when the prime minister ended informal corridor confrontations with reporters and moved instead to a system of formal news conferences.

While scholars and journalists have written extensively about political influence on the media, very little attention has been given in the Canadian context to media influence on government. What has been written tends to be speculative and to downplay media influence. For instance, Geoffrey Stevens, a leading columnist, argued in 1978 that the media's influence "does not extend to causing the government to follow a course that it does not want to follow or that it feels the public is not ready for it to follow." However, others said that Stevens had probably underrated the power of the media to create a climate of political and public opinion in which the government and Opposition must operate.

Attitude Toward Foreign Media

There is a tension in Canada between the belief in the libertarian ideal of an unrestricted press and the fear of dominance by the American media. This concern runs through the numerous government studies that have been conducted on the media since 1929, and was voiced as recently as 1980, by Communications Minister Francis Fox:

> We are and will remain committed to the freest possible flow of information. But...[a] balance is required in terms of protecting legitimate sovereign rights on the one hand, and ensuring the free flow of information on the other. Many of the communications issues which impact upon Canada-United States relations fall somewhere in between. The criterion should be whether a developed country such as Canada, or for that matter a developing country, has managed in its communications policies to balance competing interests in a responsible and internationally exemplary way.

It is this tension which most affects the Canadian government's attitudes toward foreign media.

The libertarian ideal, for example, is seen in the government's stance on the recent UNESCO debates on a new world information order. Officials aligned themselves with the U.S. view that government restrictions on news flow are intolerable. This belief is implemented in the treatment of foreign correspondents covering Canadian affairs; for example, there are no special accreditation procedures: those employed by recognized media are routinely granted working visas. Similarly, there is no regulation requiring approval of cables, and foreign correspondents have not been jailed. At present, 28 foreign correspondents are stationed in Canada—mainly in Ottawa, Toronto and Montreal. They represent both the communist and non-communist media—such as *Pravda*, Hsinhua News Agency and Prensa Latina on the one hand, and Agence France-Presse, the Press Trust of India and the *Los Angeles Times* on the other. Some journalists whose primary posting is in the United States are also responsible for covering Canadian news and they make periodic trips north. The federal government invites about 800 opinion makers each year to take specially arranged tours of Canada; the majority of these are journalists.

The free-flow ideal is also seen in the contacts Canadian journalists maintain internationally. Either as individuals or organizations, Canadian newsmen have links with a diversity of press organizations, such as the International Press Institute, the International Institute of Communications, and the Commonwealth Association of Broadcasters. Under the auspices of various international bodies, Canadian media—the CBC in particular—provide training and technical assistance to developing countries.

Be that as it may, however, the government has instituted provisions affecting foreign ownership and content of Canadian media. Newspapers have no such legislation, probably because only one daily, the *Red Deer Advocate* in Alberta, is controlled by foreign (in this case, British) interests. In broadcasting, however, the government has declared that 80 percent of the voting shares of any enterprise must be owned by Canadians, and that all directors must be citizens of Canada. This regulation was promulgated in 1970. At that time, 48 American and British companies, such as the Columbia Broadcasting System and Marconi, were obliged to divest themselves of Canadian holdings.

Foreign content is also restricted in the broadcast media. In AM radio, 30 percent of all records played must meet two of these criteria: the instrumentation and/or lyrics are performed principally by Canadians; the music is composed and the lyrics are written by Canadians; the performance is recorded in Canada. In television, all stations must broadcast 60 percent Canadian content between six a.m. and midnight, calculated on an annual basis. In addition, domestic fare between six p.m. and midnight must total 60 percent on the CBC's owned and operated stations, and 50 percent on private stations. Although the regulations have generally been observed, private TV programmers have slated their domestic programs in the very early and very late evening periods, when viewing is low. As a result, more than 70 percent of all programming actually seen by English-speaking viewers is of foreign, mainly American, origin. This is not likely to change soon. Public opinion on American

cultural influence has not been especially vexed. Moreover, broadcasters have incentive to make the most of imported shows; an American program costs a network about $8,000 per half hour, but returns five times that figure in advertising revenue.

In the magazine field, American periodicals sell well: *National Geographic* distributes about 700,000 copies an issue; *Family Circle,* 500,000; *Playboy* and the *National Enquirer,* 300,000 each. It is clear there is no restriction on their importation—except for the legal provisions that permit Customs officers to ban terrorist or extraordinarily pornographic material. But there is indirect support for magazines that are "Canadian," as defined by ownership and content, through tax writeoff provisions for advertisers.

News Agencies

Canada's leading news agency, the Canadian Press, has traditionally enjoyed a near monopoly in the country. A cooperative owned by most of the country's daily papers, CP operates essentially as a news exchange, similar in pattern to the Associated Press, with member papers obligated to supply news of their areas for dissemination to other members. The agency also serves as a mechanism for international news exchange, through agreements with AP, Reuters and Agence France-Presse. Through a broadcast subsidiary, Broadcast News, it services some 340 private radio and TV stations, while a second subsidiary supplies news to the publicly owned Canadian Broadcasting Corporation. Canadian Press was founded in 1917, as an amalgamation of regional agencies, and for seven years accepted parliamentary grants to cover the cost of bridging the distance between regions. Since then, the agency has been independent of government.

In recent years CP's preeminent position has been eroded by the growth of United Press Canada, formed in 1979 as a successor to United Press International of Canada and the earlier British United Press. CP remains, however, the basic infrastructure for news exchange in Canada. With some 450 employees, more than half of them editorial staff members, the agency operates on an annual budget of some $20 (US$17) million (compared with $2.3 (US$1.9) million for UPC). It has full French and English services, plus pictures, stock market news, and features. CP's head office is in Toronto, while the French-language service is based in Montreal, and it also has bureaus in Vancouver, Edmonton, Winnipeg, Ottawa, Quebec City and Halifax, plus individual correspondents in several other cities. Abroad, there are small CP bureaus in London, New York and Washington; it has frequently been criticized for overdependence on foreign agencies for its international news.

Within Canada, however, CP has expanded from a simple news exchange to the point where it generates a good part of its own news. This is especially true of Ottawa, where a staff of 30 reporters and editors covers governmental and parliamentary affairs. During the 1970s the agency also engaged in an extensive technological changeover, moving from a system based on teletypesetters to computerized news-handling. A significant part of the CP membership now receives news by what is called CP Datafile—computer-to-computer delivery of full reports at 1,200 words a minute. On a major news day, the circuit serving the larger papers delivers some 200 columns of news, or about 160,000 words. While CP does not disclose detailed rate information, members pay for the service according to a complex formula based mainly on circulation.

In contrast to the CP co-operative, United Press Canada is owned by United Press International and the Toronto *Sun* Publishing Company, with the latter holding majority control. UPC describes itself as totally separate and independent from UPI, although it works closely with the international agency in delivering its news and in providing it with coverage of Canada. The agency has 38 staff members assigned to the head office in Toronto and bureaus in Vancouver, Edmonton, Winnipeg, Ottawa, Montreal, Quebec City and Halifax. Like CP, UPC operates a computerized service, with transmission handled through UPI's computer center in Dallas, Texas. National news and sports services are delivered both at conventional speeds and at 1,200 words per minute for direct delivery to newspaper computers, or on high-speed teleprinter.

In addition to the two basic wire services and a British Columbia regional wire UPC operates a telephoto picture network, a Spanish-language wire, two UPI broadcast news wires, the UPI financial wire and CATV television news wire. UPC's three basic Canadian news wires carry some 240,000 words per day to 35 print subscribers with a total circulation of more than 20 million per week.

Broadcast subscribers include the CBC and some 40 independent radio and television stations. Rates are negotiated individually with each client and, as with CP, are not made public.

Traditionally, coverage of Canada by foreign news services has depended heavily on Canadian services, especially CP. (AP, for instance, has no staff members in Canada.) Some small and local news services also supply foreign customers, including Canadian American News Service, Canada World News and Ward News Service. Only a handful of foreign newspapers and magazines are represented in Ottawa.

Studies on news flow in and out of Canada tend to reflect the national preoccupation with U.S. relations. Complaints are regularly raised (and studies supply supporting evidence) that Canada depends on U.S. sources for its foreign news, and that foreign agencies give Canada relatively little attention. One examination of American news reporting on Canada concluded that Americans receive "rather poor quality" coverage considering the social, political and economic ties (and problems) between the two countries. This was attributed primarily to the lack of American reporters, especially for the wire services, working in Canada. Another study made by Joseph Scanlon, documented the heavy attention Canadian papers give to U.S. news: content analysis of 30 Canadian dailies showed Canadian papers carried more items about the role of the United States in world affairs than they did about Canada's role. The study also showed that, in terms of items printed, the Canadian papers were more concerned about local matters in the United States than about affairs in their own section of Canada.

Electronic News Media

In theory, and for the most part in practice, Canadian governments do not interfere in the news or public affairs content of broadcasting stations, even though they have a large role in shaping broadcasting structures. The broadcast media are regulated by the Canadian Radio-television and Telecommunications Commission (CRTC), set up by the federal Broadcasting Act of 1968 to "regulate and supervise" all aspects of the national broadcasting system. The act defines the supervisory role in very general terms, saying, for instance, that programming should provide "reasonable, balanced opportunity for the expression of differing views" and "should be of high standard, using predominantly Canadian creative and other resources."

While the commission's mandate is thus rather vague, and while the commissioners' appointment by government leaves room for vulnerability to pressure, in practice both government and commission give allegiance to the credo that neither should interfere directly with content. Historically, there have been occasional controversies over covert or overt government interference, notably before the 1960s and particularly in connection with the publicly owned Canadian Broadcasting Corporation and its predecessor, the Canadian Radio-Broadcasting Commission. The CBC was especially open to government influence during its weak early days in the 1930s. During the Second World War, the network became almost an arm of government. In the 1950s, when the CBC dominated national broadcasting on both radio and television, government interference was alleged in several cases. In 1959 there were charges, never proven, that then Prime Minister John Diefenbaker had intervened to bring about cancellation of a public affairs radio show, "Preview Commentary," that had carried a good deal of criticism of government. (The program was reinstated following a mass resignation of CBC producers.) In the same year a parliamentary committee heard firm evidence that a cabinet minister had, following a protest from the French government, put pressure on the CBC to ban interviews with Algerian rebels.

Such incidents seemed to disappear in the late 1960s as broadcast organs, including the CBC, developed an independent and even adversary tone. That trend was best shown by the CBC-TV program "This Hour Has Seven Days," a radical, probing and extremely popular public affairs show that regularly embarrassed the government. It was eventually curbed by the CBC management, which accused the programmers of irresponsibility, but there were no charges of government interference.

The October crisis of 1970 over FLQ terrorism was particularly traumatic to the broadcast media, in that some apparently felt more vulnerable than newspapers to restrictions of the anti-terrorist War Measures Act. Some English-language private broadcasters were especially timid. For instance, Montreal radio station CJAD suspended staff member Rod Dewar for criticizing the War Measures Act on the air, and broadcast a statement, cited in *Content* magazine, revealing of the mood among broadcasters:

> Events of recent weeks have changed the climate of our country, our province and our city. The federal government...has imposed legislation which temporarily deprives us of many freedoms we have taken for granted.

> Along with all communications media, CJAD has lost some of its freedom to air divergent opinions. CJAD recognizes the need for such sweeping legislation and endorses it wholeheartedly. To the best of our ability we will no longer air certain minority views while the present crisis exists...

While the CJAD position was widely criticized, especially by journalists, it probably reflected a pattern of overreaction to the War Measures Act. CBC postponed showing of two controversial documentaries, one on Hollywood film people blacklisted during the McCarthy era and another called *Legacy of Lenin,* because of "concern and anxiety" in the country. But broadcasters were not alone in their attitude. The Quebec Film Censorship Board, after a complaint from the Montreal mayor, banned a sex movie, "taking into account the troubled times through which the people of Quebec are now passing."

In the wake of the crisis, there were complaints that broadcasters had both slavishly upheld the authoritarian War Measures Act and that they had exaggerated the threat of the terrorists. One consequence was a series of consultations between the Canadian Association of Broadcasters and The Canadian Association of Police Chiefs on handling of news in a crisis. This led to a document described in some reports as an agreement or set of guidelines giving police greater control over news during a crisis. (The broadcasters insisted it was only a "working document" rather than an agreement.) The guidelines stated that police and media were "partners in the fight against lawlessness," that police "must have the right to make the decision on release of news for publication," and that any abuse of confidence between police and media "should be a matter for serious concern on both sides, including when necessary disciplinary action against those employees who knowingly or consistently fail to operate within the principles and ethics agreed to by the national joint committee."

Radio-TV Distribution by Household (May 1979)		
Total number of households 7,558,000		
Number of households with	Radio	TV
0 sets	121,000	170,000
1 set	2,182,000	4,706,000
2 sets (TV 2-plus)	2,417,000	2,683,000
3 sets	1,452,000	—
4-plus sets	1,385,000	—
Total with sets	7,437,000	7,388,000

Interestingly, the chairman of the broadcast regulatory agency, the CRTC, was among those who criticized broadcasters for seeming to surrender a measure of independence. He sent a message to broadcasters saying that the independent dissemination of news was a primary responsibility, and that any restraint in this area would be a matter of most serious concern. The commission also called a public hearing on the case, and afterward issued a statement saying it assumed individual broadcasters would take no steps to implement the guidelines. The project was quickly abandoned.

Quebec separatism was the focus of another issue in government interference in 1977, a year after election of a Parti Quebecois government in Quebec. Following a number of complaints from federal cabinet ministers about separatist influence in Radio-Canada, the French-language section of CBC, the government formally asked the CRTC to undertake an investigation. The resulting report was somewhat amorphous (it criticized all media for failing to contribute to national unity), but among journalists a widespread view developed that the government had succeeded in putting indirect pressure on Radio-Canada to curb news and information favorable to Quebec separatism.

In the same year another government study, this one by a royal commission appointed by the province of Ontario, raised broader questions of interference with media independence. The commission was headed by Judy LaMarsh, a former federal secretary of state, and was set up to examine violence on TV, but its report went far beyond that, to condemn the commercial values of broadcasting and suggest far-reaching solutions. Among other things, the report called for: (1) a radical restructuring of the broadcasting industry to create a common delivery system programmed in complementary rather than competitive patterns; (2) a Freedom of Information Act that would make communicators vulnerable to penalties for "promulgating information that leads to incitement of crime and violence"; (3) a national news council to hear public complaints; (4) an enforceable code of journalism ethics, and (5) a national media ombudsman with power to order retractions. Predictably, journalistic reaction to the report was hostile, and the Ontario government made no move to implement even those parts that might have fallen under provincial jurisdiction.

While the LaMarsh report probably reflected public unhappiness with the quality of broadcasting, the CRTC has not characteristically taken a strongly interventionist line. A landmark case illustrating this arose from a 1967 CBC-TV program called "Air of Death," which had been attacked as biased and irresponsible in its description of industrial air pollution. The CRTC held a hearing in 1969 to discuss not just "Air of Death" program but the whole question of balance in programming, and thereafter produced a very restrained report. While it again cautioned broadcasters to seek a reasonable balance, it defended their right to take editorial stands, and concluded: "The quality of Canadian broadcasting will not be improved by over-regulation or restrictive interpretations of the broadcasting act."

Despite this view, the commission in the past decade has occasionally censured individual stations for failure to provide balanced programming. In a 1970 case, the Halifax radio station CHNS was rebuked for its handling of an editorial criticism of a local charity fund-raising organization called Miles for Millions. The commission said the station should have advised the organization of the criticism in advance and delivered a copy of the script to organizers before asking them to reply.

A Montreal radio station, CFCF, was similarly criticized in 1977 after it mounted a campaign against Quebec's Official Languages Act. The commission found the station had, over a two-week period, devoted at least a quarter of its broadcasting time to the issue, and that viewpoints hostile to the act had predominated in a ratio of 30 to one. In its statement on the case, the commission spoke of the public's right to receive programming that dealt fairly and adequately with public issues, and added that "the denial of this right by a broadcaster...is a form of censorship." The greater the controversy, it said, the greater the need for balance.

In both cases, however, the commission took no action beyond public wrist-slapping. The same approach was taken in a different kind of case in 1971, when the commission criticized radio stations in Kitchener, Ontario, for agreeing to join a blackout of news about an impending downtown development.

The commission has thus developed a somewhat ambiguous stance that is generally respectful of media independence, but emerges occasionally as a mildly paternalistic influence that prods broadcasters either toward caution and responsibility or toward more aggressive reporting. And while it is sometimes vulnerable to government pressure, as in the Radio-Canada case, it also may be seen at times to act as a buffer between government and broadcasters.

Percentage Distribution of TV programs	
(1976—prime time—CTV and English CBC combined, 7–11 p.m.)	
Sports	2.5 hours
Variety/music/game	8 hours
Sitcom	9 hours
Action/adventure	10 hours
Western	nil
Melodrama	2 hours
Feature film/made for TV	2 hours
"Family" drama	1.5 hours
News/current affairs/ doc.	6 hours
Anthology/drama	2 hours
Serious music/special interest	1.5 hours

Education & Training

University training in journalism began in Canada at the end of the Second World War, when programs were started by Carleton University in Ottawa and the University of Western Ontario in London. A major program was also developed at Ryerson Institute of Technology (now Ryerson Polytechnical Institute) during the 1950s, but the three remained the only full-scale programs until the late 1970s, when programs were begun at King's College in Halifax (associated with Dalhousie University), at Concordia University in Montreal and at the University of Regina in Saskatchewan. In addition, a variety of journalism and communications courses are offered at community colleges across the country.

During the 1970s both Carleton and West-
ern introduced graduate programs, differing in format. Western ended its undergraduate training and introduced a 12-month preprofessional master's degree program, while Carleton initiated a program of two academic years (or one year for journalism graduates or experienced professionals).

The two major industry associations are the Canadian Association of Broadcasters and the Canadian Daily Newspaper Publishers Association. The latter has five divisions: Administration, Advertising, Circulation, Editorial and Production. Other organizations include the Centre for Investigative Journalism, the Agricultural Press Association of Canada, Canadian Business Press, Canadian Periodical Publishers' Association, Magazines Canada (The Magazine Association of Canada), the Periodical Press Association, and the Radio-Television News Directors Association.

Summary

Canadian journalism in the early 1980s was heavily preoccupied with the problem of ownership concentration of the press. The purchase in 1980 of the FP group by Thomson's left two large chains, Thomson's and Southam's, controlling 54 of Canada's 117 daily newspapers—and 48 percent of the daily circulation in the country. (There were also concerns about local monopoly, as in the case of the Irving group, which controls all English-language dailies in New Brunswick.) The concentration problem became particularly acute in August of 1980 with the simultaneous closings of the *Ottawa Journal* (Thomson's) and the *Winnipeg Tribune* (Southam's), actions that in each case left the opposing group with a daily monopoly in the respective markets. The federal government responded to this problem by appointing a royal commission on newspapers, which held hearings in late 1980 and early 1981 and received a range of briefs that called for, among other things, tougher anti-combine laws in the newspaper industry. Another pattern that brought considerable comment before the commission was the rise in several cities—including Toronto, Montreal, Quebec City, Edmonton and Calgary—of down-scale tabloid newspapers fracturing what had been a fairly uniform pattern of serious, middle-of-the-road dailies.

While Canadian journalists in both print and broadcast media continued to enjoy a high degree of independence from the state, governments at both the federal and provincial levels had considerable involvement with media structures. That involvement was expressed mainly in public mechanisms, such as the Canadian Broadcasting Corporation and the Canadian Film Development Corporation, designed to enhance Canadian culture in the face of strong penetration by American media. The pattern indicates that Canadians will continue to face the challenge of ensuring media independence in an environment where governments generally accept a responsibility for protecting and stimulating national media.

CHRONOLOGY

1975   Parliamentary committee criticizes Montreal *Gazette* for erroneously reporting that budget was improperly leaked to businessmen, but takes no punitive action.

1976   Supreme Court of Canada finds Irving newspapers of New Brunswick not guilty of monopolistic practices.
Legislation passed prohibiting advertisers from income tax deductions for advertising placed in publications not meeting requirements of domestic ownership and content.

1977   CRTC rebukes Montreal radio station CFCF for failure to provide balanced commentary on Quebec government's language legislation, but renews license.
CRTC report accuses Canadian Broadcasting Corp. of failing to contribute to national unity.
Ontario Royal Commission on Violence in the Mass Media recommends radical restructuring of broadcast industry; no government action taken.

1978   Editor and publisher of Toronto *Sun* charged under Official Secrets Act for publishing parts of confidential document on Soviet espionage; charges dismissed for lack of evidence. Supreme Court of Canada gives decision that editors must believe assertions in letters carried by their newspapers if they are to successfully plead fair comment in libel actions; some provinces have passed legislation to repair this "loophole"; legislation is pending in others.

1979   United Press Canada formed as successor to United Press International of Canada.

1980   Federal government introduces freedom of information bill. Canadian government establishes Royal Commission on Newspapers in wake of newspaper closures and corporate realignments by Thomson and Southam chains.

BIBLIOGRAPHY

Adam, G. Stuart, ed. *Journalism, Communication and the Law.* Toronto, 1976.

Babe, Robert E. *Canadian Television Broadcasting Structure.* Ottawa, 1979.

Baer, Douglas E. "Newspaper Readership in Canada." Paper presented to Association for Education in Journalism. Houston, Tex., 1979.

Black, Hawley L. "French and English Canadian Political Journalists: A Comparative Study." Unpublished paper, Royal Commission on Bilingualism and Biculturalism. September 1967.

Canada. Canadian Radio-Television Commission. "Report of the Special Committee on 'Air of Death.'" Ottawa, 9 July 1970.

———. CRTC. "Report of the Committee of Inquiry into the National Broadcasting Service." Ottawa, 14 March 1977.

———. Royal Commission on Broadcasting. *Report* (Fowler Report). Ottawa, 1957.

———. Royal Commission on National Development in the Arts and Letters. *Report* (Massey Report). Ottawa, 1951.

———. Royal Commission on Publications (O'Leary Report). Ottawa, 1961.

_____. Royal Commission on Radio Broadcasting. *Report* (Aird Report). Ottawa, n.d.

_____. Special Committee of the Senate on Mass Media. *Report.* Ottawa, 1970.

_____. Task Force on Government Information. *Report.* Ottawa, 1969.

Canadian Advertising Rates & Data. Toronto, 1980.

Canadian Radio-television and Telecommunications Commission. *Canadian Broadcasting and Telecommunications: Past Experience, Future Options.* Ottawa, 1980.

Clement, Wallace. *The Canadian Corporate Elite.* Toronto, 1975.

Cumming, Carman. "The Impact of Television on Political Journalism." *Carleton Journalism Review,* Summer 1979, p. 3.

Elkin, Frederick. "Communications Media and Identity Formation in Canada." Benjamin D. Singer, ed. *Communications in Canadian Society.* 2nd ed. Toronto, 1975.

Federation professionnelle des journalistes du Quebec. "A Summary Dossier on the Interventions of the Police Administration and the Ministry of Justice in the Work of Journalists (Dossier Z)." Unpublished paper, April 15, 1971.

Gane, Lorraine. "How Publishers Influence Daily News Coverage." *Carleton Journalism Review,* Spring 1979, p. 3.

Gordon Lusty Survey Research Ltd. *National Newspaper Readership Study—Fall 1975.* Don Mills, Ont., May 1976.

Haggart, Ron, and Golden, Aubrey E. *Rumours of War.* Toronto, 1971.

Irving, John A. *The Mass Media in Canada.* Toronto, 1962.

Johansen, Peter. "The Canadian Radio-Television Commission and the Canadianization of Broadcasting." *Federal Communications Bar Journal,* 1973, p. 183.

_____. "The CRTC and Canadian Content Regulation." *Journal of Broadcasting,* 1973, p. 465.

Kesterton, Wilfred. *A History of Journalism in Canada.* Toronto, 1967.

_____. *The Law and the Press in Canada.* Toronto, 1976.

McDayter, Walt. *A Media Mosaic.* Toronto, 1971.

McGillivray, Don. "'Poor' Nova Scotia and 'oil-rich' Alberta Stereotyped." Ottawa *Citizen,* September 21, 1979, p. 29.

Murray, J. Alex, and Gerace, Mary C. "Canadian Attitudes toward the U.S. Pres-

ence." *Public Opinion Quarterly* 1972, p. 388.

Ontario. The Royal Commission on Violence in the Communications Industry. *Report.* Toronto, 1977.

Osler, Andrew M. "An Analysis of Some Aspects of French and English Content in the Canadian Press Wire Service, May 2-6, 1977." Unpublished paper, Canadian Radio-television and Telecommunications Commission, July 1977.

Peers, Frank. *The Politics of Canadian Broadcasting.* Toronto, 1969.

_____. *The Public Eye.* Toronto, 1979.

Porter, John. *The Vertical Mosaic.* Toronto, 1965.

Powe, L.A. Jr. "The Georgia Straight and Freedom of Expression in Canada." *Canadian Bar Review* 48 (1970), p. 433.

Radio Bureau of Canada. *Radio 80.* Toronto, 1980.

Riley, Barbara. "Shared Experience in the Mass Media: A Comparative Study of Reaction Sources in French and English Canadian Newspapers." Unpublished paper, Carleton University Institute of Canadian Studies, 1969.

Rutherford, Paul. *The Making of the Canadian Media.* Toronto, 1978.

Scanlon, T. Joseph. "A Study of the Contents of 30 Canadian Daily Newspapers for Special Senate Committee on Mass Media." Unpublished paper, Carleton University School of Journalism, October 1969.

_____. "Canada Sees the World through U.S. Eyes: One Case Study in Cultural Domination." *Canadian Forum,* September 1974, p. 34.

Siegel, Arthur. "French and English Broadcasting in Canada: A Political Evaluation." *Canadian Journal of Communication,* Winter 1979, p. 1.

Simeon, Richard. "More Power to the Provinces." *Maclean's,* January 7, 1980, p. 38.

Singer, Benjamin D. *Communications in Canadian Society.* 2nd rev. ed. Toronto, 1975.

Smiley, Donald V. *Canada in Question: Federalism in the Seventies.* 2nd ed. Toronto, 1976.

Sparkes, Vernone M. "Canada in the American Press and the U.S. in the Canadian Press." *Canadian Journal of Communication,* Spring 1980, p. 18.

_____. "The Flow of News between Canada and the United States." *Journalism Quarterly,* Summer 1978, p. 260.

Stevens, Geoffrey. "The Influences and Responsibilities of the Media." Paper presented to the National Conference on the Legislative Process, University of Victoria, B.C., 1978.

Thompson, David C. "The Coverage of Canada in the U.S. News Media." *Carleton Journalism Review,* Summer 1978.

Westell, Anthony, and Cumming, Carman. "Canadian Media and the National Imperative." In Nimmo, Dan, and Michael W. Mansfield, eds., *Government and the News Media: Comparative Dimensions.*

Wolfe, Morris. "Civil Disobedience." *Saturday Night,* October 1980, p. 13.

CHILE

by Robert P. Knight

BASIC DATA

Population: 11,169,000
Area: 756,948 sq. km. (292,258 sq. mi.)
GNP: 717.6 billion pesos (US $18.4 billion) (1979)
Literacy Rate: 92%
Language(s): Spanish
Number of Dailies: 40 (1978, est.)
  Aggregate Circulation: 1 million
  Circulation per 1,000: 90
Number of Nondailies: 28
  Aggregate Circulation: NA
  Circulation per 1,000: NA
Number of Periodicals: NA

Number of Radio Stations: 195
Number of Television Stations: 31
Number of Radio Receivers: 2 million
  Radio Receivers per 1,000: 180
Number of Television Sets: 1 million
  Television Sets per 1,000: 90
Total Annual Newsprint Consumption: 44,000 metric tons
  Per Capita Newsprint Consumption: 4 kg. (8.8 lb.)
Total Newspaper Ad Receipts: NA
  As % of All Ad Expenditures: NA

Background & General Characteristics

Chile is a literate country with one of the longest records of a free press of any nation in South America. It has undergone major changes in the past decade, changes that began in a political way and that have continued in an economic way. And the Chilean press today is also quite different from what it was in 1970.

The country's literacy rate is one of the highest—92 percent—among developing nations. Affluence is also relatively high, considering a burdensome inflation rate for more than 25 years—a rate that is decelerating but which nevertheless remains in double-digit figures, well above those in the United States. The people and the language are European in character, with the greatest percentage of the population being of mestizo and/or European stock, notably Spanish, with heavy strains of English and German, and also including a number of other ethnic elements, such as Yugoslav. A native Indian population still exists but in small numbers in small areas.

Chile's strong journalistic tradition is seen in a national press of high quality, even despite the travails of the last 10 to 12 years.

While not a high-paying profession, journalism nevertheless has been an honorable calling and has tended to attract first-rate talent. However, this characteristic may be one reason why the country's press has advanced only so far: the very excellence of Chilean journalism might have created an element of overconfidence—even apathy—among publishers, editors and reporters.

Although the Chilean press has been linked historically with the intelligentsia, it has at the same time related itself to the people. The first newspaper, *La Aurora de Chile,* was founded by a Catholic priest, Fray Camilio Henriquez, in 1812. However, this does not mean that the press was closely tied to the church; in Chile there has always been a tendency toward separation of church and state. In some eras—and in some contemporary publications—links to the church might be noted but that is the exception to the rule. From the beginning the press tended to be outspoken and free of undue government influence. Not that governments, parties, and factions made no attempt to control or manage the press in one way or another. And, naturally enough, many of the earlier newspapers were linked to parties or special interests. But mainly, from the very first, the

Chilean press was noted for its biting political satire—a robustly sarcastic defiance of authority that did not begin to moderate until the new and unsettling climate of hostility surrounding the emergence of Salvador Allende and his bitter opponents in the late 1960s.

The quality of Chile's press has depended on its purpose. The established newspapers—such as *El Mercurio* and *La Tercera*—have always maintained the highest standards. The "expedient press," on the other hand, has cared less for overall quality and more for achieving short-term goals such as the election of a particular candidate or the espousal of an immediate cause. Perhaps the "expedient" papers have had a greater tendency to sensationalize—to do anything necessary to attract readership, and then get those readers to heed the real messages behind the overdramatized headlines.

Chilean journalists may fall into three categories. First are the pragmatists, who work on whatever media offer jobs, regardless of the individual journalists' own viewpoints—for example, a leftist employed by a conservative publication. In Chile today there are at least 1,100 unemployed print and broadcast journalists; they represent more than 25 percent of those employed prior to the 1973 coup that overthrew Allende. This hard fact alone can nourish the pragmatic feeling among those newspeople lucky enough to be working. Second are the idealists, who generally work for opposition media such as the magazine *Hoy*, certain radio stations or church-related magazines. Finally come those who are oriented to public relations, whose only goal is to make money, not to worry about politics. In that sense they are similar to the pragmatic journalists, although they may gravitate to organizational communications instead of news media, and use their training to reach the public for the sake of banks, businesses and private enterprise in general.

Given the factors of establishment/"expedient" press and pragmatic/idealistic/PR journalists, one might say that the Chilean media continue to do their job—reporting in their characteristic manner, for example, what is going on in the country's traditionally strained relations with Argentina. This provides good international wire news, well displayed and well edited but nevertheless an outside product, beside the more or less superficial coverage of Chile itself—in which many areas and many topics are omitted.

Investigative reporting, as such, has never taken hold, though Chilean journalists are certainly capable of it. (Some is seen in *Hoy* but not necessarily in the hard-hitting manner now more common in, say, the United States.) In brief, compared to earlier times there is a distinct mediocrity in the Chilean press today.

For the most part, Chile's press is secular in orientation and closely linked to the geographic/cultural center of the country—Santiago, the capital city, and its surroundings. Above all, however, the Chilean press is apolitical. Publications with any political leanings have not been permitted since the mid-1970s. (Some survived the 1973 coup—in which General Augusto Pinochet overthrew Allende, the first Marxist freely elected president of a Latin American country—but did not last too many years after that.) The only visible ideological tendencies are toward the right, or at least toward support of Pinochet's military government.

Almost all newspapers and magazines are in Spanish, with only a handful being printed for other language groups (there have been, for example, Arabic publications and one in Serbo-Croatian). Most of the newspapers are broadsheets, with only a few tabloids, in contrast to a greater number during the Allende and pre-Allende periods. Nor is there more than a handful of afternoon papers. Daily issues are relatively slim, with a normal maximum of perhaps 36 pages—despite an increasing volume of advertising. Most dailies have Sunday editions, whose circulation tends to be higher. The larger papers, especially those of the El Mercurio chain, have magazine sections or supplement of varied kinds.

The magazine sections are particularly popular, in limited-page editions, throughout the week. The pioneer in the supplement field was *La Tercera*, the largest-circulation paper in Chile today. *El Mercurio* also stands out, with a juvenile section and one for secondary school students. These and others like them attract young readers because they provide genuine service in the form of material students can use with their homework. Thus they are not only useful but good business. They are also, obviously, an important weapon in the stiff competition between *El Mercurio* and *La Tercera*. One of the Mercurio-group tabloids, *Las Ultimas Noticias*, basically a more sensational paper, has several sections, including a Friday highlight of weekend activities, as well as special supplements for women and students and the like. *La Tercera*'s supplements include men's and women's sections. The government-owned *La Nación*, which has changed names and formats several times, has also had several magazine sections. The best known of these sections is *El Mercurio*'s *Revista del Domingo,* a Sunday supplement that appears in all the Mercurio papers—and which on occasion even runs pieces mildly critical of government.

The major cities continue to have competing newspapers, after a fashion. In Santiago, competition definitely exists even though three of the five papers are associated with the El Mercurio chain. Most of the other large cities have more than one newspaper, although one usually predominates.

11 Largest Newspapers by Circulation (weekday)

1. *La Tercera de la Hora,* Santiago	350,000
2. *El Mercurio,* Santiago	175,000
3. *Las Ultimas Noticias,* Santiago (El Mercurio group)	100,000
4. *La Segunda,* Santiago (El Mercurio group)	75,000
5. *La Nacion,* Santiago	50,000
6. *El Mercurio,* Valparaiso (El Mercurio group)	70,000
7. *El Sur,* Concepción	35,000
8. *El Mercurio de Antofagasta* (El Mercurio group)	30,000
9. *La Estrella,* Valparaiso (El Mercurio group)	28,000
10. *La Prensa,* Osorno	26,000
11. *El Diario Austral,* Temuco	26,000

(It should be noted that circulation figures are not verified by an outside agency and are often estimates. Various sources will differ over circulation figures.)

Clearly, the country's most influential newspapers are three of the five remaining Santiago dailies. *El Mercurio,* founded by Agustin Edwards MacClure in 1900 (and based on the earlier success of Edwards's *El Mercurio* of Valparaiso) is far and away the most important although not necessarily the most widely circulated paper in the country. S.S. Koppe, Inc., Mercurio's advertising representative, actually claims the Santiago paper has a daily circulation of 325,000 and 425,000 on Sundays, but other sources cite lower figures. Its weekly airmail edition also circulates to 57 countries on a delivery schedule of 48 hours to seven days after

publication. In terms of circulation the largest newspaper is *La Tercera de la Hora* (usually called *La Tercera*), founded in 1950 by the Pico Canas brothers. It managed to survive the 1973 coup because it is basically apolitical, and this may account for some of its current appeal in a Chile that has disavowed political inclinations. Third most influential—though a distant third—may be *La Segunda de Las Ultimas Noticias* (called *La Segunda*), a Mercurio tabloid that is said to have 75,000 readers on weekdays and Sundays. The more sensational Mercurio tabloid, *Las Ultimas Noticias,* founded in 1902, is giving *La Tercera* a run for its money in circulation but not in influence, especially under a new editor known for his yellow-journalism approach. *Las Ultimas Noticias* is also attempting to be more national in its coverage and distribution.

In certain ways, the magazine *Hoy* is equal in influence to *El Mercurio.* Its circulation of 50,000 is huge in the magazine area. (*Selecciones del Reader's Digest,* always one of the country's most popular publications, has 48,000 readers.) But its influence comes from the fact that, more clearly than any other publication, even the Church publications, it represents an opposition to the military government. Other periodicials of importance are the Church-related *Mensaje, Solidaridad* and *Analisis;* as well as *Que Pasa,* a conservative but sometimes critical magazine not unlike *U.S. News & World Report,* and *Ercilla,* the leading newsmagazine until it was bought out by some financiers and its staff mutinied to form *Hoy* in 1977.

Chilean publishing firms are much less influential than they once were. By 1977, their new titles had descended to a low of 387, compared to 1,500 in the mid-1960s. Santiago, long the headquarters for well-known historians, had become known as one of the book publishing capitals of the Spanish-speaking world, and Chileans were served by "instant books"—topical treatments of current events within the country even before that type of book became so popular in the United States. There were once an estimated 700 printing houses in Chile, turning out not only books but many magazines. The largest of these, Zig Zag, had been bought by the Christian Democrats in 1967, with funds supplied by the Catholic Church. Under pressure from its Allende-inspired workers in 1970, it was forced to raise wages 67 percent. Within a month it sold its equipment to the Popular

Unity government, which renamed it Quimantu, a Chilean Indian name. Quimantu turned out Marxist works, both classic and contemporary, and a stream of popular materials such as comic books that hammered home Marxist messages in entertaining fashion. In that sense, the government sensed how to make effective use of the means of mass communication. After the 1973 coup, Quimantu was taken over by the military government and renamed Gabriela Mistral, after the Chilean Nobel Prize poetess. Its production was lowered considerably and the new government seemed interested in finding a commercial buyer for Chile's best known printing house.

Economic Framework

One of today's strongest influences on the Chilean press is that of the economic climate. Without question, Chile was in economic chaos at the time of the 1973 coup. (Coups and nondemocratic administrations—in contrast to those of most Latin American countries—have been rare in Chile's history.) Inflation was running in excess of 700 percent per year. Clearly there was no confidence in the then-existing economic system, which was attempting to bring more enterprises under state management—a trend that had accelerated to a degree under the previous Christian Democratic administration of 1964-70 (Latin America's first Christian Democratic government). By 1973 survival may have been the watchword, both for consumers and publications. Post-coup revelations showed, for example, that the United States Central Intelligence Agency had poured more than $1.6 million into *El Mercurio* to keep it afloat during the Allende years, and that it had also contributed, in varying amounts, to other journalistic enterprises for the same reason. (The underlying purpose, of course, was to keep these enterprises on the anti-Allende, anti-Marxist side.) In any case the country considered itself ready for a different economic approach after the coup. By 1975 that approach was the one espoused—and subsequently strongly defended by—University of Chicago economist Milton Friedman, who was to win the Nobel Prize in economics that very year. In his later book, *Free To Choose*, Friedman indirectly explains what has been happening in recent years both in the Chilean economy and with the Chilean media: free market principles are to apply; government is to release its hold. A

more dramatic example can be seen in television than in print media. Since 1975, Chilean television has shifted dramatically from what originally was envisioned—when TV was introduced in 1959—as an essentially educational medium to a consumer-oriented broadcast system. Instead of insisting that the universities continue to program their stations (the universities had been granted the original licenses) for educational purposes, with little emphasis on advertising, they have been told to "auto-finance"—that is, to make their own way economically, which clearly has meant a dependence on advertising, ratings, and similar factors associated with a commercial medium.

In the process, the electronic media, and especially TV, are giving an unheard-of competition to newspapers. While the press may still predominate in news dissemination—not an area of major concern for Chile's consumer-oriented TV—the audiences are beginning to lean heavily on TV not just for their entertainment, but also, despite its scarcity, for their news. In the meantime, radio is abandoning an earlier concern for news; many of the newer and now quite popular FM stations have no news departments at all. (Santiago alone has 22 AM and 16 FM stations.)

Only three types of newspaper ownership exist today: individual, corporate, and government. Before the 1973 coup, political party ownership (both incumbent and opposition) exerted great influence; such newspaper-party affiliation has been outlawed since 1974. However, powerful as the parties may have been with newspapers in terms of ownership or influence, they were not the predominant economic force in the press prior to 1973. Since the founding of *El Mercurio* of Santiago in 1900, the El Mercurio chain—not any outside group—has been the major newspaper force in the country. (The chain's mother newspaper, *El Mercurio* of Valparaiso, had been founded in that nearby coastal city in 1827, making it what today is the oldest existing Spanish-language newspaper anywhere in the world.) Others in the 11-member press empire include the Santiago morning and afternoon tabloids, *Las Ultimas Noticias* and *La Segunda* (founded in 1902 and 1931 respectively); two newspapers in the northern city of Antofagasta, *El Mercurio de Antofagasta* (1906) and *La Estrella del Norte* (1966); and the tabloid *La Estrella* of Valparaiso (1921). The chain's smaller papers are *La Prensa,* Tocopilla (1924); *La*

Estrella de Iquique (1966), *El Mercurio,* Calama; and *La Estrella,* Arica.

Indisputably, the El Mercurio chain predominates in Chile. And, it is important to note, the Edwards family is much more than a newspaper-owning family. One of many Anglo names sprinkled throughout Chilean history, Edwards has long been associated with banking and other commercial interests, making the family one of the most influential in the country. Although one might expect the family to be involved in much media cross-ownership—especially considering that radio is in the private sector—the Mercurio chain has not been very active in electronic communications. At one time it did control a radio network but its newspapers have always held top priority. Television has not yet been open to private control although there are some hints in the new constitution of 1981 that it may pass into private hands, in keeping with the free-market philosophy of the military government. Obviously, the El Mercurio group would be a prime candidate for involvement in TV were that to come to pass.

This brief description should make clear the continued ascendance of *El Mercurio* despite the fact that *La Tercera,* the Pico Canas paper, is today the country's largest. If *El Mercurio* represents anything like a monopoly, it has gone virtually unchallenged except during the Allende period, when various efforts to break up the chain's influence failed. For in a sense, the El Mercurio group exemplifies the mix of elite and popular papers that have prospered for some time in Chile. The parent papers in Valparaiso and Santiago are relatively somber, rather vertically made up, akin to *The New York Times* in appearance and tone, while the tabloids—which do indeed represent the tabloid tradition—are not unlike the New York *Daily News*, with their large photo coverage, colorful headlines and horizontal makeup.

Among other papers, the government-owned *La Nación* leans toward the Mercurio end of the continuum in appearance and content, while the Pico Canas' *La Tercera* is a tabloid that has seen even "wilder days" than the Mercurio tabs. All the tabloids, indeed, have had a tinge of yellow press about them; this was even more true of those that disappeared in the 1973 coup. (The well-produced communist tabloid *El Siglo* had been founded in 1940 and survived periods even when the Communist party was outlawed).

In distribution patterns and networks, *La Tercera* and *El Mercurio* of Santiago are naturally the papers that blanket Chile. Same-day distribution is possible, thanks to air and rail connections in this geographically difficult country, the world's longest—and one of the narrowest—with a north-south extension of some 2,600 miles. Circulation centers around Santiago, with its population of close to four million, and the largest slice of the circulation pie comes in the geographic area of the central valley. From there it spreads north to the most distant mining towns, and south to the communities in the fjord-like regions of sub-Antarctica. Altogether Chile has about 75 urban areas. Outside of the central region between Santiago and the coastal city of Valparaiso to the west, there is virtually no east-west distribution, the country being only an average of 100 miles wide. The top 11 newspapers easily account for 75 to 90 percent of the circulation in the country. This takes into consideration the fact that populations of all communities but Santiago are relatively small and that the Santiago press is so nationwide in character. Currently six of the leading-circulation papers are in the provinces but that is only because half of the metropolitan papers were closed at the time of the 1973 coup or shortly thereafter. If those that died still existed, they probably would be in the top group and the provincials would not be represented at all, except perhaps for *El Mercurio* of Valparaiso.

Chile is more fortunate than most countries (certainly more than most in South America) in that it produces much of its own newsprint and therefore depends far less on foreign sources, with their constantly escalating prices.

As in any country where the advertising ratio of advertising to news is 60/40 in favor of ads, one would expect that Chilean newspapers would feel some adverse impact from space buyers. However, it is actually no greater than in most countries with similar economic frameworks. Special interest lobbies, including the mining companies, do have influence, but they are not overtly predominant forces.

Questions of industrial relations, strikes and labor unions are largely moot because unions have not been free to operate in their usual manner since the 1973 coup. Only in mid-1981 were 10,000 miners permitted to strike for the first time since the coup, and then only under very controlled "by the numbers" circumstances. This represents a considerable contrast to the pre-1973 Chile, which had one of the strongest labor movements on the continent—no doubt a factor in its swing to the left prior to Allende. (The country also had a strong history of social legislation, dating to the 1920s.)

A factor that may be impeding circulation gains is per-copy price, recently hiked from 25 to 50 cents, a large sum in Chile. (Newsmagazines now cost two dollars, also a negative circulation factor.) More important, perhaps, are the competition for time from television and radio and the fact that Chileans no longer bother to buy two or three newspapers daily as they once did. There is no point in that practice any longer; there is no pluralism, as there once was, only monotony. The government does not release circulation figures, which—when compared to earlier days—would show this pattern of single-paper or no-paper purchase. But close examination of newsprint consumption, as done by Robert N. Pierce, makes the point vividly.

In technological terms, the Santiago papers are the most advanced, as might be expected. *La Tercera* has gone to offset and *El Mercurio,* which had been lagging in technology, is now gearing up to introduce such sophisticated elements as electronic editing.

Press Laws

A new constitution, effective March 11, 1981, was endorsed by a margin of some 67 percent of the electorate in September, 1980. It had been under discussion for at least two years, and journalists were in the forefront of those who objected to its freedom-of-the-press sections. Unlike many Latin American countries, Chile has had relatively few constitutions; even during the Allende period it had been governed under a reformist constitution of 1925. That document guaranteed "freedom to express, without prior censorship, opinions...through the medium of the press or any other form, without prejudice to liability for offenses...."

The important thing to remember in Latin America is that it is not so much the laws on the books that count as their enforcement—or lack of enforcement. Article 19 of the 1981 constitution pertains to freedom of expression but elsewhere in the instrument are several supposedly transitory rules or regulations that are meant to apply during the eight-year period of rule begun by General Pinochet with that new constitution.

One of the detested rules gaining constitutional approval was Bando 122, a regulation that had enabled the military to determine which print media could appear. Although it pertained primarily to new publications seeking permission to print, it also was considered retroactive to existing publications. Actually, for many years prior to Bando 122 Chile had required that every publication obtain a permit to print, but this was more a housekeeping regulation for the sake of the National Library, which was to receive copies of all publications for its shelves. Bando 122, on the other hand, exerted a chilling effect.

Another provision causing trouble for the press was Decree Law 2181 of December, 1975. As explained by Pierce, "any local military commander could shut down any mass medium in his district for six issues, or in the case of broadcasters, for six days. He was to be the sole judge of whether the medium committed one of the proscribed offenses. These were emitting news, opinion, or other communications which tend to 'create alarm or distrust in the population, disfiguring the true dimension of the facts, whether they be manifestly false or contravene the rules given for internal order.' Repeated offenses would lead to permanent closing. Offenders could be warned of their misdeeds before punishment, and appeals were allowed."

This provision was similar to a 1949 sedition law that allowed the government to close any of the print or electronic media for six days if internal security were threatened. Although rarely enforced, it was well known by journalists.

Emerging from the new constitution as a matter of major concern to journalists and others in Chile was the elimination of mandatory "colegios"—professional councils to determine membership in the various professions. In the case of journalism, a widely copied landmark system of licensing was established during the mid-1950s presidency of Carlos Ibáñez, supposedly as a means of insuring responsibility in the press. That stated goal caused some alarm but early fears of the system disappeared quickly. One of the licensing requirements was that journalists be trained in university journalism schools, and soon the majority of the nation's newspeople met that requirement—to the benefit of the country's mass media. Exceptions could be made—and were—to this requirement, and the government stayed fairly well out of the picture.

The colegio system was never overtly used to exclude anyone from journalism—or the reverse. It was seen by journalists as just another colegio in a country that had been inclined to license its various professionals. It was with these various other groups that the Colegio de Periodistas joined—unsuccessfully, it seems—in 1981 to protest the free-market stand on professional affiliation and its concomitant abolition of the colegio system.

Actually the new non-colegio approach still requires that a journalist have a degree from a state-approved school, such as a university or private institution established under the law. The latter provision opens up the possibility that institutions other than universities—say a group of newspapers such as El Mercurio's—might give training. The difference here is that licenses would not be monitored by a colegio, that is, by an association of journalists themselves.

The attitude of the press toward the colegio matter was not immediately clear. On the one hand, it stood to gain in economic terms from an increase in the number of job candidates, with salaries declining accordingly. (A colegio function had been to help set and maintain salaries—obviously running counter to a free-market philosophy.) On the other hand, it might lose in the professional preparation or orientation of its new employees, since a glut of schools could bring lower standards.

In a country as small as Chile, an important by-product of the colegio system has been a sense of collegiality among journalists. That may have existed to a degree even without the colegio (a more socially oriented Circulo de Periodistas, or journalists' club, had already been popular), but the colegio so greatly intensified the feeling as to touch off the already mentioned journalists' protest meeting in 1981. Hoy even ran a cover story about the anticipated problems.

In a sense, it may be said that Chile's press has gone through three periods. First were 150 years of a genuinely free press—unlike that of virtually any other Latin American country in length and reality. Then came the three years of Allende's presidency; in this period, despite fear of the government's real designs on the mass media, the press actually functioned in a free and at times even licentious manner. Finally, beginning in 1973, Pinochet's military rule has subjugated the press to the greater economic good of the country, leaving it limited freedom. Before 1970 press freedom was pretty much taken

for granted. After 1970 it seemed to be in jeopardy and had to be defended. Since 1973 journalists have begun to realize what their country has given up in exchange for a society ostensibly more peaceful politically and more stable economically.

At least theoretically, a common thread might be seen in the nation's press laws. From 1925 on, laws were intended to uphold certain standards. Agustin Edwards MacClure, founder of Santiago's El Mercurio, wrote in 1928: "The history of journalism in Chile has no dark pages but, on the contrary, is a record of integrity born of the high conception which Chilean journalists have at all times had of their mission." If his words were accurate, it is no wonder that the country's newspeople accepted a variety of laws intended to enforce stardards of journalistic conduct—starting with the constitution of 1925 and continuing through the internal security law of 1949 (together with its 1964 and 1967 amendments) and—perhaps above all—the 1956 law establishing the Colegio de Periodistas.

True, there has been dissent. The 1964 amendment was called a "muzzle law" because it attempted to impose standards on the reporting of crime (articles on individual offenses could not be longer than 500 words or broadcasts more than three minutes). It was relaxed somewhat in its 1967 version. Also, the 1964 and 1967 amendments provided for the right of ratification or correction, which permitted the government, as well as others, to obtain equal-display corrections of what they considered to be misinterpretations or errors. In general, it might be said that Chile's media legislation embodied all the more common elements of press laws in advanced societies, including provisions against libel, slander and other forms of defamation. Thanks to the strong journalists groups and the country's tradition of a free press, abuses of the laws were relatively rare although not unheard of.

The degree of independence of the judiciary is a matter of opinion. Chile has long taken pride in its courts and in their ability to uphold democratic principles. It was definitely a spirit of independence in the courts that helped save the press from falling victim to most of the anti-media moves of the Allende government. Since the 1973 coup, however, the military has prevailed, and the courts have tended not to back the press in its efforts for greater freedom.

Censorship

The government agency charged with monitoring the press is the Department of Social Communication, headed by a lawyer. (It might be noted here that many of the individuals who deal with the press come from other disciplines and therefore that they may lack understanding of the press and its traditions.) The department is said to keep track of what is said and written. Prior censorship itself lasted only a short time after the 1973 coup. The agency has a hand in authorizing or de-authorizing publications, under the previously mentioned Bando 122.

Perhaps the most effective weapon the agency has on a day-to-day basis is the fact that most government news is channeled through public relations or information offices. There is a fear of talking to journalists, and potential news sources prefer to use information offices as buffers between themselves and reporters. This situation may have been aggravated by the well-ingrained habit of Chilean newspapers, notably *El Mercurio,* of dealing essentially with official sources. It was not uncommon for *El Mercurio* to have such a source report to the newspaper offices for a formal interview.

Prior censorship is relatively rare in Chile. Only in times of crisis, such as immediately after the 1973 coup, has it been invoked. On the other hand, newspapers and broadcasting stations have been shut down, usually for short periods of a few days—but sometimes permanently—as the result of using offending material. In other words, sanctions tended to be applied after the fact rather than before, except in instances where Bando 122 was applied and publications were never permitted to appear in the first place—as in the case of the magazine *Gente Actual* of the Hoy group and a projected women's magazine by a progressive woman journalist, Delia Vergara.

For a time, the Colegio de Periodistas, the licensing/ethical body, served to some degree as a press council, in line with the legal mandate it was given to help insure journalistic responsibility. But, as the years passed and its effectiveness remained in question, its press council function became less visible and less influential with newspapers. Only when it feared for freedom of the press did it tend to speak out—and, then, to an audience somewhat ready to listen.

Under the terms of a 1971 law, all matters concerning television broadcasting at a national level, including program organization and advertising time, are dealt with by a 15-member national television council.

State-Press Relations

The Department of Social Communication, which monitors the press, is also the government information ministry. It is intended to inform the public and the press of the functions of the government and its various other ministries. Although the department is the preferred channel for dissemination of government information, its officials will send reporters to designated ministries for information that the central office does not have. As might be expected, the agency includes some former journalists, among them a number of fairly well-known *El Mercurio* staffers.

Although one does not see the heavy-handed president's-picture-on-every-newspaper-page tactics of some military governments, it may be assumed that news in Chile is managed to a degree. "Old boy networks" also contribute to this system of press control, as good manners dictate that one accede to the wishes of friends. Further cooperation comes from such journalists as society reporters and sports writers. These newspeople make it easier for the government or other interests to reach various groups and attract them with favors like tickets to horse races, social functions and similar entertainment events.

If the military government has discouraged and even punished dissent, it at least has opened the way for some types of criticism since 1978—apparently realizing that there was need for some opposition press, some safety valve. It was also recognized that Chile would look better in the eyes of the world—at a time when the military government was still being criticized for its human rights conduct—if the press seemed to be fairly open. So it is that *Hoy* and the Catholic publications and some private radio stations have been able to disclose certain events that the government would prefer to keep secret.

El Mercurio in particular has enough power to criticize a change of education ministers or even some economic matters. What it does *not* do is overtly campaign against the country's loss of democracy in general and press freedom in particular. Therefore, while its criticism does not really disturb the government it does serve to tell the world that Chile is "free"—a message that is important to the image Pinochet seeks to develop. *Hoy* is much more forthright but it has a smaller circulation and carries less weight, in and out of the country. In the long run, however, both *Hoy* and the Church publications may yet be the most influential in producing change.

But more immediately, one can say that when *El Mercurio* comes out against low pensions, it can have an effect; that when its Sunday supplement, *Revista del Domingo,* criticizes TV advertising, it can influence the hours in which alcohol is publicized or the number of the ads being played per hour. It must be remembered that *El Mercurio* is an entity in itself, and a powerful one, with connections to many enterprises and many important people. And, although it is usually in matters of lesser moments that even *El Mercurio* makes a difference, on at least one occasion the paper may have really jolted the country—and the world. This was when it published details of the Chilean secret police's involvement in the assassination in Washington of Allende's former ambassador to the United States, Orlando Letelier.

Direct measures against journalism did exist both in the Allende and in the post-Allende periods, but more so in the latter. It should be pointed out that other means besides press censorship were taken to reduce participatory democracy in the post-coup period. For example, some books were burned, even as late as 1975; bookstores were required to submit lists of the books they had for sale; films were censored (and often not permitted to be shown); and magazines were censored or confiscated. More chilling was the fact that as many as one out of every 250 Chileans were detained, at least temporarily, amounting to a minimum of some 41,000 persons. Political parties were finally outlawed in 1977 (they had been in "recess" until then but apparently that measure was considered insufficient to eliminate their influence).

It took at least three years after the coup for the stronger measures to ease, the change taking place apparently when the press became more accustomed to self-censorship.

After the coup, about 30 newspapers and magazines and 12 radio stations were permanently closed. A few of these closings supposedly came about as a result of economic conditions, such as in the case of *La Prensa,* the Christian Democratic newspaper which was a successor to *El Diario Ilustrado,* founded in 1902 and long maintaining nominally hidden contacts with the Catholic Church. Nevertheless, at least 54 full-time

journalists were arrested and as many as 11 of them may have been killed. In addition, many part-time journalists, including academicians and politicians, were arrested or detained.

During the Allende period, the newspaper suspension which aroused the greatest concern was that of *El Mercurio,* for what was to have been six days, under the internal security law but which the courts cut to one day in June 1972.

The tables illustrate the difficulties faced by news organizations and journalists alike, especially since the coup. Although many of the actions have been relatively short-term in nature, they have tended, when taken all together to exert a powerful chilling effect on the mass media, leading to self-censorship and conformity. This, together with individuals' desires to return to some degree of economic and social normalcy, has had a profound effect on Chilean journalism, moving it away from its historic traditions of freedom.

The state cannot be said to exercise control of the press directly through some of the more common means, such as subsidies, allocation of newsprint and labor union manipulation. Advertising support can play a role since state enterprises continue to be numerous—although fewer each year as the distance from the Allende period grows. Also, in keeping with the free-market concept, there has been an easing of import licenses for printing equipment. Licensing of journalists, the most common practice in Chile, has never been permitted to become a real political tool.

Attitude Toward Foreign Media

A measure of the importance of a foreign correspondent in the 1970s was how many times he or his news organization had been banned, especially in the post-coup period. The military government would prefer to be left alone, even if it means denying access to a correspondent. Such action will be taken when the journalist presents an unflattering picture of the country. An idea of how often this has happened can be gained from the table.

Today foreign publications are freely distributed in Chile, even when the government is displeased with some offending piece. About 1976, publications could be confiscated at the airport, as happened with the leftist Spanish publication, *Cambio 16.*

Suspension and Confiscation of Media Units, 1970–

Allende Period

Date	Person or Organization	Government Action	Explanation or Comment
1971	Radio Agricultura; Radio Cooperativa	Suspended 24 hours	Came during street disorders during a women's protest.
1971	*Puro Chile* (Communist)	Suspended	Libelously accused three opposition senators of conspiring against the government but appeared the next day under another name, *Dulce Patria*.
1971	Radio Balmaceda	Suspended twice (24 and 48 hours)	Charged with "serious offenses against the President and the Armed Forces." Voice of Christian Democrats.
1972	*El Mercurio*	Suspended (one day)	Reported an economic crisis; suspension lasted only one day, thanks to courts.
1972	All radio stations	Taken over	Lasted 12 days until courts said government could not force all stations into a government network.
1972	*La Mañana*, Talca	Underwent intervention	Lasted eight months until courts ordered it taken from workers and returned to owners.
1972	Radio Minería	Suspended	Broke away from the mandatory government hookup during the bitter truckers' strike.
1973	All newspapers	Censored	Lasted four days after abortive coup.
1973	*La Tercera*	Suspended	Carried ad by fleeing leaders of abortive coup.
1973	*La Tribuna*	Suspended	Carried "false and alarmist" news during failed coup.

Post-Allende Period

Date	Person or Organization	Government Action	Explanation or Comment
1973	*El Siglo, Puro Chile, Ultima Hora* and other leftist publications	Closed	Supported the ousted Allende government.
1973	Radio Corporación	Expropriated	Became Radio Nacional, in a network blanketing the country for the new military government.
1974	*Mensaje* (Jesuit magazine)	Censored	Had included quotations from President Allende, etc.
1974	*La Segunda*	Suspended	Anticipated a sharp increase in cigarette prices.
1975	*Vanguardia* (magazine)	Closed	
1975	*Politica y Espiritu* (magazine)	Closed	Treated too many taboo subjects such as secret police; economics.
1976	*Color*, Concepción	Expropriated	Supposedly acted as front for Marxist organizations.
1976	*Ercilla* (magazine)	Confiscated	March 26 issue contained "tendentious articles destined to disfigure the image of the Supreme Government" (Lost: 60,000 copies, $45,000).
1976	*La Tercera*	Suspended one day	Censored because of letter from lawyers about indifference of courts to government abuses.
1977	Radio Balmaceda	Closed	Repeatedly offended government; was suspended twice before.
1978	*Nueva Vea*	Confiscated	Discussed Argentine border dispute on eve of meeting between the two countries' heads of state.
1978	*La Segunda*	Suspended 48 hours (First closure outside the courts)	Threatened coexistence of citizens and made offensive charges against government, it was said.

Note: Most of suspensions were for six days, under existing law.

Jailings of Newsmen, 1970–

Allende Period

Date	Person	Government Action	Explanation or Comment
1971	Marcelo Maturana, *P.E.C.* (conservative weekly)	Arrested	Reported schisms in Army ranks.
1972	Mario Carneyro, *La Segunda*	Arrested	Supposedly defamed interior minister in stories about secret arms imports.

Post-Allende Period*

Date	Person	Government Action	Explanation or Comment
1973	Jorge Pacull, *Ultima Hora* Oscar Waiss, ex-*La Nacion* Alberto Gamboa, *Clarin* Jose Gomez Lopez, *Puro Chile* Alejandro Arellano, *Iba Aybat*	Detained in National Stadium	
1974	Manuel Cabieses, *Punto Final*	Threatened with execution	Sentenced to 30 years in prison.
1976	Balisario Velasco, Radio Balmaceda	Banished to remote village	Station shut down for mentioning a sugar shortage.

*These are used only as examples among the 54 believed jailed and 11 believed killed in post-coup Chile.

How much foreign material or propaganda weaves its way into Chilean publications is uncertain. More certain is the fact that the practice used to be relatively common. Once there was an active program to get U.S. materials into Chilean media—from both the U.S. government and U.S. enterprises such as the big copper companies. Such campaigns may have been relatively successful with smaller provincial papers that often needed boiler plate material to fill up their pages. Without doubt, the CIA had a fairly successful program of penetration into the media, in terms of actual articles and of cooperative journalists. During the Allende years, the CIA spent $8 million in its Chilean campaign, $1.6 million of which went to *El Mercurio*. But the penetration can be traced back as far as the early 1950s.

Several Chilean journalists have been active members of the Inter-American Press Association, including Agustin S. Edwards III who was president of IAPA just at the time Allende was coming in, and Hector Gonzalez of Rancagua, a small-newspaper owner who ran into trouble under Allende. As might be expected, the IAPA gave backing to its Chilean colleagues throughout the 1970s, and twice yearly, in its Freedom of the Press Committee reports, chastised the government for its infringements on the press. Another group, the International Press Institute, likewise reported the Chilean situation with regularity in its journal, *IPI Report*.

For its part, the Chilean government may have paid less attention to the outside groups than to its own publications. In the matter of the New World Information Order and the 1979 UNESCO Declaration, Chile stood with the developed rather than the developing nations. The debate never received much attention in Chile and may not have been well known among journalists. (Interestingly, some of the strong voices on the Third World side have been exiled Chilean journalists.)

News Agencies

At one time, even in the mid-1970s, Chile had three or four national news agencies, but they were small and did not compare in importance with the international agencies operating in the country. The Chilean agency that lasted, even if without great influence, was Orbe. Founded in 1952 as a private organization, it was bought in the late 1960s by a group of Christian Democrats. During the Allende period it came under government control and later returned to private ownership. However, it sells its space to government and other agencies, with official material forming the bulk of its file.

The four agencies that still existed after the coup but did not survive into the 1980s were Agencia Noticiosa Prensa; Radio y Cine (PYRC), founded in 1945 and the oldest of the four; Agencia Noticiosa Corporación de Periodistas (COPER), founded in 1948; and Agencia Orbe Latinoamericana, founded in

Bannings and Jailings of Correspondents, 1970–

Allende Period

Date	Person	Government Action	Explanation or Comment
1971	Martin Houseman, UPI	Expelled	Reported Chile furnished arms to Colombian guerillas. Bureau's license canceled but order quickly rescinded.

Post-Allende Period

Date	Person	Government Action	Explanation or Comment
1973	Bobi Sourander, *Dagens Nyheter,* Stockholm	Arrested, expelled	Charged with using his car as ambulance for insurgents and held for 14 days.
1973	Paul Heath Haeffel, *Boston Globe*	Arrested	Charged with staying at a different hotel than the one listed on his tourist card. Kept one week.
1973	Flavio Lara, *Opinião,* Brazil	Vanished	Disappeared at the airport.
1973	Michel Gautier, French language network of Canadian Broadcasting Corp.	Arrested	Kept two days.
1973	Lief Person, *Arbetet,* Stockholm; Philippe Labreveux, *Le Monde;* Edouard Bailby, *L'Express;* Peter Sumberg	Expelled	
1973	Peter Torbiornasson, *Aftonbladet,* Sweden; Marlise Simmons, *Washington Post;* Anton Froeck, Dutch Radio; J.M. Sanchez, Uruguay; Pierre Kalfon, *Le Monde;* Antonio Rodriguez Conceiro, EFE wire service, Spain; Mario Cervi, *Corriere della Sera;* Frank Manitsas, CBS; George Dupy, *Le Figaro;* Pino Cimo, *Il Messaggero,* Rome; Dwight Porter, *Newsweek, Business Week, Financial Times*	Detained, roughed up, or expelled	
1974	Marcel Niedergang, *Le Monde*	Denied entry	
1974	George Roth, Canadian Broadcasting Corp.	Detained	

Various Periods After the Coup

Date	Person	Government Action	Explanation or Comment
	Jonathan Kandell, Juan de Onis, *New York Times;* Joanne Omang, Joseph Novitski, *Washington Post;* Rudolph Rauch, *Time;* William Montalbano, *Miami Herald;* James Pringle, *Newsweek*	Expelled	Usually charged with "false" and "tendentious" stories

Note: This is not a comprehensive list, but indicative of the number affected. Freelance correspondents added to the number, as happens in coups.

1956. PYRC had distributed a daily national news service, plus a foreign news summary supplied on request to provincial customers. COPER served mainly provincial daily newspapers and Santiago broadcasting stations. Agencia Orbe Latinoamericana dealt primarily in foreign news, with representatives in a number of Latin American countries as well as an exchange network with Orbe and agencies in other countries. More than 20 subscribers received its domestic and foreign news service.

The major international agencies are represented in Chile: Associated Press, United Press International (which also provides a domestic service), and Reuters, plus smaller agencies like Deutsche Presse-Agentur and EFE of Spain. Major U.S. newspapers and newsmagazines also have roving correspondents who cover Chile.

As stated earlier, Chile is well served in its newspapers by the international agencies, and a high volume of such material is used. It does not necessarily represent Latin America and the Third World as well as it does the developed nations of North America and Europe.

Electronic News Media

On the one hand, government seems to be less involved than in the past with broadcasting; on the other, it is both as much and more involved. This apparent contradiction arises partly from the Friedman-type view of the electronic media—a free-market approach, with private enterprise in charge. Even so, the government remains in control of the ever-important TV because the universities still hold the licenses, as was originally desired, for educational purposes. Further, and perhaps even more significant, the government television network (originated, interestingly enough, during the presidency of Eduardo Frei in the 1960s) has now expanded to the point of having repeaters in 76 communities running the entire length of the country. Thus the government has access to the country's entire TV audience—much more than does any single station.

Similarly, the government-owned Radio Nacional has stations in 70 communities, thereby blanketing the country. It sometimes requires other stations to join its network for important announcements and speeches (This practice, however, is not new; having

existed for more than 20 years; at one time, every station in the country had to join the national network for a government newscast at eight p.m. nightly). But unlike the television system, the rest of the stations are operated commercially, rather than by the universities (which is to say the government). This is in line with the long-standing practice in many Latin American countries of having most radio commercially operated.

Education & Training

Chile's journalism education system is one of the most respected in Latin America. The Univerity of Chile School of Journalism was founded in 1953 and the Catholic University School of Journalism in 1961. Training is also offered at the University of the North and at the University of Valparaiso. (A fifth school, at the leftist-oriented University of Concepción, was closed when the university was banned after the coup). The Santiago schools graduate an average of 25 journalists per year, although the number increased to as many as 50 in the late 1970s. That was because great numbers of students who had been in social sciences switched to journalism when the former disciplines either disbanded or lost their former prestige.

The future of journalism education is uncertain. Talk continues of advanced programs and even of private organizations getting into the picture. Journalism is a discipline in demand among young people, with relatively good salaries of $600 to $900 monthly.

As mentioned earlier, one of the major changes in the profession concerns the abolishment of the Colegio de Periodistas as the legal arbiter of who gets into the field.

The National Prize in Journalism (Premio Nacional de Periodismo) is the leading journalistic award in the country, but there are also numerous specialized prizes, such as the Lenka Franulic award for women (named after a prominent woman journalist of Yugoslav descent) and prizes given by commercial concerns.

Organizations include the Colegio de Periodistas, the more social Circulo de Periodistas, and many associations for newspeople of different kinds, such as police reporters, economic writers and horse-racing reporters. Still, the colegio has been the most important. For a time after the coup, its members agreed to publish the government-owned newspaper. (For a short time it changed its name from *La Nación* to *La Patria*. It then switched to *El Cronista* and eventually back to *La Nación*.)

Summary

With a military junta firmly in power—and with a mandate from the people to remain so at least through 1988—it would seem that there will not be major changes or major growth in Chile's media or journalistic profession over the next decade. How the country will emerge from this period is uncertain. Chileans are accustomed to democracy and freedom, especially in the media. Will they return to democracy in its old form, with much fighting and in-fighting among political elements, or will they reemerge with new thoughts about what is needed for their country and its continued economic and political—but especially economic—stability?

One can attempt to listen to voices from abroad to learn whether exiled journalists or others are campaigning—as have the Cubans for so many years—for more freedom, for the release of any journalists still said to be jailed. But one cannot seem to hear many such voices. Whether this indicates that there is no real dissent or whether protest and resistance do exist is hard to say. What seems clear is that categoric predictions are not in order. One observer recalls forecasting, early in the Allende period, that freedom of the press would never suffer in Chile, that it was too firmly entrenched, that the people were too strongly committed to it. In a sense, he was correct *for the Allende period*, when the many problems concerning the press might, in retrospect, have been viewed as just that: *problems*. In contrast, freedom of the press has definitely been curbed since the 1973 coup, in a variety of what some might fear are irreversible methods. Much hinges on what happens with the economy. If the government succeeds in curbing inflation in a permanent or quasi-permanent way, and if the country comes to enjoy relative economic health, then it is less likely that the people will raise a hue and cry about press freedom, about the growing trend to commercialism in Chilean society and about other profound changes now taking place throughout the nation. Hence, what is good for the country's economy may not be so good for the country's press.

CHRONOLOGY

1976   *Ercilla* magazine's March 26 issue confiscated.

La Tercera suspended one day because of letter from lawyers about indifference of courts toward government abuses.

Belisario Velasco of Radio Balmaceda banished to remote village and station shut down for mentioning a sugar shortage.

1977   Radio Balmaceda closed permanently.

Bando 122 enacted, permitting military to determine which publications can appear.

Political parties banned instead of just being "in recess."

1978   *Nueva Vea* confiscated for discussing Argentine border dispute on eve of meeting between the two countries' heads of state.

La Segunda suspended 48 hours in first closure outside courts.

1980   Electorate approves by 67 percent a new constitution incorporating previous restrictions, including Bando 122.

1981   New constitution goes into effect in March.

Colegio de Periodistas abolished as legal monitor of licenses for journalists.

BIBLIOGRAPHY

Alexander, Robert J. "Chile's Cultural Dusk." *Christian Science Monitor,* January 21, 1975.

Dinges, John. "Chile Silences 2 Main Voices of Once Independent Media." *Washington Post,* February 3, 1977.

Fagen, Patricia. "The Media in Allende's Chile." *Journal of Communications,* Winter 1974, p. 59.

"Freer Press in Chile." *Index on Censorship,* January-February 1979, p. 51.

Goodsell, James Nelson. "Chilean Junta Censors Traditional Free Press." *Christian Science Monitor,* April 4, 1974.

Landis, Fred. "How 20 Chileans Overthrew Allende for the CIA." *Inquiry,* February 19, 1979, p. 16.

McHale, Tomas P. *El Frente de la Libertad de Expresion.* Santiago, 1972.

"Media No Longer Function Independently." *IPI Report,* November 1975, p. 1.

Merrill, John C., Bryan, Carter R., and Alisky, Marvin. *The Foreign Press.* Baton Rouge, La., 1970.

Moreno Laval, Jaime, "Libertad de Prensa: Un Legado en Entredicho." *Hoy,* February 11, 1981, p. 24.

1980 Editor & Publisher International Year Book. New York, 1980.

Pierce, Robert N. *Keeping the Flame.* New York, 1979.

_____. "Lights Out in Santiago." *Quill,* January 1974, p. 17.

Silva Castro, Raul. *Prensa y Periodismo en Chile (1812-1956).* Santiago, 1958.

Sobel, Lester A., ed. *Chile and Allende.* New York, 1974.

Stanley, Diane. "The Press in Chile—The Rectification Law." *Nieman Reports,* January 1961, p. 27.

UNESCO Statistical Yearbook 1978-79. Paris, 1980.

_____. *World Communications* (Paris, 1975).

United States Department of State, Bureau of Public Affairs. *Background Notes: Chile.* Washington, D.C., 1980.

U.S. Senate, Select Committee to Study Government Operations with Respect to Intelligence Operations. *Covert Action in Chile: 1963-1973.* Washington, D.C., 1975.

Valdebenito, Alfonso. *Historia del Periodismo Chileno (1812-1955).* Santiago, 1956.

Weil, Thomas E. *Area Handbook for Chile.* Washington, D.C., 1969.

PEOPLE'S REPUBLIC OF CHINA

by Min Chen and James Chu

BASIC DATA

Population: 1.02 billion (est.)
Area: 9,560,990 sq. km. (3,691,502 sq. mi.)
GNP: 666 billion yuans (US$444 billion) (1978)
Literacy Rate: 20-25%
Language(s): Mandarin Chinese; Shanghai, Canton, Fukien, Hakka dialects
Number of Dailies: 43 (1978)
  Aggregate Circulation: 32,353,000 (1978)
  Circulation per 1,000: 33.8 (1978)
Number of Nondailies: NA
  Aggregate Circulation: NA
  Circulation per 1,000: NA
Number of Periodicals: 1,600

Number of Radio Stations: 93
Number of Television Stations: 47
Number of Radio Receivers: NA
  Radio Receivers per 1,000: NA
Number of Television Sets: 3 million
  Television Sets per 1,000: 3.1
Total Annual Newsprint Consumption: 1,183,000 metric tons
Per Capita Newsprint Consumption: 1.3 kg. (2.9 lb.)
Total Newspaper Ad Receipts: NA
  As % of All Ad Expenditures: NA

Background & General Characteristics

The theory of the press in China flows directly from Marxist-Leninist doctrine, which emphasizes the effective manipulation of coercive and persuasive mass media as an instrument of national development. Marxism-Leninism holds that the press is a tool of class struggle. To be an effective tool, as such, the press must assume a militant role. Lenin said: "A newspaper is not merely a collective propagandist and collective agitator, it is also a collective organizer." In essence, the press is regarded as a primary vehicle not only for persuading and educating the masses, for recruiting their support, but also for mobilizing them to carry out policies of the party and of the government.

Mao Tse-tung rigidly followed and stressed this doctrine. In a talk with the editors of the *Shansi-Suiyuan Daily* in 1948, Mao said: "The role and power of the press consists in its ability to bring the Party program, the Party line, the Party's general and specific policies, its tasks and methods of work before the masses in the quickest and most extensive way." More specifically, the functions of the press are to publicize the Party decisions, to educate the masses and to form a link between the Party and the masses. Obviously, Mao stressed the importance of the Party-masses relationship. Through the press, the Party strives to organize the masses, to mobilize the masses and to develop in the masses the proletarian characteristics that will make them loyal and useful citizens of the country. To achieve these missions—as the *People's Daily* put it in 1960—the press must become the Party's "loyal eyes, ears and tongue," and "an important bridge for daily contact between the Party and innumerable people and a powerful tool for the Party to guide revolutionary struggle and construction."

According to Mao's concept of the press, a "proletarian journalist" should take part in mass movements to enrich his practical knowledge and to gain experience. Only when journalists understand problems of the masses and become experienced in mass movements will they be able to shoulder the task of organizing, agitating and educating the masses.

Censorship is too mild a term to describe the political control of the press when one examines the scope of the purge during the Cultural Revolution. The Propaganda Department of the Central Committee of the Communist Party, the command center for the mass media, sustained heavy losses in the political turmoil. Those purged included Lu Ting-yi, director of the department until 1967, Hu Chiao-mu, one of the deputy directors, and Wu Leng-hsi, editor in chief of the *People's Daily*. Casualties among the top journalist cadres were numerous. Imprisonment was common and a few lost their lives. The latter included Teng To, editor of the *People's Daily*, and Tao Chu, the propaganda chief of Guangdong Province. They were dubbed "capitalist roaders" because of following the prevailing party line approved by Liu Shao-chi, then chief of state of the People's Republic of China; this line was presently denounced by Chairman Mao. In his "confession" at a Red Guard rally, Wu Leng-hsi spoke of his dilemma as editor-in-chief of the *People's Daily*:

In the summer of 1956, Liu Shao-chi approved a *People's Daily* editorial opposing "reckless advance." The editorial was first drafted by Teng To, then revised by Hu Chiao-mu and Lu Ting-yi, and finally reviewed and approved by Liu Shao-chi. In the Nanning Conference in early 1958, Chairman Mao pointed out that this editorial was erroneous, that opposing "reckless advance" was erroneous, and that the editorial undermined the initiative and creativity of the masses and cadres, and resulted in the "U-shaped" development of our national economy. At that time I did not understand what this was all about, so I telephoned Peking to send for the manuscript of that editorial and discovered the development explained above. Liu Shao-chi wrote in the manuscript, which he had reviewed and approved, that it was to be presented to Chairman Mao for review and approval. Chairman Mao wrote three words, *pu kan le* ["I don't want to read it further"], on it. I informed Hu Chiao-mu, and remarked that Liu Shao-chi would be implicated. Hu told me not to make these facts public at the conference, so I did not. Thus did I cover up for Liu Shao-chi.

Since the demise of the "Gang of Four," the Chinese press has strived to improve its writing style and to publish articles reflecting the "real voices of the people." But the basic functions of the press remain unchanged. Newspapers remain a "propagandist tool of the proletarian class." As such, they must maintain rigid disciplines, and must not enjoy press freedom.

In general, the Chinese Communist press can be analyzed in terms of its administrative levels and its specialized functions.

Administratively, two levels of the press exist: the central, or national, press and the local press. Major newspapers at the central level include the *People's Daily*, organ of the National Central Committee of the Party; the *Enlightenment Daily*, the *Worker's Daily*, the *Liberation Army Daily* and *China Youth Daily*. The local-level press includes provincial, district and county newspapers. Each of the 29 provinces and big municipalities publishes a daily paper under the direct supervision of the local Party committee.

The major national newspapers serve various specific functions to meet the needs of various readers. The *People's Daily* is the mouthpiece of the Party Central Committee and is under the direct supervision of the Politburo. The editorial content of this paper, widely reprinted by other newspapers throughout the country, is required reading for all Party members. The *Enlightenment Daily*, operated by the Department of Propaganda of the Party's Central Committee, focuses its coverage on cultural, educational and scientific events. The *Worker's Daily* is an organ of the National Workers Union; another paper, *Wenhui Bao,* is the teachers' organ. The *Liberation Army Daily*, operated by the General Political Department of the Ministry of Defense, circulates in military units and state institutions. The paper allows no individual subcriptions. The Central Committee of the Chinese Communist Youth League publishes the *China Youth Daily* and the *China Pioneers Daily*, both for young readers.

The *People's Daily* can function as a good example to illustrate the organization of a Chinese newspaper. The paper has a staff of 1,600, of which some 500 work for the editorial department. The rest are on the staffs of the departments of administration and printing. The editorial department consists of ten units:

1. Mass Work. This unit handles letters to the editor. More than 1,000 such letters arrive at the paper each day. They are carefully studied by a staff of 80 journalists. Only a small proportion are published in the paper. Other letters are compiled, edited, and forwarded to the Central Committee of the Party or referred to an appropriate office of the government. Based on information collected from these letters, the mass work unit dispatches its staff to investigate events. At times, findings of these investigations are published in the *People's Daily*. However, publication of the findings is not the major concern of the paper. The *People's Daily* serves as a vital channel through which feedback of the public to Party policies flows from the lowest to the top levels of the political structure.

2. *International News.* It includes more than 100 journalists, including staff correspondents in the United States, England, Japan, North Korea, Rumania and Yugoslavia. The *People's Daily* normally devotes a full page to international news, averaging one-sixth of its news space each day.

3. *Domestic Politics.* This unit is responsible for the coverage of major political and Party matters in the country.

4. *Science and Technology.* Responsible for reporting developments in modernization at home, and scientific and technology innovations abroad. This unit functions to keep the subject of science and technology on the agenda of mass education.

5. *Agriculture.* Successful modernization of China to a great extent hinges on the growth of agricultural production. In recent years, the Chinese authorities have promoted greater intensity of land use, further mechanization and other measures to keep food supplies ahead of population growth, including a nationwide effort to limit birth rates. Staff correspondents of the agriculture unit in the *People's Daily* play a significant role in propagating these policies.

6. *Industry and Commerce.* This unit is charged with the responsibility of reporting the production of new goods and of marketing these products. To carry out these tasks, the *People's Daily* actually becomes an advertising agency, providing free publicity for all industries and businesses in the country.

7. *Theoretical Propagation.* To propagate the doctrines of Marxism, Leninism and Maoism is the pivotal function of the press in China. The press is considered the instrument of collective propaganda, agitation and organization—an instrument being used as a weapon in the struggle to build the "socialist state." The essential role of the press, in the words of the *People's Daily*, is "to educate the population in socialist thought, to propagandize the Communist Party's plans and policies, and to tighten up the close relationship between the Party and masses."

8. *Literature and Art.* Cultural liberation is an important part of the efforts of the current Chinese Communist leadership to rally the support of the population. Articles on classic Chinese art and literature have reappeared in periodicals throughout the nation. Lighter folk music gradually replaces highly revolutionary operas, and humorous, adventure-filled epics about empresses and heroic generals compete with the long, serious films that chronicle the arduous effort of idealistic peasants and factory workers. Foreign literature, art, movies and music have also found their way into China. It is not clear yet how far this permissiveness will be allowed to go, but the literature and art unit of the *People's Daily* plays an important part in carrying out policies dealing with cultural liberalization in today's China.

9. *Reporters.* This unit consists of "professional journalists" and amateur correspondents. The missions of staff journalists are to visit news sources to investigate events reported by unpaid amateur correspondents, and to supervise staff reporters stationed in each province of the country.

The distinct difference between the duties of Chinese reporters and their Western counterparts is in the amount of newsgathering and writing they are expected to do. While Western reporters are employed to gather and write news, staff reporters of a Chinese newspaper spend most of their time helping amateur correspondents—government employees, workers, teachers, soldiers, peasants —write articles for the paper. At times staff reporters write news stories on the basis of the information provided by the amateur correspondents. At other times they go out to work on stories in cooperation with the amateurs. According to the Chinese Communist concept of journalism, the correspondents are the ones who know the local situation best, being able to supply leads and clues that a professional reporter may not find readily available.

10. *Commentary.* Editorials and commentaries of the *People's Daily* reflect the policies of the Party. Most topics of the editorials and commentaries are determined by the staff of the commentary unit. But topics dealing with important policies are dictated by the Party's Central Committee. To ensure a faithful implementation of Party policies, the editor-in-chief of the *People's Daily* and his five deputies are appointed by the Department of Propaganda of the Central Committee.

Having survived the straightjacket Cultural Revolution, the Chinese press is going through stages of recuperation, resurrection and rapid expansion. Staff personnel as well as editorial policy, from the *People's Daily* down to the sub-provincial newspapers, has changed dramatically. Those who followed the anti-intellectual, anti-Western "Gang of Four" lines have been dismissed, and a new era of pragmatism and profit-oriented thinking has set in. Also resurrected are once-defunct newspapers and magazines, notably *The Peking Evening News* and *The Yangcheng Evening News* of Canton. Conspicuously absent, however, is *The Takung Pao of Peking*, a newspaper formerly associated with non-Party intellectuals.

The great mass audience of China is out there for the print media to reach. Even at the most conservative estimate of 20 percent literacy, China should have roughly 200 million readers waiting to be served. And a large portion of them are city dwellers with higher consumption power. Ever since the government relaxed its publication and subscription rules in 1978, a rapid expansion of readership has occurred in China.

The total circulation of national and provincial dailies for 1978—in which the latest statistics were given by the central government—was 11 billion copies (this figure is derived by multiplying the average circulation by 365 days). However, a second and more recent set of statistics, also given by the authorities, provides a much brighter picture. In September 1980 the postal administration reported that the country's more than 1,700 newspapers and periodicals had a combined average circulation of 150 million. As sole agent of distribution for all magazines and newspapers across the land, the postal authority is in a position to provide such figures. The authority also reported that on the average there was one copy of a newspaper or periodical for every 7.7 persons in China, and one for every two persons living in the urban areas.

Based on the September 1980 circulation figure of 150 million copies for the 1,700 newspapers and periodicals, China has a combined circulation of about 146 copies for every 1,000 inhabitants.

At present, 59 newspapers are known to be publishing in China. The following is a list of the papers, their location and, where available, their latest circulation figures.

National Newspapers

The People's Daily, East Changan Road, Peking —6,300,000
Guangming Ribao (Enlightenment Daily), Peking
Gongren Ribao (Worker's Daily), Peking, daily except Sundays
Reference News (CanKao Xiaoxi), tabloid daily, Peking—9,000,000
Beijing Ribao (Peking Daily), Peking
Beijing Wanbao (Peking Evening News), Peking
Tiyu Bao (Physical Education News), triweekly
Jiankang Bao (Health News), semiweekly

Zhongguo Nongmin Bao (China's Farmers' Newspaper), weekly, Peking—230,000
Zhonggao Chingnian Bao (China's Teenagers News), triweekly
Zhongguo Shaonian Bao (China's Youngsters), every Wednesday
Jiefang Ribao (Liberation Daily), Shanghai
Wen Hui Bao (Literary Gazette), Shanghai—900,000
Jiefangjun Bao (Liberation Army Daily), Peking

Provincial and Municipal Newspapers

Tianjing Ribao, Tianjing, Tianjing Municipality
Nanfang Ribao (Southern Daily), Canton, Guangdong Province
Guangzhow Ribao (Canton Daily), Canton
Yangcheng Wanbao (Goats City Evening News), Canton—300,000
Xinhwa Ribao (New China Daily), Nanjing, Jiangsu Province
Sichuan Ribao (Szechwan Daily), Chengdu, Sichuan Province
Dazhong Ribao (The Masses Daily), Jinan, Shandong Province
Zhejiang Ribao (Chekiang Daily), Hangchow, Chienciang Province
Guangxi Ribao (Kwangsi Daily), Guiling, Guangxi Province
Helongjiang Ribao (Helongjiang Daily), Harbin, Helongjiang Province
Mudanjiang Ribao (Mudanjiang Daily), Mudanjiang, Helongjiang Province
Guizhou Ribao (Kweichow Daily), Guiyang, Guizhow Province
Hebei Ribao (Hebei Daily), Hebei Province
Xingtai Ribao (Xingtai Daily), Xingtai City, Hebei Province
Hubei Ribao (Hubei Daily), Hankow, Hubei Province
Changjiang Ribao (Yangtze Daily), Wuhan, Hubei Province
Henan Ribao (Henan Daily), Cheng Zhou, Henan Province
Liaoning Ribao (Liaoning Daily), Liaoning, Liaoning Province—300,000 (1974)
Liaohwa Bao (Liaohwa News), Liaohwa, Liaoning Province
Jiling Ribao (Kirin Daily), Jiling, Jiling Province
Nei Mongol Ribao (Inner Mongolia Daily), Hohhot, Nei Monggol
Yunnan Ribao (Yunnan Daily), Kunming, Yunnan Province
Jiangxi Ribao (Chiangsi Daily), Nanchang, Chiangxi Province
Shanxi Ribao (Shansi Daily), Taiyuan, Shanxi Province
Fujian Ribao (Fujian Daily), Fuchou, Fujian Province
Shaanxi Ribao (Shensi Daily), Xian, Shaanxi Province
Xian Ribao (Xian Daily), Xian, Shaanxi Province
Gansu Ribao (Kansu Daily), Lanzhou, Gansu Province
Anhui Ribao (Anhwei Daily), Hefei, Anhui Province
Qinghai Ribao (Tsinghai Daily), Xining, Qinghai Province

Ningxia Ribao (Ninghsia Daily), Yinchuan, Ningxia Autonomous Region

Sinjiang Uygur Ribao (Sinkiang Daily), Urumqi, Xinjiang Autonomous Region

Xizang Ribao (Tibet Daily), Lhasa, Xizang Autonomous Region

Ala Shan Bao (Ala Shan News), Bayinhot, Inner Mongolia, weekly—2,500 (in Mongolian)

Cang Zhou Ribao (Tsangchow Daily), Tsangchow, Hopeh Province

Gansu Nunming Bao (Kansu Farmers' News), Lanchow, Kansu

Guangdong Nongmin Bao (Kwangtung Farmers' News), Canton, founded March 1980

Hofei Wanbao (Hofei Evening News), Hofei, Anhwei

Hangzhou Ribao (Hangchow Daily), Hangchow, Chekiang

Jinzhong Bao (Tsinchung News), Shansi

Luda Ribao (Luta Daily), Dairen, Liaoning

Renmin Tiedao Bao (People's Railroad News)

Shanxi Nongmin Bao (Shansi Farmers' News), Shansi Province

Qing Nian Bao (Youth News), Shanghai

Shenyang Ribao (Shenyang Daily), Shenyang (Mukden), Liaoning

Tangshan Ribao (Tangshan Daily), Tangshan, Hopeh

Yenan Bao (Yenan News), Yenan, Shensi (resurrected since April 1979)

Newspaper & Periodical Categories	
Popular knowledge	23
Sports and recreation	7
Pictorials and dailies, nondailies	24
Political	11
Economics and trade	5
Philosophy and social sciences	21
Education and Chinese and foreign linguistics	13
News, publishing and library science	6
Literature	31
History, archaeology	12
Music, dance	8
Fine arts, calligraphy and photography	8
Drama and cinema	12
Juvenile and children	11
Natural sciences	14
Mathematics, physics and chemistry	22
Astronomy and geography	14
Biology and biosciences	15
Agriculture and ag sciences	7
Industry and technology	30
Chinese medicine and Chinese herbal pharmacy	7
Western medicine and Western pharmacy	34

Among the more than 1,700 newspapers and periodicals distributed through the Chinese postal system, 331 in the Chinese language are open for overseas subscription. Each is identifiable by its publisher, location and frequency. Sixteen are daily and nondaily national and provincial newspapers. The rest are semi-monthly (eight), monthly (100), bimonthly (80), quarterly (126) and one unspecified (*Communique from the State Council*).

A breakdown of the 335 newspapers and periodicals by the Joint Publishing Company of Hong Kong, the overseas arm of the monopoly New China Book Store of China, appears in the accompanying table.

All of these periodicals are sponsored by national or provincial institutions. The subprovincial periodicals are for internal circulation only, and they are often of inferior quality. The State Council issued an order in July 1980 forbidding any unregistered periodicals to utilize the postal system to solicit or distribute.

Economic Framework

Private ownership of the press does not exist in China. Instead, ownership depends on the type of publication. All dailies are owned either by the Central Committee of the Communist Party (*People's Daily* is one such) or by the provincial Communist Party committees. When there is more than one daily in a city, such as Peking, Canton and Shanghai, one is owned by the municipal Party committee, in which case the paper usually appears in the evening so as not to compete with the morning daily, which is the product of the provincial Party committee. *Yangcheng Wanbao* ("Canton Evening News") and *Peking Wanbao* ("Peking Evening News") both belong to their respective municipal Party committees. Nondailies are owned either by district Party committees or county Party committees, districts being administrative units that are composed of several counties under the provincial government.

Some more prosperous or populous administrative units between the provincial and county level and cities that are district seats may also have their own dailies, such as *Xintai Ribao* in Xingtai, Hebei, about 400 kilometers (250 miles) south of Peking. They are generally nondailies, such as Shanxi Province's *Jin Chong Bao*, which was identified by the *People's Daily* as the "organ of the Party committee of Jinchong District."

The numerous departments and committees of the State Council, the Party's administrative arm that runs the country, may publish their own nondailies, weeklies or periodicals. *Tiyu Bao*, for instance, is owned by the Athletics Committee and Jiankang Bao by the Health Department.

All dailies or nondailies identified with the title "Ching Nian" ("Youth") belong to the Chinese Youth League.

Periodicals can be published by academic institutions and government agencies with the approval of the Party committee of the district.

Distribution of all the print media, dailies, nondailies and periodicals is handled by the post offices. Distribution of books of various sizes is handled by the New China Book Store. To the post office workers, more business does not mean higher pay but heavier mailbags. This is reason enough to cause consumer frustration over the tardiness of mail service. Readers in the countryside often complain that dailies are delivered in bundles several times a month.

Two recent "improvements" announced by the post office give the outside world a glimpse of the state of the newspaper distribution system in China. They were hailed by the postal administration and the newspapers as a major breakthrough when the *Guizhow Ribao* in Guiyang, Guizhou Province, and the *Shanxi Ribao* in Taiyuan, Shanxi Province, promised to finish printing by 6:30 a.m., and when the post office promised to deliver the newspapers to the government offices before 8 a.m.

The world's most populous Communist economy has begun to realize its need for commercial advertising. As a result, advertising reappeared in China's mass media in 1979, after its absence for more than a decade since 1966.

In January 1979, in celebration of the Lunar New Year, a Shanghai radio station started broadcasting commercial spots. In the same year Canton Television pioneered the venture of TV commercials in China, followed by Shanghai Television, which aired a commercial for a Chinese cola. Also in 1979, when Shanghai Television telecast "live" the performance of the visiting Boston Symphony Orchestra, two 60-second spots for a Swiss watch, all in English, were broadcast during an intermission. These English commercials indicate a typical intent of foreign commercials in Chinese mass media: to show the good will of the advertiser to the

Chinese public. In the March 1979 issue of the English weekly journal, *Beijing* (Peking) *Review*, the official Shanghai Advertising Corporation announced it would "offer full and efficient services" to its clients. In December 1979 the *People's Daily* made its own announcement: that it would accept paid space from foreign concerns—another breakthrough in Chinese advertising.

Advertising in China is not designed to create society's wants—at least not just yet. It is considered trade stimulus to facilitate the flow of commodities and provide a vehicle to enhance the quality of products.

Press Laws, Censorship & State-Press Relations

As there is no press law, and since the judicial system has just begun the process of reconstruction, censorship is practiced by the Party committees at various levels. Two levels of the committees are involved in monitoring the press: the Party committee of the city where the newspaper is located, and the committee that has direct jurisdiction over the location. Thus *Peking Daily* is monitored by both the municipal Party committee and the Central Committee of the Chinese Communist Party. On the other hand, the *Yangcheng Evening News* of Canton is monitored by the municipal committee of Canton and the provincial committee in Guangdong. The official in charge of the propaganda department of a Party committee at an appropriate level controls the press.

Unlike the Russian system, where Glavlit censors sit in the editorial rooms of the *Pravda*, *Izvestia* and other papers, Chinese journalism practices a self-imposed censorship, which is carried out subtly in the following manner:

1. Journalists are recruited by the Party from graduates of journalism departments or short-term journalism workshops. While they need not be Party members, they must be loyalists. Vacancies are not open for competition but are filled by appointment through the local Party committees. Promotion, demotion, transfer and termination may all be experienced by the same person in a short time, as in the case of a reporter for the *Yangcheng Evening News*. During the Cultural Revolution, the arrest and demotion of hundreds of journalists, and their subsequent rehabilitation after the political turmoil indicated the breadth and depth of press censorship via personnel control.

2. While routine material does not require "clarification" (meaning approval) from Party authorities, important editorials and news stories all require prior endorsement by the upper-ladder Party committees. For instance, editorials appearing in the *People's Daily, Red Flag* and the *Liberation Army Daily* on the Chinese National Day (October 1), New Year's Day and Laborers' Day (May 1) are jointly written by the editorial staffs of the three journals, in close consultation with the Central Committee of the CCP. Similar procedures are applied to editorials that announce new policies or reinforce the current Party line. The publication of such important editorials requires prior approval of the chairman or a vice-chairman of the Central Committee.

Attitude Toward Foreign Media

A vast gulf exists between the Chinese and Western concepts of how a journalist operates. For journalists of non-Communist countries, their job is to secure information and report it to their readers. From the Chinese point of view, the press is an arm of the government, which tells the press exactly what to say and do. These different concepts of the journalism function underline the relationship between the Chinese government and foreign correspondents in China.

While cables are not censored in Peking, a system of subtle censorship does exist. Foreign correspondents may find that their cables are promptly dispatched, but when a story offends, its author is summoned to the Information Department of the Foreign Ministry, lectured, and perhaps given a "serious warning." The correspondent may find that his/her privilege is being delayed if not revoked. This may include a long wait for permission to import a car. The more serious offender will find his/her visa simply not renewed. Politics plays an important part in the treatment of foreign correspondents. Normally, each of the correspondents, especially those from non-Communist countries, is in Peking in exchange for a Chinese correspondent in his/her country. The Chinese are reluctant to risk any reciprocal action against their own newspeople.

Because of the housing shortage, many foreign correspondents live in high-rise hotels —sanitized ghettoes for aliens. This naturally sets up a formidable barrier between the foreign reporters and the ordinary Chinese, who are forbidden to enter without first being screened and registered. The isolation also makes it extremely difficult for correspondents to keep up with the flow of events, and causes them to rely heavily, if not entirely, on the official reports and text statements released by the information officials at the Foreign Ministry and on the New China News Agency wire.

Another source of information is Chinese newspapers, although non-Chinese-speaking correspondents must rely on the interpreter assigned by the Chinese government to translate articles into English and other languages. They also need the interpreter when they are trying to cover a story. Obviously, questions of loyalty can arise when it comes to news deemed controversial.

News Agencies

There are two news agencies in China: the New China News Agency (NCNA) and China News Service, which supplies feature stories. NCNA is an active arm of the Chinese Communist Party. It personnel are on the Party payroll, and its director usually serves as a deputy director of the Propaganda Department of the Central Committee of the CCP. It is the sole foreign news distributor in China, and joins with China News Service in reporting domestic news to the outside world. But China News Service does not serve any client inside China; only NCNA can distribute domestic news throughout the country.

In 1979 NCNA sent three reporters to the University of Missouri, and others to European nations to learn modern newsgathering techniques. It has established a News Research Institute within the agency to seek methods of better news writing.

One NCNA provincial branch has given some visiting journalists a glimpse at its domestic operations. In 1979 this particular branch had a director, a deputy director, an editor, twelve reporters and three photographers. News originated from this branch was statistically broken down into three types: (1) for public consumption, (2) for reference only, (3) important stories. The best reporter had 37 stories published. Twenty-five was the average. A total of 308 photographs were released in the year.

NCNA uses voicecast, teletype, Morse code and satellite transmission facilities to reach its clients. Measuring by scope and magnitude, however, voicecast is the most widely used channel. One United States government publication reported that, in 1972, 46 shortwave stations in Peking were assigned to the China News Service for transmitting NCNA's daily newsfile to both domestic and international listeners—using 12 indigenous languages and dialects and 11 foreign languages. NCNA acquires news sources through domestic branches, overseas bureaus, news exchange agreements with other news agencies, and monitoring of foreign news services. Since 1972 NCNA has signed exchange agreements with almost all major news agencies in the world, including Reuters, AFP, Tass, AP, UPI and Kyodo. With the radioteletype and Morse code, NCNA's Peking headquarters is also capable of monitoring almost all foreign news services. It should be noted, however, that although NCNA has access to all news around the world, only a few carefully selected items are released. Much of the deleted material is available only to high ranking officials for reference in policy making—an old practice dating back to the earliest days of the People's Republic.

Electronic News Media

The history of the Chinese Communist broadcasting enterprise dates back to 1941, when the Yenan Hsin Hua (New China) Broadcasting Station began its broadcasting on an experimental basis. Called XNCR, the station was not officially established and made only two-hour-a-day broadcasts until 1945. It beamed its programs into the Nationalist Chinese-controlled territories in the northwestern part of the country. The Communists claimed that their broadcasting had a demoralizing effect on the enemy forces, causing a great number of Nationalist officers and soldiers to join the People's Liberation Army.

Radio and television are valuable tools of national development in China. The organizational structure of the electronic media resembles that of the press, that is to say, on three levels—central, provincial and local. With the establishment of the People's Republic of China on October 1, 1949, the Yenan station was officially renamed the Central People's Broadcasting Station. Under the supervision of the Central Broadcasting Administration, the central station—actually a radio network—consists of four stations, all located in Peking. Stations I and II broadcast in Mandarin, the main dialect of China. Station I, on the air 21 hours and 35 minutes a day, focuses its programs on news and commentaries, while Station II, broadcasting 18 hours and 25 minutes daily, features music, drama, literature and history. Station III aims its programs at listeners in Taiwan and is on the air 20 hours a day. The fourth station provides programs to the minorities in languages such as Tibetan, Kazakh, Uighur and Mongolian. A total of 10 hours of programs each day is devoted to the minorities. They account for only six percent of China's nearly one billion population, but occupy nearly 60 percent of its total land.

Also under the supervision of the Central Broadcasting Administration is Radio Peking, one of the five largest international radio stations in the world. Radio Peking broadcasts 39 different languages for a total of 120 hours of air time each day; programs in Japanese, Russian and English account for 50 percent of this time. Radio Peking also exchanges pretaped programs with stations in 20 countries and receives more than 100,000 letters each year from listeners throughout the world.

The provincial broadcasting stations consist of at least one station in each of the provincial capitals. In addition, in larger cities like Shanghai, municipal radio stations serve the needs of the local listeners. Generally, the provincial and city stations relay programs from Peking and add local news, entertainment, sports and weather reports. As of June 1979, 93 radio stations and 455 transmitting and relay stations were in operation.

The local broadcasting system in China is characterized by the wired operation. In the early 1950s the Chinese began developing "radio-receiver networks" at county and municipal levels to solve the problems of insufficient radio facilities and limited numbers of receivers. The central government ordered county and municipal governments, military units, schools, factories and all other organizations at the local levels to appoint broadcasting monitors. Their duties included listening to and recording news, political instructions and other important programming broadcast by central and provincial stations, with a view to organizing people to listen to programs collectively. As part of this monitoring system, the Chinese developed "wired broadcasting networks," patterned after the Soviet Union radio-diffusion exchange system. The system uses a central receiver, with an amplifier and a switchboard housed in the studio. Stations' broadcasts are picked up by the receiver, amplified and sent through the switchboard to loudspeakers installed in village squares, school playgrounds, marketplaces, rice paddies, factories, mines, communal mess halls, dormitories, households and even on treetops and telephone poles. Today, although China no longer has a shortage of radio receivers, the wired broadcasting system remains in operation at more than 95 percent of local communes because of its effectiveness in mass persuasion.

The Central People's Broadcasting Station in Peking initiated television in 1958. Today 47 stations serve every province and autonomous region except Tibet. Two channels are in operation in Peking. Channel 2 televises its news programs through a microwave network of 169 relay stations to television sets all over the country. Its typical broadcasting day starts at 5:30 p.m. and ends at 11 p.m. On special occasions such as national holidays, Channel 2 extends its programming to midnight. Chinese television demonstrates clearly the use of broadcasting to serve the public interest. In a variety of forms, programs provide information and understanding about the world in which the audiences live; they report news of the policies and activities of the national government; they present live coverage of important events; they broadcast lectures on modern technology, on life and cultures of foreign lands, on family health; they dramatize revolutionary events through theater, opera and films. Channel 8 in Peking aims its programs at the local audience. On Mondays, Wednesdays and Fridays, Channel 8 devotes its air time exclusively to broadcasting college-level courses. On weekdays, Channel 2 also uses its morning hours—9 a.m. until 12 noon—to telecast educational programs. These programs are the essence of the curriculum of the Television University.

The history of educational television in China dates back to 1960, but it was suspended during the Cultural Revolution. Special lectures on television resumed in 1977 but it was not until 1979 that the Television

University was inaugurated in Peking. With 600,000 enrolled—and countless nonenrolled—students, Television University claims to be the country's, and perhaps the world's, biggest educational undertaking, offering courses in mathematics, physics, chemistry and English. Students watch lectures and demonstrations on television in their homes and in 18,000 centers specially set aside for that purpose. Lessons are given by professors from institutes of higher learning and by other specialists. Person-to-person instruction and laboratory activities are available at learning centers. Students are mainly workers in factories, middle-school teachers, and men and women of the People's Liberation Army. Recipients of the Television University degree are recognized as college graduates by the state.

No official statistics about the number of television receivers in China have been released. As of January 1980 it was estimated that three million sets, 3.1 for every 1,000 people, were available. In 1980 also reports claimed 35 percent of the families in Peking and 25 percent of those in Shanghai had television sets. Most factories, schools and government offices had at least one set. The figures may not sound impressive to Westerners, but considering the cost of even the cheapest black-and-white television sets in China, it is extraordinarily high. The average factory worker would have to invest five to eight months' salary to pay the 300 to 450 yuan ($200 to $300) for a standard Chinese set. Despite the sets' prohibitive cost, however, the government cannot manufacture and import them fast enough to meet the demand. For one reason, the mere appearance of a television antenna on the top of a roof adds social prestige to the family. More significantly, television provides a heavy dose of educational programs to the viewers (although the entertainment programs are primitive).

Education & Training

Chinese journalists are fighters on the ideological front. They are regarded as revolutionaries and in fact are "cadres" in the bureaucratic system. Hence the training of journalists in China is conceived as moral-political. The curriculum of journalism education is designed, in Mao's words, to produce proletarian newspeople "imbued with socialist consciousness."

The curriculum consists of three categories:

1. Political theories. Students are required to study Marxism-Leninism, dialectical materialism, political economics and the history of the Communist movement and of the Chinese Communist Party. In these classes, journalism students learn the body of principles and practices that underlie the operation and behavior of the Chinese Communist political system, of which the press is an integral part. One of the authors of this chapter has written:

> These courses determine the nature of news. According to Marxism-Leninism, news is the factual description of man's struggle in the society and man's struggle against the natural environment. Facts are used to support the political thoughts of the leadership upon which a policy is formulated. Thus, facts must be analyzed, selected and consolidated by the journalist to record the history of proletarian revolution and to help the people grasp the political thoughts of the party leadership.

2. Literature and history. Courses in this category, from the viewpoint of Chinese journalism educators, are fundamental to the development of the student's writing skills. Students are introduced to—and are required to write—essays, novels, short stories, commentaries and other forms. The courses cover ancient and contemporary Chinese literature, foreign literature and Chinese and world history, together with introductions to literature and basic writing.

3. Professional courses. In addition to gaining professional skills in newsgathering, writing and editing, students study the socialist ideology and practice of newsgathering, foreign press systems, and current events and issues. Course titles include "Principles of Journalism," "News Reporting and Writing," "Newspaper Editing," "Press Photography," "Political Propaganda," "History of Chinese Newspapers and Periodicals" and "The Foreign Press."

One foreign language is required for all journalism majors. Most students take English; others learn German, Japanese, Russian and Spanish.

In today's China, four universities—the People's University in Peking, Fun Tan University in Shanghai, Chi Nan University in Canton and Amoy University in Fukien—offer four-year journalism programs accredited by the Ministry of Education. Other universities, such as Kwangsi University, Yunnan University, Shangtung University, Kiangsi University and Nanking Normal College, also offer journalism courses. Peking Broadcast College is the only four-year institution in China that trains technicians, radio and television broadcasters and foreign correspondents for the electronic media. The college consists of three departments: electronic technology, broadcast journalism and foreign languages.

News establishments and propaganda committees at various levels also conduct short-term training workshops. Candidates are mostly selected from part-time correspondents, young Party members, Liberation Army soldiers, high school students, workers and even peasants who have acquired "correct political thoughts." These "indigenously trained" newspeople are grass-roots journalist cadres serving as "ears and eyes of the Party."

Summary

The theory of the press in China is derived from the Marxist-Leninist doctrine that integrates the press with the political communication machinery. Both Lenin and Mao stressed the role of the press as educator, organizer and agitator of the mass movement. But because of the socioeconomic conditions of Chinese society—as well as Mao's personal experience as a proletarian revolutionary—Mao himself placed even greater emphasis on the role of the press as a bridge between the Party and the masses. Throughout his life he strove to use the press as the spearhead in developing the proletarian characteristics in the masses. This concept explains why the Chinese press has suffered so greatly in each major political campaign—particularly during the Cultural Revolution, which demanded that the press be the "loyal eyes, ears and tongue" of the leadership. Chinese Communists believed then and believe now that without the service of such organs the country's leadership cannot take any effective action and will be toppled inevitably by "counterrevolutionaries." Mao's death and the arrest of the "Gang of Four" have not altered the basic concept of the press in the mind of the current leadership. Propaganda officials purged during the Cultural Revolution have been "rehabilitated" and placed back in key positions in the nation's mass persuasive effort under the new leadership of Deng Xiaoping (Teng Hsiao-ping). Today the task of strengthening the Party's political and ideological work is now in the hands of the veteran Teng supporters, the "capitalist roaders" during the Cultural Revolution. But Mao's concept of the Chinese press remains basically intact.

Two administrative levels of newspapers exist in China: the national press and the local press. Major national newspapers serve various specific functions and focus their coverage on different subject matters. At the local level each province and big municipality publishes a daily newspaper under the direct supervision of its local Party committee.

Although the rate of illiteracy remains high, China may well have at least 200 million readers served by the print media. It was estimated in September 1980 that the total circulation of the 1,800 Chinese newspapers and periodicals was 150 million, or about 150 copies for every 1,000 inhabitants.

Official statistics on the number of radios are not available. As of January 1980, it was estimated that three million television sets, one for every 319.4 people, were available. TV sets are in great demand, despite their prohibitive cost. Possession of a TV carries social prestige and viewing provides one of the rare leisure activities in China's regimented society.

One of the most significant developments in the Chinese media in recent years has been the reappearance, in 1979, of advertising, after its absence for more than a decade since the beginning of the Cultural Revolution in 1966. The Chinese experience in advertising suggests that advertising in this country is another form of political propaganda, promoting not only goods and services but, more importantly, the nation's progress toward modernization.

The reappearance of classic Chinese and Western art and literature in the Chinese mass media indicates another significant development in the press policy of the current leadership. In line with this is the tacit permission to listen to foreign radio broadcast. The Voice of America, BBC and even the Voice of Free China from Taiwan are no longer jammed.

No foreign ownership of mass media in China is permitted. The government authorizes only a few foreign publications or their Chinese editions for sale in the country. Among them is the Chinese edition of *Reader's Digest*. But at least government officials and party cadres are adequately informed of foreign events through the *Reference News* Chinese translations of world news dispatches. This eight-page daily report is highly popular reading material among intellectuals. Its current circulation is nine million.

To help inform foreign residents in China of major news events in the country, the Chinese Communist Party published its first English-language newspaper, *China Daily*, on June 1, 1981. A sister publication of the *People's Daily*, the paper publishes Tuesday through Saturday in Peking and Hong Kong. It has a circulation of 18,000.

These developments seem to demonstrate that the Chinese government adopts a very restricted policy toward international information flow. As members of the foreign press corps in Peking increase, so does the competition for news coverage. Before Nixon visited China in 1972, the government permitted only a few selected journalists or writers to visit the vast land for a short period of time under well-planned itineraries. For the most part, the results of such tours were favorable reports about the host country. Now China is experiencing different foreign coverages: up-to-the-minute accounts of major events in the country and in-depth analyses of the nation's problems and issues. Peking's foreign press corps is under criticism from the Chinese authorities for being too negative in its reports. A Dutch correspondent, William van Kemenade of NRC Handelsblad, left China in June 1981 at the request of the Foreign Ministry for behaving "inappropriately." It was the second case in four years that an accredited foreign journalist was expelled. In 1977 Ross Munro, then a correspondent for the Toronto *Globe and Mail* and *Time* magazine, was asked to leave after he wrote a five-part series on human rights violations in China.

In conclusion, the command roles of the Chinese press remain a mouthpiece of the Party, a powerful weapon in fighting against the "people's enemies," and a textbook of the people.

CHRONOLOGY

1972   Associated Press and New China News Agency (Hsinhua) reach agreement on exchange of news and photos, establishing first regular news and photo channel between China and United States in 22 years.

1976   China's first television transmission via satellite offers films of Premier Chou En-lai's (Zhou Enlai's funeral; previous satellite transmissions were made by foreign networks, starting with President Richard Nixon's trip to China in 1972.

1979   Television University estab-

lished; Central Broadcasting and Television University first opened in 1960 but was disrupted during Cultural Revolution.

Wei Jingsheng, editor of underground publication *Exploration*, sentenced to 15 years imprisonment after being found guilty of providing military secrets to a foreigner and engaging in counter-revolutionary activities.

1981   First English-language newspaper, *China Daily*, published.

BIBLIOGRAPHY

Aronson, James. "By Your Pupils You'll Be Taught." *Columbia Journalism Review*, January–February 1980.

Barnett, A. Doak. *China on the Eve of Communist Takeover*. New York, 1962.

Bauer, Raymond A. *The New Man in Soviet Psychology*. Cambridge, Mass., 1952.

Beijing Review, Peking.

Brown, Robert U. "Newspapers in China." *Editor & Publisher*, December 9, 1972.

Canako Xiaoxi ("Reference News").

Chang, Parris H. *Power and Policy in China*. University Park, Pa., 1975.

Chao, Tse-jen. "A Study of Chinese Communist Broadcasting." *Ta-lu Fei-chin Chipao*, July–September 1962.

Chen, Jo-hsi. *The Execution of Mayor Yin*. Bloomington, Ind., 1978.

China Quarterly.

China Reconstructs, Peking.

Christian Science Monitor.

Chu, Godwin, ed. *Popular Media in China*. Honolulu, 1978.

_____. *Radical Change through Communication in Mao's China*. Honolulu, 1977.

Chu, James. "Broadcasting in the People's Republic of China." In *Broadcasting in Asia and the Pacific*. Ed. John A. Lent. Philadelphia, 1978.

_____. "China Is 'Back to Basics' in Journalism Education." *Journalism Educator*, January 1980.

_____. "Chinese Advertising: Its Policy, Practice and Evolution." *Journalism Quarterly*, Spring 1972.

_____. "How China's Media Train Foreign Correspondents." *Editor & Publisher*, September 1, 1979.

_____. "Mainland China Too Has a Television Industry." *Television International*, March–April 1977.

_____. "The PRC Journalist as a Cadre." *Current Scene*, November 1975.

_____, and Fang, William. "The Training of Journalists in Communist China." *Journalism Quarterly*, Autumn 1972.

Current Scene.

Far Eastern Economic Review.

Guangming Ribao ("The Enlightenment Daily").

Hiniker, Paul. *Revolutionary Ideology and Chinese Reality*. Beverly Hills, Calif., 1977.

Inkeles, Alex. *Public Opinion in Soviet Russia*. Cambridge, Mass., 1968.

Isaacs, Norman E. "China: Casting Off the Myths." *Columbia Journalism Review*, January–February 1973.

Issues and Studies, Taipei.

Jiefang Ribao ("The Liberation Daily").

Kecskemeti, Paul. "Totalitarian Communications as a Means of Control: A Note on the Sociology of Propaganda." *Public Opinion Quarterly*, Summer 1950.

Liu, Alan P. L. *Communications and National Integration in Communicast China*. New enlarged edition. Berkeley, Calif., 1971.

MacFarquhar, Roderick. *The Hundred Flowers Campaign and the Chinese Intellectuals*. New York, 1960.

Mao Tse-tung. *Selected Works of Mao Tse-tung.* Peking, 1965 and 1967.

Markham, James W. *Voices of the Red Giants.* Ames, Iowa, 1967.

Myrdal, Jan. *Report from a Chinese Village.* New York, 1966.

Nanfang Ribao ("Southern Daily").

Nunn, Raymond. *Publishing in Communist China.* Cambridge, Mass., 1966.

Pool, Itheil de Sola, et al., ed. *Handbook of Communication.* Chicago, 1973

Pye, Lucian W. *Communication and Political Development.* Princeton, N.J., 1963.

Renmin Ribao ("People's Daily").

Schell, Orville. "Dateline Peking: Competitive as Hell." *Columbia Journalism Review,* January–February 1980.

Schurmann, Franz. *Ideology and Organization in Communist China.* Berkeley, Calif., 1966.

Schwartz, Benjamin I. "The Reign of Virtue: Some Broad Perspectives on Leader and Party in the Cultural Revolution." *The China Quarterly,* July–September 1968.

Sterba, James P. "China Publishes Its First Newspaper in English." *San Francisco Chronicle,* June 2, 1981.

The New York Times.

Topping, Seymour. "China Denounces Party Journalist." *The New York Times,* May 9, 1966.

Townsend, James R. *Political Participation in Communist China.* Berkeley, Calif., 1967.

Wen Hui Bao ("The Literary Gazette").

Worthy, William. "Reporting in Communist China." *The New Republic,* March 26, 1957.

Xinwen Yenjiu Tzeliao ("Research Material of the Press"), Peking.

Xinwen Zhanxian ("News Front"), Peking.

Yu, Frederick T. C. *Mass Persuasion in Communist China.* New York, 1964.

COLOMBIA

by Robert N. Pierce

BASIC DATA

Population: 26,476,000
Area: 1,139,600 sq. km. (439,886 sq. mi.)
GNP: 1.16 trillion pesos (US$26.39 billion) (1979)
Literacy Rate: 72%
Language(s): Spanish
Number of Dailies: 42
  Aggregate Circulation: 1.33 million
  Circulation per 1,000: 105
Number of Nondailies: 8
  Aggregate Circulation: 125,000
  Circulation per 1,000: 5
Number of Periodicals: 300

Number of Radio Stations: 231
Number of Television Stations: 18
Number of Radio Receivers: 2.85 million
  Radio Receivers per 1,000: 117
Number of Television Sets: 1.7 million
  Television Sets per 1,000: 70
Total Annual Newsprint Consumption: 44,400 metric tons
  Per Capita Newsprint Consumption: 1.8 kg. (4 lb.)
Total Newspaper Ad Receipts: 1.73 billion pesos (US$39.4 million) (1979)
  As % of all Ad Expenditures: 25.3

Background & General Characteristics

One of the earliest parts of Latin America to be explored by the conquistadores, Colombia likes to claim that it is the most Spanish country in the Western Hemisphere. This approaches reality only for the most educated elite, however. Taken as a whole, Colombia could more truly be thought of as a microcosm of Latin America.

Perhaps in no other country can one find so many of the varied and often opposite factors that make up the region. It is placed where South America, the Caribbean and Central America meet. It has mountains and seacoasts; snows and swamps; white, brown and black people and mixtures of all; super-rich, super-poor and a strong middle class; the continent's most famous novelist and pathetic illiteracy; oil, coffee and marijuana as major products; absolutist politicians, communist terrorists and a working democracy.

Predictably, this has resulted in a media system that does not fit neatly into any category. The media are among the more modern in Latin America, but in most types—newspapers, television, magazines—

they are outranked in hemispheric influence by one or more other countries, even though Colombia itself is one of the four Latin American nations with a population over 25 million.

Nevertheless, Colombian mass communication has at least three aspects that set it apart from its neighbors: No other country as large—or even half its size—has press freedom. By 1980 Colombia had maintained substantial liberty of printed media for nearly a quarter of a century. On the other hand, Colombia is the only large Latin American country with a television system completely owned by the government. Colombia's TV differs from that of any other state system in the world, in the way it allows private enterprise to participate.

But perhaps of greatest significance, the largest and most successful rural education program through mass media is found in Colombia. There also is a vigorous adult education program in the cities. Since the 1950s, Colombia has waged an almost feverish campaign to reach all its citizens—children and adults—with literacy and other basic skills. University students, soldiers and members of religious and business groups for years have donated time to achieve this elementary goal.

And yet, while official estimates of adult literacy have risen to 81 percent, cities remain islands surrounded by peasants, about half of whom cannot read. Perhaps the greatest difficulty is that many peasants do not have easy access to reading material and thus soon forget the skills they learn in brief periods of schooling.

At the other end of the spectrum, Colombia maintains a tradition of high culture that is rooted in the earliest colonial days. Revering purity in the language, Colombians like to speak of Bogotá as "the Athens of America," and their penchant for the humanities is reflected in the saying that for every 100 people in Bogotá, there are 200 poets.

Colombia is one of the most regionalized countries in Latin America, perhaps more so even than Mexico and Brazil. It has seven cities of more than 200,000 population, scattered widely through the country; three cities—Bogotá, Medellin and Cali—have over a million each. Although the capital—unlike Brazil's—clearly outranks the other cities, it must contend with fierce provincial identities and jealousies.

Until recent decades Colombia was chopped up into pockets and valleys isolated by the twin ranges of the Andes. Railroad construction was difficult and confined to narrow-gauge track, rivers had limited navigation and mountain trails were traversed mostly by pack mules. Only the coming of air transport has made possible a relatively free flow of people and goods.

Despite the high position that cultural matters have always held in Colombia, it was not among the first Latin American countries to produce the printed word. The first printing press arrived in 1737, two centuries after such an event in Mexico. Even so, another half-century passed before a newspaper called *Papel Periódico de la Ciudad de Santa Fé de Bogotá* emerged in 1791. As in most neighboring lands, the real outburst of journalism came with the wars of independence in the early 1800s.

Journalism in the next century also followed the standard Latin American path of the time, as power oscillated between the business class (Liberals) and the landed gentry (Conservatives), the one proclaiming press freedom in its constitutions, the other curbing it in its own. Colombia's oldest major newspaper today, *El Espectador* of Bogotá, was founded in 1887 as a Liberal organ, but its first quarter-century saw five closings.

During this period there began the practice—more pronounced in Colombia than in any Latin American country—of national leaders mixing careers as politicians and newspaper directors. The two best-known affiliations of recent times have been those of Presidents Laureano Gómez with *El Siglo* and Eduardo Santos with *El Tiempo*.

Most existing dailies were founded in the first two decades of the 20th century, and they underwent their greatest ordeal during the 1948-57 civil war known as *La Violencía*—nominally a struggle between the two political parties, although guerrilla warfare pitted neighbor against neighbor. By the time national revulsion won out and the fighting ended, at least 200,000 persons had been killed. Newspapers were symbols, vehicles and victims of the conflict, since they too were staunch partisans of one party or the other. The high point of their drama came in 1951, when Gómez closed several leading Liberal papers. They soon reopened, but this angered the Conservatives so much that mobs burned and sacked the plants of *El Tiempo* and *El Espectador*. Gómez's own newspaper applauded the destruction.

In a reform move, General Gustavo Rojas Pinilla ousted Gómez in 1953. At first press freedom returned, but Rojas soon chafed at criticism from both Liberal and Conservative papers, and controls on the press (and radio) steadily mounted until *El Tiempo, El Espectador* and *Diario Gráfico* were suspended. They presently resumed publication under new names and greater restrictions.

Rojas Pinilla used many of the conventional forms of media control—such as suspensions, censorship and jailings—but also added some less common ones. He set up a central agency to import newsprint and used its allocations as a weapon to reward or punish. He also overtly fostered propaganda, and became widely known for his law of *desacato,* which forbade statements "directly or indirectly disrespectful to the president of the republic or the head of a friendly nation."

All sectors of Colombian life rose up—in what was called the National Front—to overthrow Rojas Pinilla in 1957, and they also devised a cautious and complex plan to defuse the partisan conflict. Offices as high as the presidency would be rotated and apportioned between the two main parties for 20 years in a transition to a hoped-for normality of political competition. Although no laws restricted the press, the major newspapers bowed to the will of the parties they had supported and joined in a generally muted political life. They criticized governments, but with such restraint that they tended to become boring. Even so, the various presidents eyed the press with distrust, frequently using subtle pressures on radical organs and muzzling broadcasters under repeated declarations of states of emergency and siege.

The principal differences among Colombian printed media are in politics, regional outlooks and levels of appeal (elite vs. mass readerships). The population is 95 percent Catholic and a concordat is maintained with the Vatican, so religious minorities are insignificant in journalism. The use of Spanish in media also is almost universal, although broadcast stations on the black-populated Caribbean islands of San Andrés and Providencia carry the dominant English language there. English-language weeklies, primarily for Anglo-U.S. residents, have spasmodic lives in Bogotá and Cali. One of the best established was *The Chronicle,* which started in 1965 and suspended publication for economic reasons in 1980.

Colombia has 32 daily newspapers and 16 nondailies. They are approximately evenly divided between two groups: serious, standard-sized morning dailies with Sunday editions; and sensational, tabloid evening dailies without Sunday editions. Bogotá alone has six dailies, four of them in the morning group. By the beginning of the 1980s the two major papers in the country, *El Tiempo* and *El Espectador,* were engaged in a battle of special sections, running them three to four times a week and increasing the sale price about five cents on those days. The 32 dailies are found in only 12 cities, including all the provincial capitals, so there may be as many as three and four dailies in cities outside Bogotá.

The number of newspapers in the country has fallen from 44 in the mid-1960s to the present 32, although the level seems to be stabilizing there, as some new units have been started to compensate for closings. Circulation, which increased 66 percent between 1965 and 1975, also seemed headed for a level-off. Total circulation of daily newspapers is figured at 2,369,400 or 105 copies for each 1,000 inhabitants.

The wide range of levels of appeal found in some media systems is not present in Colombia. It is not as middle-of-the-road as Costa Rica, but neither does it have the extremes of seriousness and sensation to be noted in Great Britain. Most of the serious newspapers such as *El Tiempo* and *El Espectador* pay obvious attention to consumer tastes and

emerge with an attractive product. Type faces, color photography and layout techniques showed dramatic improvements in the 1970s.

Afternoon tabloids sold mostly in the street are familiar sights throughout Colombia, notably three in Bogotá—*El Bogotano, El Espacio* and *El Vespertino. El Bogotano,* the most lurid, goes in heavily for crime, disasters, human interest and soccer, although stopping short of extremes in bloodiness and lust. It is published by an advertising executive, Consuelo de Montejo, who is generally ostracized by the publishing and political establishments. She takes shrilly populist positions and is often accused of being communist.

To Colombians, the most important classification of a newspaper is whether it supports the Liberal or Conservative party. Both groups are well represented among the country's dailies, although *El Tiempo* and *El Espectador* of Bogotá, the two most prestigious, both are Liberal. The most respected Conservative voice is *El Colombiano,* in the provincial city of Medellin.

El Tiempo has been controlled by the Santos family since its founding in 1911, and this has given it much continuity of tradition. (One of its directors, Eduardo Santos, was president of the republic in 1938-42.) It frequently appears on lists of the most influential papers in the world, and ranks among the half-dozen best in Latin America. Largely centrist in the political spectrum, it defends traditional liberal values such as human rights and international cooperation. As the most fervent standard-bearer of the coalition between the Liberals and Conservatives during the National Front period, *El Tiempo* lost some credibility and reader interest, but in recent years the editors have been working hard to overcome this with bright makeup, modern newswriting styles and a broad array of content. The paper occupies a luxurious new building in the suburbs.

With circulation of about 200,000 daily, *El Tiempo* lags slightly behind *El Espectador* in total sales. Although it leads in Bogotá, its rival is substantially ahead in provincial cities. It has been trying to increase both its total circulation and the proportion of its sales covered by subscriptions. With the start of three special sections at various times in the week, *El Tiempo's* circulation went up more than 15 percent in a year.

El Tiempo has about 200 employees in the news and editorial operation, out of a total of 1,500. The management tries to require that its employees work only at *El Tiempo,* but an average pay of about $500 a month makes this nearly impossible.

Despite the strength of provincial dailies, *El Espectador* comes closest to being a national newspaper. Its circulation ranks a strong second to the local dailies in several major cities and even outsells the leaders in Cartagena and Pereira. It prints four editions daily—for Bogotá, the coastal area, the west and the east. Total circulation runs 220,000 daily, 280,000 Sundays.

Like *El Tiempo* and most other Colombian newspapers, *El Espectador* is a family-owned enterprise, founded in 1887 and in the hands of Cano family members ever since. They tend more toward business and less toward political participation as compared with the Santos family of *El Tiempo,* and their paper was a trendsetter in technical modernization. Occupying a gracefully designed building in Bogotá's suburbs in 1963, it set about acquiring cold-type composition, computers and, later, display terminals in the newsroom. This has not only allowed it to gradually reduce its production staff and effect savings, but also permitted two extra hours for deadlines.

Despite its larger circulation, *El Espectador* lags behind *El Tiempo* in advertising revenues. It is trying to overcome this by producing special sections on sports, television and the home.

El Colombiano of Medellin, although more old-fashioned in methods than its Liberal competitors in the capital, has a wide following even outside its own city. This is because of its preeminence as a Conservative spokesman and also because it speaks for the fiercely proud region of Antioquia, a bastion of industry and free enterprise that could be compared with São Paulo in Brazil. The paper upholds a long tradition of erudition in its columns, boasting more college graduates on its staff than any other Colombian daily.

Magazines in Colombia have always trailed behind the other media in circulation and advertising. *Cromos,* a variety publication leaning heavily on pictures, is far and away the most important. Other widely circulated periodicals are *Vea,* a sensational newspaper-type weekly; and *Vanidades, Buen Hogar* and *Selecciones del Reader's Digest,* all domestic reprints of foreign magazines. Although usually not considered magazines, comic books and *fotonovelas* (still-picture melodramas) make up a vast publishing industry in Colombia, selling 100 million copies

a year. About 40 percent of the output is exported to Venezuela, Ecuador, Chile and Central America. Colombia also produces many small, high-quality specialized magazines. An innovative undertaking called the *Latin American Times,* a weekly published in English for export to the United States and other English-speaking areas, was launched in Bogotá in 1979.

Colombia has always lacked a newsmagazine of stature similar to Venezuela's *Resumen* or Brazil's *Veja.* At the beginning of the 1980s this deficiency was being overcome by a weekly called *Guión.* It was founded in 1976 as a vehicle of Conservative opinion, published by a foundation and backed by party stalwarts associated with Misael Pastrana Borrero, former national president. But under the editorship of Juan Carlos Pastrana, his son, the magazine turned more toward news and analysis modeled after *Time* and *Newsweek. Guión* carried departmentalized coverage of subjects ranging from bullfighting to humor, but most emphasis was on public affairs. A distinguishing mark was the highly original cover cartoons by Hugo Cano. It also introduced a breezy writing style, a departure from the ponderous prose that charaterizes Colombian magazines.

Economic Framework

Latin America as a whole was making healthy economic gains in the 1970s, even outpacing the population growth, and Colombia hovered near the average rate for the area. Coffee traditionally has been the mainstay of the country's export earnings, but by the end of the decade manufactured goods had edged it out of first place. The country produces 70 percent of its petroleum needs and apparently has the capacity to increase this.

Like the oil-rich Arab states, Colombia has an excess of dollars, but for a different reason. The massive drug traffic with the United States, though illegal, has become so important financially that it is called "the parallel economy" and is estimated to equal all other exports in value. However, this has had a harmful effect on domestic trade, as the drug barons tend to invest in land, thus driving up its cost—along with the cost of everything else—and producing annual inflation of about 30 percent.

The sudden availability of wealth has

brought a pattern familiar in emergent countries—heavy foreign investment in industry and urban buildings, a flight of poor people to the cities in a vain search for betterment, a rapid increase in the middle class, consumerism and mass marketing facilities like brand names and supermarkets, and unexpected energy problems (Colombia was self-sufficient in oil until 1975).

Colombia's economic progress has had a dramatic impact on advertising money going into the mass media. Until the late 1970s the Colombian press had suffered from all the weaknesses and frustrations associated with financial malnutrition—small size, outdated equipment, severely underpaid staff, niggardly outlays on content and hesitance to try new directions. A key producer of newspaper advertising revenues in advanced countries—mass retailing through department stores and supermarkets—was almost nonexistent. Advertising investment in dollar terms was going up to 10 percent a year, just meeting inflation levels.

Then in 1977 a bonanza in world coffee prices, combined with a surge in industrial production and building construction, heated up the economy. Advertisements placed through agencies went up 45 percent in 1977 and 47 percent the next year. Only in 1979 did it slacken off to 23 percent. Even then, however, total advertising expenditure in mass media (excluding many privately placed ads) was $159,533,000*—three and one-half times what was spent in 1973.

The major beneficiaries of this trend are the newspapers, although all media have gained. Television had made its major incursion on newspapers and radio by the middle of the 1970s, but the two latter were recovering ground by 1980. This was particularly true in major newspapers with an attraction for classified advertising; it was not uncommon for a dozen or more such pages to be sold daily in *El Tiempo*. Numbers of pages in newspapers had increased about 50 percent in the decade, despite huge increases in newsprint prices.

Competition within and between media is probably as robust as anywhere in the world, except for television. Although some afternoon papers are published by morning affiliates and occasionally joint printing arrangements are made, there is multiple ownership of dailies in all the large cities. Chain owner-

ship between cities is unheard of and would be anathema amid Colombia's regional jealousies. Nor does the country have a large magazine group such as De Armas in Venezuela.

Although group ownership and affiliation pervades the radio system, this generates competition because the major contenders have the strength of numbers. There are three major commercial networks—Caracol with 58 stations, Todelar with 63 and Radio Cadena Nacional (RCN) with 63; some of these are owned by the chains while others are affiliated. A government network, Radio Nacional, reaches about half the country's population, mostly with educational and cultural programs.

Colombian newspapers have no central distribution system. They contract with dealers operating through an association or syndicate. This, however, has posed some financial problems because the dealers by law must be given the same benefits as the newspapers' employees.

The cost of newsprint is a serious problem for Colombian newspapers; it stood at about $700/per metric ton delivered in Bogotá in 1980, most of it from Canada. Only $420 of the price was paid to the sellers, the rest allocated to shipping from abroad and from a Caribbean port. Poor port facilities add to the problems, and a shortage of warehouses means ships have to wait to unload, thus driving up the price. The government has helped by lowering newsprint taxes, and publishers are trying to cut costs more by asking the government also to eliminate consular fees on the exports.

Party affiliations remain the most important outside influence on editorial policy, although editors are trying to shed their reputation for slavishness. Advertiser influence counts for little, except in the case of financially weak publications. It was widely believed that desertion by advertisers pressured by the government caused the 1980 death of *Alternativa,* a respected leftist weekly edited by famed novelist Gabriel Garcia Márquez. Advertising ratios in dailies range from almost no ads in the afternoon tabloids to 60 percent in the largest morning papers.

Unionism in Colombian media is splintered and, from a bargaining standpoint, weak. Most employers deal only with their

---

*The rate of exchange in August 1980 was 48 pesos-US$1.00

company's in-house union (syndicate), and strikes are extremely rare, partly because of a willingness of both sides to compromise. *El Espectador* had a one-day stoppage in 1979, the first in its 92 years. The National Federation of Journalists has been trying for several years to unite enough local unions to meet the minimum required by law for industrywide negotiation. Its organizers hope to put some professional autonomy into the hands of professional newsmen and protect their work from owners who know nothing about journalism.

Press Laws

The Colombian Constitution provides the kind of protection that depends largely on the good intentions of the government in power. It guarantees freedom of the press only in times of peace and requires the journalist to respect the integrity of the individual, social stability and public order. Furthermore, no publication may be supported, without government permission, by foreign governments or companies.

In 1975, in an effort to raise the educational level of journalists, the Liberal government of Alfonso López Míchelson put through the Law of the Journalist, very similar to *colegio* laws passed in other countries. Some of the main points are:

1. To practice journalism, a person must have a journalism degree from a school approved by the government, have worked five years as a journalist before the law was passed, or worked three years and passed an examination on Colombian culture and journalistic methods, drawn up by the Ministry of Education. Those with foreign degrees must take the examination unless their government has a treaty on the matter with Colombia.

2. Any journalist who works without a license card—or anyone who hires him—can be fined $115 to $230.

3. The law covers journalists working in public relations, news agencies, radio or television. Opinion writers and journalists for free-distribution publications are exempt.

4. Journalists cannot be made to reveal their sources, although they are responsible legally for their writings.

5. Public officials must guarantee journalists access to information.

6. Foreign journalists working for news agencies, diplomatic missions or interna-

tional groups may apply for accreditation by the Ministry of Education if they are accredited abroad.

7. The Ministry of Education can suspend or cancel a license if the holder breaks laws related to journalism or is convicted of damaging third parties in his work.

8. The National Council of Journalism is created to consult with the government about press freedom, union freedom, protection of journalistic interests, and ethics. The council is made up of three government ministers and three representatives of journalistic groups.

Colombia also has the usual laws on libel and privacy, but they are little used. Although the judiciary is generally recognized as of high integrity, litigation on journalistic matters is rarely undertaken.

Censorship

Despite frequent periods of censorship during the years of *La Violencia*, this practice has largely fallen into disuse in Colombia. Until 1979 it had been common practice in radio and television.

In radio, station operators had to censor themselves against content that told about "crime against the family or against sexual liberty and honor"; impeded police work; was nonobjective about or defended crime; attacked the constitution, laws, foreign relations, institutions, "life, honor and goods" of citizens, or respect due authorities"; incited lawbreaking or breach of peace; or reported political speeches without 48 hours' notice to the government. Violation of the radio rules could cost a station its license for two years or more.

In television, news scripts and films had to be submitted for government inspection at least 30 minutes in advance. Although direct censorship in television removed the need for direct punishment, packagers of news programs had another goad to stay on guard—they had to bid regularly for lease of the television time, and lapses from propriety could count against them.

Soon after its election, the Liberal government of President Julio César Turbay announced in 1979 that it was lifting all restrictions from radio and television news. Turbay said the only criterion for broadcast news would be "the responsibility and patriotism" of the newscaster. The next year, however, during the long terrorist occupation of an embassy, it was proved that radio news still could be shut down during a crisis.

Colombia has had several presidents who have used all the pressures they could enlist against the press, notably López Michelson in 1974-78. However, this did not cause any monolithic resistance to the press by the national government. Officials remain remarkably easy to get news from, particularly to confirm stories gathered elsewhere.

State-Press Relations

Owing to memories of *La Violencia,* alignments with parties that make up the National Front, and continued danger from leftist terrorists, the major media have only slowly eased away from collaboration with the government in sensitive matters. Even with the cautious reintroduction of political competition as the National Front has been dismantled, the media put themselves in the role of spokesmen or loyal opponents of the government in power, depending on their affiliation.

The same caution is extended toward two other major institutions—the military and the Catholic Church. The press knows that danger of a military takeover is ever-present and wants to prevent an open confrontation. Editors also rarely criticize the church, although they may take issue with some points of the concordat, the agreement between the government and the Vatican.

The presidential press office is in charge of the government's minor efforts toward propaganda. It sends a daily bulletin by messenger to the media, distributes news releases from the ministries and signals the headlines of coming official stories by telex.

Despite the general hesitancy to stir up conflict, the media do report some stories embarrassing to the government. The corruption and failures of the police campaign against the drug traffic has been extensively revealed. Involvement of presidential relatives in conflict of interest also has come under fire.

No newspaper has been shut down overtly in recent years, although several radical publications have suffered harassment. *Alternativa* came under fire from military leaders in 1976, and only after a formal protest from the Bogotá Journalists' Circle did President López Michelson declare that the weekly would be protected during his term. But after his departure from office, *Alternativa* closed for financial reasons, believed to be due to an advertiser boycott prompted by government pressures.

The state of siege, in effect off and on during 20 of the 25 years before 1980, has been the usual rationale for restrictions on broadcasters. The 1980 seizure of the Dominican Embassy by M-19 terrorists demonstrated the differences among the media as to government policy. The press covered the event thoroughly but was untouched because copies of the papers, unlike broadcast signals, did not get inside the embassy. Television newscasts were generally cautious, but radio networks went live, suspending regular programs—and its reporters launched a barrage of aggressive and often confused coverage. The government acted decisively, shutting down radio news on the grounds that it was most easily received by the kidnappers and thus could upset negotiations. Later the radio ruling was lifted with the proviso that only what had appeared in newspapers could be aired. One radio network's newscasts were suspended for two days as a punishment. After the siege ended, television showed films made inside the building during the crisis.

One sign that the government had risen above its nervousness over television came in 1977 when a series about *La Violencia* was scheduled for showing. Written by García Márquez, the series depicted the civil war killings in all their cruelty and horror. The Conservative party attacked the project on the grounds that it had been defamed and that passions would be stirred up during the upcoming presidential election. López's cabinet discussed the issue at length but refused to prohibit the showing.

Other forms of control such as jailings, union manipulation and licensing abuses are notably absent. Despite a storm of criticism of the licensing system when the 1975 law was passed, the issue has disappeared from the public arena. In fact, the only complaint now is that the license cards are too easy to obtain.

Attitude Toward Foreign Media

In no respect is the Colombian political establishment's distrust of the press more pronounced than in the matter of foreign correspondents. Bogotá—almost equidistant from the farthest capitals and blessed with convenient air routes—is nearly an ideal home base for coverage of Latin America.

Foreign reporters also cover Colombia, and various governments have always shown extreme touchiness toward what they write.

All correspondents must apply for accreditation by the Ministry of Education. Those who operate bureaus with teletypes must also seek a permit from the Ministry of Communications for technical reasons. Because correspondents are usually in a hurry and also because of the general air of freedom, foreigners often neglect to go through these formalities, or to renew applicable documents when they expire. Although officials usually do not insist on enforcing the regulations, even when they are angered by what they perceive as an offensive story, they have been known to become suddenly punctilious about the law.

Harassment of foreign correspondents has long been a possibility, although not on the scale of situations in Chile or the Soviet Union. The international journal *Index on Censorship* recounted these incidents it said happened in Colombia in the mid-1970s:

1. British reporter Timothy Ross had trouble with his visa extension after he reported on Bogotá's crime problem. He alleged later that in separate incidents he was interrogated five hours by police and escaped from a kidnap attempt.

2. Ross was summoned for a tongue-lashing by President López Michelson and later was shunned in quests for information.

3. A reporter for the *National Enquirer* had his transport taken by police, was questioned a full day and was told not to write anything.

4. Fast-exit visas, traditionally given to foreign correspondents, were lifted temporarily.

5. Two foreign reporters were beaten by police during student demonstrations even though they showed their credentials.

6. United Press International was ordered to close its bureau after it distributed a false report that the president had been assassinated. The order was canceled after UPI transferred its bureau chief out of the country.

UPI's brush with the law came through what appeared to be an accident. A young Chilean reporter who was to be hired for the Bogotá bureau came in two days early to learn procedures. He was practicing on a supposedly unconnected teletype, typing out imaginary stories. One of them was a "flash" that President López had been assassinated. Before UPI discovered the flash had gone out on its worldwide wires and ordered its withdrawal, a number of media in various countries had publicized it.

Top UPI officials rushed to Bogotá to apologize to López. Although most Colombians were riled at the wire service, many public expressions, including editorials, implied that López had been too harsh. Within a week, the order was lifted. (UPI had continued operations during that time.)

Three years later the Associated Press got into the same trouble, again over a news report it had transmitted. López's cabinet had adopted a measure authorizing the jailing of persons without a warrant, as a response to embarrassing successes by the terrorist M-19 group. AP reported this was a suspension of constitutional rights, and the presidential press office issued a heated denial. Then the Ministry of Communications discovered that AP's accreditation was not in order (which was true of many correspondents), so the government shut down the agency on the legal grounds, also noting that it was transmitting "frankly tendentious and inexact" news. Again, the local press, including leftists, rose up in protest, and the government dropped the matter. Actually, it had left AP an escape hatch by making the suspension effective only until it got its papers in order.

Foreign ownership of media has never been an issue in Colombia because no serious attempts have been made in that direction. However, a law covering radio prohibits more than 25 percent of the ownership of any station in the hands of foreigners. Laws also set maxima for foreign programs and recordings in broadcasting; they are generally ignored and unenforced.

Colombia has largely stayed out of international press disputes such as those initiated within UNESCO. Partly because its ownership of television already meets one of the goals of the UNESCO reformers, the proposals have excited little interest in Colombia.

News Agencies

Colombia usually has three or four national news agencies in competition at any one time, although they die and are replaced with great frequency. The oldest, Colombia Press, founded in 1955, decided to go out of business in 1980 because of the government's practice of sending free government press releases by telex to provincial newspapers, undercutting one of the agency's main sources of income. Another agency, CIEP, exists to cover Bogotá for the daily *El Pais* of Cali, although it sells its news to papers in other cities. Colprensa is operated by the Catholic organization Opus Dei and distributes articles by mail; it is trying to achieve an electronic distribution system. Alaprensa, another agency, also has some provincial clients.

AP and UPI each has about six of the leading Colombian newspapers as clients, plus a number of broadcast stations. They gather and distribute domestic news as well as sending news abroad and selling international coverage to Colombian media.

Other agencies with bureaus in Bogotá either sell their news cheaply or give it away. They are Reuters of Britain, Agence France-Press, EFE of Spain, Inter Press of Rome, Tass and Novosti of the Soviet Union, New China News Agency, Deutsche Presse-Agentur of West Germany, and Prensa Latina of Cuba.

Electronic News Media

Colombia has the curious combination of a radio system which is conventional but of relatively high quality, along with an innovative television system which draws criticism from many sides. Changes are being proposed for television with increasing frequency.

Radio in Colombia started in 1930 with an experimental station in Bogotá and soon spread to the whole country, capitalizing on its ability to leap the mountain barriers, particularly with short wave, which one-fifth of the approximately 350 stations use along with the standard medium wave. Although the bulk of the programming is conventional popular music and sports coverage, radio has shown much vigor in news programs. Competition can drive it to unusual enterprise, such as live coverage of both the U.S. Republican and Democratic 1980 conventions. Most radio activity is commercial, although the government maintains a network that programs cultural and educational material.

Radio has developed with little interference from the government. The main participation by the state is its operation of Radio Nacional, a cultural and educational service reaching about half the national population. Using programs provided by the Ministry of

Education, Radio Nacional airs four hours daily of systematic education, allowing listeners to work toward a high school diploma. About 50 percent of its time is used for music, 10 percent for news, and the rest for various other programs. The government never has used radio extensively for propaganda, confining such activities to an occasional speech by the president and daily spot announcements for civic improvement campaigns.

Commercial radio goes out over almost 350 stations, the largest total in Latin America except for Brazil and México, much larger countries. In some cases its news is highly regarded by professionals, and international coverage is frequent. Surveys show that radio is the medium preferred as a news source by 40 percent of the population, as compared with 28 for television and 26 for newspapers. However, this dominance is mostly accounted for by the large lower economic class. In the middle class, all three media are about even, and the rankings are reversed in the upper class, where 46 percent prefer newspapers to 18 percent for radio.

Television has been totally owned by the national government since its inception in 1954. Although its main purpose is to educate, inform and elevate the Colombian public, it has conceded the need for entertainment and commercial revenues. Instead of securing these directly it uses a familiar Latin American device—hiring out broadcast time to contractors. However, its method here is distinctive: a flat rate is set for the air time to be allocated and bids are received from contractors as to the quality of programs they will use along with their commercials. The system, called Inravisión, operates only three channels, Channel 7 (national), which reaches nearly all the population, Channel 9 for the major cities or about 60 percent of the people, and Channel 11, an educational service to reach adults in Bogotá and the central plateau. Channel 9 is being increased to approximate the coverage of Channel 7.

Although all television transmission facilities are government owned, most activity takes place in approximately 30 programming and production companies (packagers), which put out three or more hours of programs per week; many more small operations produce less. The three largest packagers are Punch, RTI and Caracol, and other serious competitors include Colvision, Promec, Cempero and RCN. All get their revenue from sale of advertisements which they sprinkle among entertainment and news, either locally produced or imported in form of films and tapes.

Despite the unique combination of state and private participation in TV, the results have won little applause. There is widespread belief that the process of bidding for air-time rental has been corrupted by favoritism toward friends of the various governments and that this leads to a lower quality of programs. At the beginning of the 1980s much public discussion was probing into the system and searching for new solutions. As the public grew more dissatisfied with the content, the medium's share of the advertising market was going down.

One complaint against the government ownership system is that it has prevented any geographical decentralization. In a large country with strong regional consciousness, all program origination remains in Bogotá. Only one channel reaches most of the country, and for many years Bogotá had two more channels almost to itself. While Inravisión, the television authority, is trying to spread the second commercial channel and the educational channel to more cities, the fact that all programs are made in the capital still rankles the residents of cities such as Medellín and Cali. Only occasionally do cameras go outside Bogotá for events such as international soccer games or Holy Week in Popoyán.

Until 1979 the Colombian government staunchly refused to allow color television. Many groups concerned over the plight of the poor people struggling to ward off starvation had supported the ban. The reasoning primarily was that the spending spree accompanying introduction of color sets would set off new bursts of inflation, and that increased advertising would push up prices of consumer goods. This would make the already impossible burden on the poor even heavier.

However, incoming President Turbay, who had campaigned against color TV, reversed his field and called for its adoption. After lengthy public hearings over whether to adopt the U.S., West German or Japanese transmission methods, the government opted for the U.S. system, mainly on grounds that so many of its imported programs come in that form.

But even the advent of color did not satisfy viewers who were critical of program quality; the imports tended to be the cheapest and most outdated shows. This in turn led to a proliferation of videocassette recorders among the more affluent (a complete system with a color viewing set costs about $2,000). Once the system is in place the operation is relatively inexpensive. Viewers can rent a tape for less than $2, or about the price of two cinema admissions.

The aspect of Colombian broadcasting most admired in other countries is its contributions to adult education. This takes place through Acción Cultural Popular (ACPO) for the rural population and the Fondo de Capacitación Popular for city-dwellers. ACPO has often been rated as the most successful peasant education project in Latin America, perhaps in the world. It is better known as Radio Sutatenza, named for the remote mountain hamlet served in 1947 by a young priest named José Salcedo. He despaired of reaching his 5,500 parishioners scattered through the hills, and also saw that they needed practical education as well as spiritual guidance. For his first transmitter, he hauled a 100-watt device up the mountainside by horseback. For more equipment, he sold his parishioners' chickens in the city. His first goals were to teach reading, writing and arithmetic to villagers in remote areas. He found the peasants eager to learn, but soon discovered also that they would go much faster and retain more if the radio lessons were combined with personal contact. So he developed a corps of volunteers called monitors who would encourage the learners and explain the radio message.

Father Salcedo further learned that the most important—and really necessary—educational phase for the peasants was to acquire the desire to change their lifestyles. The aim of ACPO became "to form men who want to better themselves individually and socially, and who are consciously committed to the tasks of development." This in turn led to training needed for a better life—hygiene, nutrition, use of medical services, farming practices, consumer knowledge, sports and recreation, problem solving, ethics and religion, family relations, birth control, community activities and political consciousness.

Although Father Salcedo's tiny 100-watt unit has now become five powerful transmitters reaching an audience of nearly 14 million persons, ACPO has spread into other media. A weekly newspaper aimed at reinforcing the reading skills learned by radio has an average circulation of 41,000, with an estimated four persons reading each copy. It prints a variety of textbooks and guides and distributes phonograph records as study aids. But the focus of ACPO's activities remains small radio schools led by volunteer workers. By 1976 these amounted to more than 17,000. ACPO has a full-time staff of more than 1,000, whose work is directed from the national headquarters in an 11-story building in Bogotá.

ACPO was closely identified with the Catholic Church and the Colombian government in earlier years, but it now derives its revenues from other sources—60 percent from its profitable commercial printing operations, and the rest from donors, mostly foreign foundations. Its next expansion of operations is expected to come in education through television.

Education & Training

Five universities in Colombia—two in Bogotá and others in Medellin, Cali and Barranquilla—offer degrees in journalism. They have received a large stimulus from the 1975 Law of the Journalist, which requires new entrants into the field to have a university journalism degree. Although older journalists who were grandfathered by the law complain that most graduates have little practical training, resistance is fading as a younger generation begins to fill up the ranks of media staffs.

Colombia has three major organizations of working journalists. The Círculo de Periodistas de Bogotá (Bogotá Journalists' Circle), the most serious, owns two downtown office buildings and provides many welfare services to members. The Federación Nacional de Periodistas (National Journalists' Federation) represents an attempt to tie together journalistic organizations into a nationwide labor union, although thus far it has fallen short. The Asociación Nacional de Periodistas (National Journalists' Association) is largely a social group.

Summary

In most respects, the media of Colombia are, like the country as a whole, making slow and sometimes stumbling progress toward freedom, prosperity and professionalism. Newspapers are not suffering from competition with electronic media, and television has reached a point where the public is demanding improvement. The magazine industry remains somewhat behind other media, although it is coming up fast.

Colombia also has survived several political waves affecting the media. The violence and oppression of the 1950s still haunt memories, but a 20-year solution to that problem apparently has been completed. The social engineering tendencies of the 1970s produced a complicated press law and a form of licensing for journalists, but this has not proved to be the menace many publishers saw in it.

Since the economy is growing, the prospects remain bright for the coming years. This no doubt will combine with responsibility in journalism and politics to provide enough resilience to cope with problems as they arise.

CHRONOLOGY

1957-58	Rojas dictatorship overthrown. Liberals and Conservatives end nine-year civil war by agreeing to rotate public offices between the two parties for 16 years. Leading newspapers join tacitly in National Front pact to keep the peace.
1974	Media participate in orderly campaigns in first open electoral competition since formation of National Front. Efforts to introduce color television banned.
1976	Law establishes *colegio* (guild), requires all journalists to have university journalism degree or pass examination. UPI threatened with expulsion after spreading false report of Colombian president's murder; UPI apologizes, is pardoned.
1976-77	Conservative party protests historical series on television by leftist writer Gabriel Garcia Márquez; Cabinet declines to ban it.

1978   Adoption of color television approved by government; U.S. technology chosen after lengthy competition.
Minimum of 25 percent Colombian music required of radio stations.

1979   Government briefly suspends operations of AP bureau in Bogotá over supposedly false story.
Regional magazine in English, *Latin American Times,* founded in Bogotà.

BIBLIOGRAPHY

Blutstein, Howard I., et al. *Area Handbook for Colombia.* Washington, D.C., 1977.

Causa Común. *Communication Policies in Colombia.* Paris, 1977.

Corr, Edwin G. *The Political Process in Colombia.* Denver, 1972.

Ortíz, Gabriel, ed. *La Prensa Entre la Lealtad y el Miedo.* Bogotá, 1976.

Pierce, Robert N. *Keeping the Flame.* New York, 1979.

Smith, T. Lynn. *Colombia: Social Structures and Process of Development.* Gainesville, Fla., 1967.

UNESCO. *World Communications.* 1975.

COSTA RICA

by Robert N. Pierce

BASIC DATA

Population: 2,193,000
Area: 51,000 sq. km. (20,247 sq. mi.)
GNP: 33.4 billion colons (US$3.9 billion) (1979)
Literacy Rate: 90%
Language(s): Spanish
Number of Dailies: 6
  Aggregate Circulation: 210,000
  Circulation per 1,000: 104
Number of Nondailies: 7
  Aggregate Circulation: NA
  Circulation per 1,000: NA
Number of Periodicals: NA
Number of Radio Stations: 33–38

Number of Television Stations: 11
Number of Radio Receivers: 156,000
  Radio Receivers per 1,000: 75
Number of Television Sets: 160,000
  Television Sets per 1,000: 77
Total Annual Newsprint Consumption: 11,200 metric tons
Per Capita Newsprint Consumption: 5.4 kg. (11.88 lbs.)
Total Newspaper Ad Receipts: 63.4 million (US $7.4 million) (1976)
  As % of All Ad Expenditures: 19.9 (1976)

Background & General Characteristics

Descriptions of many Latin American countries and their mass media systems often take on the contours of Greek tragedy: Despite many positive aspects, they are dragged down by bad fortune and their own follies to an inexorable fate of falling back two steps for each one they climb.

Such is not the case in Costa Rica. Its level of democracy, both political and economic, is clearly the highest in Latin America and compares favorably with the most fortunate nations in the Western world. While it suffers from most of the same problems that its neighbors do, it has developed ways to cope as well as could be expected in these times.

One of the most important such correctives is citizen commitment to political issues, more than personalities and partisanships. Although the latter loom large on the Costa Rican scene, they do not prevent the electorate from facing the difficult if less exciting questions of how to improve programs without overthrowing governments.

Clearly such resolution of conflict must depend on public discussion, both to give needed facts and to provide a forum for competing solutions. And there must be vehicles and promoters of this discussion. The norms of journalism say the mass media should fill this role, and in Costa Rica they have done so to a remarkable extent.

History has shaped this interplay of politics and journalism, and one sees more of the substance than the symbolism of the national traditions. Costa Rica has had no literary artists of world rank to hymn its cultural virtues, and there are almost no statues of war heroes because it has had almost no wars to speak of, its army having been disbanded in 1948. Its patriotism, which actually exists, is nearly transparent, lacking the coloration of holy causes and jealously guarded quirks and foibles.

While today's constantly arriving tourists do not complain of drabness, this quality of life was the bedrock on which today's Costa Rica is built. Columbus touched its territory on his fourth voyage, and it was named for having a supposedly rich coast. This proved a mistake, as there were few minerals and the Indians resisted enslavement to work the land. As the conquistadores moved on to quicker riches in other countries, Costa Rica was settled by Spanish peasants who tilled small holdings and shared in a dull but not miserable poverty. Hemmed in by two mountain ranges on a central plateau, they communicated as equals on neighboring farms; the few towns were almost in sight of each other.

Thus the colonial settlers worked out ideas about journalism close to those of Jefferson; certainly their character was closer to his ideal of the yeoman-citizen than that of Jefferson's own countrymen. When Spanish rule collapsed without a fight in 1821, a sort of town-meeting democracy soon replaced it. Not only did the government permit the founding of vigorous newspapers but even demanded it, even though they had to be handwritten because the first printing press did not arrive until 1830. An early law, notable not only because it is eloquent but also because it was enforced, expressed what had already become a tradition:

> Liberty of thought and expression is so absolute that no prior censorship, no regulation, no special or common tribunal shall restrict it. Neither the very overthrow of the constitutional order, armed rebellion nor civil war shall be a motive to repress it.

Aside from the handwritten publications, the main sources of newspapers were the presses of Guatemala City, the capital of the colonial captaincy that included Costa Rica and of the Central American Federation which succeeded it. Such papers were *La Gaceta de Guatemala, El Editor Constitucional* and *El Amigo de la Patria.* There were only 57,000 inhabitants, and they relied on Guatemala and Nicaragua for most of their leadership in larger matters.

After the Republic of Costa Rica replaced the federation government, the burgeoning newspapers were ready to educate the people in the ways of independence and self-government. In the words of an editor of the time, "Freedom without enlightenment or knowledge seems to be an absurdity," echoing a similar dictum of Jefferson. By the middle of the century, 21 handmade wooden presses churned out a wide variety of documents and weekly newspapers selling from 500 to 600 copies to a population that was estimated at 42 percent literate.

The smallholder farming economy had led to little outreach to the rest of the world other than Central America, but two developments toward the mid-1800s changed this. First, large plantations of export crops such as coffee began to supplement the peasant farms. This promoted the rise of a landed aristocracy with an appetite for both foreign fashions and the "modern" trappings of cities. The elites saw to it that all sorts of conveniences, from railroads to an opera house, were provided, and this called for dealings with suppliers in Europe and the United States. Soon foreign bankers were competing to lend money on futures of coffee production.

Also, in 1856 Costa Rica took part in its first and only real foreign war, a brief campaign to oust the U.S. filibuster William Walker from his Nicaraguan base, where he hoped to imperialize Central America. Costa Rica's military role was relatively small, but it was a striking success and raised the people's patriotic spirits and gave them a cosmopolitan sense.

The press responded to this growth in Costa Rica's relationships with the outside world by providing more information and more editorial debate over the best way to cope with the new problems. Important, often commercially oriented papers began to replace the parochial gossip sheets of earlier years, and the first dailies were founded in the 1870s. Some of the titles now carried by dailies in the capital, San José, were born during this period. The oldest existing paper, *La Prensa Libre,* was founded in 1889.

Dictatorships have emerged briefly three times in the last century, in 1890-94, 1917-18 and 1948-49. In each case, an enraged public opinion abetted by a vigorous press brought down the usurper. Unlike most other Latin American countries, Costa Rica has not had instability as its norm.

During the 20th century, class conflict—planters and business people pitted against the working sector—has shaped Costa Rican politics and, to some extent, the press. Extremism has been avoided, though, and the two sides have evolved into a mild social democracy and a progressive conservatism. Both communists and far-rightists have their organizations but so far have not been important in politics or journalism.

The country's two most important newspapers reflect this struggle. Both were founded near the time that the most recent phase of political rivalry started in the late 1940s. *La Nación,* which clearly dominates the field, was started in 1946 as a profit-making enterprise, and generally has defended the viewpoint of the country's most important commercial bloc, the National Association of Business Federations (ANFE). *La República* followed in 1950 as the organ of the reformist politicians headed by José (Pepe) Figueres, although in recent years it has become more nonpartisan. To fill the void left by *La República's* political withdrawal, Figueres's wing of the National Liberation Party founded another daily, *Excélsior,* in 1974. However, it died in 1978, having lost money ever since its start.

Broadcasting has always been primarily a commercial activity, although political viewpoints have much ventilation on talk shows and purchased time. Radio started in the 1920s, and the first television station came in 1960.

The 1970s saw a drastic transformation of Costa Rican journalism from quaint amateurishness to vigorous, competitive professionalism. While it still has not achieved the polish found in some large cities of Latin America, it is not far away. Furthermore, the factors impelling the improvement—high ethics, economic growth, professional education and freedom of expression—are clearly more favorable than anywhere else in the region.

Another important factor in this growth is the audiences of the media themselves. They do not have the intellectual sophistication that would come with a center of high culture such as Buenos Aires or Mexico City, but the general level of adaptation to public affairs is higher. Adult literacy is nearly complete, at about 90 percent, and nearly all children have some schooling, although they get an average of only four years because their families need them to work.

The lower class, consisting of those who are so poor they make little use of the print media, is estimated at one-third to one-half of the population. However, the remainder, nearly all in the middle class, make up an ambitious, upwardly mobile market for the media. The per-capita income of $1,600* (1980 estimate) ranks among the highest in Latin America, and clearly Costa Rica has one of the most evenly distributed national wealths among the world's developing nations.

As the growth rate of population falls and industry becomes the largest contributor to the gross domestic product, the country is making small but significant forward steps in its economy. Inflation remains at about the same level as that of the United States,

although the balance of payments remains a critical problem.

A population profile of Costa Rica shows a large head with a small body: The San José metropolitan area includes a fourth of the country's 2.2 million inhabitants. Furthermore, the Central Plateau (Meseta Central) has three-fifths of the total population although it covers only one-fifth of the space. Media distribution is far greater in this area than in the more tropical lowlands; the Meseta has one copy of a newspaper for each eight inhabitants, while the lowlands have one for each 100.

The population is remarkably homogeneous in both race and language. About 25,000 aboriginal Indians live on remote reservations, and about the same number of Jamaican-descended blacks are found mostly in the Atlantic port of Limón. Although English is the first language of the blacks, they are almost all bilingual and are increasingly integrating into the national life.

While class consciousness has increased steadily since the middle of the 20th century, it has not divided the country into hostile political camps. Communist and other far-left papers circulate freely, but they have never achieved a serious acceptance from the bulk of the population.

Costa Rica has a variety of languages spoken by ethnic subgroups, mostly Europeans and U.S. citizens; the only one used by enough persons to justify substantial publications is English. There have been short-lived, badly produced papers catering to the social interests of U.S. residents in the country. Only in the 1970s did there emerge a consistently serious form of journalism in English. By far the most professional example has been *The Tico Times,* a semi-weekly in San José. Another weekly, the *San José News,* also had improved greatly by the end of the decade, but it was far behind the *Times.* It ran only 12 pages, the printing was deficient, and much of the copy was reprint material from U.S. publications.

At any one time there are usually two or three widely sold publications other than the major dailies. These typically appeal to special audiences or interests, and the life span of most has been short. By the start of the 1980s these included *Extra,* a very small daily seeking the small market for sensationalism; *Semanario Universidad,* an in-

---

The rate of exchange in August 1980 was 8.57 colons-US$1.00.

creasingly professional weekly published by students at the University of Costa Rica; and *Cancha,* a lively though amateurish sports weekly. The country has no magazine of major stature, although there are several agricultural, social, religious, cultural and political journals.

It is easy to see a spectrum of appeals in Costa Rica's press, from the moderately serious in *La Nación* to the moderately frivolous in *Extra.* However, the country has never supported an outrightly sensational publication of the type so popular in Mexico City. Reasons advanced for this range from the smallness of the population to its relatively high education.

In physical terms, the most distinctive aspect of the Costa Rican press is its addiction to the tabloid format. All of its newspapers—even the giant of the field, *La Nación*—print in this size, and the only explanation offered is the tradition to do so, plus the Costa Rican's disdain for largeness in all things. One newspaper that tried to go against the norm, *Excélsior,* lasted only four years with its full-sized imitation of British popular papers' layout.

An exception to the tabloid rule is more a matter of necessity: *The Tico Times's* Tuesday edition, which is a reprint of *The New York Times*'s "Week in Review" section, with two pages of local copy inserted by the San José paper.

Because of the small page size, the number of pages can be relatively high. *La Nación* usually ranges near 100, while *La República, La Prensa Libre, The Tico Times* and *Semanario Universidad* normally run 24–32.

No daily newspapers are printed outside San José. Even the few weeklies that appear in provincial cities usually are ephemeral and short lived.

In circulation, *La Nación* clearly dominates the field, maintaining 60 to 70 percent of total sales of dailies. Its reported 110,000 circulation is confirmed by outside sources. *La República's* is credited with 25,000 to 30,000 by advertising authorities, although its management reports 45,000. The estimate for *La Prensa Libre* is 15,000 to 20,000 and for *Extra* less than 5,000.

Clearly the most prominent newspaper in Central America, *La Nación* epitomizes the aspirations of Costa Rica's middle and upper classes. It is prosperous, consumerist, political without being polemic, and concerned about the world outside Costa Rica while devoting most of its attention to domestic problems.

The dominant tone of *La Nación* is soberness even to the point of dullness, particularly on the main news pages. While reporting techniques have improved steadily in recent years, news stories often still are only slightly rewritten pronouncements by government and other leaders.

One unusual tradition that *La Nación* maintains is to devote its small, tabloid front page to summaries of the day's news, set in large body type and carrying modest headlines. These help the reader to get the gist of the somewhat turgid and lengthy stories inside. The paper's sheer size also is notable; with nearly 100 pages, it has space for a fairly wide range of coverage, even though advertisements fill about 65 percent of the total.

La Nación's main journalistic strengths come out in its editorial and feature pages. A daily article by Enrique Benevides at the upper left of the editorial page, entitled simply *La Columna* ("The Column"), is a national institution because of its acuteness. The daily editorial also is highly respected, and many of the best writers and thinkers of the country contribute to the page and to the op-ed.

Feature pages inside, however, have been increasingly filled with brightly written, well-researched investigative and social reporting. This has ranged from politics to market-basket coverage. The paper also has developed a series of daily special sections dealing with cultural affairs, sports, children's interests, farming, automobiles, tourism and homemaking. It also runs a normal complement of comics, daily features such as horoscopes, and a moderate reportage of sports.

La Nación's stock is publicly traded and is held by more than 400 persons, although the board is closely identified with the National Association of Business Federations (ANFE). It has 470 employees, 36 in the editorial operation. Of its 110,000 circulation (1980 level), 63 percent is in San José Province.

Architect of *La Nación's* modern form was Guido Fernández, who served as director for 12 years, beginning when he was 34. Having graduated in law from the University of Costa Rica, he went on to study in major U.S. universities. He also acquired a conservative though not reactionary economic outlook, and this persuaded the business-minded board of the paper to hire him.

Fernández constantly tried to infuse modern reporting and editing methods into *La Nación,* although he was limited by the shortage of trained journalists. He cooperated with the university's School of Journalism in an effort to upgrade his staff, but later became disheartened with the school as its professors became more politicized.

Turning more to on-the-job training, Fernández sought to correct what he called "a deformation of the press"—its over-reliance on government sources and the neglect of popular and private information, plus excessive emphasis on economic matters. He also set out to improve the coverage of local communities and of provincial regions, rather than dealing exclusively with national news.

Fernández worked steadily to improve the production aspects of the paper. He persuaded the reluctant board to build an attractive new plant in the suburbs, covering 48,000 square feet. He also invested $1.5 million in new presses, relieving a shortage of printing capacity and permitting 128 black-and-white pages daily.

After years of strained relations with his board, Fernández resigned in 1980 following disputes over editorial policy regarding the Nicaraguan revolution. He went into television news and became journalism chairman at the Autonomous University of Central America (UACA) in San José.

La República, born in the political ferment following the troubles of 1948–49, was intended to be the organ of the new National Liberation Party founded by Pepe Figueres. It served this purpose decreasingly until, with ownership going into the hands of investors, it became independent in the late 1970s. Significantly, it started making profit in 1979 after three decades of losses.

Journalists with *La República* have always realized their paper was secondary to *La Nación* in prestige. In fact, it moved into third place for four years beginning in 1974 with the vigorous efforts by the Figueres faction, U.S. financier Robert Vesco and others to launch the daily *Excélsior.* Although *Excélsior* did not damage *La Nación* significantly, it did take away circulation and advertising from the other dailies, notably *La República,* and took over the number-two position.

Excélsior's death in 1978 for economic reasons came at a period when *La República* was expanding its ambitions. It moved into a modern new plant with advanced equipment and contracted to print five other papers. A new director took over, and the front-page format changed entirely to pictures, resulting in no jumps for stories, although sensational-ism was avoided. Such supplements as a children's section and a travel section were added, and one province was emphasized each week on a rotating basis. Better-trained journalists were hired, and more good writing and reporting resulted. Circulation rose from 15,000 or 20,000 to a reported 45,000 (other observers place the figure at 30,000).

Almost all Latin American countries have some type of English-language news publication, ranging from highly professional dailies to miserably poor publicity and gossip sheets; the latter are the most common form and are all that most small countries have in English. Costa Rica, one of the smallest, is an exception, with a semiweekly that has long achieved respect and stability: *The Tico Times,* its name referring to the nickname for Costa Ricans.

Like most nondailies, the *Times* does not undertake to present a full spectrum of foreign and national news but rather emphasizes angles of most interest to foreigners resident in Costa Rica, or to those who, living in their own countries, have concerns about that nation. However, this does not consist of the social trivia so often found. The *Times's* content indicates that it feels its readers are—or should be—interested in a wide range of serious news about Costa Rica. Although its staff consists mostly of footloose young U.S. citizens, its spot-event, depth and interpretive coverage are on a par with the best in small U.S. communities.

The *Times* is neatly laid out and makes frequent use of full-color photography. As mentioned above, its Tuesday edition, selling 2,500, consists largely of *The New York Times's* Sunday "Week in Review." The main edition, on Friday, sells 6,500. About half the sales are by subscription, and about half of those are sent overseas, although delays and expenses in foreign mailing are a major problem. The paper is printed by contract in *La República's* plant. It sells for 17 cents on the street, or about $6.50 per year by subscription. The plant has been owned and operated by two generations of the Dyer family since its founding in 1956.

Economic Framework

Although far short of a "boom" or "miracle," the growth of Costa Rica's economy managed to bring it healthily through the petroleum crisis of the 1970s, which was particularly acute because the country produces no oil of its own. (Nearby Venezuela, however, has played the role of the big brother and has given Costa Rica favorable terms on imported fuel.)

Real economic growth was staying close to five percent annually in the late 1970s, helped by two factors. First, the population growth, once one of the highest in the world, was being reduced markedly by birth control acceptance. Next, inflation was staying safely near 10 percent, even though Costa Rica is closely dependent on the economic systems of larger countries.

The most serious problems have been related to Costa Rica's ties with the United States, which accounts for a third of both its exports and its imports. These problems are an unfavorable balance of payments due to a trade deficit, resulting in a chronic shortage of dollars; and the fluctuating price of coffee, the main export, which was falling steadily toward the end of the decade after an earlier bonanza.

All this moderate but steady growth has been reflected in measured commercial progress for the mass media. With some variations, the total advertising outlay has risen between 10 and 15 percent annually. Newspapers and television each have about two-fifths of this, radio one-fifth. After a decade in the doldrums, television came out with strong competition for the advertising dollar in the 1970s, but toward the end newspapers were recovering, largely because they were trying to fill the void of good magazines. (Central America remains a desert for domestic magazines, although some multinational ones are considering regional editions.) Circulation of daily newspapers is low—only about 150,000 for a population of 2.2 million—and thus the cost per thousand is higher than that for television and radio, but the prestige of the printed word retains some attraction for advertisers.

Advertising material must be produced in Costa Rica to avoid a 100 percent import tax on its cost.

Both political and family ownerships have largely disappeared among the major media, and investment for profit-making purposes has become the norm. *Excélsior*'s bid was even damaged by its appeal to liberal followers of Figueres, some analysts believe, and another attempt to start a party newspaper shortly after its death also met with quick failure. Weeklies, which come and go every few years, remain a possible outlet for political factions.

The only clear representation by a family is that of the Borrasés, owners of the two small dailies, *La Prensa Libre* and *Extra*. They have shown a notable lack of desire for change in their methods.

Concentration in ownership has never been a problem in Costa Rica, even though the profit motive is strong. Occasionally one newspaper publisher will put out a smaller companion edition, such as the current pair owned by the Borrasés, but this has had little importance in the total picture. The only form of concentration that often stirs criticism is the predominance of *La Nación* in both circulation and advertising, but no serious proposals to limit this by law have been made. Legislation limiting ownership consists only of a rule prohibiting foreign ownership.

All the newspapers seek the economic security of converting their sales to the form of subscriptions, but only *La Nación* has made large headway here, with subscriptions accounting for 59 percent of its circulation. Per-copy sales for all the papers are largely in downtown San José; because the capital's center is intensely overcompacted, sales to pedestrians are thriving. Each newspaper maintains its own distribution network. Although new highways in recent years have opened access to all population centers in the country, the dominance of the Meseta remains in newspaper sale patterns.

Newsprint, imported mostly from Canada, is in ready supply at about $550 a ton, and import duties are negligible. There is some complaint over the country having only one newsprint wholesaler.

According to a 1974 survey, *La Nación* was running 66 percent of its space in advertising, *La República* 49 percent and *La Prensa Libre* 37 percent; there are no indications that these ratios have changed substantially.

Costa Rica's newspapers have achieved a remarkable degree of independence from influence by individual advertisers and other special-interest groups, with the notable exception of the business and planter control of *La Nación* (during Fernández's directorship he often took editorial stands that disturbed his board members). Much concern has been voiced by lawmakers and others that advertisers exert a different sort of influence on readers. This is the rampant promotion of imported luxury goods, which strains the economy beyond its capacity and destroys the simple virtues of Costa Rican traditions.

Pressure from unions and threats of strikes also are an insignificant factor for Costa

Rican publishers. Labor laws set rudimentary minima for pay and working conditions, but these have little relevance to the needs of workers. Editorial salaries at *La Nación* in 1980 were varying from $160 to $400 per week; those at other newspapers range lower.

Per-copy costs of San José newspapers have remained little changed for a decade due to the strong competition. In 1980 the smaller dailies were charging the equivalent of 11 cents. *La Nación*, like *The Tico Times*, was charging 17 cents.

All San José papers have made a successful transition to offset printing through the plants of *La Nación* and *La República*. *La Nación* is beginning to adapt to computer typesetting methods.

Press Laws & Censorship

Journalists in Costa Rica enjoy a freedom that is seldom surpassed anywhere else in the world. This exists not so much because of laws, which are not notably protective, but because of a general consensus that information and discussion must be free to carry on a democratic government.

The basic laws affecting the media are the Constitution of 1949; the Press Law of 1902 (often amended and expanded); the Radio Law of 1954, (with later regulations for television); and the Colegio de Periodistas (Guild of Journalists) Law of 1969. The last has by far been the most controversial.

The constitution contains a guarantee of freedom of expression, largely nullified with exceptions, although not as many as are usually found in Latin American charters. Some of the exceptions are endangering public morality or order, injuring third parties and political propaganda "invoking religious motives."

The Press Law is largely concerned with procedural matters, and with defamation, for which a prison term of up to six months is provided. It also makes punishable the intentional subversion of friendly relations with another nation. There is a stipulation that when someone's honor is offended he may demand and get a retraction.

A potent safeguard in the Press Law is the requirement that defamation cases be tried by a special section of the Supreme Court, and that judges should act according to their consciences in such cases. Leniency is prescribed if the defendant has acted with the public interest in mind.

Free access to public information is promised in the constitution. State secrets are excepted.

A related law sets up a censorship board operating through the Ministry of the Interior. It is required to screen all printed or graphic material consisting of "obscene or pornographic texts,... the disemination of antisocial customs, and the presentation of scenes which may lead to vice, criminality, sexual aberrations and the use of drugs or which are contrary to the country's social values."

The laws governing radio and television are limited in scope. They set defamation norms similar to those for the press and require half-hour weekly donations of air time to the Education Ministry and, during elections, to the Supreme Tribunal of Elections. Other broadcast prohibitions cover false news, vulgar language, anything "contrary to public morality," insults "prejudicial to personal honor or interests," pirating of programs, disclosure of private correspondence, and giving information to an enemy during war.

The Colegio law of 1969 has been making waves on the normally placid surface of Costa Rican journalism since its passage. It had widespread support because it was intended to upgrade professionalism among journalists. To achieve this, the law required that all persons working as reporters on domestic media must be graduates of the University of Costa Rica's School of Journalism, which was founded just the year before. Two exceptions to this were that journalists then practicing could be grandfathered into membership, and degrees from other universities approved by the UCR would be accepted, taking care of those working in Costa Rica with foreign degrees. Since the UCR was the only university in Costa Rica, no domestic competition existed.

In the early years of the law, the complaints came from young persons who wanted to go to work without completing university studies—and from those who wanted to hire them, often at relatively low salaries. The claim that the Colegio system consisted of government "licensing" was often heard, although experience showed that the state would not interfere in any way.

At first there were very few UCR journalism graduates available, but soon the situation reversed itself as the enrollment boomed. Instead of being the despised minority, UCR alumni became the majority, with a vested interest in protecting the exclusivity of their degrees.

This led to the next phase of the controversy. During the 1970s four new universities were founded, all eager for recognition of their professional degrees, not only in journalism but in law and other fields. U.S. journalists working in Costa Rica typically are wanderers without journalism training, and several sought to meet at least the spirit of the Colegio law by enrolling for a new 18-month graduate program at the Autonomous University of Central America (UACA), a private institution with departments scattered through San José. Studying under some of the best-qualified Costa Rican journalists, they felt their training was sounder than the five-year program at UCR, largely taught by nonjournalists.

Although UACA was founded and run by Costa Rican educators, the dispute gradually took on unaccustomed overtones of Yankee-Tico antagonism. The only previous enforcement of the Colegio law had involved Joe Phillips, editor of the weekly *San José News*. He was not a UACA graduate, and he did not challenge the law, although he was convicted, given a suspended sentence and automatically barred from practicing journalism.

Ironically, the next full-blown case also concerned a U.S. national, Stephen Schmidt, a reporter for *The Tico Times*. Colegio backers had generally avoided a confrontation over the law, allowing some UACA graduates to work in violation of it. However, during a 1980 meeting of the Inter American Press Association in San José, Schmidt stood up and publicly admitted he was working illegally and dared the law's supporters to do something about it. The Colegio filed suit, and the case began a long-range procession through the courts. At the same time, efforts began to reform the law in the national Legislative Assembly.

Although not resembling the more repressive aspects of many Latin American systems, the Colegio case in Costa Rica did bring into focus issues lying at the heart of media-government relations elsewhere. On the one hand, it pointed up the movements in many Latin American countries to bring—by force of law—professionalism to an occupation that has traditionally suffered indignities, incompetence and miserable pay. On the other hand, it gives ammunition to worldwide opposition to the Colegio concept by demonstrating that it can be used not to build the profession but rather to expel valuable members. (Schmidt and Phillips are generally conceded to be two of the best journalists who have practiced recently in Costa Rica.)

Another aspect with global implications is that, unlike Phillips, Schmidt based his defense on the broadest possible basis of law. He claimed that the courts should place international human rights agreements above national law and recognize the right of anyone to be a journalist. Such a principle, if taken seriously by the courts of other countries, could reverberate in political jails throughout the world.

Furthermore, there was talk of the possibility that the U.S. government would exert diplomatic pressure on Costa Rica to protect Schmidt under a long-standing commercial agreement. If this should occur, it also would have implications for other countries.

Apart from the Colegio law, a vast array of other legislation implying a social responsibility of the media was proposed in the 1970s, particularly during the Liberation party presidencies that ended in 1978. The only major change that resulted was the above-mentioned law forbidding foreign ownership in the media—aimed primarily at fugitive U.S. financier Robert Vesco, who helped found *Excélsior*. Many of the other proposals were highly innovative, particularly in their attempt to control sex, violence and other exploitation in television. Although they failed final passage, the media were put on notice that abuses would be opposed.

The censorship board's strengthening did result from the effort. Its mandate, which extended to the print media, and was broad and vague, excited much criticism because of its potential for political use. In the field of morality, however, the board was fighting a slowly losing battle as pornographic films gradually increased.

Other types of control are relatively insignificant in Costa Rica.

State-Press Relations

Government agencies, many of them separated from the president's control, put out a large amount of advertising related to their function, such as liquor manufacturing, insurance, banking, homebuilding, tourism and air travel. Although their content rarely is political, such ads can sometimes be given unevenly to friends of the party in power, as occurred when the Liberationists tried to help *Excélsior*.

The degree to which journalists are paid for government "public relations" work is probably the lowest in Latin America. In part this is controlled by the fact that such payments appear in the official gazette, and in Costa Rica they are considered an embarrassment.

Although law guarantees the public access to documents, this is largely a myth in practice. However, enterprising reporters usually can get such documents clandestinely from friends in official positions.

After long avoiding anything resembling a propaganda ministry, the government under conservative President Rodrigo Carazo set up an Office of Information in 1980. It was born out of politicians' accustomed complaint that the press does not inform the public adequately. However, in its early stages it was entangled in bureaucracy and had little effect on journalism, even though it attempted to gain some coordination over publications put out by a number of ministries. The most widely read state organ, the official gazette, sells about 6,000 copies daily because it prints all the laws and legal notices.

Attitude Toward Foreign Media

Costa Rica produces no news of revolutions, street violence and political turmoil, so it is off the beaten path for the foreign press. Reporters drop in occasionally for an international meeting or to do a situation story on the country's rather calm and parochial conflicts. When they visit, journalists find no obstacle other than the lack of excitement. Sources talk freely, telephone and cable offices are uncontrolled, and no permits are needed.

News Agencies

The country has no national news agency, although *La Nación* and *La Prensa Libre* cooperate in the Central American News Agency (ACAN), sponsored by the Spanish agency EFE. *La Nación*'s other agencies are Associated Press, United Press International and Agence France-Presse. *La República* has AP and Deutsche Presse Agentur. *La Prensa Libre* also has AP.

Electronic News Media

Like the press, broadcasting made an impressive expansion in its professional services in the 1970s. This occurred mostly in television, as radio had already reached a plateau before the decade started. By the end of the 1970s there were five television channels operating, all in San José; one was an over-the-air pay channel. This vastly overcrowds the market, and only Channels 6 and 7 are considered important journalistically.

Channel 7 is the oldest, and until the 1970s had the field largely to itself, although this advantage did not result in much development on its part. It made profits and was partly owned by the American Broadcasting Company. Its newscasts consisted mostly of reading news on camera and adding a few films furnished by public relations offices.

Competition began to improve the country's TV news with the arrival of Channel 6, particularly when it greatly expanded its new operations in 1976.

The number of radio stations originating programs fluctuates between 33 and 38, with about 15 having repeater stations. Eight stations, all of them small, are in towns outside San José. One short-wave station beaming its signal to much of Middle America is El Faro del Caribe, which broadcasts Protestant evangelical material in English and Spanish.

A few of the leading radio stations have long been active in the news field, maintaining staffs of nearly a dozen and programming several hours a day of public affairs. Traditionally the most active has been Radio Reloj, which has nine staffers; its trademark is giving the exact time every minute.

Trying for a more sophisticated, analytical approach in recent years has been Radio Monumental. Radio Columbia goes in heavily for sports along with other types of news.

As for content, radio resembles other Latin American countries in its great emphasis on music and sports, plus some soap operas. In television, programming reflects the fact that Costa Rica is prosperous enough to generate a good market for the medium but not large enough to produce much material. A 1976 survey showed that U.S. series and specials filled 31 percent of the time, locally produced programs 24 percent, movies 19, soap operas 9 and other material 17. Aside from the United States, Mexico furnishes a great part of the programs, with some from Venezuela.

A great outpouring of protest and planning about television took place in the mid-1970s. Among the reforms proposed were one that the government buy 51 percent of all broadcasting companies and that foreign investment be banned. The latter did become law, but none of the more sweeping projects succeeded. Advertising is controlled as to the quantity of its import and whether it endangers health, but otherwise the commercial clutter continues unabated; spot advertisements may take up more than 15 minutes at program breaks.

Surveyors have found that radio can reach virtually the entire population, with a penetration of 93 percent of the homes, even though some of the reach is by short wave. The latest available data show 81 television receivers per 1,000 population, although this ranges from 182 in San José and the provincial capitals to 29 outside these urban areas. Since Costa Rican families are large, a relatively small number of sets can reach a large part of the population. Penetration into homes in San José and the provincial capitals is set at 90 percent.

Education & Training

Journalism education in Costa Rica, discussed above in regard to the Colegio law, has received perhaps more concentrated attention from the profession, the lawmaking establishment, and the public than anywhere else in Latin America. It was born in the hope that it would solve all the nation's journalistic ills, but then disillusionment and bitter complaining set in. There has always been a shortage of qualified professors. The result, at least at the principal center, the University of Costa Rica, has been that the two or three full-time professors have always been teachers with no training or experience in the profession, but with degrees in other fields, which make them academically acceptable. Much of the teaching is done by part-time faculty members whose preparation has been entirely on the job. The private university, UACA, has tried to improve on this slightly by putting all the training in the hands of respected professionals. Another problem for UCR has been the influx of political refugees from other countries who get jobs on the journalism school faculty. They invariably are doctrinal firebrands and tend to politicize their teaching, usually on the Marxist side.

The UCR school's early orientation was toward newspapers, but in 1975 it got its first television studio and expanded into broadcasting, and in 1979 into advertising and public relations. It now has about 500 students, but continues to be handicapped by lack of space and adequate faculty pay. None of its professors have offices, and other facilities are scattered about the campus. The UCR school offers scholarships for its graduates to earn master's and doctoral degrees abroad.

Professional organizations except for the Colegio de Periodistas play little role. There is a Sindicato de Periodistas (Journalists' Union), a Cámara Nacional de Radio (National Chamber of Radio Stations) and a sports announcers' association.

Summary

Through the end of the 1970s the mass media in Costa Rica had been conditioned by the nation's small size, its democratic way of life and the relative scarcity of public controversy. These have given the media system a chance to progress as best it could without government interference, while limiting the scope of its operation because of the country's cultural dependence on other areas. One remarkable newspaper, *La Nación*, has emerged, with adequate competition from others. Broadcast journalism, while still provincial, has moved ahead to rival and surpass newspapers in some instances.

As Costa Rica has stayed on its present path for at least the last three decades, there is little to indicate that it will deviate severely in the near future. It may encounter serious strains, such as the challenge from the radical social reforms proposed in the 1970s. Middle-class values have largely won out, and so long as the poor maintain some hope of moving upward economically a confrontation with implications for the media may be avoided.

Costa Ricas's greatest danger appears to be its own middle-class prosperity. It is easy to measure the effects of this on the nation's international balance of payments, as more and more consumer imports from large countries are demanded. While this benefits the media in the short run through advertising, it could damage them in the long run if it results in a wrecked economy.

Another effect has been a sacrifice of traditional Costa Rican social values in favor of the U.S. and Mexican norms that come along with the imports. The media, particularly television, have been seen as the principal vehicles for this cultural invasion, and serious attempts to prevent this, even through government ownership, have been made.

These have been turned away for the moment, but such pressures could return if the media do not change and the public rebels again.

CHRONOLOGY

1968 School of Journalism founded at the University of Costa Rica.
1969 Colegio de Periodistas founded under new law.
1974 *Excélsior,* new daily, founded to challenge domination of *La Nación* and advance the Liberation party. Intervention of U.S. financier Robert Vesco becomes an issue.
1975-78 Wave of reformist legislation aimed at curbing social abuses by the media is debated in Legislative Assembly; largely ends with election of conservative Rodrigo Carazo as president.
1978 *Excélsior* dies in financial chaos.
1980 Colegio sues U.S. journalist Stephen Schmidt, working in Costa Rica, on criminal charge of acting as journalist without being a Colegio member.
Guido Fernández, who led *La Nación*'s rise to professional prominence, resigns as director to go into television news.

BIBLIOGRAPHY

Blutstein, Howart I. et al. *Area Handbook for Costa Rica.* Washington, D.C., 1970.

Flowers, George A. Jr. "Television in Costa Rica: A Response to Picture-Tube Imperialism?" Unpublished paper, University of Texas, 1977.

Fonseca, Jaime M. *Communication Policies in Costa Rica.* Paris, 1977.

McNelly, John T., and Deutschmann, Paul J. "Media Use and Socioeconomic Status in a Latin American Capital." *Gazette* no. 1, (1963): p. 1.

Pierce, Robert N. "Costa Rica's Contemporary Media Show High Popular Participation." *Journalism Quarterly.* Autumn 1970, p. 544.

Pierce, Robert N. *Keeping the Flame: Media and Government in Latin America.* New York, 1979.

UNESCO. *World Communications.* Paris, 1975.

Waisanen, F. B., and Durlak, Jerome T. "A Survey of Attitudes Related to Costa Rican Population Dynamics." American International Association for Economic and Social Development, August 1966.

REPUBLIC OF CUBA*

by John Spicer Nichols

BASIC DATA

Population: 9.8 million
Area: 119,900 sq. km. (46,300 sq. mi.)
GNP: 9.36–8.64 billion pesos (US$12–13 billion) (est.)
Literacy Rate: 94-98%
Language(s): Spanish
Number of Dailies: 12
  Aggregate Circulation: 912,000
  Circulation per 1,000: 93
Number of Nondailies: NA
  Aggregate Circulation: 300,000 plus
  Circulation per 1,000: NA

Number of Periodicals: 100 plus
Number of Radio Stations: 51
Number of Television Stations: 2
Number of Radio Receivers: 2 million
  Radio Receivers per 1,000: 204
Number of Television Sets: 800,000
  Television Sets per 1,000: 82
Total Annual Newsprint Consumption: NA
Per Capita Newsprint Consumption: NA
Total Newspaper Ad Receipts: NA
  As % of All Ad Expenditures: NA

Background & General Characteristics

When Fidel Castro and his guerrilla army came down from their mountain stronghold to take control of the Cuban government in 1959, one of their earliest and most widely criticized acts was the swift takeover of the country's mass communication system. In the 18 months following Castro's victory, all mass media opposing the revolutionary government were closed down or starved out of business, and by 1961 all Cuban media, regardless of political stance, were owned or controlled by Castro forces.

Government control of the media served two major purposes. The most obvious was to eliminate open opposition to the revolution. As the fervor that accompanied the transfer of governments waned, as Cubans faced the realities of economic chaos, political upheaval and a host of diplomatic crises, Castro felt that an adversary media system was not contributing to revolutionary goals and had to be silenced.

Even more important in Castro's view, monopoly allowed the government to use the mass media to achieve the major revolutionary goals of mass integration, education and mobilization. "[I]f we want to overcome the gap which separates us from the developed nations," he said, "... our resources [must be] used in a rational, organized way. There is no room for waste. We don't have the luxury of following the path of free competition to achieve economic development."

Castro had learned, through his effective use of a clandestine press and radio station during the guerrilla campaign, that the mass media are precious resources for fostering revolution. When he came to power in 1959, Cuba's broadcast media were among the few useful assets in that extremely poor country. Most homes outside of Havana lacked running water but not a radio receiver. Cuba also

---

*The research for this chapter was funded in part by the College of the Liberal Arts (Thomas F. Magner, associate dean for Research and Graduate Studies) and the School of Journalism (Robert O. Blanchard, director) of The Pennsylvania State University. The author also wishes to thank Mr. Orville L. Freeman, president of Business International Corporation, and Professor R. Thomas Berner of Penn State. Portions of this chapter were adapted from the author's *Journalism Monograph* titled "Organization, Control and Functions of the Cuban Mass Media"; his contributions to *Keeping the Flame: Media and Government in Latin America* by Robert N. Pierce; and *Case Studies of Mass Media in the Third World*, edited by John A. Lent.

had more television sets per capita than any other Latin American country. Castro believed that those resources could not be left to the helter-skelter management of private owners under a libertarian media system. Rather, they had to be used as a government tool for national development. "What is freedom to write and to speak for a man who doesn't know how to write, who doesn't know how to read?" Castro would ask those who questioned his decision.

Castro frequently is charged with the destruction of a free press in Cuba; in reality, however, he merely substituted one form of strict government control for another. The pre-revolutionary media were seedy, censored, venal puppets of government and industry. Every Cuban president from the time of independence to the revolution either had overtly censored or more subtly bribed editors and reporters into submission. In the period immediately before the overthrow of dictator Fulgencio Batista in 1959, press censorship and corruption reached their worst. The government was paying the press approximately $450,000 a month in bribes, allowing some prominent journalists to pocket tens of thousands of dollars per month. Only six of the 58 newspapers publishing in Cuba in 1958 were surviving without government advertising and subsidies, and many of the papers that did not cooperate with the government were forced out of business through trumped-up taxes or restrictions on vital imports such as newsprint and equipment. Still other newspapers were owned outright by Batista and his collaborators.

In the long run, though, government censorship worked in favor of Castro's revolutionary movement. Cuban audiences eager to hear news not censored by the Batista government consequently tuned in to Radio Rebelde, the guerrillas' clandestine radio station. Radio Rebelde, which was inaugurated in February 1958 by Ernesto (Che) Guevara, eventually became one of the most listened-to voices in Cuba and much of the Caribbean. Each night, a growing number of Cubans would tune in to the station and hear a barrage of reports of guerrilla victories, manifestos, patriotic poems and music. Castro frequently polished his oratorical skills over the air, and by the time the revolutionaries took control of the government he had refined his ability to the point that many analysts considered him the world's greatest political speaker of the era.

Castro's successful use of the mass media as a propaganda tool during the insurrection has had a tremendous impact on the current Cuban government's philosophy toward the media. In contrast to many countries where the media are institutions to be tolerated, manipulated or perhaps repressed, the Cuban media are viewed as an essential public utility to be used in accomplishing revolutionary goals. However, it must be remembered that revolution is a process of rapid social change; thus the Cuban revolution, like most true social revolutions, has zigzagged through distinct phases. Accordingly, Cuban communication policy also has changed frequently.

In 1959, the new revolutionary government immediately ended bribes and subsidies to the press (except to the official newspaper, *Revolución*), and as a result, most newspapers shortly went out of business. Even those newspapers not dependent on government subsidies for their survival also had financial difficulties. As the government rapidly nationalized private industry and business, the remaining media found it increasingly difficult to find advertising revenues to support themselves.

Despite the economic problems, the few privately owned media were not censored by the government for a year or so, and had considerable latitude to criticize Castro and his government. But as the revolution gathered steam, the adversary press became progressively more cautious, and in late 1960, by intimidation, expropriation and increased economic pressure, the revolutionary government had closed almost all of the privately owned print media and gained complete ownership of the broadcast media.

In the early 1960s the Cubans introduced a Marxist media system, in which criticism of revolutionary goals was increasingly repressed, and Castro laid down the dictum that was to govern the role of the mass media in the new Cuban society: "For those within the Revolution, complete freedom; for those against the Revolution, no freedom." Despite government intervention, the controls were not monolithic, and a considerable amount of debate still could be found in the Cuban media, particularly the print media. Two groups, one headed by the revolutionary Che Guevara and the other by old-line, Soviet-style communists, argued over the future path of the revolution. Some of the ideological debate spilled onto the pages of Havana's two major newspapers, each controlled by a contending group.

By 1966 Cuba had entered a phase of mobilization and radicalization of the media under the newly adopted policies of Guevara, the victor in the debate. The revolutionary elite moved to consolidate their direct control over the media, starting by merging the warring newspapers of the preceding years into *Granma,* the single and official voice of the Cuban Communist party. It was Guevara's strategy that a "new Cuban man" would be forged in an egalitarian society and mobilized behind revolutionary goals. To do that, the mass media would be used to educate the masses and not be allowed to deviate from official policy.

This new phase of the revolution proved a disaster. Cuban-Soviet relations were strained, Guevara was killed in Bolivia while trying to transplant his ideology, and the Cuban economy was in chaos. Castro responded by returning to Soviet-style centralization of his government and continuing tight control on all forms of expression until the revolution was consolidated. That period lasted until about 1975, when Cuba emerged from five years of international isolation, economic hardship and considerable repression. The revived Cuban revolution was able to boast of numerous social gains in the area of education, housing and health care, greater economic stability and a new constitution that granted the masses increased participation in the government. Corresponding to these changes, the Cuban media assumed a critical new function, in which they served as channels for citizens' complaints about the tactical operation of the government. However, no criticism of the strategic goals of the revolution was permitted.

A new stage of the revolution seemed to be evolving as Cuba entered the 1980s. Severe economic difficulties returned, mostly as the result of the failure of the island's critical sugar harvest and the financial drain of supporting Cuban combat troops in Africa. Increased absenteeism, black market activity, corruption, shortages of basic products and general unrest were reported in the country. (Despite recent problems and tension, however, the majority of Cubans continue to support Castro, and according to U.S. intelligence estimates, he would win in a landslide if a general election for president were held in the country.) To cope with the problems, the Castro government took two major actions. First, the top levels of the administration were reorganized, resulting in a greater centralization of control of important divisions, such as the Ministry of Interior, which is in charge of the police and courts. In the other action, Castro relieved the tension caused by dissidents by allowing them—indeed in many cases forcing them—to leave Cuba. In the spring of 1980, officials opened the port of Mariel, precipitating a disorderly boat-exodus of more than 125,000 Cubans to the United States. The effect of this new stage in the Cuban revolution on media policy cannot yet be determined.

Given the Cuban philosophy that the media are public utilities and that their content must be centrally planned for political formation and social and economic development, the Cuban media's greatest success has been in education. In 1961 the government made universal literacy its top priority and mobilized the entire Cuban society, including the mass media, to achieve that goal. The media served three important functions in the literacy campaign. First, they helped to recruit an army of literacy teachers by blanketing the country with a highly nationalistic appeal. Second, they were used in direct instruction of illiterates and in the training of the volunteer literacy teachers. The printing presses of the expropriated newspapers were consolidated into an official book publisher called the National Press. Millions of copies of a learner's primer and a teacher's manual were produced in a few months to support the campaign. Radio and television schools also were organized to supplement the lessons of the teachers in the countryside. And third, the Cuban mass media attempted to bring nationwide honor to the campaign by eliciting the support of Cubans not directly participating.

Although the crash teaching program of 1961 brought the country's population over the threshold of literacy, Cuba was far from an educated society. To consolidate and further the early gains, the government established a permanent adult education program and national school system in which the media continued to contribute significantly. Although radio and television are the most important educational media, the Cuban print media also continued to play an essential educational role. Since the National Press was organized during the literacy campaign, more than 360 million copies of 11,800 titles have been printed in the country. In 1974, 20 times more books were printed in Cuba than in any year prior to the revolution. More than half of those books were for education. The general-circulation newspapers and magazines still publish educational material, but currently are used largely for news transmission and political formation. However, some specialized magazines, mostly directed at children, are intended for educational purposes, and others published by the Ministry of Education assist in teacher training. Owing in part to the use of centralized mass media in literacy and other educational programs, illiteracy has by now been virtually eliminated in Cuba, and the country has one of the highest levels of education in the region. In 1980, between 94 and 98 percent of the population could read and write in Spanish—one of the highest literacy rates in the Western Hemisphere.

Centralized control of the mass media has also resulted in a substantial growth in media hardware, and thus, unduplicated media audiences. The party newspaper Granma publishes three times as many copies each day as the total circulation of all daily newspapers published in Cuba in 1958. Granma and other newspapers and magazines are distributed throughout the country.

Although Cuban radio and television were relatively well developed before the revolution, the growth of the post-revolutionary broadcast media has been unprecedented. The government claims that more than 2 million radio receivers, about double the number of receivers before the revolution, and about 800,000 TV sets, two to three times the pre-revolutionary number, were in use on the island in 1980. (Both pre-revolutionary and post-revolutionary Cuban media statistics are unaudited and, therefore, should be used with caution.) During the same two-decade period, the total number of radio and television transmitters decreased, but the overall amount of programming increased, and signal coverage was extended to almost all of the island.

To some extent the distribution of print media and the transmitters and receivers of the broadcast media are concentrated in the capital city of Havana and other large cities, but compared to the pre-revolutionary period —and to other countries in the world—media concentration in Cuba is relatively minor. In sum, Cuban audiences are media rich, at least quantitatively, compared to people in countries with similar levels of economic development. This fact is consistent with the communist perspective that the media are essential tools for social and economic development as well as for integrating the entire population under one ideological banner.

For the most part, Cuban newspapers are organs of various divisions of the Cuban Communist party and have similar staff organization, format and content. Granma, the highest-circulation daily, is the official voice of the party and is organized as a political division of the party's Central Committee, one of the most powerful entities in the Cuban leadership. The newspaper (named for the vessel that transported Castro's guerrilla force from Mexico to Cuba to begin jungle warfare against Batista) has an estimated daily circulation of more than 560,000. In addition, a weekly digest of Granma is published in Spanish, French and English, with more than 100,000 copies distributed worldwide. Granma was founded in October 1965 when Castro merged Revolución and Hoy, the newspapers representing the debating factions of the revolution. The editor of Granma since 1967 has been Jorge Enrique Mendoza, a member of the Central Committee, former propagandist for Castro's pre-revolutionary guerrilla forces and one of the most influential leaders in Cuban government.

The other national daily, Juventud Rebelde, is published by the Union of Young Communists, technically a mass organization but actually nothing more than the youth division of the party. The newspaper circulates about 230,000 copies Monday through Friday and 325,000 copies on Sunday. Both Granma and Juventud Rebelde are distributed throughout the nation—the morning Granma is circulated outside Havana in the afternoons and vice versa for the afternoon Juventud Rebelde. Each is widely read by party workers and government bureaucrats—and also frequently read aloud, along with other revolutionary literature, over the public address systems in many Cuban factories. The third national newspaper, Los Trabajadores, is published three times a week by the Central Union of Cuban Workers. Its circulation is estimated at 300,000.

In addition, the party committees of 10 provinces publish daily newspapers that are closely modeled after Granma. Although the circulation and influence of these regional papers are limited, they appear to have greater leeway to comment on local affairs than the national dailies have to comment on

Cuban Regional Dailies		
Newspaper	Province	Est. Circulation
El Guerrillero	Pinar de Río	13,000
Girón	Matanzas	19,000
Vanguardia	Villa Clara	22,000
Adelante	Camagüey	26,000
Sierra Maestra	Santiago de Cuba	10,000
Ahora	Holguín	14,000
Venceremos	Guantánamo	6,000
Siempre 26 Es	Las Tunas	6,000
La Demajagua	Granma	6,000
Las Tunas	Granma	6,000

national issues. The total press run for these provincial dailies is about 122,000.

Granma and its provincial imitations are modeled, especially in typography, after the Soviet Union's *Pravda*. All are standard-size newspapers with usually six and a maximum of 12 pages. The Cuban papers tend to be slightly more flamboyant than the Soviet ones in their use of color and special graphics. Most of the content is devoted to transcripts of speeches by Castro and other important officials, the goings and comings of foreign leaders and delegations, reports of developmental successes, industrial production figures, photos of exemplary workers, a heavy dose of sports and culture and, recently, an increasing number of letters to the editor. Crime, conflict and bad-news reporting common in Western papers is rare in the Cuban press. According to a content analysis published by the Cuban journalists union in 1975, Granma's general content breaks down as follows: social issues, 54.5 percent; international affairs, 12 percent; domestic politics, government and administration, 11 percent; economics, 9.3 percent; science and technology, 6.1 percent; military, 2.9 percent; and miscellaneous, 3.2 percent.

Cuban media content is extremely dull. According to surveys conducted by Cuban researchers, the vast majority of the Cuban population disapprove of media content, and top government officials and media policymakers have called for improvements. In a speech to the Fourth Congress of the Union of Cuban Journalists in 1980, Raúl Castro, Fidel's brother, commander of the military

and second in command of the Cuban government, chided the group for the low quality of Cuban journalism. He criticized the journalists for being "boring" in their style, failing to "delve deeper into basic problems" and practicing self-censorship. He called on the journalists to criticize malfunctions of government operations, although *not* the revolution itself. "Criticism within our ranks is a political duty and social responsibility," he said. And after he finished his address and was walking off stage, he shouted, "Criticize all you want! The party is behind you!"

The principle of democratic centralism, in which journalists are encouraged to criticize the tactical operations but not the strategic goals of government, is basic to communist systems. So is the effort to dress up and make more palatable the generally dry material appearing in the communist press. However, the problem is probably endemic to a system that has mostly political and educational content. Even audiences of the Western media who consider news, public affairs and education content useful and interesting would find a steady diet of it tedious.

Another reason for the low quality of Cuban journalism is the limited number of trained journalists. The number of full-time newspeople probably is only several hundred, and most of them have been selected for their ideological commitment rather than their journalistic skill or educational training. Their work is supplemented by several thousand volunteer correspondents stationed around the country.

More than 100 magazines, journals and specialized newspapers are published in Cuba, and each is governed by a specific sector of Cuban government or one of the mass organizations. Examples are *Mujeres,* Cuban Federation of Women; *Política Internacional,* Ministry of Foreign Relations; *Cuba Azúcar,* Ministry of the Sugar Industry; and *El Deporte,* National Institute of Sports. The sponsoring group has the sole responsibility for the organization, editorial policy and operation of its publication, although party ideological planners and central government officials have coordinating powers and considerable influence on matters of policy. Because of the diversification of control of the periodical press and its insulation from direct supervision, most magazines and journals enjoy increasing latitude to comment on issues, although mostly from the perspective of their sponsoring organizations or their constituencies. Not surprisingly, the most influential magazine, *Verde Olivo,* is published by the Revolutionary Armed Forces, probably the most powerful sector in Cuban government.

A new periodical, *Opina,* is Cuba's largest-selling magazine. *Opina,* which is published by the Cuba Institute for Consumer Research and Planning and is filled with relatively lively articles about consumer products and affairs, current events and cultural activities, usually sells its entire press run of 500,000 copies within hours after it reaches the newsstands. Other Cuban magazines of hemispheric influence are *Bohemia, Casa de las Americas* and *Tricontinenal.*

Economic Framework

All mass media are owned and operated by the Cuban Communist party, the government or their constituent organizations. Consequently, the media operate almost entirely on state funds. Some income is generated by the print media from newsstand sales—five cents (US) for a daily newspaper—and international subscriptions. The Cuban print media also carry advertising, although it does not produce revenue. The international editions of *Granma* and other publications distributed abroad increasingly have been carrying ads for Cuban tourism, manufactured goods and other items that might build Cuban foreign trade. The domestic editions of *Granma* do not carry advertising, but a few Cuban magazines have classified ad sections. Most classified ads offer or ask for apartments, cars, furniture and personal services such as radio and TV repair.

On one hand, the Cuban revolution has been successful in redistributing the economic wealth of the nation more equally among all sectors of the population. On the other hand, the revolution has failed to build a healthy, stable economy that can produce the basic goods and services needed by the Cuban people. The many causes of this economic stagnation include the U.S. trade embargo, vulnerability to fluctuating world prices for sugar (Cuba's major export and source of foreign exchange), government mismanagement, and considerable cost of maintaining Cuban expeditionary forces in Africa. Thus, despite two decades of revolutionary government, Cuba remains a very poor country, heavily dependent on the Soviet Union for its financial survival.

Cuba's economic situation and media policy are reciprocally related. The allocation of scarce financial resources to develop the Cuban mass media system has contributed to widespread shortages in other sectors of the economy. While television sets are plentiful in both urban and rural areas, basic commodities such as food and clothing are in short supply, severely rationed and can be bought only after standing in lines for hours—or through the flourishing black market.

The extent of the Cuban government's commitment to developing the television system, for example, is apparent from studying Cuba's five-year plan ending in 1980. One of the highest priorities was the importation from the Soviet Union of about 100,000 television sets per year. This goal was particularly costly to meet because Cuban television operates on a 525-line system built by U.S. companies in the 1950s, and therefore the regular TV sets manufactured by Cuba's socialist trading partners for use on their 625-line system are not compatible. As a result, the Soviet Union builds 525-line sets—at substantially higher prices—solely for sale to Cuba. Another major goal in Cuba's 1975–80 five-year plan was the construction of a plant that would convert bagasse, a by-product of sugar cane, into newsprint. But economic problems have kept the plant from full production, thus perpetuating a chronic shortage of paper and forcing Cuba to continue importing it.

Clearly, the Cuban leadership considers the mass media, especially TV, to be a crucial communication link needed to maintain revolutionary cohesion among the people. But its heavy media-investment requires postponing other important development projects and making other economic sacrifices. In turn, the sluggish economy does not produce exports to earn the foreign exchange needed to purchase newsprint, ink and replacement parts for presses and the archaic broadcasting equipment, almost none of which is manufactured in Cuba.

Labor is represented in the media by the Union of Cuban Journalists, founded in 1963. In 1980 the union had nearly 3,000 members, working both full time and part time.

Press Laws

Cuban press law is predicated on the socialist principle that the rights of the collective take precedence over the rights of the individual. Professor Adamantia Pollis argues that the historical experience of Cuba fostered a very different notion of freedom and human dignity. The developed countries of North America and Western Europe, having gone through an industrial revolution, developed a philosophy of political and civil rights as the core of human dignity. But when transferred to Cuba and other developing states that same philosophy allowed the colonial powers and local elites to politically and economically exploit the underdeveloped nations. As a result, according to Pollis, the people of Cuba began to view freedom and human dignity as social and economic rights rather than civil and political rights. "Freedom from starvation, the right for all to enjoy the material benefits of an advanced developed economy, and freedom from exploitation became the articulated goals," she says.

In the view of the Cuban leadership, social and economic equality is a precondition to civil and political rights, such as the Western concept of freedom of the press; therefore, society has the right to use the mass media as tools to achieving collective goals. The new Cuban constitution, ratified by popular referendum in 1976, legitimizes the concept that a citizen's right to speak freely is subordinate to the good of the state. Article 52 states:

> Citizens have freedom of speech and of the press in keeping with the objectives of socialist society. Material conditions for the exercise of that right are provided by the fact that the press, radio, television, movies, and other organs of the mass media are state or social property and can never be private property. This assures their use for the exclusive service of the working people and in the interest of society.

Those rights are further limited by Article 61:

> None of the freedoms which are recognized for the citizens can be exercised contrary to what is established in the Constitution and the law, or contrary to the existence and objectives of the socialist state, or contrary to the decision of the Cuban people to build socialism and communism. Violations of this principle can be punished by law.

Although the punishment of Cuban journalists guilty of counterrevolutionary behavior is legitimized by the new constitution, the legal provisions are, as in most Latin American countries, largely a matter of form, and other means of media control are more significant. Subtle controls over the operation of the mass media are so effective that jailings, censorship and other forms of overt repression are comparatively rare.

Nevertheless, the Inter American Press Association has listed about a dozen journalists as among the 2,000 to 5,000 political prisoners held in Cuban jails in the late 1970s. Despite several recent releases of political prisoners, including some media people, several Cuban journalists still are imprisoned, a few since the early 1960s. (While the Cuban government concedes that former journalists are in Cuban jails, it also says that they were imprisoned for ordinary criminal behavior rather than for what they wrote.)

Censorship

Formal government censorship has been practiced in Cuba and, to a limited extent, continues today, but its use as a media control is grossly overestimated by observers outside of Cuba. The reason that censorship and other overt controls generally are not required is that Cuban journalists, with rare exceptions, are ideologically aligned with the goals of the revolution and, in numerous instances, also hold top leadership positions in the government and party. For example, Jorge Enrique Mendoza, the editor of *Granma,* also is a member of the Central Committee and a deputy in the national assembly, formerly held several top ministerial posts in the government, and was one of Castro's top propagandists in the pre-1959 guerrilla warfare. And Mendoza is not an exception. A study by this author published in *Journalism Monographs* documents that at least 71 percent of Cuban editors and other top media policy-makers also hold leadership positions in the party and the government and/or were pre-revolutionary allies of Castro. Under these circumstances, it is highly unlikely that the government would find much need to censor the press. The overlap between the Cuban media and officialdom is so complete that, if the government censored the press, it would, in effect, be censoring itself.

The control of rank-and-file journalists is almost as complete as for their editors. More than 40 percent of all Cuban journalists are members of the Cuban Communist party or the Communist Youth Union. Only a few sectors of Cuban society, such as the police force and military officers, have a higher percentage of membership. In addition, all journalists must be members of the Union of Cuban Journalists, which establishes and strictly enforces standards that govern the media and, to some extent, the private behavior of all its members. Those who violate union policy can lose their accreditation, and thus, their right to publish.

Despite the effectiveness of these controls, the Cuban government on occasion has been forced to resort to more overt methods. The most sensational case was that of Cuban writer Heberto Padilla. Padilla was a correspondent for the Cuban news agency Prensa Latina and for *Granma* in both Prague and Moscow, but lost his job following a run-in with the government in 1968. The disgruntled Padilla continued, as a poet and novelist, to write what some considered veiled criticism of the government.

In March 1971 Padilla was jailed without charges. The word of his arrest filtered abroad, and in April a large group of European and Latin American leftist writers and intellectuals (among them Jean-Paul Sartre, Gabriel Garcia Márquez, Carlos Fuentes, Octavio Paz and Mario Vargas Llosa) published an open letter to Castro expressing concern over the imprisonment and "the use of repressive methods against intellectuals and writers who exercise the right of criticism." After being held incommunicado for more than a month—and after writing a long, abject confession of his "errors against the Revolution"—Padilla was released from jail. Two days later, he appeared before the Cuban Congress on Education and Culture and read his letter of self-criticism. The congress responded with a hard-line declaration on the mass media and cultural affairs. Among other things, the assembled writers and artists said that the mass media "are powerful instruments of ideological education whose utilization and development should not be left to spontaneity and improvisation."

A month later, the international group of writers wrote Castro and his congress a second letter charging that Padilla's confession had been obtained through torture, and likened the episode to "the most sordid moments of Stalinism." Both Castro and Padilla denied the charge, but worldwide criticism of the affair continued.

Afterwards Padilla worked in obscurity as a translator in Havana, but was not allowed to publish his own works. In 1980, after a year of petitioning the government and with the sponsorship of U.S. Senator Edward M. Kennedy, Padilla was allowed to emigrate to the United States, where he is scheduled to publish several of his literary works.

State-Press Relations

The Cuban government has no information ministry that administers all, most, or even a large share of the country's mass media. At least a dozen government divisions have some administrative control over the media. All broadcasting media are supervised by the Cuban Institute of Radio and Television, which in turn, is administered directly by one of the vice-presidents of the Council of Ministers. Although the broadcasting institute reports to the Ministry of Communication on mostly technical matters and coordinates with other agencies of government, the fact that the institute is supervised by such a high official—thus bypassing lower levels of government that supervise the other media—demonstrates the importance that the Cuban government places on broadcasting.

Although the broadcasting media are highly centralized, the remaining media are relatively decentralized and the type of supervision varies greatly. As previously discussed, newspapers and magazines are attached to various mass organizations or divisions of the party and government, and are organized and controlled to best represent each group's interests in the national forum. The Cuban Institute of Cinema Art and Industry, a division of the Ministry of Culture, controls all filmmaking, including newsreels and documentaries. The Ministry of Culture also shares with the Ministry of Education in the supervision of editing, printing and distribution of all books in Cuba. The Cuban news agency, Prensa Latina, claims to be autonomous of offical supervision.

Despite this hodgepodge of organizational controls, some centralized supervision does exist. The Department of Revolutionary Orientation, a division of the Central Committee of the party, seems to have some authority to coordinate Cuba's propaganda activities and to set general media policy. According to the limited evidence available, the department's authority has fluctuated greatly in past years and has frequently been contested by other agencies. In the 1960s the department had great power in matters of ideology and was often referred to as the "censorship board," but in the 1980s its power seems to have deteriorated and its responsibilities today are less policy-setting and more operational—implementing policy determined elsewhere in the Cuban hierarchy.

Of course, the relationship of the government and the press is reciprocal—even in a communist system such as Cuba's. Not only does the Cuban government affect the media, but the media also affect the Cuban government. The best example is the increasing ability of the Cuban press to criticize the government and force changes in its tactical operations. In 1975, when Cuba broke out of its long siege of isolation from the world, the Cuban government was markedly changed. It had become far more complex—structures in the political system were more differentiated, an expanded bureaucracy was increasingly making and enforcing rules (previously the providence of Castro and his inner circle), and the means of public representation in decision making had increased. Cuban scholars call this the process of "institutionalization."

The showpiece of Castro's new Cuba is *poder popular* (people's power), a political structure designed to link the people more directly to the government. Established by the new Cuban constitution, which was approved by popular referendum in 1976, *poder popular* is a system of elected bodies beginning at the neighborhood level and continuing up to a national assembly. The elected representatives are required to hold regular meetings of the neighborhood groups to hear grievances and to report back about progress in solving previous complaints. Such meetings observed by the author were attended by a large number of citizens and the discussion was frequently enthusiastic and critical. However, the meetings were not concerned with questions of policy but rather with the efficiency with which established policy was being implemented. Thus, consistent with the Marxist principle of democratic centralism, the people have the opportunity to criticize the performance of government agencies and bureaucrats at a local level without challenging the central government's overall authority.

In 1974 the Cuban press began publishing reports of these meetings, and in the following year *Granma* launched a "consumer action" column, to force bureaucrats to account for their mistakes and inefficiency and to relay reader concerns to the government. Editors of the column, titled "By Return Mail," invite readers to blow the whistle on unresponsive administrators, long waits in the local hospital, lack of garbage collection or any other cases of negligence and waste. A team of reporters is then assigned to investigate the charges and report on their findings. As the column continues to build a reputation and wide readership, it increasingly has been demanding "accountability," in essence fixing blame for the abuses that are uncovered. For example, an investigation initiated by the column staffers led to the firing of three top officials in Havana's sanitation department after a reader reported that two department vehicles were abandoned for months on a city street.

The column was so successful and popular with the readers that Havana's other daily, *Juventud Rebelde,* started one of its own, and the idea is now spreading to newspapers in the providences. *Juventud Rebelde* receives between 800 and 900 letters a week.

In addition to vertical feedback, in which the press registers a sample of public grievances as a form of intelligence for the government and a release for the masses, the press also serves a feedback function on a horizontal plane. As the Cuban government became larger and more complex, disputes among the numerous administrative divisions could no longer be solved interpersonally. Increasingly, the mass media have the expanded role of relaying information from one branch of government to another, and publications controlled by these branches tend to advocate their positions in the national forum. That is not to say that these publications will deviate from stated national policies; however, they do tend to hype matters of greatest concern to their branches while offering only an obligatory nod to matters more relevant to others.

Attitude Toward Foreign Media

The foreign press was an essential ingredient in the Cuban revolutionary movement. During the first several months of guerrilla warfare, Castro's handful of poorly fed and poorly armed troops operated in obscurity and with neither military nor political success. A United Press dispatch reporting that Castro had been killed when his invasion force landed in Cuba was widely published throughout the island. There was no hope of expanding the guerrilla activity until he was able to demonstrate that he and his group were alive and active. Castro had no access to the corrupt and heavily censored Cuban press; thus the solution was to be interviewed by a foreign correspondent. So in February 1957, Herbert Matthews of *The New York Times* was brought to the rebel stronghold in the Sierra Maestra to interview Castro.

To some extent, Castro sought to gain international support for the revolution, but he was more concerned with circumventing the censored Cuban press by using the international press for its internal impact. The domestic effect was as Castro predicted. The publication of Matthews' articles in the *Times* brought a roar of disbelief from Batista's incumbent government while snowballing publicity at home and abroad, a steady stream of new recruits into the mountains, and more foreign newsmen. As a result of this early experience, Castro has developed a strong respect for the power of the foreign press in both helping and hurting the Cuban revolution. Consequently his treatment of the foreign press corps is usually indicative of his broader foreign affairs strategies.

In the early 1960s, as relations with the United States rapidly deteriorated and Cuba began to close its doors to the outside world, treatment of the foreign press grew increasingly hostile. The few Western correspondents permitted to enter Cuba were severely restricted and harassed by everybody from government officials to bellhops in hotels. During his marathon speeches to the Cuban people, Castro reserved some of his most acid criticism for the Western press, and in 1969 he closed down the bureaus of the Associated Press and United Press International, expelling their correspondents. Only correspondents from Communist publications and news agencies were allowed to remain in Havana.

In 1975, as tension with the United States eased and Cuba emerged from its long isolation and initiated an aggressive foreign policy, Cuban treatment of the foreign press swung in the opposite direction. In contrast to the limited access and harassment of previous years, Western reporters received a cordial welcome in Cuba. Many prominent U.S. reporters (including Dan Rather, Bill Moyers, Frank Mankiewicz and Barbara Walters), previously personae non gratae, reported receiving lavish treatment—extensive press briefings, a blizzard of publicity material, escorted tours of development projects and tourist spots and, frequently, interviews with Castro and other top Cuban leaders. The reporters had wide access to news sources and government documents, and traveled without government control or surveillance. Foreign policy analysts say that Castro's improved treatment of Western journalists is only a part of Cuba's overall drive for expanded international relations.

In addition to a political motive, the Cuban government has economic reasons for courting U.S. correspondents. Following an influx of more favorable U.S. news coverage of Cuba, North American tourism, an important source of foreign exchange for Cuba's troubled economy, increased substantially in the late 1970s.

Even after the trend toward normalization of relations between Cuba and the United States faltered in 1978 and 1979 over questions about Soviet troops in Cuba and Cuban troops in Africa, Cuba's international public relations campaign continued. In 1979, both AP and UPI signed exchange agreements with Prensa Latina, the Cuban world news agency, for distribution of each other's service, and Castro, while visiting New York to give a speech to the United Nations, hosted an elaborate dinner party for the elite of U.S. journalism, including Katharine Graham, chairman of the board of the Washington *Post;* Ben Bradlee, the *Post*'s editor; Roone Arledge, president of ABC news; Lester Bernstein, editor of *Newsweek;* and Henry Grunwald, editor of *Time.*

Despite the markedly improved situation, Cuba is by no means entirely open to the foreign press. The government continues to exercise some control over visiting correspondents and clearly attempts to manage the news that is reported about the country. Many reporters still have difficulty obtaining visas to enter Cuba, and some foreign newspeople have had to supply clippings of their newspapers' editorial stances on Cuba before visas were issued.

Despite the exchange agreements, the U.S. wire services are not allowed to establish bureaus in Cuba, although Cuban officials ignore arrangements in which correspondents for Canadian and European media also are stringers for U.S. media.

On isolated occasions authorities have confiscated film footage of critical industries and military personnel, and in one recent incident, local police detained a U.S. correspondent for three hours while his credentials were checked with military intelligence. Virtually all correspondents report having taken mandatory tours of showcase schools and experimental farms before being allowed to interview important news sources.

Probably the most important medium in Cuba's international communication activities is Radio Havana, the country's short-wave service. Since its founding in 1961, Radio Havana has become one of the most listened-to voices in the hemisphere. Its eight transmitters air more than 54 hours of programming daily in English, Spanish, French, Arabic, Portuguese, Guarani, Quechua and Creole. Most of the content is news and commentary with a heavy emphasis on Latin America. Radio Havana has also served as a repeater for Radio Moscow and Radio Sandino, voice of the Sandinista guerrillas before they took control of the Nicaraguan government.

During the 1960s and the early 1970s, the Cuban external broadcasting system was saturated with shrill anti-American propaganda. The Voice of America countered with the most concentrated propaganda campaign in its history—including programming designed specifically for Cuban audiences and more generally to counteract Radio Havana's effect elsewhere in Latin America. In 1974, the United States ended its special Cuban programming, and there was a slight deescalation of the war of words from both sides of the Straits of Florida.

Despite the Voice of America campaign, U.S. commercial radio has had a much greater impact on Cuban audiences. A large number of Cubans can and frequently do listen to Miami radio stations (only 225 miles away) on standard medium-wave receivers, and with a good antenna and favorable weather conditions can pick up U.S. television programming in their homes. Cuban officials have argued that the commercial lure of Miami broadcasting was a major cause of the Cuban exodus of 1980. Although the officials express great concern about the problem, they have never attempted to jam foreign broadcast signals, even during the midst of Cuba's isolation in the 1960s and early 1970s.

Numerous Soviet-bloc publications are available at Cuban newsstands, and an occasional Western publication, such as *The New York Times,* can be found in Cuban libraries, although not on the newsstands. First-run U.S. films such as *The Godfather* and *The Way We Were* have been shown in Havana theaters since 1975. Although films from the USSR, Czechoslovakia, England, Spain and Mexico are shown more frequently, the lines for the U.S. films are usually longest. In addition, old Hollywood films, primarily from the 1940s and 1950s, regularly are shown on Cuban television.

As part of its increased international activities, Cuba has been extremely active in the politics of developing countries. Cuba hosted the Conference of Non-Aligned Nations in 1979, and Castro serves as chairman of the movement through 1981. Consequently, Cuba has strongly advocated the nonaligned-nation positions on international news-flow issues and has consistently voted with that bloc. Furthermore, Cuba has been a major supporter of the new Non-Aligned New Agencies Pool. Prensa Latina, Cuba's world news agency, also serves as a redistribution facility for the nonaligned pool, and Cuba contributes 6 percent of all items used in the pool. Only Yugoslavia, Egypt and Iraq contribute a greater percentage.

The Union of Cuban Journalists also maintains close contact with international, regional and Soviet-bloc media organizations. For example, Ernesto Vera, president of the union, is vice-president of the Prague-based International Organization of Journalists and a leader of the Latin American Federation of Journalists.

News Agencies

Prensa Latina, Cuba's world news service, is the major source of foreign news for most of the Cuban mass media. The agency, founded in 1959, has about 400 staffers stationed in the central office in Havana and 34 bureaus around the world. Many of the correspondents in its bureaus are local stringers. In addition, Prensa Latina has exchange agreements with 50 news agencies, photo services and other news organizations. The agency claims to distribute daily about 250 to 300 items of news and analysis in Spanish, English and French to approximately 1,000 clients, including both national and international subscribers. It also claims it receives no government subsidy but pays all its expenses with fees charged from the subscribers. However, relatively few of the world's major media regularly use the Prensa Latina file. Prensa Latina also publishes and distributes to its clients various magazines and bulletins, including *Cuba International.*

There have been several instances in which Prensa Latina correspondents were expelled from host countries for questionable political activities, or were observed performing diplomatic functions for the Cuban government in addition to their journalistic function for the news agency.

In 1974 the National Information Agency was formed as the domestic complement to Prensa Latina. Little is known about the agency, but apparently it has its own staff and transmission facilities, and in addition to carrying news and commentaries to and from the Cuban provinces, it also serves the public relations function of organizing press coverage of major national ceremonies and visiting delegations.

Electronic News Media

Radio and television are the most important media in Cuba. Owing largely to Castro's early success with his guerrilla radio station, the government relies heavily on its broadcasting system as a means of information transmission and national integration. In the early years of the revolution, Castro would appear on national radio and television, often daily, to explain revolutionary goals and encourage popular cooperation. The media became so crucial to the revolutionary process that Herbert Matthews of *The New York Times* coined the phrase "government by television." Although Castro speaks less frequently on Cuban radio and television today, the broadcasting system continues to shoulder a large portion of the educational and political responsibilities for the nation.

Cuba has two national television channels. One of the channels, as a carryover from the early use of the media in literacy training, is an educational channel designed for direct classroom use and more general professional training for teachers, technicians and other specialists. The other channel is intended for popular consumption and carries programming heavily weighted toward cultural affairs, news and political events and commentaries.

The five national radio channels are centered in Havana and are supplemented by an extensive system of local stations and repeaters blanketing the island. The major news channel is Radio Reloj (Clock), which broadcasts news 24 hours per day and announces the time each minute.

All facets of the broadcast media are centrally administered by the Cuban Institute of Radio and Television, and although directors of individual stations claim considerable programming autonomy, in-country research indicates that radio and television are the most tightly controlled of all Cuban media. Nonetheless, University of Texas researchers Elizabeth Mahan and Jorge Reina Schement noted several important similarities to the U.S. broadcasting system, and argued that much of the greater diversity in U.S. broadcast content was merely the product of the larger scale of that system.

Education & Training

Cuban officials and editors have deplored the low quality of the nation's journalists, and as a result some effort has been made recently to upgrade journalism education and training in Cuba. The country has two journalism programs, at the University of Havana and the University of the Oriente, but both emphasize ideological training over reporting and writing techniques. Approximately 500 students are enrolled in the four-and-a-half year programs. However, editors and directors of major Cuban media report that few university-trained journalists find their way into Cuban newsrooms, and those who do are inadequately trained. The vast majority of Cuban journalists learn their professions on the job.

The Union of Cuban Journalists also carries out educational activities through its pubications (such as *UPEC* and *Fototecnica*), political seminars and refresher courses. In recent years, the union has empowered its local divisions to evaluate the effectiveness of its courses and the professional quality of its members and to hold journalism contests to encourage improvement of the media content.

Summary

Cuban mass media policy is a highly flexible adaptation of the Marxist philosophy of the press. While all media are owned, operated and at the service of the state, in accordance with Marxist principles, they also have many characteristics that set them apart from other Soviet-bloc nations. Their individuality results from the country's early revolutionary experience, frequent modifications to adjust to the changing winds of international affairs and domestic problems during the past two decades, and the flamboyant yet pragmatic nature of Cuban President Fidel Castro.

The Cuban media are viewed by the government and party as essential tools for solving the basic problems of society, but their centralized use in education, development programs and political formation has been a mixed blessing for Cuba. On one hand, the Cuban government replaced the pre-revolutionary media system, which by all accounts was seedy, corrupt and U.S.-dominated, with one of the most developed media systems among countries at the same level of economic development. With the substantial growth in media hardware and unduplicated media audiences, the Cuban leadership has been able to eradicate illiteracy in the country, implement other educational and developmental programs and forge a national political consensus, the recent domestic turmoil notwithstanding.

On the other hand, the Cuban approach means the automatic end of libertarian media practices. Individuals and dissident sectors of Cuban society have only limited opportunities to discuss the tactical operation of the government and no opportunities to criticize the revolution itself in the mass media. And, although in contradiction to official policy, the Cuban leadership, especially the second-echelon bureaucrats, tend to conceal and distort facts that they feel might tarnish their image with the public. The result is rigid government control of media content. The top leadership is concerned about these maladies and has issued directives intended to cure them, but the prognosis is guarded.

It is often said that the one thing to expect in Castro's Cuba is the unexpected. That is probably true for the Cuban press. Nevertheless, whatever media structures or policies evolve in the future will certainly be constrained by the country's revolutionary ideology and harsh economic realities. Within those limits, a continuation of the post-1975 trend toward greater press criticism of lower-level government operations would be expected. However, no attacks on the basic principles of the revolution and its top leaders will be tolerated, and some consolidation within the media would be expected to occur during times of turmoil, such as during the exodus of 1980. Cuba's improved treatment of the international press is also expected to continue. To the extent that Cuba is able to reduce tension with the United States via the foreign press, and to improve relations with the nonaligned nations, it gains leverage with the Soviet Union, and thus can maximize Russian economic and military aid while minimizing attached strings. In sum, Castro will use the press to balance both domestic and external forces so that he has greater power to conduct the Cuban revolution as he deems best for the Cuban people.

CHRONOLOGY

1975   *Granma,* official newspaper of the Cuban Communist party, begins publishing "By Return Mail," consumer-action column in which citizens can complain about the tactical operation of the Cuban government, although not about general revolutionary goals. Other major publications add citizen feedback columns shortly afterwards.

1976   New Cuban constitution, approved by popular referendum, provides for various elected bodies, including a national assembly, and legitimizes concept that the individual citizen's right to free speech is subordinate to the rights of the collective in the socialist state. Cuban press serves as a forum for public discussion of a limited number of articles to the draft constitution.

1977   A greatly increased number of U.S. and other Western journalists, previously personae non gratae, are permitted to enter Cuba, receiving lavish treatment. Change in attitude toward foreign correspondents reflects part of Cuban efforts to reduce tensions with the United States and to play a more active role in international affairs.

1978   Alfredo Izaguirre, former editor of the Havana daily *El Crisol,* is released from jail and allowed to emigrate to the United States as part of a release program for an estimated 3,000 Cuban political prisoners. Izaguirre had been arrested in 1960 for "counterrevolutionary activities." Several other journalists imprisoned early in the revolution remain in Cuban jails.

1979 Associated Press signs exchange agreement with Prensa Latina, Cuban international news agency. Contract provides for redistribution rights for each other's dispatches. United Press International signs a similar agreement a few months later. AP and other Western wire services had been expelled from Cuba in 1969.

1979-1980 In private speech to the national assembly, President Fidel Castro reports severe economic problems caused, in part, by crop failures, worker absenteeism and official corruption. As a result he reorganizes Cuban government, extending his control over key ministries. A high level of tension and dissatisfaction is reported on the island.

1980 Heberto Padilla, former Cuban journalist and dissident writer whose brief imprisonment and public confession of sins against the revolution in 1971 made him an international *cause célèbre*, is allowed to emigrate to the United States. Since 1971, he had worked as a translator in Cuba but was not allowed to publish his own works.

Raúl Castro, second in command to his brother Fidel in the Cuban leadership, addresses Fourth Congress of the Union of Cuban Journalists, charging that Cuban media are dull and that Cuban journalists must delve deeper into basic problems. "Criticize all you want," he says. "The party is behind you!"

Economic problems and domestic unrest lead to disorderly exodus of more than 125,000 refugees from Cuba to the United States. A few journalists are sprinkled among the refugees, mostly unemployed workers plus a sizable number of criminals and other outcasts.

BIBLIOGRAPHY

Carty, James W. *Cuban Communications.* Bethany, W.Va., 1978.

Dominguez, Jorge I. *Cuba: Order and Revolution.* Cambridge, Mass., 1978.

Fernández Moya, Rafael. *La Propaganda y la Guerra.* Havana, 1977.

Knippers Black, Jan, et al. *Area Handbook for Cuba.* Washington, D.C., 1976.

Knudson, Jerry W. "Herbert L. Matthews and the Cuban Story." *Journalism Monographs,* Lexington, Ky., 1978.

Mahan, Elizabeth and Reina Schement, Jorge. "Broadcasting in Cuba and the United States: Systems, Structures, and Practices." Paper to International Communication Association, 1980.

Martinez Victores, Ricardo. *7RR: La Historia de Radio Rebelde.* Havana, 1978.

Matthews, Herbert L. *Revolution in Cuba: Essay in Understanding.* New York, 1975.

Morgan, Ted. "The Press in Cuba." *Columbia Journalism Review,* March–April 1975, pp. 13–16.

Nichols, John Spicer. "Dateline Havana: September 1979." *The Quill,* September 1979, pp. 12–13, 38.

————. "The Havana Hustle: A New Phase in Cuba's International Communication Activities." In *Case Studies of Mass Media in the Third World,* John A. Lent, ed., no. 10 in Studies in Third World Societies. Williamsburg, Va., 1980.

————. "Organization, Control and Functions of the Cuban Mass Media." *Journalism Monographs,* Lexington, Ky., in press.

Pierce, Robert N. with Nichols, John Spicer. *Keeping the Flame: Media and Government in Latin America.* New York, 1979.

Pollis, Adamantia. "The Context of Human Rights and the Case of Cuba." Paper to National Conference on Cuba, 1979.

Rodríguez, Ernesto E. "Public Opinion and the Press in Cuba." *Cuban Studies/Estudios Cubanos,* July 1978, pp. 51-65.

Soto Acosta, Jesús. *Bibliografia "Prensa Clandestina Revolucionaria" (1952-1958).* Havana, 1965.

Thomas, Hugh. *The Cuban Revolution.* New York, 1977.

Vera, Ernesto. "Mass Media in Cuba." *The Democratic Journalist,* 1979, no. 11, pp. 12-16.

Werthein, Jorge. "Televisión Educativa y Empleo de los Medios Masivos para Educación en Cuba." *Revista del Centro de Estudios Educativos.* 1976, no. 4, pp. 91-114.

CZECHOSLOVAKIA

by Paul Underwood

BASIC DATA

Population: 15.291 million (1980)
Area: 127,946 sq. km. (49,400 sq. mi.)
GNP: 840.4 billion koruna (US$80.5 billion) (1979)
Literacy Rate: 99%
Language(s): Czech, Slovak
Number of Dailies: 30
  Aggregate Circulation: 4.453 million
  Circulation per 1,000: 296
Number of Nondailies: 111
  Aggregate Circulation: 981,400
  Circulation per 1,000: 65
Number of Periodicals: 1,500

Number of Radio Stations: 14
Number of Television Stations: 2
Number of Radio Receivers: 3,778,000
  Radio Receivers per 1,000: 248
Number of Television Sets: 4,048,000
  Television Sets per 1,000: 266
Total Annual Newsprint Consumption:
71,000 metric tons
Per Capita Newsprint Consumption: 4.8 kg. (10.6 lb.)
Total Newspaper Ad Receipts: NA
  As % of All Ad Expenditures: NA

Background & General Characteristics

Communist-ruled Czechoslovakia occupies a strategic position in the heartland of Central Europe, having common frontiers with Poland, the Soviet Union, Hungary, Austria and both East and West Germany. Its almost 50,000 square miles incorporate the historic Czech lands of Bohemia and Moravia and Slovakia, which lies between Moravia and the Soviet border. The Slovaks, who make up about 30 percent of the population, consider themselves distinct from the Czechs, but the two peoples are closely related, both ethnically and linguistically. About 65 percent of the population is Czech and the remaining five percent is composed of groups of minorities living mainly in border areas—Hungarians and Ukranians in Slovakia, Poles in Moravia, Germans in Bohemia. Both Czech and Slovak are official languages. Literacy is virtually complete.

Bismarck once declared that "He who is master of Bohemia is master of Europe." Their geographical position has condemned the Czechs to become involved in almost every historic upheaval, both East and West.

Modern Czechoslovakia has existed only since the end of World War I, when the country was established from parts of the old Austro-Hungarian Empire. Nevertheless, before 1948 she had enjoyed the longest tradition of parliamentary government in Eastern Europe and a special status as the most industrialized nation of the area. She is still one of the most industrialized, with one of the highest standards of living among the Soviet-bloc states. Despite recurring shortages of some foodstuffs and the high cost of consumer durables, consumption levels are fairly close to those of Italy.

The ancestors of the present-day Czechoslovaks participated in the great movement of the Slav peoples from their original homeland into the areas vacated by the various peoples that harassed the Roman Empire in its dying days. From the very beginning these people led a precarious existence, constantly menaced by German expansion from the west and would-be conquerors from the east. It is perhaps indicative that during the ninth century this early empire was the scene of a struggle between western Roman Catholicism and eastern Orthodoxy for the control of the people's spiritual life—a struggle that ended with the triumph of the West.

The Czech lands became a commercial crossroads. German merchants and German craftsmen settled in the towns, and the development of city life in the modern sense was due to them. German settlers poured in to tame the outlying wildernesses. Medieval Bohemia became almost a half-Germanic, half-Slavonic state. Rich silver mines were exploited and the Kingdom of Bohemia, which had remained under the rule of its native dynasty, became one of the richest states in Europe. It reached an apogee under Charles IV, who was also Holy Roman Emperor. He made Prague the capital of the empire, beautifying it with monuments that even today help make it one of the most beautiful cities in Europe. He also made it a center of learning, founding in 1348 the first university in Central Europe—still called Charles University—and encourging artists and writers. Most literary works of the time were in Latin since that was the common language of the clergy and the learned, but the first buds of a Czech national literature began to swell during his reign. By the next century those buds had developed into fruit: patriotic poems, songs and hymns, translations of the Scriptures and religious treatises, works on science and practical matters.

Printing was introduced from Germany soon after Gutenberg printed his Bibles. The first book was produced in Pilsen in 1468. Another press was established in Prague in 1486 and many others followed, earning Bohemia a continent-wide name for itself as a center of the new craft. The development of printing owed much to the spread of Protestantism, particularly to the Hussite movement, which began as an effort to reform Roman Catholicism but became also a drive for social justice and a protest against the Germanization of the land.

Hus was burned at the stake in 1415 and his followers rose in fury. By 1431 they had crushed five "crusades" organized by the Germans and the Roman church. Both sides eventually wearied of the struggle and when the Emperor Sigismund promised to respect Czech autonomy and Hussite principles in the Church, the fight was over. Sigismund was crowned King of Bohemia in 1435. Nevertheless, the struggle was decisive for the development of a Czech national consciousness and the Czech language.

Hus himself had composed a Czech grammar and worked on improving the literary language. He invented a Latin orthography for the Slav languages, with special marks over letters to indicate certain sounds. Although many changes have been made since then, this system is still used by the Czechs, Slovaks, Slovenes and Croats. Furthermore, wherever the Hussites had held power they had founded schools in which the instruction was in Czech.

Meanwhile, in 1526, the Hapsburgs had claimed and won the throne of Bohemia, beginning a reign that was to last until 1918. Only a few weeks earlier, the Turks had crushed neighboring Hungary at the Battle of Mohac, an event reported in the first news sheets we know of to have circulated in Prague. (At least two historians assert there had been newspapers issued in 1515, but no indication of what they were like has come down to us.)

Many more newsheets followed, however, for this was the time of Luther and the Reformation, as well as the Counter-Reformation. Both sides enlisted printers and their presses in the struggle, which raged for more than a century. The climax came when the Hapsburg Emperor Ferdinand II decided to Germanize the Czechs and force Catholicism on them once and for all. A national revolt broke out. It was crushed so thoroughly that the spirit of the nation appeared broken for nearly 200 years.

The re-Catholicization was carried out by executions, fines and prisons. Schools were closed and the great university and all public instruction were turned over to the Jesuits. Members of the nobility were executed or exiled, as were the Protestant clergy. German functionaries ran the government. German was imposed as an official language. Czech became the language of just the village and the countryside. In 1622 censorship was imposed, and not lifted again until 1848.

The so-called Thirty Years War, of which this struggle in Bohemia was one aspect, continued until 1648. During all this time, foreign armies marched and countermarched across Bohemia. By the time peace finally came, the population of the kingdom had fallen from the three million counted in 1618 to a mere 800,000. More than 500 towns had disappeared.

The first signs of a national revival appeared in the 18th century. Newspapers began with a twice-weekly journal, the *Prazske Noviny* ("Prague News"), the origins of which can be traced to 1719. German-language papers had started even earlier, but the *Prazske Noviny* was the first to be printed in Czech. This did not necessarily make it popular, however, since, like the German papers, it was the voice of the Hapsburg administration.

The first attempt at publishing a newspaper in Hungarian-ruled Slovakia was made in 1783, when Daniel Tallyai issued the *Prespurske Noviny* ("Pressberger News"). Pressburg was the German name of the city now known as Bratislava, the present Slovak capital. After four years Tallyai had to close his paper up for lack of subscribers; almost 25 years passed before the second, *Tydennik* ("Weekly"), came on the market.

As the ideas of the 18th century Enlightenment spread to Bohemia, efforts began to revive the Czech language. A chair in Czech was founded at the university. The Emperor Joseph II lifted the censorship briefly, encouraging the efforts, which continued in the face of the revived absolutism of subsequent rulers. The ideas of the French Revolution spread. This revival movement was led by five scholars: Joseph Dobrovsky, the founder of Slavonic philology; Josef Jungmann, the author of the first history of Czech literature; Jan Kollar, a poet; Pavel Safarik, the founder of Slavic archeology, and Frantisek Palacky, a political leader and the first great Czech historian. His *History of the Bohemian People* has been called the Bible of the revival.

The important publications of the day were journals and magazines; their editors included some of these leaders of the cultural revival. Safarik was the editor of a popular illustrated magazine called *Svetozor* ("World Outlook"). But far and away the most important was one called *Casopis Cheoeho Museum* ("Journal of the Czech Museum"). Its founder and editor was Palacky, and he made it into a showpiece of Czech scholarship.

The role played by Palacky and his colleagues was taken in Slovakia by Ludovit Stur, a teacher, journalist and writer. From 1845 to 1848 he published a paper called *Slovenskyi Narodne Noviny* ("Slovak National Newspaper") that became the voice of the Slovak revival movement. But equally important was his work in unifying the various Slovak dialects into a uniform written language.

Meanwhile, in Prague, the old *Prazske Noviny* acquired a new editor in 1846. He was Karol Havlicek, who was to become known as the father of Czech journalism. Havlicek enlarged the format of the paper and improved the coverage so much that in the first year he doubled the number of subscribers,

despite the censorship and the tax that had to be paid on each issue. The idea of this tax was to keep down circulations because it, of course, increased the price.

The wave of revolutions that swept Europe in 1848 forced the Hapsburgs to abolish the censorship. This marked the real beginning of Czech journalism. The first move was made by Havlicek, who left *Prazske Noviny* to begin publishing the first Czech-language daily, the *Narodni Noviny* ("National News"). Existing journals began publishing political news and other papers sprang up. Havlicek's paper became recognized as the spokesman of the middle class liberals. The principal voice of the opposition radical democrats was *Prazsky Vecerni List* ("Prague Evening Page"), which began operations two months after *Narodni Noviny* but soon became the most widely circulated paper in Prague, with a press run of 5,000.

This taste of freedom soon ended. Hapsburg military forces restored absolutism, taking over the Czech capital just two months after the ending of censorship. The old controls were not reestablished immediately, however. By the end of 1848, 66 newspapers and periodicals were being published in Prague alone, some printing both German and Czech editions. The crackdown began the next year when a decree required all political publications to put down a deposit, called a *kaution*. Havlicek was one of the few able to gather together the required amount by the deadline. Most of the papers had to stop publication but some survived by avoiding politics.

Three months later the military authorities suspended *Narodni Noviny*. Havlicek appealed to Vienna and got the ban lifted, but six months later the paper was ordered closed. Havlicek moved to the old silver mining center of Kutna Hora, where he published a twice-weekly called *Slovan* ("The Slav"), which was distributed all over Bohemia and Moravia. At first the Imperial authorities replied by setting up their own Czech language paper, called *Vidensky Dennik* ("Vienna Daily"). But they also continued to harass Havlicek, who finally shut down *Slovan* to avoid an official closure. Havlicek and others of the 1848 editors were arrested and convicted of sedition. The others were sent to prison; Havlicek was sentenced to internal exile in the Tyrol and was allowed to return only just before his death.

In 1852 the authorities further restricted the press by requiring licensing and increasing the amount of the *kaution*. By the end of that year, only two Czech-language papers were still being published in Prague, as well as one in Moravia. The capital had six German-language papers, which, like those in Czech, operated under strict government control. Even so, the authorities were not content. In 1857, they reinstated the old tax on each issue of any periodical. By the end of that decade the only surviving Czech language daily in Prague was the official *Prazske Noviny*, and its circulation was a mere 2,000 copies. The four German-language papers together sold just 14,000.

The authorities had consistently denied any application to start a new paper but in 1860 relented enough to permit two. The first approval went to Alois Krasa, who established *Cas* ("Time") in October that year, and the second to Julius Gregr, who founded *Narodni Listy* ("National Pages") in 1861. *Cas* represented the conservative upper classes, but *Narodni Listy* was the voice of the patriots grouped around Palacky. It was to become one of the principal forums of Czech politics and succeeded in surviving until 1941. An ally appeared in 1862 when a group of writers began publishing *Hlas* ("The Voice"). It merged with *Narodni Listy* in 1865.

Meanwhile, the authorities began slowly demolishing the control structure. Supervision was transferred from the police to the courts and the censorship commission was dissolved. The papers were far from free, however. They were still subject to fines and confiscations, even suspension orders. A tax on advertising was lifted only in 1874 and the *kaution* only in 1894. Even then the issue tax was continued; it was not ended until 1899.

Despite all these hurdles, the last quarter of the 19th century witnessed a considerable growth in the press, which was spurred by the organization of modern political parties, like the Social Democrats and the Agrarians, who quickly established papers to promote their ideas. Several of these grew to national significance, like *Pravo Lidu* ("Peoples' Right"), which became the official voice of the Social Democrats. There were also a few non-party papers, the most important of which was *Lidovi Noviny* ("People's News"), which was founded in Bruno in 1893 and went on to become recognized as probably the nation's best.

By 1900 the number of dailies in Bohemia and Moravia had reached 37. In addition, 329 other periodicals were classified as political publications. Ten years later the number of dailies had increased to 45, and by 1913, on the eve of World War I, to 59. The figure for all periodicals that year was 1,946, of which 702 were considered political.

The war brought censorship and other restrictions. Sentiment for independence grew, particularly after 1917 when a writers' manifesto called for a democratic Europe made up of independent states. This dream was realized when the peace treaty provided for an independent Czechoslovakia. Thomas Masaryk, its first president, praised the efforts of the press during the war, saying: "In our case leadership was supplied by the press, particularly those journals which, with tactical skill, withstood the military terrorism. By purposeful adroitness they revived sinking spirits using language incomprehensible to the enemy though comprehensible to every Czech."

The constitution for the new state guaranteed press freedom, but a 1923 press law provided for legal restrictions under certain circumstances. Under its provisions a newspaper could be banned, and later amendments added the limiting of distribution and even the imposition of prior censorship.

The state faced many problems, the most serious of which involved the relationship between the Czech lands and Slovakia as well as relations with various minority peoples, particularly the Germans. The Slovaks feared domination by the Czechs and kept struggling for greater autonomy. The Germans were to play a central role in Hitler's breakup of the state in 1939.

The old political parties and their papers were joined by new ones. The important political dailies included, in addition to *Pravo Lidu*, *Cheske Slovo* ("Czech World"), representing the National Socialists; *Venkov* ("Countryside"), of the Agrarian Party, *Lidove Listy* ("People's Pages"), the organ of the Catholic Populist party, and *Rude Pravo*, of the Communists. The Social Democrats, Populists, National Democrats, Agrarians and National Socialists were the most important parties.

Not all the papers were political, however. The old *Lidove Noviny* continued its independent way, by now recognized as one of Europe's best. Its circulation reached 100,000 in the 1930s. Another politically unattached daily was *Narodni Politika* ("National Politics"). By 1930 the Czechoslovak press included 115 dailies, 88 other papers published every other day and 423 weeklies. Some of the largest claimed circulations of 200,000 and more.

The worldwide economic depression of the

1930s brought trouble that was compounded into disaster with Hitler's rise to power in Germany. German and Slovak extremist groups, along with the Communists, did their best to break up the republic. In its struggle to cope with the situation the Prague government resorted to censorship, confiscations and bannings of the publications of all three groups. Even some pro-government papers were restricted in what they could print. But it was to no avail. Under the Munich Agreement of 1938, the Western powers forced the government to cede certain border areas to Hitler and other neighboring states. A few months later Bohemia became a Nazi protectorate and Slovakia was set up as a puppet republic.

Newspapers closed voluntarily or were seized. More than 1,000 ceased publication in the first 18 months of the occupation and were replaced by Nazi organs. The few Czech papers permitted to continue operations were heavily censored; the Germans dictated even headlines and placement of stories. An underground press sprang up, both Communist and non-Communist. At least 112 of the people responsible were caught and were either executed or died in concentration camps. Another 126 were imprisoned but survived to see the liberation of their country in 1945.

A coalition of political parties, including the Communists, took power after the war. Private ownership of the press was forbidden. Only authorized parties included in the National Front and official organizations such as the trade unions, rural cooperatives, the national youth organization and some government ministries could publish papers. This provision did not appear significant since all but two of the major prewar papers had been published by parties, but its effect was to give the Ministry of Information control of licensing and other press affairs. And the Ministry of Information was held by the Communists.

Through it they also directed Ceteka, the national wire service, and supervised broadcasting. They moved first in broadcasting, filling all key positions with their own people. Since the ministry's Bureau of Publications had the power to regulate the number, size and location of all periodicals, as well as the number of copies printed, and controlled as well the allocation of newsprint, the Communists were able to shape the entire postwar press even before they actually seized sole political power in 1948.

Their final pre-coup move came in 1947 when, at their insistence, a law was passed that made membership in the Communist-controlled Czech or Slovak Journalist Unions a condition of employment. So there was not much left to do when they did take open control. The papers that had refused to toe their line were muzzled in one way or another. Some were simply suppressed. Of the 44 dailies published at the start of 1948, only half survived, and those were reorganized on the Soviet model. *Rude Pravo* came to be as close a copy of Moscow's *Pravda* as possible; the other papers followed its lead.

No break in the monolith appeared until 1956 when, in the wake of Khrushchev's denunciation of Stalin, some Czech papers acknowledged that things were not as they had presented them. But the regime almost immediately cracked down, ending any thought of change. Only in the early 1960s did things begin to move. The Czech economy turned sour and, apparently as a kind of compensation, the regime began to allow a slow but rigidly controlled liberalization. This gathered steam on its own, fueled by dissent and disillusionment both within and without the Party. Pushed by intellectuals, the movement led to the ouster of the old hard-line leadership of the Party and government at the beginning of 1968.

A new reform-minded group of Communists led by Alexander Dubcek took control and began practical steps toward political, economic and social changes that seemed to hold out the prospect for a better life for the people. Censorship was lifted. The news media were set free and put in the hands of people sympathetic to the changes embodied in an "Action Program," which promised freedom of the press, independent courts, secret-ballot elections, effective economic reforms and the separation of Party and government, along with many other steps.

All this obviously was anathema to the Soviets. In August 1968 Soviet and Soviet-bloc forces invaded Czechoslovakia and occupied the country. Censorship was reimposed and the whole reform process canceled. A quiet but desperate struggle continued between the people attempting to preserve the reforms and the Party hard-liners doing Moscow's bidding in attempting to turn the clock back.

The latter finally carried the day. News style and content reverted to that of the old Stalinist days, featuring the worst banalities of Communist propaganda. The writers, journalists and artists who had formed the vanguard of the Prague Spring were fired, exiled or otherwise silenced. At the 1972 congress of the Journalists' Union it was disclosed that more than 1,200 members had been expelled. There has been no return to the wholesale terror of the 1950s but, except for the fact that it is permitted a greater measure of liveliness, the press generally looks as if there had been.

The Czech and Slovak papers are organized in almost parallel fashion. Thus, *Rude Pravo* is the organ of the Czech Communist Party's Central Committee, and Bratislava's *Pravda* fills the same role for the Slovak Party organization.

Official statistics list 30 dailies, but circulation figures and other details are provided for only 28 of these. Nine are published in Prague and nine in Bratislava, although one of the latter is printed in Hungarian rather than Slovak. The parallel breaks down when it comes to the smaller provincial papers, where the Czechs, since they comprise about 60 percent of the population, have more.

Over all, 11 dailies are printed in Slovak, one in Hungarian and the rest in Czech. All are full size; there are no tabloids. *Rude Pravo* and the other major papers usually run eight pages an issue, with the smaller provincials averaging only four. All are published by the Communist Party and government, approved organizations, or captive parties that have been permitted a paper existence.

About 500 other periodicals and magazines appear weekly and more than 1,000 at less frequent intervals. Organized religions recognized by the regime have their own publications, but they too are censored and stick strictly to church affairs.

Most of the important dailies are published in the morning, although both Prague and Bratislava have popular evening papers. The others are generally due out about noon, a fairly common schedule in Central Europe since the days of the Austro-Hungarian Empire.

Except for *Uj Szo* ("New World"), the Hungarian-language daily in Bratislava, and *Prager Volkszeitung,* a German-language weekly published in Prague, all major publications are printed in either Czech or Slovak. Most appear every day of the week, although a few skip Mondays. There are no special Sunday editions and no magazine sections on the Western pattern.

Only Prague and Bratislava have more than one daily but even in those cities the papers are not considered competitors. As in other Soviet-bloc countries, the press is structured so that each paper is designed for a specific audience.

By far the largest in terms of circulation is *Rude Pravo*, which claims 900,000 copies in two editions, one printed in Czech and the other in Slovak. *Pravda*, its Bratislava twin, has 330,000. Two Prague dailies—*Prace* ("Labor," the principal trade union paper) and *Zemedelske Noviny* ("Farmers' News"), published by the Agriculture Ministry—claim 317,000 and 342,000 respectively.

Others in the top 10 in terms of circulation are: *Lidove Demokracie* ("Peoples' Democracy"), of the Peoples' Party (Catholic), 217,000; *Mlada Fronta*, published by the Central Committee of the Socialist Union of Youth, 239,000; *Svobodne Slovo* ("Free Word"), the organ of the puppet Czech Socialist Party, 228,000; *Praca* of Bratislava, the organ of the Slovak trade union organization, 190,000; *Nova Svoboda* ("New Freedom"), the biggest of the provincials, which is published in the coal and steel center of Ostrava, 198,000; and *Czechoslovensky Sport*, published by the Czech Association for Physical Training, 185,000.

Three other dailies distribute more than 100,000 copies, 10 between 50,000 and 100,000, three between 25,000 and 50,000 and two between 10,000 and 25,000. In addition, hundreds of factories and enterprises produce their own news sheets, some daily and others weekly.

Rude Pravo is far and away the most influential paper in the country simply because it is the official voice of the regime. Bratislava's *Pravda* and *Prace*, the trade union paper, are usually ranked next.

Economic Framework

The Czech economy is fundamentally a replica of the Soviet central control and command model. It has had its ups and downs since it was first imposed in the 1950s. It functioned fairly well at first but in the early 1960s developed serious problems. Recurring failures sparked dissent that led directly to the 1968 events. An economic reform plan drawn up during the middle 1960s that provided for a kind of decentralized market socialism had only started to be implemented when the Soviet invasion cut all changes short. During most of the 1970s the recentralized economy did not do badly, thanks in part to Western credits, but by the end of the decade unfavorable trends had again become apparent. These threaten the standard of living—the one success the Moscow-backed regime of Party chief Gustav Husek has had

—and raise the possibility of new political and social unrest.

In the short run, the nation's economic situation had little impact on the media. Since their purpose is not to make money but to serve the government and Party, they continue to operate in their usual fashion regardless of economic ups and downs. But as the 1960s proved, economic difficulties can spark public discontent and turn the media into a true reflector of public opinion.

As in all Soviet-bloc countries, newspapers are the regime's principal communication link with the Party's cadres on all levels and are, therefore, of major importance. But for the general public, broadcasting is more important in Czechoslovakia. Practically every Czech family has both radio and television and relies on them for information, as well as entertainment, more than on the papers.

Private ownership of any media is forbidden by law. Broadcasting is a government monopoly, and all newspapers and periodicals are published by the Party, the government, or affiliated organizations. The two afternooners, *Vecerni Praha* of Prague and *Vecernik* of Bratislava, are more popular in style and content, but all dailies are basically very serious publications. Sensationalism is unheard of.

Distribution of all newspapers and periodicals is handled by the government's Postal Press Distribution Agency. The supply of newsprint is controlled and allocated by the government's Office for Press and Information. Czechoslovakia produced 75 million tons of newsprint in 1978.

More advertising is in evidence than in the past but probably no paper devotes as much as a third of its total space to ads. Most of what does appear is placed by state enterprises, although there is some by foreign companies. No groups outside the party have any influence on the media. In times of difficulties differences can appear in the media but these reflect factional differences inside the Party itself rather than outside interest groups.

Strikes have been used in the past, both for and against press freedom. They were one of the weapons the Communists used in the 1947-48 period to get rid of recalcitrant editors. In 1968 a similar kind of pressure was used by liberal journalists to get rid of hard-line editors, but this sort of thing can happen only in times of particular stress.

The Czech and Slovak Journalist Unions have about 5,000 members—the 1977 figures were 4,762 full members plus 219 candidates.

Significantly, 14.3 percent of those were under 30 years of age, a considerable increase over the 1967 figures, which showed only 8.6 percent under 30.

Wages are not high; the regime has consistently followed a policy of not allowing much of a gap between blue- and white-collar wages. There is a good deal of what in the West would be called free-lancing in order to increase incomes.

Press Laws

Both the 1948 constitution, adopted when the Communists seized power, and its 1960 revision guaranteed freedom of speech but added that its exercise could be restricted in the "interests of the working people," meaning the Communist Party. Publication of newspapers and periodicals was restricted to official organizations, and all other media were placed under the direct control of the state.

A press law promulgated in 1966 noted that freedom of the press was guaranteed by the fact that press organizations had been "placed at the disposal of the working people and their organizations."

Both the 1948 constitution and its revision included the customary provisions against libel and the publication of official secrets but also barred disclosure of what were referred to as state and economic secrets. These apparently can include any information that has not been officially made public.

All papers must be registered with the government's Office for Press and Information. Papers may be suspended if, in the judgment of the office, they have failed to observe the conditions under which their permission to publish was granted.

The 1966 law declared that the media were to provide timely, truthful, comprehensive and as complete information as possible about events "both at home and abroad," something the press was able to do only for the brief period of the Prague Spring.

It provided for precensorship, or, more properly, it legally defined the practice, which had been standard for more than 20 years. It also provided the possibility of appeal of censorship rulings to the courts, but, in fact, the judiciary is a tool of the ruling party.

The same measure made editors responsible for libelous material. Previously, despite the legal provision against libel, there was no possibility of a successful suit since responsibility lay with the Party. Editors also were required to publish retractions of published information proven to be false.

The law gave the press a new weapon against bureaucracy. It stated that state and other institutions were bound to provide editors with information upon request, provided this information did not involve those undefined state, economic and official secrets. Except for changes in the censorship requirements and other amendments, this 1966 code still is the basic press law of the country.

Two amendments to the criminal code in 1973 could impact on media personnel. One provided that anyone "who spreads untrue reports about the international position" of the country "which could harm the interests of the republic, or who causes such reports to be spread abroad" is liable to three years in prison. A second amendment upped the minimum sentence for disclosing a state secret from 10 to 12 years.

Another law, also approved in 1973, gave authorities the right to seize mail. All foreign mail is processed in a special facility in Prague, and according to some sources, all letters both coming in and going out of the country are read and copies are kept.

Censorship

At the present time there is no official precensorship of the media in Czechoslovakia. This does not mean there has been any relaxation of control, however. Editors, all of whom must be trusted members of the Party, have been made responsible for the contents of their publications. They are kept well informed of the Party's ideas of proper coverage and interpretation. Any variation could mean dismissal.

This was the system originally used by the Communists when they took power in 1948. But in 1953 a secret government decree established a prior censorship procedure under an office labelled Chief Authority for Press Supervision. This at first was directly responsible to the Council of Ministers but later was placed under the Interior Ministry, which also controlled the police.

That arrangement continued until 1967, when the new press law went into effect. It legalized the procedure and set up a Central Publication Authority with precensorship powers. Then, in June 1968, an amendment repealed the censorship authority. However, it also provided for confiscation of printed

matter if its publication constituted a criminal offense. In other words, it set up a post-censorship system.

After the Soviet invasion this was changed again to require precensorship, but the responsibility was placed on the chief editors. The following April official prior censorship was resumed, but again was lifted a few months later in favor of editorial responsibility.

State-Press Relations

The Press and Information Ministry has complete supervision of all media, broadcast and print alike. Publications must register with it and be approved, making it, in effect, a licensing authority. It also is responsible for the allocation of newsprint and other supplies.

Under the Czech system, the Party's Central Committee and its supporting agit-prop staffs are responsible for the preparation of plans and directives to the media. Party and government officials hold regular briefing sessions with editors of the leading newspapers and broadcast officials so there should be no mistake as to what the regime wants or does not want printed or broadcast. The smaller papers follow the line of the majors, and provincial editors are briefed by regional officials.

In addition, the national news agency, which is an arm of the government, issues a twice-weekly bulletin to editors that makes clear the line they should be taking in coverage and interpretation.

By such means the media have been forcibly transformed back into a tightly controlled instrument of propaganda on the old Soviet model. A Journalist Union congress in 1972 defined the duties of members as that of "political workers, a segment of the Party,... responsible to the Party"—an echo of the Stalinist past.

Newspapers and other periodicals are allowed some scope in criticizing official actions, but not regarding matters of fundamental policy. As a result, about the only criticisms that can be found concern how policies are carried out and not the policies themselves.

During the 1963–68 period the media had considerable influence on government policies. Many of the economic changes envisaged in the 1968 Action Program had been first argued in the press. Even more to the point is the fact that it was the continued opposition of editors, journalists and writers that rendered the whole censorship system unworkable.

In the wake of the Soviet invasion, all the journals that represented the vanguard of the Prague Spring were revamped or closed. Staffs of newspapers and periodicals were purged wholesale; an estimated 2,000 lost their jobs. Since then the influence has been completely the other way. The media have returned to their old role of serving merely as a transmission belt from the leadership down. As far as is known there have been no suspensions or confiscations in recent years and only one editorial misstep. In 1976 Jiri Hayek, the editor of a journal called *Tvorba*, was dismissed for recommending that at least some of the people purged after 1968 be allowed to return to their previous work.

Many of the most prominent of these have been jailed—some exiled—for a variety of alleged offenses ranging from making critical remarks about the internal situation in Czechoslovakia to foreign news people, to publishing "unauthorized" material abroad, to distributing clandestine leaflets at home.

State control over the media is virtually absolute.

Attitude Toward Foreign Media

The official attitude toward foreign media has followed the same up-and-down course noted with respect to other aspects of the society. Following the 1948 Communist coup, the importation of all foreign publications, except some scientific and technical works and those from the Soviet bloc, was banned. Listening to foreign broadcasts became a crime.

Foreign correspondents who attempted to report on internal developments beyond official announcements were expelled, or worse. In 1951 AP correspondent William N. Oatis was arrested on spying charges and sentenced to prison. He was not released until 1953.

From that time on until the mid-1950s no Western journalists were permitted. When they finally were readmitted their activities were closely supervised. This situation changed only slightly up to 1963, when the various restrictions began to be relaxed. But it was not until some time after that that editorial offices were given permission to subscribe to a few Western papers—provided

copies were not made available to the public.

Jamming of foreign broadcasts, which had been standard during the 1950s, was halted in 1963, except for those made by Radio Free Europe. Three years later a few Western publications were allowed to be imported for public consumption. The number of these was increased gradually over the next few months.

Freer access to Western media was one of the demands of the reformers, and after the Dubcek regime took over in January 1968, most of the barriers were lifted. But they clanked down again as tight as ever after the Soviet invasion. Within weeks at least eight Western correspondents stationed in Prague had been expelled, and others soon followed. Jamming resumed. Western media disappeared from public sale, including even some of the papers published by Western European Communist parties. They have not reappeared.

Newspeople wishing to report on developments in Czechoslovakia must obtain special visas authorizing their activity from the Ministry of Foreign Affairs. Applications for accreditation for permanent correspondents must be made to the same office. Correspondents have reported the authorities are now demanding, as a condition for granting applications for either temporary visits or accreditation, a promise not to contact any political dissident.

The attention paid to dissidents by correspondents has been a sore point with the regime ever since 1968 and has resulted in numerous cases of expulsions, bannings and general harassment of newspeople. Every year since 1970 there has been at least one such case reported; most years there have been several. Even representatives of the Communist press have not been exempt. In 1972 the editor of the principal Italian Communist newspaper, *L'Unita*, was kicked out. Another Italian journalist was arrested that same year and held for 43 days before being expelled.

There is no official count anywhere of the number of correspondents who have been refused visas. Most cases are never reported, but enough have been publicized to suggest that the total in the last 10 years probably runs into the hundreds.

Foreign broadcasting still has an impact despite the jamming, which is effective only in a small area around the jamming facility. But it is difficult to measure. Some foreign broadcasters estimate that the majority of the Czech people listen to foreign radio and see foreign TV broadcasts on a more or less regular basis. Both West German and Austrian TV can be received in the border areas. One indication of their popularity is the fact that so many rooftop aerials in the Slovak capital of Bratislava are turned to receive Austrian TV signals that they are referred to locally as "the Vienna woods."

Even this limited access has an impact on Czech broadcasting, which, in order to hold the audience, has had to diversify and lighten its programming. While its freedom has been trimmed considerably since 1968, it still is less ideologically dominated than the print media.

Prague is the seat of the Soviet bloc's International Union of Journalists and virtually all meaningful Czech contacts with international journalists' organizations are conducted through or in connection with it. The Czechs, of course, supported the Soviet position on the 1978 UNESCO Declaration.

News Agencies

The official news agency, Ceskoslovenska Tiskova Kancelar (CTK), better known as Ceteka, is an arm of the government. It functions under the Press and Information Office and serves as the government's official voice.

The original Ceteka was founded in 1918 as a government agency. The Communists got control of it when they were assigned the Ministry of Information after World War II. It did little beyond relaying government announcements and the foreign news file of Tass to the Czech press.

Beginning in the late 1950s, however, Ceteka was given a freer hand in picking up information from other agencies, and by the early 1960s the proportion of Tass news in its daily file had fallen from about 80 percent to around 30 percent. Although this has changed back in the other direction since 1968, the Tass share has not returned to the earlier figure, principally because Ceteka provides more coverage on its own.

During the 1950s the agency had no correspondents abroad, but by the end of 1962 it had 28 working in various foreign capitals, mainly in the Soviet bloc but also in various Western centers. In addition, in some places it shared correspondents with *Rude Pravo*, the only individual paper authorized to station newspeople abroad.

At the present time it has 14 bureaus throughout Czechoslovakia and 30 bureaus or individual correspondents abroad. Headquartered in Prague, it supplies news and pictures to the broadcasting services as well as to newspapers and periodicals. Payments for these services are supplemented by a state subsidy. It has working agreements with all the major international agencies for the purchase or exchange of news and pictures, as well as with the agencies of neighboring Communist-ruled countries.

Its daily service to the domestic press runs about 40,000 words, in both Czech and Slovak. It also relays a certain amount of foreign agency product in the original language: English, French, German, Russian. In addition to the advisory bulletins it distributes to editors, it publishes others on science, etc., for the general public. For the most part, it is the sole distributor of foreign agency material in the country.

There are two other minor agencies set up to deal with foreign media on a commercial basis and to distribute feature information abroad: Pragopress and Tatrapress. The latter is a Slovakian operation that is primarily charged with gathering and distributing features and materials on tourism for audiences abroad. Pragopress does the same thing but also contracts with foreign media to make films, recordings and the like on Czechoslovak subjects.

Electronic News Media

All broadcasting is a state monopoly. Radio is operated by Czechoslovak Radio and television by Czechoslovak Television, both of which are state organizations under the supervision and control of the Press and Information Office.

Domestic radio is divided into five networks: Radio Prague, which broadcasts in Czech to Bohemia and Moravia; Radio Bratislava, which broadcasts in Slovak to Slovakia; Radio Hvezda, which covers the whole country, programming in both languages, and Radio Vltava and Radio Devin. The latter two, one for the Czechs and the other for the Slovaks, feature high quality programming on the order of the British Broadcasting Corporation's Third Programme.

Radio Prague and Radio Bratislava are heavy on propaganda and informational programs, official news broadcasts and political commentaries. Hvezda features light entertainment, pop music and the like. It is the one service that is on the air 24 hours a day. There are also some regional and local services, including programs in both Polish and German.

Television broadcasting started on an experimental basis in 1953 and regular programming began the following year. Development was slow, and it was the end of the decade before it could be considered truly a mass medium.

Originally, radio and television were administered jointly. They were not split into the two independent operations until 1964.

A second television service, this one in color, went on the air in 1970. As with the first network, development has taken some time because of equipment shortages and the slowness of setting up studios and transmitting facilities.

The principal TV programming centers are in Prague, Brno, Ostrava, Bratislava and Kosice. Both the latter are in Slovakia. The first service is on the air most of the day, with morning programs for night-shift workers and for schools. School programs also take part of the afternoons. On weekdays, the regular programming begins in midafternoon and continues until 11 or 12 p.m. On weekends it runs from 9 a.m. to near midnight, with a break in the early afternoon. Except on special occasions, the second channel operates only in the evenings.

About a third of the total TV broadcast time is devoted to news and information. Both services are supported by license fees paid on receivers and by state subsidies. Official statistics for 1978 listed 4,048,000 TV licenses and 3,778,000 radio permits. However, this latter figure does not include the large number of wired receivers still in use around the country and probably also does not include many of the transistors carried around by the youth.

Both radio and television carry advertising, although the income from it is reported to be small. The advertisements, almost all of which are placed by state enterprises, are grouped in 15-minute blocks scattered throughout the broadcast day.

Broadcasting in Czechoslovakia has always been in the hands of the government. Radio transmissions began in 1923 and listening quickly became more widespread than in any of the other Eastern European countries. The Communists moved to get control of the service immediately after World War II, by putting trusted members in all key positions. At the time they actually seized the government, the remaining non-Communist employes were removed, completing the hold. They immediately converted all operations into propaganda weapons, or, in the words of a *Rude Pravo* editorial, into "an instrument of political education of the masses."

In their zeal for indoctrination, they overshot the mark. The programming became so dull and monotonous that people simply failed to listen. Spurred by complaints and the challenge posed by Western broadcasts, the regime in the mid 1950s began to allow more time for music, light entertainment and sports. Ideology, although it remained the primary ingredient, was peddled in smaller doses. The 1960s brought still more changes: extended reports of Party activities gave way to abbreviated newscast coverage. The music component, particularly the pop music the youth wanted, was expanded. Call-in broadcasts on radio became widely popular and Western TV series, including some from the United States, became familiar.

The role of Czech radio and TV in the aftermath of the Soviet takeover is a more familiar story. Operating from secret and mobile transmitters, broadcasters kept reporting the news fully, relaying accounts of developments—and even TV pictures—not only to the home audience but also abroad. It took the Soviets nine days to locate and silence all the various transmitters. It took an even longer time to get programming back on the old track, but by 1971 observers reported it was once again heavily larded with political ideology. Radio, however, still devotes more time to light entertainment than to any other single type of programming.

Czech television is linked with the Soviet bloc's Intervision network. Through it, it receives not only programs from other bloc countries but also some Western programming relayed from the Eurovision network. It imports other TV features not only from "friendly socialist" countries but also from Western Europe and even the United States so long as they are not, as one official explained, "anti-socialistic."

The Czechoslovak Radio also operates a shortwave foreign broadcast service in English, French, German, Italian, Spanish Arabic, Portuguese, Czech and Slovak. It is directed mainly to other European countries but also is beamed to Africa, South Asia, the Far East and Australia and to North and South America.

Education & Training

Formal journalism education began in 1953 when a Department of Journalism was created, along with an Institute of Journalism, at Charles University. It is now called the Faculty of Social Sciences and Journalism. A journalism program is also offered at Comenius University in Bratislava. Both programs take five years to complete and both institutions award degrees upon completion of the required courses.

It is not clear what has happened to the graduates of these two programs, however. Statistics published in 1974 showed that less than 42 percent of the nation's journalists held diplomas of any kind from institutions of higher learning. Ten percent actually had no more than the basic public school education.

One inference is that Party loyalty is more important than professional training when it comes to hiring journalists. This may have been underlined by a government decree published in 1973 requiring all journalists, whether Party members or not, to complete a course in Marxism-Leninism if they had not already done so.

Like the Kremlin, the Czech regime distributes state prizes each year to people it considers to have rendered special service in the arts and sciences, including journalism. The principal criterion, however, is Party loyalty, not necessarily outstanding work.

As with almost all major organizations in the country, there is both a Czech and a Slovak Journalists' Union. The two have a common umbrella body in the Journalists' Center of Czechoslovakia, which is headquartered in Prague. All three sponsor congresses of members, publish periodicals that deal primarily with journalistic matters, and help in drawing up journalistic codes.

Summary

The history of the Czech press is one of recurring oppression and freedom, repression again, and again freedom. A new cycle is under way and how it will turn depends in the final analysis on the ability of the Husek regime to hold its position, which has never been strong and which has been shaken by recent unfavorable economic trends.

Much will also depend on the course of the changes now underway in neighboring Poland. If the Poles can win a considerable degree of freedom for their mass media—as they currently appear to be doing—without Soviet intervention, the Czechs may very well try once again to bring "socialism with a human face" to their land, including a press that is more representative and more responsive to the real needs of its audience.

CHRONOLOGY

1966 New press law promulgated "placing press organizations at the disposal of the working people."

1967 Precensorship imposed on all publications.

1968 Precensorship repealed and replaced by postcensorship; new law provides for confiscation of printed matter contrary to state interests.
Alexander Dubcek lifts censorship and promises freedom of press as part of liberalization program; Soviet-bloc forces invade Czechoslovakia, occupy country and reimpose censorship.

1972 At annual congress of Journalists Union it is disclosed that over 1,200 journalists had been dismissed from union and profession. Correspondent of *L'Unita*, Italian Communist daily, expelled from country.

1973 New government decree requires all journalists to complete courses in Marxism-Leninism. Amendment to Criminal Code provides prison terms for journalists "who spread untrue reports."

1976 Jiri Hayek, editor of *Tvorba*, dismissed.

BIBLIOGRAPHY

Dvornik, Francis. *The Slavs in European History and Civilization.* New Brunswick, N.J., 1962.

International Press Institute. *The Press in Authoritarian Countries.* Zurich, 1959.

"Journalists Purged." *East Europe*, May 1972, p. 36.

Kaplan, Frank L. *The Czech and Slovak Press: The First 100 Years. Journalism Monographs*, no. 47, January 1977.

_____. *Winter Into Spring 1963–1968.* Boulder, Colo., 1977.

Merrill, John C., Bryan, Carter R., and Alisky, Marvin. *The Foreign Press.* Baton Rouge, La., 1970.

Olson, Kenneth E. *The History Makers.* Baton Rouge, La., 1966.

Palmer, Alan. *The Lands Between.* New York, 1970.

Paulu, Burton. *Broadcasting in Eastern Europe.* Minneapolis, 1974.

Portal, Roger. *The Slavs, A Cultural and Historical Survey of the Slavonic Peoples.* New York, 1969.

Pribichevich, Stoyan. *World Without End.* New York, 1939.

Radio Free Europe. *"The Cultural Scene in Czechoslovakia." RFE Research Report,* January 14, 1974.

_____. "New Machinery for the Administration of Criminal Law." *RFE Research Report,* June 27, 1973.

_____. "Pre-February 1948 Press Regulation Restored." *RFE Research Report,* August 9, 1968.

Schopflin, George, ed. *The Soviet Union and Eastern Europe.* New York, 1970.

Seton-Watson, Hugh. *Eastern Europe Between the Wars.* New York, 1962.

Taborsky, Edward. *Communism in Czechoslovakia.* Princeton, N.J., 1961.

UNESCO. *World Communications, A 200 Nation Survey of Press, Radio and Television.* Paris and New York, 1975.

DENMARK

by Harold A. Fisher

BASIC DATA

Population: 5,111,534 (1979, est.)
Area: 43,075 sq. km. (16,631 sq. mi.)
GNP: 326.35 billion krone (US$60.83 billion) (1979)
Literacy Rate: over 90%
Language(s): Danish
Number of Dailies: 49 (1979)
  Aggregate Circulation: 1,832,000
  Circulation per 1,000: 280
Number of Nondailies: 336 (1977)
  Aggregate Circulation: 5.9 million
  Circulation per 1,000: 1,156
Number of Periodicals: (same category as nondailies)

Number of Radio Stations: 44
Number of Television Stations: 30
Number of Radio Receivers: 4.2 million (1977)
  Radio Receivers per 1,000: 823 (1977)
Number of Television Sets: 1,771,000 (1977)
  Television Sets per 1,000: 333 (1977)
Total Annual Newsprint Consumption: 133,700 metric tons (1977)
  Per Capita Newsprint Consumption: 26.27 kg. (57.8 lb.)
Total Newspaper Ad Receipts: 1.9 billion Krone (US$352.2 million) (1979)
  As % of All Ad Expenditures: 46.1 (1979)

Background & General Characteristics

The press has long been an important and integral part of Danish life. Its history extends back to 1666, but it was not until press freedom was guaranteed by law in 1849 that newspapers gained prominence. Although the number of newspapers has been falling, circulation has remained stable enough to allow Denmark to claim one of the world's highest per capita circulations of newspapers.

There are daily newspapers, mostly concentrated in the larger cities and largely aligned to a political-party point of view. These dailies are unquestionably the Danes' best general forum for information and debate. There are illustrated weeklies and district weeklies, both gaining importance as vehicles of local advertising and information. There is also a growing number of local advertising sheets and handbills, which bring advertising directly to the consumer and drain financial support from the dailies and weeklies. Only a few small serious cultural or political journals exist. Growing competition for the audience has come from

Denmark's Radio, which has sole rights to radio and television broadcasting. In recent years, it has expanded its news services and has begun developing regional radio. However, it does not compete with print publications for advertising revenues; its support derives entirely from license fees.

There is no truly national press. Most dailies are concentrated in Denmark's largest city, Copenhagen (population about 1,250,000), which claims roughly 16 percent of all dailies and about half of the nation's total newspaper circulation.

Any consideration of the Danish media must take into account the fact that the Kingdom of Denmark consists of the penninsula of Jutland, five large islands and 480 smaller islands between the North Sea and the Baltic, and the outlying territories of Greenland and the Faeroe Islands in the North Atlantic. This geographical spread and the sparse population in some regions affect the organization and distribution of newspapers and radio programs.

The Danish media audience is sophisticated, generally well educated and affluent. All citizens must receive at least nine years of formal education or attend school until they are 16 years of age. The state is required to offer a tenth voluntary year, and plans are being laid to extend compulsory education to a 12-year system. About 90 percent of all students attend public schools; the remainder are enrolled in state-subsidized private schools. In 1978 primary and secondary schools reported a total enrollment of 831,803 students. In addition, youth are increasingly encouraged to attend Denmark's five universities and three technical colleges. In the 1977–78 academic year, the five universities had enrollments totalling 52,264. These figures imply that one of every 16 lower-level students attends a university. The result is a highly literate media audience, interested in a wide range of political and social affairs.

Although Denmark has industrialized considerably since 1945, it remains an agricultural-based society. Farmers and smallholders have formed cooperative societies that market their produce and conduct research. This has helped to make Danish farm products—especially butter, beef and bacon—internationally competitive. Meanwhile, industrial production has risen to the point where, despite critical shortages of certain raw materials, it now accounts for two-thirds of the country's exports. Denmark's major industries include iron, shipbuilding, fishing, chemicals, engineering, furniture, electronics, porcelain, textiles and metal goods; these, like their agricultural counterparts, have been finding larger markets abroad. Because of its trade, its exposure to the sea and its tourism, Danes have long had an international world-view, which results in keen interest in international affairs, a fact that is reflected in the high proportion of foreign news in Danish dailies.

Although in the past most Danes lived in small villages, today three-quarters of the population reside in town and urbanized districts. Copenhagen accounts for more than a quarter of the population, and it is the country's single large metropolitan center. Aarhus, the next largest city, has a population of less than 250,000. Only two other cities have populations over 100,000—Odense (170,000) and Alborg-Norresundby (155,000). All other cities are small. Farms, meanwhile, have been dwindling in number and increasing in size.

The national language is Danish, taught in the schools and employed as the medium of communication. Most Danes also speak and read English. Some publications appear in both languages. Many Danes also speak Swedish and/or German.

With the exception of the specialized *Børsen*, urban dailies and provincial papers alike seek to appeal to all educational and interest levels. All Danish papers also display a balance of hard news, commentary and background material. The district papers add to that balance good reporting of local news and information. The typical Danish newspaper avoids extremes; neither excessive sensationalism nor stuffy intellectualism is tolerated. The nearest approaches to the sensational are the light and popular midday tabloids, *B.T.* and *Ekstra Bladet*, while the "heaviest" and most serious reading matter may be found in limited amounts in *Information* and *Aktuelt's* Sunday edition. This middle-of-the-road approach has resulted in a press with few high-quality elite papers and equally few sensational "popular" papers.

In general, Danish papers have a neat and warm appearance. They are informal but dignified. Their makeup is pleasing, typography is attractive, use of white space effective, employment of pictures generous and interesting. The language employed is conversational and friendly.

The first Danish paper, *Dèn Danske Mercurius*, was founded in 1666 by the Crown to publish official bulletins and to laud the king and the government. Press censorship existed until 1849, but since then the Danish press has been one of the world's freest. Four early papers founded in the 18th Century still thrive today: *Berlingske Tidende* (1749), Aalborg *Stiftstidende* (1767), Fyens *Stiftstidende* (1772) and Aarhus *Stiftstidende* (1794).

As indicated above, the press is composed of larger urban dailies and smaller provincial papers, the latter interested in publishing district news and information. About half of the newspapers published in rural areas are local editions of the larger papers. Newspapers in Denmark still largely stress opinions of the editors and offer friendly advice in preference to providing objective news and factual information. But they are not gossip sheets. Recently, as the Danish press has become larger and concentrated into groups, the move has been toward more straight, factual news reporting.

Danes established their reputation for being avid newspaper readers early. In 1970 the proportion of newspaper circulation to population ranked as the world's highest, with about 400 copies of dailies published for each 1,000 Danes. Although the smallest farm house in the most remote rural area still gets at least one newspaper each day, circulation and readership have been declining during the past several decades.

Ownership of newspapers by private families or limited liability companies is another cherished tradition. Ownership has usually been restricted in number or confined to residents of the areas in which a newspaper circulates. But that phenomenon has been breaking down in recent years; since 1945, there has been increased concentration of ownership into the hands of a few publishing houses or chains, and the number of dailies has declined accordingly.

All papers published in Denmark are in Danish. One paper, the *Statstidende*, contains only official government announcements. Another deals exclusively with building-trade information. However, papers are normally general interest dailies.

A special daily, the independent *Kristeligt Dagblad* (Christian Daily), represents the Folk Church, the major religious group in the country. A strong Lutheran country, Denmark also has a specialized religious news organization, the Kristeligt Pressebureau, which distributes church-related information to Danish papers.

With the arrival of press freedom in Denmark in 1849 and concurrent social and political development, four groups of newspapers arose, each associated with a definite political party and a distinct social grouping. The earliest group, eventually to include some 60 papers, represented the middle-class Conservatives. A few years later (1865-90), a similar number of papers were founded to promulgate the farmers' Liberal party. In 1872 the first Social Democratic daily appeared in Copenhagen, and by the turn of the century, 20 other papers championed the Social Democratic cause in the provinces. The fourth grouping was formed in 1905, when the Radicals, mostly composed of small landholders and the intelligensia, broke away from the Liberal party to form one of their own. They got the support of a dozen older newspapers, among them the *Politiken* (founded 1884) and another dozen new ones founded quickly thereafter.

By 1913 there were 143 independent dailies, and at least 30 cities and towns had papers representing three or four different parties. Some of these political journals were owned by the parties themselves, others by sympathetic independent publishers. The rivalry between party-oriented newspaper groups has continued to the present. In Copenhagen, for example, *Berlingske Tidende* continues to represent the Conservatives, *Politiken* the Radicals and *Aktuelt* the Social Democrats.

Since World War II, the number of dailies has been reduced steadily by economic and other problems—together with concentration of ownership—from 130 to 48, and in the process each party has lost press support. When a number of independent Social Democratic newspapers went out of business in the 1960s, *Aktuelt* moved to fill the vacuum by publishing regional editions. Today, the Social Democratic party owns only *Aktuelt* and two provincial papers.

Circulation figures further illustrate the dwindling support for party newspapers. Compared with 1968, Conservative papers today have 10 percent less of the total circulation, Social Democratic papers only half as much, Liberal papers about the same and Radical papers about two percent more. Over the past few decades, many papers have also loosened their political ties. In fact, 25 of Denmark's 48 remaining dailies now indicate they think of themselves as independent.

But not all are totally independent. With changes in ownership and pressures to survive economically, papers are making new alliances. Particular interests, causes or ideologies have spurred circulation growth for several specialized papers at a time when the general trend in the number of newspapers and in circulation has been downward. Two independent papers that have done well are the serious *Information* (originally a Resistance paper) and *Børsen*, a business daily. The religious *Kristeligt Dagblad* has done well because of its specialization. *Land og Folk*, founded as another Resistance paper, has advanced in recent years as the voice of the Communist party. Denmark's only new paper since World War II days, *Minavisen* (founded 1970) has grown because it serves more as a membership paper of the Socialist People's party than as a general daily.

Even with the last two examples, however, Danish newspapers in general are less openly political than in the past. Political opponents are given fairer treatment. There is less editorializing and greater objectivity. And with the modification of strict party-line policies, the Danish press has lost some of the political influence it once held.

The shift away from newspaper affiliation with parties and the worsening economic milieu for the Danish press have served to reduce sharply the number of cities with competing newspapers. Copenhagen remains the home of nine rival dailies, four of which have circulations of over 100,000. Only four other provincial cities have two competing dailies: Aarhus, Holbaek, Kolding and Odense. And only one town, Rønne on the Baltic Island of Bornholm, has two distinctly local competing papers.

As a result of these forces of change, Denmark's present 49 dailies might better be reclassified according to political views as follows: Social-Democratic, three; Social-Liberal, three; Independent Social-Liberal, two; Conservative, two; Independent Conservative, two; Liberal, fifteen; Independent, Liberal, seven; Communist or Socialist, two; and Independent or apolitical, thirteen.

Most Danish dailies have a similar size and format—a 22 x 5.5 inch seven- or eight-column page with up to 40 pages for the larger dailies, 20 pages for provincials and 12 to 14 for smaller papers. (The exceptions are Copenhagen's two tabloid-size publications, B.T. and Ekstra Bladet.) In all papers, headlines are bold. Advertisements take up one-third to two-thirds of space, with ads even on front pages. Numerous pictures are used effectively. Satirical, informational and political cartoons add grace, variety and intelligent humor. Color is employed well. In general, makeup is lively but not lurid, and light without undue loss of seriousness.

In Copenhagen, all dailies are now either morning or midday papers. The biggest of the morning papers—Berlingske Tidende (circulation 127,000), Politiken (140,000) and Aktuelt (60,000)—have all lost circulation ground to the more popular midday tabloids, B.T. (225,000) and Ekstra Bladet (238,0000) in recent years, but they are struggling to regain that lost readership. Sunday editions, which the tabloids do not run, possibly help here. Berlingske Tidende claims a Sunday circulation of about 207,000, Politiken some 204,000 and Aktuelt about 125,000.

Among provincial dailies, evening papers predominate. Only four important provincials publish mornings: Aarhus's Jyllands-Posten (The Jutland Post), Hillerød's Frederiksborg Amts Avis, Kolding's Jydske Tidende and Odense's Fyns Tidende (Times of Funen). Provincial papers with higher weekday circulations also publish on Sundays in Aalborg, Aarhus, Hillerød, Hjørring, Kolding and Odense. Total Sunday circulation in the provinces comes to about 653,000 copies.

In 1979 the distribution of newspapers by size of circulation was as follows: over 100,000, four dailies in Copenhagen and none elsewhere; 50,000 to 100,000, one in Copenhagen and five in the provinces; 25,000 to 50,000, two in Copenhagen and 10 in the provinces; under 25,000, two in Copenhagen and 24 elsewhere.

According to recent official Danish statistics, Denmark's 10 largest newspapers are:

Ten Largest Newspapers by Circulation	
1. Ekstra Bladet	250,000
2. B.T.	222,000
3. Politiken	138,000
4. Berlingske Tidende	122,000
5. Jyllands-Posten	88,000
6. Stiftstidende	76,000
7. Stiftstidende	75,000
8. Aktuelt	61,000
9. Vestkysten	60,000
10. Fyens Stiftstidende	55,000

Historically, by virtue of their solid reportage, range of topics, emphasis on politics, literature and other serious matters, Copenhagen's Berlingske Tidende, Politiken and Aktuelt have all ranked as the country's most influential newspapers. Berlingske Tidende is especially notable for its emphasis on foreign news, well balanced with Danish coverage, and its special pages each week of Scandinavian news. From the standpoint of weighty matter, the ultraserious Information would have a place of its own. From a national outlook and wide-circulation point of view, the Jyllands-Posten must also be regarded as quite important. However, if popularity and a wide range of subject matter are to be considered, both tabloids carry influence.

Denmark's largest weekly magazine is Billed-Bladet, with a circulation of about 395,000. It is followed by the family magazine, Illustreret Familie Journal (352,000) and the Se og Hør ("He and She") with 278,000.

Because of Denmark's geographical location and because Danes believe in the free flow of information, newspapers from surrounding countries are easily available, especially in German, Swedish and English.

Economic Framework

Denmark's economy rests on two foundations, its agriculture and its industrial output. Agriculture has been healthy. But inflation, unemployment, escalating oil prices and soaring costs of raw materials that must be imported, added to increased consumer demand for imported goods, have resulted in lowered industrial production and an unfavorable trade balance in the past few years. In 1975 the government took measures to increase consumption and investment. Other recent measures include devaluation of the Danish krone in 1977 and limitation of pay increases. But unemployment and inflation have continued to climb. Recently, the Social Democratic/Liberal coalition government increased taxes on energy and slashed public spending in a further attempt to control the economy.

These economic strictures have affected the media in several ways—and not merely in the decrease in the number of dailies from 130 in 1945 to 49 today. Except for a rise in 1976, circulations have declined, having failed over the years to keep pace with population growth. Advertising income and net profits have decreased while wages and production costs have risen. And once-private ownership has not only become concentrated but concentrated in larger units.

Some 25 percent of the total circulation of all dailies plus two large weeklies, numerous district papers, a book publishing business and a print shop are controlled by the Berlingske group. The other large newspaper chain is owned by the Berg group, which publishes six dailies. Concentration is also conspicuous among district papers.

A fair portion of the Danish press operates on a nonprofit basis. In some cases, such as that of *Information*, the staff has taken over responsibility for running the paper. The Social Democratic press is owned and run by trade unions, which actually subsidize it. At least 16 small Liberal and Radical provincial papers are published by nonprofit companies with several hundred stockholders. In fact, only 10 small papers are privately owned by a single person or family today.

In the interests of efficient operation, Danish papers cooperate in several ways. The Copenhagen media jointly own the A/S Bladkompagniet for cooperative distribution and delivery of their newspapers, most periodicals and a number of foreign papers. The company operates with small profits and uses only about one-fourth the personnel that would be necessary if each paper set up its own distribution network. Danish papers have also set up a joint purchasing agency to import newsprint and to secure equipment.

Denmark must import all its newsprint. Imports have been declining, as has consumption, due in part to decreasing numbers and circulations of dailies. In 1970 Danes used 149 million metric tons of newsprint; by 1977, consumption was down to less than 134 million metric tons. But meanwhile the cost of newsprint has climbed.

The big morning papers and provincial newspapers get between 55 and 65 percent of their revenue from advertising, while the urban midday and smaller rural papers typically receive 30 to 40 percent. Ads take up about half of the space, with the proportion rising in recent years to help keep pace with rising costs of production.

Because of the strained Danish economy, newspapers must operate with low profit margins. In 1975 *Berlingske Tidende* had a net surplus of income over costs of less than $200,000. *Politiken*'s surplus in 1976 was 2.2 percent, while *Aktuelt* reported a gross business of just over $18.6 million with a net loss of $2.2. million.

Denmark's most serious labor conflict in 30 years took place in 1977 with a strike that represented life or death for both labor and management. In the 1950s and 1960s, Danish newspaper organizations, especially the Berlingske group, took on larger staffs as circulations grew. Featherbedding, fictitious overtime pay and other practices were devised by the typographers' unions to assure full, continued employment of its members. At the time, printers were highly paid.

With the 1970s came rising costs of newsprint and production, inflation, lowered circulations, fewer newspapers, and talk by management of moving to new technologies —all threats to printers. The Berlingske group found itself with 50 percent overstaffing—900 printers and typographers where 600 were needed. Early retirement, generous preretirement, no replacement of retirees and cancellation of certain benefits were all plans invoked in attempts to economize and continue as in the past. But the strong left-wing typographer's union conceded nothing.

Then, in December 1976, the labor court upheld Berlingske's right to offer pre-pension payment to each of its redundant staff, and Berlingske gave six weeks' notice that a new staffing schedule would become effective on January 30, 1977, at which time 300 employees would become redundant.

During January 1977, printers systematically obstructed Berlingske production. Advertising was boycotted and circulation hit. When the printing staff failed to appear for work on January 30, Berlingske locked its gates on the union. Lengthy, futile negotiations ensued. The government tried to intervene, to no avail. A labor court ruled the obstruction by the printers unlawful and ordered them to return to work. But the strike continued.

Then, on April 1, sympathy strikes closed down all Danish newspapers that were members of the Association of Danish Newspaper Employers. For three weeks, Danes had little to read. Meanwhile all other employees received full pay. Newspapers made plans to bypass the unions by going immediately to photo-offset machines run by nonunion laborers. The unions began to see the need to concede. On April 24, all union workers but those of Berlingske compromised and other newspapers resumed publishing. Finally, on May 21, agreement was reached between the Berlingske management and its printers, with both sides making concessions. At minimum, the Berlingske group lost readers and profits, while the unions lost a minimum of 250 jobs.

In addition to the typographers' and printers' unions referred to above, over 2,000 working journalists are organized in the Danish Union of Journalists (Dansk Journalistforbund) to represent their economic and professional interests. This union has been instrumental in getting salary raises for newsmen. On the management side, practically all newspapers now belong to the Danish Newspaper Publisher's Union (Danske Dagblades Udgiverforening), which looks after their common economic interests. The Association of Danish Newspaper Employers represents the publishers in wage agreements with typographers and printers. There are also other unions or associations of editors and publishers that have now come together into the Joint Council of Danish Newspapers to speak on behalf of the press with governmental authorities and the general public. Among other things, the council has established a code of ethics for reporting of criminal cases. The Danish Press Council, composed of members of the Joint Council, rules on violations of this code.

Today, about 63 percent of the circulation of Denmark's entire press is accounted for by the top 10 dailies. Virtually all Danish papers have either converted or are in the process of conversion to photo-offset and to electronic newsrooms.

Press Law

Article 77 of the Constitutional Act of the Kingdom of Denmark states: "Any person shall be at liberty to publish his ideas in print, in writing, and in speech, subject to his being held responsible in a court of law."

Freedom of the press has been in effect since 1849, when the introduction of the liberal constitution abolished nearly two centuries of censorship. Since then, the Danish press has been among the freest in the world. The legal limits of fair comment in speech and writing are wide, with the main constraints imposed by laws protecting individual honor and good reputation. Because of this sanctity of the individual, newsmen and editors have lost some cases, and have occasionally also faced short prison sentences (none over three months).

Press freedom in Denmark hinges on the official view of democracy, which in turn is based on the citizen's right to form his own opinions. According to this view, democracy simply ceases to function without freedom of the press, and for this very reason, the press must be independent of government. Press freedom, therefore, is not a privilege guaranteed to Danish newspapers, but an obligation. This principle has been extended even to pornographic publications.

Journalists are not required to observe professional secrecy, but most consider it an unwritten code that they should keep secret their sources, and that any expressed desire for anonymity by a source must be strictly honored. To date, no Danish journalist has revealed his source and the courts have respected this stance.

No law exists requiring either newspapers or journalists to register or to become licensed. Nor is an import license required for equipment or newsprint.

Censorship

Article 77 of the Danish Constitution also states that "censorship and other preventive measures shall never again be introduced." During its occupation by Nazi Germany from 1940 to 1945, the Danish press was strictly controlled. In the last two years of that period, German censorship was total and the press was forced to publish articles against its will. Otherwise, as already mentioned, there has been no censorship in Denmark since 1849.

Even military information can be published unless the government requests secrecy or has been traditionally maintaining secrecy of certain defense oeprations.

The Danish Press Council does interpret and pass judgments related to the press's voluntary code of ethics on reporting criminal cases. But compliance with this code is voluntary rather than mandatory.

State-Press Relations

In Denmark, the government makes no attempt to control the press or the flow of government news and information to the public. In 1970 it passed a law guaranteeing the principle of publicity in the administration, except for matters involving security.

The press considers itself responsible to provide information about legislation. It regards itself as essential to the processes of democracy, especially in assuring that new legislation is well explained as is information about legislation that may be needed. At the same time, the press considers itself to have a distinct role in the democratic process at the electoral level.

In only one area has there been a hint of possible government intervention, and this presumably has been in the interests of maintaining a multi-voice press, a principle that is considered a mainstay of democratic political life in Denmark. Since the mid-1970's the question of government subsidies for the press has arisen repeatedly as more and more newspapers have failed or have merged into chains or groups. The government has subsidized the press in several ways—through low-interest loans to publishers; relief from value-added taxes; postal, telephone and telegraph concessions, and by submitting advertising to inform the public about its governmental and municipal activities. Publishers agree the last is healthy, and are inviting more such ads.

Since 1975, the government has also been putting four million Krone ($800,000) annually into the Financial Institution of the Daily Press so the institute can grant assistance for market research and product development. But to date, publishers have rejected any form of direct subsidy because they wish to avoid any precedent that would compromise their full independence from government. The Union of Journalists wants public support only if it can be administered in such a way that it will encourage the establishment of new papers.

Attitude Toward Foreign Media

Denmark imposes no restrictions on foreign media or foreign correspondents. Stories can be moved out of the country without hindrance. Foreign journalists are treated with deference, in keeping with the Danes' high respect for their own press.

News Agencies

Danish newspapers depend for most of their foreign news on the Ritzaus Bureau, the country's national news agency. Founded in 1866 by E. N. Ritzau, it serves government departments but is not state controlled. Since World War II, the Danish press has cooperatively owned the bureau. It works in conjunction with Reuters, Agence France-Presse, Deutsche Presse-Agentur and European national agencies. It releases about 14,000 words of foreign copy per day, 50 percent of which is based on Reuters reports, 30 percent on AFP and 10 to 15 percent from DPA. It also has excellent service for the provincial papers and supplies news to Danish radio and television. Its general manager and editorial staff are responsible to a governing board of directors.

Foreign news bureaus operating regularly and freely in Denmark, in addition to those mentioned above, include Tass and Novosti (USSR), ANSA (Italy), ADN (East Germany) and AP and UPI (United States).

Electronic News Media

Danmarks Radio, which has sole rights for Danish radio and television broadcasting, began operations in 1925, when it took over services previously operated by amateurs. Although a monopoly, it is an independent and public institution interested in serving the people with news, information, entertainment and artistic programs. It also acts as a forum for free expression of a wide range of opinions.

Danmarks Radio is governed by a Radio Council consisting of 27 members elected by the Folketing, (lower chamber of parliament). Under the direction of the minister for cultural affairs, the council sets up the principles for national radio and television activities and assures that those principles conform to Danish law. But the council is not dominated by government. Although the chairman and vice-chairman are nominated by the minister of cultural affairs and one member is named by the minister for public works, the remainder are nominated to represent the listeners and viewers in the general public.

Danmarks Radio has a Press Department that is directly responsible to the director general, who has sole responsibility to the Radio Council. Among the program departments there are a News and Current Affairs Department for radio, and a Television Current Affairs Department, the latter covering news, home and foreign political affairs, current-affairs programs on social and economic problems, and discussions and reportage from home and abroad.

In 1977 Danmarks Radio broadcast 14,034 hours of radio programs from one long-wave, three medium-wave and 40 VHF transmitters, and 2,344 hours of television programming from its 30 color transmitters. About half of the telecasts were imports.

All revenue for Danmarks Radio derives from licensing; there is no income from advertising. Total budgetary income from the 4.2 million radio receivers and 5.45 million television sets amounted in 1977 to about $160 million. A home pays only one fee for a license. Faroese Radio and Greenland Radio are not subject to Danmarks Radio, but there is close cooperation. Greenland's television is cable only.

Danmarks Radio focuses on information and cultural affairs. On the radio side it has a Music Department, Children and Young People's Department, Education Department, News and Cultural Affairs Department, Cultural and Social Affairs and a Theater and Literature Department. Television also has a Cultural Department, a Current Affairs Department and a Theater Department. The News Service (Pressens Radioavis) is administered by a committee consisting of five members of the Radio Council and five representatives of the press. This committee oversees the finances of the news service and appoints its editor in chief.

Education & Training

Formerly, a journalist normally spent two to three years of on-the-job training as an apprentice to a senior journalist before entering the profession. Then, in 1962, that training was supplemented by a six-month theoretical course at the Danish College of Journalism at the University of Aarhus. In 1971, this system was reorganized: trainees are now sent directly to the college, where they spend two and one-half years in liberal arts and journalistic training before entering an 18-month apprenticeship on a daily newspaper. Journalists from other Scandinavian countries also attend this college.

Summary

The Danish press has a long tradition of freedom and independence from government, which is preserved to this day. Although Danes continue to be avid newspaper readers, in recent years the number of papers has been dwindling quite rapidly and circulation has decreased gradually. Since World War II, the number of independent dailies has dropped from 130 to 49, causing chains and groups to be formed for survival. In addition, newspapers were hit with a crippling strike in 1977 by typographers and printers fearful of losing their jobs to new technologies.

The Danish government has attempted to assist ailing papers with subsidies, concessions and low-interest loans. It has made no attempt to interfere with the free press, but publishers continue to reject any form of direct subsidy.

Danmarks Radio, an independent and public institution that gets all its support from license fees, provides a healthy radio and television counterpart to the press. Its fare is rich in news, public affairs and informational and cultural programming. In the strictest sense of the word, Denmark's radio and TV—being government supported—do not compete with the press, but they must inevitably make inroads into newspaper circulation. This in turn could prove an incentive to changes in print-media style and format, thus giving a new image to the country's entire mass-communications apparatus.

CHRONOLOGY

1970 Danish government passes law guaranteeing open publicity of administrative affairs, except in cases involving national security.

Denmark's only new newspaper in recent years, *Minavisen*, founded in Copenhagen.

1973 Danmarks Radio given sole right to radio and television broadcasting under Radio and Television Service Act.

1975 Government begins annual grant to Financial Institution of the Daily Press for market research. Government also provides subsidies to papers in form of tax and other concessions and government advertising in newspapers.

1977 Typographers and printers' unions strike the Berlingske group in attempt to save jobs obtained through earlier featherbedding practices. Entire Danish press shut down for three weeks until an agreement is reached.

BIBLIOGRAPHY

Danish Association of Advertising Agencies. *Media Scandinavia, 1980.* Copenhagen, 1980.

Europa Yearbook, 1980. Vol. 1. London, 1980.

"IPI Affairs: Northern European Members Discuss Current Issues." *IPI Report.* October 1978, p. 8.

Merrill, John, Bryan, Carter R., and Alisky, Marvin. *The Foreign Press.* Baton Rouge, La., 1970.

Merrill, John, and Fisher, Harold A. *The World's Great Dailies: Profiles of 50 Newspapers.* New York, 1980.

Nielsen, Lars. "Democracy and Information." *Danish Journal,* February 1978, p. 3.

Norlund, Neils. "Why Papers are Scarce in Copenhagen." *IPI Report,* March 1977, p. 9.

Press and Information Department, Ministry of Foreign Affairs. *Denmark: An Official Handbook.* Copenhagen, 1970.

Statistical Yearbook, 1980. Copenhagen: Danmarks Statistik, 1980.

"Subsidy Principle Accepted, but..." *IPI Report.* November 1975, pp. 9–10.

"The Battle of the Newspapers." *Danish Journal,* March 1977, pp. 6–7.

UNESCO. *Statistical Yearbook, 1978–79.* Paris, 1980.

"Who's Afraid of Handouts?" *IPI Report.* May–June 1977, pp. 21–22.

DOMINICAN REPUBLIC

by Robert N. Pierce

BASIC DATA

Population: 5,621,000
Area: 48,692 sq. km. (18,800 sq. mi.)
GNP: 4.8 billion pesos (US$4.8 billion)
Literacy Rate: 68%
Language(s): Spanish
Number of Dailies: 10
  Aggregate Circulation: 208,000
  Circulation per 1,000: 37
Number of Nondailies: 30
  Aggregate Circulation: NA
  Circulation per 1,000: NA
Number of Periodicals: 17

Number of Radio Stations: 106
Number of Television Stations: 5
Number of Radio Receivers: 2 million
  Radio Receivers per 1,000: 356
Number of Television Sets: 500,000
  Television Sets per 1,000: 90
Total Annual Newsprint Consumption: 2.6 metric tons
  Per Capita Newsprint Consumption: 0.5 kg. (1.1 lb.)
Total Newspaper Ad Receipts: NA
  As % of All Ad Expenditures: NA

Background & General Characteristics

As the only Spanish-speaking nation among the Caribbean Islands to follow Western patterns, the Dominican Republic stands somewhat alone. But this uniqueness has not produced isolation. Openness to foreign influence has always prevailed.

The Spanish influence came first, and even today Dominicans like to point out that their capital, Santo Domingo, was the first permanent Spanish settlement in the New World. Spaniards soon lost interest in it, however, when it could not provide the riches they sought. Next came two decades of domination by newly freed black slaves from Haiti; this tore apart the Spanish institutions and left little in their place.

Since then, while some efforts have been made to rebuild the Spanish way of life, most leading Dominicans have seen their future lying in the U.S. sphere of influence. U.S. Marines occupied the country for eight years (1916–24) and did much to modernize it. Their departure was followed soon by the 31-year dictatorship of Rafael Leónidas Trujillo. Even in the uneasily democratic period since Trujillo's death in 1961, there has not been the serious effort to throw off North American influence that other Latin countries have witnessed.

The growth of Dominican journalism was affected by outside forces much as were other institutions. But the press could gain little benefit from these models during Trujillo's era; he brutally prevented any editorial initiative. Since then, however, the media have surged forward in quality and scope, to the point where they rank favorably among other Latin countries' systems. This is partly due to nearness to Puerto Rico, the U.S. island commonwealth, that has developed rapidly at the same time; the two systems are friendly rivals and have stimulated each other's ambitions.

The Dominican Republic remains one of the least developed countries in the hemisphere, and in many ways the media have progressed more than the populace. Adult literacy has reached only about 60 percent, and per-capita income was estimated in 1978 at $849, poorly distributed and concentrated among elites, with a narrow although growing middle class. Santo Domingo dominates the country, one of every four inhabitants calling it home. Only one other city, Santiago de los Caballeros, is large enough to support mass media, and it is only a fourth the size of the capital. In all, only a third of the people live in the nine largest cities, the rest having their homes on farms or in towns of 45,000 or fewer.

Spanish is almost universal among Dominicans, and thus language poses no problem for the media. Nor does race create any rigid social boundaries. Three-fourths of the people are mulatto, an evidence of the colonial importations of Africans to work plantations, while an estimated 16 percent are white. While nearly all Dominicans try to marry so as to lighten their children's skin color, mulattoes are found in every level of public life.

Nor does religion or ideology create serious schisms. Catholicism is the nominal faith of about 95 percent, and politics largely follows the lines of personal loyalties to leaders. Even so, the country has long displayed a remarkable tolerance, with Protestants, communists, foreigners and other fringe groups finding a relatively easy accommodation. It was the only nation in the world to be completely open to Jewish refugees from Nazism.

Dominicans have a variety of daily newspapers to choose from—seven in the capital and one in Santiago. Morning papers are all full-sized, afternoon ones tabloid. Two are published on Sundays, and Saturday editions of others tend to be larger and in some cases include color comics. The two major ones generally range from 40 to 60 pages, and most days the tabloids have 20 to 32 pages. Supplements and magazine sections have become commonplace. About 30 nondaily papers are found in various cities, including a minor English-language publication, but these count for little in the national life.

In prestige and advertising, two of Santo Domingo's morning dailies—*Listin Diario* ("The Little List") and *El Caribe* ("The Caribbean")—rank well above the other papers and are staunchly competitive. Both are serious in their approach to news but attractively designed and well printed with cold type. *Listin* is offset, and *El Caribe* letterpress.

Listín Diario was born in 1889 as a one-page bulletin of commercial items published by a shipping company as a giveaway. It steadily became more newsy, gained foreign news from the French agency Havas when a cable was laid, and turned into a commercial success when it began to be sold instead of given away. When Trujillo came to power the paper tried to survive by accommodating him, but even so he set about starving it by founding his own paper, *La Nación*, which he made sure got the bulk of advertising. In 1942, because of failing income, its owners had to suspend *Listín* and to sell its equipment. Two years after Trujillo's assassination in 1961, they repurchased the equipment and resumed publication. The paper defended the radical reforms of Juan Bosch, who was elected president to succeed Trujillo. It suspended publication during the 1965 civil war.

Listín is steeped in traditions fostered by the owning family, the Ricart-Pellegrano clan. Its director is Rafael Herrera, a lively 77-year-old active in hemispheric affairs. Nowadays the paper tries to be independent, although it maintained a moderate opposition to Joaquín Balaguer, the president who was in power 13 years after the 1965 war. "We try to take a national position, defending human liberties and conserving human decency," Herrera says. He particularly won distinction during the 1978 crisis when the army tried to maintain Balaguer in power by voiding election results. He mediated personally between the two sides while keeping up a drumfire of editorials supporting the constitution. "Perhaps more than any other man," a *New York Times* reporter wrote, "Mr. Herrera kept the fragile system free when it was under the most extreme stress."

Daily Newspapers by Circulation	
Listín Diario	58,000
El Caribe	52,000
El Nacional	45,000
La Noticia	28,000
La Informacion	15,000
Periodico El Tiempo	10,000
El Diario de Macoris	3,500
*Circulation of *El Sol* and *Ultima Hora* not available.*	

El Caribe has long been identified with German Ornes, an aggressively conservative lawyer prominent in international press groups. It was founded in 1948 for commercial purposes under Trujillo's control. Ornes bought it from the government in 1954 and had to flee the country the next year; he regained control after Trujillo's death in 1961. Ownership has stayed in the Ornes family; Antonio Ornes, a son of German trained in journalism at Columbia University, is managing editor. German Ornes takes fierce pride in the news operation. "No one in the Dominican Republic is considered to be a newsman until he has gone through our newsroom," he declares. Of more than 200 employees, about 50 are editorial workers.

Both *Listin Diario* and *El Caribe* receive Associated Press and United Press International, plus several supplementary services from the United States, and *Listin* also carries Agence France-Presse. UPI, AFP and the Spanish agency EFE are favored among smaller papers.

Economic Framework

A combination of political stability, a ready market for its products in the United States, and enlightened economic planning by the government has given the Dominican Republic one of the highest and steadiest rates of economic growth in Latin America, despite also having one of the highest population growth rates. While the country remains in deep poverty as a whole, the steady expansion in the late 1970s opened new vistas of prosperity for the mass media.

The element of the growth most important for the media was a boom in the size of the middle class and an explosion in consumerism. By the decade's end this class was estimated to have risen to 35 percent, with 15 in the upper bracket and 50 in the lower. The new middle class, if not affluent, still could grasp at symbols of modernity, particularly on credit. New cars, new homes and a host of household gadgets were suddenly to be seen, at least in the capital city. To be marketed, all these must be advertised. Newspapers—particularly the two full-sized ones, *Listin Diario* and *El Caribe*—have reaped much of the advertising bonanza, and they have one of the most impressive advertising-to-editorial space ratios in the hemisphere. Both *Listin* and *El Caribe* have spacious new buildings, and several papers are rapidly moving toward advanced printing techniques.

Dominican media also have been taking advantage of the best in business management techniques learned in foreign and local universities. The practice of big-business families of sending their sons abroad for such training is growing rapidly.

A sure indication of the prospects for making money in the press is the willingness of investors to buy into it. This has been happening in Santo Domingo, and plans for two new dailies and a television station have

been rumored. The reasons for the financial attractiveness most often offered are the political prominence available to media directors, the fact that one can make a quick profit on a relatively small investment and the prolific growth of government advertising. Political ambition has been diminishing as a motive for owning media, in comparison with other motives. *Listin* and *El Caribe* are owned by families actively engaged in running them; while they seek to influence the political process, neither is closely identified with a party. Most of the other media are in the hands of men who look on them primarily as investments.

Santo Domingo also has witnessed a phenomenon rarer in Latin America than in other areas—widespread group or interlocking ownership of media. *Listin Diario* is associated with an afternoon newspaper, *Última Hora,* and a radio station. *El Caribe* has links with a television and a radio station. *El Nacional,* the leading afternoon daily, is jointly owned with the principal magazine, *Ahora;* an afternoon daily, *El Sol;* and a television and a radio station. The latter group was bought in 1980 by Pepín Corripio, who planned to found still another daily.

The income of broadcast stations was rising much more slowly than that for newspapers as the 1980s began. This has been laid to the relatively high cost of producing commercials, as few are imported. Nevertheless, the country has five television stations in the capital. These are Channel 2, Tele Antillas; 4, Radio Televisión Dominicana (government); 7, Rahintel; 9, Color Visión, and 11, Telesistema. Channel 13, Tele-Inde, was put out of operation by Hurricane David in 1979. All transmit in color.

Newspapers operate their own circulation systems through agents. The larger papers sell as many as 40 percent of their copies in the interior of the country, although this is not economical because the advertising market is in the capital. They also sell as many as 2,000 abroad—in New York, San Juan and Miami—because of the massive Dominican emigration in recent decades. Morning papers can reach New York the day of publication.

Most advertising in newspapers continues to be for brand or company names rather than for sale items. The ratios of advertising to total space range from about 30 percent in the afternoon tabloids to about 60 in the full-sized morning papers. The Latin American custom of individuals buying news space for personal announcements—weddings, birthdays, funerals, etc.—persists.

Since most media exist for the profit and personal ambitions of the owners, there is little evidence of their truckling to the demands of outside interests. Gulf and Western, the U.S. company that owns a large part of the agricultural and tourist sectors, considered getting into television but decided against it.

Despite a slowly increasing dissatisfaction among media employees, labor problems have been almost nonexistent in Dominican media. The only strike of consequence was against *El Nacional* in 1973. Staff members, not supported by their union, tried to influence the paper's editorial policy and were refused by management. They picketed for several days and then left to found *La Noticia,* an afternoon tabloid. By 1980 *Listin Diario* was the only daily with a union.

The media's growing prosperity has not resulted in professional-level salaries for editorial workers, except for top editors. Experienced reporters typically earn about $350 a month, so they must work at two or more jobs in government or commercial public relations, in other media such as television or radio, or in string work for foreign media.

Dominican newspapers have long been among the leaders in Latin America in adopting new printing techniques, and *Listin* is believed to be the first in the region to go completely offset. Photographic (cold type) composition is almost universal, although *El Caribe* maintains the letterpress printing process through improved, nonmetal plates.

Press Laws & Censorship

The 26 constitutions the Dominican Republic has had all have contained a guaranty of free expression, but they have had little to do with reality. The only exception was the 1963 version, adopted during the presidency of leftist Juan Bosch; it prohibited "any type of coercion or censorship" of the press. After Bosch's overthrow that year by forces close to the earlier Trujillo dictatorship, the constitution reverted to less protection of press freedom, banning Communist propaganda and making it a crime to broadcast material from blacklisted organizations.

Laws relating to the media have reflected the policy of the government in power rather than the constitution. Trujillo, after his take-over in 1932, dealt with the media mostly through coercion at various levels, including political and economic. However, he later solidified his control through a series of laws, basically the Communications Law of 1938. Another, passed in 1944, established formal censorship of printed matter by the Interior Ministry, with fines, confiscation and imprisonment as penalties. In 1949 the National Commission of Public Spectacles was set up with powers over broadcasting, stage and cinema. It was responsible for seeing that no performance critical of the government or offensive to good customers was presented. An unusual variation came in 1961, just before Trujillo's assassination, requiring that merchants selling television or radio sets report the names of all buyers to the director general of telecommunications.

The current press law dates to 1962, during the unelected and generally conservative government that replaced the dictatorship. It prohibits "all preventive measures, all intervention and all administrative control over expression of ideas or communication of facts." It then allows exceptions for offenses against "the honor of persons, social order or public peace"; it maintains that the stipulating of these exceptions will protect the press from arbitrary repression. Although many punitive measures are authorized, it must be noted that none constitute prior restraint; also, possible penalties are relatively light.

In some detail, the law seeks to make the direction of newspapers aboveboard and trustworthy. The director must be an adult Dominican citizen without a criminal record, and receiving of foreign funds except for advertising is prohibited. The newspaper must report its purpose to officials, list its stockholders and report its finances and its circulation, subject to government audit. Advertising must be clearly identified.

One of the earliest instances of right of reply was enacted by the law. This specifies that errors must be corrected without charge. Also punishable are incitement to attempted or actual crime and incitement of military or police personnel to disobedience or neglect of duty. A section using rather vague terms forbids "offenses" to the country's president, false news that "perturbs the public peace," and "outrage against good customs." It permits obscene materials of all types to be seized.

The law also forbids publication of facts about paternity suits, divorce, abortion cases, internal court discussions, or suicide of minors. Sight or sound recording is banned from courtrooms unless a judge permits it. All speeches in the legislature are privileged and cannot be the grounds for any legal action because of publication. The same is true of official documents.

The most extensive section of the law pertains to various forms of libel, which it defines as any allegation that attacks the honor or reputation of a person or organization, even if the identity is only hinted. The punishment is much heavier if the attack is against a government official, a court witness, or another country's ambassador or highest leaders. Truth is allowed as a defense if the aggrieved party is a public officeholder, but not if the matter concerns his private life or pardoned crimes.

Aside from this law, no important legal weapons exist, and censorship has not been employed since the Trujillo period. Dominican officials are quite open to reporters, and press conferences by government ministers are common.

State-Press Relations

Like Colombia, the Dominican Republic has emerged from the dual ordeals of dictatorship and civil war since the middle of the century, and its government has walked unsteadily down the democratic path. The Dominican media have not adopted the voluntary self-censorship Colombia has known, but they do show signs of avoiding excesses that might cause a political relapse.

Nevertheless, the posture of nearly all the news media has been one of criticism. None is openly affiliated with a political party, but their sympathies range across the spectrum from communist to rigid conservatism. This diversity does not prevent them from closing ranks against any incursion by the government against press freedom.

Relations between government and press were particularly tense during the presidency of Joaquín Balaguer (1966–78). The press suspected him because, although he was freely elected three times, he had been associated with the dictator Trujillo. He in turn repeatedly showed distrust of the media, although the conflict often blew hot and cold. The press avoided an all-out declaration of war because of two factors: Balaguer was notably successful in bringing justice and prosperity to the country, and he never mounted a sustained persecution of the print media.

The most serious media repression under Balaguer was against radio. The minister of telecommunications would periodically shut down either a single news program or a whole station, citing some aspect of the law. Invariably these actions would be reversed, either by court action or by the president, after a campaign of protest by the press.

Radio is a favorite forum for out-of-office politicians, and it was used eloquently by the fallen hero of the leftists, Juan Bosch. While Bosch himself was not banned from the airwaves, two leaders of his movement, the Dominican Revolutionary Party (PRD), were. In 1975 they were deprived of their rights to broadcast, and their program, "Tribuna Democrática," was separately banned. While their case was pending in court, Balaguer lifted both bans, although the release of the program was indirect, as it was allowed to return under a new name. His action followed an outcry from press and public.

The severity of the law regarding defamation has encouraged several flurries of libel actions against newspapers and political spokesmen. Several of these have been against *Listin Diario,* although all have eventually failed in the courts. Another involved José Francisco Peña Gómez, secretary general of PRD, in 1977. He was charged for accusing the army of being responsible for the death of a policeman at a riot-torn university campus. Peña Gómez said that before being charged he was called in for questioning by several military leaders who accused him of being "an enemy of the armed forces." The politician later was acquitted, but he had faced the possibility of two years in prison and a $1,000 fine.

The political conflict entered a tragic phase in 1972 with a series of murders of journalists. Gregorio García Castro, news editor of the afternoon daily *Última Hora,* was killed that year as he left his office. Three policemen were arrested. Orlando Martínez, the executive director of the leading magazine, *Ahora,* was murdered in 1975 by gunmen who drove past his car as he was going home. Also a columnist for the daily *El Nacional,* he had been defending himself from charges made on radio by Juan Bosch that he was a communist. That year was not over before Martínez' brother Eduardo was cut down by bullets at the door of his apartment. He also was a columnist for *El Nacional.* No one has ever been convicted in any of these killings.

Brief jailings also were an occasional hazard for journalists during the Balaguer period, although the action always was under the cloak of law. This was the case of two editors of *La Noticia* during the 1974 siege of the Venezuelan consulate by terrorists. The paper had published such an enterprising photograph, taken inside the consulate, that the police reasoned that it could only have been made with prior knowledge of the terrorists' plan by the journalists.

The power of the press and the vulnerability of the broadcast media was demonstrated during the constitutional crisis of 1978, when PRD candidate Antonio Guzmán defeated Balaguer in the presidential election. When the voting results were coming clear, the armed forces stopped them, and it appeared that a repeat of the 1963 overthrow of Bosch was coming. The generals shut down television and radio, but the newspapers editorialized strongly against the outrage. The personal mediation by *Listín* editor Rafael Herrera also was credited with bringing the final solution.

Attitude Toward Foreign Media

Foreign correspondents have never made the Dominican Republic a full-time base of operations, so their coverage usually concerns either political crises or long-term trends. The country has nearly always had centrist or conservative leaders who depend heavily on the outside world, and they have not been inclined to antagonize trade partners by giving trouble to citizens who come as visiting reporters. This was not a problem even during the Trujillo dictatorship. Correspondents covering the 1965 war had to undergo much danger because the fighting consisted largely of sniper fire and took place in the crowded center of Santo Domingo.

Other than English-language tourist guides, the only foreign-oriented publication of general distribution is the *Santo Domingo News,* published variously as a weekly and as a five-day-per-week daily. It is published by a Dominican family and is far below the Spanish-language press in editorial and production quality.

The country's geographical position puts it at the crossroads of radio signals, and shortwave listening to foreign government stations is often found. Voice of America, Radio Havana and the British Broadcasting Corporation are the most popular, although Dominican listeners tend to find the Cuban programs boring. Medium-wave radio can be received from Cuba and the United States in the northern part of the country, and Puerto Rican stations come in from the south. Dominican television watchers on the south coast also can see programs from Puerto Rican stations when their own go off the air.

Dominican press leaders have been active in international organizations. German Ornes, director of *El Caribe,* has been president of the Inter American Press Association and is current chairman of its freedom of the press committee; he has frequently spoken for the group on government-press relations. Rafael Herrera and Carlos A. Ricart of *Listín Diario* and Rafael Molina Morillo, formerly director of *El Nacional,* also have been active in IAPA. Herrera has been the Dominican delegate to UNESCO, particularly in meetings concerning communication policies. The Dominican government has avoided taking an extreme position on such debates, although Herrera has been a wittily eloquent speaker for the conservative position.

News Agencies

The country has no full-fledged domestic news agencies nor full-time bureaus maintained by international agencies, which cover it either with stringers or with correspondents sent in from elsewhere. All the dailies and television stations and the 10 to 12 largest radio stations subscribe to international agencies, with the Associated Press, United Press International, Agence France-Presse and Editors Press Service being the most common.

Electronic News Media

One of the oldest and most active broadcasting industries in Latin America is found in the Dominican Republic. Commercial radio started in 1927, and the government station followed in 1934. Government television began in 1952, and the first commercial station, Rahintel, initiated operations in 1959; color transmission came in 1964. By 1980 there were five television stations, all in color, and 106 radio stations, about 30 in the capital and 15 in the second city, Santiago. One station, Radio Santa María de la Vega, transmits adult education programs involving more than 10,000 students.

Broadcasting is almost universally accessible to Dominican citizens. Rahintel and

Radio-Televisión Dominicana carry television signals to about 90 percent of the population, and the others reach about 75 percent. The government has placed some public television sets in villages, and those villagers with sets of their own often sell admission to their neighbors. Qualified estimates tend to agree that there are about 500,000 television sets and 2 million radios in the country.

Stations have always been quick to adopt new forms of equipment such as mobile units, videocassettes and cartridge radio. Television uses the U.S.-type 525-line definition, and a large part of the programs comes from the United States and major Latin American countries.

Education & Training

Journalism education has existed in Santo Domingo since 1953, when the Autonomous University founded a three-year course leading to a professional degree. In 1969 a private school, the Dominican Institute of Journalism, was started. In addition, the major newspapers have long seen their role as training grounds for young journalists, introducing the latest in North American techniques. This was most notable in the case of *El Caribe,* founded by Stanley Ross from the United States.

While facilities at the schools are rudimentary and most students must hold jobs to support themselves, the academic influence is beginning to be felt in the newsrooms. This is true not only in the quality of work but also in the drive for professional prerogatives.

Summary

In terms of professional and economic growth, the journalistic media of the Dominican Republic represent one of the most notable success stories in the hemisphere. Operating in a free-enterprise context, they display prosperity and competence to a far greater degree than would be expected in a country that is generally underdeveloped. The professionalism in the newspapers is notably advanced. Press freedom has been mostly stable since the mid 1960s, although incursions into broadcasting have been persistent.

The country's strategic position and natural resources hold out prospects for continued economic progress, and the fact that political democracy has weathered severe tests indicates that more and more of the population will share in the increasing wealth. With an orderly enhancement of education, all this can indicate only a hopeful future for the media.

CHRONOLOGY

1973	Strike against *El Nacional,* leading daily, results in founding of *La Noticia,* another daily.
1974	Police briefly arrest two leading officials of daily *La Noticia* for supposedly trafficking with terrorists.
1974-75	*El Caribe* and *Listín Diario,* two leading dailies, occupy new publishing plants.
1975	In separate incidents nine months apart, brothers Orlando and Eduardo Martínez, prominent journalists connected with *Ahora-El Nacional* group, are killed by assassins.
1979	*Ahora-El Nacional* company sold to commercial entrepreneur.
1980	National congress considers licensing bill for journalists.

BIBLIOGRAPHY

Draper, Theodore. *The Dominican Revolt: A Case Study in American Policy.* New York, 1968.

Rodman, Selden. *Quisqueya: A History of the Dominican Republic.* Seattle, 1964.

Weil, Thomas E. et al. *Area Handbook for the Dominican Republic.* Washington, D.C., 1973.

Wiarda, Howard J. *The Dominican Republic: Nation in Transition.* New York, 1969.

ECUADOR

by George Kurian

BASIC DATA

Population: 7,901,000 (1980)
Area: 274,540 sq. km. (106,000 sq. mi.)
GNP: 180 billion sucre (US$7.2 billion) (1978)
Literacy Rate: 57%
Language(s): Spanish
Number of Dailies: 37
  Aggregate Circulation: 550,000
  Circulation per 1,000: 78
Number of Nondailies: 101
  Aggregate Circulation: 19,200
  Circulation per 1,000: 3
Number of Periodicals: 284

Number of Radio Stations: 250
Number of Television Stations: 10
Number of Radio Receivers: 2.85 million
  Radio Receivers per 1,000: 360
Number of Television Sets: 550,000
  Television Sets per 1,000: 70
Total Annual Newsprint Consumption: 10,800 metric tons (1978)
  Per Capita Newsprint Consumption: 2.2 kg. (4.9 lb.)
Total Newspaper Ad Receipts: NA
  As % of All Ad Expenditures: NA

Background & General Characteristics

The founding father of the Ecuadorian press is also one of the national heroes of the country: Francisco Javier Eugenio de Santa Cruz y Espejo. His publication *Primicias de la Cultura de Quito,* founded in 1792, provided the impetus to the movement for independence from Spain. Imprisoned twice, he died in jail where a plaque still honors him as "our first journalist." Most of the periodicals that followed were short-lived political diatribes, such as Juan Montalvo's *El Cosmopolita,* in which Montalvo mounted his attacks on the authoritarian rule of Garcia Moreno, his archenemy. Montalvo is regarded as one of the greatest 19th-century literary figures in Latin America. Hailed as the voice of the Liberal opposition, *El Cosmopolita* was suppressed by Garcia, who forced Montalvo to seek refuge in Colombia. When Garcia met his death at the hands of an assassin in 1875, Montalvo took credit for the act, exclaiming, "My pen killed him." Returning to Ecuador, Montalvo edited a new periodical, *El Regenerador,* until the rise of a new dictator, Gen. Ignacio de Veintimilla, put an end to it. From Montalvo, Ecuadorian press is said to have acquired its permanent

cast: a flair for journalistic polemics and a style to match it.

However, the first true newspaper in which editorial concerns and the reporting of news transcended political jousting was the daily *El Telegrafo,* founded in Guayaquil in 1884 and published uninterruptedly since. If *El Telegrafo* is the oldest, *El Comercio* is the largest and best selling. Founded in 1904 at Quito, it sells over 115,000 copies daily; its evening satellite, *Ultimas Noticias,* has a circulation of 65,000. *El Universo* of Guayaquil is the only other major daily founded before World War II. *La Razon* of Guayaquil and *El Tiempo* of Quito were both founded in 1965, while the more recent *Expreso* of Guayaquil was founded in 1973. In a different category is the official gazette, *Registro Oficial,* founded in 1830, which contains only announcements of laws and decrees.

All dailies in Quito and Guayaquil are morning papers except for *Ultimas Noticias* in Quito and *La Razon* in Guayaquil. All papers describe themselves as independent.

Beside the Guayaquil and Quito dailies, some 29 provincial dailies are published in nine other cities, such as Ambato, Loja and Portoviejo, giving the Ecuadorian daily press a total strength of 37 newspapers (out of the more than 200 newspapers, according to historian Carlos de la Torre Reyes, founded since the Battle of Pichincha). The total circulation of these dailies, according to UNESCO, is 550,000, or 78 per 1,000 inhabitants, placing Ecuador in the above-average category for Latin America and in 72nd rank in the world. Of the total circulation, Quito and Guayaquil papers account for 405,000, or 74 percent. The 29 regional papers thus have an average circulation of no more than 5,000. With such a small circulation, their impact on national life is minimal, and most discussions of Ecuadorian press ignore them altogether. UNESCO also reports 101 nondailies (of which 32 are published from once to three times a week) and 284 periodicals of all kinds but without citing circulation figures. Editores Nacionales is perhaps the nation's largest magazine publisher.

As noted, the Ecuadorian press is notably apolitical, and no major daily acknowledges political affiliations. This has led to the publication of regular newsletters or occasional newspapers by the nation's 13 political parties. Quito and Guayaquil newspapers, reflecting strong regional traditions, emphasize local interests although they provide substantial coverage of domestic and international news. The country has thus no national daily, but *El Comercio* comes close to being one. Its owners have been long involved in national affairs at the highest levels; Carlos Mantilla Ortiga was Ecuadorian ambassador to the United States and his brother Jorge Mantilla Ortega was ambassador to the Court of St. James. In Guayaquil, *El Telegrafo* is considered the voice of the Costa, or the coastal plain.

Economic Framework

The Ecuadorian press is still privately owned. Each newspaper is closely identified with and owned by a noted family: *El Comercio* (and its evening satellite, *Ultimas Noticias*) by the Mantilla family, *El Telegrafo* by the Castillo family and *El Universo* by the Perez family. Ownership has been fairly stable and there have been no changes in ownership for many decades.

While internewspaper competition is intense in both Quito and Guayaquil, both cities have a dominant newspaper; *El Comercio* claims 55 percent of daily circulation in Quito and *El Universo* 46.5 percent of daily circulation in Guayaquil. When

Ultimas Noticias's 65,000 copies are added to *El Comercio*'s total, the El Comercio company enjoys a virtual monopoly in Quito; the only other Quito daily, *El Tiempo,* offers only token competition with a circulation of 28,000. The situation is better in Guayaquil, where both *El Telegrafo* and *Expreso* have managed to trim *El Universo*'s lead to less than formidable proportions. While *El Telegrafo* remains patrician in its format, most Ecuadorian dailies are contemporary in both typography and coverage of news. The more popular ones display a certain liveliness and a sensitivity to reader interests commonly associated with U.S. and European dailies.

The impact of journalism on society and its professional maturity is evidenced by the number of journalistic organizations in the country: the National Union of Journalists, the National Confederation of Journalists, the Association of Democratic Journalists, the Guayaquil Association of Journalists and the Press Circles of Quito and Guayaquil. Strikes have been rare, not because of government restrictions on union activity but because disputes are often settled through mediation.

Press Laws, Censorship & State-Press Relations

Every constitution since the early days of the republic has contained a clause guaranteeing freedom of expression. This in itself is not unusual; what is unusual is that by and large these guarantees have been respected. From time to time, however, governments have not hesitated to flaunt the big stick, citing the constitutional phrase "contrary to national interest" to threaten or penalize those papers which overstepped the accepted bounds of criticism. Nevertheless, the track record has been good. The University of Missouri Press Freedom Index in the late 1960s ranked Ecuador 25th in the world, while K. Q. Hill and P. A. Hurley in their 30-year survey of press freedom in Latin America have rated Ecuador good during two five-year intervals and average for the other four five-year periods. The IPI and IAPA annual reports devote very little space to Ecuador in their survey of threats to press freedom. In the judgment of most media watchers, Ecuador stands among the top 10 countries in Latin America with respect to press freedom.

Such a tradition has not exempted the Ecuadorian press from the usual vicissitudes of its neighbors. In 1953, under the presidency of Jose Maria Velasco Ibarra, *El Comercio* and *Ultimas Noticias* and their affiliated radio station were closed down for 44 days for refusing to publish a government announcement that severe newspaper criticisms would not be tolerated. There were no apparent conflicts between 1956 and 1960 but they resumed when Velasco Ibarra returned to office in 1960. Under the military government that assumed power in 1963 the anti-Communist *El Clarin* was closed for a few days and its editor jailed because of a critical article in its pages. When *El Clarin* resumed publication it carried an official communique requiring all radio stations, news publications and other information media to submit all programs or articles for prior approval to the civil and military chief. In 1965 the military government closed *El Tiempo* on the grounds that it had persistently maligned the government and fostered a climate of subversion and public disorder. In 1969, again under Velasco Ibarra, the editor of the magazine *Vistazo* was summoned for hours of questioning about certain articles that had offended the regime, but no other action was taken against the publication. From 1970 to 1972 the Communist weekly *Manana* was closed. In 1972 the government of Guillermo Rodriguez Lara revived Section 10 of Article 141 of the 1945 constitution guaranteeing freedom of opinion regardless of the means of expression. But the law went on to state that journalism would be regulated by law and that the primary objective of journalism is the defense of national interests. The Rodriguez regime, like many of its contemporaries, did not see any conflict between these two statements but assumed that what is good for the state is good for the press.

In 1973 President Rodriguez passed a decree requiring all newspapers to publish official notices. In the same year the government arrested a reporter for refusing to reveal his source, although the law specifically shields journalists against disclosure of sources under coercion. The reporter was released following protests by the publishers as well as journalists. In 1979 *Nueva,* a Quito monthly, was banned for reporting "facts which are against the reasonable exercise of freedom of expression and are injurious to the dignity of the state."

Ecuador's return to the democratic fold in 1980 under popularly elected President Jaime Roldos was accompanied by a reaffirmation of the constitutional guarantees of press freedom. Since then there has been only one

minor breach of this freedom. It occurred toward the end of 1980 when the president of the magazine *Kaskabel* was placed under arrest for publishing an article the authorities described as insulting and slanderous. The minister of government was later asked to appear before Congress to explain his action. The minister said that the incident was a criminal matter and that it had nothing to do with the freedom of the press.

Since 1968 Ecuadorian journalists have been regulated by licensing procedures. The Law for the Professional Defense of the Journalist lays down the conditions of licensing. Candidates must have completed a course supervised by the ministry of education as well as possess five years' on-the-job experience. Journalists with 10 years' experience can be licensed by the National Union of Journalists without taking the course.

Attitude Toward Foreign Media

The relative freedom of the Ecuadorian press is best proved by the freedom enjoyed by foreign media in Ecuador. There have been few incidents where foreign reporters have been harassed, imprisoned or expelled. One of the last reported such incidents was in 1972 when two resident correspondents of Prensa Latina, the Cuban News Agency, were arrested on suspicion of being involved in terrorist activities. They were expelled, but Prensa Latina was allowed to continue operations.

Ecuador has refrained from going along with the rest of the Third World in supporting the 1978 UNESCO Declaration on the Media without, however, denying the primacy of national interests in defining the role of the media. Ecuador has also taken an active role in regional and international press organizations, such as IPI and IAPA.

News Agencies

Ecuador has no national news agency. At least seven foreign news agencies are represented in either Quito or Guayaquil, including AP, UPI, Reuters, Deutsche Presse-Agentur and Tass.

Electronic News Media

In 1980 Ecuador had approximately 290 originating radio stations; of these 200 transmitted on medium wave and the remaining on shortwave and FM frequencies. One hundred of these stations belong to five major networks. The government operates one transmitter, the National Broadcasting Station of Ecuador, broadcasting on both medium and shortwave. Five networks are made up of a number of loosely affiliated but individually owned and operated (O & O) stations. The largest of these networks is Cadena Nacional Equatoriana, with 29 stations. The others are Cadena Amarillo, Cadena Circuito, Cadena Radio Equatoriana and Cadena Catolica. But the best known of the commercial stations is the Voice of the Andes ("La Voz de los Andes") owned and operated by the World Radio Missionary Fellowship, a group supported by evangelical Protestant sects in the United States. Its programs in 15 languages reach as far as Australia, Europe and Southeast Asia.

One television channel (Channel 10) in Guayaquil covers most of the country through a relay system. There are 10 stations: three in Quito, three in Guayaquil, three in Cuenca and one in Ambato. About 73 percent of the programs are imported, mostly from the United States. All stations are required to devote at least five minutes per day to literacy programs.

Education & Training

Schools of Journalism at the Universities of Guayaquil, Quito and Cuenca offer four-year courses in journalism.

Quito is the location of the best-known school of media studies in Latin America: Centro Internacional de Estudios Superiores de Periodismo para America Latina (CIESPAL), established in 1958 under the auspices of UNESCO. CIESPAL offers short-course training for journalists and broadcasters, conducts research and publishes *Chasqui,* a research journal.

Summary

Although it shares many common characteristics with its neighbors, the Ecuadorian press also offers sharp contrasts. While still subject to nagging and periodical irritants, state-press relations have been free of major crises. Even President Velasco Ibarra, who was fond of lecturing the press (even occasionally telling them how to edit their stories), never went so far as to erase the thin red line that divides the state from the media. As a result, Ecuadorian papers continue to offer a lively commentary on the state of the nation without rancor and without fear.

CHRONOLOGY

1979 The monthly *Nueva* banned for circulating reports "injurious to the dignity of the state."

1980 Newly elected President Jaime Roldos reaffirms constitutional guarantees of press freedom. President of the magazine *Kaskabel* arrested for slander of public authorities.

BIBLIOGRAPHY

Arciniegas, G. C. "Development of Mass Communication Media in Ecuador." *Democratic Journalist,* 1973:4.

Hill, K. Q., and Hurley, P. A. "Freedom of the Press in Latin America: A Thirty-Year Survey." *Latin American Research Review,* 15:2, 1980.

Reyes, C. "Prensa Ecuatoriana: Influencia y Hegemonia." *Opiniones Latinoamericanas,* February 1979.

EGYPT

by Harold A. Fisher

BASIC DATA

Population: 42 million (est.)
Area: 1,000,258 sq. km. (386,200 sq. mi.)
GNP: NA
Literacy Rate: 30%
Language(s): Arabic
Number of Dailies: 17
  Aggregate Circulation: 3,012,000
  Circulation per 1,000: 79
Number of Nondailies: 25
  Aggregate Circulation: 1,338,000
  Circulation per 1,000: 32
Number of Periodicals: 38

Number of Radio Stations: 30
Number of Television Stations: 1
Number of Radio Receivers: 5,275,000 (1977)
  Radio Receivers per 1,000: 125 (1977)
Number of Television Sets: 1.4 million
  Television Sets per 1,000: 33
Total Annual Newsprint Consumption: 75,000
metric tons (1977)
  Per Capita Newsprint Consumption: 2 kg.
(4.4 lb.) (1977)
Total Newspaper Ad Receipts: NA
  As % of All Ad Expenditures: NA

Background & General Characteristics

The Egyptian press dates back over a century and a half and has experienced six distinct phases of development. The country's first paper, *Al Waka'e,* served as a ruler's journal, devoting its news to government and civil service activities. Currently *Al Waka'e* is the government's official journal, publishing new decrees and regulations.

Although the earliest papers were official mouthpieces, public opinion finally pressured Khedive Ismail to permit the publication of truly independent papers. As a result, *Al Ahram* was born as a weekly in 1875, and *Al Watan,* another independent weekly, appeared two years later. The independent papers of this period fought injustices in the political system and even went so far as to attack the Khedive himself and openly encourage popular revolution. Later several openly revolutionary papers joined in the fray.

The revolution against Ottoman domination ended in British occupation, the second phase in the life of the Egyptian press. During this period the press played a decisive role resisting the British and shaping public opinion against the occupation.

During the third period, between the World Wars, the press became highly partisan, reflecting the opposing political forces vying for attention. Considerable press coverage also went to social reforms, such as women's emancipation and the fight against prostitution and narcotics. To survive, a number of papers went underground.

During the pre-Revolution phase (1939–52), the press witnessed the birth of numerous papers and magazines, mostly party organs: *Misr El-Fatah* (1944) for the Misr El-Fatah Party, *Al Assas* (1947) for the Saadist Party, *Sawt El Umaa* (1946) for the Wafd Party and *Akhbar El Yom* (1944), an anti-Wafd organ. The pre-Revolution press again mobilized public opinion against foreign occupation and gave considerable attention to Arab unity and to championing the Palestinian cause. In this period foreign sales of papers fell off sharply, a decline that continued throughout the Revolution.

During the Egyptian Revolution (1952–73), with the suppression of all political parties except the Arab Socialist Union, party papers disappeared. The press suffered heavy censorship from the Nasser government, and foreign news was rigidly restricted. In fact, Nasser did not nationalize the press until

1960, but its spirit had been broken long before by censorship and by the suppression of those that showed any independence, such as the pro-Wafdist *Al Misr*. Thus the Revolution made the press a tool for propagating Nasser's Arab socialism and for rallying the masses to the government's causes.

In the present, sixth phase—since the October (1973) War—press has regained a strong measure of freedom. Press censorship has been lifted, constructive criticism has found its way back into the papers and political issues are again discussed freely. These developments began under the presidency of Anwar Sadat, but not without some problems.

Today, Egypt's newspaper industry exhibits its vitality and some diversity in style and viewpoint. Although the Sadat government owns the majority of the stock in the major papers (at least 51 percent) and exercises considerable influence over their operation, the Egyptian press does not feel strong pressure to follow the governmental line and even carries some gentle criticism.

Since more than 90 percent of Egypt is desert, about 99 percent of her 42 million people live in the valley and delta of the Nile. About one-third of the population lives in large urban centers, Cairo being the most populous with over eight million residents. Nearly all the remainder live in the country's numerous rural villages.

Approximately 90 percent of the populace is Muslim (mostly Sunni), with the remainder predominantly Coptic Christians. Fairly large Greek and Armenian minority communities exist in Cairo and Alexandria.

Arabic is the language of nearly all Egyptians, and the single language has done much to unify the country. A few Berber-speaking villages are found in the western oases. Most educated Egyptians also speak either French or English, often with a preference for the former because of long Egyptian association with France. Government papers and laws are often published both in Arabic and in French. These foreign-language papers also provide daily news and information for the sizeable expatriate communities of Europeans and Americans residing in Egypt.

Primary education is compulsory for all children between six and twelve years of age, and state education through the university level is free of charge. Although about eight million children and adults are enrolled in schools, adult illiteracy still runs high, particularly in the nation's approximately 4,000 rural villages. This illiteracy, estimated to be 69.7 percent overall and over 75 percent in the villages, keeps circulation of newspapers low in the rural areas. However, there is a good amount of group readership of papers—a literate reading to illiterates—found there. Newspaper and magazine circulation is thus heaviest among the educated urban elite.

Under President Anwar Sadat's predecessor, Gamal Abdul Nasser, socialism prevailed, and wealthy landowners, businesspeople and manufacturers were stripped of much of their financial power by land and wealth redistribution. President Sadat, on the other hand, encouraged individual enterprise so that today there is a small elite of the wealthy and a growing middle class with some purchasing power. The latter includes many of the country's numerous civil servants and members of a rapidly growing professional class.

All of the largest, most significant newspapers, nondailies and periodicals are published in Arabic, Egypt's official and principal language. But other linguistic communities are well represented, too. Of Egypt's 17 dailies, nine are published in Arabic, four in French, two in Greek, and one each in English and Armenian. Among the more important nondailies and periodicals, 28 are published in Arabic, 15 in French, 10 in English and one in Italian, plus nine bilingual (Arabic-French or Arabic-English) and trilingual (Arabic-French-English) publications.

Perhaps the best known religious paper is the monthly *Al-Daoua*, the organ or the Muslim Brotherhood. There are small periodicals, however, that represent the Islamic faith and the Christian churches. Although the Coptic Orthodox and Coptic Evangelical churches are a minority, they have freedom to produce their own publications.

President Sadat allowed party papers to reappear in the 1970s, and political issues have been discussed quite freely in papers. But purely party organs are few because supporters of the small parties lack the funding for regular publication. Those that remain take definite political stances. Among such papers, *Al-Shaab* (The People) serves as the organ of the Socialist Labour Party, *Arev* as the official voice of the Armenian Liberal Democratic Party, and *Misr* as the paper of the Arab Socialist Party. Among the weeklies, the Liberal Socialist Party has its *Al-Ahra*, the Arab Socialist Union its *Al-Hurriya* and the National Progressive Unionist party its *Al-Tuqaddam*.

Egyptian dailies all tend to cover about the same news and give items similar priorities. Yet, there is considerable diversity in their approach and style. Most of the press reflects serious journalistic principles. The largest paper, *Al Akhbar*, employs a popular, lively approach, but it is far from sensational. *Al Gomhouriya* espouses Arab socialist and leftist causes, focusing more on political commentary than on hard news. Some of the periodicals appeal to popular interests, but most aim serious materials at special-interest segments of the public.

Since most Egyptians live along the Nile River or in its delta, readership clusters in those areas. Most magazines and papers are published in Cairo, in the heart of the delta, and in Alexandria, on the Mediterranean coast. Six dailies, five weeklies and 13 of the more important periodicals originate in Alexandria. All the rest—eleven dailies, 20 weeklies and 25 of the most important periodicals—appear in Cairo. The majority of Egyptian newspapers use standard-size format. They employ bold headlines and subheads, often in a different color. Photos are used effectively. Two or three pictures typically take the lead page, while numerous photographs appear on the inside pages. *Al Ahram* typically publishes 16- or 18-page weekday editions, as do the other leading dailies.

Most Alexandrian dailies are afternoon publications: four appear in the evening, one at noon and just one in the morning. In Cairo the opposite holds, with eight morning and three evening dailies. All of Egypt's high circulation dailies, *Al Ahram, Al Akhbar* and *Al Gomhouriya*, are morning editions.

Several weekly editions cover Friday, the official Muslim holiday. *Al Ahram*'s Friday edition is *Ahram El Gomaa*, with a circulation of over 700,000. *Al Akhbar*'s weekend newspaper, *Akhbar El Yom*, appears Saturdays in over 750,000 copies. *Al Gomhouriya* publishes a Thursday paper, *Gomhouriyet El Khamis*, in about 200,000 copies.

Until the mid-1950s, the weekly and periodical press actively published illustrated party papers, social or economic journals and illustrated entertainment magazines. During the Revolution, the first two disappeared, but the entertainment magazines survived, with the official political line grafted on.

There are still numerous popular weeklies and periodicals, plus a number of serious professional or special-interest journals. Three illustrated weeklies of general interest in 1979 were *Al-Mussawar* (162,000), *Akher Saa* (183,817) and *Sabah El Kheir* (about 100,000). Popular special interest weeklies include *Hawaa* and *Al Maraa* for women. The politically oriented weekly, *Rose Al-Youssef*, has a large circulation both in Egypt and in the rest of the Middle East. During the presidency of Gamal Abdul Nasser, *Rose Al-Youssef* became guilty of carrying the government's anti-imperialist and restrictive measures too far. More recently, its political commentary has toned down, but its sarcasm and satire remain. A popular entertainment weekly is the *Al-Izaa Wal-Television* (circ. 120,000). *Mickey, Tan Tan* and *Samir* are published for children.

More serious journals include the *Arab Observer* (weekly), the *Middle East Observer* (weekly), *October* (monthly), *Al-Hilal* (a literary monthly), *Al-Fussoul* (monthly), *Deserat Ishterakia* (monthly) and *L'Économiste Egyptien*.

Egypt's three largest papers enjoy daily circulations of well over 400,000. In a considerable drop of circulation, the next three range between 60,000 and 70,000 copies.

10 Largest Newspapers by Circulation

Name	Language	Place of Publication	Circulation
1. *Al Akhbar*	Arabic	Cairo	695,000
2. *Al Ahram*	Arabic	Cairo	410,000
3. *Al Gomhouriya*	Arabic	Cairo	400,000
4. *Al Messaa*	Arabic	Cairo	70,000
5. *Le Journal D'Egypte*	French	Cairo	63,000
6. *Al-Shaab*	Arabic	Cairo	60,000
7. *Phos*	Greek	Cairo	20,000
8. *Egyptian Gazette*	English	Cairo	19,000
9. *Le Progrès Egyptien*	French	Cairo	15,000
10. *Barid Al-Charikat*	Arabic	Alexandria	15,000

After another drop, the next four only claim circulations between 15,000 and 20,000.

Unquestionably, the three most influential papers are *Al Ahram, Al Akhbar* and *Al Gomhouriya*. All have high circulations, all are similar in content, all treat stories with about the same priority. But each has its special sphere of influence and appeal. *Al Akhbar* has the highest circulation, and its appeal is popular, light-hearted, sometimes bordering on the sensational. It claims students, bureaucrats, housewives and professionals among its readership. *Al Ahram* is more a "newspaper of record," reporting fully on official events. It is also much more serious in its approach. Its commentary is geared to the intellectuals, and it has its greatest strength among the educated, government officials, business and university people. *Al Gomhouriya* is at the opposite end of the spectrum, appealing to the villager, to workers and to the less educated. Since before the Revolution, it has tended to stress leftist ideological and political goals, while the latter two focus more on straight news.

Egypt's most elite newspaper is *Al Ahram*. Its excellent coverage of foreign and national news, its attention to social issues and the arts, its insightful editorial commentary and its production quality have justified the paper's claim to be "the newspaper of the Arab world." Its editors verify all news items before publication to avoid rumor or false news. Its format and approach are serious and businesslike. Its news analyses, editorials, commentary and features are among the best in the Arab world. Its cartoons convey incisive political views cleverly. As Egypt's most prestigious and authoritative paper, *Al Ahram,* sets the pace for serious, elite journalism for the entire Middle East.

Economic Framework

As a developing country, Egypt is far from wealthy. Its only fertile soil is the narrow strip bordering the Nile and its delta, where cotton, onions, wheat, maize, millet, rice and sugar cane form the chief crops. Save for recently discovered oil reserves, there are few mineral deposits. In its recent history, the country has been bankrupted by four wars with Israel. Until 1973 socialism prevailed, and industry suffered. Under Sadat, however, foreign investment was encouraged, and the nation embarked on a development plan. But help did not arrive quickly enough,

and by the late 1970s inflation, huge debts, an adverse balance of payments, food imports and a burgeoning population combined to produce severe economic difficulties. About the same time, other Arab nations were cutting off relations with Egypt because of Sadat's peace initiatives with Israel. Consequently, annual per capita income has remained low (less than US $250) and individual purchasing power weak.

National economic problems and low individual purchasing power have coupled with the nation's low literacy rate to restrict both purchases of newspapers and television sets and attendance at the cinema. Nonetheless, the media exercise a tremendous influence on the Egyptian people. Radio was a particularly effective political tool during Nasser's rule, and it remains so today, especially among the millions of village dwellers. Though the cinema has been mainly an entertainment medium, radio and television have always been tools used by the government to arouse loyalty and nationalist fervor. Newspapers on the other hand have had a degree of autonomy. They are considered a "fourth authority" by some.

Today papers discuss political matters freely and gently criticize government, but they never openly oppose it. In terms of popularity and credibility among the masses, radio is most important, followed by dailies (especially *Al Gomhouriya*) and a few weeklies. Newspapers exercise the greatest influence in the urban areas, while radio reigns in the villages.

Most papers are produced by the five big publishing houses. The Dar El Hilal Press Organization produces *Al Mussawar, Hawaa, El Hilal* and some children's weeklies and popular monthlies. The Rose El-Youssef Press does not publish a daily, but the popular weekly of the same name as well as the weekly *Sabah El Kheir*. The Al Ahram Press Organization publishes *Al Ahram, Ahram El Gomaa, Al Ahram El-Ektesady* (an economic journal), *Al Maarifa* (a weekly) and women's, economic, political, and children's magazines. The Al Akhbar Publishing House produces *Al Akhbar, Akhbar El Yom* (Saturdays) and *Akher Saa,* an illustrated weekly. The Dar El Tahrir Press Organization publishes *Al Gomhouriya* and its Thursday special paper, *Al Messaa* (Egypt's largest evening daily), two French dailies (*Le Progrès* and *Le Journal d'Egypte*) and the *Egyptian Gazette* (English). All these publishing houses operate as separate entities and compete with one another commercially.

Most papers circulate in the urban areas, either along the north-south axis of the Nile, along the Suez Canal or along the Mediterranean shore. Papers are delivered by air, rail and road transport.

Egypt must import all the newsprint that it consumes. In 1978 it imported 75,000 metric tons of newsprint, or an average of about two kilograms per person. Import of newsprint is under government control.

Egypt, particularly Cairo, is now the publishing center of the Middle East, and many of the presses are fully up-to-date. *Al Ahram,* for example, uses computers to store data and to feed and control the photo typesetting and hot metal printing processes, a computerized photo-composing system, photopolymer plates and facsimile transmission and reception of text and photos from all over the world. It microfilms all issues of its papers. The Al Ahram Management and Computer Center also provides commercial research services for companies desiring them.

Press Laws

The 1971 Constitution of the Arab Republic of Egypt upholds individual rights and freedoms. Article 47 guarantees freedom of individual opinion and the right to publicize such opinion verbally, in writing, by photography or by other means. It recognizes the vital importance of constructive self-criticism to the national structure.

Article 48 states:

Freedom of the press, printing, publication and mass media shall be guaranteed. Censorship of newspapers is forbidden.... In a state of emergency or in time of war, a limited censorship may be imposed on the newspapers, publications and mass media in matters related to public safety or purposes of national security in accordance with the law.

In 1974 President Sadat ended the censorship restrictions in effect during the Revolution except on military matters affecting the state security.

In 1975, under Decree Number Four, he established the Higher or Supreme Press Council. The decree states:

The Egyptian press is an independent national institution [which] takes a role in serving the popular powers, in achieving the goals and objectives of the society, and in public surveillance through the free word and constructive criticism under the supervision of the Supreme Press Council.

The Press Council is under the chairmanship of the First Secretary of the Arab Socialist Union. Legally, all publications in Egypt come under the control of this Higher Press Council.

A little later in July 1975 the Arab Socialist Union established the Charter of the Press Honour, which states that the Egyptian press is "responsible for defending the country, respecting the society morals and values, protecting liberty, supporting democratic socialism and maintaining national unity."

In 1978 President Sadat abolished the Ministry of Culture and Information, which had owned and controlled all newspapers up to that time. However, all the major papers remained under government ownership.

The Press Law of July 1980 provided the major papers more freedom through a liberalization of the press organizations. The government, however, continues to hold 51 percent ownership in newspapers under a new Shura (Advisory) Council. Employees of the papers have first option to hold the remaining 49 percent of the stocks in their papers, with a set limit on the amount any one employee may own.

According to Egyptian Press Law, destructive criticism, defamation, libel, sensation in sex or in crime news, indecency, obscenity, sedition, treason and invasion into personal and family affairs are forbidden. Public prosecution for such offenses is headed by the attorney general. The courts in Egypt, however, are essentially free from the administrative and legislative branches of government.

Censorship

The Egyptian press has undergone considerable repression and censorship, first at the hands of colonial overlords and later from the Revolutionary government. In the late 19th century newspapers were restricted severely by the British colonial government. For nearly two years during the British occupation of 1882–1919, most Egyptian newspapers were closed down. After World War I, British censorship was lifted, but was imposed again during World War II.

The 1952 Revolution abolished the monarchy and suppressed political parties, causing all party papers to close. Then the military officers who had seized power established their own publishing house (Dar Al Tahrir), which founded the daily *Al Gomhouriya* in 1953. The same year, President Naguib officially banned all party papers and increased press censorship. Colonel Nasser tried to lift this censorship when he emerged as president in 1954, but the freed press became so outspoken that he quickly reimposed restrictions. All during Nasser's regime, censorship was periodically imposed; severe limitations were set during each of the four wars with Israel. In 1954, when the paper *Al Misr* openly criticized Nasser for usurping the rights of the people, the Revolutionary Command Council revoked its publishing license, closed it down and tried and sentenced its publishers to 10-15 years in prison. In 1960 Law Number 156 was passed which regulated press affairs and transferred the ownership of the Al Ahram, Akhbar El Yom, Rose El-Youssef and Dar El Hilal Press organizations to the Arab Socialist Union. During the Revolution, censorship and a monopoly political party discouraged diversity among papers. After the October War in 1973, censorship was lifted and the Egyptian press began a new era of relative freedom.

State-Press Relations

During the Revolution, the media were owned and controlled by the Ministry of Culture and Information. In 1975 President Anwar Sadat created the Higher Press Council mentioned above, making the press an independent national institution or "fourth authority." Three years later, Sadat abolished the Ministry of Culture and Information, but kept the major papers under government ownership.

Since 1974 the government has eased press restrictions. Columnists have debated over the need for political parties, have criticized Nasser, have discussed student and popular discontent and have even investigated official corruption. Nondailies have been more outspoken than the dailies. Party papers sprang up again in the mid-1970s. But there have been limits. Theoretically, journalists have full rights to criticize the government openly, but in practice such criticism remains gentle and constructive, and it has taken the press some time to understand fully just where these limits lie. The Progressive

Party's weekly *Al Ahali* was seized for too much antidemocratic content. Most party papers failed, however, because of financial difficulties.

As one authority points out, the Egyptian press is not by any means an independent Fourth Estate. When Muhammad Heikal, the most powerful journalist under President Nasser and then the editor of *Al Ahram,* spoke out too strongly against Sadat's policy in 1974, the president gently took his power away by offering Heikal the position of personal press secretary, a role Heikal declined. Although President Sadat has verbally attacked his critics publicly, he has not imprisoned or banned them as Nasser had done. In 1973, for example, when a number of journalists were suspended, they continued to receive their salaries. When they were reinstated, Sadat explained his actions by saying that he sought a dedicated press.

President Sadat has consistently held that position to this day. He endorses press freedom, but he wants a responsible press. In 1977 he told the People's Assembly that "the press is the property of the people and will remain so." His attitude has been that the press needs to be restrained—ideally by itself.

Perhaps the most obvious example of editorial influence on government policies occurred during Muhammad Heikal's editorship of *Al Ahram.* President Nasser sought his advice, and Heikal's weekly column "Bisuraha" ("Speaking Frankly") was a barometer of official attitudes, a forum in which Heikal occasionally disagreed with government policy and a platform through which he influenced Nasser's decision-making.

After Anwar Sadat became president in 1970, newspaper suspensions were few. The weekly *Sabah El Kheir* was seized briefly in 1975. In 1978 several issues of the Progressive Party's *Al Ahali* were banned. The next year an issue of the leftist paper *Al Taquaddam* was confiscated, as well as the paper's presses and office equipment. But usually more subtle pressures have been employed; for example, in 1977 when the political weekly *Rose Al-Youssef* became too radical in its support of popular disaffection, its editor was replaced by another more favorable to official views. About the same time, government pressure forced the Al Ahram Publishing House to close down the Marxist monthly *Al Talia* for a similar editorial line.

In 1978 President Sadat's internal policies and peace initiatives with Israel resulted in problems and at least one disaster for the press. The editor of *Al Ahram,* Youssef El Sebai, was assassinated by those who opposed the Camp David accords. In a referendum, Sadat got power to ban outspoken critics from writing in the press. Several journalists were subsequently banned, among them Mustafa Amin of *Al Akhbar* who had criticized members of the People's Assembly for joining Sadat's new program without knowing its contents. Muhammad Heikal was effectively silenced by being prohibited from foreign travel. Five journalists were tried for publishing materials that allegedly had helped instigate the 1977 riots against rising food costs. Several other journalists living in Egypt, in other Arab countries and in Europe were investigated and condemned. President Sadat said that his anger with these accused journalists was not a matter of press freedom—and certainly no journalist was put behind bars—but a matter of positive support for Egypt, particularly in the foreign media. By October 1978 the president had abolished the Ministry of Culture and Information and had promised full freedom of the press.

Under Sadat the government's most effective means of controlling the press was either suspension or removal of offending journalists. It assured its control by owning the majority of the stock in the publishing houses.

Attitude Toward Foreign Media

In 1974, when President Sadat ended censorship of the Egyptian press, he also eliminated the requirement that foreign correspondents submit their stories for censorship prior to dispatching them.

The government under Sadat generally welcomed and encouraged the foreign press. There were a few isolated incidents involving foreign correspondents during the past decade. In 1977, for example, the *Guardian* correspondent was expelled. On the whole, however foreign correspondents have been able to enter Egypt freely and have had open access to all information except that on sensitive military matters.

Some of Egypt's smaller papers are published by individuals in their own cultural language (Greek, Armenian), but all such publishers are Egyptian citizens. Egyptian law requires that all property must be owned by bona fide citizens.

The Egyptian people have long been under strong foreign influences. The first paper, *Al Waka'e,* was published as a propaganda device by Mohammad Aly. Some of the other early papers were used in a propaganda war against Khedive Ismail. Newspapers established out of literary, commercial, political or personal motives soon found themselves either mouthpieces for the colonial French or English or as tools of the opposition. During the Revolution, Gamal Abdul Nasser used the press to win converts in other Arab countries to his socialistic ideas.

Egyptian journalists have long been active in international organizations such as the International Press Institute (IPI) and the International Institute of Communications (IIC). The IPI has frequently intervened with government on behalf of Egyptian journalists and newspapers. In 1979, for instance, the IPI expressed concern over prosecutions against a number of journalists.

As a leader of the Third World, Egypt has supported a balanced flow of world information and the idea of a Non-Aligned News Agency pool. The Middle East News Agency (MENA) has worked closely with other Third World news agencies to provide an alternative to the Western services, while at the same time cooperating with the Western "Big Five." The Coordination Committee of the Non-Aligned News Agency held its initial meeting in Cairo early in 1977, and in that year MENA was second only to the Yugoslav agency Tanjug in the amount of stories contributed to the pool.

News Agencies

Egypt's only news agency, the Middle East News Agency (MENA), began operations in February 1956. It was established as a joint creation of Cairo's largest publishing houses just before the Suez crisis to counter Western agencies' biases. The founders also wanted to improve dissemination of Egyptian national news. MENA was taken over by the Egyptian government in 1962, when the Revolutionary Council assumed control of newspapers. In contrast to other Arab national news services, MENA developed an international capability. By the late 1970s MENA had a staff of over 300 journalists and offices in every other Arab country until Sadat's peace initiatives with Israel forced the shutdown of some of them.

MENA's Arabic, French and English newscasts have run for 18 hours per day. It has correspondents in all the principal foreign capitals and agreements with the news agencies of France, England, Iran, Saudi Arabia, the Philippines, East Germany, Qatar and Oman to transmit their copy over its own network. It exchanges television materials with ten Arab and three Western organizations and photographs with 21 agencies.

Ten foreign news agencies had bureaus in Cairo in 1980: AFP (France), EFE (Spain), ANSA (Italy), ADN (East Germany), Reuters (U.K.), BTA (Bulgaria), dpa (West Germany), Kyodo Tsushin (Japan), and AP and UPI (U.S.).

Electronic News Media

Egyptian radio broadcasts programs to Egyptians in eight languages, and has foreign services outside the country in 30 languages. It is the most important information medium to the villagers. There are several services designed for the Egyptian populace, among them the Main or General Service Program, the European or Second Program, People's Service, Sudan Corner, the Music Program and the Alexandria Domestic Service. All offer a good proportion of news. About 18 percent of the General Service programs are news-related. The Second Program is noted for its excellent informational features. The People's Service is devoted to a heavy diet of internal news and information.

In 1970 President Nasser developed objectives for the Broadcasting Service that included the concept of ethical news broadcasting and of meeting the people's daily needs. Nasser made Egyptian broadcasting what some have called a "mobilization system" to reach the masses and to propagate official policies. President Sadat has continued the service much as his predecessor envisioned it.

Television, first developed in 1960, broadcasts about 20 hours per day on two VHF channels. Both have schedules that include a variety of news and commentary programs. The news, news interpretation, press reviews and political commentaries occupy about 15 percent of the schedule on both television programs. Television, like radio, is considered a mobilization tool.

Education & Training

Egyptian universities have long had journalism training programs. A degree program in journalism was founded at the American University in Cairo in 1935 and at Cairo University just four years later. Both began offering degrees in mass communication studies in the 1970s. Until recently, however, university training has been theoretically oriented. It was not until the mid-1970s that the American University in Cairo began offering practical training in broadcast journalism and that Cairo University initiated courses that give students direct experience with broadcast program planning, writing and production. Both universities now offer undergradute and graduate degrees in journalism and mass communication.

Meanwhile, many of the older professional journalists and broadcasters have been trained in workshop-type institutes or as apprentices. Until the late 1950s, Egypt had few such institutes. The government first founded a radio institute and then, in 1963, it started a TV training institute that has offered a variety of courses, including news writing and production. In Egypt radio and TV reporters are regarded not as journalists, but as government officials.

Summary

Egypt's press, established over a century ago, is well developed. Many fine nondailies and periodicals supplement daily newspapers. The press has gone through six phases of growth, during which it has repeatedly faced censorship and oppression, first from colonial rulers and later from the national government. The press was nationalized during the presidency of Gamal Abdul Nasser.

President Anwar Sadat lifted censorship in 1974 and a year later set up the Supreme Press Council to supervise the press. In 1978, he abolished the Ministry of Culture and Information, but kept major papers under government ownership. He issued a decree in 1980 that liberalized the organization of major newspapers and arranged to transfer the government's majority ownership from the defunct Arab Socialist Union to a new Advisory Council. Government ownership of the majority of shares in the press organizations appears likely to continue for some time.

Egypt's press, like those of most Middle Eastern countries, is subject to changes in the area's political climate. However, the Egyptian press should continue to thrive under Sadat's successor, Hosni Mubarak.

Readership is rising steadily. If the press continues to be supportive of the government, it could play a key role in national development and should continue to gain increased freedom.

CHRONOLOGY

1975	Sadat establishes new Higher Press Council to supervise press.
1977	Law bans Marxist political activity, including news reporting. Sadat makes clear public control over press is necessary and stresses importance of free, but responsible press. Party newspapers allowed to appear but disappear within few months because of financial difficulties.
1978	Sadat abolishes Ministry of Culture and Information, but major papers remain under government ownership.

Youssef El Sebai, editor of *Al Ahram*, assassinated by opponents of Sadat's peace initiatives with Israel.

1979	Several journalists arrested for strong opposition to government policies. Two jailed for antifeminist articles. Middle East News Agency boycotted by other Arab countries in retaliation for Sadat's peace moves with Israel. Several Arab countries, including Saudi Arabia, ban all Egyptian media.
1981	Sadat assassinated.

BIBLIOGRAPHY

Boyd, Douglas A. "Egyptian Radio: Tool of Political and National Development." *Journalism Monographs,* no. 48, February 1977.

"Egypt Relaxes." *IPI Report,* April 1977, p. 2.

"IPI in Action: Egypt." *IPI Report,* July 1979, p. 9.

Issawi, Charles. *Egypt in Revolution: An Economic Analysis.* London, 1963.

"MENA Closures Deplored." *IPI Report,* May 1979, p. 3.

"Middle East: Egypt." *IPI Report,* January 1973, p. 8.

Ministry of Information, State Information Service. Arab Republic of Egypt. *Yearbook, 1977.* Cairo, 1977.

Nasser, Munir K. *Press, Politics and Power: Egypt's Heikal and Al Ahram.* Ames, Iowa, 1979.

"Press Freedom Report, 1975: Egypt." *IPI Report,* December 1975, p. 14.

"The Press Under Pressure: Egypt." *IPI Report,* April/May 1974, p. 14.

Rugh, William A. *The Arab Press.* Syracuse, 1979.

"Six are Banned, but Quizzed." *IPI Report,* September 1978, p. 2.

Talaat, Shahinaz. "Egyptian Mass Media." Unpublished paper, American University in Cairo, 1975.

"Will Words Regain Freedom in Sadat's New Press Council?" *IPI Report,* October 1975, p. 4.

"World Press Freedom Review, 1978: Egypt." *IPI Report,* January 1979, p. 4.

"World Press Freedom Review, 1979: Egypt." *IPI Report,* December 1979, p. 4.

"The World Press Score: Egypt." *IPI Report,* February 1973, p. 7.

EL SALVADOR*

by John Spicer Nichols and Charles T. Salmon

BASIC DATA

Population: 4.7 million
Area: 20,935 sq. km. (8,083 sq. mi.)
GNP: 7.4 billion colons (US$2.96 billion) (1979)
Literacy Rate: 62%
Language(s): Spanish
Number of Dailies: 13
  Aggregate Circulation: NA
  Circulation per 1,000: NA
Number of Nondailies: NA
  Aggregate Circulation: NA
  Circulation per 1,000: NA

Number of Periodicals: NA
Number of Radio Stations: 60
Number of Television Stations: 5
Number of Radio Receivers: 3 million (est.)
  Radio Receivers per 1,000: 638 (est.)
Number of Television Sets: 300,000 (est.)
  Television Sets per 1,000: 64 (est.)
Total Annual Newsprint Consumption: NA
  Per Capita Newsprint Consumption: NA
Total Newspaper Ad Receipts: NA
  As % of All Ad Expenditures: NA

Background & General Characteristics

Nearly 10,000 people were killed in El Salvador during 1980 in political violence hedging on full-scale civil war. In the beginning days of 1981, the leftist guerrillas launched a "final offensive" that failed to overthrow the ruling military-civilian junta but claimed thousands more lives. As the result of the fighting, normal operation of all sectors of Salvadoran society, including the mass media, had ceased, and with the rapid escalation of violence and the growing complexity of the problems underlying the violence, there seemed little likelihood that the country would return to normality.

Although a virtual blackout of news about military operations and the political dynamics was in effect in El Salvador, the local news media were filled with the carnage. Television newscasts routinely aired scenes such as a housewife calmly hosing the blood off the sidewalk in front of her home after a daylight assassination, and newspapers displayed banner headlines such as "50 More Killed Yesterday!" Salvadoran and foreign journalists attempting to cover what was becoming a major world crisis were the prime targets of both the security forces and an assortment of terrorist groups. "If you are not on the leftists' death list, you are surely on the rightists' list," said a Salvadoran journalist. "There is no middle ground in this country." Scores of domestic and foreign journalists were arrested, kidnapped, expelled from the country, wounded or killed in 1980. The offices of foreign news agencies and local media were repeatedly ransacked, machine-gunned or bombed. Consequently, modern journalism—in which important public affairs are soberly and dispassionately reported and analyzed to enlighten the population and clarify issues for national decision-making—was impossible to practice in El Salvador.

*Research for this chapter was funded in part by the College of the Liberal Arts, Pennsylvania State University (Thomas F. Magner, associate dean for Research and Graduate Studies). The authors also wish to thank Professor R. Thomas Berner, Penn State, for his considerable assistance in this project.

NOTE: Most published statistics on the media in El Salvador have been overtaken by recent events there. The above were believed accurate in 1980.

The bloodletting is largely the result of long-festering social and economic problems. Rigid class structure and maldistribution of national wealth is commonplace in Latin America, but the inequities in El Salvador are extreme even by regional standards. For generations, El Salvador has been tightly controlled by a tiny landowning and business elite, known as "the 14 families." Although the actual number of families in the Salvadoran oligarchy is probably a few hundred, the wealth still is extremely concentrated. The top five percent of the population receives 38 percent of the income, and the bottom 40 percent receives two percent.

More important is control of the land, the most valuable resource in the largely agricultural economy. El Salvador is the smallest and most overcrowded nation on the American mainland—more than four million people live in just over 8,000 square miles. Until 1980, less than two percent of the population owned between 60 and 85 percent of that scarce land, and as a result, most Salvadorans have traditionally earned subsistence incomes by working on the large plantations of the oligarchy. Unemployment, disease, malnutrition and illiteracy are endemic, especially in the rural areas.

A long succession of military governments ruling in behalf of the so-called 14 families have firmly enforced the status quo and undercut any attempts at significant social and economic reform. Their record of repression, corruption and incompetence also was extreme by regional standards. After the reform-minded Christian Democratic party was blocked from power in election frauds in 1972 and 1977, many Salvadorans, particularly the rural poor, concluded that armed insurrection was the only remaining course of action. Increased activity by Marxists guerrillas who, in comparison to revolutionary groups in neighboring Nicaragua and Guatemala, were unusually ruthless and arbitrary in their use of terror, only brought violent retaliation from the government security forces and private armies hired by the oligarchy.

In the wake of the Nicaraguan revolution in 1979, a group of young army officers encouraged by the United States overthrew the government of General Carlos Humberto Romero and announced sweeping reforms and free elections in the hope that they would prevent all-out revolution. Nationalization of the banks and an ambitious land reform program were decreed. The reforms not only failed to check the violence but further polarized the political forces in El Salvador. The ruling military-civilian junta that eventually evolved after the coup had the support of neither the dogmatic left or rabid right and was powerless to stem the chaos.

The assassination of Archbishop Oscar Arnulfo Romero in March 1980 best demonstrates the viciousness of the struggle. The activist archbishop, who had been critical of the violence and counterviolence, particularly by the government, was shot by right-wing gunmen in front of his church altar while performing a funeral mass. At the archbishop's funeral, another 35 Salvadorans were killed by gunfire and the subsequent stampede probably triggered by leftist gunmen.

The repression of the press in the 1980s is not unique in the history of El Salvador. The bloody rule of General Maximiliano Hernández Martinez, beginning in 1932, set the standard followed in varying degrees since. General Hernández overthrew a constitutional but inept civilian government following a communist-led peasant uprising that endangered the landed oligarchy. He crushed the revolt, but more than 30,000 Salvadorans died in the process. Those newsmen who dared criticize the general's tactics were lucky if they were only fined or jailed. Many were summarily shot. By 1934, when Hernández was "re-elected" in balloting supervised by the army, all of Salvadoran news media were dutifully supporting him.

The army, backed by the conservative economic elite, ruled without interruption thereafter. The resulting monolithic political system, in which any opposition was fiercely repressed, prevented the development of a highly politicized press common elsewhere in Central America. Most Salvadoran newspapers were founded as profit-making enterprises and not as voices of political causes. The limited opposition found refuge in the Catholic Church, the only institution with some insulation against government repression. The church became the forum for grievances of the poor, and by the 1970s a sizable percentage of the priests had become radicalized supporters of the leftist revolutionaries. In addition, the early opposition resorted to printing crude handbills and pamphlets on clandestine presses and distributing them hand to hand throughout the countryside. The church media and the underground press continued as important opposition voices in the early 1980s.

In 1980 the national press, although more

San Salvador Dailies (1980)

Newspaper	Circulation in 1979	Director	Founding Date	Description
El Diario de Hoy	86,617 Weekday 109,540 Sunday (audited)	Enrique Altamirano Madriz	1936	AM tabloid; offset
La Prensa Gráfica	76,709 Weekday 121,560 Sunday (audited)	Rosalio Hernández Colorado	1903	AM tabloid
Diario Latino	50,000	Guillermo Machon de la Paz	1890	Midday except Sunday
El Mundo	50,990	Cristobal Igleslas	1967	PM except Sunday; offset
La Crónica del Pueblo	10–20,000	José Napoleón González	1968	PM tabloid; except Sunday
El Independiente	NA	Jorge Pinto Hijo	NA	PM Standard
Diario Oficial	2,100	NA	NA	Official government gazette

politicized than previously, was not carrying the polemical political columns and editorials that frequent newspapers in other Central American countries. About 70 percent of the content of large-circulation dailies was advertising, and the remaining 30 percent—the editorial content—was dominated by sports news, social notes, comics, puzzles and other banalities. Although editions often exceeded 70 pages, no more than two pages were devoted to national news and two pages to international news. "The [Salvadoran] press is an insult to human intelligence," a Salvadoran academic concluded.

Despite the dubious editorial quality, the newspapers had a highly polished physical appearance. Many were composed with computers, printed on high-speed offset presses, had modern typography and design, frequently used color and in comparison to other Central American newspapers were well written and carefully edited.

Seven daily newspapers were being published in San Salvador, the capital city, in 1980.

Six other daily newspapers of limited circulation and importance were published outside of the capital city in 1979. They were: *Diario de Occidente,* published in Santa Ana; *Diario Ahuachapan,* Ahuachapan; *Diario de Oriente,* San Miguel; *Excélsior* and *Heraldo de Sonsonate,* Sonsonate; and *La Tribuna,* Usulutan. Whether they have survived the heavy fighting in the rural areas is unknown. Several nondailies also were published, the most important of which were *El Salvador News-Gazette,* an English-language newspaper, and *Orientación,* weekly newspaper of the Catholic church.

The potential audience for the Salvadoran press is small but proportionately larger than other countries with similar historical background and level of economic development. Almost all Salvadorans are Spanish-speaking *mestizos.* The literacy rate of approximately 62 percent is significantly higher than for the northern neighbors, Guatemala and Honduras, and the terrain permits much easier distribution. Despite these relative advantages, the press has not been particularly significant in most Salvadorans' lives. Compared to coping with economic deprivation and the political chaos, reading a daily newspaper does not seem particularly important. And to the extent that Salvadorans do use media content, it is mostly music and other entertainment—not news and public affairs—via cheap transistor radios.

Economic Framework

Reflecting El Salvador's strongly capitalistic orientation, the vast majority of the media are privately owned, usually by family businesses. The only major exceptions are the official gazette, one radio station, and two educational television channels operated by the government, and one radio station and a few publications owned by the Catholic church. Also reflecting the economy, ownership of the media, particularly broadcasting, is extremely concentrated. One man, Boris Eserski, a Salvadoran citizen living in Miami, owns two television channels and 48 percent of the third commercial channel, in addition to the controlling interest in one of the largest radio networks.

The media traditionally have been very profitable businesses, owing to high revenues and unusually low costs. Most income came from generous amounts of advertising placed by major business interests and, to a lesser degree, the government. On the other side of the ledger, the owners have had few labor costs. In 1980 most newspaper reporters were paid about $120 per month and supplemented their incomes with bribes from their news sources—again, primarily business and government. In addition, lenient tax laws prohibit taxes on all printing operations, including newspapers, and the importation of production equipment, newsprint and other supplies.

However, in 1980 and 1981 the Salvadoran economy was on the verge of collapse. Leftist guerrillas were attempting to destroy the economy as a major part of its military strategy, and the right wing's response compounded the economic damage. As a result, foreign and domestic investment ceased, domestic capital was tucked away in foreign banks, and a large share of the business and technical class fled to Guatemala, Mexico and the United States. Under those conditions, the financial survival of most Salvadoran media was in doubt.

Press Law & Censorship

In 1981, having suspended the constitution and declared a state of seige, the military-civilian junta was ruling under martial law. However, in the unlikely possibility that El Salvador will return to normal constitutional law, the following articles of the 1962 Constitution apply to the national press:

Article 158, first paragraph, states: "Every person may freely express and disseminate his thoughts provided they are not injurious to morals or to the private lives of persons. The exercise of this right shall not be subject to previous examination, censorship, or bond; but anyone who violates the law thereby shall be liable for the offense committed."

Article 158, second paragraph, states: "Propaganda advocating anarchistic or anti-democratic doctrines is prohibited."

Article 158, fourth paragraph, states: "In no event may the press, its accessories, or any other material means devoted to the dissemination of thought be confiscated as an instrument of crime."

Article 157, second paragraph, states: "Neither the clergy nor laymen may engage in political propaganda of any kind based on religious motives or making use of religious beliefs of the people. Likewise, the laws of the state, its government, or public officials may not be criticized in religious rights or sermons in places of worship."

The greatest legal restrictions on the press are provided for in the Law on Defense and Guarantee of Public Order, which was decreed by General Carlos Humberto Romero and approved by the nominal congress in 1978. Under this law, the following individuals who have "committed an offense against the constitutional public order" can be imprisoned for three years: "Those who propagate by the spoken or written word, or by any other means within the country, or send abroad, tendentious or false news or information designed to disrupt the constitutional or legal order, the tranquility or security of the country, the economic or monetary systems, or the stability or public values and property; those who publish such news and information in the mass communication media; and those citizens of El Salvador who, while abroad, disseminate news and information of that kind...."

The ruling junta declared its state of siege on March 6, 1980, and has periodically renewed it ever since. Under the state-of-siege provisions, the Defense Ministry is empowered to censor the press, open personal mail, tap telephone lines, restrict foreign and domestic travel, ban meetings and other associations without a permit, establish curfews, and make arrests and searches without a warrant. Previous Salvadoran governments often have resorted to martial law to rule the country.

State-Press Relations

Despite the array of laws and other government powers to restrict the press, a certain anarchical freedom existed in El Salvador in 1980. The military-civilian junta, having little or no political and popular support and domestically backed only by an army deeply divided between reformist junior officers and hard-line senior officers, was apparently powerless to enforce its policies. The law of terrorism—enforced by both the left-wing guerrillas and the right-wing private armies of the oligarchy—was the only effective means of governing the press. Those news media that were willing to risk terrorist attacks were generally free to criticize their opponents without official censorship.

San Salvador's two leading newspapers, *Diario de Hoy* and *La Prensa Gráfica,* were firmly under the control of and spokesmen for the landed and business elite but also were subject to frequent attacks from the leftists. Both dailies had been seriously damaged by bombs planted by the guerrillas. Many of the papers' editors and staff were threatened, attacked, kidnapped or killed. All of El Salvador's television system and most of the radio stations were in the hands of the right but similarly were attacked. Particularly in the rural areas, the guerrillas seized radio stations long enough to broadcast their manifestos and communiqués.

Although the major media were mostly under the control of the oligarchy, the opposition forces (including both Marxists guerrillas and more moderate opponents) also had considerable access to the media. In 1980 two opposition dailies, *La Crónica de Pueblo* and *El Independiente,* were published in San Salvador. *El Independiente,* a crudely produced afternoon newspaper that was not submitted for censorship, usually was filled with seditious editorial content and paid pronouncements from a variety of leftist opposition groups. Its staff was frequently a target for right-wing hit squads, and in 1980 its printing plant was twice destroyed by incendiary bombs. In both cases, the newspaper continued to publish after contracting other printing facilities. Its newsroom has been attacked with machine guns, and the editor-publisher, Jorge Pinto, a radicalized member of a wealthy Salvadoran family, narrowly escaped several assassination attempts. *La Crónica,* while more moderate in its opposition, also suffered official government repression as well as attacks from clandestine right-wing groups. The Romero government ordered banks not to give credit to and state agencies not to advertise in *La Crónica* and, subsequently, closed it down. Since reopening, the newspaper's offices and the home of its publisher-editor, Dr. José Napoleón González, were bombed. Several of *La Crónica*'s staff were kidnapped and killed.

Probably the most important opposition media in El Salvador were the radio station of the Catholic Church and its various publications, especially *Orientación.* Until his assassination, Archbishop Romero delivered two-hour homilies weekly over YSAX radio, in which he would appeal for basic social and economic reforms, an end to the violence, and respect for other human rights. His radio sermons had the highest ratings in national history. The government responded by prohibiting newscasts, commentaries and cultural programming that it said endangered public order, and organized a boycott of major advertisers. In 1979 and 1980 the studios of YSAX were bombed three times—one attack destroying the facilities. The church station was rebuilt with small donations from parishioners and foreign church groups and returned to the air. In the interim, most parishes sent representatives to tape-record the archbishop's homily each Sunday, and a powerful transmitter in neighboring Costa Rica also broadcast the tapes.

In late 1980 the guerrillas added a clandestine radio transmitter, probably located in Nicaragua, to their already sizable propaganda arsenal of underground newspapers, pamphlets and handbills.

Attitude Toward Foreign Media

Most foreign correspondents would agree that El Salvador was the most dangerous reporting assignment in the world in 1980 and 1981. Correspondents reported the military and political aspects of the story under wartime conditions—with no battle lines to hide behind and little or no protection from the government security forces. In 1980 numerous foreign correspondents were arrested, expelled or wounded, and a few were killed or were missing and presumed dead. Virtually all foreign correspondents received death threats, and many wore bulletproof vests. Several had been kidnapped by guerrillas, taken to secret press conferences, directed to report them favorably and eventually released. Many U.S. correspondents expressed the fear that both the left and the right were attempting to kill them in hopes that their deaths would have an international political impact similar to the execution of ABC-TV newsman Bill Stewart during the Nicaraguan revolution. The danger was so great that representatives of some major news media would no longer return to El Salvador; they reported the story from Mexico City and other regional capitals via telephone contacts with in-country sources.

Before the government lost control, the army was zealous in restricting the importation of leftist publications or others it believed were subversive. In 1980, however, the flow of foreign media into El Salvador seemed to be limited only by finances and threat of violence. Marxist-oriented books and periodicals were readily available in San Salvador along with *The New York Times, Miami Herald,* and an assortment of Spanish-language translations of Hearst magazines. Radio Moscow and Radio Havana were clearly heard and had large audiences. There was a smaller listenership for Voice of America.

News Agencies

The Salvadoran print and broadcast media subscribed to a variety of international news agencies. AP and UPI were most frequently used. Latin-Reuter, AFP, dpa, and ACAN were also used. El Salvador does not have its own news agency.

Electronic News Media

The radio system in El Salvador is the most highly developed in Central America and the most influential news medium in the country. Although almost all radio stations are privately owned commercial operations, the first station in the country and in all of Central America—National Radio of El Salvador (YSS)—was established by the government in 1926 and managed by the chief cabinet officer for Dr. Alfonso Quiñonez Molina, then president of the country. (The station originally operated with the call letters AQM, the president's initials.) By 1979, radio had reached virtually the entire country. Sixty originating stations—only 26 of them located in the capital city—and 21 relay stations were on the air, while the number of radio receivers tripled during the 1970s. An estimated three million receivers were in use, with approximately 90 percent of all Salvadoran homes having at least one.

The vast majority of radio content was normally music—mostly popular fare from the United States, but news and public-affairs programming were fairly good compared to neighboring Central American countries. Channel YSU was one of the most widely listened-to stations in the country, and in addition to its own news programming carried daily feeds from the Voice of America. However, during the guerrilla offensive in 1981 all stations were operating under a news blackout and broadcasting non-stop music.

All private stations are licensed every five years and administered by a special division of the Ministry of Interior. Licenses can be revoked for minor violations of the national telecommunications law, which deals with allocation of frequencies and other technical aspects of broadcasting. Although government threats are said to be frequent, actual license revocations are rare.

Television began in El Salvador in 1956 and—also compared to other Central American countries—was well developed in 1979. The Ministry of Education operated two educational channels developed in the early 1970s with financial support of the United States. These channels, the most advanced in the region, were carrying programming in basic education, advanced technical training, and cultural affairs. All three commercial stations had modern studios, used up-to-date electronic newsgathering equipment and aired regular news and public affairs programming. The news programs tended to dwell on the national violence by frequently using graphic footage of dismembered bodies, but the majority of the content was soap operas and reruns from Mexico, Venezuela and the United States. Approximately 300,000 TV sets were in use in the country, 70 percent of which were located in San Salvador.

Education & Training

Journalism in El Salvador, like other Central American countries, is a low-paying, low-prestige, part-time job, and as a result, journalistic quality and professional standards are very low. Two communication training programs were offered in El Salvador in the late 1970s: a five-year mass communication program at the School of Journalism of the National Autonomous University and a two-year social communication program at the private Central American University. However, virtually none of the graduates entered journalism. In 1980 only three Salvadoran journalists had a university degree in communication, journalism or a related field. Media personnel learn their work on the job or in brief visits to the United States, mostly to observe production techniques.

Summary

Assessing the recent past, predicting the near future of El Salvador and the remnants of its press is extremely difficult. Reflecting the ideological and economic cleavages in the country, the media tend to support either the left-wing or right-wing combatants and are the targets of violent attacks from their opposition. The Salvadoran press has never served the needs of the large majority of the people, but in the early 1980s—with the escalation of violence and the growing tendency by world powers to make El Salvador an international battlefield—journalism is even less relevant to the needs of the impoverished Salvadoran peasants. There appears to be no easy solution to the political and economic problems underlying the violence. Consequently, the only thing certain about El Salvador's future is that the violence will continue, and foreign and domestic journalists attempting to describe, explain or interpret the fighting will continue to die.

CHRONOLOGY

1978 General Carlos Humberto Romero decrees Law on Defense and Guarantee of Public Order, approved by nominal Salvadoran congress. Law restricts written and oral communication that government believes upsets existing political and economic order, and provides severe penalties for offenders.

1979 Young army officers overthrow Romero's right-wing government, form military-civilian junta to carry out sweeping reforms and oversee elections. Three months later, junta collapses, is replaced by another junta dominated by hard-line officers.

1980 Military-civilian junta suspends constitution, declares state of siege, allowing government to censor press, suspend most civil. rights. Archbishop Oscar Arnulfo Romero, human-rights advocate, shot by right-wing gunmen while performing mass. YSAX radio, church station over which Archbishop Romero frequently called for social-economic reform, bombed off air. Rodolfo Dutriz, owner of rightist *La Prensa Gráfica,* severely wounded, his bodyguard killed when left-wing guerrillas open fire on them from speeding car; Dutriz is only one of many Salvadoran journalists killed or wounded by assailants of both left and right.

1981 News blackout in effect as guerrillas launch "final offensive" to overthrow military-civilian junta. Offensive fails to bring down government, but thousands more combatants and innocent civilians killed in fighting. French photojournalist Olivier Rebbot, on assignment for *Newsweek* magazine, shot in chest while covering "final offensive"; fellow photojournalist Harry Mattison, on assignment for *Time* magazine, drapes himself over wounded Rebbot until help arrives; Rebbot dies a month later in U.S. hospital, is one of several foreign correspondents killed, wounded, kidnapped or missing and presumed dead in El Salvador.

BIBLIOGRAPHY

Alisky, Marvin. "The Mass Media in Central America." *Journalism Quarterly* (Fall 1955), pp. 479-86.

Blutstein, Howard I., et al. *Area Handbook for El Salvador.* Washington, D.C., 1971.

Dickey, Christopher. "El Salvador's Shadowy War: Political Center Vanishing as Bullets Fly." *Washington Post,* June 30, 1980, p. 1.

González, José Napoleón. "El Salvador—A Silenced Voice." *Index on Censorship* (November-December 1977), pp. 20-23.

Mayo, John K., Hornik, Robert, and McAnany, Emile. *Educational Reform with Television: The El Salvador Experience.* Palo Alto, Calif., 1976.

Nissen, Beth. "Reporters in Bulletproof Vests." *Columbia Journalism Review* (July-August 1980), pp. 9-10.

Organization of American States. *Report on the Situation of Human Rights in El Salvador.* Washington, D.C., 1978.

Riding, Alan. "El Salvador's Troubles May be Entering a New Phase." *The New York Times,* October 21, 1979, p. 2E.

_____. "El Salvador's Junta Unable to Halt the Killing." *The New York Times,* March 23, 1980, p. 4E.

ETHIOPIA

by Harold A. Fisher

BASIC DATA

Population: 29,705,000 (1978)
Area: 1,223,600 sq. km. (472,435 sq. mi.)
GNP: 8.29 billion birr (US$3.98 billion) (1979)
Literacy Rate: 10%
Language(s): Amharic
Number of Dailies: 3 (1979)
  Aggregate Circulation: 43,000
  Circulation per 1,000: 1.4
Number of Nondailies: 4 (1979)
  Aggregate Circulation: 31,000
  Circulation per 1,000: 1
Number of Periodicals: 8

Number of Radio Stations: 2
Number of Television Stations: 1
Number of Radio Receivers: 215,000 (1979)
  Radio Receivers per 1,000: 143
Number of Television Sets: 25,000 (1979)
  Television Sets per 1,000: 0.8
Total Annual Newsprint Consumption: 1,000 metric tons
  Per Capita Newsprint Consumption: .04 kg. (.09 lb.) (1978)
Total Newspaper Ad Receipts: NA
  As % of All Ad Expenditures: NA

Background & General Characteristics

Ethiopia's press may be characterized as small, weak and a mouthpiece of the government. In recent years, since Marxist and socialist influences have become predominant in Ethiopia, the press has taken on all the characteristics that mark a controlled and owned propaganda arm of communist government.

Ethiopia is a rural society, where illiteracy still runs at 90 percent among the general populace and at least 94 percent in the rural areas. Shortly after Emperor Haile Selassie was overthrown, the socialist government launched a crash literacy program. However, amidst the ravages of civil strife and with the population growth rate averaging over 2.5 percent per annum, little progress has been made toward eradicating illiteracy. While education is free, there simply are not enough schools or trained teachers to meet the basic educational needs of the country's numerous children. Except for the Amharic areas, which were favored during the reign of the Emperor, there are very few schools in the rural districts. Most primary and secondary schools have hardly functioned since they were nationalized in 1975; since September 1976, most have been controlled by local urban dwellers' associations and peasant associations with little appreciation of the importance of education. As a result, in the 1976-77 academic year, there were only 4,853 primary and secondary schools, with 33,252 teachers, for a nation with a population of about 29 million. Because the universities and teacher training colleges have operated only intermittently since 1975, few new teachers have been certified to meet the nation's urgent educational needs.

The socialist revolution has virtually eliminated the former support infrastructure for education by expelling missionary educators and by seizing the lands of the Ethiopian Orthodox Church during the land reform program. Today there is little affluence in Ethiopia; the growth of small private industries was halted by the revolution, and even those farmers who benefitted from the land distribution lack the capital, equipment and expertise to operate much above the subsistence level. Consequently, in 1979 half of Ethiopian farming was still at subsistence level, and lack of incentive, poor agricultural techniques and adverse weather conditions in the form of an extended drought were causing the abandonment of some 200,000 hectares every year.

Private industry, still in its fledgling stage,

was dealt a heavy blow by the Marxist regime. Along with banks and insurance companies, most private industries were nationalized in 1976. Now confined mostly to food processing and manufacture of textiles, it contributes less than six percent to the total national income.

The nation has been further crippled since 1975 by the brutality of the revolutionary Marxist government and by secessionist wars in Eritrea. The government has ruthlessly eliminated or caused to flee thousands of its political enemies, including many of the country's best educated and capable persons. The wars have brought death to thousands of other potential leaders, have divided the nation's limited resources and have nearly destroyed the nation's economy.

Ethiopia is densely populated, with nearly 70 persons per square mile. Because parts of the terrain are mountainous, deserts or barren plateau, the populace is concentrated in rather small areas. No adequate transportation system exists, so isolation of communities remains a severe problem. This, combined with the high rural illiteracy and subsistence economy, confines newspaper circulation almost entirely to the urban areas. There are only two cities of significant size: Addis Ababa, the capital, has about one and one-quarter million inhabitants, and Asmara, in the north, has about 300,000 residents.

The distribution of tribal and ethnic groupings has always presented a problem for Ethiopia. Despite the nation's geographic isolation, these lingual groupings have remained diverse, with Nilotic tribes located in the south and west, the Gallas and the Amharrs (the ruling tribe under Haile Selassie I) in the central plateau regions, the Somalis in the east, and the Tigre and Tigrinya and Arab-speaking peoples in the north. This pattern has been overlaid with two expatriate languages, Italian and English, neither of which has had the influence to become the lingua franca of the country. Much of recent education, however, has been in English, leading to the development of an English-language press for the educated urban elite.

Ethiopia's communications and media systems have never been fully developed. During the rule of Emperor Haile Selassie, the nation's media were among the world's most oppressed. Journalists could be fined as much as one-third of their monthly pay for even a trivial offense, such as printing a picture of a prize-winning bull on the same page as a

minister's speech. Young liberal intellectuals were unable to gain access to the press. Nonetheless, there were some hopeful signs. In 1963, for example, the government permitted the operation of a powerful shortwave radio station, Radio Voice of the Gospel, on Ethiopian soil and placed relatively few restrictions on its operations. The military government that took over after the Emperor's overthrow in 1974 first allowed considerable press freedom. But as it tightened its grip on political power in the country in 1975, all vestiges of press freedom began to disappear. Today the media have become mere official propaganda tools, and even loyal journalists are being harassed and ill treated.

The earliest development of the press in Ethiopia was spurred by external influences on the otherwise isolated country. Italian influences in Asmara led to the publication of two Italian-language dailies, the *Giornale Dell'Eritrea* and *Quotidians*, for a period of time. English and American influences resulted in the publication of two English-language dailies, the *Ethiopian Herald* and the *Voice of Ethiopia*, in Addis Ababa. For a time a French daily, *Addis Soir*, also appeared in the capital. In 1970 five dailies in three languages, with a total circulation of 37,000, were being published in Addis Ababa, with four others in three languages in Asmara. All five of the dailies in Addis Ababa were published in an expatriate language. Thus, foreign residents in the country accounted for a high percentage of the readership.

Today the nation's two leading dailies are published in Addis Ababa. *Addis Zemen* publishes about 37,000 copies in Amharic, the nation's official language. The English-language *Ethiopian Herald,* with a daily circulation of about 6,000, also originates in the capital. Together these two papers account for about 90 percent of all the country's circulation of dailies. A Tigrigna-language daily, *Hebret*, circulates about 2,000 copies from its Asmara base. A small Arabic daily, *Al-Wahda* (circulation about 1,000), also originates in Asmara.

Ethiopian newspapers have always been interested in the serious side of the news. Little sensationalism marks their pages. There have been good editorials, particularly in the *Ethiopian Herald.* However, official views have seldom been opposed, since the papers have either been controlled by or under the close surveillance of the government. Dailies have carried a high proportion of international news. But because of the weak internal communication networks, news of the provinces has been sparse in the dailies.

All the dailies are small, typically four or six pages in length. The *Ethiopian Herald* has appeared in a six-column broadsheet format, with a daily editorial by a representative of the Ministry of Information and a generous amount of commercial retail advertising. Generally, photographs have been few in number.

The Ministry of Information and National Guidance publishes all four of the country's weeklies in Addis Ababa. The largest is the Amharic *Yezareitu Ethiopia*, with a circulation of about 30,000. A smaller Amharic weekly, *Ethiopia*, is published in 2,000 copies. The other two weeklies also report low circulations: the Arabic *Al-Alem* publishes 2,500 copies, and the Oromogna *Berisa* circulates about 2,000 copies.

Most of the remaining periodicals are also published by some official arm of the government. The official gazette of laws, orders and notices is *Negarit Gazzetta,* published fortnightly in English and Amharic. The fortnightly Amharic police journal is *Police Ena Ermijaw*. The Ministry of Defense publishes *Wetaderma Alamaw* in Amharic every two weeks. Another fortnightly is the Amharic *Negadras*, published by the Addis Ababa Chamber of Commerce; still another Amharic fortnightly is *Abyotawit Ethiopia*. The leading monthly is the *Birhan Family Magazine*, with 15,000 copies in Amharic. The lone privately published magazine is *Addis Fana*, an Amharic monthly.

Economic Framework

Ethiopia has long been considered one of the world's poorest nations. But the political disruptions of the past decade have brought additional suffering to the country's largely agricultural economy. Production of food has been hindered further by the absence of good farm-to-market roads, by an inefficient marketing system, by poor seed and by outdated farming methods. Transportation and exports of foodstuffs have been severely hampered by the factional wars. Poor production of agricultural products has been matched by slumps in all of Ethiopia's small manufacturing sector except for the maufacture of cotton yarn.

Because of these failures, the present government has fallen deeply into debt. The

country has run a balance of trade deficit continuously since 1974. By 1978 it owed the USSR an estimated $1 billion. In the late 1970s only the extraordinarily high world market prices for coffee, one of Ethiopia's principal export commodities, kept the deficit from becoming unmanageable. Given the subsistence farming characteristic of much of the nation's agriculture and the persistence of civil war, there is little hope for rapid improvement.

Although they are now run by the government and so production expenses can be met to keep them operational, the media are adversely affected by the bleak economy. Few citizens can afford to purchase subscriptions, or radio or television receivers.

Distribution of newspapers and other publications has been largely confined to the principal cities. This has been due partly to the fact that most of the educated elite with sufficient financial resources to buy and read publications have lived and worked in Addis Ababa, Asmara, Jimma, Dessie, Harrar and Gondar. The rugged terrain, poor roads and a slow, inadequate rail system have made speedy delivery outside the cities virtually impossible. Air transport, while good, has been limited to interconnections between the largest cities.

Ethiopia has also had to rely entirely upon expensive imported newsprint, a factor that has boosted prices and deterred wide circulations. Nor have publications been able to depend heavily on good advertising revenues for support. Advertising has been primarily limited to small retail ads.

Press Laws, Censorship & State-Press Relations

Article 25 of the Ethiopian Constitution provides all subjects with freedom of expression of their ideas orally or in writing and the right to disseminate such ideas by whatever means are available. However, in practice, the government closely controls individual access to the media.

While Haile Selassie was in power, considerable space was given to general news besides reporting on the activities and affairs of governmental agencies. Since the Dergue has taken over, the newspapers have devoted most of their space to official propaganda and to discussions of the finer points of Marxism-Leninism. While Selassie ruled, the powerful Christian station Radio Voice of the Gospel was given freedom to broadcast programs as it wished and had only limited censorship of news. At the time of its takeover from the Selassie government, the provisional military government used radio and television to incite citizens to violence against the Emperor. Then, on March 12, 1977, the Dergue accused Radio Voice of the Gospel of spreading bourgeoise ideology, took it over and renamed it Radio Voice of Revolutionary Ethiopia, announcing that it would thereafter be used for the intensification and advancement of the revolution of the broad masses. On January 23, 1978 the Provisional Military Administrative Council (PMAC) merged the station with Radio Ethiopia so that they could "agitate the broad masses to enable the revolution to achieve its objectives." At the same time, it extended broadcasts in Oromigna (Galligna) to four hours per day and increased programs in Tigrigna and Tigre so more pro-government materials could be aired in the rebellious north. Radio Voice of the Gospel's foreign staff of some 20 Europeans and Africans left. The radio medium, like the newspapers before it, became propaganda tools of the Marxist Government, providing only the information the government wishes the masses to receive.

Attitude Toward Foreign Media

Ethiopia has always been sensitive to the activities of foreign news agencies and correspondents. Under Haile Selassie they were encouraged to report information freely, unless it placed the country in an unfavorable light or suggested enemies were getting the upper hand. During the Somali border disputes in the mid-1960s, for example, the Emperor chastised Radio Voice of the Gospel for reporting Somali successes too freely.

After the overthrow of the Selassie government in 1974, the new revolutionary military government became increasingly restrictive of foreign journalistic activities. At first it seemed the media would be open to the people and conditions would improve for foreign journalists, then increasing pressure mounted to ban the foreign press. Early in 1975 Agence France-Presse, Reuters and *Time* correspondents were expelled. The Reuters correspondent was first questioned about the sources for his story about the execution of five officers; the others were expelled without reason. Next, any foreign reporting of the secessionist wars in Eritrea

was banned. Then, on April 25, 1977, the PMAC expelled the last resident Western journalists; representatives of *The Washington Post*, Reuters and AFP were given 48 hours to leave the country. Since that time only a limited number of correspondents have been allowed in and then only on occasion, for brief periods and under close surveillance. By contrast, during the same period the number of the Soviet-bloc journalists increased, and the Cuban news agency, Prensa Latina, opened a bureau in Addis Ababa in January 1978.

In March 1976 the Dergue announced that only correspondents accredited with the official Ethiopian News Agency (ENA) would be able to report Ethiopian news or to use the government-run telecommunications system. All foreign journalists on a temporary visit to the country were closely watched by official "guides" and their reports were censored by ENA before transmission. Such acts led to a near total blackout of news about Ethiopia to the outside world. Further restrictive steps were taken in 1979, when the Ministry of Information and National Guidance, which is in charge of the media, closed down the Chinese Hsinhua news agency office in Addis Ababa and ordered its personnel to leave the country. The ministry accused the agency of spreading malicious propaganda against the Ethiopian revolution and its friends (presumably the Russians). Today, only media representatives of the pro-Soviet Marxist countries are allowed access to Ethiopia.

Ethiopia supports the UNESCO Declaration on the Media.

News Agencies

The International Press Agency (IPA) was established as a national news agency in 1961 to distribute all foreign and domestic news to the mass media. In its early days it subscribed to Reuters, AP and Agence France-Presse. AFP had correspondents in both Addis Ababa and Asmara, while AP, Reuters, Tass and UPI each kept one in the capital.

Later, the IPA became the Ethiopian News Agency (ENA). As the Marxist Dergue gained a firm political power base in the mid-1970s, it began banning all Western agencies, and in 1979 Hsinhua, the Chinese news agency, was expelled. Today the only agencies providing service ENA are Tass, Prensa Latina and those of the Eastern European Communist satellites. Much of the material is propagandistic.

Electronic News Media

Radio has always been Ethiopia's most effective medium for the masses. Since illiteracy has ranged highest in the rural areas, few could read and newspapers have had little influence on farmers; television has been for the favored few urbanites who could afford sets. Haile Selassie considered radio an important medium, and the present Marxist-dominated government has seized upon radio to indoctrinate the masses.

Television services commenced in 1964, operating evenings from 8 to 10:30 p.m. for a total of about 19 hours per week, plus a daytime service to schools. Evening programs have been commercially sponsored.

The government currently operates three 100-kw national services; two are shortwave and the other medium wave. These stations broadcast in Amharic, English, Tigrigna and Oromigna. Several regional services supplement the national services: 100-kw medium-wave station at Harrar broadcasts in Oromigna and Somali and another at Asmara in Tigre and Tigrigna. The Voice's international service beams programs to East Africa and to Somalia. The Ethiopian Television Service covers Addis Ababa and the immediate vicinity with black and white signals for four hours each day. All services broadcast only government-approved news.

Education & Training

During the Emperor's rule, Haile Selassie I University in Addis Ababa established a Mass Communications department. But before the Emperor's overthrow the university became a hotbed of ferment, and classes were disrupted. When the present PMAC came to power, it assigned students to a crash literacy training and rural education program in the provinces, and many university training programs were abandoned.

Prior to the change of government, some Ethiopian journalists were trained in the International Press Institute's Africa training program. Such activity ceased when Haile Selassie was deposed.

Summary

The media in Ethiopia have always been under the dominance of the government. Strictures were firm during the reign of Emperor Haile Selassie I; since the present PMAC government took power, they have become oppressive.

The press has always been small and weak. Its circulation has been limited by illiteracy of over 90 percent, poor economic conditions among the masses, lack of a middle class, inadequate infrastructures, and a poor transportation network. As a result, circulation of dailies and magazines has been and continues to be confined to the educated urban elite in the nation's largest cities.

The future of Ethiopia's media appears dismal. They are—and it appears they will continue to be—mere propaganda tools of the government. Press freedom is nonexistent, as evidenced by recent reports that Ethiopian journalists are being harassed and treated poorly. The media will almost certainly remain enslaved to the government as long as it is in power. The facts that agrarian reforms have been only partially successful, that illiteracy runs about as high as in the past, and that the nation is closed to outside aid except that prescribed by the pro-Marxist government—all indicate a long, hard struggle for the media to become economically viable, vital information tools for the populace to better understand and contribute to the society.

CHRONOLOGY

1974	Military takes over media and uses them to foment hatred of Emperor Haile Selassie.
1975	Reuters, AFP and *Time* correspondents expelled from country.
1977	PMAC government takes over Radio Voice of the Gospel, renames it Voice of Revolutionary Ethiopia. Last Western correspondents expelled from the country.

1978   PMAC government merges Radio Voice of Gospel with Radio Ethiopia to make it propaganda tool.
Cuban news agency, Prensa Latina, opened bureau in Addis Ababa.

1979   Office of Hsinhua News Agency closed, personnel expelled.
Ethiopian daily *Addis Zemen* indicates national journalists being harassed and ill treated and cannot perform their duties well.

BIBLIOGRAPHY

"Addis Ababa." *IPI Report*, May 1979, p. 3.

Africa South of the Sahara, 1979-1980. London, 1979.

"Churches Plug a News Gap." *IPI Report*, June 1979, p. 10.

"Digest." *IPI Report*, August 1979, p. 16.

"Ethiopia One Year after the Emperor's Overthrow." *Christian Science Monitor*, September 23, 1975, pp. 14-15.

"Ethiopians Stop Student Protest." *The New York Times*, September 17, 1974.

"Ethiopia Tightens Its Controls over Foreign Journalists." *Christian Science Monitor*, February 17, 1976, p. 4.

Head, Sydney W. *Broadcasting in Africa.* Philadelphia, 1974.

"IPI in Action: Ethiopia." *IPI Report*, February/March 1975, p. 7.

Legum, Colin L. (ed.) *Africa Contemporary Record.* London, 1977–78.

Merrill, John C., Bryan, Carter R., and Alisky, Marvin. *The Foreign Press.* Baton Rouge, La., 1970.

"News of the World's Press in Brief." *IPI Report*, May 1976, p. 6.

"News of the World's Press in Brief." *IPI Report*, June 1976, p. 7.

"Press Freedom Report, 1974: Ethiopia." *IPI Report*, January 1975, p. 15.

"Press Freedom Report, 1975: Ethiopia." *IPI Report*, December 1975, p. 8.

"The Press Under Pressure: Ethiopia." *IPI Report,* April/May 1975, p. 12; June 1975, p. 6.

"World Press Freedom Review, 1979: Ethiopia." *IPI Report*, December 1979, p. 6.

FINLAND

by George Kurian

BASIC DATA

Population: 4.76 million
Area: 336,700 sq. km. (130,000 sq. mi.)
GNP: 129.58 billion markka (US$31 billion)
Literacy Rate: 99.1%
Language(s): Finnish, Swedish
Number of Dailies: 93
  Aggregate Circulation: 2.8 million
  Circulation per 1,000: 585
Number of Nondailies: 140
  Aggregate Circulation: 700,000
  Circulation per 1,000: 689
Number of Periodicals: 1,070
Number of Radio Stations: 1

Number of Television Stations: 2
Number of Radio Receivers: 2.5 million
  Radio Receivers per 1,000: 524
Number of Television Sets: 1.5 million
  Television Sets per 1,000: 315
Total Annual Newsprint Consumption: 120,000 metric tons
  Per Capita Newsprint Consumption: 27 kg. (59.4 lb.)
Total Newspaper Ad Receipts: 2.56 billion markka (US$700 million)
  As % of All Ad Expenditures: 57

Background & General Characteristics

The Finnish press has a long tradition. The first newspaper appeared in Swedish in 1771 when the country was under Swedish rule. Called *Tidningar Utgifne Af Et Sallskap i Abo* ("News published by a Society in Abo") it was put out by Aurora, a patriotic literary group whose members were drawn from the Abo Akademi, at that time Finland's sole university, and edited by Professor Henrik Gabriel Porthan. Four years later, the first Finnish-language publication appeared in the city of Turku; called *Suomenkieliset Tietosanomat* ("News in the Finnish Language"), it was edited by a rural clergyman. Finland's press beginnings differed from those of other Scandinavian countries, where the first newspapers were founded either by the postmaster or by book printers, that is, by those with access to news or the technical ability to duplicate it. Later, however, book printers took over newspaper publishing in the country. Many of the newspapers published during these early years (in the 19th century Finland was a semi-independent grand duchy of Russia) had young idealists from academic circles as editors. Some of the prominent literary figures worked for a time as newspapermen; among them, J. L. Runeberg, the national poet of Finland, Z. Topelius, a popular poet, who was editor of *Helsingfors Tidningar* for 20 years; E Lonnrot, the great folklorist; and J. V. Snellman, philosopher-statesman and the leading light in the Finnish national revival.

By 1840 Helsinki (then Helsingfors) began to emerge as the main center of Finnish journalism, and in 1847 the first Finnish-language newspaper was founded in this essentially Swedish-speaking city. Called *Suometar* (with reference to Suomi, the Finnish name for Finland), the paper was among the first to emphasize news. Helsinki newspapers increased in importance as the capital became the focal point of Finnish society and culture. Although the educated class still spoke Swedish, many also subscribed to papers in Finnish because of a growing national spirit. By the end of the 1840s the Finnish-language press had not only struck roots but also displayed vigorous growth. Of the 16 newspapers in 1860 one half were in Finnish. At the beginning of the 1850s Finnish newspapers had only one tenth as many subscribers as the Swedish press, but by 1860 the relative proportion had risen to one-half. Although newspaper reading became comparatively widespread during this period, Finland's readership compared unfavorably with that of other European countries. In 1866, 32 papers were published in the country, or one per 57,000 inhabitants, placing Finland among the bottom five in Europe, only higher than Russia (which had 200 newspapers, or one for every 300,000). In contrast, Switzerland had 300 newspapers (one for every 7,000), Norway 150 (one for every 34,700) while Denmark, England and France (with 100, 1,260 and 1,640 newspapers respectively) each had a ratio of 1:20,000. The average edition of a Finnish newspaper in the 1860s was only 774 copies. Of the 16 newspapers published in 1860, only five had editions exceeding 1,000 copies, *Helsingfors Tidningar,* with 2,356 subscribers, being far in the lead. Only one of the papers could be considered a daily newspaper in the strict sense of the term. This was the official Swedish-language *Finlands Allmanna Tidning,* appearing six times a week from 1831. Of the seven Swedish-language newspapers, four were published twice a week while the sole Finnish-language newspaper appeared semi-weekly.

The 1860s were a time of vigorous press activity following the brief thaw in the repressive rule of the tsars. The reign of Tsar Alexander 11 (1855–81) was initially liberal and effected several important reforms. The liberals and the Young Pro-Finns grew bolder, and although they had little political influence were responsible for the creation of Finland's first modern newspaper, *Helsingfors Dagblad.* Published every day of the week, it was edited by Robert Lagerborg, the first full-time professional journalist in Finnish press history. After Lagerborg's early death in 1882, the paper began to decline; seven years later it ceased publication. One reason for its death was its adoption of a neutral attitude toward the Swedish-Finnish controversy, which had become the central concern of the 1880s. The Pro-Finns pressed their claims through a new newspaper known as *Uusi Suometar* ("The New Suometar"), which soon assumed leadership of the Finnish-language press. Because *Uusi Suometar* espoused conservative causes (Conservatives were indeed known as Suometarians), radicals broke with it and around 1890 founded their own organ, *Paivalehti,* ("Daily News"), the country's first liberal newspaper. Accordingly, by the 1890s the Finnish press had clearly split along party lines, with the three main groups—the Swedish nationalists, the

Conservatives or the Old Finns, and the Young Finns—having their own newspapers. A fourth group was added in the 1890s when the Social Democrats began establishing newspapers within the labor movement. *Tyomies* ("The Workman"), founded as a weekly in 1895 and converted into a daily in 1899, developed into the leading spokesman of Finnish socialism. By the turn of the century it was the country's largest newspaper in circulation if not in influence. In any case, Finland entered the 20th century with a vigorous press, sharply divided in ideology but economically sound and intellectually dynamic.

Alongside the newspapers proper, there also came into existence a number of educational and commercial publications that shunned controversial issues like politics and language. But even the most unbiased newspaper acquired a political color in due course. An example was *Hufvudstadsbladet* ("News of the Capital"), for many decades the largest newspaper for advertising in Helsinki as well as in the provinces. Apolitical at first, it drifted into politics by 1890 and soon became a moderate proponent of Swedish interests.

The total number of newspapers grew continuously in the latter decades of the 19th century, as the accompanying table shows. The turnover of publications during this period was also great, as is apparent from the fact that during 1890 to 1900 alone 153 publications were founded whereas only 81 survived to the end of the century. The table also illustrates the faster growth of the Finnish-language press as compared to Swedish papers; by 1890 the former had overtaken the latter in both the number of newspapers and issues per week. Ownership and editorial patterns were also changing: the private printer-publisher was being replaced by the joint stock company, while the academics who moonlighted as journalists were being replaced by permanent and full-time professional newspeople.

The press also gained access to more rapid means of communication, such as the telephone and telegraph. In 1887 Finland acquired its own news agency, followed by a second agency in 1898. The first rotary press was acquired by *Hufvudstadsbladet* in 1896, followed by *Uusi Suometar* in 1899, but the old hand presses remained in use, especially in rural areas, well into the 20th century. In makeup the papers presented a medieval appearance—with black gothic letters and heavy borders. At the turn of the century

Newspaper Growth from 1860 to 1900					
Finnish		Swedish		Total	
# Newspapers	# Issues	# Newspapers	# Issues	Newspapers	Issues
1860	6	7	7	19	13	26
1870	9	12	9	28	18	40
1880	20	33	14	59	34	92
1890	32	92	23	85	55	177
1900	53	159	28	100	81	259

Paivalehti made an attempt to change over to roman but was forced by readers to revert to the gothic with which they were familiar. It was not until 1912 that *Uusi Suometar* set all its text in roman. Violent protests were raised but gradually the example was followed by other major newspapers.

The years from 1899 to 1905 are known in Finland's history as the Years of Oppression. The publication of the February Manifesto in 1899 and the appointment of Nicholas Ivanovitch Bobrikov as governor general of Finland signaled fresh Russian efforts to revoke the autonomy of the country and convert it into a Russian province. For Bobrikov, freedom of the press was anathema; he saw in the Finnish papers the most formidable obstacle in the path of Russification. Believing that the National Press Board and the censors were too indulgent, his first official measures included instructions on rigorous supervision of the news: against 97 cases of censor intervention in 1898 there were 375 cases in 1899. Instead of merely having articles and news items deleted, newspapers were confiscated and newsmen were deported as a matter of practice. During these years 24 publications were closed down and 47 suspended for varying lengths of time.

When the repression came to an end in 1905 (following Bobrikov's assassination and the November Manifesto of 1905) the press began to experience another period of vigorous growth. The period before World War I also witnessed the founding of the Agrarian party and its organ, *Ilkka*, established by Santeri Alkio. As the party grew it established more papers, of which *Maakansa* was the most notable. (Founded in Viipuri, it was later moved to Helsinki; when the Agrarian party changed its name to the Centre party the paper's name was also changed—to *Suomenmaa:* Finland.) In 1917, the last year of Russian sovereignty, 382 papers were published in Finland, while over the previous 17 years the aggregate circulation of newspapers and magazines had grown six times.

That newspapers had come into their own was attested to by the establishment in 1916 of the Newspaper Publishers Association (Sanomalehtien Liitto-Tidningarnas Forbund) with a membership of 60. A year later Finland became independent.

The major development in the press of sovereign Finland was the growth of party organs. Until the end of the Second World War, the largest group comprised right-wing papers generally supporting the Coalition party. As late as 1946 nearly 22 newspapers characterized themselves as Conservative, but of these 10 have ceased publication and five have declared their neutrality. In the 1970s there were only seven papers in the Conservative category, all of them old and stable, and with larger circulations than others. The Agrarian party claimed 19 newspapers at its zenith in 1932. From 1965, when it changed its name to the Centre party, it began to follow more moderate politics. In the 1970s it claimed the allegiance of 14 papers, two of them relatively large, with a total circulation only slightly smaller than that of the Conservative press. The Social Democratic press, which numbered 26 papers at independence, by 1971 had declined to 11, all of them small except for *Suomen Sosialidemokraatti*, the only daily in the group, which claimed a circulation of 38,000. One of the reasons for this decline was the breakaway, in 1957, of the Workers and Smallholders Social Democratic Union, with its own daily, *Paivan Sanomat*, published from Helsinki. The Communist press dates from 1946, when *Tyokansan Sanomat* was founded. In 1957 this paper merged with *Vapaa Sana* to form *Kansan Uutiset*, which sells over 44,000 copies daily.

In the 1970s the party press profile was as shown in the table on the following page. The party press has declined in number by two-thirds: from 105 in 1918 to 38 in the 1970s. The trend is toward even fewer party papers, especially within the leftist press.

It is difficult to measure the political influence exerted by party newspapers. At the time of the 1970 elections, non-socialist newspapers claimed 89.1 percent of the aggregate circulation, but non-socialist parties received only 58.5 percent of the votes, while the left-wing parties gained 41.4 percent of the votes although their papers represented only 10.9 percent of the circulation. The entire party press, however, represented only 41.4 percent of the total circulation.

In addition to newspapers, parties run their own news agencies: the Lehdiston Sanomapalvelu Pressens Nyhetstjanst (LSP) of the Coalition party, Uutiskeskus Nyhetscentralen of the Centre Party, Tyovaen Sanomalehtien Tietotoimisto Arbetartidningarnas Notisbyra of the Social Democrats, and Demokraattinen Lehtipalvelu Demokratisk Presstjanst of the People's Democratic party. All these agencies receive state appropriations from the national budget.

As a nation with total literacy, Finland ranks high both in newspaper circulation and newsprint consumption per capita. In 1980, 93 newspapers were published in the country, with an aggregate circulation of 2.8 million, or 585 copies per 1,000 inhabitants. In addition, 140 nondailies (published one to three times a week) and 85 advertising papers (distributed free of charge) with aggregate circulations of 0.7 million and 2.4 million respectively (689 and 1,000 copies respectively per 1,000 inhabitants). These figures place Finland sixth in the world in newspaper circulation per capita. Twelve of the dailies are published in Swedish, accounting for 7 percent of sales.

Circulation figures are relatively reliable because they are audited by Levikintarkastus Oy-Upplagekntroll Ab (Circulation Inspection Company), to which most newspapers belong. Recent trends indicate that newspaper readership is approaching saturation point and further gains will be slow.

Finland is the second largest exporter of newsprint in the world, and during the past decade domestic consumption has generally accounted for only about 7 percent of the production. Because of the export priorities, newspapers are forced to pay comparatively high newsprint prices. Nevertheless, there is no shortage of newsprint and the average number of pages in each issue has steadily risen. Finland's per capita newsprint consumption of 29.4 kg is the world's fifth highest.

Dailies are published in 57 towns and cities; in terms of population, 29 are in cities with populations of less than 10,000; 34 in cities with between 10,000 and 25,000; 14 with between 25,000 and 50,000; 11 with between 50,000 and 100,000 and five with over 100,000. There are 18 cities with competing dailies. The center of the nation's press is still Helsinki, with the most influential national dailies, but its dominance is being challenged by the provincial press, which has exhibited a greater growth rate during the 1970s. During the five-year period from 1965 to 1970 the 19 largest provincial dailies increased their circulations by 14.9 percent while the combined circulations of Helsinki papers increased by only 2.8 percent. This trend follows the emergence of provinces as cultural and industrial centers in their own right.

From a journalistic point of view, Finnish newspapers tend to be rather staid and sober rather than sensationalist or lively. Crime and sex are usually downplayed and scandals are shunned. Even political criticism is gentle and moderate. Typographically the papers have a slightly old-fashioned appearance, with only small concessions to modernity in layout and makeup.

Too many stories are crammed onto the main news page and continued inside after a few sentences. More often than not letters to the editor are banal. An amusing feature is

Political Press						Total No. of Publications
	Days of Publication					
	7	6	5	4	3	
National Coalition	6	1				7
Centre	6	7	1			14
Social Democratic	1	3	2	1	3	10
Social Democratic Union			1			1
People's Democrats (communist)	1		2		3	6
Total						38

the birthday list, where the birthdays of all notables are noted with brief biographical details; to avoid inclusion in this list, biographees are required to notify the Finnish News Agency that they do not wish their birthdays to be announced. Sports and cultural events are usually described in detail. One unique feature is the daily summary in each newspaper of the editorial comments of its competitors. Another is the relatively objective and lengthy coverage of foreign news, as a result of which the average Finnish newspaper reader is better informed about world affairs than his counterpart in other European countries. The news style of Finnish journalism has been the subject of much criticism. Owing to their low rates of pay and poor professional training many reporters tend to use handouts and avoid doing their homework before going out on a story. Because newsprint is easily available, stories are usually too long and badly edited.

Evening newspapers play a minor role in Finnish journalism. Only one evening paper appears in Helsinki, down from three in the early 1970s. Morning papers are usually delivered to the homes by 7 a. m. enabling readers to complete reading before they go off to work. There are no special Sunday papers.

Only one newspaper in Finland can claim a national character and circulation: *Helsingin Sanomat,* which appears among the *World's Fifty Dailies.* With a total circulation of 368,350, *Helsingin Sanomat* is read by every fourth adult in the country. About 97 percent of its readers are subscribers and about two-thirds live outside of the capital. Owned by the Erkko family (which also controls an afternoon newspaper, periodicals, a book publishing firm, two print plants, a newspaper distribution company and a newspaper circulation control company), it is an independent paper that usually comes out on the side of liberal and democratic ideas. The daily averages about 38 pages on weekdays and 54 pages on Sundays (with one issue running to 92 pages). Its editorial staff includes 180 reporters and photographers in addition to regional reporters and six foreign correspondents.

Economic Framework

As in other countries, the Finnish press represents only a small fraction of the industrial sector: aggregate assets of newspaper companies account for 1.4 percent of all industrial assets. As newspaper publishing by itself is not financially profitable, many press enterprises have other diversified interests, which provide nearly 70 percent of their total annual revenues. Even so, only 65 percent of the companies report a profit while 31 percent report a loss. Furthermore, the larger newspapers account for the lion's share of the profits, leaving the small- and medium-sized papers in dire financial straits. Of the total 1977 revenues of 1.045 billion markka ($250 million), 73 percent came from advertisements and 27 percent from subscriptions and single-copy sales. (Of the latter, subscriptions accounted for 90 percent and newsstand sales 10 percent.) The economic structure of newspapers is thus doubly skewed: there is an overdependence on advertising and on subscriptions. Subscriptions and single-copy prices have not kept up with inflation. Newspapers are still comparatively cheap, with single copies selling at 50 cents. More than 60 percent of all advertising is channeled through newspapers and local publications, and in this respect newspapers have a clear edge over television, which receives only 10 percent. There is no commercial radio system. The significant economic development since the mid 1950s has been the large increment in advertising volume and the constant increase in advertising rates, although the former has not kept pace with the rise in industrial production. On the other side of the ledger, the same period has witnessed steep increases in salaries and wages, which account for 41.1 percent of revenues (as compared with 22.8 percent for the rest of industry) as well as in costs of newsprint, transportation and machinery. As a result of rapid technological changes in the printing industry, a number of newspapers are faced with the task of financing the acquisition of costly equipment from their ordinary revenues.

About 11,000 people were employed by the Finnish press in 1978 and another 19,000 by the printing industry. The principal labor union is the Suomen Sanomalehtimiesten Liitto-Finlands Journalistforbund (Association of Finnish Journalists), founded in 1921. Over the years, the association has evolved into a welfare society with a well-developed social and fraternal program. Strikes have been few; the most recent, in 1980, lasted for three weeks and was settled following lengthy negotiations.

Finland has no chains except in one or two cases where a newspaper issues a part-edition or a partly re-edited version under another name in a neighboring locality, similar to the Kopfblatt system in West Germany. There is also very little concentration in ownership. The largest company, Sanoma Oy (publisher of *Helsingin Sanomat* and *Ilta-Sanomat*) accounts for only 10 percent of total press circulation. Likewise, the 10 largest dailies have only 46 percent of the national circulation. However, there is a strong geographic concentration in the south, with publishing in the northern areas comparatively underdeveloped.

Most papers are being printed by offset. Modern computer-based systems are used only by the large national dailies, but their extension has been hampered by labor opposition.

Press Laws

When Finland became independent in 1917 one of the first laws of the new government was a Press Freedom Act. It came into effect in 1919 and has since then remained the foundation of the country's free press. Its basic principle, contained in Section I, guarantees every Finnish citizen the right to publish printed material "without public authorities being allowed to set any obstacles to this in advance as long as the provisions of this Act are observed." All citizens are also granted the right to carry on a printing business after notifying the authorities, to sell or circulate books, newspapers and publications without hindrance, and to edit publications. Chapters six and seven of the act deal with the forfeiture and seizure of criminal printed works and the suspension of periodicals and newspapers—applying particularly to obscene publications, both domestic and imported, a subject of lively discussion in the 1960s. The law also provides for the right of rectification for individuals and institutions who wish to correct false statements about themselves. Newspapers are required by law to print these corrections in one of the two issues that appear immediately subsequent to the receipt of the correction, in the main section and in the same typeface as the items to which they are a reply. If a paper neglects to do so, it is liable to a fine not exceeding 500 markka ($120), but this provision is being enforced rather leniently.

Subsequent legislation has also safeguarded freedom in the acquisition of information. The Act On Publicity of Official Documents of 1951 confirms the right of Finnish citizens to obtain access to any public official document, although this right is subject to government discretion in the case of requests from foreign nationals. The act defined categories of secret documents excluded from public access but most official documents come automatically into the public domain 25 years following their dates.

An amendment to the Code of Procedure in 1966 accorded to journalists the right, except in serious criminal cases, to refuse to divulge to the court the source of their information. This right of anonymity has been extended—through a 1971 supplement to the act—to radio and television. Another amendment in 1974 stipulated punishment for publications that discriminated against (or incited such discrimination against) any population or group of defined race, color, nationality or religious affiliation. Chapter 24 prohibits illicit eavesdropping and illicit surveillance by both public officials and private citizens. Chapter 27 deals with libel in print, for which the specified penalty is a prison term of not less than two months and not more than two years. Violation of privacy is also classified as a crime, but publication of details concerning a person's actions in public life or in public office or any other comparable activity is not regarded as an invasion of privacy. A new act in 1970 revised the old regulations relating to blasphemy, but punishment is still stipulated for public blasphemy of God and for crimes against religious faith. The Criminal Code contains provisions dealing with defamation, especially, insults and abuse directed against a dead person. The punishment for such a crime is more severe if it appears in printed materials. Other restrictions on the press include the duty to maintain secrecy in matters relating to national defense, and to report only facts and not comments on matters that are sub judice. High treason is considered a crime and so also is defamation of foreign heads of state. The last is a specific reference to the Soviet Union, which is extremely sensitive to opinions voiced in the Finnish press.

Finnish legislation does not contain a theoretical formulation of press freedom as found in the constitutions of other countries, but under normal circumstances the press enjoys adequate guarantees in practice. If freedom of the press is interpreted as the reader's freedom to choose his means of information, it can be claimed that Finland has full press freedom. However, the old liberal assumption that press freedom is principally freedom from state control does not hold good in such a complex economic and social system as that of Finland's. Press monopolies constitute an equally important constraint. Fortunately, Finland is free of such chains and concentration of media power.

Efforts at self-regulation by the Finnish press began in 1957 when the Finnish Association of Journalists established a code of conduct known as Rules for Journalists. Following the examples of Sweden and Norway, the Finnish media established an ombudsman or "Court of Honor" known as Board of Opinion for Mass Media, (Julkisen Sanan Neuvosto, JSN). The Finnish body operates in the same way as the press councils in other countries except that, unlike many of them, it also handles broadcasting. Between 1969 and 1978 the council received 597 complaints, of which 145 led to the censure of the medium concerned.

Censorship

Censorship is prohibited by the same laws that guarantee freedom of speech and expression. Consequently, there are no censorship agencies in the country.

State-Press Relations

Finland has no information ministry or department and the government plays a low-key role in information and news management. The principal element of state-press relations is the subsidy system.

Partly because of the high casualty rate among newspapers and partly because of increasing production costs that medium and small newspapers were unable to meet, the question of state subsidies to the press was raised in 1965. The newspapers of three parties supported the idea but the rest opposed it as a possible threat to press freedom and as a backdoor attempt by the state to influence print media and dilute their integrity. Because of this opposition the bill introducing direct state subsidies was defeated in Parliament in 1966, but the government went ahead anyway, granting subsidies to political parties to use as they saw fit.

In 1980 the media received four types of subsidies from the government. The so-called General Subsidy for Transportation of Newspapers reimbursed the postal service for re-duced newspaper-postage rates. In 1978 this allocation totaled 201 million markka ($48 million). In addition, newspapers received a direct Transportation and Delivery Subsidy amounting to 25 million Finnish marks in 1978. In that year 44 regular newspapers were eligible for the subsidy; party papers received 84 percent and independents 16 percent; among the party papers 54 percent of the subsidy went to the socialist press and 45 percent to the non-socialist papers. Since 1971 news agencies have been granted a special subsidy toward their telecommunication expenses. Seventy three newspapers also received this subsidy. The bulk of the grant went to the national news agency (Suomen Tietotoimisto) representing 61 newspapers. The rest of the subsidy went to five minor political party news agencies.

The fourth subsidy—through the political parties—remains the most important means of media support by the state. It is distributed to the parties according to their percentage of seats in Parliament. Thus, in 1978, the Social Democratic party received 27 percent, the People's Democratic party (front name for the Communist party) 20 percent, the Centre Party 19.5 percent, the Coalition or Conservative Party 17.5 percent and three minor parties 4.5 percent each.

Attitude Toward Foreign Media

For historical reasons, Finland has attracted very little foreign media attention. For more or less the same reasons, few Finnish papers maintain foreign correspondents, except in the major news centers like London, Paris, Washington, Moscow, Bonn and Stockholm. There are no special accreditation procedures for foreign correspondents nor do they require special visas. There are no import restrictions on foreign publications.

The quantity of foreign films, magazines, television shows and recordings is substantial. Approximately 40 percent of all television programming is foreign made; 95 percent of all films shown in Finland come from abroad, as do 60 percent of phonograph records. Materials from the United States and Western Europe predominate but the Soviet bloc claims a respectable 30 percent of the film market. On television an average of three U.S. shows are broadcast each season, and the Voice of America is received more than 15 hours a day in most parts of the country.

Finland has adopted an ambivalent attitude toward the UNESCO Declaration on the Media, perhaps out of deference to Soviet wishes in this matter.

News Agencies

The national news agency is Suomen Tietotoimisto/Finska Notisbyran (STT), founded in 1915 through the merger of three news services, and owned cooperatively by Finnish newspapers and the Finnish Radio Company. STT has a direct teleprinter service from Reuters, AFP, Tass and the Scandinavian news agencies. Some of the bigger dailies also subscribe to AP and UPI. Foreign materials of interest to Finnish readers are translated—but not edited—and sent to all client newspapers.

The four major political parties—Coalition, Center, Social Democratic and People's Democratic—maintain their own news agencies, all subsidized by the state.

Electronic News Media

The sole licensed broadcasting company is the Finnish Broadcasting Corporation (Oy Yleisradio Ab: YLE), owned 99.9 percent by the state with the remaining 0.1 percent of the shares divided among 58 shareholders. The operations of YLE are supervised on behalf of the Council of State by the minister of communications. The highest executive authority is the Administrative Council, elected by Parliament for four-year terms. The council nominates the Programme Councils and elects the Board of Directors. Because its members are chosen by Parliament, its composition usually reflects the ideological makeup of the national legislature.

While YLE has a monopoly over radio broadcasting, it is assisted by OY Mainos-TV-Reklam Ab (MTV), a joint stock company that broadcasts over 900 hours of commercials on the YLE networks annually. MTV pays YLE for broadcasting time and technical services.

Finnish broadcasting legislation goes back to 1927, a year after YLE began full-scale operations, but it is sadly outdated and makes no reference to television. Several reforms have been proposed over the years but none of them has obtained the necessary political backing. The latest significant change was effected in 1948 when the election of the Administrative Council was transferred from the stockholders' meeting to Parliament.

There are three Finnish programming councils, one for radio, one for television and one for all Swedish-language broadcasting. The law guarantees Swedish programming a position relative to the size of the Swedish-speaking population and although that population is only 7 percent of the national total, Swedish programs account for 20 percent of all programs.

Broadcasting funds derive from two major sources: radio and television license fees and commercial advertising; the former provides 80 percent of the company's operating expenditures and the latter 20 percent. Advertising is limited to a maximum of 15 percent of air time.

In the early 1970s YLE attempted, under the guidance of a left-dominated parliament, to introduce a radical slant to the content of programming. This led to the so-called Information War, in which conservative elements, backed by the church and the small farmers, successfully reversed the trend and brought YLE back to its middle-of-the-road, neutral position.

Education & Training

Organized training for journalists did not begin until the 1920s. The first step was the introduction of a special newspaper examination by the School of Social Studies (now the University of Tampere) in 1925. Nevertheless, a lecturer in the subject was not appointed until 1943 and the first professor until 1949. For Swedish-speaking Finns, training is provided at the Swedish Social and Communal College in Helsinki. The University of Helsinki has training programs for information studies but not in journalism.

By tradition, the major newspapers train volunteers in practical newspaper work. Sanoma Osakeyhtio, the newspaper concern, established a private school for journalists in 1967. Many Finnish journalists also attend courses at Arhus, Denmark, arranged by the Nordic Publishers' Organization. Nevertheless, the percentage of trained journalists in the profession is small; only 34 percent are believed to have passed beyond the secondary school.

Summary

The Finnish press is relatively healthy. Very few papers have died during the past 10 years. Newspaper circulation has been growing continuously during the same period. Finnish newspapers have also been among the first in Scandinavia to apply computer-based printing and typesetting technology. Freedom of the press has never been ser-iously threatened in Finland and the country has never been mentioned in IPI reports. In neither ownership nor circulation is the Finnish press as concentrated as in other European countries.

CHRONOLOGY

1971   Government introduces selective subsidy system for ailing newspapers through political party organizations.

1980   Journalist strike lasting three weeks is settled through direct negotiations.

BIBLIOGRAPHY

Steinby, Torsten. *In Quest of Freedom.* Helsinki, 1971.

FRANCE

by Charles R. Eisendrath

BASIC DATA

Population: 53,522,000
Area: 551,670 sq. km. (212,945 sq. mi.)
GNP: Fr 213 trillion (US$531 billion) (1979)
Literacy Rate: 97%
Language(s): French
Number of Dailies: 96
   Aggregate Circulation: 10,863,000
   Circulation per 1,000: 205
Number of Nondailies: 694
   Aggregate Circulation: 15,451
   Circulation per 1,000: 291
Number of Periodicals: 13,716
Number of Radio Stations: 34

Number of Television Stations: 3,135
Number of Radio Receivers: 17,441,000
   Radio Receivers per 1,000: 330
Number of Television Sets: 14,693,000
   Television Sets per 1,000: 278
Total Annual Newsprint Consumption: 581,400 metric tons
   Per Capita Newsprint Consumption: 11 kg. (24.2 lb.)
Total Newspaper Ad Receipts: Fr 4.55 billion (US$968.5 million) (1976)
As % of All Ad Expenditures: 61.5

Background & General Characteristics

By any world standard, the press in France peaked early. Total newspaper circulation had reached its all-time high by 1946, and stood in the mid-1970s at the level of 1939—with a much-reduced readership per thousand. Only one-sixth as many dailies were publishing in Paris in 1974 as in 1914, for example, and fewer than half the number of 1946. Accounting for the pattern were a number of explosive political and technical developments.

The press mirrored the slow growth common elsewhere from the 1631 founding of Theophraste Renaudot's *La Gazette,* France's first newspaper, until the Revolution of 1789. That period of prolonged social upheaval provided ideal growing conditions for fertile editorial and publishing concepts. Journals of information such as *Le Moniteur Universel* and *Journal des Débats* appeared along with the first great precursors of the opinion press, which was to dominate European journalism for 150 years: Jean-Paul Marat's *l'Ami du Peuple,* Jacques-René Hebert's *Père Duchêne,* Nicolas Bonneville's *Tribun. Le Moniteur* illustrated the frequent fate of

newspapers caught in political crossfires by being converted under Napoleon into a personal propaganda sheet after its competitors were suppressed.

Beginning with the Restoration of 1815 and continuing until the 1880s, the most important developments were technical. Introduction of the telegraph in 1845 and the telephone in 1876 not only permitted rapid transmission of news but coincided with enlargement of the nation's literacy. Creative entrepreneurs sensed a lucrative demand. Between 1867 and 1872 Marinoni and Derriey developed the rotary press, capable of using the new wood-pulp paper for producing large editions at a fraction of the cost of the rag stock printed by hand-operated machinery. Railroads also permitted rapid delivery anywhere in the country.

And as the industrial revolution came to printing and delivery systems, democratization spread readership. Building circulation had been a difficult—and not always high-priority—goal when journals were high-quality, elegantly written products for the upper classes. In 1836 Émile de Gerardin launched *La Presse* at half the price of his rivals, and French journalism was never the same. Charles Havas, a sometime newsman and banker ruined by the downfall of Napoleon, contributed to the rapid-dissemination process by creating the first news agency in 1832, a full 14 years before the Associated Press took shape in the United States.

These lessons in the profit potential of mass media were refined in 1863 with creation of *Le Petit Journal.* By reaching below the middle class with simple writing in an informal, familiar tone, that paper scored stupendous gains in circulation, which topped 300,000 within five years. For European societies benefiting from new public literacy laws, *Le Petit Journal* became a model imitated across Europe. As a whole, the press thrived on the freedom brought by liberal regimes, and generally supported them. As University of Paris historian Pierre Albert puts it, the press "provoked the revolution of 1830, contributed to the one of 1848, enfeebled the second Empire after 1860 and assured the triumph of the republicans in the elections of 1876 and 1877."

The golden age of the French press from 1881 to 1914 was as spectacular as it was brief. In terms of quality, the law of July 29, 1881, with its ringing statement that "the press...is free," represented a dramatic return to the principles of 1789 and the Declaration o. the Rights of Man. The most liberal press law in Europe, it fostered a luxurious range of viewpoint. Among the 80 newspapers of Paris in 1914, *Le Temps* was the serious paper of record, *Le Figaro* was read by moderates, *La Croix* by militant Catholics, *L'Intransigeant* by nationalists, *L'Action Française* by monarchists and *L'Humanité* by socialists. In circulation, all of these trailed *Le Petit Journal, Le Matin* and *Le Journal,* which, with *Le Petit Parisien,* the biggest newspaper in the world, reached 4.5 million readers. This meant that Paris alone accounted for 60 percent of the national market. But the provincial press was also booming. Even small hamlets had their own newspapers, and in the cities, a dozen dailies boasted circulations surpassing 100,000. As First World War censorship approached, market penetration for French daily newspapers stood at 244 per thousand of population, never again to be sustained.

"Venal" is the word most often used to describe the French press between the two world wars. Responses to the patriotism and the often capricious censorship of "The Great War" cost newspapers much of their credibility. After the Armistice, a continual round of political, economic and social crises caught the press in intellectual crossfires it was unable to escape. Inflation and introduction of photographs increased production costs at a time when advertising revenues fell precipitously. Professional integrity was heavily mortgaged to the politics of publishers, most of them right wing. To satisfy the appetite for more serious political news, politico-literary weeklies such as the moderate *Candidate, Gringoire* of the right and *Vendredi* of the left became a mark of the era.

By 1939 more than half the Paris dailies published in 1914 had folded. The "big four," which had become mouthpieces of the political right, had lost circulation significantly, in part because of the rise of opposition from various leftist positions in *Le Populair* (Socialist), *L'Oeuvre* (Radical), *L'Humanité* and *Le Soir* (Communist). The most significant innovations of the 1930s were contributed by industrialist Jean Prouvost with his illustrated weekly *Match* and the daily *Paris-Soir.* Using British popular-press formats and American management techniques, Prouvost lifted circulation from 60,000 in 1930 to 1.8 million by the end of the decade.

The German conquest of France and occupation of its northern half demolished what credibility remained in the press. From the successful invasion of June 1940, newspapers in the north either ceased publication or became outright propaganda organs. Some in the Vichy sector temporarily managed a sort of bland neutrality, but only until the Allied landings in North Africa in November 1942, at which time they went the way of those in occupied territory. This process wrenched long-established habits. The public's reliance on the print media was broken. In its place, the relatively new medium of radio brought the French the only uncensored news available.

In the immediate postwar years, French journalism flowered in a universal, if brief, renaissance. Intense interest in events following the Allied victory shot readership to a momentary peak of 15.1 million, or 379 per thousand of population. A generation of journalists who had broken into the profession in the slatternly 1930s—many of them matured on clandestine underground papers during the Occupation—suddenly "sensed freedom to print the truth," as Françoise Giroud, a founder of *l'Express* and one of their number, phrased it; "For the first time in our lives, it seemed possible to do what we wanted to do." It did not last. By 1952 newspaper circulation had fallen to 1914 levels. Seventy-two newspapers had folded in six years; fewer remained than there had been at the turn of the century.

Some of the causes of these developments merit attention. The heady sense that "everything is possible," enthralling to Giroud and hundreds of others in 1946, soon was threatened. The Ordinances of August 1944, drafted during the heady months of liberation, reestablished the press on a new basis designed to avoid the indulgences of the 1930s. They established regulated ownership and subsidies intended to encourage diversity. But when threats of Communist takeover, defeat in Indo-China and disaster in Algeria thoroughly frightened politicians, the system came to be used to gain influence for the party in power. The de Gaulle constitution for the Fifth Republic completed the process by handing the chief executive preemptory powers over the press.

---

10 Largest Daily Newspapers by Circulation (1979)

1.	*Ouest-France* (Rennes)	750,000
2.	*France-Soir* (Paris)	497,900
3.	*Le Monde* (Paris)	437,800
4.	*La Voix du Nord* (Lille)	371,900
5.	*Le Progrés* (Lyons)	371,300
6.	*Sud-Ouest* (Bordeaux)	355,700
7.	*Le Parisien Libéré* (Paris)	336,700
8.	*Le Dauphiné Libéré* (Grenoble)	315,100
9.	*Le Figaro* (Paris)	313,500
10.	*La Nouvelle République du Centre-Ouest* (Tours)	276,200

---

9 Largest Magazines by Circulation (1979)

1.	*Paris-Match*	813,900
2.	*l'Express*	645,300
3.	*Marie-Claire*	635,700
4.	*Jours de France*	590,400
5.	*Figaro Magazine*	555,000
6.	*Elle*	462,600
7.	*Le Nouvel Observateur*	454,800
8.	*Le Point*	359,400
9.	*Nouvel Economiste*	140,800

In terms of national influence, the two most potent organizations in French print journalism are the Paris daily *Le Monde* and Agence France-Presse (AFP), the national wire service.

The people who run France, study it and report it to the rest of the world read *Le Monde*. Doubts about that statement, and the unique position it implies, would be quelled by the sight of the limousines that queue up every working day at about noon to pick up copies fresh from the presses. One goes to the president, others to government ministers. No strategy of private business would be deemed sound unless formulated with information drawn from *Le Monde*. Its pages set the news agenda for French radio and television as well as the nation's other newspapers. No foreign correspondent files a report on France in ignorance of what *Le Monde* has to say on the subject.

Editorially, *Le Monde* leans somewhat to the left of the political center, and stylistically shares as much with newsmagazines as with newspapers. Its elegantly written prose concerns itself more with analysis than abundant facts, with thoroughness rather than immediacy of reporting. Its 180 journalists are assigned to a dozen "rubriques" ranging from politics to education and "Equipment and Regions," forming specialized news compartments blurred only in a small "General Information" section and the front page, which also carries the daily, one-column editorial in boldface. The ways in which it breaks the usual rules are instructive. Unlike other French dailies, *Le Monde* makes use of graphics seldom and newsphotos never. It treats foreign news much more comprehensively than other French dailies, and has the most complete staff of foreign correspondents. In contrast to other dailies of its size, it is a cooperative in which journalists own 40 percent of the shares, can block selection of a new editor and each year divide 25 percent of the profits. Nearly alone among Paris dailies through much of the 1970's, *Le Monde* had profits to divide.

The paper was set up with de Gaulle's assistance in 1944 by Hubert Beuve-Méry, who had been a foreign correspondent. De Gaulle's hopes of having secured a docile mouthpiece, however, were soon destroyed by *Le Monde*'s independence. When Beuve-Méry retired in 1969, leadership passed to Jacques Fauvet. In 1976 a former staffer wrote a stinging best-selling book accusing *Le Monde* of adapting truth "to its own purposes...specializing in pseudo-truth." The paper's position, however, remained undamaged. In 1980 it once again demonstrated sufficient independence of government wishes to have incurred a criminal suit against Fauvet by the minister of justice for criticizing the courts.

Economic Framework

The decade of the 1970s brought remarkable changes to the French economy. High-technology manufactures began to replace luxury and agricultural products in overall importance. Long-range planning introduced rational priorities, while the coming of age of the nation's first generation undecimated by war since 1914 quickened the pace of innovation. In 1976 Prime Minister Raymond Barre jolted the traditionally heavily protected industrial sector by withdrawing price controls, weakening job guarantees and refusing to devalue the franc to rescue uncompetitive companies.

The results, while aggravating relatively high unemployment, have helped restructure the industrial base. In the last two years of the 1970s, corporate profits jumped nearly 40 percent. Growth stood near the top of the European Economic Community. Exports increased 30 percent in four years. These short-term impacts, however, were probably less important than the government's decision to commit enormous resources—Fr104 billion ($25 billion)—to seven new "strategic" growth sectors to replace ailing heavy industries such as steel, shipbuilding and bulk textiles. Through mergers, selective credit and investment incentives, the Barre Plan pumped energy into telecommunications, microelectronics, office equipment, nuclear power, aerospace, biotechnology and undersea research.

While the press shared in the general prosperity, it was pushed ever more quickly to effect economies of scale in production. This meant further concentration of ownership across the board, with special undercurrents in the agitated flow of Parisian publishing.

From its high point in 1892, the number of daily papers had fallen steadily from 414 to 90 in 1976. But even that figure, modest for a nation of 54 million people, is misleading. Estimates of how many editorial operations retain *real* independence range from 42 to 67. There is little doubt, however, about two implications of those low figures: (1) 10 large chains control the vast majority of readership; (2) the provinces are in the hands of "ducs de la presse," with monopoly powers over local news.

Concentration began earlier in the provinces than in Paris, and went further, faster. Of 37 takeovers between 1959 (when the movement gathered force) and 1972, 66 percent were bought off by the eight largest "dukedoms." The principal mechanisms for acquisition are *couplage,* in which papers share advertising revenues, or "absorption," when they merge production. Frequently, as a bow to law limiting ownership to one daily, vestigial traces of the established local paper are left in place, typically as four-page inserts to the main provincial edition. In 1978 *Ouest-France,* the Rennes-based giant with the country's largest circulation (800,000), was publishing 30 local editions across 12 departments (roughly the equivalent of U.S. states); *Sud-Ouest,* which dominates the Aquitaine from Bordeaux, was putting out 16 of them in eight *departments.*

Typically, papers such as these faced less demanding head-on competition in their circulation areas than Paris counterparts, and so were able to grow more easily. Union restrictions on management were not as tight, production costs somewhat lower. The incentives toward merger were also strong. France's centralized broadcasting system, with its heavy emphasis on national and international news, left nearly untouched the local markets, where demand for hometown coverage ran strong as the French economy entered a period of rapid, sustained growth. At the same time, magazines strongly invaded newspaper advertising revenues, lending further impulse to economies of scale. From 1959 to 1963 alone, for example, the proportion of expenditures going to dailies and magazines shifted from 60–40 percent in favor of newspapers to a 65–35 percent lead for the latter.

Benefiting from these advantages and capitalizing on the opportunities, provincial papers gained a telling advantage in the technical innovations of the period, installing computers, photo-offset and facsimile production methods. The man and organization that best exemplify the benefits and fears generated by the concentration process is a former specialty magazine publisher with a controversial past, Robert Hersant.

Hersant began in 1950 with *Auto-Journal,* a car magazine. Six years later he acquired local newspapers and used them to gain election to the National Assembly, retaining a seat for more than 20 years despite frequent protest by liberals and organized labor. By the time he took over *Paris-Normandie* in 1971, Hersant had already absorbed dailies from *Nante* in the west to *Nord-Matin* in the north, *Le Berry Républicain* and *Centre Presse* in the heartland to *France-Antilles* on the French Caribbean Island of Guadeloupe.

His methods were well established: use of facsimile to reduce freight costs, merge advertising operations, install computer editing and photocomposition to cut editorial expenses, and reduce staffing drastically. The move at *Paris-Normandie* produced mass firings, strikes and national publicity, but did nothing to stop Hersant. Even critics who call him "The French Hearst" and "Citizen Hersant" acknowledge his contributions to sound newspaper financing and management.

Five years later Hersant carried his spectacular offensive to Paris. *Le Figaro,* which for more than 150 years had occupied the middle of the high-quality road in Parisian newspapering with the solid, gray uprightness of an obelisk, was losing more than $5 million annually. Hersant took control in 1975. Within months, some of *Figaro's* nationally recognized journalists concluded that they could not work for him. Editor Jean d'Ormesson resigned publicly in a front page editorial accusing Hersant of manipulating staff and news policies. The new *patron* answered in the same space, cooly replying that he rescued the paper by carrying out his convictions. The paper's best known columnist soon followed its editor. Raymond Aron, a prestigious economics columnist, quit in 1977, charging Hersant with being unable to gain the confidence of his staff.

France-Soir was next. For years the capital's biggest daily and one of its liveliest, it had lost nearly half of its onetime circulation of more than a million. Hersant bought a commanding interest and used it to turn the paper around, ignoring the barrage of protest and strikes attending his purchases. His empire stood at an even dozen papers, reaching one in every five of the 12 million readers of French newspapers.

Within the Paris daily press, the movement toward consolidation has been accompanied by interesting subthemes. The capital still has 9 papers, a luxuriant variety not matched elsewhere and, quite possibly, unaffordable. Generally, the higher quality journals have gained at the expense of the popular press, in large part because of prolonged urbanization of the country and democratization of the educational system, which extended the period of schooling for millions of Parisians. *Le Monde, La Croix* and *Figaro* all grew, for example, while, *France-Soir, L'Aurore* and *Le Parisien Libéré* lost readers.

Concentration has also been flanked by rejuvenation, through creation of new titles, or with new organizations using old ones. In 1973, for example, Jean-Paul Sartre founded the present *Libération,* resuscitating a name that had disappeared from the scene with the death of a former *Libération* in 1964. *Le Populaire, 24 Heures, Paris-Press, La Nation* and *Combat* all perished in the 15 years following 1960, but a whole family of others were born in that period. Besides *Libération,* there came *Le Quotidien de Paris, L'Humanité Rouge, Le Quotidien du Peuple* and *Rouge.* Most of the newcomers developed only modest followings, and one, *J'Inform,* folded within three months of its founding in 1977. However, *Le Matin,* an offshoot of the highly successful *Nouvel Observateur* group, maintained healthy growth after starting that same year.

The 1970s brought substantial change to the structure of the French press. The group headed by Jean Prouvost, considered the father of the modern newspaper-magazine industry, was obliged by financial difficulties to sell off most of its shares in 1974, including 50 percent interests in major publications such as *Paris-Match,* France's largest magazine, the women's *Marie-Claire* and the television guide *Télé-7-Jours.* The latter was taken over by another group that underwent considerable reshuffling. Hachette, a giant conglomerate built around a book publishing company with strong government links, also founded the high-quality newsweekly *Le Point* to compete with the dominant *L'Express,* which itself was sold by Jean-Jacques Servan-Schreiber to Anglo-French Financier Sir James Goldsmith. Hachette still publishes several other magazines, including *Elle* and the weekend *France Dimanche.* The main theme of its reorganization, however, was to sell off troubled periodicals. In late 1980 Hachette came under the control of Matra, an electronics-defense conglomerate.

The longest strike in French newspaper history shook the group headed by Emilien Amaury by crippling its flagship publication *Parisien Libéré.* However, neither the strike nor Amaury's death in 1977 destroyed the company. Although another firm bought 25 percent of its stock, it still publishes *Parisien Libéré,* with its 23 local editions in the Paris metropolitan area, the sports magazine *L'Equipe* and the women's monthly *Marie-France,* among others.

Chains with declared ideological commitments include Bayard-Presse, an important Catholic group that publishes the Paris daily *La Croix* as well as 18 other family, youth and religious periodicals. The Communist party puts out *Humanité* (circulation 151,000) in Paris, other dailies in Limoges, Lille and Marseille and 522 weeklies across the country.

In the ranks of the newly powerful in the French press, Robert Hersant has been joined by Daniel Filipachi, a onetime photographer for *Paris-Match* who bought the magazine from Hachette in 1975. He owns a dozen others, all of them geared to entertainment and the young. They include *Salut Les Copains,* the rough equivalent of the U.S. weekly *Rolling Stone,* and the French edition of *Playboy.* An attempt to enter the American market with a recreated *Look,* however, failed after three issues. On a smaller scale, Jean-Louis Servan-Schreiber, younger brother of the former *l'Express* publisher Jean-Jacques, built *l'Expansion* into the nation's most influential business magazine, and started the successful *"F"* for women. A venture into a trendy sort of city journalism with *Paris-Hebdo,* however, proved unsustainable.

More than 200 periodicals officially characterized as "foreign or international" are edited in France, the most influential of them being the American *International Herald Tribune* (IHT). Jointly owned by the New York Times, Washington Post and Whitney Communications companies, the IHT is universally regarded as one of the world's best papers despite a minuscule editorial staff of less than 30. The keys to its high quality are tight editing, broad outlook and access to all the best available news services, both U.S. and foreign. Six days a week, the European edition, averaging 16 pages, is published simultaneously in Paris, Zurich and London, then distributed by air and surface transport to 140,000 readers, about 45 percent of whom are American citizens. The paper, whose audience includes decision makers in both multinational business and diplomacy, added a facsimile Asian edition in 1980. Published in Hong Kong, its circulation within several months had reached 12,000, and also brought IHT's distribution network to 143 countries.

Television, so often the scapegoat of publishers explaining their failures, was less truly a threat in France than elsewhere. Indeed, during the 1960–67 peak years of its introduction, with more than one million new sets going on line each year, daily newspaper circulation steadily increased. For several years the French regarded television more as

a toy than a transformer of attitudes. The "mortal venom," in the words of Yves L'Her, editor in chief of the industry's authoritative *Presse-Actualité,* was inflation. The vast majority of French newspapers are sold on newsstands instead of by subscription, making them vulnerable to reader rejection when prices are raised suddenly. Although from 1959 to 1967 the kiosk price went up only negligibly, thanks to decisions by the finance ministry, which must grant approval, the next period was altogether different. Between 1967 and 1975, readers saw the price of their favorite papers rise almost every year, quadrupling in the process. Each time, newspaper sales decreased by five to 10 percent. L'Her points out that publishers seldom explained the reasons for the increased costs, even in a year such as 1974, when newsprint shot up 82 percent, further aggravating the situation.

Whenever possible, publishers sought to offset increased production costs with advertising rather than price increases, but faced obstacles of both law and tradition. One condition qualifying periodicals for lucrative state aid is that no more than two-thirds of their surface areas be taken by advertising. By custom, a relatively small proportion of total advertising goes to the press (half that of Germany, for example). The situation is particularly critical in Paris, where daily newspaper advertising revenues rose at less than half the rate of provincial counterparts in the first six years following the introduction of television commercials in 1969. With television quickly taking 15 percent of national advertising—primarily at the expense of magazines—Paris newspapers fell back on their trump card. From 1970 to 1974, sales staffs worked on boosting classified advertising, which at principal periodicals in the capital climbed between 20 and 50 percent. At some national newspapers, classifieds (primarily covering jobs and real estate) accounted for more than 60 percent of total advertising revenues.

Becoming a journalist involves far more than getting a job with a periodical, or having work published on a regular basis. Strict national regulations cover who may enter the profession, how they do so, what duties they will perform for how much money, and whether they will be permitted to maintain the considerable benefits that attend their status as certified practitioners. All these things are contained in the National Collective Labor Contract for Journalists, renegotiated biennially by journalists' and publishers' organizations, with active participation by state representatives.

In 1977, the most recent year for which figures are available, France had 14,673 registered journalists; among those 3,089 were women, an increase of 280 percent over 1960.

9,695 full-status journalists
2,003 trainees
568 freelance writers
303 interns
628 photojournalists
208 freelance news photographers
266 layout editors
138 TV cameramen

As a group, journalists occupy a somewhat contradictory position in French society. Their pay is relatively good, job security matches that of tenured professors, yet their unemployment rate, 14 to 18 percent, stays stubbornly among the highest of any sector. From their ranks have come a significant number of national figures (from Jean-Paul Marat to Georges Clemenceau to Claude Estier, Françoise Giroud and President François Mitterand) as well as influential writers (such as Émile Zola and Albert Camus). Grandeur, however, has not rubbed off on the profession. Asked to rank the prestige of journalists by personal experience in lieu of polls on the subject, Olivier Todd, when he was the editor of *L'Express,* replied only half-mockingly "somewhere between press-agents and prostitutes." He pointed for contrast to the United States, where Gallup surveys of public "confidence ratings" in the late 1970s pegged the press just below the public schools, considerably above the U.S. Supreme Court.

The national contract divides French journalism into 14 job "functions," each with a set minimum salary, and includes some ranks that in other sectors denote management. Coverage extends, for example, to editors in chief, section heads, plumes-a-tout-faire on general assignment and researchers. Nor is compartmentalization limited to the nature of work performed. In the case of newspapers, each category is further broken down for salary purposes by location of the enterprise. Under the 1976 contract, a top editor in Paris was assured slightly less than his counterparts on regional dailies (some of which are larger than any paper in the capital), but one-third more than those directing coverage on local papers. Renumeration

is similarly subdivided, but with important provisions cutting across the board. Seniority and company-loyalty raises are built into the system for a full 20 years and come in addition to cost-of-living adjustments, which are automatic. One sort of bonus, in fact, has been codified. Every journalist by law receives a late December *la treizième,* or "thirteenth month," amounting to a month's pay at the highest level earned that year. At some large publications, contracts "extend" the salary year to 16 months.

National agreements spell out working conditions in no less detail. In the rapidly changing, frequently chaotic world of publishing, management often finds it convenient to shift junior employees into jobs of greater responsibility on a fill-in basis. French law adds financial reward to the opportunity to demonstrate competence. A young person lifted from lowly legwork to rewrite, for example, must be given a raise equal to the difference between what he was getting before the tryout and the contract minimum for the new work. Another aspect of this provision illustrates the comprehensive nature of the entire employment arrangement. While protecting *débutants* against exploitation, the law also tries to prevent management from using tryouts to humiliate more senior employees, by stipulating that the person coming into a job cannot make more than his predecessor.

Night work receives 15 percent more pay; hazardous assignment (defined as anything from domestic riots and foreign wars to epidemics, spelunking and "underwater reporting") carries an automatic guarantee of additional life insurance, which must range between a sum not less than 10 times the reporter's salary, and not more than 10 times the editor in chief's. No circumstance is overlooked. If somebody is injured in the line of duty, he receives full salary for a year; if permanently maimed, full retirement benefits. The family of an employee killed on the job, in addition to generous payment, is assured that the employer will pay the cost of returning the body to his residence or anywhere else "an equivalent distance away" from the scene of the tragedy.

Leaves of absence are treated with similar generosity. Maternity adjustments are guaranteed. "Call or recall to the flag," as the contract colorfully describes military conscription, constitutes a break in employment, but if management fails to find work *acceptable to the journalist* upon his return, a full year's pay is due, complete with the *treizième*. Special provisions grant protection from being required to do promotion work, and from being refused permission to freelance for other publications if such would not do the employer "professional or moral prejudice." Continuing education comes free of charge. A 1974 law designed to upgrade the profession requires publishers to set aside one percent of their profits to support studies pursued by their employees at the Centre de Perfectionnement des Journalistes.

Vacations and other time off are spelled out in luxurious detail. All bearers of a press card get a full month off after one year on the job. Traditionally, this means August; another twelve-day vacation comes in winter. France being a Catholic country, and having the longest national history in the West, official holidays commemorating religious sanctity and political tumult ring the calendar—at least one in every month except February. Family life is encouraged. Journalists get a week's leave when they marry, three days if they become parents, two days when they move or become parents-in-law. Death merits equal reverence, requiring one day off if it claims journalists' brothers or sisters-in-law, two days for a brother, sister or grandchild, four for a spouse, parent, grandparent or parent-in-law.

The centerpiece of negotiated amelioration, however, is job security. Article L761-5 says flatly that "If an employer dismisses an employee, indemnity is due." If the cause for firing is "grave or repeated" faults on the part of a journalist, a special commission may reduce severance pay. Otherwise it is fixed by law as equivalent to one month's pay for each year or fraction of a year's work at the publication. In the case of anyone with 15 years' seniority, special boards decide *how much more* than the legal formula must be paid. Cost to employers can be considerable. In August 1980, firing a Fr50,000- ($12,000-) a-year journalist with 10 years' on the job, for instance, would mean paying him Fr500,000 ($120,000). These benefits are the more remarkable for being obtainable in some circumstances at an employee's discretion through the "conscience clause" of the National Labor Code.

Relative to other kinds of work in France, journalism is heavily unionized. Throughout the 1970s, union members holding press cards numbered around 60 percent, the figure being highest at large dailies, lowest on weeklies and small papers in the provinces.

Of the six unions scattered across the political spectrum, by far the largest is the Syndicat National des Journalists, Autonome, (SNJA) founded in 1918. Unlike its rivals, the SNJA maintains its independence from labor federations and political parties, and in 1978 listed a membership of 3,600. In contrast, the next largest, the Syndicat des Journalistes Français (CFDT), was half CFDT's size, and the Syndicat National des Journalistes C.G.T. had only 1,200 members. For purposes of negotiating the national contract, four of the unions band together in a union of unions of journalism—L'Union Nationale des Syndicats de Journalisme—but otherwise maintain separate representation at each paper.

Although strikes are common in the French press, most concern local issues and are limited to 24-hour protests. In the 1970s the most significant strikes focused on publishers' editorial interventions and job security rather than traditional wage demands. Both of Hersant's Paris takeovers, for example, met protest strikes. The editorial staff of *L'Express* struck briefly to register dismay over Jean-Jacques Servan-Schreiber's thrust into electoral politics. The real threat to the unions, however, was far less personal.

From the turn of the century until the 1960s, French newspaper technology remained relatively stable. But the computer and photo-offset printing with its "astonishing progress," as *Le Monde*'s "presse" commentator put it, brought wrenching dislocations to a deeply entrenched sector of the business. Journalists were affected, of course, but mostly indirectly as workers in the production trades struck to protect their jobs—and shut down papers in the process. Strikes attended modernization efforts of leading papers such as *Ouest-France* and *Sud-Ouest,* but the longest strike in the history of the French press hit *le Parisien Libéré,* one of the largest, most prosperous dailies in the capital. The paper, part of the Amaury group, wanted to introduce computerized offset printing, and a printer's union (Syndicat du Livre C.G.T.) sensed the challenge. The resulting 29-month crisis, from March 1975 to August 1977, involved disruptions at the chain's other properties, attempts to publish outside of Paris (from Chartres to Brussels), several national sympathy strikes, protests in the National Assembly, on the floor of the Paris stock exchange, and in a tower of Notre Dame Cathedral, from which tracts were thrown. Settled with government intervention, the strike cost *Le Parisien Libéré* nearly one-third of its circulation.

Press Laws

On August 24, 1789 France became the first country in the world to formally adopt press freedom as a fundamental written tenet of government. The National Assembly that day approved article XI of the Declaration of the Rights of Man and of Citizens:

The free communication of thoughts and opinions is one of the most precious rights of mankind. Each citizen may therefore speak, write, print in liberty, except in abusing this freedom in cases set forth by the law.

It is the final six words that has bedevilled the history of press freedom in France. Far more than the First Amendment to the U.S. Constitution (adopted two years after the French declaration), the effect of Article XI has been blunted by a host of "cases set forth by the law."

French free-speech law lies scattered through the Penal Code, Code of Penal Procedure, the Code of Military Justice, the Law of 29 July 1881 and a host of special edicts. Together, they form a web of remarkable stickiness and breadth, one capable of entrapping an extremely wide variety of free-flying comment.

Some of the important restrictions involve punishment categories. For instance, criminal sanctions for offenses by writing, unknown in current American precedent, are readily available in France. Libel is merely one of the several causes of action involving fines and imprisonment up to one year. While it might be argued that from a monetary standpoint, damages differ little from fines, one dimension looms so large in free-speech issues that it blots out all seeming similarity. Criminal actions bring in the intimidating factor of the full power of the state, with its investigative, policy and punitive resources —an awesome opponent even to the most powerful publisher. Civil actions allow a more manageable equation, as well as freedom from the potential stigma of a criminal record. The state merely provides an unbiased tribunal to resolve disputes between journalists and those they describe.

Other procedural aspects of French law makes its frequently criminal character all the more intimidating. In defamation cases, for instance, the usual presumption of innocence is reversed, shifting the burden of proof from accuser to the accused. Four tests of good faith must be established for an alleged libel to be judged unintentional. The deep exposure available for use against the press also mitigates against adventurousness in print. Writers stand third in a ranking of *responsables* that extends down to street vendors. The prime target is the director, who by inclination and responsibility is usually far less willing to risk jail for what his employees write than are the journalists themselves.

In Western societies, most legal limitations on free speech stem from the core idea of defamation, the harming of some person, institution or interest by things said publicly without consent. *Diffamation* itself refers to damage involving some establishable fact. *Injure,* however, covers epithets and insults with no particular factual content. The separate crimes of *offense* and *outrage* are still more broadly construed; although both relate to expression that damages the well-being of society, the former mostly concerns journalistic comment on public officials, the latter some more general transgression, such as pornography or interference with the course of justice. They are highly refined doctrines, full of niceties and ambiguity. Present purposes require the more modest concentration on the gross categories of permitted and outlawed expression.

Some differences in French and American libel law are largely of degree, albeit of generous magnitude. Most startling is that the French law designates a significant field of "no-fault" libel, in which publications may be fined, or their personnel imprisoned, for expressing *facts*. The test of culpability has nothing to do with rectitude—merely whether the statements were made, and if so, damaging, in three areas:

—Virtually anything potentially diminishing a person's honor, said without permission, provides a potential cause of action. Not satisfied with already stringent provisions of the Penal Code, the National Assembly by the law of 17 July 1970 made it a crime to publish any "word or image" from a private place without consent. The same law amended the Penal Code to allow steps ranging up to seizure of any publication which, for instance, ran classified documents or pictures of a starlet behind a garden wall.

—Facts more than 10 years old may not be mentioned without risk of libel, if they can be shown to damage an individual's reputation.

—Reference to crimes specifically pardoned, or which took place in a period officially amnestied, or off-limits, is actionable. This provision takes on particular importance with knowledge that incoming national leaders, borrowing from royal tradition, routinely amnesty ordinary crimes and, frequently, particularly troublesome historical episodes such as the Dreyfus case, World War II and the Algerian crisis. The law formally seals them off from further discussion in the press by making all references to them vulnerable to civil and/or criminal pursuit.

Beyond libel law lie other imposing barriers to free speech. Authorities Jean Marie Auby and Robert Ducos-Ader relate some of them to a generalized "public interest" and the repression of reports deemed harmful to it. In their book, *The Law of Information,* they identify four areas clearly stamped "no trespassing" to the press:

1. *Provocation to commit crimes.* Journalists may be held accountable not only if they *knowingly* assist criminal action, but also for a host of far more ambiguous actions. Provocations can be direct, indirect, or fall into one of nine categories of "special provocations"; all carry criminal sanctions, journalists being treated as accomplices. In punishing direct incitements (for example, urging opponents of nuclear power to join an illegal demonstration). French law distinguishes between "provocations followed by the effect" and those that are not. Direct provocation, of course, implies editorialization rather than straight reporting.

When the charge accuses an article of having *indirectly* encouraged theft, murder, pillage, arson, grievous bodily injury, harm to or destruction of property, or crimes and misdemeanors against state security, the press finds itself on more subjective, less defensible ground. The law punishes what a court finds to be "apology" for lawbreaking, apology defined as presenting it in a "praise-worthy, meritorious or legitimate light," whether in civil, administrative or military contexts.

2. *Offenses against public authorities, official bodies and protected persons.* The more powerful the person, the more protection is granted. This begins with the president of the republic and the doctrine of "offense," defined by Auby and Ducos-Ader, as

…much broader than the notion of injury of defamation it encompasses. Thus, it does not require [even] a precise imputation against honor, nor the presence of profanity, but simply an assault on the dignity or the authority of the president of the republic.

French law also extends the president's red-carpet insulation to members of foreign governments. The aggrieved need not lower themselves to actually bringing suit; that may be left to the prosecutor's office.

Lesser institutions must rely on ordinary libel law, but nonetheless can force publications to prove the truth of articles written about them. The rationale: "to grant special protection to institutions playing an important role in public life," which the law defines as including chambers of commerce, *"Les Grandes Écoles,"* academic councils and the Legion of Honor, in addition, of course, to all the courts and branches of the armed services.

Although institutional safeguards also shield the people who run the offices, the doctrine of "protected persons" grants another layer of armor to virtually anyone doing anything, permanently or temporarily, for the state. To be sure, members of the Council of State, the Senate and National Assembly get special consideration in disputes with the press. But no more so than regional, municipal and local authorities, whose status also rubs off on their part-time employees (including court juries and witnesses), all of whom receive partial immunity as a perquisite of the job.

Nor need the designation be as concrete as a living person performing a public task. Members of religious or ethnic groups may be "protected persons," as are all the deceased of France. The dead take their honor to the grave. Heirs may sue to throw off aspersions cast by the press on the good name of their predecessors, or on their own reputations through alleged ancestral antics.

3. *Outrage.* "Any scornful expression that diminishes respect for the moral authority of a public function, or the purpose for which it is exercised," falls under the mantle of legal *outrage.* Even broader than *injure,* it may concern anything from facts to "ironic or insolent" statements down to mere gestures. In the eyes of French law, these are the most serious of press offenses. They draw the most stringent penalties from the workings of what Auby and Ducos-Ader call "the most supple" procedures.

The French judiciary has adopted *outrage* as its chief bulwark against press scrutiny. Article 226 of the Penal Code specifically bans anything that "throws discredit on a judicial act or decision...," or which "aims to strip judicial acts or their authors of the consideration inherent in their function." Nor does interpretation leave much room for maneuver. "It is not necessary in terms of recent jurisprudence," write Auby and Ducos-Ader, "that the accused intend to attack the authority of justice; it suffices that the act *could have had* this result."

Comment before decisions are handed down is covered by the "Forbidden Disclosures" doctrine contained in the press laws of 27 July 1849, 29 July 1881 and 30 October 1935, which collectively provide that:

—Before trial, nothing may be said or shown of "circumstances of a crime of blood," or of anything capable of pressuring witnesses or revealing court procedures before official announcement.

—During litigation, personal privacy for all participants remains intact. The mere fact of statements having been made in open court gives French reporters no privilege to make them public. This includes, of course, all references to private life, facts more than ten years old and previous crimes amnestied or pardoned.

4. *Exempted Subjects.* In addition to defamation, privacy and protected public authority provisions, French law bans certain subjects outright. The following list, while by no means complete, suffices to suggest the size and tone of the dossier. Without previous authorization, periodicals may not report (a) anything concerning the military that might damage its "effectiveness or morale"; (b) anything that might "attack the credit of the nation, whether undermining confidence in its currency or the value of public funds"; (c) anything relating to parliamentary investigations or commissions; (d) anything that might "outrage public morals" or attract "undue attention to debauchery."

One of the most imaginative features of French press law operates on a plane quite independent of fines, imprisonment or the paying of civil damages. It requires forced insertions of editorial material—and not simply when journalists make mistakes, nor in their own paper. French law awards the ability to force retraction to persons dissatisfied with coverage involving them. The press, in other words, can be forced to run specific editorial material against its will. A "Right of Rectification" grants "any embodiment of public authority" accused in the press of misperformance to demand a free insertion.

The only restrictions on the correction, which the periodical must run in a prominent position in its next issue, is that it be no longer than twice the length of the original article.

By contrast, the "Right of Reply" gives any persons or organizations, public or private, the ability to force insertion whether or not the piece written about them was correct. The only requirements are that the plaintiff be identified and discussed. That alone grants access to "reply," which can be anything from denial to simple amplification. The publication must print it within three days of receiving the complaint—in precisely the same position as the original and in the same typeface. Frequently, judges extend the reply to other periodicals, requiring editors to pay for insertions 50 to 250 lines long in competing papers as well as in their own. Compliance has nothing to do with mitigating damages. It simply allows the publication to escape the fine that might otherwise be levied.

Censorship

There is no government censorship in France. Government policies however, contribute greatly to what the French call "autocensure," or self-censorship. References to it are frequent and open. Even the government's *Cahiers Française* quoted a leading journalist on the subject in a 1976 report on the daily press. An important part of the profession, said Claude Durieux of *Le Monde,* involves occasional "prudent conformism... the silence of complicity." Founded deeply in tradition, self-censorship is reinforced by the seductive pull of state subsidies and the deterrent weight of laws limiting freedom of expression. Like mighty weapons, the press laws achieve their end most effectively by *threatening* targets rather than by actual use. The 1970s brought some striking insights into the workings of the system, many of them provided by a publication whose very existence says a great deal about French attitudes toward a free press.

Roger Fressoz, director-general of the satirical weekly *Le Canard Enchainé* refers to it as France's *fou de roi,* or court jester. The term perfectly fits a publication that regularly manages to bring out information no other dares touch, and get away with it because, although deadly serious, its form and tone are joking. Examples of stories it broke in the 1970s include a prime minister's nonpayment of income tax, the government's attempted bugging of its offices ("water-gaffe," *Canard* called it) and reports of the president's acceptance of diamonds from an African emperor.

The paper's charade begins with its name. It means "chained duck," duck being the argot word for rag, and chained referring to its origins under World War I censorship. Its foppish layout includes the print equivalents of tasseled caps and shoe-bells: caricatures, color and puns galore. *Canard*'s "quack" converts a language famous for clarity into an opaque babble revealing no more than a shadowed outline of subjects discussed. Editor Claude Angeli says his political section's lisping sibilance permits its authors to be "aggressive with nuance." More than 450,000 readers across the country miss not a reference, although to anyone lacking an up-to-the minute understanding of French politics, the reports can be incomprehensible.

These elaborate stylistic precautions, however, are merely *Canard*'s surface protections. The court jester is entirely owned by its staff, whose stock reverts to the collective when members leave or die. This measure is designed to eliminate political pressures from a publisher, and is complemented by another provision that bolsters the paper's independence in a way no other national periodical finds affordable. *Canard* shields itself from manipulative advertisers (both state and privately owned) by accepting no advertising whatever. All of its considerable profit flows from the kiosk price.

The prime importance of *Le Canard Enchaîné* is not how it plays its part, but rather that there exists a role for a court jester. *Canard*'s existence and prestige measure repression, not tolerance. As the 1970s closed, there were indications of a narrowing scope of free comment.

Demonstrating "auto-censure" in reporting is of course difficult because by definition what is withheld does not appear. Yet it could be plainly traced in the treatment the French press gave several major stories, which the following three exemplify:

One was the death of President Georges Pompidou, whose condition was diagnosed fatal in 1971, and became increasingly widely known thereafter. Yet first mention of it in the press did not come until April, 1974, and only after his pathetically bloated appearance had been commented on by foreign newspapers during a summit meeting with U.S. President Richard Nixon in Reykjavik, Iceland.

There was also the war in Chad. Throughout the 1970s, French troops battled guerrillas in their former African colony, sometimes in regimental strength. As with President Pompidou's illness, detailed coverage was strongly resisted, and with considerable success. The press reported the war only intermittently, with little detail or discussion of the issues.

Finally, the Bokassa affair. Governmental response to an extremely rare instance of sustained investigation by the press provoked a response seldom deemed necessary. Embarrassing reports that President Giscard d'Estaing had accepted diamonds from Emperor Jean-Bedel Bokassa (ruler of the Central African Empire, once the French colony of Ubangi-Shari), broken by *Le Canard Enchaîné,* were followed up by *Le Monde.* Significantly, the government chose not to sue the "jester," but criminal charges against the top editor of the country's leading daily in 1980 alleged "discredit" to the courts in articles criticizing judicial decisions in five cases involving the Bokassa affair and other matters.

Government interference in Agence France-Presse's management provided a less spectacular, but more characteristic example of the pattern of indirect state-influence. Just as AFP's highly respected chief operating officer was about to resume the usual second, three-year term in the summer of 1978, the minister of culture intervened and the incumbent was forced out, replaced not for any failing but because the new designee was of undeniable value to a political coalition that had only narrowly managed survival at the polls a few months earlier. The new designee was director-general of the Syndicat National de la Presse Quotidienne, whose publisher-members determine which candidates receive how much coverage, and of what kind.

The coup was unambiguous and AFP President-Director Hubert Beuve-Méry would have none of it. A towering figure in French journalism—among other things founder and retired director of *Le Monde*—Beuve-Méry thundered, "whether in terms of principle or any other consideration, I cannot associate myself with a procedure that amounts to a grave attack on the spirit, if not the letter, of the agency's statute." That was his resignation statement. But with those few words and eloquent action, the encounter closed. There were no screaming headlines. No publication questioned the ministry or the president. Even *Le Monde* buried its founder's remarks under the *Presse* rubric deep inside the paper. Government meddling just isn't page-one news.

State-Press Relations

No discussion of the press's legal or economic structure in France can be considered complete without examining the points at which the state enters both. To a degree unmatched elsewhere in the West, the two are fused in a system French historians call *Colbertisme,* after Louis XIV's inventive comptroller and state financier. In essence, *Colbertisme* is a symbiotic relationship between the public and private sectors in which government assists business in return for representation in its councils—and for the resulting opportunity to guide it in desired directions. The genius of the arrangement lies in its ability to resolve disputes before they come to open, public test. This is also what critics find insidious about it.

Appropriately, one of the first steps in newspaper production provides an apt example of *Colbertisme* in action: registration, through obtaining a *numéro paritaire*. It is typical of the system's guiding ambiguities that this registration is neither legally mandatory nor issued directly by the state. Instead, approval must come from the Commission Partitaire des Publications et Agences de Presse, composed of seven government officials and seven publishers. Together they verify that the periodical will appear at least monthly and will devote no more than one-third of its space to advertising, preconditions that augment 11 other stipulations including requirements that owners be French nationals of legal age and without police records. Why would any publisher go through this theoretically optional political process? Because of economics. The *numéro paritaire* enables newspapers and magazines to receive their proportional share of state subsidies, which amount to about 12 percent of total print-media revenues, and without which most Paris dailies would quickly go under.

Other points of press-state contact involve legal deposition requirements and a host of special commissions for services ranging from setting the price of newsprint through delivery to guaranteeing the independence of Agence France-Presse. Two copies of every issue, signed by the publisher, must be left with the district attorney, 10 with the ministry of information, prefecture, subprefecture and mayor in the district circulated. Others go to the national archives and the Ministry of the Interior. State officials appear on the boards responsible for distributing ad lineage (through Havas, the state-controlled advertising agency) from Renault, Air France and other nationalized companies, which in turn rank among the largest advertisers in the country. They are indirectly represented in trade cooperatives such as the Nouvelles Messageries de la Presse Parisienne, distributor of all but a few of the 3.7 million newspapers read in metropolitan Paris. One-third of the members of AFP's administrative council, the supreme body charged with guarding the news service against "influences capable of compromising the exactness or the objectivity of its information" are government functionaries.

Every autumn, the 491 deputies of the National Assembly take one of their few scarcely contested votes of the year. They give away large amounts of public money— over Fr2 billion ($500 million)—to the profit-making enterprises of the press. In a country that regularly casts nearly half its votes for some form of socialism, this might seem surprising. The explanation, however, is simple: the aid is actually being distributed proportionately across the political board. This accounts for its parliamentary popularity both in the fractious atmosphere of Paris, where newspapers maintain distinct political stances, and in the provinces, where the press is generally politically bland and regionally monopolistic. Opposing aid to the press would constitute "political suicide," as the assembly's subcommittee chairman once put it.

Another reason why press subsidies are so popular is that they are not considered aid to the publishers. Officially, newspaper aid is reader aid. The theory is that without it, there would be fewer newspapers, hence a narrower range of opinion, and that editorial resources would then be too feeble to provide quality journalism. Only once since the Second World War has this reasoning been challenged, and it provoked an irresistible counterthrust from the office of the prime minister. "If the objective of subsidization is the reader of the paper," wrote Jean Serisé, who led government's defense of its policy in 1972, "the immediate assignee is necessarily the newspaper enterprise, which must reflect back to the reader, whether through expanded or improved content, the benefit provided." The law, however, does not require that public funds be used for particular uses. Publishers may treat the benefits as they would ordinary resources.

About 90 percent of the state's aid is carried on government books as "indirect" assistance. University of Paris II Professor Nadine Toussaint, a leading authority, calls it "not...aid which is given, but rather resources which are not taken away." Half-price postal rates, for instance, saved the press Fr 1,530,000,000 (nearly $364 million) in 1978, and while preferential mail rates are common for the press in many countries, they are only one among several conduits for assistance in France. Exoneration from value-added tax (TVA) levied at each production stage was worth Fr·245,000,000 ($58 million), being excused from the professional tax another Fr·180,000,000 ($43 million). Smaller but more controversial tax breaks for profits reinvested in productive capacity within five years of being earned came to a mere Fr 46.2 million ($11 million), but are so appreciated that publishers fondly call the tax code provision "Our 39-b." Despite attacks as "an anomaly" and a "shocking financial heresy" in the 1972 report, it survived intact.

Unlike indirect aid, which the government calculates in terms of the amount treasury receipts are diminished by exemptions, direct underwriting is both easier to measure and more controversial. National Assembly Deputy Roger Vivien, a Gaullist proponent of subsidies, felt obliged to scold fellow legislators in 1978 for refusing to increase subsidies for overseas distribution of French publications, for example. "One has every right to ask the powers that be" he wrote in the

official budget document that year, "to explain their reasons. If they accept the aid policy (by maintaining it) it is indispensable that they support it with funds sufficient for proper execution." No publisher could have said it with more feeling.

Other direct aid ranges from reimbursement for telephone calls to payments equaling 14 percent of composing- and printing-equipment purchase costs and preferential TVA rates. The latter merits brief discussion because it suggests how complex the system became and how unexpected are some of its results. Under the Fiscal Reform Act of December 29, 1976, publications other than dailies were given a choice. They could either pay less tax or be reimbursed for the tax they were paying on newsprint, printing and other news-service costs. All but 414 of 9,900 publications found it more profitable to pay *higher* taxes. Subsidies coming back to corporate coffers more than made up the difference.

Aside from TVA, the table below illustrates another kind of double accounting in favor of the press. In addition to the common forms of mail subsidies, France extends the principle of assisted distribution to railroad bulk freight, traditionally the main transport of national papers printed in Paris for circulation across the country. Because the state owns the railroads, it finds itself paying the press to utilize its services. No such help is available for shipments on privately controlled transportation—trucks, for example.

The institutional aspects of implementing state information initiatives proved far less stable in the 1970s than the policies themselves. In 1968 the Inter-Ministerial Committee for Information was set up under the auspices of the prime minister to "coordinate information" with the government, and to "better disseminate" news about it. In 1974 it

Indirect Government Press Subsidies (in francs)		
	1977*	1978**
Press telegrams	70,000	70,000
Other telegraphic service	2,800,000	3,000,000
Preferential postage	1,402,000,000	1,530,000,000
TVA exoneration	230,000,000	245,000,000
Profit reinvestment (39-b)	46,000,000	50,000,000
Professional tax exoneration	180,000,000	215,000,000
Total	1,860,870,000	2,043,070,000

*The rate of exchange in 1977 was Fr 4.7 = US$1.00.
**The rate of exchange in 1978 was Fr 4.2 = US$1.00.

Direct Government Press Subsidies (in francs)

	1977*	1978**
Telephone calls	8,178,000	9,978,000
Subsidized printing	13,840,000	6,000,000
Railroad reimbursement	33,850,000	38,160,000
International distribution	10,670,000	10,670,000
TVA reimbursement for publications choosing to pay increased taxes	220,000,000	235,000,000
Total	286,538,000	299,808,000

*The rate of exchange in 1977 was Fr 4.7 = US$1.00.
**The rate of exchange in 1978 was Fr 4.2 = US$1.00.

was replaced by a General Delegation for Information, whose chief was picked by the Council of Ministers. A press service specifically at the disposition of journalists was established the next year. Shortly thereafter, however, another reorganization brought the roles of spokesman and broadcast overseer to a newly created Ministry of Culture and Communication. No such upheavals came to the bureau charged with coordinating and implementing state technical and judicial policies such as aid to the print press and public service in broadcasting. Le Service Juridique et Technique de l'Information continued to perform those functions, assigned to it in 1956.

Unlike aid to publishers, the help given by the French state to individual journalists is neither officially acknowledged as such, nor given regular legislative review. Payment, however, is subject to the same sorts of conditions, *Colbertisme* exerts as strong an influence on the employed as on their employers, and begins at the same point.

A *carte professionelle d'identité* performs the same functions for journalists as does *numéro paritaire* registry for publishers. It is a screening device for entry into a realm enriched and protected by the state; a reminder of public participation in the otherwise private councils of the press. Striking similarities appear both in obtaining these forms of state sanction and the reasons for wishing to do so. The Commission de la Carte d'Identité professionelle (CCIP), composed of seven working journalists and seven government officials, determines each applicant's "high moral standards," financial arrangements and standing in the profession. Disputes on entry qualifications, any change in a journalist's annual renewal application, or working status (all of which must be registered with CCIP) are referred to a Superior

Council. There, state representation is decisive: it includes two judges, one journalist. Denials are not uncommon, often on grounds that someone does not meet the definition of "journalist" stipulated in the National Labor Code.

These provisions clearly indicate that press cards more closely resemble a license to practice than a mere formality. The reasons why keeping them stand high among personal professional priorities are the same ones that impel publishers into their form of partnership with the state: money and security. Only those with press cards are protected by the generous terms of the national labor contract, biennial renegotiation of which takes place under government supervision. As a practical matter, nobody without a card stands a chance of being hired by established newspapers.

But two other benefits are more immediate and more directly spelled out in government (as opposed to labor contract) terms:

—A 30 percent tax reduction comes automatically to each of France's 14,000 registered journalists.

—Professional integrity becomes a matter of state protection under the "conscience clause" of the National Labor Code. This remarkable provision protects journalists against summary, unindemnified firings, guaranteeing full severance benefits for those who quit or are forced to resign because of a change in a newspaper's political orientation that constitutes "an attempt on their honor, or reputation, or general integrity." Its use is commonplace.

Evidence of the interventionist effect of *Colbertisme* surfaced frequently in the 1970s, perhaps most importantly in the previously mentioned emergence of controversial publisher Robert Hersant as "the new French Hearst." Resenting Hersant's conservative politics and penchant for weaving them into newspaper policy, much of the staff of one provincial paper he acquired availed itself of the "conscience clause" in conjunction with quitting or being fired. The pattern was to be repeated, most spectacularly in Paris. Neither press "baronies" nor an owner's editorial influence is anything new in France. But Hersant's perceived relationship with government focused attention on the Gaullists as well as the publisher.

Hersant took control of *Le Figaro* and *France Soir* just in time to assure their support of Valery Giscard d'Estaing's political coalition, which was flagging badly in election campaigning. It was broadly rumored that government influence had aided Hersant's empire-building in order to secure friendly coverage in what were respectively the oldest and largest dailies in the capital. France's nationalized banking system permits control over many categories of credits, with the party in power able to extend funds to allies and withhold them from enemies. Critics also charged the Gaullists with failing to prosecute under antitrust and anti-Collaborationist statutes. Admirers countered that government policies permitted Hersant to inject technology and badly needed capital into the daily newspapers. Because of *Colbertisme*'s many points of state-press contact, a professional controversy quickly gathered political coloration.

Attitude Toward Foreign Media

No special visa is required to enter France as a journalist, but foreign correspondents based there for more than three months must register with the government to obtain a residency permit. They are also required to complete accreditation procedures with the Ministry of Foreign Affairs, which may order a background check through local consulates in their home countries. Beyond that, if they plan to cover presidential press conferences, they must join the presidential press association for further documentation.

There is no prior censorship of foreign media or screening of cables. Distribution of foreign periodicals, however, can be stopped rather easily. Single issues may be seized (if imported) or suppressed (if printed in France) by simple order of the Interior Ministry. Permanent banning of foreign media requires approval of the Council of Ministers. Distribution of foreign propaganda and for-

eign ownership of domestic media are both strictly forbidden (the *International Herald Tribune*, for example, is organized as a French corporation). Importing periodicals is subject to the same laws covering other goods; approval must come from the Ministry of Commerce and prefect of the circulation district, a process that normally takes a year.

All major international press organizations are represented in France, which voted with the United States and other Western countries against restrictions on newsgathering proposed by UNESCO.

News Agencies

Agence France-Presse (AFP) holds its own with the West's three other major wire services (AP, UPI and Reuters) with the aid of government subsidies, which in 1978 amounted to FR 161,215,000 ($38.4 million). The state's aid, which also includes partial reimbursement of the costs of taking its service, makes AFP a relative bargain for French periodicals. Its 850 journalists provide the vast majority of non-local news to the nation.

News flows into AFP's central office in Paris from 14 bureaus in the provinces and French possessions, from 84 principal overseas bureaus and from stringer representation in 163 countries. As of 1979 AFP was filing 600,000 words daily (equivalent to 12 issues of a French newspaper), in French, English, Spanish and German, to 1,400 subscribers in 154 countries. Of these, 355 were newspapers, 192 were broadcast facilities and 750 were French government agencies: ministries, embassies, administrative units. More than 80 national news agencies take AFP services, and relay it to an additional 12,000 newspapers around the world. Dispatches are transmitted by teletype, cable and, for Asia, Latin America and West Africa, via two satellites in stationary orbit 30 miles above the equatorial zones of the Indian and Atlantic oceans.

Electronic News Media

While the print press of France was undergoing profound centralization, with increased opportunities for indirect state involvement, the broadcast media undertook modest experiments in another direction. Radio and television had long been a state monopoly; in the 1970s government dominance remained, but with more room for independence.

The social role of radio and television had been clear from the start to the administration of President Charles de Gaulle. His minister of information, André Malraux, was frank about state requirements during a conversation with Pierre Salinger, then President John F. Kennedy's press secretary. "How can you govern," wondered the Frenchman, "without controlling the TV networks?" The Gaullists did not leave this to chance. The policy was to use television to balance the criticism of the written press. Before the student revolt of May, 1968, l'Office de Radiodiffusion-Television Française (ORTF) was linked directly to the government through an "Inter-Ministerial Service of Liaison and Information." Each morning, four broadcast journalists met with representatives from the ministries of finance, information, education, culture and foreign affairs. The emphasis was to be on proper "orientation" of programming. Critics such as Sanche de Gramont, a senior journalist and author, summarized a widely-held judgment in his book *The French*, published in 1969:

> [The French] are treated to a sunshine image of France as a world leader with no domestic problems.... They live in a world of bicycle racers, Olympic ski teams, pop singers and other innocuous miscellania.... The crude slant on domestic news is one reason why the May–June events of 1968 took public opinion by surprise. It was like learning that the plague has hit Camelot.

Frivolous programming and distrusted news are often cited as explanations for television's relatively slow start in France. Partially in response to reforms taken in the 1970s, the size of the audience grew almost explosively. In that decade alone, the number of sets nearly doubled, to 14 million. After 10 years in operation, the unwieldy bureaucracy of ORTF seemed intolerable to government, journalists and public alike. The Act of August 7, 1974 divided its functions among no fewer than seven separate entities, in hope that smaller units would increase performance quality. Specifically, the act charged ORTF's successors with "...ensuring that only the general interest of the people prevails...[taking] part in the diffusion of French culture throughout the world...safeguard[ing] the quality and high standing of the French language." An Institut National

de l'Audiovisuel (INA) is responsible for professional training, research, archive maintenance and overseas distribution. TéléDiffusion de France operates the broadcast installations. The Société Française de Production et Création Audio-visuelle is the state-controlled production company.

The structure of the four government-owned programming companies established by the 1974 statute shows both the desire for independence and the difficulty of nurturing it within the context of a state monopoly. Radio France and France-Regions 3 are straightforward entities designed respectively to compete with quasi-private radio stations ringing France, and to foster cultural and political diversity. Télévision Française 1 (TF1) and Antenne 2 (A2), however, occupy more ambiguous ground. They were established as direct rivals, to develop distinct scheduling, with none of ORTF's former programatic "harmonization." Yet they operate under identical guidelines, with the same management structure. The administrative council of each is made up of two representatives of the state and one each from Parliament, the press, "the cultural world" and the company's own staff.

Only small exceptions limit the state's monopoly status. For transmission and programming it is complete, but production is exempted: the national broadcast companies can produce their own material or buy it elsewhere, from public or private sources. Nor does the 1974 law cover reception, which makes possible the "peripheral" broadcasters that operate under the laws of their nations of corporate registry: Radio-Télévision Luxembourg, Radio-Télévision Monte Carlo, Europe 1, Radio Andorre and Sud-Radio. The organization of these broadcasters is complex. Although in principle foreign companies, much of their programming is accomplished in Paris offices; while theoretically "private," the French state exerts powerful influence on them. Sofirad (Société Financière de Radiodiffusion), a state-controlled holding company, in turn owns 97 percent of Sud-Radio, 83 percent of Radio Monte Carlo and 35 percent of Europe 1. Additionally, through Havas, the state-controlled advertising agency, the government has a say in Radio Luxembourg, the most popular station in France. Havas owns a controlling interest.

The history of broadcast advertising is similarly complex. In 1951 authorization was given for commercials aimed at increasing the sale of agricultural products and in 1959 ads for some industrial goods were allowed. Not until 1968 was trade advertising permitted, and even then, it was limited to two minutes a day. The reform legislation of 1974 fixes the trade-advertising limit at 25 percent of the total revenues of all public broadcast facilities. Since only two program companies (TF1 and A2) are permitted to air commercials, the total proportion of advertising revenue in their budgets as of 1980 was 60 percent and 45 percent respectively.

These stringent limitations have implications far beyond any convenience to viewers. They hold television to a modest 14 percent share in the nation's total advertising expenditures—which means a large, if indirect, protection for print media.

Education & Training

Although the opening of the École Superieure de Journalisme de Lille (ESJ) in 1924 equipped France with Europe's first journalism school, leadership in the field did not follow. Lille remained a small outpost largely ignored by the profession. Not until the Liberation in World War II did the idea of academic preparation take hold, largely as part of a general admiration for Anglo-American ways of encouraging pluralism and political liberty. But important, too, was a new optimism among journalists who had fought their way through the clandestine press of the Resistance to leadership positions in established journals after the war. For the first time since early in the century, the times seemed right for free expression and professional self-respect.

This "green light" for journalists lasted from 1945 to the Algerian crisis, when political stress again closed in. The postwar period produced a greatly polished professional pride, but not much in the way of specialized education. That was left to the newly reconstituted Agence France-Presse, which attracted the best journalists in the country and for nearly 20 years operated as a sort of national journalism school for young staffers. As late as 1964, a mere six percent of French journalists had any academic training in the field.

By 1971, however, the proportion of journalism graduates had jumped to 20 percent within the ranks of official press-card holders. Fifteen years of "new style" journalism had taken effect, as had new institutions

capable of extending it. The Centre de Formation des Journalistes opened quickly after the liberation of Paris in 1946. The Institute Universitaire de Technologie de Bordeaux (IUT) and a variety of IUT's elsewhere were designed to answer student demands in the late 1960s for democratization of education. The national labor contract also made professional education more attractive by decreasing the number of years of apprenticeship at newspapers for journalism graduates. After the first large increase, however, the number of graduate professionals leveled off. In 1975, even in broadcast journalism, magnet for the highest proportion of professionally trained people, those with specialized education made up only 26 percent of the staffs. The most important schools are:

—*École Superieure de Journalisme de Lille.* A private institution attached to the Catholic University of Lille, the ESJ accepts 30 students for a two-year course of study.

—*Centre de Formation des Journalistes, Paris.* Each year it graduates 45 students after two or three years' work, depending on the field of specialization. It has added a Centre de Perfectionment des Journalistes for mid-career professional training.

—*Université de Bordeaux* III. Two institutions here have received national recognition. The Unité Pluridisciplinaire des Techniques d'Expression et de Communication concentrates on research, while the Institut Universitaire de Technologie trains professional journalists.

—*Centre Universitaire d'Enseignement du Journalisme de Strasbourg.* Affiliated with the University of Strasbourg III, the Center accepts 120 students for three years' study, placing most of them in the regional media.

—*Institut Française de Press et des Sciences de l'Information.* The institute is associated with the University of Paris II and concentrates on scholarly research on the media.

Summary

Neither Watergate nor the Gulag Archipelago's secrecy would be conceivable in France. In terms of the press, the country occupies a mid-ground between the extremes of nearly complete U.S. financial independence and constitutional freedom on one hand, and Soviet state ownership and control on the other. The exact position of France in this regard, however, is more easily described than defined.

While French broadcasting is effectively state controlled, some advertising is permitted and some effort made to assure a variety of reportorial viewpoint. The situation is quite the opposite in the print media, though state participation makes its position somewhat ambiguous. For example, although French newspapers are privately owned profit-seeking enterprises, few would survive without massive government subsidies. Representatives of the French state occupy positions on the boards that set newsprint prices, distribute Paris newspapers and assign advertising from large nationalized companies. They appear in the administrative councils of the theoretically independent national news service (Agence France-Presse), and even within the organizations charged with accrediting journalists. The latter is more important than it might immediately appear. Without an official press card, it is virtually impossible to work for an established journal, or to obtain the 30 percent break in income tax liability that comes with the document.

French press law begins with Article XI of the Declaration of the Rights of Man, a document roughly contemporaneous and synonymous with the First Amendment of the U.S. Constitution. Over the years, however, a succession of democracies, dictatorships, monarchies and republics have added hundreds of abridgments to free speech. (By one count, there were 660 in 1978.) Provisions strictly limit press comment on some subjects, ban it outright on others.

Why, then, does the French press remain lively and vital in many areas most of the time? Because it has learned to censor itself to a degree, and because the draconian laws are enforced only selectively. When a certain line is crossed, however, Gaullist administrations have not hesitated to install wiretaps in newspaper offices (*Le Canard Enchaîné* in 1973), or to bring criminal suits against the most respected newspaper in the country for what would pass in the United States for routine coverage of court cases involving politics (*Le Monde* in 1980).

CHRONOLOGY

1977   *Le Matin,* a moderate socialist offshoot of the Nouvel-Observateur Group, founded.
29-month-old strike at *La Parisien Libéré* settled but paper loses one-third of its circulation.

1978   Robert Hersant, "Citizen Hearst" of French publishing, takes control of his third Paris daily, *l'Aurore.*
Hubert Heuve-Méry, founder and director-emeritus of Agence France-Presse, resigns in protest against official interference and manipulations.

1980   Government brings criminal libel suit against *Le Monde* for articles concerning President Giscard d'Estaing's acceptance of diamonds from former Emperor Bokassa I of Central African Empire (Republic).

BIBLIOGRAPHY

Albert, P. "De la Gazette a Paris-Soir." *La Presse Quotidienne, Cahiers Français.* Paris, 1976.

_____. *La Presse.* Paris, 1976.

Alix, F-X, assistant editor, *Ouest-France.* Interview, June 1978.

Ambassade de France. "Legislation Governing the Press in France." Service de Press et d'Information. New York, 1977.

Ambassade de France. "Radio and Television in France." Service de Presse et d'Information. New York, 1980.

Ambassade de France. "The Printed Press in France." Service de Press et d'Information. New York, 1977.

Ammai, Alain. "Comment Devient-On Journaliste en France?" *Journal de la Presse,* October 9, 1977.

Auby, J-M, and Ducos-Ader, R. *Droit de l'Information.* Paris, 1976.

Balle, F. "The French Broadcasting System: Public Service and Competition." *Studies of Broadcasting,* 1980.

Bellanger, C., et al. *Histoire générale de la Presse Française.* Vol. 5. Paris, 1976.

Beuve-Méry, H., founder, *Le Monde,* former director, AFP. Interview, June 1978.

Billington, J.H. *Fire in the Minds of Men.* New York, 1980.

Boucher, M. "Les Syndicas de la Presse Quotidienne," *La Presse Quotidienne, Cahiers Français.*

Bourges, H., director, Journalism School of Lille. Interview, June 1978.

Brimo, N. *Le Dossier Hersant.* Paris, 1977.

Chevrillon, O., publisher, *Le Point.* Interview, June 1978.

"Cinq Écoles Reconnues." *Le Monde,* July 3, 1976.

de Gramont, S. *The French.* London, 1970.

Devevey, F. "L'Aide de L'Etat." *La Presse Quotidienne, Cahiers Francais.*

Egen, J. *Messieurs du Canard.* Paris, 1973.

Escarpit, R., founder, University of Bordeaux III Journalism School. Interview, May 1978.

Fauvet, J., editor in chief, *Le Monde.* Interview, June 1978.

Fitchett, J. "Hersant: The Press Baron of France." *International Herald Tribune,* January 27-28, 1979.

_____. "Paris Papers from Right to Left." *International Herald Tribune,* 27-28 January 1979.

Fressoz, R., editor in chief, *Le Canard Enchaîné.* Interview, June 1978.

Gentôt, D. *Convention Collective Nationale de Travail des Journalistes,* Paris, 1976.

_____. As president, Syndicat National des Journalistes (Autonome). Interview, May 1978.

Giroud, F., founder, *L'Express.* Interview, June 1978.

Giroux, P., lawyer specializing in press affairs. Interview, June 1978.

Guide du Droit de la Press. Paris, 1976.

Hollstein, M. "The Changing Press of Paris." *Journalism Quarterly,* Autumn 1978.

Jeanneney, J-N, and Julliard, J. *Le Monde de Beuve-Méry.* Paris, 1979.

Le Gendre, B. "L'Enseignement du Journalisme." *Le Monde,* July 3, 1975.

Legris, M. *Le Monde, tel qu'il est.* Plon, 1976.

Lemoine, Jean-François, publisher, *Sud-Ouest.* Interview, May 1978.

L'Her, Y. "L'Evolution des Quotidiens Depuis 1945." *La Presse Quotidienne, Cahiers Français.*

Lepape, P. *La Presse.* Paris, 1972.

Maupin, Françoise. "L'Agence France-Presse." *La Presse Quotidienne, Cahiers Français.*

Picollec, J. *Dossier H...Comme Hersant.* Paris, 1977.

Provost, R. *Le Monde.* Paris, 1977.

Servan-Schreiber, J-L. *Le Pouvoir d'informer.* Paris, 1972.

_____. As publisher, *L'Expansion.* Interview, June 1978.

Smith, A. *Subsidies and the Press in Europe.* London, 1977.

Thibau, J. *Le Monde.* Paris, 1978.

Todd, O., editor, *L'Express.* Interview, June 1978.

Toussaint, N. "La Concentration." *La Presse Quotidienne, Cahiers Français.*

_____. *L'Economie de l'Information.* Paris, 1978.

_____. "Le Métier Journaliste." *La Presse Quotidienne, Cahiers Français.*

_____. "Les Couts de Production et les Recettes." *La Presse Quotidienne, Cahiers Français.*

Vivien, R-A, "Rapport No. 3131, Assemblée Nationale." Imprimerie de l'Assemblée Nationale, November 8, 1977.

_____. As chairman, National Assembly subcommittee on aid to the press. Interview, June 1978.

EAST GERMANY

by Paul Underwood

BASIC DATA

Population: 16,756,000
Area: 108,262 sq. km. (41,789 sq. mi.)
GNP: 149.2 billion marks (US$81 billion) (1978)
Literacy Rate: 99.1%
Language(s): German, Wendish (Sorb)
Number of Dailies: 39
   Aggregate Circulation: 8,317,000
   Circulation per 1,000: 496
Number of Nondailies: 32
   Aggregate Circulation: 8,913,000
   Circulation per 1,000: 532
Number of Periodicals: 1,162

Number of Radio Stations: 5
Number of Television Stations: 2
Number of Radio Receivers: 15 million
   Radio Receivers per 1,000: 895
Number of Television Sets: 5,451,000
   Television Sets per 1,000: 325
Total Annual Newsprint Consumption:
145,600 metric tons
   Per Capita Newsprint Consumption: 8.7 kg.
(19.14 lb.)
Total Newspaper Ad Receipts: NA
   As % of All Ad Expenditures: NA

Background & General Characteristics

Though only a rump of Germany, with half the size and one-third the population of the western part of Germany, East Germany is one of the ten most industrialized nations of the world. It is easily the most heavily industrialized and prosperous of the Soviet bloc countries.

Formed from the Soviet zone of occupation following World War II, plus East Berlin, it covers most of the traditional German provinces of Brandenberg, Mechlenburg, Saxony, Saxony-Anhalt and Thuringia. Two-thirds of the country form part of the great North European Plain. In the south, the land rises up to the Harz Mountains, the Thüringer Wald and the Erzgebirge (Ore Mountains), which form the border with Czechoslovakia.

The approximately 17 million East Germans are about 99 percent literate and 75 percent urban dwellers. They are ethnically very homogeneous, counting only one small minority group, the Sorbs—or Wends, as they are sometimes called—who make up about 0.2 percent of the total population. Per capita income is between $4,000 and $5,000 a year.

The government is controlled by the Com-munist Party, which is officially known as the Socialist Unity party (SED). It not only has the administrative machinery in its hands but also directs the economy, which, like the Soviets', is planned and centrally controlled. The Party dictates virtually all aspects of political, economic and social life, including the media.

The principal role of the media in the German Democratic Republic—the official name of the country—is *not* the reporting of the day's events but the shaping of public opinion and attitudes to the interests and desires of the Party. It is not uncommon for days to elapse before an event is reported, and it may never appear. Facts and interpretation that do see print are selected and presented from an overtly partisan viewpoint that fits within the ideological framework prescribed by the Party.

Medieval Germany was the birthplace not only of Western printing but of newspapers. Organized dissemination of news had existed earlier but was limited to letters, handwritten news sheets and word-of-mouth communication. Audiences were limited and information about even important events spread only slowly. Printing presses were established in several German cities soon after the development of moveable metal type by Johann Gutenberg in the 1440s. Religious works and copies of classic literature constituted the bulk of the output at first but by the 16th century production included an ever-increasing number of broadsheets and pamphlets dealing with current events. These were produced only when there was something noteworthy to report, and it was not until the beginning of the 17th century that the first publications fitting the definition of a newspaper emerged. The earliest on record are three weeklies published in Augsburg, Strasbourg and Wolfenbuttel in 1609. The first daily newspaper appeared in Leipzig, now in East Germany, in 1650.

By this time most German cities supported newspapers of one kind or another for at least short periods. But conditions were not favorable for development. Germany was then a collection of independent states and principalities, many of them quite small. Censorship was endemic and hampered growth until well into the 19th century. Magazines flourished, however. From only about 50 in 1700, their numbers increased steadily to over 1,200 at the end of the century. And despite the difficulties, newspapers also continued to appear in various centers, including several that were destined to survive and prosper. Among these was the world-famous *Allgemeine Zeitung,* which was founded by Johann Cotta in Tübingen in 1798 and lasted until killed off by the Hitler regime.

The revolutionary movements of 1830 and 1848 that swept through much of Europe gave birth to a new German journalism—in the form of the politically partisan paper. Many such publications appeared during these periods, almost all of them small, speaking for one political faction or another. An example was the *Rheinische Zeitung für Politik, Handel and Gewerbe,* Germany's first socialist paper. Edited by Karl Marx, it lasted one year, from 1848 to 1849. Most of these papers were equally short-lived. The 1848 revolution fizzled out and the old order was restored, with an even stricter censorship in some states. Restrictions eased slowly in the latter half of the century. The triumph of Prussia in the Franco-Prussian War and the establishment of the German Empire brought an end to pre-censorship.

This was the most important gain from Germany's press law of 1874. However, that law still permitted suppression of papers publishing articles considered inflamatory or seditious. Another measure, in effect from 1878 to 1890, outlawed the publication of socialist or communist views. In addition, the German Chancellor Bismarck had a healthy respect for the power of the press, if not for journalists, and he maintained a firm hand through a variety of measures including control of the nation's big news agency, Wolff's Telegraphic Bureau, as well as through bribes to editors and even purchases of newspapers.

During this period, Germany was developing into a major industrial power and the press grew with the country. By the turn of the century about 3,500 newspapers were appearing regularly throughout the Empire. These could be divided roughly into three types: the quality press—represented by the *Allgemeine Zeitung*—independent papers distinguished by the high level of their reporting and comment; the party press, descendants of those publications that had sprung up in the 1830s and 1840s, published by or for particular political parties or groupings: and the mass press, which aimed at attracting the largest possible audiences by emphasizing human interest, sensation and entertainment.

One important bloc of party papers was published by the Social Democrats. Although its first blooming in the 1840s had been cut short, the socialist press revived in the 1860s and 1870s. By 1878, when the ban on such publications went into effect, 42 Social Democratic papers, with a total circulation of 150,000, were in existence. After the lifting of the ban in 1890, the numbers jumped to more than 60, including 19 dailies. By 1914, these had increased to 90 dailies with a total circulation of about three million.

Other papers also flourished. Although the most prestigious publications, like the *Frankfurter Allgemeine Zeitung* and the *Kölnische Zeitung,* never succeeded in attracting large audiences—both had circulations of less than 100,000—the mass press, particularly the cheap *Boulevardblatter,* which peddled sensation and relied on advertising for survival, took over the streets of German cities, particularly Berlin. Local and regional papers were generally more sedate but their journalistic standards were not much higher.

Just prior to World War I the country boasted 4,036 dailies and about 3,000 weekly and monthly publications. With the outbreak of hostilities the press, despite some initial wobbling, united behind the government.

Even the Socialist papers, along with the party's representatives in Parliament, supported the request for war credits, a decision that was to haunt the party later.

The war and the subsequent disastrous inflation temporarily slowed development but, at the same time, German newspapers enjoyed a greater measure of freedom under the Weimar republic than they had ever known. By 1932, 4,700 newspapers were being published throughout the country; 70 percent of them dailies. The largest circulation was claimed by the *Berliner Morgenpost,* with 600,000. Despite the popularity of the sensational mass press in the cities, it was the "gruppenpresse"—the papers that represented political, social or religious groups,—that dominated countrywide.

The rise of Hitler and the Nazis in 1933 brought an abrupt change. The Nazis had been publishing their own papers, one of the 100 or more organizations or groups doing so, since 1920, when the first issue of the *Völkischer Beobachter* appeared in Munich. But as late as 1932, their papers had gained only about a million of the 26 million circulation counted by the nation's press as a whole. On their accession to power, the Nazis wasted little time in moving towards taking over the whole industry. A month after Hitler was named chancellor all Social Democrat and Communist papers were outlawed, their printing facilities being seized and turned over to Nazi publications. Two years later, new laws resulted in further confiscations and closings. Still other papers were brought under control through the forced sale of majority shares to the Nazis' central publishing house.

Some non-Nazi papers survived, only to be shut down during World War II, ostensibly for economy reasons. By 1944, those still in existence had a circulation of under 4.5 million, compared to the 21 million claimed by the Nazi press.

All papers were under tight control. Editors had to be approved by the government. Journalists could work only with official authorization. The state-controlled national news agency relayed to all papers precise daily instructions from Goebbels's propaganda office as to selection and presentation of stories.

Eventually the war destroyed all the press. By early 1945, many had been wiped out by Allied bombings. Newsprint shortages had reduced the survivors to little more than handbills. The last *Völkischer Beobachter* was printed in Munich on April 30, 1945, but could not be distributed because U.S. troops had occupied the city.

With the Nazi surrender the four major Allied powers—France, Britain, the United States and the Soviet Union—divided Germany into zones of occupation. The Soviet forces took control of the northeastern part of the country. But Berlin, which was in the middle of the Soviet zone, was separated from it and put under four-power control.

The Allies agreed on a licensing system for a new press but differences in application soon became apparent. While the Western powers granted publishing licenses to private individuals and groups as well as to new political parties, the Soviets issued them only to parties and approved mass organizations. Censorship existed in both the Soviet and Western zones at the start of the occupation but was soon eased in the West, where the whole control system was abolished in 1949; the East Germans enjoyed only a brief period of relative freedom.

Soviet forces issued the first paper in their area on May 15, 1945. Called the *Tägliche Rundschau,* it was printed on the presses of the former *Völkischer Beobachter* and remained the Soviet voice in the country until it stopped publication in 1955. Shortly afterward, the Russians also started the *Berliner Zeitung,* which they subsequently turned over to the city's government.

In the summer of 1945 Russian authorities gave permission for the establishment of political parties and trade union organizations as long as they were anti-fascist. This led to the recognition of four parties: the Communists (of course), the Social Democrats (SPD), the Liberal Democrats (LDPD) and the Christian Democrats (CDU). Less than a year later, the Communists and the Social Democrats combined to form the Socialist Unity party (SED), which, under Communist control, has governed the state ever since.

In the meanwhile the Communists had begun publishing their own paper, the *Deutsche Völkszeitung.* Shortly afterwards, the Social Democrats put out theirs, called *Das Volk.* In April 1946 these two were joined, with the merger of the two parties, and became *Neues Deutschland,* which is still the country's leading daily. Papers representing the other two approved parties soon made their appearances as well: *Neue Zeit,* the organ of the Christian Democrats, and

Der Morgen, the voice of the Liberal Democrats. However, both of these suffered under stricter censorship and smaller newsprint allocations than the SED press. In subsequent years, several non-party papers were also licensed but similar controls ensured that they did not become of major importance.

Two more officially recognized parties were organized in 1948, the National Democrats and the Democratic Farmers' party. Each obtained the right to publish a daily: the National Democrats started the *National Zeitung* and the Farmers' party the *Bauern-Echo.* None of the other parties had real political power. All were part of a Communist-front organization: the United Front of Anti-Fascist and Democratic Parties.

With the establishment of regional papers and the addition of two more national dailies —*Tribune,* the official organ of the trade unions, and *Junge Welt,* the voice of the party's youth organization, the Freie Deutsche Jungend—the East German press took on the typical shape of a Soviet bloc media system. Since then it has changed little in structure, except for a reorganization in 1952-53 that resulted in the merging of some publications and the replacement of others. Probably most significant was the closing down of *Nacht-Express,* one of the last of the more or less independent papers, and its replacement by *BZ am Abend.*

About the only subsequent developments have involved variations in the tightness of official controls. These were relatively easy until 1950, when the Party decided it needed a centrally controlled concentration of reporting on subjects preselected for special emphasis. But the death of Stalin in 1953 brought a thaw to East Germany as it did to other East European states. The press showed a more varied face and assumed a more critical stance toward domestic issues, particularly after the 1953 uprising in East Berlin, which had to be put down by Soviet forces. However, this lasted only until 1956, when the old order returned in force. Another slight liberalization began after the completion of the Berlin Wall in 1961 and lasted until 1966. Another came in the wake of a SED party congress in 1971, and continued until another crackdown in 1976 brought back tight controls that are still in force.

This on-off pattern probably reflects both internal concerns and external developments. The regime's major problem has been—and continues to be—how to establish a genuine sense of national identity distinct from the "Germanness" common to both parts of the divided country.

While East Germany must compete with the West economically—in terms of jobs and living standards—it emphasizes political and ideological differences and even seeks to profit from them. For example, a constant theme of East German internal propaganda is the historic contrast between a Spartan-minded, Protestant Prussia and cosmopolitan, Catholic Rhineland and Bavaria. The aim, of course, is to identify the Communist-ruled state with the past—with the "real" Germany—while portraying the West as false to the old Germanic ideals. This means, however, that any changes that might appear to be moving the state toward a system more like that of the West—and this includes even revisionist ideas from other Communist-ruled states—must be blocked out as far as the general public is concerned. As a result, not only are Western publications—even fashion magazines—barred but developments within the Soviet bloc like the 1980-81 unrest in Poland are largely ignored in the mass media.

All East German newspapers except one are printed in German. The exception is a small daily, with a circulation of about 5,000, that is published in Bautzen, Saxony, for the Sorb minority. There are also a number of religious publications, including at least six daily newspapers. All are subject to precensorship as well as other official controls.

A listing of other papers suggests that they might be divided on the basis of political ideology, since each of the four recognized political parties publishes at least one. This is largely an illusion, however. The apparently non-Communist parties are actually nothing but inconsequential appendages of the ruling SED and their papers do not represent different points of view. The daily press is dominated by the nationally distributed papers published in East Berlin; in fact, a quarter of the nation's total circulation is accounted for by nine of the ten Berlin dailies. However, political parties also publish local and regional dailies, some of which have larger circulations than the less prominent national papers, probably because they tend to devote more space to entertainment and less to propaganda.

Most of the nondaily papers are published by factories or other enterprises, primarily for their own workers, although there are 32 weeklies that have a general readership. The nation's periodical press includes more than

Breakdown of Press by Type of Publication (December 1979)		
Type of Publication	Number	Average Circulation
Dailies	39	8,316,807
Weeklies	32	8,912,687
Factory newspapers	643	c. 2,000,000
Journals & periodicals	519	18,524,169
Communication gazettes & central press services	152	1,570,800

500 titles with a total circulation of about 16 million. An East German study published in 1979 by UNESCO gave the accompanying statistics.

The dailies usually have 40 to 60 pages per week. The journals are published weekly or quarterly and run from 24 to 400 pages.

Most East German papers are morning publications, although one of the larger Berlin dailies, *BZ am Abend,* and several of the regionals are afternooners. Many publish several editions. In fact, all 39 dailies together print nearly 300 separate editions. Most of these are issued by the SED papers, which are far and away the predominant force in the print field. They have about 90 percent of the total circulation in the country. One reason for this is that these papers are heavily favored by the regime in the allocation of newsprint, which is centrally controlled. As a result, they are not only larger—averaging six to eight pages compared to four to six for the others—but can print more of the popular local editions.

There are no Sunday editions and no magazine sections in the Western sense, although the majority of the dailies publish extended weekend supplements on Saturdays.

Most dailies are full-size papers, generally sober in appearance as in content. Two of the Berlin dailies, *Berliner Zeitung* and *Berliner am Abend,* jazz up their makeup a bit by using two-color headlines on page one, a variety of photos and varied typographical gimmicks. These two are, strictly speaking, not SED papers although they are put out by a publishing house that is to all intents and purposes an arm of the Party. So while they may look different, their content is virtually the same as that of the Party's official publications.

The major dailies follow an almost standard pattern of story presentation. Discussions of ideological problems and reports and analyses of international political and economic developments dominate their pages. A good deal of space is devoted to party affairs—pronouncements, meetings, receptions of foreign guests. Letters to the editor are encouraged, even critical ones. But as in other Soviet bloc countries, criticism must deal only with the operations of the system; it dare not question the system itself.

As noted previously, the regional papers, particularly the non-SED ones, are less heavy. They also carry much more advertising space. One study indicated that as much as one-quarter of the total space in some papers was given over to ads, the bulk of which were of the classified type.

In the East German scheme of things, each of the papers has a particular role to play and is designed to appeal to a specific audience. For example, the *Bauern-Echo* is addressed to farmers, the *National Zeitung* to former professional soldiers and ex-Nazis. The target for *Der Morgen* and *Neue Zeit* is seen as the former middle classes and the intelligensia. Although the regular dailies carry reports on sports, one, *Deutsche Sport-Echo,* is devoted solely to that subject. One other national paper, *Junge Welt,* is designed to appeal to young people.

In addition to Berlin, seven East German cities have more than one daily: Dresden, Halle, Karl Marx Stadt, Leipzig, Potsdam, Rostock and Schwerin. However, these newspapers do not compete with each other, either for readers or advertising. Indeed, they do not exist to make money but to further the purposes of the Party and state. There are no statistics to indicate whether or not they do show profits, and it is possible that no one knows for certain, since accounts would not be kept in that fashion.

Until recently, circulation figures were difficult to come by and even now are not available for some of the regional dailies. In the case of the nondailies, only overall totals have been reported.

The largest and most important paper in the country is *Neues Deutschland,* principal organ of the SED, with a circulation of 800,000. It is the East German equivalent of

Newspapers According to Topics		
Topic	Number of Titles	Average Circulation No. of copies
Politics & society	101	3,576,504
Cultural policy, literature & arts	31	746,892
Education & training systems, including:	74	5,405,213
periodicals for children & youth	14	4,318,652
health & social service system	59	722,377
sports & leisure time activities	17	2,047,721
mathematics/natural sciences	61	255,466
economics & technology of sectors of economy	99	1,661,446
agriculture, forestry & foodstuffs economy	33	894,935
fashion & homemaking	13	2,864,591
periodicals dealing with church policy	31	349,024

Moscow's *Pravda.* One other capital-city paper, the *Berliner Zeitung,* claims 500,000. Eleven other dailies, including seven of the regional papers, print from 100,000 to 500,000 copies, while five fall in the 50,000 to 100,000 bracket. Most of the others for which figures are available fall in the 25,000 to 50,000 class, although two regionals report less than 25,000 circulation.

As far as influence is concerned, *Neues Deutschland* is in a class by itself, since it serves as a guide for the rest of the press and is essential reading for all SED members and officials.

Next in importance for the general public is the *Berliner Zeitung.* Beyond these two, influence is difficult to assess. It is probable that several of the larger regional papers, such as the *Freie Presse* of Karl Marx Stadt, the *Sachsische Zeitung* of Dresden, *Freiheit* of Halle and the *Leipziger Völkzeitung* of Leipzig, all of which have circulations of 300,000 or more, carry greater weight than the other Berlin papers, none of which claims more than 175,000.

With an overall circulation of 17,229,494 for the nation's dailies and weeklies combined, plus the two million estimated for the factory papers, East Germany boasts an impressive 445 copies per 1,000 of population, one of the highest in Europe.

Economic Framework

The East German economy is a planned and centrally controlled command system, generally like those of other Soviet bloc countries but with some significant differences. It is not unfair to say that the Communists simply took over the already existing Nazi economy and adapted it to their own ideology and purposes. Both in general principles and in organization, the system is a direct descendant of the Nazi operation. The Russians also kept on the personnel involved, except those who were top-level Nazis or declared war criminals. As a result, the Communist regime has been able to profit from the enterpreneurial talents of the old managerial class, unlike neighboring Communist-ruled states where such people were replaced by party bureaucrats, most of whom lacked skills and training for the jobs.

As a result of this and other factors, the East German economy has been administered generally on a more realistic, pragmatic basis than is characteristic of Soviet bloc states. And it has been this pragmatism, plus the discipline of the East German worker, that has brought the state from the devastation of 1945 to the ranking it now enjoys among the world's industrial nations.

Most industry is state-owned. Agriculture is operated primarily by collectives and there are also collectives in industry and construction. A significant private sector exists as well; it was even more important in the 1950s and 1960s but is slowly being eradicated. Under a reform plan adopted in 1963, the economy is organized into vast vertical trusts, groups of enterprises with similar lines of production or services. There are about 100 of these trusts, all of which operate under the control and direction of 16 government ministries. These ministries, in turn, are under the supervision of the government's Council of Ministers. A few very large enterprises, known as combines, are not a part of any of the trusts but are run directly by the 16 ministries.

Although the goal of the 1963 reform was

stated to be greater efficiency through decentralization of authority, the system is still obviously highly centralized. The principal changes have involved the substitution of profit and other economic criteria for gross output as a measure of performance, and the delegation of some responsibility for planning, production and other activities to lower levels.

Except for the fact that the relative prosperity undoubtedly has led to increased sales of periodicals, all this elaborate economic structure has little impact on the media. Newspapers, periodicals and broadcasting exist for political, not economic, reasons, and economic considerations have no bearing on their function.

The regime considers the print media of primary importance in the task of promoting domestic and foreign policy objectives as well as keeping all elements of the party and the general population informed of central decisions and directives. Informational programming is also an important aspect of broadcasting but its role is seen as "stirring people to activity" and promoting "socialist consciousness."

As suggested earlier, private ownership of any part of the media structure does not exist. Nothing in the constitution forbids it but various laws and regulations make it impossible. All periodicals are published by various parties or authorized organizations; all are essentially sober, serious journals, with only the *Berliner Zeitung* and *BZ am Abend* making any attempt to put a more popular gloss on their products.

Production as well as political control is highly centralized. The SED's publishing enterprise, Zentrag, not only supervises all of the party's papers but also the operations of the Berlin-Verlag organization, which puts out at least 10 newspapers, including the *Berliner Zeitung* and *BZ am Abend* and a number of periodicals.

Zentrag also oversees publishing enterprises that produce some of the papers produced by the allied parties, as well as those responsible for both the trade union and youth organization dailies. In all, this huge trust controls about 94 percent of the nation's daily press circulation. But its tentacles stretch even further. Associated with it are two of the nation's largest paper mills, an enterprise that controls the export and import of all books, another organization holding a monopoly of all the country's advertising and publicity, and more than 100 printing offices. This whole complex operation is directed by high-ranking Party figures.

All newspapers and other periodicals are distributed through the postal system, the Deutsche Post. About 80 percent of all newspapers are sold by subscription, but the postal authorities are also responsible for the rest because they operate all newsstands from which street sales are made.

Newsprint is not available on the open market. Supplies are allocated to the various publishing enterprises by the Presseamt beim Vorsitzenden des Ministerrats—the Press Office of the President of the Council of Ministers—the all-powerful government bureau that, along with the Party, supervises all media activities. The nation has a fairly extensive timber and paper industry that supplies enough newsprint to meet all allocations and even provide an exportable surplus.

Advertising exists in both print and broadcast but is not an influential factor with either. Of all the newspapers, only the regionals, along with the *Berliner Zeitung* and *BZ am Abend,* devote much space to ads. Short periods of time are allocated for advertising on the broadcast media but totals are still relatively small. Most of the advertisers are state enterprises whose only chance for any influence over the media would be through political leverage with the state-Party control structure.

All newspeople must be members of the GDR Union of Journalists and the Party must approve all applications for membership in that organization. In addition, editors of SED papers must be approved by the Agitation and Propaganda section of the Party's Central Committee, and editors of non-SED papers by the government Press Office. Journalists are regarded as members of a profession with a vital role to play in the society and are ranked among the intellectual elite, being favored in terms of pay and privileges.

Press Laws

The 1968 East German Constitution, which replaced one promulgated in 1949, contains the usual guarantees of freedom of speech and the press. But these are qualified by various provisions requiring such personal rights to be exercised in accordance with the aims and spirit of the whole document, which specifically states that the nation is a socialist state and the "political organization of the working people...who are jointly implementing socialism under the leadership of the working class and its Marxist-Leninist party."

Since this makes the SED in fact the sole interpreter of what is proper in the implementation of socialism, it has, ipso facto, complete control over all forms of mass communication.

Press laws specify that all publications must have a license to operate. For national publications, licenses are issued by the Press Office. In the case of regional papers, this responsibility is that of the chairmen of provincial councils.

Controls over what is presented, and how, are very thorough. The main lines of publishing policy are drawn up by the Agitation and Propaganda section of the SED Central Committee, with the cooperation of other elements of the Party leadership. Broad outlines cover a five-year period and these are supplemented by more specific annual plans. On the basis of these, editors draw up quarterly plans for their operations, but they must be approved by higher-ups. Editors of SED papers must get theirs cleared by the Party's Agit-Prop section. Plans for non-SED papers have to be approved by the Press Office. Once these quarterly plans are endorsed, editors are further responsible for drawing up monthly plans, which must go through the same approval process. However, the editors themselves are solely responsible for planning on short-term bases—weekly and daily.

The first two pages of any newspaper, including any devoted specifically to local news, are exempt from all this planning, but that does not mean the papers are free to do what they please with the space. All papers receive daily directives from the Party or the Press Office concerning both the play of the news and any comment on it. These directives also go to responsible officials of the broadcast operations. In addition, themes to be emphasized are frequently spelled out by *Neues Deutschland* or one of the other major Party periodicals. These are supposed to be taken up by the regional and local papers, as well as by SED functionaries throughout the country.

The extent of state control is also widened by the fact that both broadcasting and the national news agency, which has a monopoly on internal distribution of news, are government agencies—and, further, because no one can work as a journalist without state and Party approval.

Laws exist that ostensibly protect the privacy of the ordinary citizen, but they are hedged with the same kind of caveat noted in regard to press freedom. One article in the 1968 constitution states that "postal and telecommunication is inviolable"; but immediately adds: "It may be limited only on a legal basis if it is necessary for the security of the socialist state or for criminal prosecution."

The courts are an arm of the government but the degree of independence they enjoy is not really germane. Since there is no legal definition of what might be harmful to the state, the regime is the sole arbiter and almost any citizen accused of harmful activity would almost automatically be found guilty.

Censorship

There is no pre-censorship of the press in the ordinary sense of the word. It is not needed because most of what appears in print has been dictated by the leadership. For news not specifically covered by directives, editors are expected to abide by the general guidelines laid down by the Party-state control bodies.

Post-publication analyses and critiques are conducted by these same control bodies, and woe betide any editor whose work does not match the expected result. An International Press Institute study several years ago cited the case of one East German editor who lost his job and had to flee to West Germany in 1957 because he had printed an exchange of letters between British Prime Minister Anthony Eden and Marshal Bulganin, then Chairman of the Soviet Council of Ministers, concerning the 1956 Suez affair and the Hungarian uprising that same year.

There have also been cases in the past in which entire issues of publications that happened to stray from the official line were seized and destroyed. However, no such incidents have been reported in recent years. Despite its complexity, the system seems to have been working smoothly and according to prescription. No specific rules exist that forbid officials to give information to the press, but since the system is designed to advertise the achievements of the Communist world, only "good news" appears in print.

State-Press Relations

The state and Party leaderships in East

Germany are tightly interlocked, and it is normal for top people to hold offices in both simultaneously. For that reason, the Press Office, although structurally under the chairman of the Council of Ministers (the premier, in other words), is also responsible to the SED Central Committee.

In addition to issuing publishing licenses and directing the work of the non-SED papers, the Press Office is in charge of newsprint allocations as well as the supply of other essential materials. It also runs the national news agency.

As in other Soviet bloc countries, East Germans can and do criticize the actions of officials, the operations of enterprise or other factors that make life difficult. There are even programs on radio and TV in which officials appear to answer written questions and complaints from listeners or viewers. However, all criticism must be "constructive." No one may challenge the basic tenets of the socialist society or the state. The case of Dr. Robert Havemann illustrates the limited range allowed. A prominent East German scientist, Dr. Havemann was expelled from the SED and fired from his professorship at Humboldt University for publicly calling for scientific and political liberties.

All news is managed in an openly partisan fashion to make the Communist system appear in the best possible light and the West generally—but particularly West Germany and the United States—in the worst. Problems or controversies in the Communist world are barely mentioned, if noted at all, but the picture portrayed of the West is of trouble and strife. A comparison of the stories about the United States in the March 11, 1981 issues of the West German newspaper *Die Welt* and of *Neues Deutschland* in East Germany illustrates the technique. Here are brief summaries of some of the stories:

Die Welt	*Neues Deutschland*
Haig says new letter from Brezhnev has new and interesting aspects.	U.S. building up military presence in Near and Middle East.
Reagan calls Afghans "freedom fighters," not rebels. Will U.S. send them weapons?	Crime and violence increasing dramatically in U.S., due largely to drugs and unemployment.

Die Welt	*Neues Deutschland*
Large photo and story about meeting between Haig and West Germany's Genscher. Haig complements Genscher for courage and far-sightedness.	Physicians for Social Responsibility say U.S. is leading way to nuclear war. Also national campaign in U.S. to oppose MX missile.
Reagan administration offers friendship to Chilean regime, not as strict as Carter.	Millions are budgeted by U.S. for chemical warfare research and new nerve gas factory.
	Reagan cuts social benefit programs, mostly health and unemployment benefits.

The controls over the media are absolute. A onetime editor of *Neues Deutschland* has been quoted as saying: "Our newspapers are not published to entertain the public or to earn money, but for political reasons. They are a political institution which assumes the form of a newspaper for reasons of convenience."

Attitude Toward Foreign Media

News correspondents from other countries desiring to report on East Germany on a short-term basis must obtain special visas from the press section of the Foreign Ministry. Organizations wishing to base correspondents in the country must apply to the ministry for accreditation for each individual. During most of the 1970s such applications were usually approved unless a particular candidate was on the regime's blacklist because of previous reporting. But the government began tightening up in 1979, when it imposed unusually stringent restrictions on correspondents. These required correspondents to give the Foreign Ministry at least 24 hours' notice of any plans to travel inside the country, stating their destination and reasons for the trip. In addition, they were required to obtain prior permission to interview or ask questions of anyone. Previously, permission had been required only for interviews with officials of the government, the Party and the state-run economic enterprises. The regulations also require correspondents to account for all income and expenditures in East Germany. At the time they were announced, *Neues Deutschland* said violators would be warned once, then expelled. It was generally assumed the restrictions were aimed primarily at correspondents of West German news organizations, who made up the majority of the 18 Western reporters actually stationed in East Germany. The others accredited are stationed elsewhere, mostly in West Berlin or West Germany, and make regular trips into East Germany.

Another measure later in 1979 was also clearly aimed at trying to restrict contacts between correspondents and East German citizens. An amendment to the criminal code made it a crime, punishable by two to 12 years in prison, to disseminate any news or information deemed by the regime to be detrimental to state interests.

Almost all non-Communist publications— the only exceptions being technical journals —are barred from the country by laws that prohibit the entry of works "which contract the moral and political views of the working people" or that are "likely to arouse in young people tendencies to racial hatred, cruelty, contempt for humanity, violence or murder or other illegal acts and sexual deviations."

Nevertheless, all East Germans can listen to Western radio broadcasts, and about 70 percent of the population can watch West German television. This fact has highly significant political consequences. For years, the regime made desperate efforts to block reception. Radio frequencies were jammed. Search squads checked antennas to make certain they were turned to receive on domestic TV broadcasts. But it was all in vain. Now, listening to Western radio and viewing West German TV is tolerated even though officially frowned on. And it is believed that a majority of the East Germans do listen and/or watch, at least part of the time. They still must be careful, however. Passing on to someone else information learned from a foreign broadcast is a criminal offense.

The regime implicitly acknowledges the extent of such listening and viewing by devoting considerable time and space in its own media to answering or attempting to counteract Western broadcasts, which not only keep East German listeners informed about world events they cannot get from their own media but also analyze and comment on developments inside East Germany itself. In a sense, therefore, this Western broadcasting is a substitute for the nonexistent free press in East Germany, and actually exercises some measure of control over East German politics.

Western correspondents who offend the regime in their reporting are usually expelled, and this happens more or less regularly, particularly to West German reporters —and most particularly to those representing West German TV. And at least two have been imprisoned on spy charges during the last two years.

News Agencies

The official news agency, Allgemeine Deutsche Nachrichtendienst (ADN), has held a monopoly of internal news distribution since it was formed in 1946. Originally set up by the Soviet military administration, it was turned over to East German control in 1953. At that time it was declared a state institution and placed under the Press Office. In 1956 it absorbed the national photo agency, Centralbild, which had previously enjoyed the same status as ADN.

Headquartered in East Berlin, ADN has bureaus in each of the nation's 14 district government centers. It also has 40 foreign bureaus and claims its correspondents are accredited in 62 foreign countries. It maintains exchange relations with 68 other agencies, nearly half of which are in Asia and Africa, and it receives the regular services of all the larger international agencies, including Reuters, AP, UPI, AFP and Tass.

To ADN the most important of these is Tass, whose reports make up the largest share of the foreign news supplied by the agency to newsrooms throughout the country. Of the big Western agencies, only Reuters maintains a bureau in East Berlin. These Western services go only to ADN, where their stories are selected and reformulated according to the desired pattern before being relayed to newspapers and broadcast operations.

ADN distributes via domestic teletype services about 40,000 words a day of both domestic and foreign news. It also provides a variety of feature services as well as both color and black-and-white photos. The staff includes about 600 journalists and is headed by a director general who is directly responsible to the Press Office. Operational costs are part of the state budget.

Electronic News Media

Like ADN, radio and television are state agencies, responsible to the Council of Ministers, but, like the press, under the guidance of the Agit-Prop section of the SED Central Committee. Broadcasting is very popular in the country. East Germans own about 19 million radios and more than 4.5 million TV sets.

Because of its entertainment aspects, broadcasting is less obviously political than the newspapers, but political orientation does come through immediately in news broadcasts, commentaries and even some documentaries and educational programs. The view of the world presented in these is unambiguously that of the SED leadership, which considers broadcasting an important tool in the further development of the socialist state.

The first postwar radio station in East Germany was set up with Russian help. Known as the Berliner Rundfunk, or Berlin Radio, it went on the air in May 1945. Transmitters were soon put in operation in other major cities and by 1946 two networks had been established. The following year a supervising office under the aegis of the SED took over control of the whole operation. In 1952 this function was turned over to a new State Broadcasting Committee, which imposed a more closely coordinated structure, eliminating the last vestiges of independence for the regional transmitters.

When regular TV service first began in 1956 it was administered by the same State Committee. In 1968 the two services and their administrations were split up, the governing body for radio becoming the State Committee for Radio of the Council of Ministers, with TV being run by the State Committee for Television of the Council of Ministers.

The State Committee for Radio is headed by a chairman who is responsible for all five radio services: Radio DDR I and Radio DDR II, the Berliner Rundfunk, the Stimme (Voice) der DDR and Radio Berlin International, a short-wave service for overseas listeners.

Berliner Rundfunk's programming is directed mainly at the population of East Berlin and its environs. Radio DDR I and DDR II are the principal national services. They are linked with the provincial transmitters, eight of which also provide regional programming during certain hours of the day. One also provides special programs for the Sorb minority. DDR I stresses information and light entertainment and broadcasts news every half hour. DDR II is more highbrow, stressing educational and cultural material, including classical music.

The Stimme der DDR is a 24-hour information and entertainment service, addressed to Western listeners as well as to residents of the country. It has been described as the principal mouthpiece of the regime because it attempts to explain the East German position on various international issues and events.

One other radio service in the country, Radio Volga, is operated by the Soviet military authorities for the thousands of Soviet troops—more than 20 divisions—stationed in East Germany.

The State Committee for Television now directs two regular programming channels and an educational service. Programs are produced in the TV Center in Berlin as well as in regional studios in other cities. It is a highly sophisticated operation, the best in the Soviet bloc and on a par with any of the Western European systems.

Transmissions begin early in the morning with signoff generally around 11 p.m. News is broadcast at least three times during the day: early in the morning, at 7:30 p.m. and just before shutdown. The 7:30 p.m. show is the main newscast and is broadcast on both channels simultaneously. It includes a general news review, sports, comment and the weather.

Programming has a consistent anti-West, anti-capitalist tone and news is selected and interpreted to support the regime's goals. Even the entertainment aspect is weighted: 75 percent of it must be from the communist world.

One particular program, "Der Schwarze Kanal" (The Black Canal), indicates the degree of the regime's concern over the influence of Western broadcasting. This consists of selected extracts of West German television, which are portrayed as misleading propaganda or illustrative of the sins and inequities of Western capitalism.

An East German study reported that in 1977 the radio services transmitted 64,773 hours of programming divided among various categories.

The same study reported that the total number of broadcasting hours for the two TV channels then in operation was 6,905, of which 5,289 hours were in color.

Hours of Radio Programming by Category

Spoken broadcasts	Hours
Politics and economics	24,748
Sports	692
New service	4,542
Children and youth broadcasts	1,160
Cultural policy, entertainment, plays	2,972
TOTAL SPOKEN BROADCASTS	34,114
Music	**Hours**
Classical music	6,035
Light music	5,666
Dance music	16,737
Folk music	2,221
TOTAL MUSIC	30,659

The same study reported that the total number of broadcasting hours for the two TV channels then in operation was 6,905, of which 5,289 hours were in color.

Hours of TV Programming by Category

Category	Hours
Political information	830
Features	1,099
Sports	661
Education	415
Drama	1,799
Entertainment	1,001
Children's programs	419
Youth programs	45
Advertisements	190
Miscellaneous	446

Education & Training

All East German newspeople must have journalism training. Those desiring to enter the profession must spend a year's internship with some news organization. Then, on the recommendation of the organization, they go to one of two schools at the University of Leipzig. The first is the Fachschule für Journalistik (Professional School for Journalism), which trains the rank-and-file personnel. It also conducts special courses for persons already on the job.

Trainees with university entrance qualifications can go to the Sektion Journalistik. The three-and-a-half year program there leads to a diploma that qualifies the holder for editorships and other higher-ranking posts. The basic outlines of the training are determined by the Journalists' Union, which also operates a journalism institute in East Berlin for newspeople from Asia and Africa.

There are a number of public opinion research institutes at various universities and technical institutions around the country.

East German journalists are affiliated through their union with the International Organization of Journalists, headquartered in Prague, Czechoslovakia.

Summary

The East German media structure has been very stable in recent years and there is no reason to expect significant change in the absence of a revolutionary shift in the society as a whole. While the regime has not been particularly successful in its goal of inculcating a sense of separate nationality in the people, they do have a considerable pride in the nation's accomplishments, particularly the impressive industrial growth. Most observers agree that they tend to be apolitical, willing to accept things as they are as long as the physical conditions of their lives remain relatively good.

CHRONOLOGY

1976
May — West German TV correspondent Peter van Loyen expelled after interviewing dissident writer.

December — West German TV correspondent Lothar Loewe has his accreditation withdrawn and is ordered to leave country within 48 hours on charges of "scandalous slander."

1978
January — Government closes East Berlin office of West German newsmagazine *Der Spiegel* after magazine publishes document it says was compiled by opposition group inside East Germany.

August — West German TV correspondent Lutz Lehmann forbidden by Foreign Ministry to continue work on report about condition of writers in East Germany.

1979
April — Government announces new restrictions on foreign journalists, including prohibition of interviews without official permission and requirement of 24-hour advance notice of any trips outside East Berlin; new rules also required accounting for all income and expenditures in East Germany.

June — Parliament unanimously approves new law making it an offense for anyone to supply "foreign organizations" with "information damaging to the interests of the country that does not come under the rules of secrecy," punishable by two to 12 years' imprisonment. Companion measure makes passing of manuscripts or written statements considered damaging to state interests an offense punishable by five years in prison.

1980
June — Horst Hering, correspondent for West German economics magazine, sentenced to life imprisonment on spy charges.

November — Manfred Bartz, former member of Writers' Union, arrested in East Berlin on charges of distributing unpublished texts critical of the state—the first arrest under the new law. West German TV producer Ralph Giordano refused entry into East Germany; a TV series he had made earlier about East German opposition groups had been broadcast in West Germany the previous month.

December — Peter Felten, correspondent of West Germany's *Kölnische Rundschau,* sentenced to 12 years in prison on spy charges by military court in East Berlin.

BIBLIOGRAPHY

Croan, Melvin. "East Germany." In *The Communist States at the Crossroads.* Adam Bromke, ed. New York, 1965.

Dusiska, Emil. "Historical Development of Media Systems: The German Democratic Republic." Summary of a study published as a pamphlet by UNESCO, December 20, 1979.

"East Berlin Curbs Access to News." *The New York Times,* April 15, 1979.

"GDR Unusually Sensitive to Western Press Criticism." Radio Free Europe. Research Report of May 13, 1966.

Index on Censorship. All issues since the beginning of 1976.

International Press Institute. *The Press in Authoritarian Countries.* Zurich, 1959.

Kraus, Wolfgang H. "Crisis and Revolt in a Satellite." In *Eastern Europe in Transition.* Kurt London, ed. Baltimore, Md., 1966.

Merrill, John C., Bryan, Carter R., and Alisky, Marvin. *The Foreign Press.* Baton Rouge, La., 1970.

Mond, Georges H. "Press Concentration in Socialist Countries." *Gazette,* vol. 20, no. 3, 1974.

Olson, Kenneth E. *The History Makers.* Baton Rouge, La., 1966.

Paulu, Burton. *Broadcasting in Eastern Europe.* Minneapolis, 1974.

"Recent East German Opinion Research." Radio Free Europe. Research Report of May 20, 1965.

Sanford, John. *The Mass Media of the German Speaking Countries.* London, 1976.

Schopflin, George, ed. *The Soviet Union and Eastern Europe.* New York, 1970.

Selucky, Radoslav. *Economic Reforms in Eastern Europe.* New York, 1972.

Smith, Jean Edward. *Germany Beyond the Wall.* Boston, 1969.

Stern, Carola. "Tradition and History of the German Communist Party." In *Communism in Europe.* Vol. 2. William E. Griffith, ed. Cambridge, Mass., 1967.

UNESCO. *World Communications.* New York and Paris, 1975.

WEST GERMANY

by George Kurian*

BASIC DATA

Population: 61.193 million
Area: 248,640 sq. km. (95,975 sq. mi.)
GNP: DM 1,276.2 trillion (US$638.1 billion)
  (1978)
Literacy Rate: 99%
Language(s): German
Number of Dailies: 1,229
  Aggregate Circulation: 19,298,000
  Circulation per 1,000: 312
Number of Nondailies: 41
  Aggregate Circulation: 3.375 million
  Circulation per 1,000: 55
Number of Periodicals: 867

Number of Radio Stations: 9
Number of Television Stations: 9
Number of Radio Receivers: 22,583,000
  Radio Receivers per 1,000: 370
Number of Television Sets: 20,613,000
  Television Sets per 1,000: 338
Total Annual Newsprint Consumption: 1.103
  million metric tons
Per Capita Newsprint Consumption:
  17.9 kg. (39.4 lbs.)
Total Newspaper Ad Receipts: DM 1.6 billion
  (US$880 million) (1976)
  As % of All Ad Expenditures: 47.9 (1976)

Background & General Characteristics

The contemporary West German press dates from 1949, when licensing restrictions were abolished by the occupation forces of the United States, Britain and France. In the course of the next decade the number of newspapers jumped from 160 to more than 1,500. Growth was slower from 1960, and during the late 1970s the number of publications actually declined.

In 1979 more than 1,250 editions of daily newspapers were published in West Germany and West Berlin by 400 publishers. Although the daily circulation of 20.5 million is the largest in continental Europe outside of the Soviet Union, the West German press has not yet reached the record set in 1932 when, within the same area, there were 2,889 dailies with a total circulation of 25 million and the ratio of newspapers to population (1 for every 2.6 persons) was the highest in the world.

In addition, about 50 weeklies are published in the republic, along with some 250 consumer magazines and about 700 specialized publications. On the whole, 5,000 publications of all types appear in West Germany with a combined circulation of more than 75 million. Two out of three West Germans read

a newspaper daily and nine out of 10 read a newspaper at least once a week. The average adult German also reads at least one periodical; in fact, mass magazines continue to grow in circulation despite declines in other areas of publishing.

The West German press has not regained the kind of prestige it enjoyed before World War II, when the *Frankfurter Zeitung* and the *Berliner Tageblatt* were considered to be two of the finest newspapers in the world, in the same class as *The Times* of London and Argentina's *La Prensa*. Today West Germany has eight or nine nationally respected newspapers and only three of international reputation: *Frankfurter Allgemeine, Suddeutsche Zeitung* and *Die Welt*.

The early German newspapers were the so-called "Einblattdrucke" (one-copy printings) of the Middle Ages. First distributed around 1450, they recorded war, peace, catastrophe and other news, and were passed from hand to hand among the people. Modern German journalism originated toward the end of the 18th century in the capitals of the numerous German states. Newspapers grew in importance as the states were unified after 1848, and especially after the foundation of the German Reich in 1871. The press center of

---

*The author thanks Oskar Bezold of German Information Center in New York for his help.

the country was Berlin, but newspapers flourished in the state (land) capitals, especially Frankfurt, Cologne, Hamburg, Munich and Leipzig, which were the centers of international trade. Most of these papers had middle-class background.

After World War I, a new type of paper with strong party affiliations appeared. The Socialist, Communist and National Socialist press exchanged violent polemics until 1933, when the Nazis took over the media. The party papers of the Social Democrats and the Communists were prohibited while all others were strictly controlled. Many journalists were forced to emigrate and others were arrested. During the course of World War II all papers that did not belong to the Nazi party went out of circulation simply because of the lack of newsprint. The present West German press is, much like Germany itself, built almost entirely anew from the ruins of World War II.

The majority of West German newspapers are regional and local and almost every large town has its own daily. Over 40 cities publish one or more dailies with circulations of over 100,000. The largest publishing center is Hamburg, which accounts for over a quarter of the daily circulation.

West German newspapers can be divided into four categories. First of all, there are the local "boilerplate" editions of metropolitan papers, most of them politically independent (generalanzeiger), such as the *Hamburger Abendblatt.* Second are the "boulevard" or entertainment papers, of which *Bild Zeitung* is the best example. Then come papers that lean toward one or the other of the main political parties—Christian Democratic Union, Christian Social Union, Social Democratic party, and the Free Democratic party. Finally, there are the so-called national papers, such as the *Frankfurter Allgemeine.*

Even among the provincial newspapers there are two distinct types: the "ring" papers (Kopfblatter), which are similar to the U.S. chain papers except that they are printed centrally with the masthead made over for each community and local news and advertising added; and community (Gemeinschaft) papers, usually printed in a central plant to save money. The latter are individually owned, however, and are not controlled by one company as in the case of ring newspapers.

Typical of the vast majority of West German newspapers is the *Rhein-Neckar-Zeitung* of Heidelberg. Founded shortly after

the end of the war, it claims a circulation of 99,300 for its main edition and eight subsidiary editions. The first page and about two-thirds of the editorial page are devoted to national and international news. About the same amount of space is devoted to local news, three pages to sports, a page to economic, financial and market news, and about three pages to features and entertainment. Four and a half to five pages of advertising complete the 16 to 20 pages of its average main edition.

West German papers have no standard format. They average about four to six columns in regular and tabloid size with six columns as the maximum. There is a general tendency toward horizontal display, with many one-line-spread headlines giving the appearance of a magazine. The six-day newspaper is the norm, with large weekend editions published on Saturdays. Most of the dailies appear in the morning. Afternoon papers are rare, the *Hamburger Abendblatt* being the only one in that category with a sizeable circulation. The three main Sunday papers are *Bild am Sonntag,* and *Welt am Sonntag,* both published by the Axel Springer concerns, and the Sunday edition of the *Stuttgarter Zeitung* and its affiliates.

After World War II West German journalism was oriented toward American and British models. However, the ideal for many West German journalists is not the reporter but the commentator or the columnist. Their intellectual and professional standards are high, their salaries generous and their communication skills well honed.

Unlike in pre-World War II days, the party press is very small. Almost 90 percent of the newspapers published in the Federal Republic describe themselves as nonpolitical and fewer than 10 percent follow definite party lines. Of the dailies only 30 admit to any political leanings. Indeed, the larger the publishing organization, the more ambivalent its politics. An example is Axel Springer, West Germany's most powerful publisher, who calls himself an independent but who is sometimes accused of being a Christian Democrat by the Socialists. In cities where political parties have no official organs, they are represented by independent newspapers (as they call themselves) whose editors are loosely affiliated to some party or consistently support its point of view. Although not party subsidized, these papers usually give wide coverage to party interests. Among the most influential of such papers are the

Rheinische Post (Christian Democrat) of Düsseldorf, *Westfälische Nachrichten* (Christian Democrat) of Munster, *NRZ-Neue Ruhr Zeitung* (Social Democrat) of Essen, *Westfälische Rundschau* (Social Democrat) of Dortmund and the *Aachener Volkszeitung* (Christian Democrat) of Aachen. The largest, by far, of these is the *Rheinische Post,* with a daily circulation of 24,000 in the heavily Catholic Rhineland. Communist papers are legal but exert little influence. Newspapers in West Berlin are more anti-communist than others, the most vehement being the *Berliner Morgenpost, Der Tagesspiegel* and *BZ.*

Until recently there was only one paper in West Germany printed in a language other than German: the *Flensborg Avis* of the Danish-speaking minority in Flensborg near the Danish border. Following the influx of "guest workers"—predominantly Turks— into West Germany, Turkish papers appeared in Berlin and Frankfurt. Other immigrant groups such as Russians and Ukrainians publish their own periodicals. Because there are no import restrictions, many foreign newspapers circulate freely in West Germany. Of these the most popular are the Swiss papers, such as *Neue Zürcher Zeitung* and *Die Weltwoche. Le Monde* is the most popular of the French newspapers, *The Guardian* among the British, *Corriere de la Sera* among the Italian and *The New York Times,* the *Christian Science Monitor* and the Paris-based *International Herald Tribune* among the American.

In the last 15 years there has been a dramatic increase in the number and sales of pictorial papers in West Germany. The phenomenal success of *Bild-Zeitung* (Europe's largest-selling newspaper, with a circulation of five million) indicates that German readers are satisfied neither with the conventional "viewspaper" nor with the U.S.-type information-oriented, objective publication. German editors prefer subjective stories that they believe give proper perspective and background to news presentation. The style is often stodgy by American standards.

Weekly newspapers exert a great influence on the intelligentsia compared to most dailies. They provide more detailed analysis of political events and often have superior staffs of journalists. The weeklies conduct polemical disputes and ideological discussions, as often take place between the Social Democratic *Vörwarts* and the Christian Social *Bayern-Kurier,* or between the liberal *Die Zeit* and the Conservative *Rheinische Merkur. Der Spie-*

gel occupies a special place in this category. It calls itself a newsmagazine and is patterned after *Time,* but unlike *Time* often involves itself in controversial issues and political exposés. It is particularly noted for the radical flavor of its essays. Although the number of general illustrated magazines has declined to four—*Stern, Bunte Illustrierte, Neue Revue* and *Quick*— they have stood up well to the competition of television.

The so-called yellow press (known in West Germany as "Regenbogenpress"—rainbow press, for its colorful makeup) is mainly concerned with gossip, fashion, recipes and beauty, and directed mainly toward female readers.

Three West German newspapers are represented in *The World's Great Dailies* by John Merrill and Harold Fisher: *Frankfurter Allgemeine Zeitung, Suddeutsche Zeitung* and *Die Welt.* The *Frankfurter Allgemeine Zeitung,* rated by *Newsweek* as among the 10 best in the world, is the country's most influential paper, with the most important decision-makers in West Germany constituting 90 percent of its readership. Of its 300,000 circulation (75 percent by subscription, the balance in street sales) nearly 10 percent goes abroad to more than 130 countries. A Time-Life study of the Common Market countries found that 29 percent of businessmen polled read *Frankfurter Allgemeine Zeitung* regularly. It was founded in 1949 by a group of dedicated journalists associated with the prewar *Frankfurter Zeitung,* which had been closed down by Hitler. Although there is no official connection between the two, the founders tried to make F.A.Z. independent in the best traditions of the older paper—designed to speak for the whole of Germany. Indeed, its subtitle, "Zeitung Fur Deutschland" ("Newspaper for Germany") defines the paper's principal mission.

F.A.Z. is heavy and serious in its makeup and writing and staid in appearance. Although it does use some pictures on its inside pages, they are small; the headlines are conservative and the type closely set. But what it lacks in flair it makes up in organization. Every day, the makeup and format follow a predictable pattern that is never changed. The main part of the paper is divided into three principal sections or "books": politics, economics and feuilleton (light literature), totaling between 20 and 32 pages on weekdays. National and international news account for 13 percent, editorials and op-ed articles for 7 percent, business news for 12 percent, sports 3 percent and the feuilleton 8 percent. Another 50 percent is devoted to advertising and the remaining 7 percent to features and entertainment materials. The weekend (Saturday) edition generally runs to 180 pages with an additional "Bilder und Zeitung" ("Pictures and Time") section, printed on slick paper. Special supplementary sections on science, books, travel and records are carried on certain days of the week.

To produce all this, F.A. Z. employs a staff of 161 full-time editorial personnel and 689 other employees. Its network of foreign correspondents, the largest of any West German publication, includes 31 full-time foreign correspondents in 22 foreign capitals and 25 part-time stringers. Among its distinguished foreign reporters are Jan Reifenberg in Washington, D.C., Sabina Lietzmann and Hans Jurgensen in New York, Ulrich Grudinski, Hans-Joachim Rudolph and Karl Heinz Bohrer in London, Karl Jetter, Thankmar Freiherr von Münchhausen and Andreas Graf Razumovsky in Paris, Leo Wieland in Moscow, Walter Haubrich in Madrid, and Josef Schmitz van Vorst in Rome. Besides the full-time staff, more than 450 journalists and 500 specialists are regular contributors to the paper.

F.A.Z. is incorporated as a nonprofit limited liability company, the majority of the stock being controlled by Professor Helmut Diedrich, Jurgen Eick, Professor Walter Hamm, and Professor Erich Welter. Because of its conservative financial policies F.A. Z. managed to break even or make a profit during the troubled 1970s.

Described as a paper of the middle, F.A.Z. is unattached to any political party, although it was a strong supporter of Konrad Adenauer and continues to be a vigorous advocate of private enterprise. On critical issues it tends to veer to the right, as in 1970, when Jurgen Tern, a member of the publishing board, was dismissed for sympathizing with Willy Brandt's "Ost-Politik" line against the conservative inclinations of Editor Erich Welter.

With a circulation slightly exceeding *Frankfurter Allgemeine*'s, *Suddeutsche Zeitung* (SZ) is West Germany's largest quality daily. *Stern* rates it the country's best daily and Sweden's *Dagens Nyheter* has called it "a German *Manchester Guardian:* open, fresh, reliable, and well-written." A thick paper, usually containing 40 to 50 pages on weekdays, its principal appeal is to the intelligentsia of left-wing liberalism. Founded

in 1949 by three partners—Edmund Goldschagg, Franz Joseph Schoningh and August Schwingenstein—SZ is now part of a media conglomerate that includes one of West Germany's largest book publishing companies. Although it enjoys a daily circulation of around 310,000 (80 percent by subscription and the balance by street sales), SZ faced considerable financial difficulties in the 1970s and suffered losses in many years.

SZ has a pleasing typographical format, with five wide columns, paragraphs of heavy type that highlight leading stories, and well distributed white space. The leader appears at the top of the front page's left-hand column. Pictures are not generally related to the stories on the page. A normal issue contains about two pages of international news, another two of national news, three to four pages of state news, a page of news analysis and editorials, two of features and entertainment items, five to six of business information, and one to eight (depending on the day) of sports. It carries relatively less advertising than other quality papers; the advertising ratio is around 45 percent on weekdays and 55 percent in weekend editions.

SZ has a total staff of 1,800, including 150 editors (16 of whom are in seven branch offices), 60 reporters and 14 full-time foreign correspondents. Part of SZ's success may be attributed to its highly qualified personnel—which includes 45 Ph.Ds—and to a strong sense of responsibility for presenting thoroughly researched and accurate news.

West Germany's third national daily is Axel Springer's *Die Welt,* a highly controversial but interesting and readable paper. Published from Bonn, *Die Welt* has had a troubled history and has been a loss-maker for the Springer empire. Its circulation, which reached over one million copies daily in 1949, has stabilized at around 230,000 copies on weekdays and 295,000 on Saturdays. About 80 percent are sold by subscription and the remainder on newsstands. Although Springer is staunchly conservative, *Die Welt* describes itself in its subtitle as "An Independent Newspaper for Germany." The average issue features four or more sections (or books) each of six or more pages; news and articles are grouped together on a single topic in no particular order. By percentage of the total news hole space, international news occupies 14 percent, national news 20 percent, analysis and editorials 6 percent, features and entertainments 14 percent, sports 7 percent, business 25 percent, travel 3 percent, home 6 percent and public service 5 percent. Advertising takes up 48 percent of the total space. *Die Welt* is a lively paper, designed to be read rapidly. Photographs are used liberally and the stories employ zingy, clear language, with the more interesting paragraphs highlighted in darker type. As the only paper in Bonn, its coverage of the federal government is unmatched, but it pays equal attention to foreign news. It has 34 full-time foreign correspondents and 11 part-timers, in addition to Springer's own foreign syndicated service, Springer Auslandsdienst (SAD). Its total staff of 940 includes 220 editors, 240 managers and 440 technical personnel.

Although *Die Welt* has toned down much of its former strong right-wing political views, it remains anathema to many German liberals. Nevertheless, it is a unique and distinctive paper with a reputation that transcends German borders.

Economic Framework

In general, the press in West Germany enjoys good financial health. A shakedown process in the 1950s and 1960s fostered stronger and bigger press groupings. The considerable capital investment necessary for technical innovation has furthered the process of concentration. At the same time, because there are no privately owned radio or TV stations in West Germany, newspapers have been unable to expand laterally through cross-media ownership. Several attempts by publishers to change this situation have failed.

More than a third of West German papers are printed in editions of less than 10,000, placing a considerable economic strain on publishers. Therefore, a number of publishers have established joint editorial staffs on a cooperative basis. Sometimes, smaller publishers bring out regional editions of metropolitan papers with local sections added on.

Only one-third of the newspaper sales is accounted for by newsstands; the balance of nearly 13 million copies is sold by subscription and delivered by employees or through the mail. However, the percentage of non-subscription sales is steadily increasing. Rising production and distribution costs have resulted in higher newsstand and subscription prices. A national daily on weekdays cost DM 1 (50 cents) on an average in December 1980; the weekly edition DM 1.20 (60 cents). The price of a monthly subscription to the *Frankfurter Allgemeine Zeitung,* for example, is DM 27 ($13.50); one copy of the political weekly *Die Zeit* costs DM 3 ($1.50) and the annual subscription DM 129.50 ($64.75).

West German press laws stipulate a clear separation between editorials and news on the one hand and advertising on the other. In general, advertisers do not attempt to pressure editors, although there are occasional exceptions, such as when cinema owners stop advertising their movies in papers that give them bad reviews. Large-scale advertisers operate through agencies, which are reluctant to antagonize publishers, thus in effect shielding the press from manipulation by advertisers.

The ratio between editorial and news pages and advertising varies considerably. On weekdays, it is relatively small; it is much higher on Friday and Saturday: up to 50 percent and more. The illustrated magazines have a ratio of 1:1 of editorial to advertising pages, while *Der Spiegel* has 2:1 ratio.

Lobbying in the American sense is not very common in West Germany. On the other hand, large organizations such as political parties, trade unions, trade associations, churches and others, wield great influence through their press and public relations divisions, which invite newsmen to their press conferences and tours.

IG Druck und Papier (The Press and Paper Union) represents most noneditorial personnel and printing-plant employees in West Germany, especially those involved in the technical side of production. Other publishing-house employees are members of the German Employees Union, Deutsche Angestellten Gewerkschaft (DAG). Journalists are mainly represented by Deutscher Journalisten Verband (DJV), although recently a subdivision of the IG Druck und Papier by the name of Deutsche Journalisten Union has come into existence. Among West German trade unions, IG Druck und Papier is considered somewhat radical. It is opposed to private ownership of the media and seeks to place all newspapers under public control.

In general, industrial relations in the newspaper industry are good, following the principles laid down in the Betriebsverfassungsgesetz (Law for the Constitution of Industry). Hiring and firing (more so the latter) has to be approved by the Betriebsrat (industry council) as also changes in the organization of the firm, working hours, vacation plans and the like.

The last newspaper strike in 1978 was a test of strength between IG Druck und Papier and the publishers organizations. It ended in a compromise. In principle, IG Druck und Papier is not opposed to technical innovation so long as it does not endanger jobs. Usually the trade union conforms to democratic practices even during strikes, but in a few cases has required its members not to print and typeset editorials opposed to its own political persuasions.

The wages and salaries of journalists are governed by annual agreements between the Federal Association of German Newspaper Publishers on the one hand, and the German Journalists Association, IG Druck und Papier, and the German Salaried Employees Union on the other. The 1978 agreement provided for a maximum of DM 1,368 ($684) per month for trainees in their second training year and DM 3,446 ($1,723) per month for editors with at least 15 years of service on a paper with a circulation over 30,000. Sole editors received from DM 2,614 ($1,307) per month from their third year on a paper with a circulation of below 10,000 to DM 3,782 ($1,891) per month from their 15th year on a paper with circulation of over 30,000. In larger papers, editors receive up to DM 4,124 ($2,062) per month, depending on their professional standing.

While all dailies are privately owned, the current trend is toward concentration of ownership and there is a lively debate on the dangers of such concentration. Axel Springer and his publishing group have been at the center of this controversy but the trend is not limited to Springer. The number of dailies with full editorial staffs has declined from 225 in 1954 to 126 today. The number of newspaper publishers has also declined, from 624 to around 400 over the same period. Other newspaper groups have enlarged their market share at an equal pace, with Axel Springer alone claiming 22.9 percent and the next four groups 11.4 percent as follows: Suddeutscher Verlag 3.0 percent, Westdeutsche Allgemeine Zeitung 2.9 percent, Verlag Dumont-Schauberg 2.9 percent and Societats-Verlag Frankfurter Allgemeine 2.6 percent. In addition, a number of publishers have achieved a position of local or regional prominence. As a result, 153 out of 393 municipalities with newspapers are one-paper towns. In 1954 11 out of 12 towns had a choice of papers but by the late 1950s this figure had declined to three out of five.

Popular magazines have also undergone a process of concentration. At present there are. four large publishing houses, accounting for 64 percent of all magazine circulation as follows: Bauer Group 28.3 percent, Springer Group 13.9 percent, Burda Group 11.9 percent, Gruner & Jahr Group 10.1 percent. Some groups have already expanded into the electronic-media and the entertainment industry. One such concern is the Bertelsmann AG at Gutersloh, which includes Europe's largest book club, eight printing plants and companies for the production of TV and advertising films as well as records and specialized magazines. Bertelsmann also owns 74.9 percent of the Gruner & Jahr group. The Springer group, too, has extensive and diversified holdings in cassettes, magazines, printing and training programs for different professions.

Competition between the various forms of the media is intense but newspapers have managed to hold their own both in circulation and share of advertising revenue. During a recent survey 69 percent of those polled preferred the newspaper as their source of international information and 61 percent specified newspapers when asked what medium of information they would least want to give up. The accompanying tables trace the development of the major media and the growth of advertising expenditure among them from 1973 to 1978.

Until recently West German papers were usually produced by rotary printing presses. In the last few years there has been a rapid change to offset printing. Illustrated magazines are generally printed in rotogravure. More and more newspapers are switching from hot type to photo or electronic typesetting and editorial rooms from typewriters and ballpoints to videoterminals. The large investment necessary for such a conversion is one of the main reasons behind the trend toward concentration.

Press Laws

Formal guarantees for freedom of the press are laid down in the West German Constitution (the Grundgesetz, or Basic Law), which states:

Everyone has the right to freely express and disseminate his views by word of mouth, in writing, and in images, and to inform himself, without restriction, from generally accessible sources. Freedom of the press and freedom of reporting by radio and film are guaranteed. There shall be no censorship.

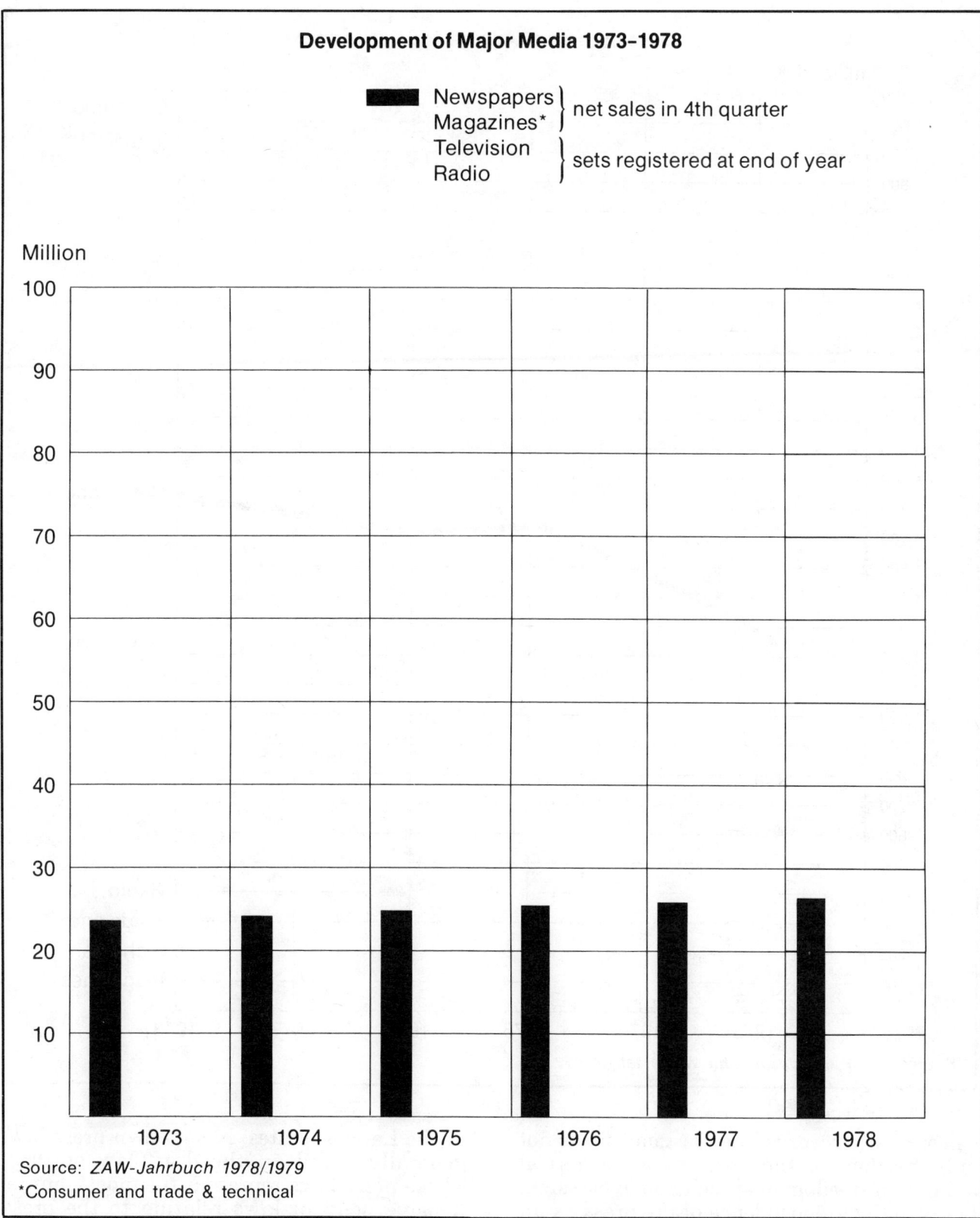

Development of Major Media 1973-1978

Newspapers } net sales in 4th quarter
Magazines*
Television } sets registered at end of year
Radio

Source: *ZAW-Jahrbuch 1978/1979*
*Consumer and trade & technical

Two basic restraints have been written into the law: the first provides for the lifting of the constitutional protection of the press in case of subversion; the second requires the press to observe the general laws protecting personal honor and general propriety. The ul- timate judge of the legality of the specific applications of these restraints is the Federal Constitutional Court. The court has enlarged the application of the law to cover not only the publications but also the technical pro- cesses of production, transportation and

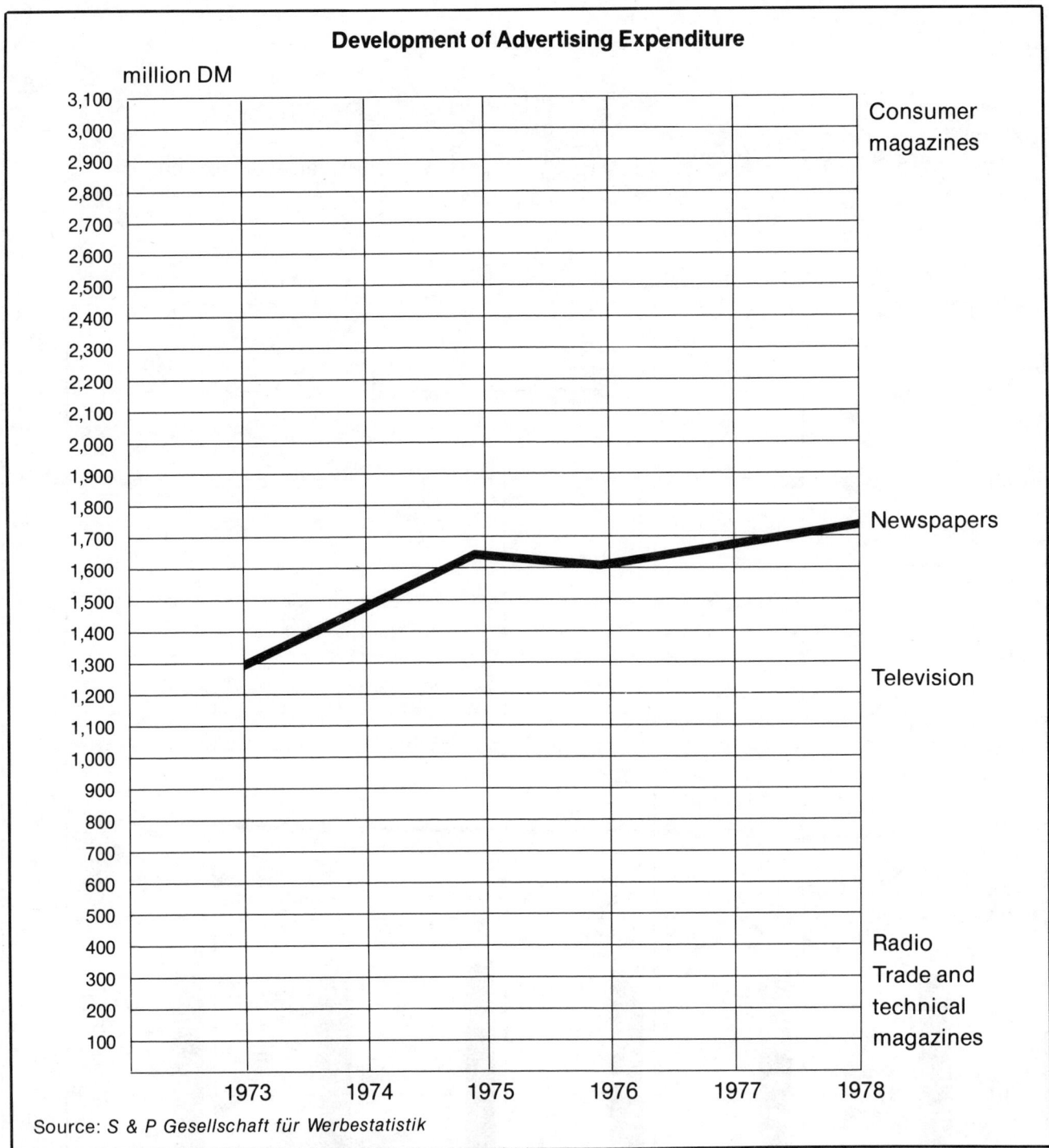

Development of Advertising Expenditure

million DM

Consumer magazines

Newspapers

Television

Radio
Trade and technical magazines

1973 1974 1975 1976 1977 1978

Source: *S & P Gesellschaft für Werbestatistik*

sales. In other words, the law guarantees not only freedom of the press as a theoretical adjunct of freedom of speech and expression, but also the independence of the press as an intellectual and business institution. Thus the press is on a par with other national institutions with clearly defined legal status and functions. Furthermore, the state is not allowed to restrict, abridge or even indirectly interfere with this freedom.

In addition to the federal guarantee, each of the Länder (states) has its own press law, generally based on the draft law of 1963. These press laws represent the most comprehensive body of laws relating to the press enacted in modern times. The press laws of some states, such as Hesse, are often cited as being among the most liberal in Europe. The Länder press laws apply not only to the printed word but also to radio and television transmissions, the projections of films, contributions of news agencies, matrix services and photo archives. On the other hand certain printed material is excluded, such as price lists, advertising copy, operating manuals and annual reports of business firms.

The press laws of every federal state except Lower Saxony include in their first paragraph a reinforcing regulation prohibiting all forms of special measures that encroach on press freedom. In the Hesse law these special measures are defined as including special taxation of the press or press products, control of the supply of newsprint, artificial increases in the price of newsprint and awarding or withholding of official advertisements. The laws also provide protection against a particular threat to press freedom that existed under the Nazis: compulsory professional organizations of journalists.

As in other democracies, press freedom in West Germany is subordinate to the laws of the land, or as the Bavarian law puts it, "To laws which apply to every one the press is also subject." The constitution also specifies the limits of press freedom. Article 18 lays down that "Whosoever misuses the freedom of expression, especially the freedom of the press to oppose free democratic institutions, forfeits these rights."

Another significant innovation of the German press law is the express reference to the social role of the newspaper and the magazine. The Rhineland-Palatinate law states: "The press is fulfilling a social function if, where subjects of public interest are concerned, it gathers and passes on news, comments, criticizes, or helps in the formation of opinion in other ways." This function of the press was acknowledged by the Constitutional Court in 1959 when it declared: "It must be conceded...that the press is competent to act in the public interest especially in dealing with political affairs in fulfillment of its social role." Article 18 of the constitution assigns to the press the duty of defending free democratic order, and all state laws incorporate the statement that "the press serves free democratic institutions."

In addition to these broad guarantees the West German press enjoys certain special rights, first being the right to publish or to run a publishing house or any other form of printing enterprise without a special permission or license from the state. Second is the right of access to official information dealing with matters of special public interest. This right, however, extends only to official information. The law of Hesse actually requires

state authorities to give newsmen such information as they might require in order to fulfill their political functions. The Hesse law also forbids discrimination against individual papers regarding information or the conditions governing its release. Other Länder limit the right, citing circumstances in which official information may be denied, particularly where it exceeds reasonable limits, relates to cases that are sub judice, is in conflict with laws of privacy, or may threaten national security. Foreign journalists have the same right of access of official information as West Germans.

Third is the protection of editorial secrecy. The right to keep sources of information secret, one of the bulwarks of press freedom, is granted journalists both in civil and in press law. The Code of Civil Procedure gives the right to refuse evidence "to those who by virtue of their office, position or profession are entrusted with facts which by their nature or by law are secret." Evidence may also be refused if it would reveal a trade secret. All the states, too, have laws protecting editorial secrecy. The Hesse law, for example, states: "Editors, journalists, proprietors, publishers, printers, and others who have been professionally concerned in the preparation, production, or publication of a printed work are entitled to refuse evidence on the identity of the author, supplier or informant, and information on its contents and on the contents of documents." A closely allied right is the protection given by the state press laws against seizure of editorial documents and police searches of editorial offices. This statute defends publications against harassment conducted under the guise of legal investigation.

The fourth right is protection against seizure of printed works, historically the most effective weapon for silencing unwelcome opinions. According to the model draft law of 1963 only a judge may order a seizure. Such seizure is prohibited if the public interest served by the publication is deemed greater than the interest which a seizure is supposed to protect. Seizure is also prohibited if the damage it causes is considered disproportionate to the importance of the case. Only undistributed copies and materials still under the control of the publisher may be seized and they may not be taken away from customers or readers. The state is liable for damage caused by unjustified seizures. At the same time state laws permit temporary impounding of copies of publications suspected of inciting violence, treason, obscenity and attacks on human dignity. However, in such cases the police must inform the state attorney within 12 hours, the state attorney must apply for a court order for confiscation within 24 hours and the court itself must decide within another 24 hours.

Despite its special position and privileges, the press may risk prosecution in a number of areas under the Criminal Code. Among these are defamation, false accusation, publication of indecent matter, acts against foreign powers, acts against national security, and treason. Paragraph 84 of the Criminal Code provides penalties for treasonable publications even if the publication was distributed without treasonable intent and even if the state secret revealed was false. These offenses, often called journalistic treason, are subject not to the press law but to the penal law.

Under the penal code slander and defamation in print entail severe penalties. Political slander often results in even more severe penalties. In the case of newspapers and periodicals the legal responsibility lies with the editor, and with the publisher in other publications.

The press laws define not only the rights but also the responsibilities of the press. These include the need to check the accuracy and source of all news before publication. This regulation is only a warning to exercise reasonable care, and carries with it no legal sanction to compel compliance. Provided the sources are clearly defined, even recognizably false news may be published.

Further, the press laws require newspapers to publish replies by any reader aggrieved by a news item or editorial and wishing to protest. In certain states the word used is *Berichtigung* (correction) while in others it is *Gegendarstellung* (reply). In fact, the right to reply is independent of the relative accuracy of the original published item or the reply. If the reply is received within three months of the publication of the offending statement and if it is restricted to facts, it must be published in the same section and in the same typeface and not as a letter to the editor. Refusal to publish a reply or a correction is punishable by fine or jail. Newspapers, however, have the right to publish a simultaneous rejoinder, commonly known as an editorial tag.

All publications are also required to list their editors who assume legal responsibility for what is published. According to the Bavarian Press Law, at least one "respon-

sible" editor must be designated for each paper. This "responsible" editor must be a permanent resident of the Federal Republic enjoying all civil rights.

Another basic law requires that if the publisher has "received, requested or been promised payment" for the publication of any material he must make it recognizable as an advertisement by printing it in a typographically distinct manner.

Finally, most of the state laws require voucher or compulsory copies of each work printed within their jurisdiction, to be supplied to a specified official body.

Quite distinct from the state press laws are federal regulations. These involve the independence of the publications from economic pressures and from takeover attempts by monopolies. Press enterprises are subject to the anti-cartel laws of the Federal Republic but because they do not normally attain the revenue and employment levels of other businesses, new criteria have to be developed, taking into account the special legal situation of the press. An independent body, known as the Gunther Commission, suggested fixing market shares (with 40 percent as the maximum), but this did not turn out to be practicable. The Press Statistic Law of 1975 enables the government to monitor ownership and concentration patterns in the West German press more closely than before. The press regulations of Bavaria and Hesse require publishing houses to reveal details of their owners and shareholders quarterly. Single or private firms must give the names, addresses and occupations of the owners and all associates; public companies must give the same details for all shareholders who own more than 25 percent of the capital. Relations between publishers and their editors are also closely regulated. If a journalist does not agree with a fundamental change in a newspaper's political views as demanded by the publisher, he cannot be forced to write against his convictions or be dismissed. (In many publishing enterprises there are editorial committees that have an important voice in decisions affecting the staff work).

Freedom of the press and its legal guarantees have not been severely tested in West Germany because of the relative stability of the government. Nevertheless, there have been at least three incidents that have brought the state and the press into confrontation. The first was the seizure of an entire issue of *Der Spiegel* by Chancellor Konrad Adenauer in 1953. The second was the "*Spiegel* Affair" of 1962, in which Rudolf Augstein and other members of the *Spiegel* staff were arrested under instructions from Defense Minister Josef Strauss in retaliation for personal attacks on Strauss. (Incidentally, the Constitutional Court ruled in favor of the state in this case.) The third was the controversy surrounding the so-called Lex Soraya, which would have amended the press laws in order to provide greater protection for foreign heads of state against journalistic intrusion into their private lives. The controversy was triggered by published reports about the private life of Princess Soraya, the former empress of Iran. The proposed amendment was later dropped because of the opposition of the German publishers and journalist association.

The German Press Council is the newspaper industry's principal organ of self-discipline. It also functions as an ombudsman, channeling and scrutinizing complaints against newspapers and periodicals. It was founded in 1962 to forestall attempts by the federal Ministry of the Interior to set up a supervisory authority to monitor the press. The council has set itself four main tasks:

• Safeguarding the press freedom and ensuring unrestricted access to news sources.
• Pinpointing and eliminating abuses within the press itself.
• Keeping an eye on the development of the press structure and guarding against the growth of combines and monopolies that would jeopardize independence and diversity.
• Representing the press vis-à-vis the government, the Parliament and the public.

The council is composed of 20 members nominated by four press associations: Bundersverband Deutscher Zeitungsverleger e. V. (BDZV), Deutscher Journalisten-Verband e. V. (DJV), Verband Deutscher Zeitschriftenverleger e. V. (VDZ) and Deutsche Journalisten Union (DJU). The council's main weakness is that its role is purely advisory and that its strongest weapon is only a public reprimand issued when its Grievance Committee considers a complaint to be justified. But the council does carry some weight with both the public and the government, and often uses its influences to dissuade both the government and the press from courses of action which it considers detrimental to a free press. The best example of this influence are its intervention in the Lex Soraya controversy and its success in convincing *Quick*

to discontinue a lurid series about the murder of a prostitute in Frankfurt.

The council has formulated a 15-point code of conduct for West German journalists. Ten of the salient guidelines are:

1. News and photos must be carefully checked and must not be distorted or falsified through editing. Unconfirmed reports, rumors and assumptions must be cited as such.

2. Published assertions or reports that subsequently turn out to be incorrect must be promptly corrected in an appropriate manner.

3. Dishonest methods must not be employed to acquire pictures or information.

4. Journalists will observe professional secrecy and will not disclose the identity of informants without their agreement.

5. The press will respect individual privacy.

6. Publishers will not print news and pictures that offend the religious susceptibilities of their readers.

7. Publishers will avoid overly sensational portrayal of violence and brutality.

8. There will be no discrimination on religious, racial or national grounds in the presentation of news.

9. Reports on medical subjects will avoid sensationalism.

10. Journalists will not accept any privileges, bribes or gifts that could in any way influence their editorial decisions.

Censorship

Article 5 of the West German constitution states specifically: "There shall be no censorship." Accordingly, there is no form of preventive censorship in the Federal Republic.

However, the recent wave of pornography has led to demands for some curbs on the sale of obscene literature to young people. Under the Schmutz and Schundgesetz (dirt and trash) law, the Federal Control Board for Publications Endangering Young People can intervene against abuses in this sphere. The board may require the offending publications to be removed from public display but has no strictly censorial powers.

State-Press Relations

Twelve years of Nazi propaganda under Goebbels conditioned many Germans to discount the government as a source of facts. Both the press and the public have consistently rebuffed government efforts to expand its own information activities and impose control over the information media. The only official outlet for news is the Presse-und Informationsamt der Bundesregierung (BPA, Press and Information Office of the Federal Government), directly under the chancellor's office. The head of the BPA holds the rank of a state secretary. The office is organized in four sections: (1) Administration, (2) News, (3) Domestic, and (4) Foreign. Its duties are limited to liaison between the government and the public. It publishes a weekly information bulletin and sponsors other publications.

Within the framework of Article 5 of the Grundgesetz (Basic Law), the media have the undisputed right to criticize the government and expose government failures or wrongdoings. The International Press Institute has not reported any retaliatory jailings of newsmen or confiscation of newspapers or periodicals since 1965.

Attitude Toward Foreign Media

There is little foreign ownership of West German media. Among newspapers there are no foreign owners, except the Swiss publisher of the Hamburg tabloid *HamburgerMorgenpost*. A few magazines, especially women's magazines, are foreign owned, mostly by Swiss, Dutch or Danish concerns. Their influence over the West German media is negligible.

Under the Länder press laws, foreign newsmen have the same right of access to official news sources as nationals. The importation and distribution of foreign newspapers and periodicals is also unrestricted by legislation. No special visas are required for foreign correspondents, nor is prior approval required for cables. Journalists from abroad do not need special accreditation unless they wish to take part in official press conferences and receptions.

The federal government has consistently backed U.S. efforts against institutionalizing state controls over the media as proposed in the UNESCO 1978 Declaration.

News Agencies

The Federal Republic of Germany has over 500 information or news agencies, of which some 145 are concerned with political news-

gathering in a broad sense. The largest is the national news agency, Deutsche Presse-Agentur (dpa, German News Agency) founded in 1949. Together with the German Dispatch Service (Deutscher Depeschen Dienst, DDP), it offers both foreign and comprehensive national reporting. All but two West German newspapers subscribe to DPA. Owned cooperatively by newspaper publishers and radio stations, its capital is split up in such a way that no individual publisher or publishing group owns more than 1 percent and all the radio stations together not more than 10 percent. The agency charges members according to their circulation; the agency's charge in 1980 was DM 0.11 (.055 cents) per monthly unit. From its headquarters in Hamburg DPA controls a large network of reporters in West Germany and correspondents in 75 foreign countries.

The Associated Press with 70 customers and Reuters with 22 are the most active foreign news agencies in West Germany. Other foreign bureaus include Agence France-Presse, ANSA, ADN, Bulgarian Telegraph Agency, Central News Agency, CTK, Jiji, Kyodo News Service, Middle East News Agency, UPI and Tass. DPA has recently established the Vereinigte Wirtschaftsdienste (VWD) for supplying economic news. Reuters offers a similar news service.

All special-interest groups and lobbies maintain their own news agencies, sometimes called "correspondence bureaus." The two largest are the Catholic News Agency (Katholische Nachrichten Agentur, KNA) and the Protestant Press Service (Evangelischer Pressdienst, EPD).

Electronic News Media

The West German radio and TV stations do not belong to the state, nor are they privately owned; rather they are *offentlich rechtlich*: publicly owned and controlled. Nine radio stations are involved in the radio network, seven of them on the basis of individual state laws. The North German Radio in Hamburg is based on agreement between Hamburg, Lower Saxony and Schleswig-Holstein and South-West Radio on an agreement between Rhine-Palatinate and Baden-Wurttemberg. Under the control of the federal government is the Deutsche Welle (German Wave), which now broadcasts in 38 languages, and Deutschlandfunk, which transmits to Europe. There is also RIAS (Radio in the American Sector) in West Berlin, which is run by West Germans even though the board of directors is appointed by the U.S. International Communications Agency. In addition, two private American setups (Radio Free Europe and Radio Liberty), a French enterprise (Europe I) and British and U.S. forces also broadcast programs from West Germany.

Two television programs are transmitted all over the Federal Republic. The first, composed of contributions produced by nine individual stations, is transmitted as a joint program, in which station shares range from three to 25 percent. The division largely corresponds to the distribution of viewers between the various stations. However, news transmissions are always the responsibility of North German Radio and sports programs of the West German Radio. The second program is produced by Zweites Deutsches Fernsehen (ZDF, Second German Television), established in Mainz in 1961 as a public-utility corporation on the basis of an agreement between all the federal states. It receives 30 percent of its income from license fees and is obliged to obtain additional earnings from commercial charges. Nearly 75 percent of the programs are transmitted in color.

Radio and television stations and programs are subject to supervision by the government of the Länder but are not bound by its directives. Management generally rests in each case on two bodies: a Radio Council and a Board of Management. The radio councils are appointed either by the Länder parliaments or directly by institutions such as churches, universities, trade unions, political parties and the press. All the stations work together in the Arbeitsgemeinschaft der offentlich-rechtlichen Rundfunkanstalten der Bundesrepublik Deutschland (ARD, Standing Conference of German Broadcasting Stations), which coordinates programs, regulates finances and deals with other shared tasks, such as planning the First Television Program.

Radio and television stations are financed through license fees; the Deutsche Welle and the Deutschelandfunk are funded by the national budget. There are considerable differences in the financial positions of individual radio stations. The ARD, therefore, has introduced a system of compensatory financing that enables even small stations to produce competitive programs. Allotment of fre-

quencies is made by the federal post office.

Program content varies from station to station and from year to year but in general the ratio between word and music in West German radio is 48 percent to 52 percent while the ratio of news (including documentaries and sports) to entertainment on television is 50–50.

Education & Training

On the basis of a survey published in 1977, some 25,000 journalists are working for the West German media, as follows:

Distribution of Journalists in Media	
Daily & weekly newspapers	6,500
Periodicals & press services	3,900
Press & news agencies	500
Radio & TV	2,800
Newsreels & audiovisuals	300
Commercial publications, associations etc.	5,000
Freelance journalists	4,700
Trainees	1,700

State press laws prohibit compulsory registration of journalists and ensure free access to the profession. Basic to the freedom of the West German press is so-called *Zulassungfreiheit* (freedom from statutory approval) for entering or practicing the profession of journalism.

Some 75 percent of the journalists in the Federal Republic enter the profession through a basic training program known as *Volontariat.* The *Volontare,* or trainees, are trained in-house by newspaper concerns in accordance with the Agreement on Training Guidelines for Editorial Trainees on Daily Newspapers between the Federal Association of German Newspaper Publishers on the one hand, and on the other the German Journalists Association, the IG Druck und Papier and the German Salaried Employees Union. Some 6.1 percent of the trainees hold a university degree and 2.3 percent a doctorate. The basic training period is two years and is generally followed by further training at any of the following institutions: Institut für Kommunikationswissenschaft of the University of Munich; Institut für Publizistik of the Free University of Berlin; Pädagogische Hochschule Ruhr of the Comprehensive University of Dortmund; Institut für Sozialwissenschaften, Kommunikationswissenschaft of the Stuttgart Hohenheim University; Institut für Publizistik of the Johannes Gutenberg University at Mainz; the Catholic Institut zur Forderung des Publizistischen Nachwuchses; the Protestant Christliche Presse-Akademie; and the German School of Journalists at Munich. Foreign journalists are trained at the International Institute of Journalism in Berlin.

As in many other countries, West German journalists are held in poor esteem by the public. According to a survey by the Institute of Public Opinion Research in Allensbach, only 13 percent of the German public held the profession in high regard, as compared with 77 percent for doctors, 60 percent for engineers, 47 percent for the clergy, and even 42 percent for coal miners. Journalists are often described as nosey mudslingers. Further, the fact that anyone with a pen can describe himself as a journalist has given rise to the saying, "If you become nothing, you become a journalist."

Summary

The West German press, reborn after the fiery ordeal of World War II, is now legally and economically more secure than ever before. Technology has enabled it to surmount some of the more serious problems posed by competition from televison, and the process of consolidation that began in the 1950s has enabled it to survive the economic pressures of the marketplace.

Two factors will exert a decisive influence on the future of the press in West Germany: developments in technology and in communications policy. Actually, one flows into the other, because technical developments exert considerable influence on communications policy. As the investment required for new technological systems is so great, the number of small and independent publishers will continue to decline and local press monopolies will grow. This may require state intervention of one form or another, affecting—at least marginally—the existence of a free press.

CHRONOLOGY

1975   West German Parliament approves law giving newsmen unlimited right to refuse to divulge sources of their information.

1976   West German printers' union, IG Druck und Papier, strikes against nation's largest newspapers for 12 days before strike is settled for 6 percent pay increase.

1978   IG Druck und Papier strikes over issue of introduction of computer technology and video display terminals that could displace some workers; publishers declare nationwide lockout; strike settled by compromise agreement: skilled hot-metal printers will operate video terminals for next 10 years.

West German company Vereinigte Wirtschaftsdienste and UNICOM News, joint venture of UPI and Commodity News Service, announce news and information exchange agreement. West German Cartel Office prohibits Axel Springer Verlag from acquiring a majority holding in the Muenchener Zeitungs-Verlag on grounds that acquisition with result in monopoly situation.

Alice Schwartzer, publisher of *Emma,* loses lawsuit against use of pictures of nude women on covers of *Stern* but claims moral victory.

1979   London-based *Financial Times* prints first issue from Frankfurt.

Plans to issue Frankfurt edition of strike-bound *Times* of London abandoned in face of opposition from IG Druck und Papier.

BIBLIOGRAPHY

Hofsahs, Rudolf, and Hans Pollman. *Das Presse-und Informationsamt der Bundesregierung.* Düsseldorf, 1977.
Jerschke, Hans-Ulrich. *Offentlichkeitspflicht der Exekutive und Informationsrecht der Presse.* Berlin, 1971.
Kruger, Wolfgang. *Probleme der Informationspolitik.* Hamburg, 1973.

GHANA

By Callix Udofia

BASIC DATA

Population: 11,936,000
Area: 238,280 sq. km. (92,000 sq. mi.)
GNP: 12.48 billion cedi (US$4.54 billion)(1979)
Literacy Rate: 25%
Language(s): English
Number of Dailies: 4
  Aggregate Circulation: 435,000
  Circulation per 1,000: 42
Number of Nondailies: 6
  Aggregate Circulation: 597,400
  Circulation per 1,000: 58
Number of Periodicals: 74
Number of Radio Stations: 23

Number of Television Stations: 4
Number of Radio Receivers: 1.8 billion
  Radio Receivers per 1,000: 164
Number of Television Sets: 35,000
  Television Sets per 1,000: 3
Total Annual Newsprint Consumption: 7,300
  metric tons
  Per Capita Newsprint Consumption: 0.7 kg.
  (1.5 lb.)
Total Newspaper Ad Receipts: 7.15 cedi
  (US$2.6 million)
  As % of All Ad Expenditures: NA

Background & General Characteristics

The Royal Gold Coast Gazette, an official paper founded in 1822 by Sir Charles McCarthy, the first British governor of the then Gold Coast settlements, marked the beginning of print journalism in Ghana. African initiative came thirty years later when the Bannerman brothers ran the *West African Herald,* which died in 1873. Another African venture during the same period was the *Gold Coast Times.* Other African initiatives, mostly small polemical news sheets, appeared and disappeared during the period. A majority of the newspapers that appeared in the 19th and early 20th centuries were weeklies. However, the most sustained African effort was shown by Dr. J. B. Danquah, who founded the first daily—the *Times of West Africa*—in 1931. Since then the number of dailies has steadily increased.

The British used the press to extend and consolidate authority and influence and model the few literate Ghanaians then perceived as heirs to power and authority. Then the indigenous press was stridently critical of the British rule. Criticism soon turned to unrestrained abuses of colonial rulers.

In 1957 Ghana emerged from colonial rule with 11 papers. Dr. Francis Kwame Nkrumah, himself a journalist, spared no time and effort in reorientating the press to socialism and the socialist approach to politics and development. He believed that the mass media should be completely under government control to assure their full utilization and commitment to the urgent aims of national integration and modernization. Unhappy with the adversary role of the independent and foreign-owned Mirror group of newspapers and the stridently critical Ashanti *Pioneer,* Nkrumah established the Guinea Press Ltd., the publishers of the government-owned *Ghanaian Times* and *Evening News,* and later introduced censorship in 1960. Before he was ousted in 1966, government corporations had been organized to publish state-owned papers and manage radio and television broadcasting, a legacy he bequeathed to successive Ghanaian governments.

Although the developments of the first year of the National Liberation Council headed by Lt. General Joseph Ankrah promised a return to nominal press freedom, Kofi Abrefa Busia's period was perhaps the freest in the history of the Ghanaian press since independence. More independent newspapers, such as the *Palaver Tribune,* the *Voice of the People* and the *Spokesman,* were established.

Private and independent press barely existed during General Acheampong's regime, 1972 to 1978. However, this period witnessed the birth of an underground press such as the *Believer* and the *Catholic Standard.* Then came General Fred Akuffo and his policy of national reconciliation, which among other things gave the press and the Ghanaian journalists a new lease on life.

There are currently four daily newspapers in Ghana: the *Daily Graphic, The Ghanaian Times,* the *People's Evening News* and the *Pioneer.* All are based in Accra, except for the *Pioneer,* published in Kumasi; all are published in English. With circulations of 200,000 for the *Daily Graphic,* 150,000 for *The Ghanaian Times,* 40,000 for the *People's Evening News,* and an estimated 50,000 for the *Pioneer,* their aggregate and per capita circulations are 435,000 and 42 copies per 1,000 Ghanaians, respectively.

Fourteen weeklies are published: *The Believer, Business Weekly, Champion, Echo, The Mirror, The Palaver Tribune, Punch, Radio and TV Times, The Scope, Sporting News, The Standard, Star, The Statesman* and the *Weekly Spectator.* Estimated total circulation is 597,400 and per capita circulation is 18.

The 74 periodicals include four fortnightlies, 27 monthlies, four quarterlies and two others, the *Economic Bulletin of Ghana* and the *Health Digest,* which come out once every two months. Their circulations range from 40,000 in the case of the *Christian Messenger,* a monthly founded in 1883 and published in English, Twi and Ga, to 2,000 for *Kabaare,* one of the eight local-language periodicals put out by the Ghana Information Services. Since most of the papers are published in English, they only appeal to the 25 percent of Ghanaians who can read and write. With a minimum wage of C4 (about $1.45) a day and an inflation rate of 54.4 percent, only the affluent sectors of the Ghanaian society and the foreign community can afford papers.

The government plays the most active role in the newspaper industry. The better-equipped, -staffed and -financed government-owned papers occupy the top echelon in the industry, while the struggling independent and private papers continue to look for some way to make their presence felt. Although the quality of journalism is among the highest in Africa, most of the papers lack good investigative, hard-hitting, straight-ahead pieces. Pre-independence combative journalism has given way to toothless and bland reportage with no definite ideology.

The format, design and makeup of Ghanaian newspapers basically reflect the traditional colonial tabloid era, except for the *Pioneer,* which appears in a standard broadsheet format. The body type is usually small and without much leading. They have fixed column widths and a limited range of headline forms, and traditional faces; usually they have single-column heads with occasional two- and three-column heads for variety. Variations in makeup patterns are limited. Issues normally contain twelve folios of 15″ x 11″ size. Sometimes they publish a sixteen-folio supplement, but supplements are not a regular feature of Ghanaian newspapers. Most are morning papers.

With a circulation of 180,000, *The Sunday Mirror,* the Sunday edition of the *Daily Graphic,* is the largest of the eighteen weeklies. Most of the weeklies and periodicals are special-interest publications. *Radio and TV Times,* put out by the Ghana Broadcasting Corporation, *Sporting News,* and *The Students' World* belong to this category. *Kpodoga,* a local-language periodical, is co-published by the Institute of Education and UNESCO. The Ghana Information Services publishes monthly papers in eight local languages; these have an aggregate circulation of about 150,000.

Almost all the papers are based in the Accra region, Ghana's capital with a population of over half a million. The *Pioneer* and the *Garden City News* come out of Kumasi, while *The Scope* and *The Symbol,* with circulations of 20,000 and 10,000 respectively, are published in Tema, the fourth largest city. Two local-language monthlies, *Kasem Labie* and *Lahabili Tsugu,* are based in Tamale. The much respected *Legon Observer,* the independent political journal put out by the Legon Society of National Affairs, the *Ghana Journal of Science* and the *Economic Bulletin of Ghana* are based in the university town of Legon, near Accra.

The three most influential and important newspapers in the country are *The Daily Graphic, The Ghanaian Times* and the *Pioneer;* they are also the largest newspapers by circulation. The *People's Evening News* is the fourth largest daily, followed by weeklies: *The Sunday Mirror* (circulation 180,000), the *Weekly Spectator* (165,000), *The Palaver Tri-*

bune (100,000), *The Standard* (30,400), *Echo* (30,000), *The Scope* (20,000) and *Radio and TV Times* (20,000).

Economic Framework

For most Ghanaians, the electronic media continue to be the main sources of news and information—particularly the radio with its national coverage and variety of local-language programs. This has been enhanced by the availability of inexpensive transistor radios. But with the increase in cost of living and the high inflation rate, the influence of television on the lives of ordinary Ghanaians may not be fully felt in the next decade. The cost of a television set is far beyond the means of the average Ghanaian. Newspapers, though not as important to a crosssection of the Ghanaian society, are and will continue to appeal to the literate Ghanaians. The nine local-language papers have small circulations, considering the size of their potential audiences. The print media need a more effective, efficient and decentralized distribution network.

A majority of Ghanaian papers are government-owned. Their circulations and influence are comparatively higher than either independent newspapers such as the *Palavar Tribune* or political party paper the *Star*. Almost all except a few local-language papers are elitist in content and approach. They all seem to emphasize the importance of power, formal authority and rewards of being "a loyal, good and law-abiding Ghanaian."

Distribution concentrates in and originates from Accra. From one third to one half of the total circulation of most Ghanaian papers is in the Accra region, an area with about one-ninth of the population of Ghana. Company vehicles, in the case of government-owned papers, or commercial vehicles hired by independent and private media organizations, convey papers to agents in the principal towns—Kumasi, Tamale, Tema, Takoradi, Cape Coast and Sekondi—from where vendors extend distribution by bicycle and on foot to the villages. Delays of one to three days are normal. It is not unusual for the Monday edition of a paper such as the *Graphic* to be available in Tamale on Wednesday morning.

Like other African countries, Ghana experiences a shortage of newsprint. Partly because of the scarcity of foreign reserves, the government imposes restrictions on many items, including newsprint and type faces. Newsprint importation is regulated through the government's three-monthly quota system. In 1977 the total consumption of newsprint was 7,300 metric tons or 0.7 kg per capita. In 1976 Ghana imported 5,803 metric tons of newsprint valued at $206,700, i.e., $356 per kilogram.

Publishing equipment is imported. It is costly, cumbersome and difficult to maintain. The new offset presses with cold type or photo typesetting are in use. They greatly improve the quality of printing, especially photoreproduction, and also reduce cost and maintenance requirements.

With these costs and other financial obligations, little or no advertising revenue, and selling prices of 50 pesewas and C1.50 for a newspaper or magazine respectively, newspapering in Ghana cannot be regarded as a profitable economic endeavor.

Ghana has no journalist or press-related unions at the national level, but trade-union rights are guaranteed under the Industrial Relations Act of 1965.

Press Laws

Fundamental human rights and freedoms, including freedom of religion, expression, assembly and association, are entrenched in the new Ghanaian constitution. The section on freedom of expression states that state-owned media "shall afford equal opportunities and facilities for the representation of opposing or differing views." The proclamation by the president, acting in accordance with the advice of the Council of State, of a state of emergency limiting the operation of these guarantees shall be subject to Parliamentary approval within 72 hours, and procedures are laid down for subsequent prolongation by a majority vote of all members of Parliament. Other constitutional provisions relating to the media are closely associated with the responsibilities of the newly established Press Commission.

Ghana's press-related laws date back to colonial times. The extent of British control of newspapers and books was defined by the Newspaper Registration Ordinance of 1894 and the Book and Newspaper Registration Ordinance of 1897. These laws required a newspaper editor to send returns of the total circulation as well as the title of the newspaper, the location of its offices, printers and publishers to the then colonial secretary. The printer was expected to print his name and address on the first and last pages of the newspaper. These regulations are still followed.

In 1934 the Criminal Code (Amendment) Ordinance, sometimes referred to as the Sedition Ordinance (Ordinance No. 21 of 1934), specified new categories of offenses constituting sedition: raising discontent or disaffection; prompting feelings of ill-will between classes or of "one color" against another; printing, selling or distributing seditious matter. Dr. Francis Kwame Nkrumah, the first president of Ghana, in 1957 inherited these press laws and introduced more.

In 1963 a Newspaper Licensing Act was passed requiring newspaper publishers to obtain a license, renewable annually, from the government. This act was repealed in 1970 by Dr. K. A. Busia, only to be reinstituted by Colonel Ignatius Acheampong in 1973. Acheampong, immediately after assuming power in 1972, promulgated a decree indemnifying the government-controlled newspapers against libel suits filed by the members of Busia's government who felt they had been defamed by press attacks. Private newspaper editors and independent journalists generally felt free to write and publish news and information during General Fred Akuffo's rule. Such an atmosphere was a byproduct of Akuffo's policy of national reconciliation, one element of which was press freedom.

Chapter 12 of the new constitution stipulates that the judiciary is to be subject only to the constitution and not to the control or direction of any other person or authority. The 1977 Constituent Assembly stipulated that the appointment of the Chief Justice and members of the Supreme Court was subject to parliamentary approval. Parliament's 71–0 rejection, for nonpayment of income taxes, of Mr. Justice Fred Apaloo as the Chief Justice and Judge of the Supreme Court provided a test of judicial independence. The Ghanaian Court of Appeal ruled that Mr. Justice Apaloo should continue in office as Chief Justice and by virtue of that office should automatically become the President of the Supreme Court. President Limann accepted the ruling.

Censorship

Chapter 22 of Ghana's new constitution provides for the establishment of an independent Press Commission. Its responsibilities include: (1) the appointment of the governing bodies of public corporations in charge of mass communications or information, including the print and electronic media; (2) ensuring "the procurement and distribution on an equitable and nondiscriminatory basis of the facilities and services required for the efficient and independent operation of the press and other media"; (3) formulating regulations for the registration of newspapers and the licensing of other media (in respect to which Parliament will be specifically debarred from legislating); (4) taking "measures to ensure the preservation of press freedom," and (5) taking measures to ensure the maintenance of professional standards in the mass media, including the adjudication of complaints.

The 12-member commission is to include one representative each from the Association of Recognized Professional Bodies, the Ghana Bar Association, the National Development Commission, the Ghana National Association of Teachers, the universities, the Ghana Association of Writers, the owners and proprietors of the private press, and the Christian Council/National Catholic Secretariat; two representatives of the Ghana Journalists' Association, and "two other members, one of whom shall be a woman." Seven of the current members have been identified as People's National Party (PNP) loyalists, while the remaining five are not. The fear is that the PNP majority would pack the boards of newspapers and appoint party hacks to management, thereby controlling the media and hindering real freedom of the press. However, in an inauguration speech, President Limann assured members of the commission and Ghanaian journalists that his government would do everything to help the commission discharge its obligations in the overall interest of the public and provide an independent institutional framework within which the Ghanaian press will operate in an atmosphere of responsible freedom.

State-Press Relations

The Ministry of Information is the information and public relations organ of the government. It is headed by a commissioner directly appointed by the president, subject to parliamentary approval. Its Information Services Department publishes eight local-language periodicals (aggregate circulation

150,000) and a variety of other English-language information materials such as *Ghana Today* (a quarterly), *The Post* (a fortnightly) and *Ghana Review* (a monthly). In conjunction with the British Council, the Information Services Department operates about 50 mobile cinema units. It makes its facilities and services available to other government departments.

Ghanaian newspapers and journalists have experienced various forms of harassment, from civilian and military regimes alike. The *Ashanti Pioneer,* an independent newspaper founded in 1939 and published in Kumasi-Ashanti by John and Nancy Tsiboe, was very critical of Nkrumah's administration. Beginning in 1960 it was subjected to intermittent government censorship; on October 19, 1962, the government decided to take it over. Both the paper's editor, A. D. Appea, and its city editor, Kwame Kesse-Adu, had been arrested earlier. Kesse-Adu spent four and a half years in detention in the Fort Ussher prison for "destructive criticism of the government" and Appea was detained for seven months.

The Pioneer resumed publication, only to be shut down in July 1972 by General Acheampong for being critical of the government. The paper was permitted to resume publication after its two top editors were forced to resign, to be replaced immediately by a government-appointed editor. As if this wasn't enough, the general put a familiar economic obstacle in the way of *The Pioneer:* the denial of an import license for the importation of newsprint.

Dr. Busia, generally regarded as a fervent believer in democracy, the rule of law, and free speech, dismissed the editor of the state-owned *Daily Graphic* in 1970 when the latter opposed the government on the issue of the need for African countries to have a dialogue with South Africa.

The editor of the independent weekly the *Echo* was detained more than once by the military authorities. This, and problems over permission to obtain an import license for newsprint, forced the *Echo* to close down. The biweekly *Legon Observer* was similarly compelled to cease publication in July 1974. Two months after General Acheampong was forced to resign in May 1978, the license of the *Legon Observer* was granted by the Ministry of Information; the periodical resumed publication on September 1, 1978. The *Believer,* which started as a religious organ

in the dying days of Acheampong, resumed publication immediately after its editor, G. A. B. Akrong, was released from detention.

Attitude Toward Foreign Media

Since 1966 Ghana has had liberal policies toward foreign media and their agents. Its exchange agreements with foreign press agencies—Reuters, AFP, CTK, Tass, ANSA and Tanjug—attest to this. As a matter of routine, visa applications of foreign correspondents outside Africa are usually referred by Ghanaian embassies and High Commissions abroad to the home government for processing and approval.

Until the 1966 military coup, the government censored outgoing press messages and a number of foreign correspondents were banned. At the beginning of September 1966 the National Liberation Council lifted the censorship and revoked the ban. Since then, Ghana has had a clean record in regards to harassment of foreign correspondents. Its liberal policies are extended not only to outgoing international press cables but also to the importation and sale of a wide array of foreign publications. However, the latter is subject to availability of foreign exchange, which has been scarce for the past eight years.

Foreign information is available to the general public. British magazines and newspapers are sold at newsstands, as are the international editions of such U.S. publications as *Time* and *Newsweek.* Although Ghanaian papers regularly carry foreign news considered of interest, foreign propaganda has little or no influence on the domestic media. Many Ghanaian journalists have been exposed to international press organizations, such as the International Organization of Journalists (IOJ), which is Soviet-backed and Czech-sponsored. Ghanaian journalists trained in the United States maintain their nominal membership in many U.S. press organizations such as Sigma Delta Chi.

Ghana, like other African countries, is committed to the 1978 UNESCO's "New World Information Order," which among other things called for greater reciprocity in the global flow of information and the support of mass media in economically less-developed countries, thereby correcting the inequalities in the flow of information to, from and between economically less-developed countries.

News Agencies

The Ghana News Agency (GNA) is the main source of both local and foreign news. Established in 1957 within the Information Services Department, it became a statutory corporation in 1960, with a board appointed by the head of state. The agency operates almost exclusively on government subventions.

Its head office is in Accra, with permanent regional bureaus in Koforidua, Kumasi, Sunyani, Tamale, Bolgatanga, Cape Coast, Sekondi and Ho, and 17 offices in district centers, and news bureaus in New York, London and Nairobi. Its six main services are home news service, foreign news, Africa/Europe service, features, daily/weekly summary and advertising services. The regional printed news service is subscribed to by 140 organizations and diplomatic missions. It employs a total of 371 editorial, administrative and technical staff and 380 stringers.

The Ghana News Agency has news-exchange agreements with Reuters, AFP, CTK, Tass, ANSA and Tanjug, which have offices in Accra. The Deutsche Presse-Agentur (dpa) is also represented in Accra.

Electronic News Media

Broadcasting began in Ghana on July 31, 1935, when a small wired relay station known as ZOY was opened in Accra to relay BBC programs. The Gold Coast Broadcasting System was established in 1954. Broadcasting became a department separate from the Information Service, to which it was formerly attached. External Service was inaugurated on June 1, 1961. Six years later the Commercial (radio-TV) Service was launched. The Ghana Broadcasting Corporation was formally incorporated on March 1, 1968.

The corporation operates three simultaneous networks on its national service. GBC-1 is the local-languages channel; programs are put out in six Ghana languages—Akan, Ga, Ewe, Nzema, Dagbani, Hausa—and English. GBC-2 (commercial radio service) broadcasts for moderate charges announcements covering trade items, entertainments, deaths and funerals, marriages and weddings, festivals and functions of charitable organizations.

GBC-3 is a channel for serious English programs for domestic listeners. There are sixteen shortwave transmitters, of 10, 20, 100 and 250 kw. These transmitters cover about 99 percent of the Ghanaian territory, operating from Accra, Ejura and Tema. In 1979 there were 1.8 million radio receivers, or 164 per 1000.

Broadcasting hours total 221 a week, of which 38 percent is light entertainment, 20 percent news and information, 20 percent cultural and scientific programs, 10 percent special audiences programs, 7 percent education and 3 percent advertising and announcements.

The External Service of Radio Ghana broadcasts in Swahili, Hausa, Arabic, Portuguese, French and English on four 100-kw transmitters sited at Tema, beaming to the whole of Africa, North America, the Caribbean, Europe and the Middle East, and two high-powered transmitters, 250 kw each, at Ejura in Ashanti.

The Ghana Broadcasting Corporation-Television (GBC-TV) was inaugurated on July 31, 1965. GBC-TV has two studios in Accra, with transmitters at Ajangote near Accra, Kissi near Cape Coast in the Central Region, Jamasi near Kumasi in Ashanti, and Tamale in the Northern Region. GBC-TV operates a 625-line system on four channels— 2, 3, 4, and 5—transmitting an effective radiation power of about 15 kw from its main transmitter at Ajangote and transmitters at Kissi and Jamasi. The Tamale station with 2 kw radiation power serves Tamale and the surrounding areas in the Northern Region; programs on film and video tape are flown daily from Accra for retransmission from Tamale.

Broadcasting time totals 47 hours a week. Twenty-six percent is light entertainment, 24 percent educational, 23 percent special audiences broadcasts, 19 percent news and information, 2 percent science and culture, 1 percent commercials and 5 percent programs for schools, usually telecast for two hours in the mornings Monday to Friday when schools and colleges are in session.

More than 85 percent of the GBC-TV programs are of local origin. In the case of TV Schools, all the programs are of local origin and there is no use of foreign film or material. Through the Programme Exchange Centre in Nairobi, Kenya, Ghana exchanges its locally produced programs with other members of the Union of Radio and Television Organizations in Africa (URTNA). Ghana imports about 10 percent of its television programs from the UK and the United States.

Both radio and television broadcasting are a state monopoly operated and controlled by the Ghana Broadcasting Corporation.

The corporation now consists of eleven main divisions: Sound (programs), Television (programs), Engineering, Music and Culture, Film Production, News and Current Affairs, Publications and Public Relations, Technical Services, Commercial Services, Administration and Accounts. The corporation, administered by a board, operates with funds derived from its wired broadcast service, from commercial broadcasting (radio and television), from television license fees and, primarily, from the government.

Education & Training

The School of Journalism and Communication is a part of the University of Ghana in Legon near Accra. Run by five indigenous faculty members, it provides both a diploma course and a master's degree course in journalism and mass communication, open to graduates and competent journalists of long experience. The diploma course is one year of full time or two years of part-time studies, after an appropriate first degree has been earned; the master's degree program requires a minimum of two years of full-time studies or three years of part-time studies. In 1976-77, seven postgraduate diplomas were awarded. Many new reporters have been trained on the job. Many Ghanaian journalists have participated in seminars, workshops and many other crash programs either supported or organized by the following international organizations: The International Organization of Journalists (IOJ), International Press Institute (IPI), International Federation of Journalists (IFJ), African-American Institute (AAI), Ford Foundation, the Thomson Foundation, African Scholarship Program of American Universities (ASPAU), Agency for International Development (AID), the Commonwealth Press Union, London, the National Union of Journalists in Britain, the Regent Polytechnic, London, and the Berlin Institute for Mass Communication in Developing Countries. In addition, many Ghanaian journalists have been trained in journalism and mass communication schools in the

United States or worked as apprentices or interns on newspapers in England or the United States. The major journalistic associations in Ghana are the Ghana Association of Writers, the Ghana Journalists Association, the Independent Newspapers Association and the Guild of Ghana Editors.

Summary

Whether government control on the newspaper press will be relaxed or tightened under President Hilla Limann will probably depend more on political situations than on how fearlessly and judiciously the newly established independent Press Commission will discharge its obligations.

Certainly broadcasting will continue to remain a state monopoly. In addition Ghana Sanyo, established in 1964 to make television and radio sets, plans to break new grounds by building a color television factory as part of Ghana's efforts to switch its network to color. But the spending power of most Ghanaians is currently down due to a shattered economy. Given such circumstances, it is doubtful whether in the next decade there will be a substantial increase in the number of radio and television sets Ghanaians own.

Ghana, like other countries in Africa, is hard hit by newsprint shortages. Even if the condition were to improve, it is unlikely that Ghana would commit its scarce foreign exchange to more kilograms of newsprint rather than the food she badly needs. Chances are that state-owned papers, to maintain their circulation rates and attract substantial advertising, will continue to be accorded preferential treatment in newsprint allocation. For the unsubsidized independent papers the future is bleak, not necessarily in terms of press freedom but in regards to an unfavorable economic climate. Most of them will die; some diversity will be unfortunately lost. Nevertheless, literate Ghanaians will continue to take newspapers seriously.

It is not likely that Ghana's economy in the next decade will experience much substantial growth. And for political reasons, chances are that the government will prefer not to disturb the status quo in mass-media ownership in the country.

CHRONOLOGY

1975 A new independent daily, the *People's Evening News,* first published in June 1974 as a biweekly, appears.
Information Commissioner Colonel Tachie expresses government's determination to assist the private sector of the mass media to expand.

1976 General Acheampong releases from detention Adolphus Anang Patterson and Kwame Kesse-Adu, both free-lance journalists locked in for six months for destructive criticism of the government.
Brig. Gen. Robert Kotei lays foundation stone of the Northern Regional Head Office of the Ghana News Agency in Tamale.
The National Youth Council puts out *Ghana Youth,* a 32-page quarterly.

1977 The National Redemption Council (NRC) promulgates "Prohibition of Rumours Decree." Under the decree, any person who by print, writing, painting or word of mouth, publishes or reproduces any statement, rumor, or report which is false and likely to cause fear or alarm or despondence to the public or disturb the public peace or cause disaffection against the Supreme Military Council or NRC, among the public or members of the armed and police forces shall be guilty of an offense punishable upon conviction by imprisonment of not less than five years or more than ten years without the option of a fine.

1978 Commander G. E. Osei, the Ashanti Regional Commissioner, on May 10 bans the *Pioneer,* Kumasi-based weekly newspaper, for running "University Closed Down," story considered detrimental to the interest of the state. Commander Osei lifts ban in June.
Inaugural meeting of the Guild of Ghana Editors.
Lieutenant-General Akuffo announces government's intention of setting up an independent press council "to provide a suitable framework within which the media, Ghanaian and foreign journalists could practice their profession."

1980 Twelve-member Press Commission is inaugurated.
Press Commission upholds T. K. Addo-Twum's claim to the editorship of the state-owned daily *The Daily Graphic.*
Information Services Department launches a new state-owned English newspaper, the *Post.*

BIBLIOGRAPHY

Ainslie, Rosalynde. "Efforts to Establish a Popular Press in Independent Africa." *The Democratic Journalist,* September 1966, p. 121.
_____. *The Press in Africa.* London, 1966.
Alsbrook, James E. "Reaction of the World's Press to the Overthrow of Nkrumah." *Journalism Quarterly,* Summer 1967, p. 307.
"An African Press Survey: West Africa." *New Commonwealth,* July 22, 1954, p. 62.
_____. *The Press in Africa.* London, 1966.
"Apaloo is Chief Justice: Limann Accepts Ruling." *Ghana News,* Ghanaian Embassy, Washington, D.C., October 1980 pp. 3, 4.
Apter, David E. *Ghana in Transition.* New York, 1968.
Austin, Dennis. *Politics in Ghana: 1946–1960.* London, 1964.
Bentsi-Enchill, Nii K. "President Limann's First Year." *West Africa,* September 22, 1980, p. 1809.
_____. "The Road to Press Freedom in Ghana." *West Africa,* October 23, 1978, p. 2079.

Bretton, Henry L. *The Rise and Fall of Kwame Nkrumah.* New York, 1966.

Committee on Inter-African Relations. *Report on the Press in West Africa.* Nigeria, 1960.

"Daily Graphic Goes to Court." *West Africa,* March 10, 1980, p. 456.

Dorkenoo, M. S. "How Ghana Censors the Press." *IPI Report,* October 1962, p. 3.

"Editor Returns to Graphic." *West Africa,* September 8, 1980, p. 1733.

"Editorial Authority of President." *West Africa,* March 3, 1980, p. 417.

"The Essah Report: Let the Media Do Their Work." *West Africa,* October 23, 1978, p. 2110.

Essilfie-Conduah, Nana. "Catalogue of Unfinished Business Facing Limann." *West Africa,* October 6, 1980, p. 1954.

"Ghana: A Year's Black Record." *IPI Report,* November 1962, p. 11.

"Ghana: The Justice Affairs." *West Africa* September 8, 1980, p. 1689.

"Ghana's Basic Problem of Growth." *West Africa,* February 11, 1980, p. 243.

"Ghana's Press Commission at Last." *West Africa,* August 11, 1980, p. 1484.

"Graphic Editor Reverts to Post." *Ghana News,* Ghanaian Embassy, Washington, D.C., September 1980, pp. 2, 5, 8.

Hachten, William A. *Muffled Drums: The News Media in Africa.* Ames, Iowa, 1971.

―――. "Newspapers in Africa: Change or Decay?" *Africa Report,* December 1970, p. 25.

Hopkinson, Tom. "A New Age of Newspapers in Africa." *Gazette.* Vol. 14, No. 2, 1968, p. 79.

Katz, Elihu, and Wedell, George. *Broadcasting in the Third World: Promise and Performance.* Cambridge, Mass., 1977.

Kitchen, Helen. *The Press in Africa.* Washington, D. C., 1956.

Mukupo, Titus. "What Role for the Government in the Development of an African Press." *Africa Report,* January 1966, p. 39.

"My Duty: President Limann." *West Africa,* July 21, 1980, p. 1321.

"New Government Newspaper." *West Africa,* January 14, 1980, p. 84.

Omu, Fred I.A., "The Dilemma of Press Freedom in Colonial Africa: The West African Example." *Journal of African History,* Vol. 9, No. 2, 1968, p. 279.

"Pioneer Banned." *West Africa,* May 29, 1978, p. 1042.

"Press Commission Appointed." *West Africa,* June 30, 1980, p. 1204.

"Press Freedom." *West Africa,* October 18, 1976, p. 1556.

"Press Freedom." *West Africa,* August 14, 1978, p. 1613.

"Progress, Trials and Tribulations for the Press in Ghana." *West Africa,* October 16, 1978, p. 2066.

"Protecting the Press." *West Africa,* December 18, 1980, p. 2526.

"Role for Communicators." *West Africa,* October 6, 1980, p. 1943.

"Rumour Decree." *West Africa,* June 20, 1977, p. 1240.

"Shock and Dismay at Takeover of 'Ashanti Pioneer.'" *IPI Report,* November 1962, p. 11.

Timothy, Bankole. *Kwame Nkrumah: His Rise to Power.* Britain, 1963.

Twumasi, Yaw. "The Newspaper and Political Leadership in Developing Nations: The Case of Ghana, 1964-1978." *Gazette,* Vol. 26, No. 1, 1980, p. 1.

Udofia, Callix., "Content and Situational Relevance of Agricultural News in the Ghanaian Times and the Lagos Daily Times." *Rural Africana,* Spring 1978, p. 51.

"Why Apaloo and Abban Were Rejected." *West Africa,* September 1, 1980, p. 1677.

Wilcox, Dennis L. *Mass Media in Black Africa: Philosophy and Control.* New York, 1975.

GREECE

by Manny Paraschos

BASIC DATA

Population: 9,200,000 (1977)
Area: 131,990 sq. km. (50,960 sq. mi.)
GNP: 1.70 trillion drachmas (US$37.8 billion)
Literacy Rate: 91%
Language(s): Greek
Number of Dailies: 118
   Aggregate Circulation: 1,200,000
   Circulation per 1,000: 130
Number of Nondailies: 875
   Aggregate Circulation: 138,000
   Circulation per 1,000: 15
Number of Periodicals: 907
Number of Radio Stations: 8

Number of Television Stations: 3
Number of Radio Receivers: 2,900,000
   Radio Receivers per 1,000: 316
Number of Television Sets: 2,000,000
   Television Sets per 1,000: 217
Total Annual Newsprint Consumption: 70,000 metric tons
   Per Capita Newsprint Consumption: 7.6 kg. (16.7 lb.)
Total Newspaper Ad Receipts: 8.84 billion drachmas (US$23,088,000) (1979)
   As % of All Ad Expenditures: 28

Background & General Characteristics

The first Greek newspapers were published in the late 18th century outside Greece, because at the time Greece was under the rule of the Ottoman Empire. George Vendotis published the first Greek newspaper in 1784 in Vienna, Austria; other Greek papers appeared later in Paris and London. This expatriate Greek press was instrumental in preparing the Greeks to revolt and in keeping the Greek language and value system alive.

The first paper in mainland Greece appeared in Kalamata on August 1, 1821, approximately five months after the Greek revolution against the Turks had started. Other early Greek papers on the mainland were published in Ydra, Galaxidi, Mesologgi, Agrinion and Athens. The oldest Greek paper still in publication (*Elfimeris tis Kiverniseos*) was started in Nafplion in 1825 as the medium of the government, which operates it to this day.

One of the earliest characteristics of the mainland Greek press was its partisanship, which dates to the reconstruction era of the mid-1800s. Another was the personal journalism that prevailed in the latter part of the 19th century and the early part of the 20th. A third was the large number of publications devoted to literary work—the most important type of print journalism that appeared in Greece, next to political journalism.

As the Greek press evolved in the last half century, two points have become clear: Greek newspapers still represent the most dynamic element of the Greek news media; the Athens national political dailies dominate the press scene. References to the press, unless otherwise noted, apply to the Athens national political dailies.

In the fall of 1980 there were 13 national political dailies published in Athens, with an average daily combined circulation of 720,427. The seven morning papers had an average daily circulation of 167,444 (or approximately 24 percent of total circulation), while the six evening papers had an average daily circulation of 552,983 (or 76 percent). Most of that circulation (approximately 65 percent) takes place in the Athens metropolitan area: the morning papers sell 94,303 copies in the metropolitan area and 73,141 in the rest of the country; the evening papers sell 377,949 in the metropolitan area and 175,034 in the rest of Greece.

The 38 dailies in the Athens metropolitan area include 20 general circulation papers, 12 financials, three foreign language papers, two sports papers, and one government-owned. There are 80 dailies in the rest of Greece, including six in Iraklion, five in Kerkyra, four each in Alexandroupoulis, Ioannina, Rethymno and Hania, and three each in Thessaloniki, Patras, Arta, Kavala, Karditsa and Trikala. There are two Athens dailies in English and one in Armenian, and one Athens nondaily each in English, French and Armenian. Five nondailies in Turkish are published in northeastern Greece; 26 magazines are published in English, one in German and one in Italian.

Regional publications account for 488, or 27 percent, of the nondaily press; legal-orientation publications for 110, or six percent; agricultural publications for 70, or four percent; religious publications for 65, or four percent; industrial publications for 60, or three percent; politically orientated publications for 65, or four percent; industrial publications for 60, or three percent; politically orientated publications for 65, or four percent; and medical publications for 40, or two percent.

Greece's national political dailies, their circulation (as of September 1980) and their political orientation are: Morning: *Akropolis,* 48,416, conservative; *To Vima,* 40,599, liberal; *Rizospastis,* 38,973, organ of the Greek Communist Party; *Kathimerini,* 18,291, conservative; *Eleftheros Kosmos,* 13,246, conservative; *Avgi,* 7,919, organ of a faction of the Greek Communist Party. Evening: *Ta Nea,* 168,419, liberal; *Apogevmatini,* 130,000, conservative; *Eleftherotypia,* 135,000, liberal; *Avriani,* 93,201, liberal; *Vradyni,* 47,367, conservative; *Mesimvrini,* 20,353, conservative; *Estia,* 7,047, conservative.

Although Greece's national political dailies have much improved since the pre-1967 days, most of them still are heavily partisan in the coverage of news, loudly promotional of their favorite political ideology, sensational in news selection and presentation, and obtrusive in typography and design. Of the papers mentioned above, only *To Vima, Ta Nea, Kathimerini* and *Eleftherotypia* seem to practice a consistent, responsible, quality journalism. Most of the rest are either too partisan or too sensational to be credible news media.

The most influential Greek papers are: *Apogevmatini* (conservative) and *Eleftherotypia* (liberal). Both have circulations of around 130,000 copies daily. The largest-selling evening tabloid, *Ta Nea,* is also liberal. The English-language *Athens Daily Post,* despite its small circulation, reaches a very important segment of the reading public.

The number of pages in Athens dailies ranges from four to 32 on the average day, with some Sunday editions having more than 48 pages per issue. A typical Athens daily may average 16 pages per day.

There are no true Sunday magazines as inserts in newspapers. Some newspapers add special sections for their Sunday editions, and many of them may feature the television schedule as a special foldout. Most papers simply increase the number of pages and features for their Sunday editions; some evening papers combine their Saturday-Sunday papers into a separate Sunday publication. Morning papers do not normally publish on Mondays and evening papers do not normally publish on Sundays.

Magazines are a major part of the print media in today's Greece. The great variety in theme and quality of magazines has resulted in their capturing a good part of the entertainment market and the advertising drachma. Unfortunately, the most popular Greek magazines tend to be of low quality. Since the bulk of their circulation depends on newsstand sales, they resort to sensational covers and content. Many successful magazines, for example, devote most of their issues to translations of cheap love stories from foreign magazines, sexy photo-romances (pictorial soap operas) and gossip.

The most popular magazines are *Domino* (weekly), Athens circulation 45,000, rest of Greece 86,000; *Romantso* (weekly), 75,000, 97,000; *Tahidromos,* 51,000, 48,000; *Fantazio,* 52,000, 54,000; *Gynaika,* 74,000, 47,000.

Of the more serious, news-features magazines, the biggest are *Gynaika, Tahidromos* and *Epikaira.* The first appeals primarily to women, with articles about feminine hygiene, professional women and homemaking. The other two offer a variety of news and features along with entertainment material, gossip columns, comics, puzzles, TV schedules, etc. These three magazines seem to absorb most of the print advertising money; about one-quarter to one-third of their space is taken up by advertisements.

The three major political magazines, *Anti, Politika Themata* and *Ikonomikos Tahi-*

dromos, are lively, informative and serious, but have very small circulation figures and advertising revenue.

Economic Framework

Although the press in Greece, both print and electronic, plays a significant role in the country's life, the profession does not generally enjoy a prestigious status among the citizenry. The main reasons for that may be the mostly sensational and partisan journalism practiced and the relatively difficult financial state of the media. Many factors contribute to the latter, including the country's financial instability (the 1980 inflation rate was 24.41); the competition for advertising revenues between the print and electronic media, with the print media at a disadvantage because radio and television are government-owned and -operated; the large number of political dailies, which may be good for political pluralism but spreads thin both the readership and advertising funds; and the large number of journalists who cannot be satisfactorily absorbed by the media.

Although Greek journalists are innovative and hardworking, most usually come to their positions through apprenticeship and lack a broad professional education. To make ends meet, many of them resort to moonlighting for other papers or television; a few even take part-time jobs as public relations consultants with the very agencies or institutions they normally cover.

The best-paid professionals seem to be those who belong to the Union of Journalists of Athens Dailies, which has succeeded in obtaining good settlements with the publishers for about the last quarter century. The average UJAD member's salary is about 50,000 dr. ($1,100) per month, while the technical union membership averages, with overtimes, 70,000–100,000 dr. ($1,555–$2,222) per month. (These figures reflect salaries in the metropolitan areas and primarily in Athens.) There have been no strikes by the editorial personnel of newspapers in the last five years, but there was a several-month-long strike of technical personnel in the summer of 1980 which was followed by a publishers' "lockout."

There are about 2,000 full-time professional newspersons in Greece today. More than half of them belong to the various unions—the Athens union has about 875 members, the

Thessaloniki union about 80, the Patras-Ipiros about 70 and the Thessalian about 70. Almost 900 journalists belong to no union.

Greece's professionals' unions are the Union of Journalists of Athens Dailies (Athens); the Union of Journalists of Dailies of Macedonia-Thrace (Thessaloniki); the Union of Journalists of Dailies of Peloponnisos-Ipiros-Islands (Patras); the Union of Journalists of Dailies of Thessalia-Sterea Ellas-Evoia (Volos); the Union of Journalists of Periodical Press (Athens); the Union of Publishers of Athens Dailies (Athens); the Union of Publishers of Rural Newspapers (Athens); the Union of Publishers of Rural Press (Athens); the Union of Publishers of Periodical Press (Athens); the Union of Correspondents of Greek Press Abroad (Athens); the Union of Foreign Correspondents (Athens); the Union of Personnel of Athens Dailies (Athens); the Union of Athens Newspaper Vendors (Athens); the Union of Personnel of Athens Newspaper Distribution Agencies (Athens); the Union of Photoreporters of Greece (Athens); the Union of Television Cameramen (Athens) and the Union of Technicians of Athens Daily and Periodical Press (Athens).

The print media dominate news reporting. The electronic media are owned and operated by the government, which in the last few years has resulted in some accusations of incompetent administration and biased reporting. Progovernment news items seem to dominate the newscasts. Although its growth rate seems to have slowed, television is still the main medium in the entertainment field. Its novelty (TV was started in Greece in 1966) and uniqueness, however, have been hampered by programming problems and the inexperience of technical personnel. Yet the electronic media absorb most of the advertising revenues. The media's versatility potential and their newness to Greek life are great attractions to advertisers. Magazines give newspapers a good fight for the rest of the advertising money.

In spite of the plethora of newspapers, Greece seems to be free of newspaper monopolies. Twenty-six of the country's 34 cities with daily newspapers have directly competitive situations. There are two newspaper chains among the Athens national political dailies: *To Vima-Ta Nea,* owned by Christos Lambrakis, and *Akropolis-Apogevmatini,* owned by the Botsis brothers (one of the brothers died recently and his heirs reportedly may sell one or both publications). A third major publisher is G. Athanasiadis, who owns the political daily *Vradyni* and the financial daily *Naftemboriki*.

Advertising pressures are not dissimilar to those on American papers. Stronger pressures on editorial content stem from the papers' political affiliation. Publishers, who are usually politically active, have strict control over their editors and, through them, over news content.

Almost all Greek papers use hot-type machines and cylindrical presses. Few magazines and two newspapers (one in Thessaloniki) are using cold-type reproduction methods. The new technology is available but still financially prohibitive for the large majority of newspapers.

The Athens Newspaper Distribution Agency is the main distributor of the national political dailies, which sell for 15 dr. (33 cents) per copy. The distribution system is government refereed, although not directly government controlled, and the complex legal system under which distribution takes place has been a source of serious controversy in post-dictatorship Greece.

Press Laws & Censorship

Except for the colonels' regime (1967–74), modern Greece has consistently outlawed censorship, bond posting, licensing of papers or journalists, and other means of press control. But the country's media are still governed by an antiquated, awkward and burdensome set of laws that in the hands of antagonistic prosecutors may—and often do —inhibit the operation of a free press. In recent years the press's major legal problems seem to have clustered around four broad areas of contention: disseminating ideas, insulting the authorities, spreading false or alarming news, and libel.

The 1975 Greek constitution in article 14 protects every citizen's right to "express and disseminate by word of mouth, in writing or through the Press, his ideas obeying the laws of the state." The same article outlaws "censorship and any other form of prior restraint" but allows seizure of the publication if the publication has insulted "the Christian or any other known religion" or "the person of the President of the Republic"; if it has revealed national security information or intended to cause the violent overthrow of the political system or to harm "the nation's

territorial integrity," or if it has offended public morality. Article 14 is complemented by article 5, which provides for the "free development of the citizen's personality," article 4, which provides for the citizens' "equality before the law," and article 25, which provides for the protection of "human rights of the individual" by the government.

The constitution does guarantee the right to publish and disseminate ideas—an improvement over the 1952 version that guaranteed only the "right to publish"—but dissemination is an area of legal as well as physical confrontation in today's Greece. Distributors of nonestablishment or underground publications have faced serious difficulties with police and prosecutors in the last six years. The plethora of small political movements born after the 1967–74 dictatorship contributed to the large number of confrontations between members of the press and the state.

The state's main legal weapon is a set of laws, Obligatory Law 582/45, which empowered the undersecretary of Press and Information to oversee the newspaper circulation system, and Legislative Order 2943/54, which set up the newspaper circulation system and defined the requirements for the licensing of newspaper sellers. Most distributors of minority viewpoint publications are unpaid volunteers who hope their publication will promote their political ideology and therefore do not meet these requirements— thus the confrontation. It is ironic that these legal gymnastics take place in the face of a law that aims at protecting the free circulation of publications. Obligatory Law 265/ 1945 states: "Whoever in whatever manner hinders the distribution or sale of legally published newspapers, magazines or other publications...is punished with at least three-month imprisonment and a 5,000- 10,000 drachmas fine [$112–$224]." "It is a much more serious violation" if the guilty party happens to be "a member of the military or an organ of public safety...." Article 181 of the Penal Code says: "Whoever publicly insults public authority, municipal authority, state authority or the Parliament-recognized head of a political party in the Country, is punished with up to three years imprisonment." Over the years this has been a notorious law.

Another law that has been used often in recent years deals with the dissemination of "false news." Article 191 of the Penal Code (amended by Legislative Order 2493/1953) says: "Whoever disseminates, in any manner, false news or rumors aiming to bring unrest or fear to the citizens or [aiming] to disturb the public faith or [aiming] to shake trust in the national currency or the armed forces or [aiming] to disturb the nation's international relations is punished with a minimum three-year imprisonment and a fine." The sentence is doubled if this is not a first offense. The law also states, "Whoever causes the above acts through negligence is punished with a maximum one-year imprisonment or a fine."

Libel is probably the most common case brought against the press, but rarely will the legal confrontation reach the last phases of litigation; most people settle out of court. It is worth noting, however, that the Penal Code describes meticulously the various types of libel ("insulting the honor of a person," "slandering the reputation of a person," "simple or malicious insult to the memory of the dead," and so forth), defines the difference between a public and a private person, and sets punishment. Truth is acceptable as a defense against libel. A newspaper or a magazine found guilty of libel must print the court decision verbatim and if the "guilty" article made reference to a public servant in the performance of his or her duty, he or she has a right to a court-supervised retraction, full in both content and appearance.

Source confidentiality is not a viable legal concept in today's Greece, but two major cases have helped to define it better. One involved the publication in a political review of a secret government document. When the editors refused to give the prosecutor the name of their source, the publication was sued under the Espionage Act (Obligatory Law 375/1936) and the main press law. The press law forbids the publication of "any military information without prior written approval of the appropriate military authority." (The press law, in fact, makes it illegal to comment on the readiness or quality of the armed forces and specifically requires the article writer to name his or her sources if they are members of the military community!) The publication was found not guilty.

Source confidentiality received some legal acceptability in the trial of the author of a book on neofascism in Greece. He was acquitted of making false accusations about persons allegedly involved in torturing many Greek citizens during the seven years of dictatorship. Many prominent politicians and journalists assisted in the defense of the

author, and the court accepted that his refusal to name his sources "in these particular circumstances was justifiable."

Freedom of information has never been an attainable cause among Greek journalists because there are so many laws protective of government actions and documents that, unless there is an obvious and major scandal involved, any free-access campaign on the part of the media is doomed to failure. In addition, government positions have been consistently endorsed by court gag orders.

In spite of the licentious appearance of movie advertisement pages and magazine covers in post-junta Greece, both society and government are rather conservative in their treatment of sexually oriented media. Obscenity is considered anything that "according to public sentiment insults decency." All obscene materials or their distribution and possession are punishable by law; the crime is especially serious if it is committed by a newspaper or a magazine.

Finally, it should be noted that there have been some instances in the last few years when journalists have been physically harmed by political opponents of their publications. Most of the confrontations have taken place during rightist organization meetings from which unsympathetic newsmen were violently expelled by the organizers. The Union of Journalists of Athens Dailies took a strong protest to the press minister in May 1976, but reportedly with little success.

Other laws affecting the press:
• Require that in order for someone to become a publisher he or she must be a Greek citizen with no criminal record.
• Require that all machinery, including typographical equipment, imported from abroad have importation licenses. (If the equipment is destined for a daily newspaper, a special license allows it to be imported duty-free.)
• Permit, under a September 1980 law, the press minister to set: (1) the minimum sale price for the metropolitan dailies (today's price is 15 dr. or 33 cents); (2) the maximum number of pages per week for these papers; and (3) the maximum number of extra copies, based on the paper's circulation figures, actually printed on duty-free newsprint.

Questions on journalistic ethics or professional practices that may extend beyond the reach of the law are usually handled by the disciplinary councils of the various professional unions. The last kind of major case these councils handled was that of journalists accused of assisting the junta in its press censorship apparatus, etc.

State-Press Relations

Newspapers are free to regularly criticize the various branches of government, and many of them do, with the executive branch the main target. Although investigative reporting and legislation for open meetings and records are in their infancy, criticism of the government by the print media is abundant and strong. According to some Greek editors government sources traditionally have been reluctant to talk openly to the media, although leaks to the press are common. Of course the political orientation of both the press and the government sources are instrumental in any exchange or publication of information.

The ideological pluralism of modern Greece has resulted in a complementary press system: political parties need an outlet to the public, and newspapers need a committed audience to survive. Over the years this mutually beneficial process has resulted in an abundance of rumors about politically motivated, inaccurate and unfair reporting that, on one hand, hurt the media's credibility while, on the other, help them among their like-minded readers. In fact it is not unusual for prominent publishers or editors to sit in top-level political meetings to help plan strategy. Helen Vlachos, one of the best-known Greek publishers, was a member of the Parliament for a few years following the fall of the junta, and Constantine, Mitsotakis, the current Minister of Foreign Affairs, owns a prominent paper in his native Crete.

Most affairs concerning the press are handled through the "press ministry," actually a department of the Ministry of the Premier. This ministry is closely related to the prime minister's office and coordinates the government's public communications, press attachés to Greek embassies abroad, foreign correspondents in Greece, Greek press problems, etc.

The main ways through which the government can exercise control over the press (excluding the legal weapons at its disposal) are government advertising (primarily for banking institutions, almost all of which are government owned), and newsprint pricing (revocation of a newspaper's import-duty-free license is one of the main punitive provisions of the Greek press laws). There are often rumors about various ministers making "deals" with publishers for loans, "grants," etc., but none of them has ever been legally substantiated.

The Greek judiciary is supposed to be an independent arm of the government. Judges become eligible for their bench after passing sophisticated examinations administered by the Ministry of Justice. Of course, as elsewhere, some judges are more appreciative of the press's function than others, and verdicts and sentences vary accordingly. In recent years, in spite of some government prosecutors' efforts to harass some members of the press, judges, especially on the appellate level, have been handing down opinions that show some understanding of the role of the press in a democracy.

In the last five years there has been only one instance of a newsman's incarceration, the case of a Cretan newspaper editor who refused as a matter of principle to pay his sentence's redemption fee and therefore stayed in jail for five weeks in the fall of 1976. During the same period there were reportedly no confiscations of publications. It should be noted here, however, that during the 1967–74 dictatorship there were numerous jailings and confiscations.

Attitude Toward Foreign Media

There are no restrictions on news flow abroad or on foreign media and their representatives: no formal accreditation procedure (a letter from the foreign publication's editor to the press minister is sufficient), no special visa requirements, no approval of cables and no import restrictions on foreign media. There have been no reported jailings or confiscations of foreign publications in post-junta Greece. (During the 1967–74 junta, foreign correspondents did face difficulties that included arrest, deportation, etc.) There are no foreign owners of major Greek media.

Greece's professional journalists are active in international press associations such as the International Press Institute, the International Federation of Journalists, the World Press Institute, UNESCO, etc.

The Greek government has opposed the 1978 UNESCO Declaration on the grounds that it would bestow the appearance of legitimacy on efforts by authoritarian governments to nationalize the press.

News Agencies

Greece's national news agency is the Athens News Agency, formed in 1905. It has correspondents in all large Greek cities and several foreign capitals. Where it can afford no representative, it sometimes uses the Greek embassies' press attachés. ANA is the main supplier of news to Greek media and has cooperative agreements with most of the major world news organizations. Some Greek papers receive additional wire services and hire translators for such copy. ANA also has an English service, distributed to about 600 customers.

The foreign news agencies represented in Greece are: Agence France-Press (French), Deutsche Presse-Agentur(West German), Associated Press and United Press International (both American), Reuter's (British), Financial Times (British), Springer Auslandsdienst (West German), Hsinhua (People's Republic of China), Turk Haberler Asansi (Turkish), Tanjug (Yugoslavian), Novosti (Soviet), Tass (Soviet), Ansa (Italian) and BTA (Bulgarian).

Electronic News Media

Greek television and radio, constitutionally entrusted to the government, aim at the "objective and equal dissemination of news and information and literary and artistic works, making every effort to ensure the program quality level that is appropriate for [the program's] social mission and the civic progress of the State." None of the constitutional press provisions applies to either radio or television.

Four radio networks, one operated by the armed forces, are transmitted from Athens. ERT, the national network, spends about 13 percent of its air time on news, including 15 minutes of news in foreign languages; YENED, the Armed Forces network, spends about 7 percent of its time on news.

Two national television networks exist. ERT covers about 85 percent of the territory and 90 percent of the people; its schedule is 50 percent entertainment, 16 percent news, 15 percent educational and 19 percent other programs. YENED covers about 70 percent of the territory and 75 percent of the people; its schedule is 50 percent entertainment, 16 percent news, 10 percent education and 24 percent other programs. About 50 percent of the news films on both networks is imported from Eurovision, American networks, etc.; about 36 percent of the entertainment schedule is imported.

With the exception of some outstanding folk tradition and cultural shows, Greek television is filled with old American shows ("Bonanza," "Kojak," "I Love Lucy," "Charlie's Angels," and so forth), Eurovision or American network news clips and very little local news. Unfortunately, the overwhelming majority of local news items center around government activity and present primarily the government side of events.

The progovernment attitude of the news presentation and the generally low quality of local programming have caused a sharp decrease in the number of television viewers. A poll taken by the weekly *Tahidromos* revealed that the number of television owners who do not watch television "at all" went from 11 percent in 1976 to 25 percent in 1979. The least-watched program was the news, which attracted 3 percent of the audience at 7 p.m. and four percent at 11 p.m.

Political pressures, stemming from the crude politicizing of news and a failure to produce worthwhile programming, have resulted in frequent changes in top management.

Generous salary ranges, aimed primarily at drawing newsmen from the newspapers and the magazines, liberal overtime contractual provisions, and general ignorance of the medium resulted in a huge financial mismanagement scandal in the fall of 1979. A report by two independent government consultants revealed that Greek television was in the red by $17.5 million.

Education & Training

In the last 20 years several attempts have been made, including one by the USIA in the 1950s, to teach journalism in an organized fashion. All met with little success.

There are several small "institutes" of journalism education in Greece today. Most are located in Athens; a few are in Thessaloniki. They tend to be evening schools with curricula of expository writing, reporting, press history, ethics, sociology, political science, typography, publishing, literature, criminology, public relations, advertising and foreign languages. The efforts of these private journalism schools, although admirable, seem doomed to failure: the schools are not recognized by the Education Ministry as institutions of higher education and so carry no academic weight; publishers base their hiring on patronage rather than talent; and perhaps most important, the profession is facing an economic crisis and its growth has been stunted.

Summary

The present Greek press system does not exhibit the signs of wisdom a system of its age and history ought to have acquired over the years. Although they are unmistakably a large part of modern Greek life, print and electonic news media in Greece do not enjoy the credibility or respect their European counterparts do. The press is dynamic, vocal and ubiquitous, but also sensational, partisan and often irresponsible.

The battle of print and electronic media over advertising money, coupled with the country's financial instability, have increased to a critical point the economic difficulties faced by the press. As the partisan competition continues among politicians and newspapers, the financial condition of most journalists is not expected to improve.

The outlook for the 1980s is more of the same. That may soon translate into newspaper closings or the emergence of various forms of consolidation or chain ownerships.

In either case, the present media pluralism is expected to diminish.

One major puzzle is the future of Greek television. Because of government support neither network is likely to face critical financial difficulties, but one wonders what may happen if the medium comes under new leadership—indeed, under a different government. Will it ever compete for news on equal footing with newspapers? Will its progovernment coverage continue regardless of regime? Will programming improve as Greek artists and technicians master the medium?

Finally, the future well-being of the professional journalist is questionable. In spite of the respectability of some professionals' salaries, most newspersons still face difficulties making ends meet. To a great degree journalism in Greece is still a "service" profession—a profession by and large populated by idealists with a yearning for "news" and the instinct or talent to get it. Recent changes in living conditions, however, have made some of that thinking impractical and many professionals have had to look for different solutions to their financial plights. Second and third jobs are becoming the rule and not the exception among Greek journalists as inflation makes money (and such jobs) more easily available and necessary.

Perhaps this loss of human resource and the threat it poses to the replenishment of the profession may be the most alarming aspect of today's Greek journalism.

CHRONOLOGY

1975	Two-week strike of editorial staffs of Athens dailies. *Christianiki* editor loses case of allegedly insulting Supreme Court. New Greek Constitution approved containing two articles with updated provisions on news media and free expression. *Alithia* sued for disseminating false news.
1976	*Eleftheros Kosmos* publishers convicted for allegedly slandering Armed Forces. *Christianiki* loses case of allegedly insulting authorities. Author of book *Birth of Neofascism in Greece* wins court

approval to keep his sources secret.
Exhibitor of movie *Emmanuela* loses case on obscenity grounds.
Eleftheros Kosmos editors convicted for allegedly insulting authorities.
Prosecutors impose gag order to protect military police records concerning an alleged plot by army to overthrow government.
Editors of six Athens dailies found not guilty of violating a gag order on news concerning the assassination of alleged CIA agent in Athens.
UJAD formally protests to government physical harass-

ment of newsmen by rightist groups with police tolerance.

Avgi loses case of allegedly disseminating false news on labor strikes.

Exhibitor of *Lola's Basement* loses case on obscenity grounds.

Alithia loses police slander case but wins another on alleged false news reporting on status of American bases in Crete.

Press Ministry issues Executive Decision on newspaper distribution.

1977 *Deep Throat* film exhibitor loses on obscenity grounds.

Kathimerini publisher Helen Vlachos wins France's Legion d'Honneur.

Anti found not guilty of publishing classified information.

Supreme Court hands down three different decisions on newspaper distribution.

1978 Parliament deliberates and finally cancels junta press law.

Over 60 persons arrested for allegedly illegally distributing Communist literature in Athens streets.

1979 Radio and television personnel stage a four-hour strike for labor reasons.

Official government accoun-

tant reports that financial mismanagement has taken place in state-run radio and television.

Radio and television directors approve a song censorship plan but tone it down as public and press protest.

Parliament approves updated version of newspaper distributors' rights and responsibilities.

Eleftheros Kosmos loses alleged alarming news case for saying USSR gained favor in Greek government.

1980 Parliament approves updated guidelines for posters, billboards.

Newspaper technical personnel strikes; publishers enforce lockout.

Parliament approves new guidelines on newspaper price setting and on maximum number of pages.

Avriani publishers found guilty of allegedly insulting the premier and face additional charges of slandering the president.

Akropolis faces extinction due to publishers' infighting.

1981 *Avriani* publishers flee to Italy to avoid imprisonment.

BIBLIOGRAPHY*

Aidalis, B. *The Abuses of the Press.* Thessaloniki, 1966.

Anagnostopoulos, N. *The Illegal Press.* Athens, 1960.

Androulakis, N. *Authority and Insult.* Athens, 1978.

Antonopoulos, N. *Freedom of the Press in Greece.* Athens, 1965.

Filia, B. *The Constitutional Right of Press Freedom.* Athens, 1966.

Georgopoulos, K. *Freedom of Circulation and Distribution of Publications.* Athens, 1963.

Giannakopoulos, Th. *Tax Law for the Press.* Athens, 1967.

Glynou, Athena. "How They Threw Away 700 Million." *Tahidromos,* November 7, 1979, p. 12.

Greek Press Agency. *Yearbook 1979.* Athens, 1979.

_____. *Yearbook 1980.* Athens, 1980.

"Journalism School." *Bulletin to UJAD Members,* June-August 1979, p. 19.

Karamountzou, A. *Competent Authority for Press Abuses.* Thessaloniki, 1963.

Koumarianou, A. *The Press in the Revolution.* Athens, 1971.

Leonardos, G. "The 7-year Rape." *Eleftherotypia,* November 1974, p. 20.

*Titles are English translations from the Greek.

Mayer, K. *History of the Greek Press.* Athens, 1957.

Ministry of the Prime Minister. *Commemoration of the Greek Press.* Athens, 1965, 1968, 1970, 1978.

National Printing Office. *The Constitution of Greece.* Athens, 1975.

"New Levels of Press Responsibility in the Birthplace of Liberty." *International Press Institute Report,* May 1979, p. 5.

"Newspaper Circulations." *Tahidromos,* December 11, 1980, p. 14.

Papalexandrou, K. *Freedom Castles.* Athens, 1971.

Papaspiliopoulos, S. "The Last Twenty Years." *Europe,* January-February 1981, p. 15.

Paraschos, E. "Constitutional Press Provisions: A World Profile." *Nieman Reports,* Summer 1978, p. 41.

———. "Numerous Obstacles Hinder Formal Training in Greece." *Journalism Educator,* January 1979, p. 114.

Research and Publicity Center, KEDE. *Greece, a Portrait.* Athens, 1979.

"The School Ghost." *Eleftherotypia,* December 1974, p. 68.

Stathatos, N. *Law of the Press.* Athens, 1966.

UNESCO. *World Communications.* Paris, 1975.

"Vertical Drop of TV Audience." *Tahidromos,* October 21, 1979, p. 12.

GUATEMALA*

John Spicer Nichols

BASIC DATA

Population: 6.6 million
Area: 109,309 sq. km. (42,042 sq. mi.)
GNP: 6.93 billion quetzals (US$6.93 billion)
Literacy Rate: 45%
Language(s): Spanish
Number of Dailies: 8
  Aggregate Circulation: 194,000 (est.)
  Circulation per 1,000: 29
Number of Nondailies: NA
  Aggregate Circulation: NA
  Circulation per 1,000: NA
Number of Periodicals: NA

Number of Radio Stations: 101
Number of Television Stations: 5
Number of Radio Receivers: NA
  Radio Receivers per 1,000: NA
Number of Television Sets: NA
  Television Sets per 1,000: NA
Total Annual Newsprint Consumption: NA
  Per Capita Newsprint Consumption: NA
Total Newspaper Ad Receipts: 8.9 million
  quetzals (US$8.9 million) (1979)
  As % of All Ad Expenditures: 15.1 (1979)

Background & General Characteristics

Guatemala is polarized by political forces fighting for control of the government. On the left stands a variety of opposition groups, including Marxists, nationalists and other guerrilla organizations, that have been fighting since the 1960s to overthrow the established political order. Opposing them on the right, is a hard-line government backed by the oligarchy and clandestine paramilitary groups that operate with the acquiescence if not the support and direction of the government. Effective voices of moderation in Guatemala have virtually disappeared.

Terror and propaganda are the prime weapons of both groups in their battle for national power. Amnesty International documented over 40 serious incidents, occurring between May 1978 and May 1979, involving Guatemalan journalism, including killings, kidnappings, detentions and forced exile of journalists, forced publications of manifestos, and bombings and other violent attacks on Guatemalan newsrooms. In 1980 alone, at least 14 Guatemalan journalists were known

to have been killed in the political violence. For those and other reasons (primarily economic), the basic journalistic functions of disseminating meaningful information about important national problems, and discussion or criticism of public policy from a variety of perspectives, for the most part do not occur.

In all such highly charged political crises, the evaluations of the function of the national press also tend to be politically polarized. In the case of Guatemala, some conservative media watchdog organizations agree with the government that the press of Guatemala is "generally free," while expressing concern about the growing violence directed at journalists. They argue that ownership of the Guatemalan press is mostly private, that no medium recently has been closed down or censored by the government, that no journalists have been jailed by authorities and, therefore, that the civil right of a free press exists in the country. However, several more liberal world and regional human rights groups vehemently disagree. They argue that official government restraint results only in the fictional right of a free press and that

---

*Research for this chapter was funded in part by the College of the Liberal Arts, Pennsylvania State University (Thomas F. Magner, associate dean for Research and Graduate Studies). The author also wishes to thank Professor R. Thomas Berner, Penn State, and Charles T. Salmon, University of Minnesota.

covert controls abrogate that right in reality. They note that the media are owned only by government supporters and that right-wing terrorist groups are a more effective control than official censorship. One of the groups, the Council of Hemispheric Affairs, labels the Guatemalan government as "the region's worst human rights violator."

Regardless of political perspective and definitional problems, all sources agree that whatever freedom does exist in Guatemala is largely a freedom for the media—not the audiences. Press, radio and TV, which are centered in the capital city, do not reach the vast majority of the Guatemalan people, and most rural Guatemalans who might at least have access radio do not speak or read Spanish, the language that predominates in all media. In sum, the Guatemalan press is a political battlefield for the nation's power contenders and generally not a source of news, opinion leadership or education for the impoverished masses.

Guatemala is a land of rare beauty—dramatic scenery, colorful Indians, fascinating Spanish colonial history and Maya prehistory. It is also the most populous, most economically developed, most politically influential and militarily powerful nation in Central America.

But the wealth and power in this relatively advanced society are reserved for a tiny minority. While a few live in comfort benefiting from the nation's expanding economy, most Guatemalans live in abject poverty. Among the majority are the 3 to 4 million culturally rich but economically poor Guatemalan Indians. Although they are all descended from the ancient Maya, these Indians speak 23 languages and 100 local dialects and wear more than 300 distinguishable local costumes. Nearly 80 percent are illiterate in the national language of Spanish. Adequate housing, health care and education are virtually nonexistent. The infant mortality rate exceeds 100 per 1,000 live births, and about four out of five Indian children are undernourished. Underemployment is chronic. Many scratch out a meager existence by farming tiny plots of land, but most survive by working in virtual servitude as laborers on the large plantations. (Two percent of the population owns 70 percent of the land, and most of the remaining 30 percent is unfit for cultivation.)

In addition to the Indians, the majority of Ladinos (Guatemalans who are not pure-blooded Indians), while more integrated into modern society, also live in dismal conditions. In all, 55 percent of the population is illiterate, but many of those considered literate are only marginally so. For most Guatemalans, the purchase of a yearly newspaper subscription or cheap transistor radio is far beyond their financial means. Under such conditions, therefore, the news media are not relevant parts of the lives of most Guatemalans.

Guatemala City was the colonial capital of the Captaincy General of Guatemala, the Spanish colonial state that included all five of the modern Central American republics. As the political center of the region, Guatemala was predictably the birthplace of Central American journalism. In November 1729, only seven years after the first newspaper in the New World was published in Mexico City, *Gazeta de Goatemala* was published in Guatemala City. But while Guatemala's status as the center of political and religious power allowed it early access to printing technology, it also meant that the press was subjected to greater official control. All Guatemalan colonial newspapers were licensed and under the watchful eye of local governors and, by extension, the Spanish crown. The content of the newspapers usually was confined to official announcements, information on religious festivals and other local news or news from Spain, approved by the local government and religious leaders. From this early history, the Guatemalan media today maintain a tradition of journalistic self-restraint in which the press rarely confronts the government and never criticizes by name the president or national political and economic leaders.

After Guatemala became independent of Spain in 1821, the press became the captive of a succession of *caudillos,* large landholders (commonly referred to as the "old families") and the two major political parties, the Liberals and Conservatives, which acted more out of expediency than political ideology. Founded during this period (in 1880) was *Diario de Centro América,* which survives today as the official government publication and the oldest daily newspaper in Central America.

The exception to the captive press was *El Imparcial,* which was founded by Alejandro Córdova in June 1922 and operated independently of the government and other sources of national power for many years. In the early 1940s, *El Imparcial* joined the growing reform movement and became an opposition newspaper, but in the late 1940s and early 1950s, as the reform movement turned to the political left, the newspaper became stridently anti-government and anti-communist. *El Imparcial* continues to publish today, but it generally supports the conservative policies of the government.

Despite the early founding of *El Imparcial,* serious development of the Guatemalan press did not begin until 1944, after a period of political turmoil. In that year, Guatemalans elected a leftist president, Juan José Arévalo, and a constituent assembly—a change of government significantly different from the usual routine of revolving-door dictatorships. Introducing a series of reformist programs and laws, the new president also initiated a more open debate of national policy. Many daily newspapers were founded during this period—three of which are still published in Guatemala today—and most quickly divided into pro- or anti-government camps. The amount of criticism of the government and the established order and the range of political opinions have not returned to the Guatemalan press since that period—which ended in 1954 when the communist-backed government of Jacobo Arbenz Guzmán was overthrown by an invasion force covertly supported by the U.S. Central Intelligence Agency. Repression of the press had begun well before the coup, but official government censorship went into force immediately afterward.

Since the overthrow of Arbenz, extremist violence and military repression, including rigid control of the press, have been endemic in Guatemala. Following a serious escalation of guerrilla activity and numerous political assassinations (including those of the U.S. ambassador in 1968 and the German ambassador in 1970), Guatemala's president, Colonel Carlos Arana Osorio, declared a state of siege and launched a counterinsurgency campaign to crush the guerrillas and their sympathizers. With the help of right-wing terror groups known as the White Hand and An Eye for an Eye, Arana was successful in consolidating his government and crushing the guerrilla force and all other opposition, even including verbal dissent. However, the cost was tremendous. Amnesty International estimates that 20,000 people were killed during the counterinsurgency campaign of 1966-74. Some of the dead were guerrillas and a few soldiers, but most were innocent peasants.

Elections have been held in Guatemala every four years since 1966, but in each one the army used electoral fraud to block the opposition, the media were warned that reporting "misleading" information about election results was subversive, and a different general was installed as president. The presi-

Guatemalan Dailies

Title	Circulation	Director	Founding Date	Description
Diario de Céntro América	10–12,000 (claimed)	Federico Zelaya Blocker	1880	PM Tabloid, ex. Saturday & Sunday; Official government pub.
Prensa Libre	56,000 (audited)	Pedro Julio García	1951	AM Tabloid, ex. Sunday
Diario El Grafico	56,000 weekday 73,000 Sunday (audited)	Jorge Carpio Nicolle	1963	AM Tabloid
La Tarde	?	Jorge Carpio Nicolle	1970	PM Tabloid, ex. Sunday; same ownership as *El Gráfico*
El Imparcial	20–34,000 (claimed)	David Vela	1922	PM Standard Size; ex. Sunday
La Hora	10–28,000 (claimed)	Oscar Marroquín Rojas	1944	PM Standard Size
Impacto	12,000 (claimed)	Oscar Marroquín Rojas	1959	Tabloid; Same ownership as *La Hora*
La Nación	30,000 (claimed)	Héctor Cifuentes	1970	AM Tabloid

dent in 1981 was General Romeo Lucas García. Despite military control, guerrilla activity resurfaced in 1975, and became a serious threat in 1979 and 1980 after an escalation of right-wing assassinations of moderate politicians, labor leaders and journalists—and also of widening revolutionary activity elsewhere in Central America.

One government and seven privately owned daily newspapers are published in Guatemala—all in the capital city.

The Guatemalan newspaper business has a long tradition of family ownership that continues today. The newspaper publishers—such as the Marroquins and the Carpios, which own four of the eight dailies—are among the nation's most distinguished families, and are an integral part of the economic and political elite. The financial affairs of the newspaper families are said to be intertwined with those of the so-called old families, although no public records exist to document these investments. The political role of the newspaper families is more overt. For example, the late Clemente Marroquin, founder of *La Hora* and one of the best-known and highly regarded journalists in Guatemala, served as vice-president of the country from 1966 to 1970; the Carpio brothers, Roberto and Jorge, of *El Gráfico*, have been candidates for several important city and national political offices; Roberto Girón Lemus, founder and principal owner of *La Nación*, served as presidential press secretary in the Laugerud administration; and Mario Ribas Montes, general manager of *El Imparcial* until his assassination in 1980, was formerly Guatemalan ambassador to Honduras. In addition to being close to the government, the newspaper families are close to one another. They are often described as "friendly rivals," who meet frequently to discuss "matters of common interest," including potential editorial positions on important political issues.

Despite the upper-class background of the newspaper owners and directors, journalism in Guatemala is a low-prestige occupation. Most working journalists are from the lower middle class, have only rudimentary education or journalistic training, express little long-term professional commitment, and are poorly paid even by national standards. In 1975 the minimum wage was substantially raised to $253 (US) per month for a reporter-editor, $200 for a reporter and $152 for a photographer. However, few media employers actually pay as much as the minimum wage. Those who are willing to accept these low-status, poorly paid positions in journalism usually see them as secondary, part-time jobs that will give them access to the leaders of government and private business. In exchange for plugging the interest of the government and business leaders in the news columns, the reporters expect to receive better-paying jobs in public relations, a variety of goods and services, and often outright cash bribes, known as *fafa*.

As a result of this system of newspaper ownership, remuneration and staffing, the content of the Guatemalan press is rarely controversial, never in direct conflict with the interests of the business and political elite, and usually of low journalistic quality. No newspaper is published in Guatemala that is critical of the government, has a liberal editorial policy or supports any opposition group. All dailies have conservative, pro-government editorial policies. Almost all editorial attacks are against a common enemy, such as President Carter's human rights policy, which resulted in the suspension of important U.S. foreign aid to Guatemala. Debates on domestic issues appear in the Guatemalan press, according to Mario Carpio, a member of one of the country's newspaper families, only when special interest groups within the national elite squabble over smaller matters that will not endanger the status quo.

There have been few attempts to publish a mass-circulation daily that is critical of the government but not seditious. The most recent attempt was *Nuevo Diario*, which in the late 1970s probed cautiously into some political and economic issues not reported in the other Guatemala City dailies. But the newspaper, as all such experiments, was short lived. In 1979, Mario Solórzano, editor of *Nuevo Diario*, and several staffers received death threats from the Secret Anti-Communist Army, a relatively new right-wing terrorist group, and fled into exile. Other reporters were kidnapped or beaten. In addition, the newspaper was boycotted by most advertisers. Under combined political and economic pressure, *Nuevo Diario* folded in 1980, although local journalists said that it was likely to reappear in 1981 with financing from more conservative interests and a traditional editorial policy.

Guatemalan dailies use an unusually large amount of wire copy from the international news agencies, primarily because it is cheaper and less controversial than local news, but also because it reflects Guatemala's political and economic dependency on other nations. The local news is dominated by sports, social notes, bulletins from official sources and graphic depictions of terrorist victims and other violence. The front pages of most newspapers on most days have at least one photograph of a mangled body. In contrast to the standard fare, the newspapers also publish a variety of reasonably stimulating columns, often by writers who are not regularly employed by the papers. However, these columnists, who generally are much more educated and literate than the regular reporters, tend to write on very abstract and philosophical topics that only by extension can be related to current, local problems. A general breakdown of one day of Guatemalan daily newspaper content, tabulated from unpublished data collected by the U.S. Embassy in Guatemala in January 1978, appears on this page.

El Imparcial is the most influential of the dailies, probably because of the newspaper's long and volatile history, its regular literary page, which attracts the best creative writers in the country, and the somewhat higher quality of its news staff. The two circulation leaders, *Prensa Libre* and *Diario El Gráfico*, are fatter, more modern and more typographically attractive than *El Imparcial*, but do not seem to command the same respect of the economic and political decision makers of the nation.

A few dozen nondailies are published throughout the country. Most are crude, irregularly issued newspapers of dubious journalistic quality. Two significant weeklies are published in Guatemala City—the English-language *Guatemala News*, which caters to the rapidly dwindling number of North American tourists, and *La Hora Dominical*, a Sunday feature supplement published by *La Hora-Impacto*. Two expensively produced magazines dealing mostly with economic subjects—*Competencia* and *Gerencia*—also are published in the capital city.

Economic Framework

The political stability created by General Arana and the discovery of oil fueled rapid economic growth in Guatemala during the 1970s. The per capita income in 1979 was $1,043, double the figure of 1974 and substantially greater than that of other Central American countries. In turn, the economic growth has led to a larger advertising base for existing media and increased investment in new media, particularly broadcasting. However, in 1980 and 1981 a slight economic downturn in Guatemala, an increase in guerrilla activity, and high interest rates in the United States precipitated serious capital flight that was expected to undercut domestic development, including further expansion of the mass media.

Regardless of the general economic conditions, the media continue under strict control of both government and private business. Only right-wing terrorist acts are more effective in limiting the range of discussion in the Guatemalan media. Other economically powerful families who are not directly invested in the media also exercise significant power by withholding advertising. While most of the advertising in both print and broadcast comes from commerical sources,

			Percent of Non-Ad Content [A]			
Guatemalan Newspaper Content						
Newspaper	**Total Number of Pages**	**Percent of Advertising**	**Domestic News**	**International News**	**Sports**	**Entertainment**
Prensa Libre	96	68.8	46.8	25.1	19.4	8.7
Diario El Gráfico	72[B]	62.9	47.6	19.9	18.7	13.9
La Nación	32	37.5	32.5	30.0	32.5	5
Diario de Centro América	48	66.7[C]	55.0	38.8	6.3	0
Impacto	16	13.1	56.1	29.5	14.4	0
El Imparcial	32[D]	39.4	63.9	19.6	10.3	6.2
La Hora	16[D]	27.6	69.0	19.0	12.1	0
La Tarde	24[D]	5.8	42.5	22.1	26.5	8.8

[A] Subject to rounding error
[B] With 16-page supplement
[C] Mostly legal ads and announcements required by law
[D] Tabloid page equivalency

government advertising constitutes a significant share of media revenues. Throughout the 1970s, the government selectively withheld its advertising from offending media.

In addition to ownership and withholding advertising, the previously mentioned *fafa* system is an effective press curb. Estimates on the number of Guatemalan journalists who receive cash bribes or other benefits from their news sources and the amount of money they regularly collect vary widely and, of course, can never be accurately documented. It is, however, safe to say that the vast majority of journalists receive *fafa* and that the usual amount is at least equal to their regular salaries. This system of bribery, common in most Latin American countries, is so ritualized that precise amounts of money openly change hands much as a sales tax would be collected in a department store in North America. Each news beat is known to yield a certain amount of *fafa,* and the journalists who collects the bribe and writes the story favorable to the news source must kick back a percentage of the proceeds to the public relations man who conducts the transaction for the news source, while the remainder is split with the reporter's editor. (In many cases, the reporter never writes a word. Instead, he merely delivers the news source's press release to the newspaper for publication.)

Many North American observers view the process as an ethical deficiency resulting from low professional development. But Mario Carpio points out that *fafa* is the effect—not the cause—of a media system created to prevent the open discussion of public affairs. He says that Guatemalan journalists have the choice of submitting to official government censorship, being shot by semi-official terror squads, or accepting payment to write the government propaganda. Remaining independent of and criticizing the Guatemalan power holders are *not* viable options for Guatemalan journalists. Under these conditions, accepting *fafa* is not an ethical question—it is a mechanism of media control over which individual journalists have little say.

Unions are not a significant factor in the Guatemala media. After several important branches of the trade union movement in Guatemala united in the 1970s and began to pressure the government and business leaders for better working conditions, many union leaders, organizers and newsletter editors became prime targets for the Secret Anti-Communist Army. In 1979 and 1980 the union movement was forced underground, after many of its moderate leaders were killed, went into exile or disappeared. In November 1979, the secretary general of the Mass Media Workers' Union, Jose Leon Castaneda, was abducted near his place of work, Radio Nuevo Mundo, and found the next morning with his chest crushed. He died later from internal bleeding.

Press Laws & Censorship

Reflecting Guatemala's checked history of dictatorships and upheaval, the country has adopted four basic constitutions—in 1879, 1945, 1956 and 1966—and numerous laws guaranteeing individual rights and freedoms, none of which have been particularly significant in limiting government actions that have in reality abrogated those rights and freedoms. The present Guatemalan constitution (1966) guarantees the expression of thoughts free from prior censorship, specifically precludes the punishment of those who criticize public officials for their official acts and prohibits confiscation or closure of any medium of communication of any crime or for expression of thoughts. The basic principles are elaborated in the Law of Expression of Thought (1966). According to Mary Gardner, the press law:

- Guarantees journalists access to all sources of information.
- Requires that directors of Guatemalan publications covering national politics must be Guatemalans.
- Guarantees to offended individuals the right of reply in the press.
- Requires that authors sign their articles and be held responsible for them on publication.
- Establishes a Press Court to hear cases relating to the press law and a Court of Honor through which public officials can redress false accusations in the media.
- Provides for the formation of a *colegio,* which sets standards of practice and requirements for membership for all journalists. (However, the *colegio* has not yet been established.)

In addition to the extralegal means discussed elsewhere in this chapter, the government can circumvent the constitutional principle of press freedom with legal means as well. The Law of Public Order allows the president of the country, without the concurrence of the congress, to declare a state of siege under which prior censorship, forced publication of government bulletins and suspension of media are legal. The Law of Public Order has been used to censor the press during times of political turmoil, such as the period immediately after the assassination of the U.S. ambassador in 1968. In that instance, the Public Relations Service of the army was empowered to censor all matter intended for publication, including news collected by international wire services for publication outside of the country. However, the law has not been used since 1971 because the extralegal means of media control have proved more effective and attract less foreign criticism.

State-Press Relations

In 1979 representatives of the International Commission of Jurists and Amnesty International visited Guatemala and subsequently published reports highly critical of the government's human rights record. The International Commission of Jurists said:

> ...since its accession to power in 1978 the current government has embarked on a systematic campaign to suppress dissent which has, in fact, generated a widespread climate of fear, demoralization, and the growth of clandestine opposition.

Amnesty International attributed the responsibility for the escalation of violence "to government, military and security forces and to semi-clandestine 'death squads,' some of which operate with apparent government complicity." Both organizations concluded that freedom of expression was impossible under these conditions.

The Guatemalan government has angrily denied the charges of those and other human rights organizations, and has characterized international reporting of the human rights situation in Guatemala as distorted and irresponsible. In 1980, Carlos Tolego Vielman, presidential public relations secretary, disputed the conclusion that press freedom did not exist in Guatemala:

> ...President Lucas has repeatedly said his government maintains and will continue to maintain the most freedom of information, press and thought, a commitment which he has kept and the Guatemalan media has [sic] been witness to.

He pointed out that the government had not censored the press recently and that no media have been seized or journalists arrested.

Government denials and differing definitions of press freedom aside, violence and threats of violence by semi-official terror squads in Guatemala—not overt government actions—have virtually ended substantive domestic criticism of the regime. Foremost among these right-wing terror groups is the Secret Anti-Communist Army, the heir to a long legacy of similar groups. Numerous attacks on journalists, bombings of newsrooms and other violence against the press have been claimed by or attributed to the Secret Anti-Communist Army in the late 1970s and early 1980s. However, the threat of violence has become equally effective in eliminating opposition voices in Guatemala. The Secret Anti-Communist Army periodically releases a "hit list" of people whom it has "tried and sentenced to death." Journalists usually appear on the lists along with trade union, student, peasant, church and moderate political leaders, and most go into exile immediately. Some of those on the "hit lists" who have not left the country have been subsequently assassinated. In other instances, journalists have been kidnapped by the terrorist group, warned not to write articles sympathetic to moderate or leftist political groups, sometimes tortured, and eventually released.

Although most of the violence against journalists is carried out by right-wing terror groups that are either directed or tolerated by the government, terrorism by the Marxist-dominated revolutionary forces has increased since the late 1970s and added to the gang warfare atmosphere in Guatemala. In August 1980, in apparent retaliation for the assassination of left-leaning journalists, the Marxist guerrillas killed Mario Ribas Montes, conservative general manager of *El Imparcial*. However, outright assassination has not been the usual action of the guerrillas. More common has been what is called "kidnapping the media." On several occasions in the late 1970s the guerrillas kidnapped government officials, wealthy businessmen or members of their families, and released them only after lengthy manifestos written by the guerrillas were published in Guatemalan and foreign newspapers and sizable ransoms were paid.

Other guerrilla propaganda activities include publishing and distributing a variety of clandestine newsletters; occasionally seizing rural radio stations for a few hours in order to broadcast manifestos; arranging for journalists to visit jungle hideouts for interviews with guerrilla leaders; and setting off "propaganda bombs," so-called because they are loud but relatively harmless, at times and places most likely to attract press coverage. In addition, the left-wing groups have had some success in forcing Guatemalan newspapers to publish their manifestos by threatening to bomb the papers' newsrooms. Although Guatemalan law prohibits the publication of subversive material, the government has not taken official action against newspapers that have submitted to guerrilla pressure.

Although the Marxist guerrilla groups, dominated by the Guerrilla Army of the Poor and Organization of People in Arms, constitute serious opposition to the government, they are ideologically divided and militarily uncoordinated, lack significant moderate or middle-class support, and therefore, according to most analysts, are not immediately able to overthrow the government. With neither side able to win a decisive victory, the terrorist activity is likely to continue escalating. "Guatemala is a blood bath waiting to happen," outgoing U.S. Ambassador Frank V. Ortiz, Jr. said in 1980. Under these conditions, meaningful journalism is unlikely to flourish.

Attitude Toward Foreign Media

The Guatemalan government has criticized the world press for what it believes are exaggerations of political instability in Guatemala and sympathetic reporting of the guerrilla movement, and has mounted a public relations campaign in North America and Europe to discredit the stories. Nevertheless, while the government has not resorted to official control of foreign correspondents to stem unfavorable reporting, many of the covert controls used against domestic journalists also are used against the foreign press corps. For example, José Calderón Salazar, correspondent for the Mexican newspaper *Excélsior,* fled the country after narrowly escaping a kidnapping attempt and later being named on a terrorist group's "hit list." Other foreign correspondents report that they have received threatening phone calls and mail or have been intimidated by Guatemalan officials, but in contrast to other Central American countries, no correspondent has been killed or seriously harmed.

News flow in the reverse direction—from the outside world into Guatemala—also is relatively unrestrained. Although Guatemalans report that innocuous reading materials from abroad, especially on political subjects, have been confiscated by the army, the standard fare of Western newspapers and newsmagazines appears on most Guatemalan newsstands. Guatemalan newspapers also make heavy use of foreign news services. According to a U.S. Embassy study, foreign news coverage carried in Guatemala City dailies in January 1978 came from the following international news agencies: dpa, carrying 30.4 percent of the total foreign coverage; AFP, 17.4; Latin/Reuters, 16.5; AP, 15.2; ACAN/EFE, 10.8; UPI, 6.4; ANSA, 2.1; and others, 1.2. Only ACAN/EFE maintains a full-time correspondent in Guatemala; the other news agencies are represented by stringers. However, regular correspondents for major Western media make frequent trips to Guatemala to cover the increasing political violence. From all the foreign news selected by the Guatemalan papers, the largest percent (36.4) had datelines from Latin American countries, 36.3 percent from Europe and only 9.2 percent from the United States.

Although news coverage of the United States is fairly light, U.S. investment in the Guatemalan media is said to be substantial. For example, Channel 3, one of four privately owned television channels in Guatemala, is owned by a U.S. citizen and carries considerable programming produced in the United States. Another large amount of TV programming comes from Televisa, the Mexican national television monopoly.

News Agencies

Guatemala does not have a domestic news agency, although the Public Relations Service of the army effectively reaches most media with official announcements and government interpretations of domestic events.

Electronic News Media

Over 100 radio stations operate in Guatemala. Six are government channels, all of which have national reach. Another two are operated by the army. The remainder are mostly small, low-wattage local stations clustered in and around Guatemala City. One of the five television channels in Guatemala is operated by the government and another by the army. All TV chanels are headquartered in the capital city, but programming is distributed to other major population centers by a system of repeaters.

The government founded the first radio station in Guatemala in the early 1930s and one of the first two television stations in 1956, and although the great majority of stations are privately owned today, strict federal control of broadcasting continues. All radio and television stations must have licenses issued by the General Directorate of National Radio and Television, and risk suspension of their licenses if their programming offends the government. However, suspension of stations (usually under the pretext that the stations violated frequency rights) has been infrequent, because the mere threat of suspension is generally sufficient to persuade the private owners to collaborate with the government and thereby protect their investments.

Radio is by far the most important medium in Guatemala. Even the tradition of family ownership extends into this medium: the largest radio network, which has 10 stations and numerous repeaters in the interior, is owned by the Archila family. But radio's impact is not as great as in the other Central American countries. A huge percentage of the unintegrated rural Indians are not reached by the predominantly Spanish-language radio stations concentrated in the cities. Church groups sponsor most of the limited amount of Indian-language broadcasting in Guatemala, but the government has increased its efforts since the rise of guerrilla activity in the 1960s. Critics charge, however, that just as the government has been fairly good at building schools and hospitals in the rural areas but poor at staffing them with teachers and doctors, the government's development of Indian-language broadcasting has emphasized hardware versus software. Because most of the Indian-language programming by both the government and church groups is broadcast via short wave, listenership is further limited. Short-wave receivers costing about $30 are far too expensive for an Indian family to purchase; therefore, irregular listening in large groups is the norm. Government, church or other development agencies install radio receivers in central locations, such as a village plaza, rural schools or community centers, and conduct "radio schools" in which a "local change agent" reinforces programming dealing with such topics as health care, agricultural innovations and literacy.

In addition, Radio Havana broadcasts special Indian-language programming to Guatemala, and U.S. Embassy officials in Guatemala estimate that the listenership to the Cuban broadcasts is relatively high in the rural areas.

The major ingredient in Guatemalan radio programming is music, mostly pop music from the United States and neighboring Mexico. However, a fair amount of news and public affairs is broadcast. Many of the major stations, such as Radio Mundial and Radio Imperador, carry regular newscasts prepared by their own news staffs. The smaller stations, however, usually rely on "radio newspapers," news programs prepared by independent contractors. These independents buy choice air time, usually at mealtimes, from radio station owners and produce programs containing news, commentaries and public service announcements. In turn, the independent producers sell advertising spots on their programs to large commercial advertisers as well as to individuals who are looking for lost items, announcing deaths in the family or offering or looking for jobs. The income is usually enough for the producers to cover their costs to the station owners and make a profit.

Some of the "radio newspapers" have their own reporting staffs, subscribe to international wire services and prepare substantive newscasts. However, most are one- or two-person operations that merely rewrite government bulletins and newspaper clips. Guatemalan print journalists charge that the "radio newspapers" are most vulnerable to *fafa* payments and therefore broadcast little more than propaganda for the government and business.

In 1979 two of the commercial television stations began daily newscasts, "Teleprensa" on Channel 11 and "Aqui El Mundo" on Channel 3. Both programs use modern production techniques and frequently replay videotapes of world news events supplied by ABC International. In addition, the channels have sent crews using modern electronic newsgathering equipment outside of the country to cover major news events of interest to Guatemalan TV viewers. The other TV channels have only irregular news programs or public affairs talk shows. Most popular among the talk shows is "Valores de Guatemala," aired on Channel 5 (the government channel) and hosted by Federico Zelaya Blocker, editor of *Diario de Centro América* (the government newspaper). Films and TV reruns from the United States dominate

Guatemalan programming, but soap operas and other entertainment programs from Televisa of Mexico and other Latin American countries are challenging the U.S. producers for dominance in this market. Very little of the programming is locally produced.

Education & Training

The Central American School of Journalism at San Carlos University in Guatemala was founded in 1952 and has since served as the country's major journalism training center. The journalism program, which was being restructured in the late 1970s, offers a three-year Professional Journalist degree and a six-year master's in Communication Science degree.

In the late 1970s, San Carlos University became the focal point of urban violence in Guatemala. During a two-and-a-half year period ending in 1980, nearly 200 students and professors were killed on or near the campus battlefield. Bombings, kidnappings, beatings and torture were also commonplace on campus. Consequently, normal university functions, including journalism education, have come to a halt.

However, the campus violence has had little direct impact on Guatemalan journalism. Enrollments in San Carlos' journalism school always have been small, and the few who do graduate from the program seldom become journalists. Unwilling to accept the low-paying and low-prestige jobs in journalism, the university graduates take public relations positions or other lucrative jobs.

Another relatively new journalism program in Guatemala is the School of Communication at Rafael Landivar University. This private school, catering to upper-class students, is much more conservative and more academically sound than San Carlos. But similarly, few of its graduates enter journalism.

Guatemalan journalists traditionally have had active professional lives, but under the current circumstances, journalism associations also have become highly politicized. Most influential among the various associations and unions for owners, editors, reporters and production people are the Chamber of Journalists and the Association of Guatemalan Journalists (APG). The Chamber is a more conservative organization, dominated by media owners and directors, and has supported the government. APG, which was

founded in 1947, has a more diverse membership including a large percentage of rank-and-file reporters. Until the late 1970s APG remained somewhat independent of the government, landowners and other vested interests, and Guatemalan journalists expressed hope that the organization would serve as an effective shield against outside pressure and as a tool for professionalization. On several occasions, APG confronted the government and demanded an end to attacks on and intimidation of journalists by "clandestine groups which enjoy complete impunity of action." However, the APG's vocal campaign against the apparent government complicity in the attacks on journalists ended in the late 1970s as the association became co-opted by the government. According to a Guatemalan newspaper, General Lucas Garcia, the country's president in 1981, personally attended the APG elections along with a retinue of government officials, retired journalists and others intended to influence the outcome of the voting. Not surprisingly, the new APG president, Fernando Molina Nanini, has vigorously defended the government and criticized those within his organization wishing to speak out on the growing political repression.

Summary

Guatemala has a long tradition of strict government control of the press, dating back to colonial times when the second newspaper in Spanish America was established in Guatemala City. Throughout the 19th century and much of the 20th, a succession of dictators and other powerful political forces routinely censored the press, jailed journalists or intimidated them so that they would not dare criticize the government.

In recent years, the generals running the country have avoided using overt measures to control the press. But despite the absence of censorship, jailings and other official repression, the Guatemalan press is one of the most tightly controlled in the hemisphere. The media are owned entirely by an economic elite that supports the government, and rank-and-file journalists are bribed into submission. Those few journalists who, for some reason, do not submit to the economic pressures and do attempt to criticize the government or write sympathetically about the Marxist guerrillas and other opposition groups, are targets for clandestine terrorist groups that operate with the complicity of the government and the large landowners. Numerous Guatemalan journalists recently have been killed, kidnapped or attacked, or have gone into exile after receiving death threats.

"There is freedom of the press...in everything which does not affect the interests of the government...," writes Mario Carpio; "...for the 'rebels,' for those who despite everything dare to say the truth and speak freely, there is always a bullet or machinegun blast."

The concept or the reality of press freedom is not relevant to the majority of Guatemalan people. They live outside of the money economy and are illiterate in Spanish, the language of the Guatemalan media; therefore, virtually all of the print media and most of the broadcast media serve the upper classes of Guatemala City and other major population centers.

The outlook for Guatemalan journalism in the 1980s is bleak. Although internal developments are closely tied to unpredictable events elsewhere in Central America, and to foreign policy decisions made in the United States, the escalation of violence and repression seems likely to continue. Under those conditions, all-out civil war will be difficult to avoid, and a politically stable, economically just society that can tolerate an open discussion of public affairs will be impossible to nurture.

CHRONOLOGY

1978 General Romeo Luca Garcia elected president of Guatemala, defeating another general and a colonel. Sixty percent of Guatemala's registered voters abstain, 20 percent spoil their ballots in protest over exclusion of leftist political groups from election. Military warns local journalists not to report "misleading" information on possible electoral irregularities.

1979 In August, Guatemalan newspapers publish, radio/television stations broadcast 1,700-word manifesto by Rebel Armed Forces as part of ransom demand paid by family of Alonso Lima, Guatemala's deputy foreign minister. Leftist manifesto scores repression of press, universities, labor leaders and peasants by government and clandestine paramilitary groups, and ends with a call for country to unite in struggle against imperialism, repression and exploitation—to "overcome or die for Guatemala, the revolution, and socialism." Lima, kidnapped in July, is soon released unharmed.

Similar "kidnapping of the media" takes place shortly afterwards. Manifesto of the Guerrilla Army of the Poor is published not only in Guatemalan press but also papers in United State, Canada, Europe and elsewhere in Latin America. Advertisements displaying manifesto are paid for by Raul Garcia Granado, wealthy landowner and distant relative of President Lucas Garcia, for release of his kidnapped son. Cost of ad in *The New York Times* alone is over $24,000.

1979 More than a dozen men with machine guns shoot up editorial offices of *El Gráfico,* Guatemala City daily—the fourth attack on the newspaper by right-wing terror groups in as many months, and only one of many against Guatemalan newspapers and radio studios during year.

1980 *Nuevo Diario,* newspaper founded to offer some criticism of the government, folds after editors and reporters are kidnapped, threatened and forced into exile while government and large commercial advertisers boycotted the paper.

Charles A. Perlik, Jr., president of 33,000-member Newspaper Guild in the United States, sends letter to Guatemalan President Romeo Lucas Garcia denouncing violence against journalists in that country. Perlik charges Lucas Garcia with "insensitivity to the problems of journalists working in Guatemala—both for national and foreign newspapers," and adds that "the near-total lack of press freedom in Guatemala today provides clear justification for the growing international criticism your government has received on human rights grounds."

"Despite the atrocities which have been committed and the publication of death lists of journalists' names by terrorist organizations known to operate with impunity in Guatemala," Perlik also writes, "your government has refused to provide protection for journalists or contribute to creating a situation in which they can work freely. In fact, there are strong indications that some of the organizations which have claimed responsibility for many of these crimes against newsmen receive official sanction and support."

In August, Mario Ribas Montes, general manager of conservative daily *El Imparcial,* is assassinated by leftists in apparent retaliation for killings, by right-wing paramilitary groups, of several journalists sympathetic to opposition. Ribas Montes's death is the 14th of a Guatemalan journalist in 1980.

BIBLIOGRAPHY

Carpio, Mario. *El Negocio de la Prensa: Un Ensayo Sobre El Periodismo Guatemalteco.* Guatemala, 1979.

Dombrowski, John, et al. *Area Handbook for Guatemala.* Washington, D.C., 1970.

Gallagher, Jack W. "Content Analysis of Guatemalan Newspapers." Unpublished study by U.S. International Communication Agency. Guatemala, January 1978.

Gardner, Mary A. "The Press of Guatemala." In *Journalism Monographs,* no. 18. Lexington, Kentucky, 1971.

"Guatemala: Journalists in Peril." *Index on Censorship.* April 1980, pp. 63-64.

Martz, John D. "Guatemala: The Search for Political Identity." In *Political Systems of Latin America,* Martin C. Needler, ed. New York, 1970.

Plant, Roger, "Guatemala—Violence and the Press." *Index on Censorship,* November-December 1977, pp. 15-20.

Real, Michael R. "Media and Freedom in the Third World: Theory Versus Practice in Guatemala." Paper to the International Communication Association, May 1980.

Riding, Alan. "Guatemala: State of Siege," *The New York Times Magazine,* August 24, 1980, p. 16.

U.S. Department of State. *Country Reports on Human Rights Practices for 1979.* Washington, D.C., 1980, pp. 326-32.

GUYANA

by G. Paul Smeyak

BASIC DATA

Population: 829,000
Area: 214,970 sq. km. (82,978 sq. mi)
GNP: G$1,055,000,000 (US$ 422 million) (1976)
Literacy Rate: 86%
Language(s): English
Number of Dailies: 2
  Aggregate Circulation: 50,000
  Circulation per 1,000: 63
Number of Nondailies: 8
  Aggregate Circulation: 236,200
  Circulation per 1,000: 305
Number of Periodicals: NA

Number of Radio Stations: 8
Number of Television Stations: 0
Number of Radio Receivers: 275,000
  Radio Receivers per 1,000: 351
Number of Television Sets: 0
  Television Sets per 1,000: 0
Total Annual Newsprint Consumption: 1,800 metric tons
  Per Capita Newsprint Consumption: 2.2 kg. (4.8 lb.)
Total Newspaper Ad Receipts: NA
  As % of All Ad Expenditures: NA

Background & General Characteristics

The Cooperative Republic of Guyana is a nation searching for an identity and a place in the community of nations amid some complex historical, cultural, legal, economic and political events. Although a part of South America, the nation is culturally linked with the English-speaking, black-ruled nations of the Caribbean.

Guyana is a small tropical country (approximately 83,000 square miles) on the northeast shoulder of South America. The coastal plain facing the Caribbean is approximately 240 miles long and ranges in width from 10 to 40 miles. This belt is the agricultural heart of the country and, while comprising only four percent of the total area, it holds 90 percent of the population. Georgetown, the capital and only major city, is in this coastal zone and serves as the principal port facility. The forest zone contains most of Guyana's mineral wealth—notably the large bauxite-mining operations. Two arid savannah areas lie in the southwest and northeast sections of the country and support sparse grasses used for cattle grazing.

Although Guyana—once called Guiana—was originally settled by the Dutch, Great Britain conquered the region and it was a British colony from 1781 to 1966, when it became independent. The British and Dutch established a plantation economy that relied on labor supplied by the African slave trade, but when slavery was abolished in 1833, the blacks left the plantations, refusing to work for their former owners. By thus withholding labor from the important agricultural sector, this action was designed to bring the colony to its knees economically. However, the British brought in Chinese, Portuguese and large numbers of indentured East Indians to work on the plantations; this broke the boycott and created the basis for racial distrust between the East Indians and blacks.

In 1975 the government estimated the population at 800,000, with a work force of 200,000. The people are ethnically diverse, although all newspapers and periodicals are published in English, the official language. East Indians, the largest ethnic group, comprise 51 percent of the population, blacks and mulattos make up 43 percent and the remaining 6 percent is composed of Chinese, Caucasians and Amerindians. Education is modeled on the British school system with primary, technical and university training available. The literacy rate is 86 percent.

When independence came the country's name was changed to the Cooperative Republic of Guyana, although political parties and a parliamentary system had developed under British rule. There is a figurehead president and a National Assembly, which holds most of the legislative power. Politically, Guyana is divided along racial lines, with the ruling People's National Congress (PNC) having managed to acquire the largest political base. The socialistic PNC is the party of the Afro-Guyanese, but it has attracted some support from other ethnic groups and has managed to retain power since 1966 despite charges of election rigging and political repression. Opposition to the PNC has traditionally come from the conservative United Force, a relatively small political group, and from the Marxist People's Progressive Party (PPP), which was until recently the main Opposition. The PPP's support has come primarily from the agrarian East Indians. Recently, however, a new political party, the Working People's Alliance (WPA) has established itself as the main Opposition to the PNC. WPA's support is mostly among the young urban dwellers, and it has cut across existing party and racial lines. It has also suffered some setbacks recently: several WPA leaders were jailed on charges of arson and three others were killed under unusual circumstances.

The size of the newspaper industry in Guyana has steadily contracted since independence in 1966 and the emergence of the ruling PNC as the dominant political force. Newspapers opposing or not directly supporting the government in power have been forced out of operation by the government's economic policies, or because they have not been able to obtain government licenses to purchase printing equipment or newsprint. PNC policy appears to be to eliminate opposition or neutral newspapers through various methods, or to control the content of those papers that remain in operation.

The technical quality of Guyanese newspapers ranges from good to poor, depending on the availability of newsprint and printing facilities. The large-circulation government-owned newspapers are technically good because they have sufficient newsprint and relatively modern offset printing equipment. Newspapers not supported by the government have an irregular newsprint supply and make a poor appearance because they are printed on older rotary presses.

Even opposition newspapers in Guyana do not engage in investigative reporting, and press credibility must be considered low. As a matter of policy, government newspaper and radio journalists have moved away from the old idea of "scoop" exclusivity and now concentrate on political news. They make no attempt to criticize or analyze governmental policies or actions. The only opposition comes from the few remaining politically oriented newspapers, or special interest periodicals, which are not published regularly and have limited circulation.

Before independence Guyana's press followed the British colonial tradition, with prestige newspapers serving the European expatriates and maintaining ties with the mother country. To fill the obvious void, a popular press grew up, appealing to the indigenous population who considered Guyana their home country. But the British style of journalism prevailed, and as independence approached, the local newspapers became more forthright in reporting, investigating and criticizing. When Guyana became a sovereign nation, it had a well-developed newspaper industry with three dailies, four Sunday editions, five weeklies, and a number of specialized journals or newsletters that were printed monthly or quarterly.

Since independence, however, the newspaper industry in Guyana has shrunk to only one daily newspaper, the government-owned *Daily Chronicle*, purchased in 1971 for a reported G$3 million dollars. In 1973 the government also purchased what was then the country's leading daily newspaper, the *Guyana Graphic*, from the Thomson newspaper group for an undisclosed price. The *Graphic* was then merged with the *Daily Chronicle* into the official Guyana National Newspaper Limited (GNNL) publishing firm. In 1974 another daily, the *Evening Post*, went out of business because of financial problems. Thus by 1980 the country's only two general-circulation newspapers were the *Daily Chronicle* and the *Sunday Chronicle*.

Both the daily and Sunday *Chronicle* are six-column tabloid newspapers and, being printed on GNNL offset presses in Georgetown, are similar in layout, type face and content. Both papers are highly visual and utilize a good blend of photographs, type and white space. Each carries display and classified advertisements, features, PNC-released government news, crossword puzzles, radio listings, personal announcements and job vacancies. The *Sunday Chronicle* also runs a two- to six-page section, "In Memoriam," where family and friends of deceased persons can publish photographs, poems or memorial messages. The *Sunday Chronicle* generally has 28 to 36 pages, the *Daily Chronicle* 16 to 24.

The GNNL company also prints *New Nation,* weekly organ of the PNC. *New Nation* is used to explain and defend PNC policies and to criticize opposition parties. It is a tabloid four to eight pages long, published on Sundays, with a circulation of 32,000. In addition, GNNL presses run off a number of weekly, monthly or quarterly publications for the government or government-owned businesses. These do not normally deal with general news unless a publication's target audience is affected. The *Official Gazette*, for example, is a weekly containing all legal notices and reporting legislation passed by the National Assembly. Its circulation is approximately 1,200, mostly scholars, politicians, lawyers and civil servants. Other publications such as *Guymine News, Guyana Today, Guyana News, Sugar News, GRP (Rice) News* and *The Copper* cater to groups interested in mining, agriculture, tourism and business.

One evening daily that has recently halted publication temporarily is the *Mirror*, the organ of the Opposition PPP. As with most party publications, the *Mirror's* content has been quite political, stressing the alleged failures and corruptions of the ruling PNC government and the desirability of PPP policies, plans and political candidates. Content selection has been highly purposeful, and timely or hard news less important than PPP political reports or news matching the party line. The *Mirror* claimed a circulation of 12,000 prior to its publication halt, caused by a failure to obtain newsprint. Its editors also assert that they were forced to stop publication six times because of newsprint problems caused by government actions. Prior to 1977, the *Mirror* purchased newsprint directly from foreign suppliers under special government-granted licenses, but subsequently it had to buy newsprint from the government-owned GNNL. PPP leaders and *Mirror* editors state that their efforts to buy a new offset press were thwarted by government officials and that the government has applied pressure on businesses to stop advertising in the paper. When the *Mirror* does publish, it does so on an old letterpress unit in Georgetown.

The Working People's Alliance does not publish a newspaper. Citing the technical problems of opposition publishers, WPA has printed newspapers in the nearby island nation of Trinidad and then tried to import them into Guyana. In 1974 10,000 copies of *Dayclean*, the WPA organ, were impounded by Guyanese Customs and eventually burned. PPP has claimed that the WPA was unable to find a Guyanese printing house for its newspaper because PNC harassed printers who produced anti-government publications.

Besides *New Nation*, the only other widely circulated weekly in Guyana is the *Catholic Standard*, published by the church with a circulation of 15,000, the *Standard* concentrates on religious news and pro-government information. In 1973, following the parliamentary elections that kept the PNC in power, the *Standard* published an article criticizing those elections, and the editor was fired by the church hierarchy. PPP claims the action was taken because of government pressure.

Economic Framework

The economy of Guyana is almost totally in the hands of the government. The ruling PNC party intends to establish Guyana as the first "orthodox socialist state" in South America, and it has nationalized foreign investments in communications, agriculture, mining and business. Because of state intervention, the government controls 80 percent of the physical capital in production and employs more than one-third of the work force. The prime minister, L. Forbes Burnham, has stated that private enterprise has a limited future in Guyana and that all major segments of the economy will come under government control.

Yet despite PNC domination of the economy, Guyana is very susceptible to outside forces, such as rapidly rising oil prices or a depressed world market for Guyanese products. Since 1975 the economy has stagnated because private investors, fearing nationalization, are not forming new businesses and because production has decreased in rice, sugar and bauxite, the nation's primary exports. Coupled with high inflation and rising oil prices, this situation has created a severe shortage of foreign exchange in the face of increasing needs to import more goods and demands to pay off existing loans. Government actions to ban imports and cut back public works and other capital development programs have not helped the foreign exchange problem, and Guyana still imports more than it exports.

The unstable economy and apparently ineffective government actions to correct the balance have had a profound effect on the economic health of newspapers and radio. Foreign advertising, which comprises 60 percent of Guyana's total advertising revenue, stopped coming into the country as soon as overseas products were banned. Local merchants, who now had a monopoly, did not feel the need to advertise once their foreign competition was stopped. Reduced advertising revenues, coupled with government pressure to advertise in official media, have placed privately owned newspapers and radio stations at a severe economic disadvantage, thereby reducing media competition.

Thus, the only newspapers and private media able to survive must have an economic base independent of advertising. And the only newspapers in Guyana today are owned either by the government, a church or a political party that uses advertising as partial support for its party organ.

Distribution of Guyana newspapers is limited primarily to the metropolitan area of Georgetown (population 167,000) or to two minor communities, New Amsterdam (20,000) and Linden (30,000). Road and rail transportation outside the three urban centers is limited, and newspaper distribution to rural areas is late and infrequent.

While there have been some major agricultural strikes in Guyana, relations between publishers and employees appear good or at least stable. One reason for this might be that since most Guyanese newspapers are politically oriented the reporters and editors generally share the publisher's social, economic or political beliefs, which may override some labor concerns. Since the number of newspapers in Guyana has declined, there are more journalists than there are jobs. Only the best newsmen have much ability to move, and internal movement in Guyana is very limited. And even prestigious radio and newspaper reporters must be wary of what they write or say. There have been at least three instances in which journalists who did not follow the government line or who criticized the government were fired or were not hired when their newspapers were purchased by the government.

Journalists in Guyana are considered part of the social and economic elite, even though they have little personal power and most are without formal journalistic training. In 1969 the United States Information Service evaluated press and broadcasting in Guyana and found that journalism played "little part in advancing the process of social and economic development largely due to inadequate education and training...." Reporters are generally paid more than the average per capita income of $G582.00 a year (as of 1980, G$2.54 = US$1.00). Still, in a nation where the majority of the people are unskilled or work in agriculture, newspaper and radio journalists must be ranked high in prestige—although as a group they stand below the professions of teaching, law, engineering and medicine.

Press Laws

Article 12 of the Constitution of Guyana promises certain freedoms for the press. While seemingly broad in scope, the article also lists areas where press protection is limited or can be limited. It specifically states that the government has the right to make laws restricting press freedoms that are "reasonably required in the interests of defence, public safety, public order, public morality or public health...." Protection is also limited in cases of defamation, invasion of privacy, private information received in legal proceedings, "disclosure of information received in confidence," or publishing of information which would "undermine the authority and independence of the court or regulating the technical administration of telephony, telegraphy, posts, wireless broadcasting or television...."

Much of the legal system of Guyana is still based on the laws passed during the colonial period. The Defamation Act delineates libel and slander, and even defines defamation by wireless or broadcasting as publication in permanent form or libel. The traditional press defenses of fair comment and privilege are granted to journalists providing fair and accurate reports of public meetings and judicial proceedings.

The original Publication and Newspaper Act of 1839 remains in force, although it has been amended several times. The original act requires everyone printing a newspaper or book to legibly include his name and usual place of business or residence on every publication. In 1972 the act was amended and now requires that all newspapers be delivered to the national archivist within 24 hours, with the publisher or printer's name and place of abode written and signed on the newspaper. The amendment further requires that newspaper and pamphlet publishers/printers execute and deliver to the registrar of deeds a G$5,000 bond with two G$5,000 sureties to guarantee damages in any defamation action. The amendment also expanded liability in defamation actions. Individuals serving as corporate officers or directors are now liable for any corporate acts of defamation and may, depending on the circumstances, be held civilly or criminally liable.

Censorship

Because of the size of Guyana and the decline of privately owned media, control of the Guyanese press is not difficult. There is not one specific agency or government bureau publicly charged with press censorship. However, the Ministry of Information and Culture is central in any attempt at press control. Most control of remaining private media is through self-censorship, and those newspapers that do not censor themselves find it impossible to obtain newsprint or equipment for printing. Moreover, with the 1972 Amendment to the Defamation Act expanding liability to individual publishers and printers for corporate acts, printing houses must now be responsible for the content of whatever is printed at their facilities. This certainly must have a chilling effect on press freedoms, as it makes printers wary of taking on political printing jobs that might offend the government.

Even legitimate acts can be dealt with summarily. After the Working People's Alliance newspaper, *Dayclean*, was seized by Guyanese Customs in 1974, a government order gave a cabinet minister retroactive power to seize or ban printed material that "is prejudicial to the defense of Guyana, public safety or to public order."

State-Press Relations

The government has embarked on a course of national development that requires it to utilize the press as a developmental tool to explain, defend and support official actions and policies. This means that the only newspapers or publications that will be allowed to exist unimpeded in Guyana are those owned by the government or those that pose no threat to government actions. Minister of State Kit Nascimento, a former journalist and public relations specialist, says "the

truth is that the cherished Western concepts of media ownership and communications freedoms die hard...in developing nations. But die they must." It must be assumed that as a cabinet member and longtime PNC supporter, Nascimento was expressing the government and PNC position. Similar statements have subsequently been made by the prime minister and other officials.

The Ministry of Information and Culture is the government's internal public information arm. The minister is a political appointee of the prime minister and therefore must reflect and support government policy and that of the ruling party. Under the minister are two career civil servants, the permanent secretary and the chief information officer, who coordinate the day-to-day activities of the ministry and its departments.

While journalists have the legal right to criticize government actions, this seldom occurs, and if it does, the offending journalists may lose their jobs or be forced to resign. The government does not want conflicting or opposition voices, and is prepared to eliminate or mitigate commercial influences that might not support PNC policies. Nascimento states that when media are privately owned one sees the "sad spectacle of editors and programme directors failing to support and often actively opposing government policies and programmes which are nationalistic and/or socialistic," because of commercial influences.

While there are no documented instances of journalists in Guyana being jailed for their political or opposition views, the journalistic function is controlled by selection of personnel for the government media, import licenses, surety bonds, judicial actions, allocation of newsprint and confiscation of opposing publications.

Attitude Toward Foreign Media

The current government appears insecure with its position, as evidenced by attempts to limit the Opposition press or news sources not under govenment control. Foreign journalists must be accredited, and must obtain a special entry permit prior to arrival in Guyana. There have been no reports of foreign journalists being jailed, but the government has applied pressure on those who have not covered official actions in a manner considered proper. During 1979, the government-owned *Daily Chronicle* ran a front-page story castigating a Caribbean News Agency (CANA) reporter for not covering a public meeting between the prime minister and residents of South Georgetown. The *Chronicle* termed the failure to cover the story a "manifestation of political bias...shameful and shocking...and atrocious." The newspaper quoted a Ministry of Information and Culture spokesman who protested the lack of coverage and said that "CANA representatives have failed to participate in various visits planned by the Ministry for media personnel." This indicates the government's desire to have the media cover only those events it plans or controls.

Through nationalization policies and other government actions, all foreign media in Guyana have either come under state ownership and control or they have ceased publication. The government has also controlled the types of publication that enter the country and have destroyed those disapproving of it or the PNC. Because of this seizure policy, foreign publications critical of the government rarely get into the country and therefore have little impact on existing domestic media.

News Agencies

There are no domestic news agencies in Guyana. Most news comes from Georgetown or its immediate vicinity. There is a loose network of stringers outside the Georgetown area, but most rural news goes uncovered.

CANA maintains a full-time representative in Guyana, the current correspondent being a former Guyanese journalist who lost his job and had to find employment sources outside the country. The Sunday and daily *Chronicle* subscribe to CANA, which concentrates on Caribbean news. The government newspapers and radio station also have access to Reuters, AP and UPI wire services. However, the newspapers and radio stations concentrate their coverage on Guyana, the Caribbean and developing nations.

Electronic News Media

In 1969 the United States Information Service declared that broadcasting had become the main medium of communication in Guyana. Newspapers were primarily confined to the urban areas, where two-fifths of the population live, whereas broadcasting had be-

come national. With broadcasting having such an impact and being such an important communication channel, it was inevitable, in light of existing government policy, that the state would take over complete control of the country's broadcast facilities.

As of 1980 Guyana had only one radio station operational and no television transmitting facilities. The radio station, Guyana Broadcast Service (GBS) was taken over by the government in 1968 from Rediffusion Limited, a foreign company, Rediffusion owned two radio stations in Guyana and let the government take GBS to secure a 15-year franchise for its other station, Radio Demerara. Rafig Khan, former Radio Demerara general manager, said in 1972 that Guyana would eventually take over that station because of the government's communication and nationalization policies. Rediffusion continued to operate Radio Demerara until 1979, when the government bought it—under extremely favorable terms payable over a 12-year period. Radio Demerara officials reported they were unable to continue operations because of economic problems arising from a lack of advertising. As of 1980 Guyana had taken Radio Demerara off the air and only GBS was providing the nation with an internal radio service. The government reports that closing the station down was the result of maintenance and foreign exchange problems.

Both GBS and Radio Demerara are public corporations under the administrative control of the Guyana State Corporation, a holding company established in 1971 to own, manage and control the assets and business practices of all official corporations.

Broadcasting in Guyana is authorized by the Guyana (British Guiana) Post and Telegraphy Ordinance (1894) and the Wireless Station Regulations (1927), which gave direction and control of wireless to the post office and power to grant broadcast licenses to the governor or his administrative agent, the postmaster general. When commercial operations existed in Guyana, the stations were run under an agreement with the government. This stipulated the government's broad authority in programming and also formalized its role, which, prior to 1950, had been accomplished on an ad hoc basis.

Since GBS changed hands in 1968, its program goals have grown to reflect the political, social and economic needs of Guyana as they are ascertained by government officials. The 1972 *GBS Programme Objectives* noted three problem areas that the official information media had to address: national development, expansion into the interior, and racism.

GBS is self-supporting through the sale of advertising. At times this has been difficult, due to competition from Radio Demerara and state demands for broadcast time. Despite the fact that GBS has had to pay for itself, government departments enjoy free air time, which reduces the time available for sale to advertisers. In addition, there are numerous public service broadcasts, such as education and religious programs, which are carried free.

The government licenses radio receivers, although there is no effective system for determining who buys a radio receiver or who has an unlicensed set. Official estimates are that only half of the receivers in Guyana are licensed, which means a significant annual loss to the national treasury. The government reports 182,000 licensed radio receivers, from which the treasury collects G$273,000 annually. This goes to general expenditures and not to GBS.

Education & Training

Journalism education in Guyana is a recent venture of the state, which apparently sees a need for trained personnel in all government media functions. Short-term training sessions (two to three weeks) are offered for government public relations officers, information personnel and working journalists. This brief training is supplemented by a 12-month course at the University of Guyana, which grants a diploma in public communications. The university program is designed to give participants a broad social sciences background and emphasizes "Development Support Communication (DSC) against the background of the National Philosophy of Co-Operative Socialism." The DSC program is a method of utilizing media to support and become an active part of government development policies. A communication component, utilizing trained journalists, is built into all developmental projects providing linkage between the state and the people.

Summary

Newspaper and radio communication in Guyana is firmly under government control. The Guyanese government has indicated, both by word and action, that there is no place for private or competing media systems in the country and that communications facilities must be owned and controlled by the state.

The media outlook for the 1980s is a continuation of the present situation, which is authoritarian government control. The only possibility for change would be if the ruling PNC lost its dominant political position in Guyana. Opposition to the current government at this point, however, does not seem capable of attaining control through the democratic process.

CHRONOLOGY

1968   Government of Guyana assumes control of one of two private commercial radio stations owned by Rediffusion Limited, a foreign company, Government station named Guyana Broadcast Service.

1971   Government purchases *Daily Chronicle* and enters newspaper publishing field.

1972   Publication and Newspaper Act amended, giving government greater control over privately owned newspapers.

1973   Government purchases *Guyana Graphic*, merges it with *Daily Chronicle* and creates Guyana National Newspaper Limited publishing company.

1974   Customs officials confiscate and destroy 10,000 copies of *Dayclean*, political newspaper critical of Guyanese government.

1979   Privately owned Radio Demerara ceases broadcasting; government broadcasting monopoly is complete.

BIBLIOGRAPHY

American University. *Area Handbook for Guyana*. Washington, D.C., 1969.

Bonell, Frank J., and Jameson, Kenneth P. *A Macroeconomic Assessment of the Economy of Guyana*. Bureau for Latin America and the Caribbean, Agency for International Development, April 1978.

Briggs, Asa. *The History of Broadcasting in the United Kingdom*. Vol. 1: *The Birth of Broadcasting*. London, 1962.

Burnham, L. F. S. *A Destiny to Mould*. New York, 1970.

Cholmondely, Hugh. *Communication and Information for Development Purposes in the Caribbean Area*. Report to the International Broadcast Institute, December 1-8, 1974. Georgetown, Guyana, 1975.

_____, and Nascimento, Christopher A. *The Development of a National Broadcasting System for Guyana*. Georgetown, Guyana, 1967.

Despres, Leo. *Cultural Pluralism and National Politics in British Guiana*. Chicago, 1967.

Dizard, Wilson P. *Television: A World View*. Syracuse, 1966.

Forsythe, Victor. *Trends Toward a National Communication Policy in the Co-Operative Republic of Guyana*. Report to the UNESCO Intergovernmental Conference on Communication Policies in Latin America and The Caribbean. Kingston, Jamaica, December 6-11, 1976.

Frost, J. M. *1970 World Radio-TV Handbook*. 24th ed. Denmark, 1970.

Gorham, Maurice. *Broadcasting and Television Since 1900*. London, 1948.

Nagatootoo, Moses, and Jagan, Cheddi. *The State of the Free Press in Guyana*. Georgetown, Guyana, 1979.

Nascimento, Christopher. "Guyana: Choosing a Relevent Broadcasting System." In *Communications Policy*. London, n.d.

_____. "Using Communications to Support Development: The Guyanan Experience." In *Issues In Communication*. London, 1977.

Paulu, Burton. *British Broadcasting*. Minneapolis, 1956.

Schmacke, Ernst. *The Press in Latin America*. 2nd ed. West Germany, 1973.

Simms, Peter. *Trouble in Guyana*. London, 1966.

Smeyak, Gerald P. "The History and Development of Broadcasting in Guyana, South America." Unpublished Ph.D. dissertation, 1973.

United States Information Service. "Rockefeller Foundation Report." Unpublished report prepared for the Rockefeller tour of Latin and South American countries in 1969. July 1969.

U.S. Department of State. "Background Notes: Guyana" (Publication 8095). Washington, March 1979.

Webber, A. R. F. *Centenary History and Handbook of British Guiana*. Georgetown, British Guiana, 1931.

HAITI

by Robert N. Pierce

BASIC DATA

Population: 5.739 million
Area: 27,713 sq. km. (10,697 sq. mi.)
GNP: 2.6 billion gourdes (US$ 1.3 billion)
Literacy Rate: 10–12%
Language(s): French, Creole; a little English and Spanish
Number of Dailies: 6
  Aggregate Circulation: 92,000
  Circulation per 1,000: 20
Number of Nondailies: 6
  Aggregate Circulation: 8,000
  Circulation per 1,000: 2
Number of Periodicals: NA

Number of Radio Stations: 57
Number of Television Stations: 1
Number of Radio Receivers: 95,000
  Radio Receivers per 1,000: 20
Number of Television Sets: 14,000
  Television Sets per 1,000: 3
Total Annual Newsprint Consumption: 700 metric tons
Per Capita Newsprint Consumption: 0.1 kg. (.22 lb.)
Total Newspaper Ad Receipts: NA
  As % of All Ad Expenditures: NA

Background & General Characteristics

News media generally depend on certain outside factors to form an environment in which they can grow. Among these are a substantial middle class, a consumption-oriented economy and widely available education.

To appreciate how important these are, one must look at a society lacking them. Such a case is Haiti. Its newspapers, both in content and personnel, resemble the sheets published during the colonial period in all parts of the New World, including North America. They share the same ease of access for nonprofessional contributors, and they have a personalism and unpredictable content that lend them some charm. On the negative side, they can be tedious, sycophantic, poorly printed and ill adapted for modern information needs.

Furthermore, in most respects the Haitian press shows little sign of the changes reshaping newspapers throughout the world. One could compare a 1980 issue with one of a decade or two earlier and find it difficult to distinguish them.

One aspect—perhaps the least obvious to the casual observer—is changing, however. This is the courage and determination to insert honest reporting into the press, no matter how slowly. That this is coming despite one of the most pervasive government control systems in the world makes it even more remarkable.

Other handicaps also make the task formidable. An adult literacy rate of only 20 percent is complicated by the fact that only about a tenth of the population speak French, the language of the press, as their primary tongue. The growing need for Haitians to know English because of U.S. commercial influence also puts a strain on their linguistic capacity.

An annual per capita income of about $250 makes Haiti the poorest country in the Western Hemisphere, but the problem becomes graver when one considers that a small elite earns much of the cash. The national income was doing little better than keeping up with the two percent population growth in the 1970s, and there were built-in limitations on how much the situation could improve. For example, 80 percent of the labor force was self-employed in agriculture, and the density per square mile was the highest in the Americas. Most of the land is in small farming tracts, and this plus the cutting of wood for charcoal has led to depletion and erosion of the soil. The only resource offering hope of economic expansion is the hands of the people, and some foreign industries have been founding labor-intensive factories in the country.

Population distribution is definitely unfavorable for newspaper circulation, with 79 percent of Haitians living outside cities. Thus the capital, Port-au-Prince, with 700,000 population, is the only newspaper market. Although there are three other cities with 30,000 to 75,000 people, they do not support regular publications.

The 1970s saw the beginning of a Creole-language upsurge among intellectuals, but it still does not find a place in daily newspapers. Radio and television have moved ahead rapidly in devoting more programming to this idiom, while the written word retains a cachet that only the status of French can match.

The only important differentiation among Haitian newspapers concerns the degree to which they collaborate with the government or, to a limited degree, criticize its actions. A tentative start at formation of political parties was allowed in 1979, only to be reversed soon; however, the incipient parties had no direct connection with printed organs. Above all, neither politicians nor editors would think of publicly questioning the legitimacy of Haiti's Duvalier regime.

Rarely in its history had the press of Haiti had a better opportunity to develop independently than in the late 1970s. The nearest it had ever come before to a period of flourishing was in the latter half of the 18th century, the last years of royal French rule. Between 1750 and 1775 a total of about 50 publications operated at one time or another; they were issued weekly or less frequently; one, the monthly *Journal de Saint-Dominque*, ran as many as 64 pages.

The French Revolution and the subsequent Haitian war of independence left the former royalist press in a shambles. When the island's former slaves founded a republic in 1804 they also started an official publication, the *Gazette Politique et Commerciale d'Haiti*. The 19th century was filled with hundreds of papers of short duration, frequently persecuted or suppressed by governments. Although the United States imposed a democratic constitution on the country during the 1915-23 occupation, the protection of press freedom it included soon was removed because of journalistic attacks on the Haitian and U.S. governments. Censorship and jailings followed.

This pattern was instructive for the Haitian presidents who ran the country after the U.S. withdrawal, and all of them used various combinations of jailings, closures and censorship, with the treatment being extended to radio after it came along. One president, Paul Magloire, had the presses of an opposition paper, *Haiti Democratique*, physically destroyed.

Under the most brutal dictatorship Haiti has seen in modern times—the 1957-71 rule of Dr. Francois Duvalier—all traces of journalistic independence were stamped out. Leading figures on two newspapers, *Haiti-Miroir* and *Independance*, were arrested, and their plants—along with those of a third, *Le Matin*—were wrecked. The bombing of the offices of another paper, *Le Patriote*, caused injury to staff members and failure of the enterprise. *La Phalange*, a Catholic paper, was closed in 1961. Other tactics used by the Francois Duvalier government were control of staff appointments, subsidies and forced publication of editorials lauding state officials.

The list of papers that survived into the 1980s includes four dailies, three weeklies and one biweekly in the entire country; all but one, a weekly in Cap Haitien, are located in the capital. The dailies, printed in full-size sheets, range from four to eight pages. The others tend to adopt magazine formats with smaller but more pages, ranging up to 32. Only one daily, *Le Nouveau Monde*, offers a magazine-type supplement with a weekend literary-cultural section.

No general-audience publications are issued primarily in languages other than French. One biweekly comes out in English for U.S readers, and specialized intellectual, commercial, touristic and religious journals are printed in English, Creole and Spanish. One general weekly, *Le Petit Samedi Soir*, includes an occasional article in Creole.

All newspapers are under 11,000 in circulation and can range as low as 2,000. Among the dailies, *Le Matin* has 10,000, *Le Nouveau Monde* 7,500, *Le Nouvelliste* 5,500 and *Panorama* 2,000. The weeklies include *Le Petit Samedi Soir*, 11,000; *Regard* 5,000, and *Le Septentrion* (Cap Haitien) 2,000. *Fraternité*, a biweekly, has 5,000.

Le Matin was founded in 1907 by Clement Magloire and still is owned by his son,

Franck. Its editor is Dumayric Charlier, a dignified elderly man who also is the unelected secretary-general of a loose grouping called the Haitian Journalists' Association. The paper has strongly backed the Duvalier regime since its troubles in the early days; in many ways it is more supportive than the official mouthpiece, *Le Nouveau Monde. Le Matin* has 20 employees, including six editorial workers, all of whom have law degrees and also hold other jobs. It gets its foreign news from Agence France-Presse (AFP) as a gift from the French Embassy; it also uses dispatches provided by the U.S. government's International Communication Agency. Printed in offset, *Le Matin* is nearly always inked clearly, unlike most others. However, it does not take advantage of offset's easy printing of photographs and, like all the papers, has almost no pictures.

Le Nouveau Monde, the government's official voice, dates from the beginning of the Duvalier regime. It shares many characteristics with *Le Matin* but has a special value because the government's official statements always appear there first, and this lends to its news appeal. Stiff formal pictures of President Duvalier, his son, Jean-Claude—the incumbent president—and other dignitaries, along with unedited announcements from various offices, throng its pages.

Trade unions are generally discouraged under the Duvalier regime, and organized labor is particularly weak in the newspaper industry.

Panorama and *Le Nouvelliste* both direct their appeal to the most literate audiences. *Panorama*—edited by Jules Blanchet, an elderly intellectual who is widely respected for his integrity—is the most independent of the dailies, although it rarely takes chances. Both papers have ancient letterpress printing plants and are extremely deficient in visual qualities.

Economic Framework

Newspapers are relevant economically at only the narrow stratum of Haitian society with money to spend at its option. Not only is the language used a discriminating factor, but the very act of buying newspapers—and certainly responding to the advertisements for luxury goods in them—is outside the realm of possibility for most Haitians. One newspaper on a randomly chosen day included advertisements for a ballet school, a nightclub, an airline (excursions to Disney World), a plumbing and electrical contractor and a violin recital—together with institutional notices for a sugar mill and a bauxite mine. The only ads in the issue approaching a general consumer appeal were those for a new supermarket and brands of rum, cigarettes and coffee.

Television has not made serious inroads into advertising, but radio has. Enterprising station owners are finding they can make profits by appealing to all social classes and selling ads accordingly. They also take advantage of the access to listeners that use of Creole provides; one advertiser of headache pills quintupled his sales in one year through radio commercials in Creole.

However, no mass medium in Haiti other than television earns enough to attract profit-seeking investors, so ownership is in the hands of people who either want to make their ideas known publicly or seek the prestige that journalism brings. The restricted market also means that Haiti has not developed newspapers stratified by a sensational-to-elite range of appeals; except for some weeklies that aim more for younger, freer-thinking readers, all the publications seek basically the same audience. It also means that there has been no movement toward concentration of ownership; with no such economic power among media owners, the government has not felt moved to regulate them.

Closeness to the United States and Canada brings an ample supply of newsprint, although the extremely low financial resources of Haitian publishers have been cut into by soaring prices in the 1970s. This makes printing paper the largest expense for a newspaper, since labor is relatively cheap. There are no unions among Haitian newspapers and therefore no strikes.

The purchase price of a newspaper ranges from 20 cents for dailies to 60 cents for weeklies. This relatively high figure keeps circulation totals to low levels, so publishers must gain most of their income from advertising. A spot check of the dailies in 1980 showed *Le Matin* with 59 percent of its space in ads, *Le Nouvelliste* 43, *Panorama* 41 and *Le Nouveau Monde* 33.

Press Laws

Late in 1979, Jean-Claude Duvalier took the advice of some hard-line aides and decreed a press law that put in writing some of the most restrictive practices of journalistic control. Among the most feared was a licensing provision requiring that any journalist applying for a license give extensive information about his family. This would have put not only the applicant but also his relatives in severe danger of persecution.

Announcement of the law set off a furor inside and outside the country; the Inter-American Press Association and the U.S. government made stiff protests. President Duvalier implicitly conceded that he had received bad advice, and formed a blue-ribbon commission of respected citizens, including journalists. They met for two months, made their recommendations, and the government rewrote the law largely following the commission's advice.

Thus, the only vestige of the original licensing provision was a requirement that a journalist carry a press card issued by his employer and countersigned by a government information official. Foreign journalists were also required to get press cards from the government, to be issued with proof of identity.

The new version, proclaimed March 31, 1980, mostly concerned trivia. One provision that had attracted much attention in the earlier draft survived into the second. It sets a three-year prison term for anyone who commits an "outrage" against the president or the first lady.

Other requirements include:
• Local managers of press agencies must be Haitians. Such agencies must send out "complete, exact, impartial and trustworthy" news.
• Bookstores must insure the "popularization of thought" in offering those Haitian and foreign works that are not prohibited.
• Publication of criminal proceedings before their official announcement is forbidden. This applies also to jury deliberations or arguments in divorce, paternity and defamation trials; publicly seeking donations to pay off fines; reporting parliamentary debates dealing with national defense; and receiving subsidies from a foreign government.
• Persons attacked or criticized in the press must be given a right of reply in the same place where the item appeared.
• Publication of defenses in criminal trials, material that corrupts children, and encouragement of drug use is forbidden.

The law also promises to help the media in two minor ways. These are in requirements that the press receive a 25 percent mail rate reduction and that the government form a commission to help foreign companies make films in Haiti.

Despite this law, the apparatus for press control has always been and remains rather simple. It operates through the Ministry of the Interior, the office in charge of police work—and therefore the most important ministry in Haiti. No elaborate list of prohibited subjects is given out, but when a journalist displeases some dignitary he hears about it. This notice comes in two forms—by telephone and by summons to the ministry. The first is considered sufficient for minor offenses and for pliant persons. In the second, government agents are sent to pick up the offender and take him to the ministry. He is told his journalism is considered harmful to the nation. If he repeats his offense, it is suggested, he may face either official or "popular" action. The latter, on the surface, implies retaliation by irate citizens supporting the government. In reality it means hoodlums on official subsidies.

Censorship

Diligent, systematic censorship exists only for foreign imports and new publications. One official at the international airport has the formidable job of inspecting all incoming printed matter. At times he is told to stop *all* material about Haiti, at others he must watch only for critical reporting. Magazines such as *Time* and *Newsweek* typically are handled by slicing the relevant page or pages from each copy. Newspapers with problem material—usually the *Miami Herald* and *The New York Times*—are simply destroyed for that day, with the explanation offered subscribers that they "did not arrive." Embassies in Port-au-Prince receive the publications unhindered, by diplomatic pouch, and the gist of the sensitive articles gets quickly circulated by *telediol,* a local idiom for oral communication. Also, news from abroad comes back with travelers, and by telephone and letters. The censors do not have the capacity to handle mail.

When a new daily or weekly publication proposes to start, the government usually demands galley proofs in advance. In more than one case, this has resulted in a stillbirth for the enterprise.

An effective and pervasive form of control

is the financial payoff. Some of this is in the form of legitimate official advertising, but in several cases it involves a direct salary for a newspaper editor from the government. One paper, *Le Nouveau Monde,* is publicly considered no more than a strong supporter of the government; privately it is deemed to be directly owned by the state, which also appoints it editor. Even an opposition paper, *Le Petit Samedi Soir,* has earned much of its upkeep from government printing.

State-Press Relations

When 19-year-old Jean-Claude Duvalier took over the presidency in 1971 as the chosen successor of his late father, there was a general expectation abroad that the Duvalier police state with all its attendant terror and economic injustice would continue. Underscoring this feeling was the fact that the youth was following directions of his mother, who took over the leadership of the black conservative elite and repressed the more modern mulatto establishment.

However, in fits and starts the government has moved away from the brutality of the old regime. As the son has matured he has sought to show more independence and modernism, as well as a sensitivity to foreign opinion, particularly in the United States. In 1980 he even went so far as to marry— against his mother's wishes— a divorcee clearly identified with the mulatto power structure. The tension between the two political forces continues, although rarely manifested publicly.

These changes have been reflected in Haiti's communication systems, both mass and interpersonal. A pervasive spy network for monitoring incautious if not subversive conversations has always been an integral part of the Duvalier controls. In earlier years an upper-class Haitian would speak unguardedly only in a moving car with a confidant of long standing; lower-class persons would not make such conversation at all. Toward the mid-1970s both the repression and the caution began lessening, and impertinence was to be heard at cocktail parties and in offices and homes.

This method of passing along information and criticizing governmental developments does not represent a temporary substitute for mass media channels, which would normally be expected to carry the messages. Rather, it is a natural outgrowth of the oral tradition of

the tribal and slave societies upon which the Haitian nation was founded. In its modern form it is called *telediol,* which some observers believe is the dominant form of societal communication. It has many of the norms of modern mass media lacking in the Haitian newspapers, such as credibility, independence, access to all classes, and speed. Although the president has publicly complained about the practice, the government itself often announces its actions through this channel.

Thus the most significant gropings toward freer expression have been oral and outside the normal media, and they remain the target of government surveillance to make sure they do not go too far. This was the case in a celebrated incident on November 9, 1979, at an orderly but daring session of the Haitian League of Human Rights. About 60 armed men broke up the meeting and physically assaulted a number of people including several foreign diplomats. The U.S. Embassy delivered a sharp protest, and the government expressed regret while denying responsibility.

A similar incident came in August 1980, when uniformed police dispersed a street demonstration against a new educational policy. About 300 students were the protestors, and, facing the danger from the police, took refuge in the nearby offices of Radio Haiti-Inter, one of the leading critical media. Only after the station owner, Jean Dominique, negotiated with the police did the students leave.

International revulsion was stirred in an earlier event, the near-fatal beating in late 1977 of the Rev. Luc Neree, a Baptist minister and father of Bob Neree, who published a weekly paper called *La Jeune Presse.* The paper, generally critical of official action, had run an article saying that the presidential private guard called the Tontons Macoutes, which has been disbanded after years of brutality against prisoners, had really been the basis for its sucessor, the Volunteers for National Security (VSN).

The beating took place on a public street, when two former Tontons Macoutes forced the clergyman's car off the road and dragged him from it. The son suspended publication of his paper in protest and later left for the United States. Under pressure of international criticism, the government brought the two assailants to trial and gave them four-month sentences, but they quickly were out of jail.

The Haitian government's policy toward the media has largely reflected its perception of the official U.S. stand in the matter. A mild liberalization, particularly stimulated by the influence of Nelson Rockefeller, took place in the second Nixon administration and that of Gerald Ford. After the election of Jimmy Carter, the movement drastically accelerated, with maverick weekly papers and radio stations leading the shift toward investigative reporting and criticism. It reached a crescendo in the final year of the Carter presidency.

This was illustrated by the openness with which a campaign for the Legislative Assembly—the first such since the elder Duvalier took office—was conducted early in 1979. Widespread public discussion of issues took place, although all but one of the 58 winners were Duvalierists, and the lone oppositionist quickly changed sides.

The Haitian government has always been concerned not only with what is said about it inside the country but also outside. It has not hesitated to use the utmost brutality to intimidate critics whose complaints might be heard abroad. But it risked just such exposure in November 1980 when it carried out the most severe reversal of liberalization in Jean-Claude Duvalier's regime.

Resentment against criticism had been building up among the old-line leaders, particularly because of the controversial seaborne migration of Haitian refugees and their treatment after being returned from the Bahamas. This was proving not only an embarrassment but also a potentially destabilizing factor for the regime.

After a cabinet meeting, police began a roundup of journalists and reformist politicians; their number was variously estimated at 40 to 150 persons. Particularly hard hit were staffs of weeklies such as *Le Petit Samedi Soir* and *Fraternité,* and of radio stations. Among the latter, radios Haiti-Inter, Metropole, Progres and Cacique were suspended. Prominent political leaders who had been sources for statements considered dangerous and caught in the net were Gregorie Eugene of the Social Christian Party and Gerard Gourgue, president of the league that had arranged the 1979 human-rights meeting which had been broken up.

However, rather than throwing the detainees in prison and keeping them there incommunicado, the government expelled most of them from the country. They headed for Miami and New York, where, surrounded by earlier exiles, they promptly raised an even louder outcry against the Duvalierists.

As for other forms of information control, government propaganda does not take the form of planned, systematic promotion of determined programs. Rather, it is adulation for the first family and copious praise for government actions. The Ministry of Information has no clearly defined function, so only part of the official propaganda comes from it. Much of this material originates in the office of *Le Nouveau Monde,* and the other media are expected to republish it from there.

Attitude Toward Foreign Media

The Haitian government, usually sensitive to its dependence on foreign and international powers, does not choose to openly antagonize visiting correspondents. They do meet with problems, however, through an elaborate system of runarounds; the maze of red tape among various official agencies can be maddening. Agence France-Presse maintains a correspondent in Port-au-Prince, and United Press International has a stringer. Both are mostly deferential to officialdom.

The government has not participated actively in the UNESCO debate over the "New World Information Order."

News Agencies

Since all the media of consequence are in the capital, no economic need for a national news agency has emerged. There are no resources for Haitian media to have their own foreign correspondents, although extensive news of a superficial sort is published from the major interior towns.

Agence France-Presse is clearly the major source of foreign news, not only because of Haiti's historic relationship to French affairs but also because of the French government's concerted effort to keep the country oriented to Paris. Most of AFP's material is free or at nominal fees. Some media also subscribe to service by UPI.

Electronic News Media

Radio is by far Haiti's most important mass medium, not only in entertainment but also in journalism. Despite the status conferred by use of a written medium such as newspapers, even the upper classes rely heavily on radio in Haiti. Because of this, radio also serves as the country's primary unifying medium, giving the rich matron and her cook a common viewpoint on public affairs.

Radio newscasts and commentary programs are frequent through the day and night, and the journalistic staffs compare well in size and quality with those of the newspapers. As there is growth in set ownership and as consumerism and civic concern emerge, radio entrepreneurs find an inviting market, and the larger units are making profits. Their popularity in political and commercial areas stems partly from the fact that they have led the "revolution" in the use of Creole in recent years. By the end of the 1970s the best-known station, Haiti-Inter, was airing about four hours of entertainment and one of news daily (of a total of 19) in Creole.

With less dignity to maintain than the newspapers, radio stations can interact better with the public. After Haiti-Inter's owner, Jean Dominique, was fined $30,000 for libel, thousands of people came to the station to contribute to a fund to pay off the fine; they circumvented the law against such subscriptions by buying cassette tapes from Dominique's company.

Unlike other developing countries, Haiti makes it relatively easy to count the radio stations because there are so few of them. The total was 22 in 1980, with an estimated one million receivers in use. Thus the exposure to radio dwarfs that of any other medium.

The four most noted stations are privately owned: Haiti-Inter, Metropole, Progres and Caraibe. Also prominent are one government station, Nationale; and two religious outlets, Lumiere (Protestant) and Soleil (Catholic). The government station is surprisingly well thought of, as its news sometimes does not reflect well on the regime. It also carries much public educational material.

Television is still in the rudimentary stage in Haiti. From 1959 to 1979 it had only one station, TéléHaiti, operating via cable with one channel in French and the other in English. The English-language channel was started as a marketing entry into tourist hotels. It later began to appeal to English-speaking alien residents and educated native Haitians. TV went to color transmission in 1971, being one of the first such in Latin America. TéléHaiti's ownership is dominated by Americans, who get most of their income from cable fees paid by about 19,000 subscribers, only in the capital area. The quality of the picture often suffers from the drain of power caused when nonsubscribers pirate the signal from lines. Many poor people watch the programs in open-air sets in public squares; merchants selling the sets typically contribute these facilities.

The country's first over-the-air television came in December 1979, with the founding of Télévision Nationale. Its all-new, sophisticated equipment and superior signal gave it some competitive appeal over the cable station; occasionally it makes use of Haiti's satellite ground station. With financial assistance from the Vatican, Télévision Nationale brings live coverage of Holy Week and Christmas ceremonies from Rome. It also sometimes airs important international soccer games.

With a staff of 140, Télévision Nationale is making a spirited effort to produce original programs for public improvement in such areas as farming, birth control, hygiene and child care. It has shown a flair for fusing the Haitian flair for humor and spectacle with modern educational techniques. It expects to get repeater stations shortly to take the signal to Cap Haitien, on the northern end of the island.

Despite its initial endowment with good equipment, Télévision Nationale operates on a very tight budget. It manages to get U.S. films at low rates—$100 to $150—because of its nonprofit status. It has increased the percentage of programming originating in Haiti to about 40 percent and is trying to enlarge its audiences by increasing its use of Creole.

Education & Training

All journalistic training in Haiti is on the job, although editors prefer that reporters have university education, with law being the favored field. All such recruits come from the University of Haiti, the country's only one, with about 3,000 students. In the 1950s the university had a journalism program which lasted several years. By the start of the 1980s journalistic leaders were trying to reactivate the program.

Summary

The rapidly increasing ferment in the Caribbean region means that Haiti no longer can stagnate under a reactionary regime as it has in various degrees for more than two decades. Regional influences are much more infectious than before, when the principal concern from outside was tourism. The old regime cannot prevent the political and economic changes in the other islands from becoming known in Haiti, regardless of how it tries to control the mass media.

Even the fact that such pulses of change had been felt faintly in the media by the start of the 1980s portended a growing tendency to discuss the good and the bad in Haitian public life. These challenges had not reached the question of whether the dictatorship should remain, and whether they do so seems to depend mostly on the regime itself. If it continues a cautious but steady liberalization, as it did in the late 1970s, it could contain and absorb the reformism being advocated. If, however, it lurches back to the absolutism of Francois Duvalier's rule—as was indicated in the massive purge of journalists in late 1980—the extreme left would perceive a field ripe for harvest.

CHRONOLOGY

1971   Francois Duvalier, dictator-president of Haiti, dies and bequeaths presidency to his 19-year-old son, Jean-Claude.

1974   Experiments begun to elevate use of written and spoken Creole, Haiti's native language. Government revokes exclusive franchise previously granted to a commercial television station in preparation for its own telecasting.

1977   Haitian journalists attend Inter-American Press Association meeting for first time in decades, signaling new tendencies toward independence in media. Reformist weekly, *La Jeune Presse*, shut down by its owner after his father is beaten by government thugs. Government censors stop two weeklies before they circulate their first issues.

1978   Culprits in 1977 beating convicted, sentenced to four months, but soon released from jail. Boldness of journalistic criticism increases. Government hires New York public relations firm, Edelman International Corp.

1979   Government officials warn media not to publish reports of election irregularities. Book encouraging political parties published; three parties formed. Government writes stern new press law, including licensing of journalists. It soon backs down under domestic and foreign criticism and reforms law in much milder version.

1980   Several dozen journalists arrested and 18 expelled from the country in largest crackdown on newspeople in Haiti's history.

BIBLIOGRAPHY

Leyburn, James G. *The Haitian People*. New Haven, Conn., 1966.

Logan, Rayford W. *Latin American Studies: Haiti and the Dominican Republic*. New York, 1968.

UNESCO. *World Communications*. Paris, 1975.

Weil, Thomas E., *et al. Area Handbook for Haiti*. Washington, D.C., 1973.

HONDURAS*

by John Spicer Nichols

BASIC DATA

Population: 3,691,000
Area: 112,088 sq. km. (43,277 sq. mi.)
GNP: 330 billion lempiras (US$165 billion)
(1978)
Literacy Rate: 50–57%
Language(s): Spanish
Number of Dailies: 6
   Aggregate Circulation: 130,400
   Circulation per 1,000: 35
Number of Nondailies: 15
   Aggregate Circulation: 30,000 (est.)
   Circulation per 1,000: 8
Number of Periodicals: 40

Number of Radio Stations: 110
Number of Television Stations: 3
Number of Radio Receivers: 520,000
   Radio Receivers per 1,000: 141
Number of Television Sets: 142,200
   Television Sets per 1,000: 39
Total Annual Newsprint Consumption: 2,584
   metric tons
Per Capita Newsprint Consumption: 0.7 kg.
   (1.54 lb.)
Total Newspaper Ad Receipts: NA
   As % of All Ad Expenditures: NA

Background & General Characteristics

Honduras is the second poorest country in the Americas. The majority of its people are subsistence farmers who suffer from malnutrition, illiteracy and lack of health care. The country has been plagued by scores of unscheduled changes of government, border wars with its neighbors, economic underdevelopment and devastating natural disasters.

Despite those conditions, Honduras has made considerable political and economic progress in the past decade, and, as a result, has been able to avoid most of the violence, chaos and repression that have consumed neighboring El Salvador, Guatemala and Nicaragua. During the 1970s, a succession of reform-minded military governments carried out a land reform program, a literacy campaign and ambitious public works construction—including roads, hospitals and schools. These governments enacted a series of relatively progressive labor and social security laws. At the same time, the military tolerated opposition political parties, including a small

Communist Party, generally respected human rights (which are routinely violated elsewhere in the region); and allowed the press to criticize, within a surprisingly wide range, government and other powerful sectors of society.

The unique combination of conditions in Honduras challenges many North American notions about democracy and military dictatorship and their effects on the development and control of a national press system.

The Honduran newspaper business is small, underdeveloped, of very low quality, and, for the most part, not a very important factor in the lives of the Honduran people. Most Hondurans, who live scattered throughout the rough countryside with little access to modern communications and transportation, are concerned primarily with daily survival. Even if newspapers could be distributed in the rural areas and even if the contents of those newspapers were remotely relevant to the daily lives of the peasants, the vast majority would be unable to read them. Overall, only 50 percent of the nation is literate,

---

*Research for this chapter was funded in part by the College of the Liberal Arts, Pennsylvania State University (Thomas F. Magner, Associate Dean for Research and Graduate Studies). The author also wishes to thank Professor R. Thomas Berner, Penn State; Professor James A. Morris, University of Texas–El Paso; Cresencio Arcos, Public Affairs Officer, United States Embassy in Honduras; and Charles T. Salmon, University of Minnesota.

Honduran Dailies			
Newspaper	Place of Publication	Founding Date	Est. Circulation
La Tribuna	Tegucigalpa	1977	40,000
El Cronista	Tegucigalpa	1911	7,000
El Heraldo	Tegucigalpa	1979	unknown
La Gaceta	Tegucigalpa	1830	2,400
La Prensa	San Pedro Sula	1964	45,000
El Tiempo	San Pedro Sula	1970	36,000

despite the fact that Honduras has a demographically homogeneous population of Spanish-speaking *mestizos* (mixed Spanish and Indian ancestry), and has only small pockets of blacks and unintegrated Indians. In rural areas, the literacy rate is even lower—30 percent.

Consequently, only six daily newspapers are published in Honduras—four in the capital city of Tegucigalpa and two in the major industrial city of San Pedro Sula.

La Gaceta is the official bulletin of the government and carries decrees, speeches of the military leaders and legal notices. The daily newspapers are supplemented by a handful of generally undistinguished nondailies, which have low circulations, irregular publication schedules and short life spans. The most important nondaily is *Presencia,* a biweekly publication of the national university, which deals mainly with political themes including frequent criticism of the military government. In addition, about 40 magazines, journals and specialized periodicals are published in Honduras. All are limited in circulation, and, with the possible exception of *Revista Militar* (a magazine published by the army), have limited influence on the Honduran readership.

Almost all Honduran newspapers are privately owned family businesses. Despite the long tradition of a political press in Honduras and in contrast to the highly politicized press elsewhere in Central America, the Honduran dailies have not taken strident political positions since the government was reorganized under the military in the 1970s. Their editorial positions range from moderate to far right, and, for the most part, support the military government and economic elite. Typically, they publish between 30 and 50 pages per day in tabloid format. (*El Heraldo* is the only daily that does not publish on Sunday.) The editorial content is mostly sports, social notes, crime and other highly sensational news stories. The small amount of serious journalism that appears in these newspapers deals with local and national issues, and the sparse foreign coverage is usually about either the political problems of Honduras' Central American neighbors or events in the United States.

The exception is the standard-sized, low-circulation *El Cronista,* which carries little news or advertising and shuns sensationalism. *El Cronista* concentrates on analysis and political opinions, which, local observers say, swing from the radical left to the radical right. The newspaper, a hobby of the prominent Valladares family for nearly 80 years, is probably best described as eccentric.

The best newspaper in Honduras, both technically and editorially, is *La Prensa.* This slick offset publication uses liberal amounts of color and has modern typography and layout. The highlight of *La Prensa* is its editorial and op-ed pages, which are noted for their relatively probing and insightful analyses of public affairs. The editor of *La Prensa* and the nation's most highly regarded journalist is Amilcar Santamaría.

To the extent that the Honduran press serves a news function, it is only for the educated elite in the urban areas. The Honduran press cannot be considered a *mass* medium. However, within those limits, the nation's newspapers carry on a lively political debate that is unusual among underdeveloped states ruled by military governments. Virtually all political parties and organized interest groups have access to the news media. In 1980 the leaders of the small Honduran Communist Party and other splinter groups frequently were interviewed in the daily newspapers and on radio. Recent exposés in the Honduran press have dealt with the use of unnecessary force by the local police in arresting suspects or quelling student demonstrations, the potential involvement of the military with drug trafficking and the continuation of serious corruption in all sectors and at all levels of society. Editorialists lambaste the military leadership, occasionally by name. The military reacts with expressions of annoyance, threats of formal action and subtle economic pressures, but only rarely imposes overt controls.

The range of the political debate, the frequency of press criticism and the military's restraint in muzzling public discussion are indications of a relatively stable national system, especially when compared to the extreme volatility throughout Central America. Some of the reasons for the stability are:

• Because the country is so underdeveloped, the Hondurans have demanded comparatively few social and economic resources. To the extent that the demands have increased, the substantial economic growth of the 1970s encouraged by military-backed development programs and high prices for coffee and other crops and raw materials exported by Honduras has met those demands.

• In spite of an unequal distribution of wealth, differences between rich and poor are not as pronounced as elsewhere in Central America. Honduras does not have a family dynasty, oligarchy or small class of multimillionaire businessmen, such as in Guatemala or El Salvador. "Our poverty is better distributed," the Honduran foreign minister once said only half jokingly.

• The population is more homogeneous and sustains fewer radicalizing pressures, such as overpopulation or cultural differences, than its neighbors.

• The military government has a comparatively broad base of political participation. Sectors such as organized labor, peasant and agricultural groups, and small business and professional associations, previously denied access to government under civilian leadership, have been made institutionalized participants in public life. The increasing number of special-interest groups represented in the government guarantees that an increasing range of political opinions is expressed in the public forum.

• Military leaders periodically have carried out modest reforms that have served as a release valve for accumulated social pressure and dissatisfaction with the government. The most recent and perhaps significant of these changes was to hold elections in 1980, a time of increasing public disgust over corruption in the military. Honduran voters elected a national assembly that was expected to write a new constitution and call for direct elections in 1981 for a new civilian president.

Economic Framework

Despite recent economic advances, Honduras remains a poverty-stricken country. The per capita gross national product was less than $500 in 1980, because Honduras still has an agriculture-based economy that did not begin substantive modernization until after the 1950s. For example, the first paved road between Tegucigalpa, the capital city, and San Pedro Sula, the nation's economic center, was not built until 1967.

Under these economic conditions, the number of commercial media outlets in Honduras is predictably small and ownership is extremely concentrated. One family, headed by Jorge Larach, owns two of Honduras' six daily newspapers; and a combination of two families, headed by Valleda Toledo and Rafael Ferrari, owns all three television stations in Honduras and *Emisores Unidas,* the largest of two major radio networks that controls 13 individual stations. These and other media families have also heavily invested in other important sectors of the Honduran economy. The daily newspaper *El Tiempo*— owned by a consortium of businessmen, banks and insurance companies—is the only major medium that is not dominated by prominent Honduran families. And with the exception of *El Cronista,* all are said to be fairly profitable businesses.

Due to economic conditions, the advertising base to support the commercial media system is very thin, giving advertisers considerable influence over the editorial content of the major media. The Honduran economic elite and the military government routinely have used their proportionately large advertising budgets to influence the media. The military tends to reward friendly media with increased advertising allotments and punish its opponents by withdrawing official advertising.

In addition to advertising pressures on publishers, other economic controls are exercised on the news personnel. Virtually every journalist in Honduras receives *mordidas* (cash payments from news sources intended to influence reporting). The *mordida* system is not unique to Honduras. It is practiced to some degree in almost every Latin American country and has been institutionalized to the point that journalists do not view the mordida—as it would be viewed, for example, in the United States—as unethical. However, the practice is unusually widespread in Honduras. Other economic controls used in addition to or in lieu of direct cash bribes are high-paying part-time jobs in government ministries and public relations offices of businesses, special advertising commissions, and a wide variety of goods and services. Regardless of the form of economic control, the effect is the same. Only wealthy individuals or organized sectors of the society having sufficient funds can buy access to the news media, and the common people of Honduras who lack the financial resources are excluded.

Perhaps because of the tradition of buying access in the news media, the liveliest political debates often take place in the advertising columns of Honduran newspapers. Instead of trusting the whims of news personnel, Honduran political parties, labor unions, agriculture associations and other organized groups write their own *pronunciamientos* and publish them in paid advertising space, thereby fulfilling the basic news function of informing the public and government of their position on important issues. Even the military purchases ad space or air time for this reason. In the period before the 1980 elections, Honduran newspapers were filled with *pronunciamientos* from a wide variety of mainline and splinter groups, and there was no evidence that the military or any other power holder attempted to limit the freewheeling use of this communication tool.

In 1980 slightly less than 50 percent of content of the major Honduran newspapers was advertising. In addition to advertising from the military, corporate and family interests and the various political organizations, a modest amount of advertising came from professionals, small businesses such as movie houses, shops and the general public through the classified sections. Given the small circulations, newsstand sales at the standard price of 10 cents per copy do not generate much revenue.

Despite the fact that one of Honduras' most plentiful resources is timber, virtually all of the nation's newsprint must be imported at considerable cost. With U.S. economic aid, Honduras has started construction of a pulp and paper plant to end the need for expensive imports. Completion of the project is scheduled for the mid-1980s.

Economic factors clearly are the most significant means of limiting the range of political discussion and generally controlling the content of the Honduran media. Concentrated ownership, withholding of official advertising and outright cash payments to journalists are also effective in maintaining leverage over the media that the military and other power holders only rarely have had to resort to formal censorship, jailing of journalists and other forms of overt repression that are common in the region. The military's success in using the carrot has obviated its use of the stick.

Press Laws & Censorship

The legal status of the Honduran press is somewhat unusual for Latin America. Many Latin American countries have broad constitutional guarantees of freedom of the press modeled after the constitutions of the United States and France but routinely suspend or ignore those guarantees. Honduras' constitutional guarantee of press freedom is heavily qualified by statutes, yet the military government generally respects the broader principle and does not zealously enforce the various legal exceptions. Honduran press laws, however, like those of most Latin American countries, are not very meaningful in explaining the relationship between the media and the government. As discussed previously, more effective control is found elsewhere.

The dubious importance of Honduran press law is compounded by the tenuous nature of the current constitution during the transition to a civilian government. The recently elected national assembly is supposed to rewrite the constitution before the end of 1981. Although the timetable is questionable because of political squabbling, nothing indicates that the constitution eventually drafted will substantially change the current legal status of the press.

Currently, the Constitution of 1965 and the Law of Expression of Thought, which codify the basic principles, are the basis of Honduran press law. Article 2 of the law states: "The liberties of expression of thought and information are inviolate"; and Article 5 expands the principle as follows:

All inhabitants of the Republic can freely, without prior censorship, express their thoughts, give and receive information and discuss their opinions of those of others by media of written or spoken word or by whatever other graphic, oral or visual method.

However, Article 6 qualifies those principles:

The circulation of publications that preach or make public doctrines that undermine the fundamentals of the State and of the family and those that provoke, advise or stimulate the commission of crime against people or property is not permitted.

Article 38 specifies some of these exceptions. The following types of media content are prohibited and those who publish such material may be punished:

1. Content that is in "interests contrary to the defense of National Sov-

ereignty, territorial integrity and the democratic institutions of the Republic."

2. Defamation and insults.

3. Knowingly deceptive advertising.

4. "The capricious attack without proof against commercial or industrial enterprises, national or foreign, for the sole purpose to avenge grievances or to discredit people or institutions."

5. Blackmail.

6. Pornography.

In addition, the Constitution, Law of Expression of Thought and accumulated case law provide for the following:

• Right of reply. Those who feel that they are unjustly criticized in the press have the right to publish their reply in the medium that criticized them. The response must be published within three days in the same location and under the same size headline as the offending article.

• Individual responsibility. If material forbidden in Article 38 and elsewhere is published, the author of the material, not the medium in which it is published, is liable.

• Restriction on foreign influence. No foreign government or foreign political party may subsidize Honduran media; further, the Honduran media must be financially controlled by Honduran citizens. Foreigners are not permitted to be editors or directors of Honduran media.

• Source confidentiality. Journalists are constitutionally protected from having to divulge news sources to government officials.

• Restrictions on economic reporting. Law 92 of the penal code provides for fines and imprisonment for a journalist or another "within the country or abroad who publishes or otherwise divulges false, exaggerated or tendentious news which endangers or impairs the national economy or public credit."

Clearly, the most significant legal development in the Honduran press is the formation by national law in 1979 of a closed-shop union—the Academy *(Colegio)* of Honduran Journalists. All regularly employed, salaried journalists must be members of the *colegio* in order to practice journalism in Honduras. Similar to licensing laws recently adopted in Costa Rica, Nicaragua and other Latin American countries, the major requirement for membership in the Honduran *colegio* is a degree in journalism or communication from any university recognized by the National Autonomous University of Honduras or five years of uninterrupted professional experience before enactment of the law. The *colegio's* activities are concentrated in four areas:

1. Professional protection. The law prevents journalists from being fired unless they violate the *colegio's* code of ethics. Expulsion from the *colegio* can take place only after a hearing panel documents "grave violations" of the code of ethics, such as accepting a bribe. No journalist can be fired for what he writes. Journalists expelled from the *colegio* have the right of appeal to the Ministry of Government.

2. Labor relations. The *colegio* has had a major impact on improving pay and benefits such as health care, pensions and life insurance. For example, before recent *colegio* negotiations with media owners, the minimum pay for reporters was $75 per month without benefits; the minimum now is $350 with benefits.

3. Professional standards. The *colegio* has written a code of ethics and with it is attempting to weed out journalists who are more concerned with procuring bribes than professional responsibilities.

4. Education. The *colegio* has been active in designing an improved curriculum for university journalism programs, founded its own journalism training center to upgrade the skills of "grandfathered" members not trained at the universities and regularly offers short courses for all its members.

The *colegio* activities are funded by a one-percent tax on all advertising in the Honduran media and an entry and monthly membership fee.

The Inter American Press Association (IAPA), an organization of publishers in the hemisphere, and other media watchdog organizations have made blanket condemnations of all licensing laws as threats to freedom of the press; however, such attacks do not take into account unique conditions in Honduras. Virtually all journalists interviewed in Honduras in 1980 enthusiastically endorsed the *colegio* and felt that it had tangible benefits for rank-and-file journalists and the public at large. They argue that the owners of the media are the same people or allied with those who own most of the other economic resources of the country, and, as a result, have been the major actors in limiting the flow of information in the country. The reporters said that before 1979 the owners often prevented them from writing about social, political and economic subjects that were not consonant with views of the national economic elite. The journalists said that since the *colegio* law they have had much greater latitude in writing about labor unions, left-of-center political parties and other previously taboo topics. Of course, the owners, at least two of whom are IAPA members, are not happy with the law.

On the other hand, the military government has had a better record than civilian governments backed by the economic elite in its treatment of the press. While civilian governments have traditionally used heavy-handed tactics to silence publications representing opposition political parties, the military is generally more tolerant of publication of most points of view including those with criticism of the military government. Further, labor unions have deep roots in Honduras and have been important instruments of social reform in the country. These labor unions, often in alliance with the military, have been responsible for some of the most progressive social, economic and political programs in Honduras. In sum, from the perspective of Honduran journalists, a closed-shop union in alliance with the military government, anathema to the IAPA, seems to be a means of liberating the press from stiff economic controls without exposing it to a significant increase in political controls.

State-Press Relations

Typically, the North American view is that civilian government is preferable to military government and that the former better serves the needs of the people. However, as Professor James L. Busey, a Central American specialist from the University of Colorado, has written, "The symbolism of politics often disguises the reality of gangsterism." Clearly, civilian political parties have not served Honduras well and have a tradition of repressing the nation's press.

Honduras' two major political parties, Nationalists and Liberals, do not represent distinct political ideologies or sectors of society. Rather, according to Professor James A. Morris of the University of Texas-El Paso, a leading Honduras specialist, they are merely factions of the urban elite fighting over who divides the national wealth. At election time the infamous *Mancha Brava*, goon squads organized by the political parties, would cover the countryside to round up (often by force) voters for their respective

political parties. The goon squad of the victor would be allowed to share in the spoils of office. That system bred widespread corruption, and participation in public affairs by various sectors of society —labor, agricultural groups, professional organizations— was virtually nonexistent under civilian government.

The situation carried over into the press. When the Nationalists were in power, journalists in the Liberal press were harassed, censored, jailed or bribed into submission. When the Liberals were in power, the Nationalist press endured the same treatment. But in neither case did the various sectors not represented by those political parties have access to the media.

In 1972 when the military under the leadership of General Oswaldo López Arellano seized control of the government, most Hondurans, with the exception of the politicians, supported the *coup*. The major labor and peasant groups and, to some extent, the small businessmen and professionals, who had long been starved out of power, felt that the old political-party system was beyond repair and backed the new military government. In turn the military gave these groups access to the government and responded to some of their demands for reform. While López Arellano was not a paragon of virtue, he was more of a social reformer than his civilian predecessors. Under his military regime, there was a modest land-reform program, literacy campaign, union reform and public-health improvements.

Predictably, once the previously excluded groups gained access to the military government, they demanded control of the media. For example, in 1974, the national peasant organization petitioned the government to expropriate *La Prensa* and the now-defunct daily *La Noticia* because of their antiworker editorial policies. López Arellano rejected the proposal, saying that the newspapers had the right to promote whatever viewpoint they wished, adding that the military would uphold the principle of press freedom.

Oddly enough, the strongest criticism of López Arellano's relatively liberal policies came from the so-called freely elected presidents of neighboring countries—General Kjell Laugerud Garcia of Guatemala, General Anastasio Somoza Debayle of Nicaragua and Colonel Arturo Molina Barraza of El Salvador. At a meeting of regional heads of state, the presidents cautioned López Arellano that his liberal programs, especially the land-reform program, would create instability and encouraged him to stop.

One reform that López Arellano did not institute was to end, or even modestly reduce, the widespread corruption in government. In 1975 he was toppled as a result of his alleged involvement in "Bananagate," a scandal in which the United States company United Brands admitted paying $1.25 million in bribes to Honduran officials in exchange for a reduction in the banana-export tax. Although his replacement, General Juan Alberto Melgar Castro, continued some of the reforms, most of the progressive officers allied with López Arellano were purged by being forced into the diplomatic service.

Melgar Castro was removed from office abruptly in 1978, apparently as the result of an incident involving one of Honduras' most prominent journalists. Manuel Gamero, editor of *El Tiempo* and local stringer for the United Press International, published in June of that year an interview with a fugitive in a drug-related kidnap–murder case. That interview and a series of other stories implied that the military leadership was involved in the drug smuggling. It is believed, although not documented, that the conservative wing of the military was upset that Melgar Castro did not defend the honor of the military by taking strong action against the press. Gamero was arrested in July and charged with harboring a murder suspect. He pleaded that the confidentiality of his news sources was protected by the Honduran constitution and was released two weeks later. In August, Melgar Castro was replaced by a three-man junta headed by General Policarpo Paz Garcia.

Despite this recent incident and a more strident attitude toward the press by the ruling junta, prior censorship and other overt media controls are not practiced. Open debate on most topics of public concern continues in Honduras. Criticism of the military government and its individual leaders also continues, although perhaps more circumspectly. The government continues to exercise economic controls over the media and to practice standard news-management techniques. Two military officials—the press secretary of the military junta and the secretary of public relations for the armed forces—are primarily responsible for media control. In addition to usual public relations activities such as publishing magazines and newsletters, they also exercise some punitive power—usually cutting off government

advertising from uncooperative media, such as Gamero's *El Tiempo,* and denying access to official news sources for uncooperative reporters.

In 1980 under considerable diplomatic pressure from the United States and in an attempt to ward off the escalating problems of its neighbors, the Honduran military held national elections for a constituent assembly in preparation for a direct election in 1981 to replace Paz Garcia with a civilian president. Just as the Honduran people were disgusted in 1972 with the chaos and corruption of the political parties, the vote eight years later was a repudiation of the corrupt and increasingly unpopular military government. In the election, in which 82 percent of the registered voters went to the polls, the party that the military apparently preferred, the Nationalists, was badly defeated, the Liberals winning a clear majority in the assembly.

Attitude Toward Foreign Media

The United States has dominated Honduras politically and economically for more than a century. U.S. Troops have intervened in Honduran politics on six occasions, and although troops are no longer used, the U.S. embassy in Tegucigalpa remains the focal point of Honduran politics. About 85 percent of all foreign investment in Honduras comes from the United States, and about two-thirds of all Honduran exports, primarily bananas and coffee, are bought by the United States. As such, it is not surprising that U.S. interests are deeply entrenched in the Honduran media:

• Honduran newspapers subscribe to the Associated Press, United Press International and United Feature Service.
• American Broadcasting Company International, the foreign arm of the U.S. television network, has heavy investments in Honduran television. The vast majority of the medium's content is old, second-rate serials from the United States.
• Most Honduran radio content is music produced in the United States, and the little news that is aired often is supplied by the U.S. International Communication Agency.
• Numerous U.S. publications, such as *The New York Times, Miami Herald, The Wall Street Journal, Time, Newsweek* and several Spanish-language translations of Hearst magazines, are readily available on newsstands in Honduran cities.

• An estimated 70 percent of all commercial films shown in Honduras are made in the United States.

The Honduran media also use information and entertainment from other countries. After the United States, Mexico is the major supplier. Televisa, the Mexican national television monopoly, supplies a wide range of content for Honduran television—especially soap operas—and dubs the Spanish translations for programs coming from other countries, including those from United States. In addition, the press occasionally prints dispatches from EFE of Spain; ACAN, the new Central American news agency affiliated with EFE; and Agence France-Presse.

In 1979 there were a few instances in which government officials occasionally confiscated, in apparent violation of Honduran law, books and other reading material from travelers returning from Communist countries. These confiscations were denounced vigorously in the Honduran press and have not been repeated recently.

Honduras is not well covered by the foreign media. Only ACAN-EFE maintains a full-time correspondent in the country; AP, UPI, Latin-Reuters, AFP and Deutsche Presse-Agentur of Germany have local stringers. Major events, such as the 1980 election or the devastating hurricane of 1974, usually are covered by correspondents stationed at the bureaus of major media in Mexico City, Miami and New Orleans.

In 1979 the International Press Institute reported:

> Foreign correspondents complained that they were frequently told to report to military intelligence officers and attempts were made to intimidate them, with accusations being made of distorted reports intended to damage the interests of the army and government.

In-country interviews in 1980 and discussions with U.S. foreign correspondents who regularly cover Honduras, including reporters from *The New York Times* and *The Washington Post*, produced no evidence of such a problem. However, Honduran military officials frequently have applied oral pressure to local journalists, a practice not uncommon even in the United States and other Western countries. Even if this practice has been carried over to foreign correspondents—in comparison to the neighboring countries of Central America where foreign correspondents frequently are threatened with physical harm and occasionally are beaten, shot at or killed—the problem in Honduras seems to be neither widespread nor serious.

News Agencies

Honduras does not have a domestic news agency.

Electronic News Media

Given the widespread illiteracy and poor transportation, radio is unquestionably the most important medium in Honduras. Despite tremendous growth in 1970s during which both the number of transmitters and receivers nearly doubled, very little is known about the listenership, the content and the impact of Honduran radio.

With the exception of a military radio station, all Honduran radio stations are privately owned, and, with a few other exceptions, are operated as commercial enterprises. Most of the content is music, time breaks and society notes. The remainder consists of editorial commentary and analysis but only rarely straight news. The few noncommercial stations are operated by religious organizations and tend to have more substantive content. The most important is Radio Católica, which has a major transmitter in Tegucigalpa and repeaters throughout the country. The signals of the more than 100 radio stations are believed to cover most of the national territory and to reach regularly about two million Hondurans, over half of the total population.

Although powerful stations from the major cities and large networks continue to be dominant, the largest growth seems to be among low-power local stations outside the major cities. However, except for the small local listenership, nobody (probably including the government) seems to know much about the programming of local radio. If the other Central American countries are accurate indicators, radio is a powerful force in Honduras, but to what end is uncertain. Officials in the capital city express some concern that Radio Havana and Radio Sandino from revolutionary Nicaragua can be heard clearly throughout Honduras. Said one former official:

> Our people may be illiterate but they're not ignorant. The radio news starts at 5 a.m., and you can see campesinos plowing with transistor radios hanging from their necks. One of the best businesses here is radio batteries.

Television is far less important, despite substantial development during the 1970s. One national channel (5), headquartered in Tegucigalpa and supplemented by five regional repeaters, and two local channels (3 and 7) in Tegucigalpa and San Pedro Sula, respectively, reach an estimated total audience of 670,000. Channel 3 has a daily news program, "Hoy Mismo" ("This Very Day"), the only one in the country. An eight-hour program, "Domingo" ("Sunday"), airs on Channel 5 each week. The host, Jacobo Goldstein, a wealthy and popular national opinion leader, describes his program as a combination of "60 Minutes" and "The Tonight Show." Serious features and interviews with a wide range of national world leaders are mixed with sports, music, games, stunts and other banalities. Before the election, spokesmen for the two major political parties and one smaller party were given 15 minutes of air time to explain the platforms of their parties. The program also broadcast live (via microwave from a satellite facility in Panama) segments of the Pope's visit to Latin America in 1980. "Domingo" has the largest audience of any locally produced program.

Government supervision of both radio and television is delegated to the National Directorate of Electric Communications.

Education & Training

There has been formal journalism training at the National Autonomous University of Honduras since 1969. In 1979 two private universities—José Cecilio del Valle University in Tegucigalpa and another in San Pedro Sula—started new four-year journalism programs. Because of the education requirement of the new *colegio* law, considerable effort has been made to upgrade the local journalism programs, but by all accounts, including those of university officials in Tegucigalpa, Honduran journalism education is sadly lacking.

The Honduran Press Association, a social-professional organization which has been largely replaced by the new *colegio,* annually honors its top journalists with two awards—the Paulino Vallardes Award for news writing and the Alejandro Castro Award for editorial writing, both named for distinguished former Honduran journalists.

Summary

Honduras is an economically undeveloped, socially unequal and corrupt nation ruled by a military government. Despite its flaws, the military has conducted modest social reforms and generally respected basic human rights in the country. Consequently, the Honduran news media have had during the 1970s great latitude to conduct a lively open debate on controversial topics, to publish the opinions of opposition parties and political dissidents and even to criticize the military government and its individual leaders.

However, the flow of news in Honduras is not without numerous controls. The military and the economic elite of the country wield heavy influence over the news media— usually by withholding advertising or bribing reporters. And as a last resort, the military has infrequently used overt repression, such as jailing editors and closing down radio stations, to maintain its control over the media. Despite those controls, most Honduran journalists feel that the military government, on balance, has respected the news and criticism function of the media far more than the civilian governments that preceded it.

The foundation built by this reformist military offers Honduras a chance to find a peaceful alternative to the spiral of violence, chaos and repression that has swept through Central America. However, whether Honduras will be able to take advantage of that opportunity is an open question. The 1980 national election that the United States forcefully urged on the corrupt Honduran military will return civilian politicians to power in 1981. But the political-party system has not served Honduras well. Civilian governments do not have good records of effective national leadership, toleration of opposition political parties, social reform for the impoverished majority and respect for basic human rights. Whether the new government is capable of responding to the complex problems of Honduras, and, if so, whether it can act soon enough to prevent impending violence are not certain. Nonetheless, it is clear that at the outset of the 1980s the Honduran political system, and, by extension, its national press system are at a turning point that may determine their course for several decades to come.

CHRONOLOGY

1978   Manuel Gamero, editor of daily newspaper *El Tiempo,* jailed for two weeks by military government for allegedly harboring murder suspect; Fugitive was a source for series of articles that Gamero wrote about possible involvement of military officers in Honduran drug trade. Gamero argues that Honduran press law protects source confidentiality and is released after two weeks in jail. Editorial cartoonist for paper is held for longer period on related charges.

1979   Jesuit-operated radio station closed down for broadcasting material that military government labels subversive. Honduran press strongly criticizes government action, and after two months, station returns to air. While media concedes there may have been substance to government's charges, they argue that Honduran law directs charges must be brought against responsible individual rather than entire station.
Colegio of Honduran Journalists, a closed-shop union, formed by national law. In order to be licensed, Honduran journalists must meet education requirements and obey *colegio's* code of ethics.

1980   Military government holds elections for national assembly that is scheduled to rewrite constitution by end of 1981 in preparation for direct elections of a civilian president. During election campaign, Honduran news media conducts freewheeling debate on political issues and gives open access, in both news and advertising columns, to major political parties and splinter groups, including small Communist Party.

BIBLIOGRAPHY

Blutstein, Howard I., et al. *Area Handbook for Honduras.* Washington, 1971.

Gardner, Mary A. "The Press in Honduras: A Portrait of Five Dailies." *Journalism Quarterly,* no. 1, 1963, pp. 75–82.

Mejia, Medardo. "El Periodismo de la 'Illustration' como Periodismo Legitimo de Honduras," *El Heraldo,* May 24, 1980, pp. 17–18.

Morris, James A., and Ropp, Steve C. "Corporatism and Dependent Development: A Honduran Case Study." *Latin American Research Review,* no. 2, 1977, pp. 27–68.

Republica de Honduras. *Ley de Emision del Pensamiento.* Tegucigalpa, 1963.

Riding, Alan. "Hondurans Chafe as Graft, but Little Else, Thrives," *The New York Times,* December 23, 1980, p. A2.

U.S. Department of State. *Country Reports on Human Rights Practices for 1979.* Washington, 1980.

White, Robert A. *Mass Communications and the Popular Promotion Strategy of Rural Development in Honduras.* Stanford, 1976.

HONG KONG

by Elliott S. Parker

BASIC DATA

Population: 5 million (1979, est.)
Area: 1,057 sq. km. (408 sq. mi.)
GNP: HK$61.21 billion (US$12.7 billion)
Literacy Rate: 74%
Language(s): Cantonese and other Chinese dialects; English
Number of Dailies: 126
  Aggregate Circulation: 1.7 million
  Circulation per 1,000: 362
Number of Nondailies: NA
  Aggregate Circulation: NA
  Circulation per 1,000: NA
Number of Periodicals: 296

Number of Radio Stations: 2
Number of Television Stations: 3
Number of Radio Receivers: NA
  Radio Receivers per 1,000: NA
Number of Television Sets: NA
  Television Sets per 1,000: NA
Total Annual Newsprint Consumption: 63,600 metric tons (1979, est.)
  Per Capita Newsprint Consumption: 14.6 kg. (32.2 lb.)
Total Newspaper Ad Receipts: HK$130 million (US$26 million)
  As % of All Ad Expenditures: NA

Background & General Characteristics

Situated off the southeast corner of the Chinese mainland, Hong Kong maintains a political and financial uniqueness in Asia. Both the economy and government are marked by freedom rarely found in Asia outside Japan. The newspapers reflect this freedom and are the least fettered papers in the region. Not only does this result in a lively—some say sensational—press for local consumption, but in Hong Kong as a steadily growing center for regional distribution of news and information.

Hong Kong was founded as a British colony in 1841, a status it still retains. Part of the Kowloon peninsula was ceded to the British in 1860 and a 99-year lease was signed in 1898 for the New Territories. The three areas are slightly over 400 square miles. One of the highest population densities in the world results from the pressure of 5 million people living on less than 16 percent of this area.

This population is 98 percent Chinese. The remaining two percent is composed primarily of British, Indians and Americans, plus smaller representations from Singapore, Thailand, Portugal, Pakistan and the Philippines. Of this population, 52 percent are male and about 40 percent are under 20 years of age. About 40 percent of the population is composed of immigrants, primarily from Guangdong province in the People's Republic of China. Recently, significant numbers of ethnic Chinese and others have been arriving from Vietnam as refugees.

Eighty-eight percent of the population speaks Cantonese, the main language of southern China. Ten percent of the population speak other Chinese dialects, and English is widely understood among the middle and upper classes.

The overall quality of journalism on larger papers is fairly high: however, there are a large number of so-called mosquito Chinese-languge papers that specialize in sensationalism, horse racing results and crime. Newspapers such as the *South China Morning Post, Ming Pao (Ming Bao)** or *Sing Tao Jih Pao (Xing Dao Ri Bao),* devote significant

---

*Names of Chinese-language papers in this chapter are given first in the form that they appear on the nameplate followed by the *pinyin* transliteration.

amounts of space to international affairs—as might be expected given the Colony's dependence on trade and commerce.

Recently, a few papers have begun to carry in-depth investigative articles. Due to the very poor salaries on some papers, some editors and reporters write about certain products or people in return for favors. Literary pages with serials, novels and poems tend to remain under the dictatorship of the page editor, who many times has personal, rather than professional reasons, for deciding which stories to run.

The history of the press in the colony is intertwined with the history of the press in Canton and Macao. The earliest papers were published in Canton and it was the mid-19th century before newspapers began to be published in Hong Kong proper after foreigners were banned from residing in Canton.

Sometime between 1852 and 1858 the first Chinese-language paper appeared, *Chung Ngoi San Po (Zhong Wai Xin Bao)*, based primarily on translations from the *China Mail*. The earliest English-language publication in Hong Kong was the semimonthly *Government Gazette*, a four-page paper started in 1841. In 1842 it combined with the *Friend of China* and was renamed *Friend of China and Hongkong Gazette*. A year later the *Eastern Globe* was established, but it soon ran afoul of the governor and ceased publication. The *China Mail* was begun in 1845 and continued until 1974. The oldest Chinese paper still being published is *Wah Kiu Yat Po (Hua Qiao Ri Bao)*, which started in 1925.

The first half of the 20th century was an extremely fluid period for Hong Kong journalism. Editors and publishers came to Hong Kong from China when their views fell out of favor there. During the 1930s and 1940s some papers moved from Hong Kong to the mainland to continue publishing during the Japanese occupation of Hong Kong and northern China.

In 1979 there were 126 newspapers registered in Hong Kong. They included four English dailies, eight other English papers, 110 Chinese papers, three bilingual (Chinese-English) papers and one Japanese paper.

Although the profusion of papers forces hawkers to periodically ask government to allow them to increase the size of their kiosks, the larger papers account for the bulk of circulation and readership.

The fastest-growing Chinese newspaper, the *Oriental Daily News (Dong Fang Ri Bao)*,

claims a circulation of 450,000 and 27 percent of the readership. The next two largest papers, *Sing Pao (Cheng Bao)* and *Sing Tao Jih Pao,* report circulations at 245,000 and 75,000 respectively. These three papers have 53 percent of the readership while the next seven largest have only 29 percent of the readership.

Each of the two largest Chinese papers has more circulation and readership than all the English papers combined. The largest English paper is the *South China Morning Post,* with a circulation of 65,000 and three percent of the readership. This circulation is about twice that of the nearest competitor, the *Hong Kong Standard.* There are two English tabloid papers: the *Star* and the *Sun.* The *Sun* began publishing in 1979. The English papers are read by less than five percent of the readers.

The most influential papers are important to different constituencies. The *South China Morning Post* is of value not only to tourists and students desiring to improve their English but also to the businessman who needs to follow the thinking of the government. The *Oriental Daily News* is influential because of the large readership, although the *Ming Pao* is considered more intellectual and independent. *Sing Tao Jih Pao* and *Wah Kiu Yat Po* carry weight in the business community.

Some newspapers are important out of proportion to their circulation. Unhampered by domestic restrictions, these papers reflect the thinking of Peking or Taipei. *Ta Kung Pao (Da Gong Bao),* for instance, started in Tientsin in 1902, identifies with the People's Republic of China. It has good access to sources there, often publishing information before it is published in the official Chinese press. At the same time, lying beyond domestic control, these papers are often critical of policies or personnel. *Ta Kung Pao* is noted for its journalistic excellence in writing and layout. *Wen Wei Pao (Wen Hui Bao)* reflects Peking policies, while the *Kung Sheung Daily News (Gong Shang Ri Bao)* and the *Hong Kong Times (Xiang Gang Shi Bao)* speak with the voice of Taiwan.

As a communications hub enjoying a high degree of freedom, Hong Kong is a major center of publications with circulation throughout the Southeast- and East-Asian region. The premier publication of this type is the weekly *Far Eastern Economic Review.* *Asiaweek,* begun in 1975, is a general-interest newsmagazine. Publications with special interests range from art *(Arts of Asia)* and travel *(Orientations)* to computers *(Computer Age)* and communications and advertising *(Media).* The colony is also headquarters for the *Asian Wall Street Journal* and the *Asia Magazine,* a four-color supplement that is distributed to various newspapers in the region. The Chinese edition of the *Reader's Digest* is edited and published in Hong Kong, while the editorial pages of both *Time* and *Newsweek* are transmitted by satellite for printing and distribution from Hong Kong. The most recent publication to take advantage of satellite transmission is the Paris-based *International Herald-Tribune,* which began printing in Hong Kong in September 1980.

A rapidly expanding area of publications is directed to the People's Republic of China. With the opening of the country to more outside information, many new periodicals have sprung up to cater to this market. In addition, many links and cooperative arrangements have been forged between media institutions in Hong Kong and on the mainland.

The opening of the People's Republic has, at the same time, greatly diminished the number and importance of "China watchers." Some of the larger institutions, such as the Union Research Institute, and publications, such as *China News Analysis,* still maintain an active publishing program, but many other monitoring and research services, such as the United States Consulate General, have cut back drastically, and wire services now staff Peking directly.

Economic Framework

Although the colony, to some extent, shared the economic problems of the rest of the world in the latter half of the 1970s, in general, it is true that "when the rest of the world suffers from recession, Hong Kong has only a hiccup." Both the domestic economy—measured by the rise in the standard of living—and international trading remain strong.

This is reflected in the growing advertising revenue of larger newspapers. Smaller newspapers continue to fight for the increasingly smaller part of the advertising revenue.

In this free-market setting most newspapers are owned by individuals while the largest are owned by corporations. There is little concentration of ownership. Some of the smaller papers have substantial financial backing from interested outsiders. Even publicly quoted papers are required to publish only a minimum of financial information under Hong Kong statutes.

The largest and most far-reaching chain is the New York-based Dow-Jones Company. In Hong Kong, it has financial interests in the *Asia Magazine,* the *Asian Wall Street Journal, Far Eastern Economic Review* and the *South China Morning Post.* In the region, it has links and financial interests with the *Straits Times* group in Singapore, the *New Straits Times* in Malaysia, the *Bangkok Post* and the *Borneo Bulletin* in east Malaysia.

The major regional chain is the Sing Tao group. The chain was formed in 1938 by Au Boon-haw with the original purpose of carrying advertising for his Tiger Balm, a Chinese proprietary salve which he manufactured and distributed. The group now owns the *Hong Kong Standard, Sing Tao Jih Pao,* the tabloid *Star* and Chinese-language *Star (Xing Bao).* Not only does the parent company have interests in other papers in the region, but it also publishes *Sing Tao Jih Pao* in North America.

Transmitting copy by satellite, *Sing Tao* is printed in San Francisco, Vancouver, Toronto and New York, where some local news is added. These editions find high readership among newly arrived immigrants, most of whom have recently arrived from Hong Kong or southern China. The North American editions also include the weekly Sunday supplement, *Sing Tao Weekly,* printed in Hong Kong and also distributed there.

A free port, Hong Kong has no restrictive policies on the importation of newsprint. In 1980 the average price was about HK $2,300 (US $460)* per ton.

More than 90 percent of the newspapers are sold on newsstands. Home distribution accounts for relatively little of the circulation. Morning papers are bought by the earliest workers on the way to work, while the other papers are bought by office workers during lunch or on the way home.

The cost of most Chinese papers is about six cents. The broadsheet English papers sell for 20 cents, and the tabloid English papers sell for 10 cents.

Advertisers have relatively little influence

---

*Local currency throughout the rest of this chapter has been converted into U.S. equivalents at the rate of HK$5-US$1.

on broad editorial policies of the larger papers, but the problems of writers and columnists mentioning names of products and accepting gifts remains. On the smaller papers, the problems of influence from outsiders is much less, as most of them were started in the first place to advocate certain points of view.

The Hong Kong Journalists Association is the journalists' union, but until recently it did not actively engage in pursuing demands for increased salaries or better working conditions.

The salary structure is a two-tier system. At the bottom of the system are the smaller Chinese papers, which may pay high school graduates $100 a month and journalism graduates of a local university about twice as much. The second tier is composed of the English papers and larger Chinese papers. On the larger English papers, a senior journalist may make $2,000 per month.

Only about 20 percent of the local university journalism graduates work on Chinese papers, preferring to go into advertising or public relations, or work with the Government Information Services—all of which pay significantly higher salaries. Some papers prefer to hire graduates from universities on Taiwan, who, since their degrees are not recognized in Hong Kong, cannot work for the government.

The 10 largest Chinese newspapers have more than 80 percent of the readership, with the top three accounting for about 53 percent. The fastest-growing circulation belongs to the *Oriental Daily News.* Among the English newspapers, the *South China Morning Post* has about 75 percent of the readership of the four English papers.

Only a few smaller papers are still being printed by letterpress; most papers are printed offset. Due to the complexities of the Chinese language, none of the Chinese papers use computerized front-end systems, although some use Japanese phototypesetting machines to set camera-ready copy.

Press Laws

Legally, Hong Kong has one of the more restrictive sets of press laws. In practice, Hong Kong enjoys one of the freest press systems in the world.

Hong Kong is administered by the Hong Kong government and organized along lines traditional for a British colony. The local head of government is the governor, appointed by the Queen. The governor regulates the registration of local newspapers, distribution, any supplements to newspapers, the registration and control of printing presses, and the identification of journalists. He can also prohibit the importation of any publication. In practice, these broad powers are seldom used, and the Hong Kong papers enjoy an extremely high degree of freedom.

Newspapers are governed by three main regulations and ordinances: Control of Publications Consolidation Ordinance (1979), the Newspapers Registration and Distribution Regulations (1979) and the Printed Documents (Control) Regulations (1964).

Under the Control of Publications Consolidation Ordinance, it is illegal to print or publish "any publication" tending to induce people to "commit an offence" or to support or proselytize for secret societies or other organizations deemed "prejudicial to the security of the Colony" or to the "maintenance ...of public order or safety." "False news" is also prohibited. Newspapers may be suspended or deregistered and the proprietor or printer may be fined or imprisoned for violating any of these provisions.

All newspapers must be registered and either a $2,000 bond must be posted or two guarantors acceptable to the registrar of newspapers in the Home Affairs Office must be furnished. Newspapers are also required to pay a $20 fee annually.

Printing presses are also required to be licensed, as are news agencies and newspaper distributors.

Other ordinances prohibit any writing of seditious matter, publication of any intimidation or libel. Medical advertisements for the prevention, relief or cure of a long list of diseases—such as kidney stones, smallpox, venereal disease and trachoma—are also prohibited. Advertisements relating to abortion are not allowed. Neither photography or sketching is permitted in courtrooms, or of anyone involved in court proceedings.

English law is closely followed, with alterations applicable to the colony. The judiciary is independent of both the executive and legislative organs of government. Cases may be appealed to the Privy Council in London.

Censorship

The colony does not censor newspapers, but the system of licensing and bonds could be used to control the press. The governor does appoint censors for cinema, television, radio, posters, billboards and other means of mass communication.

There is no "D-notice" system as in England. Editors and publishers have occasionally agreed, through the "old boy" network, on deemphasizing or not covering certain stories. In the past this usually involved coverage of the "two Chinas." The Hong Kong government wants to remain as neutral as possible and local journalists know how far they can go in criticizing or advocating a specific policy.

A case of censorship that was not initiated by government occurred in 1976 when the Chinese University of Hong Kong suspended the campus newspaper, the *Shatin News,* for publishing an investigative report on the fate of university graduates.

State-Press Relations

The Government Information Services (GIS) not only fulfills the expected purpose of sending out news releases and setting up press meetings with government officials but is also directed to convey to government what the public is thinking.

The GIS has three sections: the news division, the public relations division and the publicity division. In 1979 the Information Branch of the government Secretariat was created to coordinate the work of the GIS, Radio-Television Hong Kong and the Television and Entertainment Licensing Authority.

The news division is responsible for channeling government information to the media. A daily information bulletin is published and a teletype service is offered to newspapers and broadcasting stations. The Chinese papers subscribe to a complementary facsimile service. A 24-hour telephone inquiry service is maintained to answer questions from any journalist about government affairs or policy.

The public relations division assists visiting correspondents and works with news agencies and correspondents based in Hong Kong, and, further, creates an image of modern Hong Kong in potential overseas markets. This section makes the GIS different from many government information operations. As a colony, Hong Kong has no elected government and lacks any formal opposition in the parliamentary sense. To

keep government informed of the public mood and desires, a daily newssheet of items translated from Chinese newspapers is distributed to government officials in addition to a weekly review of Chinese editorials and press comment. The division also publishes occasional Green Papers to elicit comment before major policy changes are implemented. It also publishes a fortnightly newspaper in Chinese, *Hong Kong News Digest,* to keep Chinese living in the United Kingdom informed of events in the colony, especially the New Territories.

The publicity section is essentially a government advertising agency. It produces editorial matter such as books, fact sheets and films for documentation and briefings. It also handles the publicity for public events like the Fine Arts Festival and for such government campaigns as Keep Hong Kong Clean, Fight Crime, Community Against Drugs and Road Safety Campaign. This section is also in charge of trade advertising campaigns in other countries.

During natural or civil emergencies, the GIS further serves as a communications center.

The GIS has information officers with 20 government departments. In the past, local journalists have accused the GIS of hindering, rather than helping, in getting news from government sources, or of giving special opportunities to the government-funded Radio-Television Hong Kong.

There is little direct influence by the press on broad government policy. The English-language papers, especially, have extended letters-to-the-editor pages, where the merits and implications of policy are debated at length. The Chinese papers, read by the majority of Hong Kong residents, place much less emphasis on editorials and editorial comment.

Newspapers have done little investigative reporting in the past, although some are beginning to give reporters time and support to tackle complicated subjects.

In a press situation as effectively free as Hong Kong's, suspension or confiscation of newspapers is rare. The last such acts occurred in the late 1960s, when the Cultural Revolution in China spilled over and the colony suffered riots and demonstrations. Several papers—*Ta Kung Pao, Wen Wei Pao* and the *New Evening Post (Xin Wan Bao)*— were suspended for a short time.

No publications have been banned and no journalists have been jailed. Papers have been fined, however, for violating the regulations governing obscenity.

Attitude Toward Foreign Media

Due to the lack of controls over the media, and especially foreign correspondents, Hong Kong has become home base to more and more reporters covering the general area.

Special visas are not needed by correspondents; accreditation is required only when the journalist desires to have a mail box at the GIS to receive all releases and handouts. Prior cable approval is not required, nor have any correspondents been banned or jailed.

The government has the power to ban foreign publications, but this power has rarely, if ever, been used.

Little foreign propaganda is directed at Hong Kong, although the government is sensitive to the image that Hong Kong presents abroad through the media, because of its dependence on free trade and the desire to portray a stable, progressive appearance to potential investors and businessmen.

The Hong Kong chapter of the International Press Institute is vigorous. The Chinese Press Institute is headquartered in Hong Kong, and holds an international conference of Chinese newspapers every other year.

Among institutions that maintain bureas or offices in the Colony are: *Der Spiegel, The Economist*, McGraw-Hill, *Newsweek*, Time-Life, *Asahi Shimbun, Baltimore Sun, Dong-A Ilbo, Financial Times* (London), *Herald & Weekly Times* of Melbourne, *Los Angeles Times*, Mainichi Newspapers, *Miami Herald, The New York Times, Yomiuri Shimbun* and *The Times* of London.

News Agencies

With the exception of the teletype link between the GIS and the papers and broadcasting stations, Hong Kong has no domestic news agency.

Most major foreign agencies maintain bureaus in the colony. Both Reuters and United Press International maintain regional headquarters, while one of the three main offices of Agence France Press is located in Hong Kong. New China News Agency (Xinhua News Agency) maintains its largest office outside the mainland on the island. The Republic of China's Central News Agency also staffs a bureau.

Other agencies represented in Hong Kong are: Antara, The Chinese Overseas News Agency (Taiwan), Jiji Press News Agency, Kyodo News Service, National Catholic News Service.

Radio and television services represented in Hong Kong are: the American Broadcasting Corporation, All India Radio, the Australian Broadcasting Commission, British Broadcasting Corporation, Columbia Broadcasting System, German Radio and Television, Korean Broadcasting System, Nippon Hoso Kyokai (NHK), National Broadcasting Company, Radio New Zealand, Swedish National Radio and Visnews.

During the late 1960s and early 1970s many correspondents used Hong Kong as a base to cover the Vietnam war. Since then, there has been a precipitous decline in resident correspondents.

Electronic News Media

The commissioner for television and entertainment licensing administers the Television Ordinance, under which the two television stations are licensed. Both stations are commercial and transmit in both Chinese (mainly Cantonese) and English.

Hong Kong's first television was started in 1957. Of the two current companies presently operating, Television Broadcasts Ltd. (TVB) is the oldest, having started in 1967. TVB broadcasts 133 hours per week on the Chinese channel (Jade) and 82 hours per week on the English channel (Pearl) and has about 70 percent of the audience for each service. More than two million people may watch the daily, locally produced drama and variety shows on TVB-Jade.

Rediffusion (Hong Kong) Ltd. started the first cable television in 1957. It reorganized in 1973, and the new Rediffusion Television Ltd. (RTV) applied for and was granted a license for a second dual-channel service. RTV-1 (Chinese) started transmission in 1973 and the English service started in 1974. The most popular programs on RTV-2 are imported daytime serials and dramas.

Compared to the more than 2 million viewers of the daily, locally produced drama and variety shows in Chinese, fewer than 100,000 people view English-language programs. On the English networks, the most popular programs are news and weather.

Part of the requirements of licensing is that the commercial stations transmit eight hours of educational television to schools each school day. Programs are produced by the government Educational Television Service.

Hong Kong has two public radio stations, both broadcasting in Chinese and English. One is a commercial station, the other a government station.

The government station, Radio Hong Kong, broadcasts almost 600 hours of programs each week on five channels. Since most of the Hong Kong population speaks Cantonese, the station broadcasts mostly in Cantonese rather than Mandarin, the official language of China. There are two channels of Chinese, two in English, and one providing a dual language service. Since 1967 there have been no license fees for radio or television receivers. The station is financed from general revenue. No commercials are carried.

Commercial radio broadcasts 19 hours a day on each of two Chinese channels and one English channel. Under terms of the license issued by the government, the only newscasts permitted are those from the GIS, because of the sensitive political situation surrounding Hong Kong. During the 1970s this requirement was very loosely enforced. The license also limits commercial announcements to 10 percent of program time. Content is the responsibility of the station.

The British Forces Broadcasting Services operates a station designed to serve the particular requirements of British and Gurkha forces stationed in the New Territories. The station is on the air almost 80 hours a week, broadcasting mainly in Nepali.

Education & Training

The largest journalism program is found in the Department of Communications at Hong Kong Baptist College, a private religious university. The first students graduated in 1971. The college graduates about 60 journalism students every year in four sequences: journalism (Chinese and English stream), radio and television, film, and public relations and advertising. Students in the department publish a weekly student newspaper, alternating Chinese and English editions, broadcast a closed-circuit radio-television station and run an advertising agency.

The Center for Communication Studies at the Chinese University of Hong Kong was formed in 1974 and coordinates a master's degree program in communications and an undergraduate program in journalism. The Center graduates about 15 to 20 students a year. Hong Kong Shue Yan College, started in 1976, graduates about 30 to 40 students in journalism every year in its undergraduate program. Chu Hai College in Kowloon has a department of journalism, which graduates about a dozen students a year, but the degrees are not "recognized" by the Hong Kong government.

Many local newspapers have internships available to journalism students. Recently, the Hong Kong government announced the establishment of a Journalism Training Board to look into the various facets of journalism training and recommend future directions.

The very active Chinese Language Press Institute has its headquarters in Hong Kong and meets every other year. The Foreign Correspondents' Club plays an important part in local journalism. Although basically a social club, it offers the large corps of itinerant correspondents a place to gather.

Other associations in Hong Kong are the Hong Kong Chinese Press Association, the Hong Kong Press Club and the Newspaper Society of Hong Kong.

Summary

Just as Hong Kong has been a commercial gateway to China for more than a century, it

Percentage Distribution of Radio Programs (1972, est.)

Entertainment	78%
News	10
Education	3
Other	6
Advertisements	3

Percentage Distribution of Television Programs (1972, est.)

Entertainment	73%
News	14
Education	4
Other	5
Advertisements	4
Percentage of television programs imported: 50%	

is now becoming a media gateway. More and more agencies and organizations are using the colony as a base for entering China. In the 1980s this relatively new and potentially very lucrative aspect will become a larger part of the Hong Kong media scene as the mainland uses media to encourage industrialization, modernization and tourism.

Local newspapers will see more rationalization and modernization. Even though two-thirds of the reading population read a daily paper, there remains a dearth of very small, marginally viable newspapers for the population. Because of rising affluence, overall circulation will continue to rise as more people find it possible to buy several papers, and separate households, requiring their own papers, increase faster than the overall rate of population growth. Pass-along readerships is declining.

Newspapers will be forced to find better ways to distribute the product and to use more color printing in order to appeal to advertisers. Some advertising money will be inevitably diverted to the posters of the new rapid transit system.

Magazines remain an underdeveloped area in Hong Kong. There are few magazines with reasonable circulation dealing with serious issues. The six magazines with the largest circulation emphasize entertainment.

Hong Kong will retain its status as a center of regional publishing and home base for many correspondents covering Asia for regional and international publications. Not only are there communication advantages in this arrangement, but there is also stability and little government control of press or correspondents.

CHRONOLOGY

1975	*Asiaweek* begins publication.	**1979**	Journalism Training Board set up.
1976	*Asian Wall Street Journal* starts publishing.		*Sun* begins publication.
	Chinese University of Hong Kong suspends campus paper.	**1980**	*Time* begins satellite transmission of pages.
1978	Commercial Television closes.		*International Herald-Tribune* starts publishing.

BIBLIOGRAPHY

Allen, Charles L. *Communication Patterns in Hong Kong.* Hong Kong, 1970.

"An Institution Turns '30.'" *Asiaweek,* March 31, 1978, p. 46.

Anson, Robert Sam. "The Wall Street Journal's Asian Adventure." *Institutional Investor,* October 1979, p. 201.

Asian Press & Media Directory. Hong Kong, annual.

Chan, Yue-ping. "A Study on *Sing Tao Jih Pao* and its Position in Hong Kong Journalism." Master's thesis, University of Missouri, 1962.

Chang Chih Kang, ed. *Journal of Journalism and Communication Society 1979.* Hong Kong, 1979 (?).

Chang Kuo-sin. *A Survey of the Chinese Language Daily Press.* Hong Kong, 1968.

Cheung, Wellington W. K. *"Kung Sheung Daily News* and Its Position in Hong Kong Journalism." Master's Thesis, University of Missouri, 1958.

Chu, Godwin C., ed. *Research on Mass Communication in Taiwan and Hong Kong: Selected Abstracts.* Honolulu, 1977.

Clayton, Charles C. "Hong Kong." In *The Asian Newspapers' Revolution,* ed. John A. Lent. Ames, Iowa, 1971.

Donald, W. H. "The Press," in *Twentieth Century Impressions of Hongkong, Shanghai, and Other Treaty Ports of China,* ed. Arnold Wright. London, 1908.

Gigot, Paul. "Asia's War of Words (and Ads)," *Far Eastern Economic Review,* July 4, 1980, pp. 87–91.

Guild, Frazer. "Better, Brighter Papers But Still a Lack of Well-Trained Journalists." *Hongkong Standard 30th Anniversary Magazine,* March 1, 1979, pp. 34–36.

Hong Kong. *Control of Publications Consolidation Ordinance, Chapter 268.* Hong Kong, 1979.

Kao, Irving Ke-yung, "Ta Kung Pao: Before and After Communism." Master's thesis, University of Missouri, 1951.

Lent, John A. *Asian Mass Communication: A Comprehensive Bibliography and Supplement.* Philadelphia, 1975, 1978.

Liu, Melinda. "How to be First With the News." *Far Eastern Economic Review,* December 22, 1978, pp. 21-23.

Mitchell, Robert Edward. "How Hong Kong Newspapers Have Responded to 15 Years of Rapid Social Change." *Asian Survey,* September 1969, pp. 669-81.

Moss, Peter. "Unaccustomed as We Were to Public Speaking." *Media* (Hong Kong), July 1980, pp. 19-20.

Nathan, P. Viswa. "The Difference Between the Freedom to Publish and a Free Press." *Hongkong Standard 30th Anniversary Magazine,* March 1, 1979, pp. 37-38.

O'Neill, Michael. "China Mail, 1845-1974." *Media* (Hong Kong), September 1974, pp. 22-25.

Parker, Elliott S., and Parker, Emelia M. *Asian Journalism: A Selected Bibliography of Sources on Journalism in China and Southeast Asia.* Metuchen, N.J., 1979.

Shen, James C. Y. *The Law and Mass Media in Hong Kong.* Hong Kong, 1972.

"The Trib is Aiming to Beat the Clock." *Media* (Hong Kong), June 1980, p. 14.

Tsui, Anthony. "Hong Kong's Strong Preference for Local Productions." *Media Asia,* 1975, pp. 117-21.

Yu, Timothy L. M., ed. *Mass Communication in Hong Kong and Macao: An Annotated Bibliography.* Singapore, 1976.

HUNGARY

by Paul Underwood

BASIC DATA

Population: 10,727,000
Area: 92,981 sq. km. (35,890 sq. mi.)
GNP: 609.6 billion florints (US$32 billion) (1978, est.)
Literacy Rate: 97%
Language(s): Hungarian, German, Rumanian, Serbo-Croat
Number of Dailies: 27
  Aggregate Circulation: 2,585,000
  Circulation per 1,000: 243
Number of Nondailies: 86
  Aggregate Circulation: 5,820,400
  Circulation per 1,000: 547

Number of Periodicals: 898
Number of Radio Stations: 3
Number of Television Stations: 1
Number of Radio Receivers: 2.59 million
  Radio Receivers per 1,000: 241
Number of Television Sets: 2,667,000
  Television Sets per 1,000: 249
Total Annual Newsprint Consumption: 45,000 metric tons
Per Capita Newsprint Consumption: 4.2 kg. (9.24 lb.)
Total Newspaper Ad Receipts: NA
  As % of All Ad Expenditures: NA

Background & General Characteristics

Hungary is the smallest of the Eastern European Soviet-bloc nations, both in area and population. Its more than 10 million people are spread over an area slightly smaller than the state of Indiana. Although the north and west are hilly, most of the countryside is aptly described by the picturesque old peasant saying: "Stand on a pumpkin and see Budapest."

Budapest is the capital and the center of trade and industry as well as government. The city was formed in the 19th century by the union of Buda, the old royal capital on the west bank of the Danube, with Pest, the commercial market town that had grown up on the opposite bank. The city boasts more than two million inhabitants, about a fifth of the country's total.

More than 95 percent of the population is Magyar (Hungarian). There are small German, Slovak, Yugoslav and Romanian minorities. Literacy is about 98 percent. The per capita income is just over $2,000 a year, which puts Hungary in the mid-range of Soviet-bloc nations, and her people are able to enjoy a fairly wide assortment of consumer goods.

As in all USSR-dominated countries, the media in Hungary are organized on the Soviet model, centrally controlled and directed to serve the interests of the Hungarian Socialist Workers (Communist) Party and the state. However, since the early 1960s the comparatively relaxed policies of Party chief Janos Kadar have given the press greater freedom from constraints than is characteristic of the rest of the bloc, with the exception of Poland.

The history of Hungary began in the winter of A.D. 895-96, when a group of Magyar tribes—tradition says there were seven—under the leadership of a chief named Arpad crossed the Carpathian Mountains and established themselves in the Middle Danube basin. A Turki people, the Magyars had originally lived east of the Ural Mountains but had wandered, or been pushed, from that homeland down to just north of the Caspian Sea. Under pressure from other migrating nations, these seven tribes moved westward, finally reaching the broad Danubian plains that had been left virtually deserted as a result of barbarian invasions and wars.

From this strategic heartland, the Magyars ravaged Europe for more than 50 years, until the Holy Roman Emperor annihilated one of their armies and reorganized the empire's Eastmark (now Austria) as a bastion against them. Chastened, the Magyars settled down to build up their new lands and gradually deserted their pagan faith for the Roman Catholic form of Christianity.

Their first great king, Stephen I, who came to the throne in 997, was the real founder of the Hungarian kingdom. He not only abolished the old tribal organization but established direct contact with Pope Sylvester II, who sent him a special crown; it eventually came to be the symbol of both the throne and the whole nation.

With Christianity came the monastic orders, particularly the Benedictines, who were given vast estates by the king. The monks became the nation's teachers. They cleared the land, introduced modern agricultural techniques, invented a Latin alphabet for the Magyar language and generally served as a Westernizing yeast in the country's developing culture.

Despite recurring wars, Hungary grew in size and power. Immigrants were welcomed, and often given special privileges. Among these were large groups of Germans who settled in the border areas of Transylvania and built the famous Seibenburgen (Seven Cities), which still retain a definite German flavor. Early in the 13th Century the king granted a charter of liberties similar to England's Magna Charta. Known as the Golden Bull, it has ever since been considered a cornerstone of Hungarian law and government.

However, the 13th Century also witnessed the frightful Mongol invasion of 1241-42, which left the country ravaged and in many areas almost depopulated. But although normal life soon resumed and prosperity returned, an even greater threat began to appear to the south, as the Turks expanded their empire from Anatolia into the Balkans. One by one the various states of the Balkans fell under the Turkish yoke, until Hungary became the lone bastion of Western civilization against the Moslem tide.

Meanwhile Hungary's throne had become elective, each occupant being chosen by a vote of the nobles. A series of good choices enabled the nation to continue prospering despite the steady Turkish advance. This halcyon period culminated in the reign of Matthias Corvinus, who proved himself not only as a warrior but also as a patron of learning. King Matthias fostered education and the arts, founded universities—and also

arranged for the establishment of the country's first printing press. The maiden publishing venture of that press, the *Chronica Hungarorum,* issued in 1472, was followed by a variety of religious books, typical of the age.

But those days of Hungary's glory faded with Matthias's death. The next king was weak and the nobles did pretty much as they pleased. A large peasant revolt in 1514 was put down with great cruelty, leading to the virtual enslavement of the country. Then, 12 years later, the Turks struck, almost annihilating the Hungarians at the famous battle of Mohacs. Nothing could stop the Turkish armies from sweeping on to take Buda, the capital, before returning home.

The Hungarian king had been killed at Mohacs and a dispute arose immediately over the succession, one side supporting John Zapolya, ruler of Transylvania, the other, Ferdinand of Hapsburg. In the struggle, Ferdinand had the better of it until the Turks intervened again, on Zapolya's side. This time they not only took Buda but pushed on up the Danube to lay siege to Vienna. And although that assault failed, the three-way struggle continued off and on until 1533, when a treaty between the Turks and the Austrians divided the country. The Austrians took over the westernmost areas, while the Turks controlled the central and southern regions, with Transylvania in the east being set up as a autonomous principality under Turkish suzerainty.

For 150 years, the Turks ruled over the heart of Hungary. Printing had long since been banned and the history of the nation during this period remains virtually a blank. Once again, wide areas had become depopulated as the bloody struggle continued unceasingly in the border lands. It was not until the 17th Century that the tide of battle turned. The Turks were beaten back a second time—and for good—from the walls of Vienna, and Buda was also recaptured. The final peace treaty of 1699 left the Austrian Hapsburg emperor in possession of all Hungary.

But the triumph brought new conflicts in its wake. The Hapsburgs proved intent on a policy of Germanization that infuriated the Hungarians, who resisted fiercely. A long revolt ended with a truce in which the emperor generally recognized the ancient rights and privileges of the Magyars. Only at this time did a national press begin to appear.

Hungarian press historians consider a

publication called *Mercurius Hungaricus,* which was printed in Latin between 1705 and 1710, as the nations's first newspaper. However, other authorities reserve this title for a weekly, also in Latin, called *Nova Poseoniensis* ("Pozsony News"), which first appeared in 1721. (Pozsony is the Hungarian name for the city of Bratislava, which, although now in Czechoslovakia, was the Hungarian capital during the time the Turks ruled over most of Hungary.) But although the first newspaper published in Hungarian did not come out until 1780, the next few years saw the birth of a variety of Hungarian-language periodicals. However, most of these were actually published in Vienna or Pozsony, rather than Budapest.

At this time, Hungary was enjoying a period of relative freedom under the liberal-minded Hapsburg emperor Joseph II, who had abolished press censorship on taking the throne. But things changed all too soon and Joseph restored tight censorship, hampering development of a political press. Only literary annuals and some periodicals were generally left alone. A new struggle with Vienna was brewing, a struggle that was to culminate in the revolution of 1848. This ferment caused the birth of a number of short-lived but politically significant publications, including *Orsaggyulesi Tudositasok* ("Parliamentary Information"), a regular report of the proceedings of the Hungarian Diet published by Lajos Kossuth, who later led the 1848 uprising. Kossuth also founded a regular journal called *Pesti Hirlap* ("News of Pest") in the early 1840's. Although suppressed in 1845, it was reborn later and became one of Hungary's leading newspapers.

One of the first achievements of the 1848 revolution was the abolition of censorship and promulgation of a new press law. Although this law declared that anyone was free to publish and express his thoughts through the press, it required publishers to obtain a license, which could be had only on payment of a fairly sizable liability deposit. The law also barred agitation for forced change of religion or the constitution. This act remained in force until 1914.

The revolution also gave enormous impetus to press development. Only 33 Hungarian-language and 19 German-language periodicals were available in the country before March 1848, but shortly afterwards the total was 86—an increase of 34. But the eventual suppression of the revolution was a serious setback. Only nine of the new papers survived and journalism generally stagnated under Austrian occupation until 1867, when a compromise with Vienna set up the so-called Dual Monarchy, with Hungary as a separate state under the Hapsburg emperor. Now the Austrian restrictions were done away with and the press was once again relatively free. An even greater and longer-lasting expansion period commenced, and by 1906 a total of 1,787 periodicals were being published throughout the country, compared to the 1867 figure of only 109. In Budapest, a reader had his choice among 39 dailies—30 in Hungarian and nine in German. This period also witnessed the birth not only of the first inexpensive, large-circulation newspaper that earned most of its revenues from advertising, but of the sensational papers. And all this growth took place even though only a small part of the population was literate.

Most of the press at this time was concentrated in the Hungarian-speaking parts of the country. Hungary then included large areas of what are now parts of Yugoslavia, Czechoslovakia and Romania. The non-Hugarian peoples of these lands were subjected to a ferocious Magyarization drive, which in many cases included denying them the use of their own languages. As a result, newspapers in these areas were not only few but subject to severe restrictions and censorship.

At the onset of World War I in 1914, the Budapest government made certain changes in the 1848 press law—restricting freedoms to some degree—to help keep the opposition press in check. These were lifted following the 1918 revolution that declared Hungary an independent republic, but within only six months communists seized power. A Hungarian Soviet-style republic was proclaimed and a Moscow-type press system imposed, with centralized control. Many newspapers were seized or simply put out of business.

This regime, in its turn, lasted only a few months. It was overthrown by a counterrevolution led by Admiral Miklos Horthy, who proclaimed reestablishment of the monarchy, but without a king. Instead, supported by right-wing forces, he ruled as a personal dictator. Prior censorship was imposed. Communist papers were forced underground and a good part of the Social Democratic press was eliminated. Newspapers had to have permits from the government to operate and security forces maintained tight control over what was printed. Government did not merely have the legal power to proscribe or suspend any publication deemed detrimental to the state or the "national cause"; it controlled the newsprint supply and also used subsidies to keep papers in line. These subsidies came from a so-called "press fund" for which ministers did not have to account to Parliament. It was widely believed that even the nation's largest surviving Social Democratic paper, the well-regarded *Nepszava* ("People's Voice") received money from the "press fund."

All this took a heavy toll. Less than a third of the number of papers that had flourished before 1914 were still being published in 1921.

During succeeding years, the Horthy regime became more and more openly dictatorial, it carrying out successions of "purifications" of both publications and journalists. Most of the older papers were weeded out, one by one. In fact, only two independent dailies survived the last of these "purifications," which followed the Nazi occupation of the country in 1944.

Despite all the restrictions, the pre-World War II Hungarian press was probably the most diverse and most interesting in southeastern Europe. The Budapest papers—most of the Hungarian print media were published in the capital—represented a range of political interests unusual for the area. The principal independent daily, *Magyar Nemzet* ("Hungarian Nation"), was known throughout the continent, especially for its economic, sociological and historical articles. *Nepszava*'s reputation also extended beyond Hungary.

Hungary entered the war on the Axis side but was able to maintain her own institutions and a measure of freedom of action during the early years of the struggle. Nevertheless, the screws were tightened on the press. A decree published in October 1942 required papers to publish speeches and statements by government ministers in a prescribed way that involved the time of publication, position in the paper and even the type size. The end came in March 1944, when Hitler, having learned that Horthy officials were attempting to contact the Allies to surrender, occupied the country and installed a puppet government. It took months of hard fighting to clear Nazi troops from the country. Budapest, which underwent a winter-long siege, with the Germans entrenched in the Buda hills and Soviet forces in Pest, was devastated.

In early 1945 Soviet troops finally succeeded in expelling the Nazis, and a coalition of old political parties set up a provisional government. However, control was actually in the hands of the Soviet occupation forces. A new electoral law, approved later in 1945, set the stages for elections to choose a National Assembly. Six political parties, ranging from the Conservatives to the Communists, participated in the campaign. The centrist Smallholders' party won about half the five million votes cast, while the Communists and Social Democrats, the two leftist groups, polled only about a million and a half together. A coalition government was now formed with nine members of the Smallholders and four each from the Social Democratic and Communist parties. Arpad Szakasits of the Social Democrats and Matyas Rakosi of the Communists became deputy premiers. In February 1946 the newly elected National Assembly declared Hungary a republic.

During the next few months, the Communists appeared content to remain simply part of the governing coalition. However, early in 1947 charges of a plot to overthrow the government led to a campaign—masterminded by the left—against the Smallholders. In the midst of the ensuing turmoil Rakosi demanded new elections, which were held that August. Again, despite widespread intimidation, the Communists and the Social Democrats—who had now become integrated—failed to win an absolute majority. (The Communists themselves received just 22 percent of the vote.) It was the last such election in the country. In 1948 the Communists forced a merger with the Social Democrats, many of whose former leaders were expelled. Later that same year, Zoltan Tildy, a Smallholder who had been named president of the nation, was forced to resign. Step by step, a complete Soviet-style regime took power. A constitution, promulgated in 1949, declared Hungary a "people's democracy" and, in effect, a one-party state.

Meanwhile the press had burgeoned once again. In the days immediately following the war old newspapers reappeared, new ones were opened. At first, the provisional government allowed only four papers to be published, one for each of the parties in the coalition, but others, including a reborn *Magyar Nemzet,* came later. The tone of most of the reporting and comment was moderate, even in the Communist periodicals. But this soon changed. Within a short time most papers had become stridently pro-Soviet, anti-Western. Although a few, including *Magyar Nemzet,* managed to resist the pressure for a while longer, they too were eventually forced into the Communist mold. By the end of 1948, the last remnants of press freedom had been eliminated. Ownership of all printing plants had been "transferred to the people," meaning, of course, to Communist control. The press had been forced into the role of the regime's principal medium of mass propaganda.

As of February, 1953, 22 dailies and 88 weeklies were being published in the country, with a total combined circulation of more than three million copies. Most important was the official Communist daily, then called *Szabad Nep* ("Free People"), which was modeled closely on Moscow's *Pravda.* All the other papers took their lead from it—which could hardly have been otherwise, since all operated under the tight control of the Information Bureau, an arm of the government's Council of Ministers, and under the supervision of the Agitation and Propaganda Section of the Party's Central Committee.

In Hungary, as in other Soviet-bloc nations, the harsh police rule and difficult economic conditions sparked unrest in the wake of Stalin's death in 1953. Led by *Irodalmi Ujsag* ("Literary Gazette"), the journal of the Hungarian Writers Association, both writers and journalists began to protest against censorship. The complaints increased as the party vacillated between repression and conciliation. Things reached such a state that in 1956 the leadership of the Federation of Journalists planned an assembly aimed openly at confronting "the system which hitherto has been based on lies." But the assembly never took place: the Party had turned back to repression. Budapest and the nation rose in revolt. For 10 bloody days, freedom was the word. New papers appeared, uncensored. But then Soviet tanks rumbled back into the capital, reimposed tight controls and put Janos Kadar in power as the new Party chief.

Journalists received a great deal of the blame for the uprising; one high government official went so far as to say they were primarily responsible. And many paid a high price: arrests, imprisonments, deportations to Russia, even death. Trials were still taking place as late as 1958. Incidents reflecting continued resistance on the part of newsmen and others continued for some time afterward, but it was in vain. The old rules were emphasized once again in 1958 by a top government official, who warned: "The press has the duty of defending the policies of the Communist party and the interests of Socialist construction against their enemies and against those who do not carry out the policy of the party or who distort it. The press thus has the duty of criticizing those who seek to retard our progress. There is no place for any other kind of criticism in our regime."

This warning came on the heels of a purge of journalists that cut their number by about one thousand, as well as a reconstitution of the press's professional organizations. Nevertheless, despite these actions and harsh words, conditions for the press did not go all the way back to the grim times before 1953. The revolution had a profound effect on the Communist Party and government and, therefore, on the press as well.

The Kadar regime realized that it badly needed to build public support, and that this would require some freedom of expression. At the same time, it was impelled by its situation to try to identify in the public mind the future of the Party with that of the nation. Control over the mass media was seen as one means to that end. The result has been a degree of tolerance that is felt, not just in the media but throughout the society. And while cautious but firm control is retained over all communication, particularly the newspapers, the Hungarian press has become lively, interesting and even entertaining. (Some independent papers, notably two Catholic publications, received printing licenses early.) There has been a marked decline in dogmatic, ideological writing. The regime appears to feel that a certain amount of free exchange is healthy, as long as it is kept within prescribed limits. But criticism of the Soviet Union is outside those limits, as is anything that might be considered to be advocating change in Hungary's Communist system. In fact, a 1972 revision of the constitution added new, more restrictive phrases in connection with freedom of speech and the press.

Hungary has 30 daily newspapers, eight of which are printed in Budapest, the others in provincial capitals or industrial centers. Most of the Budapest papers circulate nationally. All major papers are printed in Hungarian, although one relatively small-circulation Budapest daily, called *Daily News/Neuste Nachrichten,* appears in both English and German editions. There is also an English-language edition of a paper called *Vilaggazdasag* ("World Economy"). In addition, each of the national minority groups—German, Slovak, Serbian and Romanian—has a publication in its own language. (All these are weeklies except the Romanian, which is fortnightly.) There are also at least 12 religious publications representing the Roman Catholics, Greek Orthodox, Baptists, Calvinists, Lutherans, Jews and Unitarians. All, of course, are subject to Party controls.

In the Hungarian context, the Western distinctions of elite, popular and yellow journalism are meaningless. All papers are serious publications, emphasizing political, economic and cultural news. The differences between them are largely a result of editorial perceptions as to the interests of the specific audiences for which each is designed.

The largest and most important Hungarian paper, *Nepsabadsag* ("People's Freedom"), is the party's principal organ, setting the tone for the rest of the press. *Nepsabadsag* is actually the former *Szabad Nep,* revamped and renamed after 1956. Its circulation is listed at 810,000. Following in importance (by circulation) are *Nepsava* ("People's Voice"), published by the national Trade Union Council (300,000); *Esti Hirlap* ("Evening Herald"), sponsored by Budapest's Party committee (251,000); *Magyar Nemzet,* published by the Patriotic People's Front—the Party's mass organization—as a paper for intellectuals (127,000); *Nepsports* ("People's Sport") (170,000); and *Magyar Hirlap* ("Hungarian Herald"), a relatively new paper, established in 1968 as the government's organ (just over 50,000). Of these top six, which account for about 70 percent of the country's total circulation, *Nepsabadsag, Nepsava* and *Magyar Nemzet* are probably the most influential.

None of the provincial dailies has more than 100,000 circulation. The largest is *Dunantuli Naplo* ("Transdanubian Journal") of Baranya County with 86,000. Ten others print over 50,000 copies daily, eight circulate between 25,000 and 50,000 and only two print fewer than 25,000.

Most dailies run six to 12 pages, usually broadsheet size although some are tabloids. (Only one, *Esti Hirlap,* is specifically an evening paper.) Most also publish six days a week, printing on Sundays but skipping Mondays. The Sunday issues, which generally boast larger circulations than the weekday editions, are also larger in size, having special sections dealing with cultural and social questions.

There is also a wide variety of special interest publications, including at least nine literary reviews and 57 trade union journals. The weekly *Radio es Televizio Usag* ("Radio and Television News") has the largest circulation of any nondaily periodical. Other leading weeklies include *Nok Lapja* ("Women's Magazine"), an illustrated publication produced by the National Council of Hungarian Women; *Orszag-Vilag* ("Country and World"), an illustrated paper of the Hungarian-Soviet Friendship Society; *Ludas Matyi,* a highly popular satirical journal; and *Elet es Irodalom* ("Life and Literature"), an important literary and political review.

Economic Framework

The Communist takeover in Hungary brought the imposition of a typical Soviet-style centralized economic system. Its shortcomings began to appear in the 1950s—and helped cause the 1956 revolt. The post-1956 regime spent some years trying to adjust the system to the realities, a process that culminated in 1968 with the introduction of what was called the New Economic Model (NEM). Under NEM, the state retained final say, but economic enterprises were free to decide for themselves on such aspects of production as output and number of employes. The aim of the restructuring was to rationalize the economy by making it responsive to market imperatives—in other words, to let the market be the deciding factor. The hope was that this would enable the nation to participate more effectively in international trade, particularly with the West. Hungary is particularly dependent on trade, not only because of its size but also because—except for bauxite and some low-quality coal—it lacks industrial raw materials. The reform has worked well enough to lead Hungarian economic experts to predict that the nation's currency will become fully convertible sometime in the 1980s.

Although the new system is unique in the Soviet bloc, it has had little impact on the media, largely because of the continued importance of public financing in their operations. The Kadar regime has consistently argued that culture is one aspect of life that should not be determined solely by the market. About the only important change the system has brought to the media has been an increased interest in advertising as a source of revenue. This became evident when the regime, as part of its effort to mesh domestic prices with world market levels, increased distribution charges as well as prices of paper and other materials.

However, the regime also limits the amount of space or time that can be devoted to advertising. A Hungarian study notes that although *Nepsava* was losing money in 1971 it was not allowed more advertising space than it had been in 1970.

Nevertheless, in comparison with other Soviet-bloc capitals, Budapest seems a sea of ads. Neon signs and mass-transit poster ads are close to Western European levels. Newspapers carry whole pages, mainly of the small, classified type. Advertising also exists on radio and television, although to a much smaller extent and limited to specific time periods. Most of the obvious advertising is for consumer products, including such Western items as Pepsi-Cola and Chanel perfumes, but industrial marketing is said to be a growing field.

The director general of the Hungarian Advertising Agency—known as Mahir—reporting in 1979 on the activities of his enterprise during the previous year, noted 6,500 ads for radio, broadcast over a total of 3,200 minutes; 160 30-second TV spots, three million copies of advertising posters, eight million circulars and prospectuses, and newspaper ads worth a total of 28 million forints ($1.47 million).

Mahir, it should be added, is not a monopoly: all enterprises have the right to advertise their own products. Moreover, editors are responsible for determining what is acceptable as far as advertising is concerned; there is no censorship. But the realities of control are such that none of the media can greatly expand the proportion of space or time now devoted to ads. Thus Mahir handles about a third of all advertising in Hungary.

No private person may own a newspaper or broadcast facility. Broadcast is a government monopoly and newspapers can only be published by political or social organizations. All media institutions in Hungary are either publicly financed, as in radio and television, or function as part of a larger economic enterprise, as with most national newspapers. The latter are produced by publishing houses, which are also responsible for other types of publications: magazines, journals and even some books.

Since the 1968 reform, each enterprise as a whole has to be profit-minded—except, in most cases, for the individual newspaper. As the above mentioned Hungarian study explained, the publishing house "plays the role

of a 'buffer' which absorbs possible economic shocks and enables the editorial boards to work free of market considerations, directing their full energy toward the realization of cultural and communication policies.

As in other Soviet-bloc countries, the press is highly concentrated. One government publishing enterprise is responsible for 30 percent of all the country's newspapers and periodicals. If the operations of similar organizations controlled by the Party, the trade union organization and the official youth organization are added, the total output represents 98 percent of the Hungarian periodical press.

Distribution—in the hands of the postal authorities—is even more concentrated. More than 80 percent of all Hungarian dailies are sold on a subscription basis.

Hungary produces only a relatively small amount of newsprint, so most must be imported, chiefly from the other Soviet-bloc countries or from Scandinavia. Both the import and allocation of supplies are controlled by the government. Prices now are generally at world levels.

The Hungarian Journalist Association has about 3,000 members, including all professionals working on regular newspapers. About 25 percent of them are women. In addition, print news people belong to the Printing, Paper and Press Workers Union, while most of the broadcast staffs are members of the Art Workers Union. The leaderships of all three organizations meet periodically to assure coordination of efforts.

Historically, newspaper salaries have tended to be low, particularly when compared with those of managers and technical people in industry. When incentive bonuses became common under the NEM reform, they were so large in relation to wages that they caused considerable fluctuations in income and a good deal of discontent. As a result, in the early 1970s all wages were raised and bonuses reduced to even out income.

Since then, journalists, like most others in the society, have received additional wage adjustments as the government has sought to balance incomes with price increases necessary to coordinate the internal economy with world prices. In this process, prices of all periodicals have gone up but, in the case of newspapers, not high enough to cover the increased costs. It is widely assumed that all papers are subsidized to some degree in one way or another.

The new electronic technology in printing

is just beginning to affect Hungarian journalism. The national news agency, Magyar
Tavirati Iroda (MTI) began installing the
first such system in the country—and the
first anywhere in the Soviet bloc—in 1979. At
that time, the trade magazine *Magyar Import* reported that similar systems were also
to be installed in "the central press organizations," presumably meaning the big publishing houses that produce the national
dailies, as well as in broadcast operations.

Press Laws

Unlike the 1949 constitution, which declared all media the property of the state, the
1972 revision puts only radio and television
in that category. The earlier version also
guaranteed freedom of speech and the press,
even though the reality was something else.
Now, both are guaranteed if "in accordance
with the interests of socialism." Provisions of
a government decree dealing with mass
communication require publishers of newspapers or other periodicals to have a license.
Distribution is also through official channels.

Incitement, warmongering, dissemination
of rumors, defamation and libel against persons living or dead are offenses under the
criminal code. The "misuse of the likeness or
the recorded voice" of a person is also forbidden. Correction of false or misleading
statements is required by law. Under its
provisions a person or organization so offended "may demand a qualifying statement
to be published by the said periodical, or by
the Hungarian Radio and Television, within
30 days following the date of publication or
transmission." If the correction is not made,
the complainant may "place a claim"
against the responsible editor or broadcast
organization.

Another government decree requires government offices to answer written requests
from the media for information. This measure says in part that if any news organization "has published a proposition or criticism, submits the text and asks for an
answer within five days after publication,
the direct supervisory authority of the state
organ concerned is required to examine the
proposition or criticism and give the editor
an answer." If the authority approached is
not authorized to answer, it must so inform
the editor within five days; otherwise it must
give its formal reply within 30 days. However, penalties for failure to do so are not

specified. The law says only that in such a
case the editor should report to the next
highest authority, and adds: "the competent
minister is obliged to proceed in the matter
without delay to give an answer and, depending on the circumstances, may call the person in default to account."

Censorship

There is no specific censorship office in
Hungary and no mandatory pre-censorship.
That does not mean there are no controls,
however. Editors, who are obviously carefully chosen, are responsible for what is
published or broadcast. Policy on public information and propaganda is formulated by
the Party, whose members hold the top positions in the media. The party's agitprop
section closely supervises the performance of
both print and broadcast media. Even so,
some published criticisms sound surprisingly
like those heard in Western nations. For a
Soviet-bloc regime, the Hungarian Party and
government are surprisingly tolerant. Kadar
himself has been satirized on national TV
and been made the butt of cartoons. Satirical
comments on topics that would be taboo in
neighboring countries escape censure. As a
result, the restrictions that do exist—no criticism of the Soviet Union, no questioning of
the essential basis of Communist rule—are
not violated if for no other reasons than the
fear that any alternative to the present situation would be worse.

There are indications that the provincial
papers may be more restricted than the
larger national dailies, partly because they
are under the control of the county Party
committees as well as the central organizations. A case in point was provided several
years ago when an official of a timber farm
who was also a member of the local county
Party committee was removed from office for
corruption. The case was reported in full by
Nepszabadsag but not mentioned by the
paper in the county where the farm was
located. When asked about the lack of coverage, the editor indicated he had not received
authorization "from the appropriate quarters."

State-Press Relations

In addition to their Party supervision, the
media are under the control of the Informa-

tion Bureau of the Council of Ministers. This office is responsible for the organization of all public information and its dissemination to the media, and also has direct authority over both the radio and television operations and the national news agency, MTI. It issues publishing licenses and distributes the newsprint supply. It takes part in the preparation of laws and decrees affecting the press, and also in policy decisions on financial, wage, price and labor questions in the whole mass-communications field. Various government ministries also have their own press offices and press spokesmen, but the Information Bureau has overall responsibility, being specifically charged with organizing "information and propaganda relating to the work of the supreme legislative and administrative bodies."

Obviously, in such a system news is managed in conformity with the propaganda aims of the Party and government. As already indicated, Hungarian media have a greater measure of freedom than is generally true elsewhere in the Soviet bloc, but the control over the media—by government and Party together—is complete. No one else decides what papers will be published, the share of newsprint allocation, who may work as a newsman—and pretty much what will be printed.

Attitude Toward Foreign Media

Foreign correspondents wishing to report on Hungary must obtain special visas from the press section of the Foreign Ministry. Newsmen working in the area who cover the country on a more or less regular basis can obtain accreditation for periods of time, ranging up to a year, with multiple exit and reentry visas. A correspondent faces relatively few official hurdles. He may file when, how and what he pleases—although, of course, consistently unfavorable reporting may result in a rejection of a subsequent visa request.

Foreign publications are available in Hungary, although not in sufficient quantities to be easily available to the general public. Newspapers occasionally carry articles warning of the danger of the "intellectual contraband" contained in such materials, as well as in foreign radio and TV broadcasts. Nevertheless, there is no jamming of foreign broadcasting, even by Radio Free Europe, and newspapers in Western

Hungary actually carry regularly the schedule of the Austrian TV programs for the benefit of readers close enough to the border to pick them up.

This apparent ambivalance pervades the whole of the media scene. For example, in 1972, Hungarian students took the occasion of the anniversary of the 1848 revolution to demonstrate against the government. In a commentary, *Nepszabadsag* described the demonstration itself as "tolerable," but also objected strongly to Western coverage.

The Hungarian Association of Journalists is affiliated with a number of international press organizations but its principal tie is with the International Union of Journalists, headquartered in Prague, Czechoslovakia.

On international issues, the Hungarian regime stands with the Soviet Union and questions relating to the media, like the 1978 UNESCO declaration, are no exception.

News Agencies

MTI, the official news agency, is an arm of the government, responsible to the Council of Ministers' Information Bureau. Its director general and his deputies are appointed with government approval. As the principal supplier of news and news photos to the Hungarian press, radio and television, MTI also serves official publications. Two subsidiaries, the Office of Broadcasting and Interphoto, prepare material for foreign readers.

MTI also publishes one of the Budapest dailies—the bilingual *Daily News/Neuste Nachrichten*—and a number of bulletins dealing with developments in such fields as trade, economy and management. It has exclusive distribution rights for foreign agency news inside the country, and receives the regular services of about 20 foreign agencies, including Reuters, AP, UPI, AFP and Tass. Of these, it relies mainly on Tass, particularly concerning international foreign policy issues. In addition, it has exchange arrangements with about 30 other national and regional agencies throughout the world, from which it occasionally picks up material.

MTI has correspondents in major cities and towns throughout Hungary and in 16 foreign cities including London, Paris and Washington, and also in all the Soviet-bloc capitals. A 1974 report said the daily file for the Hungarian press consisted of about 40,000 words of both domestic and foreign news. The agency distributes an average of 2,000 photographs a month. It also operates a service that monitors foreign broadcasts, the material from which is used to supplement the news file.

All this is handled by a staff of 1,000 employes, of whom 180 are journalists and 44 press photographers. A note in a 1979 issue of *Magyar Import,* the journal of the Hungarian Chamber of Commerce, said that on the average it took an hour for a news item to go through MTI processing and reach editorial offices. Speeding up this distribution process was one of the reasons given for the purchase of electronic editing equipment announced that same year. The guidelines issued in December 1979, for the 12th Party congress called on the media to devote greater attention to accurate and quick information.

Electronic News Media

As already noted, broadcasting in Hungary is a government monopoly. Magyar Radio es Televizo (Hungarian Radio and Television Service: MRT) is responsible to the Council of Ministers' Information Bureau, which prepares material and provides the equipment needed for broadcasting operations. The technical aspects—transmitters, stations, relays, etc.—are the responsibility of the Ministry of Transportation and Postal Affairs.

MRT's income and expenses are part of the state budget. The president of the service holds ministerial rank in the government, while his top aides are also government appointees. By statute, the advisory board that supervises operations includes one of the Party secretaries.

Although MRT gets some income from advertising, its major source of revenue is from license fees paid by owners of radios and television sets. In 1976 there were about 2.5 million licensed TV sets in the country and about the same number of radios.

A statement of purpose drawn up by the service noted that broadcast programming "proceeds on the principle that socialist values will be supported." It added that "ideologically ambiguous" works are tolerated provided they are not anti-socialistic, but that anything which might be construed as anti-socialistic is forbidden. The statement also spelled out MRT's aim: "a realistic representation of the life and concerns of working class people; proving the interde-

pendence of workers and peasants; the further strengthening of confidence in the Party, its politics and the social system..."

News/public affairs programming is a prominent feature of both radio and television. News bulletins are broadcast every hour on radio, while TV news programs can be seen in the early evening and just before the day's signoff. MRT has its own correspondents both at home and abroad, and of course draws material from the national news agency. It also receives programming from both Intervision, the Soviet bloc's exchange network, and Euro-vision, the West European equivalent. However, pickups from the West are—not surprisingly—far less frequent than from the East. Indeed, Hungarian broadcast people are quite frank about their roles. One was quoted several years ago as acknowledging that "TV news is part of the political broadcasts of the propaganda department."

The 1968 economic reform gave publicly financed institutions, for the first time, the right to form economic enterprises—in other words, to make money. The Radio and TV Service seized on the opportunity to set up a Commercial Bureau, which handles advertising, publishes books, sells tapes and goes in for other similar ventures. Most of the income is left with MRT to use in projects aimed at benefiting broadcasting personnel.

Education & Training

The National Association of Hungarian Journalists is the professional organization for newspeople. It has 27 specialized sections whose functions include the evaluation and criticism of the work of individual journalists and suggestions as to editorial policy.

The association operates the International Center for the Training of Journalists in Budapest, which offers courses of four to six months, chiefly for people from other countries. Most newcomers to the profession are university graduates who have completed the two-year program of the Hungarian Center for Training of Journalists. There is also a special course for editors.

In addition, the Mass Communication Research Center of Hungarian Radio and Television deals—despite its name—with all branches of the media and conducts a great amount of public opinion research. It is primarily concerned with examining the impact of programs and reporting.

Summary

The general trend of the media in Hungary since the 1968 economic reform has been toward a significant growth in the regional press and a virtual standstill in the national papers—apparently a reflection of the general decentralization of the economy. It is assumed this will continue, although probably not at the pace set earlier. Development plans emphasize increasing the circulation of existing papers, rather than starting new ones. Improvements in layout, appearance and even reporting are also called for in the plans.

Given the present international situation, there is no prospect of any significant change in the structure or operations of the Hungarian media. Whether Hungarians generally favor the governing regime or not, most seem to be convinced that given the realities of their geographical situation, it represents the best of possible alternatives.

CHRONOLOGY

1956 Government Information Office set up.

1967 *Daily News* founded by Hungarian Telegraph Agency.

1968 *Magyar Hirlap* founded as Budapest daily.

1972 Constitutional revision excludes print media from category of state property.

1979 Magyar Tavirati Iroda, national news agency, installs country's first electronic news editing and distribution system.

BIBLIOGRAPHY

Binder, David. "Hungary's Currency Strategy." *The New York Times,* December 26, 1980, Sec. Y, p. 21.

Browne, Malcolm W. "Austrian TV a Hit with Hungarians." *The New York Times,* January 28, 1975, p. 4.

"Change in Hungary: Kadar is Satirized." Washington Post, February 4, 1975, p. A12.

Hanson, Philip. *Advertising and Socialism.* White Plains, N.Y., 1974.

Krokovay, Zsolt. "Reflections on Censorship." *Index on Censorship,* April 1980, p. 17.

Lengyel, Emil. *100 Years of Hungary.* New York, 1958.

Merrill, John C., Bryan, Carter R., and Alisky, Marvin. *The Foreign Press.* Baton Rouge, La., 1970.

Mond, Georges H., "Press Concentration in Socialist Countries." *Gazette,* 20:3 (1974): 145.

"MTI to Install U.S.-Japanese Video Display Terminals." Radio Free Europe. *Hungarian Situation Report,* March 6, 1979, p. 4.

Olson, Kenneth E. *The History Makers.* Baton Rouge, La., 1966.

Palmer, Alan. *The Lands Between.* New York, 1970.

"Party Control of Provincial Media." Radio Free Europe. *Hungarian Situation Report,* February 5, 1975, p. 2.

Paulu, Burton. *Broadcasting in Eastern Europe.* Minneapolis, Minn., 1974.

Press in Authoritarian Countries. Zurich: International Press Institute, 1959.

Rab, Balonzs. "Samisdat Sackings." *Index on Censorship,* April 1980, p. 13.

Schopflin, George, ed. *The Soviet Union and Eastern Europe: A Handbook.* New York, 1970.

Selucky, Radoslav. *Economic Reforms in Eastern Europe: Political Background and Economic Significance.* New York, 1972.

Szecsko, Tomas, and Fodor, Gabor. *Communication Policies in Hungary.* Paris, 1974.

UNESCO. *World Communications, A 200-Country Survey of Press, Radio and Television.* Paris and New York, 1975.

INDIA

by Whitney R. Mundt

BASIC DATA

Population: 659 million (est.)
Area: 3,287,782 sq. km. (1,269,083 sq. mi.)
GNP: Rs 995.4 billion (US$126 billion) (1979)
Literacy Rate: 34%
Language(s): Hindi, English, Urdu, Punjabi, others
Number of Dailies: 929 (1977)
  Aggregate Circulation: 10,672,000 (1977)
  Circulation per 1,000: 17.3 (1977)
Number of Nondailies: 4,303 (1977)
  Aggregate Circulation: 10,290,000 (1977)
  Circulation per 1,000: 16.7 (1977)
Number of Periodicals: 12,371 (1977, est.)

Number of Radio Stations: 84
Number of Television Stations: 17
Number of Radio Receivers: 24 million
  Radio Receivers per 1,000: 36
Number of Television Sets: 1 million
  Television Sets per 1,000: 1.5
Total Annual Newsprint Consumption: 235,813 metric tons
  Per Capita Newsprint Consumption: 3.8 kg. (8.4 lb.)
Total Newspaper Ad Receipts: Rs 675 million (US$81 million) (1977, est.)
  As % of All Ad Expenditures: 54 (1977, est.)

Background & General Characteristics

India is well served by its mass media. In any democracy, where the political and social health of a people depends upon the free flow of information, freedom of the press is essential. India is no exception, and with one brief but extraordinary interruption—Prime Minister Indira Gandhi's abortive experiment in dictatorship between 1975 and 1977—its press has enjoyed a degree of independence that has made it the envy of many other Asian nations.

At the same time, the Indian press is beset by the same pressures that afflict the press in other free nations: political pressures applied by a government which occasionally finds its course of conduct challenged by media critics; social pressures from a people diverse in ethnic and religious background; and economic pressures brought by the need to compete in a free market.

Other problems confronting the press of India relate to the literacy, affluence and language diversity of its audience. The literacy rate of India's millions, although showing steady gains, continues to lag behind that of most nations. Present estimates place literacy at approximately 34 percent, an ap-

preciable increase over the figure of 29 percent in 1971 and 24 percent in 1961. Still, this is a rather low rate, and it depresses newspaper circulation figures; India's 1.6 copies per 100 persons falls well below the figure of 10 per 100—regarded by UNESCO as appropriate for developing countries. Newspaper reading, however, is an afternoon activity in the villages, and even in some of the larger towns, of India. Perhaps 15 of 20 persons hear news from the press through oral communication.

India's affluence—or lack of it—places the nation among the low-income countries of the world. The gross domestic product per capita remains below $150, although the annual GDP growth rate—a negative figure between 1970 and 1974—has nudged into the plus side of the ledger since 1975. But distribution of income is uneven: 5 percent of the national income was received by the bottom 20 percent of the population, while 25 percent was received by the top 5 percent. The simple truth is that great masses of people cannot afford to buy newpapers.

The language diversity of India's 659 million citizens constitutes one of the newspaper industry's continuing problems. It is perhaps best illustrated in Delhi street signs, which are printed in four languages and four scripts: English, in roman script; Urdu, in Perso-Arabic script for Muslims; Punjabi, in Gurumukhi script for Sikhs; and Hindi, in Devanagari script for Hindus. Hindi is the official language of the nation, but it is spoken by a majority of citizens in only six of India's 22 states. English is the "link" language—the tongue common to all areas of India, though spoken familiarly only by the well educated. Other than English, there are 15 tongues spoken by large segments of the population. In Delhi alone, newspapers are published in 13 of those 15 languages as well as in English.

Population distribution—although perhaps not a problem in the same sense that literacy, affluence, and language diversity are problems—is a factor that affects newspaper circulation in India. The 1981 census will surely disclose a population in excess of 650 million persons. This figure will place India second only to China in size of population, and will rank the country among the world's leaders in population density. At the time of the last census, 18 cities held over 500,000 residents, and nine of these were over one million. India has four major metropolitan areas: Calcutta, Bombay, Delhi and Madras. Their populations range from just over three million in Madras to more than seven million in Calcutta. Those four cities alone publish nearly 32 percent of the newspapers printed in India—4,220 out of 13,320.

Of those 13,320 newspapers, 875 were dailies and 3,801 were weeklies as of January 1977—the most recent date for which official figures are available. The remainder were published at less frequent intervals but come within the definition of newspapers as printed periodical works containing public news or comments on the news. The quality of journalism practiced by the leading newspapers among the dailies may be described as responsible. Text, headlines, and layout all tend to confirm this evaluation. Indeed, India's press is not faced with the problem confronting her former master, Britain: the gap between the so-called elite newspapers and the popular press—those papers that subsist on a steady diet of sex and lowbrow features. In Britain, newspapers like the revered *Times* and the intellectual *Guardian* exist alongside sex-oriented tabloids like the *Daily Mirror*. But in India, even soft pornography would arouse popular indignation. It is fair to say that the Indian press is almost uniformly highbrow, although occasionally a tabloid-sized paper like *Blitz* will capitalize

on a scandal, and use red ink, large headlines and front-page artwork to express an editorial point of view. In this manner such a newspaper begins to resemble the "yellow" journalism so well exemplified in the United States at the turn of the century.

Generally speaking, however, news in India's papers is reported with very little hyperbole, headlines are small and non-sensational, and layout is generally "gray"—conservative, with few pictures. Human interest features are rare. Story selection tends to favor official sources, and it is not uncommon to find the same photograph—a government release—on the front pages of several newspapers. This deference to official wisdom suggests a timidity that may reflect the vestiges of that 19-month period of curbed journalistic freedom under Mrs. Gandhi—know as the Emergency.

Historically, the Indian press is emerging from a period of English influence. It began during the British Raj, or rule, when James Augustus Hicky started the *Bengal Gazette* in 1780. His two-sheet *Gazette* was a "weekly political and commercial paper open to all parties but influenced by none." Hicky was sued for libel and imprisoned in poverty. In ensuing years of colonial experience, a number of still-existing, important newspapers were founded. *The Times of India* was begun as an English language weekly in 1838 and converted into a daily in 1850. *The Statesman* was founded in 1875, and *The Hindu* celebrated its centenary in 1978. *The Tribune* observed its 100th anniversary on February 1, 1981. These are English language papers, confirming the British influence on the Indian press. But the vernacular press grew alongside the Anglo-Indian newspapers. *Bombay Samachar,* a daily newspaper in Gujarati, was founded in 1822 and is the oldest existing local-language paper.

The spirit of nationalism stimulated the growth of the Indian press. Jawaharlal Nehru and Mohandas Gandhi both wrote for or started newspapers. Gandhi founded two weeklies in India—*Young India* in 1919 and *Harijan* in 1933. Nehru became chairman of the board of directors of the *National Herald* when that paper was founded in 1938. Gandhi and Nehru guided the independence movement to its culmination in 1947, when the British parliament granted full independence to India and Pakistan.

India's British heritage and her spirit of independence are evident in that nation's press today. The British influence may be seen in the number of English-language newspapers: 2,765, including 89 dailies; the total is exceeded only by the 3,289 Hindi-language papers. More than 500 newpapers are published in each of six other languages: Urdu, 975; Bengali, 855; Marathi, 806; Tamil, 618; Gujarati, 580; and Malayalam, 539. Counting only dailies—newspapers published at least four times a week—the English-language papers (89) fall to fifth place, exceeded by Hindi, 252; Urdu, 94; Marathi, 94; and Malayalam, 91. Other dailies are in Tamil (58); Kannada (53); Gujarati (37); Bengali (22); and Telugu (17).

English leads all other languages in numbers of newspapers issued monthly, quarterly, and annually. The table on the next page summarizes the data available officially at the beginning of 1977.

The political independence of India's press is suggested by the fact that 92 newspapers were published by political parties as 1977 began. Their political ideologies are difficult to identify because there were 18 parties that published newspapers, and this fragmentation tends to defeat attempts at classification. However, only four of those parties circulated their papers among significant numbers of readers. The Communist Party of India published 26 newspapers in 1976, and circulation figures were available for 19 of those; their readers totaled 81,515. Another 58,719 readers subscribed to 12 of the 15 newspapers published by the splinter Communist Party of India (Marxist), which broke with the Communist Party of India in 1964. The Socialist Unity Centre of India claimed 27,608 readers for two of its three newspapers, including 21,443 subscribers to *Ganadabi*, a Bengali fortnightly published from Calcutta. It was the largest circulated publication among political party newspapers. Finally, the Indian Party Congress claimed 22,966 readers for 11 of its 25 newspapers. Circulation figures for newspapers published by other parties were relatively small.

In India's swiftly moving political waters a number of new alignments and realignments have taken place since 1977. Party affiliations and party publications verified at that time may have little relevance to today's political scene. In fact, the Election Commission accorded recognition to six national parties for the 1980 election: Janata; Lok Dal, or Janata; Indira Congress, or Congress; Communist Party of India; Communist Party of India (Marxist); and Congress.

In addition to the diverse political loyalties in India, there are diverse ethnic and religious orientations. The basic racial stock is Caucasoid, onto which have been grafted Proto-Mongoloid, Australoid and Negrito elements. About three percent of the population are aboriginal inhabitants of India. There are three alien ethnic groups, numerically insignificant: the Parsis, descendants of refugees who fled Muslim persecution in Persia in the eighth Century; Jews, descendants of settlers who fled their respective countries in the first, seventh, and 19th Centuries; and Anglo-Indians, descendants of mixed marriages between Europeans and Indians. These ethnic groups are not significantly represented as such in the mass media of India.

The major religious communities of India are the Hindus, Muslims, Christians, Sikhs, Buddhists, Jains and Zoroastrians. The Hindus account for nearly 83 percent of the population, while the Muslims comprise about 11 percent and the Christians less than three, the Sikhs less than two, the Buddhists less than one, and the Jains about one-half of one percent. The Zoroastrians number below one million, thus representing an almost insignificant percentage, but they are concentrated in Bombay, where they are influential socially and economically. Publications of various religious groups are numerous; in 1976, out of a total of 12,371 periodicals published in India, 1,304 were devoted to religion and philosophy.

In some instances, these religious organizations publish commercial newspapers. In Kerala, where the Christian sects are strong—particularly Roman Catholics—the first daily newspaper was founded in 1887 by a Catholic priest who was a member of the Carmelites of Mary Immaculate. His newspaper, *Deepika*, was also the first published in the Malayalam language. Today *Deepika* circulates about 78,000 copies per issue and maintains correspondents in all the major cities of Kerala as well as in New Delhi.

In terms of competition, newspapers are concentrated in India's 15 major cities—particularly in the four metropolitan centers. Madras leads in the number of papers appearing at least twice weekly with 44. Bombay follows with 40, then Delhi with 38 and Calcutta with 35. Delhi leads all major cities in the number of weekly newspapers with 230. Hyderabad follows with 187, Bombay is third with 130, Calcutta fourth with 121, Bangalore fifth with 92 and Madras sixth with 75.

At the beginning of 1977 India's 15 major cities each published 100 newspapers or more —a total of 6,478 papers out of the national

Number of Newspapers and Periodicals (Language and Periodicity as of December 31, 1976)

Language	Dailies	Tri-bi/weeklies	Weeklies	Fortnightlies	Monthlies	Quarterlies	Other Periodicities	Annuals	Total 1976	Total 1975	Total 1974
English	89	5	324	208	1,176	609	283	71	2,765	2,559	2,453
Hindi	252	27	1,456	439	919	144	37	15	3,289	3,142	3,200
Assamese	3	1	12	11	9	9	4	—	49	38	32
Bengali	22	7	231	109	295	140	49	2	855	771	739
Gujarati	37	3	139	71	275	37	12	6	580	567	569
Kannada	53	3	122	60	126	20	7	1	392	348	331
Kashmiri			1						1		
Malayalam	91	2	82	65	277	13	5	4	539	498	465
Marathi	94	9	252	67	292	46	18	28	806	748	717
Oriya	10		17	15	77	17	1	1	138	135	128
Punjabi	12	1	109	21	103	18	14		278	259	268
Sanskrit	1		2	1	9	8	2		23	22	22
Sindhi	4		19	4	27	3	1		58	55	59
Tamil	58		94	130	314	18	4		618	556	527
Telugu	17	1	122	73	213	11	4		441	418	425
Urdu	94	6	482	127	233	26	6	1	975	929	915
Bilingual	18	9	262	123	471	123	60	21	1,087	992	989
Multilingual	4		46	20	124	44	20	6	264	247	224
Others	16		29	22	53	34	8		162	138	121
TOTAL:											
1976	875	74	3,801	1,556	4,993	1,320	535	156	13,320		
1975	835	70	3,628	1,450	4,617	1,197	479	147		12,423	
1974	822	68	3,666	1,411	4,491	1,124	458	144			12,185

total of 13,320. Delhi and Bombay had more than 1,000 each. As mentioned above, those two cities, combined with Calcutta and Madras, published nearly 32 percent of all newspapers in the country—a total of 4,220. Other cities with at least 100,000 population each published another 30 percent, or 4,051 papers, while towns with less than 100,000 population brought out nearly 22 percent, or 2,914. State capitals other than metropolitan cities had the remaining 16 percent—2,135 newspapers.

This concentration of the press in the cities is natural, of course. But to say that it is natural is no consolation to the rural dweller. He finds himself deprived of access to news of current affairs, and logical explanations are of no value to him. As Ramesh Chander pointed out during a 1978 seminar at Agra on the problems of caring for India's rural readership: "eighty percent of the population resides in 576,000 villages; and though overall literacy is 34 to 35 percent, in the villages it is as low as 27 to 28 percent; means of communication are so scarce that hardly 30 percent of the villages are connected by serviceable roads." As a result, Chander concluded, "What may truly be called a rural press is yet to be born."

In size, newspapers vary, within reasonable ranges, in area of the printed page. A survey in 1976 of 417 daily newspapers revealed that among "big" papers—those circulating more than 50,000 copies per publishing day—the average page size was 2,466 square centimeters, or perhaps 16 by 24 inches. There were 40 respondents in the "big" paper category. Among "medium" papers—those circulating between 15,000 and 50,000 copies daily—the average page size was only slightly smaller: 2,343 square centimeters, the most common dimension. There were 72 respondents in this "medium" paper category. Among "small" papers—those circulating fewer than 15,000 copies daily—the average page size was much smaller: 1,740 square centimeters, or perhaps a fairly even distribution of tabloid and regular-size papers among the 305 respondents. The "big" newspapers responding to the survey averaged 8.54 pages per issue; the "medium" newspapers averaged 7.71 pages; the "small" newspapers 4.04.

The average price per issue for "medium" and "big" newspapers was about four cents. For "small" papers the average price was substantially lower—two and a half cents. For the laborer, however, buying a single

issue of a newspaper would be a costly proposition.

Most of the daily newspapers published in India are morning editions, and the larger papers appear daily, including Sunday. Some, like *The Times of India,* publish magazines as well as standard newspapers. Besides the highly regarded *Illustrated Weekly of India,* the *Times* also publishes *Dharmayug,* a pictorial weekly, and *Dinaman,* a newsweekly, both in Hindi. *Sarika,* a forthnightly magazine in Hindi, carries short stories, while *Madhuri,* another Hindi fortnightly, carries stories and pictures about film stars. *Filmfare* is also a fortnightly film magazine, but is published in English. Two other fortnightlies in English are *Femina,* a magazine that "reflects the art of womancraft," and *Youth Times,* which provides young people with "a platform for airing views on the changing cultural and social values." The *Times* also publishes two monthlies: *Parag,* a Hindi magazine for children; *Science Today,* articles in English about science for the average reader; a comic book in English, Hindi and Bengali; and a newspaper in Marathi. The *Times* also issues several annuals. Obviously, such diversity from one publisher is atypical, but there are a number of other newspapers that have magazines and magazine sections for their readers.

The multilingual fluency of *Times* publications illustrates a special problem for the Indian publishing industry: the multiplicity of languages and their mutual unintelligibility. Besides English and 15 languages accorded constitutional status, there were 42 other languages in which newspapers were published in 1976. In those 42 languages 162 papers were printed, totaling 124,000 copies —a substantial circulation, though perhaps miniscule in relation to industrywide figures. More than 10 newspapers were published in each of the following languages: Lushai, 19 (circulation 11,000); Konkani, 18 (22,000); Nepali, 16 (10,000); Khasi, 11 (7,000); and Manipuri, 11 (9,000). Other languages included Arabic, Portuguese, Chinese, French, Italian, Swahili, Spanish, German and Latin.

Foreign mission publications represent a significant portion of the press in India, while serving the special interests of their respective nations. In 1976, there were 109 publications brought out by 26 foreign missions; 67 of these commanded a circulation of 904,801. Approximately 78 percent of the total readership was devoted to Soviet publications, while the United States garnered about 12 percent.

The USSR distributed 50 periodicals among more than 707,000 recipients. The largest of these was *Soviet Bhumi,* a Hindi fortnightly issued in Delhi. The United States was next, with eight publications serving over 111,000 readers. The American showcase, *Span*—an English monthly, also published in Delhi, with a circulation of nearly 80,000—is a slickly produced, glossy magazine with a smorgasbord of articles, stories, and cartoons reprinted from popular U.S. magazines, along with occasional original pieces like the conversation between U.S. Ambassador Robert Goheen and Indian journalists Pran Chopra and S. Nihal Singh in the August 1980 issue. Other countries offering their own publications included East and West Germany, with five and seven respectively, followed by the Arab League, Bulgaria, France, Republic of Korea and the United Kingdom, with three each.

Geographically speaking, India's newspapers are fairly well distributed among 22 states and nine union territories—although, as pointed out earlier, publication is heavily concentrated within the cities. Only the union territories of Arunachal Pradesh and Lakshadweep were without newspapers in 1977. Maharashtra had the largest number of papers of any state (2,051) followed by Uttar Pradesh (1,832), West Bengal (1,542), Tamil Nadu (1,021), and Andhra Pradesh (905). The union territory of Delhi published 1,745 papers in 1977. Counting only dailies, the largest number published in any state was in Uttar Pradesh, which had 138. The states of Himachal Pradesh and Nagaland published no daily newspapers in 1977, nor did the union territories of Arunachal Pradesh, Dadra and Nagar Haveli, Lakshadweep, and Pondicherry. The table below provides a comparison.

Distribution of Newspapers						
State/Union Territory	Dailies	Tri-/Bi-Weeklies	Weeklies	Others	Total 1977	Total 1976
Andhra Pradesh	43	2	337	523	905	860
Assam	6	2	36	63	107	96
Bihar	20	4	179	177	380	345
Gujarat	33	3	142	393	571	534
Haryana	5	1	102	160	268	236
Himachal Pradesh	—	—	19	53	72	70
Jammu and Kashmir	20	—	104	32	156	143
Karnataka	80	3	184	437	704	658
Kerala	93	1	101	552	747	709
Madhya Pradesh	84	7	285	176	552	505
Maharashtra	132	16	476	1,427	2,051	1,948
Manipur	12	—	3	29	44	40
Meghalaya	1	4	16	19	40	34
Nagaland	—	—	3	1	4	4
Orissa	11	1	25	152	188	167
Punjab	29	1	170	301	501	459
Rajasthan	46	1	347	402	796	692
Tamil Nadu	66	2	125	828	1,021	965
Tripura	11	3	28	5	47	43
Uttar Pradesh	138	19	912	763	1,832	1,597
West Bengal	36	7	327	1,172	1,542	1,347
Arunachal Pradesh	—	—	—	—	—	—
Andaman, Nicobar Islands	2	—	2	5	9	8
Chandigarh	5	—	28	108	141	120
Dadra and Nagar Haveli	—	—	1	—	1	1
Delhi	40	1	251	1,453	1,745	1,637
Goa, Daman and Diu	7	—	6	23	36	35
Lakshadweep	—	—	—	—	—	—
Mizoram	9	—	10	4	23	17
Pondicherry	—	1	6	41	48	50
TOTAL	929	78	4,225	9,299	14,531	13,320

Circulation figures for these newspapers reveal clearly that while most papers fall in the "small" category, with fewer than 15,000 subscribers, the bulk of the nation's newspaper readers subscribe to one or more of a very few "big" papers—those circulating over 50,000 copies. This generalization holds true for both the daily newspaper category (including papers published at least twice weekly) and the periodical category (published weekly or less frequently). In 1976 there were 23 daily newspapers (less than four percent of the total) that controlled nearly 34 percent of the circulation, while 352 dailies (about 55 percent of the total) controlled only eight percent. In 1977 only one Indian newspaper achieved a circulation over 300,000: *Ananda Bazar Patrika*, a Bengali-language paper published in Calcutta. Four others reported circulation figures exceeding 200,000, and another 22 counted over 100,000 in 1977.

The newspapers with the greatest circulation are not necessarily the newspapers with the greatest weight. Three papers are credited, generally, with exerting influence that exceeds their circulation and extends even beyond their nation's borders. They are *The Times of India, The Statesman,* and *The Hindu*.

The *Times* began as a weekly in 1838 and was called the *Bombay Times*. It became a daily in 1850, and in 1861 it changed its name to *The Times of India* to reflect its growing status and influence. It was purchased by Thomas Bennett, a journalist, who thereupon brought F.M. Coleman, a printer, into the business. Thus the firm acquired the corporate name by which it is known today: Bennett Coleman & Co. Ltd.

The firm has expanded until today it consists of 14 news-interest publications and 14 focusing on other interests. The news publications include the flagship paper in Bombay and two sister newspapers of the same name, one published in New Delhi and the other in Ahmedabad. They operate under common management but with separate editorial staffs and are therefore competitive. According to General Manager Ram S. Tarneja, the papers must follow a policy of objective and impartial coverage, with no partisan political philosophy. Critics, however, maintain that the *Times* has always been an establishment newspaper—an unabashed champion of colonialism under the British Raj, a backer of Indira Gandhi during her first term, a supporter of the Janata Party when it came to power. Tarneja responds that the press is part of society and cannot act against the will of the people. During the Emergency the *Times* chose voluntary self-censorship over the alternative: government-exercised pre-censorship.

The *Times's* influence is due in part to its status as the oldest English-language daily in India, to its role as spokesman for the national interest of India, to its social conscience and its journalistic excellence—and its sheer success, as demonstrated in a circulation of over 400,000 readers.

The Stateman is also an institution in India. It was founded in 1875 by Robert Knight, whose sons, in 1922, formed the newspaper's corporate owner, Statesman Ltd. Today the firm publishes five news-interest publications, the most important of which are the flagship newspaper, published at the firm's headquarters in Calcutta, and its sister of the same name, published in New Delhi.

The newspaper's influence exceeds its circulation, which in 1977 was just over 173,000. Part of that influence may be due to the quality of its reporting, which is highly regarded for its accuracy, and its editorials, which are serious and thoughtful. *The Statesman* has had the good fortune to be blessed with excellent editors in Kuldip Nayar, Pran Chopra and S. Nihal Singh.

The Statesman lost none of its prestige during the Emergency, when it fought the imposition of pre-censorship and the restriction of press freedom. Generally credited with leading that fight is C. R. Irani, the managing director, who received the Freedom House Award for his opposition to government attempts to control the press.

Irani feels that *The Statesman* has earned the respect of its readers because it has always believed in giving fair coverage to all points of view and because it has set a standard for responsible journalism.

A third newspaper generally considered influential is *The Hindu*—actually, five dailies of that name published from Madras, Coimbatore, Madurai, Bangalore and Hyderabad. They are family-operated papers owned by Kasturi and Sons Ltd. Other than the above-mentioned five, there is the *Hindu International Edition*, a weekly from Madras that was founded in 1975.

The Hindu's editor is G. Kasturi, who assumed his post in 1965. He is one of a long line of editor-proprietors from the same family who have guided the paper to its present status as one of India's most influential, and certainly its most up to date. Kasturi's innovations include a full complement of video display terminals in the newsroom, generous use of color in a modern offset printing plant, and a facsimile transmission facility. He is also responsible for the international edition, which extended *The Hindu's* readership abroad, and for a number of special sections which improved its readability.

The newspaper's influence stems in part from its venerable status as one of the nation's century-old papers, in part from its enviable geographical position in South India, where Madras is the lone metropolitan center, and in part from its identification with Indian nationalism during British rule. *The Hindu* maintains its position today through its wide-ranging coverage of news, obtained from foreign correspondents in London, Washington, Tokyo, and Singapore, and through its liberal philosophy—"not left, not reactionary, not progressive, but freedom-believing."

Other newspapers with a significant following include *The Indian Express,* which like *The Statesman,* fought the imposition of Emergency restrictions and salvaged its credibility while other newspapers lost theirs. Today the *Express* has a circulation of 543,341 for all editions published from 10 cities—the largest circulation of any multicity newspaper. *The Tribune,* with main offices in Chandigarh, is respected for its independence and its social conscience.

Among the language newspapers, *Ananda Bazar Patrika,* a Bengali paper published from Calcutta, has the highest circulation of any single edition daily, and *Malayala Manorama* claims over a half-million readers in the highly literate state of Kerala.

Even the big newspapers, with their large press runs, do not employ the latest technology—except, perhaps, for *The Hindu.* The full range of technology exists in India, but most newspapers are produced by methods outdated in Europe and the United States—such as "hot metal" machinery and handset type that are obsolescent if not obsolete in the West. In the composing rooms of leading Indian newspapers pressmen will demonstrate with pride the operation of Linotype machines that were abandoned for scrap in some small American newspapers. India has 130,000 hand compositors employed in the industry, and at least 15 newspapers are produced by calligraphists. A survey of 452 dailies revealed that nearly one-third did not

possess printing presses and were required to contract with commercial printers.

Part of the problem lies in India's reluctance to import machinery and goods that the nation is capable of producing at home. And—no less significant—the new technology is labor-saving technology, and India does not wish to employ modern methods at the expense of jobs.

Economic Framework

The old cliché that "The rich get richer and the poor have children" is, like all generalizations, fallacious. But it seems to have some relevance to the economic climate in the Indian press industry. The well established, financially diversified newspapers continue to prosper, while smaller papers are born, live brief lives and die. Government of India figures show that although 286 newspapers went out of existence in 1976 there was an overall increase of 7.2 percent in the number of newspapers. Circulation was up marginally in 1976 from the previous year—34.08 million as compared with 33.88 million. But that is a growth rate of only 0.7 percent—down from 2.2 percent the previous year.

Small newspapers were the chief casualties. Their numbers diminished by 379 titles, their circulation fell from 15.6 million to 14.86 million, and their share of the market shrank to 43.6 percent from 46.1 percent. But medium newspapers did not fare well, either. Their numbers decreased by six titles, their circulation dropped from 6.46 to 6.22 million, and their share of the market slipped from 19.1 percent to 18.3 percent.

On the other hand, big newspapers increased to 115 from 107, their circulation climbed from 11.75 million to 12.98 million, and their share of the market went up from 34.8 percent to 38.1 percent.

Probe India, a monthly English-language magazine specializing in investigative journalism, published an in-depth study of the role of the big press in its January 1980 issue. The exposé claims that *The Times of India* and its allied publications made a profit of about Rs30 ($3.6) million in 1978-79, as compared with about Rs7.5 million ($900,000) in 1970-71. *Probe India* places net profits for *The Hindustan Times* group at Rs5 million ($600,000) in 1977-78, compared with just over Rs1 million in 1972-73; profits for *Malayala Manorama* at Rs1.8 million ($216,000) in 1977-78, up from Rs0.2 million

($24,000) in 1970-71; and for Kasturi and Sons Ltd. a profit of over Rs2.5 million ($300,000) in 1977-78, up from just over Rs1 million ($120,000) in 1970-71. If *Probe's* figures are accurate, or even reasonably close, they reveal a trend that suggests a healthy future—at least for the industry's giants.

Newspapers are free to grow and prosper— or to wither and die—because they are, by and large, private enterprises. But radio and television in India are state-owned and must fit into a governmental system, with all the political inertia natural to a bureaucracy. Broadcasting has not developed in India as rapidly as it might have done. The government-owned All India Radio has entered its 50th year and television its 23rd, but neither has realized its potential.

The press, on the other hand, has reached maturity in everything but technology. One suspects that it is private ownership which has assisted the process of growth. A majority of the newspapers in India—62.4 percent, or 9,073 publications—are owned by individuals. Societies and associations own another 18.5 percent, or 2,682 papers, while central and state governments together own 3.6 percent, or 516.

In percentage of circulation, joint-stock companies place first, with 38.9 percent of the total. The table below displays the ownership pattern for those newspapers whose circulation figures are known. It reveals clearly that six percent of the nation's newspapers control nearly 39 percent of the nation's readers —a serious concentration of opinion-making power.

As mentioned earlier, "popular" or "yellow" journalism poses no problem in India; but the same cannot be said for "chain" journalism— the linking of several newspapers in a number of cities under a single corporate umbrella. In July 1980 the Ministry of Information and Broadcasting announced that the newly reconstituted Press Commission would add to its terms of reference a study of "Chain newspapers; links with industry, their effect on competition and on the readers' right to objective news and free comments." Earlier, the Lok Sabha (the lower house of Parliament) had heard testimony indicating that the question of diffusion of ownership of newspapers and their links with big industrial houses needed to be studied in depth because some newpapers published versions of political views in line with the thinking of the large companies' proprietors.

There is a genuine concern that as large newspapers become associated with industries, those newspapers will come to reflect the views of business. As those newspapers acquire new properties, adding links in the chain, readers will have access to fewer opinions—or so the argument goes. And if those fewer opinions are the opinions of big business, which is vulnerable to the dictates of government, then the potential for mischief exists. For example, if a newspaper is owned by an industrialist with interests in concrete plants, and if that industrialist must obtain a license to operate the plant, then—hypothetically—the government could exert subtle pressure to obtain favorable publicity.

The table on the next page lists eight of the larger chains, the number of dailies owned by each, and the percentage of total circulation claimed by each.

The Monopolies and Restrictive Trade

Pattern of Newspaper Ownership (1977)			
Form of Ownership	Number of Papers*	Circulation ('000)	Percentage of Total Circulation
Government	240	1,131	3.0
Individual	4,490	11,263	30.1
Joint Stock Companies	449	14,561	38.9
Firm/Partnerships	447	3,721	10.0
Trusts	230	2,369	6.3
Cooperative Societies	69	138	0.4
Societies/Associations	1,618	3,514	9.4
Educational Institutions	158	454	1.2
International Organizations	4	7	—
Political Parties	58	279	0.7
TOTAL	7,763	37,437	100.0

*Represents newspapers whose circulation data were available.

Chain Ownership of Dailies and Their Circulation				
Chains*	Dailies	Circulation ('000)	Percentage of Circulation of All Metropolitan Dailies	
			1976	1975
1. Bennett Coleman and Company	9	846	23.1	21.8
2. Express Newspapers	7	455	12.4	13.5
3. Ananda Bazar Patrika	5	317	8.7	9.3
4. Hindustan Times & Allied Publications	4	347	9.5	9.9
5. Amrita Bazar Patrika Pvt. Ltd.	3	297	8.1	8.8
6. Statesman Ltd.	2	189	5.2	5.4
7. Kasturi & Sons Ltd.	1	167	4.6	4.8
8. Indian National Press (Bombay) Ltd.	4	134	3.6	4.1
Total	35	2,752	75.2	77.6

*Having Circulation of over 100,000

Practices Act of 1969 was passed to protect against such concentration of power, and against monopolistic and restrictive trade practices. It governs expansions, mergers, and amalgamations of a specified value; the starting of new business projects that would become interconnected with existing undertakings of a specified value; and monopolistic and restrictive trade practices prejudicial to the public interest. The act applies to the whole of India except the state of Jammu and Kashmir.

From the viewpoint of the publisher, a problem more pressing than merger or amalgamation is the simple task of distributing his newspapers. In a nation of perhaps 650 million people, spread over 575,936 villages and 2,643 urban centers, the difficulty of transport assumes major proportions. Punjab may be the only state in which nearly every village is connected by link roads to the main road network. Buses, motorcycles, scooters and even bicycles are used to transport newspapers. Milkmen and postmen generally deliver them, and students and teachers going to schools in the towns bring them back to their villages.

Motor delivery may be suspended during the summer monsoon season, according to Chunibhai Vaidya, editor of *Bhoomiputra* in Baroda. Over half of Gujarat's 14,222 villages are without bus service, he says, between the first shower and completion of road repair following the five-month rains.

Urban centers are linked with rail service, which is extensive in India. Romesh Chander, publisher of *Hind Samachar* in Jullundur, Punjab, tells of a newspaper distributor with a seasonal railway pass between two stations who picks up papers at one station, then throws them from the running train at fixed

points agreed upon earlier with his rural customers.

Other means of transport include air, although the cost of air delivery is nearly prohibitive. For a while, G. Kasturi, editor of *The Hindu,* had his own fleet of small aircraft delivering papers, but later adopted facsimile transmission from Madras for editions in Coimbatore, Madurai, Bangalore and Hyderabad. However, most newspapers publishing from more than one center distribute news and other textual material between centers by means of teleprinters.

Newsprint availability must also concern publishers. The requirements of newspapers and periodicals for newsprint are met through imports, plus local production of the National Newsprint and Paper Mills at Nepa Nagar in Madhya Pradesh. Total indigenous production for 1977–78 was 54,000 metric tons. Because perhaps 75 percent of newsprint must be imported, and because India wishes to maintain a favorable balance of trade, newsprint rationing, based on government allocation, must be tolerated. As a result, newspapers in India are relatively thin.

A newsprint advisory committee advises the government on import and allocation policy for newsprint (and newsprint machinery). Committee members include the minister of information and broadcasting as chairman, one representative of the Indian and Eastern Newspaper Society, one representative of the Indian Language Newspapers Association, one each from the Indian Federation of Working Journalists and the National Union of Journalists (India), three members of Parliament, and six persons selected by the government.

Allocation of newsprint is based on consumption the previous year, with an allowance for growth. Various other provisions govern allowance for waste, increased or decreased circulation, and compliance with regulations.

At present, newsprint supply does not appear to be a problem, but during the Emergency publishers found themselves vulnerable to government pressure because the government was able to order banks to lower credit limits against newsprint quotas. Even now newsprint may be stored on a newspaper's premises, but in a locked storage room behind a door on which there is displayed the name of the creditor bank. The newsprint may be released only on completion of satisfactory financial arrangements.

Government influence is exerted through advertisements as well as newprint allocation. The government's advertising policy, expressed through the Directorate of Advertising and Visual Publicity, implicitly insists on the right to demand space from newspapers at rates fixed by the DAVP. "Patronage" of small newspapers is one of the elements of that advertising policy, although the government maintains that choice of media in which to place its advertising is made on merit.

Government-sector advertising has been estimated at Rs320 ($38.4) million, representing nearly 24 percent of the country's total advertising business. The accompanying table tallies advertising income derived from government sources for 418 daily newspapers divided into "big," "medium" and "small" categories. Nearly half of the "big" newspapers derived 10 to 24 percent of their advertising income from the government, while over one-fourth of the "small" papers depended on government for 50 to 74 percent.

The percentage of advertising to news matter is a point of concern to the government, which considers an ideal ratio to be 40 percent advertising to 60 percent news. Not all of the daily newspapers achieve that ideal. *The Times of India* (Bombay) devoted 63 percent of its space to advertising in 1976. *The Na-*

tional Herald in Lucknow carried 60 percent advertising, while *The Hindustan Times* in Delhi was close behind with 59 percent. These were followed by *The Hindu* in Madras and *The Statesman* in Calcutta with 55 percent advertising, *Ananda Bazar Patrika,* a Bengali language daily in Calcutta, with 53 percent, *The Indian Express* (Bombay) and *The Tribune* (Chandigarh) with 47 percent each, and *Malayala Manorama* (Kottayam) with 44 percent. Clearly, practically none of the major English-language dailies in India reaches the ideal ratio.

Another source of concern to the government, as it is to publishers, is the possibility of employee strikes. As sole proprietor of the broadcast industry, the government must deal with work stoppages such as the hunger strike by the staff and employees of Bombay Doordarshan (television) in November 1980. This was planned to protest what the workers called "deplorable working conditions" at the TV center and the "indifferent attitude adopted by authorities." The strikers threatened to halt the daily four-hour transmission from Bombay if demands were not met.

Strikes are generally of the wildcat variety, affecting individual papers, although occasionally token national strikes occur. G. Kasturi, editor of *The Hindu,* can recall only three strikes in nearly 25 years at his newspaper: in 1968 *The Hindu* was shut down for two and a half months; in 1967 a short walkout followed the paper's statement of support for the Congress Party; and in 1957, when the paper took a stand *against* the Congress Party it was struck for five days. More recently *The Times of India* in Bombay staged a lockout for nearly two weeks in October 1980 following a strike called by the Mumbai Mazdoor Sabha to protest suspension of six members.

In March 1977 newspaper employees went on a national one-day token strike to press their demands for interim relief pending the awards of two wage tribunals. The labor minister responded by granting relief rang-

Advertising Income Derived from Government Sources (Percentage of Total Income)							
Category	Nil	Below 10%	Between 10 to 24%	Between 25 and 49%	Between 50 and 74%	75% and Above	Total Number of Papers
Big	1	9	19	7	0	0	41
Medium	6	7	28	25	5	—	73
Small	25	24	45	96	76	27	304
Total	32	40	92	128	81	27	418

ing from Rs85 ($10.20) to Rs131 ($15.72) per month for working journalists and Rs23 ($2.76) to Rs85 ($10.20) for other newpaper employees, depending on the class of paper.

Employers' representatives withdrew from the boards of directors in December 1977, bringing about a year-long deadlock in their operation. Subsequently, a one-man tribunal consisting of G. D. Palekar, former justice of the Supreme Court, was set up to study the issue of wage revision. Both editorial and non-editorial employee wages are governed by national statute, which would be affected by the Palekar recommendations. The last wage revision took place in 1967, although bilateral negotiations with unions have introduced ad hoc adjustments, and there have been cost-of-living adjustments.

Palekar proposed substantial increases after studying the circulation figures of 16 newspapers for the years 1965 and 1979 and learning that *The Hindu* had increased its circulation by 135 percent, *The Hindustan Times* by 147 percent and *Malayala Manorama* by 214 percent. Those proposals were scaled down in the final recommendations to the government, and workers' groups were prepared to organize public protests to dramatize their dissatisfaction with the modifications. The government had not made a decision as late as November 1980.

The current starting wage for a beginning journalist is in the Rs600–700 ($72–84) range. In addition, there are allowances for housing and night duty, as well as compensatory allowances.

The two major labor unions whose members will be affected by the negotiations are the Indian Federation of Working Journalists (IFWJ) and the National Union of Journalists (India). IFWJ is a federal all-India body representing journalists and trade unions and is recognized by the government as the representative of journalists on the wage board. Its membership includes working journalists from editor to freelancer to proofreader. The National Union of Journalists is a federation of journalists' unions, with affiliated units in almost all states. NUJ publishes *Inkworld,* a monthly journal on professional and trade union matters. IFWJ has a strong element of the Communist party leading it.

Newspapers, too, would be variously affected by the negotiations, depending on their circulations. They are classified by size into nine groups for purposes of the wage adjustment, which is both retrospective and prospective. The table below, while it does not classify newspapers into the nine groups, does classify by circulation and number and gives some idea of the number of papers that would be most seriously affected by the award.

As the table shows, there are 23 newspapers circulating over 100,000 copies on a daily basis. These 23 boast a combined circulation of 3,473,000. This means that about 3.5 percent of the daily newspapers in India account for nearly 37 percent of the daily circulation.

Press Laws

The Constitution of India guarantees to all citizens the right to freedom of speech and expression. While freedom of the press is not explicitly guaranteed, it has been judicially determined that the freedom of speech and expression clause—Article 19(1)(a)—includes press freedom. However, it is not an absolute freedom, for Article 19(2) qualifies it somewhat: "Nothing in sub-clause (a) of Clause (1) shall affect the operation of any existing law, or prevent the State from making any law,

Circulation Pattern of Newspapers (1976)							('000)
Category	Circulation Ranges	Dailies*		Periodicals		Total	
		Number	Circulation	Number	Circulation	Number	Circulation
Big	One lakh† and above	23	3,473,000	33	5,419,000	56	8,892,000
	50,001 to 1,00,000	19	1,272,000	40	2,821,000	59	4,093,000
Medium	15,001 to 50,000	89	2,531,000	145	3,697,000	234	6,228,000
	5,001 to 15,000	158	1,428,000	499	4,279,000	657	5,707,000
Small	5,000 and below	352	757,000	6,179	8,398,000	6,531	9,155,000
	TOTAL	641	9,461,000	6,896	24,614,000	7,537	34,075,000

*Including Tri/bi-weeklies.
†1 lakh = 100,000

insofar as such law imposes reasonable restrictions on the exercise of the right conferred by the said sub-clause in the interests of the security of the State, friendly relations with foreign states, public order, decency or morality or in relations to contempt of court, defamation or incitement to an offence." Thus the government can restrict freedom of the press with cause, subject to judicial interpretation of the reasonableness of that restriction.

Statutory enactments directly reinforcing freedom of the press in India include The Parliamentary Proceedings (Protection of Publication) Act, 1977, and the Prevention of Publication of Objectionable Matter (Repeal) Act, 1977. The first gives newspapers protection against action in the courts for publishing the proceedings of Parliament. Similar protection was first granted in 1956 but then repealed during the period of the Emergency. This 1977 act simply restores the original protection. The second statute repeals the Prevention of Publication of Objectionable Matter Act, 1976—another measure of the Emergency. That act made punishable any words which, among other things, excited disaffection towards the government, promoted disharmony, caused fear or alarm, incited others to commit offenses, defamed certain public officials or were indecent or intended for blackmail. The act also gave the government power to demand a security deposit and to order forfeiture of the deposit, to seize and destroy newspapers, and to seize presses and order them forfeited.

Other press laws in force include (1) Newspaper (Price and Page) Act, 1956, providing for the regulation of the price charged for newspapers in relation to their pages for the purpose of preventing unfair competition; (2) Newspaper (Price Control) Act, 1972, providing for the control, in the public interest, of newspaper prices; (3) Press and Registration of Books Act, 1867, regulating printing presses and newspapers, placing a duty on publishers to furnish annual statements; (4) Working Journalists (Fixation of Rates of Wages) Act, 1958, allowing the government to set wages for working journalists and to regulate hours of work, holidays, notice period for termination of service, and so on; and (5) Working Journalists (Conditions of Service) and Miscellaneous Provision (Amendment) Act, 1974, empowering the government to set wage rates and working conditions for nonjournalist newspaper employees.

Certain press-related laws also apply to others. They include (1) Contempt of Courts Act, 1952, providing that the High Court can punish for contempt of itself and subordinate courts; (2) Contempt of Legislature, penalizing newspapers that commit breaches of privilege; (3) Copyright Act, 1957, protecting the rights of authors of original works in certain categories; (4) Code of Criminal Procedure, enabling the government to order forfeited every issue of a newspaper if it appears to contain material that brings hatred or contempt or excites disaffection towards the government; (5) Indian Penal Code, 1868, defining and prohibiting obscenity, applies to works that are lascivious or appeal to the prurient interest or might tend to deprave and corrupt persons who are likely to read, see, or hear the material; (6) Indian Post Office Act, 1898, prohibiting the mailing of lottery materials, obscene matter and newspapers published contrary to the provisions of the Press and Registration of Books Act of 1867; and also empowering postal authorities to detain any newspaper containing any seditious matter; (7) Prize Competition Act, 1955, regulating prize competitions and providing that newspapers which promote or conduct competitions in violation of the law may find those copies forfeited to the government; (8) Drug and Magic Remedies (Objectionable Advertisements) Act, 1954, to control the number of advertisements published in newspapers for alleged cures for venereal diseases, sexual stimulants and alleged cures for diseases and conditions peculiar to women.

Although there is no law that restrains the press from publishing information which might constitute an invasion of the privacy of private citizens, Indian newspapers generally are conscientious about observing the right of privacy. For example, *Malayala Manorama* as a matter of policy does not reveal the names of rape victims. The recently revised terms of reference of the Press Commission now include consideration of the "constitutional and legal safeguards to protect the citizen's right to privacy."

All newspapers must register with the central government before beginning operation. The declaration to be filed must indicate the proposed title, the language, the periodicity, and other particulars. If the title is already in use, the publisher must propose alternate choices. Within 48 hours of the publication of each issue the publisher must send a copy to the Registrar of Newspapers. When the registrar has received the first issue he will allot a registration number and issue a registration certificate. Licenses must be obtained for imports, but will not be granted for second-hand and rebuilt machinery.

Special accreditation procedures are required for journalists who cover events in the capital. The Central Press Accreditation Committee, a body composed of journalists, reviews requests for accreditation accompanied by photographs of the applicant and particulars of his professional career. A press identity card will be issued to accredited journalists. This status entitles them to such special considerations as publicity material, invitations to press conferences, concessional travel within the country, meetings with officials, housing, telephone connections, membership in the central government health service, entry to government of India offices and to the press gallery of Parliament.

At the present time, neither reporters nor publishers need to post compulsory bonds or security deposits—a notorious weapon of intimidation under the British Raj. The posting of such bonds was required during the Emergency under authority of The Prevention of Publication of Objectionable Matter Act, 1976. Chapter three of the act empowered the government to direct the keeper of the press to deposit as security "such amount as the competent authority may think to require" if the newspaper had published objectionable matter.

One of the newspapers required during the Emergency to deposit a security bond was *Himmat,* a Bombay weekly edited by Rajmohan Gandhi, grandson of Mahatma Gandhi, which was ordered to deposit Rs25,000. *Himmat,* which means "courage," took the censor to court to challenge the legality of the order.

The courts must interpret the law, and the period of the Emergency provided a severe test of their independence. By and large, they demonstrated their integrity. In one instance, Kuldip Nayar, a senior editor of *The Indian Express,* was detained under the Maintenance of Internal Security Act (MISA). Nayar filed a writ petition of habeas corpus, and the government, fearing an adverse judgment, released him. The Delhi High Court nevertheless issued its opinion that orders of detention were not outside the pale of review and chided government lawyers for seeking to avoid a judgment by releasing Nayar before an order for his release had been issued. The following year, however, the courts suspended the writ of habeas corpus.

In another instance George Verghese, editor of *The Hindustan Times,* was fired from his post by K. K. Birla, the owner, on suggestion of Birla's political friends. The suggestion followed publication of a series of articles critical of Indira Gandhi's government. The Press Council of India, established in 1966 to uphold editorial independence, news objectivity and fairness of comments, prepared to hear the dispute. Birla challenged the jurisdiction of the Press Council, but the Delhi High Court ruled that the council was the proper forum to consider charges of interference in the editorial process or pressure by the government. The government's response was simple. It abolished the Press Council.

There were a number of similar cases in which courts in India demonstrated their independence from the political process, although severe pressures were placed on individual judges through such measures as involuntary transfers.

Censorship

The Ministry of Information and Broadcasting is the agency concerned with monitoring the press. At present there is no prepublication censorship in India. There is, however, a timidity, or self-censorship, which may reflect the vestiges of the Emergency, a time of tribulation for many journalists. According to a white paper issued by the Ministry of Information and Broadcasting in August 1977, as many as 259 journalists were detained. Instances of censorship during the Emergency also abounded; the case of Ramnath Goenka's *Indian Express* will serve to illustrate.

The first act was the proclamation of Emergency on June 25, 1975, on the ground that the security of India was threatened by internal disturbances. The following day a censorship order was issued, providing that "no news, comments, rumours or other report, relating to [any of nine specified items] shall be published in any newspaper, periodical or other document unless such news, comments, rumour or other report has been submitted for scrutiny to an authorised officer and the publication thereof is authorised in writing by such officer...[and that] no such publication shall be made except in accordance with such conditions or restrictions as such officer may impose."

Shortly after that order was issued, the *Statesman* editor in Delhi, S. Nihal Singh, was asked by the Information and Broadcasting Ministry to publish certain photographs in a particular manner. He responded that the censorship order did not give the government authority to order certain items printed, but merely to order that such items go unpublished.

The government then ordered the *Statesman* to show cause why an unspecified number of government directors should not be added to the paper's board of directors on grounds of mismanagement. The paper responded by obtaining an injunction against the government's move.

Shortly thereafter, the government revoked the passport of C. R. Irani, managing director of the *Statesman,* thereby preventing him from attending a meeting of the International Press Institute in the United States. The government also withdrew advertising, confiscated the *Statesman's* press in Delhi, saw to it that concessional postal rates for newspapers were not available to the *Statesman,* and attempted to obtain control by buying shares in the company from private shareholders. The *Statesman* countered this last move by acquiring other private shares and placing them with loyal members of the staff. Finally, the government sent officials to the homes of *Statesman* journalists with warnings that they should do something to change the paper's attitude if they were interested in keeping their jobs.

Ramnath Goenka's *Indian Express* was similarly treated. In July 1975 Goenka learned that his son might be detained by the government under the Maintenance of Internal Security Act (MISA), which permitted arrest without grounds and without trial for one year. The son, B. D. Goenka, was a heart patient; the threat to detain him under MISA was a preliminary step in a plan by the government to assume control of the *Express* chain. Through an intermediary Goenka sought protection for his son. Soon, however, the Goenkas were informed that unless the *Express* papers were relinquished, the government would seek control through use of income tax authorities and court action. Goenka delayed by posing questions relating to transfer of ownership, then set a price of $30 million at which the government balked.

Next the government sought to gain control of the board of directors. Goenka threatened to take the matter to court, and in the ensuing process of negotiation he agreed to permit the government to name six members of the board, including the new chairman, K. K. Birla, who was to supervise editorial policy only. However, Birla attempted to order the transfer of Ajit Bhattacharjea, a senior editor, because of the editor's criticism of the government's suspension of habeas corpus. Goenka reminded Birla of his limited authority, but shortly thereafter Goenka was informed that if he did not agree to an extension of Birla's powers, he and his son and his daughter-in-law would all be detained under MISA. Goenka protested by a letter to the prime minister's secretary, outlining the threats received from V. C. Shukla, the minister of information and broadcasting. Shukla later denied making any threats.

Four days later the Press Information Bureau issued statements containing allegations about "Large scale tax evasion and fraud by a newspaper tycoon." After Goenka issued a rebuttal, the Press Information Bureau issued a new release, repeating the charges and naming Goenka. When Goenka complained again to the prime minister's secretary, the Ministry of Industry and Civil Supplies responded six days later by taking over control of Goenka's jute mill.

Meanwhile, government interference in the operation of the newspaper delayed its appearance, leading to a loss of circulation. When Goenka sought redress in court, the government stopped all advertisements in the *Indian Express* group of newspapers, and also in *The Tribune* and *The Statesman.*

Other actions against the *Express* included an attempt by the government to appoint an acting editor-in-chief, to which Goenka objected, contending that the government had not honored its side of an agreement to allow a committee to decide such matters. The next day the electric supply of the Delhi *Express* was cut off—padlocked at the switchbox. The Delhi High Court ordered power restored on Goenka's petition. Two days later police came to the *Express* offices in Delhi and sealed the press without warning, and while this was being done an announcement was placed in *The National Herald* that *The Indian Express* air conditioning equipment was to be sold at public auction to satisfy municipal taxes in arrears. Subsequently the bank notified the paper that it would no longer finance the purchase of newsprint.

By December 1976 it was clear that *The Indian Express* could not hold out much longer. In January 1977 the president dissolved the Lok Sabha, and the government relaxed the rules of Emergency. In March Indira Gandhi was defeated in elections. To understate the case, the change of government was most propitious for the *Express.*

During the Emergency the Press Council

was dissolved. Thus it could not exercise its function of protecting the press from external pressure. In 1979, the council was reconstituted, its function to "build up" a code of conduct for newsmen through case law, to hold hearings on complaints made against newspapers and news agencies, and to consider complaints against the government, with the right to criticize governmental action.

The Press Council consists of a chairman and 28 members, including 13 from among working journalists. Six others come from the management side of the newspaper business, five are members of Parliament, one is a representative of the news agencies, and three are public members. The chairman is chosen by a special panel of parliamentarians and council members.

Like the Press Council that was dissolved, the current council has no power to impose legal penalties. Unlike its predecessor, however, the current council levies fees on newspapers and news agencies, whereas the former council relied on the government for grants. The new funding arrangement increases the council's independence.

The current council owes its existence to the Press Council Act, 1978, which gave members status as public servants, with the power of subpoena, just as in the case of the former council.

Of 91 cases brought before the reconstituted Press Council between April 1979, when it came into existence, and August 1980, 47 dealt with events of the period between 1975 and 1979, when the council was not functioning; The council has refused to hear those 47. Of the remainder, most cases (perhaps 20 to 25) involve the financial viability of small newspapers—for example, government-withheld advertising for political purposes. Others are common complaints, such as the failure of an editor to publish a letter.

The Press Council cannot accept a complaint that is being heard concurrently by a court of law. And once it accepts a complaint, its sole power is to issue an opinion. Thus it relies on vindication to soothe the victor, and publicity to castigate the vanquished.

Unlike the Press Council, which is a statutory body, the Press Commission is an ad hoc group that will go out of existence after it renders it report. The present commission was formed in July 1978, consisting of 10 members, all appointed by government. It meets *in camera* to insure that persons invited to appear may speak freely.

The commission is charged with the responsibility to inquire into the growth and status of the press since 1954, when the first Press Commission submitted suggestions on future development. Its terms of reference consist of 18 items: (1) the role of the press in a developing and democratic society; (2) the present constitutional guarantee regarding freedom of speech and expression and whether this is sufficient to ensure press freedom; and adequacy and efficacy of the laws, rules and regulations for maintaining this freedom; (3) constitutional and legal safeguards to protect the citizen's right to privacy; (4) means of safeguarding the independence of the press against economic and political pressures and pressures from proprietors and management; (5) role of the press and the responsibilities it should assume in developmental policies; (6) the press as an industry, a social institution and a forum for informed discussion of public affairs; (7) ownership patterns, management practices and financial structures of the press, and their relation to growth, editorial independence and professional integrity; (8) chain newspapers, links with industry, and their effect on competition and on the readers' right to objective news and free comments; (9) economics of the newspaper industry: newsprint, printing machinery and other inputs; (10) advertising: government, private, educational and commercial; (11) government-press relations and the role of official agencies; (12) relations that should subsist between different elements of the press, namely, publishers, managers, editors and professional journalists, and others; (13) growth of small and medium papers and of the language press; (14) development of the periodical press and specialized journals; (15) news coverage and news values, structure and functioning of news agencies and feature agencies, flow of news to and from India; (16) training of professional manpower, steps to improve professional standards and performance, research in journalism and mass communication; (17) journalism as a means of better mutual understanding in the context of proposals for a new international information order; (18) perspective of newspaper development.

Initially the commission sent out 50,000 questionnaires; 7,000 were returned. Then 3,000 persons were invited to appear before the commission; 850 did so. None was subpoenaed. Another 1,000 persons were interviewed to determine how the press was run.

Finally, a number of studies were assigned to be written. Thus far 175 have been completed and another 150 are in progress; more may be added to the schedule.

Although the Press Commission meets *in camera* with those who appear before it, there are no administrative rules to restrict commissioners or other public officials from giving information to the press. There is, however, the Indian Official Secrets Act, 1963, which makes it an offense for any person for any purpose prejudicial to the safety or interest of the state to publish (among other things) or communicate to any other person any information that might be useful to an enemy.

Nor is there a freedom of information act that might be used by newsmen or other citizens to gain access to documents or records that a public official might wish to remain hidden.

With the general exception of the Emergency, during which heavy-handed censorship dampened journalistic ardor, the Indian press has not been unwilling to criticize government. As mentioned above, however, even during periods of peace between press and government there has been some self-censorship. The Indian press has not yet reached the ethos of "Publish and see what happens." Although intellectually they are as capable of debating government policies as any nation's journalists, they have been unwilling to test their freedom. Thus in theory the right to criticize government exists in India just as it does in the United States. But in practice there is a demonstrable reluctance to exercise that right beyond a point.

The closest thing to "managed" news takes place, oddly enough, at the local theater. Every cinema house is required by law to show newsreel films supplied by the government. The films are about 20 minutes each in length, and each contains several stories. The newsreels are produced once every two weeks by government filmmakers who travel about the countryside in mobile vans, shooting 35mm film which is reduced to 16mm for distribution. Some journalists feel the films were slanted during the Emergency.

The government also is said to have managed the news over All India Radio during the Emergency. This was achieved simply by omitting certain items from broadcasts. For example, if there was a riot in Old Delhi, it might not be reported over AIR. But BBC would carry a story, and listeners would thus discover the omission from AIR.

State-Press Relations

The Ministry of Information and Broadcasting is designed to inform the public about government programs, plans and policies, and to inform the government about public reaction. The ministry also provides liaison with state governments and other organizations working in the field of information and publicity. Regional and branch offices as well as mobile units assist in the operation of the ministry.

The ministry is assisted by 14 media units: (1) Akashvani, or All India Radio (AIR); (2) Doordarshan (television); (3) Press Information Bureau, (4) Publications Division, (5) Research and Reference Division. (6) Directorate of Advertising and Visual Publicity, (7) Registrar of Newspapers for India, (8) Directorate of Field Publicity, (9) Photo Division, (10) Song and Drama Division, (11) Films Division, (12) Central Board of Film Censors, (13) Directorate of Film Festivals, (14) National Film Archive of India.

In addition to these 14 media units, seven public-sector undertakings and autonomous societies aid the ministry: (1) Indian Institute of Mass Communication; (2) Film and Television Institute of India; (3) Children's Film Society; (4) Film Finance Corporation; (5) Indian Motion Pictures Export Corporation; (6) National Film Development Corporation; (7) Directorate of Evaluation.

Of these 21, several should be singled out for brief description:

The Indian Institute of Mass Communication was established in 1965 as an autonomous society to provide training and research in communication. It trains government information personnel through refresher courses and offers a postgraduate course in journalism for developing countries and a diploma course in news agency journalism for nonaligned countries. The institute also undertakes communication research projects, media performance evaluation projects and special seminars, and maintains the largest library in India on the subject of mass communication, with 12,346 books and subscriptions to about 267 periodicals as of March 1980. In addition, the institute publishes a quarterly journal, *Communicator*, and has published a number of books. Its director, H. Y. Sharada Prasad, also serves as information adviser to Prime Minister Indira Gandhi (who was returned to office in 1980 despite her earlier conduct).

The Film and Television Institute of India,

organized in 1960, is an autonomous body that offers training in the art and craft of TV and filmmaking. It provides in-service television training for Doordarshan employees and a two-year common course in cinema.

The Children's Film Society was set up as an autonomous body in 1955 to promote and produce films suitable for children and adolescents. In its first 21 years, the society produced or acquired 157 films, 12 of which have won national and international awards.

Akashvani (All India Radio or AIR; the Hindi word means "sound from sky") has in its network 84 broadcasting centers covering over 89 percent of the population and 77.6 percent of India's land area. It began in 1927 with the establishment of two private transmitters, which the government took over in 1930. Broadcasting has been a state monopoly since that time. Today the government broadcasts from 157 transmitters in its home service programs, which are received by about 24 million radio sets. Over 38 percent of the broadcast time is devoted to music, while nearly 35 percent is news. The central news organization puts out news in 19 languages, using reports sent in by 319 AIR correspondents in India and abroad. AIR also broadcasts to foreign countries through its external service in 25 languages, including 17 foreign and 8 Indian.

Doordarshan (television; the Hindi word means "seeing from distance") was created in 1976 when it was delinked from All India Radio and set up as a full-fledged directorate. It now has 17 transmitters covering over 14 percent of the population and 5.7 percent of the land area, with reception on about 700,000 sets. The broadcast schedule includes about four hours daily of general programming, of which perhaps one-half hour is devoted to news. Another two hours daily of educational programming is piped into the schools. All signals are black and white, although experimental color has been transmitted successfully. In October 1980 the government was debating whether to invest in color equipment. Income for both Doordashan and Akashvani is derived from commercial fees and from license fees. For radio the annual fee is $1.80; for television the fee is $6.00. The broadcast services were reportedly ready to announce a record income of over $19.2 million for the fiscal year 1979–80.

In 1978 a study group recommended that India's radio and television services be granted autonomy; the proposal was not accepted.

The Press Information Bureau handles public relations for the government—disseminating information to the press and other media, acting as a clearinghouse for official data and providing feedback to the government on public reactions to official policies. For small and medium newspapers, PIB offers special services such as a weekly news digest and illustrated articles covering development activities. The bureau also assists accredited correspondents with facilities and publicity material. A single-sheet weekly wall newspaper produced by PIB is posted at key points, particularly in remote areas.

The Directorate of Advertising and Visual Publicity undertakes advertising campaigns, selects newspapers for placement of government advertising and regulates accreditation of advertising agencies.

The Registrar of Newspapers for India maintains a register of data concerning newspapers, issues registration certificates, approves proposed titles, oversees regularity of publication, verifies circulation claims in order to allocate newsprint and prepares an annual report with statistics on the press in India.

The Research and Reference Division provides a reference service to media units of the ministry, including *India—A Reference Annual,* a standard reference source that is found in scholarly libraries around the world.

The Central Board of Film Censors certifies films for showing in India. Without certification, a film may not be exhibited. The Board may refuse a certificate if the film or any part of it is against the interest of the security of the state, friendly relations with foreign states, public order, decency or morality; if it involves defamation or contempt of court or is likely to incite the commission of an offense. In 1977 the board granted certificates to 1,763 Indian films and 1,142 foreign films. Certificates were denied to 30 foreign films and one trailer of an Indian film. In 1975 *Kissa Kursi Ka,* a satirical film about an unqualified president of a mythical country, was denied a certificate. The film's producer asked the Supreme Court to order the government to issue a certificate. Meanwhile, V. C. Shukla, the minister of information and broadcasting, ordered the film seized. The producer again appealed to the court, which ordered the government to preserve the film during the course of litigation. When the court ordered a showing of the film, the government claimed that it could not be found. In February 1979 Shukla and the prime minister's son, Sanjay Gandhi, were sentenced to two years in jail for destroying the film.

State control over the press was intensified during the 19-month Emergency, but the potential for control existed before that time and exists today, notably in the allocation of newsprint, which is handled through the State Trading Corporation, a government monopoly. Potential for control is also seen in government advertising. Of 400 daily newspapers submitting data, 108 reported receiving at least half of their income from government advertising in 1976. A third source of potential control lies in government licensing of imports such as machinery, spare parts and photographic materials. Application for permission to import must be made on an annual basis to the Chief Controller of Imports and Exports. The Registrar of Newspapers determines the entitlement of each publisher. A fourth source of control is the accreditation procedure for correspondents, and the special considerations, such as housing, that accrue to those who are accredited. Loss of accreditation during the Emergency resulted in genuine hardship for some journalists who were dispossessed of their low-cost housing. Still another source of government control lies in the credit arrangements publishers must make with nationalized banks. The state is also the largest customer of the news agencies, and they were forced into massive reorganization at government direction in part because of dependence on income from the state. And of course direct control exists in radio and television which are government monopolies.

Attitude Toward Foreign Media

Foreign correspondents in India must work through the Ministry of External Affairs, which is charged with explaining and interpreting the policies of the government of India to overseas newsmen. In 1977–78, assistance was provided to 208 foreign journalists and to 38 foreign television teams. These correspondents in most cases must have visas to enter India, but not to travel about the country. However, they are asked to notify the government of their travel plans, and they may be advised not to visit certain areas.

Prior approval for cables is not required at present, but officially the government has authority under the Indian Telegraph Act of

1885 to take temporary possession of any telegraph and to order that any message not be transmitted. Under the act the government may intercept any message and require that it be disclosed. If the sender knows the message to be false or fabricated, he may be fined and/or imprisoned.

During the Emergency seven foreign correspondents were expelled and another 29 barred from entry. One of those ousted has described the circumstances of his expulsion in "Dateline Delhi—For the Last Time," an article published in the *Far Eastern Economic Review* for February 20, 1976. Lawrence Lifschultz speculates in that article that he was expelled because of official dissatisfaction with an earlier article in the same magazine, on the *Indian Express* affair, which appeared without the government's version. That view appeared a week later in an article entitled "The 'Express' Affair: New Delhi's Story," but the denials were printed too late to preserve Lifschultz's accreditation, if in fact his expulsion was the result of the earlier story.

Import restrictions may be imposed by authority of the Sea Customs Act of 1878 on goods of any specified description. In practice such restrictions are imposed routinely only on "obscene" publications such as *Playboy* and *Hustler*. Occasionally a book or magazine may be banned on religious grounds. The December 3, 1979 issue of *Newsweek* was disallowed for containing Muhammad's picture, which is proscribed by Islam. The magazine had been admitted, but then was confiscated. In one instance a book was admitted with a disclaimer rubber-stamped by the government in each copy. The book was an atlas published by the London *Times* showing national boundaries not recognized by India.

Foreign ownership of domestic media is also forbidden. For example, if Americans or foreigners wanted to establish a wholly-owned *Wall Street Journal*, it would not be permitted. But *Reader's Digest* publishes an Indian edition, which is acceptable. The prohibition is founded on concern over the flow of foreign exchange rather than the content of communications. Multinational-corporation operations are restricted in India. Coca-Cola was forced to close its 22 bottling plants in 1977 after it had captured 60 percent of the Indian soft drink market.

The most prestigious of the international press organizations are based not in India, but elsewhere in the world. This fact is a matter of convenience, not of inhospitability by the Indian government. Many Indian journalists are members of such organizations as the International Federation of Newspaper Publishers, the International Press Institute and various UNESCO committees. For example, Mohammed Yunus Dehlvi, editor and general manager of *Shama,* served on the executive committee of the International Federation of Newspaper Publishers (FIEJ) and is a member of the International Press Institute (IPI). U. L. Baruah, director general of All India Radio, served in the administrative council of the Asia Pacific Broadcasting Union, and B. G. Verghese, former editor of *The Hindustan Times,* is a member of the UNESCO International Commission on Communications Policy.

The UNESCO Declaration on Fundamental Principles concerning the Contribution of the Mass Media was fully supported by the government of India, whose representative voted for it. But opinion in the editorial columns of Indian newspapers was by no means unanimous. D. R. Mankekar, writing in *The Indian Express,* called it an important document of special significance to developing countries. On the other hand, Abu Abraham, argued in *The Times of India* that the danger of the UNESCO proposals is that they pay obeisance to liberalism but are calculated in practice to undermine it.

News Agencies

There are four domestic news agencies in India: the Press Trust of India (PTI), United News of India (UNI), Hindustan Samachar and Samachar Bharati. PTI was formed in 1948 out of Associated Press of India, owned and operated by Reuters. Today it maintains 81 offices, employs 500 staff members and serves 450 subscribers. Full-time correspondents are stationed in New York, London, Moscow, Katmandu (Nepal), and Colombo (Sri Lanka). PTI files 60,000 words daily by teleprinter, including news from the Soviet Union (Tass), France, (AFP), and United Kingdom (Reuters). Its rates are based on the circulation of the subscriber and on the number of words the subscriber (A, B, or C service) desires.

UNI started operations in 1961, three years after the failure of United Press of India. Today it operates 75 branch offices, employs

560 staff members and serves 450 subscribers. It maintains correspondents in New York, London, Katmandu, Dacca (Bangladesh), Singapore, Hong Kong, Dubai, Qatar, Kuwait and Nairobi. UNI leases 60,000 kilometers of telephone lines for its subscribers, who receive news from the Soviet Union, United States and West Germany through the agency's agreements with Tass, AP, and d p a, respectively. UNI rates are based on circulation, with a minimum charge of Rs1,070 ($128.40) monthly for newspapers with less than 5,000 copies sold per issue. All UNI newspaper subscribers receive the same number of words.

Both PTI and UNI serve customers other than newspapers. In fact, UNI receives 42 percent of its revenue from non-newspaper sources, including 13 percent from All India Radio. Some of UNI's 450 teleprinters are leased by government ministries, state governments, hotels, banks and airports.

Hindustan Samachar (Indian News) is a multilingual news agency that began service in 1948. It provides service in Hindi, Marathi and Gujarati on teleprinters using Devanagari script. At its peak of operation, prior to the Emergency, it had a teleprinter circuit connecting a network of 21 offices to serve 135 subscribers in 10 Indian languages.

Samachar Bharati (News India) is also a language agency (that is, an agency serving language papers primarily). It was inaugurated in 1966 and provides service in 10 languages to 150 subscribers. It has an agreement with United Press International for its world news service, which it supplies via teleprinter to 30 offices. Samachar Bharati maintains correspondents in New York, London and Bonn, and another 400 correspondents and stringers in India.

The four agencies were merged by the government during the Emergency into a single agency called simply Samachar. The government maintained publicly that the merger was voluntary, but G. G. Mirchandani, editor and general manager of UNI, opposed it openly. As a result, All India Radio stopped taking UNI's service, cutting the agency's revenue drastically. Then UNI was notified that payment for its needs would have to be made in advance. Next, the teleprinters at the 18 government ministries were cut. Finally, pressure was applied by the government through UNI's subscribers. The four agencies were merged in February 1976, and Mirchandani was out of a job. After the formation of the new government in March 1977, a committee was formed to examine the functioning of Samachar. Partly as a result of the Kuldip Nayar committee report, the agencies were able to begin their separate operations in April 1978, and Mirchandani was rehired to direct UNI.

Eleven foreign news services maintain offices in India. They include Agence France Presse (AFP), Associated Press, Reuters, Tass, United Press International, Allgemeiner Deutscher Nachrichtendienst (ADN) of the German Democratic Republic, Deutsche Presse-Agentur (DPA) of the Federal Republic of Germany, and news agencies from Poland and Yugoslavia.

The government of India accredits these and other foreign news agencies to work in India, but since 1948 all foreign news agencies have been required to route all traffic through one domestic agency only. (Tass has been permitted an exception; both PTI and UNI take the Tass news service.) The purpose of channeling news through a single agency is financial. Individual newspapers are spared the expense of subscribing to different news agencies and thus duplicating services while increasing the cash flow out of India. Some newspapers, like *The Times of India,* have foreign news-agency teleprinters in. their newsrooms, but pay a domestic agency for the service. While foreign news agencies thus have, in effect, only one subscriber in India, domestic agencies are free to sell their services to newspapers which also take the services of competing domestic agencies. About 20 to 30 Indian newspapers subscribe to PTI only, 130 only to UNI, and another 150 to both.

Another special arrangement affecting the flow of news from abroad is the nonaligned news-agency pool. In 1975 the foreign ministers of nonaligned countries decided to form such a pool. Information ministers and news agency representatives from 62 countries met in New Delhi to frame a news-exchange agreement. India arranged a two-way flow of news with 14 so-called nonaligned countries: Cuba, Indonesia, Vietnam, Yugoslavia, Bangladesh, Iraq, Sudan, Algeria, Qatar, Morocco, Kenya, Ethiopia, Zambia and Malaysia. The exchange began in August 1976 by telex, teleprinter and telegram, depending on facilities available. India supplied four or five news items daily to each of its pool partners, who were free to use or to decline the material. PTI handled the ex-

change, but dropped out of the pool four years later after observing that the nonaligned group appeared to serve primarily political purposes.

Electronic News Media

Because broadcasting is a state monopoly in India, state policies relating to radio and television news are, in fact, the policies employed by the media. All India Radio permits its stations to operate freely except for broad program patterns and language ratio. For example, six to 10 percent of programming must be devoted to such "development" broadcasts as family planning, cultivation and health care. Crime may not be reported. The central news organization sends out 67 news bulletins daily in 19 languages. Over the entire network, news is broadcast daily through 242 bulletins in 37 languages and 34 local dialects. When Parliament is in session, daily commentaries in English and Hindi review the proceedings in both houses. Reviews of legislative proceedings in the states are broadcast from state capitals.

Unlike AIR, India's television system does not have a newscasting network. There is no national news bulletin telecast collectively by all Doordarshan kendras (studios); each kendra prepares and presents its own bulletins. A major goal of television broadcasting is the dissemination of social education—agricultural information, health and hygiene, and family planning.

Education & Training

Journalism education in India is, by common admission, deficient. But in the academic scheme of things, it is new. The first department of journalism was established in 1941 at Panjab University in Lahore, transferred to Delhi in 1947 after partition, and finally to Chandigarh in 1962. Madras University established a journalism department in 1947, followed by the universities of Calcutta in 1950, Mysore in 1951, Nagpur in 1952 and Osmania in 1954. More recently, programs have been instituted at Punjabi University, Jabalpur University, Ravishankar University, University of Poona, and Banaras Hindu University. The University of Kerala in Trivandrum has begun a department of journalism headed by Dr. K. E. Eapen, who holds a Ph.D. from the University of Wisconsin. Programs in mass communication are offered at Bangalore University and at the Rajendra Prasad Institute of Communication & Management. In all, there are about 50 schools offering journalism courses, with an enrollment of perhaps 1,500 students.

Osmania University's program in Hyderabad has achieved a good reputation among journalism professionals. Headed by Professor S. Bashiruddin, the Department of Communication & Journalism offers a one-year master's degree and a one-year postgraduate bachelor's degree.

Banaras Hindu University's one-year bachelor's program, headed by Professor Anjan Kumar Banerji, is also well regarded. It is one of the few schools to teach language journalism, with instruction in Hindi as well as in English. (Bangalore and Mysore universities teach in Kannada and English.) The student newspaper at Banaras Hindu, *Parisar,* is a Hindi-language paper. Professor Banerji also serves as president of the Indian Journalism Education Association. All faculty members are graduates of the Indian Institute of Mass Communications.

The Rajendra Prasad Institute offers a number of one-year diploma courses in such areas as journalism, public relations, advertising and photography, and a two-year diploma in printing; instruction is offered by colleges in 19 cities. The institute publishes *Alpha,* a communications monthly magazine, and *The Word,* an annual magazine designed "to promote mass communication arts and media."

The Press Institute of India is an autonomous institution set up by Indian newspapers in 1963. Its director is Chanchal Sarkar, a former Nieman Fellow at Harvard, and the assistant director, K. Bhupal, served with *The Statesman* in Delhi. PII holds seminars, workshops and refresher courses for newspaper and periodical staff-members, and also organizes symposia for interdisciplinary and foreign groups. The institute has brought out over two dozen publications and publishes *Vidura,* a bimonthly journal devoted to the mass media, which circulates in 26 foreign countries. PII also runs an annual prize contest for news photographers.

Other awards in the field of journalism include an all-India competition, sponsored by the Directorate of Advertising and Visual Publicity, for excellence in printing and designing of books and publications, including newspapers. The Chandrakant Vora Memorial Award consists of three annual cash prizes—one each for the best report published in Gujarati, Marathi and English newspapers. The Durgadas Ratan Devi Trust gives five awards to (1) the editor whose advocacy of a cause has made greatest impact on the public mind, (2) the outstanding columnist, (3) the best investigative report, (4) the outstanding news story and (5) the outstanding portrayal of an event through pictorial reproduction or cartoon.

The most important journalistic associations and organizations include:

Indian and Eastern Newspaper Society. IENS is the newspaper publishers' group, founded in 1939. It publishes a monthly journal, *Indian Press.*

All India Newspaper Editors' Conference. AINEC is an organization of newspapers and periodicals as represented by their editors. It was founded in 1940.

All India Small and Medium Newspapers Federation. Founded in 1968, AISMNF deals with the problems of proprietors and editors of small and medium newspapers. It publishes a journal entitled *Editor.*

Indian Language Newspapers' Association. Any newspaper or periodical published in any of the Indian languages is eligible for membership in the ILNA, which was founded in 1941.

Editors Guild of India. The Editors Guild met at its first national convention in 1978. Membership is on an individual basis—no institutions are eligible, nor are editors of house journals and trade magazines. The guild is to be a forum of editors of general interest newspapers, news agencies and periodicals, who will meet to seek solutions to professional problems.

Summary

As a nation India is young. As a civilization it is old, but with a proud history. In the midst of this paradox the press of India finds itself with an uncertain identity—rather like an adolescent torn between the urgings of independent young manhood and the desire to please one's elders.

The colonial experience was rather like growing up in the care of a paternalistic guardian; India benefited immensely from a British sense of order and propriety and reason, but it was denied that which only a natural father can give: the love that bestows self-confidence.

Thus India, on achieving its inheritance, which was its independence, came of age; but its voice, which was its press, had not found its proper pitch. Today that voice has deepened, but its message is not yet always clear.

The range of journalistic ability in India encompasses the entire spectrum. At the upper end there are journalists who can compete—and have done so—among the world's elite. At the other end are those without the self-respect that distinguishes journalists from hacks. As L. K. Advani, former minister of information and broadcasting, was reported to have said to certain publishers shortly after the Emergency ended: "The government asked you to bow and you crawled."

Prospects for the future are good, however equivocal or regrettable the past may have been. The experience of the Emergency has sharpened the senses of India's press like a whiff of ammonia. The difference between freedom to speak and freedom to repeat is now more clearly defined. Essentially that is the difference between adolescence and maturity.

As a leader among developing nations, India recognizes that in one world there are many voices. This recognition carries with it the capacity to tolerate dissent. The press in India has the intellectual capacity for dissent, if not yet the total willingness. As the press acquires that willingness, and as India acquires that toleration, both will achieve greatness.

CHRONOLOGY

1975

June — Declaration of national emergency. Pre-censorship imposed on newspapers. Mrs. Gandhi tells National Union of Journalists that some newspapers are not concerned with national interest but are building a vicious atmosphere and that censorship is necessary to prevent incitement to defy law.

August — Satellite Instructional Television Experiment (SITE) begins in 2,400 villages in six states.

December — Government issues three ordinances: (1) Dissolution of Press Council Ordinance, abolishing Press Council on grounds it had failed to set out and enforce code of conduct and to build body of case law; (2) Repeal of Parliamentary Proceedings (Protection of Publication) Act Ordinance, removing immunity from prosecution for "substantially true report of any proceedings of either House of Parliament or State Legislature unless publication was proved to have been made with malice"; (3) Prevention of Objectionable Matter Ordinance, empowering government to prohibit prejudicial reports in newspapers and to demand and forfeit securities from keepers of presses and editors and publishers of objectionable matter.

1976

February — Four major news agencies of India are merged into single agency, Samachar.

1977

January — Government announces relaxation of rules of Emergency, decides not to enforce press censorship.

March — Indira Gandhi resigns; Morari Desai becomes Prime Minister.

April — Parliament repeals Prevention of Publication of Objectionable Matter Act, reenacts Parliamentary Proceedings (Protection of Publication) Act.

November — The Cabinet announces decision to break up Samachar into its four original constituents. Government revokes ban on government advertising in more than 80 newspapers; political affiliations of newspapers and periodicals will not be considered in placing advertisements.

December — Parliament is told that as many as 208 dailies, 1,434 weeklies, 362 fortnightlies, and 518 monthlies were closed between June 24, 1975 and January 29, 1976, on various grounds, including non-submission of material for pre-censorship, arrests of editors, and seizure of printing presses. According to the Annual Report of the Ministry of Information and Broadcasting, 440 newspapers and periodicals were pre-censored during the Emergency, 51 newsmen lost their accreditation, and the declarations of 2,649 newspapers were cancelled. Advertisements were denied to 98 newspapers and periodicals.

1978
May   Central Government announces appointment of second Press Commission to go into development of Indian press in past 25 years and make recommendations on its future.

August   Parliament passes Press Council Bill. Membership to consist of 28 persons appointed by the government, including five members of Parliament; others are to be members of the press, representing broad spectrum.

1979
May   Government rejects bill to convert state-owned radio and television into autonomous corporation, prefers "functional autonomy" over statutory autonomy.

1980
January   Mrs. Indira Gandhi returns to power.
           President Neelam Sanjiva Reddy assures Parliament that "The government reiterates its commitment to the freeedom of the Press."

February   Minister for Information and Broadcasting V. P. Sathe, announces that India's four news agencies may be reunited into a single agency—Samachar—as they were during the Emergency.
           UNESCO publishes report of Commission on International Communication Problems, condemning press censorship and endorsing free access for journalists to both official and nonofficial sources, India approves report through vote of its representative on the 16-member commission.

September Ordinance announced by President Reddi gives union and state governments power to detain any person for up to 12 months without trial.

BIBLIOGRAPHY

Bhattacharjee, Arun. *The Indian Press: Profession to Industry.* Delhi, 1972.

Desai, M. V. *Communication Policies in India.* Paris, 1977.

Franda, Marcus F. "Curbing the Indian Press." *Fieldstaff Reports: South Asia Series* Vol. 20, nos. 12, 13, 14 (February 1977).

Frost, J. M., ed. *World Radio TV Handbook.* New York, 1980.

Henderson, Michael. *Experiment with Untruth.* Delhi, 1977.

India. *India: A Reference Annual 1979.* New Delhi, 1979.

———. *Mass Media in India 1978.* New Delhi, 1978.

———. *Press in India 1977.* New Delhi, 1979.

———. *Report 1978-79.* New Delhi, 1979.

"India." *Encyclopedia of the Third World.* Vol 1. 1978.

Indian News and Feature Alliance. *Press And Advertisers Year Book 1979.* New Delhi, 1979.

Jones, Graham. *The Toiling Word.* London, 1979.

Katzen, May. *Mass Communication: Teaching and Studies at Universities.* Paris, 1975.

Mankekar, D. R., and Mankekar, Kamla. *Decline and Fall of Indira Gandhi.* New Delhi, 1977.

Mathew, K. M., ed. *Manorama Yearbook 1980.* Kottayam, India, 1980.

Mehrotra, R. K., coordinator. *Mass Communication in India: An Annotated Bibliography.* Singapore, 1976.

Mehta, D. S. *Mass Communication and Journalism in India.* New Delhi, 1979.

Merrill, John C., and Fisher, Harold A. *The World's Great Dailies: Profiles of Fifty Newspapers.* New York, 1980.

Parthasarathy, Rangaswami. *A Hundred Years of the Hindu.* Madras, n.d.

Raghavan, G. N. S. "Do Mass Media Reach the Masses? The Indian Experience." *Prospects.* 10, no. 1 (1980), p. 90.

Rau, M. Charapathi. *The Press.* New Delhi, 1974.

Sorabjee, Soli J. *Law of Press Censorship in India.* Bombay, 1976.

———. *The Emergency, Censorship and the Press in India, 1975-77.* New Delhi, 1977.

"The Press Under Pressures." *Probe India.* January 1980, p. 6.

Winsbury, Rex. "India's Technology Dilemma." *World Press Review.* February 1981, p. 60.

INDONESIA

by Elliott S. Parker

BASIC DATA

Population: 138.3 million (est.)
Area: 1,906,240 sq. km. (736,000 sq. mi.)
GNP: Rp 32.73 trillion (1979) (US$52.2 billion) (1979)
Literacy Rate: 50% (est.)
Language(s): bahasa Indonesia (Malay), Chinese, Dutch, some 200 local dialects
Number of Dailies: 84
  Aggregate Circulation: 2,281,000
  Circulation per 1,000: 16.5
Number of Nondailies: 76
  Aggregate Circulation: 800,000
  Circulation per 1,000: 5.8

Number of Periodicals: 91
Number of Radio Stations: 517 (1978)
Number of Television Stations: 1
Number of Radio Receivers: 6.5 million (est.)
  Radio Receivers per 1,000: 47 (est.)
Number of Television Sets: 700,000 (est.)
  Television Sets per 1,000: 5.1 (est.)
Total Annual Newsprint Consumption: 56,100 metric tons
  Per Capita Newsprint Consumption: 0.4 kg. (.08 lb.)
Total Newspaper Ad Receipts: NA
  As % of All Ad Expenditures: NA

Background & General Characteristics

Indonesia, the fifth most populous nation in the world, lies athwart geographical, cultural, social, economic and strategic networks extending from the southern part of Asia to the island continent of Australia.

Crossing three time zones and 3,200 miles, the archipelago consists of more than 13,000 islands, of which about 6,000 are inhabited. The nation straddles the equator and lies between the Indian and Pacific oceans. Historically Indonesia has been a crossroads of trading and social interchange, and this has helped make the contemporary nation a composite of peoples and cultures deposited by successive waves of migration.

Sundanese, Javanese, Balinese, Batak and Ambonese are only a few of the 200 languages or dialects spoken in the archipelago. This multiplicity of tongues demonstrates both the heterogeneity of the islands and the difficulty of treating the press, radio and television as broad-based "mass" media.

The five main islands are Sumatra; Kalimantan (on the island of Borneo, which also includes Brunei and the Malaysian states of Sabah and Sarawak); Sulawesi (formerly Celebes); Irian Jaya (formerly Dutch New Guinea); and the most populous, Java, where about two-thirds of the population live.

Outside the major cities, an already low level of literacy drops precipitously and the use of the national language declines in rural areas. In the villages, the language of daily communication is the local tongue.

The history of journalism in Indonesia follows the disparate streams of the various languages. The first paper published in the Dutch East Indies was the *Bataviasche Nouvelles,* a Dutch-language paper which appeared in 1744. Its editor was a Dutch official. The paper survived only two years. During the remainder of the century various Dutch journals appeared and disappeared. Few were concerned with local events; most were rewrites of news in papers received from Holland. A publication was started to cover activities in the local real estate market, in 1810 the *Bataviasche Koloniale Courant* appeared as an official paper, lasting until the following year when the British occupied the islands and started the English-language *Java Government Gazette. The Gazette* lasted only until 1816, when Dutch rule was reimposed. Also in that year the Dutch-language *Bataviasche Courant* was founded as the islands' first general-interest paper. It changed its name to *Javasche Courant* in 1828, and survived until the Japanese occupation in 1942.

Other Dutch publications in Jakarta (then Batavia) included *Java-Bode,* which existed from 1852 until the early 1950s, the *Bataviasche Nieuwsblad,* and the *Het Algemeen Dagblad van Nederlandsch-Indie.* By the middle of the 19th century, about 30 newspapers were being published in the colony. At the end of the century Dutch papers had been or were being published outside Jakarta. There were *De Locomotief* in Semarang, *Mataram* in Jokjakarta, *De Preanger Bode* in Bandung, and the *Deli Courant* on Sumatra.

This period, between about 1850 and 1870, also marked the appearance of the first Indonesian-language papers. These included *Bromartani,* published in Surakarta in 1855; *Soerat Chabar Betawie* (1858); and *Bientang Timoer* (1862). *Bromartani,* in common with several other publications, was printed in Javanese rather than Malay. The first Malay-language paper, *Soerat Kabar Bahasa Melajoe,* was started in 1856 in Surabaya. In general, the editors of these early publications, and their financing, were Eurasian.

The first Indonesian newspaper edited by Indonesians and financed by local capital was *Medan Prijaji,* which started publishing sometime between 1907 and 1910. Other papers of this period in Java were *Darmo-Kondo* (Surakarta), *Sinar Hindia* (Semarang) and *Oetoesan Hindia* (Surabaya). Outside Java, papers were published in Pontianak *(Oetoesan Borneo),* Medan *(Benih Mardika),* and *Tjaja-Soematra* in Padang (the two latter in Sumatra). These papers became the means of communicating and expressing the sense of nationalism and anticolonialism that had begun with the Budi Utomo independence movement in 1908.

Such papers were different from their predecessors. Profit was not a motive; they were designed to further the aims of various nationalistically inclined groups around the islands. Because only about five percent of the population were estimated to be literate in the Indonesian language, circulations were small—few papers had circulations over 1,000—and advertising was minimal.

At the turn of the century, Medan, Padang and Atjeh were pockets of publishing for the Malayo-Muslim world that centered on Singapore. Religious and secular publications—including newspapers—flourished, and correspondence columns became important modes of communication between communities in Java, Sumatra, Sarawak and peninsular Malaya. Ultimately, the social, religious and political influence of these papers was felt more in Singapore and Malaysia than in Indonesia.

Papers directed to the immigrant Indonesian-Chinese community were in a much stronger financial position, occupying the cultural middle ground between the Dutch and the Indonesians. Like all the countries of Southeast Asia, Indonesia has a significant Chinese community; the best known of its papers include *Ik Po,* started in Surakarta (1904), *Sin Po,* Jakarta (1910) and *Tjhoen Tjhiou,* Surabaya (1914). The Surabaya-based *Sin Tit Po* considered itself a leader of the nationalist movement. Although *Ik Po* was published using Chinese characters, most Indonesian-Chinese papers were written in Batavian Malay, a combination of Bazaar Malay and the Hokkien dialect of Chinese.

The Indonesian-Chinese papers generally were in much better financial condition than the indigenous Indonesian press. They also had a wider circulation than the Dutch papers. At one time, *Sin Po* claimed a circulation of 10,000.

About 1920, the number of Indonesian-Chinese papers increased dramatically and began to develop into two types, one emphasizing Chinese culture and China, the other focusing on the place of Chinese in the local society.

All Dutch and most Indonesian papers were banned during the Japanese occupation between 1942 and 1945. The press became a tool of the military government, which published five papers including *Djawa Shinbun* in Jakarta and *Sinar Matahari* in Jokjakarta. An underground press, represented by *Merah Putih* in Surakarta, also appeared.

By prohibiting the use of Dutch, the Japanese forced the population to speak, write and read Indonesian (later to be codified as "bahasa Indonesia") as the lingua franca throughout the islands. Prior to this time, Indonesian had been only a trading language that facilitated maritime commerce across an area from southern Thailand through Malaysia and Indonesia to the Philippines. When the war ended, Indonesian was well positioned to become a national language, slowly displacing regional dialects.

In 1973 Indonesia and Malaysia signed an agreement that rationalized the spelling and use of bahasa Malaysia and bahasa Indonesia. Although deriving from the same root, the languages had developed differently due to colonial influence—Dutch in Indonesia and English in Malaysia.

Days before the Japanese surrendered, Indonesia proclaimed its independence. The Dutch did not accept the independence proclamation, returned, and finally were forced out in 1949. Meanwhile, however, the Indonesian press blossomed. Between 1949 and the Guided Democracy concept introduced by Indonesia's first president, Sukarno, in 1956, the press increased in numbers and circulation. More Indonesian-language papers were founded, English-language papers were started, and the Chinese press entered a period of relative prosperity. Although independent, most papers were owned or subsidized by the myriad political parties and ethnic groups that had begun to vie for power after independence.

Under Guided Democracy, Sukarno abandoned the parliamentary style of government in favor of reaching consensus by the traditional Indonesian means of discussion rather than voting. Society was represented by function and region as well as by party. Power was in the unlikely three-handed grip of Sukarno, right-wing military groups, and the Communist Party of Indonesia (*Partai Komunis Indonesia* or PKI). Although Sukarno attempted to use the two other groups as counterbalances, the PKI continued to grow, and by the mid-1960s had the largest membership of any communist organization outside China or the Soviet bloc.

Sukarno also initiated broad and stringent regulations against the press. Newspapers were required to actively support any government policy, with criticism not allowed. Mochtar Lubis, Indonesia's most respected and well-known journalist, was jailed for almost ten years. Left-wing and Communist papers became dominant, claiming half the circulation. At this time, Sukarno also took over Antara, the national news agency, which was already actively supporting the government line. "In a revolution," Sukarno said, "there should be no press freedom." In just a few years, the number of papers and circulation dropped by half.

Tension between the army and the PKI grew as the PKI aligned itself with China, culminating in the "Gestapu affair," an attempted takeover by the PKI, which was foiled by the army in September 1965. In the aftermath of the abortive coup, thousands of people were killed or imprisoned, right-wing and communist papers were banned or closed and the leftist-dominated Antara closed for a time and reorganized. Later in the year, papers published in Chinese were also closed because of a belief that they were pro-communist. To replace these papers, the government began *Harian Indonesia*.

In 1966 Sukarno was forced to hand over control to President (then General) Suharto. Papers that had been closed or voluntarily suspended publication began to publish again. The problems of distribution, scarcity of newsprint and advertising and lack of trained professionals remained, but the outlook for the press was optimistic.

Newspapers were enabled to operate under Suharto's pragmatic New Order (*orde baru*). Individual publications consolidated or became stronger, and circulation showed yearly increases. Writing was lively, political cartoons common. In 1966, a Basic Law of the Press was passed by the legislature; it seemed to return the press to the pre-Sukarno days. Some newspapers took more independent stances and the government tolerated increasingly severe stands against its policies. Newspapers commented on—and criticized—sensitive issues that had previously been ignored. These included the elections of 1971, the questions of the political prisoners of the abortive 1965 coup, the business practices of Tien Suharto, the president's wife, and also the role of *pribumi*, or indigenous Indonesian businessmen vis-a-vis Indonesians of Chinese descent.

However, press freedom still balanced between government control and self-restraint. In January 1974 the former became dominant. In that month, coincident with the visit of the Japanese prime minister, riots and demonstrations broke out in Jakarta. Later Suharto instituted some reforms and revoked the publishing permits of at least five major newspapers, including the one most well known overseas, Mochtar Lubis's *Indonesia Raya*. Several weeklies also were closed. It was further announced that journalists on the banned papers would be required to undergo security screening by *Kopkamtib* (the army command for internal security), and that the papers themselves must support both the New Order and "Pancasila," the national ideology promulgated by Suharto. The latter consisted of five (*panca*) principles (*sila*): belief in one God, humanitarianism, national unity, democracy, and social justice.

In the wake of this "Malari affair" (from

the Indonesian *Malapetaka Lima Belas Januari,* or January 15 Disaster), Mochtar Lubis and several other people were not allowed to leave the country. (Lubis was presently jailed for two and a half months during the investigation of the demonstrations.) Four years later, in January 1978, seven papers were closed for two weeks and 240 critics arrested. Among the papers were the prestigious *Merdeka* and *Kompas,* the latter closed for the first time since its formation in 1965. The general newsmagazine, *Ekspres,* was also banned. The result of these crackdowns can be seen even today. With the exception of *Merdeka,* whose editor, B. M. Diah, is a former minister of information, the daily press avoids overtly controversial editorial stands. *Tempo,* a weekly magazine along the lines of *Time,* is well known for publishing provocative editorials and columns.

Most Indonesian papers are broadsheet size, published in Jakarta, and use bahasa Indonesia. Two, the *Indonesian Observer* and the *Indonesia Times,* are in English. The government-owned *Harian Indonesia* is the only Chinese-language publication, although about half its content is in bahasa Indonesia.

In 1980 Indonesia had 84 daily papers, 76 weeklies; 33 weekly, 32 biweekly and 22 monthly magazines, and five "bulletins." The total circulation of all these publications, according to the Ministry of Information, was 5.2 million. Of this total, daily papers accounted for 2.3 million on an average day. Sixty-two percent of this circulation is in Jakarta, where the press is heavily concentrated; 25 percent of the daily papers are published in Jakarta, including the nation's six largest dailies, which account for 77 percent of the circulation in the capital. In 1979, 43 percent of the adult population read a daily.

The largest paper (305,000 daily), and one of the most respected, is *Kompas.* Both *Kompas* and the second largest daily, *Sinar Harapan* (200,000), are commonly considered "Christian" papers, a seeming anomaly in a country where 85 percent of the population is nominally Muslim. But although the two newspapers do represent Christian (Catholic in *Kompas,* Protestant in *Sinar Harapan*) interests, they also speak to a wider urban, educated public with what has been called "Western rationality." Their serious and well-written content makes them two of Indonesia's most influential papers, with circulation primarily among the elite strata of Jakarta. Joining them in influence is the much older, intensely nationalistic *Merdeka* ("Independence"), formed during the fight for independence in 1945. Its circulation is now about 89,000.

Two other leading Jakarta dailies are *Suara Karya,* the organ of Golkar, the government-sponsored "functional group," with a circulation of 128,000; and *Berita Buana,* a sensation paper known for "circus-type" graphics, with 125,000 readers. Indonesia's fastest-growing paper is *Pos Kota,* formed in 1971, with a current circulation of 150,000. Like *Berita Buana,* it is known as sensational: no political news is run; the emphasis is on crime and local coverage. Circulation is limited almost entirely to the capital and the paper is read by *becak* ("trishaw") drivers, *jagas* ("watchmen") and other workers. Readership is estimated at between five and ten people per copy.

The two English-language papers, *The Indonesia Times* and *Indonesian Observer,* are also published in Jakarta, with respective circulations of 40,000 and 30,000. They are read primarily by the diplomatic community, tourists, and foreigners working in Indonesia. The single Chinese-language paper, *Harian Indonesia,* has a circulation of about 40,000.

Outside Jakarta, dailies have little circulation, except for four provincial papers, each appearing in a traditionally strong newspaper center: *Harian Analisa* (75,000 readers) in Medan, with the *Suryabaya Post* (70,000) in East Java, *Suara Merdeka* (100,000) in Semarang and *Pikiran Rakyat* (85,000) in Bandung.

In addition to daily papers (usually six days a week), the Ministy of Information lists 1,000 relatively small magazines directed to specific audiences. These range from the general newsmagazines such as *Tempo* and *Topik* to the satiric, comic-style *Stop,* reminiscent of *Mad* magazine. *Kartini, Violeta* and *Femina* highlight fashion, entertainment, and movie stars.

The quality of the largest Indonesian-language papers is high, but the majority suffer from lack of trained journalists, old equipment, problems of distribution, and tenuous financial conditions.

Economic Framework

Indonesia's economic and political instability affects the press as well as every other institution. Advertising is not well developed, newsprint is costly, equipment old and inefficient. Only in the last decade have publishers begun to look at papers as profit-making enterprises. Before, most papers were organs of particular political parties or groups and profit was secondary. Given the political situation, the high capital costs required to start a publication, and relatively low profits compared to other investments, press entrepreneurs have been reluctant investors. One estimate is that only a third of the dailies are in good financial condition.

Further, the potential reading audience is relatively small. Until the 1960s, there was little emphasis on education in bahasa Indonesia. One estimate is that only 15 percent of the population is literate in the national language. Nonetheless, this means 20 million potential readers.

Actual readership, compared to circulation, varies according to economic class. Many workers read papers in coffee shops or on bulletin boards; several people may buy one and pass it around. In the higher economic classes, many buy one major, serious paper and a copy of the local daily or weekly. Most papers are sold by street vendors rather than subscriptions.

Indonesia has been called a "listening" society. In Jakarta, slightly over 40 percent of the adults read a daily newspaper—about the same number that listen to radio. But in the outlying areas, radio is much more popular than reading. Price is also a factor. A month's subscription to a daily paper would be about five dollars, while a locally made transistor radio (good for many months if not years) can be purchased for slightly more than eight dollars.*

Ownership of papers is by limited corporations. There are usually links with political parties, which may either support or oppose the government. The few chains that exist are small, usually including a paper and several magazines. The Merdeka group, for instance, also publishes the *Indonesian Observer,* as well as the weekly newsmagazine *Topik* and a women's magazine, *Keluarga.* The Selecta group of weeklies includes *Yunior, Senang, Ideal, Detekif & Romantika* and *Stop.*

The many islands and lack of transportation infrastructure limits national distribution of publications, especially in the outer islands. *Kompas, Sinar Harapan* and *Merdeka* have the only significant circulation outside the capital. But even if distribution were to be drastically improved, the villages would still have little interest in the major papers, since most of their content concerns international affairs or events in Jakarta and a few other large cities. Hardly any other papers move beyond their individual cities of publication, nor can they even afford to cover the many small, isolated villages in their own circulation areas.

In 1980, however, the government began a "Newspapers for Villages" (*Koran Masuk Desa,* or KMD) program in an attempt to bring newspapers to the 80 percent of Indonesian villagers whose doings are not covered in the main papers, radio, or television. Under this program, the government provides a three-and-one-half-cent-per-copy subsidy for the first 5,000 copies of the village editions during the first year of publication. These are four-page, weekly papers usually in bahasa Indonesia, but occasionally bilingual or in the local language, such as Sundanese or Balinese, and distributed with an existing daily paper. Some papers use Jawi, the Arabic script-based version of bahasa Indonesia. There are 20 KMD regional papers distributing a total of 150,000 copies. Thirty-seven papers in 13 provinces have signed up for the program.

The government's desire to limit foreign exchange affects newsprint availability. The first 65,000 metric tons of newsprint is imported free of import tax by a special government agency, Pancaniaga, which has a monopoly on bulk newsprint. Distribution to individual newspapers is decided by the Newspaper Publishers' Association, SPS (Serikat Penerbit Suratkabar). Publishers wanting newsprint in excess of their 65,000-ton allotment must buy on the open market and pay a 20 percent import tax. In mid-1980, the price of newsprint was about $500 per metric ton. A newsprint mill is under construction, but at present most newsprint comes from Canada and the Scandinavian countries.

A rupiah devaluation of almost 34 percent in late 1978 severely affected many papers, especially the smaller ones. This resulted in newsprint prices increasing 50 percent, while printing and transport costs rose 25 percent. To counter rising costs, publishers raised per-copy prices about one-third, to 17 cents, or about the cost of a cup of coffee, and many papers showed circulation declines of five to

*In this chapter, all prices are given in U.S. dollars and converted at the rate of $1=Rp 600.

30 percent. Advertising rates were also raised 20 to 30 percent. The net result was that the larger papers became stronger and the smaller papers weaker. A number of the latter, together with provincial journals, found it difficult to survive, and some went under.

In its effort to support a non-monopoly policy and help the smaller-circulation press by directing some advertising away from the larger papers, the government has placed a limit of 12 pages on all dailies, which may contain only 30 percent advertising. Although overall advertising expenditures have declined, the percentage going to the larger papers has nevertheless remained constant and accounts for about half of their income.

Monthly salaries for reporters and editors on larger papers range from $250 to $833, and on smaller ones from $166 to $500. Supplements include such items as rice allotment, transport subsidies, or payment of medical costs for the reporter and family.

Indonesian unions are organized along industrial rather than craft lines and most local unions are affiliated through both regional and national unions to multi-industry national federations. The newspaper industry is not fully represented by a single union but rather by a number of locals, each tied to a political or religious group. The largest of these is Persatuan Wartawan Indonesia (2,300 members). Certain types of trade union activity are permitted, including strikes, in the private sector. Illegal strikes are also common.

The state of the economy has not allowed much improvement in printing or pre-press technology. *Berita Buana* was the first daily to install offset presses, in 1971, and the larger papers today are also offset, but the majority still use letterpress. The smaller printing establishments have few complete fonts of type, resulting in many wrong-font errors when particular letters are unavailable. Few small papers print their own publications, so they must wait until their turn comes up, and days can go by before a paper is actually on the streets.

Press Laws

Indonesia has no major body of law or precedent dealing with the media, although the constitution of 1945 guarantees and explains "freedom of assembly, association and expression of thoughts."

Prior to 1966, regulation of the press was by decree—colonial decrees under the Dutch and presidential decrees by Sukarno. The Press Act of 1966 (No. 11) entitled "The Basic Principles of the Press," was the first—and so far the only—formal legislation to define the principles of the printed media. Implementation and administration of the act is by the minister of information.

In the 1966 law, the function of the press is stated to be "an instrument of the revolution constituting an active, dynamic, creative, educative, informative mass medium with the social function of stimulating...progressive thinking." The press is expected to "safeguard, defend, uphold and implement *Pancasila* and the 1945 constitution...fight for truth and justice...foster the unity of progressive-revolutionary forces in the struggles opposing imperialism, colonialism,...communism and fascist-dictatorship"; and to "become the channel of constructive, progressive and revolutionary public opinion."

The press also has the right of constructive "control, criticism, and correction."

Press freedom is based on acceptance of the "responsibility and the implementation" of the functions described above. Publications based on the ideology of Communism/Marxism-Leninism are prohibited.

Under the 1966 law, publication permits are not required, but this provision has been delayed during a transition period; about 250 permits for daily papers have been issued. This is more than the actual number of papers currently being published: because there is a limited number of permits, businessmen prefer to retain the permit so as to retain the option of publishing in the future. A permit is valid for an indefinite period and priority is given to papers to be published in the provinces. No bond is required.

The law also permits the government to establish a news agency and publish one daily in bahasa Indonesia and one in a foreign language. Where "necessary," it says, "the government shall give aid to the national press."

Publications must be organized as corporations, "putting stress on ideal qualities, regulated in a "*gotong-royong*" (mutual help) way and guided by "the familial system." Foreign capital is not allowed in the corporation and all founders and board members must be Indonesian. The management must "not have been involved in any counter-revolutionary action." The chairman of the board is responsible for editorial execution and is obliged to exercise the right of reply and correction.

The act also specifies the requirements for a journalist: to be an Indonesian national, to understand fully the functions and obligations of the press as defined by the act, and to be "imbued with the spirit of *Pancasila*... never having betrayed the revolution." Journalists must also possess "skill, experience, training, high morals, and responsibility."

Under the guidelines of the state policy, the press act of 1966 and the mass media are to be reviewed during the third five-year plan (Repelita III) which began in 1979. The purpose of the review is said to guarantee and intensify "the growth of a sound, free and responsible press."

No body of law deals with libel or obscenity. In the absence of legal precedents, some cases of libel have been decided by the Dewan Kehormatan (Court of Honor), a part of the Journalists' Association.

The Indonesian press tends to see itself as a privileged institution. A 1973 study showed that only 60 percent of the press thought it necessary to follow government regulations, with only half considering the law of the country to be binding on them.

Censorship

Kopkamtib, the internal security organization, is the primary agency that monitors the press. Until 1977, domestic newspapers were required to obtain a permit from Kopkamtib in addition to the publishing permit from the Ministry of Information. Kopkamtib also holds briefings, as does the Ministry of Information, indicating what kind of news should be printed.

In 1980, for example, editors meeting with the commander of Kopkamtib and the head of Bakin (the intelligence coordinating board) were told not to report on a "Petition of 50" from retired military officers and former public officials to Parliament. The petition claimed that President Suharto had misrepresented Pancasila in two recent speeches.

Generally, particular issues of a publication are not censored since editors are usually aware of sensitive subjects. Some papers closed in 1978 were allowed to reopen only after agreeing to certain terms set by the government. The 1978 closings followed reports allegedly exaggerating student discontent and opposition to the reelection of Suharto (who was reelected without opposition). Before being permitted to start operating again, editors were required to sign letters saying each paper was willing to engage in "introspection and internal improvements" to develop a free and "responsible" press. Each editor pledged to bear in mind that his paper would help maintain national stability, put the interests of the public above those of the paper, maintain good relations with the government and the national leadership, and respect the law governing the press and stipulations laid down by the Press Council and government agencies. They were also advised not to cover student political activities or quote prominent people who had been critical of the administration.

Under the 1966 Press Act, a Press Council was formed "to assist the government in fostering jointly the growth and the development of the national press." The Press Council is composed of 17 members, with the minister of information as chairman. The remainder of the council includes five members of the general public, two government officials and nine members of the Press Society, an umbrella group composed of the Indonesian Newspaper Publishers' Association (Serikat Penerbit Suratkabar—SPS), Indonesian Journalists' Association (Persatuan Wartawan Indonesia—PWI), Association of Press Printing Enterprises (Serikat Grafika Pers) and the Association of Advertising Agencies (Persatuan Perusahaan Periklanan Indonesia—PPPI).

The Ministry of Information also includes a Film Censorship Board, composed of representatives from such fields as foreign relations, cinematography and culture. All films must be viewed and passed by this board, which considers educational, informational and entertainment values. In 1977-78, 650 films, both domestic and imported, were submitted to the board. Twenty six were rejected. Each provincial governor also has authority to reject films if he feels them to be offensive to local values.

State-Press Relations

The Ministry of Information controls and monitors the print media. The main divisions of the ministry are General Information, Radio and Television, and Press and Graphics.

The current minister of information, Ali Murtopo, who took over in 1978 after service in military intelligence, once said, "I am not a defender of the free press." He added: "The press of the developing countries is free but must also be responsible. Our society is not strong enough." This type of doctrine, with its cyclic crackdowns on the press, masks a more delicate, uniquely Indonesian approach to editorial freedom and criticism of official policies. One editor has said that "a feeling for subtle hints and signals has proved more important for the continuation of a functioning press than open and formal statements, or even written law."

The Indonesian press is very much of the Javanese social fabric. The social norms value circumspection, self-restraint and the practice of "saying the truth gently... and with as little purpose to hurt as possible." In this environment, aggressive journalism is considered insensitive and crude.

For the most part, criticism is couched in very subtle terms, depending on obscurantist language, the use of new words, or the use of old words in slightly different contexts. Readers are used to, and comfortable with, reading between the lines.

Press conferences may be small gatherings among editors and government officials where journalists are given certain information, but asked to postpone or refrain from using it. When this informal communication breaks down, confrontation occurs and the government reacts sharply, as it did after the 1974 Malari affair, which led to the closing of several papers for their reportage of harsh student statements about the President's wife and corruption among government officials. After the closings, however, some of the student statements about the president's wife remedied by the government.

Most papers banned were in Jakarta, and represented a new type of aggressive journalism, written for an urban, cosmopolitan elite. This was partly the result of the 1965 "Gestapu" episode, when many journalists and editors were barred from working in their profession, and replaced by a younger group, less committed to a Javanese "shadow play" approach.

Many journalists were arrested or detained after the abortive coup of 1965-66, but none remain in jail. No foreign journalists have been jailed.

State control of the press is implemented in various ways. In the case of the "Newspapers for Villages" program there is a formal subsidy to papers. With publications like *AB (Angkatan Bersenjata),* run by the army, control is direct and subsidized through the device of buying up much of the press run.

The government may also threaten to withdraw advertisements. For some papers, such advertising is not only considerable but essential to solvency. Further, the government may buy papers, particularly small provincial journals, for the use of office workers.

Under the 1966 Press Law, journalists must also meet certain requirements. These requirements, both political and professional, can be interpreted in various ways. Kopkamtib has warned publishers against hiring journalists fired or jailed during "Gestapu," and some newsmen were blacklisted after the 1974 Malari affair.

Attitude Toward Foreign Media

A supplement to the Press Act of 1966, enacted in 1972, regulates the foreign press and journalists in Indonesia. To become accredited foreign correspondents must first have their home offices furnish letters of introduction to the Directorate for the Guidance of the Press in the Ministry of Information. A correspondent should also apply for a visa from the nearest Indonesian diplomatic post three months ahead of the time he expects to arrive in Indonesia.

Once the correspondent is approved by the Ministry of Information, he is issued a visa and a press card, both good for one year, with possible extension.

Indonesian nationals working for foreign journalists or bureaus also must obtain accreditation. They too apply to the Ministry of Information, but must include a statement of "good conduct" from the local police. They are also required to join the Indonesian Journalists' Association.

The two most sensitive subjects for the correspondent—as well as for the domestic press—are the Indonesian presence in East Timor and criticism of the Suharto family. Several correspondents were expelled in 1980 and early 1981 for dealing with such touchy issues. The most recent case in which a visa was not renewed was that of Paul Zach, a writer for *Reuters* and *The Washington Post.* A few weeks earlier, the correspondent for the *Sydney Morning Herald,* Peter Rodgers, also was forced to leave when he was denied a visa renewal. This made him the last resident correspondent for an Australian media organization. Earlier, in 1980, Radio Australia correspondent Warwick Beutler also lost his visa. The information ministry indicated that Beutler's expulsion was for unbalanced reporting of the Indonesian invasion of Portuguese Timor in 1975. The visa refusal, however, had been preceded, in early 1980, by Radio Australia's Indonesian-language broadcasts reporting on the "Petition of 50" and criticism of President Suharto.

In 1977 a photojournalist for *Paris-Match* was deported from Timor. (Two years earlier, during the 1975 Indonesian invasion of Portuguese Timor, six journalists were killed in two separate incidents.) In mid-1980 the *Asian Wall Street Journal* had articles blacked out when it carried stories alleging corruption at high levels of government. In 1978 journalists' visa applications were held up until after the elections and Suharto's reinstallment. In 1976 an issue of *Newsweek* and its Asian regional editor were banned when the magazine ran a story critical of Suharto and alleging upper-tier government corruption. The local (foreign) correspondent in Jakarta was officially reprimanded.

Foreign publications require government permission to circulate, and those "which harm or endanger the society, state and the Indonesian revolution" are prohibited. So too are foreign publications that have aspects of "Marxism, Leninism, Communism, pornography, sadism and other concepts ... contrary to *Pancasila* principles." The minister of information, with the assistance of the attorney general, may prohibit or take other measures against foreign publications, under regulations decided in 1972.

Local distributors voluntarily black out with paint any article or photograph that might cause foreign periodicals to be prohibited by the attorney general. Any publications or items bearing Chinese characters are prohibited, but almost all materials censored are in English.

Time magazine is typical. *Time* has a circulation of approximately 17,000 in Indonesia. Towards the end of the week, according to Indonesia's *Tempo*, advance copies of *Time* are sent to the local distributors from Hong Kong, and submitted to the attorney general's office, which then will issue a permit. If only certain items are excised or blacked out, cables are sent to Hong Kong to send the full shipment. It is then met at the airport and transferred under security conditions to a warehouse where carefully screened employees, who cannot read English, black out the offending parts.

After the student demonstrations of 1978 and the crackdown on local papers, wire service accounts in incoming Singapore papers were blacked out.

Publications bearing pictures of Mao Tsetung now are allowed to enter, but a few years ago, all pictures of the Chinese leader would have been blacked out. Any images of Muhammad are blacked out since the majority of the population is Muslim. It is held that no person can know what the Prophet actually looked like.

Domestic journalists have contact with international press groups through local organizations. The Indonesian Journalists' Association is a member of the Confederation of ASEAN Journalists, composed of representatives from parallel organizations in the ASEAN countries (Singapore, Malaysia, Thailand, and the Philippines). The association also has agreements with the national journalists' associations in Australia, Japan and Yugoslavia. The Indonesian Publishers' Association is affiliated with FIEJ, the International Federation of Newspaper Publishers headquartered in Paris. Antara, Indonesia's news agency, is a member of the Non-Aligned News Pool and OANA, Organization of Asian News Agencies.

In September 1980, Indonesia hosted the first Islamic World Mass Media Conference.

Organizations with correspondents in Indonesia include *Asahi Shimbun, Asian Wall Street Journal*, Depthnews Asia, Deutsche Presse-Agentur (dpa), *Far Eastern Economic Review, Mainichi Shimbun*, and Nippon Hoso Kyokai.

News Agencies

The earliest Indonesian news agencies were formed by nationalists, who sought to furnish news independently of the Dutch suppliers. The first of this type was formed, not in what would become Indonesia, but Holland, in 1913. It was called Indonesische Pers Bureau.

The first agency in Indonesia was ANETA (Het Algemeen Nieuws-en Telegraaf-Agentschap), formed in 1917. It became a semi-official arm of the colonial government. After independence, ANETA was taken over by Indonesian journalists and renamed Persbiro Indonesia (PIA). PIA merged with Antara in 1962.

Antara ("between" in bahasa Indonesia) is the major agency. It was founded in 1937 by, among others, Adam Malik, now Indonesia's vice-president. The full name is Lembaga Kantor Berita Nasional Antara (LKBN Antara). It became the official agency in 1962, and is governed through a council composed of representatives from government and the private sector.

Antara provides news, feature and photo services to newspapers, commercial institutions and diplomatic missions. Output consists of twice-daily news bulletins, comment, weekly press reviews and various financial and economic bulletins.

The agency has correspondents or bureaus in 43 locations around the islands, bureaus in Hamburg and Tokyo, and correspondents in Kuala Lumpur, Rangoon and Hong Kong. Direct telex links have been established with Bernama, the Malaysian news agency in Kuala Lumpur, and the Philippines News Agency in Manila. Antara also serves as the secretariat of OANA.

The newest agency, KNI (Kantorberita Nasional Indonesia) was formed in 1966 by 11 newspapers that wanted an independent service free of government or political ties. KNI has bureaus and correspondents throughout Indonesia, but no overseas staff. It distributes the Associated Press file, news bulletins in English and bahasa Indonesia, and a petroleum and mining report.

A third agency, PAB (Pusat Pemberitaan Angkatan Bersenjata) handles primarily army news, but its scope extends beyond the strictly military into economic and political areas. It was formed in 1965 as a counter to the, at that time, leftist-oriented Antara. PAB also distributes news bulletins in English and bahasa Indonesia, in addition to features.

News from international agencies must be channelled through Antara or KNI. Foreign news-services distributed are United Press International, Deutsche Presse Agentur, Reuters, Agence France-Presse, and occasionally Tass. Some 25 national agencies have exchange agreements with Antara; these include Central News Agency (Taiwan), Kyodo News Service, Hapdong and Orient Press of Korea, Tanjug, Novosti, Press Trust of India, Saudi Arab News Agency, Iraqi News Agency, ANSA (Italy), and EFE (Spain).

UPI, AP, Reuters, Agence France-Presse and Tass have bureaus in Jakarta. Permits for bureaus, as distinct from those for correspondents, must be obtained from the Ministry of Information. These are valid for one year and may be renewed. They also can be revoked at any time.

In August 1980 news agencies were asked not to distribute stories of Indonesian origin within the country itself. Deselectors were installed by the telecommunications authority to filter all copy datelined Jakarta. The ruling followed reporting by foreign agencies and newspapers critical of high government officials. It does not affect news from other countries.

Electronic News Media

During the 1920s and 1930s, the Dutch opened a few radio stations, mainly oriented to their local interests and to keep in touch with the Netherlands. During the occupation years of 1942–45, the Japanese modernized broadcasting facilities and demonstrated how radio could be used as propaganda. Within days of declaring independence in 1945, Radio Republik Indonesia (RRI) was formed. It broadcast from underground transmitters during the four-year fight for independence.

Radio is the only medium in Indonesia that might be called "mass." The low literacy level, isolated islands scattered across thousands of miles of water, and the influx of cheap transistor sets all combine to make radio the most widely used method of communication.

RRI is part of the Ministry of Information. The main studio is in Jakarta, but the system also has five "Nusantara" relay stations and approximately 45 local or regional stations. The Nusantara relay stations—in Medan, Jokjakarta, Banjarmasin, Udjung Pandang and Jayapura—coordinate the local stations. National broadcasts, usually news, originate in Jakarta and are relayed, but the majority of local stations produce their own programs. Although the productions of the main national station in Jakarta are usually in bahasa Indonesia, these programs also use a significant precentage of local languages.

In many areas, reception of RRI is weak. People listen to external broadcasts from the culturally similar Radio Malaysia, Radio Netherlands and the widely respected Radio Australia. Radio Australia, in fact, is estimated to have 30 million Indonesian listeners. All of these organizations broadcast in bahasa Indonesia.

Currently, RRI is stressing programs oriented toward the rural audience. In 1969 it started radio forums with listener groups around the country. School programs are also broadcast.

Several hundred "amateur" stations supplement the official RRI outlets. These are approved by the Ministry of Information and the authority that oversees telecommunications, and usually are heard only in circumscribed areas, since transmitter power is limited. Amateur stations were started by student activists during the post-"Gestapu" period of 1966. Today they are owned by a variety of private groups. Their programming is primarily entertainment, although they must also relay RRI news, and at least 10 percent of the content must be of the public service type. Political activities are not allowed. Although for the most part these are very small operations, some amateur stations have an extremely high level of programming and transmitting.

The overseas service, Voice of Indonesia, broadcasts in English, bahasa Indonesia, Chinese, Arabic, bahasa Malaysia, French, Hindu and Urdu.

Television also is part of the Ministry of Information. Televisi Republik Indonesia (TVRI) was introduced to the country in 1961, but did not become operational until a year later. By 1979 TVRI had 110 relay stations around the archipelago. All programming originates from Jakarta. Thirty-two percent of the budget comes from the 15 percent of time devoted to advertisements, and 65 percent from license fees. The remainder comes from a government subsidy.

The majority of television sets are in Jakarta. Ownership increased about 20 percent in 1977, while the number of people watching on an average day rose from 38 percent—or 1.4 million—in 1976 to 45 percent—or 1.7 million—in 1979.

During the same period, radio listenership remained relatively constant, while newspaper readership increased slightly more slowly than TV viewing. A content analysis of this three-year period showed that more than 60 percent of all printed or broadcast news concerned happenings in or around Jakarta.

Unity is of paramount importance in Indonesia's heterogeneous society. All media take particular care against offending any religious or ethnic group. When TV first became available in rural villages via satellite in 1976, TVRI scheduled commercials so they would be seen in Jakarta, but not in the rural *kampongs* (villages), so as not to exacerbate tensions between the relatively affluent city and the poorer areas that did not aspire to the material desires shown in the advertisements—mainly for foreign products. (Later, for commercial reasons, this approach was

dropped and the villages saw the same ads as the cities.) Nor was sex appeal allowed in commercials. TVRI followed a strict moral code, in which marriage was sacred and premarital sex banned. And crime could not be shown to "pay." In January 1981, in a major policy change, President Suharto announced that no commercials whatever would be allowed on TVRI after March. Revenue lost would be made up by additional government subsidy.

All local TV programs use bahasa Indonesia. Because of financial constraints, foreign programs are not dubbed or subtitled in the national language.

Indonesia was the first developing nation (and the fourth country, after Canada, the Soviet Union and the United States) to establish its own domestic communications satellite system. The first satellite, Palapa I (named after a 14th-century prime minister who vowed not to eat until the whole country was united), was launched in 1976. A second was launched a year later. As a result, television may be received in the most isolated villages, although more importance is given to using the satellites for upgrading and installing telephone, telex and cable service. Contracts have been signed to buy two more satellites in 1984.

Education & Training

Journalism education, like journalism itself, is not widespread in Indonesia. Most programs at the university level stress an interdisciplinary approach to training, aimed at producing "opinion leaders" rather than students skilled only in techniques. All but a few programs are located on the main island of Java.

The earliest university program was started in 1948 at Gadjah Mada University in Jokjakarta as the Department of Information. In 1956 this department was superseded by the Department of Mass Communication in the Faculty of Social and Political Science. The University of Indonesia in Jakarta started a Department of Mass Communication in the Faculty of Social Sciences in 1959. This was followed by the establishment of communication departments at Hasanuddin University in Udjung Pandang, on Sulawesi in 1960, Pajajaran University in Bandung in 1965 and Diponegoro University in Semarang in 1967.

Each university program is a five-year

series of courses leading to a master's degree. Within the journalism program students take the same general curriculum. There are no specializations, although some electives are available. Most require a thesis to complete the program.

In addition, private institutions train journalists. The Newspaper Publishers' Association supports the Jakarta Perguruan Tinggi Publisistik (Graduate School of Mass Communications), which offers a five-year program leading to a master's degree. Lembaga Pendidkan dan Konsultasi Pers (The Indonesian Institute for Press Training and Consultancy) is also in Jakarta. The Surabaya Journalism Academy is located in east Java.

The Indonesian Journalists' Association, in cooperation with the government, offers working journalists one- to two-week courses and seminars in specific subjects. The Ministry of Information operates the Academy of Information (Akademi Penerangan) for its own personnel, and TVRI operates a training center (Pusat Latihan TVRI). Pendidikan Periklanan Jakarta offers short courses in advertising and public relations.

In addition to the organizations already noted, several are devoted to specific interests: Yayasan Pembina Pers Indonesia (Press Foundation of Indonesia), Himpunan Penulis Ilmiah Indonesia (Indonesian Science Writers Society), Ikatan Penulis Keluarga Berencana (Association of Family Planning Writers), Jakarta Foreign Correspondents Club, Badan Periklana dan Media Pers Nasional (National Board on Advertising and Media), Bakohumas (Badan Koordinasi Hubungan Masyarakat Pemerintah: Coordination of Government Public Relations), Perhumas (Perhimpunan Hubungan Masyarakat Indonesia; Public Relations Association of Indonesia) and Ikatan Pers Mahasiswa Indonesia (Students' Press Association.)

Summary

Journalism in Indonesia is a textbook example of mass communications in a developing country in degrees not found in most countries.

Indonesia is composed of an unassimilated population of almost 140 million people spread across thousands of miles of islands—although concentrated on one island—speaking a variety of mutually unintelligible languages, with not one tongue predominating, and low literacy in any language. The nation is improving economically, but the economy remains unstable, and although a sense of unity is developing, the population still has widely differing religious, cultural and ethnic backgrounds.

In media terms, these characteristics translate into a communications system that is heavily concentrated on one island reflecting one ethnic group, and a relatively small potential audience for reading newspapers or listening to the radio.

Since the fight for independence is still a living memory, most editors and journalists have an automatic opposition to any authority, whether colonial or local. In the absence of a body of law and tradition, both the government-army authority and the press tend to react to short-term expedients with little understanding of long-term results. The military in particular tend to be overenthusiastic about controlling the press in its jurisdiction. Once independence from the Dutch was achieved, the press embarked on a period, under Sukarno, when it sought to define an identity, just as Sukarno was forcing the country to develop an Indonesian sense of unity and purpose. Under the New Order of Suharto, the country turned to a pragmatic road, emphasizing economic and material development, not only in cities and towns but in the rural areas. The press found that opposition and politics alone did not constitute the sole function of the press. Professional journalists began to displace some of the former politicians on editorial staffs and papers were started in the rural areas. Journalism education changed from theory, inherited from the Dutch, to practical concerns and concerns with the uniqueness—and requirements—of Indonesian mass communications.

Economics remains the central problem of the country and the press. Modern print communication requires major capital expenditure; strong papers must have the support of both local and national advertisers; and, major circulation increases are limited by the available newsprint.

The Indonesian press, it has been said, "is among the freest in Asia." But—given the character of the press in most of the Far East—such a statement also implies a high degree of censorship. Although censorship is a fact of life, writers and editors have developed methods for circumventing external limitations and repression.

CHRONOLOGY

1974	Repelita II (Second five-year plan) starts.		Rupiah devalued.
1975	Six correspondents killed during invasion of Portuguese East Timor.	**1979**	Repelita III begins.
		1980	"Newspapers for Villages" program starts.
1976	First domestic satellite launched.		Islamic World Mass Media Conference held in Jakarta.
1977	National elections held. Second satellite launched.		Radio Australia journalist banned.
1978	Government cracks down on press following student demonstrations.		International news agencies ordered not to "play back" local stories.

BIBLIOGRAPHY

Adam, Ahmat. "The Vernacular Press in Padang, 1865-1913." *Akademika,* July 1975, pp. 75-99.

Adinegoro. *Publisistik & Djurnalistik* [Mass Communications and Journalism], 2 vols. Jakarta, 1963.

Agassi, Judith B. *Mass Media in Indonesia.* Cambridge, Mass., 1969.

Anderson, Benedict R. O'G. "Cartoons and Monuments: The Evolution of Political Communication under the New Order." In Karl D. Jackson and Lucian W. Pye, eds. *Political Power and Communications in Indonesia.* Berkeley, Calif., 1978.

Anderson, Michael H. "The Guided Press of Indonesia: Freedom Versus Responsibility." In John A. Lent, ed. *Guided Press in Southeast Asia: National Development vs. Freedom of Expression.* Amherst, N.Y., 1976.

Antara. *Almanak Pers Antara 1977.* Jakarta, 1977.

Chu, Godwin C. and Alfian. "Programming Development in Indonesia." *Journal of Communication,* Autumn 1980, pp. 50-57.

Crawford, Robert. "Indonesia." In John A. Lent, ed. *The Asian Newspapers' Reluctant Revolution.* Ames, Iowa, 1971.

Dekker, E. F. E. Douwes. "The Press." In Arnold Wright, ed. *Twentieth Century Impressions of Netherlands India.* London, 1909.

Eapen, K. E. "Communication—Indonesian Style." *Media Asia,* 1974, pp. 35-44.

Hanna, Willard A. "Indonesian *Komik.*" *American University Field Staff Reports,* 1979, pp. 1-11.

Indonesia. Department of Information. *Press Act of Indonesia.* Jakarta, n.d.

Indonesia. Museum Pusat. *Katalogus Surat-Kabar.* Jakarta, 1973.

———. "The Media and an Inside Story." *Far Eastern Economic Review,* June 15, 1979, pp. 48, 51.

Lent, John A. *Asian Mass Communication: A Comprehensive Bibliography* and *Supplement.* Philadelphia, 1975, 1978.

Markarim, Nono Anwar. "The Indonesian Press: An Editor's Perspective." In Karl D. Jackson and Lucian W. Pye, eds. *Political Power and Communications in Indonesia.* Berkeley, Calif., 1978.

Moertopo, Ali. "Communication Planning: Some Thoughts." *Media Asia,* 1980, pp. 21-24.

Nunn, G. Raymond, comp. *Indonesian Newspapers: An International Union List.* Taipei, 1971.

Oetama, Jacob. "Mass Media in Indonesia." *Media Asia,* 1978, pp. 82-85.

Oey Hong Lee. *Indonesian Government and Press During Guided Democracy.* Hull, England, 1971.

Prakoso, Mastini Hardjo, comp. *Mass Communication In Indonesia: An Annotated Bibliography.* Singapore, 1978.

Soebagijo, I. N. [Notodidjojo, Subagijo Ilham]. *Sejarah Pers Indonesia* [History of the Press in Indonesia]. Jakarta, 1977.

Suryadinata, Leo. *The Pre-World War II Peranakan Chinese Press of Java: A Preliminary Survey.* Athens, Ohio, 1971.

Susanto, Astrid. "The Mass Communications System in Indonesia." In Karl D. Jackson and Lucian W. Pye, eds. *Political Power and Communications in Indonesia.* Berkeley, Calif., 1978.

IRELAND

by Paul Ashdown

BASIC DATA

Population: 3.4 million
Area: 68,894 sq. km. (25,490 sq. mi.)
GNP: Ir£5.9 billion (US$12.1 billion) (1978)
Literacy Rate: 98-99%
Language(s): English, Gaelic
Number of Dailies: 7
  Aggregate Circulation: 748,000
  Circulation per 1,000: 220
Number of Nondailies: 54
  Aggregate Circulation: 1,672,000
  Circulation per 1,000: 524
Number of Periodicals: 159
Number of Radio Stations: 2

Number of Television Stations: 1
Number of Radio Receivers: 949,000
  Radio Receivers per 1,000: 300
Number of Television Sets: 655,000
  Television Sets per 1,000: 207
Total Annual Newsprint Consumption: 45,300
  metric tons
Per Capita Newsprint Consumption: 14.2 kg.
  (31.2 lb.)
Total Newspaper Ad Receipts: Ir£14.7 million
  (US$25.3 million) (1976)
  As % of All Ad Expenditures: 50.9

Background & General Characteristics

The Republic of Ireland is a nation of 3.4 million people, living in the ancient Irish provinces of Munster, Connacht and Leinster and three of the nine counties of Ulster. Ireland became a British dominion in 1922 and declared its sovereignty in 1937. Six counties of Ulster remain part of the United Kingdom, although that division is not recognized by the republic.

Ireland's four morning newspapers have a combined circulation of 416,000. Three evening newspapers have a circulation of 332,000. Fifty-four percent of the adult population read a morning newspaper, and 45 percent an evening paper. The percentage of daily-newspaper readers is lower in Connacht and Ulster than elsewhere. While the percentage of adult readers of morning newspapers has decreased in the past decade, circulations have increased. Sunday newspapers have a circulation exceeding one million and are read by 87 percent of the adult population. Three out of five Irish adults read a provincial newspaper.

Because Ireland's population is small, newspapers must have broad appeal if they are to survive economically. Accordingly, the Irish press is comparatively homogeneous, without the ethnic, partisan, religious, economic or social constituencies sometimes characteristic of the press in other European countries.

All Irish media must be examined within the context of Ireland's location and its historic, political and economic dependence on its much more populous eastern neighbor. The daily circulation of British newspapers in Ireland is estimated to be 231,000, and at least 40 percent of the population regularly read a British Sunday newspaper. British books dominate the domestic market and British television penetrates throughout the north and east of the country.

Ireland has the lowest population density of any member of the European Economic Community. Slightly more than half the population is urban, with about 30 percent living in and around Dublin. The population is 94 percent Roman Catholic and has a 98 percent literacy rate. An ambitious program of bilingualism preserves Ireland's ancient Gaelic tongue. About one-third of the population can speak Gaelic but only a few thousand people, primarily in the counties along the west coast, use the language regularly.

Irish newspapers reflect the nation's conservative, homogeneous, democratic population. Irish morning newspapers traditionally have paid more attention to political, social and economic news than their British counterparts, but considerably less than some other European newspapers, especially in their coverage of foreign news. Criticism of the government and the church is vigorous, while the use of salacious material and coverage of crime and violence are circumspect. Athletic events are given extensive coverage.

Irish readers may obtain a broad spectrum of viewpoints on most issues, although Irish laws and customs to a degree determine what newspapers are willing to print. Many newspapers are attractively designed and competently edited, but typically lack adequate attribution, consistently good news judgment, and investigative reporting. Many Irish journalists see the Irish press as provincial, proprietary and preoccupied with trivialities, and there is a general lament about the lack of adequate research or professional training available to journalists.

The printing press was first used in Ireland in 1550, but it was not until 1659 that the first newssheet circulated. The first commerical newspaper, the *Irish Intelligencer*, was published in 1662, followed by the *Dublin Newsletter* in 1685 and the *Dublin Intelligence* in 1693. In 1725 George Faulkner founded the *Dublin Journal*, which lasted for a century. This was followed in 1763 by the *Freeman's Journal*, which became the organ of the Irish Parliamentary party. In 1766 a provincial press emerged with the publication of the *Limerick Chronicle*, which is still publishing. *The Nation*, started in 1842 after Catholic emancipation, was Ireland's first popular newspaper, and also among the first papers to articulate a truly nationalistic viewpoint. Its publishers, Thomas David, Charles Duffy and John Dillon, explained how Irish nationhood "was relevant to contemporary events rather than simply to the country's vast and romantic history," wrote newspaper historian Anthony Smith. Increasing literacy and education aided the penny press after 1859, when the *Irish Times* appeared. Its rival, the *Irish Independent*, was published in 1891 to counter the *Freeman's Journal*, and became linked with nationalist Charles Parnell. By 1880 Ireland had 17 dailies.

While many Irish newspapers were established ostensibly for political purposes, their publishers also had strong commercial motivations. As was the case in England, a pros-

perous free press developed in Ireland in the 19th century to serve the needs of the mercantile class in an emerging democratic state.

In 1931 the *Irish Press* was founded by Eamon de Valera, hero of the rebellion, and later president and prime minister, in opposition to the pro-treaty coalitions that supported the Irish Free State.

Today's largest newspapers, exclusive of Sunday editions, are listed in the accompanying table.

10 Largest Newspapers by Circulation	
1. *Irish Independent*	174,276
2. *Evening Press*	171,780
3. *Evening Herald*	117,595
4. *Irish Press*	98,790
5. *Irish Times*	75,009
6. *Cork Examiner*	67,968
7. *The Kerryman* (weekly)	43,781
8. *Evening Echo*	42,705
9. *Limerick Leader*	33,500
10. *Connaught Times*	30,158

The *Sunday Press* has a circulation of 384,521, followed by the *Sunday World*, 319,218, and the *Sunday Independent*, 276,217.

Ireland's daily morning newspapers average 16 pence (27 cents) in price; the evening newspapers average 12 pence (20 cents) and the Sunday papers 18 pence (30 cents).

The *Irish Times*, which sells most heavily in Dublin, is regularly read by about half the professional and managerial classes, and is considered the nation's most influential paper. Originally the voice of the Protestant and unionist minority, it is now a politically independent, liberal newspaper devoting about 20 percent of its columns to social, political and economic news, with extensive parliamentary reports, foreign news and coverage of the arts. The *Irish Times* had been a commercial public company but in 1974 was converted into a newspaper trust. Reportedly the *Times* is looking at plans for a quality Sunday newspaper but is moving towards it cautiously.

The *Irish Independent* is loosely identified with the Fine Gael party, and appeals to a largely bourgeois, Catholic and rural constituency consistent with is greater circulation.

It is controlled by the family of its original owner, William Martin Murphy. The *Irish Press* has declined in circulation slightly since 1967 but continues its leadership in the Sunday market. It is still identified with the de Valera family and the Fianna Fail party, but is balanced in its political coverage.

The *Independent* and the *Press* use larger display devices than does the *Times*. The dailies devote an average of about 33 percent of their space to advertising. All morning and evening papers are full-size and average about 18 pages. The *Sunday Press* and *Sunday Independent* usually run 28 pages with spot color. The *Sunday World*, a tabloid, uses color extensively, and runs about 48 pages. A new tabloid competitor, the *Sunday Journal*, runs about 40 pages. Both *World* and *Journal* are gossipy and sensational; KILLER COP'S WIFE SPEAKS would be a representative tabloid headline. The *Sunday Press* and *Sunday Independent* use multi-column pictures and large headlines on an eight-column format, and display large front-page advertisements. Their content is more serious than that of the tabloids, but still emphasizes personalities, news features and athletics. The *Press* and *Independent* have lost circulation to the tabloids, as well as to the British newspapers. The Sunday and evening papers aspire to a popular audience.

The *Evening Press*, unlike the *Evening Herald,* has increased steadily in circulation. In 1968 the *Evening Press* had a circulation of 149,000, the *Evening Herald* 145,000. The *Evening Herald* is owned by the Independent Group. Both papers are full size with large headlines and generous use of two- and three-column pictures. They are less serious in intent than the morning newspapers and use more spot news and features. The *Evening Herald* is considering changing to a tabloid format.

While competition is spirited in Dublin, fewer than 10 Irish cities have competing newspapers. Most provincial newspapers have circulations between 10,000 and 25,000, with about an equal number above or below that range. The daily *Cork Examiner*, first published in 1841, has increased in circulation some 28 percent since 1968, and is the nation's most significant non-Dublin paper. More than 90 percent of its circulation is in the province of Munster, the republic's second most populous. The newspaper also publishes the *Irish Weekly Examiner*, a sprightly tabloid that uses some color and devotes attention to the arts, and the *Evening Echo*.

Provincial newspapers vary in quality, but are read thoroughly within their communities. A number of provincial papers not only supply news to the Dublin papers, but a few of the larger provincials use their own writers to cover national affairs. Some provincials also carry features in the Irish language. A provincial paper is usually based in its chief county town or city, which, in earlier times, was likely to be a British garrison town. Traditionally, therefore, such papers tended to support political union with Britain. During the late 19th century, however, many provincial newspapers were founded to advocate nationalist policies. After the Easter Rising of 1916, most of the provincials began supporting the Sinn Fein independence movement and were frequently harassed for their views. In number they are about half what they were in 1870, but their circulation is more than four times as great. Most provincial newspapers carry little national news and avoid partisan analysis.

Some 247 magazines are published in Ireland, broadly categorized as follows: academic, cultural and historical, 16; agricultural, 28; business and public affairs, 15; education, 20; Irish language, 5; medical, 16; religious, 44; sport and leisure, 26; trade and technical, 63; women, 5; youth, 9. Ireland's best current affairs magazine is *Magill*, edited in Dublin by Vincent Browne. *Magill* created a furor in 1980 by reopening the 1969 arms crisis controversy, which implicated the taoiseach (prime minister), Charles Haughey, in the smuggling of weapons into Ulster.

Economic Framework

Ireland's newspapers face continuing competitive pressures from the British press and from government-sponsored radio and television. Daily newspaper readership declined from 60 percent of all adults in 1972 to 54 percent in 1978. In Dublin alone the reduction was an alarming 11 percent. From 1973 to 1978 the readership of evening newspapers dropped from 48 to 45 percent, while readership of weekly magazines decreased by 38 percent during that period. All categories, except housewives without children, people above age 45 and the middle-class socioeconomic group, decreased their readership of morning and evening newspapers. Analysts attribute some of the decline to increasing penetration of the British *Daily Mirror* and other popular tabloids. Television viewing has increased considerably since 1973, and at least 80 percent of the adult population now watches TV on a regular basis. This figure undoubtedly will increase with recent improvements in channel selection and penetration. Of even greater concern is the fact that television news is overwhelmingly considered more reliable than that of newspapers.

While these conditions have not led to newspaper failures, they probably have contributed to increasing ownership concentration. The *Sunday World*, with its immense circulation, was acquired recently by the Independent Group, which also publishes the *Evening Herald* and *Sunday Independent*. Dublin-based newspapers have increased their holdings of provincial newspapers, and the Independent Group alone controls three newspaper groups. Other major concentrations seemed likely as 1980 ended, but no public outcry has resulted.

Irish newspapers carry the highest rate of value added tax in Europe, and the tax is levied on both advertising and newspaper sales. The government does not tax newsprint directly. Irish publishers have requested a zero-rated VAT, newsprint subsidies and capital equipment grants, but have had limited success. While the per capita consumption of newsprint is about average for European countries, Ireland is a large consumer of newspapers in relation to its wealth. Ireland imports almost all its newsprint from Finland, Canada and Sweden, and this has become increasingly expensive. Before the 1973 oil crisis Ireland imported 52,931 metric tons, valued at £4,405,000 ($7,400,400). In 1979 it imported 54,131 metric tons, but the value increased to £16,656,000 ($27,982,080) as the cost of newsprint increased 287 percent. In 1979 Ireland exported 286 metric tons, valued at £70,000 ($117,600).

Because of its limited economy and small population, Ireland is unable to support either an exclusively commercial or noncommercial broadcasting system. The Wireless Telegraphy Act of 1926 provided for a state broadcasting service to be financed by license fees and import duties on wireless sets and components. The act also permitted the broadcasting of advertising matter and Ireland became one of the few nations to finance its service by selling time. The national service first became Radio Eireann and, with the addition of television in 1961, Radio Tele-

fís Éireann. One RTE radio channel, Radio na Gaeltachta, broadcasts exclusively in the Irish language.

From 1958 to 1968 the volume of advertising about doubled and its value quadrupled until it was 1 percent of the GNP. Most of the increase was spent on television. In 1976 radio and television was attracting more than 40 percent of Ireland's advertising expenditures, a matter of increasing concern for the newspaper industry. In 1978 a second RTE television channel went on the air, also to be financed in part by advertising revenues. Between 1970 and 1976 advertising revenue, as a percentage of total RTE earnings, declined from 61 percent to 46 percent, primarily due to the fact that RTE costs rose faster than its advertising rates. RTE officials hope to increase combined advertising revenue on the two channels by about 15 percent to bring revenues more in line with expenses. Traditionally advertisers have had less influence on programming than have community interest groups.

Unions play an important role in Irish industry. Ireland has more than 90 unions, representing 75 percent of the non-farm labor force, and no law governs collective bargaining. Newspapers generally do not have closed shops and union membership is not a condition for employment for journalists as it is for mechanical operatives. Nevertheless, about 1,600 Irish journalists belong to the British-based National Union of Journalists, while only about 30 journalists elect to remain outside the union. Many of these are special writers whose work does not appear regularly. Some public relations practitioners also are union members.

The NUJ expresses great concern with the new technology at Irish newspapers. Among the dailies only the *Cork Examiner* and the *Irish Times* have made the complete transition to photocomposition, as have about half the provincial newspapers. Few papers have introduced direct input systems and no editorial terminals have been installed. High interest rates on loans have been as much of a deterrent as union opposition. The *Irish Times* had the benefit of an EEC training grant and some government assistance in making its conversion, which incorporated an integrated editorial, administrative and commercial computer system. The NUJ contends this led to unanticipated financial problems arising from a lower productivity than was expected in the new caserooms, and an extra workload for journalists. The NUJ pressed this claim to negotiate additional benefits, including a four-day work week.

Although continuing loss of craft jobs from the introduction of computer-based systems is anticipated, the total number of printing jobs is expected to increase during the next decade. The NUJ contends computerized production methods will gradually blur the distinction between journalists and some production workers, and urges its "chapels" (associations of printing-office employees) to press for appropriate compensation. Strikes have been uncommon.

Irish newspapers are domestically owned and attempts at foreign control have been opposed. When a foreign buyer was reportedly negotiating with the Independent Group in 1973, the government minister for industry and commerce declared that "a situation in which ownership or control of Irish newspapers passed into non-Irish hands would be unacceptable." The Committee on Industrial Progress has urged that some formal policy be initiated to prevent foreign control of newspapers.

Press Laws & Censorship

The Irish Constitution guarantees free speech, but also specifies that the press "shall not be used to undermine public order or morality or the authority of the State." This extends to publication or utterance of "blasphemous, seditious or indecent matter." In practice, censorship in Ireland, when it exists at all, is largely counteracted by the penetration of news media in Britain and Northern Ireland.

Censorship laws were rather strictly enforced during World War II to prevent publication of anything that might jeopardize Ireland's neutrality. Catholic morality is ostensibly protected by the Censorship of Publications Act forbidding publication of matter that is indecent, obscene, or advocates birth control. Although newspapers have largely been exempted from the provisions of such laws they have refrained from flouting them. But newspapers have been fined heavily for publishing certain judicial proceedings for divorce—also proscribed by the censorship law. The Offences Against the State Acts prohibits newspapers from referring to the Provisional IRA, although newspapers and magazines have ignored the acts in the last

20 years on the grounds that obeying them would make it impossible to report anything substantive about the continuing disturbances in Ulster. In late 1980 *Magill* published statements by an unidentified "leading member" of the Provisional IRA, who said the IRA will step up its efforts to kill leading Britons, including the former secretary for Northern Ireland and the head of the British judiciary. Since the intended victims were identified, the magazine would have been remiss in not publishing the interview. In 1979 Lord Mountbatten was killed by a bomb blast in Mullaghmore, and terrorism remains a major national concern. Most newspapers have worked out a modus vivendi with the state by not carrying lengthy interviews or profiles of IRA members, and by reporting incidents and statements with restraint.

The state-controlled broadcast media, however, have great difficulty in reporting similar statements and have remained circumspect in their coverage of the IRA. After RTE broadcast a reporter's summary of an interview with a Provisional IRA chief of staff in 1972, the government dismissed RTE's entire administrative body. In 1976 the government again ordered RTE to stop broadcasting interviews with Provisional IRA members, and also banned interviews with spokesmen for the IRA's legal political party, the Provisional Sinn Fein. The ban followed a radio interview with a Sinn Fein official that had been broadcast the previous day. Despite such difficulties, the electronic media have continued to seek more freedom to speak out on controversial issues.

Of greater importance to the Irish media are the nation's libel and contempt laws. Dublin newspapers have been prosecuted for contempt in recent years for criticism of the Special Criminal Court, which sits with three judges but no jury. *Hibernia,* an outspoken, irreverent Dublin weekly newspaper with investigative instincts, has been throttled repeatedly by libel judgments. The publication recently settled a suit by Royal Ulster Constabulary personnel whom *Hibernia* accused of abusing prisoners. The *Irish Times,* which prints *Hibernia,* was a co-defendant in the suit. When *Hibernia* libeled a priest, its editor, John Mulcahy, argued that an editor should have the same limited liability enjoyed by a corporate officer of a company that is sued. But the court rejected the defense and levied a heavy fine. The *Sunday*

World lost a sizable judgment when it was found guilty of libeling an Irish senator in a front-page story. Recently the *Sunday World* was enjoined from publishing an article on a stock exchange inquiry into allegations made by a former employee against government brokers. Such prior restraint is uncommon but is mandated in some cases by Irish law.

State-Press Relations

Irish journalists have no right of professional secrecy, as do lawyers, physicians and clergy, and journalists have on occasion been detained for not revealing their sources. The government itself has sub-rosa tendencies. Under the Criminal Procedures Act, a journalist may not publish evidence of preliminary hearings of indictable offenses other than to report that such proceedings occurred, unless permission to publish further details is requested by the accused and approved by the judge. Cabinet meetings and certain parliamentary committee meetings are closed to the press. There is also continuing indirect pressure on journalists from government officials to restrict political information. To the extent that editors succumb to social pressures inherent in a closely knit society, these attempts are successful. A tradition of secrecy evolved from Ireland's civil wars and external domination, and a belief remains that the government knows best. But there is still aggressive criticism of government officials, discussion of political, economic and religious policies and continuing pressure for greater freedom of information.

The Government Information Bureau issues statements on behalf of state offices, arranges access to officials, coordinates public information programs, accredits and briefs foreign journalists and publishes government documents. The bureau has generally good relations with the Irish media. It is headed by a full-time press officer appointed by the political party in power.

Rather than explicit controls over the press, there is in Ireland an elitist news perspective deriving from shared newsgathering practices. The national newspapers are similar in their news judgments and editing. Political correspondents take turns in the press gallery of the Oireachtas, or Parliament. They attend the same functions, talk to the same sources, arrive at the same conclusions and generate similar political responses.

This type of reporting runs a high risk, as was apparent during the national elections in 1977. The media simply assumed a victory for the National Coalition of Fine Gael and Labour. This proved spurious when the opposition Fianna Fáil elected the largest majority of parliamentary seats in the history of the republic. Journalists ignored public opinion polls that repeatedly called their judgments into question. As Brian Farrell explained in his excellent study of the election, "The political correspondents and other senior journalists who play the gatekeeper role sensed and shared the perception of a majority of senior politicians that experienced observation was a more reliable guide to public opinion, in all its rich variety, than any 'outsider's' survey. The two sets fed each other, the journalist's reports, based on their assessment of the politicians' moods, in turn coloring the politicians' own views of the course of the campaign ... as the two sets of insiders concentrated their attention on each other, too many messages failed to reach them from the mass of outsiders. A wide range of shared assumptions and expectations was no substitute for an objective and dispassionate examination of what was actually happening."

Attitude Toward Foreign Media

Foreign coverage of Ireland is inadequate, and also preoccupied with the conflict in Northern Ireland. Very few full-time foreign correspondents are based in Ireland, although British-based journalists report Irish affairs. Irish governments and industrial associations have been concerned about foreign perceptions of Ireland as a nation in constant turmoil, and declines in tourism have been attributed to continuing publicity about IRA activities as well as rising prices. The Department of Foreign Affairs is responsible for external publicity, and the government engages international publicists to promote Irish interests.

Ireland has a leadership role in addressing such world communication issues, with Irish statesman Sean MacBride heading UNESCO's 16-member International Commission for the Study of Communication Problems. The commission's report was debated in 1980 in Belgrade at UNESCO's 21st General Conference, and was reported in the Irish press. The report called for free access for reporters to the entire spectrum of opinion within any country and denounced arbitrary control of information, licensing of journalists or special protection for reporters. The report was criticized for what some contended was its bias against the commercial press of advanced countries, not necessarily excluding Ireland.

News Agencies

An Irish News Agency was established in 1949 in part to promote Irish interests abroad and gather information for domestic consumption, but was closed in 1957. Irish newspapers publish some reports supplied by the Associated Press, United Press International, Reuters and Agence France-Presse, and also use some foreign syndicated material, but the source of these British, French and American wire-service reports is seldom provided. Television is supplied by British Visnews, UPITN and CBS. There is a free flow of information between the republic and Northern Ireland and correspondents are maintained in both Dublin and Belfast. The *Irish Times* has correspondents in Brussels and London, as does RTE. Ireland is otherwise dependent on foreign sources for news and information. This is a matter of concern in Ireland, which is more dependent on international news agencies than other small European nations of comparable size.

Electronic News Media

Irish broadcasting began in 1926 in a tiny studio called Dublin Broadcasting Station with the call signal 2RN. In 1960 it was converted into Radio Telefis Eireann, an autonomous statutory corporation under the Broadcasting Authority Act. It is governed by a seven-member authority with separate controllers for radio and television. Under the terms of the Act, the authority is directed to ensure that "any information, news or feature which relates to matters of public controversy or is the subject of public debate ...is presented objectively and impartially." However, political party broadcasts are permitted. The Authority is also charged with furthering the Irish language and the national culture. A separate station, funded by Radio Telefis Eireann, broadcasts entirely in Gaelic from its station in Casla in Connemara County.

Education & Training

Education for journalists in Ireland is unsystematic and may now be in a transitional period from which a more orderly approach could emerge. RTE usually hires journalists from the newspaper industry, but has offered them only very limited training in broadcast writing and editing. Broadcast journalists belong to the NUJ, which has encouraged a more systematic approach to the recruitment and training of journalists. A 1974 government report sharply criticized RTE's lack of training facilities for journalists, but no policy changes were forthcoming. The Catholic Communications Institute established a Communications Centre in Dublin in 1965 and began media training in 1967. The Centre offers a nine-unit broadcasting course that also attracts students from many developing countries. Courses in publishing, cinematography and journalism are available to both clergy and lay persons of all faiths. Government officials and business executives have availed themselves of a course covering the skills of appearing on television and responding to questions.

A two-year course of study for journalists is offered by the School of Journalism at the College of Commerce in Rathmines, Dublin. Newspapers have assigned their junior reporters and editors to take the course, and shared the cost with the NUJ. A pre-entry training course is available and graduates about 20 potential journalists a year. No training in journalism is offered at Irish universities. Some media people are university graduates, but they are in the minority. There continues to be a disdain for formal journalism training, especially among the provincial newspapers, which prefer on-the-job training to programs of instruction. Accordingly, there is no academically based communications research center in Ireland, although the School of Journalism at Rathmines is interested in developing one. The school is also expanding into block-release courses, a crash program attempted successfully in England, in which journalists go into residence at a college during a vacation period. Several Irish political scientists and sociologists have expressed interest in the communications media, and have written engagingly about them.

There are no professional organizations for journalists in Ireland. The NUJ serves as a forum for some matters of professional concern. Newspaper publishers have two groups;

the Provincial Newspapers Association of Ireland and the Dublin News Managers' Committee. Advertisers belong to the Association of Advertisers in Ireland Ltd., and produced a code of advertising standards in 1967.

Summary

Although troubled by economic difficulties, high taxation and competition from electronic and foreign media, the press in Ireland remains a powerful vehicle of expression in the nation's society. While readership studies suggest increasing informational preferences for the electronic media, which is dominated by foreign-produced programs, it is evident that the press plays a unique part in the lives of most Irish people, and is still the preferred medium of opinion leaders. The character of Irish newspapers reflects the robustness of Irish life. Newspapers mirror Irish affinity for language and discourse, athletic competition, traditional values and institutions, politics and nationalism.

Television has brought a great change in Irish life. As Brian Farrell noted, among a new generation of broadcasters there was "a conscious iconoclasm that breached at least some of the conventions of Irish society. The mere fact that those in authority were seen to be asked questions (no matter how deferentially) was an important advance."

Unquestionably Ireland is becoming less insular and more open to changing roles for women and young people. A growing population, with the problems and opportunities it presents, reverses the unhappy situation that existed when Ireland's most prominent export was its people. Yet the continuing tensions in the north of Ireland and the seeming intractability of centuries-old disputes clearly divert attention from social and economic matters, and sap the energies of a sizable percentage of the island's residents. The final resolution of the Irish partition will bring about further changes in Irish life.

Changes in Irish society seem to require more freedom of information, and the next decade will probably lead to some softening of the laws of libel and contempt, and also to the limitation of executive secrecy. At the same time, a greater concentration of media may offset gains in freedom of communication. Journalists will change as the press builds an investigative tradition and establishes professional training opportunities.

CHRONOLOGY

1976   Irish government orders RTE to stop broadcasting interviews with members of Provisional IRA and Sinn Fein.

1978   Second RTE television channel begins broadcasting. *Sunday World* taken over by Independent Group.

1979   *Hibernia* loses libel suits.

1980   MacBride Commission issues report. *Magill* publishes revelations on 1969 arms crisis. Court enjoins *Sunday World* from publishing article on stock market.

BIBLIOGRAPHY

Adams, Michael. *Censorship: The Irish Experience.* Totowa, N.J., 1968.

Browne, S. J. *The Press in Ireland.* London, 1937.

Chubb, Basil. *The Government and Politics of Ireland.* London, 1970.

Encyclopedia of Ireland. Dublin, 1968.

ISRAEL

by Samuel R. Moore

BASIC DATA

Population: 3.69 million
Area: 21,287 sq. km. (8,219 sq. mi.)
GNP: 24.14 billion shekels ($12.7 billion) (1978)
Literacy Rate: 90%
Language(s): Hebrew, Yiddish, Ladino, English, Arabic
Number of Dailies: 24
  Aggregate Circulation: 1,337,000
  Circulation per 1,000: 362
Number of Nondailies: NA
  Aggregate Circulation: NA
  Circulation per 1,000: NA
Number of Periodicals: NA

Number of Radio Stations: 4
Number of Television Stations: 3
Number of Radio Receivers: 660,000
  Radio Receivers per 1,000: 179
Number of Television Sets: 356,000
  Television Sets per 1,000: 96
Total Annual Newsprint Consumption: 31,000 metric tons
  Per Capita Newsprint Consumption: 8 kg. (17.6 lbs.)
Total Newspaper Ad Receipts: NA
  As % of All Ad Expenditures: NA

Background & General Characteristics

Israel has a well-developed network of communications media. The 24 daily newspapers are available even in remote areas. Papers are privately owned and are free to express a variety of political, ideological and religious views. They are responsive to government guidance, however, in matters relating to national security and to foreign relations. With a national literacy rate of 90 percent, the press provides intellectual stimulation for political debates and offers a wide range of educational and cultural information. Standards of journalism are high. Coverage is extensive, including international news. Because of the objections of religious groups to stories involving violence and scandal, most papers avoid sensational reporting. Dailies print six to 20 pages, with supplements on Friday. No paper publishes a Saturday edition. Photographs are rarely used.

The first Hebrew newspapers in Israel (then part of the Ottoman Empire), *Ha-Levanon* and *Havazzelet,* were established as weeklies in 1863 by founders of the first Hebrew printing presses in Jerusalem. They differed from the Hebrew periodicals that had already begun to appear in Europe in that news and current events were central and the language was livelier and simpler. Eventually the Jerusalem papers exerted considerable influence on the early stages of the revival of spoken Hebrew. Both papers were closed by the Turkish authorities within a year, but *Havazzelet* was reopened in 1870 and continued to appear until 1911.

After World War I, the press (now in Palestine, a League of Nations mandate under British administration) underwent a process of modernization. A number of daily papers made their appearance, and a clear distinction emerged between the dailies and the weeklies. The important dailies engaged in general publishing. Coverage of literary, scientific and artistic developments tended to be concentrated in the Friday supplement, which became a regular feature of most papers. The weeklies dropped their coverage of straight news, placing their emphasis on signed articles, while the daily papers devoted themselves to topical material and refrained from specialization. This left room for the development of professional periodicals. A further postwar innovation was the introduction of afternoon papers. These were generally of a more popular nature than the morning press. Another development was a growing distinction between the formal writer and the journalist. Previously the dividing line had been blurred, but now there emerged the journalist-reporter type, familiar in Western journalism.

The post-World War I period was also marked by a move away from Jerusalem to Tel Aviv, which became the center of Hebrew-language newspaper publishing.

In 1925 the labor movement decided to publish its own paper, *Davar,* which became the most widely circulated morning paper. The increase in the number of political parties led to a parallel growth in the number of papers, as each group sought to propagate its views through its own organ. Today, although the press is privately owned and does not rely heavily on governmental funding, many papers do receive subsidies from political parties and religious groups. As a result, a large number of dailies in Israel are organs of these supporting groups.

Despite the rapid growth of cities since its creation three decades ago, Israel has no local dailies; only one city has a local weekly. An excellent transportation system and the small size of the country lend themselves to this phenomenon of complete dominance by national newspapers. No city is so far from the communications center of Tel Aviv that it could start a local newspaper without strong outside competition. The two largest-circulation newspapers, for example, use air transport to deliver their first papers to Haifa within one hour of press time.

In addition to Israel's small area, there are other reasons for the popularity of national papers. The many party newspapers have loyalists throughout the country. Also, the average Israeli is conditioned to look outside his town or city for the factors affecting his daily life. The highly centralized nature of the national government accounts for a deeper interest in nationwide political affairs than in local politics. Parties and central government play a determining role in such municipal concerns as budgets, officials and law enforcement.

The influence of outside forces on Israeli life largely accounts for the interest of Israelis in international news. As a small, isolated land, Israel is dependent upon the economic and political decisions of numerous foreign powers. The nation also looks to Jews in many of the Western countries for a good deal of its tourism and philanthropic support. Further, a majority of the Jewish population is foreign born. These immigrants have families, friends and experiential attachments in a variety of nations, and news from their former home-countries is of primary interest to them. Israeli newspapers satisfy this demand for national and international news, particularly of a political nature. Each daily also tries to cover the entire nation by publishing local and regional stories sent in both by correspondents and by ITIM, the national news agency. But such reports remain only a small part of the daily news fare.

Twenty daily newspapers are published in Tel Aviv and four in Jerusalem. They are mainly in Hebrew, but also in Yiddish, English, Arabic, Hungarian, French, Polish, Bulgarian, Rumanian and German. All consider themselves national, not local. Evening dailies have the largest circulations, although morning papers are considered more influential. The nondaily press is mainly in Hebrew, although titles do appear in several other languages.

Most Hebrew morning dailies have strong political or religious affiliations. *Al Hamishmar* is affiliated with the Mapam party, *Hatzofeh* with the National Religious Front. *Davar* is the long-established organ of Histadrut, the nationally powerful labor organization. The Mapai party publishes the weekly *Ot.*

The most influential and respected dailies, for both quality of news coverage and commentary, are *Ha'aretz,* with a daily circulation of 80,000, and *Davar,* with 44,850. These are the most widely read of the morning papers, exceeded only by the popular afternoon *Ma'ariv* (260,000) and *Yedioth Aharonoth* (180,000). *The Jerusalem Post* gives detailed and sound news coverage in English. (It also has some 30,000 readers in the United States and Canada.)

National newsprint consumption amounts to approximately 31,000 metric tons annually, of which some 9,400 are produced domestically.

Economic Framework

The media of Israel work within an economic framework of adjustment and reform. In 1973 Israel's growing economy slowed sharply, caused by the world energy crisis and the Yom Kippur War. The government launched an emergency plan to revive the economy. To increase confidence in Israel's currency, a fixed rate of exchange for the pound was made, but was abandoned in 1977.

Advertising plays a large part in the economic framework of Israel, with a total annual expenditure for all media of more than 894,784,000 IL (nearly $100 million). Newspapers receive 55.9 percent of the advertising revenue, with magazines next at 11.3 percent. Other types receiving revenue are outdoor displays, radio, exhibitions, direct mail and cinema, but television has no commercial advertising. The high number of dailies makes newspapers the most desirable advertising media. Radio is also effective, reaching 90 percent of the population. Israeli advertisers are represented by approximately 65 officially recognized agents. There are also 10 public relations companies, although most public relations work is carried out by the advertising agents.

There are several laws, controls and restrictions governing advertising. Billboards and cinema commercials and slides are subject to taxation. A statutory law, however, prohibits billboard advertising on interurban highways. Advertisers are subject to two codes of standards. The Israel Consumerism Council has put forth standards based on the International Chamber of Commerce code, and a code of ethics has been established by the Advertisers Association of Israel. A "truth in advertising" agreement has also been accepted by all major advertising associations. Other groups concerned with the advertising industry are the Israel Advertising Association, the Daily Newspapers Publishers Association and the Israel Public Relations Association. Several private companies and academic institutions offer market research facilities in Israel.

Press Laws

The government of Israel oversees the media through two offices: the Central Office of Information and the Government Press Office. Both are under the Prime Minister's Office and are supervised by a minister in charge of information services, who is actually a minister of information. To coordinate information policies, meetings are held between officials of the Government Press Office, the Information Division of the Ministry of Foreign Affairs and representatives of the Kol Broadcasting Authority. Close contact is maintained between government agencies dealing with news media and with members of the press represented by its Committee of

Editors. During these briefings, the press is occasionally asked to treat certain items of information as background only and refrain from publishing them.

An important press law—one of the few in the nation—concerns the Knesset, the Israeli Parliament. Section 28 of Fundamental Law states, "The publication of proceedings taken and anything said at an open session is unrestricted and does not entail any criminal or civil liability." But it further states, "The Chairman of such meeting may (in the manner authorized in the Knesset Procedural Code) forbid the publication of any matter which in his opinion may endanger the security of the State." Section 29 provides that "proceedings in a closed session may not be published save in the manner laid down in the Knesset Procedural Code."

In July 1965 a Defamation Law was passed. It provides that persons publishing, writing or distributing information regarded as defamatory must furnish proof that such information is true and that it was published in the public interest. In case of conviction, penalties are imposed not only on journalists and publishers but also on newspaper-office employees, printers and news vendors.

Censorship & State-Press Relations

De jure censorship is relatively lenient. However, because of the extreme importance of the Israeli Army, strict censorship governs the publication of material relating to national security, including military operations, activities in occupied areas and matters relating to foreign affairs. Provisions and procedures are handled by censorship laws that were passed by British authorities in 1945. Articles dealing with national security are reviewed by a board of military censors. Material regarded as endangering the nation's safety is deleted; offending newspapers are often fined. The Committee of Editors represents the press before the military censors. Appeals against the actions of the censors may be lodged with a committee composed of an army officer, a newspaper editor and the president of the Bar Association.

Despite the existing laws, however, foreign newsmen often file their stories without first submitting them to the proper censorship committees, drawing the ire of the Israeli government. In late 1970 *Time* reported that a secret meeting had taken place in Israel between King Hussein of Jordan and the

Israeli deputy prime minister, and the attorney general's office considered taking action against three foreign journalists who had filed the reports without submitting them to censorship. In 1969 Israel withdrew the press accreditation of Anthony Hatch, CBS correspondent in Jerusalem, for broadcasting news of Israel's invasion of Egypt before the official announcement.

In 1970 in Jerusalem, the Foreign Press Association in Israel demanded the abolition of military censorship on outgoing news material. The government said it would look into the matter; however, nothing was changed. On October 20, 1973, at the height of the Yom Kippur War, Philip Caputo of the *Chicago Tribune* became the first American newsman to reach the bridgehead that Israeli troops had thrown across the Suez Canal. Caputo saw that the task force which Israeli officials had said was operating in Egypt was in reality a full-scale counteroffensive, involving at least three divisions. When Caputo routinely turned in his story for clearance at the end of the day, he found that it was heavily censored.

While military censorship has been imposed strictly for the good of national security, Israeli spokesmen have suffered a lapse of credibility among citizens as a result, especially since the Yom Kippur War. Previously, official statements enjoyed a high reputation for accuracy and thoroughness. They did not tell everything, but whatever version they gave of a story usually proved to be the correct one. After the 1973 war, however, it was disclosed that military censorship had killed a number of important news stories. There have since been charges against the Army's information services, Opposition politicians claiming that overly strict and irrational censorship brought about the surprise and demoralization of the Israeli public, newspaper editorials calling for a thorough revision of Israel's security laws. In late 1973 the public was suddenly notified that oil wells in the Gulf of Suez, occupied by Israel since 1967, were set on fire under mysterious circumstances. This resulted in a wave of speculations, with the assumption that Arab commandos had penetrated Israeli defense lines. However, the real reason soon spread across the country by word of mouth—an Israeli Hawk missile had mistakenly hit an oil rig and set off the fires. It was almost a month before military authorities allowed the real reasons to be published, and only after an American NBC correspondent flew

out of Israel and cabled the story from Europe without going through the mandatory censorship.

As already shown, Israel's censorship reaches the foreign media. In 1974 the Sinai and the Suez Canal area were closed to foreign reporters. Also, while he was defense minister, Moshe Dayan issued orders that each request for a press interview with military personnel—regardless of rank—must go through him. Dayan admitted that he took this course of action after a series of interviews published in American newspapers in which then-General Arik Sharon, who commanded the successful crossing of the Suez Canal, heavily criticized military leaders for letting politics interfere with their judgment.

In November 1980 the Israeli military government in the occupied West Bank started a new crackdown on foreign journalists in an effort to prevent them from reporting firsthand on clashes between Arab demonstrators and Israeli soldiers. The Israelis arrested and charged one American reporter and confiscated the film and notes of others. The measures were introduced after a television crew videotaped troops firing from a rooftop during a demonstration in which Arab teenagers were shot in the legs.

Since then, the Army has moved strongly against journalists. It has declared entire Arab towns to be military zones, closing them as soon as demonstrations begin and detaining reporters caught on the scene. Criminal charges were filed against Howard Arenstein of United Press International for his presence "in a closed military zone"—the campus of Bir Zeit University—during a demonstration.

Several journalists experienced situations in which they were detained by troops and had their film or tape confiscated—and often exposed. The Army's Lieutenant Colonel Amir Cheshin and Zev Chafets, head of the Government Press Office, claimed that the steps were very necessary because of heightened tension. "As soon as a camera appears, a rock is picked up," Chafets said. "TV cameras tend to have an inciting effect very often, particularly in the case of political demonstrators who are anxious to make a point. It is very well known that cameras need pictures and rock-throwing needs pictures."

For the past couple of years, a growing number of people have been claiming that not only military but political considerations are often at the basis of a refusal to allow a story to be published. In 1976 in East Jerusalem, the Arab newspaper *Asch-Schaab* was closed for two weeks for violating military censorship regulations; however, it is believed that it was actually shut down because it supports the Palestine Liberation Organization. In another instance, the daily *Ha'aretz* was fined for publishing an article critical of the army's chief of staff, General Mordechai Gur. While the story involved the military, it apparently did not jeopardize Israel's national security.

A shaky situation exists between the Israeli government and the Arab-language press, particularly when concerning the West Bank. Under an order published after the 1967 War, no Arab newspaper may be delivered to the occupied territories without a permit from the military government. Any article, picture or advertisement deemed a security risk is deleted. It is also illegal for the Arab papers to show anybody who has been subject to censorship.

Lieutenant Colonel Ami Gulska, the Israeli military spokesman in Jerusalem (his authority extends to the West Bank), has admitted that there is at times a thin line between military and political censorship. "There is a very sensitive situation in the territories," he said. "Sometimes you only need a match to make a big explosion. Censorship is necessary to prevent such explosions.... Unfortunately, we are in a state of war with the PLO. Their basic ideology is the destruction of Israel. It's no secret that Palestinians in general, and the Arab press, support the PLO. We try to be as liberal as we can, but we cannot afford to help our enemy."

Of the three Arabic newspapers published in East Jerusalem, *Al-Fajr* and *Al-Sha'ab* most clearly speak for the self-determination of the Palestinian people. They are therefore more heavily censored than *Al-Quds,* which is less nationalist in tone, underscoring the thin line between political and military considerations in the censorship of Arab newspapers.

According to high-ranking sources, there is a growing debate in Israeli military circles over the Arab press censorship issue. Some argue that unless the material is blatantly anti-security, censorship is not practical. They point out that the Palestinians in the occupied territories cannot be isolated from the outside world. West Bankers, for example, receive television from Amman and pick up radio stations from across the Arab world. Since the Arabs are part of the global village,

the argument goes, nonmilitary censorship is not only nonsensical but also frustrating to the Arabs. This frustration leads to violence.

While military censorship has been openly criticized in many Israeli newspapers, the government in 1976 tried to extend its censorship to diplomacy. In January 1976 the Israeli cabinet approved a law banning press reports of secret diplomatic exchanges between Israel and other states. The regulations followed a 1975 Israeli newspaper leak of a message President Gerald Ford had sent to Premier Yitzhak Rabin, protesting plans to establish new settlements on the Golan Heights. Israel had rejected the protest. The law would have carried a 15-year prison sentence to any person found guilty of divulging messages marked "top secret" and seven years in prison for the newsman who published the leak. But after intensive protests by the Editors Committee, the Israeli Press Council and foreign news organizations, the government decided against implementation and sought a voluntary arrangement with the newspaper editors regarding certain sensitive issues, the publication of which might prove detrimental to Israel's national interests. The measures would have been an extension of the 1957 State Security, Foreign Relations & Official Secrets Law.

In some instances the Committee of Editors has decided to apply voluntary self-censorship. Among other things it has made an effort to avoid sensational stories by refraining from reporting cases of suicide and rape as such. Under the formula accepted by the committee a person does not commit suicide in Israel, but "dies in tragic circumstances"; no woman is raped, but "attacked." This decision on the part of the Israeli press testifies to its will to maintain a certain standard of character, of public responsibility, instead of catering to a lower common-denominator of taste.

Censorship has also played a part in Israeli television. In 1978 several Knesset members demanded that a film scheduled for television be banned because it would harm Israeli national interests at an awkward time in international affairs. Based on "Hirbet Hiz'a," an Israeli short story about the heart-searchings of a company of Jewish soldiers ordered to evacuate an Arab village toward the end of the 1948–49 Arab-Israeli War, it created scandal when it was first published, only months after the war, because it contradicted the official line that every Arab who left his home did so on orders from his own leaders. On a directive by the education minister, television screens were blacked out for an hour when the program was scheduled. This episode brought up the issue of the freedom of Israeli broadcasting. Under the former Labour government, decisions on what to broadcast and how were left to professional broadcasters.

Attitude Toward Foreign Media

Despite their problems, foreign journalists have found Israel a much better place to report from than the Arab nations. Compared with their lack of freedom with Arab military forces, American correspondents in Israel have had more access to fighting, surprisingly fast communications and relatively liberal censors. In the Arab countries, censorship has been heavy and officials obstinate in keeping the press from the fronts. In Egypt, U.S. correspondents were confined to hotels and then expelled after the diplomatic break with the United States in the 1960s. As a result, the American press got a much more complete picture of Israel's side of the 1967 War; the Arab side of the story had to wait, for the most part, until correspondents could file from other countries. American newsmen with the Israeli Army hitched rides to the front and wrote full accounts of what they saw, subject to the needs of military security. In Egypt, Syria and Jordan, they could not.

This freedom of movement Israel permitted was welcomed by the foreign newsmen in Israel, but it also brought danger. Two American correspondents—Ted Yates of NBC and Paul Schutzer of *Life*—were killed while accompanying Israeli troops in combat. Hearst correspondent Serge Fliegers was wounded in a mine explosion that killed an Israeli correspondent.

News Agencies

Domestic news is furnished to the press by ITIM, also known as the Associated Israel Press Limited. It is the country's national news agency, with bureaus in Tel Aviv and Jerusalem. Founded in 1950 by a group of newspapermen, ITIM is controlled by a board of managers representing the dailies that hold shares in the agency. Local news to the newspapers and to the Kol Israel Broadcasting Authority are furnished by a network of staff reporters who cover various areas of the country. Some of ITIM's news material originates with the Government Press Office.

The agency publishes a weekly "Airmail Bulletin" and a daily "Financial Bulletin," both in English.

The Jewish Telegraphic Agency, Israel's oldest and best known news agency, has overseas bureaus in New York, Paris, Buenos Aires, Johannesburg and stringers all over the world. It services 70 publications in the United States and Canada alone. In Israel, its copy is transmitted by ITIM.

For international news coverage, the press relies on Reuters, Agence France-Press, Associated Press and United Press International. UPI has its own fully staffed bureau. Reuters is the one most widely used. The other news services are represented by local correspondents.

Electronic News Media

Broadcasting was inaugurated in 1936 when the British mandate authorities started the Palestine Broadcasting Service. The programs were in English, Arabic and Hebrew, and the studios were situated in Jerusalem. (The following year saw the foundation of the Palestine Broadcasting Symphony Orchestra.)

During the last months of the Mandate, the Haganah guerrilla army maintained an illegal broadcasting station called Kol Israel ("Voice of Israel"). When Israel became a state in 1948, Jerusalem was cut off during the siege by Arab forces, and only a skeleton service could be maintained there. The broadcasting center was established in Tel Aviv; Kol Israel's first legal program was a relay of the Declaration of Independence. Initially constituted as part of the Ministry of the Interior, Kol Israel was later transferred to the Prime Minister's Office. Early in 1950 the Jerusalem Broadcasting Center was reestablished and most of the departments transferred there, although studios continued to be maintained in Tel Aviv, and later in Haifa.

Although initially confined to a single wavelength, the broadcasting service gradually expanded to four simultaneous broadcasts. Network A, broadcasting in Hebrew, presents a variety of programs, including news and current events, symphony concerts, plays, school broadcasts and higher education. Network B, which broadcasts commercials, also concentrates on entertainment and light music. Some of its programs are in non-Hebrew languages for new immigrants and tourists. It also has a daily program in simple

Hebrew for listeners with a limited vocabulary. Network C is a short-wave service to other countries. It was originally founded in 1950 by the World Zionist Organization as Kol Zion la-Golah ("The Voice of Zion to the Diaspora"), and was incorporated into Kol Israel's external services in 1959. It broadcasts in Hebrew, English, French, Yiddish, Russian, Hungarian, Rumanian, Ladino, Mograbi and Persian. Network D broadcasts in Arabic for Arabs in Israel, the Israel-held Arab areas and other Middle Eastern countries.

Certain safeguards were provided to prevent Kol Israel from becoming a government mouthpiece. Although its budget is controlled by Parliament, it is also financed by license and announcement fees, advertisements and state grants. A Public Advisory Committee was constituted, consisting of leading figures in various political groups and also in the arts. While this committee had a useful function as a safety valve, it failed to evolve a satisfactory method of work. Members of the broadcasting staff, although civil servants, are also independent individuals who have been pressing for the reconstitution of the broadcasting charter to make Kol Israel a corporation, so as to combine maximum independence with minimum official ties.

Inevitably, from time to time, the governmental approach is stressed, but every effort is made to ensure a democratic broadcasting system: to report all viewpoints on controversial issues through studio discussions in such series as "Pro and Con," "Round Table Discussion" and "Meet the Press." Before elections, spokesmen of all parties are invited to state their cases over the air, although—since nearly 20 parties put up candidates—it is impossible to give them equal time. Accordingly, time is divided according to the strength of the party, with a minimum period allotted to parties not previously represented in Parliament. Party broadcasts before elections are coordinated with the Elections Committee under the supervision of its chairman, a justice of the High Court.

The only alternative to Kol Israel inside the country is provided by the Army radio station, Galei Zahal, which broadcasts from 6 to 10:30 each evening. This station is operated on a small budget and is run by Army personnel (including both conscripts and reservists). Its objective is twofold: to provide light fare for soldiers, and to broadcast features on Army life for the Army and for the general public.

Television was late in coming to Israel, and is now only in its beginning stages. The delay was due partly to an assessment of economic priorities that put television comparatively low on the list. When an effort was first made to introduce television, the reaction from a major portion of the population was almost violent in its intensity. It came mainly from cinema owners, educators, trade union and government leaders. The population as a whole entered into what became known as "the great debate," reaching to university student meetings, assemblies of agriculturists, and at one time occupying the cabinet for about an hour during its regular weekly sessions. Despite this opposition, a certain amount of underground activity was being carried out. The Army chief of staff sent a small military mission to the United States to check on the possibility of establishing a purely military television service, which might be used for tactical and strategic training and also be interwoven into the Army's educational system. A number of investors in many parts of the world sent in proposals for TV investment. Government authorities finally agreed to lay the groundwork for a television industry.

A major breakthrough came when the Rothschild Foundation offered to finance classroom teaching on television through an open network. This was directed primarily to schools in development areas with large new immigrant populations which had difficulties in obtaining teachers. A pilot project went into operation in 1965, presently developed into a regular daily service.

Pressure for general television increased as a result of the presence in the country of tens of thousands of TV sets, mostly in areas populated by Arabs who were intensively watching programs from the neighboring Arab countries. The problem became even more acute as a result of the Six-Day War of 1967, after which it was decided to inaugurate general television. The transmission of programs in Hebrew and Arabic began in 1968 and rapidly attracted a wide and growing audience.

Color telecasts were to have started in 1979, and most sets and stations have been equipped for color. However, because of decisions by the Ministry of Energy and Communications, engineers had to install special systems to wipe color out. Television importers further complicated the situation. In an effort to boost sales, they equipped their sets with anti-wipe systems that restored color partially. Israeli television will stop wiping the color, but no attempt to maintain color standards will be operational until all required equipment is installed. Color sets in Israel cost approximately $2,000.

TV programming includes news, which is popular, foreign thrillers, feature films, local and foreign entertainment programs, discussions on current affairs, and documentaries. But there have recently been several complaints that there is too much talking and too little entertainment. Also, major American film companies are boycotting Israeli television because of pressure from the country's Theater Owners Association. A member of the Knesset has attempted to bypass these problems and have features purchased through the government.

Education & Training

Most Israeli journalists have completed academic secondary schools, and some have university educations. Modern news-reporting techniques are learned mostly on the job, although many journalists were employed on the staffs of newspapers in other countries before coming to Israel. Courses in journalism are offered at Tel Aviv University and at Hebrew University in Jerusalem.

The professional interests of newspapermen are represented by the Israeli Journalists Association. The Israeli Press Council, established in 1963, deals with matters relating to press freedom and professional ethics. The Daily Newspaper Publishers' Association of Israel, an affiliate of the International Federation of Newspaper Publishers, negotiates on behalf of publishers with official groups and with labor unions. It is also in charge of the purchase and distribution of newsprint.

Summary

Censorship, however justified, is always an infringement of the basic democratic princi-ple of freedom of the press. However, even in a democracy, there may be general agreement on the need for voluntary censorship in time of war without prejudice to the principle of free expression. The success of voluntary censorship requires a general agreement that it is justified by the presence of a national emergency.

The existence of a national emergency in Israel has been acknowledged by almost everyone, including the press, since the state was established. This has forced both the press and the government officials to take the nation into their confidence and explain the reasons for their actions. They have also had to establish a means of preventing publication of information that could harm national security.

Throughout the years there have been fluctuations regarding the awareness of a national emergency. Restrictions on the press were not always accepted with the same degree of readiness. However, the fact that the condition of emergency in Israel has proved to be of such lasting duration has in turn eroded, at least partly, the initial aversion to the very existence of censorship. Protests made against restrictions when they were first introduced were eventually forgotten. Thus, temporary defense measures were gradually consolidated into permanent routine.

This is the paradox under which the press system of Israel must work. The country is supposedly a democracy, where freedom of the press is practiced. Yet the Israelis must fight to maintain their democratic principles—and for the very survival of the nation—with the press often suffering as a result. However, it is the view of most observers that, taking everything into consideration, the situation could be much worse. In a country that has known nothing but fighting since its birth the press of Israel enjoys opportunities not available to those in many more-peaceful nations.

CHRONOLOGY

1975

February   Aharon Yariv resigns as Israel's information minister, charging Premier Yitzhak Rabin's operation of government is "inappropriate and inadequate."

1976

January   After protests from press against cabinet plan to place political matters under censorship, Premier Rabin and Justice Minister Chaim Zadok announce proposal is being withdrawn "for the moment following a pledge by newspaper editors to show greater restraint before publishing material that could seriously harm Israel's diplomatic relations."

February   Arab newspaper *A Shaab* shut down for eight days, after publishing censored material.

May   In East Jerusalem Arab newspaper *Asch-Schaab* closed for violating military censorship regulations; some observers believe real reason for closing is paper's support of PLO.

1978

February   Government bars showing of TV film version of play depicting Israeli forces expelling residents of Arab village in 1948 war.

BIBLIOGRAPHY

Alcalay, Reuven. *Israel Government Yearbook, 1967.* Jerusalem, 1967.

Democracy. Jerusalem, 1974.

"Free to Tell It Like It Is?" *The Economist,* February 11, 1978, p. 62.

Friedman, Robert. "The Arab Press and Israel's Dilemma." *The Press,* April 1981, p. 22.

Goren, Dina. *Secrecy and the Right to Know.* Tel Aviv, 1979.

"IPI in Action." *IPI Report,* December 1970, p. 7.

"Israel's Newspaper Economically Independent." *IPI Report,* July 1976, p. 9.

"Israel's TV Finally Will Switch to Color." *Variety,* August 22, 1979, p. 2.

Likhovski, Eliahu S. *Israel's Parliament.* Oxford, 1971.

Lowenstein, Ralph L. "The Daily Press in Israel: an Appraisal after Twenty Years." *Journalism Quarterly,* Summer 1969, p. 326.

Merrill, John C., Bryan, Carter R., and Alisky, Marvin. *The Foreign Press.* Baton Rouge, La., 1964.

Merrill, John C., and Fisher, Harold A. *The World's Great Dailies.* New York, 1980.

"Military Censorship Cuts Israel Credibility." *IPI Report,* April–May 1974, p. 6.

"Newscasts Are Peak Viewing." *IPI Report,* May–June 1973, p. 4.

Shanon, Donald. "Israel Won Reporting War, Too." *Quill,* August 1967, p. 7.

Smith, Harvey H. *Area Handbook for Israel.* Washington, D.C., 1970.

"The Press Under Pressure." *IPI Report,* October 1974, p. 6.

"The Press Under Pressure." *IPI Report,* March 1976, p. 6.

"U.S. Films 'Not Available' to TV in Israel—not at $800 per Pic." *Variety,* February 28, 1979, p. 49.

Wigoder, Geoffrey. "Radio in Israel." *Gazette.* No. 1, 1961, p. 130.

World Communications. Paris, 1975.

Yuenger, James. "Dateline: The Middle East (Both Sides)." *Quill,* January 1974, p. 12.

Zak, Moshe. "The Contemporary Press of Israel." *Gazette.* No. 1, 1961, p. 4.

Zinder, Harry, "Television in Israel." *Gazette.* No. 1, 1961, p. 138.

ITALY

by William Porter

BASIC DATA

Population: 57,056,000 (1980)
Area: 301,217 sq. km. (116,300 sq. mi.)
GNP: 239.75 trillion lira (US$ 298.2 billion) (1979)
Literacy Rate: 95%
Language(s): Italian
Number of Dailies: 72
   Aggregate Circulation: 5,491,000
   Circulation per 1,000: 97
Number of Nondailies: 122
   Aggregate Circulation: NA
   Circulation per 1,000: NA
Number of Periodicals: 7,390

Number of Radio Stations: NA
Number of Television Stations: NA
Number of Radio Receivers: 13,439,650 (1979)
   Radio Receivers per 1,000: 235
Number of Television Sets: 12,862,944 (1979)
   Television Sets per 1,000: 225
Total Annual Newsprint Consumption: 216,400 metric tons
Per Capita Newsprint Consumption: 3.8 kg. (8.4 lbs.)
Total Newspaper Ad Receipts: 245.7 billion lira (US$ 305.6 million) (1979)
   As % of All Ad Expenditures: 28.4

Background & General Characteristics

Daily newspapers in Italy have several characteristics that set them apart from those of most of the rest of the western world. As a group, they reach only a small part of the country's people, circulating about 100 copies per 1000 of population. Traditionally their content has been highly political and their approach politicized; although there has been some dilution of that coloration since the 1960s, enough remains that some parts of the major papers can be fully comprehended only by political insiders. An eminent journalist, Enzo Forcella, once contended that there were only 1500 of those in Italy, most of them members of parliament or the apparatus of political parties.

In addition to some arcane content, Italian newspapers lose many readers because of the character of their prose. Most Italians have a secondary education or less, and newspaper language is heavy going for them. This is not so much a matter of literary elegance, although journalists do tend to take pains with and pride in their writing, as of mannerisms and special vocabulary, the tendency, for example, to coin neologisms based on for-

eign words—*absentismo, demoralizzare, attualitá,* etc.

The newspaper distribution system also tends to impede circulation. As in most of continental Europe, there is no home delivery of newspapers and only negligible distribution by mail, which means that the reader must buy his paper at a newsstand. That has become increasingly difficult in Italy since the 1960s. Operation of a newsstand requires a permit, and permits are issued by a commission dominated by the association of newsstand operators. There is every reason, of course, for current operators to keep the number of competitors down, and the result of this system has been that new dealers are younger relatives of those already in the business. At the beginning of the 1970s Italy had one newsstand for each 2670 inhabitants; France had one for each 1250, West Germany one for each 1000. In addition, Italy has a great number of flashy, highly competitive magazines, and newsdealers tend to feature these in their displays; at many newsstands newspapers are not even visible and must be asked for.

All newspapers sell at the same per-copy price, a figure set by a government-industry committee. The government's interest derives from the fact that newspapers are used in calculating the cost of living, to which is tied, in turn, the wage contracts of millions of Italian workers. Price increases thus have been permitted reluctantly but inevitably; at the time of this writing (1981) the price was set at an all-time high of 300 lire, or about 37 cents.

Accessibility and cost are not the total explanation. When a national sample of the Italian population was asked why so few people read newspapers, the most common explanation was the availability of television; in second place, the use in newspapers of language that only a few understand; listed third, the belief that political and economic forces distort the presentation of the news, even though journalists are basically honest.

The first and second of these obviously are related. Communication research repeatedly has demonstrated that people tend to use the least demanding medium; the old principle of least effort clearly applies to use of the mass media. Add to that the vague compulsion that people in most cultures seem to feel toward being well-informed, and television automatically becomes the major medium; Americans have identified it as such for twenty years.

Finally, there is the probability that most Italians do not consider their newspapers altogether trustworthy. Studies made in the late 1970s indicate that about a third of Italian newspaper readers—not, it should be noted, the nine-tenths of the population who are nonreaders—believe that newspapers manipulate the news to steer public opinion.

Whatever the explanations, the facts remain striking. Angelo Del Boca pointed out in 1967 that 19 million Italians—about 35 percent of the population at that time—who had both the means and the education to acquire and read newspapers never did so. Considering the increment in population and a continuing slow decline in total newspaper circulation, that percentage probably still holds.

It is impossible to make a simple summary judgment about the quality of Italian newspaper journalism. Like the journalism of all other countries, its quality varies from rubric to rubric (although not greatly from paper to paper, because of the homogenizing effects of the carefully specified route through which all Italian journalists become professionals). A tentative generalization might be offered that Italian journalism is excellent in those areas where style and spirit are most important, but frequently poor where quality and accuracy of information is the central consideration.

Thus the editorial opinion traditionally set out in column one, page 1—the *articolo di fondo*—almost invariably is well crafted, and has been done with elegance by such editors as Arrigo Levi, Indro Montanelli, Giovanni Spadolini, Alberto Ronchey and others. In the 19th century the tradition of the "third page" arose; for many years the major papers made that page a showcase, with short personal essays, social criticism, historical analysis, fiction and oddments from some of the best minds in the country. Although some of that quality has been diluted in the attempt to broaden the newspaper audience, the work of such people as Alberto Moravia still appears on page 3. There is nothing like it in English-language journalism.

Predictably, given the Italian passion for them, sports are well done, within the ritualistic limitations of the form. So is criticism, across a wide range of the arts. Journalists working within these forms take them seriously, and the product generally is carefully and stylishly done.

This comes in part from the tradition of leaving total control of their work in the hands of the journalists. With a rare exception or two, there are no copy editors on Italian newspapers. Journalists, whatever the subject, usually are assigned a length to which to write; the rest is up to them. This system, or lack of it, works well when style is immutably tied to substance, but it also perpetuates the inadequacies of Italian reporting in areas where substance would seem to be more important. Despite its quantity, political writing tends to be not only arcane but downright windy. Many observers consider foreign correspondence to be as bad. For years the major dailies have made it a point of pride to have correspondents in Paris, London, Moscow and either Washington or New York (sometimes in both). They also have sent staff, for varying lengths of time, to Bonn and Peking, along with Latin America. Most "hard" news from these countries comes from international wire services to which the papers belong. The material filed by each paper's own correspondents resembles the "diplomatic letters" of the elite British papers of the 19th century, consisting largely of interpretation and commentary, most of it not very informative or perceptive. There have been exceptions, such as Ugo Stille from Washington for *Corriere della Sera* and *La Stampa*'s Arrigo Levi, but for the most part there has been little to justify the extraordinary expense involved in the maintenance of journalists in these posts.

Thus far there has been little significant tradition of investigative reporting in Italian newspapers, although there are indicators of change. But the expose style, which has produced some of the best, and certainly the most dramatic, journalism elsewhere has never been a part of the Italian journalist's professional inheritance.

This lack may be partly explained by the universal assumption that the corruption widespread in Italian affairs still operates in journalism. The highly politicized character of the country's dailies also tends to induce discounting of investigation in the most fertile ground, government; presumably the reader may say to himself something like "it's just those reporters after the Christian Democrats again." Nevertheless, during the late 1970s there was solid reporting of scandals in the military and the secret service, particularly in weekly newsmagazines, and the trend seems to be growing.

At present there are only three foreign-language newspapers published in Italy, none of more than local importance: *Primorski Dnevnik*, a Slovenian paper published in Trieste; *Dolomiten*, a German-language paper published in Bolzano, and the *Rome Daily American*.

Four daily papers refer to themselves formally as Catholic, including, of course, *L'Osservatore Romano*. None of these have much influence beyond the institutional structure of the Catholic Church, a reflection of the fact that Italy has become an increasingly secularized state in the 20th century. The failure of the state church to counteract pro-divorce and pro-abortion movements has something to do with the fact that *L'Osservatore Romano* seldom has been cited or quoted in the Italian press in recent years. Obviously this is not to say that the Vatican is no longer a major force in Italian society and Italian affairs; its official voice simply has weakened.

It also is true that the Christian Democrat Party, despite its dominance of Italian politics and government for more than thirty years, has not had during that period an official newspaper that commanded national attention. *Il Popolo* is a modest, spare and by any standards pedestrian exponent of the party line with small circulation.

Press critics sometimes point out that the Christian Democrats do not need a powerful paper of their own, since a large part of the press that formally declares itself independent hews to the CD line. In any case, Italy's other political parties take the matter of a party newspaper much more seriously.

L'Unitá, official paper of the *Partito Communista Italiano*, has been one of the country's largest-circulating papers since the end of World War II. From 1944 to 1957 separate editions were published in Rome, Milan, Genoa and Turin. During these years it was a comprehensive newspaper, including such innovations as a women's section and comic strips; it also emphasized local news more than most Italian dailies of the time.

It always had financial problems, however; it carried almost no advertising, and various money-raising events such as the regular "*L'Unitá* festivals" failed to provide support for a full-scale operation. In 1962 the paper was cut back to a more conventional political organ, eliminating the comics, women's pages and some regional news. Its circulation apparently had drifted downward, but with something over 400,000 it is still among the country's largest dailies.

It thus is the most visible and important of a weak lot, the official party papers. In 1980 the old names were hanging on—the Socialists' *Avanti!*, the far-right MSI's *Il Secolo*, the Social Democrats' *L'Umanitá* and the others—but both their circulation and their influence were slight. Their continued existence seems to be largely a matter of the sponsoring party's willingness to continue to pour money into them. Perhaps the most influential of party papers after *L'Unitá*, interestingly, is the voice of the miniscule PSDUP, radical schismatics of the Communists, whose *Il Manifesto* is a skimpy but lively daily read particularly by the activist young.

Some publications that call themselves independent are commonly read as providing unique insight into party thinking, largely because of the position of the political stature of their management. *La Repubblica*, not only Italy's only important tabloid but generally regarded as its most important political journal, is edited by Eugenio Scalfari, an eminent Socialist who has a stature outside the formal leadership of the party.

The role of the *Partito Socialista Italiana* in both Italian politics and Italian journalism is difficult to explain in a few sentences. The party has attracted relatively few votes in recent elections, generally something between 9 and 12 percent of the total. This is far behind the vote for the Christian Democrats and the Communists, although it has been sufficient to keep the party in a distant third place in the parliament and make its participation critical to the establishment of several governments since the end of World Ward II. More importantly, it has represented for many journalists an intellectual base outside the camps of the Christian Democrats as well as that of the orthodox Communists and their increasingly numerous radical dissidents. The Socialists represent activist non-Communist leftists, including some philosophical Marxists. It is that point of view that *La Repubblica* represents; in that role it commands respect from journalists and politicians, who often set up an interview with Scalfari as a platform for major pronouncements. By the beginning of the 1980s it was often referred to as the most influential newspaper in the country.

Several papers dependably reflect the position of the Christian Democrats. Flaminio Piccoli, one of the party's leaders and head of the group of Christian Democrats deputies who also are professional journalists, is the editor of *L'Adige*, in Trento; *Il Tempo* of Rome, *La Nazione* of Florence, and *Il Resto del Carlino* of Bologna, all important regional papers, also consistently reflect the party's views. *Paese Sera* of Rome traditionally has played a similar role for the Italian Communist Party.

To an extent far greater than in other European countries, Italy is divided in half by the standard socio-economic indicators on an east-west line drawn through Rome. South of that line is a country far behind the north in almost every category from per capita income to health care; it is commonly said that the most important element in the Italian south's economy is the money sent back from southerners who have gone to Milan and Turin to work. Thus it is not surprising that most of the country's newspapers are located in the north. The number of Italian dailies varies a good deal over time, in part because of the common practice of establishing papers devoted to particular causes during pre-election periods. The number since 1950 has been between seventy and ninety. The solid core of these from the south, including Sardinia, has been about a dozen since the end of World War II, and never more than

fifteen. *Il Mattino* of Naples is the only nationally known southern daily, and its circulation, by its own claims, has stayed around a relatively modest figure of 150,000.

Standard newspaper format in Italy is full size, either eight or nine columns. Most papers tend to be gray—small type (including a great deal of italic, used for graphic variation rather than for differentiation of content), small headlines, and few photographs on the front page. The most striking exception among standard-size papers is *Il Messaggero* of Rome, which uses a "show window" front-page makeup with large photographs or other graphics and underlines referring the reader to the story inside. Major dailies publish seven days a week, with light Monday papers devoted in great part to sports. Weekday issues normally have between 20 and 26 pages; Sunday papers frequently go up to 36. Some have experimented with magazine sections, but these have not taken hold.

It also should be noted that, despite the substantial coverage given to sports in standard dailies, there has been a long national tradition of papers devoted entirely to sports, four of which, at the time of this writing, were dailies, each claiming circulations at or above 200,000.

Only 39 Italian cities have newspapers. This reflects not only the generally low readership but, as in other European countries, the saturation of the country by a few national newspapers, especially *Corriere della Sera*, *La Stampa*, *Il Giorno* and *L'Unità*, all of which can be found on almost every newsstand in the country. The province of Umbria, northeast of Rome and southwest of Florence, is the location not only of Perugia, with a population of 125,000, but also Terni, over 100,000, and cities of such cultural importance as Assisi, Urbino and Gubbio. There is not a single daily newspaper in the province; and, although *La Nazione*, of Florence, produces an Umbrian edition, there is nothing like thorough local coverage. In contrast, smaller northern cities such as Varese, with a population of about 80,000, have competitive dailies.

Obviously, most Italian newspaper circulation is in the larger cities of the north. Official figures for 1977 indicated that almost 50 percent of the circulation was in the northwest section (Milan, Turin and other industrial centers), another 11 percent in the northeast (Bologna, Venice, etc.), and about 27 percent in the country's central region

(Rome, Florence). The 10 largest papers, all located from Rome northward, circulated (by their own claims) about 53 percent of the total daily circulation.

Although Milan is generally considered the center of Italian journalism because of the presence of *Corriere, Il Giorno,* and *Il Giornale Nuovo,* Rome has the most mastheads—19, as of this writing, compared to Milan's nine. Genoa and Turin have four each, Naples three, and eight other cities, all in the north except for Palermo, have two.

In the United States, advertising rates are tied to circulation; circulation claims are monitored by an independent association, the Audit Bureau of Circulation, and inflated figures lead to quick embarrassment. There is no such constraint in Italy. Advertising other than classified is handled by one of a handful of agencies call *concessionari,* which write contracts, typically for a year in advance, purchasing a stipulated amount of space. In theory the concessionaire in turn sells this space (or time, in the case of broadcasting) to advertisers. In practice this simple process is more complicated, primarily because the major concessionaires are part of huge industrial conglomerates in which the government is a major stockholder. In effect the whole system becomes a form of subsidization and a powerful means of influencing the development and functioning of Italian media. When Indro Montanelli, a distinguished staff member of *Corriere della Sera,* broke from that paper in 1973 to begin a new daily more inclined to the political right, he was guaranteed an advertising income of around ten million dollars before the paper even began operations.

Thus there is no inducement for meticulous reporting of circulation figures. At the same time, to report other than a publication's official claims is to move into a morass of speculation. The information that follows is from 1975 claims. At that time, there were six dailies with circulations of less than 10,000; 13 with circulations between 10,000 and 25,000; 22 between 25,000 and 50,000; 18 between 50,000 and 100,000; and two with more than a half million. None reached, nor reaches, a million.

Few observers of the Italian press would argue either with the order or the relative accuracy of the figures, since newspaper circulation, although in slow decline, has been relatively stable for a good many years. Attempting to identify the next five is more difficult, but the group probably is made up

Five Largest Newspapers by Circulation	
Corriere della Sera, Milan	660,000
La Stampa, Turin	511,000
L'Unitá, Milan and Rome	450,000
Il Giorno, Milan	329,000
Il Messaggero, Rome	315,000

of *Il Tempo* (Rome), *La Repubblica* (Rome), *Il Giornale Nuovo* (Milan), *La Nazione* (Florence) and *Il Resto del Carlino* (Bologna), all with circulations over a quarter million but under 300,000.

Of this presumptive top ten, only the Communist *L'Unitá* is a party paper. The others are, in the Italian phrase, *giornali d'informazione,* and most, although they have a clearly perceptible partisan stance, formally refer to themselves as independent.

Almost any Italian would automatically reply *"Corriere della Sera"* when asked to name the country's most important newspaper. *Corriere* has a national status not unlike that of *Le Monde* in France or the *New York Times* in the United States. That kind of status implies something about influence, particularly in national agenda-making, but is hardly synonymous with it. Another kind of evidence indicates that Montanelli's somewhat cynically conservative *Il Giornale Nuovo* ("Hold your nose and vote Christian Democrat," he told readers in 1976) has great influence upon the Italian middle and upper-middle class; after the Friuli earthquake of 1976, *Il Giornale Nuovo* raised more money for relief than *Corriere* and *La Stampa* combined, and when the paper itself faced an early financial crisis, readers contributed more than one million dollars in outright gifts to sustain it. Certainly a case could be made for *L'Unitá* as the daily channel for communication from leaders to the grass roots of the second largest political party in the country, and for *La Repubblica,* with its unique role in the functioning of the political system—and so it goes.

Economic Framework

Since the end of World War II, the financial condition of Italy's newspaper industry has moved from critical to catastrophic. Most Italian papers in modern times have never made a profit and have been kept alive by subsidies, open or covert. (The latter are described, in a phrase common in the business, as coming from *padri ignoti*—"unknown fathers.")

In the early 1950s three papers were generally regarded as profitable (out of about 90 at that time); although hard data were unavailable because all three were owned by wealthy families who kept such information private, everybody knew that *Corriere, La Stampa* and *Il Messaggero* made money. By the early 1970s these also had become money-losers, and during that decade their losses increased dramatically. By 1978, losses for the industry as a whole were about $250 million a year. A few small dailies in the north, such as *L'Arena* of Verona, were making profits of a few thousand dollars a year, but the industry as a whole was in a desperate state.

Furthermore, the symbiotic tie between the media business and the general state of the economy is much more tenuous in Italy than in most industrialized countries. Italy has had for years an "underground economy," so called because it operates on cash or barter and without records, particularly records relating to taxation. This unreported commercial activity undergirds a surprisingly viable Italy economy that on paper is in a state of collapse. The Italian press benefits very little from this hidden strength, however, nor did its fortunes improve greatly during the 1950s and early 1960s, the period of the "economic miracle" that saw Italy move from a country of motor scooters, two-burner stoves in kitchens without refrigerators, and cheap radios to one of automobiles, home freezers and color television sets. The newspaper business, in particular, has doggedly slid downward, despite the general state of both the official and unofficial economy. In most industrialized countries publications are sensitive barometers of the general state of the economy because advertising expenditures reflect managements' ability to afford it; most Italian advertising is essentially institutional, not retail, with a government-subsidy role involved that detaches it from the market.

The most visible outlet for consumer retail advertising is Italy's lively, multitudinous magazine industry. Although Italians are among the industrialized world's most indifferent newspaper readers, they are among Europe's top magazine readers. In 1979 there were seven weekly newsmagazines alone, with a full panoply of other types (including, since about 1975, both hard- and soft-core pornography). Such magazines as *Panorama* and *L'Espresso,* of the *Newsweek-Der Spie-*gel-*L'Express* genre, are packed with advertising. These expenditures, it can be reasonably assumed, do have an impact on the amount carried by newspapers, although there is no way of knowing how much. Such advertising is not local retail, which makes up the great bulk of advertising in the English-language press.

It would be even more difficult to assess the present impact of broadcast advertising. Radiotelevisione Italiana (RAI), from the beginning of the broadcast era the official monopoly entity, always has carried commercial announcements, but severely restricted them both in number and placement, in part to avoid cutting into print media revenues. In 1974, however, Italian courts, in a ruling on "outlaw" broadcasting stations, defined the government monopoly as applying only to nationwide broadcasting—a move that opened the door to the explosive growth of completely unregulated local stations. By 1977 there were an estimated 60 television stations in the Milan market area alone, with similar concentrations around other major cities. These carry advertising, of course, but there are almost no standardized procedures as yet to provide dependable data; Italy's first commercial television rating service began only in 1979, and in any case, hard information about sales, profits and ownership in all sectors of the Italian economy is hard to come by.

Until 1970 Italy's major *giornali d'informazione* were owned by single families. *La Stampa* of Turin still belongs to the Agnellis, who also are the principal stockholders of Fiat. Since 1974 *Corriere della Sera* has been part of Corriere della Sera Editoriale, owned by Rizzoli Editore, S.p.A., the biggest communication conglomerate in Italy. The name Rizzoli became well-known throughout the world because of books published under that imprint and an international chain of bookstores. In the early 1970s one of the founder's nephews, Angelo Rizzoli, began an aggressive campaign to acquire media properties, with the *Corriere* papers (*Corriere d'Informazione* is the evening masthead), which he acquired in 1974, as the corporate jewel. By 1979 the group included five weekly publications, three monthly magazines and a quarterly. The Rizzoli firm also holds part ownership (and in most cases, control) of five smaller dailies, including the biggest paper of sourthern Italy, *Il Mattino* of Naples, six magazines, a television broadcasting system based on Malta, and a variety of incidentals, including exclusive Italian rights to "Peanuts" comic books.

Il Giorno, Corriere's chief competition in Milan, represents another kind of ownership. It never has been a family-owned enterprise, although it always has been associated with Enrico Mattei and the enormous conglomerate he built, ENI (Ente Nazionale Idrocarburi). ENI is one of a group of industrial conglomerates that dominate Italy's economic activity. These are owned jointly by government and private stockholders. The largest is IRI (Istituto per la Ricostruzione Industriale). This organization, as its name implies, was established shortly after World War II, and is the holding company for a wide variety of enterprises, including the government broadcasting system. ENI, which directly owns and controls *Il Giorno,* came into being through the efforts of an unconventional entrepreneur, Enrico Mattei, whose base was the chemical industry; it now counts among its subsidiaries a major advertising agency, hotels and tourist properties, and a chain of failed variety stores. (Government practice since the early 1960s has been to attach enterprises whose complete collapse would lead to major economic distress to an *ente statali* that can provide a government subsidy.) Although *Il Giorno* is the only major daily official owned by ENI, it also owns, through a subsidiary, *Il Messaggero* of Rome.

About a half-dozen of the largest newspapers are, on the face of it, competitive. They have nationwide, or at least wide-ranging regional, distribution, and appear simultaneously on the same newsstands. Milan, Turin, Rome, Naples and a few smaller towns have competitive local papers. Despite frequent expressions of concern about the growth of monopolies on the part of newspaper trade unions, however, competition always has been less than meets the eye. In great part because of the politicization of Italian journalism, papers have a pronounced individual character with a finely delimited audience. When Indro Montanelli left *Corriere della Sera* to start his *Il Giornale Nuovo,* he openly intended to take away a damaging portion of *Corriere*'s audience. He did achieve substantial circulation quickly, but almost none of it was lured away from *Corriere.* He apparently tapped instead a lode of people who simply had not been reading newspapers at all.

The city with the most competitors is Rome, which since 1950 has had between 15 and 20 dailies, including specialized papers in sports and finance. Competition is pretty much limited, however, to the specialized fields; it is difficult to imagine a reader of *Il Messaggero* (brash, gaudy, erratically radical) being tempted to shift to *Il Tempo* (conservative, Catholic and gray) or even *Paese Sera* (orthodox Communist fellow-traveller, cautious in makeup). And certainly nothing like the competition between the *Washington Post* and the *New York Times* exists between *Corriere* and *La Stampa.*

To this point no major publication acquired by a chain such as Rizzoli has been merged with another masthead. There is little to be gained by eliminating a putative competitor for advertising; thus far, multiple publications, each with their own contracts, seem to produce more total income through the concessionaire system that could be negotiated by a single paper, however aggrandized through merger.

Why, it might be asked, should Rizzoli—or anyone else—mount an agressive campaign to buy money-losing newspapers? The answer seems to lie in the prospect of government subsidies, already built into the Scandanavian press and under serious consideration in several other countries. A speech commission of the Italian parliament, headed by Senator Giovanni Spadolini, former editor of *Corriere,* in 1975 began shaping a plan for massive support. There has been no political opposton in principle, but much negotiating about details. By late 1979 the plan included provisions for a substantial increase in the long-standing subsidy for newsprint purchases; a 50 percent reduction in the cost of telex, telephone and postage; loan guarantees for investments in machinery, equipment, construction and the purchase of building sites; a government assumption of a part of the companies' interest charges, rising from about three million dollars the first fiscal year to about six million for the next eight years, and then back to three for two more. About $2.7 million also was set aside for the first fiscal year to aid new publications. In exchange for this assistance, the plan imposed controls on concentration: aid would not be available to any company that had more than 20 percent of the total daily newspaper circulation, or more than 50 percent within its basic zone of circulation. Publication of yearly profit and loss statements, including indentification of all stockholders, would be required.

The constraints upon ownership in this

proposal represent pressure brought by the Italian national journalists' trade union, certainly the strongest such organization within media industries in the industrialized world. The Federazione Nazionale della Stampa Italiana is unique in its authority, its legal status and its role in the profession. In contrast to most countries, where for whatever reason journalists are the equivalent of skilled workers or at best members of a quasi-profession, journalists in Italy have had a special status under law since 1906, when a law was passed providing for reduced railway fares. Mussolini, himself a journalist, combined the carrot and the stick to achieve control of the profession, establishing an Order of Journalists to which all practitioners had to belong, meaning, of course, that those unacceptable to fascism were excluded. The carrot has a larger role in labor negotiations, including control of entry to the profession. A national assembly of journalists at the end of World War II voted, despite spirited opposition, to retain the device of a national Order and set a committee to work to draft comprehensive legislation and get it through parliament. The process was laborious, but in 1963 the Order of Journalists was officially established under Italian law, setting it alongside 11 other legally defined and protected professions (including medicine, law, veterinarian medicine, etc.). The procedures through which an aspirant becomes a professional journalist are described and defined in the statutes. The process begins with apprenticeship, which leads at the end of 18 months to an examination, administered and graded nationally twice a year by a committee made up of senior professionals and chaired by a judge from the appeals court level. The exam is both written (professional competence) and oral (education and intellectual breadth). It also is demanding; failure rates run from 9 to around 15 percent. The candidate who fails can try again after another 18 months; another failure removes him from the profession. Careful analysis seems to indicate a loose correlation between failure rates and the number of entry-level jobs in the field. Upon passing the exams, the candidate receives the *tessera*—the membership card for the Order, which constitutes a license to practice the profession. National legislation provides various kinds of disciplinary action that may be taken against members, as well as criminal penalties against those who practice the profession without a license. The disciplining of erring

members is in most cases the province of the Order, which releases no information; prosecution of those practicing without a license is within the court system, however, and Italian media carry, infrequently but recurringly, news of nonprofessionals fined or jailed.

The Order is the protector and monitor of the profession. It is not, however, the negotiator of labor contracts or the representative of the employees in conflicts with the owners. That role belongs to a closely parallel organization, the Federazione Nazionale della Stampa Italiana—the trade union, whose essential role is advocacy. Membership in FNSI is not obligatory for members of the Order, but more than 90 percent belong, and the geographical structure of the union parallels that of the Order. A single detailed contract covers the profession nationwide, specifying minimums for vacation, leave, severance, medical and death benefits. It also defines, again in great detail, the role in both broadcast and the print media of newsroom administrators and the "Journalists Committees" *(comitato di redazione)*.

The "reporter power" movement, which generally is considered to have begun in 1954 with the uprising of the staff of Le Monde to retain Beuve-Mery as editor, is now more active in Italy than in France. Under the provisions of the Italian contract there is an elected Journalists Committee, normally made up of three members, in every newsroom in the country. Their agressiveness varies greatly from shop to shop; at one point during the middle 1970s *Il Messaggero* of Rome was all but controlled by the committee, but its equivalent on Montanelli's *Il Giornale Nuovo* for example, was completely passive.

The active Journalists Committees generally have concerned themselves with five aspects of the enterprise's affairs: changes in ownership; changes in the top editorial posts; the political line; "fair and complete" treatment of the news; and, finally, conventional trade union concerns about hiring, firing and fringes. In larger shops, both newspapers and magazines, the guidelines for these activities are set out in an in-house contract negotiated between management and the Journalists Committee, then ratified by the full staff.

It has been a major objective of both FNSI and most of the committees to establish a right of veto over the appointment of new editors and the substantial transfer of stock to new owners. They have failed thus far, but have established contractually the right to be consulted, and frequently have brought pressure, including both the threats and the calling of strikes, to obtain promises and concessions from new bosses. During the most active period of this movement, between 1971 and 1978, Journalists Committees on such papers as *Corriere* and *Il Messaggero* had much to do with news selection and the writing (and rewriting) of headlines. During the 1976 election they succeeded in keeping out of the major papers news about, and advertising from, the Movimento Sociale Italiano, which they considered fascist. At the national level FNSI had a good deal of influence on the provisions of subsidization legislation.

Beyond contractual rights, the ultimate weapon in the hands of the news staff and their frequent allies, the printers, is the strike. Strikes within the industry in recent times have been frequent but short-lived, work stoppages ranging from a few hours to two days. Almost always they are what Italians call "hiccup" strikes, called on very short notice and aimed at a very specific issue. This is the modern Italian labor tradition, of course, rather than long, bitter standoffs.

Most of these strikes involve politics in the broad sense, rather than economic issues. The strike is the most common form of social protest; sometimes it simply reflects unfocussed anger—for example, the first reaction to the kidnapping of Aldo Moro was a general work stoppage. Strikes have been called over headlines, over one-sided news, over refusals to carry official statements from labor unions, even over problems on other newspapers not on strike themselves. There have been dozens, perhaps even hundreds, since 1975.

Economic issues are less common because, according to a proud boast in the profession, Italian journalists are second only to those of the United States in the compensation they receive, far ahead of other countries in Europe. The contractual minimums are modest, ranging, under the 1979–81 contract, from about $280 per month during the first six months of apprenticeship to about $600 for editors-in-chief. But in practice all salaries are much higher; apprentices now begin at about $600 per month in major cities. Italian journalists officially work a 35-hour week; if they work more, and everybody else does, they draw overtime, which, in the case

of some holidays, may be double. Since the journalist also receives 18 paid holidays a year, in addition to a generous vacation, the operating figure is far higher even than their stated basic rate. A rule of thumb occasionally referred to in the profession is that the actual compensation is 50 percent more than the stipulated figure. It is a reasonable estimate that in 1980 a veteran journalist on a daily in Rome or Milan was making somewhere around $30,000 a year.

Apart from "consulting fees," one perquisite of the profession that makes salary go further is the tradition of discounts from businesses. An Italian journalist who works at it seldom pays full price in a restaurant or a shop. This practice may be an extension of a law passed early in the century providing major discounts on rail fares for journalists, later extended to include airlines and other forms of transport; journalists also carry a card permitting free travel on the country's expensive superhighways.

Finally, remarkably generous retirement, medical, and severance pay provisions must be considered a part of compensation. A journalist leaving his post gets a month's pay for every year he has worked for the company, plus a bonus of seven months more. Severance pay is even higher for someone who is fired, but in practice this never happens anymore; legislation passed in 1971 protects most Italian workers, including journalists from dismissal except for "just cause," meaning blatant moral turpitude.

Press Laws & Censorship

Italian press laws closely resemble those of France and other continental countries: the constitution affirms freedom of expression as a principle, and then provides for exceptions. Article 21 of the 1947 constitution provides that "All are entitled freely to express their thoughts by word of mouth, in writing, and by all other means of communication. The press may not be subjected to authority or censorship." Restraints are "allowed only by the order of judicial authorities," who are required to cite reasons based upon press laws, which exist as part of both civil and criminal codes. In conditions of absolute urgency, however, and when the "intervention of judicial authorities is not possible," the police may enforce restraints (generally sequestration) for 24 hours. Again, as a matter of principle, "manifestations contrary to morality are forbidden."

Beyond these basics, Italian press law is made up of special provisions scattered through the whole body of Italian law—in the Albertine edict of 1848, in the Penal Code, the laws relating to Public Security, and in the 1963 legislation establishing the Order of Journalists. This last sets out the anatomy of the profession. It established two categories, "professionals," those who are full-time on one staff, and *pubblicisti,* which roughly means free-lancers; a third "special list" was set up in the late 1970s to accommodate such functionaries as the editors of technical and scientific magazines. It also specifies the process leading from apprenticeship to professional, licensed status; provides penalties under the law for certain violations, and delegates to the Order a considerable range of disciplinary powers. A 1968 law provides stipulations about the organization of the press, the most important of which is the familiar European concept of a *direttore responsabile* ("responsible editor"), the single individual who is responsible to the authorities for what goes on in the publication.

Other provisions scattered through Italian statutes define and provide penalties for offenses against the heads of state of foreign countries, slander against the state religion, attacks upon common morality, espionage, etc.—a list essentially the same in most legal systems on the Continent or otherwise based on Roman law. And as in most countries with similar legislation, these provisions have been used only in highly selective ways. There have been, rarely, sequestrations of publications, generally for offenses against morality and sometimes for political reasons related to civil unrest.

But all these potential restrictions have not prevented the rise of some of the most devastating and vicious political cartoons in the world, including fierce attacks on the Vatican and the person of the Pope; nor have they prevented assaults on every imaginable political leader (including the President of the Republic) at the level of billingsgate; nor have they prevented the rise, since about 1970, of openly available pornographic publications as gross as any in the world. It is accurate to say that the Italian journalist or publisher seldom worries about the response of the civil authorities to what is written or sketched to go on a front page, or between covers or on a poster.

The most clear-cut recent example of state action was in the spring of 1980 during the investigations of Red Brigades terrorism. *Il Messaggero* published excerpts of the testimony of an informer during a secret pretrial hearing; both the reporter involved and a law enforcement officer were convicted and given, by Italian standards, heavy prison sentences—one 18, the other 32 months. The case was uncommon enough to provoke great outcry in the country's press.

State-Press Relations

The important methods of government influence on the media in Italy are indirect: the placement of advertising, the licensing of journalists, the allocation of both advertising and subsidies, and others more subtle. There is no precensorship of the press. There is no cabinet-level Ministry of Information, nor is there any agency comparable to the office of the presidential press secretary in the United States, although there is a parliamentary press office. Careful monitoring of the press and broadcasting undoubtedly goes on, but as a function of decentralized agencies such as the armed forces and the top echelons of political parties. There is no arcane management of the news; there is little effort to project a favorable image abroad, other than through special treatment of the foreign press.

Nor are there cases of editorial influence on government affairs comparable to, for example, the role of the *Washington Post* in the Watergate affair. No paper, even *Corriere della Sera* or *La Stampa,* is perceived by the public as having the credibility achieved through objectivity sufficient to bring a government down. This also is true of RAI's broadcast journalism, although in a different contex; RAI is so sapped by political influence on all sides that it has never initiated journalism of consequence.

A familiar taxonomy of press systems throughout the world places them in either the political order or the economic order of a given nation. Within these categories, the Italian media are in a subsection of the first; they are, indeed, a part of the political order, but of the *partisan* political order, in which political advantage is all-important and government authority is of minor weight. There is evidence that the Italian press may be moving toward the economic order; in no case has it represented, since the end of fascism, subservience to the government in terms of conceding it unquestioned authority.

Attitude Toward Foreign Media

The foreign correspondent stationed in Italy not only is free from pressure by that country's government, but the recipient of favors that are almost embarrassing in their generosity. There is a special office building for the foreign press in Rome, subsidization of some expenses, and a range of special privileges, including discounts in shops. Visas, registration and other formalities are expedited. Correspondents who work up to retirement in Italy frequently choose to stay on permanently.

This outgoing attitude toward the foreign press carries over into the international press organizations. There is substantial Italian membership in the International Press Institute, and IPI's 1976 meeting was held in Italy. There are frequent meetings between groups of Italian journalists and those of other countries in the interest of better understanding, and Italy has consistently backed the U.S. position on the UNESCO 1978 declaration.

The extent to which cooperation across national borders extends to foreign ownership is, not surprisingly, unclear. There always are rumors about foreign money; there was a rumor that Rizzoli was backed by West Germans, and another that, in fact, the Rothschilds owned 51 percent of Rizzoli. Beyond question, however, is the fact that in 1977 the Libyan government of Muammar el-Qaddafi bought, in a complex transaction, what amounted to 15 percent of the stock of Fiat, which owns *La Stampa.*

News Agencies

As of 1977, 520 organizations called themselves "news agencies" in Italy. Most of these were generators and distributors of press releases in behalf of special causes, including, in addition to corporations and trade associations, many governments. A critic might contend that the largest and most important of all, ANSA, is very much like the other hand-out organizations, but ANSA officially is Italy's national news agency.

ANSA (Agenzia Nazionale Stampa Associata) was founded in early 1945 on the cooperative model common in postwar continental Europe, committing itself to rigorous standards of "independence, impartiality, and objectivity." While it never formally renounced those principles, economics forced it to move away from them by 1949, when it began to receive government subsidies from both the Council of Ministers and the foreign ministry. (It became the distributor for AP, Reuters, and AFP at the same time.) With the subsidy the government acquired the privilege of naming the agency's directors (which, at one point, included Giulio Andreotti), and openly began using it as a primary source of government information.

ANSA now is received by all Italian dailies; a large percentage of its copy is progovernment news, but it also carries substantial amounts of routine internal Italian news. It has a modest foreign staff—24 bureaus in Europe, ten in Africa, 11 in Asia, 18 in Latin America, 4 in North America, and 1 in Australia—which give particular attention to emigrant Italian colonies. It also has an exchange agreement with the Associated Press. Since all the major international agencies are available to Italian papers at low prices (a typical middle-size daily receives AP, Reuters, AFP, UPI and Tass), ANSA plays an essentially specialized role.

Electronic News Media

Until the early 1970s broadcast journalism in Italy was both scant and dull. There was a single major television news broadcast of the day, at eight p.m., the script for which was cleared by a committee representing the major political parties. The most available common ground was the elimination of anything that might have political overtones—civil disturbances, strikes and the like—and the reduction of the unavoidably political—negotiations for a new government, for example—to a stylized ballet in which the sound of politicians' voices went unheard; they were seen talking into microphones, but the words were voice-over summaries carefully sanitized by a political committee. Much that most journalists would consider news never was covered at all. "Talking heads," RAI's foreign correspondents talking pedantically about other countries' politics, made up a major segment each evening, surrounded by bland, generally upbeat, domestic news.

The system thus produced, despite the lack of blatant political bias, a continuing picture of a placid nation perpetually improving—an image that by inference made the Christian Democrat goverment look admirable. Various attempts at reform, beginning in the

1960s, finally led to substantial changes in early 1976. Broadcast journalism was divided into two categories, one Christian Democrat (*Telegiornale* 1 and the second radio network) and the other essentially Socialist, although it was commonly described as "secular" (*Telegiornale* 2 and radio 1). This arrangement produced more competition and the abandonment of many taboos; RAI began to cover a wider range of material, to be more realistic about politics, and to play a larger role in the life of the country. Broadcast journalism remains severely limited in time available, however. News staffs are large, considering this factor, and broadcast journalists must be members of the Order of Journalists. RAI newsrooms have Journalists Committees and are covered by the same contract as print journalists; they have tended to concentrate on contract matters rather than broad political or professional issues.

The explosive growth of private broadcasting in recent years has made little change in the national picture as a whole. News on these stations tends to be either negligible or tendentious political reports, depending upon the owners. Serious journalism is rare and, at least to this point, of little consequence.

Education & Training

Mussolini proposed the establishment of four journalism schools during facism; there are varying accounts of the extent to which these became operational but, in any event, they were wiped out with World War II. Since then there has been a smattering of programs, most of them short-lived—small programs in religious colleges, another at the University of Rome in the 1950s with American Fulbright professors serving on the staff, and currently some proprietary schools aimed largely at preparing for public relations careers. The Order of Journalists set the establishment of a major journalism school among its objectives in 1948 and has discussed the idea since, but no action has been taken by the organization. There were reports in 1979 that a major Italian foundation was interested in establishing a full-scale school, including a mass communication research arm.

Two factors would seem to work against the development of journalism education on a major scale. The first is the lack of jobs; Italian newsrooms already are overstaffed,

reduction seems inevitable, and there already are many candidates for each apprenticeship. There is no prospect of the kind of need or acceptance that leads U.S. publications to recruit at journalism schools. Secondly, the current professions, through the institution of the Order and their trade union, have total control over professional preparation and with it entry into the field. They are unlikely to give those perogatives up.

Summary

There are great ironies within the Italian press system. Journalists in Italy are perhaps at the top of the profession worldwide; they are highly paid, have total job security, social status, and fringe benefits unmatched anywhere. Italian publications, on the other hand, are chronic money-losers forever on the edge of ruin, in the case of newspapers increasingly rejected by their potential audience, hard to read and apparently even harder to believe.

That seems to suggest that major changes must lie ahead. Some already are underway. Future prospects can be put under four headings:

1. Economics: the shifting pattern of ownership since the early 1970s seems to indicate that businessmen, not ideologues, are taking over publishing, and that they are more interested in profit than persuasion. State subsidization of the press will probably increase over the years. With the rise of managers, the media industries will be better run. Although substantial subsidies would seem to be a real threat of government control, Italian newspapers have been subsidized by somebody for years.

One change that seems underway in the country's marketing system might provide new sources of income for the media. The growth of supermarkets and other large retailers, in place of Italy's traditional small specialized shops, may lead to development of local retail advertising, the rock upon which much of the industrialized world's press is based.

2. It has frequently been observed that the more commercial a media system becomes, the more it becomes depoliticized. Other forces in Italy are beginning to have the same influence—the growth of a sense of common concern about terrorism, the continuing revelations of political scandals that have contributed to an endemic sense of contempt for

all politicians, the decline of a sense of social class with the development of a consumer-oriented economy. There seems to have been a decline in both the amount and the fervor of Italian political journalism since 1975, although politics continues to be central to Italian affairs.

3. Changes may occur in the profession of journalist. There always has been resistance to the idea of the Order and its licensure, but dissenters have been few. The numbers may be growing. The president of FNSI, the journalists' trade union, has declared that he is against it on grounds of freedom of the press. Publishers and owners almost uniformly oppose it, and so do many politicians.

On the other hand, almost all working journalists approve the idea and want it retained. Even if there is a disestablishment of the Order, it seems unlikely that the trade union FNSI will either lose members or relinquish a significant share of its powers.

4. Finally, there is the possibility that, given the changes hypothesized above, the Italian people will have more confidence in Italian journalism and attend to it more. Judgment on that matter, however, has to be more a matter of faith than the evaluation of evidence presently available.

CHRONOLOGY

1977   Libyan government buys 15 percent stock in Fiat, which owns *La Stampa.*

1979   Italy's first commercial television rating service begins operation.

1980   *Il Messaggero* reporter given 18 months' jail sentence for publishing excerpts of testimony of informer during trial of Red Brigades.

BIBLIOGRAPHY

Anon. "Come valuta i quotadiani e come giudica i giornalisti il lettore italiana." *Prima Communicazione,* May 1977, p. 52.

Anon. "The Periodical Press in Italy in 1975-1976-1977." *Italy: Documents and Notes.* September-November 1979, p. 493.

Berti, Angiolo, et al. *L'Ordine Dei Giornalisti.* Rome, 1974.

Castronuovo, V., and Tranfaglia, N. *La Stampa Italiana del Neocapitalismo.* Bari, 1976.

Del Boca, Angelo. *Giornali in Crisi.* Turin, 1968.

Forcella, Enzo. "Millecinquecento lettori." *Tempo Presente,* November 1959, p. 451.

Levi, Arrigo. *Televisione all' Italiana.* Milan, 1969.

Murialdi, Paolo. *La Stampa Italiano del dopoguerra, 1943-1972.* Bari, 1974.

Pansa, Giampaolo. *Comprati e venduti.* Milan, 1977.

Penniman, Howard, ed. *Italy at the Polls.* Washington, 1977.

JAMAICA*

by Marlene Cuthbert

BASIC DATA

Population: 2.25 million
Area: 11,422 sq. km. (4,410 sq. mi.)
GNP: $4.19 billion (US$2.54 billion)
Literacy Rate: 60%
Language(s): English
Number of Dailies: 3
   Aggregate Circulation: 108,000
   Circulation per 1,000: 5
Number of Nondailies: 12
   Aggregate Circulation: 336,500
   Circulation per 1,000: 16
Number of Periodicals: 5
Number of Radio Stations: 2

Number of Television Stations: 1
Number of Radio Receivers: 600,000
   Radio Receivers per 1,000: 286
Number of Television Sets: 200,000
   Television Sets per 1,000: 95
Total Annual Newsprint Consumption: 8,700 metric tons
   Per Capita Newsprint Consumption: 4.2 kg. (9.24 lbs.)
Total Newspaper Ad Receipts: $18,447,520 (US$20,272,000)
   As % of All Ad Expenditures: NA

Background & General Characteristics

The press of Jamaica prints in English, the only official language of the country. The quality of journalism is, in general, quite high by international standards, except for an afternoon newspaper with a very sensational approach. When the three daily papers are classified into the categories elite, popular and yellow, the *Daily Gleaner* falls into the first category, the *Daily News* into the second, and the *Star* verges on the third.

In 1717, with the publication of the *Weekly Courant,* Jamaica became the first British colony in the Caribbean to establish a newspaper. Several newspapers made brief appearances during the next century, but these were usually pamphlets with only a few news items on subjects such as runaway slaves and events in Britain. The first enduring newspaper did not appear until 1834. This was the *Gleaner,* a private organ initially published as a weekly but later the first daily on the island. Other papers have appeared during the *Gleaner's* life—which predates that of *The New York Times* by four years—but the *Gleaner* has always maintained its position as Jamaica's most influential print medium.

The paper's first owners were the de Cordova family—wealthy Jamaican merchants —and the paper remained in their control until 1897, when shares were offered to the public. The company is managed by a 10-person board of directors.

Since 1951 the Gleaner Company has also published a daily tabloid, the *Star,* the island's only afternoon paper, as well as the *Weekend Star;* both are written in a more lively and sensational style than the *Gleaner.* In addition the company publishes the *Sunday Gleaner*—which has a magazine section —and several other publications, listed in the accompanying table.

The *Jamaica Daily News* began in 1973 as a private morning tabloid published by Communications Corporation of Jamaica. The principal shareholders were the National Continental Corporation, in which ITT had an interest, and another local company,

*The author wishes to express particular gratitude to Hugh Daley for making available some primary data which he had collected for *UNESCO: Mass Media Survey: Jamaica* (REQ/Comm/MD/20, 1980).

Frequency, Average Number of Pages/Issue and Circulation of Jamaican Newspapers, 1980		
Newspaper	Frequency and Average Number of Pages/Issue	Circulation
		50–100,000
Sunday Gleaner	Daily (14)	91,000
Weekend Star	Weekly (28)	70,000
Children's Own	Weekly in school term	84,000
		25–50,000
Daily Gleaner	Daily (28)	47,000
Star	Daily (16)	45,000
		10–25,000
Tourist Guide	18 issues per year	20,000
Merry-go-round (entertainment)	Fortnightly	10,000
Jamaica Daily News	Daily (20)	16,000
Sunday Sun	Weekly (36)	20,000
Struggle	Weekly (8)	20,000
		under 10,000
Western Mirror	Biweekly (16)	6,000
Catholic Opinion	Monthly	7,000
Jamaica Churchman (Anglican)	Monthly	6,000
Workers Time	Monthly (8)	2,000
New York Times "Week in Review" (Gleaner Co.)	Weekly (8) (broadsheet)	550

Desnoes & Geddes. Together the two owned over 40 percent of shares, with additional financing by public subscription. Although designed as a competitor to the *Gleaner,* the *Daily News* did not affect the older paper's popularity and was usually purchased along with it rather than instead of it. The Communications Corporation also published a Sunday tabloid, the *Sunday Sun,* which has its own magazine section.

By 1978, after a period of serious financial problems that included skyrocketing newsprint costs, the company went into receivership. To prevent its closure, a new company, Daily News Ltd., was formed with shares held for the government through the Jamaica Development Bank, which made the company a substantial loan. The same staff members were maintained and the government stated that it planned to have the paper owned by workers and community-based organizations, similar to the ownership of Radio Jamaica.

Ownership of Jamaica's print media is concentrated in the hands of the Gleaner Company, which owns the two largest circulation dailies comprising about 85 percent of daily circulation as well as half of the nondailies. The Gleaner Company and the *Western Mirror* are corporately owned. As mentioned above, the *Daily News* changed from corporate to government ownership when the government rescued it from receivership in 1978.

In 1980 four other newspapers were being published on a biweekly, weekly or monthly basis. These were the biweekly *Western Mirror* in Montego Bay, aimed at citizens of western Jamaica and started by the staff of the *Beacon* newspaper, which went into receivership in 1980; *Struggle,* the publication of the Workers Party of Jamaica (WPJ), a communist party; and two monthly church newspapers. During the 1970s two weeklies allied to the major political parties and trade unions, *Public Opinion* and *The Voice,* begun in 1937 and 1952 respectively, had ceased publication, along with several other small papers.

Except for *Struggle,* the press reflects a Christian religious orientation since this is the country's only numerically significant faith.

Politically, the Gleaner Company newspapers are right of center. The company's policy statement asserts:

Gleaner policy is founded in the philosophy that human progress springs from the effort and enterprise of individuals exerted singly or in groups; and in the conviction that there is no system of Government or human relationships which provides any effective and satisfactory substitute for the hard work and ingenuity of individuals competitively applied....

The "Statement of Principles" of the *Daily News* reads:

The Paper must be progressive. That is, it must not support reaction.... The paper must support the Third World in the North/South dialogue towards a New International Economic Order.... It must retain its freedom to support or criticize positions and postures of political parties or interest groups from the standpoint of basic policy of the paper and the national interest of the country.

According to the editor of the *Western Mirror* in a 1980 interview, the policy of the paper is to be politically independent, and the paper wants "to make sure that the voice of the people is heard at all times."

All three dailies are published in the capital and distributed island-wide, as are most nondailies. There is no foreign language or minority-owned press. The special interest press includes Gleaner Company publications such as *Children's Own,* distributed weekly during school term; *Tourist Guide,* published 18 times a year; *Merry-go-round,* a fortnightly entertainment paper; and the *New York Times* "Week in Review." The last and the *Gleaner* are broadsheets while other papers are tabloid.

Economic Framework

Jamaica's economic climate deteriorated rapidly after the mid-1970s due to oil price increases and lack of investment by the private sector, which objected to the policy of democratic socialism declared by the government in 1974. The Jamaica dollar was devalued by about 45 percent between 1977 and 1979.

The Gleaner Company showed a net loss from 1977 to 1979, after having made only a very small profit in 1976. In 1978 it had to issue debenture stock to raise $4 million (US$2,240,000) the stock was oversubscribed by $500,000 (US$280,000). The 1979 Gleaner Company Report stated that the country's economic conditions hurt the company's financial position, particularly in advertising

and importation of raw materials where issue of licenses was slow. The company report stressed an effort to make its publications more viable by cutting back on newsprint wastage.

The Gleaner Company's financial problems reflect the effect of Jamaica's weakened economic condition on the press in general. Although, as noted above, the *Daily News* and the *Beacon* went into receivership, they have survived under new ownership, but other small papers closed down completely during the 1970s.

The electronic media were also adversely affected, but to a lesser degree. The government-owned Jamaica Broadcasting Corporation had a deficit of over half a million U.S. dollars in 1979, but Radio Jamaica Ltd. continued to make a profit.

During the late 1970s newsprint has been less readily available, as licenses have been granted more slowly due to the shortage of foreign exchange. Like all other imports, newsprint requires a license from the Trade Administrator's Department. The 1979 Gleaner Company Report stated that the company had reduced its average number of pages from 21 to 17. Newsprint costs in 1980 were about US$700 per short ton.

Advertising ratios show the daily and Sunday *Gleaner* ads occupying between 46 percent and 62 percent of space in 1979–80, while average space of the *Daily News* in 1980 was 35 percent. There is no obvious influence of advertising on editorial policies.

Between 1977 and 1980 the cost of both the *Daily Gleaner* and the *Daily News* doubled, moving from 20 cents (US11 cents) to 40 cents (US22 cents) per copy.

Total employment in the newspaper industry in 1980 was approximately 550 persons, of whom about 225 were journalists. The approximate wage scale in U.S. dollars is: executive management, $19,000; junior management, $12,000; sub-editors and reporters, $5,000.

The Gleaner Company has a Viscount letterpress, purchased in 1967, and a four-unit standard (Crabtree) letterpress purchased in 1961. A computer is used for typesetting, and also has text-editing capacity. The *Daily News* is printed on a Cottrell V-15A offset press capable of producing 15,000, 48-page newspapers per hour. The *Western Mirror* rents a small offset press.

A Jamaica Union of Journalists (JUJ) was formed in 1956 by journalists, most of whom worked for the Gleaner Company. The JUJ turned for guidance to the National Workers Union, an affiliate of the People's National party. The *Public Opinion* newspaper recognized the JUJ immediately but the Gleaner Company said that because of its "solis position" (it was the only daily) it could not tolerate its workers being represented by any union with affiliation to the union of a major political party. A fight ensued between the journalists and the Gleaner Company but after several months of nonrecognition the company eventually acknowledged the union. However, the JUJ survived only about 18 months, largely because the Gleaner Company was able to disperse the membership via promotion, and by transfer of union officers to newly created rural bureaus. Journalists did not unionize again until the 1970s.

By 1980 Jamaica had no trade unions exclusive to journalists, but three unions represented various categories of workers employed in print media organizations. The one closest to being a bona fide journalist union was the Union of Journalists and Allied Employees (UJAE). This union was not restricted to professionals, however, as it could also represent other media workers such as typists. At the Gleaner Company most journalists and allied workers were represented by the UJAE, while the Union of Technical and Supervisory Personnel (UTASP) covered journalists in supervisory positions. At the *Jamaica Daily News,* the National Workers Union (NWU), an affiliate of the People's National party, one of the island's two major parties, represented journalists and other workers.

The UJAE had been formed in 1974 after *Daily Gleaner* editorial workers sought representation by the Bustamante Industrial Trade Union (BITU), an affiliate of the Jamaica Labour Party, the island's other major political party. When the Gleaner Company reiterated its unwillingness to negotiate through any politically affiliated trade union, the editorial workers formed the UJAE, and after an eight-week strike gained recognition under the Labour Relations and Industrial Disputes Act, which had recently been passed.

The UJAE strike was the first general work-stoppage of reporters and sub-editors in the history of Jamaica's print media. It was followed by several other brief strikes and slowdowns. In February 1977 workers at the Gleaner Company walked out for two days to support demands for pay increases to certain workers affected by the changeover from hot to cold type printing machinery. Between June 1977 and February 1978, 121 workers were laid off at the Gleaner Company because of both the changeover to cold type and the company's poor financial position following devaluation of the Jamaican dollar. The result was a one-day sick-out by unionized editorial workers to show solidarity. The dispute went to the Ministry of Labour, but the workers were not reinstated. The company directors' report for 1977 also stated that when a number of employees were made redundant, there was a slowdown of editorial and production workers, which led to the closing of the plant from July 25 to August 3 and the loss of several days of publication. As a result, the minister of labour and employment appointed a board of inquiry, which confirmed the company's serious financial state. However, Gleaner management-labor disputes continued through 1980.

Nor was labor unrest confined to the *Gleaner.* A one-day strike was called by the National Workers Union at the *Jamaica Daily News* in August 1977 over the dismissal of Editor Canute James, who was eventually reinstated. James had been discharged because of disagreement between himself and the managing director over the composition of an editorial committee and guidelines relating to editorial operation and authority, including the editor's right to select editorial page columnists. The dispute went to the Ministry of Labour, which appointed a three-man board of inquiry.While acknowledging the company's right to set editorial policy, the board ruled in favor of the dismissed editor, although its recommendation of an editorial committee was never implemented.

Press Laws*

The laws of Jamaica, including its press laws, like those of most other Commonwealth Caribbean countries, were derived from British law and passed while those countries were still colonies. Although the Jamaican Constitution of 1962 makes no special mention of freedom of the press, it provides for protection of freedom of expression. Thus the Jamaican press occupies the same constitu-

*This section and the Censorship section rely very heavily on the pioneer work by Dorcas White of the Faculty of Law, University of the West Indies, *The Press and the Law in the Caribbean.*

tional position as does an individual citizen, press freedom being guaranteed by implication since the constitution specifically permits "freedom to hold opinions and to receive and impart ideas and information without interference."

Of course, however, there are restraints. In Jamaica seditious libel is an offense in common law. A person charged with publishing seditious libel could also be charged with effecting a public mischief. In Jamaica it is a misdemeanor, punishable by two years imprisonment, to incite "disaffection amongst members of the police force or to do any act calculated to induce any member of the force to withhold his services or to commit breaches of discipline." Clearly, this can affect press criticism of the police.

Blasphemous libel is another common-law offense in Jamaica, while defamatory libel has two aspects: criminal and civil. However, there are some instances in which a newspaper can publish without fear of civil or criminal action for defamation. These are called "privileged occasions." It has been said that "the reason for this is expediency [because] there are certain occasions when it is in public interest that people should be able to...write with complete freedom unhampered by any underlying fear, real or imaginary that subsequently they may have to answer for what they have said."

There is also a law on obscenity, designed to protect public morals and public decency; indeed, publication of obscene matter is an offense not only in Jamaica, but in all the Caribbean islands.

The law of contempt has two aspects: contempt of court and contempt of Parliament. Contempt of court, a common-law offense, has been defined as "words or acts obstructing or tending to obstruct the administration of Justice," and has also been held to include "any act done of writing" in this respect. Further, the publication in a newspaper of an article containing "scurrilous personal abuse of a judge, with reference to his conduct as a judge in a judicial proceeding which has terminated is a contempt." It is also in contempt of court to publish matter abusing persons who are involved in proceedings before that court.

Contempt of Parliament has been defined as (1) interference with parliamentary privilege, and (2) "words or acts which cast aspersions on the dignity of either House." More specifically it is an offense, punishable by a fine of $100 (US$56) or 12 months imprison-

ment, for anyone to "publish any false or scandalous libel on either House."

The press can also be barred from attendance at sittings of both parliamentary houses. The constitution indicates that each legislature has the power to regulate its own proceedings besides being able to determine its own privileges. The penalty for contravention of these regulations is a maximum fine of $1,000 (US$560) "or in default of payment thereof to imprisonment with or without hard labour for a period not exceeding twelve months."

Registration of newspapers and periodicals in Jamaica follows the same procedure as that of any other trade or business. Under the Licences on Trade and Business Act a license can be obtained after payment of duty, which is payable annually thereafter. The act does not require the name and address of the publisher or printer to be included. There is no requirement for compulsory posting of bonds.

Censorship

Jamaica has no agency for monitoring the press. There are no prepublication censorship procedures, nor is there a press council, although Jamaicans may put cases before the Caribbean Press Council. The law of Jamaica does not tell newspapers what to print except that each paper must include the name and address of the proprietor, the place where the newspaper is published and the date of publication; and the Printers Act makes it mandatory for the printer to print his name and address on the newspaper.

The law does, however, indicate what must *not* be printed, although this might not be called censorship in the ordinary meaning of the word. The Censorship (Press and Postal) Act empowers the governor general in times of emergency to forbid by proclamation the publication of "all information with respect to troops, ships, aircraft, or war materials etc....or to any measures taken for or connected with the defence of the Commonwealth...." The governor general can also forbid the publication of any statement, comment or suggestion calculated directly or indirectly to convey such information.

The Official Secrets Act places restrictions on the type of information that government officials can disclose. This act was passed by the British Parliament and extended to all parts of the then Colonial Empire. The parliaments of territories that became independent have the power to amend or repeal any imperial act extended prior to independence but no independent Caribbean Commonwealth nation has amended or repealed the Official Secrets Act.

The act itself makes it a felony for anyone "for any purpose prejudicial to the safety or interest of the State" to "obtain or communicate to any other person any sketch, plan, model, article...or information which is calculated to be or might be or is intended to be directly or indirectly useful to an enemy." This is an offence punishable by a minimum of three years and a maximum of seven years' imprisonment. Also under the act, it is a misdemeanor for any state functionary to disclose official information to "any person other than a person to whom he is authorised to communicate it...," and the recipient of any such information can be found guilty of a misdemeanor and "liable to imprisonment with or without hard labour for a term not exceeding two years," or to both a fine and imprisonment. Although the recipient can attempt to prove that the communication to him of the information was "contrary to his desire," Dorcas White, a Caribbean legal expert, has pointed out that if a reporter had solicited information that had been published it would be difficult if not impossible to prove that his desire was disregarded.

According to the aforementioned legal expert, the effect of the Official Secrets Act "is to deprive the public of the right of access to public information." However, as already mentioned, no Commonwealth Caribbean nation—including Jamaica—has seen fit to change this law.

State-Press Relations

Criticism of the government by sections of the press in Jamaica has been intense and unrestricted. From 1974, when the People's National party (PNP) government declared a policy of democratic socialism, the Gleaner Company publications became increasingly hostile, and the government complained frequently about the Gleaner's criticisms. Although no official action was taken against the Gleaner, the company felt harassed by, for example, a march on its premises on September 24, 1979, led by Prime Minister Michael Manley, who expressed the governing party's objection to the Gleaner with the

seemingly veiled threat, "Next time...next time." The PNP had been angered by the Gleaner's campaign against the new Cuban ambassador, Ulises Estrada, whom the paper described as an intelligence officer, guilty of undiplomatic interference in Jamaica's internal affairs. On the day before the march, the Gleaner had bannered "Mounting Tourist Cancellations" across three columns linking a speech by Manley with alleged tourist falloff. Next to this story was a large chart reporting a Gleaner poll that showed PNP trailing the Jamaica Labour party (JLP) in popular support; and inside, a full-page advertisement called Manley a "Judas" who had "sold out Jamaica to the Cubans for less than 30 pieces of silver!" According to the Columbia Journalism Review, this ad was signed by a spurious organization assumed to be a JLP creation.

A few weeks later Oliver Clarke, managing director and chairman of the Gleaner Company, stated that at PNP's request the Gleaner Company board of directors met with a deputation of 12 persons from PNP. At this meeting, according to Clarke, PNP accused the Gleaner of "giving respectability to rumours, of a partisan stance and of breaching the ethical practices of journalism." The Gleaner board cited instances considered intimidating towards the paper's future operations. PNP for its part "assured the Gleaner Board that there was no intention to intimidate the Gleaner." Clarke's report concluded that in spite of this assurance "there now exists a concerted and well organized programme designed to—even by the most moderate interpretation—influence the activities of the Gleaner Company and its publications."

Almost a year later, on October 13, 1980, the Jamaica Daily News reported on an exclusive interview with Minister of Finance Hugh Small, under the headline "Gleaner Subversive to National Development—Small." The Daily News quoted Small as saying: "The 'Gleaner' does not want Jamaica to change, it does everything to prevent change. It is an openly partisan paper presenting the world as an embattled place in which the struggle is between communism and capitalism. It has taken the side of capitalism. The 'Gleaner' has shut off the Third Estate of the world's dispossessed...." In a speech at PNP's 42nd annual conference, Small also said that in the third term of office, which the party hoped to win, the media would have to be viewed as a tool in the development of the people and not as a subverting agent.

PNP did not win a third term, however, as the general election on October 30, 1980 gave the JLP, led by Edward Seaga, more than 50 out of 60 seats. Prime Minister Seaga also became minister of information and culture in the new government, which had already made its media policy clear in its election manifesto:

> Jamaicans have always exhibited strong preference for the programmes and publications of the private media...[whose] views enjoy much greater support than those of the [government] media which are considered heavily biased in favour of Government policies and programmes.

The manifesto also emphasized that the JLP did not favor public ownership or control of the *Jamaica Daily News,* and concluded with the statement that "the JLP supports the free media and its right to operate freely in the manner guaranteed by the Constitution of Jamaica." In effect, this was a green light for the *Gleaner* in particular and an unfettered Jamaican press in general.

However, under any Jamaican government since independence, newspapers have never been suspended or confiscated, nor have newsmen, local or foreign, ever been jailed or banned for reporting activities. As described earlier, when the *Jamaica Daily News* went into receivership in 1978 the government made it a loan to prevent its closure, and stated that, when the loan was repaid, *Daily News* shares would be made available to its workers and to community-based organizations on the model of Radio Jamaica. More than a year after the government loan a *Daily News* editorial maintained that there had been no government interference with editorial operations.

Attitude Toward Foreign Media

Correspondents who come to Jamaica to work are required to obtain a work permit from the Ministry of Labour if they are going to live on the island for an extended period of time. If they are on short visits, not exceeding 30 days in a given calendar year, they need a letter of exemption from the ministry. Correspondents must have a local address to obtain a work permit since the permits are not issued to companies or firms outside of Jamaica.

Although no prior submission of cables is required, the Telegrams (Production of) Act could affect newspapers since its enforcement would prevent journalists from filing reports to the outside world. The act has never been invoked, but it does give the government the right to receive all foreign cables, and further states that incoming cables can be confiscated if the minister considers this is in the public interest. The only restriction on foreign periodicals stems from the Undesirable Publications (Prohibition of Importation) Act, which empowers the relevant minister "if he is of opinion that the importation of any publication would be contrary to the public interest" to ban its import after declaring it an "undesirable publication."

There is no longer any foreign ownership of domestic media in Jamaica.

The major issue concerning foreign propaganda has been the perception of the government, between 1975 and 1980, that the foreign press, particularly in the United States, was giving Jamaica unduly negative coverage. Serious declines in tourism to Jamaica were blamed on this. The *Gleaner* newspaper reprinted the negative foreign articles very frequently.

Contacts with international press organizations are maintained through the Press Association's affiliation with the International Organization of Journalists and the Latin American Federation of Journalists, and the Gleaner Company's membership in the Inter-American Press Association (IAPA). The Gleaner's managing director, an IAPA executive, is also regional vice-chairman of its Committee on Freedom of the Press.

Jamaica supported the UNESCO Declaration on the Media in 1978.

News Agencies

Jamaica has no domestic news agency, although in 1978 a small operation, JAMPRESS, was begun in the national Agency for Public Information as part of ASIN, a Latin American service through which 10 countries exchange information in an attempt to implement the new international information order. However, JAMPRESS reached a much larger number of countries because it used the telex facilities of Inter-Press Service (IPS) for dispatching stories, and IPS distributed JAMPRESS releases to about 400 subscribers throughout the world. Each week one staff person was responsible for submitting a small number of articles on subjects of national interest, many of them government releases. In November 1980 the new JLP government suspended the operation of JAMPRESS, stating that the suspension was temporary.

Although Jamaica and most other English-speaking Caribbean countries are too small to support national news agencies, they co-operated during the 1970s to form a Caribbean News Agency (CANA). CANA was incorporated in 1976 as an independent, non-profit company jointly owned by its share-holders, 15 private and public mass media of the Caribbean Commonwealth. By 1980 CANA had expanded, maintained its independence and achieved moderate financial success. CANA was unique in providing the model of a developing world-news agency, which, in a region where the majority of media were publicly owned, was independent of direct control by governments and, in addition, had no financial, editorial or managerial support from foreign news agencies.

Jamaican media comprise three of CANA's fifteen shareholders, the greatest number from a single country; the *Daily Gleaner* controls the largest number of shares, 10.5 percent. In 1980 CANA had a staff of 14 at its headquarters in Barbados and maintained full-time correspondents in Jamaica and three other larger territories, as well as stringers in the smaller islands. CANA obtains international news from Reuters World Service, with which it has an exclusive contract. Thus Reuters cannot sell to Caribbean media other than through CANA.

In the foreword to CANA's Guidebook, the general manager stated that CANA reporters were to be objective, as "CANA does not take sides, grind axes, promote viewpoints or editorialise." Although CANA aimed to gather news with and from a Caribbean perspective, CANA journalists were not to act as the voice of any special interest group.

During CANA's formative years concerns were expressed that the agency would have difficulty maintaining political independence. However, by 1980, after four years of operation, no evidence of political control had materialized. Observers both inside and outside the agency expressed the view that CANA had functioned independently of Ca-

ribbean governments. In fact, any concerted manipulation of CANA by governments would be very difficult, due to the diversity of the countries from which its shareholders come. No single government among the widely-scattered autonomous countries could easily exert enough pressure on CANA to undermine the agency.

The news agencies operating full-time bureaus in the island are CANA; Prensa Latina (PRELA), the Cuban news agency, which has two full-time correspondents, both Cuban nationals, and two subscribers in Jamaica, the *Daily News* and the government radio-TV station; and Inter-Press Service (IPS), which has four subscribers in Jamaica: the *Daily News,* the two broadcast stations and the Agency for Public Information. Other news agencies—AFP, AP, UPI, Reuters and EFE—operate with part-time correspondents and stringers, most of whom are employees of other media in Jamaica. Of these agencies, Reuters (through the contract with CANA described above) has four subscribers in Jamaica. None of the other agencies has subscribers, largely because the mass media cannot afford another international news source.

Electronic News Media

Jamaica has two radio stations, JBC-AM and FM and RJR-AM and FM, and one television station, JBC-TV. The Jamaica Broadcasting Corporation (JBC) began in 1959 as a statutory corporation wholly owned by the government and operated on semi-commercial lines. The corporation is responsible to the minister of information and culture, but ministerial approval is needed only for obtaining loans and appointing or dismissing the general manager. The Jamaica Broadcasting Corporation Act of 1959 states two potentially contradictory aims for the station: to provide the public with programs of information, instruction and entertainment; and to earn enough money to continue operations.

Radio Jamaica (RJR) was set up in 1950 by Rediffusion of England, which owned 70 percent of the shares; 28 percent were owned by other foreign investors and only 2 percent by Jamaicans. In 1977 the government acquired majority interests in the company but stated that it did not wish to own a second radio station and appointed an interim board to set up guidelines for transferring ownership to workers and "organizations with a mass-representative base." This was accomplished in early 1980 and 50.1 percent of shares were offered to such organizations as trade unions, teachers' and nurses' associations, cooperatives, building societies and church associations. Government retained 25.1 percent of shares, while 24.8 percent went to RJR workers. Not all shares were taken by the first group, and the Jamaica Development Bank (which underwrote the share issue) holds these until such time as organizations take them up.

Education & Training

In 1974 the University of the West Indies established a Caribbean Institute of Mass Communication on its campus in Jamaica. The institute offers a one-year diploma course for about 30 Caribbean journalists, and a B. A.-degree course that accepts 30 students a year. Each year some Jamaicans receive regional training in a four-month course for Caribbean journalists begun in 1972 and sponsored by the Caribbean Conference of Churches and Codrington College, Barbados. Many still receive training in North America and Europe.

Locally, the Press Association of Jamaica annually presents the Seprod Awards for outstanding journalism.

The major local journalistic organization is the Press Association of Jamaica (PAJ), formed in 1943 and having 120 fully paid members in 1980.

The major print media of Jamaica are members of the Caribbean Publishers and Broadcasters Association (CPBA), which was formed mainly to facilitate a joint contract with Reuters News Agency. Members of the CPBA helped to bring about the Caribbean News Agency (CANA) in 1976, and only CPBA members were allowed to become CANA shareholders.

Summary

For nearly two decades since independence, the press in Jamaica has played a vibrant role in the society. Legal controls, part of the country's British legal heritage, are the major constraint on press operation. In the late 1970s economic restraints surfaced, leading to some scarcity of newsprint, causing layoffs and forcing one daily and one nondaily to go into receivership. Fortunately, both of these papers were able to continue under new ownership, but other nondailies that had closed during the 1970s have not resumed publication. Economic problems will undoubtedly continue into the 1980s, though possibly with less severity than in the 1970s. It is to be hoped that the government will lift the recent restrictions on foreign exchange, which affect the importation of newsprint, or else exempt newsprint from these restrictions. In any case, the press will almost certainly continue to occupy a significant role as Jamaica struggles to become a nation that is economically as well as politically independent.

CHRONOLOGY

1974 Caribbean Institute of Mass Communication, University of the West Indies, Jamaica established; Union of Journalists and Allied Employees (UJAE) formed.

1976 Caribbean News Agency (CANA) founded.

1977 Jamaica's first regional radio station, JBC Radio West, created.

1978 *Jamaica Daily News* goes into receivership but enabled to continue by formation of new company financed by government loan through Jamaica Development Bank. Government buys Radio Jamaica from foreign ownership (Rediffusion) and announces plans to divest shares to workers and community organizations.

1979 People's National Party (PNP) marches on Gleaner Company. Board of directors of Gleaner Company meets with PNP.

1980 Public citizens inquiry into the media held by Press Association of Jamaica. PNP government divests majority of Radio Jamaica shares to workers and community-based organizations. *Beacon* newspaper goes into receivership; its staff forms the *Western Mirror*.

BIBLIOGRAPHY

Brown, Aggrey. "The Mass Media of Communications and Socialist Change in The Caribbean: A Case Study of Jamaica." *Caribbean Quarterly* 22:4 (December 1976): 43.

Carter-Ruck, P. F. *Libel and Slander.* 1972.

Cuthbert, Marlene, "Canadian Newspaper Treatment of a Developing Country." *Canadian Journal of Communication* 7:1 (Summer 1980): 16.

_____. "The Caribbean News Agency: Third World Model." *Journalism Monographs,* February 1981.

_____ and Sparkes, Vernon. "Coverage of Jamaica in the U.S. and Canadian Press in 1976: A Study of Press Bias and Effect." *Journal of Social and Economic Studies,* ISER, Mona, Jamaica, 27:2 (June 1978): 204. Abstracted by SOCIAL SCISEARCH, Institute for Scientific Information 090294 and by ERIC, ED 168 001.

_____. "Interpersonal Versus Mass Media Channels as Influences on Tourism to the Caribbean: An Empirical Study." *Caribbean Quarterly,* vol. 26, no. 4, 1980.

_____. "Mass Media in National Development: Governmental Perspectives in Jamaica and Guyana." *Caribbean Quarterly* 23:4 (December 1977): 90.

_____. "News Selection and News Values: Jamaica in the Foreign Press." *Caribbean Studies* 19:2 (July 1979): 93.

Daley, Hugh. *UNESCO Mass Media Survey: Jamaica.* REQ/Comm/MD/20, 1980.

Gleaner Company Limited. *Report 1977, Report 1978, Report 1979.*

Kopkind, Andrew. "Trouble in Paradise." *Columbia Journalism Review,* March–April 1980, p. 41.

Lent, John. *Third World Mass Media and Their Search for Modernity.* Lewisburg, Pa., 1977.

Ponder, Rhinold Lamar. "The Role of the Press in National Development: Conflict in Jamaica." Princeton University, January 1980, unpublished.

Press Association of Jamaica. Secretary's Report, 37th Annual General Meeting of the Press Association of Jamaica. September 7, 1980.

White, Dorcas. *The Press and the Law in the Caribbean.* Barbados, 1977.

JAPAN

by John Lent

BASIC DATA

Population: 114.276 million
Area: 380,730 sq. km. (147,000 sq. mi.)
GNP: Y190.71 trillion (US $980 billion) (1978)
Literacy Rate: 99%
Language(s): Japanese
Number of Dailies: 126
  Aggregate Circulation: 65,880,502
  Circulation per 1,000: 571
Number of Nondailies: NA
  Aggregate Circulation: NA
  Circulation per 1,000: NA
Number of Periodicals: 1,640

Number of Radio Stations: 981
Number of Television Stations: 10,102
Number of Radio Receivers: 98.86 million
  Radio Receivers per 1,000: 868
Number of Television Sets: 56.08 million
  Television Sets per 1,000: 492
Total Annual Newsprint Consumption: 2.52 million metric tons
  Per Capita Newsprint Consumption: 22 kg. (48.4 lbs.)
Total Newspaper Ad Receipts: Y655.4 billion (US $2.73 billion) (1979)
  As % of All Ad Expenditures: 31.9

Background & General Characteristics

The Japanese press is relatively young, but very big and sophisticated for its age; virtually free of government restrictions, but until recently, rather timid in performing a watchdog function. It is a technologically advanced press that worries about the inroads made by technology of new media. It is uniquely successful in Asia—and possibly the world—and may be a victim of its own success.

A sidestep through history can provide some perspective on the state of the Japanese press. For example, the limiting of one newspaper per prefecture for control purposes during World War II has been partially carried over to the present, thus allowing some local newspapers to have monopolies. The timidity of the journalists in carrying out investigative assignments, along with their pro-establishment bias, may be rooted in history as well: perhaps it is a hangover of the fear experienced during the war and the subsequent Allied occupation, perhaps it goes back to the Meiji period of the 19th century when the government saw the press as a tool for educating the people in the ways of the modern world, or perhaps it is endemic to the big-business journalism that Japan

has had for nearly three quarters of a century. The party-line proclivities of the Japanese press, in all likelihood, go back to the political nature of early newspapers, and the modernity of the press is probably related to the fact that journalism and Japan's modernization as a country began simultaneously in the 1860s.

Japan's first (1861) newspaper, *Batavia Shimbun* (a duplicate in Japanese of an Indonesian Dutch publication, *Javasche Courant*), was a latecomer among Asian papers, mainly because of the closed-society nature of the country. Technologically, Japan was ready for print news media as early as the late sixteenth century, when printing from movable type was introduced almost simultaneously by Portuguese missionaries and the Japanese military—the latter learning of it while carrying out maneuvers in Korea. But, before newspapers could evolve, Japan closed its doors to the world for about two centuries.

The dawn of Meiji journalism saw two types of newspaper—*ko-shimbun* (small newspaper) and *oh-shimbun* (big newspaper). The *ko-shimbun* were mass-oriented, employing the work of folk-ballad writers, while the *oh-shinbum* were written by serious scholars who devoted prodigious amounts of space to political affairs. The latter dominated the 19th century press. However, all early newspapers were establishment-biased, because (1) they were founded by former samurai of the top levels of the class-conscious Tokugawa era, (2) nearly every daily depended on government support, and (3) the press laws, the first of which was passed in 1869, prescribed the news that should be published.

Two of the early Osaka-based political newspapers—*Asahi* (established in 1879) and *Mainichi* (1888), which have evolved into giants today—began emphasizing general news reporting, attributable to the business acumen of their respective publishers, Ryohei Murayama and Kikoichi Motoyama. Both men thought of their newspapers as commodities to sell, Motoyama introducing the budget system to *Mainichi* to give it a strong financial base. By the early 20th century, because of Japanese war news and the introduction of the "third page" (devoted to crime and social affairs), circulations soared. The 1923 earthquake that destroyed Tokyo—and its press—also boosted Osaka's two giants, *Asahi* and *Mainichi*, the latter attaining a one-million circulation by 1924. The third contemporary giant, *Yomiuri Shimbun*, began its rise immediately after the earthquake. The 50-year-old *Yomiuri* was struggling in 1924 when purchased by Matsutaro Shoriki, who popularized it by highlighting sensationalism, games and gimmicks.

As Japan became more militaristic in the early 1930s, only a handful of journalists were critical of the government, again lending support to the thesis that the press had been establishment-prone. Prominent among the few critics was Sunao (Rokko) Kikutake, editor of *Fukuoka Nichi-Nichi*, who, because of his writing, suffered reprisals of the military, including air-raid maneuver demonstrations that used *Fukuoka Nichi-Nichi's* plant as "target."

By 1937 most of the press supported the military. Laws by the Showa government, thought-control efforts of the Domei News Agency (which propagandized in China and Southeast Asia, and which, at its peak, had a staff of 3,000 and over 50 bureaus throughout the world) and the Bureau of Information (which censored and provided press guidance at home), and merging of newspapers under the National Mobilization Law of 1938, definitely brought the press into line. The concentration characteristic of the press today might be traced to the National Mobilization

Law. The number of pre-World War II newspapers dropped from 1,422 to 355 in 1941. The following year, the government policy stipulated only one newspaper per prefecture (or a total of 54 in Japan), thus easing censorship tasks. Suppression existed also because of government control of newsprint allocations after 1938, and total manipulation of war news.

The guarantees of press freedom that Japan enjoys today are traceable to the Supreme Commander of Allied Powers (SCAP) during the postwar occupation period. SCAP abolished all restrictive media legislation, declared the existence of freedom of the press and called for the disassociation of the press from government. But, in implementing this freedom, SCAP used the repressive tactics it sought to eliminate. Some individuals, especially those who had supported the Japanese military government, or those feared to be communists or leftists as the cold war intensified in the late 1940s and early 1950s, were barred from journalism. At the urging of SCAP, Shoriki was replaced as head of *Yomiuri*, as were the publishers of 43 of the other 55 postwar dailies. SCAP also banned the communist newspaper, and the censorship exercised by the occupation forces was, in the eyes of some people, as unreasonable as that of the Japanese military. One Japanese author has said that the "red purge" caused more dismissals in the press—2.3 percent—than in 18 other industries, which had an 0.38 percent dismissal rate.

Economically, some current practices and traits of the Japanese press originated in the aftermath of the war. The guarantee of press freedom at that time accounted for the establishment of 126 new newspapers by 1946. However, few of them could survive the competition, and between 1948 and 1951, most of them merged with older ones or closed. Thus, a pattern of monopolization and concentration returned with the huge national dailies dominating Japan and local dailies monopolizing their regions. Throughout the 1950s, the rivalry was extremely keen, based on promotional gimmicks that are common yet,—potential subscribers received soaps, sugar and utensils, leading to coinage of the phrase, "pot and kettle competition."

By 1960 the market approached saturation, with circulation gains barely following population increases. The Big Three— *Asahi*, *Mainichi* and *Yomiuri*—were affected most seriously, their share of aggregate circulation receding from 69.9 percent in 1942 to 59.2

percent in 1945 and 44.3 percent in 1959. The result was even more aggressive competitive strategies on their part, including the expansion of markets to the far north and experimentation with new technology.

Despite rising subscription prices, circulations have continued to increase, placing Japan second to the Soviet Union in total circulation and first in the world among major countries in number of copies per 1,000 population (571). The 65,880,502 total circulation figure of 1979 represented a 3.2 percent gain over the previous year. Japanese circulations can be looked at in at least two ways—total copies when set papers of evening and morning editions are counted as one (45,851,852), or total copies when set papers are counted as two (65,880,502). (These figures include over 5.3 million copies of sports dailies.) Morning editions are nearly twice as popular among Japanese readers, with 43,538,681 subscribers compared to 22,341,821 for evening editions. The growth rate of total newspaper circulation between 1978 and 1979 was 2.6 times that of the number of households in the country.

Most of these copies (91.9 percent) reach subscribers' homes via delivery people, while 7.5 percent are sold at newsstands, 0.1 by mail and 0.5 in other ways. More than 99 percent of the general newspapers are delivered to subscribers' homes. Japan has an elaborate delivery system, made up of 22,145 circulation agents, who are divided into three classes. Single-franchise agents handle one national newspaper and its associates; a multiple-franchise agent circulates two or three national papers, while an open agent takes care of all papers sold in a given area. The number of employees of all circulation agents in 1979 was 389,402, an increase of nearly 10,000 over the previous year. Trucks, not the normally efficient and fast train system, transport 85 to 90 percent of all newspapers to the agents.

The rapid growth of the Japanese press is closely related to such national traits as the intense curiosity, acquisitiveness and competitiveness of a people packed into an island state. Of course, other Japanese characteristics helped—including Japan's uniqueness in Asia as a nation of homogeneous people speaking one language (and geared to a highly advanced technology). Whereas the press of the Philippines, India or Malaysia must contend with numerous minority languages, in Japan, the only language other than Japanese in the print media is English. (There are four English-language papers—*Japan Times, Mainichi Daily News, Daily Yomiuri* and *Asahi Evening News*—with a total circulation of 100,000. These are looked on as a prestige element by their big owners, and used by Japanese readers to learn or upgrade their English-language skills.)

Unlike the mass-circulated press in many countries—which tends to be lowbrow—Japanese newspapers consider themselves quality dailies. The local press has a good reputation for serious professional reporting of both local and international events. International news is prominently featured and profusely used because of Japan's heavy dependence on other countries. Recent surveys of Nihon Shimbun Kyokai show that 15.4 percent of the newshole is devoted to foreign news, 60 percent of which emanates from the wire services.

In 1979 the editorial performance of the Japanese press was creditable both in volume and quality. A midyear survey by Nihon Shimbun Kyokai revealed that nationwide, 70 percent of the readers had a positive feeling of trust of their newspapers, while only 16 percent felt negatively. The public's trust in the press is especially encouraging in the context of the credibility gap that existed for a generation until the late 1970s. Credibility had been hurt by the incestuous relationships newspapers maintained with government and other institutions, and by the charges that papers lacked individuality and were too meek in performing an adversary role. Whereas numerous government favors would have been considered bribes in other societies, the Japanese press deemed them special rights built into the system. Among such favors had been exemptions from various taxes and very low rates for government property on which newspapers built their plants. The accusation that newspapers lacked individuality was related to the spirit of neutrality and impartiality in which news was reported, and to the fact that individual publications were too bureaucratized to have distinctive voices. Also, some of the blame for sameness was attributed to the *kisha* (reporters) clubs common to Japan, which exercised exclusive rights over many news sources, barring nonestablishment journalists and protecting their own news sources to the extent that stories lost their impact. The clubs—and the press in turn—were vulnerable to pressures because their facilities were provided by government and business sponsors.

Changes were forthcoming in 1977, when, after a number of complaints about press sameness and meekness, more investigative and interpretive reporting was printed. For the first time, bylines also appeared, making reporters accountable for what they wrote. By 1979 Japan's investigative journalism was exposing irregularities involving public corporations and government agencies such as Kokusai Denshin Denwa Company, Japan Housing Corporation, the Ministry of Finance, the Environment Agency and even the Prime Minister's Office. *Asahi* was credited with initiating the investigations with its stories on the irregular accounting of the Japanese National Railways Construction Corporation, but exposés by all Japanese papers were notable. Reporters got their information from employees of the organizations investigated. The papers gathered follow-up information on their own before the authorities could act. (Previously, the press had relied on the authorities to provide such material.) And active public support for the investigations was forthcoming. As the Nihon Shimbun Kyokai reported, "...This is the first real instance in Japan of investigative reporting, with newspapers competing intensely to score scoops."

Economic Framework

Although the Japanese press in 1979 was rather prosperous, showing business performances exceeding previous peaks, there was apprehension about how long the good times would last. Remembering the effects of a long recession in the 1970s, publishers are cautious. They fear the repercussions on the economy of worldwide crude oil price hikes, the steeply rising prices of coniferous-tree chips (used for newsprint) and—perhaps above all—the difficulty of coping with technological progress. As the technology of new media becomes more accessible, newspapers —despite their own highly advanced production systems—are afraid they will be made obsolescent. Believing the public's information needs will become further diversified and specialized, the press is hoping to coexist with new technology—by functioning as basic and general information purveyors, an index, so to speak, of the new media's more specialized and personalized information. Newspapers, therefore, actively participate in the many new-media experiments, and submit requests to the Ministry of Posts and Telecommunications, seeking assurances that they will be granted use and operation of new-media privileges.

Anything like the financial upsurge in 1979–80 was absent throughout most of the 1970s. Severe internecine competition and the poor economic situation nationally accounted for less-than-positive changes in the Japanese press. In 1975 and 1976 newspapers attempted to combat the recession by delaying the addition of new production technology, reducing the number of pages and dismissing workers—the latter especially difficult in light of Japan's policy of granting employees permanent status. In 1976 *Sankei Shimbun* planned to cut its 3,600 work force by one-half by 1979, while *Mainichi* had plans of reducing its 6,700 payroll to 1,200. By 1977 *Mainichi* admitted to virtual bankruptcy, with a 1976 loss of Y8.64 billion ($29.5 million) and debts of Y61.9 billion ($258) million. The company was rescued when two banks froze its interest payments. That same year, Nihon Shimbun Kyokai convinced its member newspapers that the intense circulation wars—where electric blankets, watches and pocket calculators were given to potential subscribers— were nonprofitable, and that the papers should rationalize their sales activities. Another competitive element that had to be curbed was the tendency of all national dailies to saturate remote areas with their editions.

The tide began to change in 1978, when *Asahi* led the way in upping its monthly subscription rate 18 percent—to Y162 ($8.33) for the set of a morning and an evening edition. Seventy-three other newspapers raised their rates in mid-1980, because of a 30 percent hike in the cost of newsprint, increased cost of supplies and higher wages offered delivery boys. Advertising also contributed to the growing profits. In less than four years after 1947, newspaper advertising had grown more than tenfold, while in the 1950s and 1960s, the annual growth rates averaged 24 and 14 percent respectively. In 1962, for the first time in its history, the press received more revenue from advertisements (50.4 percent) than from sales (49.6 percent). However, with the advent of commercial radio in 1951 and television in 1953, the monopolization of advertising revenue by the press was at an end. In 1950, 71.6 percent of all advertising money went to newspapers, while in 1960, the pie was split almost equally between newspapers (39.3 percent) and radio and television (32.5 percent). But since 1978 Nihon Shimbun Kyokai has carried out a publicity campaign on the advantages of newspaper advertising. In 1978, for the first time since 1973, newspaper advertising revenue topped that of television in growth rate. The 1978 advertising revenue of newspapers showed a 12.5 percent increase over the previous year.

The first six months of 1979 saw an increase not just in total advertising revenue but also in advertising volume, which rose by eight percent over the previous period. By mid-1979, therefore, advertising revenue accounted for 52.3 percent of total newspaper revenues, while the share for sales declined to 47.7 percent.

Total advertising expenditures in Japan in 1979 were almost Y2.12 trillion ($8.69 billion), a 15 percent increase over 1978. Of this total, newspapers garnered Y655.4 billion ($2.73 billion) compared to Y750.8 billion ($3.07 billion) for television, Y106.1 billion ($435 million) for radio and Y111.9 billion ($459 million) for magazines. Thus, the shares of the advertising revenue were: television 35.5 percent, newspapers 31.9, magazines 5.2 and radio 4.9. A 1979 Nihon Shimbun Kyokai survey showed that in 88 newspapers, a record total of 214,812 pages of advertising was used, averaging out to 43 percent of newspaper content.

And since 1976, a steady decline of employees in all departments except editorial has also helped profits; as of May 1979, the total employee decrease was 1,552, or 2.1 percent. This was made possible by limiting the number of recruits from among school graduates, resulting in fewer young staff members.

As a result of these efforts, the first half of 1979 saw subscription and advertising revenues up by 11.4 percent and 14.6 percent, respectively, over the corresponding period for the previous year. Total expenditures rose by 10.1 percent (eight percent of which was for personnel), but profits were up 11.7 percent. This was in sharp contrast with 1977, when one of every two newspapers suffered a deficit.

Chief characteristics of the Japanese press, besides size, are tendencies toward concentration and monopolization. The concentration is observable everywhere. Japan's huge press-circulation of over 65 million, larger than the combined daily circulations of the rest of Asia, is concentrated in 126 dailies. The top five of those newspapers—the national Asahi, Mainichi, Yomiuri, Nihon Keizai Shimbun and quasi-national Chunichi, which compete against local newspapers throughout Japan—account for about 60 percent of total national circulation. These dailies have printing plants in numerous places and publish more than 120 different regional editions daily. When sold as sets of morning and evening editions, at least seven dailies have circulations in the millions. In 1979 Yomiuri had nearly 8.4 million morning and 4.9 million evening subscribers, while Asahi figures were 7.5 and 4.7 million respectively, and Mainichi 4.6 and 2.5 million, respectively. The financial daily, Nihon Keizai Shimbun, sold 1.8 million morning and 1.1 million evening, while figures for Chunichi were 2.7 and 1.5 million, Sankei Shimbun 1.9 and 1.0 million and Hokkaido Shimbun 993,957 and 839,394. Yukan Fuji, with only an evening edition, sells over a million copies.

As an example of the concentration within a given newspaper company, Asahi employs 9,069 people in five major Japanese cities, 23 overseas offices and 281 local news bureaus. The company uses 125 company-owned cars, 82 motorcycles, 53 radio-equipped jeeps, 13 vans with radiophoto transmission facilities, three jet aircraft and four helicopters, to gather and disseminate news for its 18 major morning editions, 10 afternoon editions and 105 designated editions for various communities. In addition, Asahi publishes an English-language daily, three weeklies, three monthlies and 10 yearbooks, and has interests in 60 other enterprises, including radio-television stations, travel agencies and real estate firms.

Concentration, and in some cases monopoly, is common in the local press. In most prefectures (there are a few exceptions, as well as the big cities like Tokyo) only one newspaper is published locally. Because of such monopolization, the local press has strong business foundations and is highly profitable. Chunichi, a local in Nagoya, is becoming a giant, quasi-national newspaper stepping into the domain of the Big Three. Recently Chunichi bought Tokyo Shimbun and a local paper. Two other large local newspapers are Hokkaido Shimbun of Sapporo and Nishi Nippon Shimbun of Fukuoka. Along with Chunichi, they have become known as bloc newspapers, because they publish elsewhere besides the single prefecture to which local dailies normally limit themselves.

Press concentration is also prevalent in ownership structure. There is a strong trend for newspapers to limit shareholders to members of their own organizations. Again, the origins of this practice can be traced historically—to 1942, and the newspaper-control regulations of the wartime Japan Newspaper Association, aimed at preventing outside capital from pressuring independent editorial policies on the newspapers. After the war a "Commercial Code" stipulated that shares of all joint stock companies be made available to the public, but it was offset soon after by a "Special Law Concerning Newspapers," which said the press could limit its shares only to members. As a result, most Japanese newspapers have adopted some variant of this closed system of ownership. In 1976, a survey by Nihon Shimbun Kyokai (Japan Newspaper Publishers and Editors Association) showed that 17 newspapers (including *Asahi, Mainichi, Yomiuri* and *Nihon Keizai Shimbun*) had 100 percent internal ownership, 24 others 50 percent and 28 less than 50 percent. Significantly, the companies accounting for over 50 percent of the total newspaper circulation limit ownership of shares to their employees. This trend causes problems when companies need to raise capital, because the funds for such capital must be raised internally.

Japan is the world's third largest producer of newsprint, and ranks second in consumption. In 1979 Japan produced 2.579 million tons, a 6.2 percent increase over 1978, while domestic consumption was 2,521,000 tons, an increase of 8.9 percent. Consumption was high because of the increased advertising volume, which required more pages. As of December 1979 manufacturers held in stock a 27.9-day newsprint supply. That same year, 17.8 percent of newspapers' total outlay went to meeting costs of newprint.

Encouraging has been Japan's production of lightweight newsprint since 1977. In the production of this quality of paper, recycled scrap paper is increasingly used; by 1979, 20 percent of the raw materials used in newsprint production was scrap paper. Lightweight-paper consumption was expected to top 90 percent in 1980.

Japan's labor-management relations may not exist elsewhere in the world. Each year, companies hire graduates of universities and senior high schools after submitting them to a series of examinations. Once hired, an employee is hardly ever dismissed, being employed until retirement at 55 or 60; the dominant factors in determining pay are age and years of service. Japanese labor unions are not by crafts, but rather by companies—that is, all employees of a company belong to the same union. Labor and management work to maintain harmony; if workers strike, they do so after working hours. The aim is to let management know something is amiss with the harmonic relationship, and to expect remedies. All of this—plus the aforementioned fact that employees own shares in the newspaper companies—means more labor loyalty. Japan has been unique among industrialized nations in its ability to introduce new production systems with virtually no interference from labor. Japanese unions were not antagonistic during the technological upgrading because they did not face personnel dismissals and were assured of continued employment.

Newspaper personnel costs have been rising steadily—accounting for 40.6 percent of the total press outlay by 1979—while the number of employees has been decreasing yearly since the 1975 peak, owing primarily to retrenchment caused by mechanization. (Of course, this flies in the face of Japan's general employment policies.) Because fewer graduates have been recruited from universities and high schools in recent years, 1979 figures showed that the average newspaper employee is 36 years old and has 14.6 years of service. The advancement of the average age has caused concern among the newspapers, as indicated by Nihon Shimbun Kyokai: "The main argument under such circumstances has been over how to replace the aged employees engaged in the production process and how to revise the traditional seniority wage system."

Men make up 92.4 percent, and women 7.6 percent of the newspapers' work force. In 1979, there were 18,078 editorial personnel—compared to 17,810 in 1970—among the total 65,928 newspaper employees. (The total represents a decrease from a high of 71,412 in 1972.) Average monthly base pay of a press employee rose from Y80,000 ($361) in 1972 to nearly Y210,000 ($950) in 1979.

Despite fears of encroachments of new media and its own temporary delays in implementing technology in the mid-1970s (because of the overall economic slump), the Japanese press still ranks among the more automated and labor-saving in the world. In 1959, *Asahi* became the first newspaper in the world to use facsimile transmission, connecting Tokyo and Sapporo by microwaves, with printing by offset. Since then, facsimile transmission has become an effective and widely used method, employed by national dailies to connect their publishing plants and to speed production and delivery in remote areas. Newspapers are rapidly shifting to computer photo-typesetting and offset printing with at least 34 plants completely or partially converted to offset. In 1978 the number of web offset presses increased by nearly 30 units to a total of 127 in 114 plants. *Asahi* installed 32 web offset presses in its newly completed $100 million Tokyo plant, which some believe will affect the spread of offset in Japan. (*Asahi's* headquarters, nearly all of which is computerized, is thought to be the most modern in the world.) Thus, the 961 letterpress rotary presses still in use are likely to be converted soon. By the 1970s, in fact, newspaper plants were nearly completely computerized with systems such as *Asahi's* NELSON (News Editing and Layout System of Newspapers) and *Nihon Keizai Shimbun's* ANNECS (Automated Nikkei Newspaper Editing and Composing System).

In 1979, Japan exhibited a domestically made laser plate-maker (being tested at *Asahi,* and expected to be put into wide use), and experimented with Japan's version of Viewdata. The latter, called CAPTAINS (Character and Pattern Telephone Access Information Network System), has been tested in 1,000 Tokyo homes. The system connects home television sets to information storage centers via public telephone circuits, so that users can see requested information on their television sets. The press participated by providing information to the storage centers. Japanese newspapers have also been looking to cable television as a possible extension of their services via home facsimile, and for its two-way communication potential.

Because such sophisticated technology requires enormous amounts of energy, Nihon Shimbun Kyokai set up a Committee to Cope with Resources and Energy Problems, which will explore ways of "securing resources for the entire newspaper world on one hand, and of developing alternate resources and rationalizing newspaper production on the other."

Press Laws & Censorship

All laws restricting the press have been eliminated, except for regulations in general laws and in the special law on protection of military secrets of United States forces stationed in Japan. Before World War II, freedom of the press was safeguarded by Article 29 of the Meiji Constitution, but circumscribed "within the limits provided by laws enacted by the Diet [Parliament]." This provision made for a number of restrictions. The Potsdam Declaration of 1945, specifying Japan's surrender conditions, mentioned freedom of the press, and the Japanese Constitution of 1947 established press freedom and prohibited censorship. No limitations of this freedom were mentioned.

Among general legal considerations that may extend to the press are those of defamation, privacy, obscenity, offical secrets and freedom to gather news materials. Defamation, which can be a civil and criminal offense, was inserted into the Criminal Code after World War II, to insure harmonious relationships between press freedom and respect for individuals' honor. If truth is proved, virtually no story can be considered a punishable offense.

Since a 1964 case, however, invasion of privacy is a tort; the press is liable to damages if it injures a person's right to privacy. Although only a few cases have been tried, the public's consciousness of this right has become acute in recent times. Obscenity laws have been rather strict; translations of *Lady Chatterley's Lover* and other books have been held as obscene, and censors have been blacking out pubic areas in sex magazines when they allow them in circulation at all. Some change may be forthcoming in obscenity laws after an April 1980 court ruling held it is "unconstitutional censorship" to censor or prohibit importation of sex magazines. Magazines had long challenged Article 175 of the Criminal Code (which did not allow sales of pornographic literature) on the grounds that its definition of obscenity contradicted freedom of expression as guaranteed in the constitution.

The Criminal Code has no provisions concerning official secrets, but every public official has a duty not to reveal such information. In 1973 there was an important case of a *Mainichi* reporter who obtained Ministry of Foreign Affairs secrets by befriending, and eventually bedding, a woman employee of that office. As an aftermath of that case, the Supreme Court ruled that acquisition of national secrets by the press is not illegal as long as they are obtained through normal newsgathering activities. The court ruled it is illegal to use threats or coercion or to "trample on the dignity of the source" to get news.

Until recently, the Supreme Court said the press was obligated to disclose news sources and produce materials under court order. However, in February 1980, the Court dismissed a case against *Hokkaido Shimbun,* involving a reporter who refused to divulge his source. For the first time in Japanese history, the reporter's right to withhold information was recognized.

Still being debated in Japan is a proposed Information Disclosure Act, similar to the Freedom of Information Act in the United States. Throughout 1979, efforts were made by consumer-movement groups, opposition parties, and other organizations to legally enforce the disclosure of official documents.

A number of self-imposed limitations have often been debilitating to the Japanese press. Among these are the three so-called "institutional inhibitions"—criticism of the royal family, exposures of the intimate relationship between rightist gangsters and politicians, and exploitation of the most sensitive area of society, the "untouchables." Until the end of the 1970s, the Japanese press had been traditionally hesitant to go against the establishment. Editors did not demand investigative reporting, and newspapers took a party line, opposing communism and favoring the ruling party, big business and national progress.

In the past, such self-imposed restraints hindered Japanese newspaper reporting. The scandal that brought down the Tanaka government was not reported by dailies until they were forced to do so by an exposé in a monthly magazine, *Bungei Shunju.* For two months in 1976, *Yomiuri* sat on an important story it had on Prime Minister Takeo Miki. There have been other significant coverups.

It is still too early to predict how long the current spate of investigative stories will continue.

State-Press Relations

Still, relations between the Japanese government and mass media are relatively good. Access to officials exists and reporters do have a right to criticize government—even though they often have been hesitant to exercise that right. Credibility in newspaper reportage diminished as a result of the coverage of the Tanaka government corruption

charges of 1974, but by 1976, when it was revealed that Lockheed had donated vast sums of money to Japanese politicians, newspapers aggressively reported the events. Despite numerous protests and libel suits from many political and business leaders, the press went to great lengths to "reconcile the right of the people to know and the basic human rights of the suspected politicians," as Nihon Shimbun Kyokai noted in *The Japanese Press.* A number of these individuals, including former Prime Minister Tanaka, were arrested. The Japanese press definitely exercised editorial influence on government policies as a result of these investigations.

At other times, as in 1977, when the government proposed to revise the Criminal Code, with possible effects on press freedom, the press made its influence felt; the government said it would move with "great caution." In 1978, when the Defense Agency proposed "legislation to provide against national emergency," with implications of restricting news activities, a storm of controversy was stirred up by the press. Editorials of practically all newspapers cautioned against a seeming trend towards authoritarian government and demanded maintenance of the principle of civilian rule. The Defense Agency finally announced that the emergency would not include control of speech. Also in 1978, when the prime minister stated in the Diet that he intended to look into a law to protect secrets, the press and opposition parties criticized the plan as as control measure, and the government backed down. Thus, unlike in many countries, hasty decisions affecting freedom of the press are not tolerated in Japan.

Jailing of newsmen and suspension and confiscation of newspapers are rarities in modern Japan, and the state does not seem to control the press through subsidies, allocation of newsprint, advertising support, labor union manipulation or any other extralegal means.

Attitude Toward Foreign Media

Foreign media personnel in Japan do not face the hassles that are prevalent in other Asian countries. Virtually never does one hear of foreign correspondents being jailed, denied entry or otherwise harassed. Instead, one learns of a Foreign Press Center being inaugurated in 1976, to help in arranging interviews, translation and research materials for foreign journalists; of bilateral journalist-exchange programs being established with the United States, Soviet Union, Australia, Europe, China and ASEAN. Interdependence is a big theme in Japanese press circles, and even individual newspaper companies have arranged for foreign journalists to visit. Not that Japan has always been a foreign journalist's Utopia—or that it is one even today. The belief exists that foreign correspondents for years were shut off from many sources of news and faced difficulties in obtaining stories. This was said to have resulted from the exclusive rights to many news sources held by *kisha* clubs, which barred foreign newsmen. Moreover, the foreign press traditionally had been kept out of government briefings until some inroads were made in the 1970s. Today, foreign correspondents can attend, as observers, the nationally televised, prime minister's press conferences, as well as the formal conferences of the foreign minister—but not his briefings.

Japanese newspapers have shown concern over the proposed New International Information Order. When UNESCO originally considered the Declaration on the Contribution of Mass Media, the Japanese press opposed what it considered an attempt by UNESCO to restrict freedom of the press. The final draft of the declaration was regarded as more satisfactory because—in the words of one official—it had "been made quite harmless by consensus of the representatives of various governments." In the debates on the New International Information Order, Japan tended to side ideologically with the countries of the West.

News Agencies

Japan has two main news agencies, both post-World War II products born out of the military government's Domei News Agency. Kyodo News Service, formed in 1945, is a nonprofit organization similar to the Associated Press; from its beginning it has dealt with general news, and maintains correspondents in 37 cities around the world. Jiji Press, also started in 1945, operates as a joint stock corporation similar to United Press International. Originally handling only economic news, Jiji began disseminating general news in the 1950s. The agency has correspondents in 24 cities outside Japan.

Kyodo has survived some hard times to become one of the key news agencies in Asia, if not the world. In 1952, the agency faced its most serious crisis when Japan's three major papers, which paid one-fourth of Kyodo's revenue in membership fees, withdrew, thinking they were large enough to have their own network of correspondents in Japan and abroad. But the "big three" later reversed their decision.

Unlike many nations, Japan does not suffer from a one-way news flow from the United States and Europe, since it has its own large corps of overseas correspondents working for both news agencies and individual media. Thus there is less need for foreign news agencies. In 1979, Japan had 354 correspondents abroad, 117 of whom were in North America (111 in the United States), 103 in Europe (32 in London, 28 in Paris), 15 in Africa, 101 in Asia (17 in China, 14 in Bangkok, 11 in Hong Kong and 10 in Singapore), seven in Australia and 11 in South America (seven in Brazil).

Electronic News Media

No doubt Japan is one of the most advanced nations in the world in its development of broadcasting. The television system is among the world's largest. Nippon Hoso Kyokai (NHK), the only noncommercial public broadcasting corporation, has 6,078 television stations, 3,068 of which are general network and 3,010 educational. Among commercial television stations, 485 are VHF, owned by 48 companies, 3,534 are UHF, owned by 45 companies, and five SHF.

NHK also maintains 314 standard-wave radio stations on two networks, as well as 479 FM stations. Among commercial radio stations, 179 are standard wave, owned by 48 companies, two short wave, owned by one company, and seven FM, owned by four companies.

Concentration and monopolization trends also seem to permeate the electronic media, as the above figures show. Besides the huge number of stations concentrated within NHK, there are 115 commercial companies that have a total of 4,024 television stations and 188 radio stations. Thirty-six commercial companies own both radio and television stations, 57 only television, 17 only standard-wave radio, one only short-wave radio and four only FM radio. NHK obviously has felt the squeeze from commercial broadcasting; with deficits in 1979, it asked that viewer fees be increased.

Percentage Distribution of Television Programs

	News	Culture	Entertainment	Education	Sports	Advertising
NHK General	32.7%	25.6%	25.3%	16.4%	—	—
NHK Education	1.0	18.8	—	80.2		
Commercial	12.9	24.3	46.0	12.7	3.1	0.5

The electronic media broadcast for long periods daily. NHK AM radio networks, for example, broadcast 19 and 18.5 hours daily, while the FM network is on for 18 hours; the commercial radio stations average about 22.5 hours. NHK's first AM network splits its time by devoting 39.7 percent to news, 30.4 to culture, 28.5 to entertainment and 1.4 to education; the second AM network is made up of 77.6 percent educational matter, 12 percent news and 10.4 culture. Figures for NHK's FM stations average to 42.7 percent culture, 34.8 entertainment, 14.6 news and 7.9 education. The commercial radio stations emphasize music, with 41.1 percent, followed by culture, 20.8; entertainment, 17.5; news, 12.9; education, 5.0; sports, 1.5, and advertisements, 0.9.

Among the television stations, NHK general stations divide their fare among news, 32.7 percent, culture 25.6, entertainment 25.3 and education 16.4. NHK's educational TV network has 80.2 percent education, 18.8 culture and 1.0 news. Commercial television stations use 46 percent entertainment, 24.3 culture, 12.9 news, 12.7 education, 3.1 sports and 0.5 advertisements.

Japan also ranks very high in the world in numbers of television and radio receivers. There is a total of 56,075,000 television sets, or 492 per 1,000 people; and 98,862,000 radio receivers, or 868 per 1,000. The Japanese are probably the world's second most avid television viewers; a 1979 Nihon Shimbun Kyokai survey showed that the average person watches 3:37 hours on weekdays and 4:21 on Sundays. In one of the few requests it has made of broadcasting, the government in 1979 asked that television not be shown after midnight in an effort to save energy. However, Nihon Shimbun Kyokai reported that the real reason may have been part of a "spiritual movement to change the people's lifestyle of watching television late at night." Relatively, use of radio is low, the average person listening 42 minutes on weekdays and 30 minutes on Sundays.

In 1979 there was mounting public criticism of excessive television commercials, especially those on children's television programs. As a result, the Fair Trade Commission planned to scrutinize more closely television's possible effects on children.

Education & Training

In the early 1970s, the Asian Mass Communication Research and Information Centre listed at least 15 Japanese schools and institutes that were involved in teaching, training or research in mass communication. This is a high figure for Asia, although not as high as the number in India. The difference is that many of Japan's educational institutions devoted to journalism are involved in high-level research and training. The Institute of Journalism at Tokyo University, Department of Communications at Sophia University, the School of Mass Communication at Seijo University and the Department of Mass Communication at Kansai University have reputable programs that teach and carry out research.

Besides universities and colleges, media organizations are also prominently involved in professionalization activities such as education, training and research. Chief of these for print media is Nihon Shimbun Kyokai, which publishes 13 periodicals concerning the press, conducts research studies, trains

Percentage Distribution of Radio Programs

	News	Culture	Entertainment	Education	Music	Sports	Advertising
NHK AM 1	39.7%	30.4%	28.5%	1.4%	—	—	—
NHK AM 2	12.0	10.4	—	77.6	—	—	—
NHK FM	14.6	42.7	34.8	7.9	—	—	—
Commercial	12.9	20.8	17.5	5.0	41.1	1.5	0.9

journalists and monitors media performance and ethical standards. Among other professional organizations are the Foreign Press Centre, a nonprofit, private foundation that assists duly accredited foreign journalists in Japan, and Nippon Kisha Club (Japan National Press Club), which was founded in 1969 and has 1,631 members.

Summary

The Japanese press continues to rank extremely high in size, economic security, quality, technology, professionalization and freedom to express itself. Economic progress, efforts to identify with new media, and investigative reporting trends in the closing years of the 1970s, are encouraging signs. Japanese publishers, however, do not think they can be smug about recent economic recovery in the newspaper industry; in fact, a number of them predict financial bad times for their papers, based on the belief .that international conditions will worsen in the 1980s.

CHRONOLOGY

1975   Large national dailies begin printing their papers locally.

1976   Investigative reporting of Tanaka government corruption.
Mainichi Shimbun reporter sentenced for leaking government secrets.
Nihon Shimbun Kyokai establishes advertising code of ethics.

1977   Tokyo court rejects rights-of-rebuttal demand in opinion advertising case.
Mainichi Shimbun, in financial trouble, establishes new corporation.

1978   Opposition mounts against idea of establishing emergency law, owing to fear of speech-freedom suppression.
Circulation war subsides; subscription rates increased.
Nihon Keizai Shimbun switches to phototypesetting and computerized page-composing system.

1979   Visual information systems—Teletext and CAPTAINS—experiments conducted.
Sapporo High Court upholds district court decision that reporters have right to refuse testimony in court.

BIBLIOGRAPHY

Academia, W.S. "Mass Media: Advent of the Fifth Estate." *Japan Echo,* 3:3 (1976) pp. 32–43.

Arai, Naoyuki. *Sengoro Ayumi Shimbun Journalism.* Tokyo: Tosho Shimbun Sha, 1976.

Asian Mass Communication Institutions—A Directory. Singapore: AMIC, 1973.

Brown, Ronald G., and Jung-Bock, Lee. "The Japanese Press and the People's Right to Know." *Journalism Quarterly,* Autumn 1977, pp. 477–81.

"Confidentiality: Japanese Press Makes Headway." *Indian Press,* July 1979, pp. 25–27.

de Roy, Swadesh. "Japan Meets 'Long-Felt Obligation.'" *Media,* February 1977, p. 23.

Ejiri, Susumu. "Japan's Press: A Unique Structure." *Communicator,* April 1977, pp. 11–16.

"General Privileges." *IPI Report,* September 1974, p. 5.

"Has the Supreme Court Recognized Newsmen's Right Not to Disclose News Sources?" *NSK News Bulletin,* June 1980, p. 3.

Hazelhurst, Peter. "Tokyo Paper Switches to Full Automation." *The Times,* September 25, 1980, p. 5.

Huffman, James L. "The Meiji Roots and Contemporary Practices of the Japanese Press." *The Japan Interpreter,* Spring 1977, pp. 448–66.

Ito, Masami. "Press Freedom in Japan." Association for Asian Studies, Toronto, Canada, March 20, 1976.

Kawanaka, Yasuhiro. "The Role of Japan in the Flow of News in Asia—Desirability and Feasibility of a World News Agency in Japan." Fair Communication Policy Conference, East-West Center, Honolulu, Hawaii, March 28-April 3, 1976.

Komatsubara, Hisao. "Japan." In John A. Lent, ed. *Newspapers in Asia: Contemporary Problems and Trends*. Hong Kong: Heinemann, forthcoming.

————. "The Japanese Press and Lockheed: Speculation without Investigation." *Media*, June 1976.

Lent, John A. *Broadcasting in Asia and the Pacific*. Hong Kong and Philadelphia: Heinemann and Temple University Press, 1978.

————. "History of the Japanese Press." *Gazette*, Summer 1968, pp. 7-36.

————. "The Missionary Press of Asia, 1550-1860: Precursors of Today's Journalism." In *Proceedings of the First International Symposium on Asian Studies*. Hong Kong: Asian Research Services, 1979, pp. 659-74.

Nakamura, Koji. "The Power of Japan's Press." *Far Eastern Economic Review*, October 3, 1975, p. 28.

Saar, John. "In Japan, Competition's Keen and Cost Disregarded." *Philadelphia Inquirer*, April 8, 1977, p. 4A.

Saito, Yasaburo. "Hard Times for English Language Press in Japan." *Media*, March 1977, p. 27.

Sakurai, Yoshiko. "Japan: Circulation or Suicide." *Indian Press*, September 1975, pp. 66-67.

————. "Japanese Press Begins Massive Retrenchment." *Media*, August 1976, p. 16.

Stokes, Henry Scott. "Computers Do It All at Tokyo Paper, Asahi." *The New York Times*, October 19, 1980, p. 19.

Takagi, Noritsune. "Genron Tosei to Mass Media." In *Gendai Nihon to Mass Communication*. Vol. 2. Tokyo: Aoki Shoten, 1972.

The Japanese Press 1980. Tokyo: Nihon Shimbun Kyokai, 1980.

"The Press Clubs of Japan." *Burson-Marsteller Report*, August 1975, p. 4.

"Toppling Tanaka." *Time*, December 9, 1974, p. 78.

Werner, John R. "Japanese Newspapers Use Advanced Technology." *Editor & Publisher* (June 24, 1978), pp. 17-18.

Yamada, Maki. "Business: The Japanese Way." *Atlas*, June 1978, p. 47.

Yu, Lydia N. "Consensus-Orientation and the Indirect Style of the Japanese Press." *Philippine Journal of Public Administration*, January 1974, pp. 28-39.

JORDAN

by George Kurian

BASIC DATA

Population: 3,104,000 (1980)
Area: 96,089 sq. km. (37,100 sq. mi.) (including Israeli-occupied West Bank)
GNP: JD 625 million (US$1.9 billion) (1979)
Literacy Rate: 50.1
Language(s): Arabic (official); English widely understood
Number of Dailies: 5
    Aggregate Circulation: 125,000
    Circulation per 1,000: 41
Number of Nondailies: 4
    Aggregate Circulation: 48,000
    Circulation per 1,000: 19

Number of Periodicals: 40
Number of Radio Stations: 1
Number of Television Stations: 1
Number of Radio Receivers: 532,000
    Radio Receivers per 1,000: 191
Number of Television Sets: 165,000
Television Sets per 1,000: 45
Total Annual Newsprint Consumption: 1,700 metric tons (1977)
    Per Capita Newsprint Consumption: 0.6 kg. (1.3 lb.)
Total Newspaper Ad Receipts: NA
    As % of All Ad Expenditures: NA

Background & General Characteristics

The first newspaper in Jordan (then called Transjordan) was *Al Sharq al Arabi* ("The Arab Orient"), which appeared in 1923 as a government publication. For the first three years it published political and literary news, but later limited itself to official notices and changed its name to "Official Bulletin of the Government of Transjordan." In 1927 three weeklies were founded: *Jazirat al-Arab* ("The Arab Peninsula"), *Al-Sharia* ("The Law"), and *al-Urdon* ("Jordan"). But it was not until 1939 that the country's first daily, *Al Jazirah*, appeared at Amman; the Jordanian press is thus, strictly, only a little over 40 years old.

The development of a national press began in earnest after the annexation of East Palestine at the end of the First Arab-Israeli War of 1948 and the subsequent large-scale entry of Palestinian Arabs into the mainstream of Jordanian society. For the next decade or so, the Palestinians dominated the country as well as the media. The dailies *Filastin* and *Al Difa'a* appeared in Jerusalem in 1949. Both had originally been published from Jaffa (later renamed Yafo) and had moved to Jordan when that city became a part of the new state of Israel.

The 1950s ushered in an era of vigorous journalism reflecting the growing opposition of the Jerusalem newspapers to the Jordanian government's relatively cautious position on the Palestine issue. While Jerusalem was the center of the press activity, weeklies and dailies appeared in the capital, Amman, representing a wide range of political views. In addition to *Al-Urdon,* which had become a daily in 1948, Amman had two new dailies: *Al Jihad* and *Al Manar,* the latter supported by the Conservative Muslim Brotherhood. Jerusalem had two English-language dailies, *Jerusalem Star* and *Jerusalem Times.*

1967 marked the first serious attempts by the state to limit the size and freedom of the fourth estate. In that year six papers, one English and five Arabic, constituted the press: *Falastine, Al-Difaa, Al-Jihad, Al-Manar, Al-Urdon* and the *Jerusalem Star.* Two events, a press merger and the Six-Day War, shook the fragile foundation on which these newspapers operated. Following newspaper criticisms of the Jordanian army's response to Israeli raids, an executive order was issued reorganizing the press. The June 1967 war interrupted this reorganization, and caused dislocations of its own. The Israeli occupation of Jerusalem and the West Bank area forced the Arabic press of Jerusalem to flee eastward, just as it had done some 20 years earlier. Two new dailies emerged in Amman, *Al Destour* in 1967 and *al Difa'a* in 1968. Almost immediately the press was drawn into the regime's confrontation with the Palestinian Al Fatah and its sister movements. The civil war placed under a severe strain the loyalties of the Palestinian journalists who staffed the Amman dailies and weeklies; many became discouraged when the government closed down *al-Difa'a* for siding with the commandos and established the state-run *Al-Rai*. One result of the upheaval was to persuade many talented Jordanian journalists to leave the country and seek employment in the nascent media of the oil-rich states of the Arabian peninsula. This movement of skilled personnel, continuing well into the 1970s, further weakened the Jordanian press and reduced its competitive edge in the Arab world.

A less spirited and less varied press emerged after the 1970-71 civil war, reflecting the general weakening of political opposition and a weariness on the part of the media, evident in the editorials of this period. Newspapers no longer criticized official policies, especially those concerning foreign relations. Press treatment of the Palestinian question was more compatible with the government's view than in the past.

Even so, a bill was introduced in the National Assembly in 1963 calling for pre-publication censorship. The government found that such a measure was no longer necessary, however, and the bill was dropped.

As of 1980 the Jordanian press consisted of five dailies: *Al Rai* (50,000), *Jordan Times* (10,000), *Al Destour* (30,000), *Al Akhbar* (25,000) and *Al Urdon* (10,000). The aggregate circulation of 125,000 has remained more or less stable over the past decade. The per capita circulation of 41 per 1,000 inhabitants is about the average for the Arab world; it is lower than that of Lebanon and Kuwait but higher than that of Algeria and Tunisia. Jordan ranks 97th in the world in per capita circulation.

Jordanian newspapers exhibit more individuality than the rest of the Arab press, because private ownership is still tolerated. The most influential of the dailies is *Al Rai* ("Opinion"), which was founded by the government in 1971. In 1974 it became the mouthpiece of the Arab National Union (ANU); when ANU was dissolved in 1974 a royal decree turned the newspaper over to the

Jordan Newspaper Company, which also publishes the *Jordan Times*, the kingdom's only English-language daily. *Al Rai* comes out every day of the week and usually consists of 14 to 16 pages, while *Jordan Times* is published six days a week and consists of six to eight pages. In 1976 *Al Rai* was suspended for 10 days for publishing a communique by Jordanian authorities criticizing the Syrian intervention in Lebanon. It was suspended again in 1977 for an item concerning the army.

Al Destour is a politically conservative daily published by the Jordan Press and Publishing Company. Founded in 1967, it comes out every day of the week with an average issue of 14 pages. It was suspended in 1978 for four days for printing an unauthorized announcement of an amnesty for political prisoners.

Al Akhbar is a moderate nationalist paper founded in 1974 by a member of the influential al-Majali family. Issued every day of the week, it consists on an average of 12 pages. Its license was revoked for a time in 1975 following a dispute with the government over its comments on a symbol resembling the Star of David that appeared on the Jordanian currency. Al-Majali, the publisher, was jailed for a week. The government later issued a clarification that the star was originally Islamic. *Al Akhbar* was again suspended in 1978 for publishing an appeal by the Save Jerusalem Committee.

Al-Urdon is not only the oldest daily in publication but also the most monarchical and for this reason receives very lenient treatment from the state. Violently anti-Nasserite and anti-PLO, it has been suspended only once: in 1967 when its owner, Khalil Nasr, refused to comply with the provisional law of 1967 ordering its merger with another newspaper. Issued six days a week, it enjoys only a small circulation; it is also the smallest in size, with an average issue consisting of no more than four pages.

The daily press is complemented by a fairly well established weekly and monthly press: *Al-Liwa* ("The Flag"), which follows a moderate Islamic line, *Akhbar al-Usbu* ("The Week's News"), a progovernment newsmagazine, and the monthly *Al Fajr al-Iqtisadi* ("The Economic Dawn"). Several non-political periodicals are also published by the Armed Forces Command, the Ministries of Education, Information, Agriculture and Wakf (Religious Properties) and the Amman Chamber of Commerce.

Economic Framework

Jordan's newspapers are all privately owned, even *Al Rai*, which is believed to be owned by interests close to the palace. *Al Destour* is owned by an elite group that includes Mahmoud al-Sharif, Kamil al-Sharif, Tariq al-Massarueh and Abdessalam al-Tarauneh. *Al-Akhbar* is owned by the al-Majali family, which has played an active role in Jordanian politics. *Al Urdon* is believed to have strong connections with the state because it is distributed mainly to the armed forces and other government entities.

Of all the newspapers, *Al Rai* appears to be strongest financially and *Al Urdon* the weakest. Although *Al Rai* and *Al-Destour* are competing papers, they share joint circulation and advertising departments. All papers are reportedly operating in the black. This is not surprising in the light of Jordan's healthy economy and Amman's growing importance as a commercial center.

The Journalists' Union was dissolved in 1952, as a result of internal dissension, and reconstituted in 1969. Its political role is limited and it has never sponsored a strike. Since 1977, its leadership has contested the validity of the laws against press freedom, unsuccessfully so far.

Press Laws & Censorship

Until 1953 the law on printed matter in Jordan was the Ottoman law as amended in 1928 and 1933. An additional law for the control of publications was first decreed in 1939, later replaced by a new law in 1948 that established censorship over all written materials, including letters and telegrams. In 1953 all these laws were unified and codified. During the next 20 years four more laws were added to the statute book, in 1953, 1955, 1967 (later rejected by the National Assembly) and 1973. As cumulated in 1973, the main provisions of the law are as follows:

• The right to a press card is limited to Jordanian nationals with at least five years' experience in journalism or a university diploma and those not in the service of a foreign power.

• A license is required for the publication of any periodical. This license is granted or revoked by the cabinet on the advice of the information minister. The cabinet's decision further requires the approval of the king and may not be appealed. If a license is revoked the holder must wait at least one year before he may obtain another.

• Every periodical must name a publisher responsible for its contents. Five copies of each issue must be sent to the Department of Printed Materials before distribution to the public.

• Infractions leading to a revocation of license or temporary suspension are: publication of materials that could prejudice the security of the state, the public interest or the constitutional foundations of the kingdom; unlicensed publication; irregular publication; and delay in submitting management accounts.

• It is forbidden to publish: news concerning the king or the royal family without prior authorization of the royal cabinet; information on new military techniques; items contrary to good morals; items offensive to religion; attacks on friendly heads of state; news relating to the armed forces, the security apparatus or the intelligence services; political communiques of foreign diplomatic representatives; secret state documents; and appeals in support of suspended publications. Publication of such items is punishable by a fine of JD500 ($147) and one year's prison sentence.

• Periodicals are subject to an annual financial audit by the Ministry of Information; it is forbidden to accept financial subsidies from foreign interests.

• The prices and advertising rates are to be based on criteria determined by the Ministry of Information after consultation with the Journalists Union.

• A minimum capital of JD10,000 ($2,930) is required for a daily newspaper or news agency and of JD3,000 ($879) for other periodicals.

• All printing houses must hold a license from the Ministry of Information; name a director legally responsible for printed materials; provide the Ministry of Information with samples of all typefaces used; keep a register of all printed materials; receive the Ministry's authorization to distribute any non-periodical publication.

• The authorization of the Ministry of Information is required for the distribution of any publication from abroad.

The enforcement of these laws is the responsibility of the Ministry of Information, formerly the Department of Printed Materials. By regulations issued in 1974 this department is charged also with keeping abreast of the foreign press, facilitating the work of foreign journalists, keeping files on Jordanian and foreign journalists, controlling the flow of foreign print and non-print media into the kingdom, and publishing information about Jordan.

In addition, there are a number of other laws and regulations designed to make the profession of journalism itself difficult. For instance, physicians, lawyers, pharmacists and engineers may not engage in journalism while active in their professions; editors in chief must have at least five years of prior experience in newspaper work. Although these restrictions are enforced only haphazardly, they constitute a potential threat to free-lance journalism.

State-Press Relations

The variety and number of press-control mechanisms in the government arsenal could be presumed to ensure a subservient, even servile, press. This has not been always so. State-press relations have been marked in recent years by recurring suspensions of newspapers and imprisonment of journalists. Such incidents were most frequent during the period from 1967 to 1978. In 1967, after the press expressed dismay at the inability of the army to respond adequately to Israeli military raids across the border, Prime Minister Wasfi Tell declared that newspapers had "failed to meet the level of responsibility expected of them." He revoked all publishing licenses and then issued new licenses on condition that the four Jerusalem dailies merge into two, in each of which the government held a 25 percent interest. The conflict with the Palestinian commandos brought a fresh media crisis of even more serious proportions. The government closed two dailies, *Al Destour* and *al-Difa'a,* when they carried on their front pages a Palestinian fedaiyin communique blaming the "reactionary regime" for the conflict. When new papers appeared in place of the suspended ones, the government moved against them with equal swiftness. *Al Sabah* ("The Morning"), founded by Arafat Hijazi, was suspended in 1975 along with two weeklies, and *Al Shaab* ("The People"), founded by Ibrahim Sakejha, was suspended in 1977, the latter for having accused Prime Minister Mudir Badran of contacts with Israeli officials. All of the current newspapers except *Al-Urdon* have been suspended at least once during the past four years, even though the political climate

in the kingdom has improved and the media are no longer as restive as they were in the 1960s.

But the government's decisiveness and readiness to use its powers are beginning to pay off. The more militant Palestinian elements have been effectively excluded from the media and journalists have been forced to learn the ground rules under which they are expected to function. According to one official, "In most cases it takes only a phone call to the editor from the minister of information to suppress one news item or play up another." Thus, Jordan is one of the few countries in the developing world to achieve full control over the media without overt censorship or state ownership.

Attitude Toward Foreign Media

Jordanians of the upper class read a number of foreign, especially Arab, publications. Because the content of Jordanian publications show little variety, foreign newspapers and periodicals constitute an important source of world news presented in different perspectives. The government has been unwilling to act directly against such imported publications, perhaps out of a deference to world opinion. Communist literature is banned but still reaches certain sections of the population in clandestine form. As noted earlier, the import and distribution of foreign publications requires the permission of the Ministry of Information, and the government often persuades local distributors to stop handling offending newspapers and periodicals.

Foreign correspondents are required to be registered with the Ministry of Information but they do not require special visas nor do cables require prior approval. However, all reports are monitored by the ministry, and the authors of unfriendly reports are quietly asked to leave the country.

The Jordanian government officially endorses UNESCO 1978 Declaration on the Media and subsequent efforts to make the media subservient to the state in developing countries.

News Agencies

The national news agency is the Jordan News Agency (JNA), founded in 1965. With a permanent staff of 20 in Jordan and four abroad it supplies over 5,000 words of national and local news daily in Arabic. JNA receives the overseas services of Reuters, AFP, AP, UPI, MENA, and Tass.

Electronic News Media

Electronic media are controlled by the Hashemite Jordan Broadcasting Service (HJBS) and the Jordan Television Corporation, both under the Ministry of Communications. HJBS broadcasts a home service with two medium-wave transmitters and a foreign service using short-wave transmitters. Television potentially reaches 85 percent of the population with two main transmitters and two repeaters. News and information constitute 22.5 percent of radio programming and 21.5 percent of television programming.

Education & Training

Jordan has at present no journalism school. Efforts are under way to establish a mass communications training center in Amman.

Summary

The press of Jordan has been characterized as loyalist; it displays some of the characteristics of a free press, such as private ownership, but the government has never tried to hide its whip, and numerous press casualties during the past two decades provide effective testimony to state control. Weak and passive, the press reflects the state of the country today: it supports a traditional system which views the media as an engine of modernization and therefore deeply suspect, and in which the very word opposition is taboo.

CHRONOLOGY

1976   *Al Rai* is suspended for 10 days.
1977   *Al Rai* is again suspended.

1978   *Al Destour* is suspended.
           Al Akhbar is suspended.

BIBLIOGRAPHY

Rugh, William A. *The Arab Press*. Syracuse, N.Y., 1979.

KENYA

by Dennis L. Wilcox

BASIC DATA

Population: 15 million
Area: 582,646 sq. km. (224,960 sq. mi.)
GNP: Sh 34.4 billion (1979) (US $4.7 billion) (1979)
Literacy Rate: 25%
Language(s): Swahili, English
Number of Dailies: 3
    Aggregate Circulation: 178,326
    Circulation per 1,000: 10
Number of Nondailies: 59
    Aggregate Circulation: 574,520
    Circulation per 1,000: 40

Number of Periodicals: 28
Number of Radio Stations: 18
Number of Television Stations: 4
Number of Radio Receivers: 525,000
    Radio Receivers per 1,000: 64
Number of Television Sets: 60,000
    Television Sets per 1,000: 2
Total Annual Newsprint Consumption: NA
    Per Capita Newsprint Consumption: NA
Total Newspaper Ad Receipts: NA
    As % of All Ad Expenditures: NA

Background & General Characteristics

The Kenyan press is an anomaly among the press systems of the Black African states in that private and commercial interests still control and operate the mass and popular press. Government ownership, except for radio and television, is minimal.

The country's daily newspapers—*Daily Nation, The Standard* and *Taifa Leo* ("The Nation Today")—are not only privately owned but are the last remaining dailies in Black Africa owned and controlled by foreign interests. The English-language *Daily Nation* and the Swahili *Taifa Leo* are owned by Prince Karim Aga Khan IV, an international businessman and spiritual head of the Ismaili Moslems. *The Standard* and several other publications are part of the London-based Lonrho conglomerate that has mining interests, breweries and transport companies in many African nations.

Although—like newspapers of most developing nations—the Kenyan press faces various governmental pressures calling for "constructive criticism" and commitment to "nation building," Western observers generally agree that Kenya has one of the freest presses in the Third World and Black Africa.

Nor does the government—or even KANU, the ruling political party in this de facto one-party state—own or operate a major commercial newspaper. By the same token, ownership by an opposition party is a moot point. As one Kenyan says, "There isn't any opposition political party." The nearest thing to opposition are factions within the broad based KANU.

The government does have the power to detain journalists, confiscate newspapers and even ban publications, but these actions are always something in the background as part of the nation's legacy of English colonial laws, and are alluded to only in occasional speeches by government ministers when they have felt the brunt of editorial criticism.

For all practical purposes, reporters and editors exercise a degree of self-regulation and restraint that keeps any conflict between government and press at a low level. Journalists do feel a commitment to "nation building," but they also have enough independence to criticize government policies editorially, and even do investigative exposes. This is particularly true under the presidency of Daniel Arap Moi, who assumed leadership of the nation after the death of Jomo Kenyatta, the nation's founding father, in 1978.

The average Kenyan is well informed through the press, but there is wide disparity between urban and rural areas in terms of access to mass media. Nairobi, the capital, has at least half of the nation's radio and television sets, newspaper circulation, telephones and postal traffic—but less than 10 percent of the population.

Like most developing nations, Kenya is still a rural country. About 85 percent of the population are still farmers—and the only two urban areas are Nairobi, in the center of the country, and Mombasa on the Indian Ocean coast. Nairobi is the only city in Kenya with competing dailies, since the capital is really the hub of all journalistic activity in the country. Mombasa is a press center but only in that competing newspapers—transported by truck from Nairobi—are sold on the streets. Limited publishing activity is found in Kitale, Kijabe and Kisumu.

Kenya's literacy rate is about 25 to 30 percent—somewhat higher than most Black African states. Although the country has made major progress in literacy training over the last decade, it may be a losing battle in terms of an exploding population. Kenya probably has the world's highest birthrate and the population is growing at 4 percent annually. The average farm wife has 8.1 children, and more than half of the nation's population is now under 18 years old.

A number of languages are spoken among Kenya's six major tribal groupings, but the nation's official language is Swahili, spoken by about 65 percent of the population. Swahili replaced English as the official language in 1971, but English is still the lingua franca of journalism, commerce and higher education. English is widely understood in the urban areas, but less so in traditional rural areas. Another major language is Kikuyu, spoken by 25 percent of the people.

The quality of journalism in Kenya is on a par with the press of Nigeria—above the Black African average in writing, layout and production. The writing style reflects the fact that most Kenyan journalists have been able to take advantage of formalized training programs—either through the International Press Institute's short courses in the 1960s and the early 1970s, or by attending the University of Nairobi's School of Journalism established in 1970. Another route has been journalism training abroad in the United States or Great Britain. A great deal of effort in training programs for personnel has also been invested by the daily newspapers themselves, so that, although foreign owned, they could be operated by Kenyan nationals. Indeed, the Africanization of the staffs has probably been one reason why the government has not pressed the issue of foreign ownership and taken steps, as the other African nations have done, to ban such ownership or insist that the majority of the newspaper be owned by nationals or the government itself.

The layout of the Kenyan dailies—all are tabloids—follows the British circus style, but more ideas from the American press are being introduced. The newspapers also have modern printing plants, and the quality of the production is quite good. The three dailies are in the category of the popular press, offering a mix of news, special features, comic strips, advice columns and consumer advertising. The *Standard,* a six-column tabloid, is more sensational than *The Nation* or *Taifa Leo.* One issue had dead bodies in a four-column, page-one spread, beneath the headline, "Gangsters Die by the Gun."

The three dailies are published in Nairobi. *The Daily Nation* has the largest circulation, almost 100,000. Second in rank is *Taifa Leo* (published by the Nation group) with 50,000. It has a six-column format and runs eight pages. *The Standard* has the lowest circulation of the three, with about 33,000. It, too, uses a six-column format, and favors large headlines on most of its 28 daily pages. But the largest-circulation newspaper (about 110,000) is the *Sunday Nation.* Like the dailies, it has a tabloid format with six columns and circus makeup; its average edition runs 36 pages.

Another Sunday paper is the *Nairobi Times,* with a circulation of about 25,000. It was started in 1977 by well-known Kenyan journalist Hilary Ng'weno and is a 12-page, nine-column broadsheet. Catering to the upper middle class with features and commentary about Kenyan life and world affairs, it also has a "Weekend Review" section with movie, record, theatre and restaurant coverage, plus sections for business items, sports scores and comic strips.

At least three weeklies are worth noting. The Nation group publishes the 12-page *Taifa* for 62,000 readers, the Standard group puts out *Baraza* ("Meeting") for a readership of 40,000. Both publications are Swahili-language tabloids, written in the vein of popular journalism and offering a variety of entertainment features for readers with lower educational levels.

Kenya's prestige weekly, published by

Hilary Ng'weno since 1975, is the *Weekly Review*. It has a circulation of only 18,000, but is considered obligatory reading for high ranking government employees and the country's opinion leadership. It is printed in an 8½x11 format and many observers say it is a newsprint version of *Time*. *Weekly Review* specializes in political commentary, in-depth analysis of current issues and general news items about African and world events. It is published in English and the average edition has 48 pages.

Although English or Swahili dominates Kenyan journalism as a lingua franca, three other languages are found among the list of weekly newspapers. *African Samachar,* with a circulation of 18,000, is published in Gujarati for the nation's Indian population. Among other languages used by weekly publications for various ethnic groups are Dholuo and Kiswahili.

8 Largest Newspapers by Circulation

Newspaper	Circulation	Frequency
Sunday Nation	108,000	Weekly
Daily Nation	95,000	Daily
Taifa Weekly	62,540	Weekly
Taifa Leo	50,481	Daily
Baraza	40,000	Weekly
The Standard	32,000	Daily
Nairobi Times	25,000	Weekly
Weekly Review	18,000	Weekly

The four top-circulation papers are all part of the Nation newspaper group. From almost any standpoint—size of staffs, capital resources, editorial influence—this publishing combine is the most influential in Kenyan journalism.

Although much smaller in size and facilities, Hilary Ng'weno's publications—*The Nairobi Times* and *Weekly Review*—are making a significant impact on Kenyan print media. They represent a new and influential force because (1) they are owned and operated by a native Kenyan instead of foreign interests, (2) they are professionally edited and are a cut above the rest of the Kenyan press in news treatment and analysis, and (3) readership is concentrated among the highly educated and affluent. Ng'weno himself is Harvard educated and part of the country's elite. His publications set a new standard of journalistic excellence for the nation.

Although Ng'weno is introducing more American concepts into newspaper layout and news coverage, the nation's press remains very British in its appearance—the result of Kenya having been a British colony-protectorate for more than 80 years before independence in 1963.

This long period of colonialism (Kenya was one of the last to become independent) instilled British journalistic traditions in a number of ways. In particular, the press was geared to the European settlers. One historian has said that local news in Kenya was based mainly on settler life and the world news was about events in or affecting Great Britain. Reporters tended to be drawn from British provincial newspapers and the editors from the bigger journalism centers. And even up to the mid-1970s, British expatriates directed the operations of the major dailies in Kenya—although their titles gradually changed from "editors" to "training officers."

The British did not forbid the development of an indigenous press among the Africans, but neither did they actively encourage it. The African press had its beginnings in the 1920s, and among the first editors was one Kamau wa Ngengi, who would become known to the world as Jomo Kenyatta, the nation's first president. He produced a monthly in the Kikuyu language.

Kenya's early vernacular press was characterized by poor reproduction, limited coverage, small circulations, internal strife and often irresponsible policies—but it also played a critical role in the development of nationalism and the pressure for independence. Indeed, African publications are often credited with generating the unrest that eventually led to the Mau Mau uprisings in the late 1940s. By 1951, the British considered this press to be seditious and dangerous—to the point that under the Emergency Declaration of 1952 the British closed at least 50 African newspapers. With only a few exceptions this meant the closing down of the entire vernacular press.

For the declaration had teeth. Among them was the Printing Presses Ordinance, which empowered the government to cancel any printing license if a publisher produced any document prejudicial to peace and good order in the colony. Police were also given the right to search property and seize any printing presses they believed to have been used in the printing of seditious documents. Another edict made it a crime to have a banned publication in one's possession. Individuals could be placed in preventive detention for long periods of time without a formal judicial hearing. (One detainee was Kenyatta, although he was given a lengthy, well publicized trial.) The result of all this was a weak indigenous press at independence, but strong and healthy press combines owned by foreign interests. Both foreign and African publishers and journalists have since prospered—together.

Economic Framework

Kenya is Black Africa's leading exponent of capitalism and free enterprise; unlike the majority of African nations, the government has refrained from nationalizing major industries and does not seem particularly attracted to the concept of socialism as a vehicle of national development.

The overall annual growth of the economy is five to six percent, with the manufacturing sector increasing at the annual rate of 13 to 14 percent. The relative stability of the government, coupled with its active solicitation of foreign investors, has made Kenya a desirable location for economic development. Tourism, energetically developed in the past 15 years, is now the nation's third largest industry, bringing in much needed foreign exchange.

Kenya's major problem in the next decade will be coping adequately with its population explosion—the percentage is one of the highest among developing nations—and the pressures such a growth will create on available jobs, food and housing. Already, the expanding population has penetrated the country's splendid national parks as farmers plow under one of the world's few remaining wildlife sanctuaries. Population is also causing widespread deforestation. Further, since Kenya must import its oil, the increased costs will have a serious effect on trade deficits.

At present, Kenya's economic stability and prosperity bodes well for the continued expansion and development of the press. Population growth will also increase readership of the popular newspapers. Improved transportation and communication links within the nation will also bring the mass media to the countryside, where most Kenyans live, while the creation of an educated upper middle class opens the door for a greater number of specialty and elite publications.

Given the nation's tilt toward free enterprise and capitalism, the press will continue to be privately owned and operated, and the government probably will not succumb to the temptation of beginning its own daily—or nationalizing present publications. Foreign investment is strongly encouraged, and the present government does not seem particularly concerned that the nation's two major publishing groups are owned by foreign interests.

Several leading Kenyan journalists, including Hilary Ng'weno, have publicly called for an end to foreign ownership, and there has been some discussion of possible joint ownership by government and the foreign interests. Another idea, under consideration in some circles, is to force the foreign companies to sell at least 51 percent of a newspaper's stock to Kenyan investors. Nationalism aside, however, the Kenyan government has not made foreign ownership of the press an issue, perhaps thinking that any such action would alarm present and potential foreign investors in other industries. (The government may also feel that it already has control of the major mass media in Kenya—radio and television.) In addition, the foreign owners of the two major newspaper groups have kept a low profile and have completely Africanized their staffs. Native Kenyans now direct the operations of the newspapers—and the owners rarely intervene in editorial policy. (But intervention does occasionally surface. George Githii, editor of the *Daily Nation,* resigned in 1977 in protest against editorial interference by the Aga Khan, the paper's principal stockholder. The latter had insisted on the publication of an article refuting Githii's editorials, which had criticized the treatment of dissenters within one of Kenya's Muslim communities.)

The only trade union representing journalists is the National Union of Journalists, directed by George Odiko. The union has very little influence since strikes are almost always illegal.

At present, Kenya's newsprint is imported, but there are no quota restrictions on any publication. Newspapers must get an import license like any other business, but no attempt is made to use the licensing structure as a club over any papers not sympathetic to the government. On the other hand, some struggling newspapers may find it difficult to afford the rising newsprint costs.

There is no direct evidence that the press is subject to advertiser influence. In many African nations, government does expend a significant amount on advertising in "friendly" publications, but government advertising in Kenya is not substantial—most advertising being placed by commercial firms.

Press Laws

The Kenyan Constitution guarantees freedom of the press. Total support of this concept, however, is qualified in other sections of the constitution that call for the print media to serve Kenya's national interests. The press is also exhorted to help in the process of nation building, and in unifying the peoples of Kenya. In fact, even government officials say the constitution tends to emphasize a "responsible press" instead of a "free press." The concept, as stated by one Kenyan diplomat, is that constructive criticism is more beneficial to the country than irresponsible reporting and the sensationalizing of minor events.

Although Kenya does have one of the freest press systems on the continent, one must attribute it to the tolerance of government and its ability to get its point of view across to editors without having to invoke any number of press laws on the books. For example, police are given the power of search and seizure; in effect, a local policeman is empowered to seize any issue of a newspaper that he thinks is in violation of the law. The government also has sweeping power to arrest and detain any citizens, including journalists, for long periods—without trial or due process. Journalists may also be arrested and detained for violating the Preservation of Security Law. Sedition and libel laws, inherited largely from the British colonial government, are subject to wide interpretation. In 1976 advocates of changing the presidential succession process were warned by Kenya's attorney general that it was a capital offense "to imagine, devise, or intend the death or disposition of President Kenyatta." Even talk of who might succeed Kenyatta was declared illegal.

As for any business operating in Kenya, registration of newspapers is required. Publishers must annually submit to the government the title of their publications, names and addresses of the owners and the average yearly circulation. The government then routinely issues a license for publication. The license can also be revoked, but there has never been a situation yet where this was done to a general circulation newspaper. On the other hand, a budding opposition political party might have difficulty receiving such a license.

The Book and Newspaper Law, passed in 1960, also requires all publishers and printers to post a bond as a hedge against any libel judgments against the publication. The amount of the bond, however, is not excessive and it does not have the effect—as it does in other countries—of limiting the number of publications or making newspaper owners engage in extreme self-regulation just to ensure that the bond is not forfeited.

Journalists in Kenya are not registered or certified. The Ministry of Information does issue press cards, but they are relatively easy to get. In fact, the Kenya Union of Journalists is concerned that too many press cards are held by people who are not bona fide newsmen. In 1978, for example, 1,500 press cards were issued—and estimates of working journalists in the country are far below that figure.

The Kenyan judiciary, on paper, is relatively independent and could be a buffer between the press and the government if the latter chose to launch an active campaign of suppression. There is judicial review of the constitutionality of legislation and edicts, but the power of the judiciary to overrule government in matters concerning the press has never been thoroughly tested. Indeed, some observers say there is no substantial body of written law or case law to protect the press against arbitrary government action.

One must remember, too, that Kenya is a de facto one-party state and most members of the judiciary are also members of the party. High-court judges are appointed for life by the president but the president can also remove a judge if he receives cabinet approval. However, while removal would not be difficult, there is no precedent in the country yet for doing so.

Censorship

It is evident that the government does have a number of ways to censor the press, but only in rare instances has it seen fit to exercise its power. If pressure is applied, it is in the shadow world of indirect action: a few well-placed calls to editors from cabinet ministers—or self-regulation by journalists who have learned how far they can go.

There is no pre-publication censorship by the Kenya government, but officials often

Most newpapers in Kenya are utilizing letterpress printing techniques, but offset is becoming more popular with the modernization of production facilities.

talk to editors about major stories before they are printed. Ultimately, however, the editors decide what will be published and what play the story will be given.

Considering the government's relatively tolerant attitude toward the press, there is no agency officially charged with monitoring the press, although the Ministry of Information, the attorney general and even the President's Office may be involved occasionally, depending on the issue. At other times, a government minister will give a major speech on the responsibilities of the press or how the press should help national development.

Kenya does have a censorship board to review imported films for morality and violence, but it is now fairly inactive, and only sexually explicit films are not allowed.

At present, there is some agitation in Kenya for the establishment of a national press council. In mid-1980 the minister of information called for such a council to monitor the press for accuracy and ethics. The council would also be given power to intervene (by censure or fines) if newspapers failed to cooperate with its recommendations.

Hilary Ng'weno, probably Kenya's leading journalist-editor, has also endorsed the concept of a national press council. He suggests that the group be made up of representatives from the legal, judicial and academic communities. In his view, "The communications council should be a watchdog whose main purpose is to improve the professional standards of communication, especially in so far as they relate to professional ethics." Ng'weno elaborated further on this in July 1980, in a speech to a workshop of the Kenya Institute for Mass Communications:

The rights that as communicators we claim to have are rights which are ours by virtue of the laws and constitutions of the countries in which we work. They are no mysteriously God-given rights which somehow belong to us as communicators independent of the system of rights and obligations which govern the activities of the other citizens.... They [journalists] can challenge the system only so long as their challenge does not lead to such a destabilising of the system that all freedoms are threatened.

State-Press Relations

Jomo Kenyatta, the country's founding father and president until his death in 1978, had very definite views about the role of the press in Kenya and the rest of Africa. In his youth, as an editor of Kikuyu nationalist publications, he saw the power of the press to inform and inspire the people. His views are illustrated by what he told the 1968 meeting of the International Press Institute in Nairobi:

The influence for good exerted by the press should be rooted here in the desire to inform and inspire the people. The press should positively promote national development and growing self-respect. And the press should always seek to coalesce, rather than to isolate, the different cultures and aspirations and standards of advancement which make up our new nation.

Kenyatta's philosophy, as an ideal, finds little disagreement from Kenyan journalists; for the most part, they do feel an obligation to make a contribution to national development and, over the years, have developed a sixth sense as to how far they can go in directly criticizing governmental policies.

Early on, for example, the press learned that it was not wise to directly criticize the leadership of Kenyatta or any programs he strongly advocated. Journalists, including foreign newsmen, also learned that it was not in their best interests to explore the many Kenyatta family business dealings that bloomed as a direct result of allegedly exploiting government connections. Even in Kenya today, these dealings (said to have included profits from poached ivory) are not subject to much journalistic probing because of reverence for Kenyatta.

At the same time, the Kenya press does explore a number of social and public issues that suggest government mismanagement or incompetence. For example, Editor Michael Kabugua of *The Standard* broke a story about grain shortages in the country. He found that government officials had exported grain reserves instead of keeping them in storage. The cabinet minister responsible was removed—but was reassigned to the Ministry of Culture.

The *Nairobi Times* regularly toes the line between exposé and sedition by covering issues dealing with income distribution, government housing policy, tribal rivalries, the economics of tourism, and unemployment among university graduates. This ability of the press to talk about kinks in the system is rare among the Black African nations—even though it is tempered with journalistic support of fundamental government policy. One gets the impression in Kenya that there is a lot of cooperation between press and state, as opposed to the strong adversary relationship of white press and white government in South Africa.

The issue of managed news is subject to some disagreement, depending on one's perspective. Many Kenyan journalists contend they are free to pursue the news as they see fit, but outside observers perceive a good deal of informal government pressure on editors. "Stern warnings" are given to the press, spelling out the limits beyond which criticism will be unacceptable. Editors are also told to be "responsible," and this is enough to keep them in line. An official statement by the Kenya News Agency (KNA) a decade ago said simply, "It is only reasonable to expect the press of any country to adopt a sympathetic... attitude and any attempt to champion causes which are not at variance with the policies and needs of the country can only be regarded as open hostility. It should not be surprising therefore if action is taken to remedy the situation."

The two major newspaper groups, being owned by foreign interests, fully realize that they can only continue to operate by not openly antagonizing the government. Given the history of what has happened to other foreign-owned papers throughout Black Africa, caution does seem a good idea, from the standpoint not only of economy but survival.

Editorial influence on government policies does take place—newspapers can and do create public pressure in cases where lower-echelon officials are incompetent or corrupt. The press can also attack government programs that are not working, especially if the government realizes this and wants to change policies anyway.

The government has not suspended or confiscated any newspapers since 1970, but there have been increasing reports since 1978 of journalists being harassed by the police and even being detained for short periods of time. A former president of the Kenyan Union of Journalists has also publicly charged in the *Nairobi Times* that police often question newsmen over materials published in their papers. Another Kenyan journalist says that the government often exerts pressure on newspapers to fire certain reporters.

The best known case of jailing is not that of a journalist but of Kenya's most celebrated novelist, Ngugi wa Thiongo (formerly James Ngugi) who was arrested in 1977 under suspicion of endangering public safety. He is the author of several novels that indirectly criticize government policies and the destruction of traditional Kenyan life by industrialization. (One, *Petals of Blood,* has been received enthusiastically in Britain and the United States.) President Kenyatta had Ngugi arrested when he tried to produce a controversial play in Kikuyu. He was later released by President Moi, but the play has yet to be produced—although it is available in print.

The government also has policies that encourage the press. Many newspapers benefit from government advertising as a form of additional revenue, and loans are available if a paper wishes to purchase new equipment. Another indirect subsidy is reduced postal rates for publications.

The government does not subsidize the import of newsprint, however, and even levies a stiff import duty on it. In addition, one must get permission from the Exchange Control Commission to order newsprint, since it involves foreign exchange. In sum, newspapers may order as much newsprint as they need if they can afford it.

Attitude Toward Foreign Media

Kenya is a hospitable environment for foreign correspondents and Nairobi is the base for more of them than any other capital in independent Black Africa. Foreign newsmen appreciate not only the tolerant press attitude of the government but the modern conveniences and relatively cool climate of Nairobi. Airline connections to other African nations or Europe are also excellent.

To work in Kenya, correspondents must be accredited by the Ministry of Information but the process is relatively easy. So too is getting visas, a procedure no different from that for tourists. Nor does a foreign correspondent have trouble cabling stories; there is no government screening or censorship.

In recent years Kenya has expelled some foreign correspondents but this is the exception, not the rule. Jomo Kenyatta was relatively tolerant of the foreign press correspondents during his presidency, but most correspondents clearly understood that unflattering stories about him would not be tolerated. Once, at a dinner, Kenyatta floored a waiter with a single punch after the man accidentally spilled soup on the president's lap. The lone correspondent present at the banquet was told that he would be on the next plane if he reported the incident.

Foreign periodicals also circulate freely in the country, particularly newsmagazines— except those from South Africa or communist countries.

News Agencies

The Kenya News Agency (KNA) is operated by the Ministry of Information and is the nation's primary national news agency. It has an exclusive contract with UPI and Reuters for the distribution of foreign news within the country. Newspapers, however, are free to utilize the services of AP or other agencies if they desire. Most publications, however, rely on KNA because it is cheaper.

A number of national news agencies have bureaus in Nairobi, including Agence France-Presse (France); Agenzia Nazionale Stampa Associata (Italy); Associated Press (United States); Ceskoslovenskai Tiskoya Kancelar (Czechoslovakia); Deutsche Presse Agentur (West Germany); Ghana News Agency; Reuters (Britain); United Press International (United States); and Tass (Soviet Union).

Kenya, like most developing nations, is somewhat sensitive to how the country and its leadership are portrayed to the rest of the world. On occasion, government officials complain that the international news agencies are not covering Kenya's economic progress and national development programs. Instead, too much news is concentrated on problems in housing, unemployment and the poaching of wild game. Officialdom also resents the perception often conveyed that the nation is one large game park, or that pictures of tribespeople represent the modern Kenya.

Electronic News Media

Although newspapers in Kenya may be commercially owned—even by foreign investors—radio and television are the exclusive province of the government. Broadcasting is under the direct control of the Ministry of Information. It has operated the Voice of Kenya (VOK) since 1964, when a statutory public corporation (modeled after the BBC) was dissolved. Given the illiteracy of the nation, and the ability of radio and television to reach millions, VOK is a powerful tool for education and propaganda. It is doubtful that commercial radio and television stations will be established in Kenya for some time to come.

Commercial advertising is accepted, but the major cost of operating broadcasting services falls on government subsidy. Both radio and television combine a number of imported entertainment programs with local programming in areas of education. One radio comedy show, started with funds from UNESCO, is a major hit and gives listeners information about family planning, health care and nutrition.

Broadcast personnel are part of Kenya's civil service and are generally selected on the basis of professional competence and ability, not political considerations. Many have received training abroad or at the University of Nairobi.

Kenyans with short-wave radios can easily listen to broadcasts from the BBC, Voice of America and Radio Moscow. The two latter conduct a lot of their programming in Swahili.

Education & Training

The University of Nairobi School of Journalism opened in 1970 as a direct result of assistance from the International Press Institute (IPI) and UNESCO. It offers a two-year diploma course in newspaper and broadcasting journalism to Kenyan and other African students. Most faculty are still British or American expatriates, but the school also receives teaching assistance from many of Kenya's leading journalists.

Another organization interested in journalism training and professionalism is the Kenya Union of Journalists. This group sponsors workshops and sets professional standards for newsmen. It also is a collective vehicle for presenting the press's viewpoint to the government.

Summary

Despite the presence of several restrictive laws on the books, Kenya probably has the freest press among the Black African states. The International Press Institute, in its 1979 report on world press freedom, simply described the Kenyan press as "stable, pragmatic, and free."

Kenya is also the only nation in independent Black Africa that has its press exclusively under private ownership, and the only nation that still allows foreign interests to own the nation's major daily newspapers.

The future of the press in Kenya remains

bright. The government, under the leadership of Daniel Arap Moi, appears relatively stable and there is a growing tradition of press freedom. This will be reinforced in coming years, as Kenyan journalists become more professional and sophisticated in walking the tightrope between the needs of national development and the people's right to be informed.

As Kenya develops a larger middle class, there will be more diversity of publications, catering to specialized interests and audiences.

CHRONOLOGY

1977   George Githii, editor of *Daily Nation,* resigns because of editorial interference from newspaper's major stockholder, Prince Karim Aga Khan IV.
Ngugi wa Thiongo, Kenyan playwright and novelist, arrested and detained under suspicion of endangering public safety; previous novels indirectly criticized government.
Hilary Ng'weno, Kenya's leading journalist, begins new quality Sunday newspaper, *Nairobi Times.*

1978   Jomo Kenyatta dies in office. Orderly transition of government follows; Vice-President Daniel Arap Moi elected president in his own right in 1979.

1979   Hilary Ng'weno calls for end of foreign newspaper ownership.

1980   Kenya Union of Journalists complains that police are increasing harassment of journalists.
Minister of Information calls for establishment of national press council; Idea endorsed by Hilary Ng'weno.

BIBLIOGRAPHY

Daily Nation. Nairobi, November 12, 1978.

Gerbner, George. *Mass Media Policies in Changing Cultures.* New York, 1977.

Hachten, William. *Muffled Drums.* Ames, Iowa, 1971.

Kenyatta, Jomo. "An Address to the International Press Institute Conference in Nairobi." *Africa Today,* June–July 1969, p. 5.

Miller, Norman. "Kenya's Nationalism and the Press, 1951–1961." Unpublished master's thesis, Indiana University, 1961.

Morrison, Donald, et al. *Black Africa: A Comparative Handbook.* New York, 1972.

Nairobi Times. August 24, 1980.

Rosenblum, Mort. *Coups and Earthquakes.* New York, 1979.

Soja, Edward W. *Communication and Change: The African Experience.* Evanston, Ill., 1970.

Sunday Nation, Nairobi, July 13, 1980; July 27, 1980.

The New York Times, February 26, 1978.

Tunstall, Jeremy. *The Media Are American.* New York, 1977.

UNESCO. *World Communications.* New York, 1975.

Wall Street Journal, October 27, 1980.

Wilcox, Dennis L. *Mass Media in Black Africa: Philosophy and Control.* New York, 1975.

SOUTH KOREA

by Jae-won Lee

BASIC DATA

Population: 37,500,000 (1980)
Area: 98,966 sq. km. (38,211 sq. mi.)
GNP: 34,560 billion won (US$57.6 billion) (1980)
Literacy Rate: 93%
Language(s): Korean
Number of Dailies: 25
   Aggregate Circulation: 6,220,000
   Circulation per 1,000: 166
Number of Nondailies: NA
   Aggregate Circulation: NA
   Circulation per 1,000: NA
Number of Periodicals: 1,423 (1979)

Number of Radio Stations: 56
Number of Television Stations: 20
Number of Radio Receivers: 14,000,000 (1980)
   Radio Receivers per 1,000: 373
Number of Television Sets: 6,270,000 (1980)
   Television Sets per 1,000: 167
Total Annual Newsprint Consumption: 225,000 metric tons (1980)
   Per Capita Newsprint Consumption: 6 kg. (13.2 lb.)
Total Newspaper Ad Receipts: 99 billion won (US$165 million)
   As % of All Ad Expenditures: 36

Background & General Characteristics

The fate of the press in the Republic of Korea (South Korea) has been closely identified with the turbulent nation-building process of the country. This was especially true during the last decade, when both the nation and its press advanced on the economic front and retreated on the political road.

In the seventies South Korea scored impressive economic successes. President Park Chung-hee engineered the nation's business structure to specialize in the production of export items, processed or assembled using imported parts and raw materials. The nation's entire energy was mobilized to boost the volume of exports. Park's single-minded drive on economic development succeeded in elevating Korea to the coveted status of an NIC (newly industrialized country) from the painful stage óf an LDC (less developed country).

During the same period the press of South Korea also made great progress in business terms. Before the seventies the press had perennially experienced financial losses. Publishers kept their papers alive not necessarily for the profits to be gained but rather for the other social advantages accruing from owning news media. In the seventies, however, no publisher of a national daily complained about business losses. The public's enhanced buying power, the increased advertising volumes, the popularity of a consumption-oriented life-style were all conducive to the steady expansion of newspaper circulation. The expansion of the media business was especially marked in the electronic sector. A television set has become standard equipment in today's Korean household, while radio is being pushed aside into the kitchen or automobile.

Politically the seventies were merely an extension of the sixties and fifties, with an oppressive regime tightening its control and leaving little room for the orderly transfer of power. The strong-willed Park did not allow any criticism of the authoritarian ways in which he ruled the country, banning the press from reporting opposition movements or critical views regarding his policies.

Despite the increased satisfaction of material needs, in the late seventies those Koreans who craved more political freedom revolted on campuses and in the countryside. A series of events of this sort eventually led to Park's assassination by his own intelligence chief in October 1979. With his violent death, any dream of a peaceful restoration of democracy was again deferred. The ensuing martial law regime deprived the press of any freedom other than that of applauding and marching in line.

In November 1980 the martial law government enacted a massive restructuring of the nations's entire media industry. All the media in Korea were affected in one way or another by this drastic action, termed "revolutionary" by one daily. The restructuring took the form of merger, elimination, creation of new outlets and consolidation of related media; it also modified the structure by which national dailies reported on local news.

Despite this government-initiated action, the media did not (or, to be precise, could not) print or air even a faint complaint. Instead the restructuring had to be reported as "voluntary" to demonstrate the media's loyalty to the spirit of the "New Era," a key slogan of the new government.

The eventful year 1980 ended with the passage of a new press law, designed to "enhance press freedom and secure press responsibility," by the temporary National Assembly, a legislative organ of the martial law government. During the preceding summer, a fair number of "dissident" or "impure" journalists were expelled from the profession.

It would be a mistake to regard the government as the sole source of all the problems and troubles involving the media. In several instances the government responded to public outcries against, or professional criticism of, excessively commercialized media activities and the corrupt practices of some journalists.

The present unhappy relationship between the press and the government has a long history, though different in causes and intensity at different times. Nevertheless, the present situation involving Korea's press is all the more regrettable when compared to the splendid cultural history in which Koreans take pride.

Koreans invented and used movable metal type, the initial technology for a modern press, as early as 1241 A.D. in the publication of Yi Kyu-bo's (1168–1241) 28-volume *Sangjong Yemun*. The oldest remaining book so printed in Korea dates back to 1377, some 70 years before Gutenberg's use of movable type. In the early years of the Yi Dynasty (1392–1910) printing books with movable type became prevalent due to the court's interest in spreading Confucian classics and historical literature. A government foundry was established in 1403 to back up the work of the "department of books" in the court.

In 1443 scholars for the fourth monarch of the dynasty, King Sejong, invented Korea's own phonetic system of writing, "Hangul." The king, in promulgating the system, reasoned that the average citizen needed a simple writing system, easy to use in expressing opinions and thoughts. The invention of a Korean alphabet, a remarkable achievement in Korea's cultural history, might have liberated Koreans from the yoke of Chinese ideographs. However, the erudite ruling class of the dynasty preferred using the complex Chinese letters and frowned upon Hangul, calling it "lesser language."

The continued use of Chinese ideographs in writing was in part responsible for the eventual demise of Korea's early printing technology using movable metal type. The thousands and thousands of Chinese letters needed in printing ideographs made woodblock printing the more economically feasible mode. Thus, Hangul and movable metal type, both invented early in Korea's history, were not accorded a chance to lead Korea's culture during the next centuries.

During the dynasty years a form of court newsletter, called "Chobo," circulated for officials in the countryside, but it did not develop into a regular newsletter for the public. The weak economic base of the society, rule by a small aristocracy, the traditional reverence for Chinese influences, and the closed-door policy maintained by the dynasty all worked against the beginning of mass media at that time.

In the last decades of the dynasty, Korea awoke to the need to enlighten the masses to modernize the country and keep up with foreign nations. Groups of court officials were dispatched to Japan, which had begun to modernize, with an assignment to learn "new knowledge" and new measures necessary to keep the shaky and isolated kingdom alive. In earlier centuries Japanese had often received the superior Chinese culture via Koreans; in the 1880s the superior culture came from the West and it was Japan that transmitted it to Korea.

One of the important lessons the Korean missions obtained from the Japanese was the realization that they needed to publish newspapers. The delegates sent to Japan in 1883 returned home with a Japanese newspaper reporter and several printers. The idea of publishing newspapers for the masses, however, was a bitter pill to swallow for a dominant faction in the Korean court, which still preferred the authoritarian and elitist traditional mode of thinking. The court, nonetheless, created the bureau of publication, "Pangmun-guk," immediately.

This government bureau published Korea's first modern newspaper, *Hansong Sunbo*, in 1883. It was supposedly a government organ issued three times a month, but it also carried news on a variety of subjects, even listing the prevailing prices of major commodities. It was written in Chinese letters only, and bureau officials constituted the staff. The paper terminated publishing after a year or so because a faction in the court rebelled against this "radical" social experiment.

The government tried publishing a weekly, *Hansong Chubo*, two years later, in 1886. This weekly lasted for two and a half years. It was notable for its combined use of Chinese letters and the Korean alphabet in its news writing.

The next important development was the publication of *Tongnip Shinmun* ("The Independent") in 1896. This was a three-times-a-week publication owned and edited by an American-educated Korean. Korean journalists and news media annually observe April 7, the date of the paper's founding, as Newspaper Day. The honor and respect accorded to that particular paper recognizes its pivotal importance in modern Korean journalism: it was the first privately owned paper; it used Korean only; its editorial stance was independent.

Tongnip Shinmun became a daily in 1898 after another newspaper, *Maeil Shinmun*, emerged as Korea's first daily three months before. These papers and others published at that time did not print more than 3,000 copies each and did not last for more than a few years. Their short life span was primarily due to the relatively weak financial bases of the papers. Nonetheless, newspapers flourished in number. In 1910 22 dailies were being published. The newspaper was becoming an indispensable part of the society.

The role Korean papers played in this early period was that of social reformer and innovation. Changing a society that had been closed for centuries meant opening the society to Western knowledge. Foreign-educated Koreans and those who had exposed themselves to the world outside played key roles in journalism. Also significant at this time was the contribution made by foreign mission-

aries, especially those from the United States. In the 1880s American missionaries opened Korea's first modern schools, educating many youths who later became leaders in various sectors of the society, including journalism.

The new culture flowing into Korea this way, however, threatened the traditional social structure of Korea and the power base of the Yi Dynasty. Factional strife over the merits or demerits of the open-door policy intensified in the court. While Korea was opening its eyes to a broader world, China tried to continue wielding its traditional influence on Korea. Russia was developing a taste for this land, too.

It was Japan, the emerging Asian power, that succeeded. After defeating Russia in the Russo-Japanese War (1904-05), Japan put Korea under its "protection" in 1905 and finally ended the Korean dynasty in 1910 by colonizing the Korean peninsula.

Korean newspapers and Korea itself suffered during Japanese colonial rule (1910–45). Japan tried to replace Korea's culture with the Japanese one during the colonial rule. Japanese was made the official language. The authorities approved publication of only a few Korean newspapers, and controlled those few with stringent prepublication censorship. In 1940 the colonial rulers chose to close down the two leading nationalistic papers, *Dong-A Ilbo* and *Chosun Ilbo*. During its 20 years of existence *Dong-A Ilbo* had suffered temporary closings on four occasions; confiscation of copies 489 times; sales bans 63 times; and the killing of editorial items, 2,423 times. Arrest, imprisonment, persecution and terrorization of journalists were commonplace as well.

Korean newspapers were an important medium of Korean independence movements. Many independence fighters at one time or another in their lives worked in the press. There they kept their patriotic desire alive and tried to spread it to the public. The papers continued playing the role of social reformers in the belief that their nation had been taken over by the Japanese mainly because of old social structure and outdated mores. Additionally, the papers developed the role of champions fighting against an unjust government and for Korea's national cause, its independence.

The political ideology implicit in the roles the early Korean newspapers played was libertarian democracy, the roots of which were imported from the West. With Japan's defeat in World War II, Korea was liberated in 1945 and its independent government established in 1948. Article 1 of the Constitution declared: "The Republic of Korea is a democratic republic." It contained an additional paragraph: "The sovereignty of the Republic of Korea shall reside in the people, and all state authority shall emanate from the people."

In practice, however, the republic has usually been less than democratic, and state authority has resided more often than not in the rulers themselves. Thus the libertarian democratic press and the authoritarian governments have often been on a collision course.

The Korean press has been resilient in its fight against governmental interference. Its fighting spirit grows out of its tradition of resistance against the unjust colonial government of the Japanese, and from the influence of Western press practices, especially American. Ever since her liberation from Japan, Korea has maintained special ties with the United States for security and economic reasons. It was only natural for the Korean press to adopt the press system of the United States as a role model. Promising journalists have been trained in or exposed to American media practices and ideals.

The ideological orientation of the Korean press toward the role of watchdog and critic has never been appreciated by Korea's governments. Government's response has been direct or indirect control of the press in various forms. As is typical in authoritarian press systems, the press enjoyed only those freedoms the governments allowed it to have, in implicitly and explicitly defined areas.

In the seventies owners of the press found an expedient solution to the recurrent clashes with the government—they concentrated business expansion. Korean society was rapidly expanding industrially, and commercialism was the safest policy the press could pursue without inviting interference from the government. A trend of sensationalism and an emphasis on soft-news items were evident in media's handling of contents. The press also began providing consumer-oriented news in abundance.

The business success of the daily newspapers was most evident in their circulations. The aggregate total circulation in 1970 was about 2.94 million copies a day; there were 44 dailies at that time. The number of dailies declined from that to 37 in 1975 and to 25 in 1980. But at the same time, the size of the aggregate circulation doubled to 5.87 million copies in 1975 and rose to an estimated 6.22 million in 1980.

The primary factors conducive to this rapid growth were the economic and business conditions of Korean society in general. Next to them in importance would be the availability of a highly literate audience; a recent UNESCO publication lists Korea's literacy rate as of 1980 at 92.7 percent (97.5 percent for males and 87.9 percent for females). Also significant is the linguistic and racial homogeneity of Koreans, a factor that makes the job of the newspapers far easier than in a multilingual society.

Estimated Circulations of Dailies in Various Categories (December 1980)		
Categories	Circulations	%
6 national	4,221,000	67.0
9 specialized	965,000	15.5
10 local	1,029,800	16.6
25 dailies	6,215,800	100.0

Auditing of circulation sizes is not practiced in Korea, hence the papers tend to inflate their circulation figures in any public announcements. This bragging is accepted as a routine practice in the highly competitive newspaper industry. The figures in the circulation table are based on independent assesments from various sources in the publishing industry, not on individual claims. Some 10 percent to 15 percent are acknowledged to be free promotional copies, so the sizes of paid circulation should be smaller by that margin.

National dailies dominate Korea's newspaper industry. The six national dailies and the nine specialized dailies are all published in Seoul, the capital city. Since major parts of the country can be reached within six hours of transportation time from Seoul, the newspapers published in Seoul are delivered on the date of issue even in the countryside. In the provincial areas, those who are interested in public affairs usually subscribe to a national paper and a local.

Korea is a country oriented toward centralized government, with a minimal level of autonomy allowed to local provinces. The capital city is literally a special part of the country, critical to the working of the whole nation. Its population is huge, 8.37 million according to the 1980 census. Roughly one out of every four Koreans lives in Seoul. Seoul also is the center of almost everything conceivable in Korea—political, economic, sociocultural and educational. Psychologically, too, the residents of Seoul tend to feel superior to those in the countryside. This attitude is unconsciously perpetuated by Korea's media through their editorial orientation, rooted in the capital city. Media contents often ignore the fact that three out of every four Koreans live outside Seoul.

Local dailies are underdeveloped and qualitatively inferior to national dailies. Yet the papers published in Pusan and Taegu, the two provincial cities with several million people, made qualitative improvements in the seventies. They are exceptional cases in the group of 10 local dailies.

In early 1981, the 25 daily newspapers published in Korea—six national, 10 local and nine specialized—were all privately owned, though three of them are known to have special ties with the government. Three of the six national dailies are morning papers, and the other three are evening papers. They publish six days a week, taking Monday off.

Of the six national dailies, three announced they had reached the mark of one million copies a day late in the seventies. Their actual sizes of circulations, however, are considered to in the 800,000 to 950,000 range. These are *Chosun Ilbo, Dong-A Ilbo* and *Joong-ang Ilbo*. The remaining three—*Hankook Ilbo, Kyunghyang Shinmoon* and *Seoul Shinmun*—boast of publishing more than 500,000 copies a day each. These six national dailies, especially the first four listed above, are all recognized as Korea's prestige newspapers, and hence are engaged in fierce competition.

The *Chosun Ilbo* is considered the most influential quality paper of Korea. Its editorials show a measure of independence, and

its columns and news analyses present thoughtful reading material. For its intellectual orientation, it has clearly become the favorite of the educated and those who are serious-minded about public affairs. This qualitative strength is not a small achievement in a situation where the government applies visible and invisible pressures against the press to make its views prevail.

Up until the seventies *Chosun* was second to the *Dong-A Ilbo* in terms of prestige and influence. *Dong-A*'s pronounced opposition stance attracted intensive governmental interference in the seventies; this interference took an extensive range of harassment—jailing of reporters, summoning of editors, threatening of advertisers and so on. *Dong-A* was thus systematically shorn of its traditional characteristics, and has now become a newspaper with only a name to remind one of the glories and courage of its past days. The columns of biting criticism and the scrupulous sense of justice that once marked its personality are not there. Yet its faithful readers did not desert it in number; rather, they anticipate a time when *Dong-A* will be allowed to regain its editorial excellence.

Two relatively young newspapers have successfully solidified their positions in the competitive prestige circle of dailies; *Joong-ang Ilbo* and *Hankook Ilbo*. *Joong-ang*, founded in 1965, has succeeded in making itself a mass appeal paper by specializing in reader-oriented news and editorial matters. It is somewhat less elitist than *Chosun* and *Dong-A*. In its single-minded drive to increase circulation it has benefited from its affiliation with one of Korea's top business conglomerates, the Samsung Group.

The other young newspaper, *Hankook*, is noted for its editorial appeal to the young and the modern. Founded in 1954, *Hankook* became a legend in the Korean newspaper industry, especially for its energetic founder publisher, Chang Key-young. Chang personified *Hankook* by involving himself in every phase of its operation—he even supervised his truck drivers when he felt the newspaper delivery was not executed fast enough. *Hankook* began showing a halt in its rising readership in the mid-sixties when Chang joined the government as deputy premier. From then on its readers began suspecting a softening of its editorial independence, and symptoms of bias in favor of the government.

The remaining two general dailies of Seoul, *Kyunghyang Shinmoon* and *Seoul Shinmun*, do not share the prestige of the four men-

10 Largest Daily Newspapers by Circulation (December 1980)	
Chosun Ilbo (Seoul)	925,000
Dong-A Ilbo (Seoul)	891,000
Joong-ang Ilbo (Seoul)	837,000
Hankook Ilbo (Seoul)	628,000
Kyunghyang Shinmoon (Seoul)	525,000
Seoul Shinmun (Seoul)	415,000
Daily Sports (Seoul)	335,000
Pusan Ilbo (Pusan)	300,000
Maeil Shinmun (Taegu)	300,000
Maeil Kyungje Shinmun (Seoul)	150,000

tioned above. They survive through their affiliation with the government. *Seoul* is a government organ, carrying full texts of government policies and decisions. It is must reading for government employees and businessmen as well. *Kyunghyang* has emerged as the ideological advocate of the government. Its editorial position is usually one octave above that of other papers in favoring the government. It reads like a part of the government's political campaigns.

Though they are dwarfed by the national dailies, the 10 local papers are making a steady improvement in quality and in size of circulations. Except for Seoul, there is no town with competing newspapers. In the 1980 restructuring of the nation's media system, the government persuaded four competing papers in the countryside to merge with officially chosen papers so that the country's nine provinces and a special district, Pusan, came to have only one paper each.

The two most successful local dailies, *Pusan Ilbo* and *Maeil Shinmun,* publish around 300,000 copies a day each. They are likely to grow faster in the years ahead because their cities, Pusan and Taegu, are fast-growing metropolitan areas with no competing newspapers. The eight other local dailies are rather modest in circulation—one publishes about 150,000 copies, six enjoy a circulation between 50,000 and 25,000, and the smallest is under 20,000.

A third group of daily newspapers, the nine specialized papers, includes the *Daily Sports* (335,000 copies) and two business dailies, *Korea Economic Daily* and *Maeil Kyungje Shinmun,* each publishing about 100,000 to 150,000 copies a day. Also to be noted as specialized papers are three children's dailies, very popular in Korea's elementary and junior high school grades. These dailies for children, each enjoying a circulation of some 100,000 copies, provide extra homework and study materials related to respective school curricula as well as major news of the day tailored to children's reading levels. These papers print school news, too, provided by a large pool of student reporters from across the country.

Korea has three foreign-language dailies: two in English (*The Korea Times* and *The Korea Herald*) and one in Chinese (*Hanjung Ilbo*). Their circulations are limited to a range between 20,000 to 50,000, respectively, but they serve their relevant communities as vital sources of daily news. In the case of the English dailies, both Korean owned, roughly half of their subscribers are Koreans—mostly college students who study current English or intellectuals who want to read foreign news and syndicated columns in the original version. The *Herald* maintains a close tie with the government and thus reflects government's views in its news reporting and editorials. It reads like an English version of the *Seoul Shinmun,* the Korean-language daily acting as government's organ. The *Times* is being published as a sister paper of the *Hankook Ilbo.* It exercises an independent editorial course in its political leaning, thus becoming the favorite of critically minded foreign residents in Korea.

By and large Korea's newspapers, especially those published in Seoul, are quality papers with an elitist slant. They put a high premium on hard-news reporting, and search out contributions from experts, professionals and scholars. They fill their pages with an extensive range of subject matter—international, national and local—and cover a variety of subject areas—political, economic, societal and cultural. Ads occupy roughly one-third of the total space.

The length of each daily was eight pages, through December 1980. The number of pages increased to 12 beginning in January 1981. The space available for editorial matter is still considered scarce and competitive, owing to the rapidly growing volume of information generated by the industrializing society of Korea. Reporters and editors have developed various techniques for packing the pages with highly condensed and abbreviated forms of expressions. They also enjoy the influence accruing from the growing number of publicity seekers competing for space.

The editorial fare of a typical daily issue generally follows the same pattern: p. 1—major news, international, national and local; p. 2—follow-up stories, analysis pieces and editorials; p. 3—foreign news at large; p. 4—business, economy and economic indicators; p. 5—special contributions and in-depth reports on select subjects; p. 6—literature, arts, serial fiction and letters; p. 7—women, family, living and serial fiction; p. 8—select subject area of the day, such as science, health or education; p. 9—sports and hobbies; p. 10—metropolitan and local news; p. 11—another local page; and p. 12—entertainment (movies, travel, television program listings and so on). On each page, ads on the bottom are separated from editorial matter on the top. The newspaper format is standard broadsheet size.

Weekly and monthly magazines published by major national dailies command sizable circulations and influence. Weeklies, however, focus on sensational news events, tending to exploit the private lives of popular actresses and television celebrities. The monthlies are quality general magazines, directed toward ideas, issues and perspectives, as is evident in the *Shin Dong-A, Monthly Chosun* and *Monthly Joong-ang*.

Some other weeklies put out by less-known publishers had been excessively sensationalistic and often less than responsible in their exposé reporting. Scores of them were closed down by the martial law government in 1980 in the wake of its "cleanup campaign." This same campaign also killed several well-respected journals of opinion, an endangered species in today's Korea, including such magazines as *Literature and the Intellect* and *The Deep-Rooted Tree*. With the death of such journals, the periodicals specializing in social criticism and political advocacy have disappeared from Korea.

The preeminence enjoyed by the national dailies is in part attributable to the absence of general weekly newspapers in Korea. Instead there are numerous specialized weeklies serving a respective organization or institution. One example is the host of college campus newspapers. Because student movements have been a part of Korean politics, these student papers attract close attention from the government.

In business terms, there does not appear to be a major roadblock to further growth of the newspaper industry in the decade ahead. Domestic production of newsprint is more than adequate to meet the demand from the newspaper industry. Further, Koreans remain avid readers of newspapers; newspaper reading is such a norm and necessity that, for instance, government officials often read them even during office hours, using office copies.

At the same time, Korea's newspapers still maintain their traditional pace-setting role in news reporting. In today's newspapers, most of the nationally significant news items read like the original copies of official government announcements. Yet most Koreans continue taking news seriously, often practicing the art of reading news between the lines. In Korea, scanning the environment has been a practical necessity for survival and hence a fact of life. It is a behavior acquired through a lengthy period of political instability amid external threats that challenge the security of the country. Newspapers, whether credible or not, have to be read meticulously. This may guarantee a further expansion of Korea's newspaper industry.

Economic Framework

Korea's economy has been one of the fastest growing in the world. Per capita income jumped from a miserable $250 in 1970 to a decent $1,508 in 1980. The comparable volumes of export earnings were from $835 million to $17.5 billion, a 21-fold increase in 10 years. Korea's economy slumped in 1980, but it appeared to be a temporary slowdown caused in part by domestic political instabilities.

The one obvious benefit of the November 1980 restructuring of media organizations has been a solidified financial footing for the surviving consolidated media industries. When seen from a financial point of view, the

Per-Media Shares of Industry Advertising						
Year	Newspaper	Magazine	Radio	TV	Misc.	Total spending*
1970	46.8%	6.5%	20.6%	14.1%	12.0%	12.73
1972	35.9	7.7	15.6	24.6	16.2	19.02
1974	32.0	4.5	22.9	34.5	6.1	43.00
1976	33.7	3.8	15.8	32.5	14.2	93.50
1978	33.8	3.4	12.5	32.1	18.2	169.95
1980	35.9	3.9	12.5	29.8	17.8	275.25

*Note: Korean "won" in billion.
Sources: Lee Hwan-ey, *Mass Com Management* (Seoul, 1980), p. 82; *Dong-A Ilbo*, Feb. 14, 1981, p. 2, for the data on 1980, compiled by The First Advertising Agency of Seoul.

drastic restructuring appears likely to transform the media industries into sound businesses. The surviving national dailies—only one national daily, the weakest one, was closed down in 1980—are competitive and doing very well in promoting their circulation. They diversify their revenue sources by publishing various periodicals.

Total advertising volume has been increasing steadily, even during the economically difficult year 1980. The newspaper medium has fared very well in its competition for a share of advertising. In fact, its shares of advertising revenue showed a steady rising trend after the mid-seventies. In Korea's newspaper industries, the subscription fees still contribute the bigger proportion of revenues, about 60 percent, to a newspaper's total earnings. They have yet to tap earnings from classified advertising, a source not fully developed in Korea.

Up until the early seventies, Korea's newspapers and other news media were notorious for their low salaries for reporters. The poorly paid reporters were vulnerable to external pressures and to payoffs from agencies and others with vested interests. At a news beat the press corps would demand unofficial subsidies from the very office covered. Underpaid reporters in the provincial cities plagued honest citizens and government officials with threats and extortions.

Beginning in the mid-seventies owners began raising the salary for their employees at a rapid rate, in part to prevent trained journalists from being lured away by expanding businesses and other well-paying organizations. The situation in the countryside also improved, though at a slower pace than in Seoul. A reporter at a national daily, with five years of experience, is now paid a salary comparable to a medium-level industry executive.

The majority of journalists have high ethical standards and view the unprofessional activities of some of their colleagues as a disgrace to the profession. Yet receiving payoffs has been a habitual practice with certain reporters for many years. Whether paid enough or not, some journalists may find it very hard to shun the lure of corruption as long as there are agencies and persons willing to buy publicity and favorable treatment in news reports. Increasing the news hole in newspapers would help remedy this shameful aspect of Korean journalism.

The news media as a whole had a total of 18,703 employees as of January 1980, according to a survey reported by the *Korean Press & Broadcasting Annual 1980*. Newspapers employed 54.6 percent (10,210) of the total, broadcasting companies 37.8 percent (7,065), and news agencies 7.6 percent (1,428). Of the newspaper employees, executives accounted for 1.7 percent; editorial personnel, 30.2 percent; advertising-circulation, 14.9 percent; management-planning, 21.8 percent; production staff, 21.4 percent; miscellaneous jobs, 10.0 percent. Female employees constituted 10 percent of total media employment, 8.3 percent of newspaper staffs and 6.1 percent of editorial personnel in newspapers.

One factor impeding the speedy expansion of the newspaper industry is its antiquated production system, especially the typesetting procedure. Type is still set by hand. Newspapers insist on using Chinese characters in conjunction with the Korean script, Hangul. Chinese ideographs are now used in less than 10 percent of news content, but they are usually used for key words and frequently in headlines.

Korea's newspapers, like the Japanese, run texts in vertical column lines progressing from the right-hand side to the left. This was the time-honored way of writing in Chinese. However, the new generation is being taught with horizontally written texts in school. These young people do not have zeal for learning Chinese letters, so newspaper reading is a task for many of them. Typesetting, language and format—innovations in these areas remain a challenge to Korean newspapers as they enter the information age.

Press Laws, Censorship & State-Press Relations

The Korean press has been constrained by the government in one way or another ever since the seventies. Reporters have periodically protested against various forms of governmental interference, especially against the visible and invisible presence of intelligence agents in and around the newsrooms. Relations between the press and the government were like a never-ending tug of war, which occasionally reached the boiling point. Owners of the press generally preferred expediency, and acted as a buffer.

In the early seventies Korean politics were unstable at best. The fall of South Vietnam alarmed President Park Chung-hee and drove him to tighten his rule and revise the constitution for his reelection. His measures did not bring the intended domestic stability but rather a series of protests from the opposition, college students and intellectuals. The press, in the course of covering such events and issues, was harassed as an ally of the opposition movement. President Park began issuing "presidential emergency decrees," the most notable of which was the ninth, proclaimed in May 1975.

Presidential Emergency Decree No. 9 banned the press from "negating" or "opposing" the new constitution and also from "advocating its revision or abolition." The teeth of this decree lay in its additional stipulation that no one could criticize the decree itself. How many journalists were tried for violation of this decree is not publicly known, though at one point eight persons released from jail in 1979 and 1980 were identified as former journalists convicted in relation to the decree. The real force of this decree, however, lay in its effectiveness in controlling and intimidating the press, reducing the range of freedom in reporting and preventing the press from freely exercising its function of criticism.

The decree was abolished in December 1979 by the martial law government in the wake of President Park's assassination in October 1979. Lifting the decree was not very meaningful; the press was already under military censorship. The military censorship of the press continued through January 1981, when martial law was lifted.

Censorship of the press during a time of martial law is not a surprise in itself. Yet this martial law period, October 1979 to January 1981, proved to be a very significant chapter in the relations between the government and the press. The government used the press for its purposes or, to borrow a key slogan of the government, as "participants in the construction of a new era." The government's use of the private press was so extensive and intensive that it may leave a lasting scar on the concept of press independence in Korea. It also caused irremediable injuries to the conscience of those professional journalists who had been subjected to this treatment.

The use of the press, first, took the form of news management and distortion. The government dictated to the press how to write important items, and where to run them. Deletion of certain words or paragraphs was enough to distort incoming foreign news, and the press was forced to print such contextually distorted stories.

Second, the government used the press as a medium of propaganda. Passive reporting was not tolerated on key policies and important issues—the press was directed to stage a series of campaigns in the news and editorial columns, and often exemplary master copies of articles were given to the press. Such subjects were often related to strengthening the legitimacy of the new government and building up a favorable public image of its leadership.

Reporters did not always accept these government dictates quietly. Even under the threat of martial law, in the spring of 1980 groups of reporters at national dailies staged sit-in demonstrations inside their newsrooms. Their leaders were expelled from their jobs the following summer when the government conducted a massive "cleanup campaign" across major sectors of the society. From the press alone, some 100 to 400 employees were estimated to have been dismissed in the campaign. However, this toll did include some journalists who had been suspected of unethical practices.

Korea's reporters had staged a bigger wave of protests during 1974–75. A group of 180 reporters at the *Dong-A Ilbo* adopted a "declaration" in which they demanded that freedom and independence be allowed in media production. This movement spread throughout the country and resulted in the adoption of similar resolutions by reporters' groups at 29 other media organizations. In response to this declaration *Dong-A*'s management censured 133 of its employees, and the *Chosun Ilbo* 76. The government was not idle, either. *Dong-A* suffered a massive boycott by advertisers, presumably instigated by the government, beginning in late December 1974 and extending through early 1975.

In dealing with "targeted" journalists, the government prefers to use indirect methods of control rather than arrest and trial in open court. Indirect methods are less visible; they include temporary detention for investigation, harassment and threats. Agencies engaging in this control include the national police, the Korean CIA and certain military intelligence units. These activities are legitimized by relevant laws such as the National Security Act, the Anti-Communist Law and several procedural laws relevant to protecting military information.

Newspapers are registered with the government through the Ministry of Culture and Information upon satisfying a legally set, minimum level of facilities and assets. This ministry coordinates government information for the press, and its head acts as a government spokesman. After the lifting of the martial law in January 1981, formal censorship was not practiced anymore, except with incoming foreign publications. The government instead handed the press a "guideline for voluntary cooperation on reporting," in which it asked the press to refrain from raising questions on various measures taken by the previous martial law government. The guideline also asked the press to portray the "positive prospects" for the nation's economy "even if the condition really looked pessimistic." Even though the press is not officially censored, its performance is being monitored by a newly organized agency at the ministry, the "Publicity Coordination Office."

Also in January 1981, the government enacted a new press law giving provisions for reporters' access to information sources and for newsmen's privilege on confidentiality. A more significant feature of the law, however, is that it makes "press responsibility" a legal requirement. This unique element of the law is in accordance with a new constitutional requirement (second paragraph, Article 20, Korea's Constitution):

> Neither speech nor the press shall violate the honor or rights of other persons nor undermine public morals or social ethics. Should speech or the press violate the honor or rights of other persons, claims may be made for the damage resulting therefrom.

The president's honor is already protected by an existing law designed to prevent "crimes committed to defame the Chief Executive."

How the provisions in the Constitution and the Press Law will work in reality remains to be tested in the courts.

The version of "press responsibility" enforced by censors earlier had resulted in public's questioning of media credibility. Rumors were enjoying such a truth value that some cynics called them UPI, the "unofficial public information." A "responsible" press could have quelled the rumors; when the press was not free to do so, the government itself was hurt. During the martial law period, the government on several occasions had to publicly identify rumors, thereby only spreading them farther.

Attitude Toward Foreign Media

In early 1981 there were about 75 resident correspondents in Korea, representing some 50 foreign news media. About 20 of the 75 correspondents were foreigners and the rest Koreans. About half of them were considered active, full-time reporters. Their news media included major wire services of the West (AP, UPI, Reuters, AFP and Kyodo), major daily newspapers of Japan, and other news organizations from the rest of Asia. They either have bureaus, under approval from the government, or merely resident correspondents, who submit credentials to the government.

In news gathering and reporting, foreign correspondents enjoy the same degree of freedom, whatever it is, as do Korea's domestic media personnel at any given time. They are not placed under any special constraint; there is no official censorship of their outgoing stories. The government agency relevant to their activities is the Ministry of Culture and Information, especially its Korean Overseas Information Services.

The Korean government uses persuasion in dealing with foreign reporters. It briefs them on important news developments. Its officials phone them to emphasize government views on certain news events. The government, however, checks their reporting through feedback—by checking the stories written by them and printed by their home media. The home media often create headaches by printing stories developed by nonresident staff from non-Korean sources; stories on North Korea and analysis items negative to or critical of Korea's incumbent leadership fall into that category. The ultimate government solution for dealing with "hostile" or "undesirable" correspondents involves withdrawing its approval of bureaus or denying the extension of visas. Such drastic measures have rarely been taken, except in several cases involving Japanese media.

The ups and downs in the relations between Korea and Japan are largely attributable to the Korean government's retaliation against Japanese media. Stories compiled by some Japanese correspondents had been judged by the government as "distorted" or "malicious." Such correspondents were ordered to leave Korea within a few days, and their bureaus were closed down for a certain period. The two Japanese papers, *Mainichi Shimbun* and *Asahi Shimbun,* experienced such measures in 1979 and 1980, respectively.

There is an import restriction placed on foreign publications. The quota system is justified officially as being necessary to save the foreign exchange reserve; in reality the government's implicit policy is to curb an increase in the domestic circulation of certain foreign publications. *Time* (25,000 copies) and *Newsweek* (20,000 copies) are popular among Korean readers. High subscription costs are an additional factor explaining the small circulations of such foreign dailies as *The New York Times* (50 copies), *The Washington Post* (50 copies) and *The Wall Street Journal* (40 copies).

By law, foreign nationals are not allowed to own and operate news media in Korea. An exception is the U.S. military-run broadcasting system, AFKN (American Forces Korean Network). AFKN started its operation in the first year of the Korean War, 1950. It began television broadcasting in 1957, and has an AM radio and FM services. It covers the whole nation, and treats the American servicemen as its primary audience. Its report or transmission of news on U.S. affairs is efficient and up to the minute; for instance, AFKN-TV broadcast the 1980 presidential debate live in color.

AFKN also plays a fringe role, minor but significant, for some Koreans. To Korean students learning English, AFKN is an instructional medium; to Koreans who have returned from the United States, it is an information medium. AFKN also is generally recognized for its fast delivery of pop tunes for the younger generation. Yet its reporting on Korean affairs is minimal; even though its headquarters is situated in Seoul, AFKN usually reports news on Korea from wire service stories dispatched from Tokyo.

In principle, the Korean National Commission for UNESCO takes the position that the Third World complaints on international news flows are valid and legitimate. In practice, Korea does not play a significant role on the issue and has not yet developed a coherent national policy toward it. This inaction is in part due to a failure to coordinate various governmental agencies to work on the issue. It also is related to the status of Korea's domestic media; the Korean government is not in a proud position to make gripes about foreign media at the UNESCO level while its own media have been put under various forms of control.

News Agencies

News services were plentiful in Korea until 1980. There were six major agencies, all privately owned. Their activities, however, were mainly supplementary because major dailies all had their own networks of reporters throughout the country. Major dailies also maintained their own correspondents abroad in major capital cities such as Washington, D.C., Tokyo, Taipei, London and Paris. The activities of Korea's domestic news services were therefore redundant except for the function of receiving news from world wire services. Most of the six services were unstable.

In November 1980 the government forced them to merge into a single organization, the Yonhap News Agency. It is a cooperative agency; the previous Haptong and Tongyang services hold 49 percent of its stock and newspapers and electronic media own 51 percent. In the 1980 action the government also banned Seoul dailies from stationing resident correspondents in the countryside and prevented local dailies from keeping full-time correspondents in the capital city. In theory this action was taken in the belief that Yonhap could fully function as a domestic agent and develop as a viable news agency. The measure also was designed to eliminate redundant local reporters who had been paid meagerly and hence resorted to various unprofessional activities.

Yonhap is now functioning as the sole domestic news agency in Korea, feeding foreign news from world wire services to domestic media and distributing domestic news between Seoul and provincial cities. It receives news from AP, UPI, Reuters, AFP, Kyodo and some 20 other agencies in Asia and Middle East. It maintains its correspondents abroad in seven major capitals of the world. It is manned by some 600 staff members, an overstaffed situation resulting from the government's decision that it should absorb all the employees of the six defunct agencies.

As of early 1981 the agency had not yet worked out an efficient organizational structure. It is tentatively structured with eight departments, the two key offices being the news department (for domestic news and incoming foreign news) and the international services (for news to be transmitted abroad). One function that could be effectively executed by Yonhap is transmission of Korea's domestic news abroad, yet its activity in this area was minimal during 1981. Its international services department is manned by only 10 reporters, who translate a limited number of domestic news items into English for transmission to a limited number of foreign clients. Yonhap also provides translated versions of foreign wire stories to domestic media. Major media, especially the national dailies, receive the original versions of foreign news; domestic media save time by using Yonhap's translated stories.

The government is very sensitive to the kinds of foreign news transmitted by the world's major wire services. Items under scrutiny include stories on North Korea or those that can be construed as putting Korea as a whole or political leaders in particular in a negative light. Yonhap sorts them out, or in translation edits them along an assumed line of "safety." Domestic media can feel "safe" in using such edited translations on their pages; they assume that Yonhap has exercised the necessary care in translating sensitive items.

Yonhap is less than one year old at the time of this writing. It promises to become an efficient national news agency, owing to the major structural changes in Korea's media system that favor its growth. This positive prospect will be realized only if the government does not meddle with its operation, using it as a tool for news control or as a medium through which it can manipulate news from abroad.

Naewoe Press is a minor domestic news agency operating in Korea, though not as a competitor to Yonhap. It specializes in providing news on the Communist bloc, especially North Korea. Its news is often attributed to radio monitoring, but only government intelligence agencies are expected to monitor North Korean radio transmissions. Naewoe is thus recognized as a government apparatus, and most dailies carry a small boxed story listing Naewoe-provided news bits. Such news items attract some interest because to South Koreans they are the only daily news available on North Korean happenings.

Electronic Media

Broadcasting in Korea began in 1927 with a radio station in Seoul. Through 1980 it grew to five major networks, led by the largest, the state-run Korea Broadcasting System (KBS). KBS had 16 regional bureaus and relay stations, through which it reached virtually the whole nation. It started its television broadcasting in 1961, and it became in name a public corporation in 1973. Next in size was the Moonhwa Broadcasting Company (MBC), which had affiliate stations in 21 local areas. MBC began its television broadcasting as a commercial channel in 1969.

Another commercial network, Tongyang Broadcasting Company (TBC), was the third largest broadcasting system with three affiliate stations in the countryside; TBC began its television in 1964. The two other major broadcasting systems were the Dong-A Broadcasting Service (DBS) and the Christian Broadcasting Service (CBS), both operating radio services only. DBS served the Seoul area and its vicinity only, and CBS had four local stations. Except for two (KBS and CBS) of the five systems, the broadcasting companies were created and owned by print media industries: TBC by the *Joong-ang Ilbo,* MBC by the *Kyunghyang Shinmoon* and the DBS by *Dong-A Ilbo.*

Korea's broadcasting underwent a drastic structural transformation in the wave of the government-initiated realignment of media systems in November 1980. The government's KBS absorbed TBC and DBS, and now operates these as its own channels. CBS was stripped of its general news function and allowed to broadcast evangelic programs only. MBC purchased the majority shares (51 percent) of its local affiliates, and again KBS has obtained the majority shares (65 percent) of MBC. In effect, all the nation's broadcasting systems have been put under the control of KBS.

The two private systems, DBS and CBS, had often run into conflicts with the government. These two broadcasting services had aired enough items critical of Korea's authoritarian government to invite government's close watch to their operations. *Dong-A's* loss of DBS meant a loss of an important revenue source for that daily newspaper, never a favorite of the government.

The government argues that its 1980 action was taken as a result of growing widespread public criticism of broadcasting media practices. Viewers might have liked the status quo, but media critics and communication researchers indeed lamented the less-than-ethical commercialism and sensationalism on commercial television, charging that most of the popular television programs lacked redeeming social value. Some programs were criticized for being centered around the luxurious life-styles of the urban rich. Such programs were examined in terms of their potentially demoralizing effect upon the less affluent segments of the public.

A competing school of critics argued that the government was to blame for the way commercial television had developed. They claimed that the government did not allow commercial television to develop and produce public affairs programs that could scrutinize the government. They reasoned that commercial television's emphasis on entertainment was what the government wanted, because such programs diverted public attention away from politics and social issues.

Nonetheless, Korea's television has become a favored medium and television watching a national pastime with the mass audience. There were only 380,000 television sets used in Korea in 1970, but the distribution of sets had climbed to an estimated 6.27 million as of 1980, a figure indicating that eight out of 10 households contain a television set. A survey with a national sample, conducted by a Sogang University researcher, shows that in December 1980 some 78 percent owned one television set in their households, 19 percent two sets and 2 percent three sets or more. The same survey also revealed that some 63 percent of its respondents watched television for more than three hours daily, about 30 percent for one to three hours, and only 6 percent for less than an hour.

In 1980 some 30 percent of television programs were imported. Foreign-made movies were the leading category in viewing; next in popularity were sports programs and various serial dramas and shows.

Television watching grew into a new experience with the wholesale shift to color broadcasting in late 1980. Until that time the government had prevented television from broadcasting in color out of a belief that color television would escalate the sense of gap between the affluent and the less fortunate.

The KBS has embarked on an ambitious plan to generate quality programs in quantity, imbued with Korea's cultural identity and national aspirations. It also struggles to create a distinctive personality for each of its three channels: TV-1 as a general network, TV-2 (formerly TBC) as an entertainment channel, and TV-3 (UHF) as educational television. Its financial resources for such endeavors are relatively strong. KBS collects the mandatory license fees from owners of television sets—about $3.75 per month for a color set (which coincidentally is the amount equal to the monthly subscription fee for daily newspapers) and somewhat less for black-and-white sets. It airs commercials in blocks between programs, a second major source of its revenues.

After the restructuring and reorganization of broadcasting, as of early 1981 what was most apparent in Korean television was the uniformity in news reporting. Television, both KBS-TV and MBC-TV, acted as an agent of governmental propaganda and political campaigns. The two television systems seemed to compete in loyalty to the government.

As to radio, various channels were being reorganized in 1981. At one point the state-run KBS operated four AM channels (one of which was formerly DBS) and two FM channels (one was formerly TBC-FM). MBC has one AM channel and one FM channel. CBS functions as a channel of religious programs only. Radio sets in use were estimated at 14 million, roughly two per household, as of 1980.

Education & Training

Eleven universities offer bachelor's degrees in journalism, communication and public relations. Most of the programs started after the mid-sixties, with three beginning earlier —Joong-ang University in 1958, Ewha Womans University in 1960, and Hanyang University in 1963. They admit an average of 30 students each annually; each has three to six full-time faculty members. All but three have master's programs, and five offer doctoral course work. The major market for the graduates is in private industry, which demands a growing number of personnel skilled in advertising, publicity work, public relations and in-house publications. Only a few graduates end up working in the newsrooms of major media.

Korea's newspapers, especially the national dailies, recruit their reporting staff through open competitive examinations. Most successful candidates are college graduates in political science, law, economics and English. Through this system major media have been able to hire quality editorial personnel. An in-service educational program is felt to be needed, especially for those coming to the job without college education in the field of journalism. The media industries, in cooperation with the government, are considering a program for this purpose, and reporters are anticipating leaves with pay for refresher courses during the mid-eighties.

There are various professional associations of media employees, organized along occupational lines. These groups pursue their respective interests through meetings, joint activities and newsletter publications. There also are several fund-granting foundations set up to help journalists exclusively.

One of the better known professional associations is the Kwanhun Club. Organized in 1957, it has some 200 members, mostly mid-career and experienced journalists. A group comparable to this for resident foreign correspondents is the Seoul Correspondents Club.

The Korean Journalists Association (KJA) is the most effective and visible organization. Founded in 1964, it is affiliated with 45 chapters comprising 3,150 members working for news organizations. The largest journalism association in Korea, it draws its members from the reporting staffs at newspapers, broadcasting stations and news agencies. KJA has been very active and often very successful in resisting the infringement of press freedom and in promoting improvements in reporters' working conditions and compensation. Representing the majority of the nation's newsmen, KJA has been able to exert its influence for the welfare of its members on the owners of the press and government agencies as well. If a reporter is detained or summoned by an agency, it was this journalists' association that first attempted rescue. If a newspaper is slow in pay raises, it was KJA that applied group pressure against the owner.

KJA in principle is a professional association, not a labor union for collective bargaining and collective action. Owners of the press have not recognized collective bargaining by their reporters. Under the existing Korean laws reporters may organize to engage in collective bargaining, yet the owners have successfully resisted occasional moves initiated by their reporters. In the absence of such unions KJA has been playing the role of a collective bargaining agency for reporters.

A medium the journalists' association used effectively was its newsletter, the *Korean Journalists Association Newsletter*. It was an informative listing of the plight, problems and happiness experienced by Korean journalists. It was banned from publication in August 1981 in the wake of the "cleanup campaign" conducted by the government. Also banned was the association journal, *Journalism*.

Part of Korea's professional journalism is a press council, the Korean Press Ethics Commission. It started in 1961 and has been active in deliberating on complaints and in initiating investigations into issues of social concern. In general, it has been successful in reminding the media of the concerns informed citizens have about them.

Summary

The mass media industry of South Korea has a promising base for further growth as a business in the eighties. Korea's traditional reverence toward education and culture provides the human resources necessary to produce quality media as well as the sophisticated clients to consume such products. The improving economy should continue generating the necessary economic support.

The broadcast media will face a growing temptation toward commercialism in an era of mass culture. The super-sized Korea Broadcasting System has a promise to keep and a challenge to its ingenuity, to put its imported Western technology to creative use in providing forms and content conducive to the shaping of Korea's modern culture based on her traditional culture.

Newspapers will have to cope with the particular demands and expectations of the younger generation having a "New Education"; they constitute the majority of readers. The current language and format of newspapers will attract mounting resistance from Korea's new majority. Improvements in typesetting and editing through computerization are necessities.

The newly consolidated news service, Yonhap News Agency, can grow as a solid national news agency actively transmitting Korean news abroad as well as receiving incoming news from abroad. By strengthening its external services, Yonhap can contribute to remedying the imbalance in international news flow about Korea.

Relations between the press and the government have been turbulent and explosive in the modern history of Korea. Relations in the future will depend largely on the margin of safety the government feels toward domestic political stability and perceived external threats to Korea's security. Both the restructured media systems and the new government were initiating their first year in 1981. The new media structure is susceptible to government attempts to use the media as tools for news control and propaganda. The new press law could result in further curbs of press freedom.

The public seriously questions the credibility of the news media as a whole. To the extent that the government remains a major source of information, the media credibility problem really is a question of the credibility of the government. Restoring the media's credibility will be a key to creating a sense of trust in the society's domestic political stability.

CHRONOLOGY

1974 A series of protests by groups of reporters at the *Dong-A Ilbo* and 29 other news media organizations across the nation, leading to "declarations on freedom and independence in media production."
A massive boycott of advertising sponsorships against the *Dong-A Ilbo* follows its reporters' initiation of the protests.

1975 Presidential Emergency Decree No. 9 bans the press from opposing the new constitution allowing President Park's re-election to presidency; also bans the press from criticizing the decree itself.

1978 Thirty-seven journalists revealed to have received favors from a major business group in obtaining the rights to purchase apartments at Korea's most expensive apartment complex.

1979 Military censorship of the press under the martial law. Extensive use of news media as government's instrument of propaganda.

1980 Sit-in demonstrations by groups of reporters at national daily newspapers demanding press freedom, under the martial law.

Publication of 172 "demeaning, low-quality" periodicals banned; the blacklist also includes several well-known journals of opinions.
Forced resignation of some 100 to 400 journalists, including "unethical" reporters and "targeted" journalists.
Drastic restructuring of the nation's mass media organizations and systems through merger, consolidation and elimination: (1) The state-run Korea Broadcasting System becomes the monopoly owner of all radio and television channels; (2) the *Dong-A Ilbo* loses its radio service to KBS; (3) the Christian Broadcasting Service is prevented from airing general news; (4) seven daily newspapers are eliminated; (5) six existing news services are consolidated into a single organization, Yonhap News Agency.
New press law passed making press responsibility a legal requirement. Also stipulates provisions on reporters' access to information sources and newsmen's privilege of confidentiality.

BIBLIOGRAPHY

(Unless noted otherwise, publications originating from Seoul are in Korean.)

Academy of Korean Studies. *Political Thoughts and Korean Culture.* Seoul, 1980.
Carter, Thomas F. *The Invention of Printing in China and Its Spread Westward,* 2nd ed. New York, 1955.

Choe, Chong-ho. "Korea's Communication Culture: An Inquiry into Spoken and Written Words." *Korea Journal,* August 1980, pp. 41–52 (in English).
Choi, Chang-sup. "A National Audience Survey on the Uses of Radio and Television." A report written for the Ministry of Culture and Information, December 1980, Seoul.

Choi, Jin-woo, ed. *Readings in Journalism.* Seoul, 1979.

Choi, Joon. *A History of Korean Journalism,* rev. ed. Seoul, 1980.

Hangul Society. *The 50-Year History of Hangul Society.* Seoul, 1971.

Haptong Press. *Haptong's Korea Annual 1980.* Seoul, 1980.

Kim, Bong-gi. *Brief History of the Korean Press.* Seoul, 1965 (in English).

Korean Journalists Association. *Korean Journalists Association Newsletters,* Vol. 2 (August 1968–March 1972) and Vol. 3 (April 1972–March 1979). Seoul, 1978, 1979.

Korean Overseas Information Service. *A Handbook of Korea.* Seoul, 1979 (in English).

_____. *Constitution.* Seoul, 1980 (in English).

Korean Press Institute. *Korean Press & Broadcasting Annual 1980.* Seoul, 1980.

Lancaster, Lewis R. *The Korean Buddhist Canon: A Descriptive Catalogue.* Berkeley, Calif., 1980.

Lee, Hwan-ey. "Business Administration of Korea's Mass Media in the Seventies." *Shinmun Hakpo* (Journal of the Korean Society for Journalism and Communication Studies), no. 12 (1979), pp. 143–168.

_____. *Mass Com Management,* rev. ed. Seoul, 1980.

Lee, Kang-soo. "Mass Communication and Mass Culture." In *Korean Society,* ed. by the Korean Social Sciences Institute, Seoul, 1980, pp. 151–181.

Lee, Kang-soo, et al. "A Study of Problems with Korea's Commercial Television." *Hanyang Communication Review,* Seoul, vol. 1, 1980, pp. 1-76.

Mason, Edward S., et al. *The Economic and Social Modernization of the Republic of Korea.* Cambridge, Mass., 1980.

McMurtrie, Douglas C. *The Book: The Story of Printing and Bookmaking.* London, 1943.

Ministry of Culture and Information. "Press Law" and "Procedural Law on the Press Law." Pamphlets, Seoul, 1981.

National Bureau of Statistics, Economic Planning Board. *Korea Statistical Yearbook 1980.* Seoul, 1980.

Oh, In-hwan, and Choe Chong-ho, eds. "Developmental Communication in Korea." In *Shinmun Hakpo,* no. 10, 1978, pp. 187–285.

Park, Yong-sang. "A History of Press Laws in Korea." *Shinmun Yongu* (Journalism Studies, Seoul), 21:2, winter 1980, pp. 8–44.

"Preliminary Reports on the 1980 Census." Released by the Economic Planning Board, printed in the *Seoul Shinmun,* January 25, 1981, p. 4.

Shin, In-sup. *A History of Advertising in Korea.* Seoul, 1980.

Stokes, Henry Scott. "Seoul's Censors and Press Distort Dispatches from U.S." *The New York Times,* September 4, 1980, p. A9.

Yoo, Chang-gyun, ed. *Historical Perspectives on the Direction of Contemporary Korean Culture.* Seoul, 1980.

You, Ho-sun. "Present Status and Prospect of Korean Pulp and Paper Industries." *Asian Economies* (Seoul), no. 34, Sept. 1980, pp. 5–41 (in English).

Yun, Tae-rim. *The Structure of Korean Personality.* Seoul, 1970.

LEBANON

by Harold A. Fisher

BASIC DATA

Population: 3,100,000 (1977)
Area: 10,400 sq. km. (4,015 sq. mi.)
GNP: NA
Literacy Rate: 75%
Language(s): Arabic
Number of Dailies: 42 (1979)
   Aggregate Circulation: 650,000
   Circulation per 1,000: 200
Number of Nondailies: 26 (1979)
   Aggregate Circulation: 937,500
   Circulation per 1,000: 300
Number of Periodicals: 16 (1979)

Number of Radio Stations: 11
Number of Television Stations: 3 (1981)
Number of Radio Receivers: 1.6 million (1976)
   Radio Receivers per 1,000: 540
Number of Television Sets: 450,000 (1977)
   Television Sets per 1,000: 147
Total Annual Newsprint Consumption: 8,000 metric tons (1977)
   Per Capita Newsprint Consumption: 2.5 kg. (5.5 lb.)
Total Newspaper Ad Receipts: NA
   As % of All Ad Expenditures: NA

Background & General Characteristics

Despite numerous restrictions and limitations resulting from nearly a decade of civil war and internal strife, the Lebanese press has remained active, diverse and fairly vigorous.

In its diversity, the newspaper industry reflects the numerous specialized political, ethnic and religious interests that characterize the people of Lebanon. The size of the industry is also affected by Lebanon's geographical placement and her leadership in the Arab world. Many papers, especially nondailies and periodicals, enjoy wide circulation in other parts of the Arab world and among people of Arab extraction who reside in other parts of the world. Such popularity of Lebanese publications outside the country has been adversely affected to some degree by the continuing strife within the country.

Even during the height of the civil war, which greatly hindered the operation of the press, about two dozen newspapers and magazines reflective of a wide variety of news and opinions were appearing. Some were published in battle zones at great danger to the lives of the editorial and production personnel. Some newspaper offices and print-ing plants were destroyed by the war or by enemies of the press. Despite this a number of papers ceased publication only briefly, when the battle raged the fiercest. Then, in 1977, censorship was imposed on the press for a while, and more papers were forced to cease publication for a time. But as things eased, the newspaper industry recouped some of its former vigor.

Some authorities note that the Lebanese newspaper industry is healthy, but not wealthy. It has been hampered by a lack of sufficient funds, which has kept it from developing as fully as possible. Because of its diversity, which caters to the interests of a large number of small ethnic, political and religious groupings, circulations, and consequently profits, tend to be small. The restrictions placed on the size of newspapers and on the amount for which they can be sold further limit profits. In some cases, therefore, operation of a newspaper is sustained by a special interest group, often from outside the country.

Lebanon's newspaper readers are the most literate and the best educated in the entire Middle East. Well over 75 percent of the populace is literate, and most have had at least primary level education. There is state primary and secondary education, but privately supported institutions provide the main facilities for secondary schools and for institutions of higher education.

Because of the country's role in international commerce, many Lebanese were affluent prior to the civil war. In addition, there was a sizable merchant, retail and professional middle class. Such people were interested in national, international and cultural affairs. They were interested in national and world developments, and supported the idea of a free press.

But the press has suffered during the civil war from an increasing exodus of readers who have lost confidence in the future of the country. The exodus has affected circulations of late, which had held up admirably through a lengthy period of stress. Many of the smaller papers with marginal circulations may not be able to withstand further loss of their financial base if the exodus continues.

Lebanon's population is concentrated in Beirut, which claims about one-third of the country's three million or more residents, and in a few other major cities, such as Tripoli, Zahle and Sidon. Tripoli, for example, has about 150,000 residents. Numerous villages dot the coastal plains and the Mediterranean side of the Lebanon Mountains. The remainder of the people reside in the fertile Bekaa valley and in the rural areas of the south and extreme north.

For historical and traditional reasons the nation's varied religious and ethnic communities concentrate in certain geographical areas. Maronite Christians, the largest Christian sect, live in east Beirut and along the coast to the north of the capital. The Druze homeland is in the Lebanon range to the south of Beirut. Members of the Greek and other Eastern Orthodox communities tend to dwell in the north. Armenians are found in Beirut and in the other cities. The areas in and around Tripoli, south of Beirut and in the western quarters of the capital are inhabited by Muslims. Palestinian refugees, many still living in makeshift camps, are located in and near Beirut and Tripoli and in the regions south of Sidon down to the Israeli border. In nearly every case, each of these communities is served by newspapers and periodicals that cater first to its special interests, needs and wants.

The bulk of the population reads and speaks the Arabic language. However, the Armenian community retains its own identity and language. Lebanon was under a French mandate between the two World Wars, and French influence has remained pervasive throughout much of the country, but especially among the Christian sects. Many Lebanese still have strong ties with France, having received their education there or in French private schools in Lebanon itself. Therefore, French continues to be the lingua franca for much of the populace. English is also widely spoken and used, especially among the educated, since many of the secondary and higher educational institutions were founded by missionaries and other English-speaking supporters.

The quality of journalism emanating from Lebanon's diverse press varies widely. Although there are few papers interested only in entertainment values, quality is not generally high and objectivity is affected by political, ethnic or religious views. Some papers exhibit very high quality journalistic principles and practices, among them *Al-Jarida, L'Orient—Le Jour, Al-Hayat, An-Nahar* and *Al-Anwar*.

Lebanon's first paper, *Hadikat Al-Akhbar* ("The Garden of News") was founded in 1858 by Khalil El-Khouri. Two years later, *Nafeer Souria* ("The Call of Syria") appeared, published by Butrus Al-Bustani, famous for his literary works. Both were published in Lebanon. The year 1860 also ushered in two other Arabic papers published outside the country: *Aj-Jawa'ib* ("The Traveling News") originating in Istanbul, and *Barid Paris* ("Paris Mail"), printed in France.

Although Lebanon was part of the Ottoman Empire at the time, journalists experienced few restrictions unless they criticized the Turkish government. Later, press freedom became restricted for foreigners in Lebanon, such as missionaries who wished to publish.

The relative freedom of the press, coupled with the educational system introduced by missionaries, put Lebanon's press well ahead of those of other Arab countries, leading at least one historian to label Lebanon the "true cradle of Arab journalism." The earliest Lebanese papers, already usually associated with some religious or ethnic grouping, called the people of the country to unity. But at that time, Lebanon was still part of Syria. Most of the early papers were weeklies and did not endure long because of financial problems.

When Abdul Hamid II became the Sultan of the Ottoman Empire, the Lebanese press came under heavy restrictions. Journalists were forbidden to print commentary and the amount and kinds of publishable news were severely restricted. Such pressures forced the

Lebanese journalists to call for independence and freedom, thus establishing today's strong link in the press between journalism and politics. Because of the Ottoman oppression, many Lebanese journalists fled to Egypt, where a few founded some of Egypt's current leading papers and magazines, such as *Al-Ahram* and *Al-Musawar*. At the time Lebanese publishers were directed to give priority to the health of the Sultan in their pages, then to agricultural and commercial news. Comment on ethical and/or social issues, criticism of Turkish officials and reference to any enemies of the Sultan were all strictly forbidden. Every article was pre-censored by the Turkish Ministry of Education.

In 1908 a new Ottoman elite came to power and some of the limitations on the Lebanese press were lifted. However, the press remained far from free. When journalists became bold and used their limited new freedoms to call for a Lebanese national awakening, sixteen of them were publicly hanged for stirring public opposition to the Turkish Empire. When the French took over after World War I, they first upheld Ottoman press laws, then even increased their restrictiveness. When the Lebanese journalists opposed the 66 new laws imposed by the French, a 67th was added to allow the French government to suspend any newspaper without trial as it saw fit.

Despite the oppression, the Lebanese press thrived. By 1929 there were 271 papers, most of them calling for national independence. Many editors were imprisoned for their boldness, but each punishment made the press more determined and more credible in the eyes of the Lebanese people. Thus, a spirit of a vital, free press was fostered among the people, a spirit that remains strong today. But the taking of political positions by the press also had a long-term negative effect upon the Lebanese papers: even today there is the tendency to concentrate on editorial views and commentary rather than on hard news.

As a result of World War II, Lebanon gained her freedom. However, the first independent indigenous government actually multiplied official restrictions on the press. It considered any violation of press law a criminal offense. In a single day it suspended seven papers. But the press kept up the pressure, which finally led to a popular revolt against the new government in 1952, a new regime and more relaxed press laws. After 1952 the press again grew rapidly. Over fifty

papers were published in Beirut alone. Many of the papers were somewhat sensational in nature, and all served a particular group or faction. In 1962 the government adopted laws that made the Lebanese press essentially free.

However, the press itself continued to face its historical problems. It remained aligned with special interest groups. It often concentrated on views rather than news. It was made up of many small-circulation papers that were barely self-sustaining. It lacked proper organization and planning. And it had low professional standards for its journalists. These identical problems still plague today's press in Lebanon.

Now, however, a new generation of editors and publishers is trying to overcome such limitations, and despite the continuing war, some progress has been made. Some papers have begun to appeal to more than one ethnic or religious or political group. Managers are reorganizing. National and international advertising support has helped provide additional support. And now that the Lebanese universities have set up journalism and mass communications training programs, young journalists are starting with better training, and professional standards are improving.

Lebanese newspapers and periodicals are published in four languages. The majority of the publications are in Arabic, the country's official language. But several papers *(Ararat, Ayk, Aztag* and *Zartonk)* are published in Armenian for the sizable Armenian communities, which settled in Lebanon after the Turkish persecutions following World War I. Because of continuing French cultural and educational ties, there is a strong French-language press, represented by the *L'Orient —Le Jour, Le Soir* and *Le Reveil* newspapers. The *Daily Star* is the country's principal English-language newspaper.

Political and ethnic or religious interest, often intertwined, remain strongly represented in the Lebanese press. Some of the more obvious alignments are *Al-Amal,* published by the Phalangist Party, and *Nida,* the voice of the Lebanese Communist Party. But nearly every paper reflects some political leaning. One of the press' continuing problems is the influence of external political and monetary pressures to publish views favorable to them. With a few exceptions, newspapers and periodicals are all published in Beirut, the country's capital.

Most Lebanese dailies are standard size and format. The Press Syndicate, controlled by the publishers, limits the number of pages of newspapers to protect the smaller, financially weaker papers. The control is linked to price: a newspaper cannot increase its size beyond certain limits without increasing its sale price. Thus an eight-page newspaper, for example, sells at one price (in 1975, it was 25 Lebanese piasters, or about eight U.S. cents), while a four-page paper must sell at two-thirds as much. This ruling also curbs effectively the publication of magazine and special interest sections by newspapers. Some papers circumvent this law by taking out additional licenses to publish.

The majority of the Lebanese dailies are a.m. publications. But a few are afternoon papers, and the leading p.m. daily is the *Lisan Al-Hal* ("The Tongue of Events"), a former morning paper that now has a circulation of about 33,000. Except for an *Al-Anwar* Sunday supplement, there are no Sunday newspapers.

All the important dailies except *Journal Al-Haddis* are published in Beirut. The three largest dailies by circulation in 1979 were *An-Nahar* (circulation: 85,000), *Al-Anwar* (75,200) and *At-Tayyar* (75,000, but it was temporarily being issued as a weekly in 1979). After these three largest dailies, the circulations of other dailies drop considerably. The next largest daily in 1979 was *Ad-Destour,* with a reported circulation of 53,400. The next three dailies—*Lisan Al-Hal* (33,000), *Al-Hayat* (32,538) and *Al-Amal* (29,000)—represented another fall-off in circulation. Other papers with circulations over 10,000 in 1979 included *Ad-Dunia* (25,000), *L'Orient—Le Jour* (21,500), *Daily Star* (19,220), *Le Soir* (16,500), *An-Nass* (16,000), *Telegraf—Beirut* (15,500) and *As-Safa* (15,000).

In terms of circulation, *An-Nahar* and *Al-Anwar* are Lebanon's most influential dailies. *An-Nahar* has high credibility among most of the readers. Since most of the country's elite speak French, two of the French-language newspapers, *L'Orient—Le Jour* and *Le Soir,* are disproportionately influential. One Arabic paper that is influential out of proportion to its circulation is *Al-Jarida,* a paper staffed by some of the country's most respected journalists.

A number of weekly papers claim high circulations and are also considered influential and credible. The most noteworthy, *Al-Hawadess* (circulation 167,500 in 1979), has a strong political orientation and is published in London (it was formerly published in Beirut). Another politically oriented weekly, *Al-Ousbou' Al-Arabi* ("Arab Week") circu-

lates about 125,000 copies throughout the Arab world. *Achabaka,* specializing in society news and features, sells about 126,500 copies each week. Still other influential high-circulation weeklies are *Assayad* (94,700), *Al-Moharrer* (87,000) and *Samar* (50,000), a photorama magazine.

Economic Framework

The Lebanese economy is based on private enterprise, with most people employed in service industries and only relatively few in agriculture. About two-thirds of its traditionally free-market trade has been in transit traffic as its port cities handled transshipments of goods to other Arab and Asiatic countries. Until the civil war Lebanon was also the banking center of the Arab world and conducted a bustling tourist trade. To many Middle Easterners, Lebanon was known as the Switzerland of the Arab world.

But nearly a decade of factionalism and bloody civil war has severely crippled Lebanon's economy. Beirut's busy port was mostly destroyed in 1975 and renewed fighting closed it again for five months in 1978. The Beirut airport has lost much of its passenger and commercial cargo trade. Many of the principal banks and corporation offices that had headquarters in Beirut left as a result of the extended fighting, and some have been reluctant to return because of the lack of a permanent political settlement. The tourist trade, which was bringing in 20 percent of the country's income in 1974, was down to 7.4 percent of the national income in 1978. A rapid rise in the rate of inflation since 1979 has compounded the negative economic effects of the war. Recently, the Lebanese pound, stable in value through nearly a decade of uncertainty, has devalued considerably. Many of the Lebanese, always an enterprising people, have continued retail businesses by operating from temporary street-side stands or from the backs of their trucks or cars. But the economy continues to decline as fighting goes on and inflation continues to rise.

The country's violence and economic problems have taken their toll on the press. A number of newspaper offices and printing plants have been bombed or sabotaged. In many cases the newspaper offices have been located in battle zones, forcing shutdowns during times of open fighting. A number of journalists have been killed; others have joined one of the numerous armed factions waging battle with one another. Newsprint imports have been disrupted for long periods. Delivery of the papers has been difficult. People have had less money to spend on publications or could not get to shops to buy them. The combination of the war and economic strains has closed down a large number of papers and periodicals. Nonetheless, even during the height of the civil war in 1975–76 about two dozen newspapers and magazines were appearing regularly. And many papers were revived as soon as the intensity of the hostilities slackened.

In Lebanon the radio broadcasting service has always been part of the Ministry of Information and, as such, has represented the government's views. Nonetheless, in normal times there was considerable objectivity in its news and informational programming. Both television services are controlled by commercial interests that focus on production of entertainment programming. Television news has served as a complement but never as a serious competitor to newspapers. Educated Lebanese have traditionally depended on newspapers for in-depth national and international news and for editorial commentary. Most affluent Lebanese take one or more newspapers, read periodicals, and listen to or watch both national and foreign broadcasts.

The Lebanese press tends to be owned either by private individuals or by publishing houses. For example, *L'Orient—Le Jour* and *Al-Jarida* are owned by George Naccache, a wealthy lawyer and politician. *An-Nahar* and several magazines are published by the Press Cooperative House, which has been under the control of the Tweini family since the daily's founding in 1933. *Al-Hayat* ("The Life") and the *Daily Star* are part of the Dar Al-Hayat Publishing House, which also has a public relations firm and a marketing operation. *Al-Anwar* ("The Lights") and the weekly magazines *As-Sayyad* and *As-Shabaka* have been under the Dar Al-Sayyad Publishing House, which is owned by the Frayha family. Other papers are under similar family or small corporation ownership, as are the television services. Radio Liban is owned and operated by the government.

No Lebanese newspaper can be classified as an elite, quality daily, but several are serious journals. *An-Nahar* is considered a leader by the intelligentsia because it seeks, more than most, to report a variety of politically divergent views as fairly and objec-

tively as possible; it has acted as a watchdog for the rights of the public. *L'Orient—Le Jour* is noted for its excellent background information on news, its insightful editorials and its scholarly feature stories. *Al-Anwar* stresses excellence of production and high journalistic standards more than any other of the dailies.

A number of the other Lebanese dailies stress popular entertainment values in preference to quality news and information. Because their journalists are often poorly trained or represent a factional view, the stories in such papers are often marked by inaccuracies, rumors and bias. Because of low income from small circulations, many of these papers have turned to foreign support, often in the form of subsidies or outright bribes, and the news of such support groups is covertly or overtly slanted in their favor in the papers' contents. Such assistance may come from foreign embassies or companies, from the Lebanese government or from other sources. One business manager once bragged that his paper took bribes from both Russian and American sources for placing an item critical of China. Subsidies come in a variety of ways—from direct rental of the publication, from payments to certain programs or causes supported by the paper, through gifts of equipment or paper, or through heavy advertising. Sometimes papers are paid to keep silent on certain issues or events. When newspapers have not complied to subsidy requests, they have been retaliated against by bombings or by physical attacks on the editorial staff. Despite such questionable practices, there is little deliberate sensationalism purely for its own sake.

Although each has its own subscription clientele, most Lebanese papers depend heavily on street sales. Most newspapers circulate primarily in the cities.

All of the newsprint used must be imported. In 1978 about 8,000 metric tons were shipped in and used, an average of about two and one-half kilograms per inhabitant. The government charges a tax on newsprint. During the civil war adequate newsprint sometimes became difficult to obtain because the Beirut port was closed by hostilities and destruction for long periods of time.

Since most Lebanese papers have small circulations, income from advertising is vital. Papers must actively seek advertising; however, most concessions to advertisers appear to be to those foreign companies who heavily subsidize a paper either by large advertising contracts or in some other clandestine manner. Most Lebanese papers have an ad-to-newshole ratio of about one to one to two to one.

Press Laws

Under the Lebanese Constitution, adopted in 1926 and amended in 1947, personal freedoms and freedom of the press are guaranteed and protected.

Lebanese press law and press freedoms were born out of a background of Turkish and French colonial oppression of the press and the resultant press and public determination to gain better conditions for public information. When Lebanon first became independent a new press law actually increased restrictions on the press and made any violation of the new law a criminal offense. When the press opposed the new law, the government suspended seven papers in a single day. The press reacted by calling for a general strike. When the government, in its turn, held firm, the press boycotted all news about deputies and government leaders, a stand supported by all the opposition parties and the press syndicates of Damascus, Cairo and Baghdad. This led to public discontent and the eventual resignation of the first President of the Republic and the fall of his government.

The new regime, grateful to the press, fashioned a new press law in 1952 that lifted most press restrictions except the right of the administration to suspend papers. It also established a separate court for press offenses. A 1953 law attempted to limit the number of permits issued to operate newspapers.

But it was the passage of a 1962 press law that defined journalism and established journalists' rights and freedoms. Article Nine of the new law defined journalism as "the free profession of publishing news publications" and declared the freedom of this profession could not be limited except by the general laws of the Republic. A journalist was defined as anyone whose profession and main income were from journalistic means. It set standards for journalists, declaring they must be Lebanese, at least 21 years old, with a baccalaureate degree and having practiced journalism as an apprentice for at least four years. Older practicing journalists were exempted from the educational requirement. The law also organized all Lebanese journalists into two syndicates: the Lebanese Press Syndicate (owners) and the Lebanese Press Writers (Reporters) Syndicate for active, working journalists. The law also created a Higher Press Council and set up a special committee to draft further legislation to define the privileges of journalists and provide a retirement plan for them.

The 1962 law minimized formal state censorship and set the limits of press freedom. It declared punishable by law any news that endangered national security, the unity of the state or the sanctity of its borders, that degraded any religion or caused sectarian tension, or that brought disrepute to any foreign head of state. Publication of false news with intent to blackmail was strictly forbidden.

In the ensuing decade, the press fought for and gained further freedoms for other media. In 1967 the press succeeded in getting abolished the practice of censoring foreign publications before allowing them to enter Lebanon. In 1970, after press pressure, the government withdrew Ministry of Information censors from the television stations. The rights of advertising and public relations industries were more clearly defined. Meantime, however, radio has remained under full state control. And many of the press freedoms have been severely tested during the past decade of strife.

Under the Lebanese judicial system there is a special Press Tribunal to handle legal questions. However, it has been bypassed several times during the civil war when the rights of the press were at stake. Judges are separately chosen and a commissioner represents the government in important trial matters, so that the judicial system is essentially independent of the legislative and administrative branches of government.

Censorship & State-Press Relations

As it is deemed necessary, the Ministry of Information controls and censors all materials aired on the Lebanese Broadcasting Service. Although newspapers and television are theoretically free from censorship, there have been numerous incidents involving both local and foreign press just prior to and since the outbreak of the civil war in 1974. Such censorship has come from the Syrian occupation forces, from the Syrian government, from the Lebanese military and from the Lebanese government, especially the Ministry of Information.

In 1972, for example, Elias Abboud, manager of the daily *Beirut,* was sentenced to a month's imprisonment for publishing an article degrading the president of Libya and a similar sentence was given Baqer Sherri, manager of *Al-Kifah,* for publishing articles degrading the kings of Morocco and Jordan. Stories in local papers and some foreign papers about the state of troubles on the Israeli border were strictly censored.

On May 7, 1973 a state of emergency was declared and press censorship was again imposed. Several western journalists were arrested for trying to take out uncensored films of the fighting on the southern border. Later in 1973 the owner of *As-Shaab* and the editor of *Al-Moharrer* were arrested for publishing articles defamatory to the President of the Republic. The editor and a correspondent for *An-Nahar* were arrested for publishing the secret resolutions of the conference of Arab chiefs of state in Algeria. Both were charged under military law for endangering the security of Lebanon and for straining relations with a foreign country. Both were released after appeal from the International Press Institute. About the same time, two journalists of leftist newspapers were given prison terms for defamatory articles about the Lebanese army. In 1974 the publisher of *Al-Destour* was given six months' imprisonment for slandering King Faisal of Saudi Arabia.

The sensitivity of the authorities increased during the civil war. Early in 1975 the editors of eight Beirut newspapers were given two months' imprisonment each for publishing reports about the transfer of army officers after certain incidents in Sidon. Later in the year a number of foreign papers were seized for publishing articles and information considered harmful to the security of the country. Among the papers seized were *The Guardian,* the *Daily Telegraph,* the *Daily Mail, Le Monde,* the *New York Times,* the *International Herald Tribune, Newsweek* and several Kuwait newspapers.

Even more stringent censorship was introduced early in 1977. All foreign correspondents were required to submit five copies of every publication to the censors before their transmission abroad, plus one copy of the published report. At the time there were 13 subjects banned from publication. Most of the pressure for this regulation came from Syrian authorities. But censorship was unevenly applied: reports on Christian activities were passed, while any references to Kamal Jumblatt and his Leftist Alliance were censored. Following the imposition of this decree, Syrian troops withdrew from the offices of several papers.

In 1978 six papers were suspended for a day for stories about a Syrian army search for the murderers of Rightist leader Tony Franjieh. Although 1979 proved to be a less tense year, some censorship continued. A Kuwait paper, for example, was banned for ten days.

The Lebanese press has responded to censorship restrictions in several ways. In some cases editors simply went to jail rather than comply. In other cases blanks were left in papers where the stories were to have appeared. In others, the authorities reconsidered and either lightened the fines or shortened imprisonment. Most banned papers were allowed to return after a period of time.

The civil war has also given rise to a rash of violent actions against the press and its personnel. Because the war has produced numerous armed factions and because external forces have also tried to make gains for themselves during this period, it is often difficult to trace the sources of or motives for violent acts. In most cases the Lebanese government was either unwilling or unable to check the excesses. Even a partial listing of such acts aids understanding of the chaos that has prevailed.

In 1972 explosions partially destroyed Beirut's largest daily, *An-Nahar,* and its sister French-language publication, *L'Orient —Le Jour.* In 1973 the printing presses of the weekly *Al-Hawadess* were destroyed and the offices of the daily *Al-Moharrer* damaged. In 1978 bombs damaged the *An-Nahar* building again.

The war took its toll on the lives of journalists, too. In March 1976 a French press photographer was killed during Beirut street fighting. Two months later Edouard Saab, editor of *L'Orient—Le Jour,* was killed, again during a battle. In March 1980 *Al-Hawadess* editor-publisher Selim Al Lawzi was murdered as he was leaving Lebanon, possibly because of his outspoken articles against the Syrians and the Palestinian Liberation Organization. His writing hand was mutilated before he was shot. One Lebanese cabinet minister described his killing as "the murder of the free word," and the president of the Lebanese Reporters Association urged journalists to leave Lebanon because it could no longer be considered a haven for press freedom.

Since 1962 Lebanon has had a government-created Higher Press Council that handles problems related to journalism. It is composed of officers and members of the Lebanese Press Syndicate and the Lebanese Reporters Syndicate, and the head of the Lebanese Ministry of Information press and legal affairs department. The Council was charged with drafting the bylaws of the Lebanese Press Union, which is made up of the officers of the two press syndicates. The Higher Press Council hears only cases that relate to the press. During the recent hostilities censors have frequently bypassed both the Council and the judiciary's Press Tribunal to deal directly with individual papers and journalists.

Attitude Toward Foreign Media

In normal times foreign correspondents have been welcome in Lebanon, and their restrictions have been few. But during the past decade their travel and stories have been curtailed; some have been jailed or expelled. Such incidents include the expulsion in 1975 of Edward Hughes, an American freelance journalist for *Reader's Digest,* for allegedly working for Israel, and the arrest of Paul Delifer, the AFP bureau chief in Beirut, in 1978. In some cases, as in the kidnapping of Toronto *Star* correspondent Gerald Uttig in 1976 by Palestinian guerillas, the government was simply unable to control factions within the country.

Although censorship of foreign publications before they are admitted to Lebanon was outlawed in 1969, the war and chaos of the 1970s brought a return of the practice. Some foreign papers, especially those from France, were refused entry in 1972 because of their stories about trouble on the Israeli border. The same trouble spot led to additional censorship of some foreign papers in 1973. As indicated earlier, a number of western and Kuwaiti papers were seized in 1975 for publishing articles harmful to the security of the country and for printing pornographic materials.

News Agencies

Lebanon has a single press association, the Lebanese Press Syndicate, with 18 member papers. It was founded in 1911.

News agency foreign bureaus have abounded in a country that normally welcomes foreign journalists and serves as an excellent central residence for reporting on Middle Eastern affairs. In 1979 Agence France-Presse (France), EFE (Spain), ANSA (Italy), ADN (East Germany), CTK (Czechoslovakia), Deutsche Presse-Agentur (West Germany), Novosti (USSR), MENA (Middle East) and AP and UPI (USA) all had established foreign bureaus in Beirut. In addition, the Iraqi News Agency, Jamahiriya News Agency (Libya), Reuters (UK) and Tass (USSR) all had offices there.

Electronic News Media

The Lebanese Broadcasting Service is controlled by the government and voices official views in its news, although it has a fair amount of freedom to be objective. During the height of hostilities in 1975, one government radio news announcer restored public confidence in the nation by his thorough news reports. Television news complements printed news, but does not give detailed information.

Education & Training

Traditionally the Lebanese journalist has gained his training while serving as an apprentice on a newspaper or periodical. The 1962 press law requires four years of practical experience as an apprentice before a person may become a recognized journalist. Alternately, a candidate for the title may hold a license degree in journalism from the Lebanese University or any equivalent or higher degree in an institution acceptable to the university. Although the number of journalists trained in a professional university program is growing, many working journalists remain on the job who have had only an apprenticeship. As of this writing, the American University of Beirut has both an undergraduate and a graduate program in journalism and mass communications.

Summary

The Lebanese press is considered the freest in the Middle East, and it has a history of struggle to gain and hold that tradition. The press serves a diverse range of political, ethnic and religious views. Consequently, it has always had a tendency to concentrate on editorial views and commentary in preference to hard news. The allegiance to a particular view has led to the publication of numerous papers with small circulations. The small circulations have both encouraged the tendency to accept subsidies or bribes from big business or foreign sources to promote their own interests, and kept papers from developing fully professional staffs.

During the past near-decade of civil war, the press has endured bombings, murder and imprisonment of its journalists, censorship and other restrictions. The foreign press, traditionally given free rein, has also been restricted. Although many newspapers have survived the hostilities and readership has held up fairly well, soaring inflation and the devaluation of the Lebanese pound now threaten the economic health of the press.

As of this writing, the future of the Lebanese press remains uncertain. Much will depend on the political settlement ultimately reached—or the lack of it—and the restoration of peace to the country. If current economic conditions and the ongoing unrest continue, the press faces a rather bleak future. Smaller papers with low circulations may face shutdowns, and the press may lose some of the freedoms it fought so valiantly to gain during the past century. However, all projections of the future must be made with extreme caution, for the Lebanese remain an enterprising, resourceful people, capable of arriving at innovative solutions to problems.

CHRONOLOGY

1975 Editors of eight papers imprisoned and several foreign papers seized.

1976 Toronto *Star* correspondent kidnapped by Palestinian guerrillas.

1977 Censorship imposed. Some papers forced to cease publication. Foreign correspondents required to submit copy before transmission to home newspapers.

1978 AFP bureau chief arrested in Beirut, released shortly thereafter.

Bombings of *An-Nahar* and *Al-Hawadess* newspapers.

Six papers suspended for stories about the slaying of Rightist leader Tony Franjieh.

1980 *Al-Hawadess* editor-publisher brutally murdered.

BIBLIOGRAPHY

"Digest." *IPI Report,* July 1978, p. 16.

The Europa Yearbook, Volume II. London, 1980.

"IPI in Action: Lebanon." *IPI Report,* February 1974, p. 7.

"Lebanon." *IPI Report,* July/August 1972, p. 13.

"Lebanon." *IPI Report,* December 1972, p. 7.

"Lebanese Censorship Variable." *IPI Report,* February 1977, p. 1.

"Middle East Editor Kidnapped, Then Shot." *IPI Report,* March/April 1980, p. 3

"Middle East: Lebanon." *IPI Report,* January 1973, p. 8.

"Press Freedom Report, 1974: Lebanon." *IPI Report,* January 1975, p. 17.

"Press Freedom Report, 1975: Lebanon." *IPI Report,* December 1975, p. 15.

"The Press under Pressure: Lebanon." *IPI Report,* April/May 1975, p. 13.

"A Quick Look Around: Lebanon." *IPI Report,* July/August 1973, p. 13.

"The Risks They Run." *IPI Report,* June 1976, p. 7.

UNESCO, *Statistical Yearbook, 1978-1979.* Paris, 1980.

"World Press Freedom Review of 1978: Lebanon." *IPI Report,* January 1979, p. 5.

"World Press Freedom Review: 1979: Lebanon." *IPI Report,* December 1979, p. 5.

MALAWI

by Harold A. Fisher

BASIC DATA

Population: 5,669,000 (1978, est.)
Area: 118,484 sq. km. (45,747 sq. mi.)
GNP: 1.46 billion kwacha (US$1.17 billion)
Literacy Rate: NA
Language(s): Chichewa, English
Number of Dailies: 1
  Aggregate Circulation: 18,000
  Circulation per 1,000: 3
Number of Nondailies: 6 (1979)
  Aggregate Circulation: NA
  Circulation per 1,000: NA
Number of Periodicals: 85
Number of Radio Stations: 1

Number of Television Stations: None
Number of Radio Receivers: 1,322,000 (1977, est.)
  Radio Receivers per 1,000: 250
Number of Television Sets: None
  Television Sets per 1,000: None
Total Annual Newsprint Consumption: 100 metric tons (1978)
  Per Capita Newsprint Consumption: 0.02 kg. (0.04 lb.)
Total Newspaper Ad Receipts: NA
  As % of All Ad Expenditures: NA

Background & General Characteristics

Malawi's newspaper industry may be characterized as small, weak, struggling, somewhat powerless and dominated by the government. Its size and growth are inhibited because Malawi is composed primarily of a rural population in which adult illiteracy remains high. The low per capita income makes newspapers an unaffordable luxury to many. Circulations of all papers are low, thus reducing the capital income needed for improvements. The small newspaper reading audience has discouraged competition, always a counterpart of a healthy print industry. Limited retail advertising and lack of heavy industries depress support from advertisers. Until recently, few Malawians had received any professional training in journalism. Finally, since 1973, the press has been under the control of the Office of the President. Under Dr. Hastings Kamuze Banda's watchful eye, the local national press has been carefully monitored and the foreign press discouraged and, for long periods of time, banned.

Recent statistics on the rate of literacy in Malawi are difficult to procure. In 1966 nearly two million people—about 78 percent of the populace—were illiterate. However, since the achievement of independence in 1964, the nation has stressed education and literacy has steadily increased. Nonetheless, illiteracy continues to remain high among rural adults.

In 1975 Malawi launched a five-year education project that included construction of 22 primary schools, 22 rural education centers and a teacher-training college. By 1977-1978 there were 2,294 primary schools, in which 11,115 teachers were teaching 675,740 pupils, a ratio of one teacher for every 61 students. In 1978 the Ministry of Education reported 15,140 students were enrolled in secondary schools and more than 1,500 were attending the University of Malawi. But because of Malawi's limited economic resources, only about 45 percent of the school-age children can be taken into schools. It appears evident that Malawi's emphasis on education will slowly increase demand for newspapers and the other mass media.

Within Malawi, only a small wealthy indigenous elite and a minority middle class can afford to buy newspapers daily. This factor, plus interest in farming on the part of the majority of able-bodied adults, has led to the publication of a number of specialized magazines and papers featuring agricultural topics, and to dependence on transistorized radios for information.

As of mid-1978, the International Labour Organization estimated that slightly over two million of Malawi's 2,386,000 economically active population (or about 84 percent) were engaged in agriculture-related pursuits. One-third of those not engaged in agriculture were employed in industry, and the remaining two-thirds in services, the sector growing most rapidly. Rises in the number of building, construction, transportation and communications workers and those providing financial services were most marked of all.

Malawi's population density, 153 per square mile (1977), is about four times that of the African continent as a whole. About 99 percent of the nation's residents are African. Most whites and Asians live in the urban centers—Blantyre, Zomba and Lilongwe. History, economic development and topography have all influenced the country's uneven population distribution. In 1977 the southern region claimed 228 persons per square mile, the central region 154 and the northern only 62. An earlier movement to the urban centers in the south, Blantyre and Zomba, has been partly curtailed by the government's decision to make Lilongwe, in the central region, the capital and by the establishment of several development projects in the northern and central regions.

Lilongwe, in the heart of the nation's most agriculturally productive area, is the fastest growing city, especially since it has become the national capital and the base for a number of small industries. Its population exceeded 103,000 in 1978. Blantyre, in the south, serves as the country's chief commercial and industrial center. In 1977 it claimed 222,153 residents. Nearby Zomba, with a population of slightly over 21,000, has been developed as a university town; the main campus of the University of Malawi is located there. By comparison, the populations of urban centers in the north are small; Mzuzu, one of the largest, counts only some 16,000 residents.

English, introduced during colonial rule, serves as the medium of communication for the commercial sector, the language of instruction in schools and the lingua franca of the nation's educated elite. It has also been chosen by the government to serve as a unifying force among Malawi's segmented

and diverse makeup of ethnic and lingual groupings, most of which are too small to develop textbooks and other printed literature of their own. Chichewa is widely understood and spoken by up to 95 percent of the populace.

Several factors limit the quality of journalism in Malawi. Prior to independence in 1964, newspapers were published almost entirely by Western journalists for the colonial settlers, and few Africans had the opportunity to receive training or to work. One exception was Harvey Mlanga, who joined the African Newspaper Group in the 1950s and became editor of the *African Weekly* and who later (1973) became managing editor of Blantyre Newspapers. Although a number of training institutes have been held since independence, as yet few Malawian journalists have the benefit of in-depth training or a liberal arts degree. Other limiting factors have been governmental restrictions on journalists and on publications, the low educational levels of readers, for whom English is a second language, and the high cost of newsprint.

The earliest newspaper in the area was the *Nyasaland Times and Central African Planter,* founded in 1895. During those days, the British colonial office controlled Nyasaland. Later, the European white settlers began feeling their way of life was threatened by British control. The British-owned paper focused on settler and homeland subjects and scarcely considered Africans; it supported the controlling powers, a characteristic that remains a feature of the press in Malawi even today.

Successor to the *Nyasaland Times and Central African Planter,* the *Daily Times* serves as Malawi's only daily newspaper. During the period of the Federation of Rhodesia and Nyasaland, the Blantyre Printing and Publishing Company, Ltd., a subsidiary of Thomson Publications, Ltd., of England, took over the paper, renamed it the *Malawi Times* and published it bi-weekly (Tuesdays and Fridays). It circulated in Blantyre and Zomba and in the surrounding districts. By 1970 it was reporting a circulation of 8,400. Now published in Blantyre five times weekly, Monday through Friday, as the *Daily Times,* it claimed a circulation of over 14,000 in 1978; that number has risen since. The *Times* has always been published in English.

In 1959, shortly before Malawian independence, the Malawi Congress Party was created. The same year, the *Malawi News* came into being as the Party's official organ, published in Limbe twice weekly, on Tuesdays and Fridays. Today it is known as the *Malawi News: The Voice of The Malawi Congress Party* and appears only on Saturdays. It concentrates its coverage on Party affairs, President Banda's activities and development projects. The *News* now circulates about 16,000 copies each week in English, Nyanja and Tumbuka. Mike Kamwendo functions as editor for both the *Daily Times* and the *Malawi News,* evidence that the entire press is under control of the nation's official ruling party.

Several other publications appear weekly. The *Government Gazette,* published by the official government print shop, provides a record of government appointments, laws and regulations. The Congress of Labor produces *Malawi Labor News* once a week in Blantyre. Other weeklies include *Malawi This Week,* also originating in Blantyre, and the *Agrinform,* published in Zomba.

The government publishes several fortnightlies, monthlies and quarterlies. One especially attractive publication is *This Is Malawi.* Put out by the Department of Information, it features domestic activities and developments. The Department of Information also produces *Backgrounder,* a fortnightly, *Malawi Features,* a monthly, and several monthly periodicals in indigenous languages, including *Boma Lathu* (Chichewa), *Malawi Mizinthunzi* and *Malawi Mwezi Uno.* It also publishes an English-language quarterly, *Vision of Malawi.*

Although most Africans follow traditional beliefs, Christians comprise about a quarter of the population and various Christian faiths are active in publishing periodicals. There are two Roman Catholic fortnightlies, the *Catholic Church Newsletter,* in Limba, and *The African,* in Lilongwe, the latter a publication of the White Fathers written in English, Cinyanja and Tumbuka. The Anglicans publish *Ecclesia,* a monthly newsletter of the Church of the Province of Central Africa, on their press in Likwenu. Each month the Presbyterian Church of Central Africa produces *Kuunika* ("Light") on its press in Mkhoma for distribution in Chichewa. The Watch Tower Bible and Tract Society publishes *Gongwe La Mlinda* each month. The Seventh Day Adventists put out two quarterlies, *Kalata wa ma Mission ena* and *Kotale wa Sabata Sukulu.* The Association of Religious Institutes of Malawi circulates the monthly *ARIMA Newsletter.*

Malawi also boasts a number of official special-interest periodicals, among them *Field Newsletter, Malawi* and *Ulimi m' Malawi,* all published by the Department of Agriculture, and *Moyo,* produced by the Health Extension Service. The Malawi Broadcasting Corporation circulates *Malawi Calling: MBC Official Programme Guide,* a fortnightly. The Peace Corps produces *Here's An Idea.* The Mathematical Association publishes a special interest quarterly, as do the Tea Research Foundation and the Economics Society. Sports periodicals include the quarterly *Malawi Sportsman* and *Mulanje Mountain Club.*

Several publications emanate from the University of Malawi; including *Odi,* produced quarterly by the Writer's Group, *Poly-View,* published by the Polytechnic Institute, the monthly *Bulletin,* the *University Students' Magazine,* and the *Chronicle,* published irregularly.

Economic Framework

As indicated earlier, Malawi's economy is based primarily on agriculture. The negative import-export balance, the small industrial class, the limited number of professionals and the small core of wealthy landowners, industrial entrepreneurs and professionals restrict the expansion of the economy. Since becoming prime minister in 1963 and subsequently president-for-life, Dr. Banda has kept Malawi isolated politically from most of its neighbors. Because of trade and job opportunities to the south, Malawi has fallen under South African influence. This has served to further isolate Malawi and to limit its trading partners.

These economic and political conditions, coupled with governmental monopoly ownership and control of the media, restrict the health and growth of the media. Even if the government were to allow it, few Africans are sufficiently wealthy to own or to expand the media. At the same time, low per capita income prevents heavy consumer investment in the media. Daily newspapers and costly magazines would be too expensive for the bulk of the populace, as would frequent attendance at the cinema. These conditions have combined with other factors to make ownership of transistor radio receivers the predominant characteristic of Malawi media consumers.

Radio stands out as the most important

medium in Malawi for other reasons besides its cheap cost. Because of still-high illiteracy and the diversity of cultures and languages, the number of those who would read newspapers remains largely restricted to the educated elite who can understand English. As a result, there is a radio receiver for every four persons, but only one copy of a daily newspaper for every 333 persons.

While Malawi's broadcasting system now reaches the entire nation, the circulation of newspapers and periodicals focuses primarily in the southern and central regions, where the main urban centers are located and where the transportation and distribution systems are better developed.

Since Malawi must import all its paper, the small newspaper industry has been heavily impacted by the rising costs of newsprint. This has contributed still further to the inability of many would-be consumers to afford the regular purchase of a newspaper.

Further, the idea of consumerism has not yet fully penetrated Malawi's economy. As a result, retail advertising in the media remains modest, bringing in only limited financial support. Moreover, government ownership of the media restricts the amount and influence of advertising.

Press Laws & Censorship

Malawi is a one-party state controlled by the Malawi Congress Party and headed by President-for-Life H. Kamuzu Banda, who is both Head of State and Head of Government. The Constitution contains no guarantee of press freedoms. While there is a National Assembly, most of the nation's policy decisions are made by the President. He has the right to participate in any parliamentary debates he wishes to attend and may refuse his assent to any bill.

Consequently, President Banda has established policies vis-a-vis the media almost entirely by himself. He has also restricted the press when it has fallen short of his expectations, thus establishing national press laws by precedent on a case-by-case basis. For example, on October 23, 1967, Dr. Banda unilaterally announced the imposition of censorship on all publications, including films. Such procedures have deprived even the foreign press of freedom within the country and have led to the banning of foreign papers and journalists for long periods of time.

State-Press Relations

Since the state owns and operates practically all the media, opportunity for an adversary press-government relationship does not exist. All newspapers must be registered with the government. Officially, the law does not require pre-censorship and indicates reporters and writers may produce materials without interference. However, Dr. Banda clearly believes the domestic press should not criticize his policies or the country. When articles have been critical, publications have been banned and the persons responsible detained.

Examples of government control over and restriction of the press abound. In July 1968 the work permit of a British publisher of a monthly magazine in Blantyre was withdrawn. About the same time, the British editor of the *Malawi Times* was invited to leave Malawi by September. In 1973, after publication of reports of a Mozambique border clash between Malawian and Portuguese troops, eight Malawian journalists were jailed without trial and the government's chief information officer was arrested. A British journalist was also arrested and deported. A radio news reporter was deported for refusing to broadcast the official government version of the story because he considered it a falsification of the real truth. Shortly afterwards, Dr. Banda announced in the National Assembly that he was introducing legislation to restrict "lying" journalists and that any journalist who stepped out of line could expect a lengthy jail sentence.

The Malawi government's relations with the press have been additionally marred by several similar, smaller-scale incidents. However, as David Burnet, a former managing editor of the Blantyre Printing and Publishing Company, has pointed out, it must be remembered that Malawi has had no historical national press tradition and that the press has had to take a role in the creation of a national identity. In such situations, the press is viewed as responsible to the nation and as exercising that responsibility under the eye of the government.

At first, after independence in 1964, publications and broadcasting were responsible to the Ministry of Information. But in 1973 the Ministry of Information was abolished and its functions taken over by the Office of the President and by the Ministry of Trade and Tourism. Today, the Department of Information serves as the public relations arm of the government, charged with informing and educating Malawians and with promoting national pride and unity.

Attitude Toward Foreign Media

Ever since shortly after independence, the Malawi government has always taken decisive actions against foreign media or journalists perceived to be guilty of offending national sensitivities. In the 1960s, expatriate journalists and publishers were invited to leave the country. Individual copies of imported British papers have been banned if they contained articles critical of Malawi. Early in the 1970s the government banned a number of foreign newspapers, among them the *Rhodesian Herald* and a South African current affairs magazine, *To The Point*.

After independence, resident foreign journalists became increasingly unwelcome. By 1972 the last resident foreign correspondent in the country, Matthew White, was first jailed and then deported without explanation. Shortly before that, the editor-in-chief of the *Times of Malawi*, Norman Catternach, left after the government arrested his staff. After the 1973 reports of Mozambique-Malawi border clashes resulted in the detention of eight African journalists, free-lance British journalist John Borrell was arrested and deported for alleged implication in "malicious" reports about the incident. Shortly thereafter, the government dropped the Reuters wire service after complaining that the agency was sending out false stories about Malawi. Reuters was later re-admitted on the basis that all correspondents would have to be cleared by the agency's chief African salesman. The individual deportations of foreign journalists were followed by a 1974 decree from President Banda banning all foreign journalists from the country.

In June 1977 Dr. Banda's government embarked on a policy of liberalization. As one step in the new policy, Dr. Banda invited foreign journalists to visit Malawi for the first time since 1973. He held his first international press conference in nearly a decade in June 1978 with reporter representatives of the London *Times,* Reuters, UPI and the BBC, among others, present. However, the euphoria soon ended. A few days later, disappointed by the coverage those same journalists had given the Malawi June elections, Dr. Banda declared that as a result of their erroneous reports no foreign correspondents

would thereafter be permitted into Malawi. That policy still holds.

Reuters again came under criticism of the Malawi government in 1980 for quoting a Zambian newspaper story that said Malawi had refused to recognize national boundaries set up during colonial days.

In the UNESCO-inspired "free and balanced" information flow debate, the Malawi government clearly sides with those Third World countries who seek "balanced" information, an all-African news agency and "protection" of journalists.

News Agencies

The Malawi News Agency (MANA) serves as the news gathering and disseminating wing of the Information department. The agency gathers news through district and regional offices for distribution to the Malawi press and the Malawi Broadcasting Corporation. It monopolizes distribution of the Reuters news and sublets the stories to MBC and to the local press. It compiles from Reuters a daily news file for President Banda, for the Ministry of External Affairs and for the Malawi Congress Party. The only external news agency taken is Reuters, and it is carefully controlled by Malawians on its staff and by government.

Electronic News Media

All broadcasting in Malawi comes under the jurisdiction of the Malawi Broadcasting Corporation. Radio broadcasting operations began in 1958 when the Central African Federation established a radio studio in Blantyre. Because the signal to the area was inadequate, a relay transmitter was installed in 1960 near Zomba. In 1963 a 20-kilowatt short wave transmitter and a 250-watt medium wave transmitter were added. Until independence in 1964, programs were aimed primarily at the white settler constituency.

As one of its first acts, the Banda government created the Malawi Broadcasting Corporation (MBC), which is controlled by a Board consisting of a chairman and four to seven members appointed by the Minister in charge. Until 1973, this responsibility fell to the Minister of Information, but more recently it has been the duty of the Minister of Trade and Tourism, and President Banda is free to assign broadcasting to any minister he chooses.

The Board appoints a Director-General, who chairs the Board and administers the broadcasting service. The Corporation's constitution permits commercial advertising and commercial broadcasting. At the direction of the Minister, the service diffuses any announcements or statements of public importance to the government. Thus, in effect, the policy and output of the service is under the full control of the government.

The MBC broadcasts in English and in Chichewa. It attempts to program primarily for two major audiences: the urban dwellers and the large rural-traditional constituency. It seeks to provide listeners with a wide variety of materials, mainly designed to educate and inform the public and to build up listeners' appreciation of and loyalty to the nation.

About 12 to 15 percent of the programs are news, current affairs and public service programs. There are approximately a dozen newscasts daily, with news coming from the Malawi News Agency and its Reuters source and from foreign stations via MBC's own monitoring service. Many listeners also tune in to BBC and Voice of America for news. In addition, there is about an hour per day of programming that features national development and unity and African and international affairs.

The MBC has no plans to expand into television broadcasting.

Education & Training

Malawian journalists and broadcasters have had a variety of training experiences. Some have been educated in U.S. universities, such as Mike Kamwendo, the managing editor of the *Daily Times* and the *Malawi News*. In 1980 a number of Malawi students were studying journalism and photography in universities in West Germany, India and the United States. Some technicians have received their training at the Malawi Polytechnic College in Blantyre. But most of the personnel have received either institute-type and/or on-the-job training.

Many of the broadcasters have attended 12-week to six-month institutes operated by the BBC, the West German government or private organizations. In-country or on-the-job training for broadcasters has been conducted by expatriate advisers and senior MBC staff members. Peace Corps and British Volunteer Service Overseas specialists have assisted with staff training in Malawi.

Recently the tendency has been to hold institutes within Malawi itself. In 1978 the Information department, aided by the Thomson Foundation, mounted a three-month media course for Malawi News Agency and district information officers. In 1980 Reuters organized a short course in Malawi for journalists, and a six-week course for journalists drawn from the Malawi News Agency, the MBC and Blantyre Newspapers was held at Mpemba Staff Training College. In this African-led institute, Kenya journalist and Information Office Peter Mwaura acted as chief lecturer for the course.

Summary

Malawi's tiny press and media industry face formidable problems, located in a predominantly rural setting where education and literacy are low and only a small elite have the interest, funds and skills to support and develop the media. Moreover, the media lack historical tradition and the media personnel have not been adequately trained. In that setting, the government owns, operates and keeps a tight control on virtually all the media.

Although prospects for the future are not bright, not all is bleak. Although nothing indicates governmental ownership or controls will be lifted soon, the government is in a position to make the media serve as tools in behalf of the development of the nation. Fortunately, too, training is improving and the media operations are becoming more and more professional. However, because of the shortages of human and economic resources, the press and broadcasting in Malawi will have a long uphill battle to develop into fully professional operations and to make a maximum impact in the service of the Malawi citizenry.

CHRONOLOGY

1977   Malawi government embarks on a policy of liberalization. Foreign correspondents invited to visit Malawi for first time since 1973.

1978   President Banda holds his first international news conference since 1973.
Foreign correspondents banned from Malawi for their alleged erroneous reporting of the national elections.

1979   Mike Kamwendo becomes managing editor of *Daily Times* and *Malawi News*.

1980   Reuters wire agency criticized for quoting a Zambian story saying Malawi was refusing to recognize national boundaries.

BIBLIOGRAPHY

Crosby, Cynthia. *Historical Dictionary of Malawi*. London, 1980.

"Dr. Banda Versus the Press." *IPI Report*. September/October 1973, pp. 1-2.

Europa Yearbook, Volume II. London, 1980.

Hachten, William A. *Muffled Drums: The News Media in Africa*. Ames, Iowa, 1971.

Head, Sydney W. *Broadcasting in Africa*. Philadelphia, 1974.

"Journalists—Students for Life." *This Is Malawi*. December 1980, pp. 12-13.

"Malawi." *IPI Report*. August 1974, p. 14.

"Malawi Refutes a Reuter Report." *This Is Malawi*. November 1980, p. 16.

Malawi Yearbook, 1978. Blantyre, 1978.

Merrill, John, Bryan, Carter, and Alisky, Marvin. *The Foreign Press*. Baton Rouge, 1970.

UNESCO. *Statistical Yearbook, 1978-1979*. Paris, 1980.

MALAYSIA

by Elliott S. Parker

BASIC DATA

Population: 12.7 million (1977, est.)
Area: 329,370 sq. km. (127,170 sq. mi.)
GNP: M$35.4 billion (US$16.4 billion)
Literacy Rate: 75%
Language(s): Bahasa Malaysia (Jawi and
 Rumi); Mandarin, Hokkien and Cantonese
 Chinese; Tamil; Hindi; English
Number of Dailies: 43
 Aggregate Circulation: 1.5 million (1980, est.)
 Circulation per 1,000: 118
Number of Nondailies: NA
 Aggregate Circulation: NA
 Circulation per 1,000: NA

Number of Periodicals: NA
Number of Radio Stations: 1
Number of Television Stations: 1
Number of Radio Receivers: 1.27 million (1979,
 est.)
 Radio Receivers per 1,000: 100
Number of Television Sets: 692,017 (1979, est.)
 Television Sets per 1,000: 55
Total Annual Newsprint Consumption: NA
Per Capita Newsprint Consumption: NA
Total Newspaper Ad Receipts: M$106.9 million
 (US$48.8 million) (1979, est.)
 As % of All Ad Expenditures: 59 (1979, est.)

Background & General Characteristics

Malaysia is a diverse country. This deceptively simple but primary fact affects the country in every dimension—social, economic, political, cultural. The communications system mirrors this complexity.

Most vividly reflected in the mass media are divisions by race, language and ethnicity. There are three principal racial groups. Slightly over half the population is Malay, slightly over one-third is Chinese and about 10 percent is Indian. (Although both Chinese and Indians may be Malaysian, or citizens of Malaysia, the term "Malay" refers to the indigenous Malays or *bumiputras*.) These three groups have dramatically different cultures, religions, languages and traditions.

Dividing along linguistic lines, the Malays speak Bahasa Malaysia, the national language, and the standardized variant of classical Malay which was the lingua franca throughout the archipelago before the entrance of colonial powers. Due to religious and cultural similarities, Indonesia and Malaysia have been cooperating in developing a common form of the language for both

countries. Malay can be written in two styles: Jawi, written in Arabic script, and Rumi, written in Roman letters. Rumi is the modern and prevailing form.

The standard Chinese dialect, known as Mandarin to non-Chinese speakers, is taught in Chinese schools throughout the world. However, Chinese is also divided into a number of other mutually unintelligible dialects. These dialects use essentially the same characters for writing, which serves as a connecting thread among varying Chinese linguistic groups. Mandarin is not the mother tongue of most Chinese in Southeast Asia or Malaysia. Two-thirds of the Chinese speakers in Malaysia use either Hokkien or Cantonese, dialects from southern China. About 37 percent of the population uses some form of Chinese as a mother tongue.

About 12 percent of the population speak Tamil as the mother tongue. This south Indian language is used here, as in the other linguistic groups, for simplicity. Indians may also speak Malayalam or Hindi. Tamil is the most used language in the Indian community, but it is traditional to speak of "Malays," "Indians" or "Chinese," with the realization that within these simplistic groupings there are other very distinct divisions.

Most Malaysians also use or understand at least one other language. Urban dwellers tend to be bi- or trilingual, usually in English, Bahasa Malaysia or Chinese. In the rural areas of the east coast of the peninsula, the most commonly used language shifts dramatically to Malay. English is widely understood in urban areas. Bahasa Malaysia became the country's national language in 1957, and since 1970, language policy has been reinforced by deemphasizing English-medium schools, while retaining the teaching of English as a subject.

The country has two distinct geographic regions. Peninsular Malaysia, or West Malaysia, extends south from the Indochinese peninsula. The two states of Sabah and Sarawak are located 500 miles across the South China Sea on the northern coast of Borneo. Collectively, they are called East Malaysia and add a degree of geographic complexity to the mosaic.

In addition to the diversity of language and ethnicity, the country is divided along economic and political lines. The Chinese have been primarily small-business people, not widely represented in government administration or politics, and concentrated in cities and towns. Politics and government have been the province of the Malays, who are heavily represented in rural areas. Restructuring this demographic architecture has been a prime focus of government policy since the riots of May 13, 1969.

In 1969, following national elections, the country was shaken with race riots. Hundreds were killed, Parliament was suspended and the country was put under control of a National Operations Council for a time. In the aftermath, plans were made for the restructuring of society to eliminate economic disparities and ethnic identification by class or race. The procedures are spelled out in a series of five-year plans, the third of which ended in 1980. The philosophy is spelled out in the *Rukunegara* or National Ideology.

The *Rukunegara* sets out five goals for the country (national unity, a democratic way of life, a just society, a liberal approach to cultural traditions, and a technologically progressive society) based on five principles (belief in God, loyalty to the king, upholding of the Constitution, rule of law, and good behavior and morality).

This restructuring has a tremendous effect on the mass media. The emphasis on Bahasa Malaysia has resulted in broader use, increasing circulation, and a higher quality in publications employing it. Media are expected to cooperate with government policy and assist in development.

News content and immediacy are not always the most important considerations. Newspapers carry a high proportion of undated, timeless material about development and government activities. On the death of the prime minister it was hours before the government media carried the story. Sixty percent of the news in Malaysian papers originates from government. Reporting tends to be bland and uncritical. Opinions and editorials are usually about international subjects or noncontroversial local subjects.

There are exceptions. The first prime minister of independent Malaysia writes a column, "As I See It," for the Penang-based *Star* newspaper that is often critical, and the small weekly tabloid *Watan* has been critical of some government policies. The pseudonymous columnist Sri Delima, in her column "As I Was Passing," and cartoonist "Lat" offer perceptive scenes of Malaysian society.

A significant number of Malaysians read papers, especially in another language, not for news, but to improve or maintain their ability in the second language.

Like the population, newspapers were essentially immigrants. The first paper, the *Prince of Wales Island Gazette,* started in Penang in 1805 for the English colonial community. The first Chinese-language periodical was started in Malacca by missionaries to proselytize for converts in China, while the Malay-language press began towards the end of the century with an orientation to the overseas Arab community, widespread in this crossroads of trading. The Tamil press accompanied Indian plantation workers as Chinese papers accompanied tin miners. Newspapers related closely to their ethnic constituency and contained great amounts of news from the homeland.

Until the independence and consolidation of the three countries, the journalistic history of Malaysia, Singapore and Indonesia overlapped and intertwined. In the early years of the 20th century, papers started developing a stronger identification with the local community, but were still oriented towards ethnic concerns.

With the invasion of Malaya by the Japanese at the beginning of World War II, some (mainly Chinese-language) papers went underground while the Japanese took over others as propaganda organs.

The English left a legacy of media control. This was expanded during what was called the Emergency, the 12 years of insurgency that began in 1948, when communists were trying to gain control, posing a major threat to stability. Media campaigns were heavily used to combat the terrorists.

Advocacy is not new to Malaysian journalism. Newspapers have been used to propagate and maintain colonialism, spread Christianity, spread and modernize Islam, promote Malay literature and further the struggle for independence. After the riots of 1969, media were again seen as a major tool to restructure society and build a national consciousness.

There are four English-language papers. The oldest and most famous is the *New Straits Times* (formerly the *Straits Times*), started in 1845 as a business and shipping intelligence paper. This 182,000-circulation daily, morning broadsheet is published in Kuala Lumpur with its sister paper, the *Malay Mail,* an afternoon tabloid, which emphasizes lighter news and features. It was bought in 1952 when the then Singapore-based *Straits Times* was looking for a Malaysian property. The *Mail's* circulation is about 55,000.

The *Star,* when it was started in 1971 in Penang, was modeled on its Hong Kong cousin and the popular British tabloids. It soon became more serious, retained its format and moved to Kuala Lumpur. Circulation has grown from about 10,000 in the first year to over 63,000.

The sole English peninsular paper published outside the capital is the *National Echo* in Penang, which started early in the century as the *Straits Echo* to spread the ideas of Sun Yat-sen. It changed the name to reflect its status as a national paper, rather than a paper limited to the northern part of the country. Current circulation is 31,000.

All of the English papers have Sunday editions. Two papers have begun recently. The specialized *Business Times* was formed by splitting the shipping and financial section of the *New Straits Times* off to form a new publication in 1976. Circulation is about 7,500. A biweekly tabloid, *New Thrill,* probes

"the unknown, the mysterious and the exciting."

The oldest Malay-language paper is the *Jawi* script *Utusan Melayu* (and its Sunday edition, *Utusan Zaman*), which started in Singapore in 1939 and moved to Kuala Lumpur in 1952. Daily circulation is about 42,000. The early Malay papers catered heavily to Islamic groups, particularly those of Arab background. In the periods immediately before and following World War II the Malay papers were the primary agent in building a Malay consciousness and identity.

Like the Chinese-language papers, early Malay papers were staffed not by trained journalists but writers, essayists and politicians who needed a forum for their views. Now, as then, the Chinese and Malay papers devote a large amount of space to purely literary work, such as novels and poetry.

Launched in 1967 with a circulation of 8,000, *Utusan Malaysia* (the Sunday edition is *Mingguan Malaysia*) rapidly eclipsed the rival *Berita Harian* (and its Sunday edition, *Berita Minggu*). It now has a circulation of 148,000 compared to *Berita Harian's* 102,000. *Utusan Malaysia* is noted for knowledgeable coverage of domestic politics and human-interest features. Both papers use *Rumi.*

A new Malay paper was started in 1976 in Penang. Its name, *Bintang Timur,* is suggestive of one of the pioneer Malay papers published across the Malacca Straits in Padang, Sumatra, in 1864. Circulation of this tabloid is about 20,000.

Chinese papers include the *Sin Chew Jit Poh (Xing Zhou Ri Bao)* (daily circulation, 66,000), *Nanyang Siang Pau (Nan Yang Shang Bao)* (110,000 circulation), *China Press (Zhong Guo Bao)* (52,000 circulation), *Malayan Thung Pau (Ma Lai Ya Tong Bao)* (68,000 circulation), *Shin Min Daily News (Xin Ming Ri Bao)* (81,000 circulation), and the *New Life Post (Xin Sheng Huo Bao)* (105,000 circulation), a bi-weekly tabloid.* All of these are published in Kuala Lumpur.

Two Chinese papers are published in Penang: *Kwong Wah Jit Pao (Guang Hua Ri Bao)* (46,000 circulation) and *Sin Pin Jih Poh (Xin Pin Ri Bao)* (40,000 circulation). The *Kin Kwok Daily News (Jian Guo Ri Bao)* is published in Ipoh (6,000 circulation).

Two papers are published in Tamil—*Tamil*

---

[1]In this chapter, the translated or transliterated name as given on the nameplate is given first, if any. This is followed by the *pinyin* transliteration of the Chinese characters, where available.

Nesan and *Tamil Malar*. Both are published in Kuala Lumpur, are broadsheet size, and average eight to 10 pages. *Tamil Nesan* has a circulation of 28,000 and *Tamil Malar* 15,000. A Punjabi paper, *Malayan Samachar* (2,000 circulation), a small, weekly tabloid is also published.

All of the above papers are published in Peninsular Malaysia. Sabah and Sarawak, in comparison, are much less richly served.

Sarawak has four daily English papers: *The New Vanguard, Sarawak Herald,* the *Borneo Post,* and the oldest, the *Sarawak Tribune. The New Vanguard, Sarawak Herald* and the *Sarawak Tribune* also run pages of news in Bahasa Malaysia. Only the *Tribune* and the *Post* have circulation figures exceeding 10,000. The other two probably have less than half this.

The largest Chinese paper in Sarawak is the *See Hua Daily News,* with a claimed circulation of 21,000. The other Chinese papers are the *Chinese Daily News* (3,000 circulation), *Berita Petang Sarawak* (17,000 circulation), *Malaysia Daily News* (7,000 circulation), *Miri Daily News* (9,500 circulation), *People's Tribune* (3,000 circulation) and the *World Morning Post* (5,000 circulation).

Sabah has one small (2,000 circulation) paper in Bahasa Malaysia, *Sinar Usia.* The two English papers are the *Daily Express* and the *Kinabalu Sabah Times,* both of which use Bahasa Malaysia and Kadazan inserts. The *Daily Express* has circulation of about 40,000; the *Times'* circulation is about 7,000.

The largest Chinese paper in Sabah is the *Overseas Chinese Daily News* with a circulation of about 45,000. The *Sandakan Jih Pao* has a circulation of 25,000. There are three other Chinese papers: *Merdeka Daily News* (9,800 circulation), *Tawau Jih Pao* (1,800 circulation) and the *Asia Times* (7,000 circulation).

(Circulation figures given are not necessarily audited—many are estimates or claimed by the publisher.)

The magazine market has seen many new titles, but many last for only a few issues. Numerous inexperienced publishers start magazines to capitalize on the advertising revenue. The most successful magazines are those published by established book and newspaper organizations that have the experience, capital, and distribution networks.

In Chinese, the most popular magazines are *Women* and *New Tide*. In English, the most popular magazines are *Reader's Digest, Movie News* and *Her World*.

Unlike the English and Chinese magazine market, the Bahasa Malaysia market does not have foreign competition. The Bahasa Malaysia press has seen a profusion of magazines as advertisers target newly affluent Malay readers and non-Malays who want to practice their language skills. The most popular magazines are those dealing with fashion, women's interests and movie and television entertainment, such as *Jelita, Utusan Radio dan TV (Radio and TV Guide), Majalah Filem (Film Magazine)* and *Filem dan Fesyen (Film and Fashion)*.

The most influential newspapers are the *New Straits Times, Utusan Malaysia* and *Sin Chew Jit Poh*.

Economic Framework

Malaysia has a very strong economy, with the resilience to bounce back during the economic turbulence of the 1970s. The GNP increased in the six- to ten-percent range through most of that decade. Both the overall economic climate and redistributions called for in the Second and Third Malaysia Plans have resulted in at least the larger papers showing profits, due mainly to increased advertising.

Given the limited amount of time available for advertising, and limits on what products may be advertised on radio and television, over half the advertising revenue is spent in newspapers. Of this percentage, about half is spent in the English papers and 40 percent spent in the Chinese press. The government is considering selling more commercial time in the electronic media to shorten the waiting time for advertisers.

In Peninsular Malaysia, most newspapers are corporate entities and, by law, a majority of the ownership must be in Malaysian hands. In East Malaysia, most papers are owned by political-party leaders.

The largest publishing group is the New Straits Times Group. Under the umbrella holding-company, Fleetprint, the group is composed of the *New Straits Times,* Berita Publishing and Financial Publications. The group is 80 percent owned by government-related corporations and 20 percent by Singapore's Times Publishing. Before the separation of Malaysia and Singapore in 1965, the *Straits Times* as well as *Nanyang Siang Pau* and *Sin Chew Jit Poh* were branches of the Singapore parent papers.

The New Straits Times, in addition to publishing the newspaper, owns—along with the Singapore *Straits Times* and the *South China Morning Post* in Hong Kong—the *Asia Magazine,* a semiweekly supplement distributed with Sunday newspapers in the region.

The Berita publishing subsidiary produces a variety of periodicals, such as *Her World* and *Jelita* for women, *Fanfare* and *Malaysian Business.* It also publishes annuals aimed at the Malaysian market, such as the *New Straits Times Annual, Bumiputra Trade Directory* and *Information Malaysia,* in addition to books.

Financial Publications publishes *Business Times.*

UMNO (United Malay National Organization), the main partner in the ruling National Front party, owns two-thirds of the *Utusan Melayu/Utusan Malaysia* group, which also publishes *Utusan Radio dan TV, Selecta Femina, Wanita* and *Filem dan Fesyen.*

Star Publications is 75 percent owned by the MCA (Malayan Chinese Association), the second major partner in the National Front. It bought *Kwong Wah Jit Poh* in 1974 and publishes two magazines, *Galaxie* in English and *Shang Hai* in Chinese.

Nanyang Siang Pau is majority owned by Malaysians, although the Singapore parent of the same name retains a few shares. The primary connection between the two papers is in advertising, where common ad rates have been developed. There is some exchange of news and features and occasional combined coverage of foreign events. *Sin Chew* has similar arrangements with the parent paper in Singapore.

The owner of the *Tamil Nesan* is a high ranking official in the MIC (Malaysian Indian Congress), the third major component of the National Front.

Life Publishers is a rapidly expanding group which publishes the bi-weekly *New Life Post* paper, and the periodicals *New Tide, Mister, The Track* and *Feminine,* all in Chinese.

Much of the newspaper competition in Malaysia centers around the problems of distribution and the desire of some papers to become more "national." While the *Star* has moved south to Kuala Lumpur, the *New Straits Times* is moving both north and south. In 1977 the *Straits Times* spent R$6,825,000 (US$3.25 million)* on presses and facilities to enable them to print an edition in Prai, across from Penang. Page negatives are flown each night to the northern press. Other papers are delivered by truck to Johore Bahru in the south and Kota Bahru on the east coast. Some copies are air-delivered to East Malaysia. Other papers deliver throughout the peninsula by truck.

The *New Straits Times* owns 40 percent of Enesty, a separate company that handles delivery and distribution of the Straits Times publications.

With the exception of 1973, when newsprint was in short supply worldwide, newsprint supply has been adequate. All newsprint is imported, almost all from Canada. The late 1980 price was about $445 per ton.

Journalists are represented by the National Union of Journalists. There have been no strikes in the last few years. In West Malaysia, there are probably 3,000 people employed as journalists (writers, photographers and editors).

Circulation reflects geographical and ethnic divisions. Until the *Star* moved to Kuala Lumpur, 75 percent of the circulation was in Penang and the northern states. The *China Press* is effectively available only within Kuala Lumpur. The *Jawi Utusan Melayu* circulates widely in rural, conservative areas. English papers are read mainly in large urban areas. Few East Malaysian papers are available on the peninsula and relatively few peninsular papers circulate in East Malaysia. By law, Singapore papers are not allowed to circulate in Malaysia (and vice versa).

In West Malaysia, slightly over half of the adult population read a daily paper in 1979. About 21 percent read a Chinese paper and 12 percent an English paper. In the last five years, Chinese readership has increased slightly within a longer-term decline. English readership has decreased slightly. Readership of the Tamil papers has been increasing steadily since 1975, but still accounts for less than four percent of the total adult readers.

Readership of Bahasa Malaysia dailies has been steadily increasing since 1975, after

---

[2]Local currency throughout the rest of this chapter has been converted into U.S. equivalents at the rate of R$2.10-US$1.00.

a previous period of decline. In 1975, 12 percent of the adults read a Malay paper compared to 19 percent in 1979. The increase is in the Rumi papers, at the expense of the Jawi paper *(Utusan Melayu),* which has seen a 50 percent drop in readership in the last five years.

These figures, from Survey Research Malaysia, do not necessarily reflect circulation. "Pass-along" readership varies according to social and economic factors, depending on ethnic group. Malay papers have approximately 12 readers per copy, the Chinese and Tamil papers have about five readers per copy, while the English papers have fewer than three readers per copy.

More than 70 percent of the readers read *Utusan Malaysia,* the *New Straits Times, Nanyang Siang Pau* or *Sin Chew Jit Poh,* which account for 45 percent of the circulation.

In November 1980 the average daily price of a daily paper was increased to 17 cents from 14 cents. The last increase was in 1978, when the price had been 12 cents. Sunday editions run about three cents more.

Most major papers are printed by offset, although the *Straits Times* is the only one to use an electronic front-end system. The other offset papers use photocomposition. The remaining papers are printed by letterpress.

Press Laws

The constitution guarantees freedom of speech and expression and thus, derivatively, freedom of the press. Parliament has enacted laws deemed necessary for the security and well being of the nation.

The Printing Presses Act of 1948 requires the registration of printing presses and a permit to publish a newspaper or other serial. Both the registration and permit (called the KDN after the initials of the issuing authority, the *Kementerian Dalam Negeri* or Ministry of Home Affairs) may be withdrawn or suspended at any time. Permits must be renewed every year.

Under the original act of 1948 and subsequent amendments in 1971 and 1974, newspapers cannot publish any matter harmful to the public order, security or morality of the country, or misuse facts concerning disorders; they must insure the majority of material published is relevant to Malaysian affairs; must inform the ministry of changes in editors, printers or publishers; and must be under at least 70 percent Malaysian-citizen control. Under this act the minister of home affairs may also require a publisher to print corrections or retractions.

The 1948 Sedition Act was also amended in 1971 to prohibit the discussion of four sensitive issues: adoption of Malay as the national language; special rights granted to the Malays; the special position of the state sultans, or rulers; and citizenship policies for non-Malays.

In 1971, the editor of *Utusan Melayu,* Melan Abdullah, and an assistant editor were charged with sedition, on grounds that a headline on an editorial about the abolition of Tamil- and English-language schools, based on a speech of the now-minister of education, was seditious. On appeal, Melan was found not guilty, but the fine and conviction of his assistant was upheld.

Earlier in the year, an opposition party member (Democratic Action Party) was convicted and fined for making a seditious speech. Fan Yew Teng, the editor of the party's journal, *The Rocket,* was also convicted of sedition after publishing the speech, although he later won on appeal.

Under the Control of Imported Publications Act of 1958 and the 1971 amendment, the minister of home affairs may prohibit the importation of publications which he feels may be prejudicial to public order, morality or security.

The Cinematographic Film Ordinance of 1952, as revised in 1971, empowers a Film Censorship Board to censor all films prior to public screening in accordance with guidelines from the Ministry of Home Affairs.

Under these guidelines, the board considers the racial and religious sensitivities of the various ethnic communities. Sex scenes, nudity and "lustful" acts are not permitted, nor are films that sympathize with the criminal or show that crime pays, or films that attempt to show there is no God.

Under the Internal Security Act of 1960 (ISA), the minister of home affairs may prohibit the printing, publication, sale, issue, distribution or possession of any document or publication containing material harmful to security or public order, or that incites violence, or promotes feelings of hostility between different races or classes of the population. The ISA also allows for preventive detention of suspects for indefinite periods.

Many of these laws were amended and strengthened following the racial riots that erupted in May 1969.

Several other regulations have sections that affect the media. Under the Public Order (Preservation) Ordinance, the telecommunications authorities may withdraw or limit the right of a person or the public to use telecommunications facilities. The Copyright Act of 1969 is an attempt to limit pirating of creative works. In the past, pirating of audio materials has been especially prevalent. The Defamation Ordinance of 1957 protects the public against libel and slander. Legitimate defenses against libel suits in Malaysia are apology without malice, truth, absolute privilege and fair comment.

Politicians have been charged under the Official Secrets Act. Lim Kit Siang, the leader of the opposition, was convicted of receiving classified military information and taking no action to prevent its publication in the official party journal, *The Rocket.* On appeal, the conviction stood, but the sentence and fines were reduced, allowing him to retain his seat in Parliament.

In 1979 an East Malaysian politician, Dzulkifli bin Abdul Hamid, was charged under the Official Secrets Act for leaking a secret letter concerning Vietnamese refugees to the *Kinabalu Sabah Times.*

A writer for *Business Times,* a subsidiary of the *New Straits Times,* appealed a judgment against him concerning two articles he had written for the paper in 1977. He was charged under the Securities Industry Act for writing an article that was "false or misleading in a material particular." The charge against him was not a direct attack on the press, but gained importance to journalists when his former employer, the *Business Times,* refused to support him or pay his legal costs.

The East Malaysian states of Sabah and Sarawak have equally stringent regulations on printing and publishing.

The Printing Press Ordinance of 1939 in Sabah requires the registration of presses and a deposit. A permit to publish a paper is also required. One of the conditions of the permit is that it must surrender any documents the paper may hold if requested by the proper government official.

Printing presses must also be registered in Sarawak under the Printing Press Ordinance of 1962 and newspapers must obtain a permit under the Local Newspaper Ordinances of 1958 and 1962. A deposit is required for registration and permits are issued when the paper agrees not to publish any material that might induce a person to commit an offense, or is prejudicial to the public safety or security.

The Malaysian judiciary follows English tradition closely and is independent of the other branches of government.

Censorship

The Ministry of Information, using the Printing Presses Act, the Internal Security Act, and the Control of Imported Publications Act, censors both domestic and imported material.

The guidelines for film censors are the most explicit. In 1974, after a plethora of films like *Hot Pickup, Sexy Susan Knows How,* and violent "spaghetti Easterns" like the *One-Armed Swordsman* and *The Big Boss,* film censorship was restructured.

Established in 1966, the Film Censorship Board, as restructured, consists of a chairman, deputy chairman and 12 members. This board screens every film made in or coming into Malaysia. Films may be banned, passed or cut. Distributors unhappy with the board's decision may appeal to an 18-member Committee of Appeal. Members of both boards are appointed by the king.

If a film is turned down by the appeals committee, but is thought to have educational, historical or cultural value, a final appeal may be made to a 27-member Assessment Committee.

In 1979, 942 films were passed by the board and 66 were banned outright. All those banned were foreign films. Films that have been banned include *Jesus Christ, Superstar* and *The Godfather.*

The decision to ban *The Godfather* was made because it was felt the film encouraged the public to seek advice from criminals and this coincided with a period of increased terrorist activity. The chief police officer of the northern state of Perak had recently been assassinated.

Films to be shown on television are further vetted by television officials, although RTM is represented on the censorship board.

The guidelines are meant to control the screening of films dealing with sex, violence, crime, politics, religion, bigotry, horror and "yellow culture." The last is taken to mean, in general, the decadent parts of Western culture. Films dealing with the law must show justice being administered and must not encourage anti-government feelings. In 1971, for example, news film showing violent demonstrations in Europe was not allowed to air. Crime must never pay and there must be respect for law officers.

Films that glorify communism, oppose government policy or the *Rukunegara* are banned. Films that glorify "any particular race while degrading another would also be banned." In television, the series "Garrison's Gorillas" was dropped because the Germans were always on the losing side and this was felt to project the idea of "race supremacy." The same argument resulted in the "Tarzan" series and "Roots" being banned. And, in this Islamic country, the TV mini-series "Holocaust" was not shown because it dealt with Jews.

Films that insult "public dignity by showing an irresponsible way of life and behavior not acceptable to the Malaysian society" are banned, as are films dealing with sadism, cruelty and excessive violence, and also those that demonstrate the use of firearms.

Extending these themes to the print media, one can predict the subjects that would be avoided in print—at least those that are applicable across media lines.

Since local editors know the sensitive subjects to avoid, relatively few papers have had their publishing permits or "KDN's" suspended or revoked. If a publication strays too near sensitive subjects, the ministry will informally suggest how the story is to be played. International publications bear the brunt of censorship.

There have been government calls for a press council or advisory council, but none exist at present.

Few federal laws exist that restrict officials from giving journalists information, unless the information may affect national security or military secrets. On occasion, however, state officials have ordered department heads not to talk with writers.

More important than any formal regulations limiting the flow of information, are the lack of a tradition of investigative or in-depth reporting on the part of the newspapers, and the traditional—and strong—reticence on the part of civil servants to talk with journalists.

State-Press Relations

The Ministry of Information carries out most of the communication activities of the government through its three departments: the Department of Broadcasting, Department of Information and *Filem Negara Malaysia* (National Film Unit).

The policies and activities of the ministry are delineated by government economic policies—starting with the First Malaysia Plan in 1965 and continuing through the Third Malaysia Plan ending in 1980—and the *Rukunegara.*

Using the three departments, the ministry can command all the channels of communication. All domestic radio and television, with the exception of a small, wired network in three major cities, is run by the Broadcasting Department. The information department publishes magazines (*Sinar Zaman* in Malay, *Tou Shih* in Chinese and *Udhayam* in Tamil) as well as occasional pamphlets and other printed material to promote government objectives. The total circulation for the 30-odd publications of the department is probably around three million. It also designs billboards, posters, stage shows and exhibitions, and sends mobile film and speaking units to outlying areas. *Filem Negara Malaysia* produces and distributes documentary and nonfiction films, which are presented through the mobile units, other government agencies, TV Malaysia and commercial movie theaters. In 1979 the unit produced 95 titles with a total viewing time of 1,300 minutes. Distribution to foreign countries is handled through the Ministry of Foreign Affairs.

Within the Department of Information, the Press and Liaison Division provides the channel through which official information on government policies and activities reaches the mass media, usually through press releases. Up to 20 percent of the local news used by large newspapers is unaltered press-release material.

The division also issues full texts of speeches of officials, furnishes photographs of official functions, informs media of forthcoming events and accredits local and foreign correspondents.

Besides the mass media, person-to-person communication is handled by the Community Development Communication division. Mobile units (204 land and 45 riverine units) are equipped with public address systems, film projectors and audiovisual aids. Government officials explain policy and objectives to groups of people primarily where radio and TV reception is weak, or to emphasize particular policies such as drug abuse, *Rukunegara,* Third Malaysia Plan, the metric system or voter registration. These topics may be covered in short courses, assemblies, briefings, stage shows or house-to-house visits.

Journalists and editors not only receive

guidelines on how to play particular stories, but government officials give general advice. A former prime minister said the press "must not give rise to misunderstanding"; a deputy information minister said journalists "should persuade the people to accept national policies for their own good"; and the secretary of the National Union of Journalists asked the press to support the Second Malaysia Plan and the New Economic Policy. A police superintendent called cooperation between police and the press "vital," and suggested it be strengthened.

The minister of education in 1978 said there should be freedom of the press, "as this would help the people acquire maturity of thought." He added, however, that "it is advisable for the Malaysian press to be self-disciplined or maintain self-restraint" in a multi-racial society, where the emphasis must be on building a united nation.

Some senior government officials have asked the press to be more critical and have gone so far as to tell civil servants to emulate the journalists by talking to a broad spectrum of the public to gain information and not limit their contacts to ministers and other high officials.

In addition to general suggestions, the government manages news more directly. When Prime Minister Tun Abdul Razak died in London of leukemia in 1976, most of the Malaysian public was shocked, as it had been told only that he was suffering from exhaustion due to overwork.

Some state officials have initiated policies that prohibit government employees from talking to the press. Current federal policy dictates that public relations officers may not talk with unaccredited foreign reporters or writers unless the reporter has a special permit from the prime minister's office.

After a blackout near the capital, a spokesman for the semi-official National Electricity Board replied to a reporter's question on the subject by saying there was no reason for the public to know the origin of the blackout. If the public needed to know they would be told, the spokesman said.

Given the sensitivity of editors to government desires, few papers have been suspended or closed. Following the riots that shook the country in 1969, all papers were suspended for two days, the Chinese-language *China Press* for two weeks.

In 1973 an irregular publication, *Truth,* was banned when it did not follow the government stand on the situation in west Asia. The federal government also revoked the license of *The International Times,* a daily paper in Kuching. Two years later, one issue of *Suara Rakyat* was banned and the paper folded soon after. A successor, *Pelita Rakyat,* did not have its KDN renewed at the end of 1975. At the end of 1980, *Tamil Malar* was suspended following demonstrations against the paper after it inadvertently published a column disparaging Islam.

Since 1976 three editors have been held under the Internal Security Act. In the most famous of these cases, the managing editor of the *New Straits Times,* Abdul Samad Ismail, and the assistant editor of *Berita Harian,* Samani bin Mohamed Amin, were charged with working against the "best interests of Malaysia." In televised confessions, they stated they were tied to communist and Marxist groups in Singapore and Malaysia. Samad Ismail had been a leader in fighting for independence from England in the 1950s, and a month before his detention had received the *Hadiah Pejuang Sastra* (Literary Pioneer) award from the prime minister, for his "crucial contribution to the nation's literature" and for instilling "national consciousness in the people in their struggle for independence."

Earlier, Singapore had jailed the editor and assistant editor of the *Berita Harian* (Singapore), who, in turn, confessed that Samad was the "mastermind" of a "communist scheme" to "subvert the Malays."

Samad remains in jail. Samani was released 15 months later.

In East Malaysia, the states of Sabah and Sarawak have suspended or closed more papers. (When Malaysia was formed, Sabah and Sarawak retained rights that other states did not have.) Three employees of the *Kinabalu Sabah Times* were given 24 hours to leave the state in 1976, resulting in the paper being closed for several days. At the same time, three staff members of the *Daily Express* were allowed to return after being deported under a previous administration. The state government also banned two Chinese papers, *Sabah Shi Pao* (the Chinese edition of the *Kinabalu Sabah Times*) and the *Sandakan Jih Pao.* The Sarawak state government suspended the *See Hua Daily News* several times in the early 1970s.

Attitude Toward Foreign Media

Journalists desiring to be accredited correspondents in Malaysia must apply to the Press and Liaison Division of the Ministry of

Information. If they reside in the country they will also require an identity card and work permit. Prior approval for cables is not required.

No foreign correspondents have been jailed, although several have been banned or expelled from Sabah or Sarawak. Both states have retained their own immigration laws and even citizens from other Malaysian states must apply for visas. In 1979 K. Das, a Malaysian citizen and correspondent for the *Far Eastern Economic Review,* was forced to leave Sarawak after writing stories on local politics. The month before, Hugh Mabbett, a New Zealander who had lived many years in West Malaysia, was forced to leave Sabah. He had been hired a few months earlier to be editor of the *Kinabalu Sabah Times.* In 1970 Henry Kamm, *The New York Times* correspondent, was told to leave both states.

Foreign publications are more often banned or censored than domestic. To prevent outside information about the 1969 riots from reaching the Malaysian public, censors met planes at the airport and burned newspapers carrying coverage of the disturbances. These papers were from England *(Daily Telegraph, Sunday Times, The Observer* and *The Economist)* and Australia. Copies were made of some articles and smuggled into Malaysia from Singapore. People found in possession of the copies were arrested and fined.

The distributors of *Time* magazine were ordered to tear out a color section on the People's Republic of China in 1970 because it "could mislead the public." Newsmagazines have also been banned for reproducing an etching of Muhammad. Muslims believe no one can know what the Prophet looked like. The picture was blacked out.

Outside propaganda is not limited to publications. In the waning days of the Cultural Revolution in China, it was discovered that children's toys, cars and trucks were being imported with the slogans of Chairman Mao painted on the sides as part of the design.

Over the years, the *Far Eastern Economic Review,* as the major regional news publication, has found itself banned or censored on numerous occasions. In 1973 the *Review* was banned or cut several times for including stories dealing with a leadership crisis in the federal government, and with the Malayan Chinese Association. In 1976 it was delayed one week while eight pages on the death of Mao were torn out. In 1980 photographs of a braless Hawaiian girl were covered with black ink. In late 1979 the Amnesty Interna-

tional report on Malaysia was banned, as was the issue of *Asiaweek,* a news magazine from Hong Kong, when it carried a story on the report.

The government has been extremely sensitive about foreign coverage of Vietnamese refugees. Areas around the refugee camps have been designated "controlled areas" under the Internal Security Act. A Reuters correspondent was escorted out of one of these areas in 1979, and his notes and letters given to him by refugees were confiscated.

News Agencies

Malaysia's national news agency Bernama *(Pertubohan Berita Nasional Malaysia)* commenced operations in 1968 as a statutory body authorized by act of Parliament.

Bernama is managed by a 13-member board of governors. The chairman is appointed by the minister of information, six members represent the government mass media such as Radio-TV Malaysia and the Department of Information, and six members represent private subscribers, such as newspapers.

Bernama has five objectives: 1) to enhance the national prestige; 2) to present objective information on matters of national interest; 3) to report truthfully and fairly the views of all segments of the population; 4) to provide accurate information on Malaysia to foreign correspondents and international news agencies; and 5) to contribute to regional cooperation.

Bernama offers four services to subscribers. The general news service furnishes a daily teleprinter report in both Malay and English. The economic service provides coverage of economic, company and shipping news, and news of the Kuala Lumpur Stock Exchange. This is distributed daily to those subscribers who do not have teleprinter facilities. The foreign news service distributes the Agence France-Presse file to Malaysia media. In 1980 the agency started a pictorial service to distribute feature photos.

Almost all local papers subscribe to Bernama, as do Radio-Television Malaysia, foreign agencies, banks, corporations and education and research centers.

Bernama has various exchange agreements with other agencies including OANA (Organization of Asian News Agencies), Antara (Indonesia), International Islamic News Agency, Tanjug (Yugoslavia) and the

Middle East News Agency. It also participates in the ASEAN (Association of South East Asian Nations) news exchange network.

Twenty percent of the $2.3 million operating budget comes from private subscribers, the remainder from government media.

The agency maintains a permanent office in each state and has a network of about 500 staff writers and stringers throughout the country. Bureaus are also maintained abroad in Jakarta, Bangkok and Manila.

The Bernama wire allows smaller papers, especially those in East Malaysia, to have access both to domestic news and some foreign news. Although large papers have direct links with wire services, most papers are not on solid financial ground and cannot afford this type of hookup. It is also government policy to increase the news flow between the two parts of Malaysia.

Electronic News Media

The electronic media come under the authority of the Department of Broadcasting. The headquarters of both radio and television is at the massive, modern complex called Angkasapuri, near Kuala Lumpur. There are eight regional stations in West Malaysia and regional stations in Sabah and Sarawak.

Radio Malaysia broadcasts over six networks. Four of the networks have a general service catering to specific language groups; one each for Bahasa Malaysia (168 hours per week), English (87 hours per week), Chinese (160 hours per week) and Tamil (93 hours per week). The remaining two, *Radio Ibu Kota* (capital city radio) and an FM stereo service, broadcast mainly music and news. In addition to the four main languages, broadcasts are also made in two main aboriginal languages, Semai and Temiar. In East Malaysia, programs are aired in a variety of languages and dialects including Indonesian, Iban and Kadazan.

Television operates over two networks on the peninsula and Network III in East Malaysia. Most are broadcast in—or subtitled with—Bahasa Malaysia. English, Tamil and Mandarin Chinese are used in news programs.

Depending on geographical area, listeners may also listen to other stations. On an average day, about 20 percent of the audience will listen to Radio Singapore for music and dramatic shows. Rediffusion (Malaysia) Sdn.

Bhd. runs a wired system available to subscribers in the Kuala Lumpur area, the Penang area and Ipoh. Most of the Rediffusion broadcasting is music, although to fulfill the terms of their license, news and information programs from Radio Malaysia are used. Listeners in the northern part of the country may listen to the internal English-language broadcasts for servicemen and families at the Royal Australian Air Force base near Butterworth.

Over the last decade, television viewing has grown steadily with a particularly marked increase in 1979, after the introduction of color transmission. The most popular programs are feature films and light entertainment that draw large, ethnically integrated audiences. A feature film may draw 96 percent of the viewers. At the other extreme, only one percent of the viewers say they "never miss" programs on social or economic development.

Television has grown faster than radio listening in the last decade, and, in fact, radio listening declined over most of this period, picking up slightly in 1979. Music is the popular preference after news. Eighty-three percent of the listeners said they "never listened" to programs on development.

All radio and television sets require an annual license.

The overseas service of Radio Malaysia, *Suara Malaysia* (The Voice of Malaysia) broadcasts in eight languages: Indonesian, English, Chinese, Thai, Arabic, Burmese, Tagalog and Bahasa Malaysia.

The first satellite station was constructed at Kuantan in 1970 for international use, and a second was built in 1975 to relay live programs to East Malaysia.

The policies and operation of radio and television, being totally under government control, give a clearer view of the government's media philosophy without the distorting effects of other influences.

In a predominantly Muslim environment, certain themes contrary to Islam are not allowed; lip-to-lip kissing may not be shown, pork and pork products and liquor cannot be advertised. Cigarette ads are permitted, but only the pack may be shown—beautiful backgrounds and people cannot be used.

News items are selected for the relevance to Malaysia. In 1973 little was shown of the Watergate affair, but extensive pro-Arab coverage was given the Yom Kippur War. Local items are inevitably "good news." Murders, rapes and divorces are not covered.

Ribbon cuttings and dedications are standard fare on newscasts with voice-over narration, although this is slowly being changed. News items are hierarchically graded. If the king is to be shown on the broadcast, this will be the lead item, followed by any item on the prime minister and working down through the protocol list. Women are not permitted as news readers because they might distract the viewer. Opposition party members are not allowed to use television or radio.

Some subjects are not aired, but the ministry also looks for positive values to "build up national consciousness and unity in accordance with the principles of the *Rukunegara*." Productions should project "harmonious race relations, crime does not pay, loyalty to country, rule of law, belief in God."

"Each play," states the ministry, "must carry a message and reflect the country's multiracial society." Plays may be rewritten to emphasize these qualities, and government ministers have written plays to demonstrate what topics dramas should include. Because of this emphasis on positive values, films may be passed by the Film Censorship Board but still not be shown on television.

Non-TV drama may also be banned by the Ministry of Home Affairs. A production about the plight of Vietnamese refugees in Malaysia was not permitted to be performed because it dealt with "sensitive" issues.

Program schedules are skewed towards the rural Malay population, who retire early and have few alternative forms of entertainment. This results in the popular feature films being started earlier in the evening than urban dwellers might like.

In the early 1970s, the government launched a campaign to use more locally made commercials with the goals of portraying a more Malaysian identity on television, helping local studios and agencies and promulgating the use of Bahasa Malaysia.

Foreign-produced commercials were first assessed a five percent surcharge, which was increased in a few years to 50 percent. People and background had to be Malaysian and if the commercial was to be shot outside the country, a Malaysian crew was required. Advertisements must use—or be subtitled in—Bahasa Malaysia. Caucasians are not allowed in commercials, nor is "British- or American-English" allowed to be heard—speech must be "Malaysian-English." By 1980 almost all commercials were locally produced and several had won international awards for excellence.

Percentage distribution of radio programs (1980, average for all networks)	
Information and education	17.2%
Entertainment	51.4
News	14.0
Religious	3.6
Drama	5.1
Sports	2.5
Other	6.2

Percentage distribution of television programs (1980, average for all networks)	
Information and education	22.1%
Entertainment	7.3
News	19.6
Religious	9.9
Drama	36.4
Sports	1.9
Other	2.8

Percentage of television programs imported: 40%

Education & Training

Although the government early recognized the importance of communications in the development of the country, university-level training was slow to emerge. Administrators generally looked to the British or European tradition, which saw journalism as a trade or craft one learned by joining a newspaper as an apprentice or cadet. In some cases, large organizations such as Bernama or the *Straits Times* could afford to hire specialists for a limited time for in-house training.

The first organized courses for journalists were conducted by the South East Asia Press Center (SEAPC), which was formed in 1966 with backing from the Ministry of Information, the Press Foundation of Asia and local newspapers. It was designed to offer in-service courses to working journalists throughout the Southeast Asian area. In 1974, the SEAPC was reorganized as the Malaysian Press Institute and efforts were focused on the problems and training of Malaysian journalists. It offers a variety of short courses in specific topics such as general writing, science writing and photography.

The first university program in communications was started at Universiti Sains Malaysia (then called Penang University) in mid-1971 in the School of Humanities. It offers B.A. and M.A. degrees.

Six months later, in 1972, Institut Teknoloji Mara (ITM) took in the first students for a diploma program in mass communications, specializing in journalism, public relations or advertising. The diplomas are recognized as being equivalent to B.A. degrees from a university. Applicants to the three-year course at ITM must be *bumiputras*. The campus is located in a suburb of Kuala Lumpur.

Universiti Kebangsaan Malaysia (the National University of Malaysia) was established at Bangi, south of the capital, in 1970. In 1976 a Communication Department was added to the Faculty of Social Sciences and Humanities, offering courses in broadcasting, advertising, public relations and development communication. This is a four-year bachelor's-degree program.

All three of the above programs emphasize communication in both Bahasa Malaysia and English, and students have the opportunity to do internships with news organizations.

The University of Malaya offers graduate-level courses in the Department of English that specializes in mass-communications theory and research.

The Institut Penyiaran Tun Abdul Razak (IPTAR) (Tun Abdul Razak Training Center) at Angkaspuri is part of the Ministry of Information and offers short courses in administration and engineering subjects. It was formerly known as the National Broadcast Training Center. It is also the headquarters for the Asian Institute for Broadcasting Development, which offers training courses to students from the Pacific and Asian regions. The AIBD is partially supported by the Malaysian government and UNESCO.

The Institute of Public Relations started short courses in 1973. The first course leads to an introductory certificate in public relations, the second to a full certificate.

Journalistic associations in Malaysia include the Newspaper Publisher's Association and the National Union of Journalists (NUJ). The NUJ is affiliated with the Confederation of ASEAN Journalists.

Summary

The government of Malaysia accepts the classical view of mass communications in a developing country—loosely labeled "development journalism"—that media are to be used to help the country's growth by serving as a conduit of information and actively supporting nation-building, development and the government. Indeed, the idea of development communication found some of the earliest proponents in this country.

The nation faces a variety of problems that affect the way policymakers view the media—and the press in particular, since it is the primary independent medium. In an unstable region, while communist insurgents remain a low-level threat, all of the attendant problems of development are exacerbated in Malaysia's heterogeneous, volatile society. In the face of these problems, among others, government concern about, and control of, the mass media will continue to be a hallmark.

The Malay press, with the support and active encouragement of the government, is drawing an increasing number of readers to all periodicals in Bahasa Malaysia. Advertising revenue, although proportionately low, is increasing, again with active government encouragement. The Malay press has become more secular and professional, and shows increased confidence and viability. Malay, English and Chinese newspapers, in concert, have not only doubled readership in a decade but also increased the number of pages per copy.

English-language papers receive a disproportionate share of advertising revenue; the *New Straits Times* is still considered an elite paper by much of the population. English is seen as a bridging language between ethnic groups and a requirement for access to much technological information.

The Chinese press is also well supported by advertising, but there is a de-emphasis on Chinese education. Formal education is a necessity for literacy in Chinese, and the number of Chinese schools continues to decline, due both to government pressure and community awareness that there is a declining market for Mandarin speakers. Two factors may influence the growth of the Chinese press: next-door neighbor Singapore has recently started a major campaign to make Mandarin the primary Chinese dialect in place of the other dialects and on a par with English; and the Chinese have a long history of respect for the Chinese written language and learning in general. Over the decade, readership of Chinese papers has dropped by a third.

The Tamil press, addressing a much

smaller and generally less affluent audience, and represented by only two papers, is in a long-term decline.

All papers face the problem of attempting to gain or retain readers by using material of interest to their ethnic constituencies, and at the same time, go beyond purely ethnic concerns to the concerns and problems of the entire society.

CHRONOLOGY

1975	Third Malaysia Plan begins.		*Times* thrown out of Saban.
1976	*Sabah Shi Pao* and *Sandakan Jih Pao* suspended.		Correspondent of *Far Eastern Economic Review* banned from Sarawak.
	Samad Ismail jailed.		Yang di-Pertuan Agong dies.
	Business Times and *Bintang Timur* begin.	**1980**	*Tamil Malar* suspended.
1979	Editor of *Kinabalu Sabah*		Journalist convicted under Securities Industry Act.

BIBLIOGRAPHY

Abdul Rahman Al-Ahmadi. "Notes Towards a History of Malay Periodicals in Kelantan." In *Kelantan: Religion, Society and Politics in a Malay State*, ed. William R. Roff. Kuala Lumpur, 1974.

Amnesty International. *Report of an Amnesty International Mission to the Federation of Malaysia 18 November-30 November 1978*. London, 1979.

Coats, Howard, and Dyer, Frances. *The Print and Broadcasting Media in Malaysia*. Kuala Lumpur, 1972. Reprinted in *Leader Malaysian Journalism Review*, 1974, pp. 3-23.

Das, K. "Malaysia: The Enemies Within." *Far Eastern Economic Review*, July 2, 1976, pp. 8-9.

Dol Ramli. "Media for Development—How the Malaysian Machinery Works." *Media Asia*, 1978, pp. 10-13.

"Editors Held under ISA." *The New Straits Times*, June 23, 1976.

Fernandez, Joseph. "The Writing Is on the Wall...in Bahasa." *Media* (Hong Kong), October 1979, pp. 18-22.

Grenfell, Newell. *Switch On, Switch Off: Mass Media Audiences in Malaysia*. Petaling Jaya, 1979.

"I Played up the Communist Victories." *The New Straits Times*, June 26, 1976.

Khoo Kay Kim and Jazamuddin Baharuddin, eds. *Lembaran Akhbar Melayu (Themes in the History of Malay Journalism)*. Kuala Lumpur, 1980.

Lent, John A. *Asian Mass Communication: A Comprehensive Bibliography* and *Supplement*. Philadelphia, 1975, 1978.

———. "Malaysia's Guided Media." *Index on Censorship*, Winter 1974, pp. 65-75.

———. "True (?) Confessions—TV in Malaysia and Singapore." *Index on Censorship*, March-April 1978, pp. 9-18.

Lim Huch Tee, ed. *Mass Communication in Malaysia: An Annotated Bibliography*. Singapore, 1975.

Newman, Barry. "Malaysian Government Decides What's on TV: News of Its Own Feats." *Wall Street Journal* December 5, 1980, pp. 1, 20.

Parker, Elliott S. "The Malaysian Election of 1974: An Analysis of Newspaper Coverage." *Studies in Third World Societies*, December 1979, pp. 79-132.

Parker, Elliott S., and Parker, Emelia M. *Asian Journalism: A Selected Bibliography of Sources on Journalism in China and Southeast Asia*. Metuchen, N.J., 1979.

Parker, William C. *Communication and the May 13th Crisis*. Kuala Lumpur, 1979.

Syed Arabi Idid. "Public Relations: A Glimpse of the Practioners in Malaysia." *Media Asia*, 1978, pp. 165-70.

Wong, Eugene. "How Not to Advertise in Malaysia." *Media* (Hong Kong), May 1979, pp. 25, 26.

MEXICO

by Michael Sewell

BASIC DATA

Population: 66,633,000
Area: 1,978,800 sq. km. (764,014 sq. mi.)
GNP: 2.45 trillion pesos (US $107.6 billion) (1979)
Literacy Rate: 65.1%
Language(s): Spanish
Number of Dailies: 352
   Aggregate Circulation: 3,994,000
   Circulation per 1,000: 60
Number of Nondailies: 483
   Aggregate Circulation: NA
   Circulation per 1,000: NA
Number of Periodicals: 1,964

Number of Radio Stations: 770
Number of Television Stations: 108
Number of Radio Receivers: 17,154,000
   Radio Receivers per 1,000: 301
Number of Television Sets: 4,885,000
   Television Sets per 1,000: 84
Total Annual Newsprint Consumption: 247,300 metric tons
   Per Capita Newsprint Consumption: 3.9 kg. (8.6 lb.)
Total Newspaper Ad Receipts: 1.15 billion pesos (US$ 57.7 million) (1976)
   As % of All Ad Expenditures: 12.8

Background & General Characteristics

The cultures of Mexico are diverse, and contribute to a society about which it is difficult to generalize. The ethnic composition is 55 percent *mestizo,* a mixture of the indigenous peoples and their Spanish conquerers; 29 percent Indian, 15 percent European and one percent of other races or nationalities. Spanish, the official language, is spoken by 97.9 percent of the population, but the illiteracy rate in 1970 was 28.3 percent with over 10 million people over the age of 15 unable to read. Of the Spanish-speaking population, 7.8 percent speak both Spanish and their indigenous languages; 2.1 percent speak only their Indian tongues.

Mexico's land area of 1,972,546 square kilometers (about 750,000 square miles) makes it the fourteenth largest country in the world and the third largest in Latin America. It is approximately one-fourth the size of the United States, with a 1980 population of roughly 65 million. Mexico shares with the United States a border of over 3,000 kilometers or about 1,800 miles, and this proximity has had great political and economic influence on her history. From even before the Texas Revolution of 1836 and the Mexican War of 1845 to the present problems over illegal immigrants to the United States, Mexicans have recognized, sometimes feared, the power of the north.

The country's roots are both Indian and Spanish. The Indians lived in Mexico centuries before the Spanish conquistadores arrived in 1519. To some extent, this long cultural symbiosis has love-hate aspects. There is pride in Spanish language and history, yet some resentment toward the conquest by the Europeans and their centuries of harsh rule and exploitation.

Modern Mexico has a unique personality that stems from both the Spanish and Indian heritages and from historical occurrences, particularly the Mexican Revolution of 1910. This self-image, often referred to as *mexicanismo,* has been defined by one scholar as a social outlook—"seen by most Mexicans as a unique process of recent history beginning with the Revolution of 1910–1917. They are wont to eschew any notion that theirs is a parasite or hybrid culture in the sense of depending upon foreign ideological transfusions."

The military phase of the revolution ended in 1920 after a period of great turmoil and bloodshed. To achieve stability and to safeguard the social accomplishments, the ongoing movement was placed in the hands of the

Partido Revolucionario Institucional (Institutional Revolutionary Party) or PRI. Although there are other political parties, PRI has maintained a hegemony at all levels of government. The president, who has always been a PRI candidate, is limited to a single term of six years. Proponents of this system argue that it is a one-party democracy, while critics maintain that it is a dictatorship of sorts, by PRI.

A nebulous term for most outsiders, the revolution at any moment may be merely whatever the political leadership says it is, but it remains the central symbol, the *raison d'être,* for that leadership. In the words of one study, the rhetoric of politics in Mexico is the rhetoric of the revolution:

> Whether social security benefits are extended to a new village, a parcel of land divided, a dam inaugurated, or a steel mill expanded, it is all attributed to the Revolution.... Many Mexican intellectuals insist that the Revolution is dead, but the political leaders continue to talk in terms of its myths, and these seemingly still have enormous hold on the minds of the masses.

The populace usually makes a distinction between the politicians in power and the revolution. For them, it is a social revolution, a program of specific improvements in the standard of living and the lifestyle of the average Mexican. Thus there has often been discontent with government policies, programs and results.

In the 1970s, Mexico experienced a number of great problems—a steadily increasing population because of an annual birthrate of over three percent (and, ironically, improved health care); rural migration to the cities, particularly Mexico City, which will soon be the world's largest metropolis with a population in excess of 15 million; serious unemployment and underemployment; and a staggering inflation rate, long in double-digit figures, and expected to be at least 25 percent in 1981. Economic problems were eased a bit, at least psychologically, with the discovery of large oil deposits in August 1975, but the specter of inflation and its ravaging of the middle class still remains for leaders to contend with.

Mexico produced the Western Hemisphere's first printed materials when Juan Pablos set up a press in 1539, but his and subsequent printing shops were tightly controlled by the Spanish government and the Catholic Church. For almost two centuries only religious materials or occasional notices of remote or innocuous events appeared, and no newspaper surfaced. In 1722 Juan Ignacio de Castorena established *Gaceta de Mexico,* but neither it nor its immediate successors displayed much journalistic zeal. It was the war for independence from Spain that produced vitriolic political journalism, led by *El Despertador Americano,* which was founded in 1810. That paper awakened not only rebellion against the Spanish but a century of political journalism as well. Much of the 19th century involved battles of the pen versus the sword—as well as those of the pen allied with the sword.

Ultimately, Mexican politics and journalism divided into the relative camps of conservatism and liberalism. Throughout the century the nation's leaders were determined to either use the press or to control it. A student of Mexican history has written that the press suffered "licensing, censorship, fines, prison terms, bribes, boycotts, confiscation, closing, exile, good-behavior bonds, even personal assault and execution." The political activity of the press—and the resolve of the government to control or silence it—reached new heights during the rule of President Porfirio Díaz from 1882 to the start of the revolution. By 1910, when the revolution broke out, the press was almost wholly controlled by the Díaz administration.

The early years of the revolution resulted in the deaths of most newspapers and virtually no present newspaper predates this period. On the other hand, many of today's newspapers were born during the upheaval, including *Excélsior* and *El Universal,* two of Mexico's best-known dailies. Today, the Mexican press includes more than 220 daily newspapers with a combined circulation of about 5.7 million copies (1974 figures). There is roughly one copy of a daily newspaper for each two families. Mexico City has 27 dailies, which account for 2.3 million circulation. The content of the average daily newspaper is approximately 40 percent local news, 20 percent national, 10 percent international and 28 percent advertising. There are almost 300 nondaily newspapers.

Although most Mexican newspapers are relatively young and have grown up with the revolution, this is not to say that the masses see the press as a positive tool of the continuing revolution, any more than they would view most government officials as such. The populace has little regard, generally, for the accuracy, much less the detachment, of most newspapers or other mass media today. Most Mexicans simply do not view these media as reliable sources of important information. Historically, the press has been suspect for a number of reasons, particularly its susceptibility to a vast range of government inducements or pressures, from the *mordida* (literally, "bite," or bribe) to use of sheer physical force by authorities.

Radio began with experimental broadcasting in 1921 and expanded quickly, despite some geographical barriers, and television was introduced in 1950, making Mexico the world's sixth nation to establish television commercially.

In 1977 Mexico had 694 radio stations (584 AM and 110 FM) and 243 television stations, of which 119 were commercial. Cinema began in the early part of the century but reached its peak of popularity during World War II.

Both public relations and, especially, advertising have developed in recent decades as adjunct industries for mass communications in Mexico. In economic structure and approaches, the country's mass media have tended to model themselves after the United States, and the marketing roles of advertising and public relations have become increasingly important not only to the media but to Mexico's business world.

Historically, the press of Mexico has been small in both circulation and influence. The literacy rate of 30 percent of the population in 1910 rose to 65 percent in the 1960 census, then began to decline as the population grew faster than schools could be built or teachers trained. Additionally, such geographical barriers as mountain ranges and deserts combined with a transportation system—inferior until recent times—to virtually assure the absence of large circulation.

Even the advent of broadcasting has not changed this pattern for most of Mexico. Until very recently, with developments and investment in satellite and other telecommunications systems, broadcasting could not reach many remote areas, not only because of topography but also economic factors such as low per capita income in rural areas.

This situation has changed and continues to change with a growing urbanization rate. Because of unemployment, underemployment and other negative conditions, large numbers of persons migrate to the cities. In 1970 the population of Mexico was 48,377,000 of which 26,544,000 (or 55 percent) lived in cities of 20,000 or more. Projections for 1980

predicted a total population in excess of 68 million, of which over 40 million, or approximately 60 percent, would be urban. This urbanizing trend is conducive to larger circulations for newspapers, which are located in the larger towns and cities.

The focal point of the Mexican press and other mass media is Mexico City—not only the capital but by far the largest city, home for roughly one of every five persons in the whole country. With a population in excess of 10 million (estimates run as high as 13 million), Mexico City is fully five times larger than the next largest city, Guadalajara. Obviously Mexico City tends to dominate political, economic and social trends. A number of Mexicans see it as almost synonymous with the national ethic and spirit.

Mexico City has the same preeminence, if not domination, in mass media. Its 26 daily newspapers collectively account for about half of the national daily circulation. The press of Mexico City is the press of influence, the elite press. Several of the city's newspapers have won a reputation for literary editing, comment and leadership, although aggressive reporting of politics and criticism of government officials is not traditionally typical. Accuracy is variable from one newspaper to another, depending on the integrity and abilities of the staff.

Almost all newspapers in Mexico are published in Spanish. Most are standard size. Approximately 35 percent of the 200-plus dailies are chain-owned. The largest, not only in Mexico but the Spanish-speaking world, is the Garcia Valseca group of over 30 newspapers. Many of its newspapers can be recognized by a commonality of name: *El Sol* ("The Sun"), followed by the names of the cities in which they are published. The second largest chain, with seven newspapers, is run by the O'Farrill family, with *Novedades,* one of Mexico City's leading dailies, as its flagship paper. O'Farrill also has investments and ownership in magazines and broadcasting. Chain control in Mexico is slightly less than in the United States and occurs mostly in the larger population centers. In 1970, 49 of 75 cities in Mexico (65.3 percent) had competing daily newspapers.

While newspapers may tend to reflect a conservative political viewpoint (Garcia Valseca's *El Sol de Mexico* in the 1960s) or take a liberal stand, (*Excélsior* prior to 1976), they do not tend to be political organs. An exception would be *El Nacional* of Mexico City, which speaks for the ruling party,

Partido Revolucionario Institucional, but most of the papers support the political status quo.

Philosophies and approaches vary. As mentioned above, several Mexico City newspapers have a tradition as elite journals; among these are *Excélsior, Novedades* and *El Universal.* Others notably *El Heraldo* (Mexico City), cater to the upper and rising middle class, especially young professionals. Still others comprise the popular press and several fit the category of sensationalist (if not "yellow") journals: the country's largest tabloid, *La Prensa,* and *Ovaciones* emphasize crime coverage, mixed with sports and other features. In both tone and degree, the content of these and similar newspapers around Mexico is superficial. Most have relatively high circulations.

Most daily newspapers in Mexico are small in circulation. For the most part, the largest dailies exist in Mexico City and the bulk of their circulation is in the federal district. The 10 largest newspapers, eight of which are in Mexico City, account for about 20 percent of the national daily circulation.

10 Largest Newspapers by Circulation (1980)

La Prensa	278,000
Ovaciones	228,000
Novedades	190,000
El Heraldo	185,000
El Universal	171,000
Excelsior	160,000
El Norte	96,000
Diario de la Tarde	71,000
El Sol de Mexico	NA
El Informador	NA

It should be noted that circulation figures for most newspapers in Mexico are unavailable, outdated or unaudited, if not otherwise questionable.

The three most influential newspapers nationally are *Excélsior, Novedades* and *El Universal* of Mexico City. Influential leaders within their cities and regions are *El Norte* of Monterrey and *El Informador* of Guadalajara. *La Prensa,* the circulation leader, is a tabloid.

There are virtually no foreign-language papers; the best known is the English-language *The News,* published in Mexico City.

Economic Framework

While changing demographic patterns have altered accessibility to the mass media, such patterns have also affected the economy. The economic impact of the burgeoning urban population has been reflected in unemployment, urban problems and inflation. Serious unemployment in Mexico City and double-digit inflation that reached 25 percent in 1981 obviously are not conducive to either the economy or mass media, which must depend on reader sales and substantial advertising revenues. President José López Portillo has taken a conservative approach on economic matters: his government-spending reductions have included purchase of newspaper advertising by government agencies; this constitutes about 20 percent of the advertising revenue for most Mexico City dailies. The president also let it be known when he took office that he frowned upon purchase of news space in the press—the traditional *gacetillas* or paid publicity notices —by government officials. Thus, competition for reader and advertiser by mass media becomes more intense.

As already mentioned, concentration in ownership is not quite as great as in the United States. The fact that most of Mexico's newspapers were born during or since the Revolution and are relatively young has mitigated against concentration or monopoly generally. A couple of individuals or families have built up substantial holdings. The preeminent Garcia Valseca chain has recently fallen to another group of investors, headed by former President Luis Echeverria and the O'Farrill chain. Perhaps more important is the O'Farrills' multiple and cross-ownership: at varying times the family has owned— among other holdings—20 magazines, national radio station XEX and Mexico's first television station, XH-TV. Together with the Azcarraga family, the O'Farrills also control Televisa, S.A., a commercial combine of four networks in Mexico City and government stations, totalling 82 stations throughout Mexico. Approximately 60 percent of these stations were owned wholly by the two families in 1974. The other 40 percent were owned by other individuals or groups or partly owned by the O'Farrills and Azcarragas. But the O'Farrill family is quite probably the most influential private owner in Mexico's mass communication system.

A key institution for newspapers in Mexico is Productora e Importadora de Papel, S.A.

(Producer and Importer of Paper, Inc.). PIPSA, as it is usually called, is the government newsprint monopoly. It buys newsprint in volume and, as a collective purchasing system it can sell to client newspapers at below-market prices. Those newspapers that receive allocations generally have a plentiful, relatively inexpensive supply, but PIPSA also has the power to withhold or refuse allocations. Many Mexican journalists say that PIPSA is beneficial to the press but dissidents in the past have argued that PIPSA was used as a barrier or weapon against them. Although publishers own 40 percent of PIPSA, the government owns the controlling 60 percent.

Approximately 30 percent of the content in the Mexican press is advertising. Although advertisers might exert pressure in several ways, it is usually unnecessary, for news space is for sale in the form of the previously mentioned *gacetillas*. However, consciously or subconsciously, editors are affected by advertiser preferences. Government, usually the major advertiser or "benefactor," is the most obvious instrument of influence, enabling numerous direct and indirect controls over the press to be exerted by officialdom. Special interest lobbies also have real persuasive or political influence from time to time, especially over those publishers or newspapers with particular political leanings.

Labor unions in Mexico tend to be dominated by the government. Certainly the recent orientation of the Partido Revolucionario Institucional and of the government itself has been very favorable to labor, creating strong "reporter power" and making strikes unlikely or even unnecessary. There have been instances where this has affected freedom of the press, but generally the only result has been to tie management's hands in upgrading professional standards. Some editors maintain that it is virtually impossible, because of the labor laws, to fire an incompetent or unethical reporter.

Many of Mexico's larger newspapers, especially in Mexico City, Guadalajara and Monterrey, use offset printing and other new technologies. Most lag behind the United States in electronic editing but the Mexican press in larger urban areas is generally more modern than in most other Latin American nations.

Press Laws

The constitution of 1917 states that free-dom of press will not be limited except in regard to "private life, morals and public tranquility." There are specific laws dealing with violations of those areas, including a law—antedating the constitution by a year—that prohibits *descato,* or disrespect for authority. It is a good example of specific restriction of a general, nebulous category such as "public tranquility." The *descato* statute says journalists must not maliciously "excite hatred of the authorities, the army, the national guard, or the fundamental institutions of the country."

Actual practice has been a matter of often ignoring the specific laws but rarely the power and thought behind them: in traditional deference to the *descato* concept, the president (until very recently) has not been criticized but his cabinet ministers have. The amount of press freedom in this century has been more dependent on the president in office than on legal or constitutional protections. Some presidents have been more liberal than others and the press has always been attuned to that.

There has also existed traditionally an attitude of cooperation with government that some journalists would call self-censorship and that others would term patriotism. Whatever their perceptions, motivations and temptations, most Mexican journalists have been very much aware that the law in Mexico is usually whatever a person in power or authority says it is.

There is no licensing or registration of journalists in Mexico, as in Cuba or Chile, for example. Commercial regulations of the press are not dissimilar to those in other private enterprise systems, such as the United States. Compulsory bonds are illegal.

One editor in Mexico has stated that while there is freedom of the press, there is no freedom of information: no "shield" laws affording protection of confidentiality, or "sunshine" laws requiring access to public information. Journalists are free to seek information from government officials and agencies but there is no guarantee or requirement that they will be successful. In fact, some governmental secrecy goes unquestioned and unchallenged. Reporters do not often view themselves as having a legal or a moral right to official information, nor are they enthusiastic about pursuing an adversarial relationship.

Both the constitution and tradition regard the publishing of matters about private individuals as potentially unwise. There are exceptions, such as publicity given to persons arrested for (but not convicted of) crimes, but personal affairs are either off limits or tend to invoke libel laws and prohibition of reporting "private life [and] morals" mentioned in the constitution.

The judiciary of Mexico seems genuinely desirous of maintaining independence, but at times resorts to sidestepping politically sensitive issues. This may be done by relying on very narrow legal issues or interpretations or by merely delaying rulings until some other persons, factors or events resolve the situation.

Censorship

The government would like to appear to be democratic and to believe in press freedom; indeed, its officials may actually support it in theory. In any case, blatant direct censorship has rarely been a problem for the press in Mexico. There is no official government agency charged with monitoring the press. There are no pre-publication censorship procedures, as in Brazil or Chile. The government relies on a cooperative spirit and much more subtle techniques. Indeed, there *may* be some secret governmental agency for monitoring the press or coordinating its manipulation; the lack of an information flow tells one that this is indeed possible. But it is also unlikely because it is unnecessary. Other methods work well enough. In a nation that historically has been conservative if not authoritarian about such matters, government is apt to release only information that is either innocuous or self-serving. Nor are the majority of journalists likely to demand information, negative or not, having no freedom of information acts to shore up their courage or back their persistence.

Moreover, newsmen view the press as an instrument of the revolution, a means of promoting harmony in a poorly educated country. They fear a loss of faith in the Mexican system by readers if harsh criticism of officials is published. Typical of this attitude is the remark of a Tijuana editor:

Mexico is still a developing country and needs the cooperation of all sectors, including the press. We're not mature enough yet to permit liberties like those in the United States, where you can criticize even the President. In Mexico we would call that a lapse of discipline. We would have thought twice before publishing anything like Watergate because there are foreign countries who are just waiting for us to break.

But self-censorship by reporters is not always related to notions about the role of the press in national development. According to one observer:

Most reporters and contributors either know how far they can go, or do not feel the temptation to go very far. This enables many of them to state publicly that *they* never had anything censored. And the fact is that a great deal *can* be said in Mexico. The government is discreet in its demands.

A distinction also can be made in regard to the proximity of the journalist to the subject that he is writing about. The provincial press, distant from the federal power center of Mexico City, is a little more prone toward criticism of that faraway government's agencies and officials. On the other hand, journalists are usually sensitive to the wishes and reactions of local and state leaders in their area. Observers of the press in the city of Jalapa note that the press pays acute attention to the reaction of the state governor and there is no criticism of him, the president or their major policies. Municipal authorities are less immune, but the city government also can provide enough rewards or threats to neutralize most of the newspapers there.

Despite the presence of a fair number of benign journalists and general absence of a watchdog press, there are examples here and there of individual journalists, reportage and even a few newspapers engaged in aggressive reporting and criticism. When the nearly ubiquitous self-censorship is not embraced by these journalists, other methods are employed by government officials. It should be emphasized, however, that most of the methods are relatively subtle and many involve the rewarding of "proper" conduct more than coercion.

In broadcasting there is both a more specific regulatory framework and a more official, announced view of the role of the broadcast media. Although there were prior laws regulating communications, the Federal Law of Radio and Television of 1960 determines the nature of broadcasting today. The law emphasizes the social significance of broadcasting and stipulates that the broadcast frequency spectrum is part of the inalienable public domain. Because the airwaves belong to the people, the government is obligated to monitor and regulate broadcast stations or enterprises. Numerous specific articles of the law stipulate kinds of programming and the nature of approaches to some topics, such as a prohibition of "hard sell" in advertising of alcoholic beverages over 20 proof.

The law states that there shall be no prior restraint or censorship but numerous provisions must also be met: prohibited are broadcasts that corrupt the Spanish language, violate community customs, encourage antisocial behavior, denigrate national heroes, offend commonly held religious beliefs, or discriminate on the basis of race or color. It is also illegal to broadcast information contrary to the national security or against the public order and air time must be yielded to the government for emergency messages at the request of the president or the minister of the interior.

There are no press councils or media councils, as in Sweden or the United States, to adjudicate disputes over professional ethics or prior restraint. Why such councils do not surface is conjectural, but historical and cultural factors may well be contributing causes.

State-Press Relations

It is fair to say that the government manipulates rather than controls the Mexican media. As in most developing countries, broadcasting and cinema are officially controlled. But even though the press can be legally regulated by law, it is, in theory and reality, relatively free. Both the free enterprise system and the libertarian approaches of the United States are copied—to a degree. However, because of differing economies, as well as political, social and historical factors, the resemblance ends there.

The government's greatest single form of control over the Mexican press is the cooperative nature of most publishers, editors and reporters. Some reporters, for example, consider asking for a public budget as a slight against the treasurer who drafted it. It is true that the government has traditionally been authoritarian toward the press, but Mexico has been a conservative society traditionally. It is not unusual, then, that there are conservative journalists.

Loans for capital improvements or investments can be channeled through financing agencies such as Nacional Financiera. Newsprint allocations can be made or withheld through PIPSA, the government newsprint monopoly. Because PIPSA—as mentioned earlier—buys newsprint in volume and functions as a collective purchasing system, it can sell to client newspapers at wholesale prices. Obviously, this economic advantage is popular with the publishers—that is, with the ones who receive an allocation of paper. But some journalists have complained that PIPSA has been the government's instrument of harassment or retribution against them. The left-wing magazines *Política* and *Por Qué?* claimed in separate incidents in the 1960s and early 1970s that newsprint sales had been refused by PIPSA. Ousted *Excélsior* director Julio Scherer García decided to offer an alternative voice by starting a weekly magazine of news and critical analysis, *Proceso,* late in 1976. PIPSA informed Scherer that it could not supply paper because of "prior commitments." *Proceso* obtained paper for its early issues on the open market, and under a new administration the following year it received PIPSA allocations.

Direct ownership and investment is another way in which government may control the media. Mexico's largest newspaper chain, the García Valseca group, became the most celebrated victim when Nacional Financiera foreclosed on a loan of approximately $12 million. The exact reasons are unclear; resulting changes reflect neither revenge against the owner or his editors, nor any apparent attempt to radically alter the reporting. Gradually, the conservative flagship, *El Sol de Mexico,* has moved its position as liberal reporters and editors joined the staff in recent years. This occurred because then-President Luís Echeverría's aides quickly appeared in the chain's management when its stock was made available for purchase by private investors. It appears to be Echeverría who favored the hiring of the liberals.

What government does not lend to the press or buy outright, it may give indirectly. Government advertising, mostly for its airline, Aero México, its lottery, Lotería Nacional, and its development agency, Nacional Financiera, constitutes approximately 20 percent of the advertising revenue for most dailies in Mexico City.

Also effective is the purchase of news space in the form of the previously mentioned *gacetillas.* Since *gacetillas* are not labeled as advertisements, they appear to be impartial news and may either confuse or annoy the reader. Advertisers, including government, may choose to buy the lead (principal) news story or smaller spots. *Excélsior,* long considered by many as the top newspaper in Mexico—at least until management changes in 1976—would not sell its main story in the 1970s, but in 1972 the second headline on page one could be had for $8,000.

People and their services or allegiance can

sometimes be bought, too. In Mexico, where there are differing traditions and perceptions of morality and of journalistic ethics, such "purchases" are more common and more complex. The *mordida* of bribe is common in most of Latin America in dealing with public officials, especially bureaucrats. The concept of the journalist as guardian of truth, righteousness and public welfare has never been firmly established and is probably a ludicrous concept for most Mexicans. Thus, it does not appear unusual to the public or to most journalists when reporters and editors accept *igualas* ("stipends"). These payoffs from news sources may be to ensure preferential treatment or specifically to see that a particular story is run. The *iguala* is often thought of and referred to as a public relations fee for a journalist's services. While it's acceptance is widespread, there are journalists who would like to see an end to the practice. One U.S.-educated newspaper director in Monterrey said in 1975:

> Corruption is rampant here. It is very difficult to fight, for one gets used to it, like the slums on the outskirts of town. There are maybe four or five honest reporters—those who don't take *igualas*—in Monterrey and they work for our newspapers. We have those who do; I cannot prove it, but in my heart I know they do. I cannot fire them because of the trade unions and stiff labor laws.

Perceptions of morality aside, the acceptance of *igualas* is a matter of pragmatism for many journalists, since newspaper work pays very low wages in Mexico. In order to have even a mediocre income, reporters at small newspapers must obtain half or more of their earnings from other sources—*igualas*, second jobs, even third jobs. The second job sometimes comes from a news source, as in the case of one reporter in Monterrey who covers the police beat for his newspaper by day, then moonlights as a police radio dispatcher. In some Western countries this would be considered a conflict of interest because the second job might affect the reporter's coverage, subconsciously if not by coercion. However, the abovementioned reporter considers the job "a matter of necessity."

Interestingly, further attempts at reform in recent years have come not only from a handful of journalists, but also from President José López Portillo, who let it be known when he assumed office in December 1976 that favors for reporters and editors, and even the

purchase of space, would be drastically reduced during his term.

Other ways in which the government may build friendships with journalists or gently pressure them include the overlooking of debts due from social security payments (a discrepancy that may be discovered suddenly after displeasing coverage) and the domination of labor unions.

Traditionally the press has not seriously criticized, nor satirized the president—at least not until 1975-76, the final years of Echeverría's term. By that time, liberalization of interpretation or enforcement of the legal code permitted, perhaps encouraged, stronger expression. A 1951 penal code that mandated a 12-year prison term for "disturbing the public order" was repealed in the early 1970s, and by 1975 newspaper publishers were seeking further liberalization of the 1916 law prohibiting *descato,* or disrespect for authority. Conservatives became alarmed and little change in press law has resulted. Press freedom remains what it has been for most of this century—a nebulous guarantee that can be expanded or reduced at the whim of each new president.

In broadcasting and cinema, the government invested more and more heavily in the 1970s. The result today is a system composed of state, quasi-state and private enterprise. Some broadcasters see this "mix" as necessary, if not desirable. They believe that in the crucial area of education, for example, the government must be the leader in development. They see government as economic partner and leader, participant and monitor.

Particularly significant in the regulation of broadcasting are programming allocation requirements. One specifies that at least 30 minutes each day will be devoted to broadcasts that have educational, cultural and social orientation. Such programs are prepared by the Ministry of the Interior and supplied to radio and television stations, which must broadcast them free of charge.

The other requirement is known as "fiscal time." In 1969 the government imposed a tax of 25 percent of gross income on broadcast media. Broadcasters maintained that this was a severe economic hardship and proposed a compromise by which the government would receive program time rather than cash. The government accepted and a levy of 12.5 percent of the broadcast day—fiscal time—was implemented. The government's program time is not cumulative and the decree creating fiscal time states that the broadcaster must use the time for regular, uninterrupted programming if the government does not use it. Actually, the government has not used much of its available time in the past, primarily because the *Comisión de Radiodifusión* (Broadcasting Commission) created to provide such programming to stations was unable to produce sufficient quantities. Thus, in 1976 a quasi-state company, Productora Nacional de Radio y Televisión (National Producer of Radio and Television) began providing some of the content and is expected soon to have the capacity to program for all fiscal time.

Official control of television is relatively easy to implement, for there is a single commercial combine, Televisa, composed of four network channels in Mexico City, and a network of government stations. The government has proceeded cautiously with development of cable (CATV) television and of satellite communications. This cautious pace may be to retain control over broadcasting, or merely a wait-and-see policy toward new technologies.

If the previously discussed methods fail to produce the desired response from media, government can resort to the stronger practices found in other countries of Latin America and the rest of the world. Mexico's government seems to prefer not to use force or even crude pressure; the carrot approach is much more tidy and defensible before world opinion for a government that professes to be democratic, libertarian and compassionate. But no government long ignores what it perceives to be against its best interests.

Particularly strident dissidents in Mexico have, on occasion, been dealt with harshly by the army or the police. At such times, officials have not been pleased with the reporting of such actions, and in some instances, very displeased. In November 1974, for example, the leftist opinion journal *Por Qué?* planned to publish an embarrassing story about the recapture of a politician in Guerrero from Mexico's most famous and most pursued guerrilla leader, Lucio Cabañas. What was embarrassing was that the story maintained that the army paid a ransom, then ambushed Cabañas's men, who returned the prisoner. The army's version was that the politician was recaptured in a fierce battle with the guerrillas. Learning of the planned story, police and soldiers raided and ransacked the publication's editorial offices in Mexico City, smashing the presses, confiscating the files and arresting 33 staff mem-

bers. The editors of *Por Qué?* later said that they were threatened with death if publication resumed. Earlier, in 1971, PIPSA had cut off newsprint sales to the weekly magazine, also allegedly because of government displeasure.

Less crude, more prolonged and perhaps equally effective was the case of the so-called *Excélsior* coup. Mexico's most influential newspaper, *Excélsior* was born of the revolution in 1917. By 1976 it was known for its aggressive reporting, its criticism of government, its slightly leftist (for Mexico) positions, its literary excellence and its financial strength. In 1968, when Julio Scherer García became director, the newspaper began building on an already solid reputation and moved steadily and substantially toward international recognition.

When Echeverría took office in 1970, he eased some of the controls, both formal and informal, on the press. Scherer and *Excélsior* took the fullest advantage of this, and of a seeming similarity of political and social philosophy between Scherer and the president. For several years *Excélsior's* accelerated commentary and reporting coincided with Echeverría's views and actions, but by 1975 a schism developed from some criticisms of the administration—foremost being the newspaper's demand that the foreign minister be forced to resign for supporting a United Nations resolution equating Zionism with racism. Echeverría, eager to be elected U.N. secretary general, was forced by a Jewish boycott of Mexican resorts to renounce the resolution and, it would appear, to make the foreign minister a scapegoat and dismiss him. Although other factors were involved in the fallout with Scherer, this incident appears to have been the last straw for the president.

Early in 1976 the government began a concerted campaign to pressure, if not punish, *Excélsior*. Government agencies placed thousands of dollars of advertisements in other media, charging *Excélsior* with unpatriotic and irresponsible behavior. *Excélsior* responded with continued criticism and disclosures of information embarrassing to the administration. By summer, the attacks took on a different, more ominous form: several hundred slum dwellers occupied 218 acres of suburban land owned by the newspaper, vowing not to leave as long as Scherer remained at *Excélsior*. A cooperative since 1932, *Excélsior* intended to develop a housing project on the land, with profits to be used to build a new printing plant. Authorities did nothing, an atypical approach in a country in which squatters are almost always forcibly evicted. However, the do-nothing approach can be understood when one considers that the squatters arrived at the site on buses owned by a state governor, received hot meals and materials to build shacks from government trucks, and counted a PRI politician among their ranks.

Excélsior attorneys were appalled and frustrated by judicial foot-dragging. The attorney general told them that he would enforce the law only after a general assembly of the newspaper's cooperative members was held. The meeting on July 8 turned out to be a shouting match, with Scherer and his associates unable to keep order or even speak. Varying factions were present, including, some witnesses allege, non-members who seemed to have concealed weapons. Fearing violence and unable to speak, Scherer and his aides finally left the meeting and went to their offices. Then, by voice vote, Scherer and six associates were dismissed from their positions. Scherer called the police but none came; finally, about an hour later, he and some 200 supporters left the building.

Denied a forum from which to continue the fight, Scherer decided to launch a weekly magazine, *Proceso.* He attracted about one thousand stockholders who contributed investments ranging from $40 to $800 each, and the first issue appeared in November 1976. *Proceso* was formed in the crucible of continued controversy, however, for Echeverría was determined to halt this critical voice, at least until his presidency ended in December. Apparently among his ploys was the filing of fraud charges against Scherer by the new editors of *Excélsior.* They claimed that Scherer and several of his executives had embezzled $650,000 of the cooperative's funds. Scherer escaped the entanglement, possibly because of the international attention and criticism focused on the *Excélsior* coup and its aftermath.

Meanwhile, the "new" *Excélsior* made every effort not to appear conservative by maintaining a leftist tone on the foreign news pages. When the new foreign editor called for cancellation of Prensa Latina, the Cuban news agency service, he was instructed to forget it, for that would "look bad." It was also suggested that he might add a subscription to Tass, the Soviet news agency.

It is entirely possible that the Scherer-Echeverría dispute was more one of personalities than a government-versus-the-press matter. Both *Excélsior* and *Proceso* have criticized government policies strongly in the past couple of years. Miguel Angel Grandos Chapa, former *Excélsior* staffer and managing director of *Proceso,* noted in 1977, "In *Excélsior* you can read censures of the government that are more bitter than any we ever published. But it doesn't matter. When Scherer left, the paper lost its opinion-making image." As for *Proceso,* it now receives the PIPSA newsprint initially denied it, and has had no official reaction from the administration despite its continued criticism of President López Portillo.

Another publication was spawned by the *Excélsior* affair when the paper's former columnist Samuel I. del Villar and Miguel Grandos Chapa both departed *Proceso* to start a magazine called *Razones* in 1980. The fortnightly publication seeks to "concentrate more on detailed reportage than denunciation." The new publisher, del Villar, also serves as an adviser to various government agencies.

Attitude Toward Foreign Media

Foreign correspondents have little or no trouble with censorship or harassment in Mexico. Accreditation procedures and visas are not atypical and correspondents have a great deal of freedom and mobility within the country. As with domestic journalists, however, they have no assurances that they will obtain the information they seek.

In stark contrast with a number of Latin American nations, prior approval of cables is not required. The banning or jailing of foreign correspondents is virtually nonexistent.

Information is not readily available on any ban of sales of foreign publications but such does not appear to occur. Foreign ownership of Mexican media is negligible.

Foreign media content and propaganda are relatively substantial. The Mexican press relies heavily for its international news on such news agencies as the Associated Press, United Press International, Agence France-Presse, Latin-Reuter, Deutsche Presse Agentur, Prensa Latina and Kyodo. Mexican television transmits network news and entertainment programming from the United States, as well as satellite transmissions from Europe and elsewhere, and videotapes and films from a variety of nations. Most of the foreign content, whether in print or broadcast media, is entertainment-oriented (for example, highly popular *telenovelas*—soap opera-style televised novels) and is indirect propaganda, if that. Some Mexicans have expressed the same concern as other nonaligned-nation people about the values portrayed in such "cultural imperialism."

As noted, much of the news about the United States, Western world or even other areas of the globe comes from a handful of Western news agencies. While the impact of such dependence on these agencies for international news is debatable, it is apparent that in terms of quantity Mexico must hear about the world's news from news organizations based in a limited number of nations. However, the striking countervoice offered is Prensa Latina, the official Cuban news agency.

Members of the Mexican press, particularly publishers and editors, maintain some contact and participation in international press organizations. Their primary activity is in the Inter-American Press Association.

As a matter of policy, Mexico sides with the UNESCO position on the 1978 Declaration, claiming that national development imperatives should take precedence over issues of press freedom.

News Agencies

There are three principal domestic news agencies, all with headquarters in Mexico City. Informex is the largest, with 85 offices throughout the country. It has over 300 clients—40 percent of the daily newspapers, 50 percent of the radio stations and 10 percent of the television stations. The other major news agency is Notimex; substantially smaller than Informex, it principally supplies broadcast media with such audio-visual materials as feature film. It serves 30 radio and five television stations from its main office, and from several correspondents who provide the foreign news. Agencia Mexicana de Noticias (AMEX) has a large staff, almost equivalent to Informex in size, but the relatively new agency (1968) is not firmly established. Additionally, Julio Scherer cranked up another news agency, Centro de Información, S.A. (CISA) shortly after his ouster from *Excélsior*. In 1978 CISA was supplying some 30 daily newspapers.

Foreign news agencies operating in Mexico include AP, UPI, Agence France-Presse, Latin-Reuter, Deutsche Presse Agentur, Prensa Latina and Kyodo.

Electronic News Media

Generally speaking, there is not a great deal of difference between print and broadcast journalism in Mexico. Both have need of better education and training of journalists. In both there is an emphasis in content on politics and social activities. In 1978 Televisa, the huge commercial combine of four networks in Mexico City, devoted 13.3 percent of its transmission time to news (2,847 broadcast hours) at a cost of a little more than $5 million (about 16 percent of total programming budget). The major difference between television and radio is that radio journalism carries a larger proportion of international news and relies heavily on such foreign news agencies as AP, UPI, Latin-Reuter and others.

Besides obvious technological differences, broadcast journalism also comes under more stringent and proliferated legal controls. However, there is no overt censorship of broadcast news by government officials. The attitudes toward voluntary compliance and the pressures that apply to the press also generally relate to broadcast news media.

Education & Training

Formal education in journalism is relatively new in Mexico. The biggest criticism by professional journalists of university graduates is that many of them have few or no skills. "All they know is the theory of communication, or, maybe, of journalism," complained one editor. "A lot of them can't even type." Upgrading is under way and several journalists have received graduate degrees from U.S. or European universities.

Five-year programs include the National Autonomous University of Mexico (UNAM), Iberoamerican University and the University of Guadalajara. Three-year programs, as well as technical or parajournalism programs, are available at several universities. Non-university schools of journalism exist in Guadalajara, Mexico City and Monterrey. These training programs require university-entrance qualifications.

Many journalists in Mexico continue to be trained on the job. Until around 1960 almost no journalists were university educated in journalism or communication, and the traditional apprenticeship-training approach continues to be relied on.

Summary

The press system of Mexico, perhaps never static, seems to have changed more in the 1970s than at any time since the revolution, but thorough and reliable histories and analyses of Mexican journalism are almost nonexistent, so such a statement is at best part speculation. At any rate, criticism that was unlikely in the 1960s (because it would elicit retaliation) surfaced under Echeverría and has continued during the term of López Portillo. This state of affairs may be a function of the political system's elasticity or it may signal a limited transition of the system. It is likely to continue only to the extent that the political leadership allows it to continue. Many Mexicans often speak and think in extremes, oscillating between optimism and pessimism or between this panacea and that, but extremes *in action* are not typical of Mexico's political and social life. It is safest to judge both the political system and the media by past trends.

Technologically the press will probably continue to develop, although many newspapers already possess sophistication in equipment and in content. Broadcasting may have heightened development if the government decides to commit its resources as a full partner to one route or another in developing national telecommunications.

Education, too, will likely continue to improve and assist in the development of journalists. Changes in professional standards and ethics, as in the case of *igualas,* will probably occur through education.

CHRONOLOGY

1970	President Luis Echeverría takes office. Controls on press eased; Article 145 of Penal Code repealed. Echeverría offers "liberal" approach to governing Mexico, and journalists feel some reason for optimism.
1971-1975	Some Mexican newspapers, particularly *Excélsior,* become more independent and aggressive. *Excélsior* enhances its growing national and international reputation as independent, quality newspaper.
1975	Schism occurs between President Echeverría and *Excélsior* director Scherer; Culmination of newspaper's criticism of administration policies is demand for foreign minister's resignation; he and government had supported United Nations resolution equating Zionism with racism.
1976	Nacional Financiera, government development agency, forecloses $12 million loan to Mexico's largest newspaper chain, Garcia Valseca; government then sells shares to private investors, including Echevierría and his aides, several of whom take positions in the chain's management.

Various government agencies spend hundreds of thousands of dollars on advertising critical of *Excélsior* in competing media.

"Coup" at *Excélsior* ousts Scherer and top associates.

Scherer begins publishing *Proceso,* criticizing Echeverría during his last month in office, then immediately beginning criticism of President José López Portillo.

López Portillo takes office, continues general freedom of the press, but announces that favors for reporters and editors and purchase of publicity and news space will be sharply curtailed.

1980	S. I. del Villar, a former Scherer associate at both *Excélsior* and *Proceso,* founds magazine, *Razones,* to "concentrate more on detailed reportage than denunciation."

BIBLIOGRAPHY

Becklund, Laurie. "Press in Tijuana Gaining Independence." *Los Angeles Times,* June 12, 1978.

Bremner, Charles. "Mexico Seeking Growth, Stability." Reuters News Service, July 30, 1980.

Cole, Richard R. "The Mexican Press System: Aspects of Growth, Control and Ownership." *Gazette.* No. 2 (1975), p. 67.

Cook, Carol. "Mexican Papers Fight On Despite Editor's Ouster." *The Christian Science Monitor,* January 17, 1977.

de Noriega, Luis A., and Leach, Frances. *Broadcasting in Mexico.* London, 1979.

Editor & Publisher. *1980 Yearbook.* New York, 1980.

Fagen, Richard R., and Tuohy, William S. *Politics and Privilege in a Mexican City.* Stanford, Calif., 1972.

Fox, Robert W. *Urban Population Growth Trends in Latin America.* Washington, D.C., 1975.

Hester, Albert L., and Cole, Richard R. eds. *Mass Communication in Mexico.* Brookings, S.D., 1975.

Johnson, Kenneth. *Mexican Democracy: A Critical View.* Boston, 1971.

Merrill, John C., Bryan, Carter R., and Alisky, Marvin. *The Foreign Press: A Survey of the World's Journalism.* Baton Rouge, La., 1970.

O'Shaughnessy, Hugh. "Samuel I. del Villar." *Financial Times of London,* January 11, 1980.

Pierce, Robert N. *Keeping the Flame: Media and Government in Latin America.* New York, 1979.

Simons, Marlise. "Mexico City Editor Hits Government for 'Intimidation.'" *The Washington Post,* October 26, 1976.

Taylor, John. "Mexico: The Guessing Game." *Index on Censorship,* Winter 1976, p. 34.

UNESCO. *World Communications: A 200-Country Survey of Press, Radio, Television and Film.* 5th ed. Paris, 1975.

Vargas, Armando. "The Coup at *Excélsior*" *Columbia Journalism Review,* September-October 1976, p. 45.

MOROCCO

by George Kurian

BASIC DATA

Population: 20,667,000 (1980)
Area: 409,200 sq. km. (157,992 sq. mi.)
GNP: DH 43.65 billion (US$9.7 billion) (1978)
Literacy Rate: 20%
Language(s): Arabic, French
Number of Dailies: 10
   Aggregate Circulation: 240,000
   Circulation per 1,000: 12
Number of Nondailies: 31
   Aggregate Circulation: NA
   Circulation per 1,000: NA
Number of Periodicals: 63

Number of Radio Stations: 1
Number of Television Stations: 1
Number of Radio Receivers: 2.4 million
   Radio Receivers per 1,000: 120
Number of Television Sets: 605,000
   Television Sets per 1,000: 30.2
Total Annual Newsprint Consumption: 5,200 metric tons
   Per Capita Newsprint Consumption: 0.3 kg. (.66 lb.)
Total Newspaper Ad Receipts: NA
   As % of All Ad Expenditures: NA

Background & General Characteristics

During the French Protectorate, the Moroccan press was dominated by French newspapers. Nationalist publications appeared and were tolerated by the official authorities for brief periods. Conflicts among nationalist groups and economic difficulties contributed to the brevity of their lifespans. Censorship restrictions were introduced during World War II and remained in force until independence in 1956. The Istiqlal Party was permitted to publish *Al Alam* and the Democratic Independence Party *Al Ray al-Amm.* Both were heavily censored and intermittently suspended. After the Casablanca riots of 1952 all nationalist papers were suppressed.

The largest of the newspaper publishers in pre-independence Morocco was the Mas group, owned by Pierre Mas and his son, Yves. Their empire included the largest and most influential newspapers in the country, including the Casablanca dailies *Le Petit Marocain* and *La Vigie Marocaine,* the Fes daily *Le Courrier du Maroc,* and the Rabat daily *Echo du Maroc.* In addition, the Mas group published several periodicals and con-trolled the printing and advertising industries as well.

With independence in 1956, the native press came into its own, and after the Istiqlal Party split into factions in 1959, politically sponsored papers proliferated. The conservative, loyalist Popular Movement and the Party of Independent Liberals were each represented by three journals. The Ministry of Information, in cooperation with the royalist Front for the Defense of Constitutional Institutions, published two dailies and two weeklies, and the Moroccan Communist Party published three newspapers until its proscription in 1959.

In 1980 the national press included 10 dailies of widely differing political orientation. Although weakened by frequent government seizures, the press appears vigorous and prosperous.

It will be shown that out of an aggregate circulation of 240,000 copies, the four French dailies claim 56 percent; but readership of French dailies is confined to the upper echelons of society. Half the dailies are published from Rabat and the other half from Casablanca.

Although *Le Matin* enjoys the largest circulation, the most influential daily is Istiqlal's *Al Alam*. From its establishment in 1946 until 1979 when Istiqlal joined the government, *Al Alam* was the voice of Moroccan nationalism, faithfully reporting the vicissitudes of national life and even providing an intellectual commentary on current events. Replacing *Al Alam* as the voice of the radical opposition is *Al Muharrir,* published by the Socialist Union of Popular Forces. Critical of the government's economic and foreign policies, the paper appeals especially to university students, younger professionals and government employees. At the other end of the spectrum is *Al Anba,* which is more or less a record of court happenings, royal speeches and government communiques. Because of the close identification of the state with Islam, the paper also provides extensive coverage of religious rituals.

characterized by their editorial vehemence and therefore are frequently targets of government seizure and suspension.

Economic Framework

Most Moroccan newspapers are not commercial enterprises in the strict sense of the term but rather are political and ideological tools. The costs of publication are usually underwritten by the political party or group, or, in the case of pro-government papers, by the government itself. Of the 10 major dailies, five are pro-government, two are moderate, and three are leftist. Of the aggregate circulation of these 10 papers, pro-government dailies account for 43.7 percent, the moderate dailies for 37.5 percent, and the leftist papers for 28.8 percent. There is very little concen-

10 Largest Moroccan Daily Newspapers by Circulation (1980)

Name	Language	Founded	Circulation	Political Orientation
1. *Le Matin*	French	1971	50,000	Monarchist
2. *Al Alam*	Arabic	1944	45,000	Istiqlal
3. *L'Opinion*	French	1965	45,000	Istiqlal
4. *Al Muharrir*	Arabic	1971	40,000	Socialist
5. *Maroc Soir*	French	1971	35,000	Monarchist
6. *Al Maghrib*	Arabic	1978	8,000	Monarchist
7. *Al Anba*	Arabic	1963	7,000	Official
8. *Al Mithaq al Watani*	Arabic	1976	5,000	Monarchist
9. *Al Bayane*	French	1972	5,000	Communist
10. *Al Bayan*	Arabic	1972	2,000	Communist

The quality of the Moroccan press and journalism is not comparable to the best in the Arab world, for example that of Lebanon or Egypt. This quality seems to be inversely related to the degree of national political authoritarianism and religious fanaticism. Apart from the political diversity that has historically characterized the Moroccan press, there are few characteristics that Moroccan newspapers share with the more advanced press systems.

Of the approximately 63 periodicals recorded by UNESCO in 1977, most are publications of political parties and their affiliates. The majority are published in Arabic, in tabloid format. Almost all have small circulations and are heavily dependent on subsidies from either government or anti-government sources. Catering to a small but partisan readership, these journals are generally

tration of press power. Because of their preoccupation with politics, few papers make any effort to improve their circulations through sensationalism or through publication of popular features such as cartoons. Circulation per capita is much lower in Morocco than it is in major Arab media centers such as Lebanon and Kuwait, or even in comparable Arab countries such as Algeria, Tunisia, Jordan, Syria and the United Arab Emirates. Print media circulations are also hurt by the low literacy of the population (a characteristic that Morocco shares with all Arab countries), the pre-emptive popularity of electronic media, and the generally poor editorial and production capabilities.

There is no separate industrial union for journalists or press-related workers, but they have the right to join any local or national union and to strike against their employers.

Such strikes have been rare, perhaps because of the depressed economic state of the newspaper industry.

Press Laws & Censorship

Freedom of expression was first proclaimed in 1963 by King Muhammed V's Charter of Press Liberties, which incorporated a basic press code. The code, however, contained provisions that empowered the government to apply stringent measures to limit press freedom. Strengthened in later years, notably in 1960 and 1963, the code empowered the minister of the interior to seize copies of any newspaper or periodical that appeared to threaten public order. Furthermore, he could suspend, and the prime minister could ban, any newspaper or periodical that attacked the religious and political foundations of the country. Official measures directed against the press for other offenses had to be initiated through the courts.

Within the bounds of these press laws, the Moroccan press enjoys great freedom to criticize the powers that be, with the sole exception of the king. The law provides for fines and prison terms for offenses against the royal family, the public peace, the morale and unity of the armed forces and the police, and external security. Even the monarchy has sometimes come under fire, though the criticisms are carefully worded and sometimes only hinted.

The press's ongoing struggle to debate national issues in the open and the government's efforts to contain the vehemence of such debate has produced a virtual tug-of-war between the two. The press's darkest period was in the late 1960s, when the government made regular use of its authority to seize and censor individual opposition papers. The suspension of the Istiqlal daily, *la Nation Africaine,* in February 1965 for publishing an anti-monarchical quotation from a 19th-century Egyptian philosopher created a political crisis of sorts. The newspaper's director was sentenced to 10 months in prison and about $1,000 fine. This led to the Istiqlal using its majority in the then bicameral parliament to pass an amendment to the press code eliminating the government's power to ban or suspend a newspaper. This defeat for the government was followed by King Hassan's decision to assume personal control of the government.

All internal censorship was lifted in 1977, but the essential tension between the state and the media remains. Part of this tension is inherent in the manifest pluralism of the Moroccan political system, in which authoritarianism coexists with restraint in its actual exercise. The government has never gone so far as to silence criticism totally or to enforce total conformity, as Algeria has, for example.

State-Press Relations

In its struggle against state controls during the past two decades, the press has won some significant victories, although losing ground occasionally. In 1959 when the government decreed new regulations allowing for some penalties for press offenses, the Istiqlal Party suspended publication of its five newspapers in protest against this "infringement of a free press." In 1960 when the government announced a new press code giving it more authority to suspend newspapers, a press strike led to the rescinding of the code. Government suspensions of newspapers for specific violations of the press law continue to be a regular occurrence for opposition newspapers, such as *al Muharrir,* but they do not deter these papers from continuing on the same editorial course.

The pro-government monarchical papers enjoy open government patronage and manipulate such patronage to increase circulation and to gain political leverage. The wide-circulation dailies *le Matin* and *Maroc Soir* are run by Moulay (Prince) Ahmed Alawi, a cousin of the king. The newer *al Mithaq al Watani* represents the views of former prime minister, Ahmed Osman, a rival of Alawi. Political ambitions are not absent even in the ranks of opposition newspapers. The chief editor of *al Alam,* Abdel Karim Ghallab, is not only one of Morocco's best-known journalists but also a leading politician and a central committee member of the Istiqlal.

Attitude Toward Foreign Media

Because the influence of French culture is still strong in the country and because of historical links with the French media, the Moroccan press is essentially French in character, although nationalists will deny such a conclusion. Many educated Moroccans still prefer to read *Le Monde* or other Parisian newspapers. French newspapers are still looked upon as models to be copied in style

News Agencies

The national news agency is the Maghrib Arab Press (MAP), founded by Mehdi Bennouna in 1959 as a private and independent operation. The agency has permanent offices in Rabat, Casablanca and Tangier, correspondents in all major Moroccan cities and branches in Tunis, Algiers and Paris. MAP also obtains world news from 18 international news agencies, including Reuters, AFP and UPI.

Electronic News Media

Broadcasting is the responsibility of Radiodiffusion Television Morocaine (RTM), also known as Radio Maroc, an agency of the Ministry of Information, which controls programming and operations. With a powerful long-wave transmitter at Azilal, 22 medium-wave transmitters and six FM transmitters, RTM broadcasts three separate home-service programs, a national program in Arabic, an international program in French, English, and Spanish and a Berber program. Most of the programs originate in one of the main studios in Rabat; studios also exist at Casablanca, Tangier, Fes, Oujda and other cities. The bulk of the programs is constituted by religious and educational broadcasts. Readings and commentaries of Koranic texts are heard at least twice a day and are supplemented by lectures by prominent Islamic scholars on current social and economic problems.

and format. Until 1971, the French-owned newspapers also dominated the Moroccan press. Beginning in 1958, the Istiqlal campaigned for a Moroccanization of the press. Under Istiqlal's pressure a clause was included in the press code restricting press ownership to Moroccan nationals. The government did not enforce this provision for a number of years, despite a Moroccan Press Association law suit in 1964, upheld by the Rabat Appeals Court, against the French-owned Mas Publishing Company on the ground that it had no legal right to publish. The French-owned press, in an effort to stave off the inevitable, adopted a slavishly pro-government attitude. The day of reckoning came in 1971 when the government informed the owners of *La Vigie Morocaine, Le Petit Marocain* and *Espana* that their temporary license to publish had been terminated. In quality and journalistic flair these were among the finest newspapers ever published in the country, and their death robbed the Moroccan press of some of its outstanding publications.

Morocco has generally adopted a liberal attitude toward foreign correspondents. They do not need special visas; no prior approval is required for cables. Foreign publications are available freely. However, in common with other developing nations, Morocco has lent its support to UNESCO efforts to strengthen state control over the media.

The most densely populated areas of the country are now covered by television, with a network of nine main transmitters and five low-power repeaters. A microwave relay system connects all these transmitters and links the national network with Spain (via Tangier) and thence with Eurovision.

Education & Training

A Journalism Training Center, founded in Rabat in 1969, conducts seminars for aspiring journalists with secondary education.

Summary

The Moroccan press is characterized by a rich diversity that is unusual in the context of an authoritarian and traditional Arab state. The contradiction may be explained by the persistence of French influences in a society that is essentially Islamic, regressive and uniformitarian. Despite occasional skirmishes, there has been as yet no large-scale warfare between state and media. Both seem anxious to avoid it.

CHRONOLOGY

1977   The government lifts press censorship.

1978   Ahmed Osman founds the daily *Al Maghrib*.

BIBLIOGRAPHY

Rugh, William A. *The Arab Press.* Syracuse, N.Y., 1979.